Beham / Dederer

International and European Environmental Law

Materials

International and European Environmental Law

Materials

PD Dr. Dr. Markus P. Beham, LL.M. (Columbia)

Associate Professor, University of Passau / Adjunct Lecturer, University of Vienna

Prof. Dr. Hans-Georg Dederer

Chair of Constitutional and Administrative Law, Public International Law, European and International Economic Law, University of Passau

2024

facultas

Bibliografische Information Der Deutschen Nationalbibliothek
Die Deutsche Nationalbibliothek verzeichnet diese Publikation in der Deutschen Nationalbibliografie; detaillierte bibliografische Daten sind im Internet über http://dnb.d-nb.de abrufbar.

Satz: Auer Grafik Buch Web, 1050 Wien
Druck: Facultas Verlags- und Buchhandels AG
ISBN 978-3-7089-2451-9 (facultas Verlag, Wien)
ISBN 978-3-7560-1530-6 (Nomos Verlag, Baden-Baden)

Preface

This materials collection fills the empty space alongside the most frequently used materials collections in the field of international law by providing an equivalent format for international and European environmental law. Against the common scepticism whether such compilations have not become "démodé" in times of digitalisation, both for teaching purposes, research, and practice, experience shows how tedious – and what a waste of resources – it can be having to draw up or print the most important texts individually for use in desk research or in the classroom. Our hope is to have provided a useful *vade mecum* to avoid this necessity in the future.

The selection of materials is based on our own practice and teaching syllabi at the University of Passau ("International Environmental Law") and the University of Vienna ("International and European Environmental Law"). It covers the most relevant horizontal and sectoral texts for use in introductory and specialised courses. For both the scholar and the practitioner, it may provide a first orientation in seeking to situate issues in the broader context of international and EU law.

The first three sections lay out the basic framework of fundamental principles, procedural questions and liability. The following sections stretch across the common definition of sectoral issues: air, ozone, climate, freshwater, oceans, biodiversity, and hazardous substances. With an eye to the page number and the need to carry the book to and from the classroom, certain texts – such as the TEU, TFEU, or UNCLOS – are reproduced in excerpts. Regularly updated annexes, schedules, technical data, and other materials such as forms have mostly been omitted and should best be consulted at the time of reference directly through the respective depository. As a prime example for science-based approaches to environmental regulation, we have specifically included Annex I of the 1994 Oslo Protocol though. Equally, the texts of the 1989 Basel Convention or the 1991 Espoo Convention would hardly open themselves to the reader without annexes or appendices.

While opting for a uniform style that does not take into account individual formatting choices of the various official reproductions of materials such as bold or italic fonts, we have taken into account the respective representation of norms and tables to allow for proper reference.

Comments and suggestions for future editions are gladly received at markus.beham@univie.ac.at or hans-georg.dederer@uni-passau.de.

We would like to thank Ursula Dillig, Cecilie Reckhorn, and Katharina Schötta for their help in the compilation of materials. Emil Balbierz also diligently reviewed all texts and provided invaluable assistance with the final drafts of the manuscript.

Passau / Vienna, October 2023

Markus P. Beham
Hans-Georg Dederer

Table of Contents

1.1. Stockholm Declaration 1972

Declaration of the United Nations Conference on the Human Environment, Stockholm, 16 June 1972; Report of the United Nations Conference on the Human Environment (Stockholm, 5-16 June 1972), 1973, A/CONF.48/14/Rev.1, 3

The United Nations Conference on the Human Environment, having met at Stockholm from 5 to 16 June 1972, having considered the need for a common outlook and for common principles to inspire and guide the peoples of the world in the preservation and enhancement of the human environment,

Proclaims that:

1. Man is both creature and moulder of his environment, which gives him physical sustenance and affords him the opportunity for intellectual, moral, social and spiritual growth. In the long and tortuous evolution of the human race on this planet a stage has been reached when, through the rapid acceleration of science and technology, man has acquired the power to transform his environment in countless ways and on an unprecedented scale. Both aspects of man's environment, the natural and the man-made, are essential to his well-being and to the enjoyment of basic human rights the right to life itself.
2. The protection and improvement of the human environment is a major issue which affects the well-being of peoples and economic development throughout the world; it is the urgent desire of the peoples of the whole world and the duty of all Governments.
3. Man has constantly to sum up experience and go on discovering, inventing, creating and advancing. In our time, man's capability to transform his surroundings, if used wisely, can bring to all peoples the benefits of development and the opportunity to enhance the quality of life. Wrongly or heedlessly applied, the same power can do incalculable harm to human beings and the human environment. We see around us growing evidence of man-made harm in many regions of the earth: dangerous levels of pollution in water, air, earth and living beings; major and undesirable disturbances to the ecological balance of the biosphere; destruction and depletion of irreplaceable resources; and gross deficiencies, harmful to the physical, mental and social health of man, in the man-made environment, particularly in the living and working environment.
4. In the developing countries most of the environmental problems are caused by under-development. Millions continue to live far below the minimum levels required for a decent human existence, deprived of adequate food and clothing, shelter and education, health and sanitation. Therefore, the developing countries must direct their efforts to development, bearing in mind their priorities and the need to safeguard and improve the environment. For the same purpose, the industrialized countries should make efforts to reduce the gap themselves and the developing countries. In the industrialized countries, environmental problems are generally related to industrialization and technological development.
5. The natural growth of population continuously presents problems for the preservation of the environment, and adequate policies and measures should be adopted, as appropriate, to face these problems. Of all things in the world, people are the most precious. It is the people that propel social progress, create social wealth, develop science and technology and, through their hard work, continuously transform the human environment. Along with social progress and the advance of production, science and technology, the capability of man to improve the environment increases with each passing day.
6. A point has been reached in history when we must shape our actions throughout the world with a more prudent care for their environmental consequences. Through ignorance or indifference we can do massive and irreversible harm to the earthly environment on which our life and well being depend. Conversely, through fuller knowledge and wiser action, we can achieve for ourselves and our posterity a better life in an environment more in keeping with human needs and hopes. There are broad vistas for the enhancement of environmental quality and the creation of a good life. What is needed is an enthusiastic but calm state of mind and intense but orderly work. For the purpose of attaining freedom in the world of nature, man must use knowledge to build, in collaboration with nature, a better environment. To defend and improve the human environment for present and future generations has become an imperative goal for mankind-a goal to be pursued together with, and in harmony with, the established and fundamental goals of peace and of worldwide economic and social development.
7. To achieve this environmental goal will demand the acceptance of responsibility by citizens and communities and by enterprises and institutions at every level, all sharing equitably in common efforts. Individuals in all walks of life as well as organizations in many fields, by their values and the sum of their actions, will shape the world environment of the future.

   Local and national governments will bear the greatest burden for large-scale environmental policy and action within their jurisdictions. International cooperation is also needed in order to raise resources to support the developing countries in carrying out their responsibilities in this field. A growing class of environmental problems, because they are regional or global in extent or because they affect the common international realm, will require extensive cooperation among nations and action by international organizations in the common interest.

The Conference calls upon Governments and peoples to exert common efforts for the preservation and improvement of the human environment, for the benefit of all the people and for their posterity.

Principles

States the common conviction that:

Principle 1

Man has the fundamental right to freedom, equality and adequate conditions of life, in an environment of a quality that permits a life of dignity and well-being, and he bears a solemn responsibility to protect and improve the environment for present and future generations. In this respect, policies promoting or perpetuating apartheid, racial segregation, discrimination, colonial and other forms of oppression and foreign domination stand condemned and must be eliminated.

Principle 2

The natural resources of the earth, including the air, water, land, flora and fauna and especially representative samples of natural ecosystems, must be safeguarded for the benefit of present and future generations through careful planning or management, as appropriate.

Principle 3

The capacity of the earth to produce vital renewable resources must be maintained and, wherever practicable, restored or improved.

Principle 4

Man has a special responsibility to safeguard and wisely manage the heritage of wildlife and its habitat, which are now gravely imperilled by a combination of adverse factors. Nature conservation, including wildlife, must therefore receive importance in planning for economic development.

Principle 5

The non-renewable resources of the earth must be employed in such a way as to guard against the danger of their future exhaustion and to ensure that benefits from such employment are shared by all mankind.

Principle 6

The discharge of toxic substances or of other substances and the release of heat, in such quantities or concentrations as to exceed the capacity of the environment to render them harmless, must be halted in order to ensure that serious or irreversible damage is not inflicted upon ecosystems. The just struggle of the peoples of ill countries against pollution should be supported.

Principle 7

States shall take all possible steps to prevent pollution of the seas by substances that are liable to create hazards to human health, to harm living resources and marine life, to damage amenities or to interfere with other legitimate uses of the sea.

Principle 8

Economic and social development is essential for ensuring a favorable living and working environment for man and for creating conditions on earth that are necessary for the improvement of the quality of life.

Principle 9

Environmental deficiencies generated by the conditions of under-development and natural disasters pose grave problems and can best be remedied by accelerated development through the transfer of substantial quantities of financial and technological assistance as a supplement to the domestic effort of the developing countries and such timely assistance as may be required.

Principle 10

For the developing countries, stability of prices and adequate earnings for primary commodities and raw materials are essential to environmental management, since economic factors as well as ecological processes must be taken into account.

Principle 11

The environmental policies of all States should enhance and not adversely affect the present or future development potential of developing countries, nor should they hamper the attainment of better living conditions for all, and appropriate steps should be taken by States and international organizations with a view to reaching agreement on meeting the possible national and international economic consequences resulting from the application of environmental measures.

Principle 12

Resources should be made available to preserve and improve the environment, taking into account the circumstances and particular requirements of developing countries and any costs which may emanate- from their incorporating environmental safeguards into their development planning and the need for making available to them, upon their request, additional international technical and financial assistance for this purpose.

Principle 13

In order to achieve a more rational management of resources and thus to improve the environment, States should adopt an integrated and coordinated approach to their development planning so as to ensure that development is compatible with the need to protect and improve environment for the benefit of their population.

Principle 14

Rational planning constitutes an essential tool for reconciling any conflict between the needs of development and the need to protect and improve the environment.

Principle 15

Planning must be applied to human settlements and urbanization with a view to avoiding adverse effects on the environment and obtaining maximum social, economic and environmental benefits for all. In this respect projects which are designed for colonialist and racist domination must be abandoned.

Principle 16

Demographic policies which are without prejudice to basic human rights and which are deemed appropriate by Governments concerned should be applied in those regions where the rate of population growth or excessive population concentrations are likely to have adverse effects on the environment of the human environment and impede development.

Principle 17

Appropriate national institutions must be entrusted with the task of planning, managing or controlling the 9 environmental resources of States with a view to enhancing environmental quality.

Principle 18

Science and technology, as part of their contribution to economic and social development, must be applied to the identification, avoidance and control of environmental risks and the solution of environmental problems and for the common good of mankind.

Principle 19

Education in environmental matters, for the younger generation as well as adults, giving due consideration to the underprivileged, is essential in order to broaden the basis for an enlightened opinion and responsible conduct by individuals, enterprises and communities in protecting and improving the environment in its full human dimension. It is also essential that mass media of communications avoid contributing to the deterioration of the environment, but, on the contrary, disseminates information of an educational nature on the need to project and improve the environment in order to enable mal to develop in every respect.

Principle 20

Scientific research and development in the context of environmental problems, both national and multinational, must be promoted in all countries, especially the developing countries. In this connection, the free flow of up-to-date scientific information and transfer of experience must be supported and assisted, to facilitate the solution of environmental problems; environmental technologies should be made available to developing countries on terms which would encourage their wide dissemination without constituting an economic burden on the developing countries.

Principle 21

States have, in accordance with the Charter of the United Nations and the principles of international law, the sovereign right to exploit their own resources pursuant to their own environmental policies, and the responsibility to ensure that activities within their jurisdiction or control do not cause damage to the environment of other States or of areas beyond the limits of national jurisdiction.

Principle 22

States shall cooperate to develop further the international law regarding liability and compensation for the victims of pollution and other environmental damage caused by activities within the jurisdiction or control of such States to areas beyond their jurisdiction.

Principle 23

Without prejudice to such criteria as may be agreed upon by the international community, or to standards which will have to be determined nationally, it will be essential in all cases to consider the systems of values prevailing in each country, and the extent of the applicability of standards which are valid for the most advanced countries but which may be inappropriate and of unwarranted social cost for the developing countries.

Principle 24

International matters concerning the protection and improvement of the environment should be handled in a cooperative spirit by all countries, big and small, on an equal footing.

Cooperation through multilateral or bilateral arrangements or other appropriate means is essential to effectively control, prevent, reduce and eliminate adverse environmental effects resulting from activities conducted in all spheres, in such a way that due account is taken of the sovereignty and interests of all States.

Principle 25

States shall ensure that international organizations play a coordinated, efficient and dynamic role for the protection and improvement of the environment.

Principle 26

Man and his environment must be spared the effects of nuclear weapons and all other means of mass destruction. States must strive to reach prompt agreement, in the relevant international organs, on the elimination and complete destruction of such weapons.

1.2. Rio Declaration 1992

Report of the United Nations Conference on Environment and Development (Rio de Janeiro, 3-14 June 1992), 12 August 1992, A/CONF.151/26 (Vol. I), Annex I

The United Nations Conference on Environment and Development,

Having met at Rio de Janeiro from 3 to 14 June 1992,

Reaffirming the Declaration of the United Nations Conference on the Human Environment, adopted at Stockholm on 16 June 1972, a/ and seeking to build upon it,

With the goal of establishing a new and equitable global partnership through the creation of new levels of cooperation among States, key sectors of societies and people,

Working towards international agreements which respect the interests of all and protect the integrity of the global environmental and developmental system,

Recognizing the integral and interdependent nature of the Earth, our home,

Proclaims that:

Principle 1

Human beings are at the centre of concerns for sustainable development. They are entitled to a healthy and productive life in harmony with nature.

Principle 2

States have, in accordance with the Charter of the United Nations and the principles of international law, the sovereign right to exploit their own resources pursuant to their own environmental and developmental policies, and the responsibility to ensure that activities within their jurisdiction or control do not cause damage to the environment of other States or of areas beyond the limits of national jurisdiction.

Principle 3

The right to development must be fulfilled so as to equitably meet developmental and environmental needs of present and future generations.

Principle 4

In order to achieve sustainable development, environmental protection shall constitute an integral part of the development process and cannot be considered in isolation from it.

Principle 5

All States and all people shall cooperate in the essential task of eradicating poverty as an indispensable requirement for sustainable development, in order to decrease the disparities in standards of living and better meet the needs of the majority of the people of the world.

Principle 6

The special situation and needs of developing countries, particularly the least developed and those most environmentally vulnerable, shall be given special priority. International actions in the field of environment and development should also address the interests and needs of all countries.

Principle 7

States shall cooperate in a spirit of global partnership to conserve, protect and restore the health and integrity of the Earth's ecosystem. In view of the different contributions to global environmental degradation, States have common but differentiated responsibilities. The developed countries acknowledge the responsibility that they bear in the international pursuit of sustainable development in view of the pressures their societies place on the global environment and of the technologies and financial resources they command.

Principle 8

To achieve sustainable development and a higher quality of life for all people, States should reduce and eliminate unsustainable patterns of production and consumption and promote appropriate demographic policies.

Principle 9

States should cooperate to strengthen endogenous capacity-building for sustainable development by improving scientific understanding through exchanges of scientific and technological knowledge, and by enhancing the development, adaptation, diffusion and transfer of technologies, including new and innovative technologies.

Principle 10

Environmental issues are best handled with the participation of all concerned citizens, at the relevant level. At the national level, each individual shall have appropriate access to information concerning the environment that is held by public authorities, including information on hazardous materials and activities in their communities, and the opportunity to participate in decision-making processes. States shall facilitate and encourage public awareness and participation by making information widely available. Effective access to judicial and administrative proceedings, including redress and remedy, shall be provided.

Principle 11

States shall enact effective environmental legislation. Environmental standards, management objectives and priorities should reflect the environmental and developmental context to which they apply. Standards applied by some countries may be inappropriate and of unwarranted economic and social cost to other countries, in particular developing countries.

Principle 12

States should cooperate to promote a supportive and open international economic system that would lead to economic growth and sustainable development in all countries, to better address the problems of environmental degradation. Trade policy measures for environmental purposes should not constitute a means of arbitrary or unjustifiable discrimination or a disguised restriction on international trade. Unilateral actions to deal with environmental challenges outside the jurisdiction of the importing country should be avoided.

Environmental measures addressing transboundary or global environmental problems should, as far as possible, be based on an international consensus.

Principle 13

States shall develop national law regarding liability and compensation for the victims of pollution and other environmental damage. States shall also cooperate in an expeditious and more determined manner to develop further international law regarding liability and compensation for adverse effects of environmental damage caused by activities within their jurisdiction or control to areas beyond their jurisdiction.

Principle 14

States should effectively cooperate to discourage or prevent the relocation and transfer to other States of any activities and substances that cause severe environmental degradation or are found to be harmful to human health.

Principle 15

In order to protect the environment, the precautionary approach shall be widely applied by States according to their capabilities. Where there are threats of serious or irreversible damage, lack of full scientific certainty shall not be used as a reason for postponing cost-effective measures to prevent environmental degradation.

Principle 16

National authorities should endeavour to promote the internalization of environmental costs and the use of economic instruments, taking into account the approach that the polluter should, in principle, bear the cost of pollution, with due regard to the public interest and without distorting international trade and investment.

Principle 17

Environmental impact assessment, as a national instrument, shall be undertaken for proposed activities that are likely to have a significant adverse impact on the environment and are subject to a decision of a competent national authority.

Principle 18

States shall immediately notify other States of any natural disasters or other emergencies that are likely to produce sudden harmful effects on the environment of those States. Every effort shall be made by the international community to help States so afflicted.

Principle 19

States shall provide prior and timely notification and relevant information to potentially affected States on activities that may have a significant adverse transboundary environmental effect and shall consult with those States at an early stage and in good faith.

Principle 20

Women have a vital role in environmental management and development.

Their full participation is therefore essential to achieve sustainable development.

Principle 21

The creativity, ideals and courage of the youth of the world should be mobilized to forge a global partnership in order to achieve sustainable development and ensure a better future for all.

Principle 22

Indigenous people and their communities and other local communities have a vital role in environmental management and development because of their knowledge and traditional practices. States should recognize and duly support their identity, culture and interests and enable their effective participation in the achievement of sustainable development.

Principle 23

The environment and natural resources of people under oppression, domination and occupation shall be protected.

Principle 24

Warfare is inherently destructive of sustainable development. States shall therefore respect international law providing protection for the environment in times of armed conflict and cooperate in its further development, as necessary.

Principle 25

Peace, development and environmental protection are interdependent and indivisible.

Principle 26

States shall resolve all their environmental disputes peacefully and by appropriate means in accordance with the Charter of the United Nations.

Principle 27

States and people shall cooperate in good faith and in a spirit of partnership in the fulfilment of the principles embodied in this Declaration and in the further development of international law in the field of sustainable development.

1.3. 2030 Agenda for Sustainable Development

UN General Assembly Resolution 70/1, Transforming our World: The 2030 Agenda for Sustainable Development, 21 October 2015, A/RES/70/1

Preamble[1]

This Agenda is a plan of action for people, planet and prosperity. It also seeks to strengthen universal peace in larger freedom. We recognize that eradicating poverty in all its forms and dimensions, including extreme poverty, is the greatest global challenge and an indispensable requirement for sustainable development.

All countries and all stakeholders, acting in collaborative partnership, will implement this plan. We are resolved to free the human race from the tyranny of poverty and want and to heal and secure our planet. We are determined to take the bold and transformative steps which are urgently needed to shift the world on to a sustainable and resilient path. As we embark on this collective journey, we pledge that no one will be left behind.

The 17 Sustainable Development Goals and 169 targets which we are announcing today demonstrate the scale and ambition of this new universal Agenda. They seek to build on the Millennium Development Goals and complete what they did not achieve. They seek to realize the human rights of all and to achieve gender equality and the empowerment of all women and girls. They are integrated and indivisible and balance the three dimensions of sustainable development: the economic, social and environmental.

The Goals and targets will stimulate action over the next 15 years in areas of critical importance for humanity and the planet.

People

We are determined to end poverty and hunger, in all their forms and dimensions, and to ensure that all human beings can fulfil their potential in dignity and equality and in a healthy environment.

Planet

We are determined to protect the planet from degradation, including through sustainable consumption and production, sustainably managing its natural resources and taking urgent action on climate change, so that it can support the needs of the present and future generations.

Prosperity

We are determined to ensure that all human beings can enjoy prosperous and fulfilling lives and that economic, social and technological progress occurs in harmony with nature.

Peace

We are determined to foster peaceful, just and inclusive societies which are free from fear and violence. There can be no sustainable development without peace and no peace without sustainable development.

Partnership

We are determined to mobilize the means required to implement this Agenda through a revitalized Global Partnership for Sustainable Development, based on a spirit of strengthened global solidarity, focused in particular on the needs of the poorest and most vulnerable and with the participation of all countries, all stakeholders and all people.

The interlinkages and integrated nature of the Sustainable Development Goals are of crucial importance in ensuring that the purpose of the new Agenda is realized. If we realize our ambitions across the full extent of the Agenda, the lives of all will be profoundly improved and our world will be transformed for the better.

Declaration

Introduction

1. We, the Heads of State and Government and High Representatives, meeting at United Nations Headquarters in New York from 25 to 27 September 2015 as the Organization celebrates its seventieth anniversary, have decided today on new global Sustainable Development Goals.
2. On behalf of the peoples we serve, we have adopted a historic decision on a comprehensive, far-reaching and people-centred set of universal and transformative Goals and targets. We commit ourselves to working tirelessly for the full implementation of this Agenda by 2030. We recognize that eradicating poverty in all its forms and dimensions, including extreme poverty, is the greatest global challenge and an indispensable requirement for sustainable development. We are committed to achieving sustainable development in its three dimensions — economic, social and environmental — in a balanced and integrated manner. We will also build upon the achievements of the Millennium Development Goals and seek to address their unfinished business.
3. We resolve, between now and 2030, to end poverty and hunger everywhere; to combat inequalities within and among countries; to build peaceful, just and inclusive societies; to protect human rights and promote gender equality and the empowerment of women and girls; and to ensure the lasting protection of the planet and its natural resources. We resolve also to create conditions for sustainable, inclusive and sustained economic growth, shared prosperity and decent work for all, taking into ac-

1 Footnotes omitted [the editors].

count different levels of national development and capacities.

4. As we embark on this great collective journey, we pledge that no one will be left behind. Recognizing that the dignity of the human person is fundamental, we wish to see the Goals and targets met for all nations and peoples and for all segments of society. And we will endeavour to reach the furthest behind first.

5. This is an Agenda of unprecedented scope and significance. It is accepted by all countries and is applicable to all, taking into account different national realities, capacities and levels of development and respecting national policies and priorities. These are universal goals and targets which involve the entire world, developed and developing countries alike. They are integrated and indivisible and balance the three dimensions of sustainable development.

6. The Goals and targets are the result of over two years of intensive public consultation and engagement with civil society and other stakeholders around the world, which paid particular attention to the voices of the poorest and most vulnerable. This consultation included valuable work done by the Open Working Group of the General Assembly on Sustainable Development Goals and by the United Nations, whose Secretary-General provided a synthesis report in December 2014.

Our vision

7. In these Goals and targets, we are setting out a supremely ambitious and transformational vision. We envisage a world free of poverty, hunger, disease and want, where all life can thrive. We envisage a world free of fear and violence. A world with universal literacy. A world with equitable and universal access to quality education at all levels, to health care and social protection, where physical, mental and social well-being are assured. A world where we reaffirm our commitments regarding the human right to safe drinking water and sanitation and where there is improved hygiene; and where food is sufficient, safe, affordable and nutritious. A world where human habitats are safe, resilient and sustainable and where there is universal access to affordable, reliable and sustainable energy.

8. We envisage a world of universal respect for human rights and human dignity, the rule of law, justice, equality and non-discrimination; of respect for race, ethnicity and cultural diversity; and of equal opportunity permitting the full realization of human potential and contributing to shared prosperity. A world which invests in its children and in which every child grows up free from violence and exploitation. A world in which every woman and girl enjoys full gender equality and all legal, social and economic barriers to their empowerment have been removed. A just, equitable, tolerant, open and socially inclusive world in which the needs of the most vulnerable are met.

9. We envisage a world in which every country enjoys sustained, inclusive and sustainable economic growth and decent work for all. A world in which consumption and production patterns and use of all natural resources — from air to land, from rivers, lakes and aquifers to oceans and seas — are sustainable. One in which democracy, good governance and the rule of law, as well as an enabling environment at the national and international levels, are essential for sustainable development, including sustained and inclusive economic growth, social development, environmental protection and the eradication of poverty and hunger. One in which development and the application of technology are climate-sensitive, respect biodiversity and are resilient. One in which humanity lives in harmony with nature and in which wildlife and other living species are protected.

Our shared principles and commitments

10. The new Agenda is guided by the purposes and principles of the Charter of the United Nations, including full respect for international law. It is grounded in the Universal Declaration of Human Rights, international human rights treaties, the Millennium Declaration and the 2005 World Summit Outcome. It is informed by other instruments such as the Declaration on the Right to Development.

11. We reaffirm the outcomes of all major United Nations conferences and summits which have laid a solid foundation for sustainable development and have helped to shape the new Agenda. These include the Rio Declaration on Environment and Development, the World Summit on Sustainable Development, the World Summit for Social Development, the Programme of Action of the International Conference on Population and Development, the Beijing Platform for Action and the United Nations Conference on Sustainable Development. We also reaffirm the follow-up to these conferences, including the outcomes of the Fourth United Nations Conference on the Least Developed Countries, the third International Conference on Small Island Developing States, the second United Nations Conference on Landlocked Developing Countries and the Third United Nations World Conference on Disaster Risk Reduction.

12. We reaffirm all the principles of the Rio Declaration on Environment and Development, including, inter alia, the principle of common but differentiated responsibilities, as set out in principle 7 thereof.

13. The challenges and commitments identified at these major conferences and summits are interrelated and call for integrated solutions. To address them effectively, a new approach is needed. Sustainable development recognizes that eradicating poverty in all its forms and dimensions, combating inequality within and among countries, preserving the planet, creating sustained, inclusive and sustainable economic growth and fostering social inclusion are linked to each other and are interdependent.

Our world today

14. We are meeting at a time of immense challenges to sustainable development. Billions of our citizens

continue to live in poverty and are denied a life of dignity. There are rising inequalities within and among countries. There are enormous disparities of opportunity, wealth and power. Gender inequality remains a key challenge. Unemployment, particularly youth unemployment, is a major concern. Global health threats, more frequent and intense natural disasters, spiralling conflict, violent extremism, terrorism and related humanitarian crises and forced displacement of people threaten to reverse much of the development progress made in recent decades. Natural resource depletion and adverse impacts of environmental degradation, including desertification, drought, land degradation, freshwater scarcity and loss of biodiversity, add to and exacerbate the list of challenges which humanity faces. Climate change is one of the greatest challenges of our time and its adverse impacts undermine the ability of all countries to achieve sustainable development. Increases in global temperature, sea level rise, ocean acidification and other climate change impacts are seriously affecting coastal areas and low-lying coastal countries, including many least developed countries and small island developing States. The survival of many societies, and of the biological support systems of the planet, is at risk.

15. It is also, however, a time of immense opportunity. Significant progress has been made in meeting many development challenges. Within the past generation, hundreds of millions of people have emerged from extreme poverty. Access to education has greatly increased for both boys and girls. The spread of information and communications technology and global interconnectedness has great potential to accelerate human progress, to bridge the digital divide and to develop knowledge societies, as does scientific and technological innovation across areas as diverse as medicine and energy.

16. Almost 15 years ago, the Millennium Development Goals were agreed. These provided an important framework for development and significant progress has been made in a number of areas. But the progress has been uneven, particularly in Africa, least developed countries, landlocked developing countries and small island developing States, and some of the Millennium Development Goals remain off-track, in particular those related to maternal, newborn and child health and to reproductive health. We recommit ourselves to the full realization of all the Millennium Development Goals, including the off-track Millennium Development Goals, in particular by providing focused and scaled-up assistance to least developed countries and other countries in special situations, in line with relevant support programmes. The new Agenda builds on the Millennium Development Goals and seeks to complete what they did not achieve, particularly in reaching the most vulnerable.

17. In its scope, however, the framework we are announcing today goes far beyond the Millennium Development Goals. Alongside continuing development priorities such as poverty eradication, health, education and food security and nutrition, it sets out a wide range of economic, social and environmental objectives. It also promises more peaceful and inclusive societies. It also, crucially, defines means of implementation. Reflecting the integrated approach that we have decided on, there are deep interconnections and many cross-cutting elements across the new Goals and targets.

The new Agenda

18. We are announcing today 17 Sustainable Development Goals with 169 associated targets which are integrated and indivisible. Never before have world leaders pledged common action and endeavour across such a broad and universal policy agenda. We are setting out together on the path towards sustainable development, devoting ourselves collectively to the pursuit of global development and of "win-win" cooperation which can bring huge gains to all countries and all parts of the world. We reaffirm that every State has, and shall freely exercise, full permanent sovereignty over all its wealth, natural resources and economic activity. We will implement the Agenda for the full benefit of all, for today's generation and for future generations. In doing so, we reaffirm our commitment to international law and emphasize that the Agenda is to be implemented in a manner that is consistent with the rights and obligations of States under international law.

19. We reaffirm the importance of the Universal Declaration of Human Rights, as well as other international instruments relating to human rights and international law. We emphasize the responsibilities of all States, in conformity with the Charter of the United Nations, to respect, protect and promote human rights and fundamental freedoms for all, without distinction of any kind as to race, colour, sex, language, religion, political or other opinion, national or social origin, property, birth, disability or other status.

20. Realizing gender equality and the empowerment of women and girls will make a crucial contribution to progress across all the Goals and targets. The achievement of full human potential and of sustainable development is not possible if one half of humanity continues to be denied its full human rights and opportunities. Women and girls must enjoy equal access to quality education, economic resources and political participation as well as equal opportunities with men and boys for employment, leadership and decision-making at all levels. We will work for a significant increase in investments to close the gender gap and strengthen support for institutions in relation to gender equality and the empowerment of women at the global, regional and national levels. All forms of discrimination and violence against women and girls will be eliminated, including through the engagement of men and boys. The systematic mainstreaming of a gender perspective in the implementation of the Agenda is crucial.

21. The new Goals and targets will come into effect on 1 January 2016 and will guide the decisions we

take over the next 15 years. All of us will work to implement the Agenda within our own countries and at the regional and global levels, taking into account different national realities, capacities and levels of development and respecting national policies and priorities. We will respect national policy space for sustained, inclusive and sustainable economic growth, in particular for developing States, while remaining consistent with relevant international rules and commitments. We acknowledge also the importance of the regional and subregional dimensions, regional economic integration and interconnectivity in sustainable development. Regional and subregional frameworks can facilitate the effective translation of sustainable development policies into concrete action at the national level.

22. Each country faces specific challenges in its pursuit of sustainable development. The most vulnerable countries and, in particular, African countries, least developed countries, landlocked developing countries and small island developing States, deserve special attention, as do countries in situations of conflict and post-conflict countries. There are also serious challenges within many middle-income countries.

23. People who are vulnerable must be empowered. Those whose needs are reflected in the Agenda include all children, youth, persons with disabilities (of whom more than 80 per cent live in poverty), people living with HIV/AIDS, older persons, indigenous peoples, refugees and internally displaced persons and migrants. We resolve to take further effective measures and actions, in conformity with international law, to remove obstacles and constraints, strengthen support and meet the special needs of people living in areas affected by complex humanitarian emergencies and in areas affected by terrorism.

24. We are committed to ending poverty in all its forms and dimensions, including by eradicating extreme poverty by 2030. All people must enjoy a basic standard of living, including through social protection systems. We are also determined to end hunger and to achieve food security as a matter of priority and to end all forms of malnutrition. In this regard, we reaffirm the important role and inclusive nature of the Committee on World Food Security and welcome the Rome Declaration on Nutrition and the Framework for Action. We will devote resources to developing rural areas and sustainable agriculture and fisheries, supporting smallholder farmers, especially women farmers, herders and fishers in developing countries, particularly least developed countries.

25. We commit to providing inclusive and equitable quality education at all levels — early childhood, primary, secondary, tertiary, technical and vocational training. All people, irrespective of sex, age, race or ethnicity, and persons with disabilities, migrants, indigenous peoples, children and youth, especially those in vulnerable situations, should have access to life-long learning opportunities that help them to acquire the knowledge and skills needed to exploit opportunities and to participate fully in society. We will strive to provide children and youth with a nurturing environment for the full realization of their rights and capabilities, helping our countries to reap the demographic dividend, including through safe schools and cohesive communities and families.

26. To promote physical and mental health and well-being, and to extend life expectancy for all, we must achieve universal health coverage and access to quality health care. No one must be left behind. We commit to accelerating the progress made to date in reducing newborn, child and maternal mortality by ending all such preventable deaths before 2030. We are committed to ensuring universal access to sexual and reproductive health-care services, including for family planning, information and education. We will equally accelerate the pace of progress made in fighting malaria, HIV/AIDS, tuberculosis, hepatitis, Ebola and other communicable diseases and epidemics, including by addressing growing anti-microbial resistance and the problem of unattended diseases affecting developing countries. We are committed to the prevention and treatment of non-communicable diseases, including behavioural, developmental and neurological disorders, which constitute a major challenge for sustainable development.

27. We will seek to build strong economic foundations for all our countries. Sustained, inclusive and sustainable economic growth is essential for prosperity. This will only be possible if wealth is shared and income inequality is addressed. We will work to build dynamic, sustainable, innovative and people-centred economies, promoting youth employment and women's economic empowerment, in particular, and decent work for all. We will eradicate forced labour and human trafficking and end child labour in all its forms. All countries stand to benefit from having a healthy and well-educated workforce with the knowledge and skills needed for productive and fulfilling work and full participation in society. We will strengthen the productive capacities of least developed countries in all sectors, including through structural transformation. We will adopt policies which increase productive capacities, productivity and productive employment; financial inclusion; sustainable agriculture, pastoralist and fisheries development; sustainable industrial development; universal access to affordable, reliable, sustainable and modern energy services; sustainable transport systems; and quality and resilient infrastructure.

28. We commit to making fundamental changes in the way that our societies produce and consume goods and services. Governments, international organizations, the business sector and other non-State actors and individuals must contribute to changing unsustainable consumption and production patterns, including through the mobilization, from all sources, of financial and technical assistance to strengthen developing countries' scientific, technological and innovative capacities to move towards more sustainable patterns of consumption and

production. We encourage the implementation of the 10-Year Framework of Programmes on Sustainable Consumption and Production Patterns. All countries take action, with developed countries taking the lead, taking into account the development and capabilities of developing countries.

29. We recognize the positive contribution of migrants for inclusive growth and sustainable development. We also recognize that international migration is a multidimensional reality of major relevance for the development of countries of origin, transit and destination, which requires coherent and comprehensive responses. We will cooperate internationally to ensure safe, orderly and regular migration involving full respect for human rights and the humane treatment of migrants regardless of migration status, of refugees and of displaced persons. Such cooperation should also strengthen the resilience of communities hosting refugees, particularly in developing countries. We underline the right of migrants to return to their country of citizenship, and recall that States must ensure that their returning nationals are duly received.

30. States are strongly urged to refrain from promulgating and applying any unilateral economic, financial or trade measures not in accordance with international law and the Charter of the United Nations that impede the full achievement of economic and social development, particularly in developing countries.

31. We acknowledge that the United Nations Framework Convention on Climate Change is the primary international, intergovernmental forum for negotiating the global response to climate change. We are determined to address decisively the threat posed by climate change and environmental degradation. The global nature of climate change calls for the widest possible international cooperation aimed at accelerating the reduction of global greenhouse gas emissions and addressing adaptation to the adverse impacts of climate change. We note with grave concern the significant gap between the aggregate effect of parties' mitigation pledges in terms of global annual emissions of greenhouse gases by 2020 and aggregate emission pathways consistent with having a likely chance of holding the increase in global average temperature below 2 degrees Celsius or 1.5 degrees Celsius above pre-industrial levels.

32. Looking ahead to the twenty-first session of the Conference of the Parties in Paris, we underscore the commitment of all States to work for an ambitious and universal climate agreement. We reaffirm that the protocol, another legal instrument or agreed outcome with legal force under the Convention applicable to all parties shall address in a balanced manner, inter alia, mitigation, adaptation, finance, technology development and transfer and capacity- building; and transparency of action and support.

33. We recognize that social and economic development depends on the sustainable management of our planet's natural resources. We are therefore determined to conserve and sustainably use oceans and seas, freshwater resources, as well as forests, mountains and drylands and to protect biodiversity, ecosystems and wildlife. We are also determined to promote sustainable tourism, to tackle water scarcity and water pollution, to strengthen cooperation on desertification, dust storms, land degradation and drought and to promote resilience and disaster risk reduction. In this regard, we look forward to the thirteenth meeting of the Conference of the Parties to the Convention on Biological Diversity to be held in Mexico.

34. We recognize that sustainable urban development and management are crucial to the quality of life of our people. We will work with local authorities and communities to renew and plan our cities and human settlements so as to foster community cohesion and personal security and to stimulate innovation and employment. We will reduce the negative impacts of urban activities and of chemicals which are hazardous for human health and the environment, including through the environmentally sound management and safe use of chemicals, the reduction and recycling of waste and the more efficient use of water and energy. And we will work to minimize the impact of cities on the global climate system. We will also take account of population trends and projections in our national rural and urban development strategies and policies. We look forward to the upcoming United Nations Conference on Housing and Sustainable Urban Development to be held in Quito.

35. Sustainable development cannot be realized without peace and security; and peace and security will be at risk without sustainable development. The new Agenda recognizes the need to build peaceful, just and inclusive societies that provide equal access to justice and that are based on respect for human rights (including the right to development), on effective rule of law and good governance at all levels and on transparent, effective and accountable institutions. Factors which give rise to violence, insecurity and injustice, such as inequality, corruption, poor governance and illicit financial and arms flows, are addressed in the Agenda. We must redouble our efforts to resolve or prevent conflict and to support post-conflict countries, including through ensuring that women have a role in peacebuilding and State-building. We call for further effective measures and actions to be taken, in conformity with international law, to remove the obstacles to the full realization of the right of self-determination of peoples living under colonial and foreign occupation, which continue to adversely affect their economic and social development as well as their environment.

36. We pledge to foster intercultural understanding, tolerance, mutual respect and an ethic of global citizenship and shared responsibility. We acknowledge the natural and cultural diversity of the world and recognize that all cultures and civilizations can contribute to, and are crucial enablers of, sustainable development.

37. Sport is also an important enabler of sustainable development. We recognize the growing contribu-

tion of sport to the realization of development and peace in its promotion of tolerance and respect and the contributions it makes to the empowerment of women and of young people, individuals and communities as well as to health, education and social inclusion objectives.

38. We reaffirm, in accordance with the Charter of the United Nations, the need to respect the territorial integrity and political independence of States.

Means of implementation

39. The scale and ambition of the new Agenda requires a revitalized Global Partnership to ensure its implementation. We fully commit to this. This Partnership will work in a spirit of global solidarity, in particular solidarity with the poorest and with people in vulnerable situations. It will facilitate an intensive global engagement in support of implementation of all the Goals and targets, bringing together Governments, the private sector, civil society, the United Nations system and other actors and mobilizing all available resources.

40. The means of implementation targets under Goal 17 and under each Sustainable Development Goal are key to realizing our Agenda and are of equal importance with the other Goals and targets. The Agenda, including the Sustainable Development Goals, can be met within the framework of a revitalized Global Partnership for Sustainable Development, supported by the concrete policies and actions as outlined in the outcome document of the third International Conference on Financing for Development, held in Addis Ababa from 13 to 16 July 2015. We welcome the endorsement by the General Assembly of the Addis Ababa Action Agenda, which is an integral part of the 2030 Agenda for Sustainable Development. We recognize that the full implementation of the Addis Ababa Action Agenda is critical for the realization of the Sustainable Development Goals and targets.

41. We recognize that each country has primary responsibility for its own economic and social development. The new Agenda deals with the means required for implementation of the Goals and targets. We recognize that these will include the mobilization of financial resources as well as capacity-building and the transfer of environmentally sound technologies to developing countries on favourable terms, including on concessional and preferential terms, as mutually agreed. Public finance, both domestic and international, will play a vital role in providing essential services and public goods and in catalysing other sources of finance. We acknowledge the role of the diverse private sector, ranging from micro-enterprises to cooperatives to multinationals, and that of civil society organizations and philanthropic organizations in the implementation of the new Agenda.

42. We support the implementation of relevant strategies and programmes of action, including the Istanbul Declaration and Programme of Action, the SIDS Accelerated Modalities of Action (SAMOA) Pathway and the Vienna Programme of Action for Landlocked Developing Countries for the Decade 2014-2024, and reaffirm the importance of supporting the African Union's Agenda 2063 and the programme of the New Partnership for Africa's Development, all of which are integral to the new Agenda. We recognize the major challenge to the achievement of durable peace and sustainable development in countries in conflict and post-conflict situations.

43. We emphasize that international public finance plays an important role in complementing the efforts of countries to mobilize public resources domestically, especially in the poorest and most vulnerable countries with limited domestic resources. An important use of international public finance, including official development assistance (ODA), is to catalyse additional resource mobilization from other sources, public and private. ODA providers reaffirm their respective commitments, including the commitment by many developed countries to achieve the target of 0.7 per cent of gross national income for official development assistance (ODA/GNI) to developing countries and 0.15 per cent to 0.2 per cent of ODA/GNI to least developed countries.

44. We acknowledge the importance for international financial institutions to support, in line with their mandates, the policy space of each country, in particular developing countries. We recommit to broadening and strengthening the voice and participation of developing countries — including African countries, least developed countries, landlocked developing countries, small island developing States and middle-income countries — in international economic decision-making, norm-setting and global economic governance.

45. We acknowledge also the essential role of national parliaments through their enactment of legislation and adoption of budgets and their role in ensuring accountability for the effective implementation of our commitments. Governments and public institutions will also work closely on implementation with regional and local authorities, subregional institutions, international institutions, academia, philanthropic organizations, volunteer groups and others.

46. We underline the important role and comparative advantage of an adequately resourced, relevant, coherent, efficient and effective United Nations system in supporting the achievement of the Sustainable Development Goals and sustainable development. While stressing the importance of strengthened national ownership and leadership at the country level, we express our support for the ongoing dialogue in the Economic and Social Council on the longer-term positioning of the United Nations development system in the context of this Agenda.

Follow-up and review

47. Our Governments have the primary responsibility for follow-up and review, at the national, regional and global levels, in relation to the progress made in implementing the Goals and targets over the coming 15 years. To support accountability to our

citizens, we will provide for systematic follow-up and review at the various levels, as set out in this Agenda and the Addis Ababa Action Agenda. The high-level political forum under the auspices of the General Assembly and the Economic and Social Council will have the central role in overseeing follow-up and review at the global level.

48. Indicators are being developed to assist this work. Quality, accessible, timely and reliable disaggregated data will be needed to help with the measurement of progress and to ensure that no one is left behind. Such data is key to decision-making. Data and information from existing reporting mechanisms should be used where possible. We agree to intensify our efforts to strengthen statistical capacities in developing countries, particularly African countries, least developed countries, landlocked developing countries, small island developing States and middle-income countries. We are committed to developing broader measures of progress to complement gross domestic product.

A call for action to change our world

49. Seventy years ago, an earlier generation of world leaders came together to create the United Nations. From the ashes of war and division they fashioned this Organization and the values of peace, dialogue and international cooperation which underpin it. The supreme embodiment of those values is the Charter of the United Nations.

50. Today we are also taking a decision of great historic significance. We resolve to build a better future for all people, including the millions who have been denied the chance to lead decent, dignified and rewarding lives and to achieve their full human potential. We can be the first generation to succeed in ending poverty; just as we may be the last to have a chance of saving the planet. The world will be a better place in 2030 if we succeed in our objectives.

51. What we are announcing today — an Agenda for global action for the next 15 years — is a charter for people and planet in the twenty-first century. Children and young women and men are critical agents of change and will find in the new Goals a platform to channel their infinite capacities for activism into the creation of a better world.

52. “We the peoples” are the celebrated opening words of the Charter of the United Nations. It is “we the peoples” who are embarking today on the road to 2030. Our journey will involve Governments as well as parliaments, the United Nations system and other international institutions, local authorities, indigenous peoples, civil society, business and the private sector, the scientific and academic community — and all people. Millions have already engaged with, and will own, this Agenda. It is an Agenda of the people, by the people and for the people — and this, we believe, will ensure its success.

53. The future of humanity and of our planet lies in our hands. It lies also in the hands of today’s younger generation who will pass the torch to future generations. We have mapped the road to sustainable development; it will be for all of us to ensure that the journey is successful and its gains irreversible.

Sustainable Development Goals and targets

54. Following an inclusive process of intergovernmental negotiations, and based on the proposal of the Open Working Group on Sustainable Development Goals,1 which includes a chapeau contextualizing the latter, set out below are the Goals and targets which we have agreed.

55. The Sustainable Development Goals and targets are integrated and indivisible, global in nature and universally applicable, taking into account different national realities, capacities and levels of development and respecting national policies and priorities. Targets are defined as aspirational and global, with each Government setting its own national targets guided by the global level of ambition but taking into account national circumstances. Each Government will also decide how these aspirational and global targets should be incorporated into national planning processes, policies and strategies. It is important to recognize the link between sustainable development and other relevant ongoing processes in the economic, social and environmental fields.

56. In deciding upon these Goals and targets, we recognize that each country faces specific challenges to achieve sustainable development, and we underscore the special challenges facing the most vulnerable countries and, in particular, African countries, least developed countries, landlocked developing countries and small island developing States, as well as the specific challenges facing the middle-income countries. Countries in situations of conflict also need special attention.

57. We recognize that baseline data for several of the targets remains unavailable, and we call for increased support for strengthening data collection and capacity-building in Member States, to develop national and global baselines where they do not yet exist. We commit to addressing this gap in data collection so as to better inform the measurement of progress, in particular for those targets below which do not have clear numerical targets.

58. We encourage ongoing efforts by States in other forums to address key issues which pose potential challenges to the implementation of our Agenda, and we respect the independent mandates of those processes. We intend that the Agenda and its implementation would support, and be without prejudice to, those other processes and the decisions taken therein.

59. We recognize that there are different approaches, visions, models and tools available to each country, in accordance with its national circumstances and priorities, to achieve sustainable development; and we reaffirm that planet Earth and its ecosystems are our common home and that “Mother Earth” is a common expression in a number of countries and regions.

Sustainable Development Goals

Goal 1. End poverty in all its forms everywhere

Goal 2. End hunger, achieve food security and improved nutrition and promote sustainable agriculture

Goal 3. Ensure healthy lives and promote well-being for all at all ages

Goal 4. Ensure inclusive and equitable quality education and promote lifelong learning opportunities for all

Goal 5. Achieve gender equality and empower all women and girls

Goal 6. Ensure availability and sustainable management of water and sanitation for all

Goal 7. Ensure access to affordable, reliable, sustainable and modern energy for all

Goal 8. Promote sustained, inclusive and sustainable economic growth, full and productive employment and decent work for all

Goal 9. Build resilient infrastructure, promote inclusive and sustainable industrialization and foster innovation

Goal 10. Reduce inequality within and among countries

Goal 11. Make cities and human settlements inclusive, safe, resilient and sustainable

Goal 12. Ensure sustainable consumption and production patterns

Goal 13. Take urgent action to combat climate change and its impacts*

Goal 14. Conserve and sustainably use the oceans, seas and marine resources for sustainable development

Goal 15. Protect, restore and promote sustainable use of terrestrial ecosystems, sustainably manage forests, combat desertification, and halt and reverse land degradation and halt biodiversity loss

Goal 16. Promote peaceful and inclusive societies for sustainable development, provide access to justice for all and build effective, accountable and inclusive institutions at all levels

Goal 17. Strengthen the means of implementation and revitalize the Global Partnership for Sustainable Development

Goal 1. End poverty in all its forms everywhere

1.1 By 2030, eradicate extreme poverty for all people everywhere, currently measured as people living on less than $1.25 a day

1.2 By 2030, reduce at least by half the proportion of men, women and children of all ages living in poverty in all its dimensions according to national definitions

1.3 Implement nationally appropriate social protection systems and measures for all, including floors, and by 2030 achieve substantial coverage of the poor and the vulnerable

1.4 By 2030, ensure that all men and women, in particular the poor and the vulnerable, have equal rights to economic resources, as well as access to basic services, ownership and control over land and other forms of property, inheritance, natural resources, appropriate new technology and financial services, including microfinance

1.5 By 2030, build the resilience of the poor and those in vulnerable situations and reduce their exposure and vulnerability to climate-related extreme events and other economic, social and environmental shocks and disasters

1.a Ensure significant mobilization of resources from a variety of sources, including through enhanced development cooperation, in order to provide adequate and predictable means for developing countries, in particular least developed countries, to implement programmes and policies to end poverty in all its dimensions

1.b Create sound policy frameworks at the national, regional and international levels, based on pro-poor and gender-sensitive development strategies, to support accelerated investment in poverty eradication actions

Goal 2. End hunger, achieve food security and improved nutrition and promote sustainable agriculture

2.1 By 2030, end hunger and ensure access by all people, in particular the poor and people in vulnerable situations, including infants, to safe, nutritious and sufficient food all year round

2.2 By 2030, end all forms of malnutrition, including achieving, by 2025, the internationally agreed targets on stunting and wasting in children under 5 years of age, and address the nutritional needs of adolescent girls, pregnant and lactating women and older persons

2.3 By 2030, double the agricultural productivity and incomes of small-scale food producers, in particular women, indigenous peoples, family farmers, pastoralists and fishers, including through secure and equal access to land, other productive resources and inputs, knowledge, financial services, markets and opportunities for value addition and non-farm employment

2.4 By 2030, ensure sustainable food production systems and implement resilient agricultural practices that increase productivity and production, that help maintain ecosystems, that strengthen capacity for adaptation to climate change, extreme weather, drought, flooding and other disasters and that progressively improve land and soil quality

2.5 By 2020, maintain the genetic diversity of seeds, cultivated plants and farmed and domesticated animals and their related wild species, including through soundly managed and diver-

* Acknowledging that the United Nations Framework Convention on Climate Change is the primary international, intergovernmental forum for negotiating the global response to climate change.

sified seed and plant banks at the national, regional and international levels, and promote access to and fair and equitable sharing of benefits arising from the utilization of genetic resources and associated traditional knowledge, as internationally agreed

2.a Increase investment, including through enhanced international cooperation, in rural infrastructure, agricultural research and extension services, technology development and plant and livestock gene banks in order to enhance agricultural productive capacity in developing countries, in particular least developed countries

2.b Correct and prevent trade restrictions and distortions in world agricultural markets, including through the parallel elimination of all forms of agricultural export subsidies and all export measures with equivalent effect, in accordance with the mandate of the Doha Development Round

2.c Adopt measures to ensure the proper functioning of food commodity markets and their derivatives and facilitate timely access to market information, including on food reserves, in order to help limit extreme food price volatility

Goal 3. Ensure healthy lives and promote well-being for all at all ages

3.1 By 2030, reduce the global maternal mortality ratio to less than 70 per 100,000 live births

3.2 By 2030, end preventable deaths of newborns and children under 5 years of age, with all countries aiming to reduce neonatal mortality to at least as low as 12 per 1,000 live births and under-5 mortality to at least as low as 25 per 1,000 live births

3.3 By 2030, end the epidemics of AIDS, tuberculosis, malaria and neglected tropical diseases and combat hepatitis, water-borne diseases and other communicable diseases

3.4 By 2030, reduce by one third premature mortality from non-communicable diseases through prevention and treatment and promote mental health and well-being

3.5 Strengthen the prevention and treatment of substance abuse, including narcotic drug abuse and harmful use of alcohol

3.6 By 2020, halve the number of global deaths and injuries from road traffic accidents

3.7 By 2030, ensure universal access to sexual and reproductive health-care services, including for family planning, information and education, and the integration of reproductive health into national strategies and programmes

3.8 Achieve universal health coverage, including financial risk protection, access to quality essential health-care services and access to safe, effective, quality and affordable essential medicines and vaccines for all

3.9 By 2030, substantially reduce the number of deaths and illnesses from hazardous chemicals and air, water and soil pollution and contamination

3.a Strengthen the implementation of the World Health Organization Framework Convention on Tobacco Control in all countries, as appropriate

3.b Support the research and development of vaccines and medicines for the communicable and non-communicable diseases that primarily affect developing countries, provide access to affordable essential medicines and vaccines, in accordance with the Doha Declaration on the TRIPS Agreement and Public Health, which affirms the right of developing countries to use to the full the provisions in the Agreement on Trade-Related Aspects of Intellectual Property Rights regarding flexibilities to protect public health, and, in particular, provide access to medicines for all

3.c Substantially increase health financing and the recruitment, development, training and retention of the health workforce in developing countries, especially in least developed countries and small island developing States

3.d Strengthen the capacity of all countries, in particular developing countries, for early warning, risk reduction and management of national and global health risks

Goal 4. Ensure inclusive and equitable quality education and promote lifelong learning opportunities for all

4.1 By 2030, ensure that all girls and boys complete free, equitable and quality primary and secondary education leading to relevant and effective learning outcomes

4.2 By 2030, ensure that all girls and boys have access to quality early childhood development, care and pre-primary education so that they are ready for primary education

4.3 By 2030, ensure equal access for all women and men to affordable and quality technical, vocational and tertiary education, including university

4.4 By 2030, substantially increase the number of youth and adults who have relevant skills, including technical and vocational skills, for employment, decent jobs and entrepreneurship

4.5 By 2030, eliminate gender disparities in education and ensure equal access to all levels of education and vocational training for the vulnerable, including persons with disabilities, indigenous peoples and children in vulnerable situations

4.6 By 2030, ensure that all youth and a substantial proportion of adults, both men and women, achieve literacy and numeracy

4.7 By 2030, ensure that all learners acquire the knowledge and skills needed to promote sustainable development, including, among others, through education for sustainable development and sustainable lifestyles, human rights, gender equality, promotion of a culture of peace and non-violence, global citizenship and appreciation of cultural diversity and of culture's contribution to sustainable development

4.a Build and upgrade education facilities that are child, disability and gender sensitive and provide safe, non-violent, inclusive and effective learning environments for all

4.b By 2020, substantially expand globally the number of scholarships available to developing countries, in particular least developed countries, small island developing States and African countries, for enrolment in higher education, including vocational training and information and communications technology, technical, engineering and scientific programmes, in developed countries and other developing countries

4.c By 2030, substantially increase the supply of qualified teachers, including through international cooperation for teacher training in developing countries, especially least developed countries and small island developing States

Goal 5. Achieve gender equality and empower all women and girls

5.1 End all forms of discrimination against all women and girls everywhere

5.2 Eliminate all forms of violence against all women and girls in the public and private spheres, including trafficking and sexual and other types of exploitation

5.3 Eliminate all harmful practices, such as child, early and forced marriage and female genital mutilation

5.4 Recognize and value unpaid care and domestic work through the provision of public services, infrastructure and social protection policies and the promotion of shared responsibility within the household and the family as nationally appropriate

5.5 Ensure women's full and effective participation and equal opportunities for leadership at all levels of decision-making in political, economic and public life

5.6 Ensure universal access to sexual and reproductive health and reproductive rights as agreed in accordance with the Programme of Action of the International Conference on Population and Development and the Beijing Platform for Action and the outcome documents of their review conferences

5.a Undertake reforms to give women equal rights to economic resources, as well as access to ownership and control over land and other forms of property, financial services, inheritance and natural resources, in accordance with national laws

5.b Enhance the use of enabling technology, in particular information and communications technology, to promote the empowerment of women

5.c Adopt and strengthen sound policies and enforceable legislation for the promotion of gender equality and the empowerment of all women and girls at all levels

Goal 6. Ensure availability and sustainable management of water and sanitation for all

6.1 By 2030, achieve universal and equitable access to safe and affordable drinking water for all

6.2 By 2030, achieve access to adequate and equitable sanitation and hygiene for all and end open defecation, paying special attention to the needs of women and girls and those in vulnerable situations

6.3 By 2030, improve water quality by reducing pollution, eliminating dumping and minimizing release of hazardous chemicals and materials, halving the proportion of untreated wastewater and substantially increasing recycling and safe reuse globally

6.4 By 2030, substantially increase water-use efficiency across all sectors and ensure sustainable withdrawals and supply of freshwater to address water scarcity and substantially reduce the number of people suffering from water scarcity

6.5 By 2030, implement integrated water resources management at all levels, including through transboundary cooperation as appropriate

6.6 By 2020, protect and restore water-related ecosystems, including mountains, forests, wetlands, rivers, aquifers and lakes

6.a By 2030, expand international cooperation and capacity-building support to developing countries in water- and sanitation-related activities and programmes, including water harvesting, desalination, water efficiency, wastewater treatment, recycling and reuse technologies

6.b Support and strengthen the participation of local communities in improving water and sanitation management

Goal 7. Ensure access to affordable, reliable, sustainable and modern energy for all

7.1 By 2030, ensure universal access to affordable, reliable and modern energy services

7.2 By 2030, increase substantially the share of renewable energy in the global energy mix

7.3 By 2030, double the global rate of improvement in energy efficiency

7.a By 2030, enhance international cooperation to facilitate access to clean energy research and technology, including renewable energy, energy efficiency and advanced and cleaner fossil-fuel technology, and promote investment in energy infrastructure and clean energy technology

7.b By 2030, expand infrastructure and upgrade technology for supplying modern and sustainable energy services for all in developing countries, in particular least developed countries, small island developing States and landlocked developing countries, in accordance with their respective programmes of support

Goal 8. Promote sustained, inclusive and sustainable economic growth, full and productive employment and decent work for all

8.1 Sustain per capita economic growth in accordance with national circumstances and, in particular, at least 7 per cent gross domestic product growth per annum in the least developed countries

8.2 Achieve higher levels of economic productivity through diversification, technological upgrading and innovation, including through a focus on high-value added and labour-intensive sectors

8.3 Promote development-oriented policies that support productive activities, decent job creation, entrepreneurship, creativity and innovation, and encourage the formalization and growth of micro-, small- and medium-sized enterprises, including through access to financial services

8.4 Improve progressively, through 2030, global resource efficiency in consumption and production and endeavour to decouple economic growth from environmental degradation, in accordance with the 10JYear Framework of Programmes on Sustainable Consumption and Production, with developed countries taking the lead

8.5 By 2030, achieve full and productive employment and decent work for all women and men, including for young people and persons with disabilities, and equal pay for work of equal value

8.6 By 2020, substantially reduce the proportion of youth not in employment, education or training

8.7 Take immediate and effective measures to eradicate forced labour, end modern slavery and human trafficking and secure the prohibition and elimination of the worst forms of child labour, including recruitment and use of child soldiers, and by 2025 end child labour in all its forms

8.8 Protect labour rights and promote safe and secure working environments for all workers, including migrant workers, in particular women migrants, and those in precarious employment

8.9 By 2030, devise and implement policies to promote sustainable tourism that creates jobs and promotes local culture and products

8.10 Strengthen the capacity of domestic financial institutions to encourage and expand access to banking, insurance and financial services for all

8.a Increase Aid for Trade support for developing countries, in particular least developed countries, including through the Enhanced Integrated Framework for Trade-related Technical Assistance to Least Developed Countries

8.b By 2020, develop and operationalize a global strategy for youth employment and implement the Global Jobs Pact of the International Labour Organization

Goal 9. Build resilient infrastructure, promote inclusive and sustainable industrialization and foster innovation

9.1 Develop quality, reliable, sustainable and resilient infrastructure, including regional and transborder infrastructure, to support economic development and human well-being, with a focus on affordable and equitable access for all

9.2 Promote inclusive and sustainable industrialization and, by 2030, significantly raise industry's share of employment and gross domestic product, in line with national circumstances, and double its share in least developed countries

9.3 Increase the access of small-scale industrial and other enterprises, in particular in developing countries, to financial services, including affordable credit, and their integration into value chains and markets

9.4 By 2030, upgrade infrastructure and retrofit industries to make them sustainable, with increased resource-use efficiency and greater adoption of clean and environmentally sound technologies and industrial processes, with all countries taking action in accordance with their respective capabilities

9.5 Enhance scientific research, upgrade the technological capabilities of industrial sectors in all countries, in particular developing countries, including, by 2030, encouraging innovation and substantially increasing the number of research and development workers per 1 million people and public and private research and development spending

9.a Facilitate sustainable and resilient infrastructure development in developing countries through enhanced financial, technological and technical support to African countries, least developed countries, landlocked developing countries and small island developing States

9.b Support domestic technology development, research and innovation in developing countries, including by ensuring a conducive policy environment for, inter alia, industrial diversification and value addition to commodities

9.c Significantly increase access to information and communications technology and strive to provide universal and affordable access to the Internet in least developed countries by 2020

Goal 10. Reduce inequality within and among countries

10.1 By 2030, progressively achieve and sustain income growth of the bottom 40 per cent of the population at a rate higher than the national average

10.2 By 2030, empower and promote the social, economic and political inclusion of all, irrespective of age, sex, disability, race, ethnicity, origin, religion or economic or other status

10.3 Ensure equal opportunity and reduce inequalities of outcome, including by eliminating discriminatory laws, policies and practices and promoting appropriate legislation, policies and action in this regard

10.4 Adopt policies, especially fiscal, wage and social protection policies, and progressively achieve greater equality

10.5 Improve the regulation and monitoring of global financial markets and institutions and strengthen the implementation of such regulations

10.6 Ensure enhanced representation and voice for developing countries in decision-making in global international economic and financial institutions in order to deliver more effective, credible, accountable and legitimate institutions

10.7 Facilitate orderly, safe, regular and responsible migration and mobility of people, including through the implementation of planned and well-managed migration policies

10.a Implement the principle of special and differential treatment for developing countries, in particular least developed countries, in accordance with World Trade Organization agreements

10.b Encourage official development assistance and financial flows, including foreign direct investment, to States where the need is greatest, in particular least developed countries, African countries, small island developing States and landlocked developing countries, in accordance with their national plans and programmes

10.c By 2030, reduce to less than 3 per cent the transaction costs of migrant remittances and eliminate remittance corridors with costs higher than 5 per cent

Goal 11. Make cities and human settlements inclusive, safe, resilient and sustainable

11.1 By 2030, ensure access for all to adequate, safe and affordable housing and basic services and upgrade slums

11.2 By 2030, provide access to safe, affordable, accessible and sustainable transport systems for all, improving road safety, notably by expanding public transport, with special attention to the needs of those in vulnerable situations, women, children, persons with disabilities and older persons

11.3 By 2030, enhance inclusive and sustainable urbanization and capacity for participatory, integrated and sustainable human settlement planning and management in all countries

11.4 Strengthen efforts to protect and safeguard the world's cultural and natural heritage

11.5 By 2030, significantly reduce the number of deaths and the number of people affected and substantially decrease the direct economic losses relative to global gross domestic product caused by disasters, including water-related disasters, with a focus on protecting the poor and people in vulnerable situations

11.6 By 2030, reduce the adverse per capita environmental impact of cities, including by paying special attention to air quality and municipal and other waste management

11.7 By 2030, provide universal access to safe, inclusive and accessible, green and public spaces, in particular for women and children, older persons and persons with disabilities

11.a Support positive economic, social and environmental links between urban, peri-urban and rural areas by strengthening national and regional development planning

11.b By 2020, substantially increase the number of cities and human settlements adopting and implementing integrated policies and plans towards inclusion, resource efficiency, mitigation and adaptation to climate change, resilience to disasters, and develop and implement, in line with the Sendai Framework for Disaster Risk Reduction 2015-2030, holistic disaster risk management at all levels

11.c Support least developed countries, including through financial and technical assistance, in building sustainable and resilient buildings utilizing local materials

Goal 12. Ensure sustainable consumption and production patterns

12.1 Implement the 10JYear Framework of Programmes on Sustainable Consumption and Production Patterns, all countries taking action, with developed countries taking the lead, taking into account the development and capabilities of developing countries

12.2 By 2030, achieve the sustainable management and efficient use of natural resources

12.3 By 2030, halve per capita global food waste at the retail and consumer levels and reduce food losses along production and supply chains, including post-harvest losses

12.4 By 2020, achieve the environmentally sound management of chemicals and all wastes throughout their life cycle, in accordance with agreed international frameworks, and significantly reduce their release to air, water and soil in order to minimize their adverse impacts on human health and the environment

12.5 By 2030, substantially reduce waste generation through prevention, reduction, recycling and reuse

12.6 Encourage companies, especially large and transnational companies, to adopt sustainable practices and to integrate sustainability information into their reporting cycle

12.7 Promote public procurement practices that are sustainable, in accordance with national policies and priorities

12.8 By 2030, ensure that people everywhere have the relevant information and awareness for sustainable development and lifestyles in harmony with nature

12.a Support developing countries to strengthen their scientific and technological capacity to move towards more sustainable patterns of consumption and production

12.b Develop and implement tools to monitor sustainable development impacts for sustainable tourism that creates jobs and promotes local culture and products

12.c Rationalize inefficient fossil-fuel subsidies that encourage wasteful consumption by removing market distortions, in accordance with national circumstances, including by restructuring taxation and phasing out those harmful subsidies, where they exist, to reflect their environmental impacts, taking fully into account the specific needs and conditions of developing countries and minimizing the possible adverse impacts on their development in a manner that protects the poor and the affected communities

Goal 13. Take urgent action to combat climate change and its impacts*

13.1 Strengthen resilience and adaptive capacity to climate-related hazards and natural disasters in all countries

13.2 Integrate climate change measures into national policies, strategies and planning

13.3 Improve education, awareness-raising and human and institutional capacity on climate change mitigation, adaptation, impact reduction and early warning

13.a Implement the commitment undertaken by developed-country parties to the United Nations Framework Convention on Climate Change to a goal of mobilizing jointly $100 billion annually by 2020 from all sources to address the needs of developing countries in the context of meaningful mitigation actions and transparency on implementation and fully operationalize the Green Climate Fund through its capitalization as soon as possible

13.b Promote mechanisms for raising capacity for effective climate change-related planning and management in least developed countries and small island developing States, including focusing on women, youth and local and marginalized communities

Goal 14. Conserve and sustainably use the oceans, seas and marine resources for sustainable development

14.1 By 2025, prevent and significantly reduce marine pollution of all kinds, in particular from land-based activities, including marine debris and nutrient pollution

14.2 By 2020, sustainably manage and protect marine and coastal ecosystems to avoid significant adverse impacts, including by strengthening their resilience, and take action for their restoration in order to achieve healthy and productive oceans

14.3 Minimize and address the impacts of ocean acidification, including through enhanced scientific cooperation at all levels

14.4 By 2020, effectively regulate harvesting and end overfishing, illegal, unreported and unregulated fishing and destructive fishing practices and implement science-based management plans, in order to restore fish stocks in the shortest time feasible, at least to levels that can produce maximum sustainable yield as determined by their biological characteristics

14.5 By 2020, conserve at least 10 per cent of coastal and marine areas, consistent with national and international law and based on the best available scientific information

14.6 By 2020, prohibit certain forms of fisheries subsidies which contribute to overcapacity and overfishing, eliminate subsidies that contribute to illegal, unreported and unregulated fishing and refrain from introducing new such subsidies, recognizing that appropriate and effective special and differential treatment for developing and least developed countries should be an integral part of the World Trade Organization fisheries subsidies negotiation32

14.7 By 2030, increase the economic benefits to small island developing States and least developed countries from the sustainable use of marine resources, including through sustainable management of fisheries, aquaculture and tourism

14.a Increase scientific knowledge, develop research capacity and transfer marine technology, taking into account the Intergovernmental Oceanographic Commission Criteria and Guidelines on the Transfer of Marine Technology, in order to improve ocean health and to enhance the contribution of marine biodiversity to the development of developing countries, in particular small island developing States and least developed countries

14.b Provide access for small-scale artisanal fishers to marine resources and markets

14.c Enhance the conservation and sustainable use of oceans and their resources by implementing international law as reflected in the United Nations Convention on the Law of the Sea, which provides the legal framework for the conservation and sustainable use of oceans and their resources, as recalled in paragraph 158 of "The future we want"

* Acknowledging that the United Nations Framework Convention on Climate Change is the primary international, intergovernmental forum for negotiating the global response to climate change.

Goal 15. Protect, restore and promote sustainable use of terrestrial ecosystems, sustainably manage forests, combat desertification, and halt and reverse land degradation and halt biodiversity loss

15.1 By 2020, ensure the conservation, restoration and sustainable use of terrestrial and inland freshwater ecosystems and their services, in particular forests, wetlands, mountains and drylands, in line with obligations under international agreements

15.2 By 2020, promote the implementation of sustainable management of all types of forests, halt deforestation, restore degraded forests and substantially increase afforestation and reforestation globally

15.3 By 2030, combat desertification, restore degraded land and soil, including land affected by desertification, drought and floods, and strive to achieve a land degradation-neutral world

15.4 By 2030, ensure the conservation of mountain ecosystems, including their biodiversity, in order to enhance their capacity to provide benefits that are essential for sustainable development

15.5 Take urgent and significant action to reduce the degradation of natural habitats, halt the loss of biodiversity and, by 2020, protect and prevent the extinction of threatened species

15.6 Promote fair and equitable sharing of the benefits arising from the utilization of genetic resources and promote appropriate access to such resources, as internationally agreed

15.7 Take urgent action to end poaching and trafficking of protected species of flora and fauna and address both demand and supply of illegal wildlife products

15.8 By 2020, introduce measures to prevent the introduction and significantly reduce the impact of invasive alien species on land and water ecosystems and control or eradicate the priority species

15.9 By 2020, integrate ecosystem and biodiversity values into national and local planning, development processes, poverty reduction strategies and accounts

15.a Mobilize and significantly increase financial resources from all sources to conserve and sustainably use biodiversity and ecosystems

15.b Mobilize significant resources from all sources and at all levels to finance sustainable forest management and provide adequate incentives to developing countries to advance such management, including for conservation and reforestation

15.c Enhance global support for efforts to combat poaching and trafficking of protected species, including by increasing the capacity of local communities to pursue sustainable livelihood opportunities

Goal 16. Promote peaceful and inclusive societies for sustainable development, provide access to justice for all and build effective, accountable and inclusive institutions at all levels

16.1 Significantly reduce all forms of violence and related death rates everywhere

16.2 End abuse, exploitation, trafficking and all forms of violence against and torture of children

16.3 Promote the rule of law at the national and international levels and ensure equal access to justice for all

16.4 By 2030, significantly reduce illicit financial and arms flows, strengthen the recovery and return of stolen assets and combat all forms of organized crime

16.5 Substantially reduce corruption and bribery in all their forms

16.6 Develop effective, accountable and transparent institutions at all levels

16.7 Ensure responsive, inclusive, participatory and representative decision-making at all levels

16.8 Broaden and strengthen the participation of developing countries in the institutions of global governance

16.9 By 2030, provide legal identity for all, including birth registration

16.10 Ensure public access to information and protect fundamental freedoms, in accordance with national legislation and international agreements

16.a Strengthen relevant national institutions, including through international cooperation, for building capacity at all levels, in particular in developing countries, to prevent violence and combat terrorism and crime

16.b Promote and enforce non-discriminatory laws and policies for sustainable development

Goal 17. Strengthen the means of implementation and revitalize the Global Partnership for Sustainable Development

Finance

17.1 Strengthen domestic resource mobilization, including through international support to developing countries, to improve domestic capacity for tax and other revenue collection

17.2 Developed countries to implement fully their official development assistance commitments, including the commitment by many developed countries to achieve the target of 0.7 per cent of gross national income for official development assistance (ODA/GNI) to developing countries and 0.15 to 0.20 per cent of ODA/GNI to least developed countries; ODA providers are encouraged to consider setting a target to provide at least 0.20 per cent of ODA/GNI to least developed countries

17.3 Mobilize additional financial resources for developing countries from multiple sources

17.4 Assist developing countries in attaining long-term debt sustainability through coordinated policies aimed at fostering debt financing, debt relief and debt restructuring, as appropriate, and address the external debt of highly indebted poor countries to reduce debt distress

17.5 Adopt and implement investment promotion regimes for least developed countries

Technology

17.6 Enhance North-South, South-South and triangular regional and international cooperation on and access to science, technology and innovation and enhance knowledge sharing on mutually agreed terms, including through improved coordination among existing mechanisms, in particular at the United Nations level, and through a global technology facilitation mechanism

17.7 Promote the development, transfer, dissemination and diffusion of environmentally sound technologies to developing countries on favourable terms, including on concessional and preferential terms, as mutually agreed

17.8 Fully operationalize the technology bank and science, technology and innovation capacity-building mechanism for least developed countries by 2017 and enhance the use of enabling technology, in particular information and communications technology

Capacity-building

17.9 Enhance international support for implementing effective and targeted capacity- building in developing countries to support national plans to implement all the Sustainable Development Goals, including through North-South, South-South and triangular cooperation

Trade

17.10 Promote a universal, rules-based, open, non-discriminatory and equitable multilateral trading system under the World Trade Organization, including through the conclusion of negotiations under its Doha Development Agenda

17.11 Significantly increase the exports of developing countries, in particular with a view to doubling the least developed countries' share of global exports by 2020

17.12 Realize timely implementation of duty-free and quota-free market access on a lasting basis for all least developed countries, consistent with World Trade Organization decisions, including by ensuring that preferential rules of origin applicable to imports from least developed countries are transparent and simple, and contribute to facilitating market access

Systemic issues

Policy and institutional coherence

17.13 Enhance global macroeconomic stability, including through policy coordination and policy coherence

17.14 Enhance policy coherence for sustainable development

17.15 Respect each country's policy space and leadership to establish and implement policies for poverty eradication and sustainable development

Multi-stakeholder partnerships

17.16 Enhance the Global Partnership for Sustainable Development, complemented by multi-stakeholder partnerships that mobilize and share knowledge, expertise, technology and financial resources, to support the achievement of the Sustainable Development Goals in all countries, in particular developing countries

17.17 Encourage and promote effective public, public-private and civil society partnerships, building on the experience and resourcing strategies of partnerships

Data, monitoring and accountability

17.18 By 2020, enhance capacity-building support to developing countries, including for least developed countries and small island developing States, to increase significantly the availability of high-quality, timely and reliable data disaggregated by income, gender, age, race, ethnicity, migratory status, disability, geographic location and other characteristics relevant in national contexts

17.19 By 2030, build on existing initiatives to develop measurements of progress on sustainable development that complement gross domestic product, and support statistical capacity-building in developing countries

Means of implementation and the Global Partnership

60. We reaffirm our strong commitment to the full implementation of this new Agenda. We recognize that we will not be able to achieve our ambitious Goals and targets without a revitalized and enhanced Global Partnership and comparably ambitious means of implementation. The revitalized Global Partnership will facilitate an intensive global engagement in support of implementation of all the Goals and targets, bringing together Governments, civil society, the private sector, the United Nations system and other actors and mobilizing all available resources.

61. The Agenda's Goals and targets deal with the means required to realize our collective ambitions. The means of implementation targets under each Sustainable Development Goal and Goal 17, which are referred to above, are key to realizing our Agenda and are of equal importance with the other Goals and targets. We shall accord them equal priority in our implementation efforts and in the global indicator framework for monitoring our progress.

62. This Agenda, including the Sustainable Development Goals, can be met within the framework of a revitalized Global Partnership for Sustainable Development, supported by the concrete policies and actions outlined in the Addis Ababa Action Agenda,43 which is an integral part of the 2030

Agenda for Sustainable Development. The Addis Ababa Action Agenda supports, complements and helps to contextualize the 2030 Agenda's means of implementation targets. It relates to domestic public resources, domestic and international private business and finance, international development cooperation, international trade as an engine for development, debt and debt sustainability, addressing systemic issues and science, technology, innovation and capacity-building, and data, monitoring and follow-up.

63. Cohesive nationally owned sustainable development strategies, supported by integrated national financing frameworks, will be at the heart of our efforts. We reiterate that each country has primary responsibility for its own economic and social development and that the role of national policies and development strategies cannot be overemphasized. We will respect each country's policy space and leadership to implement policies for poverty eradication and sustainable development, while remaining consistent with relevant international rules and commitments. At the same time, national development efforts need to be supported by an enabling international economic environment, including coherent and mutually supporting world trade, monetary and financial systems, and strengthened and enhanced global economic governance. Processes to develop and facilitate the availability of appropriate knowledge and technologies globally, as well as capacity-building, are also critical. We commit to pursuing policy coherence and an enabling environment for sustainable development at all levels and by all actors, and to reinvigorating the Global Partnership for Sustainable Development.

64. We support the implementation of relevant strategies and programmes of action, including the Istanbul Declaration and Programme of Action, the SIDS Accelerated Modalities of Action (SAMOA) Pathway and the Vienna Programme of Action for Landlocked Developing Countries for the Decade 2014-2024, and reaffirm the importance of supporting the African Union's Agenda 2063 and the programme of the New Partnership for Africa's Development, all of which are integral to the new Agenda. We recognize the major challenge to the achievement of durable peace and sustainable development in countries in conflict and post-conflict situations.

65. We recognize that middle-income countries still face significant challenges to achieve sustainable development. In order to ensure that achievements made to date are sustained, efforts to address ongoing challenges should be strengthened through the exchange of experiences, improved coordination, and better and focused support of the United Nations development system, the international financial institutions, regional organizations and other stakeholders.

66. We underscore that, for all countries, public policies and the mobilization and effective use of domestic resources, underscored by the principle of national ownership, are central to our common pursuit of sustainable development, including achieving the Sustainable Development Goals. We recognize that domestic resources are first and foremost generated by economic growth, supported by an enabling environment at all levels.

67. Private business activity, investment and innovation are major drivers of productivity, inclusive economic growth and job creation. We acknowledge the diversity of the private sector, ranging from micro-enterprises to cooperatives to multinationals. We call upon all businesses to apply their creativity and innovation to solving sustainable development challenges. We will foster a dynamic and well-functioning business sector, while protecting labour rights and environmental and health standards in accordance with relevant international standards and agreements and other ongoing initiatives in this regard, such as the Guiding Principles on Business and Human Rights and the labour standards of the International Labour Organization, the Convention on the Rights of the Child and key multilateral environmental agreements, for parties to those agreements.

68. International trade is an engine for inclusive economic growth and poverty reduction, and contributes to the promotion of sustainable development. We will continue to promote a universal, rules-based, open, transparent, predictable, inclusive, non-discriminatory and equitable multilateral trading system under the World Trade Organization, as well as meaningful trade liberalization. We call upon all members of the World Trade Organization to redouble their efforts to promptly conclude the negotiations on the Doha Development Agenda. We attach great importance to providing trade-related capacity-building for developing countries, including African countries, least developed countries, landlocked developing countries, small island developing States and middle-income countries, including for the promotion of regional economic integration and interconnectivity.

69. We recognize the need to assist developing countries in attaining long-term debt sustainability through coordinated policies aimed at fostering debt financing, debt relief, debt restructuring and sound debt management, as appropriate. Many countries remain vulnerable to debt crises and some are in the midst of crises, including a number of least developed countries, small island developing States and some developed countries. We reiterate that debtors and creditors must work together to prevent and resolve unsustainable debt situations. Maintaining sustainable debt levels is the responsibility of the borrowing countries; however we acknowledge that lenders also have a responsibility to lend in a way that does not undermine a country's debt sustainability. We will support the maintenance of debt sustainability of those countries that have received debt relief and achieved sustainable debt levels.

70. We hereby launch a Technology Facilitation Mechanism which was established by the Addis Ababa Action Agenda in order to support the Sustainable Development Goals. The Technology Facilitation

Mechanism will be based on a multi-stakeholder collaboration between Member States, civil society, the private sector, the scientific community, United Nations entities and other stakeholders and will be composed of a United Nations inter-agency task team on science, technology and innovation for the Sustainable Development Goals, a collaborative multi-stakeholder forum on science, technology and innovation for the Sustainable Development Goals and an online platform.

- The United Nations inter-agency task team on science, technology and innovation for the Sustainable Development Goals will promote coordination, coherence and cooperation within the United Nations system on science, technology and innovation-related matters, enhancing synergy and efficiency, in particular to enhance capacity-building initiatives. The task team will draw on existing resources and will work with 10 representatives from civil society, the private sector and the scientific community to prepare the meetings of the multi-stakeholder forum on science, technology and innovation for the Sustainable Development Goals, as well as in the development and operationalization of the online platform, including preparing proposals for the modalities for the forum and the online platform. The 10 representatives will be appointed by the Secretary-General, for periods of two years. The task team will be open to the participation of all United Nations agencies, funds and programmes and the functional commissions of the Economic and Social Council and it will initially be composed of the entities that currently integrate the informal working group on technology facilitation, namely, the Department of Economic and Social Affairs of the Secretariat, the United Nations Environment Programme, the United Nations Industrial Development Organization, the United Nations Educational, Scientific and Cultural Organization, the United Nations Conference on Trade and Development, the International Telecommunication Union, the World Intellectual Property Organization and the World Bank.
- The online platform will be used to establish a comprehensive mapping of, and serve as a gateway for, information on existing science, technology and innovation initiatives, mechanisms and programmes, within and beyond the United Nations. The online platform will facilitate access to information, knowledge and experience, as well as best practices and lessons learned, on science, technology and innovation facilitation initiatives and policies. The online platform will also facilitate the dissemination of relevant open access scientific publications generated worldwide. The online platform will be developed on the basis of an independent technical assessment which will take into account best practices and lessons learned from other initiatives, within and beyond the United Nations, in order to ensure that it will complement, facilitate access to and provide adequate information on existing science, technology and innovation platforms, avoiding duplications and enhancing synergies.
- The multi-stakeholder forum on science, technology and innovation for the Sustainable Development Goals will be convened once a year, for a period of two days, to discuss science, technology and innovation cooperation around thematic areas for the implementation of the Sustainable Development Goals, congregating all relevant stakeholders to actively contribute in their area of expertise. The forum will provide a venue for facilitating interaction, matchmaking and the establishment of networks between relevant stakeholders and multi-stakeholder partnerships in order to identify and examine technology needs and gaps, including on scientific cooperation, innovation and capacity-building, and also in order to help to facilitate development, transfer and dissemination of relevant technologies for the Sustainable Development Goals. The meetings of the forum will be convened by the President of the Economic and Social Council before the meeting of the high-level political forum under the auspices of the Council or, alternatively, in conjunction with other forums or conferences, as appropriate, taking into account the theme to be considered and on the basis of a collaboration with the organizers of the other forums or conferences. The meetings of the forum will be co-chaired by two Member States and will result in a summary of discussions elaborated by the two co-Chairs, as an input to the meetings of the high-level political forum, in the context of the follow-up and review of the implementation of the post-2015 development agenda.
- The meetings of the high-level political forum will be informed by the summary of the multi-stakeholder forum. The themes for the subsequent multi-stakeholder forum on science, technology and innovation for the Sustainable Development Goals will be considered by the high-level political forum on sustainable development, taking into account expert inputs from the task team.

71. We reiterate that this Agenda and the Sustainable Development Goals and targets, including the means of implementation, are universal, indivisible and interlinked.

Follow-up and review

72. We commit to engaging in systematic follow-up and review of the implementation of this Agenda over the next 15 years. A robust, voluntary, effective, participatory, transparent and integrated follow-up and review framework will make a vital contribution to implementation and will help countries to maximize and track progress in implementing this Agenda in order to ensure that no one is left behind.
73. Operating at the national, regional and global levels, it will promote accountability to our citizens, support effective international cooperation

in achieving this Agenda and foster exchanges of best practices and mutual learning. It will mobilize support to overcome shared challenges and identify new and emerging issues. As this is a universal Agenda, mutual trust and understanding among all nations will be important.

74. Follow-up and review processes at all levels will be guided by the following principles:
   (a) They will be voluntary and country-led, will take into account different national realities, capacities and levels of development and will respect policy space and priorities. As national ownership is key to achieving sustainable development, the outcome from national- level processes will be the foundation for reviews at the regional and global levels, given that the global review will be primarily based on national official data sources.
   (b) They will track progress in implementing the universal Goals and targets, including the means of implementation, in all countries in a manner which respects their universal, integrated and interrelated nature and the three dimensions of sustainable development.
   (c) They will maintain a longer-term orientation, identify achievements, challenges, gaps and critical success factors and support countries in making informed policy choices. They will help to mobilize the necessary means of implementation and partnerships, support the identification of solutions and best practices and promote the coordination and effectiveness of the international development system.
   (d) They will be open, inclusive, participatory and transparent for all people and will support reporting by all relevant stakeholders.
   (e) They will be people-centred, gender-sensitive, respect human rights and have a particular focus on the poorest, most vulnerable and those furthest behind.
   (f) They will build on existing platforms and processes, where these exist, avoid duplication and respond to national circumstances, capacities, needs and priorities. They will evolve over time, taking into account emerging issues and the development of new methodologies, and will minimize the reporting burden on national administrations.
   (g) They will be rigorous and based on evidence, informed by country-led evaluations and data which is high-quality, accessible, timely, reliable and disaggregated by income, sex, age, race, ethnicity, migration status, disability and geographic location and other characteristics relevant in national contexts.
   (h) They will require enhanced capacity-building support for developing countries, including the strengthening of national data systems and evaluation programmes, particularly in African countries, least developed countries, small island developing States, landlocked developing countries and middle-income countries.
   (i) They will benefit from the active support of the United Nations system and other multilateral institutions.
75. The Goals and targets will be followed up and reviewed using a set of global indicators. These will be complemented by indicators at the regional and national levels which will be developed by Member States, in addition to the outcomes of work undertaken for the development of the baselines for those targets where national and global baseline data does not yet exist. The global indicator framework, to be developed by the Inter-Agency and Expert Group on Sustainable Development Goal Indicators, will be agreed by the Statistical Commission by March 2016 and adopted thereafter by the Economic and Social Council and the General Assembly, in line with existing mandates. This framework will be simple yet robust, address all Sustainable Development Goals and targets, including for means of implementation, and preserve the political balance, integration and ambition contained therein.
76. We will support developing countries, particularly African countries, least developed countries, small island developing States and landlocked developing countries, in strengthening the capacity of national statistical offices and data systems to ensure access to high-quality, timely, reliable and disaggregated data. We will promote transparent and accountable scaling-up of appropriate public-private cooperation to exploit the contribution to be made by a wide range of data, including earth observation and geospatial information, while ensuring national ownership in supporting and tracking progress.
77. We commit to fully engage in conducting regular and inclusive reviews of progress at the subnational, national, regional and global levels. We will draw as far as possible on the existing network of follow-up and review institutions and mechanisms. National reports will allow assessments of progress and identify challenges at the regional and global level. Along with regional dialogues and global reviews, they will inform recommendations for follow-up at various levels.

National level

78. We encourage all Member States to develop as soon as practicable ambitious national responses to the overall implementation of this Agenda. These can support the transition to the Sustainable Development Goals and build on existing planning instruments, such as national development and sustainable development strategies, as appropriate.
79. We also encourage Member States to conduct regular and inclusive reviews of progress at the national and subnational levels which are country-led and country-driven. Such reviews should draw on contributions from indigenous peoples, civil society, the private sector and other stakeholders, in line with national circumstances, policies and priorities. National parliaments as well as other institutions can also support these processes.

Regional level

80. Follow-up and review at the regional and subregional levels can, as appropriate, provide useful opportunities for peer learning, including through voluntary reviews, sharing of best practices and discussion on shared targets. We welcome in this respect the cooperation of regional and subregional commissions and organizations. Inclusive regional processes will draw on national-level reviews and contribute to follow-up and review at the global level, including at the high-level political forum on sustainable development.

81. Recognizing the importance of building on existing follow-up and review mechanisms at the regional level and allowing adequate policy space, we encourage all Member States to identify the most suitable regional forum in which to engage. United Nations regional commissions are encouraged to continue supporting Member States in this regard.

Global level

82. The high-level political forum will have a central role in overseeing a network of follow-up and review processes at the global level, working coherently with the General Assembly, the Economic and Social Council and other relevant organs and forums, in accordance with existing mandates. It will facilitate sharing of experiences, including successes, challenges and lessons learned, and provide political leadership, guidance and recommendations for follow-up. It will promote system-wide coherence and coordination of sustainable development policies. It should ensure that the Agenda remains relevant and ambitious and should focus on the assessment of progress, achievements and challenges faced by developed and developing countries as well as new and emerging issues. Effective linkages will be made with the follow-up and review arrangements of all relevant United Nations conferences and processes, including on least developed countries, small island developing States and landlocked developing countries.

83. Follow-up and review at the high-level political forum will be informed by an annual progress report on the Sustainable Development Goals to be prepared by the Secretary-General in cooperation with the United Nations system, based on the global indicator framework and data produced by national statistical systems and information collected at the regional level. The high-level political forum will also be informed by the Global Sustainable Development Report, which shall strengthen the science-policy interface and could provide a strong evidence-based instrument to support policymakers in promoting poverty eradication and sustainable development. We invite the President of the Economic and Social Council to conduct a process of consultations on the scope, methodology and frequency of the global report as well as its relation to the progress report, the outcome of which should be reflected in the ministerial declaration of the session of the high-level political forum in 2016.

84. The high-level political forum, under the auspices of the Economic and Social Council, shall carry out regular reviews, in line with General Assembly resolution 67/290 of 9 July 2013. Reviews will be voluntary, while encouraging reporting, and include developed and developing countries as well as relevant United Nations entities and other stakeholders, including civil society and the private sector. They shall be State-led, involving ministerial and other relevant high-level participants. They shall provide a platform for partnerships, including through the participation of major groups and other relevant stakeholders.

85. Thematic reviews of progress on the Sustainable Development Goals, including cross-cutting issues, will also take place at the high-level political forum. These will be supported by reviews by the functional commissions of the Economic and Social Council and other intergovernmental bodies and forums which should reflect the integrated nature of the Goals as well as the interlinkages between them. They will engage all relevant stakeholders and, where possible, feed into, and be aligned with, the cycle of the high-level political forum.

86. We welcome, as outlined in the Addis Ababa Action Agenda, the dedicated follow-up and review for the financing for development outcomes as well as all the means of implementation of the Sustainable Development Goals which is integrated with the follow-up and review framework of this Agenda. The intergovernmentally agreed conclusions and recommendations of the annual Economic and Social Council forum on financing for development will be fed into the overall follow-up and review of the implementation of this Agenda in the high-level political forum.

87. Meeting every four years under the auspices of the General Assembly, the high-level political forum will provide high-level political guidance on the Agenda and its implementation, identify progress and emerging challenges and mobilize further actions to accelerate implementation. The next high-level political forum under the auspices of the General Assembly will be held in 2019, with the cycle of meetings thus reset, in order to maximize coherence with the quadrennial comprehensive policy review process.

88. We also stress the importance of system-wide strategic planning, implementation and reporting in order to ensure coherent and integrated support to the implementation of the new Agenda by the United Nations development system. The relevant governing bodies should take action to review such support to implementation and to report on progress and obstacles. We welcome the ongoing dialogue in the Economic and Social Council on the longer-term positioning of the United Nations development system and look forward to taking action on these issues, as appropriate.

89. The high-level political forum will support participation in follow-up and review processes by the major groups and other relevant stakeholders in line with resolution 67/290. We call upon those

actors to report on their contribution to the implementation of the Agenda.

90. We request the Secretary-General, in consultation with Member States, to prepare a report, for consideration at the seventieth session of the General Assembly in preparation for the 2016 meeting of the high-level political forum, which outlines critical milestones towards coherent, efficient and inclusive follow-up and review at the global level. The report should include a proposal on the organizational arrangements for State-led reviews at the high-level political forum under the auspices of the Economic and Social Council, including recommendations on voluntary common reporting guidelines. It should clarify institutional responsibilities and provide guidance on annual themes, on a sequence of thematic reviews, and on options for periodic reviews for the high-level political forum.

91. We reaffirm our unwavering commitment to achieving this Agenda and utilizing it to the full to transform our world for the better by 2030.

1.4.1. TEU, consolidated

Consolidated Version of the Treaty on European Union, 26 October 2012, OJ C 326/13

[...] DETERMINED to promote economic and social progress for their peoples, taking into account the principle of sustainable development and within the context of the accomplishment of the internal market and of reinforced cohesion and environmental protection, and to implement policies ensuring that advances in economic integration are accompanied by parallel progress in other fields, [...]

Article 2

The Union is founded on the values of respect for human dignity, freedom, democracy, equality, the rule of law and respect for human rights, including the rights of persons belonging to minorities. These values are common to the Member States in a society in which pluralism, non-discrimination, tolerance, justice, solidarity and equality between women and men prevail.

Article 3 (ex Article 2 TEU)

1. The Union's aim is to promote peace, its values and the well-being of its peoples.
2. The Union shall offer its citizens an area of freedom, security and justice without internal frontiers, in which the free movement of persons is ensured in conjunction with appropriate measures with respect to external border controls, asylum, immigration and the prevention and combating of crime.
3. The Union shall establish an internal market. It shall work for the sustainable development of Europe based on balanced economic growth and price stability, a highly competitive social market economy, aiming at full employment and social progress, and a high level of protection and improvement of the quality of the environment. It shall promote scientific and technological advance.

   It shall combat social exclusion and discrimination, and shall promote social justice and protection, equality between women and men, solidarity between generations and protection of the rights of the child.

   It shall promote economic, social and territorial cohesion, and solidarity among Member States.

   It shall respect its rich cultural and linguistic diversity, and shall ensure that Europe's cultural heritage is safeguarded and enhanced.
4. The Union shall establish an economic and monetary union whose currency is the euro.
5. In its relations with the wider world, the Union shall uphold and promote its values and interests and contribute to the protection of its citizens. It shall contribute to peace, security, the sustainable development of the Earth, solidarity and mutual respect among peoples, free and fair trade, eradication of poverty and the protection of human rights, in particular the rights of the child, as well as to the strict observance and the development of international law, including respect for the principles of the United Nations Charter.
6. The Union shall pursue its objectives by appropriate means commensurate with the competences which are conferred upon it in the Treaties.

[...]

TITLE V

GENERAL PROVISIONS ON THE UNION'S EXTERNAL ACTION AND SPECIFIC PROVISIONS ON THE COMMON FOREIGN AND SECURITY POLICY

CHAPTER 1

GENERAL PROVISIONS ON THE UNION'S EXTERNAL ACTION

Article 21

1. The Union's action on the international scene shall be guided by the principles which have inspired its own creation, development and enlargement, and which it seeks to advance in the wider world: democracy, the rule of law, the universality and indivisibility of human rights and fundamental freedoms, respect for human dignity, the principles of equality and solidarity, and respect for the principles of the United Nations Charter and international law.

   The Union shall seek to develop relations and build partnerships with third countries, and inter national, regional or global organisations which share the principles referred to in the first subparagraph. It shall promote multilateral solutions to common problems, in particular in the framework of the United Nations.
2. The Union shall define and pursue common policies and actions, and shall work for a high degree of cooperation in all fields of international relations, in order to:
   (a) safeguard its values, fundamental interests, security, independence and integrity;
   (b) consolidate and support democracy, the rule of law, human rights and the principles of inter national law;
   (c) preserve peace, prevent conflicts and strengthen international security, in accordance with the purposes and principles of the United Nations Charter, with the principles of the Helsinki Final Act and with the aims of the Charter of Paris, including those relating to external borders;
   (d) foster the sustainable economic, social and environmental development of developing

countries, with the primary aim of eradicating poverty;

(e) encourage the integration of all countries into the world economy, including through the progressive abolition of restrictions on international trade;

(f) help develop international measures to preserve and improve the quality of the environment and the sustainable management of global natural resources, in order to ensure sustainable development;

(g) assist populations, countries and regions confronting natural or man-made disasters; and

(h) promote an international system based on stronger multilateral cooperation and good global governance.

3. The Union shall respect the principles and pursue the objectives set out in paragraphs 1 and 2 in the development and implementation of the different areas of the Union's external action covered by this Title and by Part Five of the Treaty on the Functioning of the European Union, and of the external aspects of its other policies.

The Union shall ensure consistency between the different areas of its external action and between these and its other policies. The Council and the Commission, assisted by the High Representative of the Union for Foreign Affairs and Security Policy, shall ensure that consistency and shall cooperate to that effect.

1.4.2. TFEU, consolidated

Consolidated Version of the Treaty on the Functioning of the European Union, 26 October 2012, OJ C 326/47

[...]

TITLE I – CATEGORIES AND AREAS OF UNION COMPETENCE

Article 2

1. When the Treaties confer on the Union exclusive competence in a specific area, only the Union may legislate and adopt legally binding acts, the Member States being able to do so themselves only if so empowered by the Union or for the implementation of Union acts.
2. When the Treaties confer on the Union a competence shared with the Member States in a specific area, the Union and the Member States may legislate and adopt legally binding acts in that area. The Member States shall exercise their competence to the extent that the Union has not exercised its competence. The Member States shall again exercise their competence to the extent that the Union has decided to cease exercising its competence.
3. The Member States shall coordinate their economic and employment policies within arrangements as determined by this Treaty, which the Union shall have competence to provide.
4. The Union shall have competence, in accordance with the provisions of the Treaty on European Union, to define and implement a common foreign and security policy, including the progressive framing of a common defence policy.
5. In certain areas and under the conditions laid down in the Treaties, the Union shall have competence to carry out actions to support, coordinate or supplement the actions of the Member States, without thereby superseding their competence in these areas.

   Legally binding acts of the Union adopted on the basis of the provisions of the Treaties relating to these areas shall not entail harmonisation of Member States' laws or regulations.
6. The scope of and arrangements for exercising the Union's competences shall be determined by the provisions of the Treaties relating to each area.

Article 3

1. The Union shall have exclusive competence in the following areas:
   (a) customs union;
   (b) the establishing of the competition rules necessary for the functioning of the internal market;
   (c) monetary policy for the Member States whose currency is the euro;
   (d) the conservation of marine biological resources under the common fisheries policy;
   (e) common commercial policy.
2. The Union shall also have exclusive competence for the conclusion of an international agreement when its conclusion is provided for in a legislative act of the Union or is necessary to enable the Union to exercise its internal competence, or in so far as its conclusion may affect common rules or alter their scope.

Article 4

1. The Union shall share competence with the Member States where the Treaties confer on it a competence which does not relate to the areas referred to in Articles 3 and 6.
2. Shared competence between the Union and the Member States applies in the following principal areas:
   (a) internal market;
   (b) social policy, for the aspects defined in this Treaty;
   (c) economic, social and territorial cohesion;
   (d) agriculture and fisheries, excluding the conservation of marine biological resources;
   (e) environment;
   (f) consumer protection;
   (g) transport;
   (h) trans-European networks;
   (i) energy;
   (j) area of freedom, security and justice;
   (k) common safety concerns in public health matters, for the aspects defined in this Treaty.
3. In the areas of research, technological development and space, the Union shall have competence to carry out activities, in particular to define and implement programmes; however, the exercise of that competence shall not result in Member States being prevented from exercising theirs.
4. In the areas of development cooperation and humanitarian aid, the Union shall have competence to carry out activities and conduct a common policy; however, the exercise of that competence shall not result in Member States being prevented from exercising theirs.

Article 5

1. The Member States shall coordinate their economic policies within the Union. To this end, the Council shall adopt measures, in particular broad guidelines for these policies.

Specific provisions shall apply to those Member States whose currency is the euro.

2. The Union shall take measures to ensure coordination of the employment policies of the Member States, in particular by defining guidelines for these policies.
3. The Union may take initiatives to ensure coordination of Member States' social policies.

Article 6

The Union shall have competence to carry out actions to support, coordinate or supplement the actions of the Member States. The areas of such action shall, at European level, be:

(a) protection and improvement of human health;

(b) industry;

(c) culture;

(d) tourism;

(e) education, vocational training, youth and sport;

(f) civil protection;

(g) administrative cooperation.

[...]

Article 11 (ex Article 6 TEC)

Environmental protection requirements must be integrated into the definition and implementation of the Union's policies and activities, in particular with a view to promoting sustainable development.

[...]

Article 13

In formulating and implementing the Union's agriculture, fisheries, transport, internal market, research and technological development and space policies, the Union and the Member States shall, since animals are sentient beings, pay full regard to the welfare requirements of animals, while respecting the legislative or administrative provisions and customs of the Member States relating in particular to religious rites, cultural traditions and regional heritage.

[...]

CHAPTER 3 – APPROXIMATION OF LAWS

Article 114 (ex Article 95 TEC)

1. Save where otherwise provided in the Treaties, the following provisions shall apply for the achievement of the objectives set out in Article 26. The European Parliament and the Council shall, acting in accordance with the ordinary legislative procedure and after consulting the Economic and Social Committee, adopt the measures for the approximation of the provisions laid down by law, regulation or administrative action in Member States which have as their object the establishment and functioning of the internal market.
2. Paragraph 1 shall not apply to fiscal provisions, to those relating to the free movement of persons nor to those relating to the rights and interests of employed persons.
3. The Commission, in its proposals envisaged in paragraph 1 concerning health, safety, environmental protection and consumer protection, will take as a base a high level of protection, taking account in particular of any new development based on scientific facts. Within their respective powers, the European Parliament and the Council will also seek to achieve this objective.
4. If, after the adoption of a harmonisation measure by the European Parliament and the Council, by the Council or by the Commission, a Member State deems it necessary to maintain national provisions on grounds of major needs referred to in Article 36, or relating to the protection of the environment or the working environment, it shall notify the Commission of these provisions as well as the grounds for maintaining them.
5. Moreover, without prejudice to paragraph 4, if, after the adoption of a harmonisation measure by the European Parliament and the Council, by the Council or by the Commission, a Member State deems it necessary to introduce national provisions based on new scientific evidence relating to the protection of the environment or the working environment on grounds of a problem specific to that Member State arising after the adoption of the harmonisation measure, it shall notify the Commission of the envisaged provisions as well as the grounds for introducing them. [...]

TITLE XX – ENVIRONMENT

Article 191 (ex Article 174 TEC)

1. Union policy on the environment shall contribute to pursuit of the following objectives:
   - preserving, protecting and improving the quality of the environment,
   - protecting human health,
   - prudent and rational utilisation of natural resources,
   - promoting measures at international level to deal with regional or worldwide environmental problems, and in particular combating climate change.
2. Union policy on the environment shall aim at a high level of protection taking into account the diversity of situations in the various regions of the Union. It shall be based on the precautionary principle and on the principles that preventive action should be taken, that environmental damage should as a priority be rectified at source and that the polluter should pay.

   In this context, harmonisation measures answering environmental protection requirements shall include, where appropriate, a safeguard clause allowing Member States to take provisional measures, for non-economic environmental reasons, subject to a procedure of inspection by the Union.
3. In preparing its policy on the environment, the Union shall take account of:
   - available scientific and technical data,

- environmental conditions in the various regions of the Union,
- the potential benefits and costs of action or lack of action,
- the economic and social development of the Union as a whole and the balanced development of its regions.

4. Within their respective spheres of competence, the Union and the Member States shall cooperate with third countries and with the competent international organisations. The arrangements for Union cooperation may be the subject of agreements between the Union and the third parties concerned.

   The previous subparagraph shall be without prejudice to Member States' competence to negotiate in international bodies and to conclude international agreements.

Article 192 (ex Article 175 TEC)

1. The European Parliament and the Council, acting in accordance with the ordinary legislative procedure and after consulting the Economic and Social Committee and the Committee of the Regions, shall decide what action is to be taken by the Union in order to achieve the objectives referred to in Article 191.
2. By way of derogation from the decision-making procedure provided for in paragraph 1 and without prejudice to Article 114, the Council acting unanimously in accordance with a special legislative procedure and after consulting the European Parliament, the Economic and Social Committee and the Committee of the Regions, shall adopt:

   (a) provisions primarily of a fiscal nature;

   (b) measures affecting:
   - town and country planning,
   - quantitative management of water resources or affecting, directly or indirectly, the availability of those resources,
   - land use, with the exception of waste management;

   (c) measures significantly affecting a Member State's choice between different energy sources and the general structure of its energy supply.

   The Council, acting unanimously on a proposal from the Commission and after consulting the European Parliament, the Economic and Social Committee and the Committee of the Regions, may make the ordinary legislative procedure applicable to the matters referred to in the first subparagraph.
3. General action programmes setting out priority objectives to be attained shall be adopted by the European Parliament and the Council, acting in accordance with the ordinary legislative procedure and after consulting the Economic and Social Committee and the Committee of the Regions.

   The measures necessary for the implementation of these programmes shall be adopted under the terms of paragraph 1 or 2, as the case may be.
4. Without prejudice to certain measures adopted by the Union, the Member States shall finance and implement the environment policy.
5. Without prejudice to the principle that the polluter should pay, if a measure based on the provisions of paragraph 1 involves costs deemed disproportionate for the public authorities of a Member State, such measure shall lay down appropriate provisions in the form of:
   - temporary derogations, and/or
   - financial support from the Cohesion Fund set up pursuant to Article 177.

Article 193 (ex Article 176 TEC)

The protective measures adopted pursuant to Article 192 shall not prevent any Member State from maintaining or introducing more stringent protective measures. Such measures must be compatible with the Treaties. They shall be notified to the Commission.

TITLE XXI – ENERGY

Article 194

1. In the context of the establishment and functioning of the internal market and with regard for the need to preserve and improve the environment, Union policy on energy shall aim, in a spirit of solidarity between Member States, to:

   (a) ensure the functioning of the energy market;

   (b) ensure security of energy supply in the Union;

   (c) promote energy efficiency and energy saving and the development of new and renewable forms of energy; and

   (d) promote the interconnection of energy networks.
2. Without prejudice to the application of other provisions of the Treaties, the European Parliament and the Council, acting in accordance with the ordinary legislative procedure, shall establish the measures necessary to achieve the objectives in paragraph 1. Such measures shall be adopted after consultation of the Economic and Social Committee and the Committee of the Regions.

   Such measures shall not affect a Member State's right to determine the conditions for exploiting its energy resources, its choice between different energy sources and the general structure of its energy supply, without prejudice to Article 192(2)(c).
3. By way of derogation from paragraph 2, the Council, acting in accordance with a special legislative procedure, shall unanimously and after consulting the European Parliament, establish the measures referred to therein when they are primarily of a fiscal nature.

1.5.1. European Green Deal

Communication from the Commission to the European Parliament, the European Council, the Council, the European Economic and Social Committee and the Committee of the Regions the European Green Deal, 11 December 2019, COM(2019) 640 final

1. INTRODUCTION – TURNING AN URGENT CHALLENGE INTO A UNIQUE OPPORTUNITY

This Communication sets out a European Green Deal for the European Union (EU) and its citizens. It resets the Commission's commitment to tackling climate and environmental-related challenges that is this generation's defining task. The atmosphere is warming and the climate is changing with each passing year. One million of the eight million species on the planet are at risk of being lost. Forests and oceans are being polluted and destroyed[1].

The European Green Deal is a response to these challenges. It is a new growth strategy that aims to transform the EU into a fair and prosperous society, with a modern, resource-efficient and competitive economy where there are no net emissions of greenhouse gases in 2050 and where economic growth is decoupled from resource use.

It also aims to protect, conserve and enhance the EU's natural capital, and protect the health and well-being of citizens from environment-related risks and impacts. At the same time, this transition must be just and inclusive. It must put people first, and pay attention to the regions, industries and workers who will face the greatest challenges. Since it will bring substantial change, active public participation and confidence in the transition is paramount if policies are to work and be accepted. A new pact is needed to bring together citizens in all their diversity, with national, regional, local authorities, civil society and industry working closely with the EU's institutions and consultative bodies.

The EU has the collective ability to transform its economy and society to put it on a more sustainable path. It can build on its strengths as a global leader on climate and environmental measures, consumer protection, and workers' rights. Delivering additional reductions in emissions is a challenge. It will require massive public investment and increased efforts to direct private capital towards climate and environmental action, while avoiding lock-in into unsustainable practices. The EU must be at the forefront of coordinating international efforts towards building a coherent financial system that supports sustainable solutions. This upfront investment is also an opportunity to put Europe firmly on a new path of sustainable and inclusive growth. The European Green Deal will accelerate and underpin the transition needed in all sectors.

The environmental ambition of the Green Deal will not be achieved by Europe acting alone. The drivers of climate change and biodiversity loss are global and are not limited by national borders. The EU can use its influence, expertise and financial resources to mobilise its neighbours and partners to join it on a sustainable path. The EU will continue to lead international efforts and wants to build alliances with the like-minded. It also recognises the need to maintain its security of supply and competitiveness even when others are unwilling to act.

This Communication presents an initial roadmap of the key policies and measures needed to achieve the European Green Deal. It will be updated as needs evolve and the policy responses are formulated. All EU actions and policies will have to contribute to the European Green Deal objectives. The challenges are complex and interlinked. The policy response must be bold and comprehensive and seek to maximise benefits for health, quality of life, resilience and competitiveness. It will require intense coordination to exploit the available synergies across all policy areas[2].

The Green Deal is an integral part of this Commission's strategy to implement the United Nation's 2030 Agenda and the sustainable development goals[3], and the other priorities announced in President von der Leyen's political guidelines[4]. As part of the Green Deal, the Commission will refocus the European Semester process of macroeconomic coordination to integrate the United Nations' sustainable development goals, to put sustainability and the well-being of citizens at the centre of economic policy, and the sustainable development goals at the heart of the EU's policymaking and action.

The figure below illustrates the various elements of the Green Deal. [...]

---

1 Sources: (i) Intergovernmental Panel on Climate Change (IPCC): Special Report on the impacts of global warming of 1.5°C; (ii) Intergovernmental Science-Policy Platform on Biodiversity and Ecosystem Services: 2019 Global assessment report on biodiversity and ecosystem services; (iii) The International Resource Panel: Global Resources Outlook 2019: Natural Resources for the Future We Want; (iv) European Environment Agency: the European environment — state and outlook 2020: knowledge for transition to a sustainable Europe

2 In line with the findings of the 2020 European environment — state and outlook 2020: knowledge for transition to a sustainable Europe (European Environment Agency)

3 https://sustainabledevelopment.un.org/post2015/transformingourworld

4 See Political Guidelines of President elect Ursula von der Leyen: Political guidelines for the next Commission (2019-2024) – 'A Union that strives for more: My agenda for Europe' :

2. TRANSFORMING THE EU'S ECONOMY FOR A SUSTAINABLE FUTURE

2.1. Designing a set of deeply transformative policies

To deliver the European Green Deal, there is a need to rethink policies for clean energy supply across the economy, industry, production and consumption, large-scale infrastructure, transport, food and agriculture, construction, taxation and social benefits. To achieve these aims, it is essential to increase the value given to protecting and restoring natural ecosystems, to the sustainable use of resources and to improving human health. This is where transformational change is most needed and potentially most beneficial for the EU economy, society and natural environment. The EU should also promote and invest in the necessary digital transformation and tools as these are essential enablers of the changes.

While all of these areas for action are strongly interlinked and mutually reinforcing, careful attention will have to be paid when there are potential trade-offs between economic, environmental and social objectives. The Green Deal will make consistent use of all policy levers: regulation and standardisation, investment and innovation, national reforms, dialogue with social partners and international cooperation. The European Pillar of Social Rights will guide action in ensuring that no one is left behind.

New measures on their own will not be enough to achieve the European Green Deal's objectives. In addition to launching new initiatives, the Commission will work with the Member States to step up the EU's efforts to ensure that current legislation and policies relevant to the Green Deal are enforced and effectively implemented.

2.1.1. Increasing the EU's climate ambition for 2030 and 2050

The Commission has already set out a clear vision of how to achieve climate neutrality by 2050[5]. This vision should form the basis for the long-term strategy that the EU will submit to the United Nations Framework Convention on Climate Change in early 2020. To set out clearly the conditions for an effective and fair transition, to provide predictability for investors, and to ensure that the transition is irreversible, the Commission will propose the first European 'Climate Law' by March 2020. This will enshrine the 2050 climate neutrality objective in legislation. The Climate Law will also ensure that all EU policies contribute to the climate neutrality objective and that all sectors play their part.

The EU has already started to modernise and transform the economy with the aim of climate neutrality. Between 1990 and 2018, it reduced greenhouse gas emissions by 23%, while the economy grew by 61%. However, current policies will only reduce greenhouse gas emissions by 60% by 2050. Much remains to be done, starting with more ambitious climate action in the coming decade.

By summer 2020, the Commission will present an impact assessed plan to increase the EU's greenhouse gas emission reductions target for 2030 to at least 50% and towards 55% compared with 1990 levels in a responsible way. To deliver these additional greenhouse gas emissions reductions, the Commission will, by June 2021, review and propose to revise where necessary, all relevant climate-related policy instruments. This will comprise the Emissions Trading System[6], including a possible extension of European emissions trading to new sectors, Member State targets to reduce emissions in sectors outside the Emissions Trading System[7], and the regulation on land use, land use change and forestry[8]. The Commission will propose to amend the Climate Law to update it accordingly.

These policy reforms will help to ensure effective carbon pricing throughout the economy. This will encourage changes in consumer and business behaviour, and facilitate an increase in sustainable public and private investment. The different pricing instruments must complement each other and jointly provide a coherent policy framework. Ensuring that taxation is aligned with climate objectives is also essential. The Commission will propose to revise the Energy Taxation Directive[9], focusing on environmental issues, and proposing to use the provisions in the Treaties that allow the European Parliament and the Council to adopt proposals in this area through the ordinary legislative procedure by qualified majority voting rather than by unanimity.

As long as many international partners do not share the same ambition as the EU, there is a risk of carbon leakage, either because production is transferred from the EU to other countries with lower ambition for emission reduction, or because EU products are replaced by more carbon-intensive imports. If this risk materialises, there will be no reduction in global emissions, and this will frustrate the efforts of the EU and its industries to meet the global climate objectives of the Paris Agreement.

Should differences in levels of ambition worldwide persist, as the EU increases its climate ambition, the Commission will propose a carbon border adjustment mechanism, for selected sectors, to reduce the risk of carbon leakage. This would ensure that the price of imports reflect more accurately their carbon content. This measure will be designed to comply with World Trade

5 A Clean Planet for all - A European strategic long-term vision for a prosperous, modern, competitive and climate neutral economy COM (2018) 773

6 Consolidated version of Directive 2003/87/EC of the European Parliament and of the Council establishing a scheme for greenhouse gas emission allowance trading within the Community and amending Council Directive 96/61/EC

7 Regulation (EU) 2018/842 on binding annual greenhouse gas emission reductions by Member States from 2021 to 2030 contributing to climate action to meet commitments under the Paris Agreement and amending Regulation (EU) No 525/2013

8 Regulation (EU) 2018/841 on the inclusion of greenhouse gas emissions and removals from land use, land use change and forestry in the 2030 climate and energy framework, and amending Regulation (EU) No 525/2013 and Decision No 529/2013/EU

9 Council Directive 2003/96/EC restructuring the Community framework for the taxation of energy products and electricity

Organization rules and other international obligations of the EU. It would be an alternative to the measures[10] that address the risk of carbon leakage in the EU's Emissions Trading System.

The Commission will adopt a new, more ambitious EU strategy on adaptation to climate change. This is essential, as climate change will continue to create significant stress in Europe in spite of the mitigation efforts. Strengthening the efforts on climate-proofing, resilience building, prevention and preparedness is crucial. Work on climate adaptation should continue to influence public and private investments, including on nature-based solutions. It will be important to ensure that across the EU, investors, insurers, businesses, cities and citizens are able to access data and to develop instruments to integrate climate change into their risk management practices.

2.1.2. Supplying clean, affordable and secure energy

Further decarbonising the energy system is critical to reach climate objectives in 2030 and 2050. The production and use of energy across economic sectors account for more than 75% of the EU's greenhouse gas emissions. Energy efficiency must be prioritised. A power sector must be developed that is based largely on renewable sources, complemented by the rapid phasing out of coal and decarbonising gas. At the same time, the EU's energy supply needs to be secure and affordable for consumers and businesses. For this to happen, it is essential to ensure that the European energy market is fully integrated, interconnected and digitalised, while respecting technological neutrality.

Member States will present their revised energy and climate plans by the end of 2019. In line with the Regulation on the Governance of the Energy Union and Climate Action[11], these plans should set out ambitious national contributions to EU-wide targets. The Commission will assess the ambition of the plans, and the need for additional measures if the level of ambition is not sufficient. This will feed into the process of increasing climate ambition for 2030, for which the Commission will review and propose to revise, where necessary, the relevant energy legislation by June 2021. When Member States begin updating their national energy and climate plans in 2023, they should reflect the new climate ambition. The Commission will continue to ensure that all relevant legislation is rigorously enforced.

The clean energy transition should involve and benefit consumers. Renewable energy sources will have an essential role. Increasing offshore wind production will be essential, building on regional cooperation between Member States. The smart integration of renewables, energy efficiency and other sustainable solutions across sectors will help to achieve decarbonisation at the lowest possible cost. The rapid decrease in the cost of renewables, combined with improved design of support policies, has already reduced the impact on households' energy bills of renewables deployment. The Commission will present by mid-2020 measures to help achieve smart integration. In parallel, the decarbonisation of the gas sector will be facilitated, including via enhancing support for the development of decarbonised gases, via a forward-looking design for a competitive decarbonised gas market, and by addressing the issue of energy-related methane emissions.

The risk of energy poverty must be addressed for households that cannot afford key energy services to ensure a basic standard of living. Effective programmes, such as financing schemes for households to renovate their houses, can reduce energy bills and help the environment. In 2020, the Commission will produce guidance to assist Member States in addressing the issue of energy poverty.

The transition to climate neutrality also requires smart infrastructure. Increased cross-border and regional cooperation will help achieve the benefits of the clean energy transition at affordable prices. The regulatory framework for energy infrastructure, including the TEN-E Regulation[12], will need to be reviewed to ensure consistency with the climate neutrality objective. This framework should foster the deployment of innovative technologies and infrastructure, such as smart grids, hydrogen networks or carbon capture, storage and utilisation, energy storage, also enabling sector integration. Some existing infrastructure and assets will require upgrading to remain fit for purpose and climate resilient.

2.1.3. Mobilising industry for a clean and circular economy

Achieving a climate neutral and circular economy requires the full mobilisation of industry. It takes 25 years – a generation – to transform an industrial sector and all the value chains. To be ready in 2050, decisions and actions need to be taken in the next five years.

From 1970 to 2017, the annual global extraction of materials tripled and it continues to grow[13], posing a major global risk. About half of total greenhouse gas emissions and more than 90% of biodiversity loss and water stress come from resource extraction and processing of materials, fuels and food. The EU's industry has started the shift but still accounts for 20% of the EU's greenhouse gas emissions. It remains too 'linear', and dependent on a throughput of new materials extracted, traded and processed into goods, and finally disposed of as waste or emissions. Only 12% of the materials it uses come from recycling[14].

The transition is an opportunity to expand sustainable and job-intensive economic activity. There is significant potential in global markets for low-emission technologies, sustainable products and services. Likewise, the circular economy offers great potential for new activities and jobs. However, the transformation is taking place at a too slow pace with progress neither widespread nor uniform. The European Green Deal

10 Such as the free allocation of emission allowances or compensation for the increase in electricity costs
11 Regulation (EU) 2018/1999 on the Governance of the Energy Union and Climate Action
12 Trans-European Networks - Energy (TEN-E) Regulation
13 Global Resources Outlook 2019 : Natural Resources for the Future We Want: The International Resource Panel.
14 https://ec.europa.eu/eurostat/tgm/table.do?tab=table&init=1&language=en&pcode=cei_srm030&plugin=1

will support and accelerate the EU's industry transition to a sustainable model of inclusive growth.

In March 2020, the Commission will adopt an EU industrial strategy to address the twin challenge of the green and the digital transformation. Europe must leverage the potential of the digital transformation, which is a key enabler for reaching the Green Deal objectives. Together with the industrial strategy, a new circular economy action plan will help modernise the EU's economy and draw benefit from the opportunities of the circular economy domestically and globally. A key aim of the new policy framework will be to stimulate the development of lead markets for climate neutral and circular products, in the EU and beyond.

Energy-intensive industries, such as steel, chemicals and cement, are indispensable to Europe's economy, as they supply several key value chains. The decarbonisation and modernisation of this sector is essential. The recommendations published by the High Level Group of energy-intensive industries show the industry's commitment to these objectives[15].

The circular economy action plan will include a 'sustainable products' policy to support the circular design of all products based on a common methodology and principles. It will prioritise reducing and reusing materials before recycling them. It will foster new business models and set minimum requirements to prevent environmentally harmful products from being placed on the EU market. Extended producer responsibility will also be strengthened.

While the circular economy action plan will guide the transition of all sectors, action will focus in particular on resource-intensive sectors such as textiles, construction, electronics and plastics. The Commission will follow up on the 2018 plastics strategy focusing, among other things, on measures to tackle intentionally added micro plastics and unintentional releases of plastics, for example from textiles and tyre abrasion. The Commission will develop requirements to ensure that all packaging in the EU market is reusable or recyclable in an economically viable manner by 2030, will develop a regulatory framework for biodegradable and bio-based plastics, and will implement measures on single use plastics.

The circular economy action plan will also include measures to encourage businesses to offer, and to allow consumers to choose, reusable, durable and repairable products. It will analyse the need for a 'right to repair', and curb the built-in obsolescence of devices, in particular for electronics. Consumer policy will help to empower consumers to make informed choices and play an active role in the ecological transition. New business models based on renting and sharing goods and services will play a role as long as they are truly sustainable and affordable.

Reliable, comparable and verifiable information also plays an important part in enabling buyers to make more sustainable decisions and reduces the risk of 'green washing'. Companies making 'green claims' should substantiate these against a standard methodology to assess their impact on the environment. The Commission will step up its regulatory and non-regulatory efforts to tackle false green claims. Digitalisation can also help improve the availability of information on the characteristics of products sold in the EU. For instance, an electronic product passport could provide information on a product's origin, composition, repair and dismantling possibilities, and end of life handling. Public authorities, including the EU institutions, should lead by example and ensure that their procurement is green. The Commission will propose further legislation and guidance on green public purchasing.

A sustainable product policy also has the potential to reduce waste significantly. Where waste cannot be avoided, its economic value must be recovered and its impact on the environment and on climate change avoided or minimised. This requires new legislation, including targets and measures for tackling over-packaging and waste generation. In parallel, EU companies should benefit from a robust and integrated single market for secondary raw materials and by-products. This requires deeper cooperation across value chains, as in the case of the Circular Plastics Alliance. The Commission will consider legal requirements to boost the market of secondary raw materials with mandatory recycled content (for instance for packaging, vehicles, construction materials and batteries). To simplify waste management for citizens and ensure cleaner secondary materials for businesses, the Commission will also propose an EU model for separate waste collection. The Commission is of the view that the EU should stop exporting its waste outside of the EU and will therefore revisit the rules on waste shipments and illegal exports.

Access to resources is also a strategic security question for Europe's ambition to deliver the Green Deal. Ensuring the supply of sustainable raw materials, in particular of critical raw materials necessary for clean technologies, digital, space and defence applications, by diversifying supply from both primary and secondary sources, is therefore one of the pre-requisites to make this transition happen.

EU industry needs 'climate and resource frontrunners' to develop the first commercial applications of breakthrough technologies in key industrial sectors by 2030. Priority areas include clean hydrogen, fuel cells and other alternative fuels, energy storage, and carbon capture, storage and utilisation. As an example, the Commission will support clean steel breakthrough technologies leading to a zero-carbon steel making process by 2030 and will explore whether part of the funding being liquidated under the European Coal and Steel Community can be used. More broadly, the EU Emissions Trading System Innovation Fund will help to deploy such large-scale innovative projects.

Promoting new forms of collaboration with industry and investments in strategic value chains are essential. The Commission will continue to implement the Strategic Action Plan on Batteries and support the European Battery Alliance. It will propose legislation in 2020 to ensure a safe, circular and sustainable battery value chain for all batteries, including to supply the growing market of electric vehicles. The Commission will

15 https://ec.europa.eu/commission/presscorner/detail/en/IP_19_6353

also support other initiatives leading to alliances and to a large-scale pooling of resources, for example in the form of Important Projects of Common European Interest, where targeted time-bound State aid can help build new innovative value chains.

Digital technologies are a critical enabler for attaining the sustainability goals of the Green deal in many different sectors. The Commission will explore measures to ensure that digital technologies such as artificial intelligence, 5G, cloud and edge computing and the internet of things can accelerate and maximise the impact of policies to deal with climate change and protect the environment. Digitalisation also presents new opportunities for distance monitoring of air and water pollution, or for monitoring and optimising how energy and natural resources are used. At the same time, Europe needs a digital sector that puts sustainability at its heart. The Commission will also consider measures to improve the energy efficiency and circular economy performance of the sector itself, from broadband networks to data centres and ICT devices. The Commission will assess the need for more transparency on the environmental impact of electronic communication services, more stringent measures when deploying new networks and the benefits of supporting 'take-back' schemes to incentivise people to return their unwanted devices such as mobile phones, tablets and chargers.

2.1.4. Building and renovating in an energy and resource efficient way

The construction, use and renovation of buildings require significant amounts of energy and mineral resources (e.g. sand, gravel, cement). Buildings also account for 40% of energy consumed. Today the annual renovation rate of the building stock varies from 0.4 to 1.2% in the Member States. This rate will need at least to double to reach the EU's energy efficiency and climate objectives. In parallel, 50 million consumers struggle to keep their homes adequately warm.

To address the twin challenge of energy efficiency and affordability, the EU and the Member States should engage in a 'renovation wave' of public and private buildings. While increasing renovation rates is a challenge, renovation lowers energy bills, and can reduce energy poverty. It can also boost the construction sector and is an opportunity to support SMEs and local jobs.

The Commission will rigorously enforce the legislation related to the energy performance of buildings. This will start with an assessment in 2020 of Member States' national long-term renovation strategies[16]. The Commission will also launch work on the possibility of including emissions from buildings in European emissions trading, as part of broader efforts to ensure that the relative prices of different energy sources provide the right signals for energy efficiency. In addition, the Commission will review the Construction Products Regulation[17]. It should ensure that the design of new and renovated buildings at all stages is in line with the needs of the circular economy, and lead to increased digitalisation and climate-proofing of the building stock.

In parallel, the Commission proposes to work with stakeholders on a new initiative on renovation in 2020. This will include an open platform bringing together the buildings and construction sector, architects and engineers and local authorities to address the barriers to renovation. This initiative will also include innovative financing schemes under InvestEU. These could target housing associations or energy service companies that could roll out renovation including through energy performance contracting. An essential aim would be to organise renovation efforts into larger blocks to benefit from better financing conditions and economies of scale. The Commission will also work to lift national regulatory barriers that inhibit energy efficiency investments in rented and multi-ownership buildings. Particular attention will be paid to the renovation of social housing, to help households who struggle to pay their energy bills. Focus should also be put on renovating schools and hospitals, as the money saved through building efficiency will be money available to support education and public health.

2.1.5. Accelerating the shift to sustainable and smart mobility

Transport accounts for a quarter of the EU's greenhouse gas emissions, and still growing. To achieve climate neutrality, a 90% reduction in transport emissions is needed by 2050. Road, rail, aviation, and waterborne transport will all have to contribute to the reduction. Achieving sustainable transport means putting users first and providing them with more affordable, accessible, healthier and cleaner alternatives to their current mobility habits. The Commission will adopt a strategy for sustainable and smart mobility in 2020 that will address this challenge and tackle all emission sources.

Multimodal transport needs a strong boost. This will increase the efficiency of the transport system. As a matter of priority, a substantial part of the 75% of inland freight carried today by road should shift onto rail and inland waterways. This will require measures to manage better, and to increase the capacity of railways and inland waterways, which the Commission will propose by 2021. The Commission will also consider withdrawing and presenting a new proposal to revise the Combined Transport Directive[18] to turn it into an effective tool to support multimodal freight operations involving rail and waterborne transport, including short-sea shipping. In aviation, work on adopting the Commission's proposal on a truly Single European Sky will need to restart, as this will help achieve significant reductions in aviation emissions.

Automated and connected multimodal mobility will play an increasing role, together with smart traffic management systems enabled by digitalisation. The

16 As part of the requirements under the Energy Performance of Buildings Directive

17 Regulation (EU) No 305/2011 laying down harmonised conditions for the marketing of construction products and repealing Council Directive 89/106/EEC

18 Proposal for a directive amending Directive 92/106/EEC on the establishment of common rules for certain types of combined transport of goods between Member States COM(2017) 648

EU transport system and infrastructure will be made fit to support new sustainable mobility services that can reduce congestion and pollution, especially in urban areas. The Commission will help develop smart systems for traffic management and 'Mobility as a Service' solutions, through its funding instruments, such as the Connected Europe Facility.

The price of transport must reflect the impact it has on the environment and on health. Fossil-fuel subsidies should end and, in the context of the revision of the Energy Taxation Directive, the Commission will look closely at the current tax exemptions including for aviation and maritime fuels and at how best to close any loopholes. Similarly, the Commission will propose to extend European emissions trading to the maritime sector, and to reduce the EU Emissions Trading System allowances allocated for free to airlines. This will be coordinated with action at global level, notably at the International Civil Aviation Organization and International Maritime Organization. The Commission will also give fresh political consideration as to how to achieve effective road pricing in the EU. It calls on the European Parliament and the Council to maintain the high level of ambition in the Commission's original proposal for the 'Eurovignette' Directive[19], and is ready to withdraw it if necessary and to propose alternative measures.

The EU should in parallel ramp-up the production and deployment of sustainable alternative transport fuels. By 2025, about 1 million public recharging and refuelling stations will be needed for the 13 million zero- and low-emission vehicles expected on European roads. The Commission will support the deployment of public recharging and refuelling points where persistent gaps exist, notably for long-distance travel and in less densely populated areas, and will launch as quickly as possible a new funding call to support this. These steps will complement the measures taken at national level. The Commission will consider legislative options to boost the production and uptake of sustainable alternative fuels for the different transport modes. The Commission will also review the Alternative Fuels Infrastructure Directive[20] and the TEN-T Regulation to accelerate the deployment of zero- and low-emission vehicles and vessels.

Transport should become drastically less polluting, especially in cities. A combination of measures should address emissions, urban congestion, and improved public transport. The Commission will propose more stringent air pollutant emissions standards for combustion-engine vehicles. The Commission will also propose to revise by June 2021 the legislation on CO_2 emission performance standards for cars and vans, to ensure a clear pathway from 2025 onwards towards zero-emission mobility. In parallel, it will consider applying European emissions trading to road transport, as a complement to existing and future CO_2 emission performance standards for vehicles. It will take action in relation to maritime transport, including to regulate access of the most polluting ships to EU ports and to oblige docked ships to use shore-side electricity. Similarly, air quality should be improved near airports by tackling the emissions of pollutants by aeroplanes and airport operations.

2.1.6. From 'Farm to Fork': designing a fair, healthy and environmentally-friendly food system

European food is famous for being safe, nutritious and of high quality. It should now also become the global standard for sustainability. Although the transition to more sustainable systems has started, feeding a fast-growing world population remains a challenge with current production patterns. Food production still results in air, water and soil pollution, contributes to the loss of biodiversity and climate change, and consumes excessive amounts of natural resources, while an important part of food is wasted. At the same time, low quality diets contribute to obesity and diseases such as cancer.

There are new opportunities for all operators in the food value chain. New technologies and scientific discoveries, combined with increasing public awareness and demand for sustainable food, will benefit all stakeholders. The Commission will present the 'Farm to Fork' Strategy in spring 2020 and launch a broad stakeholder debate covering all the stages of the food chain, and paving the way to formulating a more sustainable food policy.

European farmers and fishermen are key to managing the transition. The Farm to Fork Strategy will strengthen their efforts to tackle climate change, protect the environment and preserve biodiversity. The common agricultural and common fisheries policies will remain key tools to support these efforts while ensuring a decent living for farmers, fishermen and their families. The Commission's proposals for the common agricultural policy for 2021 to 2027 stipulate that at least 40% of the common agricultural policy's overall budget and at least 30% of the Maritime Fisheries Fund would contribute to climate action.

The Commission will work with the European Parliament and the Council to achieve at least this level of ambition in the proposals. Given that the start of the revised Common Agricultural Policy is likely to be delayed to the beginning of 2022, the Commission will work with the Member States and stakeholders to ensure that from the outset the national strategic plans for agriculture fully reflect the ambition of the Green Deal and the Farm to Fork Strategy. The Commission will ensure that these strategic plans are assessed against robust climate and environmental criteria. These plans should lead to the use of sustainable practices, such as precision agriculture, organic farming, agro-ecology, agro-forestry and stricter animal welfare standards. By shifting the focus from compliance to performance, measures such as eco-schemes should reward farmers for improved environmental and climate performance, including managing and storing carbon in the soil, and improved nutrient management to improve water quality and reduce emissions. The Commission will work

19 Proposal for a directive amending Directive 1999/62/EC on the charging of heavy goods vehicles for the use of certain infrastructure COM(2017) 275

20 Directive 2014/94/EU on the deployment of alternative fuels infrastructure

with the Member States to develop the potential of sustainable seafood as a source of low-carbon food.

The strategic plans will need to reflect an increased level of ambition to reduce significantly the use and risk of chemical pesticides, as well as the use of fertilisers and antibiotics. The Commission will identify the measures, including legislative, needed to bring about these reductions based on a stakeholder dialogue. The area under organic farming will also need to increase in Europe. The EU needs to develop innovative ways to protect harvests from pests and diseases and to consider the potential role of new innovative techniques to improve the sustainability of the food system, while ensuring that they are safe.

The Farm to Fork Strategy will also contribute to achieving a circular economy. It will aim to reduce the environmental impact of the food processing and retail sectors by taking action on transport, storage, packaging and food waste. This will include actions to combat food fraud, including strengthening enforcement and investigative capacity at EU level, and to launch a process to identify new innovative food and feed products, such as seafood based on algae.

Lastly, the Farm to Fork Strategy will strive to stimulate sustainable food consumption and promote affordable healthy food for all. Imported food that does not comply with relevant EU environmental standards is not allowed on EU markets. The Commission will propose actions to help consumers choose healthy and sustainable diets and reduce food waste. The Commission will explore new ways to give consumers better information, including by digital means, on details such as where the food comes from, its nutritional value, and its environmental footprint. The Farm to Fork strategy will also contain proposals to improve the position of farmers in the value chain.

2.1.7. Preserving and restoring ecosystems and biodiversity

Ecosystems provide essential services such as food, fresh water and clean air, and shelter. They mitigate natural disasters, pests and diseases and help regulate the climate. However, the EU is not meeting some of its most important environmental objectives for 2020, such as the Aichi targets under the Convention on Biological Diversity. The EU and its global partners need to halt biodiversity loss. The Intergovernmental Science-Policy Platform on Biodiversity and Ecosystem Services' 2019 Global Assessment Report[21] showed worldwide erosion of biodiversity, caused primarily by changes in how land and sea are used, direct exploitation of natural resources, and with climate change as the third most important driver of biodiversity loss.

The Conference of the Parties to the Convention on Biological Diversity in Kunming, China, in October 2020 is an opportunity for the world to adopt a robust global framework to halt biodiversity loss. To ensure that the EU plays a key role, the Commission will present a Biodiversity Strategy by March 2020, to be followed up by specific action in 2021. The strategy will outline the EU's position for the Conference of the Parties, with global targets to protect biodiversity, as well as commitments to address the main causes of biodiversity loss in the EU, underpinned by measurable objectives that address the main causes of biodiversity loss.

The biodiversity strategy will identify specific measures to meet these objectives. These could include quantified objectives, such as increasing the coverage of protected biodiversity-rich land and sea areas building on the Natura 2000 network. Member States should also reinforce cross-border cooperation to protect and restore more effectively the areas covered by the Natura 2000 network. The Commission will identify which measures, including legislation, would help Member States improve and restore damaged ecosystems to good ecological status, including carbon-rich ecosystems. The biodiversity strategy will also include proposals to green European cities and increase biodiversity in urban spaces. The Commission will consider drafting a nature restoration plan and will look at how provide funding to help Member States to reach this aim.

All EU policies should contribute to preserving and restoring Europe's natural capital[22]. The Farm to Fork Strategy, outlined in section 2.1.6, will address the use of pesticides and fertilisers in agriculture. Work will continue under the common fisheries policy to reduce the adverse impacts that fishing can have on ecosystems, especially in sensitive areas. The Commission will also support more connected and well-managed marine protected areas.

Forest ecosystems are under increasing pressure, as a result of climate change. The EU's forested area needs to improve, both in quality and quantity, for the EU to reach climate neutrality and a healthy environment. Sustainable re- and afforestation and the restoration of degraded forests can increase absorption of CO_2 while improving the resilience of forests and promoting the circular bio-economy. Building on the 2030 biodiversity strategy, the Commission will prepare a new EU forest strategy covering the whole forest cycle and promoting the many services that forests provide.

The new EU forest strategy will have as its key objectives effective afforestation, and forest preservation and restoration in Europe, to help to increase the absorption of CO_2, reduce the incidence and extent of forest fires, and promote the bio-economy, in full respect for ecological principles favourable to biodiversity. The national strategic plans under the common agricultural policy should incentivise forest managers to preserve, grow and manage forests sustainably. Building on the Communication on Stepping up EU Action to Protect and Restore the World's Forests[23], the Commission will take measures, both regulatory and otherwise, to promote imported products and value chains that do not involve deforestation and forest degradation.

A sustainable 'blue economy' will have to play a central role in alleviating the multiple demands on the

21 https://ipbes.net/news/ipbes-global-assessment-preview.
22 EU guidelines SWD (2019)305 FINAL "EU guidance on integrating ecosystems and their services into decision-making".
23 COM/2019/352 final.

EU's land resources and tackling climate change. The role of oceans in mitigating and adapting to climate change is increasingly recognised. The sector can contribute by improving the use of aquatic and marine resources and, for example, by promoting the production and use of new sources of protein that can relieve pressure on agricultural land. More generally, lasting solutions to climate change require greater attention to nature-based solutions including healthy and resilient seas and oceans. The Commission will analyse the findings of the International Panel on Climate Change special report on oceans[24] and propose measures in the maritime area. This will include ways to manage maritime space more sustainably, notably to help tap into the growing potential of offshore renewable energy. The Commission will also take a zero-tolerance approach to illegal, unreported and unregulated fishing. The 2020 United Nations Ocean Conference in Portugal will be an opportunity for the EU to highlight the importance of action on ocean issues.

2.1.8. A zero pollution ambition for a toxic-free environment

Creating a toxic-free environment requires more action to prevent pollution from being generated as well as measures to clean and remedy it. To protect Europe's citizens and ecosystems, the EU needs to better monitor, report, prevent and remedy pollution from air, water, soil, and consumer products. To achieve this, the EU and Member States will need to look more systematically at all policies and regulations. To address these interlinked challenges, the Commission will adopt in 2021 a zero pollution action plan for air, water and soil.

The natural functions of ground and surface water must be restored. This is essential to preserve and restore biodiversity in lakes, rivers, wetlands and estuaries, and to prevent and limit damage from floods. Implementing the 'Farm to Fork' strategy will reduce pollution from excess nutrients. In addition, the Commission will propose measures to address pollution from urban runoff and from new or particularly harmful sources of pollution such as micro plastics and chemicals, including pharmaceuticals. There is also a need to address the combined effects of different pollutants.

The Commission will draw on the lessons learnt from the evaluation of the current air quality legislation[25]. It will also propose to strengthen provisions on monitoring[26], modelling and air quality plans to help local authorities achieve cleaner air. The Commission will notably propose to revise air quality standards to align them more closely with the World Health Organization recommendations.

The Commission will review EU measures to address pollution from large industrial installations. It will look at the sectoral scope of the legislation and at how to make it fully consistent with climate, energy and circular economy policies. The Commission will also work with Member States to improve the prevention of industrial accidents.

To ensure a toxic-free environment, the Commission will present a chemicals strategy for sustainability. This will both help to protect citizens and the environment better against hazardous chemicals and encourage innovation for the development of safe and sustainable alternatives. All parties including industry should work together to combine better health and environmental protection and increased global competitiveness. This can be achieved by simplifying and strengthening the legal framework. The Commission will review how to use better the EU's agencies and scientific bodies to move towards a process of 'one substance – one assessment' and to provide greater transparency when prioritising action to deal with chemicals. In parallel, the regulatory framework will need to rapidly reflect scientific evidence on the risk posed by endocrine disruptors, hazardous chemicals in products including imports, combination effects of different chemicals and very persistent chemicals.

2.2. Mainstreaming sustainability in all EU policies

2.2.1. Pursuing green finance and investment and ensuring a just transition

To achieve the ambition set by the European Green Deal, there are significant investment needs. The Commission has estimated that achieving the current 2030 climate and energy targets will require €260 billion of additional annual investment[27], about 1.5% of 2018 GDP[28]. This flow of investment will need to be sustained over time. The magnitude of the investment challenge requires mobilising both the public and private sector.

The Commission will present a Sustainable Europe Investment Plan to help meet the additional funding needs. It will combine dedicated financing to support sustainable investments, and proposals for an improved enabling framework that is conducive to green investment. At the same time, it will be essential to prepare a pipeline of sustainable projects. Technical assistance and advisory services will help project promoters to identify and prepare projects and to access sources of finance.

The EU budget will play a key role. The Commission has proposed a 25% target for climate mainstreaming across all EU programmes. The EU budget will also contribute to achieving climate objectives on the revenue side. The Commission has proposed new revenue streams ("Own Resources"), one of which is based on the non-recycled plastic-packaging waste. A

24 Special Report on the Ocean and Cryosphere in a Changing Climate.
25 Fitness check of the Ambient Air Quality Directives SWD(2019) 427.
26 Including by making use of new monitoring opportunities provided by digitalisation.
27 Communication "United in delivering the Energy Union and Climate Action - Setting the foundations for a successful clean energy transition" COM(2019) 285.
28 These estimates are conservative, as they do not consider, for instance, the investment needs for climate adaptation or for other environmental challenges, such as biodiversity. They also exclude the public investment needed to address the social costs of the transition and the costs of inaction.

second revenue stream could involve allocating 20% of the revenue from the auctioning of EU Emissions Trading System to the EU budget.

At least 30% of the InvestEU Fund will contribute to fighting climate change. Moreover, projects will be subject to sustainability proofing to screen the contribution that they make to climate, environmental and social objectives. InvestEU also offers Member States the option to use the EU budgetary guarantee e.g. to deliver on climate-related cohesion policy objectives in their territories and regions. InvestEU also strengthens cooperation with national promotional banks and institutions, which can encourage an overall greening of their activities to deliver on EU policy objectives. Moreover, as part of the revision of the EU Emission Trading System, the Commission will review the role of the Innovation and Modernisation Funds, which are not financed by the EU's long-term budget. The ambition will be to strengthen their role and their effectiveness in deploying innovative and climate neutral solutions across the EU. In the revision of the EU Emissions Trading System, the allocation of additional revenues from allowances to the EU budget with a view to strengthening the financing of the just transition will also be considered.

The Commission will also work with the European Investment Bank (EIB) Group, national promotional banks and institutions, as well as with other international financial institutions. The EIB set itself the target of doubling its climate target from 25% to 50% by 2025, thus becoming Europe's climate bank.

As part of the Sustainable Europe Investment Plan, the Commission will propose a Just Transition Mechanism, including a Just Transition Fund, to leave no one behind. The transition can only succeed if it is conducted in a fair and inclusive way. The most vulnerable are the most exposed to the harmful effects of climate change and environmental degradation. At the same time, managing the transition will lead to significant structural changes in business models, skill requirements and relative prices. Citizens, depending on their social and geographic circumstances, will be affected in different ways. Not all Member States, regions and cities start the transition from the same point or have the same capacity to respond. These challenges require a strong policy response at all levels.

The Just Transition Mechanism will focus on the regions and sectors that are most affected by the transition because they depend on fossil fuels or carbon-intensive processes. It will draw on sources of funding from the EU budget as well as the EIB group to leverage the necessary private and public resources. Support will be linked to promoting a transition towards low-carbon and climate-resilient activities. It will also strive to protect the citizens and workers most vulnerable to the transition, providing access to re-skilling programmes, jobs in new economic sectors, or energy-efficient housing. The Commission will work with the Member States and regions to help them put in place territorial transition plans.

The mechanism will come in addition to the substantial contribution of the EU's budget through all programmes directly relevant to the transition, as well as other funds such as the European Regional Development Fund and the European Social Fund Plus.

In order to bring an answer to the long-term financing needs of the transition, the Commission will continue to explore with relevant partners, as part of the Sustainable Europe Investment Plan, additional sources that could be mobilised and innovative ways to do so.

The need for a socially just transition must also be reflected in policies at EU and national level. This includes investment to provide affordable solutions to those affected by carbon pricing policies, for example through public transport, as well as measures to address energy poverty and promote re-skilling. Coherence of climate and environment policies and a holistic approach are often a precondition for ensuring they are perceived as fair, as illustrated by the debate on taxation of various modes of transport. For companies and their workers, an active social dialogue helps to anticipate and successfully manage change. The European Semester process of macroeconomic coordination will support national policies on these issues.

The private sector will be key to financing the green transition. Long-term signals are needed to direct financial and capital flows to green investment and to avoid stranded assets. The Commission will present a renewed sustainable finance strategy in the third quarter of 2020 that will focus on a number of actions.

First, the strategy will strengthen the foundations for sustainable investment. This will require notably that the European Parliament and Council adopt the taxonomy for classifying environmentally sustainable activities. Sustainability should be further embedded into the corporate governance framework, as many companies still focus too much on short-term financial performance compared to their long-term development and sustainability aspects. At the same time, companies and financial institutions will need to increase their disclosure on climate and environmental data so that investors are fully informed about the sustainability of their investments. To this end, the Commission will review the Non-Financial Reporting Directive. To ensure appropriate management of environmental risks and mitigation opportunities, and reduce related transaction costs, the Commission will also support businesses and other stakeholders in developing standardised natural capital accounting practices within the EU and internationally.

Second, increased opportunities will be provided for investors and companies by making it easier for them to identify sustainable investments and ensuring that they are credible. This could be done via clear labels for retail investment products and by developing an EU green bond standard that facilitates sustainable investment in the most convenient way.

Third, climate and environmental risks will be managed and integrated into the financial system. This means better integrating such risks into the EU prudential framework and assessing the suitability of the existing capital requirements for green assets. We will also examine how our financial system can help to increase resilience to climate and environmental risks, in particular when it comes to the physical risks and damage arising from natural catastrophes.

2.2.2. Greening national budgets and sending the right price signals

National budgets play a key role in the transition. A greater use of green budgeting tools will help to redirect public investment, consumption and taxation to green priorities and away from harmful subsidies. The Commission will work with the Member States to screen and benchmark green budgeting practices. This will make it easier to assess to what extent annual budgets and medium-term fiscal plans take environmental considerations and risks into account, and learn from best practices. The review of the European economic governance framework will include a reference to green public investment in the context of the quality of public finance. This will inform a debate on how to improve EU fiscal governance. The outcome of the debate will form the basis for any possible future steps including how to treat green investments within EU fiscal rules, while preserving safeguards against risks to debt sustainability.

Well-designed tax reforms can boost economic growth and resilience to climate shocks and help contribute to a fairer society and to a just transition. They play a direct role by sending the right price signals and providing the right incentives for sustainable behaviour by producers, users and consumers. At national level, the European Green Deal will create the context for broad-based tax reforms, removing subsidies for fossil fuels, shifting the tax burden from labour to pollution, and taking into account social considerations. There is a need to ensure rapid adoption of the Commission's proposal on value added tax (VAT) rates currently on the table of the Council, so that Member States can make a more targeted use of VAT rates to reflect increased environmental ambitions, for example to support organic fruit and vegetables.

Evaluations are underway of the relevant State aid guidelines including the environmental and energy State aid guidelines. The guidelines will be revised by 2021 to reflect the policy objectives of the European Green Deal, supporting a cost-effective transition to climate neutrality by 2050, and will facilitate the phasing out of fossil fuels, in particular those that are most polluting, ensuring a level-playing field in the internal market. These revisions are also an opportunity to address market barriers to the deployment of clean products.

2.2.3. Mobilising research and fostering innovation

New technologies, sustainable solutions and disruptive innovation are critical to achieve the objectives of the European Green Deal. To keep its competitive advantage in clean technologies, the EU needs to increase significantly the large-scale deployment and demonstration of new technologies across sectors and across the single market, building new innovative value chains. This challenge is beyond the means of individual Member States. Horizon Europe, in synergy with other EU programmes, will play a pivotal role in leveraging national public and private investments. At least 35% of the budget of Horizon Europe will fund new solutions for climate, which are relevant for implementing the Green Deal.

The full range of instruments available under the Horizon Europe programme will support the research and innovation efforts needed. Four 'Green Deal Missions' will help deliver large-scale changes in areas such as adaptation to climate change, oceans, cities and soil. These missions will bring together a wide range of stakeholders including regions and citizens. Partnerships with industry and Member States will support research and innovation on transport, including batteries, clean hydrogen, low-carbon steel making, circular bio-based sectors and the built environment. The knowledge and innovation communities run by the European Institute of Innovation and Technology will continue to promote collaboration among higher education institutions, research organisations and companies on climate change, sustainable energy, food for the future, and smart, environmentally-friendly and integrated urban transport. The European Innovation Council will dedicate funding, equity investment and business acceleration services to high potential start-ups and SMEs for them to achieve breakthrough Green Deal innovation that can be scaled up rapidly on global markets.

Conventional approaches will not be sufficient. Emphasising experimentation, and working across sectors and disciplines, the EU's research and innovation agenda will take the systemic approach needed to achieve the aims of the Green Deal. The Horizon Europe programme will also involve local communities in working towards a more sustainable future, in initiatives that seek to combine societal pull and technology push.

Accessible and interoperable data are at the heart of data-driven innovation. This data, combined with digital infrastructure (e.g. supercomputers, cloud, ultra-fast networks) and artificial intelligence solutions, facilitate evidence-based decisions and expand the capacity to understand and tackle environmental challenges. The Commission will support work to unlock the full benefits of the digital transformation to support the ecological transition. An immediate priority will be to boost the EU's ability to predict and manage environmental disasters. To do this, the Commission will bring together European scientific and industrial excellence to develop a very high precision digital model of the Earth.

2.2.4. Activating education and training

Schools, training institutions and universities are well placed to engage with pupils, parents, and the wider community on the changes needed for a successful transition. The Commission will prepare a European competence framework to help develop and assess knowledge, skills and attitudes on climate change and sustainable development. It will also provide support materials and facilitate the exchange of good practices in EU networks of teacher-training programmes.

The Commission has been working to provide Member States with new financial resources to make school buildings and operations more sustainable. It has strengthened collaboration with the European Investment Bank and created stronger links between structural funds and the new financial instruments with the aim of leveraging €3 billion in investment in school infrastructure in 2020.

Pro-active re-skilling and upskilling are necessary to reap the benefits of the ecological transition. The proposed European Social Fund+ will play an important role in helping Europe's workforce to acquire the skills they need to transfer from declining sectors to growing sectors and to adapt to new processes. The Skills Agenda and the Youth Guarantee will be updated to enhance employability in the green economy.

2.2.5. A green oath: 'do no harm'

All EU actions and policies should pull together to help the EU achieve a successful and just transition towards a sustainable future. The Commission's better regulation tools provide a solid basis for this. Based on public consultations, on the identification of the environmental, social and economic impacts, and on analyses of how SMEs are affected and innovation fostered or hindered, impact assessments contribute to making efficient policy choices at minimum costs, in line with the objectives of the Green Deal. Evaluations also systematically assess coherence between current legislation and new priorities.

To support its work to identify and remedy inconsistencies in current legislation, the Commission invites stakeholders to use the available platforms[29] to simplify legislation and identify problematic cases. The Commission will consider these suggestions when preparing evaluations, impact assessments and legislative proposals for the European Green Deal.

In addition, building on the results of its recent stock taking of better regulation policy, the Commission will improve the way its better regulation guidelines and supporting tools address sustainability and innovation issues. The objective is to ensure that all Green Deal initiatives achieve their objectives in the most effective and least burdensome way and all other EU initiatives live up to a green oath to 'do no harm'. To this end, the explanatory memorandum accompanying all legislative proposals and delegated acts will include a specific section explaining how each initiative upholds this principle.

3. THE EU AS A GLOBAL LEADER

The global challenges of climate change and environmental degradation require a global response. The EU will continue to promote and implement ambitious environment, climate and energy policies across the world. It will develop a stronger 'green deal diplomacy' focused on convincing and supporting others to take on their share of promoting more sustainable development. By setting a credible example, and following-up with diplomacy, trade policy, development support and other external policies, the EU can be an effective advocate. The Commission and the High Representative will work closely with Member States to mobilise all diplomatic channels both bilateral and multilateral – including the United Nations, the G7, G20, the World Trade Organization and other relevant international fora.

The EU will continue to ensure that the Paris Agreement remains the indispensable multilateral framework for tackling climate change. As the EU's share of global emissions is falling, comparable action and increased efforts by other regions will be critical for addressing the global climate challenge in a meaningful way. The debate on climate ambition will intensify in the coming months in line with the Paris Agreement provisions for regular stocktaking and updates. The Conference of Parties in Glasgow in 2020 will be an important milestone before the global stocktake in 2023. It will assess progress towards achieving long-term goals. As it currently stands, it is clear that the level of global ambition is insufficient[30]. The EU will engage more intensely with all partners to increase the collective effort and help them to revise and implement their nationally determined contributions and devise ambitious long-term strategies. This will build on the EU's own increased ambition as outlined in section 2.

In parallel, the EU will step up bilateral engagement with partner countries and, where necessary, establish innovative forms of engagement. The EU will continue to engage with the economies of the G20 that are responsible for 80% of global greenhouse gas emissions. Stepping up the level of climate action taken by international partners requires tailor-made geographic strategies that reflect different contexts and local needs – for example for current and future big emitters, for the least developed countries, and for small island developing states. The EU is also working with global partners to develop international carbon markets as a key tool to create economic incentives for climate action.

The EU will put emphasis on supporting its immediate neighbours. The ecological transition for Europe can only be fully effective if the EU's immediate neighbourhood also takes effective action. Work is underway on a green agenda for the Western Balkans. The Commission and the High Representative are also envisaging a number of strong environment, energy and climate partnerships with the Southern Neighbourhood and within the Eastern Partnership.

The 2020 EU-China summits in Beijing and Leipzig will be an opportunity to reinforce the partnership between the EU and China on climate and environmental issues, notably ahead of the Kunming Biodiversity Conference, and the Conference of Parties in Glasgow.

Likewise, the forthcoming Comprehensive Strategy with Africa, and the 2020 summit between the African Union and the EU, should make climate and environmental issues key strands in relations between the two continents. In particular, the Africa-Europe Alliance for sustainable investment and jobs will seek to unlock Africa's potential to make rapid progress towards a green and circular economy including sustainable energy and food systems and smart cities. The EU will strengthen its engagement with Africa for the wider deployment and trade of sustainable and clean energy. Renewable energy and energy efficiency, for example

29 'Have Your Say – Lighten the Load' website: https://ec.europa.eu/info/law/better-regulation/lighten-load.
30 United Nations Environment emissions gap report 2019.

for clean cooking, are key to closing the energy access gap in Africa while delivering the required reduction in CO_2. The EU will launch a "NaturAfrica" initiative to tackle biodiversity loss by creating a network of protected areas to protect wildlife and offer opportunities in green sectors for local populations.

More generally, the EU will use its diplomatic and financial tools to ensure that green alliances are part of its relations with Africa and other partner countries and regions, particularly in Latin America, the Caribbean, Asia and the Pacific.

The EU should also reinforce current initiatives and engage with third countries on cross-cutting climate and environment issues. This may include ending global fossil fuel subsidies in line with G20 commitments, phasing-out financing by multilateral institutions of fossil fuel infrastructure, strengthening sustainable financing, phasing out all new coal plant construction, and action to reduce methane emissions.

The EU also recognises that the global climate and environmental challenges are a significant threat multiplier and a source of instability. The ecological transition will reshape geopolitics, including global economic, trade and security interests. This will create challenges for a number of states and societies. The EU will work with all partners to increase climate and environmental resilience to prevent these challenges from becoming sources of conflict, food insecurity, population displacement and forced migration, and support a just transition globally. Climate policy implications should become an integral part of the EU's thinking and action on external issues, including in the context of the Common Security and Defence Policy.

Trade policy can support the EU's ecological transition. It serves as a platform to engage with trading partners on climate and environmental action. Commitments to sustainability have been continuously strengthened in EU trade agreements, in particular with regard to enhancing climate change action. The Commission has also been stepping up efforts to implement and enforce the sustainable development commitments of EU trade agreements, and these efforts will be further enhanced with the appointment of a Chief Trade Enforcement Officer. On climate change more specifically, the EU's most recent agreements all include a binding commitment of the Parties to ratify and effectively implement the Paris Agreement. The Commission will propose to make the respect of the Paris agreement an essential element for all future comprehensive trade agreements. The EU's trade policy facilitates trade and investment in green goods and services and promotes climate-friendly public procurement. Trade policy also needs to ensure undistorted, fair trade and investment in raw materials that the EU economy needs for the green transition. It can help address harmful practices such as illegal logging, enhance regulatory cooperation promote EU standards and remove non-tariff barriers in the renewable energy sector. All chemicals, materials, food and other products that are placed on the European market must fully comply with relevant EU regulations and standards. The EU should use its expertise in "green" regulation to encourage partners to design similar rules that are as ambitious as the EU's rules, thus facilitating trade and enhancing environment protection and climate mitigation in these countries.

As the world's largest single market, the EU can set standards that apply across global value chains. The Commission will continue to work on new standards for sustainable growth and use its economic weight to shape international standards that are in line with EU environmental and climate ambitions. It will work to facilitate trade in environmental goods and services, in bilateral and multilateral forums, and in supporting open and attractive EU and global markets for sustainable products. It will work with global partners to ensure the EU's resource security and reliable access to strategic raw materials.

The EU's international cooperation and partnership policy should continue to help channel both public and private funds to achieve the transition. While the EU and its Member States remain the world's leading donors of development assistance and provide over 40% of the world's public climate finance. As public funds will not suffice, the EU and its Member States will coordinate their support to engage with partners to bridge the funding gap by mobilising private finance. The Commission proposal for a Neighbourhood, Development and International Cooperation Instrument proposes to allocate a target of 25% of its budget to climate-related objectives. The Commission will also support the commitment made by national public financial resources to improve the investment climate and achieve contributions from the private sector. This work will need to be accompanied by opportunities to de-risk investments in sustainable development through tools such as funding guarantees and blended financing.

To mobilise international investors, the EU will also remain at the forefront of efforts to set up a financial system that supports global sustainable growth. The EU will build on the International Platform on Sustainable Finance that was recently established to coordinate efforts on environmentally sustainable finance initiatives such as taxonomies, disclosures, standards and labels. The Commission will also encourage discussions at other international fora, in particular the G7 and G20.

4. TIME TO ACT – TOGETHER: A EUROPEAN CLIMATE PACT

The involvement and commitment of the public and of all stakeholders is crucial to the success of the European Green Deal. Recent political events show that game-changing policies only work if citizens are fully involved in designing them. People are concerned about jobs, heating their homes and making ends meet, and EU institutions should engage with them if the Green Deal is to succeed and deliver lasting change. Citizens are and should remain a driving force of the transition.

The Commission will launch a European Climate Pact by March 2020 to focus on three ways to engage with the public on climate action. First, it will encourage information sharing, inspiration, and foster public understanding of the threat and the challenge of climate change and environmental degradation and on how to counter it. It will use multiple channels and tools to do so, including events in Member States, on the model of the Commission's on-going citizens' dialogues. Second, there should be both real and virtual spaces for people to express their ideas and creativity and work together on ambitious action, both at individual and collective level. Participants would be encouraged to commit to specific climate action goals. Third, the Commission will work on building capacity to facilitate grassroots initiatives on climate change and environmental protection. Information, guidance and educational modules could help exchange good practice. The Commission will ensure that the green transition features prominently in the debate on the future of Europe.

The Climate Pact will build on the Commission's on-going series of citizens' dialogues and citizens' assemblies across the EU, and the role of social dialogue committees. It will continue to work to empower regional and local communities, including energy communities. The urban dimension of cohesion policy will be strengthened, and the proposed European Urban Initiative will provide assistance to cities to help them make best use of opportunities to develop sustainable urban development strategies. The EU Covenant of Mayors will continue to be a central force. The Commission will work with it to continue to provide assistance to cities and regions that want to commit to ambitious pledges on climate and energy policies. It will remain an essential platform to share good practices on how to implement change locally.

The Commission is also keen to reduce its environmental impact as an institution and as an employer. It will present a comprehensive action plan in 2020 to implement itself the objectives of the Green Deal and to become climate neutral by 2030. It calls on all the other institutions, bodies and agencies of the EU to work with it and come forward with similar ambitious measures.

In addition to the Climate Pact, the Commission and Member States should work to ensure that all available planning tools for the European Green Deal are used coherently. The most important of these are the national energy and climate plans and the proposed strategic national plans to implement the common agricultural policy. The Commission will ensure that they are fit for purpose and that Member States are implementing them effectively, and will use tools such as the European Semester as appropriate.

European funds, including for rural development, will help rural areas to harness opportunities in the circular and bio-economy. The Commission will reflect this in its long-term vision for rural areas. It will pay particular attention to the role of outermost regions in the European Green Deal, taking into account their vulnerability to climate change and natural disasters and their unique assets: biodiversity and renewable energy sources. The Commission will take forward the work on the Clean Energy for EU Islands Initiative to develop a long-term framework to accelerate the clean energy transition on all EU islands.

The Commission and the Member States must also ensure that policies and legislation are enforced and deliver effectively. The environmental implementation review will play a critical role in mapping the situation in each Member State. The Commission will also present a new environmental action programme to complement the European Green Deal that will include a new monitoring mechanism to ensure that Europe remains on track to meet its environmental objectives. The Commission will also launch a dashboard to monitor progress against all of the European Green Deal objectives.

The Commission will consider revising the Aarhus Regulation to improve access to administrative and judicial review at EU level for citizens and NGOs who have concerns about the legality of decisions with effects on the environment. The Commission will also take action to improve their access to justice before national courts in all Member States. The Commission will also promote action by the EU, its Member States and the international community to step up efforts against environmental crime.

The European Green Deal launches a new growth strategy for the EU. It supports the transition of the EU to a fair and prosperous society that responds to the challenges posed by climate change and environmental degradation, improving the quality of life of current and future generations. The Commission invites the European Parliament and the European Council to endorse the European Green Deal and to give their full weight to the measures it contains.

ANNEX to the Communication from the Commission to the European Parliament, the European Council, the Council, the European Economic and Social Committee and the Committee of the Regions – The European Green Deal

Annex to the Communication on the European Green Deal

Roadmap – Key actions

Actions	Indicative Timetable[31]
Climate ambition	
Proposal on a European 'Climate Law' enshrining the 2050 climate neutrality objective	March 2020
Comprehensive plan to increase the EU 2030 climate target to at least 50% and towards 55% in a responsible way	Summer 2020
Proposals for revisions of relevant legislative measures to deliver on the increased climate ambition, following the review of Emissions Trading System Directive; Effort Sharing Regulation; Land use, land use change and forestry Regulation; Energy Efficiency Directive; Renewable Energy Directive; CO2 emissions performance standards for cars and vans	June 2021
Proposal for a revision of the Energy Taxation Directive	June 2021
Proposal for a carbon border adjustment mechanism for selected sectors	2021
New EU Strategy on Adaptation to Climate Change	2020/2021
Clean, affordable and secure energy	
Assessment of the final National Energy and Climate Plans	June 2020
Strategy for smart sector integration	2020
'Renovation wave' initiative for the building sector	2020
Evaluation and review of the Trans-European Network – Energy Regulation	2020
Strategy on offshore wind	2020
Industrial strategy for a clean and circular economy	
EU Industrial strategy	March 2020
Circular Economy Action Plan, including a sustainable products initiative and particular focus on resource intense sectors such as textiles, construction, electronics and plastics	March 2020
Initiatives to stimulate lead markets for climate neutral and circular products in energy intensive industrial sectors	From 2020
Proposal to support zero carbon steel-making processes by 2030	2020
Legislation on batteries in support of the Strategic Action Plan on Batteries and the circular economy	October 2020
Propose legislative waste reforms	From 2020
Sustainable and smart mobility	
Strategy for sustainable and smart mobility	2020
Funding call to support the deployment of public recharging and refuelling points as part of alternative fuel infrastructure	From 2020
Assessment of legislative options to boost the production and supply of sustainable alternative fuels for the different transport modes	From 2020
Revised proposal for a Directive on Combined Transport	2021
Review of the Alternative Fuels Infrastructure Directive and the Trans European Network – Transport Regulation	2021

31 The Commission's work programme for 2020 will provide further clarity on the timing of relevant actions announced for 2020.

Initiatives to increase and better manage the capacity of railways and inland waterways	From 2021
Proposal for more stringent air pollutant emissions standards for combustion-engine vehicles	2021
Greening the Common Agricultural Policy / 'Farm to Fork' Strategy	
Examination of the draft national strategic plans, with reference to the ambitions of the European Green Deal and the Farm to Fork Strategy	2020-2021
'Farm to Fork' Strategy Measures, including legislative, to significantly reduce the use and risk of chemical pesticides, as well as the use of fertilizers and antibiotics	Spring 2020 2021
Preserving and protecting biodiversity	
EU Biodiversity Strategy for 2030	March 2020
Measures to address the main drivers of biodiversity loss	From 2021
New EU Forest Strategy	2020
Measures to support deforestation-free value chains	From 2020
Towards a zero-pollution ambition for a toxic free environment	
Chemicals strategy for sustainability	Summer 2020
Zero pollution action plan for water, air and soil	2021
Revision of measures to address pollution from large industrial installations	2021
Mainstreaming sustainability in all EU policies	
Proposal for a Just Transition Mechanism, including a Just Transition Fund, and a Sustainable Europe Investment Plan	January 2020
Renewed sustainable finance strategy	Autumn 2020
Review of the Non-Financial Reporting Directive	2020
Initiatives to screen and benchmark green budgeting practices of the Member States and of the EU	From 2020
Review of the relevant State aid guidelines, including the environment and energy State aid guidelines	2021
Align all new Commission initiatives in line with the objectives of the Green Deal and promote innovation	From 2020
Stakeholders to identify and remedy incoherent legislation that reduces the effectiveness in delivering the European Green Deal	From 2020
Integration of the Sustainable Development Goals in the European Semester	From 2020
The EU as a global leader	
EU to continue to lead the international climate and biodiversity negotiations, further strengthening the international policy framework	From 2019
Strengthen the EU's Green Deal Diplomacy in cooperation with Member States	From 2020
Bilateral efforts to induce partners to act and to ensure comparability of action and policies	From 2020
Green Agenda for the Western Balkans	From 2020
Working together – a European Climate Pact	
Launch of the European Climate Pact	March 2020
Proposal for an 8th Environmental Action Programme	2020

1.5.2. Fit for 55

Communication from the Commission to the European Parliament, the Council, the European Economic and Social Committee and the Committee of the Regions, "Fit for 55": delivering the EU's 2030 Climate Target on the way to climate neutrality, 14 July 2021, COM(2021) 550 final

1. "FIT FOR 55": DELIVERING THE EU'S 2030 CLIMATE TARGET ON THE WAY TO CLIMATE NEUTRALITY

We are at a pivotal moment in the world's response to the climate and biodiversity emergencies and we are the last generation that can still act in time. This decade is a make-or-break moment for delivering on our commitments under the Paris Agreement, in the interest of the health, wellbeing and prosperity of all. The EU has led by example in setting ambitious targets for reducing net emissions by at least 55% by 2030 compared to 1990 and for being the first climate neutral continent by 2050. These goals are no longer aspirations or ambitions but obligations laid down in the first European Climate Law that create new opportunities for innovation, investment and jobs.

In this spirit, the package of proposals aims to make the EU "fit for 55" and deliver the transformational change needed across our economy, society and industry. This is a collective responsibility and opportunity that must be open to all, whether innovators and investors, companies and cities, or consumers, households and individuals. We all share in the benefits of more space for nature, cleaner air, cooler and greener towns and cities, healthier citizens, lower energy use and bills, as well as new jobs, technologies and industrial opportunities. The challenge at the heart of the EU's green transition is how we can bring these benefits to all as quickly and as fairly as possible, while strengthening our competitiveness, creating the jobs of tomorrow and effectively addressing the costs and impacts of the transition.

Acting before we reach irreversible tipping points will allow us to design that transformation rather than react and adapt to it. While the cost of non-action is clearly higher than the cost of fulfilling our climate ambitions, sterile numbers cannot capture the stark consequences of continuing business-as-usual. Non-action could also lead to new dividing lines: between those who can afford clean, modern technologies based on renewables and those with no alternative to old-fashioned and polluting ones. Next generations will bear the brunt of more frequent– and more intense – storms, wildfires, droughts and floods, as well as the conflicts that they could trigger around the world. Tackling these crises is therefore a matter of intergenerational and international solidarity. What we achieve in the next decade will determine our children's future. This is why there is sustained and growing public support for climate ambition and action[1]. Stepping up climate action is also an appeal of especially young people, including today's teenagers, who, as agents of change, call on governments and the EU to act decisively and without delay to protect the climate and environment for next generations.

Today's proposals build on policies and legislation the European Union has already put in place. The European Green Deal set the blueprint for this transformational change. It put in place the building blocks for the economy of tomorrow with landmark strategies on biodiversity, circular economy, zero pollution, sustainable and smart mobility, renovation wave, sustainable food, hydrogen, batteries, offshore renewable energy and many others. Unprecedented resources have been earmarked to support the transition, whether through the EU's recovery plan, NextGenerationEU contributing at least 37% to the green transition, the next long-term EU budget for 2021-2027 or the continued focus on sustainable finance and unlocking private investment. And we will continue to mobilise all EU policies to support the shift to climate neutrality, including research, skills, industrial, competition and trade policies.

The package is also based on clear evidence – both on the need to reach our 2030 target but also on how to achieve it in the best and fairest way possible. The 2030 Climate Target Plan[2] assessed the opportunities and costs of the green transition, and showed that the balance is a positive one if we get our policy mix right. This builds on the knowledge that what is good for the planet is good for people and the economy, as reflected by the economy growing by over 62% since 1990 with emissions falling by 24% over the same period, thus clearly decoupling growth from CO_2 emissions.

This experience and knowledge enables this package to be the most comprehensive set of proposals the Commission has ever presented on climate and energy, setting the basis for new jobs and a resilient and sustainable European economy for the future. It lays the regulatory foundation to reach our targets in a fair, cost-efficient and competitive way. It puts a price on carbon in more sectors, which brings significant additional revenues to ensure a fair transition, and makes clean solutions cheaper. It supports greater renewable energy use and more energy savings. It facilitates growing sales of clean new vehicles and cleaner transport fuels. It ensures that industry can lead the transition and gives it the certainty it needs for boosting investment and innovation. It focuses on taxing energy sources in line with our climate goals and environmental objectives. The package translates the polluter pays

1 Special Eurobarometer on Climate Change 513 (published on 5 July 2021)https://ec.europa.eu/clima/citizens/support_en.
2 COM(2020) 381 final

principle into practice. It aims to reverse the declining trend in nature's capacity to remove carbon from the atmosphere. And it helps to ensure that our climate goals are not undermined by the threat of carbon leakage, by encouraging global climate action.

The Fit for 55 Package cements the EU's global leadership by action and by example in the fight against climate change. However, EU action alone is not enough and cannot deliver the global emission reduction the world needs. The EU remains fully committed to the multilateral global order and calls upon partners around the world to work together. This is why the EU is working with the G7, the G20 and other international partners to show that increased climate ambition, economic prosperity and sustainable growth can go hand in hand. Ahead of the crucial 26th United Nations Climate Change Conference of the Parties ("COP26") in Glasgow in November 2021, this set of proposals aims to set an agenda to work with the rest of the world towards a green transition that addresses existential threats and creates new opportunities for all.

The Fit for 55 Package is a set of interconnected proposals that together deliver our ambition. This Communication gives an overview of the different proposals as well as their linkages and explains the toolbox of policy measures chosen. It presents how the package strikes the overall balance between fairness, emissions reductions, and competitiveness and illustrates how the different policies work together.

The Fit for 55 Package: At a glance

The Fit for 55 package consists of a set of inter-connected proposals, which all drive towards the same goal of ensuring a fair, competitive and green transition by 2030 and beyond. Where possible existing legislation is made more ambitious and where needed new proposals are put on the table. Overall, the package strengthens eight existing pieces of legislation and presents five new initiatives, across a range policy areas and economic sectors: climate, energy and fuels, transport, buildings, land use and forestry.

The legislative proposals are backed by impact assessment analysis, which takes into account the interconnection of the overall package. The analysis shows that an over-reliance on strengthened regulatory policies would lead to unnecessarily high economic burdens, while carbon pricing alone would not overcome persistent market failures and non-market barriers. The chosen policy mix is therefore a careful balance between pricing, targets, standards and support measures.

Pricing	Targets	Rules
– Stronger Emissions Trading System including in aviation	– Updated Effort Sharing Regulation	– Stricter CO2 performance for cars & vans
– Extending Emissions Trading to maritime, road transport, and buildings	– Updated Land Use Land Use Change and Forestry Regulation	– New infrastructure for alternative fuels
– Updated Energy taxation Directive	– Updated Renewable Energy Directive	– ReFuelEU: More sustainable aviation fuels
– New Carbon Border Adjustment Mechanism	– Updated Energy Efficiency Directive	– FuelEU: Cleaner maritime fuels
Support Measures		
– Using revenues and regulations to promote innovation, build solidarity and mitigate impacts for the vulnerable, notably through the new Social Climate Fund and enhanced Modernisation and Innovation Funds.		

2. WHOLE-OF-ECONOMY APPROACH: FAIR, COMPETITIVE AND GREEN TRANSITION

The Fit for 55 Package aims to deliver the EU's increased emission reductions target to the benefit of all Europeans and to create opportunities to take part in the transition, help those most in need, and drive stronger overall emissions reductions. It will also support the EU's green recovery from the pandemic, help spread environmental standards beyond EU borders and boost innovation in the products and technologies of the future.

2.1 A socially fair transition: tackling inequality and energy poverty through climate action

The transition towards climate neutrality can be a unique opportunity to reduce systemic inequality. Carbon pricing instruments, for example, raise revenues that can be reinvested to address energy poverty and mobility challenges for the vulnerable, spur innovation and economic growth, and create employment. This is not just a matter of fairness and solidarity it is a wider societal necessity to tackle inequities that existed before the European Green Deal and that would worsen without resolute action against climate change and towards zero pollution.

This is why solidarity is a defining principle of the European Green Deal – between generations, Member States, regions, rural and urban areas, and different parts of society – as exemplified by the Just Transition Mechanism and a number of other instruments put in place at EU level in recent years. Reaching climate neutrality will require a shared sense of purpose, collective efforts and a recognition of different starting points and challenges. Many citizens, especially younger people, are ready to change their consumption and mobility patterns when empowered by relevant information in order to limit their carbon footprint and to live in a greener, healthier environment. However, this package also addresses the concerns of those whose employment or income are affected by the transition.

This approach is reflected across the Fit for 55 package, from sharing efforts to reach climate targets among Member States based on their relative wealth to taking into account their different capabilities when distributing revenues and to addressing inequalities within each Member State. This reflects the need for increased solidarity and social fairness to match our increased speed and ambition.

In this spirit, a new Social Climate Fund will provide dedicated funding to Member States to support European citizens most affected or at risk of energy or mobility poverty, to accompany the introduction of the Emissions Trading to road transport and buildings. Energy poverty alone affects up to 34 million people in the European Union today. The Fund will help mitigate the costs for those most exposed to fossil fuel price increases during the transition. The new Fund will promote fairness and solidarity between and within Member States while mitigating the risk of energy and mobility poverty. It will build on and complement existing solidarity mechanisms[3] The Social Climate Fund will provide €72.2 billion in current prices for the period 2025-2032 in the EU budget from the new Emissions Trading System. It will enable Member States to support vulnerable low and middle-income households, transport users, and micro-enterprises affected by the impact of the extension of emission trading to building and transport. It will entail support to investments to increase the energy efficiency and renovations of buildings, clean heating and cooling, and integrate renewable energy in a manner that can sustainably reduce both CO_2 emissions and energy bills for vulnerable households and micro enterprises. It will also finance access to zero- and low- emission mobility. Where needed and as long as it is required, the Fund can cover direct income support, while green investments through the Fund, and through a.o. the Recovery and Resilience Facility and the European Regional Development Fund, are carried out and deliver their benefit.

Its volume will in principle correspond to 25% of the expected revenues from the new emissions trading covering the building and road transport sectors, starting one year before carbon pricing comes into effect in order to be ready for the change. It will be combined with national contributions of at least to 50 percent. The Commission will shortly propose an amendment to the Own Resource Decision and the Multiannual Financial Framework 2021-2027 to accommodate this new instrument. In addition, the Commission intends to lay down further guidance to Member States through a proposal for Council Recommendation as to how best to address the social and labour aspects of the climate transition.

The Commission will assess the functioning of the Social Climate Fund in 2028, also in light of the desired effects of the Effort Sharing Regulation and the application of emission trading to the new sectors.

To strengthen the social dimension further the Commission calls on Member States to use a part of revenues generated from the auctioning of allowances for the buildings and road transport sectors to mitigate the impact on those low and low-middle-income vulnerable households and transport users, in addition to the Social Climate Fund.

Member States with a higher share of fossil fuels in the energy mix, higher greenhouse gas emissions, higher energy intensity and lower GDP per capita will also benefit from an enhanced Modernisation Fund. Resources in this fund will depend on the carbon price, but the fund will be bolstered with an additional 192,5 million allowances.

Finally, there will also be continuous solidarity under the Effort Sharing Regulation and the EU Emissions Trading System where in particular one tenth of allowances for auctions are redistributed among Member States.

2.2
A competitive transition: New opportunities through industrial and sectoral change

Achieving the 2030 target will require systemic transformation across the economy. The forthcoming revisions of National Energy and Climate Plans and Governance Regulation will ensure an integrated planning, implementation and monitoring of the green transition towards 2030. They will allow the EU and its Member States to progress in a balanced manner. The Fit for 55 proposals reflect this, with action across industry, transport, buildings and energy. Complementary and targeted policies at EU and national level will accelerate the change in behaviour, technological innovation and deployment, and development of new infrastructure. A cornerstone of the package is to build on the important achievements of the EU Emission Trading System by strengthening it and applying it to new sectors where so far emission reductions have been lacking. The experience of the last 16 years has shown that emissions trading is a highly effective mechanism to bring down emissions in a cost-effective way, while the revenues it generates can be used to support the transition to cleaner production and to stimulate innovation.

Next to a carbon price signal, clear targets are needed to drive change such as in the revised Effort Sharing Regulation (ESR), which will empower Member States to take national action to tackle emissions in the buildings, transport, agriculture, waste and small industry sectors. The proposal should deliver an EU-wide reduction of 40% in emissions from these sectors by 2030, compared to the situation in 2005. The principles for attributing the relative effort to each Member State remain the same as before. Their different capacities to take action will continue to be recognised by setting national targets based on GDP per capita, with adjustments made to take national circumstances and cost efficiency into account.

Applying emissions trading to new sectors complements the other policies of the package to drive changes in public and private investments, consumer

3 e.g. Cohesion Fund, Just Transition Fund and European Social Fund Plus.

behaviour and business practices. The Commission's impact assessments show that a decision not to apply emissions trading to these areas would require much stronger regulatory measures in all sectors than proposed in this package, notably in fuel standards, renewable energy and energy efficiency as well as taxation.

2.2.1 Industrial transformation and carbon pricing

The green transition presents a wealth of opportunity to the EU industry as the world follows our lead in developing markets for clean new technologies and products and providing sustainable, local and skilled jobs across the EU. EU industry is ready to invest, but needs predictability and a coherent regulatory framework, access to infrastructure and support for innovation.

The package includes new requirements for industry to decarbonise production processes, but also support mechanisms for the uptake of new technologies. The Innovation Fund, which supports business and SMEs' investment in clean energy, will grow its financing for innovative projects and infrastructure to decarbonize industry. Particular attention will be given to projects in sectors covered by the Carbon Border Adjustment Mechanism (CBAM).

Reflecting the need for steeper emission reductions, the Commission is today proposing that by 2030 sectors covered by the revised EU ETS[4] will need to reduce their greenhouse gas emissions by 61%, compared to 2005 levels. To achieve this, we need to lower the annual emissions cap in line with the pathway to meeting the higher 2030 ambition.

To strengthen the role of carbon pricing in the transport sector, the Commission proposes to gradually extend the current EU ETS to the maritime sector over the period 2023 to 2025. Greater efforts will also be required from aviation operators to reduce their emissions, which is why the Commission is proposing to phase out the free emissions allowances this sector currently receives. In order to also address aviation emissions at global level, the Carbon Offsetting and Reduction Scheme for International Aviation (CORSIA) will be implemented through the EU Emissions Trading System Directive. We will both pursue domestic policies and continue working with our partners at international level through the International Maritime Organization and the International Civil Aviation Organization (ICAO).

Fossil fuels used by road transport and buildings are substantial sources of emissions and pollution. As they have been very difficult to decarbonise so far, they are also full of innovation and job creating potential. For instance, emissions trading in road transport will increase incentives to supply cleaner fuels for existing vehicles. It will lead to an evolution of the available fuels on the market for the existing fleet, pushing providers to decarbonise their fuels. The carbon price in itself, however, does not guarantee a quick transition to zero emission mobility for which complementary policies, including on charging infrastructure are needed.

Similarly, applying emissions trading to fuels in the buildings sector will help bring cleaner heating fuels to the market, shorten payback periods for investments in renovation and accelerate fuel-switching in heating and cooling in existing buildings. This will be complemented by policy measures to improve the energy efficiency of buildings and energy appliances and systems so that the overall energy needs in our homes and in heating and cooling will also be reduced.

This is why the Commission proposes to start applying emissions trading from 2026 for road transport and buildings. This will be done in a separate system focused on upstream fuel suppliers, putting the responsibility on fuel producers to comply with the system, rather than requiring individual households or road transport users to take part directly. Emissions from road transport and building sectors will be capped, with the cap reduced over time so that total emissions fall.

If international partners do not share a comparable ambition to the EU, there is a risk of carbon leakage whereby production is transferred from the EU to other countries with lower ambition for emission reduction. If this risk materialises, there will be no reduction in global emissions. This is why, as outlined in further detail in Section 4 of this Communication, the Commission is proposing a Carbon Border Adjustment Mechanism putting a price on imports of a limited number of high-polluting goods based on their carbon content.

This industrial transition to 2030 – and beyond to climate neutrality – must be a collective and inclusive effort, co-designed with the industrial ecosystems. The updated Industrial Strategy announced the co-creation of transition pathways with social partners and other stakeholders to chart how best to accelerate and benefit from the twin transitions, looking at the scale, speed and conditions facing each ecosystem. The pathways will identify the scale of the needs, including reskilling, investment or technology needs and devise actions to meet them, building on inputs such as industrial strategy roadmaps. Priority is given to ecosystems that commit to the transition, face the most challenges and have been heavily affected by the crisis, such as in mobility, construction and energy intensive industries.

The Commission acknowledges that the green transition can only succeed if the EU has the skilled workforce it needs to stay competitive. Education and training are central to raising awareness and boosting skills for the green economy in the instruments such as the green strand in Erasmus+ and the Education for Climate Coalition. With the European Skills Agenda for sustainable competitiveness, social fairness and resilience the Commission is rolling out flagship actions to equip people with the right skills needed for the green and digital transition. Under the Agenda, the Commission also facilitates the development of commitments for re- and upskilling in all industrial ecosystems. Various ecosystems, including the automotive

4 Power sector, energy-intensive industry sectors including oil refineries, steel works, and production of iron, aluminum, metals, cement, lime, glass, ceramics, pulp, paper, cardboard, acids and bulk organic chemicals, as well as aviation and maritime sectors.

ecosystem, have already committed to re- and upskill their workforce across the entire value chain, as part of the Pact for Skills.

2.2.2 Cleaner mobility and transport fuels

Next to carbon pricing, other measures are needed to put transport on a firm path to zero emissions, and drive down air pollution as transport represents almost a quarter of the EU's greenhouse gas emissions and is the main cause of air pollution in cities. Emissions remain higher than in 1990 and a 90% reduction in overall transport emissions by 2050[5] will be required to reach climate neutrality.

The Fit for 55 package therefore includes four proposals promoting cleaner vehicles and fuels in a technologically neutral way. The revision of the CO_2 emission standards for new cars and vans aims at further reducing the greenhouse gas emissions of these vehicles, providing a clear and realistic pathway towards zero-emission mobility. Consumer demand for zero emission vehicles is increasing sharply already[6].

The Alternative Fuels Infrastructure Regulation will ensure the necessary deployment of interoperable and user-friendly infrastructure for recharging and refuelling cleaner vehicles across the EU, keeping pace with the development of the market and guaranteeing that rural and remote areas will also be covered. The proposed mandatory targets for alternative fuels infrastructure are key to support the penetration of cleaner vehicles and the continued growth of this market which presents extraordinary opportunities for the EU car industry.

All these measures reinforce and complement each other. Knowing that the average car lasts 10 to 15 years, putting a price on carbon for road transport is urgent to make the existing fleet drive cleaner. In addition, more ambitious CO_2 standards will help to get more zero emission vehicles on the road quickly, while infrastructure obligations will put in place the necessary charging and refuelling stations to serve the millions of new vehicles that are expected by 2030 and while we continue to build a sustainable and globally competitive battery value chain.

The transition of the automotive industry and its supply chain is already happening. This requires using financial resources such as the Innovation Fund and possibilities under State aid rules for investments to create new business opportunities in different segments of the industrial ecosystem. In addition, the European Social Fund Plus (ESF+), InvestEU and other EU funding programmes can be used to support re- and upskilling measures.

The Commission is also proposing to promote the uptake of sustainable fuels in the aviation and maritime sectors complementing the ETS for the aviation and maritime sectors which makes polluting fuels more expensive for suppliers. The ReFuelEU Aviation to promote sustainable aviation fuel will oblige fuel suppliers to blend an increasingly high level of sustainable aviation fuels into existing jet fuel uploaded at EU airports, as well as incentivise the uptake of synthetic fuels, known as e-fuels. The upcoming zero emission aviation Alliance will complement this work to ensure market readiness for disruptive aircraft configurations (e.g. hydrogen, electric). The Commission also calls on the Council and the European Parliament to agree quickly on the updated Single European Sky regulatory framework, which is estimated to help cut aviation emissions by up to 10%.

The FuelEU Maritime proposal to promote sustainable maritime fuels will create new requirements for ships, regardless of their flag, arriving to or departing from EU ports, by imposing a maximum limit on the greenhouse gas content of the energy they use and making these limits more stringent over time. The upcoming Renewable and Low-Carbon Fuels Value Chain Alliance will boost the supply and deployment of the most promising fuels for all modes of transport.

Certainty about emissions performance in these sectors can only be provided by making sure that new fuels respect the sustainability criteria for renewable energy sources. This link must be preserved and we must ensure that we promote only the cleanest advanced biofuels and novel electro-fuels with the best emissions performance. In aviation, ICAO's Carbon Offsetting and Reduction Scheme for International Aviation (CORSIA) will be implemented. These measures are complemented by the revised Energy Taxation Directive, which will make cleaner fuels more attractive in all transport modes and close loopholes for polluting fuels.

2.2.3 Energy

Energy use accounts for 75% of the EU's emissions, so the transformation of our energy system is central to our climate ambitions. Saving more energy and using more renewables in the energy we do use is a key driver for jobs, growth and emission reduction.

To reach the 2030 target, the updated Renewable Energy Directive proposes to increase the overall binding target from the current 32% to a new level of 40% of renewables in the EU energy mix. This will be complemented by indicative national contributions, showing what each Member State should contribute to reach the collective target. The proposal supports Member States in making the most of their cost-effective renewable energy potential across sectors through a combination of sectoral targets and measures. It aims at making the energy system cleaner and more efficient by fostering renewables-based electrification and, in sectors such as industry and transport where this is more difficult, it will promote the uptake of renewable fuels, such as clean hydrogen.

Reduced energy consumption allows us to bring down both emissions and energy costs for consumers and industry. The revision of the Energy Efficiency

5 As compared to 1990 levels.
6 Almost half a million new electrically chargeable vehicles (ECVs) were registered in the EU in the final quarter of 2020. This was the highest figure on record and translated into an unprecedented 17% market share. It also brought the annual total to one million new ECVs, which means that the existing electric fleet doubled in just 12 months (Quarterly Report of European Electricity Markets, Q4 2020).

Directive proposes to increase the level of ambition of the energy efficiency targets at EU level and to make them binding. This should lead to 9% reduction in energy consumption by 2030, compared to the baseline projections[7]. As part of this, national indicative benchmarks for energy efficiency calculated with a new formula will also guide Member State action. The revision of the Energy Performance of Buildings Directive, planned for later in the year, will identify specific measures to accelerate the rate of buildings renovations, contributing to energy efficiency and renewable goals and greenhouse gas emissions reductions in the buildings sector.

The tax system for energy products must both preserve the internal market and support the green transition by setting the right incentives. Therefore, a revision of the Energy Taxation Directive proposes to align the minimum tax rates for heating and transport fuels with EU climate and environmental objectives, while mitigating the social impact. The new rules will remove outdated exemptions, for example in aviation and maritime transport, and other incentives for the use of fossil fuels, while promoting the uptake of clean fuels.

2.3 A green transition: Protecting nature and increasing the EU's natural carbon sink

The twin climate and biodiversity crises cannot be treated in separately. We either solve the climate and nature crises together, or we solve neither. This also means that we should not take more resources than the planet can afford to share with us. If we help delicate land and ocean ecosystems recover, they can provide for life on the planet and fulfil their role in the fight against climate change. Restoring nature and enabling biodiversity to thrive again is essential to absorb and store more carbon.

We therefore need to increase the capacity of the EU's forests, soils, wetlands and peatlands, oceans, and water bodies to act as carbon sinks and stocks. In a modernised agricultural sector, we also need farming practices that put land and nature first and regenerate the quality of our soils to ensure our food security.

As part of the updated Land Use Land Use Change and Forestry Regulation, the Commission is proposing to set higher ambitions for the expansion of the EU's natural carbon removals, which is key for balancing out emissions and reaching climate neutrality. The new proposal looks to reverse the current trend of diminishing CO_2 removals and increase the quality and quantity of the EU's forests and other natural carbon sinks. It proposes to set an EU target of net greenhouse gas removals in the LULUCF sector of 310 million tons of CO_2 equivalent by 2030. Specific national targets are proposed to contribute to this shared goal. Beyond 2030, the Commission will assess progress and envisages proposals to set this sector on the pathway to reaching climate neutrality – considering emissions and removals from the LULUCF sector and non-CO_2 agricultural emissions.

Member States will retain a certain flexibility in dividing the effort between the Effort Sharing Regulation and LULUCF sectors, underlining again the complementarity between the different proposals in the Fit for 55 package.

The Commission is also taking multiple measures to incentivise good practices in the production of biomass, and to ensure supply and demand for woody biomass remain within the limits of sustainability[8] and are in line with our objectives of restoring biodiversity, improving the health of nature, and staying within planetary limits.

The proposal on renewable energy generation includes strengthened sustainability criteria for bioenergy by extending their scope of application and by enlarging no-go areas for sourcing. Bioenergy currently accounts for around 60% of renewable energy production and, while that share is projected to decline between 2030 and 2050, the overall demand for renewable energy will increase. The proposal confirms the cascading principle, which privileges the highest value added use of wood, and ensures that national support schemes for the use of sustainably sourced biomass are in line with it and avoid harmful impacts on biodiversity.

The new EU Forest Strategy presented together with the Fit for 55 package, as well as, the forthcoming New Soil Strategy, EU Nature Restoration Law and Carbon Farming Initiative planned for later in 2021, will further strengthen the EU's natural carbon sinks, ensure that biodiversity has a key place in the overall approach and support the crucial social and economic functions of forestry and forest-based sectors.

3. OPPORTUNITIES AND INCENTIVES: INNOVATION AND INVESTMENT FOR A COMPETITIVE TRANSITION

The transition to a climate neutral economy supports innovation. The European Green Deal is a growth strategy and as outlined in the EU's updated Industrial Strategy, the Fit for 55 proposals offer significant opportunities to develop, deploy and export low-carbon technologies and green jobs.[9]

By setting a clear policy framework with detailed targets and policies, the Commission is increasing investor certainty and reducing the risk of locking in investments in carbon intensive industries that will become obsolete before too long and lead to stranded assets. The EU gains from a first mover advantage with increasing global action on climate change. Investments in a low carbon economy can spur economic growth and jobs, accelerate the clean energy transition,

7 The reference scenario used as a baseline for defining the level of ambition of the Union's targets has been updated in the legislative proposal for the revision of the Energy Efficiency Directive. The targets will from now on be calculated using the 2020 Reference scenario baseline whereas the current energy efficiency targets were calculated using the 2007 Reference scenario baseline.

8 JRC Publications Repository - Brief on the role of the forest-based bioeconomy in mitigating climate change through carbon storage and material substitution, https://publications.jrc.ec.europa.eu/repository/handle/JRC124374.

9 See the Impact Assessment for the Communication on Stepping up Europe's 2030 climate ambition, SWD (2020) 177 final.

increase long-term competitiveness and play a role in the green recovery.

The EU's long-term budget and its recovery package NextGenerationEU are specifically tailored to supporting the green transition. 30% of programmes under the 2021-2027 Multiannual Financial Framework are dedicated to support climate action, for example through cohesion policy, agriculture, and the LIFE programme for climate and environment. The target of using 35% of research and innovation funding under Horizon Europe for green investments as well as the various partnerships and missions[10] under the programme provide necessary resources for building sustainable and innovative solutions to the green transition. Horizon Europe provides substantial support for SMEs, in particular start-ups and spinout companies to develop and scale up game-changing innovations.

In addition, Member States' national recovery and resilience plans financed under the Recovery and Resilience Facility need to contribute to the green transition with measures accounting to at least 37% of the plans' allocations. But public funding will not be sufficient. The Strategy for Financing the Transition to a Sustainable Economy will help unlock the private investment needed to finance this transition.[11]

The Commission will continue to incentivise investments in the green transition. In reviewing the environmental and energy State aid guidelines the Commission will pay particular attention to ensure that they mirror the scope and ambition of the European Green Deal. Whilst the recent evaluation of the current IPCEI Communication showed that the provisions work well, some targeted adjustments would be necessary, including to further enhance their openness and facilitate participation of SMEs and to provide guidance on the criteria to pool funds from national budgets and EU programmes.

To support this, the Fit for 55 proposals contain their own dedicated financial instruments to support a fair transition, based on the revenues generated by the extension and strengthening of emissions trading. This underlines once more the interconnection between the different parts of this package of proposals. Existing solidarity mechanisms and funds are strengthened to address distributional impacts and boost further investment in innovative low-carbon solutions. The size and scope of the Innovation Fund is extended to provide support to projects in the form of carbon contracts for difference to trigger emission reductions in industry.

4.
A SUSTAINABLE EU IN A SUSTAINABLE WORLD

While only accounting for 8% of global CO_2 emissions, the EU recognises its responsibility for a higher share of cumulative emissions. The EU is committed to decisively forge a path towards a green, competitive, inclusive, circular economy. The European Green Deal, as our growth and competitiveness strategy, is contributing to transform the global narrative, affecting political and business markets, and offering an example to follow.

Global engagement and international cooperation is key to address the climate crisis and the EU actively engages with partner countries bilaterally and multilaterally.

The Fit for 55 package is a key milestone on the road to Glasgow, where the next United Nations Climate Change Conference, also known as COP26, will be held later this year. It will be the backbone of the EU's delivery on its commitments to the planet and the world, as signed up to in the Paris Agreement.

The EU is determined to ensure that decarbonisation gains in the EU should not simply push carbon emissions outside our borders. Such carbon leakage is currently prevented by the issuance of free allowances under the Emissions Trading System (ETS). That system has been effective in addressing the risk of leakage but it also dampens the incentive to invest in greener production at home and abroad.

In this spirit, the Commission is today proposing a Carbon Border Adjustment Mechanism (CBAM). Designed as a climate action instrument, it introduces a market dynamic that protects the integrity of EU and global climate policy by reducing GHG emissions in the EU and globally, and induces the relevant sectors to modernise, become more sustainable, and drive down their carbon content.

The CBAM will be gradually introduced for a few selected products. A simplified system will apply in the first years with the objective of facilitating a smooth roll out of the mechanism. The proposal for a CBAM ensures that the same carbon price will be paid by domestic and imported products and will thus be non-discriminatory and compatible with WTO rules and other international obligations of the EU. In the sectors concerned, CBAM will be gradually phased-in while free allowances are phased out, ensuring that the new system provides stronger incentives for the EU and foreign industries to innovate and reduce emissions. Moreover, sectors and companies outside the EU that may already have lower carbon content in their production cycles or in which a similar system of carbon pricing is applied will benefit from this under CBAM. As such, it is an invitation to our international partners for jointly increasing climate ambition.

The global move away from fossil fuels is already well under way. And the effects go beyond climate and environment - they are also geopolitical. The EU must adjust its policies accordingly to ensure a stable transition, including outside of its borders. In this spirit, the European Commission will soon come forward with new legislation to minimise the EU's contribution to deforestation and forest degradation worldwide and embed sustainable corporate governance in companies' strategies.

We expect partners to fulfil their Paris commitments too and are ready to work together by strengthening EU climate diplomacy. In order to enhance cooperation with our international partners and facilitate the

10 For the green transition, the missions on Climate neutral and smart cities; Healthy oceans, seas, coastal and inland waters; Soil health and food and Adaptation to climate change, including societal transformation are particularly relevant.

11 https://ec.europa.eu/finance/docs/law/210704-communication-sustainable-finance-strategy_en.pdf.

global transition to a net zero economy, the full range of the EU's external policy instruments will be harnessed to align with these higher goals. As part of its climate diplomacy in bilateral partnerships and multilateral organizations, the EU will ensure that it consults, explains, assists and where possible accommodates partners, while keeping the main objectives as laid down in the Paris Agreement in focus. This also includes support to climate finance to help vulnerable countries adapt to climate change and invest in reducing greenhouse gas emissions. The EU and its Member States have consistently been the world's largest contributor of public climate finance to low- and middle-income countries, and this will continue, with particular attention to the needs of the least developed countries.

5. CONCLUSION

The European Union is built on the premise of developing common policies to achieve our common interests. It requires solidarity between its Member States and between its citizens to achieve these goals and enjoy its benefits, with everybody acting in line with their own capacities and competences, and respecting different national specificities and starting points in reaching the end goal. The Fit for 55 package is designed in this spirit: efforts are shared between Member States in the most cost effective way, acknowledging our differences, and support is given to those most in need, to ensure that the transition reaches everybody in a beneficial way.

The package of proposals has been carefully crafted to create the right balance of policy measures and revenues generated to design and drive a just and transformational change across the t [*sic*] EU economy. Changing the weight of each tool inevitably has knock-on effects on several others, and removing any of the proposed measures requires a tuning up of proposals in other areas. To make the European Union Fit for 55 and reduce in time our emissions by at least 55%, we need all these tools and this balance.

The Fit for 55 package recognises that the EU citizens need to be offered better information, affordable options and appropriate incentives to make the individual changes that collectively help us live in balance with our environment and our planet. Citizens of all regions and ages will be closely involved in the implementation, for instance through the European Climate Pact and citizens' panels of the Conference on the Future of Europe. It also acknowledges the effectiveness of putting a price on carbon and marshals the economic power of companies and markets to deliver structural changes to our economy that provide the cleaner, healthier products and services that we need. Finally, it enables the EU to shape long-term investments, lead markets and enforce new green standards. It is this combination that will make the EU fit for a climate neutral future.

The challenges of climate change require a global response and the EU will continue engaging actively with its partner countries to support the climate and energy transformation globally.

The Commission has now presented the necessary proposals for the EU to fulfil our commitments and targets, and to genuinely embrace the transformation that lies ahead. We invite the European Parliament and the Council to swiftly begin their legislative work on the proposals presented today, and to ensure that they are treated as a coherent package, respecting the multiple interconnections between them.

The make-or-break decade has already started. The EU needs its policy toolbox to be Fit for 55 in place as soon as possible to meet our 2030 targets and set us firmly on the pathway towards becoming the first climate-neutral continent by 2050.

2.1. Espoo Convention 1991

UNECE Convention on Environmental Impact Assessment in a Transboundary Context, Espoo, Finland, 25 February 1991, 1989 UNTS 309

The Parties to this Convention,

Aware of the interrelationship between economic activities and their environmental consequences,

Affirming the need to ensure environmentally sound and sustainable development,

Determined to enhance international cooperation in assessing environmental impact in particular in a transboundary context,

Mindful of the need and importance to develop anticipatory policies and of preventing, mitigating and monitoring significant adverse environmental impact in general and more specifically in a transboundary context,

Recalling the relevant provisions of the Charter of the United Nations, the Declaration of the Stockholm Conference on the Human Environment, the Final Act of the Conference on Security and Cooperation in Europe (CSCE) and the Concluding Documents of the Madrid and Vienna Meetings of Representatives of the Participating States of the CSCE,

Commending the ongoing activities of States to ensure that, through their national legal and administrative provisions and their national policies, environmental impact assessment is carried out,

Conscious of the need to give explicit consideration to environmental factors at an early stage in the decision-making process by applying environmental impact assessment, at all appropriate administrative levels, as a necessary tool to improve the quality of information presented to decision makers so that environmentally sound

decisions can be made paying careful attention to minimizing significant adverse impact, particularly in a transboundary context,

Mindful of the efforts of international organizations to promote the use of environmental impact assessment both at the national and international levels, and taking into account work on environmental impact assessment carried out under the auspices of the United Nations Economic Commission for Europe, in particular results achieved by the Seminar on Environmental Impact Assessment (September 1987, Warsaw, Poland) as well as noting the Goals and Principles on environmental impact assessment adopted by the Governing Council of the United Nations Environment Programme, and the Ministerial Declaration on Sustainable Development (May 1990, Bergen, Norway),

Have agreed as follows:

Article 1 – DEFINITIONS

For the purposes of this Convention,

(i) "Parties" means, unless the text otherwise indicates, the Contracting Parties to this Convention;

(ii) "Party of origin" means the Contracting Party or Parties to this Convention under whose jurisdiction a proposed activity is envisaged to take place;

(iii) "Affected Party" means the Contracting Party or Parties to this Convention likely to be affected by the transboundary impact of a proposed activity;

(iv) "Concerned Parties" means the Party of origin and the affected Party of an environmental impact assessment pursuant to this Convention;

(v) "Proposed activity" means any activity or any major change to an activity subject to a decision of a competent authority in accordance with an applicable national procedure;

(vi) "Environmental impact assessment" means a national procedure for evaluating the likely impact of a proposed activity on the environment;

(vii) "Impact" means any effect caused by a proposed activity. on the environment including human health and safety, flora, fauna, soil, air, water, climate, landscape and historical monuments or other physical structures or the interaction among these factors; it also includes effects on cultural heritage or socioeconomic conditions resulting from alterations to those factors;

(viii) "Transboundary impact" means any impact, not exclusively of a global nature, within an area under the jurisdiction of a Party caused by a proposed activity the physical origin of which is situated wholly or in part within the area under the jurisdiction of another Party;

(ix) "Competent authority" means the national authority or authorities designated by a Party as responsible for performing the tasks covered by this Convention and/or the authority or authorities entrusted by a Party with decision-making powers regarding a proposed activity;

(x) "The Public" means one or more natural or legal persons and, in accordance with national legislation or practice, their associations, organizations or groups.

Article 2 – GENERAL PROVISONS

1. The Parties shall, either individually or jointly, take all appropriate and effective measures to prevent, reduce and control significant adverse transboundary environmental impact from proposed activities.
2. Each Party shall take the necessary legal, administrative or other measures to implement the provisions of this Convention, including, with respect to proposed activities listed in appendix I that are likely to cause significant adverse transbounda-

ry impact, the establishment of an environmental impact assessment procedure that permits public participation and preparation of the environmental impact assessment documentation described in appendix II.

3. The Party of origin shall ensure that in accordance with the provisions of this Convention an environmental impact assessment is undertaken prior to a decision to authorize or undertake a proposed activity listed in appendix I that is likely to cause a significant adverse transboundary impact.
4. The Party of origin shall, consistent with the provisions of this Convention, ensure that affected Parties are notified of a proposed activity listed in appendix I that is likely to cause a significant adverse transboundary impact.
5. Concerned Parties shall, at the initiative of any such Party, enter into discussions on whether one or more proposed activities not listed in appendix I is or are likely to cause a significant adverse transboundary impact and thus should be treated as if it or they were so listed. Where those Parties so agree, the activity or activities shall be thus treated. General guidance for identifying criteria to determine significant adverse impact is set forth in appendix III.
6. The Party of origin shall provide, in accordance with the provisions of this Convention, an opportunity to the public in the areas likely to be affected to participate in relevant environmental impact assessment procedures regarding proposed activities and shall ensure that the opportunity provided to the public of the affected Party is equivalent to that provided to the public of the Party of origin.
7. Environmental impact assessments as required by this Convention shall, as a minimum requirement, be undertaken at the project level of the proposed activity. To the extent appropriate, the Parties shall endeavour to apply the principles of environmental impact assessment to policies, plans and programmes.
8. The provisions of this Convention shall not affect the right of Parties to implement national laws, regulations, administrative provisions or accepted legal practices protecting information the supply of which would be prejudicial to industrial and commercial secrecy or national security.
9. The provisions of this Convention shall not affect the right of particular Parties to implement, by bilateral or multilateral agreement where appropriate, more stringent measures than those of this Convention.
10. The provisions of this Convention shall not prejudice any obligations of the Parties under international law with regard to activities having or likely to have a transboundary impact.
11. If the Party of origin intends to carry out a procedure for the purposes of determining the content of the environmental impact assessment documentation, the affected Party should to the extent appropriate be given the opportunity to participate in this procedure.

Article 3 – NOTIFICATION

1. For a proposed activity listed in appendix I that is likely to cause a significant adverse transboundary impact, the Party of origin shall, for the purposes of ensuring adequate and effective consultations under article 5, notify any Party which it considers may be an affected Party as early as possible and no later than when informing its own public about that proposed activity.
2. This notification shall contain, inter alia:
   (a) Information on the proposed activity, including any available information on its possible transboundary impact;
   (b) Information on the nature of the possible decision; and
   (c) An indication of a reasonable time within which a response under paragraph 3 of this article is required, taking into account the nature of the proposed activity; and may include the information set out in paragraph 5 of this article.
3. The affected Party shall respond to the Party of origin within the time specified in the notification, acknowledging receipt of the notification, and shall indicate whether it intends to participate in the environmental impact assessment procedure.
4. If the affected Party indicates that it does not intend to participate in the environmental impact assessment procedure, or if it does not respond within the time specified in the notification, the provisions in paragraphs 5 to 8 of this article and in articles 4 to 7 will not apply. In such circumstances the right of a Party of origin to determine whether to carry out an environmental impact assessment on the basis of its national law and practice is not prejudiced.
5. Upon receipt of a response from the affected Party indicating its desire to participate in the environmental impact assessment procedure, the Party of origin shall, if it has not already done so, provide to the affected Party:
   (a) Relevant information regarding the environmental impact assessment procedure, including an indication of the time schedule for transmittal of comments; and
   (b) Relevant information on the proposed activity and its possible significant adverse transboundary impact.
6. The affected Party shall, at the request of the Party of origin, provide the latter with reasonably obtainable information relating to the potentially affected environment under the jurisdiction of the affected Party, where such information is necessary for the preparation of the environmental impact assessment documentation. The information shall be furnished promptly and, as appropriate, through a joint body where one exists.
7. When a Party considers that it would be affected by a significant adverse transboundary impact of a proposed activity listed in appendix I, and when no notification has taken place in accordance with paragraph 1 of this article, the concerned Parties

shall, at the request of the affected Party, exchange sufficient information for the purposes of holding discussions on whether there is likely to be a significant adverse transboundary impact. If those Parties agree that there is likely to be a significant adverse transboundary impact, the provisions of this Convention shall apply accordingly. If those Parties cannot agree whether there is likely to be a significant adverse transboundary impact, any such Party may submit that question to an inquiry commission in accordance with the provisions of appendix IV to advise on the likelihood of significant adverse transboundary impact, unless they agree on another method of settling this question.

8. The concerned Parties shall ensure that the public of the affected Party in the areas likely to be affected be informed of, and be provided with possibilities for making comments or objections on, the proposed activity, and for the transmittal of these comments or objections to the competent authority of the Party of origin, either directly to this authority or, where appropriate, through the Party of origin.

Article 4 – PREPARATION OF THE ENVIRONMENTAL IMPACT ASSESSMENT DOCUMENTATION

1. The environmental impact assessment documentation to be submitted to the competent authority of the Party of origin shall contain, as a minimum, the information described in appendix II.
2. The Party of origin shall furnish the affected Party, as appropriate through a joint body where one exists, with the environmental impact assessment documentation. The concerned Parties shall arrange for distribution of the documentation to the authorities and the public of the affected Party in the areas likely to be affected and for the submission of comments to the competent authority of the Party of origin, either directly to this authority or, where appropriate, through the Party of origin within a reasonable time before the final decision is taken on the proposed activity.

Article 5 – CONSULTATIONS OM THE BASIS OF THE ENVIRONMENTAL IMPACT ASSESSMENT DOCUMENTATION

The Party of origin shall, after completion of the environmental impact assessment documentation, without undue delay enter into consultations with the affected Party concerning, inter alia, the potential transboundary impact of the proposed activity and measures to reduce or eliminate its impact. Consultations may relate to:

(a) Possible alternatives to the proposed activity, including the no-action alternative and possible measures to mitigate significant adverse transboundary impact and to monitor the effects of such measures at the expense of the Party of origin;

(b) Other forms of possible mutual assistance in reducing any significant adverse transboundary impact of the proposed activity; and

(c) Any other appropriate matters relating to the proposed activity.

The Parties shall agree, at the commencement of such consultations, on a reasonable time frame for the duration of the consultation period. Any such consultations may be conducted through an ap- propriate joint body, where one exists.

Procedure

Article 6 – FINAL DECISION

1. The Parties shall ensure that, in the final decision on the proposed activity, due account is taken of the outcome of the environmental impact assessment, including the environmental impact assessment documentation, as well as the comments thereon received pursuant to article 3, paragraph 8, and article 4, paragraph 2, and the outcome of the consultations as referred to in article 5.
2. The Party of origin shall provide to the affected Party the final decision on the proposed activity along with the reasons and considerations on which it was based.
3. If additional information on the significant transboundary impact of a proposed activity, which was not available at the time a decision was made with respect to that activity and which could have materially affected the decision, becomes available to a concerned Party before work on that activity commences, that Party shall immediately inform the other concerned Party or Parties. If one of the concerned Parties so requests, consultations shall be held as to whether the decision needs to be revised.

Article 7 – POST-PROJECT ANALYSIS

1. The concerned Parties, at the request of any such Party, shall determine whether, and if so to what extent, a post-project analysis shall be carried out, taking into account the likely significant adverse transboundary impact of the activity for which an environmental impact assessment has been undertaken pursuant to this Convention. Any post-project analysis undertaken shall include, in particular, the surveillance of the activity and the determination of any adverse transboundary impact. Such surveillance and determination may be undertaken with a view to achieving the objectives listed in appendix V.
2. When, as a result of post-project analysis, the Party of origin or the affected Party has reasonable grounds for concluding that there is a significant adverse transboundary impact or factors have been discovered which may result in such an impact, it shall immediately inform the other Party. The concerned Parties shall then consult on necessary measures to reduce or eliminate the impact.

Article 8 – BILATERAL AND MULTILATERAL COOPERATION

The Parties may continue existing or enter into new bilateral or multilateral agreements or other arrangements in order to implement their obligations under this Convention and under any of its protocols to which they are a Party. Such agreements or other arrangements may be based on the elements listed in appendix VI.

Article 9 – RESEARCH PROGRAMMES

The Parties shall give special consideration to the setting up, or intensification of, specific research programmes aimed at:

(a) Improving existing qualitative and quantitative methods for assessing the impacts of proposed activities;

(b) Achieving a better understanding of cause-effect relationships and their role in integrated environmental management;

(c) Analysing and monitoring the efficient implementation of decisions on proposed activities with the intention of minimizing or preventing impacts;

(d) Developing methods to stimulate creative approaches in the search for environmentally sound alternatives to proposed activities, production and consumption patterns;

(e) Developing methodologies for the application of the principles of environmental impact assessment at the macroeconomic level.

The results of the programmes listed above shall be exchanged by the Parties.

Article 10 – STATUS OF THE APPENDICES

The appendices attached to this Convention form an integral part of the Convention.

Article 11 – MEETING OF THE PARTIES

1. The Parties shall meet, so far as possible, in connection with the annual sessions of the Senior Advisers to Governments of the Economic Commission for Europe on Environmental and Water Problems. The first session of the Meeting of the Parties shall be convened not later than one year after the date of the entry into force of this Convention. Thereafter, sessions of the Meeting of the Parties shall be held at such other times as may be deemed necessary by the Meeting of the Parties, or at the written request of any Party, provided that, within six months of the request being communicated to them by the secretariat, it is supported by at least one third of the Parties.
2. The Parties shall keep under continuous review the implementation of this Convention, and, with this purpose in mind, shall:

   (a) Review the policies and methodological approaches to environmental impact assessment by the Parties with a view to further improving environmental impact assessment procedures in a transboundary context;

   (b) Exchange information regarding experience gained in concluding and implementing bilateral and multilateral agreements or other arrangements regarding the use of environmental impact assessment in a transboundary context to which one or more of the Parties are party;

   (c) Seek, where appropriate, the services and cooperation of competent bodies having expertise pertinent to the achievement of the purposes of this Convention;

   (d) At their first meeting, consider and by consensus adopt rules of procedure for their meetings;

   (e) Consider and, where necessary, adopt proposals for amendments to this Convention;

   (f) Consider and undertake any additional action that may be required for the achievement of the purposes of this Convention;

   (g) Prepare, where appropriate, protocols to this Convention;

   (h) Establish such subsidiary bodies as they consider necessary for the implementation of this Convention.

Article 12 – RIGHT TO VOTE

1. Each Party to this Convention shall have one vote.
2. Except as provided for in paragraph 1 of this article, regional economic integration organizations, in matters within their competence, shall exercise their right to vote with a number of votes equal to the number of their member States which are Parties to this Convention. Such organizations shall not exercise their right to vote if their member States exercise theirs, and vice versa.

Article 13 – SECRETARIAT

The Executive Secretary of the Economic Commission for Europe shall carry out the following secretariat functions:

(a) The convening and preparing of sessions of the Meeting of the Parties;

(b) The transmission of reports and other information received in accordance with the provisions of this Convention to the Parties; and

(c) The performance of other functions as may be provided for in this Convention or as may be determined by the Parties.

Article 14 – AMENDMENTS TO THE CONVENTION

1. Any Party may propose amendments to this Convention.
2. Proposed amendments shall be submitted in writing to the secretariat, which shall communicate them to all Parties. The proposed amendments shall be discussed at the next session of the Meeting of the Parties, provided these proposals have been circulated by the secretariat to the Parties at least ninety days in advance.
3. The Parties shall make every effort to reach agreement on any proposed amendment to this Convention by consensus. If all efforts at consensus have been exhausted, and no agreement reached, the amendment shall as a last resort be adopted by a three-fourths majority vote of the Parties present and voting at the session.
4. Amendments to this Convention adopted in accordance with paragraph 3 of this article shall be submitted by the Depositary to all Parties for ratification, approval or acceptance. They shall enter

into force for Parties having ratified, approved or accepted them on the ninetieth day after the receipt by the Depositary of notification of their ratification, approval or acceptance by at least three fourths of the number of Parties at the time of their adoption. Thereafter they shall enter into force for any other Party on the ninetieth day after that Party deposits its instrument of ratification, approval or acceptance of the amendments.

5. For the purpose of this article, "Parties present and voting" means Parties present and casting an affirmative or negative vote.
6. The voting procedure set forth in paragraph 3 of this article is not intended to constitute a precedent for future agreements negotiated within the Economic Commission for Europe.

Article 14 bis – REVIEW OF COMPLIANCE

1. The Parties shall review compliance with the provisions of this Convention on the basis of the compliance procedure, as a non-adversarial and assistance-oriented procedure adopted by the Meeting of the Parties. The review shall be based on, but not limited to, regular reporting by the Parties. The Meeting of Parties shall decide on the frequency of regular reporting required by the Parties and the information to be included in those regular reports.
2. The compliance procedure shall be available for application to any protocol adopted under this Convention

Article 15 – SETTLEMENT OF DISPUTES

1. If a dispute arises between two or more Parties about the interpretation or application of this Convention, they shall seek a solution by negotiation or by any other method of dispute settlement acceptable to the parties to the dispute.
2. When signing, ratifying, accepting, approving or acceding to this Convention, or at any time thereafter, a Party may declare in writing to the Depositary that for a dispute not resolved in accordance with paragraph 1 of this article, it accepts one or both of the following means of dispute settlement as compulsory in relation to any Party accepting the same obligation:
   (a) Submission of the dispute to the International Court of Justice;
   (b) Arbitration in accordance with the procedure set out in appendix VII.
3. If the parties to the dispute have accepted both means of dispute settlement referred to in paragraph 2 of this article, the dispute may be submitted only to the International Court of Justice, unless the parties agree otherwise.

Article 16 – SIGNATURE

This Convention shall be open for signature at Espoo, Finland, from 25 February to 1 March 1991 and thereafter at United Nations Headquarters in New York until 2 September 1991 by States members of the Economic Commission for Europe as well as States having consultative status with the Economic Commission for Europe pursuant to paragraph 8 of the Economic and Social Council resolution 36 (IV) of 28 March 1947, and by regional economic integration organizations constituted by sovereign States members of the Economic Commission for Europe to which their member States have transferred competence in respect of matters governed by this Convention, including the competence to enter into treaties in respect of these matters.

Article 17 – RATIFICATION, ACCEPTANCE, APPROVAL AND ACCESSION

1. This Convention shall be subject to ratification, acceptance or approval by signatory States and regional economic integration organizations.
2. This Convention shall be open for accession as from 3 September 1991 by the States and organizations referred to in article 16.
3. Any other State, not referred to in paragraph 2 of this article, that is a Member of the United Nations may accede to the Convention upon approval by the Meeting of the Parties. The Meeting of the Parties shall not consider or approve any request for accession by such a State until this paragraph has entered into force for all the States and organizations that were Parties to the Convention on 27 February 2001.
4. The instruments of ratification, acceptance, approval or accession shall be deposited with the Secretary-General of the United Nations, who shall perform the functions of Depositary.
5. Any organization referred to in article 16 which becomes a Party to this Convention without any of its member States being a Party shall be bound by all the obligations under this Convention. In the case of such organizations, one or more of whose member States is a Party to this Convention, the organization and its member States shall decide on their respective responsibilities for the performance of their obligations under this Convention. In such cases, the organization and the member States shall not be entitled to exercise rights under this Convention concurrently.
6. In their instruments of ratification, acceptance, approval or accession, the regional economic integration organizations referred to in Article 16 shall declare the extent of their competence with respect to the matters governed by this Convention. These organizations shall also inform the Depositary of any relevant modification to the extent of their competence.
7. Any State or organization that ratifies, accepts or approves this Convention shall be deemed simultaneously to ratify, accept or approve the amendment to the Convention set out in decision II/14 taken at the second session of the Meeting of the Parties.

Article 18 – ENTRY INTO FORCE

1. This Convention shall enter into force on the ninetieth day after the date of deposit of the sixteenth instrument of ratification, acceptance, approval or accession.
2. For the purposes of paragraph 1 of this Article, any instrument deposited by a regional economic

integration organization shall not be counted as additional to those deposited by States members of such an organization.

3. For each State or organization referred to in article 16 which ratifies, accepts or approves this Convention or accedes thereto after the deposit of the sixteenth instrument of ratification, acceptance, approval or accession, this Convention shall enter into force on the ninetieth day after the date of deposit by such State or organization of its instrument of ratification, acceptance, approval or accession.

Article 19 – WITHDRAWAL

At any time after four years from the date on which this Convention has come into force with respect to a Party, that Party may withdraw from this Convention by giving written notification to the Depositary. Any such withdrawal shall take effect on the ninetieth day after the date of its receipt by the Depositary. Any such withdrawal shall not affect the application of articles 3 to 6 of this Convention to a proposed activity in respect of which a notification has been made pursuant to article 3, paragraph 1, or a request has been made pursuant to article 3, paragraph 7, before such withdrawal took effect.

Article 20 – AUTHENTIC TEXTS

The original of this Convention, of which the English, French and Russian texts are equally authentic, shall be deposited with the Secretary- General of the United Nations.

IN WITNESS WHEREOF the undersigned, being duly authorized thereto, have signed this Convention.

DONE at Espoo (Finland), this twenty-fifth day of February one thousand nine hundred and ninety- one.

Appendix I – LIST OF ACTIVITIES

1. Crude oil refineries (excluding undertakings manufacturing only lubricants from crude oil) and installations for the gasification and liquefaction of 500 metric tons or more of coal or bituminous shale per day.
2. (a) Thermal power stations and other combustion installations with a heat output of 300 megawatts or more, and
   (b) Nuclear power stations and other nuclear reactors, including the dismantling or decommissioning of such power stations or reactors[1] (except research installations for the production and conversion of fissionable and fertile materials, whose maximum power does not exceed 1 kilowatt continuous thermal load).
3. (a) Installations for the reprocessing of irradiated nuclear fuel;
   (b) Installations designed:
   - For the production or enrichment of nuclear fuel;
   - For the processing of irradiated nuclear fuel or high-level radioactive waste;
   - For the final disposal of irradiated nuclear fuel;
   - Solely for the final disposal of radioactive waste; or
   - Solely for the storage (planned for more than 10 years) of irradiated nuclear fuels or radioactive waste in a different site than the production site.
4. Major installations for the initial smelting of cast iron and steel and for the production of non- ferrous metals.
5. Installations for the extraction of asbestos and for the processing and transformation of asbestos and products containing asbestos: for asbestos- cement products, with an annual production of more than 20,000 metric tons finished product; for friction material, with an annual production of more than 50 metric tons finished product; and for other asbestos utilization of more than 200 metric tons per year.
6. Integrated chemical installations.
7. (a) Construction of motorways, express roads[2] and lines for long-distance railway traffic and of airports[3] with a basic runway length of 2,100 metres or more;
   (b) Construction of a new road of four or more lanes, or realignment and/or widening of an existing road of two lanes or less so as to provide four or more lanes, where such new road, or realigned and/or widened section of road, would be 10 km or more in a continuous length.
8. Large-diameter pipelines for the transport of oil, gas or chemicals.
9. Trading ports and also inland waterways and ports for inland-waterway traffic which permit the passage of vessels of over 1,350 metric tons.
10. (a) Waste-disposal installations for the incineration, chemical treatment or landfill of toxic and dangerous wastes;
    (b) Waste-disposal installations for the incineration or chemical treatment of non- hazardous

---

1 For the purposes of this Convention, nuclear power stations and other nuclear reactors cease to be such an installation when all nuclear fuel and other radioactively contaminated elements have been removed permanently from the installation site.

2 For the purposes of this Convention:– "Motorway" means a road specially designed and built for motor traffic, which does not serve properties bordering on it, and which: (a) Is provided, except at special points or temporarily, with separate carriageways for the two directions of traffic, separated from each other by a dividing strip not intended for traffic or, exceptionally, by other means; (b) Does not cross at level with any road, railway or tramway track, or footpath; and (c) Is specially signposted as a motorway.– "Express road" means a road reserved for motor traffic accessible only from interchanges or controlled junctions and on which, in particular, stopping and parking are prohibited on the running carriageway(s).

3 For the purposes of this Convention, "airport" means an airport which complies with the definition in the 1944 Chicago Convention setting up the International Civil Aviation Organization (annex 14).

waste with a capacity exceeding 100 metric tons per day.

11. Large dams and reservoirs.
12. Groundwater abstraction activities or artificial groundwater recharge schemes where the annual volume of water to be abstracted or recharged amounts to 10 million cubic metres or more.
13. Pulp, paper and board manufacturing of 200 air-dried metric tons or more per day.
14. Major quarries, mining, on-site extraction and processing of metal ores or coal.
15. Offshore hydrocarbon production. Extraction of petroleum and natural gas for commercial purposes where the amount extracted exceeds 500 metric tons/day in the case of petroleum and 500 000 cubic metres/day in the case of gas.
16. Major storage facilities for petroleum, petrochemical and chemical products.
17. Deforestation of large areas.
18. (a) Works for the transfer of water resources between river basins where this transfer aims at preventing possible shortages of water and where the amount of water transferred exceeds 100 million cubic metres/year; and

    (b) In all other cases, works for the transfer of water resources between river basins where the multi-annual average flow of the basin of abstraction exceeds 2 000 million cubic metres/year and where the amount of water transferred exceeds 5 per cent of this flow. In both cases transfers of piped drinking water are excluded.
19. Waste-water treatment plants with a capacity exceeding 150 000 population equivalent.
20. Installations for the intensive rearing of poultry or pigs with more than:
    - 85 000 places for broilers;
    - 60 000 places for hens;
    - 3 000 places for production pigs (over 30 kg); or
    - 900 places for sows.
21. Construction of overhead electrical power lines with a voltage of 220 kV or more and a length of more than 15 km.
22. Major installations for the harnessing of wind power for energy production (wind farms).

Appendix II – CONTENT OF THE ENVIRONMENTAL IMPACT ASSESSMENT DOCUMENTATION

Information to be included in the environmental impact assessment documentation shall, as a minimum, contain, in accordance with article 4:

(a) A description of the proposed activity and its purpose;

(b) A description, where appropriate, of reasonable alternatives (for example, locational or technological) to the proposed activity and also the no-action alternative;

(c) A description of the environment likely to be significantly affected by the proposed activity and its alternatives;

(d) A description of the potential environmental impact of the proposed activity and its alternatives and an estimation of its significance;

(e) A description of mitigation measures to keep adverse environmental impact to a minimum;

(f) An explicit indication of predictive methods and underlying assumptions as well as the relevant environmental data used;

(g) An identification of gaps in knowledge and uncertainties encountered in compiling the required information;

(h) Where appropriate, an outline for monitoring and management programmes and any plans for post-project analysis; and

(i) A non-technical summary including a visual presentation as appropriate (maps, graphs, etc.).

Appendix III – GENERAL CRITERIA TO ASSIST IN THE DETERMINATION OF THE ENVIRONMENTAL SIGNIFICANCE OF ACTIVITIES NOT LISTED IN APPENDIX I

1. In considering proposed activities to which article 2, paragraph 5, applies, the concerned Parties may consider whether the activity is likely to have a significant adverse transboundary impact in particular by virtue of one or more of the following criteria:

   (a) Size: proposed activities which are large for the type of the activity;

   (b) Location: proposed activities which are located in or close to an area of special environmental sensitivity or importance (such as wetlands designated under the Convention on Wetlands of International Importance especially as Waterfowl Habitat (Ramsar Convention), national parks, nature reserves, sites of special scientific interest, or sites of archaeological, cultural or historical importance); also, proposed activities in locations where the characteristics of proposed development would be likely to have significant effects on the population;

   (c) Effects: proposed activities with particularly complex and potentially adverse effects, including those giving rise to serious effects on humans or on valued species or organisms, those which threaten the existing or potential use of an affected area and those causing additional loading which cannot be sustained by the carrying capacity of the environment.
2. The concerned Parties shall consider for this purpose proposed activities which are located close to an international frontier as well as more remote proposed activities which could give rise to significant transboundary effects far removed from the site of development.

Appendix IV – INQUIRY PROCEDURE

1. The requesting Party or Parties shall notify the secretariat that it or they submit(s) the question of whether a proposed activity listed in appendix I is likely to have a significant adverse transboundary impact to an inquiry commission established in accordance with the provisions of this appendix. This notification shall state the subject-matter of the inquiry. The secretariat shall notify immediately all Parties to this Convention of this submission.
2. The inquiry commission shall consist of three members. Both the requesting party and the other party to the inquiry procedure shall appoint a scientific or technical expert, and the two experts so appointed shall designate by common agreement the third expert, who shall be the president of the inquiry commission. The latter shall not be a national of one of the parties to the inquiry procedure, nor have his or her usual place of residence in the territory of one of these parties, nor be employed by any of them, nor have dealt with the matter in any other capacity.
3. If the president of the inquiry commission has not been designated within two months of the appointment of the second expert, the Executive Secretary of the Economic Commission for Europe shall, at the request of either party, designate the president within a further two-month period.
4. If one of the parties to the inquiry procedure does not appoint an expert within one month of its receipt of the notification by the secretariat, the other party may inform the Executive Secretary of the Economic Commission for Europe, who shall designate the president of the inquiry commission within a further two-month period. Upon designation, the president of the inquiry commission shall request the party which has not appointed an expert to do so within one month. After such a period, the president shall inform the Executive Secretary of the Economic Commission for Europe, who shall make this appointment within a further two-month period.
5. The inquiry commission shall adopt its own rules of procedure.
6. The inquiry commission may take all appropriate measures in order to carry out its functions.
7. The parties to the inquiry procedure shall facilitate the work of the inquiry commission and, in particular, using all means at their disposal, shall:
   (a) Provide it with all relevant documents, facilities and information; and
   (b) Enable it, where necessary, to call witnesses or experts and receive their evidence.
8. The parties and the experts shall protect the confidentiality of any information they receive in confidence during the work of the inquiry commission.
9. If one of the parties to the inquiry procedure does not appear before the inquiry commission or fails to present its case, the other party may request the inquiry commission to continue the proceedings and to complete its work. Absence of a party or failure of a party to present its case shall not constitute a bar to the continuation and completion of the work of the inquiry commission.
10. Unless the inquiry commission determines otherwise because of the particular circumstances of the matter, the expenses of the inquiry commission, including the remuneration of its members, shall be borne by the parties to the inquiry procedure in equal shares. The inquiry commission shall keep a record of all its expenses, and shall furnish a final statement thereof to the parties.
11. Any Party having an interest of a factual nature in the subject-matter of the inquiry procedure, and which may be affected by an opinion in the matter, may intervene in the proceedings with the consent of the inquiry commission.
12. The decisions of the inquiry commission on matters of procedure shall be taken by majority vote of its members. The final opinion of the inquiry commission shall reflect the view of the majority of its members and shall include any dissenting view.
13. The inquiry commission shall present its final opinion within two months of the date on which it was established unless it finds it necessary to extend this time limit for a period which should not exceed two months.
14. The final opinion of the inquiry commission shall be based on accepted scientific principles. The final opinion shall be transmitted by the inquiry commission to the parties to the inquiry procedure and to the secretariat.

Appendix V – POST-PROJECT ANALYSIS

Objectives include:

(a) Monitoring compliance with the conditions as set out in the authorization or approval of the activity and the effectiveness of mitigation measures;

(b) Review of an impact for proper management and in order to cope with uncertainties;

(c) Verification of past predictions in order to transfer experience to future activities of the same type.

Appendix VI – ELEMENTS FOR THE BILATERAL AND MULTILATERAL COOPERATION

1. Concerned Parties may set up, where appropriate, institutional arrangements or enlarge the mandate of existing institutional arrangements within the framework of bilateral and multilateral agreements in order to give full effect to this Convention.
2. Bilateral and multilateral agreements or other arrangements may include:
   (a) Any additional requirements for the implementation of this Convention, taking into account the specific conditions of the subregion concerned;
   (b) Institutional, administrative and other arrangements, to be made on a reciprocal and equivalent basis;

(c) Harmonization of their policies and measures for the protection of the environment in order to attain the greatest possible similarity in standards and methods related to the implementation of environmental impact assessment;

(d) Developing, improving, and/or harmonizing methods for the identification, measurement, prediction and assessment of impacts, and for post-project analysis;

(e) Developing and/or improving methods and programmes for the collection, analysis, storage and timely dissemination of comparable data regarding environmental quality in order to provide input into environmental impact assessment;

(f) The establishment of threshold levels and more specified criteria for defining the significance of transboundary impacts related to the location, nature or size of proposed activities, for which environmental impact assessment in accordance with the provisions of this Convention shall be applied; and the establishment of critical loads of transboundary pollution;

(g) Undertaking, where appropriate, joint environmental impact assessment, development of joint monitoring programmes, intercalibration of monitoring devices and harmonization of methodologies with a view to rendering the data and information obtained compatible.

3. Paragraphs 1 and 2 may be applied, mutatis mutandis, to any protocol to the Convention.

Appendix VII – ARBITRATION

1. The claimant Party or Parties shall notify the secretariat that the Parties have agreed to submit the dispute to arbitration pursuant to article 15, paragraph 2, of this Convention. The notification shall state the subject-matter of arbitration and include, in particular, the articles of this Convention, the interpretation or application of which are at issue. The secretariat shall forward the information received to all Parties to this Convention.
2. The arbitral tribunal shall consist of three members. Both the claimant Party or Parties and the other Party or Parties to the dispute shall appoint an arbitrator, and the two arbitrators so appointed shall designate by common agreement the third arbitrator, who shall be the president of the arbitral tribunal. The latter shall not be a national of one of the parties to the dispute, nor have his or her usual place of residence in the territory of one of these parties, nor be employed by any of them, nor have dealt with the case in any other capacity.
3. If the president of the arbitral tribunal has not been designated within two months of the appointment of the second arbitrator, the Executive Secretary of the Economic Commission for Europe shall, at the request of either party to the dispute, designate the president within a further two-month period.
4. If one of the parties to the dispute does not appoint an arbitrator within two months of the receipt of the request, the other party may inform the Executive Secretary of the Economic Commission for Europe, who shall designate the president of the arbitral tribunal within a further two-month period. Upon designation, the president of the arbitral tribunal shall request the party which has not appointed an arbitrator to do so within two months. After such a period, the president shall inform the Executive Secretary of the Economic Commission for Europe, who shall make this appointment within a further two- month period.
5. The arbitral tribunal shall render its decision in accordance with international law and in accordance with the provisions of this Convention.
6. Any arbitral tribunal constituted under the provisions set out herein shall draw up its own rules of procedure.
7. The decisions of the arbitral tribunal, both on procedure and on substance, shall be taken by majority vote of its members.
8. The tribunal may take all appropriate measures in order to establish the facts.
9. The parties to the dispute shall facilitate the work of the arbitral tribunal and, in particular, using all means at their disposal, shall:
   (a) Provide it with all relevant documents, facilities and information; and
   (b) Enable it, where necessary, to call witnesses or experts and receive their evidence.
10. The parties and the arbitrators shall protect the confidentiality of any information they receive in confidence during the proceedings of the arbitral tribunal.
11. The arbitral tribunal may, at the request of one of the parties, recommend interim measures of protection.
12. If one of the parties to the dispute does not appear before the arbitral tribunal or fails to defend its case, the other party may request the tribunal to continue the proceedings and to render its final decision. Absence of a party or failure of a party to defend its case shall not constitute a bar to the proceedings. Before rendering its final decision, the arbitral tribunal must satisfy itself that the claim is well founded in fact and law.
13. The arbitral tribunal may hear and determine counter-claims arising directly out of the subject-matter of the dispute.
14. Unless the arbitral tribunal determines otherwise because of the particular circumstances of the case, the expenses of the tribunal, including the remuneration of its members, shall be borne by the parties to the dispute in equal shares. The tribunal shall keep a record of all its expenses, and shall furnish a final statement thereof to the parties.
15. Any Party to this Convention having an interest of a legal nature in the subject-matter of the dispute, and which may be affected by a decision in

the case, may intervene in the proceedings with the consent of the tribunal.

16. The arbitral tribunal shall render its award within five months of the date on which it is established unless it finds it necessary to extend the time limit for a period which should not exceed five months.

17. The award of the arbitral tribunal shall be accompanied by a statement of reasons. It shall be final and binding upon all parties to the dispute. The award will be transmitted by the arbitral tribunal to the parties to the dispute and to the secretariat. The secretariat will forward the information received to all Parties to this Convention.

18. Any dispute which may arise between the parties concerning the interpretation or execution of the award may be submitted by either party to the arbitral tribunal which made the award or, if the latter cannot be seized thereof, to another tribunal constituted for this purpose in the same manner as the first.

2.2. Helsinki Convention 1992, as amended 2015

UNECE Convention on the Transboundary Effects of Industrial Accidents, Helsinki, 17 March 1992, 2105 UNTS 457, as amended by ECE/CP.TEIA/30/Add.1 (Decision 2014/2 Amending Annex I to the Convention)

The Parties to this Convention,

Mindful of the special importance, in the interest of present and future generations, of protecting human beings and the environment against the effects of industrial accidents,

Recognizing the importance and urgency of preventing serious adverse effects of industrial accidents on human beings and the environment, and of promoting all measures that stimulate the rational, economic and efficient use of preventive, preparedness and response measures to enable environmentally sound and sustainable economic development,

Taking into account the fact that the effects of industrial accidents may make themselves felt across borders, and require cooperation among States,

Affirming the need to promote active international cooperation among the States concerned before, during and after an accident, to enhance appropriate policies and to reinforce and coordinate action at all appropriate levels for promoting the prevention of, preparedness for and response to the transboundary effects of industrial accidents,

Noting the importance and usefulness of bilateral and multilateral arrangements for the prevention of, preparedness for and response to the effects of industrial accidents,

Conscious of the role played in this respect by the United Nations Economic Commission for Europe (ECE) and recalling, inter alia, the ECE Code of Conduct on Accidental Pollution of Transboundary Inland Waters and the Convention on Environmental Impact Assessment in a Transboundary Context,

Having regard to the relevant provisions of the Final Act of the Conference on Security and Cooperation in Europe (CSCE), the Concluding Document of the Vienna Meeting of Representatives of the Participating States of the CSCE, and the outcome of the Sofia Meeting on the Protection of the Environment of the CSCE, as well as to pertinent activities and mechanisms in the United Nations Environment Programme (UNEP), in particular the APELL programme, in the International Labour Organisation (ILO), in particular the Code of Practice on the Prevention of Major Industrial Accidents, and in other relevant international organizations,

Considering the pertinent provisions of the Declaration of the United Nations Conference on the Human Environment, and in particular principle 21, according to which States have, in accordance with the Charter of the United Nations and the principles of international law, the sovereign right to exploit their own resources pursuant to their own environmental policies, and the responsibility to ensure that activities within their jurisdiction or control do not cause damage to the environment of other States or of areas beyond the limits of national jurisdiction,

Taking account of the polluter-pays principle as a general principle of international environmental law,

Underlining the principles of international law and custom, in particular the principles of good-neighbourliness, reciprocity, non-discrimination and good faith,

Have agreed as follows:

Article 1 – Definitions

For the purposes of this Convention,

(a) "Industrial accident" means an event resulting from an uncontrolled development in the course of any activity involving hazardous substances either:
   (i) In an installation, for example during manufacture, use, storage, handling, or disposal; or
   (ii) During transportation in so far as it is covered by paragraph 2 (d) of Article 2;

(b) "Hazardous activity" means any activity in which one or more hazardous substances are present or may be present in quantities at or in excess of the threshold quantities listed in Annex I hereto, and which is capable of causing transboundary effects;

(c) "Effects" means any direct or indirect, immediate or delayed adverse consequences caused by an industrial accident on, inter alia:
   (i) Human beings, flora and fauna;
   (ii) Soil, water, air and landscape;
   (iii) The interaction between the factors in (i) and (ii);
   (iv) Material assets and cultural heritage, including historical monuments;

(d) "Transboundary effects" means serious effects within the jurisdiction of a Party as a result of an industrial accident occurring within the jurisdiction of another Party;

(e) "Operator" means any natural or legal person, including public authorities, in charge of an activity, e.g. supervising, planning to carry out or carrying out an activity;

(f) "Party" means, unless the text otherwise indicates, a Contracting Party to this Convention;

(g) "Party of origin" means any Party or Parties under whose jurisdiction an industrial accident occurs or is capable of occurring;

(h) "Affected Party" means any Party or Parties affected or capable of being affected by transboundary effects of an industrial accident;

(i) "Parties concerned" means any Party of origin and any affected Party;

(j) "The public" means one or more natural or legal persons.

Article 2 – Scope

1. This Convention shall apply to the prevention of, preparedness for and response to industrial accidents capable of causing transboundary effects, including the effects of such accidents caused by natural disasters, and to international cooperation concerning mutual assistance, research and development, exchange of information and exchange of technology in the area of prevention of, preparedness for and response to industrial accidents.
2. This Convention shall not apply to:
   (a) Nuclear accidents or radiological emergencies;
   (b) Accidents at military installations;
   (c) Dam failures, with the exception of the effects of industrial accidents caused by such failures;
   (d) Land-based transport accidents with the exception of:
      (i) Emergency response to such accidents;
      (ii) Transportation on the site of the hazardous activity;
   (e) Accidental release of genetically modified organisms;
   (f) Accidents caused by activities in the marine environment, including seabed exploration or exploitation;
   (g) Spills of oil or other harmful substances at sea.

Article 3 – General provisions

1. The Parties shall, taking into account efforts already made at national and international levels, take appropriate measures and cooperate within the framework of this Convention, to protect human beings and the environment against industrial accidents by preventing such accidents as far as possible, by reducing their frequency and severity and by mitigating their effects. To this end, preventive, preparedness and response measures, including restoration measures, shall be applied.
2. The Parties shall, by means of exchange of information, consultation and other cooperative measures and without undue delay, develop and implement policies and strategies for reducing the risks of industrial accidents and improving preventive, preparedness and response measures, including restoration measures, taking into account, in order to avoid unnecessary duplication, efforts already made at national and international levels.
3. The Parties shall ensure that the operator is obliged to take all measures necessary for the safe performance of the hazardous activity and for the prevention of industrial accidents.
4. To implement the provisions of this Convention, the Parties shall take appropriate legislative, regulatory, administrative and financial measures for the prevention of, preparedness for and response to industrial accidents.
5. The provisions of this Convention shall not prejudice any obligations of the Parties under international law with regard to industrial accidents and hazardous activities.

Article 4 – Identification, consultation and advice

1. For the purpose of undertaking preventive measures and setting up preparedness measures, the Party of origin shall take measures, as appropriate, to identify hazardous activities within its jurisdiction and to ensure that affected Parties are notified of any such proposed or existing activity.
2. Parties concerned shall, at the initiative of any such Party, enter into discussions on the identification of those hazardous activities that are, reasonably, capable of causing transboundary effects. If the Parties concerned do not agree on whether an activity is such a hazardous activity, any such Party may, unless the Parties concerned agree on another method of resolving the question, submit that question to an inquiry commission in accordance with the provisions of Annex II hereto for advice.
3. The Parties shall, with respect to proposed or existing hazardous activities, apply the procedures set out in Annex III hereto.
4. When a hazardous activity is subject to an environmental impact assessment in accordance with the Convention on Environmental Impact Assessment in a Transboundary Context and that assessment includes an evaluation of the transboundary effects of industrial accidents from the hazardous activity which is performed in conformity with the terms of this Convention, the final decision taken for the purposes of the Convention on Environmental Impact Assessment in a Transboundary Context shall fulfil the relevant requirements of this Convention.

Article 5 – Voluntary extension

Parties concerned should, at the initiative of any of them, enter into discussions on whether to treat an activity not covered by Annex I as a hazardous activity. Upon mutual agreement, they may use an advisory mechanism of their choice, or an inquiry commission in accordance with Annex II, to advise them. Where the Parties concerned so agree, this Convention, or any part thereof, shall apply to the activity in question as if it were a hazardous activity

Article 6 – Prevention

1. The Parties shall take appropriate measures for the prevention of industrial accidents, including measures to induce action by operators to reduce the risk of industrial accidents. Such measures may include, but are not limited to those referred to in Annex IV hereto.
2. With regard to any hazardous activity, the Party of origin shall require the operator to demonstrate the safe performance of the hazardous activity by the provision of information such as basic details of the process, including but not limited to, analysis and evaluation as detailed in Annex V hereto.

Article 7 – Decision-making on siting

Within the framework of its legal system, the Party of origin shall, with the objective of minimizing the risk to the population and the environment of all affected Parties, seek the establishment of policies on the siting of new hazardous activities and on significant modifications to existing hazardous activities. Within the framework of their legal systems, the affected Parties shall seek the establishment of policies on significant developments in areas which could be affected by transboundary effects of an industrial accident arising out of a hazardous activity so as to minimize the risks involved. In elaborating and establishing these policies, the Parties should consider the matters set out in Annex V, paragraph 2, subparagraphs (1) to (8), and Annex VI hereto.

Article 8 – Emergency preparedness

1. The Parties shall take appropriate measures to establish and maintain adequate emergency preparedness to respond to industrial accidents. The Parties shall ensure that preparedness measures are taken to mitigate transboundary effects of such accidents, on-site duties being undertaken by operators. These measures may include, but are not limited to those referred to in Annex VII hereto. In particular, the Parties concerned shall inform each other of their contingency plans.
2. The Party of origin shall ensure for hazardous activities the preparation and implementation of on-site contingency plans, including suitable measures for response and other measures to prevent and minimize transboundary effects. The Party of origin shall provide to the other Parties concerned the elements it has for the elaboration of contingency plans.
3. Each Party shall ensure for hazardous activities the preparation and implementation of off-site contingency plans covering measures to be taken within its territory to prevent and minimize transboundary effects. In preparing these plans, account shall be taken of the conclusions of analysis and evaluation, in particular the matters set out in Annex V, paragraph 2, subparagraphs (1) to (5). Parties concerned shall endeavour to make such plans compatible. Where appropriate, joint off-site contingency plans shall be drawn up in order to facilitate the adoption of adequate response measures.
4. Contingency plans should be reviewed regularly, or when circumstances so require, taking into account the experience gained in dealing with actual emergencies.

Article 9 – Information to, and participation of the public

1. The Parties shall ensure that adequate information is given to the public in the areas capable of being affected by an industrial accident arising out of a hazardous activity. This information shall be transmitted through such channels as the Parties deem appropriate, shall include the elements contained in Annex VIII hereto and should take into account matters set out in Annex V, paragraph 2, subparagraphs (1) to (4) and (9).
2. The Party of origin shall, in accordance with the provisions of this Convention and whenever possible and appropriate, give the public in the areas capable of being affected an opportunity to participate in relevant procedures with the aim of making known its views and concerns on prevention and preparedness measures, and shall ensure that the opportunity given to the public of the affected Party is equivalent to that given to the public of the Party of origin.
3. The Parties shall, in accordance with their legal systems and, if desired, on a reciprocal basis provide natural or legal persons who are being or are capable of being adversely affected by the transboundary effects of an industrial accident in the territory of a Party, with access to, and treatment in the relevant administrative and judicial proceedings, including the possibilities of starting a legal action and appealing a decision affecting their rights, equivalent to those available to persons within their own jurisdiction.

Article 10 – Industrial accident notification systems

1. The Parties shall, with the aim of obtaining and transmitting industrial accident notifications containing information needed to counteract transboundary effects, provide for the establishment and operation of compatible and efficient industrial accident notification systems at appropriate levels.
2. In the event of an industrial accident, or imminent threat thereof, which causes or is capable of causing transboundary effects, the Party of origin shall ensure that affected Parties are, without delay, notified at appropriate levels through the industrial accident notification systems. Such notification shall include the elements contained in Annex IX hereto.
3. The Parties concerned shall ensure that, in the event of an industrial accident or imminent threat thereof, the contingency plans prepared in accordance with Article 8 are activated as soon as possible and to the extent appropriate to the circumstances.

Article 11 – Response

1. The Parties shall ensure that, in the event of an industrial accident, or imminent threat thereof, adequate response measures are taken, as soon as possible and using the most efficient practices, to contain and minimize effects.
2. In the event of an industrial accident, or imminent threat thereof, which causes or is capable of causing transboundary effects, the Parties concerned shall ensure that the effects are assessed—where appropriate, jointly for the purpose of taking adequate response measures. The Parties concerned shall endeavour to coordinate their response measures.

Article 12 – Mutual assistance

1. If a Party needs assistance in the event of an industrial accident, it may ask for assistance from other Parties, indicating the scope and type of assistance required. A Party to whom a request for assistance

is directed shall promptly decide and inform the requesting Party whether it is in a position to render the assistance required and indicate the scope and terms of the assistance that might be rendered.

2. The Parties concerned shall cooperate to facilitate the prompt provision of assistance agreed to under paragraph l of this Article, including, where appropriate, action to minimize the consequences and effects of the industrial accident, and to provide general assistance. Where Parties do not have bilateral or multilateral agreements which cover their arrangements for providing mutual assistance, the assistance shall be rendered in accordance with Annex X hereto, unless the Parties agree otherwise.

Article 13 – Responsibility and liability

The Parties shall support appropriate international efforts to elaborate rules, criteria and procedures in the field of responsibility and liability.

Article 14 – Research and development

The Parties shall, as appropriate, initiate and cooperate in the conduct of research into, and in the development of methods and technologies for the prevention of, preparedness for and response to industrial accidents. For these purposes, the Parties shall encourage and actively promote scientific and technological cooperation, including research into less hazardous processes aimed at limiting accident hazards and preventing and limiting the consequences of industrial accidents.

Article 15 – Exchange of information

The Parties shall, at the multilateral or bilateral level, exchange reasonably obtainable information, including the elements contained in Annex XI hereto.

Article 16 – Exchange of technology

1. The Parties shall, consistent with their laws, regulations and practices, facilitate the exchange of technology for the prevention of, preparedness for and response to the effects of industrial accidents, particularly through the promotion of:
   (a) Exchange of available technology on various financial bases;
   (b) Direct industrial contacts and cooperation;
   (c) Exchange of information and experience;
   (d) Provision of technical assistance.
2. In promoting the activities specified in paragraph 1, subparagraphs (a) to (d) of this Article, the Parties shall create favourable conditions by facilitating contacts and cooperation among appropriate organizations and individuals in both the private and the public sectors that are capable of providing technology, design and engineering services, equipment or finance.

Article 17 – Competent authorities and points of contact

1. Each Party shall designate or establish one or more competent authorities for the purposes of this Convention.
2. Without prejudice to other arrangements at the bilateral or multilateral level, each Party shall designate or establish one point of contact for the purpose of industrial accident notifications pursuant to Article 10, and one point of contact for the purpose of mutual assistance pursuant to Article 12. These points of contact should preferably be the same.
3. Each Party shall, within three months of the date of entry into force of this Convention for that Party, inform the other Parties, through the secretariat referred to in Article 20, which body or bodies it has designated as its point(s) of contact and as its competent authority or authorities.
4. Each Party shall, within one month of the date of decision, inform the other Parties, through the secretariat, of any changes regarding the designation(s) it has made under paragraph 3 of this Article.
5. Each Party shall keep its point of contact and industrial accident notification systems pursuant to Article 10 operational at all times.
6. Each Party shall keep its point of contact and the authorities responsible for making and receiving requests for, and accepting offers of assistance pursuant to Article 12 operational at all times.

Article 18 – Conference of the Parties

1. The representatives of the Parties shall constitute the Conference of the Parties of this Convention and hold their meetings on a regular basis. The first meeting of the Conference of the Parties shall be convened not later than one year after the date of the entry into force of this Convention. Thereafter, a meeting of the Conference of the Parties shall be held at least once a year or at the written request of any Party, provided that, within six months of the request being communicated to them by the secretariat, it is supported by at least one third of the Parties.
2. The Conference of the Parties shall:
   (a) Review the implementation of this Convention;
   (b) Carry out advisory functions aimed at strengthening the ability of Parties to prevent, prepare for and respond to the transboundary effects of industrial accidents, and at facilitating the provision of technical assistance and advice at the request of Parties faced with industrial accidents;
   (c) Establish, as appropriate, working groups and other appropriate mechanisms to consider matters related to the implementation and development of this Convention and, to this end, to prepare appropriate studies and other documentation and submit recommendations for consideration by the Conference of the Parties;
   (d) Fulfil such other functions as may be appropriate under the provisions of this Convention;
   (e) At its first meeting, consider and, by consensus, adopt rules of procedure for its meetings.
3. The Conference of the Parties, in discharging its functions, shall, when it deems appropriate, also

cooperate with other relevant international organizations.

4. The Conference of the Parties shall, at its first meeting, establish a programme of work, in particular with regard to the items contained in Annex XII hereto. The Conference of the Parties shall also decide on the method of work, including the use of national centres and cooperation with relevant international organizations and the establishment of a system with a view to facilitating the implementation of this Convention, in particular for mutual assistance in the event of an industrial accident, and building upon pertinent existing activities within relevant international organizations. As part of the programme of work, the Conference of the Parties shall review existing national, regional and international centres, and other bodies and programmes aimed at coordinating information and efforts in the prevention of, preparedness for and response to industrial accidents, with a view to determining what additional international institutions or centres may be needed to carry out the tasks listed in Annex XII.
5. The Conference of the Parties shall, at its first meeting, commence consideration of procedures to create more favourable conditions for the exchange of technology for the prevention of, preparedness for and response to the effects of industrial accidents.
6. The Conference of the Parties shall adopt guidelines and criteria to facilitate the identification of hazardous activities for the purposes of this Convention.

Article 19 – Right to vote

1. Except as provided for in paragraph 2 of this Article, each Party to this Convention shall have one vote.
2. Regional economic integration organizations as defined in Article 27 shall, in matters within their competence, exercise their right to vote with a number of votes equal to the number of their member States which are Parties to this Convention. Such organizations shall not exercise their right to vote if their member States exercise theirs, and vice versa.

Article 20 – Secretariat

The Executive Secretary of the Economic Commission for Europe shall carry out the following secretariat functions:

(a) Convene and prepare meetings of the Parties;

(b) Transmit to the Parties reports and other information received in accordance with the provisions of this Convention;

(c) Such other functions as may be determined by the Parties.

Article 21 – Settlement of disputes

1. If a dispute arises between two or more Parties about the interpretation or application of this Convention, they shall seek a solution by negotiation or by any other method of dispute settlement acceptable to the parties to the dispute.
2. When signing, ratifying, accepting, approving or acceding to this Convention, or at any time thereafter, a Party may declare in writing to the Depositary that, for a dispute not resolved in accordance with paragraph 1 of this Article, it accepts one or both of the following means of dispute settlement as compulsory in relation to any Party accepting the same obligation:

   (a) Submission of the dispute to the International Court of Justice;

   (b) Arbitration in accordance with the procedure set out in Annex XIII hereto.
3. If the parties to the dispute have accepted both means of dispute settlement referred to in paragraph 2 of this Article, the dispute may be submitted only to the International Court of Justice, unless the parties to the dispute agree otherwise.

Article 22 – Limitations on the supply of information

1. The provisions of this Convention shall not affect the rights or the obligations of Parties in accordance with their national laws, regulations, administrative provisions or accepted legal practices and applicable international regulations to protect information related to personal data, industrial and commercial secrecy, including intellectual property, or national security.
2. If a Party nevertheless decides to supply such protected information to another Party, the Party receiving such protected information shall respect the confidentiality of the information received and the conditions under which it is supplied, and shall only use that information for the purposes for which it was supplied.

Article 23 – Implementation

The Parties shall report periodically on the implementation of this Convention.

Article 24 – Bilateral and multilateral agreements

1. The Parties may, in order to implement their obligations under this Convention, continue existing or enter into new bilateral or multilateral agreements or other arrangements.
2. The provisions of this Convention shall not affect the right of Parties to take, by bilateral or multilateral agreement where appropriate, more stringent measures than those required by this Convention.

Article 25 – Status of Annexes

The Annexes to this Convention form an integral part of the Convention.

Article 26 – Amendments to the Convention

1. Any Party may propose amendments to this Convention.
2. The text of any proposed amendment to this Convention shall be submitted in writing to the Executive Secretary of the Economic Commission for

Procedure

Europe, who shall circulate it to all Parties. The Conference of the Parties shall discuss proposed amendments at its next annual meeting, provided that such proposals have been circulated to the Parties by the Executive Secretary of the Economic Commission for Europe at least ninety days in advance.

3. For amendments to this Convention other than those to Annex I, for which the procedure is described in paragraph 4 of this Article:
   (a) Amendments shall be adopted by consensus of the Parties present at the meeting and shall be submitted by the Depositary to all Parties for ratification, acceptance or approval;
   (b) Instruments of ratification, acceptance or approval of amendments shall be deposited with the Depositary. Amendments adopted in accordance with this Article shall enter into force for Parties that have accepted them on the ninetieth day following the day of receipt by the Depositary of the sixteenth instrument of ratification, acceptance or approval;
   (c) Thereafter, amendments shall enter into force for any other Party on the ninetieth day after that Party deposits its instruments of ratification, acceptance or approval of the amendments.
4. For amendments to Annex I:
   (a) The Parties shall make every effort to reach agreement by consensus. If all efforts at consensus have been exhausted and no agreement reached, the amendments shall, as a last resort, be adopted by a nine-tenths majority vote of the Parties present and voting at the meeting. If adopted by the Conference of the Parties, the amendments shall be communicated to the Parties and recommended for approval;
   (b) On the expiry of twelve months from the date of their communication by the Executive Secretary of the Economic Commission for Europe, the amendments to Annex I shall become effective for those Parties to this Convention which have not submitted a notification in accordance with the provisions of paragraph 4 (c) of this Article, provided that at least sixteen Parties have not submitted such a notification;
   (c) Any Party that is unable to approve an amendment to Annex I of this Convention shall so notify the Executive Secretary of the Economic Commission for Europe in writing within twelve months from the date of the communication of the adoption. The Executive Secretary shall without delay notify all Parties of any such notification received. A Party may at any time substitute an acceptance for its previous notification and the amendment to Annex I shall thereupon enter into force for that Party;
   (d) For the purpose of this paragraph "Parties present and voting" means Parties present and casting an affirmative or negative vote.

Article 27 – Signature

This Convention shall be open for signature at Helsinki from 17 to 18 March 1992 inclusive, and thereafter at United Nations Headquarters in New York until 18 September 1992, by States members of the Economic Commission for Europe, as well as States having consultative status with the Economic Commission for Europe pursuant to paragraph 8 of Economic and Social Council resolution 36 (IV) of 28 March 1947, and by regional economic integration organizations constituted by sovereign States members of the Economic Commission for Europe to which their member States have transferred competence in respect of matters governed by this Convention, including the competence to enter into treaties in respect of these matters.

Article 28 – Depositary

The Secretary-General of the United Nations shall act as the Depositary of this Convention.

Article 29 – Ratification, acceptance, approval and accession

1. This Convention shall be subject to ratification, acceptance or approval by the signatory States and regional economic integration organizations referred to in Article 27.
2. This Convention shall be open for accession by the States and organizations referred to in Article 27.
3. Any organization referred to in Article 27 which becomes Party to this Convention without any of its member States being a Party shall be bound by all the obligations under this Convention. In the case of such organizations, one or more of whose member States is a Party to this Convention, the organization and its member States shall decide on their respective responsibilities for the performance of their obligations under this Convention. In such cases, the organization and the member States shall not be entitled to exercise rights under this Convention concurrently.
4. In their instruments of ratification, acceptance, approval or accession, the regional economic integration organizations referred to in Article 27 shall declare the extent of their competence with respect to the matters governed by this Convention. These organizations shall also inform the Depositary of any substantial modification to the extent of their competence.

Article 30 – Entry into force

1. This Convention shall enter into force on the ninetieth day after the date of deposit of the sixteenth instrument of ratification, acceptance, approval or accession.
2. For the purposes of paragraph 1 of this Article, any instrument deposited by an organization referred to in Article 27 shall not be counted as additional to those deposited by States members of such an organization.
3. For each state or organization referred to in Article 27 which ratifies, accepts or approves this Convention or accedes thereto after the deposit

of the sixteenth instrument of ratification, acceptance, approval or accession, this Convention shall enter into force on the ninetieth day after the date of deposit by such State or organization of its instrument of ratification, acceptance, approval or accession.

Article 31 – Withdrawal

1. At any time after three years from the date on which this Convention has come into force with respect to a Party, that Party may withdraw from this Convention by giving written notification to the Depositary. Any such withdrawal shall take effect on the ninetieth day after the date of the receipt of the notification by the Depositary.
2. Any such withdrawal shall not affect the application of Article 4 to an activity in respect of which a notification has been made pursuant to Article 4, paragraph 1, or a request for discussions has been made pursuant to Article 4, paragraph 2.

Article 32 – Authentic texts

The original of this Convention, of which the English, French and Russian texts are equally authentic, shall be deposited with the Secretary-General of the United Nations.

In witness whereof the undersigned, being duly authorized thereto, have signed this Convention.

Done at Helsinki, this seventeenth day of March one thousand nine hundred and ninety-two.

ANNEX I – Hazardous substances for the purposes of defining hazardous activities[1]

Where a substance or mixture named in Part II also falls within one or more categories in Part I, the threshold quantity given in Part II shall be used.

For the identification of hazardous activities, Parties shall take into consideration the actual or anticipated hazardous properties and/or quantities of all hazardous substances present or of hazardous substances which it is reasonable to foresee may be generated during loss of control of an activity, including storage activities, within a hazardous activity.

PART I – Categories of substances and preparations not specifically named in Part II[2]

[...]

PART II – Named substances[3]

[...]

ANNEX II – Inquiry commission procedure pursuant to Articles 4 and 5

1. The requesting Party/Parties shall notify the Secretariat that it/they is/are submitting question(s) to an inquiry commission established in accordance with the provisions of this Annex. The notification shall state the subject matter of the inquiry. The Secretariat shall immediately inform all Parties to the Convention of this submission.
2. The inquiry commission shall consist of three members. Both the requesting party and the other party to the inquiry procedure shall appoint a scientific or technical expert and the two experts so appointed shall designate by common agreement a third expert, who shall be the president of the inquiry commission. The latter shall not be a national of one of the parties to the inquiry procedure, nor have dealt with the case in any other capacity.
3. If the president of the inquiry commission has not been designated within two months of the appointment of the second expert, the executive secretary of the Economic Commission for Europe shall, at the request of either party, designate the president within a further two-month period.
4. If one of the parties to the inquiry procedure does not appoint an expert within one month of its receipt of the notification by the Secretariat, the other party may inform the executive secretary of the Economic Commission for Europe, who shall designate the president of the inquiry commission within a further two-months period. Upon designation, the president of the inquiry commission shall request the party which has not appointed an expert to do so within one month. If it fails to do so within that period, the president shall inform the Executive Secretary of the Economic Commission for Europe who shall make this appointment within a further two-month period.
5. The inquiry commission shall adopt its own rules of procedure.
6. The inquiry commission may take all appropriate measures in order to carry out its functions.
7. The parties to the inquiry procedure shall facilitate the work of the inquiry commission and in particular shall, using all means at their disposal:
   (a) provide the inquiry commission with all relevant documents, facilities and information;
   (b) enable the inquiry commission, where necessary, to call witness or experts and receive their evidence.
8. The parties and the experts shall protect the confidentiality of any information they receive in confidence during the work of the inquiry commission.
9. If one of the parties to the inquiry procedure does not appear before the inquiry commission or fails

1 Criteria according the United Nations Globally Harmonized System (GHS) of Classification and Labelling of Chemicals (ST/SG/AC.10/30/Rev.4). Parties should use these criteria when classifying substances or mixtures for the purposes of Part I of this annex, unless other legally binding criteria have been adopted in the national legislation. Mixtures shall be treated in the same way as the pure substance, provided they remain within concentration limits set according to their properties in accordance with the GHS unless a percentage composition or other description is specifically given.

2 Notes on technical criteria omitted [the editors].

3 Notes on technical criteria omitted [the editors].

to present its case, the other party may request the inquiry commission to continue the proceedings and to complete its work. Absence of a party or failure of a party to present its case shall not constitute a bar to the continuation and completion of the work of the inquiry commission.

10. Unless the inquiry commission determines otherwise because of the particular circumstances of the matter, the expenses of the inquiry commission, including the remuneration of its members, shall be borne equally by the parties to the inquiry procedure. The inquiry commission shall keep a record of all its expenses and shall furnish a final statement thereof to the parties.
11. Any Party which has an interest of a factual nature in the subject matter of the inquiry procedure and which may be affected by an opinion in the matter may intervene in the proceedings with the consent of the inquiry commission.
12. The decisions of the inquiry commission on matters of the procedure shall be taken by majority vote of its members. The final opinion of the inquiry commission shall reflect the view of the majority of its members and shall include any dissenting view.
13. The inquiry commission shall present its final opinion within two months of the date on which it was established, unless it finds it necessary to extend this time limit for a period which should not exceed two months.
14. The final opinion of the inquiry commission shall be based on accepted scientific principles. The final opinion shall be transmitted by the inquiry commission to the parties to the inquiry procedure and to the Secretariat.

ANNEX III – Procedures pursuant to Article 4

1. A Party of origin may request consultations with another Party, in accordance with paragraphs 2 to 5 of this Annex, in order to determine whether that Party is an affected Party.
2. For a proposed or existing hazardous activity, the Party of origin shall, for the purposes of ensuring adequate and effective consultations, provide for the notification at appropriate levels of any Party that it considers may be an affected party as early as possible and no later than when informing its own public about that proposed or existing activity. For existing hazardous activities such notification shall be provided no later than two years after the entry into force of this Convention for a Party of origin.
3. The notification shall contain, inter alia:
   (a) information on the hazardous activity, including any available information or report, such as information produced in accordance with Article 6, on its possible transboundary effects in the event of an industrial accident;
   (b) an indication of a reasonable time within which a response under paragraph 4 of this Annex is required, taking into account the nature of the activity;

   and may include the information set out in paragraph 6 of this Annex.
4. The notified Parties shall respond to the Party of origin within the time specified in the notification, acknowledging receipt of the notification and indicating whether they intend to enter into consultation.
5. If a notified Party indicates that it does not intend to enter into consultation, or if it does not respond within the time specified in the notification, the provisions set down in the following paragraphs of this Annex shall not apply. In such circumstances, the right of a Party of origin to determine whether to carry out an assessment and analysis on the basis of its national law and practice is not prejudiced.
6. Upon receipt of a response from a notified Party indicating its desire to enter into consultation, the Party of origin shall, if it has not already done so, provide to the notified Party:
   (a) relevant information regarding the time schedule for analysis, including an indication of the time schedule for the transmittal of comments;
   (b) relevant information on the hazardous activity and its transboundary effects in the event of an industrial accident;
   (c) the opportunity to participate in evaluations of the information or any report demonstrating possible transboundary effects.
7. An affected Party shall, at the request of the Party of origin, provide the latter with reasonably obtainable information relating to the area under the jurisdiction of the affected party capable of being affected, where such information is necessary for the preparation of the assessment and analysis and measures. The information shall be furnished promptly and, as appropriate, through a joint body where one exists.
8. The Party of origin shall furnish the affected party directly, as appropriate, or, where one exists, through a joint body with the analysis and evaluation documentation as described in Annex V, paragraphs 1 and 2.
9. The Parties concerned shall inform the public in areas reasonably capable of being affected by the hazardous activity and shall arrange for the distribution of the analysis and evaluation documentation to it and to authorities in the relevant areas. The parties shall ensure them an opportunity for making comments on, or objections to, the hazardous activity and shall arrange for their views to be submitted to the competent authority of the Party of origin, either directly to that authority or, where appropriate, through the Party of origin, within a reasonable time.
10. The Party of origin shall, after completion of the analysis and evaluation documentation, enter without undue delay into consultations with the affected Party concerning, inter alia, the transboundary effects of the hazardous activity in the event of an industrial accident, and measures to reduce or

eliminate its effects. The consultations may relate to:

(a) possible alternatives to the hazardous activity, including the no-action alternative, and possible measures to mitigate transboundary effects at the expense of the Party of origin;

(b) other forms of possible mutual assistance for reducing any transboundary effects;

(c) any other appropriate matters.

The Parties concerned shall, on the commencement of such consultations, agree on a reasonable time-frame for the duration of the consultation period. Any such consultations may be conducted through an appropriate joint body, where one exists.

11. The Parties concerned shall ensure that due account is taken of the analysis and evaluation, as well as of the comments received pursuant to paragraph 9 of this Annex and of the outcome of the consultations referred to in paragraph 10 of this Annex.

12. The Party of origin shall notify the affected Parties of any decision on the activity, along with the reasons and considerations on which it was based.

13. If, after additional and relevant information concerning the transboundary effects of a hazardous activity and which was not available at the time consultations were held with respect to that activity, becomes available to a Party concerned, that Party shall immediately inform the other Party or Parties concerned. If one of the Parties concerned so requests, renewed consultations shall be held.

ANNEX IV – Preventive measures pursuant to Article 6

The following measures may be carried out, depending on national laws and practices, by Parties, competent authorities, operators, or by joint efforts:

1. the setting of general or specific safety objectives;
2. the adoption of legislative provisions or guidelines concerning safety measures and safety standards;
3. the identification of those hazardous activities which require special preventive measures, which may include a licensing or authorisation system;
4. the evaluation of risk analyses or of safety studies for hazardous activities and an action plan for the implementation of necessary measures;
5. the provision to the competent authorities of the information needed to assess risks;
6. the application of the most appropriate technology in order to prevent industrial accidents and protect human beings and the environment;
7. the undertaking, in order to prevent industrial accidents, of the appropriate education and training of all persons engaged in hazardous activities on-site under both normal and abnormal conditions;
8. the establishment of internal managerial structures and practices designed to implement and maintain safety regulations effectively;
9. the monitoring and auditing of hazardous activities and the carrying out of inspections.

ANNEX V – Analysis and evaluation

1. The analysis and evaluation of the hazardous activity should be performed with a scope and to a depth which vary depending on the purpose for which they are carried out.
2. The following table illustrates, for the purposes of the related Articles, matters which should be considered in the analysis and evaluation, for the purposes listed:

Purpose of Analysis	Matters to be considered
Emergency planning under Article 8	1. The quantities and properties of hazardous substances on the site; 2. Brief descriptive scenarios of a representative sample of industrial accidents possibly arising from the hazardous activity, including an indication of the likelihood of each; 3. For each scenario: (a) the approximate quantity of a release; (b) the extent and severity of the resulting consequences both for people and for the non-human environment in favourable and unfavourable conditions, including the extent of resulting hazard zones; (c) the time-scale within which the industrial accident could develop from the initiating event; (d) any action which could be taken to minimise the likelihood of escalation; 4. The size and distribution of the population in the vicinity, including any large concentrations of people potentially in the hazard zone; 5. The age, mobility and susceptibility of that population.
Decision-making on siting under Article 7	In addition to items 1 to 5 above: 6. The severity of the harm inflicted on people and the environment, depending on the nature and circumstances of the release 7. The distance from the location of the hazardous activity at which harmful effects on people and the environment may reasonably occur in the event of an industrial accident 8. The same information not only for the present situation but also for planned or reasonably foreseeable future developments.
Information to the public under Article 9	In addition to items 1 to 4 above: 9. The people who may be affected by an industrial accident;

Purpose of Analysis	Matters to be considered
Preventive measures under Article 6	In addition to items 4 to 9 above, more detailed versions of the descriptions and assessments set out in items 1 to 3 will be needed for preventive measures. In addition to those descriptions and assessments, the following matters should also be covered; 10. The conditions and quantities in which hazardous materials are handled; 11. A list of the scenarios for the types of industrial accidents with serious effects, to include examples covering the full range of incident size and the possibility of effects from adjacent activities; 12. For each scenario, a description of the events which could initiate an industrial accident and the steps whereby it could escalate; 13. An assessment, at least in general terms, of the likelihood of each step occurring, taking into account the arrangements in 14; 14. A description of the preventive measures in terms of both equipment and procedures designed to minimise the likelihood of each step occurring; 15. An assessment of the effects that deviations from normal operating conditions could have, and the consequent arrangements for safe shut-down of the hazardous activity or any part thereof in an emergency, and of the need for staff training to ensure that potentially serious deviations are recognised at an early stage and appropriate action taken; 16. An assessment of the extent to which modifications, repair work and maintenance work on the hazardous activity could place the control measures at risk, and the consequent arrangements to ensure that control is maintained.

ANNEX VI – Decision-making on siting pursuant to Article 7

The following illustrates the matters which should be considered pursuant to Article 7:

1. the results of risk analysis and evaluation, including an evaluation pursuant to Annex V of the physical characteristics of the area in which the hazardous activity being planned;
2. the results of consultations and public participation processes;
3. an analysis of the increase or decrease of the risk caused by any development in the territory of the affected Party in relation to an existing hazardous activity in the territory of the Party of origin;
4. the evaluation of the environmental risks, including any transboundary effects;
5. an evaluation of the new hazardous activities which could be a source of risk;
6. a consideration of the siting of new, and significant modifications to existing hazardous activities at a safe distance from existing centres of population, as well as the establishment of a safety area around hazardous activities; within such areas, developments which would increase the populations at risk, or otherwise increase the severity of the risk, should be closely examined.

ANNEX VII – Emergency preparedness measures pursuant to Article 8

1. All contingency plans, both on- and off-site, should be coordinated to provide a comprehensive and effective response to industrial accidents.
2. The contingency plans should include the actions necessary to localise emergencies and to prevent or minimise their transboundary effects. They should also include arrangements for warning people and, where appropriate, arrangements for their evacuation, other protective or rescue actions and health services.
3. Contingency plans should give on-site personnel, people who might be affected off site and rescue forces, details of technical and organisational procedures which are appropriate for response in the event of an industrial accident capable of having transboundary effects and to prevent and minimise effects on people and the environment, both on and off site.
4. Examples of matters which could be covered by on-site contingency plans include:
   (a) organisational roles and responsibilities on site for dealing with an emergency;
   (b) a description of the action which should be taken in the event of an industrial accident, or an imminent threat thereof, in order to control the

condition or event, or details of where such a description can be found;

(c) a description of the equipment and resources available;

(d) arrangements for providing early warning of industrial accidents to the public authority responsible for the off-site emergency response, including the type of information which should be included in an initial warning and the arrangements for providing more detailed information as it becomes available;

(e) arrangements for training personnel in the duties they will be expected to perform.

5. Examples of matters which could be covered by off-site contingency plans include:

(a) organisational roles and responsibilities off site for dealing with an emergency, including how integration with on-site plans is to be achieved;

(b) methods and procedures to be followed by emergency and medical personnel;

(c) methods for rapidly determining the affected area;

(d) arrangements for ensuring that prompt industrial accident notification is made to affected or potentially affected Parties and that that liaison is maintained subsequently;

(e) identification of resources necessary to implement the plan and the arrangements for coordination;

(f) arrangements for providing information to the public including, where appropriate, the arrangements for reinforcing and repeating the information provided to the public pursuant to Article 9;

(g) arrangements for training and exercises.

6. Contingency plans could include the measures for: treatment; collection; clean-up; storage; removal and safe disposal of hazardous substances and contaminated material; and restoration.

ANNEX VIII – Information to the public pursuant to Article 9

1. The name of the company, address of the hazardous activity and identification by position held of the person giving the information.
2. An explanation in simple terms of the hazardous activity, including the risks.
3. The common names or the generic names or the general danger classification of the substances and preparations which are involved in the hazardous activity, with an indication of their principal dangerous characteristics.
4. General information resulting from an environmental impact assessment, if available and relevant.
5. The general information relating to the nature of an industrial accident that could possibly occur in the hazardous activity, including its potential effects on the population and the environment.
6. Adequate information on how the affected population will be warned and kept informed in the event of an industrial accident.
7. Adequate information on the actions the affected population should take and on the behaviour they should adopt in the event of an industrial accident.
8. Adequate information on arrangements made regarding the hazardous activity, including liaison with the emergency services, to deal with industrial accidents, to reduce the severity of the industrial accidents and to mitigate their effects.
9. General information on the emergency services' off-site contingency plan, drawn up to cope with any off-site effects, including the transboundary effects of an industrial accident.
10. General information on special requirements and conditions to which the hazardous activity is subject according the relevant national regulations and/or administrative provisions, including licensing or authorisation systems;
11. Details of where further relevant information can be obtained.

ANNEX IX – Industrial accident notification systems pursuant to Article 10

1. The industrial accident notification systems shall enable the speediest possible transmission of data and forecasts according to previously determined codes using compatible data-transmission and data-treatment systems for emergency warning and response, and for measures to minimise and contain the consequences of transboundary effects, taking account of different needs at different levels.
2. The industrial accident notification shall include the following:

(a) the type and magnitude of the industrial accident, the hazardous substances involved (if known), and the severity of its possible effects;

(b) the time of occurrence and exact location of the accident;

(c) such other available information as necessary for an efficient response to the industrial accident.

3. The industrial accident notification shall be supplemented at appropriate intervals, or whenever required, by further relevant information on the development of the situation concerning transboundary effects.
4. Regular texts and reviews of the effectiveness of the industrial accident notification systems shall be undertaken, including the regular training of the personnel involved. Where appropriate, such tests, reviews and training shall be performed jointly.

ANNEX X – Mutual assistance pursuant to Article 12

1. The overall direction, control, coordination and supervision of the assistance is the responsibility of the requesting Party. The personnel involved in the assisting operation shall act in accordance with the relevant laws of the requesting Party. The appropriate authorities of the requesting Party shall cooperate with the authority designated by the assisting Party, pursuant to Article 17, as being in charge of the immediate operational supervision of the personnel and the equipment provided by the assisting Party.
2. The requesting Party shall, to the extent of its capabilities, provide local facilities and services for the proper and effective administration of the assistance, and shall ensure the protection of personnel, equipment and materials brought into its territory by, or on behalf of, the assisting Party for such a purpose.
3. Unless otherwise agreed by the Parties concerned, assistance shall be provided at the expense of the requesting Party. The assisting Party may at any time waive wholly or partly the reimbursement of costs.
4. The requesting Party shall use its best efforts to afford to the assisting Party and persons acting on its behalf the privileges, immunities or facilities necessary for the expeditious performance of their assistance functions. The requesting Party shall not be required to apply this provision to its own nationals or permanent residents or to afford them the privileges and immunities referred to above.
5. A Party shall, at the request of the requesting or assisting Party, endeavour to facilitate the transit through its territory of duly notified personnel, equipment and property involved in the assistance to and from the requesting Party.
6. The requesting Party shall facilitate the entry into, stay in and departure from its national territory of duly notified personnel and of equipment and property involved in the assistance.
7. With regard to acts resulting directly from the assistance provided, the requesting Party shall, in respect of the death of or injury to persons, damage to or loss of property, or damage to the environment caused within its territory in the course of the provision of the assistance requested, hold harmless and indemnify the assisting Party or persons acting on its behalf and compensate them for death or injury suffered by them and for loss of or damage to equipment or other property involved in the assistance. The requesting Party shall be responsible for dealing with claims brought by third parties against the assisting Party or persons acting on its behalf.
8. The Parties concerned shall cooperate closely in order to facilitate the settlement of legal proceedings and claims which could result from assistance operations.
9. Any Party may request assistance relating to the medical treatment or the temporary relocation in the territory of another Party of persons involved in an accident.
10. The affected or requesting Party may at any time, after appropriate consultations and by notification, request the termination of assistance received or provided under this Convention. Once such a request has been made, the Parties concerned shall consult one another with a view to making arrangements for the proper termination of the assistance.

ANNEX XI – Exchange of information pursuant to Article 15

Information shall include the following elements, which can also be the subject of multilateral and bilateral cooperation:

(a) legislative and administrative measures, policies, objectives and priorities for prevention, preparedness and response, scientific activities and technical measures to reduce the risk of industrial accidents from hazardous activities, including the mitigation of transboundary effects;

(b) measures and contingency plans at the appropriate level affecting other Parties;

(c) programmes for monitoring, planning, research and development, including their implementation and surveillance;

(d) measures taken regarding prevention of, preparedness for and response to industrial accidents;

(e) experience with industrial accidents and cooperation in response to industrial accidents with transboundary effects;

(f) the development and application of the best available technologies for improved environmental protection and safety;

(g) emergency preparedness and response;

(h) methods used for the prediction of risks, including criteria for the monitoring and assessment of transboundary effects.

ANNEX XII – Tasks for mutual assistance pursuant to Article 18, Paragraph 4

1. Information and data collection and dissemination
   (a) establishment and operation of an industrial accident notification system that can provide information on industrial accidents and on experts, in order to involve the experts as rapidly as possible in providing assistance;
   (b) establishment and operation of a data bank for the reception, processing and distribution of necessary information on industrial accidents, including their effects, and also on measures applied and their effectiveness;
   (c) elaboration and maintenance of a list of hazardous substances, including their relevant characteristics, and of information on how to deal with those in the event of an industrial accident;

(d) establishment and maintenance of a register of experts to provide consultative and other kinds of assistance regarding preventive, preparedness and response measures, including restoration measures;

(e) maintenance of a list of hazardous activities;

(f) production and maintenance of a list of hazardous substances covered by the provisions of Annex I, Part I.

2. Research, training and methodologies

(a) development and provision of models based on experience from industrial accidents, and scenarios for preventive, preparedness and response measures;

(b) promotion of education and training, organisation of international symposia and promotion of cooperation in research and development.

3. Technical assistance

(a) fulfillment of advisory functions aimed at strengthening the ability to apply preventive, preparedness and response measures;

(b) undertaking, at the request of a Party, of inspections of its hazardous activities and the provision of assistance in organising its national inspections according to the requirements of this Convention.

4. Assistance in the case of an emergency Provision, at the request of a Party, of assistance by, inter alia, sending experts to the site of an industrial accident to provide consultative and other kinds of assistance in response to the industrial accident.

ANNEX XIII – Arbitration

1. The claimant Party or Parties shall notify the Secretariat that the Parties have agreed to submit the dispute to arbitration pursuant to Article 21, paragraph 2 of this Convention. The notification shall state the subject matter of arbitration and include, in particular, the Articles of this Convention, the interpretation or application of which is at issue. The Secretariat shall forward the information received to all Parties to this Convention.

2. The arbitral tribunal shall consist of three members. Both the claimant Party or Parties and the other Party or Parties to the dispute shall appoint an arbitrator, and the two arbitrators so appointed shall designate by common agreement the third arbitrator, who shall be the president of the arbitral tribunal. The latter shall not be a national of one of the parties to the dispute, nor have his or her usual place of residence in the territory of one of these parties, nor be employed by any of them, nor have dealt with the case in any other capacity.

3. If the president of the arbitral tribunal has not been designated within two months of the appointment of the second arbitrator, the executive secretary of the Economic Commission for Europe shall, at the request of either party to the dispute, designate the president within a further two-month period.

4. If one of the parties to the dispute does not appoint an arbitrator within two months of the receipt of the request, the other party may so inform the executive secretary of the Economic Commission for Europe, who shall designate the president of the arbitral tribunal within a further two-month period. Upon designation, the president of the arbitral tribunal shall request the party which has not appointed an arbitrator to do so within two months. If it fails to do so within that period, the president shall inform the executive secretary of the Economic Commission for Europe, who shall make this appointment within a further two-month period.

5. The arbitral tribunal shall render its decision in accordance with international law and in accordance with the provisions of this Convention.

6. Any arbitral tribunal constituted under the provisions set out herein shall draw up its own rules of procedure.

7. The decisions of the arbitral tribunal, both on procedure and on substance, shall be taken by majority vote of its members.

8. The tribunal may take all appropriate measures to establish the facts.

9. The parties to the dispute shall facilitate the work of the arbitral tribunal and, in particular shall, using all means at their disposal:

(a) provide the tribunal with all relevant documents, facilities and information;

(b) enable the tribunal, where necessary, to call witnesses or experts and receive their evidence.

10. The parties to the dispute and the arbitrators shall protect the confidentiality of any information they receive in confidence during the proceedings of the arbitral tribunal.

11. The arbitral tribunal may, at the request of one of the parties, recommend interim measures of protection.

12. If one of the parties to the dispute does not appear before the arbitral tribunal or fails to defend its case, the other party may request the tribunal to continue the proceedings and to render its final decision. Absence of a party or failure of a party to defend its case shall not constitute a bar to the proceedings.

13. The arbitral tribunal may hear and determine counter-claims arising directly out of the subject matter of the dispute.

14. Unless the arbitral tribunal determines otherwise because of the particular circumstances of the case, the expenses of the tribunal, including the remuneration of its members, shall be borne equally by the parties to the dispute. The tribunal shall keep a record of all its expenses and shall furnish a final statement thereof to the parties to the dispute.

15. Any Party to this Convention which has an interest of a legal nature in the subject matter of the dispute and which may be affected by a decision in

the case, may intervene in the proceedings with the consent of the tribunal.

16. The arbitral tribunal shall render its award within five months of the date on which it is established unless it finds it necessary to extend the time limit for a period which should not exceed five months.
17. The award of the arbitral tribunal shall be accompanied by a statement of reasons. It shall be final and binding upon all parties to the dispute. The award will be transmitted by the arbitral tribunal to the parties to the dispute and to the Secretariat. The Secretariat will forward the information received to all Parties to this Convention.
18. Any dispute which may arise between the parties concerning the interpretation or execution of the award may be submitted by either party to the tribunal which made the award or, if the latter cannot be seized thereof, to another tribunal constituted for this purpose in the same manner as the first.

2.3. Aarhus Convention 1998

UNECE Convention on Access to Information, Public Participation in Decision-making and Access to Justice in Environmental Matters, Aarhus, Denmark, 25 June 1998, 2161 UNTS 447

The Parties to this Convention,

Recalling principle l of the Stockholm Declaration on the Human Environment,

Recalling also principle 10 of the Rio Declaration on Environment and Development,

Recalling further General Assembly resolutions 37/7 of 28 October 1982 on the World Charter for Nature and 45/94 of 14 December 1990 on the need to ensure a healthy environment for the well-being of individuals,

Recalling the European Charter on Environment and Health adopted at the First European Conference on Environment and Health of the World Health Organization in Frankfurt-am-Main, Germany, on 8 December 1989,

Affirming the need to protect, preserve and improve the state of the environment and to ensure sustainable and environmentally sound development,

Recognizing that adequate protection of the environment is essential to human well-being and the enjoyment of basic human rights, including the right to life itself,

Recognizing also that every person has the right to live in an environment adequate to his or her health and well-being, and the duty, both individually and in association with others, to protect and improve the environment for the benefit of present and future generations,

Considering that, to be able to assert this right and observe this duty, citizens must have access to information, be entitled to participate in decision-making and have access to justice in environmental matters, and acknowledging in this regard that citizens may need assistance in order to exercise their rights,

Recognizing that, in the field of the environment, improved access to information and public participation in decision-making enhance the quality and the implementation of decisions, contribute to public awareness of environmental issues, give the public the opportunity to express its concerns and enable public authorities to take due account of such concerns,

Aiming thereby to further the accountability of and transparency in decision-making and to strengthen public support for decisions on the environment,

Recognizing the desirability of transparency in all branches of government and inviting legislative bodies to implement the principles of this Convention in their proceedings,

Recognizing also that the public needs to be aware of the procedures for participation in environmental decision-making, have free access to them and know how to use them,

Recognizing further the importance of the respective roles that individual citizens, non-governmental organizations and the private sector can play in environmental protection,

Desiring to promote environmental education to further the understanding of the environment and sustainable development and to encourage widespread public awareness of, and participation in, decisions affecting the environment and sustainable development,

Noting, in this context, the importance of making use of the media and of electronic or other, future forms of communication,

Recognizing the importance of fully integrating environmental considerations in governmental decision-making and the consequent need for public authorities to be in possession of accurate, comprehensive and up-to- date environmental information,

Acknowledging that public authorities hold environmental information in the public interest,

Concerned that effective judicial mechanisms should be accessible to the public, including organizations, so that its legitimate interests are protected and the law is enforced,

Noting the importance of adequate product information being provided to consumers to enable them to make informed environmental choices,

Recognizing the concern of the public about the deliberate release of genetically modified organisms into the environment and the need for increased transparency and greater public participation in decision-making in this field,

Convinced that the implementation of this Convention will contribute to strengthening democracy in the region of the United Nations Economic Commission for Europe (ECE),

Conscious of the role played in this respect by ECE and recalling, inter alia, the ECE Guidelines on Access to Environmental Information and Public Participation in Environmental Decision-making endorsed in the Ministerial Declaration adopted at the Third Ministerial Conference "Environment for Europe" in Sofia, Bulgaria, on 25 October 1995,

Bearing in mind the relevant provisions in the Convention on Environmental Impact Assessment in a Transboundary Context, done at Espoo, Finland, on 25 February 1991, and the Convention on the Transboundary Effects of Industrial Accidents and the Convention on the Protection and Use of Transboundary Watercourses and International Lakes, both done at Helsinki on 17 March 1992, and other regional conventions,

Conscious that the adoption of this Convention will have contributed to the further strengthening of the "Environment for Europe" process and to the results of the Fourth Ministerial Conference in Aarhus, Denmark, in June 1998,

Have agreed as follows:

Article 1 – OBJECTIVE

In order to contribute to the protection of the right of every person of present and future generations to live in an environment adequate to his or her health and well-being, each Party shall guarantee the rights of access to information, public participation in decision-making, and access to justice in environmental matters in accordance with the provisions of this Convention.

Article 2 – DEFINITIONS

For the purposes of this Convention,

1. "Party" means, unless the text otherwise indicates, a Contracting Party to this Convention;
2. "Public authority" means:
   (a) Government at national, regional and other level;
   (b) Natural or legal persons performing public administrative functions under national law, including specific duties, activities or services in relation to the environment;
   (c) Any other natural or legal persons having public responsibilities or functions, or providing public services, in relation to the environment, under the control of a body or person falling within subparagraphs (a) or (b) above;
   (d) The institutions of any regional economic integration organization referred to in article 17 which is a Party to this Convention.

   This definition does not include bodies or institutions acting in a judicial or legislative capacity;
3. "Environmental information" means any information in written, visual, aural, electronic or any other material form on:
   (a) The state of elements of the environment, such as air and atmosphere, water, soil, land, landscape and natural sites, biological diversity and its components, including genetically modified organisms, and the interaction among these elements;
   (b) Factors, such as substances, energy, noise and radiation, and activities or measures, including administrative measures, environmental agreements, policies, legislation, plans and programmes, affecting or likely to affect the elements of the environment within the scope of subparagraph (a) above, and cost-benefit and other economic analyses and assumptions used in environmental decision-making;
   (c) The state of human health and safety, conditions of human life, cultural sites and built structures, inasmuch as they are or may be affected by the state of the elements of the environment or, through these elements, by the factors, activities or measures referred to in subparagraph (b) above;
4. "The public" means one or more natural or legal persons, and, in accordance with national legislation or practice, their associations, organizations or groups;
5. "The public concerned" means the public affected or likely to be affected by, or having an interest in, the environmental decision-making; for the purposes of this definition, non-governmental organizations promoting environmental protection and meeting any requirements under national law shall be deemed to have an interest.

Article 3 – GENERAL PROVISIONS

1. Each Party shall take the necessary legislative, regulatory and other measures, including measures to achieve compatibility between the provisions implementing the information, public participation and access-to-justice provisions in this Convention, as well as proper enforcement measures, to establish and maintain a clear, transparent and consistent framework to implement the provisions of this Convention.
2. Each Party shall endeavour to ensure that officials and authorities assist and provide guidance to the public in seeking access to information, in facilitating participation in decision-making and in seeking access to justice in environmental matters.
3. Each Party shall promote environmental education and environmental awareness among the public, especially on how to obtain access to information, to participate in decision-making and to obtain access to justice in environmental matters.
4. Each Party shall provide for appropriate recognition of and support to associations, organizations or groups promoting environmental protection and ensure that its national legal system is consistent with this obligation.
5. The provisions of this Convention shall not affect the right of a Party to maintain or introduce measures providing for broader access to information, more extensive public participation in decision-making and wider access to justice in environmental matters than required by this Convention.
6. This Convention shall not require any derogation from existing rights of access to information, public participation in decision-making and access to justice in environmental matters.
7. Each Party shall promote the application of the principles of this Convention in international environmental decision-making processes and within the framework of international organizations in matters relating to the environment.
8. Each Party shall ensure that persons exercising their rights in conformity with the provisions of this Convention shall not be penalized, persecuted or harassed in any way for their involvement. This provision shall not affect the powers of national courts to award reasonable costs in judicial proceedings.

9. Within the scope of the relevant provisions of this Convention, the public shall have access to information, have the possibility to participate in decision-making and have access to justice in environmental matters without discrimination as to citizenship, nationality or domicile and, in the case of a legal person, without discrimination as to where it has its registered seat or an effective centre of its activities.

Article 4 – ACCESS TO ENVIRONMENTAL INFORMATION

1. Each Party shall ensure that, subject to the following paragraphs of this article, public authorities, in response to a request for environmental information, make such information available to the public, within the framework of national legislation, including, where requested and subject to subparagraph (b) below, copies of the actual documentation containing or comprising such information:
   (a) Without an interest having to be stated;
   (b) In the form requested unless:
      (i) It is reasonable for the public authority to make it available in another form, in which case reasons shall be given for making it available in that form; or
      (ii) The information is already publicly available in another form.
2. The environmental information referred to in paragraph 1 above shall be made available as soon as possible and at the latest within one month after the request has been submitted, unless the volume and the complexity of the information justify an extension of this period up to two months after the request. The applicant shall be informed of any extension and of the reasons justifying it.
3. A request for environmental information may be refused if:
   (a) The public authority to which the request is addressed does not hold the environmental information requested;
   (b) The request is manifestly unreasonable or formulated in too general a manner; or
   (c) The request concerns material in the course of completion or concerns internal communications of public authorities where such an exemption is provided for in national law or customary practice, taking into account the public interest served by disclosure.
4. A request for environmental information may be refused if the disclosure would adversely affect:
   (a) The confidentiality of the proceedings of public authorities, where such confidentiality is provided for under national law;
   (b) International relations, national defence or public security;
   (c) The course of justice, the ability of a person to receive a fair trial or the ability of a public authority to conduct an enquiry of a criminal or disciplinary nature;
   (d) The confidentiality of commercial and industrial information, where such confidentiality is protected by law in order to protect a legitimate economic interest. Within this framework, information on emissions which is relevant for the protection of the environment shall be disclosed;
   (e) Intellectual property rights;
   (f) The confidentiality of personal data and/or files relating to a natural person where that person has not consented to the disclosure of the information to the public, where such confidentiality is provided for in national law;
   (g) The interests of a third party which has supplied the information requested without that party being under or capable of being put under a legal obligation to do so, and where that party does not consent to the release of the material; or
   (h) The environment to which the information relates, such as the breeding sites of rare species.

   The aforementioned grounds for refusal shall be interpreted in a restrictive way, taking into account the public interest served by disclosure and taking into account whether the information requested relates to emissions into the environment.
5. Where a public authority does not hold the environmental information requested, this public authority shall, as promptly as possible, inform the applicant of the public authority to which it believes it is possible to apply for the information requested or transfer the request to that authority and inform the applicant accordingly.
6. Each Party shall ensure that, if information exempted from disclosure under paragraphs 3 (c) and 4 above can be separated out without prejudice to the confidentiality of the information exempted, public authorities make available the remainder of the environmental information that has been requested.
7. A refusal of a request shall be in writing if the request was in writing or the applicant so requests. A refusal shall state the reasons for the refusal and give information on access to the review procedure provided for in accordance with article 9. The refusal shall be made as soon as possible and at the latest within one month, unless the complexity of the information justifies an extension of this period up to two months after the request. The applicant shall be informed of any extension and of the reasons justifying it.
8. Each Party may allow its public authorities to make a charge for supplying information, but such charge shall not exceed a reasonable amount. Public authorities intending to make such a charge for supplying information shall make available to applicants a schedule of charges which may be levied, indicating the circumstances in which they may be levied or waived and when the supply of information is conditional on the advance payment of such a charge.

Article 5 – COLLECTION AND DISSEMINATION OF ENVIRONMENTAL INFORMATION

1. Each Party shall ensure that:
   (a) Public authorities possess and update environmental information which is relevant to their functions;
   (b) Mandatory systems are established so that there is an adequate flow of information to public authorities about proposed and existing activities which may significantly affect the environment;
   (c) In the event of any imminent threat to human health or the environment, whether caused by human activities or due to natural causes, all information which could enable the public to take measures to prevent or mitigate harm arising from the threat and is held by a public authority is disseminated immediately and without delay to members of the public who may be affected.
2. Each Party shall ensure that, within the framework of national legislation, the way in which public authorities make environmental information available to the public is transparent and that environmental information is effectively accessible, inter alia, by:
   (a) Providing sufficient information to the public about the type and scope of environmental information held by the relevant public authorities, the basic terms and conditions under which such information is made available and accessible, and the process by which it can be obtained;
   (b) Establishing and maintaining practical arrangements, such as:
      (i) Publicly accessible lists, registers or files;
      (ii) Requiring officials to support the public in seeking access to information under this Convention; and
      (iii) The identification of points of contact; and
   (c) Providing access to the environmental information contained in lists, registers or files as referred to in subparagraph (b) (i) above free of charge.
3. Each Party shall ensure that environmental information progressively becomes available in electronic databases which are easily accessible to the public through public telecommunications networks. Information accessible in this form should include:
   (a) Reports on the state of the environment, as referred to in paragraph 4 below;
   (b) Texts of legislation on or relating to the environment;
   (c) As appropriate, policies, plans and programmes on or relating to the environment, and environmental agreements; and
   (d) Other information, to the extent that the availability of such information in this form would facilitate the application of national law implementing this Convention, provided that such information is already available in electronic form.
4. Each Party shall, at regular intervals not exceeding three or four years, publish and disseminate a national report on the state of the environment, including information on the quality of the environment and information on pressures on the environment.
5. Each Party shall take measures within the framework of its legislation for the purpose of disseminating, inter alia:
   (a) Legislation and policy documents such as documents on strategies, policies, programmes and action plans relating to the environment, and progress reports on their implementation, prepared at various levels of government;
   (b) International treaties, conventions and agreements on environmental issues; and
   (c) Other significant international documents on environmental issues, as appropriate.
6. Each Party shall encourage operators whose activities have a significant impact on the environment to inform the public regularly of the environmental impact of their activities and products, where appropriate within the framework of voluntary eco-labelling or eco-auditing schemes or by other means.
7. Each Party shall:
   (a) Publish the facts and analyses of facts which it considers relevant and important in framing major environmental policy proposals;
   (b) Publish, or otherwise make accessible, available explanatory material on its dealings with the public in matters falling within the scope of this Convention; and
   (c) Provide in an appropriate form information on the performance of public functions or the provision of public services relating to the environment by government at all levels.
8. Each Party shall develop mechanisms with a view to ensuring that sufficient product information is made available to the public in a manner which enables consumers to make informed environmental choices.
9. Each Party shall take steps to establish progressively, taking into account international processes where appropriate, a coherent, nationwide system of pollution inventories or registers on a structured, computerized and publicly accessible database compiled through standardized reporting. Such a system may include inputs, releases and transfers of a specified range of substances and products, including water, energy and resource use, from a specified range of activities to environmental media and to on-site and off- site treatment and disposal sites.
10. Nothing in this article may prejudice the right of Parties to refuse to disclose certain environmental

information in accordance with article 4, paragraphs 3 and 4.

Article 6 – PUBLIC PARTICIPATION IN DECISIONS ON SPECIFIC ACTIVITIES

1. Each Party:
   (a) Shall apply the provisions of this article with respect to decisions on whether to permit proposed activities listed in annex I;
   (b) Shall, in accordance with its national law, also apply the provisions of this article to decisions on proposed activities not listed in annex I which may have a significant effect on the environment. To this end, Parties shall determine whether such a proposed activity is subject to these provisions; and
   (c) May decide, on a case-by-case basis if so provided under national law, not to apply the provisions of this article to proposed activities serving national defence purposes, if that Party deems that such application would have an adverse effect on these purposes.
2. The public concerned shall be informed, either by public notice or individually as appropriate, early in an environmental decision-making procedure, and in an adequate, timely and effective manner, inter alia, of:
   (a) The proposed activity and the application on which a decision will be taken;
   (b) The nature of possible decisions or the draft decision;
   (c) The public authority responsible for making the decision;
   (d) The envisaged procedure, including, as and when this information can be provided:
      (i) The commencement of the procedure;
      (ii) The opportunities for the public to participate;
      (iii) The time and venue of any envisaged public hearing;
      (iv) An indication of the public authority from which relevant information can be obtained and where the relevant information has been deposited for examination by the public;
      (v) An indication of the relevant public authority or any other official body to which comments or questions can be submitted and of the time schedule for transmittal of comments or questions; and
      (vi) An indication of what environmental information relevant to the proposed activity is available; and
   (e) The fact that the activity is subject to a national or transboundary environmental impact assessment procedure.
3. The public participation procedures shall include reasonable time-frames for the different phases, allowing sufficient time for informing the public in accordance with paragraph 2 above and for the public to prepare and participate effectively during the environmental decision-making.
4. Each Party shall provide for early public participation, when all options are open and effective public participation can take place.
5. Each Party should, where appropriate, encourage prospective applicants to identify the public concerned, to enter into discussions, and to provide information regarding the objectives of their application before applying for a permit.
6. Each Party shall require the competent public authorities to give the public concerned access for examination, upon request where so required under national law, free of charge and as soon as it becomes available, to all information relevant to the decision-making referred to in this article that is available at the time of the public participation procedure, without prejudice to the right of Parties to refuse to disclose certain information in accordance with article 4, paragraphs 3 and 4. The relevant information shall include at least, and without prejudice to the provisions of article 4:
   (a) A description of the site and the physical and technical characteristics of the proposed activity, including an estimate of the expected residues and emissions;
   (b) A description of the significant effects of the proposed activity on the environment;
   (c) A description of the measures envisaged to prevent and/or reduce the effects, including emissions;
   (d) A non-technical summary of the above;
   (e) An outline of the main alternatives studied by the applicant; and
   (f) In accordance with national legislation, the main reports and advice issued to the public authority at the time when the public concerned shall be informed in accordance with paragraph 2 above.
7. Procedures for public participation shall allow the public to submit, in writing or, as appropriate, at a public hearing or inquiry with the applicant, any comments, information, analyses or opinions that it considers relevant to the proposed activity.
8. Each Party shall ensure that in the decision due account is taken of the outcome of the public participation.
9. Each Party shall ensure that, when the decision has been taken by the public authority, the public is promptly informed of the decision in accordance with the appropriate procedures. Each Party shall make accessible to the public the text of the decision along with the reasons and considerations on which the decision is based.
10. Each Party shall ensure that, when a public authority reconsiders or updates the operating conditions for an activity referred to in paragraph 1, the provisions of paragraphs 2 to 9 of this article are applied mutatis mutandis, and where appropriate.
11. Each Party shall, within the framework of its national law, apply, to the extent feasible and appro-

priate, provisions of this article to decisions on whether to permit the deliberate release of genetically modified organisms into the environment.

Article 7 – PUBLIC PARTICIPATION CONCERNING PLANS, PROGRAMMES AND POLICIES RELATING TO THE ENVIRONMENT

Each Party shall make appropriate practical and/or other provisions for the public to participate during the preparation of plans and programmes relating to the environment, within a transparent and fair framework, having provided the necessary information to the public. Within this framework, article 6, paragraphs 3, 4 and 8, shall be applied. The public which may participate shall be identified by the relevant public authority, taking into account the objectives of this Convention. To the extent appropriate, each Party shall endeavour to provide opportunities for public participation in the preparation of policies relating to the environment.

Article 8 – PUBLIC PARTICIPATION DURING THE PREPARATION OF EXECUTIVE REGULATIONS AND/OR GENERALLY APPLICABLE LEGALLY BINDING NORMATIVE INSTRUMENTS

Each Party shall strive to promote effective public participation at an appropriate stage, and while options are still open, during the preparation by public authorities of executive regulations and other generally applicable legally binding rules that may have a significant effect on the environment. To this end, the following steps should be taken:

(a) Time-frames sufficient for effective participation should be fixed;

(b) Draft rules should be published or otherwise made publicly available; and

(c) The public should be given the opportunity to comment, directly or through representative consultative bodies.

The result of the public participation shall be taken into account as far as possible.

Article 9 – ACCESS TO JUSTICE

1. Each Party shall, within the framework of its national legislation, ensure that any person who considers that his or her request for information under article 4 has been ignored, wrongfully refused, whether in part or in full, inadequately answered, or otherwise not dealt with in accordance with the provisions of that article, has access to a review procedure before a court of law or another independent and impartial body established by law.

   In the circumstances where a Party provides for such a review by a court of law, it shall ensure that such a person also has access to an expeditious procedure established by law that is free of charge or inexpensive for reconsideration by a public authority or review by an independent and impartial body other than a court of law.

   Final decisions under this paragraph 1 shall be binding on the public authority holding the information. Reasons shall be stated in writing, at least where access to information is refused under this paragraph.

2. Each Party shall, within the framework of its national legislation, ensure that members of the public concerned

   (a) Having a sufficient interest or, alternatively,

   (b) Maintaining impairment of a right, where the administrative procedural law of a Party requires this as a precondition, have access to a review procedure before a court of law and/or another independent and impartial body established by law, to challenge the substantive and procedural legality of any decision, act or omission subject to the provisions of article 6 and, where so provided for under national law and without prejudice to paragraph 3 below, of other relevant provisions of this Convention.

   What constitutes a sufficient interest and impairment of a right shall be determined in accordance with the requirements of national law and consistently with the objective of giving the public concerned wide access to justice within the scope of this Convention. To this end, the interest of any non-governmental organization meeting the requirements referred to in article 2, paragraph 5, shall be deemed sufficient for the purpose of subparagraph (a) above. Such organizations shall also be deemed to have rights capable of being impaired for the purpose of subparagraph (b) above.

   The provisions of this paragraph 2 shall not exclude the possibility of a preliminary review procedure before an administrative authority and shall not affect the requirement of exhaustion of administrative review procedures prior to recourse to judicial review procedures, where such a requirement exists under national law.

3. In addition and without prejudice to the review procedures referred to in paragraphs 1 and 2 above, each Party shall ensure that, where they meet the criteria, if any, laid down in its national law, members of the public have access to administrative or judicial procedures to challenge acts and omissions by private persons and public authorities which contravene provisions of its national law relating to the environment.

4. In addition and without prejudice to paragraph 1 above, the procedures referred to in paragraphs 1, 2 and 3 above shall provide adequate and effective remedies, including injunctive relief as appropriate, and be fair, equitable, timely and not prohibitively expensive. Decisions under this article shall be given or recorded in writing. Decisions of courts, and whenever possible of other bodies, shall be publicly accessible.

5. In order to further the effectiveness of the provisions of this article, each Party shall ensure that information is provided to the public on access to administrative and judicial review procedures and shall consider the establishment of appropriate assistance mechanisms to remove or reduce financial and other barriers to access to justice.

Article 10 – MEETING OF THE PARTIES

1. The first meeting of the Parties shall be convened no later than one year after the date of the entry into force of this Convention. Thereafter, an ordinary meeting of the Parties shall be held at least once every two years, unless otherwise decided by the Parties, or at the written request of any Party, provided that, within six months of the request being communicated to all Parties by the Executive Secretary of the Economic Commission for Europe, the said request is supported by at least one third of the Parties.
2. At their meetings, the Parties shall keep under continuous review the implementation of this Convention on the basis of regular reporting by the Parties, and, with this purpose in mind, shall:
   (a) Review the policies for and legal and methodological approaches to access to information, public participation in decision-making and access to justice in environmental matters, with a view to further improving them;
   (b) Exchange information regarding experience gained in concluding and implementing bilateral and multilateral agreements or other arrangements having relevance to the purposes of this Convention and to which one or more of the Parties are a party;
   (c) Seek, where appropriate, the services of relevant ECE bodies and other competent international bodies and specific committees in all aspects pertinent to the achievement of the purposes of this Convention;
   (d) Establish any subsidiary bodies as they deem necessary;
   (e) Prepare, where appropriate, protocols to this Convention;
   (f) Consider and adopt proposals for amendments to this Convention in accordance with the provisions of article 14;
   (g) Consider and undertake any additional action that may be required for the achievement of the purposes of this Convention;
   (h) At their first meeting, consider and by consensus adopt rules of procedure for their meetings and the meetings of subsidiary bodies;
   (i) At their first meeting, review their experience in implementing the provisions of article 5, paragraph 9, and consider what steps are necessary to develop further the system referred to in that paragraph, taking into account international processes and developments, including the elaboration of an appropriate instrument concerning pollution release and transfer registers or inventories which could be annexed to this Convention.
3. The Meeting of the Parties may, as necessary, consider establishing financial arrangements on a consensus basis.
4. The United Nations, its specialized agencies and the International Atomic Energy Agency, as well as any State or regional economic integration organization entitled under article 17 to sign this Convention but which is not a Party to this Convention, and any intergovernmental organization qualified in the fields to which this Convention relates, shall be entitled to participate as observers in the meetings of the Parties.
5. Any non-governmental organization, qualified in the fields to which this Convention relates, which has informed the Executive Secretary of the Economic Commission for Europe of its wish to be represented at a meeting of the Parties shall be entitled to participate as an observer unless at least one third of the Parties present in the meeting raise objections.
6. For the purposes of paragraphs 4 and 5 above, the rules of procedure referred to in paragraph 2 (h) above shall provide for practical arrangements for the admittance procedure and other relevant terms.

Article 11 – RIGHT TO VOTE

1. Except as provided for in paragraph 2 below, each Party to this Convention shall have one vote.
2. Regional economic integration organizations, in matters within their competence, shall exercise their right to vote with a number of votes equal to the number of their member States which are Parties to this Convention. Such organizations shall not exercise their right to vote if their member States exercise theirs, and vice versa.

Article 12 – SECRETARIAT

The Executive Secretary of the Economic Commission for Europe shall carry out the following secretariat functions:

(a) The convening and preparing of meetings of the Parties;

(b) The transmission to the Parties of reports and other information received in accordance with the provisions of this Convention; and

(c) Such other functions as may be determined by the Parties.

Article 13 – ANNEXES

The annexes to this Convention shall constitute an integral part thereof.

Article 14 – AMENDMENTS TO THE CONVENTION

1. Any Party may propose amendments to this Convention.
2. The text of any proposed amendment to this Convention shall be submitted in writing to the Executive Secretary of the Economic Commission for Europe, who shall communicate it to all Parties at least ninety days before the meeting of the Parties at which it is proposed for adoption.
3. The Parties shall make every effort to reach agreement on any proposed amendment to this Convention by consensus. If all efforts at consensus have been exhausted, and no agreement reached, the amendment shall as a last resort be adopted by a

three-fourths majority vote of the Parties present and voting at the meeting.

4. Amendments to this Convention adopted in accordance with paragraph 3 above shall be communicated by the Depositary to all Parties for ratification, approval or acceptance. Amendments to this Convention other than those to an annex shall enter into force for Parties having ratified, approved or accepted them on the ninetieth day after the receipt by the Depositary of notification of their ratification, approval or acceptance by at least three fourths of these Parties. Thereafter they shall enter into force for any other Party on the ninetieth day after that Party deposits its instrument of ratification, approval or acceptance of the amendments.
5. Any Party that is unable to approve an amendment to an annex to this Convention shall so notify the Depositary in writing within twelve months from the date of the communication of the adoption. The Depositary shall without delay notify all Parties of any such notification received. A Party may at any time substitute an acceptance for its previous notification and, upon deposit of an instrument of acceptance with the Depositary, the amendments to such an annex shall become effective for that Party.
6. On the expiry of twelve months from the date of its communication by the Depositary as provided for in paragraph 4 above an amendment to an annex shall become effective for those Parties which have not submitted a notification to the Depositary in accordance with the provisions of paragraph 5 above, provided that not more than one third of the Parties have submitted such a notification.
7. For the purposes of this article, "Parties present and voting" means Parties present and casting an affirmative or negative vote.

Article 15 – REVIEW OF COMPLIANCE

The Meeting of the Parties shall establish, on a consensus basis, optional arrangements of a non-confrontational, non-judicial and consultative nature for reviewing compliance with the provisions of this Convention. These arrangements shall allow for appropriate public involvement and may include the option of considering communications from members of the public on matters related to this Convention.

Article 16 – SETTLEMENT OF DISPUTES

1. If a dispute arises between two or more Parties about the interpretation or application of this Convention, they shall seek a solution by negotiation or by any other means of dispute settlement acceptable to the parties to the dispute.
2. When signing, ratifying, accepting, approving or acceding to this Convention, or at any time thereafter, a Party may declare in writing to the Depositary that, for a dispute not resolved in accordance with paragraph 1 above, it accepts one or both of the following means of dispute settlement as compulsory in relation to any Party accepting the same obligation:
   (a) Submission of the dispute to the International Court of Justice;
   (b) Arbitration in accordance with the procedure set out in annex II.
3. If the parties to the dispute have accepted both means of dispute settlement referred to in paragraph 2 above, the dispute may be submitted only to the International Court of Justice, unless the parties agree otherwise.

Article 17 – SIGNATURE

This Convention shall be open for signature at Aarhus (Denmark) on 25 June 1998, and thereafter at United Nations Headquarters in New York until 21 December 1998, by States members of the Economic Commission for Europe as well as States having consultative status with the Economic Commission for Europe pursuant to paragraphs 8 and 11 of Economic and Social Council resolution 36 (IV) of 28 March 1947, and by regional economic integration organizations constituted by sovereign States members of the Economic Commission for Europe to which their member States have transferred competence over matters governed by this Convention, including the competence to enter into treaties in respect of these matters.

Article 18 – DEPOSITARY

The Secretary-General of the United Nations shall act as the Depositary of this Convention.

Article 19 – RATIFICATION, ACCEPTANCE, APPROVAL AND ACCESSION

1. This Convention shall be subject to ratification, acceptance or approval by signatory States and regional economic integration organizations.
2. This Convention shall be open for accession as from 22 December 1998 by the States and regional economic integration organizations referred to in article 17.
3. Any other State, not referred to in paragraph 2 above, that is a Member of the United Nations may accede to the Convention upon approval by the Meeting of the Parties.
4. Any organization referred to in article 17 which becomes a Party to this Convention without any of its member States being a Party shall be bound by all the obligations under this Convention. If one or more of such an organization's member States is a Party to this Convention, the organization and its member States shall decide on their respective responsibilities for the performance of their obligations under this Convention. In such cases, the organization and the member States shall not be entitled to exercise rights under this Convention concurrently.
5. In their instruments of ratification, acceptance, approval or accession, the regional economic integration organizations referred to in article 17 shall declare the extent of their competence with respect to the matters governed by this Convention. These organizations shall also inform the Depositary of any substantial modification to the extent of their competence.

Article 20 – ENTRY INTO FORCE

1. This Convention shall enter into force on the ninetieth day after the date of deposit of the sixteenth instrument of ratification, acceptance, approval or accession.
2. For the purposes of paragraph 1 above, any instrument deposited by a regional economic integration organization shall not be counted as additional to those deposited by States members of such an organization.
3. For each State or organization referred to in article 17 which ratifies, accepts or approves this Convention or accedes thereto after the deposit of the sixteenth instrument of ratification, acceptance, approval or accession, the Convention shall enter into force on the ninetieth day after the date of deposit by such State or organization of its instrument of ratification, acceptance, approval or accession.

Article 21 – WITHDRAWAL

At any time after three years from the date on which this Convention has come into force with respect to a Party, that Party may withdraw from the Convention by giving written notification to the Depositary. Any such withdrawal shall take effect on the ninetieth day after the date of its receipt by the Depositary.

Article 22 – AUTHENTIC TEXTS

The original of this Convention, of which the English, French and Russian texts are equally authentic, shall be deposited with the Secretary-General of the United Nations.

IN WITNESS WHEREOF the undersigned, being duly authorized thereto, have signed this Convention.

DONE at Aarhus (Denmark), this twenty-fifth day of June, one thousand nine hundred and ninety-eight.

Annex I – LIST OF ACTIVITIES REFERRED TO IN ARTICLE 6, PARAGRAPH 1 (a)

1. Energy sector:
   - Mineral oil and gas refineries;
   - Installations for gasification and liquefaction;
   - Thermal power stations and other combustion installations with a heat input of 50 megawatts (MW)or more;
   - Coke ovens;
   - Nuclear power stations and other nuclear reactors including the dismantling or decommissioning of such power stations or reactors[1] (except research installations for the production and conversion of fissionable and fertile materials whose maximum power does not exceed 1 kW continuous thermal load);
   - Installations for the reprocessing of irradiated nuclear fuel;
   - Installations designed:
     - For the production or enrichment of nuclear fuel;
     - For the processing of irradiated nuclear fuel or high-level radioactive waste;
     - For the final disposal of irradiated nuclear fuel;
     - Solely for the final disposal of radioactive waste;
     - Solely for the storage (planned for more than 10 years) of irradiated nuclear fuels or radioactive waste in a different site than the production site.
2. Production and processing of metals:
   - Metal ore (including sulphide ore) roasting or sintering installations;
   - Installations for the production of pig-iron or steel (primary or secondary fusion) including continuous casting, with a capacity exceeding 2.5 tons per hour;
   - Installations for the processing of ferrous metals:
     (i) Hot-rolling mills with a capacity exceeding 20 tons of crude steel per hour;
     (ii) Smitheries with hammers the energy of which exceeds 50 kilojoules per hammer, where the calorific power used exceeds 20 MW;
     (iii) Application of protective fused metal coats with an input exceeding 2 tons of crude steel per hour;
   - Ferrous metal foundries with a production capacity exceeding 20 tons per day;
   - Installations:
     (i) For the production of non-ferrous crude metals from ore, concentrates or secondary raw materials by metallurgical, chemical or electrolytic processes;
     (ii) For the smelting, including the alloying, of non-ferrous metals, including recovered products (refining, foundry casting, etc.), with a melting capacity exceeding 4 tons per day for lead and cadmium or 20 tons per day for all other metals;
   - Installations for surface treatment of metals and plastic materials using an electrolytic or chemical process where the volume of the treatment vats exceeds 30 m3.
3. Mineral industry:
   - Installations for the production of cement clinker in rotary kilns with a production capacity exceeding 500 tons per day or lime in rotary kilns with a production capacity exceeding 50 tons per day or in other furnaces with a production capacity exceeding 50 tons per day;
   - Installations for the production of asbestos and the manufacture of asbestos-based products;

1 Nuclear power stations and other nuclear reactors cease to be such an installation when all nuclear fuel and other radioactively contaminated elements have been removed permanently from the installation site.

- Installations for the manufacture of glass including glass fibre with a melting capacity exceeding 20 tons per day;
- Installations for melting mineral substances including the production of mineral fibres with a melting capacity exceeding 20 tons per day;
- Installations for the manufacture of ceramic products by firing, in particular roofing tiles, bricks, refractory bricks, tiles, stoneware or porcelain, with a production capacity exceeding 75 tons per day, and/or with a kiln capacity exceeding 4 m3 and with a setting density per kiln exceeding 300 kg/m3.

4. Chemical industry: Production within the meaning of the categories of activities contained in this paragraph means the production on an industrial scale by chemical processing of substances or groups of substances listed in subparagraphs (a) to (g):
   (a) Chemical installations for the production of basic organic chemicals, such as:
      (i) Simple hydrocarbons (linear or cyclic, saturated or unsaturated, aliphatic or aromatic);
      (ii) Oxygen-containing hydrocarbons such as alcohols, aldehydes, ketones, carboxylic acids, esters, acetates, ethers, peroxides, epoxy resins;
      (iii) Sulphurous hydrocarbons;
      (iv) Nitrogenous hydrocarbons such as amines, amides, nitrous compounds, nitro compounds or nitrate compounds, nitriles, cyanates, isocyanates;
      (v) Phosphorus-containing hydrocarbons;
      (vi) Halogenic hydrocarbons;
      (vii) Organometallic compounds;
      (viii) Basic plastic materials (polymers, synthetic fibres and cellulose-based fibres);
      (ix) Synthetic rubbers;
      (x) Dyes and pigments;
      (xi) Surface-active agents and surfactants;
   (b) Chemical installations for the production of basic inorganic chemicals, such as:
      (i) Gases, such as ammonia, chlorine or hydrogen chloride, fluorine or hydrogen fluoride, carbon oxides, sulphur compounds, nitrogen oxides, hydrogen, sulphur dioxide, carbonyl chloride;
      (ii) Acids, such as chromic acid, hydrofluoric acid, phosphoric acid, nitric acid, hydrochloric acid, sulphuric acid, oleum, sulphurous acids;
      (iii) Bases, such as ammonium hydroxide, potassium hydroxide, sodium hydroxide;
      (iv) Salts, such as ammonium chloride, potassium chlorate, potassium carbonate, sodium carbonate, perborate, silver nitrate;
      (v) Non-metals, metal oxides or other inorganic compounds such as calcium carbide, silicon, silicon carbide;
   (c) Chemical installations for the production of phosphorous-, nitrogen- or potassium-based fertilizers (simple or compound fertilizers);
   (d) Chemical installations for the production of basic plant health products and of biocides;
   (e) Installations using a chemical or biological process for the production of basic pharmaceutical products;
   (f) Chemical installations for the production of explosives;
   (g) Chemical installations in which chemical or biological processing is used for the production of protein feed additives, ferments and other protein substances.
5. Waste management:
   - Installations for the incineration, recovery, chemical treatment or landfill of hazardous waste;
   - Installations for the incineration of municipal waste with a capacity exceeding 3 tons per hour;
   - Installations for the disposal of non-hazardous waste with a capacity exceeding 50 tons per day;
   - Landfills receiving more than 10 tons per day or with a total capacity exceeding 25 000 tons, excluding landfills of inert waste.
6. Waste-water treatment plants with a capacity exceeding 150 000 population equivalent.
7. Industrial plants for the:
   (a) Production of pulp from timber or similar fibrous materials;
   (b) Production of paper and board with a production capacity exceeding 20 tons per day.
8. (a) Construction of lines for long-distance railway traffic and of airports[2] with a basic runway length of 2 100 m or more;
   (b) Construction of motorways and express roads;[3]
   (c) Construction of a new road of four or more lanes, or realignment and/or widening of an existing road of two lanes or less so as to provide four or more lanes, where such new road, or realigned and/or widened section of road, would be 10 km or more in a continuous length.
9. (a) Inland waterways and ports for inland-waterway traffic which permit the passage of vessels of over 1 350 tons;

2 For the purposes of this Convention, "airport" means an airport which complies with the definition in the 1944 Chicago Convention setting up the International Civil Aviation Organization (Annex 14).

3 For the purposes of this Convention, "express road" means a road which complies with the definition in the European Agreement on Main International Traffic Arteries of 15 November 1975.

(b) Trading ports, piers for loading and unloading connected to land and outside ports (excluding ferry piers) which can take vessels of over 1 350 tons.

10. Groundwater abstraction or artificial groundwater recharge schemes where the annual volume of water abstracted or recharged is equivalent to or exceeds 10 million cubic metres.

11. (a) Works for the transfer of water resources between river basins where this transfer aims at preventing possible shortages of water and where the amount of water transferred exceeds 100 million cubic metres/year;

(b) In all other cases, works for the transfer of water resources between river basins where the multiannual average flow of the basin of abstraction exceeds 2 000 million cubic metres/year and where the amount of water transferred exceeds 5% of this flow.

In both cases transfers of piped drinking water are excluded.

12. Extraction of petroleum and natural gas for commercial purposes where the amount extracted exceeds 500 tons/day in the case of petroleum and 500 000 cubic metres/day in the case of gas.

13. Dams and other installations designed for the holding back or permanent storage of water, where a new or additional amount of water held back or stored exceeds 10 million cubic metres.

14. Pipelines for the transport of gas, oil or chemicals with a diameter of more than 800 mm and a length of more than 40 km.

15. Installations for the intensive rearing of poultry or pigs with more than:

(a) 40 000 places for poultry;

(b) 2 000 places for production pigs (over 30 kg); or

(c) 750 places for sows.

16. Quarries and opencast mining where the surface of the site exceeds 25 hectares, or peat extraction, where the surface of the site exceeds 150 hectares.

17. Construction of overhead electrical power lines with a voltage of 220 kV or more and a length of more than 15 km.

18. Installations for the storage of petroleum, petrochemical, or chemical products with a capacity of 200 000 tons or more.

19. Other activities:

- Plants for the pretreatment (operations such as washing, bleaching, mercerization) or dyeing of fibres or textiles where the treatment capacity exceeds 10 tons per day;
- Plants for the tanning of hides and skins where the treatment capacity exceeds 12 tons of finished products per day;
- (a) Slaughterhouses with a carcass production capacity greater than 50 tons per day;

  (b) Treatment and processing intended for the production of food products from:

  (i) Animal raw materials (other than milk) with a finished product production capacity greater than 75 tons per day;

  (ii) Vegetable raw materials with a finished product production capacity greater than 300 tons per day (average value on a quarterly basis);

  (c) Treatment and processing of milk, the quantity of milk received being greater than 200 tons per day (average value on an annual basis);
- Installations for the disposal or recycling of animal carcasses and animal waste with a treatment capacity exceeding 10 tons per day;
- Installations for the surface treatment of substances, objects or products using organic solvents, in particular for dressing, printing, coating, degreasing, waterproofing, sizing, painting, cleaning or impregnating, with a consumption capacity of more than 150 kg per hour or more than 200 tons per year;
- Installations for the production of carbon (hard-burnt coal) or electrographite by means of incineration or graphitization.

20. Any activity not covered by paragraphs 1-19 above where public participation is provided for under an environmental impact assessment procedure in accordance with national legislation.

21. The provision of article 6, paragraph 1 (a) of this Convention, does not apply to any of the above projects undertaken exclusively or mainly for research, development and testing of new methods or products for less than two years unless they would be likely to cause a significant adverse effect on environment or health.

22. Any change to or extension of activities, where such a change or extension in itself meets the criteria/thresholds set out in this annex, shall be subject to article 6, paragraph 1 (a) of this Convention. Any other change or extension of activities shall be subject to article 6, paragraph 1 (b) of this Convention.

Annex II – ARBITRATION

1. In the event of a dispute being submitted for arbitration pursuant to article 16, paragraph 2, of this Convention, a party or parties shall notify the secretariat of the subject matter of arbitration and indicate, in particular, the articles of this Convention whose interpretation or application is at issue. The secretariat shall forward the information received to all Parties to this Convention.

2. The arbitral tribunal shall consist of three members. Both the claimant party or parties and the other party or parties to the dispute shall appoint an arbitrator, and the two arbitrators so appointed shall designate by common agreement the third arbitrator, who shall be the president of the arbitral tribunal. The latter shall not be a national of one of the parties to the dispute, nor have his or her usual

place of residence in the territory of one of these parties, nor be employed by any of them, nor have dealt with the case in any other capacity.

3. If the president of the arbitral tribunal has not been designated within two months of the appointment of the second arbitrator, the Executive Secretary of the Economic Commission for Europe shall, at the request of either party to the dispute, designate the president within a further two-month period.
4. If one of the parties to the dispute does not appoint an arbitrator within two months of the receipt of the request, the other party may so inform the Executive Secretary of the Economic Commission for Europe, who shall designate the president of the arbitral tribunal within a further two-month period. Upon designation, the president of the arbitral tribunal shall request the party which has not appointed an arbitrator to do so within two months. If it fails to do so within that period, the president shall so inform the Executive Secretary of the Economic Commission for Europe, who shall make this appointment within a further two-month period.
5. The arbitral tribunal shall render its decision in accordance with international law and the provisions of this Convention.
6. Any arbitral tribunal constituted under the provisions set out in this annex shall draw up its own rules of procedure.
7. The decisions of the arbitral tribunal, both on procedure and on substance, shall be taken by majority vote of its members.
8. The tribunal may take all appropriate measures to establish the facts.
9. The parties to the dispute shall facilitate the work of the arbitral tribunal and, in particular, using all means at their disposal, shall:
   (a) Provide it with all relevant documents, facilities and information;
   (b) Enable it, where necessary, to call witnesses or experts and receive their evidence.
10. The parties and the arbitrators shall protect the confidentiality of any information that they receive in confidence during the proceedings of the arbitral tribunal.
11. The arbitral tribunal may, at the request of one of the parties, recommend interim measures of protection.
12. If one of the parties to the dispute does not appear before the arbitral tribunal or fails to defend its case, the other party may request the tribunal to continue the proceedings and to render its final decision. Absence of a party or failure of a party to defend its case shall not constitute a bar to the proceedings.
13. The arbitral tribunal may hear and determine counter-claims arising directly out of the subject matter of the dispute.
14. Unless the arbitral tribunal determines otherwise because of the particular circumstances of the case, the expenses of the tribunal, including the remuneration of its members, shall be borne by the parties to the dispute in equal shares. The tribunal shall keep a record of all its expenses, and shall furnish a final statement thereof to the parties.
15. Any Party to this Convention which has an interest of a legal nature in the subject matter of the dispute, and which may be affected by a decision in the case, may intervene in the proceedings with the consent of the tribunal.
16. The arbitral tribunal shall render its award within five months of the date on which it is established, unless it finds it necessary to extend the time limit for a period which should not exceed five months.
17. The award of the arbitral tribunal shall be accompanied by a statement of reasons. It shall be final and binding upon all parties to the dispute. The award will be transmitted by the arbitral tribunal to the parties to the dispute and to the secretariat. The secretariat will forward the information received to all Parties to this Convention.
18. Any dispute which may arise between the parties concerning the interpretation or execution of the award may be submitted by either party to the arbitral tribunal which made the award or, if the latter cannot be seized thereof, to another tribunal constituted for this purpose in the same manner as the first.

2.4. ILC Draft Articles on Prevention of Transboundary Harm from Hazardous Activities 2001

Draft Articles on Prevention of Transboundary Harm from Hazardous Activities, 10 August 2001, UN Doc. A/56/10

The States Parties,

Having in mind Article 13, paragraph 1 (a), of the Charter of the United Nations, which provides that the General Assembly shall initiate studies and make recommendations for the purpose of encouraging the progressive development of international law and its codification,

Bearing in mind the principle of permanent sovereignty of States over the natural resources within their territory or otherwise under their jurisdiction or control,

Bearing also in mind that the freedom of States to carry on or permit activities in their territory or otherwise under their jurisdiction or control is not unlimited,

Recalling the Rio Declaration on Environment and Development of 13 June 1992,

Recognizing the importance of promoting international cooperation,

Have agreed as follows:

Article 1 – Scope

The present articles apply to activities not prohibited by international law which involve a risk of causing significant transboundary harm through their physical consequences.

Article 2 – Use of terms

For the purposes of the present articles:

(a) "risk of causing significant transboundary harm" includes risks taking the form of a high probability of causing significant transboundary harm and a low probability of causing disastrous transboundary harm;

(b) "harm" means harm caused to persons, property or the environment;

(c) "transboundary harm" means harm caused in the territory of or in other places under the jurisdiction or control of a State other than the State of origin, whether or not the States concerned share a common border;

(d) "State of origin" means the State in the territory or otherwise under the jurisdiction or control of which the activities referred to in article 1 are planned or are carried out;

(e) "State likely to be affected" means the State or States in the territory of which there is the risk of significant transboundary harm or which have jurisdiction or control over any other place where there is such a risk;

(f) "States concerned" means the State of origin and the State likely to be affected.

Article 3 – Prevention

The State of origin shall take all appropriate measures to prevent significant transboundary harm or at any event to minimize the risk thereof.

Article 4 – Cooperation

States concerned shall cooperate in good faith and, as necessary, seek the assistance of one or more competent international organizations in preventing significant transboundary harm or at any event in minimizing the risk thereof.

Article 5 – Implementation

States concerned shall take the necessary legislative, administrative or other action, including the establishment of suitable monitoring mechanisms to implement the provisions of the present articles.

Article 6 – Authorization

1. The State of origin shall require its prior authorization for:
   (a) any activity within the scope of the present articles carried out in its territory or otherwise under its jurisdiction or control;
   (b) any major change in an activity referred to in subparagraph (a);
   (c) any plan to change an activity which may transform it into one falling within the scope of the present articles.
2. The requirement of authorization established by a State shall be made applicable in respect of all pre-existing activities within the scope of the present articles. Authorizations already issued by the State for pre-existing activities shall be reviewed in order to comply with the present articles.
3. In case of a failure to conform to the terms of the authorization, the State of origin shall take such actions as appropriate, including where necessary terminating the authorization.

Article 7 – Assessment of risk

Any decision in respect of the authorization of an activity within the scope of the present articles shall, in particular, be based on an assessment of the possible transboundary harm caused by that activity, including any environmental impact assessment.

Article 8 – Notification and information

1. If the assessment referred to in article 7 indicates a risk of causing significant transboundary harm, the State of origin shall provide the State likely to be affected with timely notification of the risk and the assessment and shall transmit to it the available technical and all other relevant information on which the assessment is based.
2. The State of origin shall not take any decision on authorization of the activity pending the receipt, within a period not exceeding six months, of the response from the State likely to be affected.

Article 9 – Consultations on preventive measures

1. The States concerned shall enter into consultations, at the request of any of them, with a view to achieving acceptable solutions regarding measures to be adopted in order to prevent significant transboundary harm or at any event to minimize the risk thereof. The States concerned shall agree, at the commencement of such consultations, on a reasonable time frame for the consultations.
2. The States concerned shall seek solutions based on an equitable balance of interests in the light of article 10.
3. If the consultations referred to in paragraph 1 fail to produce an agreed solution, the State of origin shall nevertheless take into account the interests of the State likely to be affected in case it decides to authorize the activity to be pursued, without prejudice to the rights of any State likely to be affected.

Article 10 – Factors involved in an equitable balance of interests

In order to achieve an equitable balance of interests as referred to in paragraph 2 of article 9, the States concerned shall take into account all relevant factors and circumstances, including:

(a) the degree of risk of significant transboundary harm and of the availability of means of preventing such harm, or minimizing the risk thereof or repairing the harm;

(b) the importance of the activity, taking into account its overall advantages of a social, economic and technical character for the State of origin in relation to the potential harm for the State likely to be affected;

(c) the risk of significant harm to the environment and the availability of means of preventing such harm, or minimizing the risk thereof or restoring the environment;

(d) the degree to which the State of origin and, as appropriate, the State likely to be affected are prepared to contribute to the costs of prevention;

(e) the economic viability of the activity in relation to the costs of prevention and to the possibility of carrying out the activity elsewhere or by other means or replacing it with an alternative activity;

(f) the standards of prevention which the State likely to be affected applies to the same or comparable activities and the standards applied in comparable regional or international practice.

Article 11 – Procedures in the absence of notification

1. If a State has reasonable grounds to believe that an activity planned or carried out in the State of origin may involve a risk of causing significant transboundary harm to it, it may request the State of origin to apply the provision of article 8. The request shall be accompanied by a documented explanation setting forth its grounds.
2. In the event that the State of origin nevertheless finds that it is not under an obligation to provide a notification under article 8, it shall so inform the requesting State within a reasonable time, providing a documented explanation setting forth the reasons for such finding. If this finding does not satisfy that State, at its request, the two States shall promptly enter into consultations in the manner indicated in article 9.
3. During the course of the consultations, the State of origin shall, if so requested by the other State, arrange to introduce appropriate and feasible measures to minimize the risk and, where appropriate, to suspend the activity in question for a reasonable period.

Article 12 – Exchange of information

While the activity is being carried out, the States concerned shall exchange in a timely manner all available information concerning that activity relevant to preventing significant transboundary harm or at any event minimizing the risk thereof. Such an exchange of information shall continue until such time as the States concerned consider it appropriate even after the activity is terminated.

Article 13 – Information to the public

States concerned shall, by such means as are appropriate, provide the public likely to be affected by an activity within the scope of the present articles with relevant information relating to that activity, the risk involved and the harm which might result and ascertain their views.

Article 14 – National security and industrial secrets

Data and information vital to the national security of the State of origin or to the protection of industrial secrets or concerning intellectual property may be withheld, but the State of origin shall cooperate in good faith with the State likely to be affected in providing as much information as possible under the circumstances.

Article 15 – Non-discrimination

Unless the States concerned have agreed otherwise for the protection of the interests of persons, natural or juridical, who may be or are exposed to the risk of significant transboundary harm as a result of an activity within the scope of the present articles, a State shall not discriminate on the basis of nationality or residence or place where the injury might occur, in granting to such persons, in accordance with its legal system, access to judicial or other procedures to seek protection or other appropriate redress.

Article 16 – Emergency preparedness

The State of origin shall develop contingency plans for responding to emergencies, in cooperation, where appropriate, with the State likely to be affected and competent international organizations.

Article 17 – Notification of an emergency

The State of origin shall, without delay and by the most expeditious means, at its disposal, notify the State likely to be affected of an emergency concerning an activity within the scope of the present articles and provide it with all relevant and available information.

Article 18 – Relationship to other rules of international law

The present articles are without prejudice to any obligation incurred by States under relevant treaties or rules of customary international law.

Article 19 – Settlement of disputes

1. Any dispute concerning the interpretation or application of the present articles shall be settled expeditiously through peaceful means of settlement chosen by mutual agreement of the parties to the dispute, including negotiations, mediation, conciliation, arbitration or judicial settlement.
2. Failing an agreement on the means for the peaceful settlement of the dispute within a period of six months, the parties to the dispute shall, at the request of any of them, have recourse to the establishment of an impartial fact-finding commission.
3. The Fact-finding Commission shall be composed of one member nominated by each party to the dispute and, in addition, a member not having the nationality of any of the parties to the dispute chosen by the nominated members who shall serve as Chairperson.
4. If more than one State is involved on one side of the dispute and those States do not agree on a common member of the Commission and each of them nominates a member, the other party to the dispute has the right to nominate an equal number of members of the Commission.
5. If the members nominated by the parties to the dispute are unable to agree on a Chairperson within three months of the request for the establishment of the Commission, any party to the dispute may request the Secretary-General of the United Nations to appoint the Chairperson who shall not have the nationality of any of the parties to the dispute. If one of the parties to the dispute fails to nominate a member within three months of the initial request pursuant to paragraph 2, any other party to the dispute may request the Secretary-General of the United Nations to appoint a person who shall not have the nationality of any of the parties to the dispute. The person so appointed shall constitute a single-member Commission.
6. The Commission shall adopt its report by a majority vote, unless it is a single-member Commission, and shall submit that report to the parties to the dispute setting forth its findings and recommendations, which the parties to the dispute shall consider in good faith.

3.1. Lugano Convention 1993

Convention on Civil Liability for Damage resulting from Activities Dangerous to the Environment, Lugano, 21 June 1993, ETS 150

The member States of the Council of Europe, the other States and the European Economic Community signatory hereto,

Considering that the aim of the Council of Europe is to achieve a greater unity between its members;

Noting that one of the objectives of the Council of Europe is to contribute to the quality of life of human beings, in particular by promoting a natural, healthy and agreeable environment;

Considering the wish of the Council of Europe to co-operate with other States in the field of nature conservation and protection of the environment;

Realising that man, the environment and property are exposed to specific dangers caused by certain activities;

Considering that emissions released in one country may cause damage in another country and that, therefore, the problems of adequate compensation for such damage are also of an international nature;

Having regard to the desirability of providing for strict liability in this field taking into account the "Polluter Pays" Principle;

Mindful of the work which has already been carried out at an international level, in particular to prevent damage and to deal with damage caused by nuclear substances and the carriage of dangerous goods;

Having noted Principle 13 of the 1992 Rio Declaration on Environment and Development, according to which "States shall develop national law regarding liability and compensation for the victims of pollution and other environmental damage; they shall also co-operate in an expeditious and more determined manner to develop further international law regarding liability and compensation for adverse effects of environmental damage caused by activities within their jurisdiction or control to areas beyond their jurisdiction";

Recognising the need to adopt further measures to deal with grave and imminent threats of damage from dangerous activities and to facilitate the burden of proof for persons requesting compensation for such damage,

Have agreed as follows:

Chapter I – General provisions

Article 1 – Object and purpose

This Convention aims at ensuring adequate compensation for damage resulting from activities dangerous to the environment and also provides for means of prevention and reinstatement.

Article 2 – Definitions

For the purpose of this Convention:

1 "Dangerous activity" means one or more of the following activities provided that it is performed professionally, including activities conducted by public authorities:

a the production, handling, storage, use or discharge of one or more dangerous substances or any operation of a similar nature dealing with such substances;

b the production, culturing, handling, storage, use, destruction, disposal, release or any other operation dealing with one or more:

- genetically modified organisms which as a result of the properties of the organism, the genetic modification and the conditions under which the operation is exercised, pose a significant risk for man, the environment or property;
- micro-organisms which as a result of their properties and the conditions under which the operation is exercised pose a significant risk for man, the environment or property, such as those micro-organisms which are pathogenic or which produce toxins;

c the operation of an installation or site for the incineration, treatment, handling or recycling of waste, such as those installations or sites specified in Annex II, provided that the quantities involved pose a significant risk for man, the environment or property;

d the operation of a site for the permanent deposit of waste.

2 "Dangerous substance" means:

a substances or preparations which have properties which constitute a significant risk for man, the environment or property. A substance or preparation which is ex-plosive, oxidizing, extremely flammable, highly flammable, flammable, very toxic, toxic, harmful, corrosive, irritant, sensitizing, carcinogenic, mutagenic, toxic for reproduction or dangerous for the environment within the meaning of Annex I, Part A to this Convention shall in any event be deemed to constitute such a risk;

b substances specified in Annex I, Part B to this Convention. Without prejudice to the application of sub-paragraph a above, Annex I, Part B may restrict the specification of dangerous substances to certain quantities or concentrations, certain risks or certain situations.

3 "Genetically modified organism" means any organism in which the genetic material has been altered in a way which does not occur naturally by mating and/or natural recombination.

However, the following genetically modified organisms are not covered by the Convention:

- organisms obtained by mutagenesis on condition that the genetic modification does not involve the use of genetically modified organisms as recipient organisms; and
- plants obtained by cell fusion (including protoplast fusion) if the resulting plant can also be produced by traditional breeding methods and on condition that the genetic modification does not involve the use of genetically modified organisms as parental organisms.

"Organism" refers to any biological entity capable of replication or of transferring genetic material.

4 "Micro-organism" means any microbiological entity, cellular or non-cellular, capable of replication or of transferring genetic material.

5 "Operator" means the person who exercises the control of a dangerous activity.

6 "Person" means any individual or partnership or any body governed by public or private law, whether corporate or not, including a State or any of its constituent subdivisions.

7 "Damage" means:

a loss of life or personal injury;

b loss of or damage to property other than to the installation itself or property held under the control of the operator, at the site of the dangerous activity;

c loss or damage by impairment of the environment in so far as this is not considered to be damage within the meaning of sub-paragraphs a or b above provided that compensation for impairment of the environment, other than for loss of profit from such impairment, shall be limited to the costs of measures of reinstatement actually undertaken or to be undertaken;

d the costs of preventive measures and any loss or damage caused by preventive measures, to the extent that the loss or damage referred to in sub-paragraphs a to c of this paragraph arises out of or results from the hazardous properties of the dangerous substances, genetically modified organisms or micro-organisms or arises or results from waste.

8 "Measures of reinstatement" means any reasonable measures aiming to reinstate or restore damaged or destroyed components of the environment, or to introduce, where reasonable, the equivalent of these components into the environment. Internal law may indicate who will be entitled to take such measures.

9 "Preventive measures" means any reasonable measures taken by any person, after an incident has occurred to prevent or minimise loss or damage as referred to in paragraph 7, sub-paragraphs a to c of this article.

10 "Environment" includes:

- natural resources both abiotic and biotic, such as air, water, soil, fauna and flora and the interaction between the same factors;
- property which forms part of the cultural heritage; and
- the characteristic aspects of the landscape.

11 "Incident" means any sudden occurrence or continuous occurrence or any series of occurrences having the same origin, which causes damage or creates a grave and imminent threat of causing damage.

Article 3 – Geographical scope

Without prejudice to the provisions of Chapter III, this Convention shall apply:

a when the incident occurs in the territory of a Party, as determined in accordance with Article 34, regardless of where the damage is suffered;

b when the incident occurs outside the territory referred to in sub-paragraph a above and the conflict of laws rules lead to the application of the law in force for the territory referred to in sub-paragraph a above.

Article 4 – Exceptions

1 This Convention shall not apply to damage arising from carriage; carriage includes the period from the beginning of the process of loading until the end of the process of unloading. However, the Convention shall apply to carriage by pipeline, as well as to carriage performed entirely in an installation or on a site unaccessible to the public where it is accessory to other activities and is an integral part thereof.

2 This Convention shall not apply to damage caused by a nuclear substance:

a arising from a nuclear incident the liability of which is regulated either by the Paris Convention of 29 July 1960 on third party liability in the field of nuclear energy, and its Additional Protocol of 28 January 1964, or the Vienna Convention of 21 May 1963 on civil liability for nuclear damage; or

b if liability for such damage is regulated by a specific internal law, provided that such law is as favourable, with regard to compensation for damage, as any of the instruments referred to under sub-paragraph a above.

3 This Convention shall not apply to the extent that it is incompatible with the rules of the applicable law relating to workmen's compensation or social security schemes.

Chapter II – Liability

Article 5 – Transitional provisions

1 The provisions of this chapter shall apply to incidents occurring after the entry into force of the Convention in respect of a Party. When the incident consists of a continuous occurrence or a series of occurrences having the same origin and part of these occurrences took place before the entry into force of this Convention, this chapter shall only apply to damage caused by occurrences or part of a continuous occurrence taking place after the entry into force.

2 In respect of damage caused by waste deposited at a site for the permanent deposit of waste the provisions of this chapter shall apply to damage which becomes known after the entry into force of the Convention in respect of the Party on the territory of which the site is situated. However this chapter shall not apply if:

a the site was closed in accordance with the provisions of internal law before the entry into force of the Convention;

b the operator proves, in the case where the operation of the site continues after that entry into force of the Convention, that the damage was caused solely by waste deposited there before that entry into force.

Article 6 – Liability in respect of substances, organisms and certain waste installations or sites

1 The operator in respect of a dangerous activity mentioned under Article 2, paragraph 1, sub- paragraphs a to c shall be liable for the damage caused by the activity as a result of incidents at the time or during the period when he was exercising the control of that activity.

2 If an incident consists of a continuous occurrence, all operators successively exercising the control of the dangerous activity during that occurrence shall be jointly and severally liable. However, the operator who proves that the occurrence during the period when he was exercising the control of the dangerous activity caused only a part of the damage shall be liable for that part of the damage only.

3 If an incident consists of a series of occurrences having the same origin, the operators at the time of any such occurrence shall be jointly and severally liable. However, the operator who proves that the occurrence at the time when he was exercising the control of the dangerous activity caused only a part of the damage shall be liable for that part of the damage only.

4 If the damage resulting from a dangerous activity becomes known after all such dangerous activity in the installation or on the site has ceased, the last operator of this activity shall be liable for that damage unless he or the person who suffered damage proves that all or part of the damage resulted from an incident which occurred at a time before he became the operator. If it is so proved, the provisions of paragraphs 1 to 3 of this article shall apply.

5 Nothing in this Convention shall prejudice any right of recourse of the operator against any third party.

Article 7 – Liability in respect of sites for the permanent deposit of waste

1 The operator of a site for the permanent deposit of waste at the time when damage caused by waste deposited at that site becomes known, shall be liable for this damage. Should the damage caused by waste deposited before the closure of such a site become known after that closure, the last operator shall be liable.

2 Liability under this article shall apply to the exclusion of any liability of the operator under Article 6, irrespective of the nature of the waste.

3 Liability under this article shall apply to the exclusion of any liability of the operator under Article 6 if the same operator conducts another dangerous activity on the site for the permanent deposit of waste.

However, if this operator or the person who has suffered damage proves that only a part of the damage was caused by the activity concerning the permanent deposit of waste, this article shall only apply to that part of the damage.

4 Nothing in this Convention shall prejudice any right of recourse of the operator against any third party.

Article 8 – Exemptions

The operator shall not be liable under this Convention for damage which he proves:

a was caused by an act of war, hostilities, civil war, insurrection or a natural phenomenon of an exceptional, inevitable and irresistible character;

b was caused by an act done with the intent to cause damage by a third party, despite safety measures appropriate to the type of dangerous activity in question;

c resulted necessarily from compliance with a specific order or compulsory measure of a public authority;

d was caused by pollution at tolerable levels under local relevant circumstances; or

e was caused by a dangerous activity taken lawfully in the interests of the person who suffered the damage, whereby it was reasonable towards this person to expose him to the risks of the dangerous activity.

Article 9 – Fault of the person who suffered the damage

If the person who suffered the damage or a person for whom he is responsible under internal law, has, by his own fault, contributed to the damage, the compensation may be reduced or disallowed having regard to all the circumstances.

Article 10 – Causality

When considering evidence of the causal link between the incident and the damage or, in the context of a dangerous activity as defined in Article 2, paragraph 1, sub-paragraph d, between the activity and the damage, the court shall take due account of the increased danger of causing such damage inherent in the dangerous activity.

Article 11 – Plurality of installations or sites

When damage results from incidents which have occurred in several installations or on several sites where dangerous activities are conducted or from dangerous activities under Article 2, paragraph 1, sub-paragraph d, the operators of the installations or sites concerned shall be jointly and severally liable for all such damage. However, the operator who proves that only part of the damage was caused by an incident in the installation or on the site where he conducts the dangerous activity or by a dangerous activity under Article 2, paragraph 1, sub-paragraph d, shall be liable for that part of the damage only.

Article 12 – Compulsory financial security scheme

Each Party shall ensure that where appropriate, taking due account of the risks of the activity, operators conducting a dangerous activity on its territory be required to participate in a financial security scheme or to have and maintain a financial guarantee up to a certain limit, of such type and terms as specified by internal law, to cover the liability under this Convention.

Chapter III – Access to information

Article 13 – Definition of public authorities

For the purpose of this chapter "public authorities" means any public administration of a Party at national, regional or local level with responsibilities, and possessing information relating to the environment, with the exception of bodies acting in a judicial or legislative capacity.

Article 14 – Access to information held by public authorities

1 Any person shall, at his request and without his having to prove an interest, have access to information relating to the environment held by public authorities.

The Parties shall define the practical arrangements under which such information is effectively made available.

2 The right of access may be restricted under internal law where it affects:

- the confidentiality of the proceedings of public authorities, international relations and national defence;
- public security;
- matters which are or have been sub judice, or under enquiry (including disciplinary enquiries), or which are the subject of preliminary investigation proceedings;
- commercial and industrial confidentiality, including intellectual property;
- the confidentiality of personal data and/or files;
- material supplied by a third party without that party being under a legal obligation to do so; or
- material, the disclosure of which would make it more likely that the environment to which that material related would be damaged.

Information held by public authorities shall be supplied in part where it is possible to separate out information on items concerning the interests referred to above.

3 A request for information may be refused where it would involve the supply of unfinished documents or data or internal communications, or where the request is manifestly unreasonable or formulated in too general a manner.

4 A public authority shall respond to a person requesting information as soon as possible and at the latest within two months. The reasons for a refusal to provide the information requested must be given.

5 A person who considers that his request for information has been unreasonably refused or ignored, or has been inadequately answered by a public authority, may seek a judicial or administrative review of the decision, in accordance with the relevant internal legal system.

6 The Parties may make a charge for supplying the information, but such a charge may not exceed a reasonable cost.

Article 15 – Access to information held by bodies with public responsibilities for the environment

On the same terms and conditions as those set out in Article 14 any person shall have access to information relating to the environment held by bodies with public responsibilities for the environment and under the control of a public authority. Access shall be given via the competent public administration or directly by the bodies themselves.

Article 16 – Access to specific information held by operators

1 The person who suffered the damage may, at any time, request the court to order an operator to provide him with specific information, in so far as this is necessary to establish the existence of a claim for compensation under this Convention.

2 Where, under this Convention, a claim for compensation is made to an operator, whether or not in the framework of judicial proceedings, this operator may request the court to order another operator to provide him with specific information, in so far as this is necessary to establish the extent of his possible obligation to compensate the person who has suffered the damage, or of his own right to compensation from the other operator.

3 The operator shall be required to provide information under paragraphs 1 and 2 of this article concerning the elements which are available to him and dealing essentially with the particulars of the equipment, the machinery used, the kind and concentration of the dangerous substances or waste as well as the nature of genetically modified organisms or micro-organisms.

4 These measures shall not affect measures of investigation which may legally be ordered under internal law.

5 The court may refuse a request which places a disproportionate burden on the operator, taking into account all the interests involved.

6 In addition to the restrictions under Article 14, paragraph 2 of this Convention, which shall apply mutatis mutandis, the operator may refuse to provide information where such information would incriminate him.

7 Any reasonable charge shall be paid by the person requesting the information. The operator may require an appropriate guarantee for such payment. However a court, when allowing a claim for compensation, may establish that this charge shall be borne by the operator, except to the extent that the request resulted in unnecessary costs.

Chapter IV – Actions for compensation and other claims

Article 17 – Limitation periods

1 Actions for compensation under this Convention shall be subject to a limitation period of three years from the date on which the claimant knew or ought reasonably to have known of the damage and of the identity of the operator. The laws of the Parties regulating suspension or interruption of limitation periods shall apply to the limitation period prescribed in this paragraph.

2 However, in no case shall actions be brought after thirty years from the date of the incident which caused the damage. Where the incident consists of a continuous occurrence the thirty years' period shall run from the end of that occurrence. Where the incident consists of a series of occurrences having the same origin the thirty years' period shall run from the date of the last of such occurrences. In respect of a site for the permanent deposit of waste the thirty years' period shall at the latest run from the date on which the site was closed in accordance with the provisions of internal law.

Article 18 – Requests by organisations

1 Any association or foundation which according to its statutes aims at the protection of the environment and which complies with any further conditions of internal law of the Party where the request is submitted may, at any time, request:

a the prohibition of a dangerous activity which is unlawful and poses a grave threat of damage to the environment;

b that the operator be ordered to take measures to prevent an incident or damage;

c that the operator be ordered to take measures, after an incident, to prevent damage; or

d that the operator be ordered to take measures of reinstatement.

2 Internal law may stipulate cases where the request is inadmissible.

3 Internal law may specify the body, whether administrative or judicial, before which the request referred to in paragraph 1 above should be made. In all cases provision shall be made for a right of review.

4 Before deciding upon a request mentioned under paragraph 1 above the requested body may, in view of the general interests involved, hear the competent public authorities.

5 When the internal law of a Party requires that the association or foundation has its registered seat or the effective centre of its activities in its territory, the Party may declare at any time, by means of a notification addressed to the Secretary General of the Council of Europe, that, on the basis of reciprocity, an association or foundation having its seat or centre of activities in the territory of another Party and complying in that other Party with the other conditions mentioned in paragraph 1 above shall have the right to submit requests in accordance with paragraphs 1 to 3 above. The declaration will become effective on the first day of the month following the expiration of a period of three months after the date of its reception by the Secretary General.

Article 19 – Jurisdiction

1 Actions for compensation under this Convention may only be brought within a Party at the court of the place:

a where the damage was suffered;

b where the dangerous activity was conducted; or

c where the defendant has his habitual residence.

2 Requests for access to specific information held by operators under Article 16, paragraphs 1 and 2 may only be submitted within a Party at the court of the place:

a where the dangerous activity is conducted; or

b where the operator who may be required to provide the information has his habitual residence.

3 Requests by organisations under Article 18, paragraph 1, sub-paragraph a may only be submitted within a Party at the court or, if internal law so provides, at a competent administrative authority of the place where the dangerous activity is or will be conducted.

4 Requests by organisations under Article 18, paragraph 1, sub-paragraphs b, c and d may only be submitted within a Party at the court or, if internal law so provides, at a competent administrative authority:

a of the place where the dangerous activity is or will be conducted; or

b of the place where the measures are to be taken.

Article 20 – Notification

The court shall stay the proceedings so long as it is not shown that the defendant has been able to receive the document instituting the proceedings or an equivalent document in sufficient time to enable him to arrange for his defence, or that all necessary steps have been taken to this end.

Article 21 – Lis pendens

1 Where proceedings involving the same cause of action and between the same parties are brought in the courts of different Parties, any court other than the court first seised shall of its own motion stay its proceedings until such time as the jurisdiction of the court first seised is established.

2 Where the jurisdiction of the court first seised is established, any court other than the court first seised shall decline jurisdiction in favour of that court.

Article 22 – Related actions

1 Where related actions are brought in the courts of different Parties, any court other than the court first seised may, while the actions are pending at first instance, stay its proceedings.

2 A court other than the court first seised may also, on the application of one of the parties, decline jurisdiction if the law of that court permits the consolidation of related actions and the court first seised has jurisdiction over both actions.

3 For the purposes of this article, actions are deemed to be related where they are so closely connected that it is expedient to hear and determine them together to avoid the risk of irreconcilable judgments resulting from separate proceedings.

Article 23 – Recognition and enforcement

1 Any decision given by a court with jurisdiction in accordance with Article 19 above where it is no longer subject to ordinary forms of review, shall be recognised in any Party, unless:

a such recognition is contrary to public policy in the Party in which recognition is sought;

b it was given in default of appearance and the defendant was not duly served with the document which instituted the proceedings or with an equivalent document in sufficient time to enable him to arrange for his defence;

c the decision is irreconcilable with a decision given in a dispute between the same parties in the Party in which recognition is sought; or

d the decision is irreconcilable with an earlier decision given in another State involving the same cause of action and between the same parties, provided that this latter decision fulfils the conditions necessary for its recognition in the Party addressed.

2 A decision recognised under paragraph 1 above which is enforceable in the Party of origin shall be enforceable in each Party as soon as the formalities required by that Party have been completed. The formalities shall not permit the merits of the case to be re-opened.

Article 24 – Other treaties relating to jurisdiction, recognition and enforcement

Whenever two or more Parties are bound by a treaty establishing rules of jurisdiction or providing for recognition and enforcement in a Party of decisions given in another Party, the provisions of that treaty shall replace the corresponding provisions of Articles 19 to 23.

Chapter V – Relation between this Convention and other provisions

Article 25 – Relation between this Convention and other provisions

1 Nothing in this Convention shall be construed as limiting or derogating from any of the rights of the persons who have suffered the damage or as limiting the provisions concerning the protection or reinstatement of the environment which may be provided under the laws of any Party or under any other treaty to which it is a Party.

2 In their mutual relations, Parties which are members of the European Economic Community shall apply Community rules and shall therefore not apply the rules arising from this Convention except in so far as there is no Community rule governing the particular subject concerned.

Chapter VI – The Standing Committee

Article 26 – The Standing Committee

1 For the purposes of this Convention, a Standing Committee is hereby set up.

2 Each Party may be represented on the Standing Committee by one or more delegates.

3 Each delegation shall have one vote. However, within the areas of its competence the European Economic Community shall exercise its right to vote in the Standing Committee with a number of votes equal to the number of its member States which are Parties to this Convention. It shall not exercise its right to vote in cases where the member States exercise theirs and conversely. As long as no member State of the European Economic Community is a Party, the Community as a Party shall have one vote.

4 Any State referred to in Article 32 or invited to accede to the Convention in accordance with the provisions of Article 33 which is not a Party to this Convention may be represented on the Standing Committee by an observer. If the European Economic Community is not a Party it may be represented on the Standing Committee by an observer.

5 Unless, at least one month before the meeting, a Party has informed the Secretary General of its objection, the Standing Committee may invite the following to attend as observers at all its meetings or one or part of a meeting:

- any State not referred to in paragraph 4 above;
- any international or national, governmental or non-governmental body technically qualified in the fields covered by this Convention.

6 The Standing Committee may seek the advice of experts in order to discharge its functions.

7 The Standing Committee shall be convened by the Secretary General of the Council of Europe. It shall meet whenever one-third of the Parties or the Committee of Ministers of the Council of Europe so request.

8 One-third of the Parties shall constitute a quorum for holding a meeting of the Standing Committee.

9 Decisions may only be taken in the Standing Committee if at least one-half of the Parties are present.

10 Subject to Articles 27 and 29 to 31 the decisions of the Standing Committee shall be taken by a majority of the members present.

11 Subject to the provisions of this Convention the Standing Committee shall draw up its own rules of procedure.

Article 27 – Functions of the Standing Committee

The Standing Committee shall keep under review problems relating to this Convention. It may, in particular:

a consider any question of a general nature referred to it concerning interpretation or implementation of the Convention. The Standing Committee's conclusions concerning implementation of the Convention may take the form of a recommendation; recommendations shall be adopted by a three quarters majority of the votes cast;

b propose any necessary amendments to the Convention including its annexes and examine those proposed in accordance with Articles 29 to 31.

Article 28 – Reports of the Standing Committee

After each meeting, the Standing Committee shall forward to the Parties and the Committee of Ministers of the Council of Europe a report on its discussions and any decisions taken.

Chapter VII – Amendments to the Convention

Article 29 – Amendments to the Articles

1 Any amendment to the articles of this Convention proposed by a Party or the Standing Committee shall be communicated to the Secretary General of the Council of Europe and forwarded by him at least two months before the meeting of the Standing Committee to the member States of the Council of Europe, to the European Economic Community, to any Signatory, to any Party, to any State invited to sign this Convention in accordance with the provisions of Article 32 and to any State invited to accede to it in accordance with the provisions of Article 33.

2 Any amendment proposed in accordance with the provisions of the preceding paragraph shall be examined by the Standing Committee which:

a for amendments to Articles 1 to 25 shall submit the text adopted by a three-quarters majority of the votes cast to the Parties for acceptance;

b for amendments to Articles 26 to 37 shall submit the text adopted by a three-quarters majority of the votes cast to the Committee of Ministers for approval. After its approval, this text shall be forwarded to the Parties for acceptance.

3 Any amendment to Articles 1 to 25 shall enter into force, in respect of those Parties which have accepted it, on the first day of the month following the expiration of a period of one month after the date on which three Parties, including at least two member States of the Council of Europe, have informed the Secretary General that they have accepted it.

In respect of any Party which subsequently accepts it, the amendment shall enter into force on the first day of the month following the expiration of a period of one month after the date on which that Party has informed the Secretary General of its acceptance.

4 Any amendment to Articles 26 to 37 shall enter into force on the first day of the month following the expiration of a period of one month after the date on which all Parties have informed the Secretary General that they have accepted it.

Article 30 – Amendments to the annexes

1 Any amendment to the annexes of this Convention proposed by a Party or the Standing Committee shall be communicated to the Secretary General of the Council of Europe and forwarded by him at least two months before the meeting of the Standing Committee to the member States of the Council of Europe, to the European Economic Community, to any Signatory, to any Party, to any State invited to sign this Convention in accordance with the provisions of Article 32 and to any State invited to accede to it in accordance with the provisions of Article 33.

2 Any amendment proposed in accordance with the provisions of the preceding paragraph or, where appropriate, of Article 31 shall be examined by the Standing Committee, which may adopt it by a three-quarters majority of the votes cast. The text adopted shall be forwarded to the Parties.

3 On the first day of the month following the expiration of a period of eighteen months after its adoption by the Standing Committee, unless more than one-third of the Parties have notified objections, any amendment shall enter into force for those Parties which have not notified objections.

Article 31 – Tacit amendments to Annex I, Parts A and B

1 Whenever the European Economic Community adopts an amendment to one of the annexes to the directives referred to in Annex I, Parts A and B of this Convention, the Secretary General shall communicate it to all the Parties not later than four months after its publication in the Official Journal of the European Communities.

2 Within a time limit of six months after this communication, any Party may request that the amendment be submitted to the Standing Committee, in which case the procedure under Article 30, paragraphs 2 and 3, shall be followed. If no Party requests the submission of the amendment to the Standing Committee, the provisions of paragraph 3 below shall apply.

3 On the first day of the month following the expiration of a period of eighteen months after the communication of the amendment to all Parties, and unless more than one-third of the Parties have notified objections, the amendment shall enter into

force for those Parties which have not notified objections.

However, the entry into force of the amendment shall be postponed to the date fixed for the member States of the European Economic Community for the compliance of their domestic law with the directive, if this date is later than that resulting from the time limit stated in the first part of this paragraph.

Chapter VIII – Final clauses

Article 32 – Signature, ratification and entry into force

1 This Convention shall be open for signature by the member States of the Council of Europe, the non-member States which have participated in its elaboration and by the European Economic Community.

2 This Convention is subject to ratification, acceptance or approval. Instruments of ratification, acceptance or approval shall be deposited with the Secretary General of the Council of Europe.

3 This Convention shall enter into force on the first day of the month following the expiration of a period of three months after the date on which three States, including at least two member States of the Council of Europe, have expressed their consent to be bound by the Convention in accordance with the provisions of paragraph 2 of the present article.

4 In respect of any Signatory which subsequently expresses its consent to be bound by it, the Convention shall enter into force on the first day of the month following the expiration of a period of three months after the date of the deposit of its instrument of ratification, acceptance or approval.

Article 33 – Non-member States

1 After the entry into force of this Convention, the Committee of Ministers of the Council of Europe may, on its own initiative or following a proposal from the Standing Committee and after consultation of the Parties, invite any non-member State of the Council of Europe to accede to this Convention by a decision taken by the majority provided for in Article 20, sub- paragraph d of the Statute of the Council of Europe, and by the unanimous vote of the representatives of the Contracting States entitled to sit on the Committee of Ministers.

2 In respect of any acceding State, the Convention shall enter into force on the first day of the month following the expiration of a period of three months after the date of deposit of the instrument of accession with the Secretary General of the Council of Europe.

Article 34 – Territories

1 Any Signatory may, at the time of signature or when depositing its instrument of ratification, acceptance or approval, specify the territory or territories to which this Convention shall apply. Any other State may formulate the same declaration when depositing its instrument of accession.

2 Any Party may, at any later date, by a declaration addressed to the Secretary General of the Council of Europe, extend the application of this Convention to any other territory specified in the declaration and for whose international relations it is responsible or on whose behalf it is authorised to give undertakings. In respect of such territory the Convention shall enter into force on the first day of the month following the expiration of a period of three months after the date of receipt of such declaration by the Secretary General.

3 Any declaration made under the two preceding paragraphs may, in respect of any territory specified in such declaration, be withdrawn by a notification addressed to the Secretary General. The withdrawal shall become effective on the first day of the month following the expiration of a period of three months after the date of receipt of such notification by the Secretary General.

Article 35 – Reservations

1 Any Signatory may declare, at the time of signature or when depositing its instrument of ratification, acceptance or approval, that it reserves the right:

- a to apply Article 3, sub-paragraph a, to damage suffered in the territory of the States which are not Parties to this Convention only on the basis of reciprocity;
- b to provide in its internal law that, without prejudice to Article 8, the operator shall not be liable if he proves that in the case of damage caused by a dangerous activity mentioned under Article 2, paragraph 1, sub-paragraphs a and b, the state of scientific and technical knowledge at the time of the incident was not such as to enable the existence of the dangerous properties of the substance or the significant risk involved in the operation dealing with the organism to be discovered;
- c not to apply Article 18.

Any other State may formulate the same reservations when depositing its instrument of accession.

2 Any Signatory or any other State which makes use of a reservation shall notify the Secretary General of the Council of Europe of the relevant contents of its internal law.

3 Any Party which extends the application of this Convention to a territory mentioned in the declaration referred to in Article 34, paragraph 2, may, in respect of the territory concerned, make a reservation in accordance with the provisions of the preceding paragraphs.

4 No reservation shall be made to the provisions of this Convention, except those mentioned in this article.

5 Any Party which has made one of the reservations mentioned in this article may withdraw it by means of a declaration addressed to the Secretary General of the Council of Europe. The withdrawal shall become effective on the first day of the month follow-

ing the expiration of a period of one month after the date of its receipt by the Secretary General.

Article 36 – Denunciation

1 Any Party may at any time denounce this Convention by means of a notification addressed to the Secretary General of the Council of Europe.

2 Such denunciation shall become effective on the first day of the month following the expiration of a period of three months after the date of receipt of notification by the Secretary General.

Article 37 – Notifications

The Secretary General of the Council of Europe shall notify the member States of the Council, any Signatory, any Party and any other State which has been invited to accede to this Convention of:

a any signature;

b the deposit of any instrument of ratification, acceptance, approval or accession;

c any date of entry into force of this Convention in accordance with Articles 32 or 33;

d any amendment adopted in accordance with Articles 29, 30 or 31, and the date on which such an amendment enters into force;

e any declaration made under the provisions of Articles 18 or 34;

f any reservation and withdrawal of reservation made in pursuance of the provisions of Article 35;

g any other act, notification or communication relating to this Convention.

In witness whereof the undersigned, being duly authorised thereto, have signed this Convention.

Done at Lugano, this 21st day of June 1993, in English and French, both texts being equally authentic, in a single copy which shall be deposited in the archives of the Council of Europe. The Secretary General of the Council of Europe shall transmit certified copies to each member State of the Council of Europe, to the non-member States which have participated in the elaboration of this Convention, to the European Economic Community and to any State invited to accede to this Convention.

3.2. Basel Protocol 1999

Basel Protocol on Liability and Compensation for Damage Resulting from Transboundary Movements of Hazardous Wastes and their Disposal, Basel, 10 December 1999, UN Doc. UNEP/CHW.1/WG/1/9/2

The Parties to the Protocol,

Having taken into account the relevant provisions of Principle 13 of the 1992 Rio Declaration on Environment and Development, according to which States shall develop international and national legal instruments regarding liability and compensation for the victims of pollution and other environmental damage,

Being Parties to the Basel Convention on the Control of Transboundary Movements of Hazardous Wastes and their Disposal,

Mindful of their obligations under the Convention,

Aware of the risk of damage to human health, property and the environment caused by hazardous wastes and other wastes and the transboundary movement and disposal thereof,

Concerned about the problem of illegal transboundary traffic in hazardous wastes and other wastes,

Committed to Article 12 of the Convention, and emphasizing the need to set out appropriate rules and procedures in the field of liability and compensation for damage resulting from the transboundary movement and disposal of hazardous wastes and other wastes,

Convinced of the need to provide for third party liability and environmental liability in order to ensure that adequate and prompt compensation is available for damage resulting from the transboundary movement and disposal of hazardous wastes and other wastes,

Have agreed as follows:

Article 1 – Objective

The objective of the Protocol is to provide for a comprehensive regime for liability and for adequate and prompt compensation for damage resulting from the transboundary movement of hazardous wastes and other wastes and their disposal including illegal traffic in those wastes.

Article 2 – Definitions

1. The definitions of terms contained in the Convention apply to the Protocol, unless expressly provided otherwise in the Protocol.
2. For the purposes of the Protocol:
   (a) "The Convention" means the Basel Convention on the Control of Transboundary Movements of Hazardous Wastes and their Disposal;
   (b) "Hazardous wastes and other wastes" means hazardous wastes and other wastes within the meaning of Article 1 of the Convention;
   (c) "Damage" means:
      (i) Loss of life or personal injury;
      (ii) Loss of or damage to property other than property held by the person liable in accordance with the present Protocol;
      (iii) Loss of income directly deriving from an economic interest in any use of the environment, incurred as a result of impairment of the environment, taking into account savings and costs;
      (iv) The costs of measures of reinstatement of the impaired environment, limited to the costs of measures actually taken or to be undertaken; and
      (v) The costs of preventive measures, including any loss or damage caused by such measures, to the extent that the damage arises out of or results from hazardous properties of the wastes involved in the transboundary movement and disposal of hazardous wastes and other wastes subject to the Convention;
   (d) "Measures of reinstatement" means any reasonable measures aiming to assess, reinstate or restore damaged or destroyed components of the environment. Domestic law may indicate who will be entitled to take such measures;
   (e) "Preventive measures" means any reasonable measures taken by any person in response to an incident, to prevent, minimize, or mitigate loss or damage, or to effect environmental clean-up;
   (f) "Contracting Party" means a Party to the Protocol;
   (g) "Protocol" means the present Protocol;
   (h) "Incident" means any occurrence, or series of occurrences having the same origin that causes damage or creates a grave and imminent threat of causing damage;
   (i) "Regional economic integration organization" means an organization constituted by sovereign States to which its member States have transferred competence in respect of matters governed by the Protocol and which has been duly authorized, in accordance with its internal procedures, to sign, ratify, accept, approve, formally confirm or accede to it;
   (j) "Unit of account" means the Special Drawing Right as defined by the International Monetary Fund.

Article 3 – Scope of application

1. The Protocol shall apply to damage due to an incident occurring during a transboundary movement of hazardous wastes and other wastes and their

disposal, including illegal traffic, from the point where the wastes are loaded on the means of transport in an area under the national jurisdiction of a State of expert. Any Contracting Party may by way of notification to the Depositary exclude the application of the Protocol, in respect of all transboundary movements for which it is the State of expert, for such incidents which occur in an area under its national jurisdiction, as regards damage in its area of national jurisdiction. The Secretariat shall inform all Contracting Parties of notifications received in accordance with this Article.

2. The Protocol shall apply:

   (a) In relation to movements destined for one of the operations specified in Annex IV to the Convention other than D13, D14, D15, R12 or Rl3, until the time at which the notification of completion of disposal pursuant to Article 6, paragraph 9, of the Convention has occurred, or, where such notification has not been made, completion of disposal has occurred; and

   (b) In relation to movements destined for the operations specified in D13, D14, D15, Rl2 or Rl3 of Annex IV to the Convention, until completion of the subsequent disposal operation specified in Dl to D12 and Rl to Rll of Annex IV to the Convention.

3. (a) The Protocol shall apply only to damage suffered in an area under the national jurisdiction of a Contracting Party arising from an incident as referred to in paragraph l;

   (b) When the State of import, but not the State of expert, is a Contracting Party, the Protocol shall apply only with respect to damage arising from an incident as referred to in paragraph 1 which takes place after the moment at which the disposer has taken possession of the hazardous wastes and other wastes. When the State of expert, but not the State of import, is a Contracting Party, the Protocol shall apply only with respect to damage arising from an incident as referred to in paragraph 1 which takes place prior to the moment at which the disposer takes possession of the hazardous wastes and other wastes. When neither the State of expert nor the State of irnport is a Contracting Party, the Protocol shall not apply;

   (c) Notwithstanding subparagraph (a), the Protocol shall also apply to the damages specified in Article 2, subparagraphs 2 (c) (i), (ii) and (v), of the Protocol occurring in areas beyond any national jurisdiction;

   (d) Notwithstanding subparagraph (a), the Protocol shall, in relation to rights under the Protocol, also apply to damages suffered in an area under the national jurisdiction of a State of transit which is not a Contracting Party provided that such State appears in Annex A and has acceded to a multilateral or regional agreement concerning transboundary movements of hazardous waste which is in force. Subparagraph (b) will apply mutatis mutandis.

4. Notwithstanding paragraph 1, in case of re-importation under Article 8 or Article 9, subparagraph 2 (a), and Article 9, paragraph 4, of the Convention, the provisions cf the Protocol shall apply until the hazardous wastes and other wastes reach the original State of expert.

5. Nothing in the Protocol shall affect in any way the sovereignty of States over their territorial seas and their jurisdiction and the right in their respective exclusive economic zones and continental shelves in accordance with international law.

6. Notwithstanding paragraph l and subject to paragraph 2 of this Article:

   (a) The Protocol shall not apply to damage that has arisen from a transboundary movement of hazardous wastes and other wastes that has commenced before the entry into force of the Protocol for the Contracting Party concerned;

   (b) The Protocol shall apply to damage resulting from an incident occurring during a transboundary movement of wastes falling under Article 1, subparagraph l (b), of the Convention only if those wastes have been notified in accordance with Article 3 of the Convention by the State of export or import, or both, and the damage arises in an area under the national jurisdiction of a State, including a State of transit, that has defined or considers those wastes as hazardous provided that the requirements of Article 3 of the Convention have been met. In this case strict liability shall be channelled in accordance with Article 4 of the Protocol.

7. (a) The Protocol shall not apply to damage due to an incident occurring during a transboundary movement of hazardous wastes and other wastes and their disposal pursuant to a bilateral, multilateral or regional agreement or arrangement concluded and notified in accordance with Article 11 of the Convention if:

      (i) The damage occurred in an area under the national jurisdiction of any of the Parties to the agreement or arrangement;

      (ii) There exists a liability and compensation regime, which is in force and is applicable to the damage resulting from such a transboundary movement or disposal provided it fully meets, or exceeds the objective of the Protocol by providing a high level of protection to persons who have suffered damage;

      (iii) The Party to the Article 11 agreement or arrangement in which the damage has occurred has previously notified the Depositary of the non-application of the Protocol to any damage occurring in an area under its national jurisdiction due to an incident resulting from movements or disposals referred to in this subparagraph; and

      (iv) The Parties to the Article 11 agreement or arrangement have not declared that the Protocol shall be applicable;

(b) In order to promote transparency, a Contracting Party that has notified the Depositary of the non-application of the Protocol shall notify the Secretariat of the applicable liability and compensation regime referred to in subparagraph (a) (ii) and include a description of the regirne. The Secretariat shall submit to the Meeting of the Parties, on a regular basis, summary reports on the notifications received;

(c) After a notification pursuant to subparagraph (a) (iii) is made, actions for compensation for damage to which subparagraph (a) (i) applies may not be made under the Protocol.

8. The exclusion set out in paragraph 7 of this Article shall neither affect any of the rights or obligations under the Protocol of a Contracting Party which is not party to the agreement or arrangement mentioned above, nor shall it affect rights of States of transit which are not Contracting Parties.
9. Article 3, paragraph 2, shall not affect the application of Article 16 to all Contracting Parties.

Article 4 – Strict liability

1. The person who notifies in accordance with Article 6 of the Convention, shall be liable for damage until the disposer has taken possession of the hazardous wastes and other wastes. Thereafter the disposer shall be liable for damage. If the State of expert is the notifier or if no notification has taken place, the exporter shall be liable for damage until the disposer has taken possession of the hazardous wastes and other wastes. With respect to Article 3, subparagraph 6 (b), of the Protocol, Article 6, paragraph 5, of the Convention shall apply mutatis mutandis. Thereafter the disposer shall be liable for damage.
2. Without prejudice to paragraph 1, with respect to wastes under Article l, subparagraph 1 (b), of the Convention that have been notified as hazardous by the State of import in accordance with Article 3 of the Convention but not by the State of export, the importer shall be liable until the disposer has taken possession of the wastes, if the State of import is the notifier or if no notification has taken place. Thereafter the disposer shall be liable for damage.
3. Should the hazardous wastes and other wastes be re-imported in accordance with Article 8 of the Convention, the person who notified shall be liable for damage from the time the hazardous wastes leave the disposal site, until the wastes are taken into possession by the exporter, if applicable, or by the alternate disposer.
4. Should the hazardous wastes and other wastes be re-imported under Article 9, subparagraph 2 (a), or Article 9, paragraph 4, of the Convention, subject to Article 3 of the Protocol, the person who re-imports shall be held liable for damage until the wastes are taken into possession by the exporter if applicable, or by the alternate disposer.
5. No liability in accordance with this Article shall attach to the person referred to in paragraphs 1 and 2 of this Article, if that person proves that the damage was:
   (a) The result of an act of armed conflict, hostilities, civil war or insurrection;
   (b) The result of a natural phenomenon of exceptional, inevitable, unforeseeable and irresistible character;
   (c) Wholly the result of compliance with a compulsory measure of a public authority of the State where the damage occurred; or
   (d) Wholly the result of the wrongful intentional conduct of a third party, including the person who suffered the damage.
6. If two or more persons are liable according to this Article, the claimant shall have the right to seek full compensation for the damage from any or all of the persons liable.

Article 5 – Fault-based liability

Without prejudice to Article 4, any person shall be liable for damage caused or contributed to by his lack of compliance with the provisions implementing the Convention or by his wrongful intentional, reckless or negligent acts or omissions. This Article shall not affect the domestic law of the Contracting Parties governing liability of servants and agents.

Article 6 – Preventive measures

1. Subject to any requirement of domestic law any person in operational control of hazardous wastes and other wastes at the time of an incident shall take all reasonable measures to mitigate damage arising therefrom.
2. Notwithstanding any other provision in the Protocol, any person in possession and/or control of hazardous wastes and other wastes for the sole purpose of taking preventive measures, provided that this person acted reasonably and in accordance with any domestic law regarding preventive measures, is not thereby subject to liability under the Protocol.

Article 7 – Combined cause of the damage

1. Where damage is caused by wastes covered by the Protocol and wastes not covered by the Protocol, a person otherwise liable shall only be liable according to the Protocol in proportion to the contribution made by the wastes covered by the Protocol to the damage.
2. The proportion of the contribution to the damage of the wastes referred to in paragraph 1 shall be determined with regard to the volume and properties of the wastes involved, and the type of damage occurring.
3. In respect of damage where it is not possible to distinguish between the contribution made by wastes covered by the Protocol and wastes not covered by the Protocol, all damage shall be considered to be covered by the Protocol.

Article 8 – Right of recourse

1. Any person liable under the Protocol shall be entitled to a right of recourse in accordance with the rules of procedure of the competent court:
   (a) Against any other person also liable under the Protocol; and
   (b) As expressly provided for in contractual arrangements.
2. Nothing in the Protocol shall prejudice any rights of recourse to which the person liable might be entitled pursuant to the law of the competent court.

Article 9 – Contributory fault

Compensation may be reduced or disallowed if the person who suffered the damage, or a person for whom he is responsible under the domestic law, by his own fault, has caused or contributed to the damage having regard to all circumstances.

Article 10 – Implementation

1. The Contracting Parties shall adopt the legislative, regulatory and administrative measures necessary to implement the Protocol.
2. In order to promote transparency, Contracting Parties shall inform the Secretariat of measures to implement the Protocol, including any limits of liability established pursuant to paragraph 1 of Annex B.
3. The provisions of the Protocol shall be applied without discrimination based on nationality, domicile or residence.

Article 11 – Conflicts with other liability and compensation agreements

Whenever the provisions of the Protocol and the provisions of a bilateral, multilateral or regional agreement apply to liability and compensation for damage caused by an incident arising during the same portion of a transboundary movement, the Protocol shall not apply provided the other agreement is in force for the Party or Parties concerned and had been opened for signature when the Protocol was opened for signature, even if the agreement was amended afterwards.

Article 12 – Financial limits

1. Financial limits for the liability under Article 4 of the Protocol are specified in Annex B to the Protocol. Such limits shall not include any interest or costs awarded by the competent court.
2. There shall be no financial limit on liability under Article 5.

Article 13 – Time limit of liability

1. Claims for compensation under the Protocol shall not be admissible unless they are brought within ten years from the date of the incident.
2. Claims for compensation under the Protocol shall not be admissible unless they are brought within five years from the date the claimant knew or ought reasonably to have known of the damage provided that the time limits established pursuant to paragraph 1 of this Article are not exceeded.
3. Where the incident consists of a series of occurrences having the same origin, time limits established pursuant to this Article shall run from the date of the last of such occurrences. Where the incident consists of a continuous occurrence, such time limits shall run from the end of that continuous occurrence.

Article 14 – Insurance and other financial guarantees

1. The persons liable under Article 4 shall establish and maintain during the period of the time limit of liability, insurance, bonds or other financial guarantees covering their liability under Article 4 of the Protocol for amounts not less than the minimum limits specified in paragraph 2 of Annex B. States may fulfil their obligation under this paragraph by a declaration of self-insurance. Nothing in this paragraph shall prevent the use of deductibles or co-payments as between the insurer and the insured, but the failure of the insured to pay any deductible or co-payment shall not be a defence against the person who has suffered the damage.
2. With regard to the liability of the notifier, or exporter under Article 4, paragraph 1, or of the importer under Article 4, paragraph 2, insurance, bonds or other financial guarantees referred to in paragraph 1 of this Article shall only be drawn upon in order to provide compensation for damage covered by Article 2 of the Protocol.
3. A document reflecting the coverage of the liability of the notifier or exporter under Article 4, paragraph 1, or of the importer under Article 4, paragraph 2, of the Protocol shall accompany the notification referred to in Article 6 of the Convention. Proof of coverage of the liability of the disposer shall be delivered to the competent authorities of the State of import.
4. Any claim under the Protocol may be asserted directly against any person providing insurance, bonds or other financial guarantees. The insurer or the person providing the financial guarantee shall have the right to require the person liable under Article 4 to be joined in the proceedings. Insurers and persons providing financial guarantees may invoke the defences which the person liable under Article 4 would be entitled to invoke.
5. Notwithstanding paragraph 4, a Contracting Party shall, by notification to the Depositary at the time of signature, ratification, or approval of, or accession to the Protocol, indicate if it does not provide for a right to bring a direct action pursuant to paragraph 4. The Secretariat shall maintain a record of the Contracting Parties who have given notification pursuant to this paragraph.

Article 15 – Financial mechanism

1. Where compensation under the Protocol does not cover the costs of damage, additional and supplementary measures aimed at ensuring adequate and prompt compensation may be taken using existing mechanisms.

2. The Meeting of the Parties shall keep under review the need for and possibility of improving existing mechanisms or establishing a new mechanism.

Article 16 – State responsibility

The Protocol shall not affect the rights and obligations of the Contracting Parties under the rules of general international law with respect to State responsibility.

PROCEDURES

Article 17 – Competent courts

1. Claims for compensation under the Protocol may be brought in the courts of a Contracting Party only where either:
   (a) The damage was suffered; or
   (b) The incident occurred; or
   (c) The defendant has his habitual residence, or has his principal place of business.
2. Each Contracting Party shall ensure that its courts possess the necessary competence to entertain such claims for compensation.

Article 18 – Related actions

1. Where related actions are brought in the courts of different Parties, any court other than the court first seized may, while the actions are pending at first instance, stay its proceedings.
2. A court may, on the application of one of the Parties, decline jurisdiction if the law of that court permits the consolidation of related actions and another court has jurisdiction over both actions.
3. For the purpose of this Article, actions are deemed to be related where they are so closely connected that it is expedient to hear and determine them together to avoid the risk of irreconcilable judgements resulting from separate proceedings.

Article 19 – Applicable law

All matters of substance or procedure regarding claims before the competent court which are not specifically regulated in the Protocol shall be governed by the law of that court including any rules of such law relating to conflict of laws.

Article 20 – Relation between the Protocol and the law of the competent court

1. Subject to paragraph 2, nothing in the Protocol shall be construed as limiting or derogating from any rights of persons who have suffered damage, or as limiting the protection or reinstatement of the environment which may be provided under domestic law.
2. No claims for compensation for damage based on the strict liability of the notifier or the exporter liable under Article 4, paragraph 1, or the importer liable under Article 4, paragraph 2, of the Protocol, shall be made otherwise than in accordance with the Protocol.

Article 21 – Mutual recognition and enforcement of judgements

1. Any judgement of a court having jurisdiction in accordance with Article 17 of the Protocol, which is enforceable in the State of origin and is no langer subject to ordinary forms of review, shall be recognized in any Contracting Party as soon as the formalities required in that Party have been completed, except:
   (a) Where the judgement was obtained by fraud;
   (b) Where the defendant was not given reasonable notice and a fair opportunity to present his case;
   (c) Where the judgement is irreconcilable with an earlier judgement validly pronounced in another Contracting Party with regard to the same cause of action and the same parties; or
   (d) Where the judgement is contrary to the public policy of the Contracting Party in which its recognition is sought.
2. A judgement recognized under paragraph l of this Article shall be enforceable in each Contracting Party as soon as the formalities required in that Party have been completed. The formalities shall not permit the merits of the case tobe re-opened.
3. The provisions of paragraphs land 2 of this Article shall not apply between Contracting Parties that are Parties to an agreement or arrangement in force on mutual recognition and enforcement of judgements under which the judgement would be recognizable and enforceable.

Article 22 – Relationship of the Protocol with the Basel Convention

Except as otherwise provided in the Protocol, the provisions of the Convention relating to its Protocols shall apply to the Protocol.

Article 23 – Amendment of Annex B

1. At its sixth meeting, the Conference of the Parties to the Basel Convention may amend paragraph 2 of Annex B following the procedure set out in Article 18 of the Basel Convention.
2. Such an amendment may be made before the Protocol enters into force.

FINAL CLAUSES

Article 24 – Meeting of the Parties

1. A Meeting of the Parties is hereby established. The Secretariat shall convene the first Meeting of the Parties in conjunction with the first meeting of the Conference of the Parties to the Convention after entry into force of the Protocol.
2. subsequent ordinary Meetings of the Parties shall be held in conjunction with meetings of the Conference of the Parties to the Convention unless the Meeting of the Parties decides otherwise. Extraordinary Meetings of the Parties shall be held at such other times as may be deemed necessary by a Meeting of the Parties, or at the written request of any Contracting Party, provided that within six months of such a request being communicated to

them by the Secretariat, it is supported by at least one third of the Contracting Parties.

3. The Contracting Parties, at their first meeting, shall adopt by consensus rules of procedure for their meetings as well as financial rules.
4. The functions of the Meeting of the Parties shall be:
   (a) To review the implementation of and compliance with the Protocol;
   (b) To provide for reporting and establish guidelines and procedures for such reporting where necessary;
   (c) To consider and adopt, where necessary, proposals for amendment of the Protocol or any annexes and for any new annexes; and
   (d) To consider and undertake any additional action that may be required for the purposes of the Protocol.

Article 25 – Secretariat

1. For the purposes of the Protocol, the Secretariat shall:
   (a) Arrange for and service Meetings of the Parties as provided for in Article 24;
   (b) Prepare reports, including financial data, on its activities carried out in implementation of its functions under the Protocol and present them to the Meeting of the Parties;
   (c) Ensure the necessary coordination with relevant international bodies, and in particular enter into such administrative and contractual arrangements as may be required for the effective discharge of its functions;
   (d) Compile information concerning the national laws and administrative provisions of Contracting Parties implementing the Protocol;
   (e) Cooperate with Contracting Parties and with relevant and competent international organisations and agencies in the provision of experts and equipment for the purpose of rapid assistance to States in the event of an emergency situation;
   (f) Encourage non-Parties to attend the Meetings of the Parties as observers and to act in accordance with the provisions of the Protocol; and
   (g) Perform such other functions for the achievement of the purposes of this Protocol as may be assigned to it by the Meetings of the Parties.
2. The secretariat functions shall be carried out by the Secretariat of the Basel Convention.

Article 26 – Signature

The Protocol shall be open for signature by States and by regional economic integration organizations Parties to the Basel Convention in Berne at the Federal Department of Foreign Affairs of Switzerland from 6 to 17 March 2000 and at United Nations Headquarters in New York from l April 2000 to 10 December 2000.

Article 27 – Ratification, acceptance, formal confirmation or approval

1. The Protocol shall be subject to ratification, acceptance or approval by States and to formal confirmation or approval by regional economic integration organizations. Instruments of ratification, acceptance, formal confirmation, or approval shall be deposited with the Depositary.
2. Any organization referred to in paragraph l of this Article which becomes a Contracting Party without any of its member States being a Contracting Party shall be bound by all the obligations under the Protocol. In the case of such organizations, one or more of whose member States is a Contracting Party, the organization and its member States shall decide on their respective responsibilities for the performance of their obligations under the Protocol. In such cases, the organization and the member States shall not be entitled to exercise rights under the Protocol concurrently.
3. In their instruments of formal confirmation or approval, the organizations referred to in paragraph l of this Article shall declare the extent of their competence with respect to the matters governed by the Protocol. These organizations shall also inform the Depositary, who will inform the Contracting Parties, of any substantial modification in the extent of their competence.

Article 28 – Accession

1. The Protocol shall be open for accession by any States and by any regional economic integration organization Party to the Basel Convention which has not signed the Protocol. The instruments of accession shall be deposited with the Depositary.
2. In their instruments of accession, the organizations referred to in paragraph 1 of this Article shall declare the extent of their competence with respect to the matters governed by the Protocol. These organizations shall also inform the Depositary of any substantial modification in the extent of their competence.
3. The provisions of Article 27, paragraph 2, shall apply to regional economic integration organizations which accede to the Protocol.

Article 29 – Entry into force

1. The Protocol shall enter into force on the ninetieth day after the date of deposit of the twentieth instrument of ratification, acceptance, formal confirmation, approval or accession.
2. For each State or regional economic integration organization which ratifies, accepts, approves or formally confirms the Protocol or accedes thereto after the date of the deposit of the twentieth instrument of ratification, acceptance, approval, formal confirmation or accession, it shall enter into force on the ninetieth day after the date of deposit by such State or regional economic integration organization of its instrument of ratification, acceptance, approval, formal confirmation or accession.
3. For the purpose of paragraphs 1 and 2 of this Article, any instrument deposited by a regional eco-

nomic integration organization shall not be counted as additional to those deposited by member States of such organization.

Article 30 – Reservations and declarations

1. No reservation or exception may be made to the Protocol. For the purposes of the Protocol, notifications according to Article 3, paragraph l, Article 3, paragraph 6, or Article 14, paragraph 5, shall not be regarded as reservations or exceptions.
2. Paragraph 1 of this Article does not preclude a State or a regional economic integration organization, when signing, ratifying, accepting, approving, formally confirming or acceding to the Protocol, from making declarations or statements, however phrased or named, with a view, inter alia, to the harmonization of its laws and regulations with the provisions of the Protocol, provided that such declarations or statements do not purport to exclude or to modify the legal effects of the provisions of the Protocol in their application to that State or that organization.

Article 31 – Withdrawal

1. At any time after three years from the date on which the Protocol has entered into force for a Contracting Party, that Contracting Party may withdraw from the Protocol by giving written notification to the Depositary.
2. Withdrawal shall be effective one year from receipt of notification by the Depositary, or on such later date as may be specified in the notification.

Article 32 – Depositary

The Secretary-General of the United Nations shall be the Depositary of the Protocol.

Article 33 – Authentic texts

The original Arabic, Chinese, English, French, Russian and Spanish texts of the Protocol are equally authentic.

Annex A – LIST OF STATES OF TRANSIT AS REFERRED TO IN ARTICLE 3, SUBPARAGRAPH 3 (d)

1. Antigua and Barbuda
2. Bahamas
3. Bahrain
4. Barbados
5. Cape Verde
6. Comoros
7. Cook Islands
8. Cuba
9. Cyprus
10. Dominica
11. Oominican Republic
12. Fiji
13. Grenada
14. Haiti
15. Jamaica
16. Kiribati
17. Maldives
18. Malta
19. Marshall Islands
20. Mauritius
21. Micronesia (Federated States of)
22. Nauru
23. Netherlands, on behalf of Aruba and the Netherlands Antilles
24. New Zealand, on behalf of Tokelau
25. Niue
26. Palau
27. Papua New Guinea
28. Samoa
29. Sao Tome and Principe
30. Seychelles
31. Singapore
32. Solomon Islands
33. St. Lucia
34. St. Kitts and Nevis
35. St. Vincent and the Grenadines
36. Tonga
37. Trinidad and Tobago
38. Tuvalu
39. Vanuatu

Annex B – FINANCIAL LIMITS

1. Financial limits for the liability under Article 4 of the Protocol shall be determined by domestic law.
2. The limits of liability shall:
   (a) For the notifier, exporter or importer, for any one incident, be not less than:
      (i) l million units of account for shipments up to and including 5 tonnes;
      (ii) 2 million units of account for shipments exceeding 5 tonnes, up to and including 25 tonnes;
      (iii) 4 million units of account for shipments exceeding 25 tonnes, up to and including 50 tonnes;
      (iv) 6 million units of account for shipments exceeding 50 tonnes, up to and including 1,000 tonnes;
      (v) 10 million units of account for shipments exceeding 1,000 tonnes, up to and including 10,000 tonnes;
      (vi) Plus an additional 1,000 units of account for each additional tonne up to a maximum of 30 million units of account;
   (b) For the disposer, for any one incident, be not less than 2 million units of account for any one incident.
3. The amounts referred to in paragraph 2 shall be reviewed by the Contracting Parties on a regular basis taking into account, inter alia, the potential risks posed to the environment by the movement of hazardous wastes and other wastes and their disposal, recycling, and the nature, quantity and hazardous properties of the wastes.

3.3. ILC Draft Principles on the Allocation of Loss in the Case of Transboundary Harm Arising out of Hazardous Activities 2006

Draft Principles on the Allocation of Loss in the Case of Transboundary Harm Arising Out of Hazardous Activities, 11 August 2006, UN Doc. A/61/10

The General Assembly,

Reaffirming Principles 13 and 16 of the Rio Declaration on Environment and Development,

Recalling the Draft articles on the Prevention of Transboundary Harm from Hazardous Activities,

Aware that incidents involving hazardous activities may occur despite compliance by the relevant State with its obligations concerning prevention of transboundary harm from hazardous activities,

Noting that as a result of such incidents other States and/or their nationals may suffer harm and serious loss,

Emphasizing that appropriate and effective measures should be in place to ensure that those natural and legal persons, including States, that incur harm and loss as a result of such incidents are able to obtain prompt and adequate compensation,

Concerned that prompt and effective response measures should be taken to minimize the harm and loss which may result from such incidents,

Noting that States are responsible for infringements of their obligations of prevention under international law,

Recalling the significance of existing international agreements covering specific categories of hazardous activities and stressing the importance of the conclusion of further such agreements,

Desiring to contribute to the development of international law in this field, …

Principle 1 – Scope of application

The present draft principles apply to transboundary damage caused by hazardous activities not prohibited by international law.

Principle 2 – Use of terms

For the purposes of the present draft principles:

(a) "damage" means significant damage caused to persons, property or the environment; and includes:
   (i) loss of life or personal injury;
   (ii) loss of, or damage to, property, including property which forms part of the cultural heritage;
   (iii) loss or damage by impairment of the environment;
   (iv) the costs of reasonable measures of reinstatement of the property, or environment, including natural resources;
   (v) the costs of reasonable response measures;

(b) "environment" includes natural resources, both abiotic and biotic, such as air, water, soil, fauna and flora and the interaction between the same factors, and the characteristic aspects of the landscape;

(c) "hazardous activity" means an activity which involves a risk of causing significant harm;

(d) "State of origin" means the State in the territory or otherwise under the jurisdiction or control of which the hazardous activity is carried out;

(e) "transboundary damage" means damage caused to persons, property or the environment in the territory or in other places under the jurisdiction or control of a State other than the State of origin;

(f) "victim" means any natural or legal person or State that suffers damage;

(g) "operator" means any person in command or control of the activity at the time the incident causing transboundary damage occurs.

Principle 3 – Purposes

The purposes of the present draft principles are:

(a) to ensure prompt and adequate compensation to victims of transboundary damage; and

(b) to preserve and protect the environment in the event of transboundary damage, especially with respect to mitigation of damage to the environment and its restoration or reinstatement.

Principle 4 – Prompt and adequate compensation

1. Each State should take all necessary measures to ensure that prompt and adequate compensation is available for victims of transboundary damage caused by hazardous activities located within its territory or otherwise under its jurisdiction or control.
2. These measures should include the imposition of liability on the operator or, where appropriate, other person or entity. Such liability should not require proof of fault. Any conditions, limitations or exceptions to such liability shall be consistent with draft principle 3.
3. These measures should also include the requirement on the operator or, where appropriate, other person or entity, to establish and maintain financial security such as insurance, bonds or other financial guarantees to cover claims of compensation.
4. In appropriate cases, these measures should include the requirement for the establishment of industry-wide funds at the national level.

5. In the event that the measures under the preceding paragraphs are insufficient to provide adequate compensation, the State of origin should also ensure that additional financial resources are made available.

Principle 5 – Response measures

Upon the occurrence of an incident involving a hazardous activity which results or is likely to result in transboundary damage:

(a) the State of origin shall promptly notify all States affected or likely to be affected of the incident and the possible effects of the transboundary damage;

(b) the State of origin, with the appropriate involvement of the operator, shall ensure that appropriate response measures are taken and should, for this purpose, rely upon the best available scientific data and technology;

(c) the State of origin, as appropriate, should also consult with and seek the cooperation of all States affected or likely to be affected to mitigate the effects of transboundary damage and if possible eliminate them;

(d) the States affected or likely to be affected by the transboundary damage shall take all feasible measures to mitigate and if possible to eliminate the effects of such damage;

(e) the States concerned should, where appropriate, seek the assistance of competent international organizations and other States on mutually acceptable terms and conditions.

Principle 6 – International and domestic remedies

1. States shall provide their domestic judicial and administrative bodies with the necessary jurisdiction and competence and ensure that these bodies have prompt, adequate and effective remedies available in the event of transboundary damage caused by hazardous activities located within their territory or otherwise under their jurisdiction or control.
2. Victims of transboundary damage should have access to remedies in the State of origin that are no less prompt, adequate and effective than those available to victims that suffer damage, from the same incident, within the territory of that State.
3. Paragraphs 1 and 2 are without prejudice to the right of the victims to seek remedies other than those available in the State of origin.
4. States may provide for recourse to international claims settlement procedures that are expeditious and involve minimal expenses.
5. States should guarantee appropriate access to information relevant for the pursuance of remedies, including claims for compensation.

Principle 7 – Development of specific international regimes

1. Where, in respect of particular categories of hazardous activities, specific global, regional or bilateral agreements would provide effective arrangements concerning compensation, response measures and international and domestic remedies, all efforts should be made to conclude such specific agreements.
2. Such agreements should, as appropriate, include arrangements for industry and/or State funds to provide supplementary compensation in the event that the financial resources of the operator, including financial security measures, are insufficient to cover the damage suffered as a result of an incident. Any such funds may be designed to supplement or replace national industry-based funds.

Principle 8 – Implementation

1. Each State should adopt the necessary legislative, regulatory and administrative measures to implement the present draft principles.
2. The present draft principles and the measures adopted to implement them shall be applied without any discrimination such as that based on nationality, domicile or residence.
3. States should cooperate with each other to implement the present draft principles.

4.1. LRTAP Convention 1979

UNECE Convention on Long-range Transboundary Air Pollution, Geneva, 13 November 1979, 1302 UNTS 217

The Parties to the present Convention,

Determined to promote relations and cooperation in the field of environmental protection,

Aware of the significance of the activities of the United Nations Economic Commission for Europe in strengthening such relations and cooperation, particularly in the field of air pollution including long-range transport of air pollutants,

Recognizing the contribution of the Economic Commission for Europe to the multilateral implementation of the pertinent provisions of the Final Act of the Conference on Security and Cooperation in Europe,

Cognizant of the references in the chapter on environment of the Final Act of the Conference on Security and Cooperation in Europe calling for cooperation to control air pollution and its effects, including long-range transport of air pollutants, and to the development through international cooperation of an extensive programme for the monitoring and evaluation of long-range transport of air pollutants, starting with sulphur dioxide and with possible extension to other pollutants,

Considering the pertinent provisions of the Declaration of the United Nations Conference on the Human Environment, and in particular principle 21, which expresses the common conviction that States have, in accordance with the Charter of the United Nations and the principles of international law, the sovereign right to exploit their own resources pursuant to their own environmental policies, and the responsibility to ensure that activities within their jurisdiction or control do not cause damage to the environment of other States or of areas beyond the limits of national jurisdiction, Recognizing the existence of possible adverse effects, in the short and long term, of air pollution including transboundary air pollution,

Concerned that a rise in the level of emissions of air pollutants within the region as forecast may increase such adverse effects,

Recognizing the need to study the implications of the long-range transport of air pollutants and the need to seek solutions for the problems identified,

Affirming their willingness to reinforce active international cooperation to develop appropriate national policies and by means of exchange of information, consultation, research and monitoring to co-ordinate national action for combating air pollution including long-range transboundary air pollution,

Have agreed as follows:

Article 1: DEFINITIONS

For the purposes of the present Convention:

(a) "Air Pollution" means the introduction by man, directly or indirectly, of substances or energy into the air resulting in deleterious effects of such a nature as to endanger human health, harm living resources and ecosystems and material property and impair or interfere with amenities and other legitimate uses of the environment, and "air pollutants" shall be construed accordingly;

(b) "Long-range transboundary air pollution" means air pollution whose physical origin is situated wholly or in part within the area under the national jurisdiction of one State and which has adverse effects in the area under the jurisdiction of another State at such a distance that it is not generally possible to distinguish the contribution of individual emission sources or groups of sources.

Article 2: FUNDAMENTAL PRINCIPLES

The Contracting Parties, taking due account of the facts and problems involved, are determined to protect man and his environment against air pollution and shall endeavour to limit and, as far as possible, gradually reduce and prevent air pollution including long-range transboundary air pollution.

Article 3

The Contracting Parties, within the framework of the present Convention, shall by means of exchanges of information, consultation, research and monitoring, develop without undue delay policies and strategies which shall serve as a means of combating the discharge of air pollutants, taking into account efforts already made at national and international levels.

Article 4

The Contracting Parties shall exchange information on and review their policies, scientific activities and technical measures aimed at combating, as far as possible, the discharge of air pollutants which may have adverse effects, thereby contributing to the reduction of air pollution including long- range transboundary air pollution.

Article 5

Consultations shall be held, upon request, at an early stage between, on the one hand, Contracting Parties which are actually affected by or exposed to a significant risk of long-range transboundary air pollution and, on the other hand, Contracting Parties within which and subject to whose jurisdiction a significant contribution to long-range transboundary air pollution originates, or could originate, in connection with activities carried on or contemplated therein.

Article 6: AIR QUALITY MANAGEMENT

Taking into account articles 2 to 5, the ongoing research, exchange of information and monitoring and the results thereof, the cost and effectiveness of local and other remedies and, in order to combat air pollution, in particular that originating from new or rebuilt installations, each Contracting Party undertakes to develop the best policies and strategies including air quality management systems and, as part of them, control measures compatible with balanced development, in particular by using the best available technology which is economically feasible and low- and non-waste technology.

Article 7: RESEARCH AND DEVELOPMENT

The Contracting Parties, as appropriate to their needs, shall initiate and co-operate in the conduct of research into and/or development of:

(a) Existing and proposed technologies for reducing emissions of sulphur compounds and other major air pollutants, including technical and economic feasibility, and environmental consequences;

(b) Instrumentation and other techniques for monitoring and measuring emission rates and ambient concentrations of air pollutants;

(c) Improved models for a better understanding of the transmission of long-range transboundary air pollutants;

(d) The effects of sulphur compounds and other major air pollutants on human health and the environment, including agriculture, forestry, materials, aquatic and other natural ecosystems and visibility, with a view to establishing a scientific basis for dose/effect relationships designed to protect the environment;

(e) The economic, social and environmental assessment of alternative measures for attaining environmental objectives including the reduction of long-range transboundary air pollution;

(f) Education and training programmes related to the environmental aspects of pollution by sulphur compounds and other major air pollutants.

Article 8: EXCHANGE OF INFORMATION

The Contracting Parties, within the framework of the Executive Body referred to in article 10 and bilaterally, shall, in their common interests, exchange available information on:

(a) Data on emissions at periods of time to be agreed upon, of agreed air pollutants, starting with sulphur dioxide, coming from grid-units of agreed size; or on the fluxes of agreed air pollutants, starting with sulphur dioxide, across national borders, at distances and at periods of time to be agreed upon;

(b) Major changes in national policies and in general industrial development, and their potential impact, which would be likely to cause significant changes in long-range transboundary air pollution;

(c) Control technologies for reducing air pollution relevant to long-range transboundary air pollution;

(d) The projected cost of the emission control of sulphur compounds and other major air pollutants on a national scale;

(e) Meteorological and physico-chemical data relating to the processes during transmission;

(f) Physico-chemical and biological data relating to the effects of long-range transboundary air pollution and the extent of the damage[1] which these data indicate can be attributed to long-range transboundary air pollution;

(g) National, sub-regional and regional policies and strategies for the control of sulphur compounds and other major air pollutants.

Article 9: IMPLEMENTATION AND FURTHER DEVELOPMENT OF THE COOPERATIVE PROGRAMME FOR THE MONITORING AND EVALUATION OF THE LONG-RANGE TRANSMISSION OF AIR POLLUTANTS IN EUROPE

The Contracting Parties stress the need for the implementation of the existing "Cooperative programme for the monitoring and evaluation of the long-range transmission of air pollutants in Europe" (hereinafter referred to as EMEP) and, with regard to the further development of this programme, agree to emphasize:

(a) The desirability of Contracting Parties joining in and fully implementing EMEP which, as a first step, is based on the monitoring of sulphur dioxide and related substances;

(b) The need to use comparable or standardized procedures for monitoring whenever possible;

(c) The desirability of basing the monitoring programme on the framework of both national and international programmes. The establishment of monitoring stations and the collection of data shall be carried out under the national jurisdiction of the country in which the monitoring stations are located;

(d) The desirability of establishing a framework for a cooperative environmental monitoring programme, based on and taking into account present and future national, sub-regional, regional and other international programmes;

(e) The need to exchange data on emissions at periods of time to be agreed upon, of agreed air pollutants, starting with sulphur dioxide, coming from grid-units of agreed size; or on the fluxes of agreed air pollutants, starting with sulphur dioxide, across national borders, at distances and at periods of time to be agreed upon. The method, including the model, used to determine the fluxes, as well as the method, including the model used to determine the transmission of air pollutants based on the emissions per grid-unit, shall be made available and periodically reviewed, in order to improve the methods and the models;

(f) Their willingness to continue the exchange and periodic updating of national data on total emissions of agreed air pollutants, starting with sulphur dioxide;

(g) the need to provide meteorological and physico-chemical data relating to processes during transmission;

1 The present Convention does not contain a rule on State liability as to damage.

(h) the need to monitor chemical components in other media such as water, soil and vegetation, as well as a similar monitoring programme to record effects on health and environment;

(i) the desirability of extending the national EMEP networks to make them operational for control and surveillance purposes.

Article 10: EXECUTIVE BODY

1. The representatives of the Contracting Parties shall, within the framework of the Senior Advisers to ECE Governments on Environmental Problems, constitute the Executive Body of the present Convention, and shall meet at least annually in that capacity.
2. The Executive Body shall:
   (a) Review the implementation of the present Convention;
   (b) Establish, as appropriate, working groups to consider matters related to the implementation and development of the present Convention and to this end to prepare appropriate studies and other documentation and to submit recommendations to be considered by the Executive Body;
   (c) Fulfil such other functions as may be appropriate under the provisions of the present Convention.
3. The Executive Body shall utilize the Steering Body for the EMEP to play an integral part in the operation of the present Convention, in particular with regard to data collection and scientific cooperation.
4. The Executive Body, in discharging its functions, shall, when it deems appropriate, also make use of information from other relevant international organizations.

Article 11: SECRETARIAT

The Executive Secretary of the Economic Commission for Europe shall carry out, for the Executive Body, the following secretariat functions:

(a) To convene and prepare the meetings of the Executive Body;

(b) To transmit to the Contracting Parties reports and other information received in accordance with the provisions of the present Convention;

(c) To discharge the functions assigned by the Executive Body.

Article 12: AMENDMENTS TO THE CONVENTION

1. Any Contracting Party may propose amendments to the present Convention.
2. The text of proposed amendments shall be submitted in writing to the Executive Secretary of the Economic Commission for Europe, who shall communicate them to all Contracting Parties. The Executive Body shall discuss proposed amendments at its next annual meeting provided that such proposals have been circulated by the Executive Secretary of the Economic Commission for Europe to the Contracting Parties at least ninety days in advance.
3. An amendment to the present Convention shall be adopted by consensus of the representatives of the Contracting Parties, and shall enter into force for the Contracting Parties which have accepted it on the ninetieth day after the date on which two-thirds of the Contracting Parties have deposited their instruments of acceptance with the depositary. Thereafter, the amendment shall enter into force for any other Contracting Party on the ninetieth day after the date on which that Contracting Party deposits its instrument of acceptance of the amendment.

Article 13: SETTLEMENT OF DISPUTES

If a dispute arises between two or more Contracting Parties to the present Convention as to the interpretation or application of the Convention, they shall seek a solution by negotiation or by any other method of dispute settlement acceptable to the parties to the dispute.

Article 14: SIGNATURE

1. The present Convention shall be open for signature at the United Nations Office at Geneva from 13 to 16 November 1979 on the occasion of the High-level Meeting within the framework of the Economic Commission for Europe on the Protection of the Environment, by the member States of the Economic Commission for Europe as well as States having consultative status with the Economic Commission for Europe, pursuant to paragraph 8 of Economic and Social Council resolution 36 (IV) of 28 March 1947, and by regional economic integration organizations, constituted by sovereign States members of the Economic Commission for Europe, which have competence in respect of the negotiation, conclusion and application of international agreements in matters covered by the present Convention.
2. In matters within their competence, such regional economic integration organizations shall, on their own behalf, exercise the rights and fulfil the responsibilities which the present Convention attributes to their member States. In such cases, the member States of these organizations shall not be entitled to exercise such rights individually.

Article 15: RATIFICATION, ACCEPTANCE, APPROVAL AND ACCESSION

1. The present Convention shall be subject to ratification, acceptance or approval.
2. The present Convention shall be open for accession as from 17 November 1979 by the States and organizations referred to in article 14, paragraph 1.
3. The instruments of ratification, acceptance, approval or accession shall be deposited with the Secretary-General of the United Nations, who will perform the functions of the depositary.

Article 16: ENTRY INTO FORCE

1. The present Convention shall enter into force on the ninetieth day after the date of deposit of the

twenty-fourth instrument of ratification, acceptance, approval or accession.

2. For each Contracting Party which ratifies, accepts or approves the present Convention or accedes thereto after the deposit of the twenty-fourth instrument of ratification, acceptance, approval or accession, the Convention shall enter into force on the ninetieth day after the date of deposit by such Contracting Party of its instrument of ratification, acceptance, approval or accession.

Article 17: WITHDRAWAL

At any time after five years from the date on which the present Convention has come into force with respect to a Contracting Party, that Contracting Party may withdraw from the Convention by giving written notification to the depositary. Any such withdrawal shall take effect on the ninetieth day after the date of its receipt by the depositary.

Article 18: AUTHENTIC TEXTS

The original of the present Convention, of which the English, French and Russian texts are equally authentic, shall be deposited with the Secretary-General of the United Nations.

IN WITNESS WHEREOF the undersigned, being duly authorized thereto, have signed the present Convention.

DONE at Geneva, this thirteenth day of November, one thousand nine hundred and seventy-nine.

4.2. Oslo Protocol 1994

Protocol to the 1979 Convention on Long-Range Transboundary Air Pollution on Further Reduction of Sulphur Emissions, Oslo, 14 June 1994, 2030 UNTS 122

The Parties,

Determined to implement the Convention on Long-range Transboundary Air Pollution,

Concerned that emissions of sulphur and other air pollutants continue to be transported across international boundaries and, in exposed parts of Europe and North America, are causing widespread damage to natural resources of vital environmental and economic importance, such as forests, soils and waters, and to materials, including historic monuments, and, under certain circumstances, have harmful effects on human health,

Resolved to take precautionary measures to anticipate, prevent or minimize emissions of air pollutants and mitigate their adverse effects,

Convinced that where there are threats of serious or irreversible damage, lack of full scientific certainty should not be used as a reason for postponing such measures, taking into account that such precautionary measures to deal with emissions of air pollutants should be cost-effective,

Mindful that measures to control emissions of sulphur and other air pollutants would also contribute to the protection of the sensitive Arctic environment,

Considering that the predominant sources of air pollution contributing to the acidification of the environment are the combustion of fossil fuels for energy production, and the main technological processes in various industrial sectors, as well as transport, which lead to emissions of sulphur, nitrogen oxides, and other pollutants,

Conscious of the need for a cost-effective regional approach to combating air pollution that takes account of the variations in effects and abatement costs between countries,

Desiring to take further and more effective action to control and reduce sulphur emissions,

Cognizant that any sulphur control policy, however cost-effective it may be at the regional level, will result in a relatively heavy economic burden on countries with economies that are in transition to a market economy,

Bearing in mind that measures taken to reduce sulphur emissions should not constitute a means of arbitrary or unjustifiable discrimination or a disguised restriction on international competition and trade,

Taking into consideration existing scientific and technical data on emissions, atmospheric processes and effects on the environment of sulphur oxides, as well as on abatement costs,

Aware that, in addition to emissions of sulphur, emissions of nitrogen oxides and of ammonia are also causing acidification of the environment,

Noting that under the United Nations Framework Convention on Climate Change, adopted in New York on 9 May 1992, there is agreement to establish national policies and take corresponding measures to combat climate change, which can be expected to lead to reductions of sulphur emissions,

Affirming the need to ensure environmentally sound and sustainable development,

Recognizing the need to continue scientific and technical cooperation to elaborate further the approach based on critical loads and critical levels, including efforts to assess several air pollutants and various effects on the environment, materials and human health,

Underlining that scientific and technical knowledge is developing and that it will be necessary to take such developments into account when reviewing the adequacy of the obligations entered into under the present Protocol and deciding on further action,

Acknowledging the Protocol on the Reduction of Sulphur Emissions or Their Transboundary Fluxes by at least 30 per cent, adopted in Helsinki on 8 July 1985, and the measures already taken by many countries which have had the effect of reducing sulphur emissions,

Have agreed as follows:

Article 1 – DEFINITIONS

For the purposes of the present Protocol,

1. "Convention" means the Convention on Long-range Transboundary Air Pollution, adopted in Geneva mon 13 November 1979;
2. "EMEP" means the Cooperative Programme for Monitoring and Evaluation of the Long-range Transmission of Air Pollutants in Europe;
3. "Executive Body" means the Executive Body for the Convention constituted under article 10, paragraph 1, of the Convention;
4. "Commission" means the United Nations Economic Commission for Europe;
5. "Parties" means, unless the context otherwise requires, the Parties to the present Protocol;
6. "Geographical scope of EMEP" means the area defined in article 1, paragraph 4, of the Protocol to the 1979 Convention on Long-range Transboundary Air Pollution on Long-term Financing of the Cooperative Programme for Monitoring and Evaluation of the Long-range Transmission of Air Pollutants in Europe (EMEP), adopted in Geneva on 28 September 1984;
7. "SOMA" means a sulphur oxides management area designated in annex III under the conditions laid down in article 2, paragraph 3;

8. "Critical load" means a quantitative estimate of an exposure to one or more pollutants below which significant harmful effects on specified sensitive elements of the environment do not occur, according to present knowledge;
9. "Critical levels" means the concentration of pollutants in the atmosphere above which direct adverse effects on receptors, such as human beings, plants, ecosystems or materials, may occur, according to present knowledge;
10. "Critical sulphur deposition" means a quantitative estimate of the exposure to oxidized sulphur compounds, taking into account the effects of base cation uptake and base cation deposition, below which significant harmful effects on specified sensitive elements of the environment do not occur, according to present knowledge;
11. "Emission" means the discharge of substances into the atmosphere;
12. "Sulphur emissions" means all emissions of sulphur compounds expressed as kilotonnes of sulphur dioxide (kt SO_2) to the atmosphere originating from anthropogenic sources excluding from ships in international traffic outside territorial waters;
13. "Fuel" means any solid, liquid or gaseous combustible material with the exception of domestic refuse and toxic or dangerous waste;
14. "Stationary combustion source" means any technical apparatus or group of technical apparatus that is co-located on a common site and is or could be discharging waste gases through a common stack, in which fuels are oxidized in order to use the heat generated;
15. "Major new stationary combustion source" means any stationary combustion source the construction or substantial modification of which is authorized after 31 December 1995 and the thermal input of which, when operating at rated capacity, is at least 50 MW_{th}. It is a matter for the competent national authorities to decide whether a modification is substantial or not, taking into account such factors as the environmental benefits of the modification;
16. "Major existing stationary combustion source" means any existing stationary combustion source the thermal input of which, when operating at rated capacity, is at least 50 MW_{th};
17. "Gas oil" means any petroleum product within HS 2710, or any petroleum product which, by reason of its distillation limits, falls within the category of middle distillates intended for use as fuel and of which at least 85 per cent by volume, including distillation losses, distils at 350° C;
18. "Emission limit value" means the permissible concentration of sulphur compounds expressed as sulphur dioxide in the waste gases from a stationary combustion source expressed in terms of mass per volume of the waste gases expressed in mg SO_2/Nm^3, assuming an oxygen content by volume in the waste gas of 3 per cent in the case of liquid and gaseous fuels and 6 per cent in the case of solid fuels;
19. "Emission limitation" means the permissible total quantity of sulphur compounds expressed as sulphur dioxide discharged from a combustion source or group of combustion sources located either on a common site or within a defined geographical area, expressed in kilotonnes per year;
20. "Desulphurization rate" means the ratio of the quantity of sulphur which is separated at the combustion source site over a given period to the quantity of sulphur contained in the fuel which is introduced into the combustion source facilities and which is used over the same period;
21. "Sulphur budget" means a matrix of calculated contributions to the deposition of oxidized sulphur compounds in receiving areas, originating from the emissions from specified areas.

Article 2 – BASIC OBLIGATIONS

1. The Parties shall control and reduce their sulphur emissions in order to protect human health and the environment from adverse effects, in particular acidifying effects, and to ensure, as far as possible, without entailing excessive costs, that depositions of oxidized sulphur compounds in the long term do not exceed critical loads for sulphur given, in annex I, as critical sulphur depositions, in accordance with present scientific knowledge.
2. As a first step, the Parties shall, as a minimum, reduce and maintain their annual sulphur emissions in accordance with the timing and levels specified in annex II.
3. In addition, any Party:
   (a) Whose total land area is greater than 2 million square kilometres;
   (b) Which has committed itself under paragraph 2 above to a national sulphur emission ceiling no greater than the lesser of its 1990 emissions or its obligation in the 1985 Helsinki Protocol on the Reduction of Sulphur Emissions or Their Transboundary Fluxes by at least 30 per cent, as indicated in annex II;
   (c) Whose annual sulphur emissions that contribute to acidification in areas under the jurisdiction of one or more other Parties originate only from within areas under its jurisdiction that are listed as SOMAs in annex III, and has presented documentation to this effect; and
   (d) Which has specified upon signature of, or accession to, the present Protocol its intention to act in accordance with this paragraph, shall, as a minimum, reduce and maintain its annual sulphur emissions in the area so listed in accordance with the timing and levels specified in annex II.
4. Furthermore, the Parties shall make use of the most effective measures for the reduction of sulphur emissions, appropriate in their particular circumstances, for new and existing sources, which include, inter alia:
   - Measures to increase energy efficiency;
   - Measures to increase the use of renewable energy;

- Measures to reduce the sulphur content of particular fuels and to encourage the use of fuel with a low sulphur content, including the combined use of high-sulphur with low-sulphur or sulphur-free fuel;
- Measures to apply best available control technologies not entailing excessive cost, using the guidance in annex IV.

5. Each Party, except those Parties subject to the United States/Canada Air Quality Agreement of 1991, shall as a minimum:

   (a) Apply emission limit values at least as stringent as those specified in annex V to all major new stationary combustion sources;

   (b) No later than 1 July 2004 apply, as far as possible without entailing excessive costs, emission limit values at least as stringent as those specified in annex V to those major existing stationary combustion sources the thermal input of which is above 500 MW_{th} taking into account the remaining lifetime of a plant, calculated from the date of entry into force of the present Protocol, or apply equivalent emission limitations or other appropriate provisions, provided that these achieve the sulphur emission ceilings specified in annex II and, subsequently, further approach the critical loads as given in annex I; and no later than 1 July 2004 apply emission limit values or emission limitations to those major existing stationary combustion sources the thermal input of which is between 50 and 500 MW_{th} using annex V as guidance;

   (c) No later than two years after the date of entry into force of the present Protocol apply national standards for the sulphur content of gas oil at least as stringent as those specified in annex V. In cases where the supply of gas oil cannot otherwise be ensured, a State may extend the time period given in this subparagraph to a period of to ten years. In this case it shall specify, in a declaration to be deposited together with the instrument of ratification, acceptance, approval or accession, its intention to extend the time period.

6. The Parties may, in addition, apply economic instruments to encourage the adoption of cost-effective approaches to the reduction of sulphur emissions.

7. The Parties to this Protocol may, at a session of the Executive Body, in accordance with rules and conditions which the Executive Body shall elaborate and adopt, decide whether two or more Parties may jointly implement the obligations set out in annex II. These rules and conditions shall ensure the fulfilment of the obligations set out in paragraph 2 above and also promote the achievement of the environmental objectives set out in paragraph 1 above.

8. The Parties shall, subject to the outcome of the first review provided for under article 8 and no later than one year after the completion of that review, commence negotiations on further obligations to reduce emissions.

Article 3 – EXCHANGE OF TECHNOLOGY

1. The Parties shall, consistent with their national laws, regulations and practices, facilitate the exchange of technologies and techniques, including those that increase energy efficiency, the use of renewable energy and the processing of low-sulphur fuels, to reduce sulphur emissions, particularly through the promotion of:

   (a) The commercial exchange of available technology;

   (b) Direct industrial contacts and cooperation, including joint ventures;

   (c) The exchange of information and experience;

   (d) The provision of technical assistance.

2. In promoting the activities specified in paragraph 1 above, the Parties shall create favourable conditions by facilitating contacts and cooperation among appropriate organizations and individuals in the private and public sectors that are capable of providing technology, design and engineering services, equipment or finance.

3. The Parties shall, no later than six months after the date of entry into force of the present Protocol, commence consideration of procedures to create more favourable conditions for the exchange of technology to reduce sulphur emissions.

Article 4 – NATIONAL STRATEGIES, POLICIES, PROGRAMMES, MEASURES AND INFORMATION

1. Each Party shall, in order to implement its obligations under article 2:

   (a) Adopt national strategies, policies and programmes, no later than six months after the present Protocol enters into force for it; and

   (b) Take and apply national measures to control and reduce its sulphur emissions.

2. Each Party shall collect and maintain information on:

   (a) Actual levels of sulphur emissions, and of ambient concentrations and depositions of oxidized sulphur and other acidifying compounds, taking into account, for those Parties within the geographical scope of EMEP, the work plan of EMEP; and

   (b) The effects of depositions of oxidized sulphur and other acidifying compounds.

Article 5 – REPORTING

1. Each Party shall report, through the Executive Secretary of the Commission, to the Executive Body, on a periodic basis as determined by the Executive Body, information on:

   (a) The implementation of national strategies, policies, programmes and measures referred to in article 4, paragraph 1;

   (b) The levels of national annual sulphur emissions, in accordance with guidelines adopted by the Executive Body, containing emission data for all relevant source categories; and

(c) The implementation of other obligations that it has entered into under the present Protocol, in conformity with a decision regarding format and content to be adopted by the Parties at a session of the Executive Body. The terms of this decision shall be reviewed as necessary to identify any additional elements regarding the format and/or content of the information that are to be included in the reports.

2. Each Party within the geographical scope of EMEP shall report, through the Executive Secretary of the Commission, to EMEP, on a periodic basis to be determined by the Steering Body of EMEP and approved by the Parties at a session of the Executive Body, information on the levels of sulphur emissions with temporal and spatial resolution as specified by the Steering Body of EMEP.

3. In good time before each annual session of the Executive Body, EMEP shall provide information on:

   (a) Ambient concentrations and deposition of oxidized sulphur compounds; and

   (b) Calculations of sulphur budgets.

   Parties in areas outside the geographical scope of EMEP shall make available similar information if requested to do so by the Executive Body.

4. The Executive Body shall, in accordance with article 10, paragraph 2 (b), of the Convention, arrange for the preparation of information on the effects of depositions of oxidized sulphur and other acidifying compounds.

5. The Parties shall, at sessions of the Executive Body, arrange for the preparation, at regular intervals, of revised information on calculated and internationally optimized allocations of emission reductions for the States within the geographical scope of EMEP, with integrated assessment models, with a view to reducing further, for the purposes of article 2, paragraph 1, of the present Protocol, the difference between actual depositions of oxidized sulphur compounds and critical load values.

Article 6 – RESEARCH, DEVELOPMENT AND MONITORING

The Parties shall encourage research, development, monitoring and cooperation related to:

(a) The international harmonization of methods for the establishment of critical loads and critical levels and the elaboration of procedures for such harmonization;

(b) The improvement of monitoring techniques and systems and of the modelling of transport, concentrations and deposition of sulphur compounds;

(c) Strategies for the further reduction of sulphur emissions based on critical loads and critical levels as well as on technical developments, and the improvement of integrated assessment modelling to calculate internationally optimized allocations of emission reductions taking into account an equitable distribution of abatement costs;

(d) The understanding of the wider effects of sulphur emissions on human health, the environment, in particular acidification, and materials, including historic and cultural monuments, taking into account the relationship between sulphur oxides, nitrogen oxides, ammonia, volatile organic compounds and tropospheric ozone;

(e) Emission abatement technologies, and technologies and techniques to enhance energy efficiency, energy conservation and the use of renewable energy;

(f) The economic evaluation of benefits for the environment and human health resulting from the reduction of sulphur emissions.

Article 7 – COMPLIANCE

1. An Implementation Committee is hereby established to review the implementation of the present Protocol and compliance by the Parties with their obligations. It shall report to the Parties at sessions of the Executive Body and may make such recommendations to them as it considers appropriate.

2. Upon consideration of a report, and any recommendations, of the Implementation Committee, the Parties, taking into account the circumstances of a matter and in accordance with Convention practice, may decide upon and call for action to bring about full compliance with the present Protocol, including measures to assist a Party's compliance with the Protocol, and to further the objectives of the Protocol.

3. The Parties shall, at the first session of the Executive Body after the entry into force of the present Protocol, adopt a decision that sets out the structure and functions of the Implementation Committee as well as procedures for its review of compliance.

4. The application of the compliance procedure shall be without prejudice to the provisions of article 9 of the present Protocol.

Article 8 – REVIEWS BY THE PARTIES AT SESSIONS OF THE EXECUTIVE BODY

1. The Parties shall, at sessions of the Executive Body, pursuant to article 10, paragraph 2 (a), of the Convention, review the information supplied by the Parties and EMEP, the data on the effects of depositions of sulphur and other acidifying compounds and the reports of the Implementation Committee referred to in article 7, paragraph 1, of the present Protocol.

2. (a) The Parties shall, at sessions of the Executive Body, keep under review the obligations set out in the present Protocol, including:

      (i) Their obligations in relation to their calculated and internationally optimized allocations of emission reductions referred to in article 5, paragraph 5; and

      (ii) The adequacy of the obligations and the progress made towards the achievement of the objectives of the present Protocol;

   (b) Reviews shall take into account the best available scientific information on acidification, including assessments of critical loads, technological developments, changing economic conditions and the fulfilment of the obligations on emission levels;

(c) In the context of such reviews, any Party whose obligations on sulphur emission ceilings under annex II hereto do not conform to the calculated and internationally optimized allocations of emission reductions for that Party, required to reduce the difference between depositions of sulphur in 1990 and critical sulphur depositions within the geographical scope of EMEP by at least 60 per cent, shall make every effort to undertake revised obligations;

(d) The procedures, methods and timing for such reviews shall be specified by the Parties at a session of the Executive Body. The first such review shall be completed in 1997.

Article 9 – SETTLEMENT OF DISPUTES

1. In the event of a dispute between any two or more Parties concerning the interpretation or application of the present Protocol, the Parties concerned shall seek a settlement of the dispute through negotiation or any other peaceful means of their own choice. The Parties to the dispute shall inform the Executive Body of their dispute.

2. When ratifying, accepting, approving or acceding to the present Protocol, or at any time thereafter, a Party which is not a regional economic integration organization may declare in a written instrument submitted to the Depositary that, in respect of any dispute concerning the interpretation or application of the Protocol, it recognizes one or both of the following means of dispute settlement as compulsory ipso facto and without agreement, in relation to any Party accepting the same obligation:

   (a) Submission of the dispute to the International Court of Justice;

   (b) Arbitration in accordance with procedures to be adopted by the Parties at a session of the Executive Body as soon as practicable, in an annex on arbitration.

   A Party which is a regional economic integration organization may make a declaration with like effect in relation to arbitration in accordance with the procedures referred to in subparagraph (b) above.

3. A declaration made under paragraph 2 above shall remain in force until it expires in accordance with its terms or until three months after written notice of its revocation has been deposited with the Depositary.

4. A new declaration, a notice of revocation or the expiry of a declaration shall not in any way affect proceedings pending before the International Court of Justice or the arbitral tribunal, unless the Parties to the dispute agree otherwise.

5. Except in a case where the Parties to a dispute have accepted the same means of dispute settlement under paragraph 2, if after twelve months following notification by one Party to another that a dispute exists between them, the Parties concerned have not been able to settle their dispute through the means mentioned in paragraph 1 above, the dispute shall be submitted, at the request of any of the Parties to the dispute, to conciliation.

6. For the purpose of paragraph 5, a conciliation commission shall be created. The commission shall be composed of an equal number of members appointed by each Party concerned or, where Parties in conciliation share the same interest, by the group sharing that interest, and a chairman chosen jointly by the members so appointed. The commission shall render a recommendatory award, which the Parties shall consider in good faith.

Article 10 – ANNEXES

The annexes to the present Protocol shall form an integral part of the Protocol. Annexes I and IV are recommendatory in character.

Article 11 – AMENDMENTS AND ADJUSTMENTS

1. Any Party may propose amendments to the present Protocol. Any Party to the Convention may propose an adjustment to annex II to the present Protocol to add to it its name, together with emission levels, sulphur emission ceilings and percentage emission reductions.

2. Such proposed amendments and adjustments shall be submitted in writing to the Executive Secretary of the Commission, who shall communicate them to all Parties. The Parties shall discuss the proposed amendments and adjustments at the next session of the Executive Body, provided that those proposals have been circulated by the Executive Secretary to the Parties at least ninety days in advance.

3. Amendments to the present Protocol and to its annexes II, III and V shall be adopted by consensus of the Parties present at a session of the Executive Body, and shall enter into force for the Parties which have accepted them on the ninetieth day after the date on which two thirds of the Parties have deposited with the Depositary their instruments of acceptance thereof. Amendments shall enter into force for any other Party on the ninetieth day after the date on which that Party has deposited its instrument of acceptance thereof.

4. Amendments to the annexes to the present Protocol, other than to the annexes referred to in paragraph 3 above, shall be adopted by consensus of the Parties present at a session of the Executive Body. On the expiry of ninety days from the date of its communication by the Executive Secretary of the Commission, an amendment to any such annex shall become effective for those Parties which have not submitted to the Depositary a notification in accordance with the provisions of paragraph 5 below, provided that at least sixteen Parties have not submitted such a notification.

5. Any Party that is unable to approve an amendment to an annex, other than to an annex referred to in paragraph 3 above, shall so notify the Depositary in writing within ninety days from the date of the communication of its adoption. The Depositary shall without delay notify all Parties of any such notification received. A Party may at any time sub-

stitute an acceptance for its previous notification and, upon deposit of an instrument of acceptance with the Depositary, the amendment to such an annex shall become effective for that Party.

6. Adjustments to annex II shall be adopted by consensus of the Parties present at a session of the Executive Body and shall become effective for all Parties to the present Protocol on the ninetieth day following the date on which the Executive Secretary of the Commission notifies those Parties in writing of the adoption of the adjustment.

Article 12 – SIGNATURE

1. The present Protocol shall be open for signature at Oslo on 14 June 1994, then at United Nations Headquarters in New York until 12 December 1994 by States members of the Commission as well as States having consultative status with the Commission, pursuant to paragraph 8 of Economic and Social Council resolution 36 (IV) of 28 March 1947, and by regional economic integration organizations, constituted by sovereign States members of the Commission, which have competence in respect of the negotiation, conclusion and application of international agreements in matters covered by the Protocol, provided that the States and organizations concerned are Parties to the Convention and are listed in annex II.
2. In matters within their competence, such regional economic integration organizations shall, on their own behalf, exercise the rights and fulfil the responsibilities which the present Protocol attributes to their member States. In such cases, the member States of these organizations shall not be entitled to exercise such rights individually.

Article 13 – RATIFICATION, ACCEPTANCE, APPROVAL AND ACCESSION

1. The present Protocol shall be subject to ratification, acceptance or approval by Signatories.
2. The present Protocol shall be open for accession as from 12 December 1994 by the States and organizations that meet the requirements of article 12, paragraph 1.

Article 14 – DEPOSITARY

The instruments of ratification, acceptance, approval or accession shall be deposited with the Secretary-General of the United Nations, who will perform the functions of Depositary.

Article 15 – ENTRY INTO FORCE

1. The present Protocol shall enter into force on the ninetieth day following the date on which the sixteenth instrument of ratification, acceptance, approval or accession has been deposited with the Depositary.
2. For each State and organization referred to in article 12, paragraph 1, which ratifies, accepts or approves the present Protocol or accedes thereto after the deposit of the sixteenth instrument of ratification, acceptance, approval or accession, the Protocol shall enter into force on the ninetieth day following the date of deposit by such Party of its instrument of ratification, acceptance, approval or accession.

Article 16 – WITHDRAWAL

At any time after five years from the date on which the present Protocol has come into force with respect to a Party, that Party may withdraw from it by giving written notification to the Depositary. Any such withdrawal shall take effect on the ninetieth day following the date of its receipt by the Depositary, or on such later date as may be specified in the notification of the withdrawal.

Article 17 – AUTHENTIC TEXTS

The original of the present Protocol, of which the English, French and Russian texts are equally authentic, shall be deposited with the Secretary-General of the United Nations.

IN WITNESS WHEREOF the undersigned, being duly authorized thereto, have signed the present Protocol.

DONE at Oslo, this fourteenth day of June one thousand nine hundred and ninety-four.

Annex I – CRITICAL SULPHUR DEPOSITION

(5-percentile in centigrams of sulphur per square metre per year)

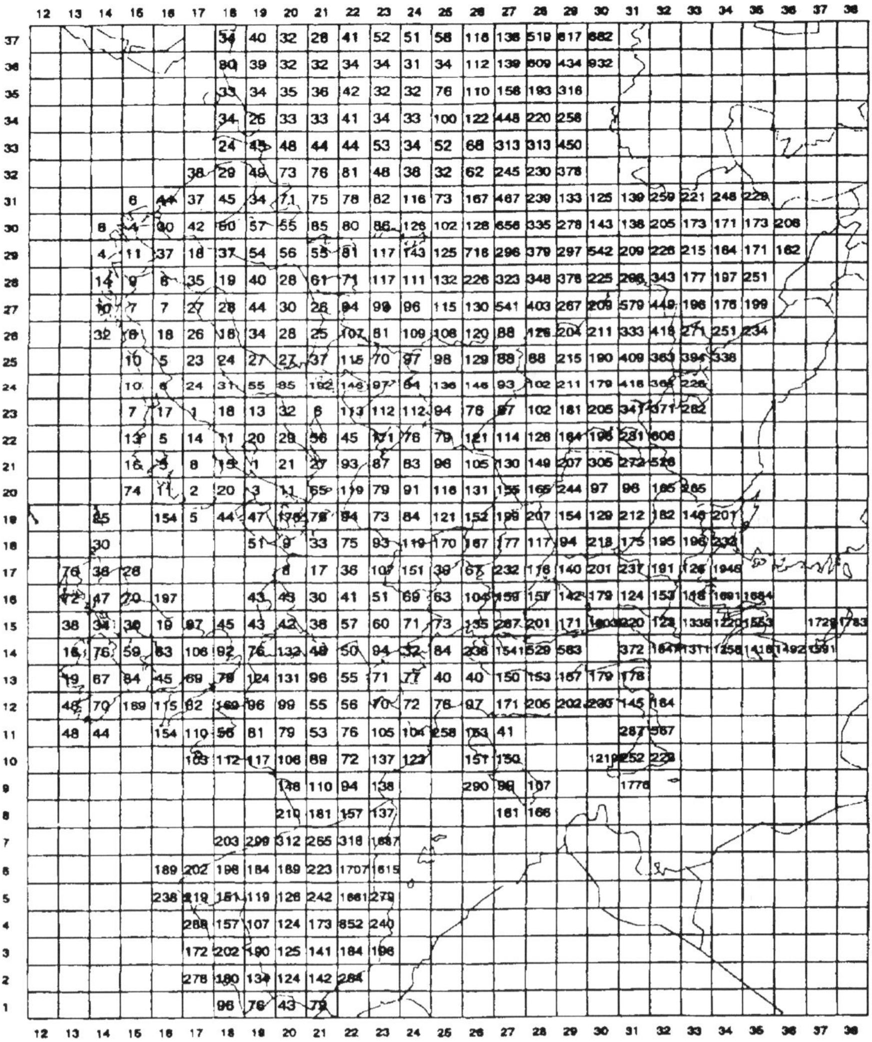

Annex II – SULPHUR EMISSION CEILINGS AND PERCENTAGE EMISSION REDUCTIONS

[...]

Annex III – DESIGNATION OF SULPHUR OXIDES MANAGEMENT AREAS (SOMAS)

The following SOMA is listed for the purposes of the present Protocol:

South-east Canada SOMA

This is an area of 1 million km2 which includes all the territory of the provinces of Prince Edward Island, Nova Scotia and New Brunswick, all the territory of the province of Quebec south of a straight line between Havre-St. Pierre on the north coast of the Gulf of Saint Lawrence and the point where the Quebec- Ontario boundary intersects the James Bay coastline, and all the territory of the province of Ontario south of a straight line between the point where the Ontario-Quebec boundary intersects the James Bay coastline and Nipigon River near the north shore of Lake Superior.

Annex IV – CONTROL TECHNOLOGIES FOR SULPHUR EMISSIONS FROM STATIONARY SOURCES

I. INTRODUCTION

1. The aim of this annex is to provide guidance for identifying sulphur control options and technologies for giving effect to the obligations of the present Protocol.
2. The annex is based on information on general options for the reduction of sulphur emissions and in particular on emission control technology performance and costs contained in official documentation of the Executive Body and its subsidiary bodies.
3. Unless otherwise indicated, the reduction measures listed are considered, on the basis of operational experience of several years in most cases, to be the most well-established and economically feasible best available technologies. However, the continuously expanding experience of low-emission measures and technologies at new plants as well as of the retrofitting of existing plants will necessitate regular review of this annex.
4. Although the annex lists a number of measures and technologies spanning a wide range of costs and efficiencies, it cannot be considered as an exhaustive statement of control options. Moreover, the choice of control measures and technologies for any particular case will depend on a number of factors, including current legislation and regulatory provisions and, in particular, control technology requirements, primary energy patterns, industrial infrastructure, economic circumstances and specific in-plant conditions.
5. The annex mainly addresses the control of oxidized sulphur emissions considered as the sum of sulphur dioxide (SO_2) and sulphur trioxide (SO_3), expressed as SO_2. The share of sulphur emitted as either sulphur oxides or other sulphur compounds from non-combustion processes and other sources is small compared to sulphur emissions from combustion.
6. When measures or technologies are planned for sulphur sources emitting other components, in particular nitrogen oxides (NO_X), particulates, heavy metals and volatile organic compounds (VOCs), it is worthwhile to consider them in conjunction with pollutant-specific control options in order to maximize the overall abatement effect and minimize the impact on the environment and, especially, to avoid the transfer of air pollution problems to other media (such as waste water and solid waste).

II. MAJOR STATIONARY SOURCES FOR SULPHUR EMISSIONS

7. Fossil fuel combustion processes are the main source of anthropogenic sulphur emissions from stationary sources. In addition, some non-combustion processes may contribute considerably to the emissions. The major stationary source categories, based on EMEP/ CORINAIR 90, include:
   (i) Public power, cogeneration and district heating plants:
      (a) Boilers;
      (b) Stationary combustion turbines and internal combustion engines;
   (ii) Commercial, institutional and residential combustion plants:
      (a) Commercial boilers;
      (b) Domestic heaters;
   (iii) Industrial combustion plants and processes with combustion:
      (a) Boilers and process heaters;
      (b) Processes, e.g. metallurgical operations such as roasting and sintering, coke oven plants, processing of titanium dioxide (TiO_2), etc.;
      (c) Pulp production;
   (iv) Non-combustion processes, e.g. sulphuric acid production, specific organic synthesis processes, treatment of metallic surfaces;
   (v) Extraction, processing and distribution of fossil fuels;
   (vi) Waste treatment and disposal, e.g. thermal treatment of municipal and industrial waste.
8. Overall data (1990) for the ECE region indicate that about 88 per cent of total sulphur emissions originate from all combustion processes (20 per cent from industrial combustion), 5 per cent from production processes and 7 per cent from oil refineries. The power plant sector in many countries is the major single contributor to sulphur emissions. In some countries, the industrial sector (including refineries) is also an important SO_2 emitter. Although emissions from refineries in the ECE region are relatively small, their impact on sulphur emissions from other sources is large due to the sulphur in the oil products. Typically 60 per cent of the sulphur intake present in the crudes remains in the products, 30 per cent is recovered as elemental sulphur and 10 per cent is emitted from refinery stacks.

III. GENERAL OPTIONS FOR REDUCTION OF SULPHUR EMISSIONS FROM COMBUSTION

9. General options for reduction of sulphur emissions are:
   (i) Energy management measures:*
      (a) Energy saving

      The rational use of energy (improved energy efficiency/process operation, cogeneration and/or demand-side management) usually results in a reduction in sulphur emissions.

      (b) Energy mix

* Options (i) (a) and (b) are integrated in the energy structure and policy of a Party. Implementation status, efficiency and costs per sector are not considered here.

In general, sulphur emissions can be reduced by increasing the proportion of non-combustion energy sources (i.e. hydro, nuclear, wind, etc.) to the energy mix. However, further environmental impacts have to be considered.

(ii) Technological options:

(a) Fuel switching

The SO2 emissions during combustion are directly related to the sulphur content of the fuel used. Fuel switching (e.g. from high- to low-sulphur coals and/or liquid fuels, or from coal to gas) leads to lower sulphur emissions, but there may be certain restrictions, such as the availability of low-sulphur fuels and the adaptability of existing combustion systems to different fuels. In many ECE countries, some coal or oil combustion plants are being replaced by gas-fired combustion plants. Dual-fuel plants may facilitate fuel switching.

(b) Fuel cleaning

Cleaning of natural gas is state-of-the-art technology and widely applied for operational reasons.

Cleaning of process gas (acid refinery gas, coke oven gas, biogas, etc.) is also state-of-the-art technology.

Desulphurization of liquid fuels (light and middle fractions) is state-of-the-art technology.

Desulphurization of heavy fractions is technically feasible; nevertheless, the crude properties should be kept in mind.

Desulphurization of atmospheric residue (bottom products from atmospheric crude distillation units) for the production of low-sulphur fuel oil is not, however, commonly practised; processing low-sulphur crude is usually preferable. Hydro-cracking and full conversion technology have matured and combine high sulphur retention with improved yield of light products. The number of full conversion refineries is as yet limited. Such refineries typically recover 80 per cent to 90 per cent of the sulphur intake and convert all residues into light products or other marketable products. For this type of refinery, energy consumption and investment costs are increased. Typical sulphur content for refinery products is given in table 1.

Current technologies to clean hard coal can remove approximately 50 per cent of the inorganic sulphur (depending on coal properties) but none of the organic sulphur. More effective technologies are being developed which, however, involve higher specific investment and costs. Thus the efficiency of sulphur removal by coal cleaning is limited compared to flue gas desulphurization. There may be a country- specific optimization potential for the best combination of fuel cleaning and flue gas cleaning.

Sulphur content from refinery products (S content (per cent))

[...]

(c) Advanced combustion technologies

These combustion technologies with improved thermal efficiency and reduced sulphur emissions include: fluidized-bed combustion (FBC): bubbling (BFBC), circulating (CFBC) and pressurized (PFBC); integrated gasification combined-cycle (IGCC); and combined-cycle gas turbines (CCGT).

Stationary combustion turbines can be integrated into combustion systems in existing conventional power plants which can increase overall efficiency by 5 per cent to 7 per cent, leading, for example, to a significant reduction in SO2 emissions. However, major alterations to the existing furnace system become necessary.

Fluidized-bed combustion is a combustion technology for burning hard coal and brown coal, but it can also burn other solid fuels such as petroleum coke and low-grade fuels such as waste, peat and wood. Emissions can additionally be reduced by integrated combustion control in the system due to the addition of lime/limestone to the bed material. The total installed capacity of FBC has reached approximately 30,000 MW_{th} (250 to 350 plants), including 8,000 MW_{th} in the capacity range of greater than 50 MW_{th}. By-products from this process may cause problems with respect to use and/or disposal, and further development is required.

The IGCC process includes coal gasification and combined-cycle power generation in a gas and steam turbine. The gasified coal is burnt in the combustion chamber of the gas turbine. Sulphur emission control is achieved by the use of state-of-the-art technology for raw gas cleaning facilities upstream of the gas turbine. The technology also exists for heavy oil residues and bitumen emulsions. The installed capacity is presently about 1,000 MW_{el} (5 plants).

Combined-cycle gas-turbine power stations using natural gas as fuel with an energy efficiency of approximately 48 per cent to 52 per cent are currently being planned.

(d) Process and combustion modifications

Combustion modifications comparable to the measures used for NOx emission control do not exist, as during combustion the organically and/or inorganically bound sulphur is almost completely oxidized (a certain percentage depending on the fuel properties and combustion technology is retained in the ash).

In this annex dry additive processes for conventional boilers are considered as process modifications due to the injection of an agent into the combustion unit. However, experience has shown that, when applying these processes, thermal capacity is lowered, the Ca/S ratio is high and sulphur removal low. Problems with the further utilization of the by-product have to be considered, so that this solution should usually be applied as an intermediate measure and for smaller units (table 2).

(e) Flue gas desulphurization (FGD) processes

These processes aim at removing already formed sulphur oxides, and are also referred to as secondary measures. The state-of-the-art technologies for flue gas treatment processes are all based on the removal of sulphur by wet, dry or semi-dry and catalytic chemical processes.

To achieve the most efficient programme for sulphur emission reductions beyond the energy management measures listed in (i) above a combination of technological options identified in (ii) above should be considered.

In some cases options for reducing sulphur emissions may also result in the reduction of emissions of CO_2, NO_X and other pollutants.

In public power, cogeneration and district heating plants, flue gas treatment processes used include: lime/limestone wet scrubbing (LWS); spray dry absorption (SDA); Wellman Lord process (WL); ammonia scrubbing (AS); and combined NO_X/SO_X removal processes (activated carbon process (AC) and combined catalytic NO_X/SO_X removal).

In the power generation sector, LWS and SDA cover 85 per cent and 10 per cent, respectively, of the installed FGD capacity.

Several new flue gas desulphurization processes, such as electron beam dry scrubbing (EBDS) and Mark 13A, have not yet passed the pilot stage.

Table 2 shows the efficiency of the above-mentioned secondary measures based on the practical experience gathered from a large number of implemented plants. The implemented capacity as well as the capacity range are also mentioned. Despite comparable characteristics for several sulphur abatement technologies, local or plant-specific influences may lead to the exclusion of a given technology.

Table 2 also includes the usual investment cost ranges for the sulphur abatement technologies listed in sections (ii) (c), (d) and (e). However, when applying these technologies to individual cases it should be noted that investment costs of emission reduction measures will depend amongst other things on the particular technologies used, the required control systems, the plant size, the extent of the required reduction and the time-scale of planned maintenance cycles. The table thus gives only a broad range of investment costs. Investment costs for retrofit generally exceed those for new plants.

TABLE 2 – Emissions of sulphur oxides obtained from the application of technological options to fossil-fuelled boilers

[...]

IV. CONTROL TECHNIQUES FOR OTHER SECTORS

10. The control techniques listed in section 9 (ii) (a) to (e) are valid not only in the power plant sector but also in various other sectors of industry. Several years of operational experience have been acquired, in most cases in the power plant sector.

11. The application of sulphur abatement technologies in the industrial sector merely depends on the process's specific limitations in the relevant sectors. Important contributors to sulphur emissions and corresponding reduction measures are presented in table 3 below.

12. In the sectors listed in table 3, process-integrated measures, including raw material changes (if necessary combined with sector-specific flue gas treatment), can be used to achieve the most effective reduction of sulphur emissions.

TABLE 3

Source	Reduction measures
Roasting of non-ferrous sulphides	Wet sulphuric acid catalytic process (WSA)
Viscose production	Double-contact process
Sulphuric acid production	Double-contact process, improved yield
Kraft pulp production	Variety of process-integrated measures

13. Reported examples are the following:
   (a) In new kraft pulp mills, sulphur emission of less than 1 kg of sulphur per tonne of pulp AD (air dried) can be achieved;**
   (b) In sulphite pulp mills, 1 to 1.5 kg of sulphur per tonne of pulp AD can be achieved;
   (c) In the case of roasting of sulphides, removal efficiencies of 80 to 99% for 10,000 to 200,000 m3/h units have been reported (depending on the process);
   (d) For one iron ore sintering plant, an FGD unit of 320,000 m3/h capacity achieves a clean gas value below 100 mg SO_X/Nm^3 at 6 per cent O_2;
   (e) Coke ovens are achieving less than 400 mg SO_X/Nm^3 at 6 per cent O_2;
   (f) Sulphuric acid plants achieve a conversion rate larger than 99 per cent;
   (g) Advanced Claus plant achieves sulphur recovery of more than 99 per cent.

** Control of sulphur-to-sodium ratio is required, i.e. removal of sulphur in the form of neutral salts and use of sulphur-free sodium make-up.

V. BY-PRODUCTS AND SIDE-EFFECTS

14. As efforts to reduce sulphur emissions from stationary sources are increased in the countries of the ECE region, the quantities of by-products will also increase.

15. Options which would lead to usable by-products should be selected. Furthermore, options that lead to increased thermal efficiency and minimize the waste disposal issue whenever possible should be selected. Although most by-products are usable or recyclable products such as gypsum, ammonia salts, sulphuric acid or sulphur, factors such as market conditions and quality standards need to be taken into account. Further utilization of FBC and SDA by-products have to be improved and investigated, as disposal sites and disposal criteria limit disposal in several countries.

16. The following side-effects will not prevent the implementation of any technology or method but should be considered when several sulphur abatement options are possible:
    (a) Energy requirements of the gas treatment processes;
    (b) Corrosion attack due to the formation of sulphuric acid by the reaction of sulphur oxides with water vapour;
    (c) Increased use of water and waste water treatment;
    (d) Reagent requirements;
    (e) Solid waste disposal.

VI. MONITORING AND REPORTING

17. The measures taken to carry out national strategies and policies for the abatement of air pollution include: legislation and regulatory provisions, economic incentives and disincentives; as well as technological requirements (best available technology).

18. In general, standards are set, per emission source, according to plant size, operating mode, combustion technology, fuel type and whether it is a new or existing plant. An alternative approach also used is to set a target for the reduction of total sulphur emissions from a group of sources and to allow a choice of where to take action to reach this target (the bubble concept).

19. Efforts to limit the sulphur emissions to the levels set out in the national framework legislation have to be controlled by a permanent monitoring and reporting system and reported to the supervising authorities.

20. Several monitoring systems, using both continuous and discontinuous measurement methods, are available. However, quality requirements vary. Measurements are to be carried out by qualified institutes using measuring and monitoring systems. To this end, a certification system can provide the best assurance.

21. In the framework of modern automated monitoring systems and process control equipment, reporting does not create a problem. The collection of data for further use is a state-of-the-art technique; however, data to be reported to competent authorities differ from case to case. To obtain better comparability, data sets and prescribing regulations should be harmonized. Harmonization is also desirable for quality assurance of measuring and monitoring systems. This should be taken into account when comparing data.

22. To avoid discrepancies and inconsistencies, key issues and parameters, including the following, must be well defined:
    (a) Definition of standards expressed as ppmv, mg/Nm^3, g/GJ, kg/h or kg/tonne of product. Most of these units need to be calculated and need specification in terms of gas temperature, humidity, pressure, oxygen content or heat input value;
    (b) Definition of the period over which standards are to be averaged, expressed as hours, months or a year;
    (c) Definition of failure times and corresponding emergency regulations regarding bypass of monitoring systems or shut-down of the installation;
    (d) Definition of methods for back-filling of data missed or lost as a result of equipment failure;
    (e) Definition of the parameter set to be measured. Depending on the type of industrial process, the necessary information may differ. This also involves the location of the measurement point within the system.

23. Quality control of measurements has to be ensured.

ANNEX V – Emission and sulphur content limit values

[...]

5.1. Vienna Convention 1985

Vienna Convention for the Protection of the Ozone Layer, Vienna, 22 March 1985, 1513 UNTS 293

The Parties to this Convention,

Aware of the potentially harmful impact on human health and the environment through modification of the ozone layer,

Recalling the pertinent provisions of the Declaration of the United Nations Conference on the Human Environment, and in particular principle 21, which provides that "States have, in accordance with the Charter of the United Nations and the principles of international law, the sovereign right to exploit their own resources pursuant to their own environmental policies, and the responsibility to ensure that activities within their jurisdiction or control do not cause damage to the environment of other States or of areas beyond the limits of national jurisdiction",

Taking into account the circumstances and particular requirements of developing countries,

Mindful of the work and studies proceeding within both international and national organizations arid, in particular, of the World Plan of Action on the Ozone Layer of the United Nations Environment Programme,

Mindful also of the precautionary measures for the protection of the ozone layer which have already been taken at the national and international levels,

Aware that measures to protect the ozone layer from modifications due to human activities require international co-operation and action, and should be based on relevant scientific and technical considerations,

Aware also of the need for further research and systematic observations to further develop scientific knowledge of the ozone layer and possible adverse effects resulting from its modification,

Determined to protect human health and the environment against adverse effects resulting from modifications of the ozone layer,

Have agreed as follows:

Article 1: DEFINITIONS

For the purposes of this Convention:

1. "The ozone layer" means the layer of atmospheric ozone above the planetary boundary layer.
2. "Adverse effects" means changes in the physical environment or biota, including changes in climate, which have significant deleterious effects on human health or on the composition, resilience and productivity of natural and managed ecosystems, or on materials useful to mankind.
3. "Alternative technologies or equipment" means technologies or equipment the use of which makes it possible to reduce or effectively eliminate emissions of substances which have or are likely to have adverse effects on the ozone layer.
4. "Alternative substances" means substances which reduce, eliminate or avoid adverse effects on the ozone layer.
5. "Parties" means, unless the text otherwise indicates, Parties to this Convention.
6. "Regional economic integration organization" means an organization constituted by sovereign States of a given region which has competence in respect of matters governed by this Convention or its protocols and has been duly authorized, in accordance with its internal procedures, to sign, ratify, accept, approve or accede to the instruments concerned.
7. "Protocols" means protocols to this Convention.

Article 2: GENERAL OBLIGATIONS

1. The Parties shall take appropriate measures in accordance with the provisions of this Convention and of those protocols in force to which they are party to protect human health and the environment against adverse effects resulting or likely to result from human activities which modify or are likely to modify the ozone layer.
2. To this end the Parties shall, in accordance with the means at their disposal and their capabilities:
   (a) Co-operate by means of systematic observations, research and information exchange in order to better understand and assess the effects of human activities on the ozone layer and the effects on human health and the environment from modification of the ozone layer;
   (b) Adopt appropriate legislative or administrative measures and co-operate in harmonizing appropriate policies to control, limit, reduce or prevent human activities under their jurisdiction or control should it be found that these activities have or are likely to have adverse effects resulting from modification or likely modification of the ozone layer;
   (c) Co-operate in the formulation of agreed measures, procedures and standards for the implementation of this Convention, with a view to the adoption of protocols and annexes;
   (d) Co-operate with competent international bodies to implement effectively this Convention and protocols to which they are party.
3. The provisions of this Convention shall in no way affect the right of Parties to adopt, in accordance with international law, domestic measures additional to those referred to in paragraphs 1 and 2 above, nor shall they affect additional domestic measures already taken by a Party, provided that these measures are not incompatible with their obligations under this Convention.

4. The application of this article shall be based on relevant scientific and technical considerations.

Article 3: RESEARCH AND SYSTEMATIC OBSERVATIONS

1. The Parties undertake, as appropriate, to initiate and co-operate in, directly or through competent international bodies, the conduct of research and scientific assessments on:
   (a) The physical and chemical processes that may affect the ozone layer;
   (b) The human health and other biological effects deriving from any modifications of the ozone layer, particularly those resulting from changes in ultra-violet solar radiation having biological effects (UV-B);
   (c) Climatic effects deriving from any modifications of the ozone layer;
   (d) Effects deriving from any modifications of the ozone layer and any consequent change in UV-B radiation or natural and synthetic materials useful to mankind;
   (e) Substances, practices, processes and activities that may affect the ozone layer, and their cumulative effects;
   (f) Alternative substances and technologies;
   (g) Related socio-economic matters;

   and as further elaborated in annexes I and II.
2. The Parties undertake to promote or establish, as appropriate, directly or through competent international bodies and taking fully into account national legislation and relevant ongoing activities at both the national and international levels, joint or complementary programmes for systematic observation of the state of the ozone layer and other relevant parameters, as elaborated in annex I.
3. The Parties undertake to co-operate, directly or through competent international bodies, in ensuring the collection, validation and transmission of research and observational data through appropriate world data centres in a regular and timely fashion.

Article 4: CO-OPERATION IN THE LEGAL, SCIENTIFIC AND TECHNICAL FIELDS

1. The Parties shall facilitate and encourage the exchange of scientific, technical, socio-economic, commercial and legal information relevant to this Convention as further elaborated in annex II. Such information shall be supplied to bodies agreed upon by the Parties. Any such body receiving information regarded as confidential by the supplying Party shall ensure that such information is not disclosed and shall aggregate it to protect its confidentiality before it is made available to all Parties.
2. The Parties shall co-operate, consistent with their national laws, regulations and practices and taking into account in particular the needs of the developing countries, in promoting, directly or through competent international bodies, the development and transfer of technology and knowledge. Such co-operation shall be carried out particularly through:
   (a) Facilitation of the acquisition of alternative technologies by other Parties;
   (b) Provision of information on alternative technologies and equipment, and supply of special manuals or guides to them;
   (c) The supply of necessary equipment and facilities for research and systematic observations;
   (d) Appropriate training of scientific and technical personnel.

Article 5: TRANSMISSION OF INFORMATION

The Parties shall transmit, through the secretariat, to the Conference of the

Parties established under article 6 information on the measures adopted by them in implementation of this Convention and of protocols to which they are party in such form and at such intervals as the meetings of the parties to the relevant instruments may determine.

Article 6: CONFERENCE OF THE PARTIES

1. A Conference of the Parties is hereby established. The first meeting of the Conference of the Parties shall be convened by the secretariat designated on an interim basis under article 7 not later than one year after entry into force of this Convention. Thereafter, ordinary meetings of the Conference of the Parties shall be held at regular intervals to be determined by the Conference at its first meeting.
2. Extraordinary meetings of the Conference of the Parties shall be held at such other times as may be deemed necessary by the Conference, or at the written request of any Party, provided that, within six months of the request being communicated to them by the secretariat, it is supported by at least one third of the Parties.
3. The Conference of the Parties shall by consensus agree upon and adopt rules of procedure and financial rules for itself and for any subsidiary bodies it may establish, as well as financial provisions governing the functioning of the secretariat.
4. The Conference of the Parties shall keep under continuous review the implementation of this Convention, and, in addition, shall:
   (a) Establish the form and the intervals for transmitting the information to be submitted in accordance with article 5 and consider such information as well as reports submitted by any subsidiary body;
   (b) Review the scientific information on the ozone layer, on its possible modification and on possible effects of any such modification;
   (c) Promote, in accordance with article 2, the harmonization of appropriate policies, strategies and measures for minimizing the release of substances causing or likely to cause modification of the ozone layer, and make recommendations on any other measures relating to this Convention;

(d) Adopt, in accordance with articles 3 and 4, programmes for research, systematic observations, scientific and technological co-operation, the exchange of information and the transfer of technology and knowledge;

(e) Consider and adopt, as required, in accordance with articles 9 and 10, amendments to this Convention and its annexes;

(f) Consider amendments to any protocol, as well as to any annexes thereto, and, if so decided, recommend their adoption to the parties to the protocol concerned;

(g) Consider and adopt, as required, in accordance with article 10, additional annexes to this Convention;

(h) Consider and adopt, as required, protocols in accordance with article 8;

(i) Establish such subsidiary bodies as are deemed necessary for the implementation of this Convention;

(j) Seek, where appropriate, the services of competent international bodies and scientific committees, in particular the World Meteorological Organization and the World Health Organization, as well as the Co-ordinating Committee on the Ozone Layer, in scientific research, systematic observations and other activities pertinent to the objectives of this Convention, and make use as appropriate of information from these bodies and committees;

(k) Consider and undertake any additional action that may be required for the achievement of the purposes of this Convention.

5. The United Nations, its specialized agencies and the International Atomic Energy Agency, as well as any State not party to this Convention, may be represented at meetings of the Conference of the Parties by observers. Any body or agency, whether national or international, governmental or non-governmental, qualified in fields relating to the protection of the ozone layer which has informed the secretariat of its wish to be represented at a meeting of the Conference of the Parties as an observer may be admitted unless at least one-third of the Parties present object. The admission and participation of observers shall be subject to the rules of procedure adopted by the Conference of the Parties.

Article 7: SECRETARIAT

1. The functions of the secretariat shall be:

(a) To arrange for and service meetings provided for in articles 6, 8,9 and 10;

(b) To prepare arid transmit reports based upon information received in accordance with articles 4 and 5, as well as upon information derived from meetings of subsidiary bodies established under article 6;

(c) To perform the functions assigned to it by any protocol;

(d) To prepare reports on its activities carried out in implementation of its functions under this Convention and present them to the Conference of the Parties;

(e) To ensure the necessary co-ordination with other relevant international bodies, and in particular to enter into such administrative and contractual arrangements as may be required for the effective discharge of its functions;

(f) To perform such other functions as may be determined by the Conference of the Parties.

2. The secretariat functions will be carried out on an interim basis by the United Nations Environment Programme until the completion of the first ordinary meeting of the Conference of the Parties held pursuant to article 6. At its first ordinary meeting, the Conference of the Parties shall designate the secretariat from amongst those existing competent international organizations which have signified their willingness to carry out the secretariat functions under this Convention.

Article 8: ADOPTION OF PROTOCOLS

1. The Conference of the Parties may at a meeting adopt protocols pursuant to article 2.

2. The text of any proposed protocol shall be communicated to the Parties by the secretariat at least six months before such a meeting.

Article 9: AMENDMENT OF THE CONVENTION OR PROTOCOLS

1. Any Party may propose amendments to this Convention or to any protocol.

   Such amendments shall take due account, inter alia, of relevant scientific and technical considerations.

2. Amendments to this Convention shall be adopted at a meeting of the Conference of the Parties. Amendments to any protocol shall be adopted at a meeting of the Parties to the protocol in question. The text of any proposed amendment to this Convention or to any protocol, except as may otherwise be provided in such protocol, shall be communicated to the Patties by the secretariat at least six months before the meeting at which it is proposed for adoption. The secretariat shall also communicate proposed amendments to the signatories to this Convention for information.

3. The Parties shall make every effort to reach agreement on any proposed amendment to this Convention by consensus. If all efforts at consensus have been exhausted, and no agreement reached., the amendment shall as a last resort be adopted by a three-fourths majority vote of the Parties present and voting at the meeting, and shall be submitted by the Depositary to all Parties for ratification, approval or acceptance.

4. The procedure mentioned in paragraph 3 above shall apply to amendments to any protocol, except that a two-thirds majority of the parties to that protocol present and voting at the meeting shall suffice for their adoption.

5. Ratification, approval or acceptance of amendments shall be notified to the Depositary in writing. Amendments adopted in accordance with paragraphs 3 or 4 above shall enter into force between parties having accepted them on the ninetieth day after the receipt by the Depositary of notification of their ratification, approval or acceptance by at least three-fourths of the Parties to this Convention or by at least two-thirds of the parties to the protocol concerned, except as may otherwise be provided in such protocol. Thereafter the amendments shall enter into force for any other Party on the ninetieth day after the Party deposits its instrument of ratification, approval or acceptance of the amendments.
6. For the purposes of this article, "Parties present and voting" means Parties present and casting an affirmative or negative vote.

Article 10: ADOPTION AND AMENDMENT OF ANNEXES

1. The annexes to this Convention or to any protocol shall form an integral part of this Convention or of such protocol, as the case may be, and, unless expressly provided otherwise, a reference to this Convention or its protocols constitutes at the same time a reference to any annexes thereto. Such annexes shall be restricted to scientific, technical and administrative matters.
2. Except as may be otherwise provided in any protocol with respect to its annexes, the following procedure shall apply to the proposal, adoption and entry into force of additional annexes to this Convention or of annexes to a protocol:
   (a) Annexes to this Convention shall be proposed and adopted according to the procedure laid down in article 9, paragraphs 2 and 3, while annexes to any protocol shall be proposed and adopted according to the procedure laid down in article 9, paragraphs 2 and 4;
   (b) Any party that is unable to approve an additional annex to this Convention or an annex to any protocol to which it is party shall so notify the Depositary, in writing, within six months from the date of the communication of the adoption by the Depositary. The Depositary shall without delay notify all Parties of any such notification received. A Party may at any time substitute an acceptance for a previous declaration of objection and the annexes shall thereupon enter into force for that Party;
   (c) On the expiry of six months from the date of the circulation of the communication by the Depositary, the annex shall become effective for all Parties to this Convention or to any protocol concerned which have not submitted a notification in accordance with the provision of subparagraph (b) above.
3. The proposal, adoption and entry into force of amendments to annexes to this Convention or to any protocol shall be subject to the same procedure as for the proposal, adoption and entry into force of annexes to the Convention or annexes to a protocol. Annexes and amendments thereto shall take due account, inter alia, of relevant scientific and technical considerations.
4. If an additional annex or an amendment to an annex involves an amendment to this Convention or to any protocol, the additional annex or amended annex shall not enter into force until such time as the amendment to this Convention or to the protocol concerned enters into force.

Article 11: SETTLEMENT OF DISPUTES

1. In the event of a dispute between Parties concerning the interpretation or application of this Convention, the parties concerned shall seek solution by negotiation.
2. If the parties concerned cannot reach agreement by negotiation, they may jointly seek the good offices of, or request mediation by, a third party.
3. When ratifying, accepting, approving or acceding to this Convention, or at any time thereafter, a State or regional economic integration organization may declare in writing to the Depositary that for a dispute not resolved in accordance with paragraph 1 or paragraph 2 above, it accepts one or both of the following means of dispute settlement as compulsory:
   (a) Arbitration in accordance with, procedures to be adopted by the Conference of the Parties at its first ordinary meeting;
   (b) Submission of the dispute to the International Court of Justice.
4. If the parties have not, in accordance with paragraph 3 above, accepted the same or any procedure, the dispute shall be submitted to conciliation in accordance with paragraph 5 below unless the parties otherwise agree.
5. A conciliation commission shall be created upon the request of one of the parties to the dispute. The commission shall be composed of an equal number of members appointed by each party concerned and a chairman chosen jointly by the members appointed by each party. The commission shall render a final and recommendatory award, which the parties shall consider in good faith.
6. The provisions of this article: shall apply with respect to any protocol except as otherwise provided in the protocol concerned.

Article 12: SIGNATURE

This Convention shall be open for signature by States and by regional economic integration organizations at the Federal Ministry for Foreign Affairs of the Republic of Austria in Vienna from 22 March 1985 to 21 September 1985 and at United Nations Headquarters in New York from 22 September 1985 to 21 March 1986.

Article 13: RATIFICATION, ACCEPTANCE OR APPROVAL

1. This Convention and any protocol shall be subject to ratification, acceptance or approval by States and by regional economic integration organiza-

tions. Instruments of ratification, acceptance or approval shall be deposited with the Depositary.

2. Any organization referred to in paragraph 1 above which becomes a Party to this Convention or any protocol without any of its member States being a Party shall be bound by all the obligations under the Convention or the protocol, as the case may be. In the case of such organizations, one or more of whose member States is a Party to the Convention or relevant protocol, the organization and its member States shall decide on their respective responsibilities for the performance of their obligation under the Convention or protocol, as the case may be. In such cases, the organization and the member States shall not be entitled to exercise rights under the Convention or relevant protocol concurrently.
3. In their instruments of ratification, acceptance or approval, the organizations referred to in paragraph 1 above shall declare the extent of their competence with respect to the matters governed by the Convention or the relevant protocol. These organizations shall also inform the Depositary of any substantial modification in the extent of their competence.

Article 14: ACCESSION

1. This Convention and any protocol shall be open for accession by States and by regional economic integration organizations from the date on which the Convention or the protocol concerned is closed for signature. The instruments of accession shall be deposited with the Depositary.
2. In their instruments of accession, the organizations referred to in paragraph 1 above shall declare the extent of their competence with respect to the matters governed by the Convention or the relevant protocol. These organizations shall also inform the Depositary of any substantial modification in the extent of their competence.
3. The provisions of article 13, paragraph 2, shall apply to regional economic integration organizations which accede to this Convention or any protocol.

Article 15: RIGHT TO VOTE

1. Each Party to this Convention or to any protocol shall have one vote.
2. Except as provided for in paragraph 1 above, regional economic integration organizations, in matters within their competence, shall exercise their right to vote with a number of votes equal to the number of their member States which are Parties to the Convention or the relevant protocol. Such organizations shall not exercise their right to vote if their member States exercise theirs, and vice versa.

Article 16: RELATIONSHIP BETWEEN THE CONVENTION AND ITS PROTOCOLS

1. A State or a regional economic integration organization may not become a party to a protocol unless it is, or becomes at the same time, a Party to the Convention.
2. Decisions concerning any protocol shall be taken only by the parties to the protocol concerned.

Article 17: ENTRY INTO FORCE

1. This Convention shall enter into force on the ninetieth day after the date of deposit of the twentieth instrument of ratification, acceptance, approval or accession.
2. Any protocol, except as otherwise provided in such protocol, shall enter into force on the ninetieth day after the date of deposit of the eleventh instrument of ratification, acceptance or approval of such protocol or accession thereto.
3. For each Party which ratifies, accepts or approves this Convention or accedes thereto after the deposit of the twentieth instrument of ratification, acceptance, approval or accession, it shall enter into force on the ninetieth day after the date of deposit by such Party of its instrument of ratification, acceptance, approval or accession.
4. Any protocol except otherwise provided in such protocol shall enter into force for a party that ratifies, accepts or approves that protocol or accedes thereto after its entry into force pursuant to paragraph 1 above, on the ninetieth day after the date on which that party deposits the instrument of ratification, acceptance, approval or accession, or on the date on which the Convention enters into force for that Party, whichever shall be the later.
5. For the purposes of paragraphs 1 and 2 above, any instrument deposited by a regional economic integration organization shall not be counted as additional to those deposited by member Statas of such organization.

Article 18: RESERVATIONS

No reservations may be made to this Convention.

Article 19: WITHDRAWAL

1. At any time after four years from the date on which this Convention bas entered into force for a Party, that Party may withdraw from the Convention by giving written notification to the Depositary.
2. Except as may be provided in any protocol, at any time after four years from the date on which such protocol has entered into force for a party, that party may withdraw from the protocol by giving written notification to the Depositary.
3. Any such withdrawal shall take effect upon expiry of one year after the date of its receipt by the Depositary, or on such later date as may be specified in the notification of the withdrawal.
4. Any Party which withdraws from this Convention shall be considered as also having withdrawn from any protocol to which it is party.

Article 20: DEPOSITARY

1. The Secretary-General of the United Nations shall assume the functions of depositary of this Convention and any protocols.
2. The Depositary shall inform the Parties, in particular, of:

   (a) The signature of this Convention and of any protocol, and the deposit of instruments of ratification, acceptance, approval or accession in accordance with articles 13 and 14;

(b) The date on which the Convention and. any protocol will come into force in accordance with article 17:

(c) Notifications of withdrawal made in accordance with article 19:

(d) Amendments adopted with respect to the Convention and any protocol, their acceptance by the parties and their date of entry into force in accordance with article 9;

(e) All communications relating to the adoption and approval of annexes and to the amendment of annexes in accordance with article 10;

(f) Notifications by regional economic integration organizations of the extent of their competence with respect to matters governed by this Convention and any protocols, and of any modifications thereof.

(g) Declarations made in accordance with article 11, paragraph 3.

Article 21: AUTHENTIC TEXTS

The original of this Convention, of which the Arabic, Chinese, English, French, Russian and Spanish texts are equally authentic, shall be deposited with the Secretary-General of the United Nations.

IN WITNESS THEREOF the undersigned, being duly authorized to that effect, have signed this Convention.

Done at Vienna on the 22nd day of March 1985.

ANNEX I: RESEARCH AND SYSTEMATIC OBSERVATIONS

1. The Parties to the Convention recognize that the major scientific issues are:

   (a) modification of the ozone layer which would result in a change in the amount of solar ultraviolet radiation having biological effects (UV-B) that reaches the Earth's surface and the potential consequences for human health, for organisms, ecosystems and materials useful to mankind;

   (b) modification of the vertical distribution of ozone, which could change the temperature structure of the atmosphere and the potential consequences for weather and climate.

2. The Parties to the Conventions in accordance with Article 3, shall cooperate in conducting research and systematic observations and in formulating recommendations for future research and observation in such areas as:

   (a) Research into the physics and chemistry of the atmosphere

      (i) comprehensive theoretical models: further development of models which consider the interaction between radiative, dynamic and chemical processes; studies of the simultaneous effects of various man-made and naturally occurring species upon atmospheric ozone; interpretation of satellite and non-satellite measurement data sets; evaluation of trends in atmospheric and geophysical parameters, and the development of methods for attributing changes in these parameters to specific causes;

      (ii) laboratory studies of: rate coefficients, absorption cross-sections and mechanisms of tropospheric and stratospheric chemical and photochemical processes; spectroscopic data to support field measurements in all relevant spectral regions;

      (iii) field measurements: the concentration and fluxes of key source gases of both natural and anthropogenic origin; atmospheric dynamics studies; simultaneous measurements of photochemically related species down to the planetary boundary layer, using in situ and remote sensing instruments; intercomparison of different sensors, including coordinated correlative measurements for satellite instrumentation; three-dimensional fields of key atmospheric trace constituents, solar spectral flux and meteorological parameters;

      (iv) instrument development, including satellite and non-satellite sensors for atmospheric trace constituents, solar flux and meteorological parameters;

   (b) Research into health, biological and photodegradation effects

      (i) the relationship between human exposure to visible and ultraviolet solar radiation and (a) the development of both non-melanoma and melanoma skin cancer and (b) the effects on the immunological system;

      (ii) effects of UV-B radiation, including the wavelength dependence, upon (a) agricultural crops, forests and other terrestrial ecosystems, and (b) the aquatic food web and fisheries, as well as possible inhibition of oxygen production by marine phytoplankton;

      (iii) the mechanisms by which UV-B radiation acts on biological materials, species and ecosystems, including: the relationship between dose, dose rate, and response; photorepair, adaptation, and protection;

      (iv) studies of biological action spectra and the spectral response using polychromatic radiation in order to include possible interactions of the various wavelength regions;

      (v) the influence of UV-B radiation on: the sensitivities and activities of biological species important to the biospheric balance; primary processes such as photosynthesis and biosynthesis;

      (vi) the influence of UV-B radiation on the photodegradation of pollutants, agricultural chemicals and other materials;

(c) Research on effects on climate

(i) theoretical and observational studies of the radiative effects of ozone and other trace species and the impact on climate parameters, such as land and ocean surface temperatures, precipitation patterns, the exchange between the troposphere and stratosphere;

(ii) the investigation of the effects of such climate impacts on various aspects of human activity;

(d) Systematic observations on:

(i) the status of the ozone layer (i.e. the spatial and temporal variability of the total column content and vertical distribution) by making the Global Ozone Observing System, based on the integration of satellite and ground-based systems, fully operational;

(ii) the tropospheric and stratospheric concentrations of source gases for the HO_x, NO_x, ClO_x and carbon families;

(iii) the temperature from the ground to the mesosphere, utilizing both ground-based and satellite systems;

(iv) wavelength-resolved solar flux reaching, and thermal radiation leaving, the Earth's atmosphere, utilizing satellite measurements;

(v) wavelength-resolved solar flux reaching the Earth's surface in the ultraviolet range having biological effects (UV-B);

(vi) aerosol properties and distribution from the ground to the mesosphere, utilizing ground-based, airborne and satellite systems;

(vii) climatically important variables by the maintenance of programmes of high-quality meteorological surface measurements;

(viii) trace species, temperatures, solar flux and aerosols utilizing improved methods for analysing global data.

3. The Parties to the Convention shall cooperate, taking into account the particular needs of the developing countries, in promoting the appropriate scientific and technical training required to participate in the research and systematic observations outlined in this annex. Particular emphasis should be given to the intercalibration of observational instrumentation and methods with a view to generating comparable or standardized scientific data sets.

4. The following chemical substances of natural and anthropogenic origin, not listed in order of priority, are thought to have the potential to modify the chemical and physical properties of the ozone layer.

(a) Carbon substances

(i) Carbon monoxide (CO)

Carbon monoxide has significant natural and anthropogenic sources, and is thought to play a major direct role in tropospheric photochemistry, and an indirect role in stratospheric photochemistry;

(ii) Carbon dioxide (CO_2)

Carbon dioxide has significant natural and anthropogenic sources, and affects stratospheric ozone by influencing the thermal structure of the atmosphere;

(iii) Methane (CH_4)

Methane has both natural and anthropogenic sources, and effects both tropospheric and stratospheric ozone;

(iv) Non-methane hydrocarbon species

Non-methane hydrocarbon species, which consist of a large number of chemical substances, have both natural and anthropogenic sources, and play a direct role in tropospheric photochemistry and an indirect role in stratospheric photochemistry;

(b) Nitrogen substances

(i) Nitrous oxide (N_2O)

The dominant sources of N_2O are natural, but anthropogenic contributions are becoming increasingly important. Nitrous oxide is the primary source of stratospheric NO_x, which play a vital role in controlling the abundance of stratospheric ozone;

(ii) Nitrogen oxides (NO_x)

Ground-level sources of NO_x play a major direct role only in tropospheric photochemical processes and an indirect role in stratospheric photochemistry, whereas injection of NO_x close to the tropopause may lead directly to a change in upper tropospheric and stratospheric ozone;

(c) Chlorine substances

(i) Fully halogenated alkanes, e.g. CCl_4, $CFCl_3$ (CFC-11), CF_2Cl_2 (CFC-12), $C_2F_3Cl_3$ (CFC-113), $C_2F_4Cl_2$ (CFC-114)

Fully halogenated alkanes are anthropogenic and act as a source of ClO_x, which plays a vital role in ozone photochemistry, especially in the 30 to 50 kilometre altitude region;

(ii) Partially halogenated alkanes, e.g. CH_3Cl, CHF_2Cl (CFC-22), CH_3CCl_3, $CHFCl_2$ (CFC-21)

The sources of CH_3Cl are natural, whereas the other partially halogenated alkanes mentioned above are anthropogenic in origin. These gases also act as a source of stratospheric ClO_x;

(d) Bromine substances

Fully halogenated alkanes, e.g. CF_3Br

Ozone

These gases are anthropogenic and act as a source of BrO_x, which behaves in a manner similar to ClO_x;

(e) Hydrogen substances

(i) Hydrogen (H_2)

Hydrogen, the source of which is natural and anthropogenic, plays a minor role in stratospheric photochemistry;

(ii) Water (H_2O)

Water, the source of which is natural, plays a vital role in both tropospheric and stratospheric photochemistry. Local sources of water vapour in the stratosphere include the oxidation of methane and, to a lesser extent, of hydrogen.

ANNEX II: INFORMATION EXCHANGE

1. The Parties to the Convention recognize that the collection and sharing of information is an important means of implementing the objectives of this Convention and of assuring that any actions that may be taken are appropriate and equitable. Therefore, Parties shall exchange scientific, technical, socio-economic, business, commercial and legal information.
2. The Parties to the Convention, in deciding what information is to be collected and exchanged, should take into account the usefulness of the information and the costs of obtaining it. The Parties further recognize that co-operation under this annex has to be consistent with national laws, regulations and practices regarding patents, trade secrets, and protection of confidential and proprietary information.
3. Scientific information

   This includes information on:

   (a) Planned and ongoing research, both governmental and private, to facilitate the coordination of research programmes so as to make the most effective use of available national and international resources;

   (b) The emission data needed for research;

   (c) Scientific results published in peer-reviewed literature on the understanding of the physics and chemistry of the Earth's atmosphere and of its susceptibility to change, in particular on the state of the ozone layer and effects on human health, environment and climate which would result from changes on all time-scales in either the total column content or the vertical distribution of ozone;

   (d) The assessment of research results and the recommendations for future research.
4. Technical information

   This includes information on:

   (a) The availability and cost of chemical substitutes and of alternative technologies to reduce the emissions of ozone-modifying substances and related planned and ongoing research;

   (b) The limitations and any risks involved in using chemical or other substitutes and alternative technologies.
5. Socio-economic and commercial information on the substances referred to in annex I

   This includes information on:

   (a) Production and production capacity;

   (b) Use and use patterns;

   (c) Imports/exports;

   (d) The costs, risks and benefits of human activities which may indirectly modify the ozone layer and of the impacts of regulatory actions taken or being considered to control these activities.
6. Legal information

   This includes information on:

   (a) National laws, administrative measures and legal research relevant to the protection of the ozone layer;

   (b) International agreements, including bilateral agreements, relevant to the protection of the ozone layer;

   (c) Methods and terms of licensing and availability of patents relevant to the protection of the ozone layer.

5.2. Montreal Protocol 1987, as amended 2018

Montreal Protocol on Substances that Deplete the Ozone Layer, Montreal, 16 September 1987, 1522 UNTS 3, C.N.181.1989.TREATIES-9 of 28 August 1989, C.N.225.1990.TREATIES-7 of 7 September 1990, C.N.246.1990.TREATIES-9 of 14 November 1990, C.N.227.1991.TREATIES-7 of 27 November 1991, C.N.428.1992. TREATIES-12 of 22 March 1993, C.N.484.1995.TREATIES-5 of 5 February 1996, C.N.468.1997.TREATIES-4/1 of 5 December 1997, C.N.1230.1999.TREATIES-7 of 28 January 2000, C.N.1096.2007.TREATIES-1 of 14 November 2007, C.N.601.2018.TREATIES-XXVII.2.a of 21 December 2018

The Parties to this Protocol,

Being Parties to the Vienna Convention for the Protection of the Ozone Layer,

Mindful of their obligation under that Convention to take appropriate measures to protect human health and the environment against adverse effects resulting or likely to result from human activities which modify or are likely to modify the ozone layer,

Recognizing that world-wide emissions of certain substances can significantly deplete and otherwise modify the ozone layer in a manner that is likely to result in adverse effects on human health and the environment,

Conscious of the potential climatic effects of emissions of these substances,

Aware that measures taken to protect the ozone layer from depletion should be based on relevant scientific knowledge, taking into account technical and economic considerations,

Determined to protect the ozone layer by taking precautionary measures to control equitably total global emissions of substances that deplete it, with the ultimate objective of their elimination on the basis of developments in scientific knowledge, taking into account technical and economic considerations,

Acknowledging that special provision is required to meet the needs of developing countries for these substances,

Noting the precautionary measures for controlling emissions of certain chlorofluorocarbons that have already been taken at national and regional levels,

Considering the importance of promoting international co-operation in the research and development of science and technology relating to the control and reduction of emissions of substances that deplete the ozone layer, bearing in mind in particular the needs of developing countries,

Have agreed as follows:

Article 1: Definitions

For the purposes of this Protocol:

1. "Convention" means the Vienna Convention for the Protection of the Ozone Layer, adopted on 22 March 1985.
2. "Parties" means, unless the text otherwise indicates, Parties to this Protocol.
3. "Secretariat" means the Secretariat of the Convention.
4. "Controlled substance" means a substance in Annex A, Annex B, Annex C, Annex E or Annex F to this Protocol, whether existing alone or in a mixture. It includes the isomers of any such substance, except as specified in the relevant Annex, but excludes any controlled substance or mixture which is in a manufactured product other than a container used for the transportation or storage of that substance.
5. "Production" means the amount of controlled substances produced, minus the amount destroyed by technologies to be approved by the Parties and minus the amount entirely used as feedstock in the manufacture of other chemicals. The amount recycled and reused is not to be considered as "production".
6. "Consumption" means production plus imports minus exports of controlled substances.
7. "Calculated levels" of production, imports, exports and consumption means levels determined in accordance with Article 3.
8. "Industrial rationalization" means the transfer of all or a portion of the calculated level of production of one Party to another, for the purpose of achieving economic efficiencies or responding to anticipated shortfalls in supply as a result of plant closures.

Article 2: Control Measures

1. Incorporated in Article 2A.
2. Replaced by Article 2B.
3. Replaced by Article 2A.
4. Replaced by Article 2A.
5. Any Party may, for one or more control periods, transfer to another Party any portion of its calculated level of production set out in Articles 2A to 2F, Articles 2H and 2J, provided that the total combined calculated levels of production of the Parties concerned for any group of controlled substances do not exceed the production limits set out in those Articles for that group. Such transfer of production shall be notified to the Secretariat by each of the Parties concerned, stating the terms of such transfer and the period for which it is to apply.

5 bis. Any Party not operating under paragraph 1 of Article 5 may, for one or more control periods, transfer to another such Party any portion of its calculated level of consumption set out in Article 2F, provided that the calculated level of consumption of controlled substances in Group I of Annex A of the Party transferring the portion of its calculated level of consumption did not exceed 0.25 kilograms per capita in 1989 and that the total combined calculated levels of consumption of the Parties concerned do not exceed the consumption limits set out in Article 2F. Such transfer of consumption shall be notified to the Secretariat by each of the Parties concerned, stating the terms of such transfer and the period for which it is to apply.

6. Any Party not operating under Article 5, that has facilities for the production of Annex A or Annex B controlled substances under construction, or contracted for, prior to 16 September 1987, and provided for in national legislation prior to 1 January 1987, may add the production from such facilities to its 1986 production of such substances for the purposes of determining its calculated level of production for 1986, provided that such facilities are completed by 31 December 1990 and that such production does not raise that Party's annual calculated level of consumption of the controlled substances above 0.5 kilograms per capita.

7. Any transfer of production pursuant to paragraph 5 or any addition of production pursuant to paragraph 6 shall be notified to the Secretariat, no later than the time of the transfer or addition.

8. (a) Any Parties which are Member States of a regional economic integration organization as defined in Article 1 (6) of the Convention may agree that they shall jointly fulfil their obligations respecting consumption under this Article and Articles 2A to 2J provided that their total combined calculated level of consumption does not exceed the levels required by this Article and Articles 2A to 2J. Any such agreement may be extended to include obligations respecting consumption or production under Article 2J provided that the total combined calculated level of consumption or production of the Parties concerned does not exceed the levels required by Article 2J.

   (b) The Parties to any such agreement shall inform the Secretariat of the terms of the agreement before the date of the reduction in consumption with which the agreement is concerned.

   (c) Such agreement will become operative only if all Member States of the regional economic integration organization and the organization concerned are Parties to the Protocol and have notified the Secretariat of their manner of implementation.

9. (a) Based on the assessments made pursuant to Article 6, the Parties may decide whether:

   (i) Adjustments to the ozone depleting potentials specified in Annex A, Annex B, Annex C and/or Annex E should be made and, if so, what the adjustments should be;

   (ii) Adjustments to the global warming potentials specified in Group I of Annex A, Annex C and Annex F should be made and, if so, what the adjustments should be; and

   (iii) Further adjustments and reductions of production or consumption of the controlled substances should be undertaken and, if so, what the scope, amount and timing of any such adjustments and reductions should be;

   (b) Proposals for such adjustments shall be communicated to the Parties by the Secretariat at least six months before the meeting of the Parties at which they are proposed for adoption;

   (c) In taking such decisions, the Parties shall make every effort to reach agreement by consensus. If all efforts at consensus have been exhausted, and no agreement reached, such decisions shall, as a last resort, be adopted by a two-thirds majority vote of the Parties present and voting representing a majority of the Parties operating under Paragraph 1 of Article 5 present and voting and a majority of the Parties not so operating present and voting;

   (d) The decisions, which shall be binding on all Parties, shall forthwith be communicated to the Parties by the Depositary. Unless otherwise provided in the decisions, they shall enter into force on the expiry of six months from the date of the circulation of the communication by the Depositary.

10. Based on the assessments made pursuant to Article 6 of this Protocol and in accordance with the procedure set out in Article 9 of the Convention, the Parties may decide:

   (a) whether any substances, and if so which, should be added to or removed from any annex to this Protocol, and

   (b) the mechanism, scope and timing of the control measures that should apply to those substances;

11. Notwithstanding the provisions contained in this Article and Articles 2A to 2J Parties may take more stringent measures than those required by this Article and Articles 2A to 2J.

Article 2A: CFCs

1. Each Party shall ensure that for the twelve-month period commencing on the first day of the seventh month following the date of entry into force of this Protocol, and in each twelve-month period thereafter, its calculated level of consumption of the controlled substances in Group I of Annex A does not exceed its calculated level of consumption in 1986. By the end of the same period, each Party producing one or more of these substances shall ensure that its calculated level of production of the substances does not exceed its calculated level of production in 1986, except that such level may have increased by no more than ten per cent based on the 1986 level. Such increase shall be permitted only so as to satisfy the basic domestic needs of the

Parties operating under Article 5 and for the purposes of industrial rationalization between Parties.

2. Each Party shall ensure that for the period from 1 July 1991 to 31 December 1992 its calculated levels of consumption and production of the controlled substances in Group I of Annex A do not exceed 150 per cent of its calculated levels of production and consumption of those substances in 1986; with effect from 1 January 1993, the twelve- month control period for these controlled substances shall run from 1 January to 31 December each year.
3. Each Party shall ensure that for the twelve-month period commencing on 1 January 1994, and in each twelve-month period thereafter, its calculated level of consumption of the controlled substances in Group I of Annex A does not exceed, annually, twenty-five per cent of its calculated level of consumption in 1986. Each Party producing one or more of these substances shall, for the same periods, ensure that its calculated level of production of the substances does not exceed, annually, twenty-five per cent of its calculated level of production in 1986. However, in order to satisfy the basic domestic needs of the Parties operating under paragraph 1 of Article 5, its calculated level of production may exceed that limit by up to ten per cent of its calculated level of production in 1986.
4. Each Party shall ensure that for the twelve-month period commencing on 1 January 1996, and in each twelve-month period thereafter, its calculated level of consumption of the controlled substances in Group I of Annex A does not exceed zero. Each Party producing one or more of these substances shall, for the same periods, ensure that its calculated level of production of the substances does not exceed zero. However, in order to satisfy the basic domestic needs of the Parties operating under paragraph 1 of Article 5, its calculated level of production may exceed that limit by a quantity equal to the annual average of its production of the controlled substances in Group I of Annex A for basic domestic needs for the period 1995 to 1997 inclusive. This paragraph will apply save to the extent that the Parties decide to permit the level of production or consumption that is necessary to satisfy uses agreed by them to be essential.
5. Each Party shall ensure that for the twelve-month period commencing on 1 January 2003 and in each twelve-month period thereafter, its calculated level of production of the controlled substances in Group I of Annex A for the basic domestic needs of the Parties operating under paragraph 1 of Article 5 does not exceed eighty per cent of the annual average of its production of those substances for basic domestic needs for the period 1995 to 1997 inclusive.
6. Each Party shall ensure that for the twelve-month period commencing on 1 January 2005 and in each twelve-month period thereafter, its calculated level of production of the controlled substances in Group I of Annex A for the basic domestic needs of the Parties operating under paragraph 1 of Article 5 does not exceed fifty per cent of the annual average of its production of those substances for basic domestic needs for the period 1995 to 1997 inclusive.
7. Each Party shall ensure that for the twelve-month period commencing on 1 January 2007 and in each twelve-month period thereafter, its calculated level of production of the controlled substances in Group I of Annex A for the basic domestic needs of the Parties operating under paragraph 1 of Article 5 does not exceed fifteen per cent of the annual average of its production of those substances for basic domestic needs for the period 1995 to 1997 inclusive.
8. Each Party shall ensure that for the twelve-month period commencing on 1 January 2010 and in each twelve-month period thereafter, its calculated level of production of the controlled substances in Group I of Annex A for the basic domestic needs of the Parties operating under paragraph 1 of Article 5 does not exceed zero.
9. For the purposes of calculating basic domestic needs under paragraphs 4 to 8 of this Article, the calculation of the annual average of production by a Party includes any production entitlements that it has transferred in accordance with paragraph 5 of Article 2, and excludes any production entitlements that it has acquired in accordance with paragraph 5 of Article 2.

Article 2B: Halons

1. Each Party shall ensure that for the twelve-month period commencing on 1 January 1992, and in each twelve-month period thereafter, its calculated level of consumption of the controlled substances in Group II of Annex A does not exceed, annually, its calculated level of consumption in 1986. Each Party producing one or more of these substances shall, for the same periods, ensure that its calculated level of production of the substances does not exceed, annually, its calculated level of production in 1986. However, in order to satisfy the basic domestic needs of the Parties operating under paragraph 1 of Article 5, its calculated level of production may exceed that limit by up to ten per cent of its calculated level of production in 1986.
2. Each Party shall ensure that for the twelve-month period commencing on 1 January 1994, and in each twelve-month period thereafter, its calculated level of consumption of the controlled substances in Group II of Annex A does not exceed zero. Each Party producing one or more of these substances shall, for the same periods, ensure that its calculated level of production of the substances does not exceed zero. However, in order to satisfy the basic domestic needs of the Parties operating under paragraph 1 of Article 5, its calculated level of production may, until 1 January 2002 exceed that limit by up to fifteen per cent of its calculated level of production in 1986; thereafter, it may exceed that limit by a quantity equal to the annual average of its production of the controlled substances in Group II of Annex A for basic domestic needs for the period 1995 to 1997 inclusive. This paragraph will apply save to the extent that the Parties decide to permit the level of production or consumption

that is necessary to satisfy uses agreed by them to be essential.

3. Each Party shall ensure that for the twelve-month period commencing on 1 January 2005 and in each twelve-month period thereafter, its calculated level of production of the controlled substances in Group II of Annex A for the basic domestic needs of the Parties operating under paragraph 1 of Article 5 does not exceed fifty per cent of the annual average of its production of those substances for basic domestic needs for the period 1995 to 1997 inclusive.
4. Each Party shall ensure that for the twelve-month period commencing on 1 January 2010 and in each twelve-month period thereafter, its calculated level of production of the controlled substances in Group II of Annex A for the basic domestic needs of the Parties operating under paragraph 1 of Article 5 does not exceed zero.

Article 2C: Other fully halogenated CFCs

1. Each Party shall ensure that for the twelve-month period commencing on 1 January 1993, its calculated level of consumption of the controlled substances in Group I of Annex B does not exceed, annually, eighty per cent of its calculated level of consumption in 1989. Each Party producing one or more of these substances shall, for the same period, ensure that its calculated level of production of the substances does not exceed, annually, eighty per cent of its calculated level of production in 1989. However, in order to satisfy the basic domestic needs of the Parties operating under paragraph 1 of Article 5, its calculated level of production may exceed that limit by up to ten per cent of its calculated level of production in 1989.
2. Each Party shall ensure that for the twelve-month period commencing on 1 January 1994, and in each twelve-month period thereafter, its calculated level of consumption of the controlled substances in 43 Article 2C Group I of Annex B does not exceed, annually, twenty-five per cent of its calculated level of consumption in 1989. Each Party producing one or more of these substances shall, for the same periods, ensure that its calculated level of production of the substances does not exceed, annually, twenty-five per cent of its calculated level of production in 1989. However, in order to satisfy the basic domestic needs of the Parties operating under paragraph 1 of Article 5, its calculated level of production may exceed that limit by up to ten per cent of its calculated level of production in 1989.
3. Each Party shall ensure that for the twelve-month period commencing on 1 January 1996, and in each twelve-month period thereafter, its calculated level of consumption of the controlled substances in Group I of Annex B does not exceed zero. Each Party producing one or more of these substances shall, for the same periods, ensure that its calculated level of production of the substances does not exceed zero. However, in order to satisfy the basic domestic needs of the Parties operating under paragraph 1 of Article 5, its calculated level of production may, until 1 January 2003 exceed that limit by up to fifteen per cent of its calculated level of production in 1989; thereafter, it may exceed that limit by a quantity equal to eighty per cent of the annual average of its production of the controlled substances in Group I of Annex B for basic domestic needs for the period 1998 to 2000 inclusive. This paragraph will apply save to the extent that the Parties decide to permit the level of production or consumption that is necessary to satisfy uses agreed by them to be essential.
4. Each Party shall ensure that for the twelve-month period commencing on 1 January 2007 and in each twelve-month period thereafter, its calculated level of production of the controlled substances in Group I of Annex B for the basic domestic needs of the Parties operating under paragraph 1 of Article 5 does not exceed fifteen per cent of the annual average of its production of those substances for basic domestic needs for the period 1998 to 2000 inclusive.
5. Each Party shall ensure that for the twelve-month period commencing on 1 January 2010 and in each twelve-month period thereafter, its calculated level of production of the controlled substances in Group I of Annex B for the basic domestic needs of the Parties operating under paragraph 1 of Article 5 does not exceed zero.

Article 2D: Carbon tetrachloride

1. Each Party shall ensure that for the twelve-month period commencing on 1 January 1995, its calculated level of consumption of the controlled substance in Group II of Annex B does not exceed, annually, fifteen per cent of its calculated level of consumption in 1989. Each Party producing the substance shall, for the same period, ensure that its calculated level of production of the substance does not exceed, annually, fifteen per cent of its calculated level of production in 1989. However, in order to satisfy the basic domestic needs of the Parties operating under paragraph 1 of Article 5, its calculated level of production may exceed that limit by up to ten per cent of its calculated level of production in 1989.
2. Each Party shall ensure that for the twelve-month period commencing on 1 January 1996, and in each twelve-month period thereafter, its calculated level of consumption of the controlled substance in Group II of Annex B does not exceed zero. Each Party producing the substance shall, for the same periods, ensure that its calculated level of production of the substance does not exceed zero. However, in order to satisfy the basic domestic needs of the Parties operating under paragraph 1 of Article 5, its calculated level of production may exceed that limit by up to fifteen per cent of its calculated level of production in 1989. This paragraph will apply save to the extent that the Parties decide to permit the level of production or consumption that is necessary to satisfy uses agreed by them to be essential.

Article 2E: 1,1,1-Trichloroethane (methyl chloroform)

1. Each Party shall ensure that for the twelve-month period commencing on 1 January 1993, its calculated level of consumption of the controlled substance in Group III of Annex B does not exceed, annually, its calculated level of consumption in 1989. Each Party producing the substance shall, for the same period, ensure that its calculated level of production of the substance does not exceed, annually, its calculated level of production in 1989. However, in order to satisfy the basic domestic needs of the Parties operating under paragraph 1 of Article 5, its calculated level of production may exceed that limit by up to ten per cent of its calculated level of production in 1989.
2. Each Party shall ensure that for the twelve-month period commencing on 1 January 1994, and in each twelve-month period thereafter, its calculated level of consumption of the controlled substance in Group III of Annex B does not exceed, annually, fifty per cent of its calculated level of consumption in 1989. Each Party producing the substance shall, for the same periods, ensure that its calculated level of production of the substance does not exceed, annually, fifty per cent of its calculated level of production in 1989. However, in order to satisfy the basic domestic needs of the Parties operating under paragraph 1 of Article 5, its calculated level of production may exceed that limit by up to ten per cent of its calculated level of production in 1989.
3. Each Party shall ensure that for the twelve-month period commencing on 1 January 1996, and in each twelve-month period thereafter, its calculated level of consumption of the controlled substance in Group III of Annex B does not exceed zero. Each Party producing the substance shall, for the same periods, ensure that its calculated level of production of the substance does not exceed zero. However, in order to satisfy the basic domestic needs of the Parties operating under paragraph 1 of Article 5, its calculated level of production may exceed that limit by up to fifteen per cent of its calculated level of production for 1989. This paragraph will apply save to the extent that the Parties decide to permit the level of production or consumption that is necessary to satisfy uses agreed by them to be essential.

Article 2F: Hydrochlorofluorocarbons

1. Each Party shall ensure that for the twelve-month period commencing on 1 January 1996, and in each twelve-month period thereafter, its calculated level of consumption of the controlled substances in Group I of Annex C does not exceed, annually, the sum of:
   (a) Two point eight per cent of its calculated level of consumption in 1989 of the controlled substances in Group I of Annex A; and
   (b) Its calculated level of consumption in 1989 of the controlled substances in Group I of Annex C.
2. Each Party producing one or more of these substances shall ensure that for the twelve-month period commencing on 1 January 2004, and in each twelve-month period thereafter, its calculated level of production of the controlled substances in Group I of Annex C does not exceed, annually, the average of:
   (a) The sum of its calculated level of consumption in 1989 of the controlled substances in Group I of Annex C and two point eight per cent of its calculated level of consumption in 1989 of the controlled substances in Group I of Annex A; and
   (b) The sum of its calculated level of production in 1989 of the controlled substances in Group I of Annex C and two point eight per cent of its calculated level of production in 1989 of the controlled substances in Group I of Annex A. However, in order to satisfy the basic domestic needs of the Parties operating under paragraph 1 of Article 5, its calculated level of production may exceed that limit by up to fifteen per cent of its calculated level of production of the controlled substances in Group I of Annex C as defined above.
3. Each Party shall ensure that for the twelve-month period commencing on 1 January 2004, and in each twelve-month period thereafter, its calculated level of consumption of the controlled substances in Group I of Annex C does not exceed, annually, sixty-five per cent of the sum referred to in paragraph 1 of this Article.
4. Each Party shall ensure that for the twelve-month period commencing on 1 January 2010, and in each twelve-month period thereafter, its calculated level of consumption of the controlled substances in Group I of Annex C does not exceed, annually, twenty-five per cent of the sum referred to in paragraph 1 of this Article. Each Party producing one or more of these substances shall, for the same periods, ensure that its calculated level of production of the controlled substances in Group I of Annex C does not exceed, annually, twenty- five per cent of the calculated level referred to in paragraph 2 of this Article. However, in order to satisfy the basic domestic needs of the Parties operating under paragraph 1 of Article 5, its calculated level of production may exceed that limit by up to ten per cent of its calculated level of production of the controlled substances in Group I of Annex C as referred to in paragraph 2.
5. Each Party shall ensure that for the twelve-month period commencing on 1 January 2015, and in each twelve-month period thereafter, its calculated level of consumption of the controlled substances in Group I of Annex C does not exceed, annually, ten per cent of the sum referred to in paragraph 1 of this Article. Each Party producing one or more of these substances shall, for the same periods, ensure that its calculated level of production of the controlled substances in Group I of Annex C does not exceed, annually, ten per cent of the calculated level referred to in paragraph 2 of this Article. However, in order to satisfy the basic domestic needs

of the Parties operating under paragraph 1 of Article 5, its calculated level of production may exceed that limit by up to ten per cent of its calculated level of production of the controlled substances in Group I of Annex C as referred to in paragraph 2.

6. Each Party shall ensure that for the twelve-month period commencing on 1 January 2020, and in each twelve-month period thereafter, its calculated level of consumption of the controlled substances in Group I of Annex C does not exceed zero. Each Party producing one or more of these substances shall, for the same periods, ensure that its calculated level of production of the controlled substances in Group I of Annex C does not exceed zero. This paragraph will apply save to the extent that the Parties decide to permit the level of production or consumption that is necessary to satisfy uses agreed by them to be essential. However:
   (a) Each Party may exceed that limit on consumption by up to zero point five per cent of the sum referred to in paragraph 1 of this Article in any such twelve-month period ending before 1 January 2030, provided that such consumption shall be restricted to:
      (i) The servicing of refrigeration and air-conditioning equipment existing on 1 January 2020;
      (ii) The servicing of fire suppression and fire protection equipment existing on 1 January 2020;
      (iii) Solvent applications in rocket engine manufacturing; and
      (iv) Topical medical aerosol applications for the specialised treatment of burns.
   (b) Each Party may exceed that limit on production by up to zero point five per cent of the average referred to in paragraph 2 of this Article in any such twelve-month period ending before 1 January 2030, provided that such production shall be restricted to:
      (i) The servicing of refrigeration and air-conditioning equipment existing on 1 January 2020;
      (ii) The servicing of fire suppression and fire protection equipment existing on 1 January 2020;
      (iii) Solvent applications in rocket engine manufacturing; and
      (iv) Topical medical aerosol applications for the specialised treatment of burns.

7. As of 1 January 1996, each Party shall endeavour to ensure that:
   (a) The use of controlled substances in Group I of Annex C is limited to those applications where other more environmentally suitable alternative substances or technologies are not available;
   (b) The use of controlled substances in Group I of Annex C is not outside the areas of application currently met by controlled substances in Annexes A, B and C, except in rare cases for the protection of human life or human health; and
   (c) Controlled substances in Group I of Annex C are selected for use in a manner that minimizes ozone depletion, in addition to meeting other environmental, safety and economic considerations.

Article 2G: Hydrobromofluorocarbons

Each Party shall ensure that for the twelve-month period commencing on 1 January 1996, and in each twelve-month period thereafter, its calculated level of consumption of the controlled substances in Group II of Annex C does not exceed zero. Each Party producing the substances shall, for the same periods, ensure that its calculated level of production of the substances does not exceed zero. This paragraph will apply save to the extent that the Parties decide to permit the level of production or consumption that is necessary to satisfy uses agreed by them to be essential.

Article 2H: Methyl bromide

1. Each Party shall ensure that for the twelve-month period commencing on 1 January 1995, and in each twelve-month period thereafter, its calculated level of consumption of the controlled substance in Annex E does not exceed, annually, its calculated level of consumption in 1991. Each Party producing the substance shall, for the same period, ensure that its calculated level of production of the substance does not exceed, annually, its calculated level of production in 1991. However, in order to satisfy the basic domestic needs of the Parties operating under paragraph 1 of Article 5, its calculated level of production may exceed that limit by up to ten per cent of its calculated level of production in 1991.

2. Each Party shall ensure that for the twelve-month period commencing on 1 January 1999, and in the twelve-month period thereafter, its calculated level of consumption of the controlled substance in Annex E does not exceed, annually, seventy-five per cent of its calculated level of consumption in 1991. Each Party producing the substance shall, for the same periods, ensure that its calculated level of production of the substance does not exceed, annually, seventy-five per cent of its calculated level of production in 1991. However, in order to satisfy the basic domestic needs of the Parties operating under paragraph 1 of Article 5, its calculated level of production may exceed that limit by up to ten per cent of its calculated level of production in 1991.

3. Each Party shall ensure that for the twelve-month period commencing on 1 January 2001, and in the twelve-month period thereafter, its calculated level of consumption of the controlled substance in Annex E does not exceed, annually, fifty per cent of its calculated level of consumption in 1991. Each Party producing the substance shall, for the same periods, ensure that its calculated level of production of the substance does not exceed, annually, fifty per cent of its calculated level of production in 1991. However, in order to satisfy the basic do-

mestic needs of the Parties operating under paragraph 1 of Article 5, its calculated level of production may exceed that limit by up to ten per cent of its calculated level of production in 1991.

4. Each Party shall ensure that for the twelve-month period commencing on 1 January 2003, and in the twelve-month period thereafter, its calculated level of consumption of the controlled substance in Annex E does not exceed, annually, thirty per cent of its calculated level of consumption in 1991. Each Party producing the substance shall, for the same periods, ensure that its calculated level of production of the substance does not exceed, annually, thirty per cent of its calculated level of production in 1991. However, in order to satisfy the basic domestic needs of the Parties operating under paragraph 1 of Article 5, its calculated level of production may exceed that limit by up to ten per cent of its calculated level of production in 1991.
5. Each Party shall ensure that for the twelve-month period commencing on 1 January 2005, and in each twelve-month period thereafter, its calculated level of consumption of the controlled substance in Annex E does not exceed zero. Each Party producing the substance shall, for the same periods, ensure that its calculated level of production of the substance does not exceed zero. However, in order to satisfy the basic domestic needs of the Parties operating under paragraph 1 of Article 5, its calculated level of production may, until 1 January 2002 exceed that limit by up to fifteen per cent of its calculated level of production in 1991; thereafter, it may exceed that limit by a quantity equal to the annual average of its production of the controlled substance in Annex E for basic domestic needs for the period 1995 to 1998 inclusive. This paragraph will apply save to the extent that the Parties decide to permit the level of production or consumption that is necessary to satisfy uses agreed by them to be critical uses.

5bis. Each Party shall ensure that for the twelve-month period commencing on 1 January 2005 and in each twelve-month period thereafter, its calculated level of production of the controlled substance in Annex E for the basic domestic needs of the Parties operating under paragraph 1 of Article 5 does not exceed eighty per cent of the annual average of its production of the substance for basic domestic needs for the period 1995 to 1998 inclusive.

5ter. Each Party shall ensure that for the twelve-month period commencing on 1 January 2015 and in each twelve-month period thereafter, its calculated level of production of the controlled substance in Annex E for the basic domestic needs of the Parties operating under paragraph 1 of Article 5 does not exceed zero.

6. The calculated levels of consumption and production under this Article shall not include the amounts used by the Party for quarantine and pre-shipment applications.

Article 2I: Bromochloromethane

Each Party shall ensure that for the twelve-month period commencing on 1 January 2002, and in each twelve-month period thereafter, its calculated level of consumption and production of the controlled substance in Group III of Annex C does not exceed zero. This paragraph will apply save to the extent that the Parties decide to permit the level of production or consumption that is necessary to satisfy uses agreed by them to be essential.

Article 2J: Hydrofluorocarbons

1. Each Party shall ensure that for the twelve-month period commencing on 1 January 2019, and in each twelve-month period thereafter, its calculated level of consumption of the controlled substances in Annex F, expressed in CO 2 equivalents, does not exceed the percentage, set out for the respective range of years specified in subparagraphs (a) to (e) below, of the annual average of its calculated levels of consumption of Annex F controlled substances for the years 2011, 2012 and 2013, plus fifteen per cent of its calculated level of consumption of Annex C, Group I, controlled substances as set out in paragraph 1 of Article 2F, expressed in CO2 equivalents:
   (a) 2019 to 2023: 90 per cent
   (b) 2024 to 2028: 60 per cent
   (c) 2029 to 2033: 30 per cent
   (d) 2034 to 2035: 20 per cent
   (e) 2036 and thereafter: 15 per cent
2. Notwithstanding paragraph 1 of this Article, the Parties may decide that a Party shall ensure that, for the twelve-month period commencing on 1 January 2020, and in each twelve-month period thereafter, its calculated level of consumption of the controlled substances in Annex F, expressed in CO 2 equivalents, does not exceed the percentage, set out for the respective range of years specified in subparagraphs (a) to (e) below, of the annual average of its calculated levels of consumption of Annex F controlled substances for the years 2011, 2012 and 2013, plus twenty-five per cent of its calculated level of consumption of Annex C, Group I, controlled substances as set out in paragraph 1 of Article 2F, expressed in CO2 equivalents:
   (a) 2020 to 2024: 95 per cent
   (b) 2025 to 2028: 65 per cent
   (c) 2029 to 2033: 30 per cent
   (d) 2034 to 2035: 20 per cent
   (e) 2036 and thereafter: 15 per cent
3. Each Party producing the controlled substances in Annex F shall ensure that for the twelve-month period commencing on 1 January 2019, and in each twelve-month period thereafter, its calculated level of production of the controlled substances in Annex F, expressed in CO 2 equivalents, does not exceed the percentage, set out for the respective range of years specified in subparagraphs (a) to (e) below, of the annual average of its calculated levels of production of Annex F controlled substances

for the years 2011, 2012 and 2013, plus fifteen per cent of its calculated level of production of Annex C, Group I, controlled substances as set out in paragraph 2 of Article 2F, expressed in CO2 equivalents:

(a) 2019 to 2023: 90 per cent

(b) 2024 to 2028: 60 per cent

(c) 2029 to 2033: 30 per cent

(d) 2034 to 2035: 20 per cent

(e) 2036 and thereafter: 15 per cent

4. Notwithstanding paragraph 3 of this Article, the Parties may decide that a Party producing the controlled substances in Annex F shall ensure that for the twelve-month period commencing on 1 January 2020, and in each twelve-month period thereafter, its calculated level of production of the controlled substances in Annex F, expressed in CO2 equivalents, does not exceed the percentage, set out for the respective range of years specified in subparagraphs (a) to (e) below, of the annual average of its calculated levels of production of Annex F controlled substances for the years 2011, 2012 and 2013, plus twenty-five per cent of its calculated level of production of Annex C, Group I, controlled substances as set out in paragraph 2 of Article 2F, expressed in CO2 equivalents:

   (a) 2020 to 2024: 95 per cent

   (b) 2025 to 2028: 65 per cent

   (c) 2029 to 2033: 30 per cent

   (d) 2034 to 2035: 20 per cent

   (e) 2036 and thereafter: 15 per cent

5. Paragraphs 1 to 4 of this Article will apply save to the extent that the Parties decide to permit the level of production or consumption that is necessary to satisfy uses agreed by the Parties to be exempted uses.

6. Each Party manufacturing Annex C, Group I, or Annex F substances shall ensure that for the twelve-month period commencing on 1 January 2020, and in each twelve-month period thereafter, its emissions of Annex F, Group II, substances generated in each production facility that manufactures Annex C, Group I, or Annex F substances are destroyed to the extent practicable using technology approved by the Parties in the same twelve-month period.

7. Each Party shall ensure that any destruction of Annex F, Group II, substances generated by facilities that produce Annex C, Group I, or Annex F substances shall occur only by technologies approved by the Parties.

Article 3: Calculation of control levels

1. For the purposes of Articles 2, 2A to 2J and 5, each Party shall, for each group of substances in Annex A, Annex B, Annex C, Annex E or Annex F, determine its calculated levels of:

   (a) Production by:

      (i) multiplying its annual production of each controlled substance by the ozone depleting potential specified in respect of it in Annex A, Annex B, Annex C or Annex E, except as otherwise specified in paragraph 2;

      (ii) adding together, for each such Group, the resulting figures;

   (b) Imports and exports, respectively, by following, Mutatis mutandis, the procedure set out in subparagraph (a); and

   (c) Consumption by adding together its calculated levels of production and imports and subtracting its calculated level of exports as determined in accordance with subparagraphs (a) and (b). However, beginning on 1 January 1993, any export of controlled substances to non-Parties shall not be subtracted in calculating the consumption level of the exporting Party; and

   (d) Emissions of Annex F, Group II, substances generated in each facility that generates Annex C, Group I, or Annex F substances by including, among other things, amounts emitted from equipment leaks, process vents and destruction devices, but excluding amounts captured for use, destruction or storage.

2. When calculating levels, expressed in CO2 equivalents, of production, consumption, imports, exports and emissions of Annex F and Annex C, Group I, substances for the purposes of Article 2J, paragraph 5 of Article 2 and paragraph 1 (d) of Article 3, each Party shall use the global warming potentials of those substances specified in Group I of Annex A, Annex C and Annex F.

Article 4: Control of trade with non-Parties

1. As of 1 January 1990, each party shall ban the import of the controlled substances in Annex A from any State not party to this Protocol.

1bis. Within one year of the date of the entry into force of this paragraph, each Party shall ban the import of the controlled substances in Annex B from any State not party to this Protocol.

1ter. Within one year of the date of entry into force of this paragraph, each Party shall ban the import of any controlled substances in Group II of Annex C from any State not party to this Protocol.

1qua. Within one year of the date of entry into force of this paragraph, each Party shall ban the import of the controlled substance in Annex E from any State not party to this Protocol.

1quin. As of 1 January 2004, each Party shall ban the import of the controlled substances in Group I of Annex C from any State not party to this Protocol.

1sex. Within one year of the date of entry into force of this paragraph, each Party shall ban the import of the controlled substance in Group III of Annex C from any State not party to this Protocol.

1sept. Upon entry into force of this paragraph, each Party shall ban the import of the controlled substances in Annex F from any State not Party to this Protocol.

2. As of 1 January 1993, each Party shall ban the export of any controlled substances in Annex A to any State not party to this Protocol.

2bis. Commencing one year after the date of entry into force of this paragraph, each Party shall ban the export of any controlled substances in Annex B to any State not party to this Protocol.

2ter. Commencing one year after the date of entry into force of this paragraph, each Party shall ban the export of any controlled substances in Group II of Annex C to any State not party to this Protocol.

2qua. Commencing one year of the date of entry into force of this paragraph, each Party shall ban the export of the controlled substance in Annex E to any State not party to this Protocol.

2quin. As of 1 January 2004, each Party shall ban the export of the controlled substances in Group I of Annex C to any State not party to this Protocol.

2sex. Within one year of the date of entry into force of this paragraph, each Party shall ban the export of the controlled substance in Group III of Annex C to any State not party to this Protocol.

2sept. Upon entry into force of this paragraph, each Party shall ban the export of the controlled substances in Annex F to any State not Party to this Protocol.

3. By 1 January 1992, the Parties shall, following the procedures in Article 10 of the Convention, elaborate in an annex a list of products containing controlled substances in Annex A. Parties that have not objected to the annex in accordance with those procedures shall ban, within one year of the annex having become effective, the import of those products from any State not party to this Protocol.

3bis. Within three years of the date of the entry into force of this paragraph, the Parties shall, following the procedures in Article 10 of the Convention, elaborate in an annex a list of products containing controlled substances in Annex B. Parties that have not objected to the annex in accordance with those procedures shall ban, within one year of the annex having become effective, the import of those products from any State not party to this Protocol.

3ter. Within three years of the date of entry into force of this paragraph, the Parties shall, following the procedures in Article 10 of the Convention, elaborate in an annex a list of products containing controlled substances in Group II of Annex C. Parties that have not objected to the annex in accordance with those procedures shall ban, within one year of the annex having become effective, the import of those products from any State not party to this Protocol.

4. By 1 January 1994, the Parties shall determine the feasibility of banning or restricting, from States not party to this Protocol, the import of products produced with, but not containing, controlled substances in Annex A. If determined feasible, the Parties shall, following the procedures in Article 10 of the Convention, elaborate in an annex a list of such products. Parties that have not objected to the annex in accordance with those procedures shall ban or restrict, within one year of the annex having become effective, the import of those products from any State not party to this Protocol.

4bis. Within five years of the date of the entry into force of this paragraph, the Parties shall determine the feasibility of banning or restricting, from States not party to this Protocol, the import of products produced with, but not containing, controlled substances in Annex B. If determined feasible, the Parties shall, following the procedures in Article 10 of the Convention, elaborate in an annex a list of such products. Parties that have not objected to the annex in accordance with those procedures shall ban or restrict, within one year of the annex having become effective, the import of those products from any State not party to this Protocol.

4ter. Within five years of the date of entry into force of this paragraph, the Parties shall determine the feasibility of banning or restricting, from States not party to this Protocol, the import of products produced with, but not containing, controlled substances in Group II of Annex C. If determined feasible, the Parties shall, following the procedures in Article 10 of the Convention, elaborate in an annex a list of such products. Parties that have not objected to the annex in accordance with those procedures shall ban or restrict, within one year of the annex having become effective, the import of those products from any State not party to this Protocol.

5. Each Party undertakes to the fullest practicable extent to discourage the export to any State not party to this Protocol of technology for producing and for utilizing controlled substances in Annexes A, B, C, E and F.

6. Each Party shall refrain from providing new subsidies, aid, credits, guarantees or insurance programmes for the export to States not party to this Protocol of products, equipment, plants or technology that would facilitate the production of controlled substances in Annexes A, B, C, E and F.

7. Paragraphs 5 and 6 shall not apply to products, equipment, plants or technology that improve the containment, recovery, recycling or destruction of controlled substances, promote the development of alternative substances, or otherwise contribute to the reduction of emissions of controlled substances in Annexes A, B, C, E and F.

8. Notwithstanding the provisions of this Article, imports and exports referred to in paragraphs 1 to 4 ter of this Article may be permitted from, or to, any State not party to this Protocol, if that State is determined, by a meeting of the Parties, to be in full compliance with Article 2, Articles 2A to 2J and this Article, and have submitted data to that effect as specified in Article 7.

9. For the purposes of this Article, the term "State not party to this Protocol" shall include, with respect to a particular controlled substance, a State or regional economic integration organization that has not agreed to be bound by the control measures in effect for that substance.

10. By 1 January 1996, the Parties shall consider whether to amend this Protocol in order to extend the measures in this Article to trade in controlled substances in Group I of Annex C and in Annex E with States not party to the Protocol.

Article 4A: Control of trade with Parties

1. Where, after the phase-out date applicable to it for a controlled substance, a Party is unable, despite having taken all practicable steps to comply with its obligation under the Protocol, to cease production of that substance for domestic consumption, other than for uses agreed by the Parties to be essential, it shall ban the export of used, recycled and reclaimed quantities of that substance, other than for the purpose of destruction.

2. Paragraph 1 of this Article shall apply without prejudice to the operation of Article 11 of the Convention and the non-compliance procedure developed under Article 8 of the Protocol.

Article 4B: Licensing

1. Each Party shall, by 1 January 2000 or within three months of the date of entry into force of this Article for it, whichever is the later, establish and implement a system for licensing the import and export of new, used, recycled and reclaimed controlled substances in Annexes A, B, C and E.

2. Notwithstanding paragraph 1 of this Article, any Party operating under paragraph 1 of Article 5 which decides it is not in a position to establish and implement a system for licensing the import and export of controlled substances in Annexes C and E, may delay taking those actions until 1 January 2005 and 1 January 2002, respectively.

2bis. Each Party shall, by 1 January 2019 or within three months of the date of entry into force of this paragraph for it, whichever is later, establish and implement a system for licensing the import and export of new, used, recycled and reclaimed controlled substances in Annex F. Any Party operating under paragraph 1 of Article 5 that decides it is not in a position to establish and implement such a system by 1 January 2019 may delay taking those actions until 1 January 2021.

3. Each Party shall, within three months of the date of introducing its licensing system, report to the Secretariat on the establishment and operation of that system.

4. The Secretariat shall periodically prepare and circulate to all Parties a list of the Parties that have reported to it on their licensing systems and shall forward this information to the Implementation Committee for consideration and appropriate recommendations to the Parties.

Article 5: Special situation of developing countries

1. Any Party that is a developing country and whose annual calculated level of consumption of the controlled substances in Annex A is less than 0.3 kilograms per capita on the date of the entry into force of the Protocol for it, or any time thereafter until 1 January 1999, shall, in order to meet its basic domestic needs, be entitled to delay for ten years its compliance with the control measures set out in Articles 2A to 2E, provided that any further amendments to the adjustments or Amendment adopted at the Second Meeting of the Parties in London, 29 June 1990, shall apply to the Parties operating under this paragraph after the review provided for in paragraph 8 of this Article has taken place and shall be based on the conclusions of that review.

1bis. The Parties shall, taking into account the review referred to in paragraph 8 of this Article, the assessments made pursuant to Article 6 and any other relevant information, decide by 1 January 1996, through the procedure set forth in paragraph 9 of Article 2:

   (a) With respect to paragraphs 1 to 6 of Article 2F, what base year, initial levels, control schedules and phase-out date for consumption of the controlled substances in Group I of Annex C will apply to Parties operating under paragraph 1 of this Article;

   (b) With respect to Article 2G, what phase-out date for production and consumption of the controlled substances in Group II of Annex C will apply to Parties operating under paragraph 1 of this Article; and

   (c) With respect to Article 2H, what base year, initial levels and control schedules for consumption and production of the controlled substance in Annex E will apply to Parties operating under paragraph 1 of this Article.

2. However, any Party operating under paragraph 1 of this Article shall exceed neither an annual calculated level of consumption of the controlled substances in Annex A of 0.3 kilograms per capita nor an annual calculated level of consumption of controlled substances of Annex B of 0.2 kilograms per capita.

3. When implementing the control measures set out in Articles 2A to 2E, any Party operating under paragraph 1 of this Article shall be entitled to use:

   (a) For controlled substances under Annex A, either the average of its annual calculated level of consumption for the period 1995 to 1997 inclusive or a calculated level of consumption of 0.3 kilograms per capita, whichever is the lower, as the basis for determining its compliance with the control measures relating to consumption.

   (b) For controlled substances under Annex B, the average of its annual calculated level of consumption for the period 1998 to 2000 inclusive or a calculated level of consumption of 0.2 kilograms per capita, whichever is the lower, as the basis for determining its compliance with the control measures relating to consumption.

(c) For controlled substances under Annex A, either the average of its annual calculated level of production for the period 1995 to 1997 inclusive or a calculated level of production of 0.3 kilograms per capita, whichever is the lower, as the basis for determining its compliance with the control measures relating to production.

(d) For controlled substances under Annex B, either the average of its annual calculated level of production for the period 1998 to 2000 inclusive or a calculated level of production of 0.2 kilograms per capita, whichever is the lower, as the basis for determining its compliance with the control measures relating to production.

4. If a Party operating under paragraph 1 of this Article, at any time before the control measures obligations in Articles 2A to 2J become applicable to it, finds itself unable to obtain an adequate supply of controlled substances, it may notify this to the Secretariat. The Secretariat shall forthwith transmit a copy of such notification to the Parties, which shall consider the matter at their next Meeting, and decide upon appropriate action to be taken.

5. Developing the capacity to fulfil the obligations of the Parties operating under paragraph 1 of this Article to comply with the control measures set out in Articles 2A to 2E and Articles 2I and 2J, and with any control measures in Articles 2F to 2H that are decided pursuant to paragraph 1 bis of this Article, and their implementation by those same Parties will depend upon the effective implementation of the financial co-operation as provided by Article 10 and the transfer of technology as provided by Article 10A.

6. Any Party operating under paragraph 1 of this Article may, at any time, notify the Secretariat in writing that, having taken all practicable steps it is unable to implement any or all of the obligations laid down in Articles 2A to 2E and Articles 2I and 2J, or any or all obligations in Articles 2F to 2H that are decided pursuant to paragraph 1 bis of this Article, due to the inadequate implementation of Articles 10 and 10A. The Secretariat shall forthwith transmit a copy of the notification to the Parties, which shall consider the matter at their next Meeting, giving due recognition to paragraph 5 of this Article and shall decide upon appropriate action to be taken.

7. During the period between notification and the Meeting of the Parties at which the appropriate action referred to in paragraph 6 above is to be decided, or for a further period if the Meeting of the Parties so decides, the non-compliance procedures referred to in Article 8 shall not be invoked against the notifying Party.

8. A Meeting of the Parties shall review, not later than 1995, the situation of the Parties operating under paragraph 1 of this Article, including the effective implementation of financial co-operation and transfer of technology to them, and adopt such revisions that may be deemed necessary regarding the schedule of control measures applicable to those Parties.

8bis. Based on the conclusions of the review referred to in paragraph 8 above:

(a) With respect to the controlled substances in Annex A, a Party operating under paragraph 1 of this Article shall, in order to meet its basic domestic needs, be entitled to delay for ten years its compliance with the control measures adopted by the Second Meeting of the Parties in London, 29 June 1990, and reference by the Protocol to Articles 2A and 2B shall be read accordingly;

(b) With respect to the controlled substances in Annex B, a Party operating under paragraph 1 of this Article shall, in order to meet its basic domestic needs, be entitled to delay for ten years its compliance with the control measures adopted by the Second Meeting of the Parties in London, 29 June 1990, and reference by the Protocol to Articles 2C to 2E shall be read accordingly.

8ter. Pursuant to paragraph 1 bis above:

(a) Each Party operating under paragraph 1 of this Article shall ensure that for the twelve-month period commencing on 1 January 2013, and in each twelve-month period thereafter, its calculated level of consumption of the controlled substances in Group I of Annex C does not exceed, annually, the average of its calculated levels of consumption in 2009 and 2010. Each Party operating under paragraph 1 of this Article shall ensure that for the twelve-month period commencing on 1 January 2013 and in each twelve-month period thereafter, its calculated level of production of the controlled substances in Group I of Annex C does not exceed, annually, the average of its calculated levels of production in 2009 and 2010;

(b) Each Party operating under paragraph 1 of this Article shall ensure that for the twelve-month period commencing on 1 January 2015, and in each twelve-month period thereafter, its calculated level of consumption of the controlled substances in Group I of Annex C does not exceed, annually, ninety per cent of the average of its calculated levels of consumption in 2009 and 2010. Each such Party producing one or more of these substances shall, for the same periods, ensure that its calculated level of production of the controlled substances in Group I of Annex C does not exceed, annually, ninety per cent of the average of its calculated levels of production in 2009 and 2010;

(c) Each Party operating under paragraph 1 of this Article shall ensure that for the twelve-month period commencing on 1 January 2020, and in each twelve-month period thereafter, its calculated level of consumption of the controlled substances in Group I of Annex C does not exceed, annually, sixty-five per cent of the average of its calculated levels of consumption in 2009 and 2010. Each such Party producing one or more of these substances shall, for the same periods, ensure that its calculated level of production of the controlled substances in Group I of Annex C does not exceed, annually, sixty-five per cent of the average of its calculated levels of production in 2009 and 2010;

(d) Each Party operating under paragraph 1 of this Article shall ensure that for the twelve-month period commencing on 1 January 2025, and in each twelve-month period thereafter, its calculated level of consumption of the controlled substances in Group I of Annex C does not exceed, annually, thirty-two point five per cent of the average of its calculated levels of consumption in 2009 and 2010. Each such Party producing one or more of these substances shall, for the same periods, ensure that its calculated level of production of the controlled substances in Group I of Annex C does not exceed, annually, thirty-two point five per cent of the average of its calculated levels of production in 2009 and 2010;

(e) Each Party operating under paragraph 1 of this Article shall ensure that for the twelve-month period commencing on 1 January 2030, and in each twelve-month period thereafter, its calculated level of consumption of the controlled substances in Group I of Annex C does not exceed zero. Each such Party producing one or more of these substances shall, for the same periods, ensure that its calculated level of production of the controlled substances in Group I of Annex C does not exceed zero. This paragraph will apply save to the extent that the Parties decide to permit the level of production or consumption that is necessary to satisfy uses agreed by them to be essential. However:

  (i) Each such Party may exceed that limit on consumption in any such twelve-month period so long as the sum of its calculated levels of consumption over the ten-year period from 1 January 2030 to 1 January 2040, divided by ten, does not exceed two point five per cent of the average of its calculated levels of consumption in 2009 and 2010, and provided that such consumption shall be restricted to:

    a. the servicing of refrigeration and air-conditioning equipment existing on 1 January 2030;

    b. The servicing of fire suppression and fire protection equipment existing on 1 January 2030;

    c. Solvent applications in rocket engine manufacturing; and

    d. Topical medical aerosol applications for the specialized treatment of burns.

  (ii) Each such Party may exceed that limit on production in any such twelve-month period so long as the sum of its calculated levels of production over the ten-year period from 1 January 2030 to 1 January 2040, divided by ten, does not exceed two point five per cent of the average of its calculated levels of production in 2009 and 2010, and provided that such production shall be restricted to:

    a. the servicing of refrigeration and air-conditioning equipment existing on 1 January 2030;

    b. The servicing of fire suppression and fire protection equipment existing on 1 January 2030;

    c. Solvent applications in rocket engine manufacturing; and

    d. Topical medical aerosol applications for the specialized treatment of burns.

(f) Each Party operating under paragraph 1 of this Article shall comply with Article 2G;

(g) With regard to the controlled substance contained in Annex E:

  (i) As of 1 January 2002 each Party operating under paragraph 1 of this Article shall comply with the control measures set out in paragraph 1 of Article 2H and, as the basis for its compliance with these control measures, it shall use the average of its annual calculated level of consumption and production, respectively, for the period of 1995 to 1998 inclusive;

  (ii) Each Party operating under paragraph 1 of this Article shall ensure that for the twelve-month period commencing on 1 January 2005, and in each twelve-month period thereafter, its calculated levels of consumption and production of the controlled substance in Annex E do not exceed, annually, eighty per cent of the average of its annual calculated levels of consumption and production, respectively, for the period of 1995 to 1998 inclusive;

  (iii) Each Party operating under paragraph 1 of this Article shall ensure that for the twelve-month period commencing on 1 January 2015 and in each twelve-month period thereafter, its calculated levels of consumption and production of the controlled substance in Annex E do not exceed zero. This paragraph will apply save to the extent that the Parties decide to permit the level of production or consumption that is necessary to satisfy uses agreed by them to be critical uses;

(iv) The calculated levels of consumption and production under this subparagraph shall not include the amounts used by the Party for quarantine and pre-shipment applications.

8qua (a) Each Party operating under paragraph 1 of this Article, subject to any adjustments made to the control measures in Article 2J in accordance with paragraph 9 of Article 2, shall be entitled to delay its compliance with the control measures set out in subparagraphs (a) to (e) of paragraph 1 of Article 2J and subparagraphs (a) to (e) of paragraph 3 of Article 2J and modify those measures as follows:

(i) 2024 to 2028: 100 per cent

(ii) 2029 to 2034: 90 per cent

(iii) 2035 to 2039: 70 per cent

(iv) 2040 to 2044: 50 per cent

(v) 2045 and thereafter: 20 per cent

(b) Notwithstanding subparagraph (a) above, the Parties may decide that a Party operating under paragraph 1 of this Article, subject to any adjustments made to the control measures in Article 2J in accordance with paragraph 9 of Article 2, shall be entitled to delay its compliance with the control measures set out in subparagraphs (a) to (e) of paragraph 1 of Article 2J and subparagraphs (a) to (e) of paragraph 3 of Article 2J and modify those measures as follows:

(i) 2028 to 2031: 100 per cent

(ii) 2032 to 2036: 90 per cent

(iii) 2037 to 2041: 80 per cent

(iv) 2042 to 2046: 70 per cent

(v) 2047 and thereafter: 15 per cent

(c) Each Party operating under paragraph 1 of this Article, for the purposes of calculating its consumption baseline under Article 2J, shall be entitled to use the average of its calculated levels of consumption of Annex F controlled substances for the years 2020, 2021 and 2022, plus sixty-five per cent of its baseline consumption of Annex C, Group I, controlled substances as set out in paragraph 8 ter of this Article.

(d) Notwithstanding subparagraph (c) above, the Parties may decide that a Party operating under paragraph 1 of this Article, for the purposes of calculating its consumption baseline under Article 2J, shall be entitled to use the average of its calculated levels of consumption of Annex F controlled substances for the years 2024, 2025 and 2026, plus sixty-five per cent of its baseline consumption of Annex C, Group I, controlled substances as set out in paragraph 8 ter of this Article.

(e) Each Party operating under paragraph 1 of this Article and producing the controlled substances in Annex F, for the purposes of calculating its production baseline under Article 2J, shall be entitled to use the average of its calculated levels of production of Annex F controlled substances for the years 2020, 2021 and 2022, plus sixty-five per cent of its baseline production of Annex C, Group I, controlled substances as set out in paragraph 8 ter of this Article.

(f) Notwithstanding subparagraph (e) above, the Parties may decide that a Party operating under paragraph 1 of this Article and producing the controlled substances in Annex F, for the purposes of calculating its production baseline under Article 2J, shall be entitled to use the average of its calculated levels of production of Annex F controlled substances for the years 2024, 2025 and 2026, plus sixty-five per cent of its baseline production of Annex C, Group I, controlled substances as set out in paragraph 8 ter of this Article.

(g) Subparagraphs (a) to (f) of this paragraph will apply to calculated levels of production and consumption save to the extent that a high-ambient-temperature exemption applies based on criteria decided by the Parties.

9. Decisions of the Parties referred to in paragraph 4, 6 and 7 of this Article shall be taken according to the same procedure applied to decision-making under Article 10.

Article 6: Assessment and review of control measures

Beginning in 1990, and at least every four years thereafter, the Parties shall assess the control measures provided for in Article 2 and Articles 2A to 2J on the basis of available scientific, environmental, technical and economic information. At least one year before each assessment, the Parties shall convene appropriate panels of experts qualified in the fields mentioned and determine the composition and terms of reference of any such panels. Within one year of being convened, the panels will report their conclusions, through the Secretariat, to the Parties.

Article 7: Reporting of data

1. Each Party shall provide to the Secretariat, within three months of becoming a Party, statistical data on its production, imports and exports of each of the controlled substances in Annex A for the year 1986, or the best possible estimates of such data where actual data are not available.
2. Each Party shall provide to the Secretariat statistical data on its production, imports and exports of each of the controlled substances
   - in Annex B and Groups I and II of Annex C for the year 1989;
   - in Annex E, for the year 1991,

- in Annex F, for the years 2011 to 2013, except that Parties operating under paragraph 1 of Article 5 shall provide such data for the years 2020 to 2022, but those Parties operating under paragraph 1 of Article 5 to which subparagraphs (d) and (f) of paragraph 8 qua of Article 5 applies shall provide such data for the years 2024 to 2026;

or the best possible estimates of such data where actual data are not available, not later than three months after the date when the provisions set out in the Protocol with regard to the substances in Annexes B, C, E and F respectively enter into force for that Party.

3. Each Party shall provide to the Secretariat statistical data on its annual production (as defined in paragraph 5 of Article 1) of each of the controlled substances listed in Annexes A, B, C, E and F and, separately, for each substance,
   - Amounts used for feedstocks,
   - Amounts destroyed by technologies approved by the Parties, and
   - Imports from and exports to Parties and non-Parties respectively,

   for the year during which provisions concerning the substances in Annexes A, B, C, E and F respectively entered into force for that Party and for each year thereafter. Each Party shall provide to the Secretariat statistical data on the annual amount of the controlled substance listed in Annex E used for quarantine and pre-shipment applications. Data shall be forwarded not later than nine months after the end of the year to which the data relate.

3bis. Each Party shall provide to the Secretariat separate statistical data of its annual imports and exports of each of the controlled substances listed in Group II of Annex A and Group I of Annex C that have been recycled.

3ter. Each Party shall provide to the Secretariat statistical data on its annual emissions of Annex F, Group II, controlled substances per facility in accordance with paragraph 1 (d) of Article 3 of the Protocol.

4. For Parties operating under the provisions of paragraph 8 (a) of Article 2, the requirements in paragraphs 1, 2, 3 and 3 bis of this Article in respect of statistical data on production, imports and exports shall be satisfied if the regional economic integration organization concerned provides data on production, imports and exports between the organization and States that are not members of that organization.

Article 8: Non-compliance

The Parties, at their first meeting, shall consider and approve procedures and institutional mechanisms for determining non-compliance with the provisions of this Protocol and for treatment of Parties found to be in non-compliance.

Article 9: Research, development, public awareness and exchange of information

1. The Parties shall co-operate, consistent with their national laws, regulations and practices and taking into account in particular the needs of developing countries, in promoting, directly or through competent international bodies, research, development and exchange of information on:
   (a) best technologies for improving the containment, recovery, recycling, or destruction of controlled substances or otherwise reducing their emissions;
   (b) possible alternatives to controlled substances, to products containing such substances, and to products manufactured with them; and
   (c) costs and benefits of relevant control strategies.
2. The Parties, individually, jointly or through competent international bodies, shall co-operate in promoting public awareness of the environmental effects of the emissions of controlled substances and other substances that deplete the ozone layer.
3. Within two years of the entry into force of this Protocol and every two years thereafter, each Party shall submit to the Secretariat a summary of the activities it has conducted pursuant to this Article.

Article 10: Financial mechanism

1. The Parties shall establish a mechanism for the purposes of providing financial and technical co-operation, including the transfer of technologies, to Parties operating under paragraph 1 of Article 5 of this Protocol to enable their compliance with the control measures set out in Articles 2A to 2E, Article 2I and Article 2J, and any control measures in Articles 2F to 2H that are decided pursuant to paragraph 1 bis of Article 5 of the Protocol. The mechanism, contributions to which shall be additional to other financial transfers to Parties operating under that paragraph, shall meet all agreed incremental costs of such Parties in order to enable their compliance with the control measures of the Protocol. An indicative list of the categories of incremental costs shall be decided by the meeting of the Parties. Where a Party operating under paragraph 1 of Article 5 chooses to avail itself of funding from any other financial mechanism that could result in meeting any part of its agreed incremental costs, that part shall not be met by the financial mechanism under Article 10 of this Protocol.
2. The mechanism established under paragraph 1 shall include a Multilateral Fund. It may also include other means of multilateral, regional and bilateral co-operation.
3. The Multilateral Fund shall:
   (a) Meet, on a grant or concessional basis as appropriate, and according to criteria to be decided upon by the Parties, the agreed incremental costs;
   (b) Finance clearing-house functions to:
      (i) Assist Parties operating under paragraph 1 of Article 5, through country specific

studies and other technical co-operation, to identify their needs for co-operation;

(ii) Facilitate technical co-operation to meet these identified needs;

(iii) Distribute, as provided for in Article 9, information and relevant materials, and hold workshops, training sessions, and other related activities, for the benefit of Parties that are developing countries; and

(iv) Facilitate and monitor other multilateral, regional and bilateral co-operation available to Parties that are developing countries;

(c) Finance the secretarial services of the Multilateral Fund and related support costs.

4. The Multilateral Fund shall operate under the authority of the Parties who shall decide on its overall policies.

5. The Parties shall establish an Executive Committee to develop and monitor the implementation of specific operational policies, guidelines and administrative arrangements, including the disbursement of resources, for the purpose of achieving the objectives of the Multilateral Fund. The Executive Committee shall discharge its tasks and responsibilities, specified in its terms of reference as agreed by the Parties, with the co-operation and assistance of the International Bank for Reconstruction and Development (World Bank), the United Nations Environment Programme, the United Nations Development Programme or other appropriate agencies depending on their respective areas of expertise. The members of the Executive Committee, which shall be selected on the basis of a balanced representation of the Parties operating under paragraph 1 of Article 5 and of the Parties not so operating, shall be endorsed by the Parties.

6. The Multilateral Fund shall be financed by contributions from Parties not operating under paragraph 1 of Article 5 in convertible currency or, in certain circumstances, in kind and/or in national currency, on the basis of the United Nations scale of assessments. Contributions by other Parties shall be encouraged. Bilateral and, in particular cases agreed by a decision of the Parties, regional co-operation may, up to a percentage and consistent with any criteria to be specified by decision of the Parties, be considered as a contribution to the Multilateral Fund, provided that such co-operation, as a minimum:

(a) Strictly relates to compliance with the provisions of this Protocol;

(b) Provides additional resources; and

(c) Meets agreed incremental costs.

7. The Parties shall decide upon the programme budget of the Multilateral Fund for each fiscal period and upon the percentage of contributions of the individual Parties thereto.

8. Resources under the Multilateral Fund shall be disbursed with the concurrence of the beneficiary Party.

9. Decisions by the Parties under this Article shall be taken by consensus whenever possible. If all efforts at consensus have been exhausted and no agreement reached, decisions shall be adopted by a two-thirds majority vote of the Parties present and voting, representing a majority of the Parties operating under paragraph 1 of Article 5 present and voting and a majority of the Parties not so operating present and voting.

10. The financial mechanism set out in this Article is without prejudice to any future arrangements that may be developed with respect to other environmental issues.

Article 10A: Transfer of technology

Each Party shall take every practicable step, consistent with the programmes supported by the financial mechanism, to ensure:

(a) that the best available, environmentally safe substitutes and related technologies are expeditiously transferred to Parties operating under paragraph 1 of Article 5; and

(b) that the transfers referred to in subparagraph (a) occur under fair and most favourable conditions.

Article 11: Meetings of the Parties

1. The Parties shall hold meetings at regular intervals. The Secretariat shall convene the first meeting of the Parties not later than one year after the date of the entry into force of this Protocol and in conjunction with a meeting of the Conference of the Parties to the Convention, if a meeting of the latter is scheduled within that period.

2. Subsequent ordinary meetings of the parties shall be held, unless the Parties otherwise decide, in conjunction with meetings of the Conference of the Parties to the Convention. Extraordinary meetings of the Parties shall be held at such other times as may be deemed necessary by a meeting of the Parties, or at the written request of any Party, provided that within six months of such a request being communicated to them by the Secretariat, it is supported by at least one third of the Parties.

3. The Parties, at their first meeting, shall:

(a) adopt by consensus rules of procedure for their meetings;

(b) adopt by consensus the financial rules referred to in paragraph 2 of Article 13;

(c) establish the panels and determine the terms of reference referred to in Article 6;

(d) consider and approve the procedures and institutional mechanisms specified in Article 8; and

(e) begin preparation of workplans pursuant to paragraph 3 of Article 10.

[The Article 10 in question is that of the original Protocol adopted in 1987.]

4. The functions of the meetings of the Parties shall be to:

(a) review the implementation of this Protocol;

(b) decide on any adjustments or reductions referred to in paragraph 9 of Article 2;

(c) decide on any addition to, insertion in or removal from any annex of substances and on related control measures in accordance with paragraph 10 of Article 2;

(d) establish, where necessary, guidelines or procedures for reporting of information as provided for in Article 7 and paragraph 3 of Article 9;

(e) review requests for technical assistance submitted pursuant to paragraph 2 of Article 10;

(f) review reports prepared by the secretariat pursuant to subparagraph (c) of Article 12;

(g) assess, in accordance with Article 6, the control measures;

(h) consider and adopt, as required, proposals for amendment of this Protocol or any annex and for any new annex;

(i) consider and adopt the budget for implementing this Protocol; and

(j) consider and undertake any additional action that may be required for the achievement of the purposes of this Protocol.

5. The United Nations, its specialized agencies and the International Atomic Energy Agency, as well as any State not party to this Protocol, may be represented at meetings of the Parties as observers. Anybody or agency, whether national or international, governmental or non-governmental, qualified in fields relating to the protection of the ozone layer which has informed the secretariat of its wish to be represented at a meeting of the Parties as an observer may be admitted unless at least one third of the Parties present object. The admission and participation of observers shall be subject to the rules of procedure adopted by the Parties.

Article 12: Secretariat

For the purposes of this Protocol, the Secretariat shall:

(a) arrange for and service meetings of the Parties as provided for in Article 11;

(b) receive and make available, upon request by a Party, data provided pursuant to Article 7;

(c) prepare and distribute regularly to the Parties reports based on information received pursuant to Articles 7 and 9;

(d) notify the Parties of any request for technical assistance received pursuant to Article 10 so as to facilitate the provision of such assistance;

(e) encourage non-Parties to attend the meetings of the Parties as observers and to act in accordance with the provisions of this Protocol;

(f) provide, as appropriate, the information and requests referred to in subparagraphs (c) and (d) to such non-party observers; and

(g) perform such other functions for the achievement of the purposes of this Protocol as may be assigned to it by the Parties.

Article 13: Financial provisions

1. The funds required for the operation of this Protocol, including those for the functioning of the Secretariat related to this Protocol, shall be charged exclusively against contributions from the Parties.
2. The Parties, at their first meeting, shall adopt by consensus financial rules for the operation of this Protocol.

Article 14: Relationship of this Protocol to the Convention

Except as otherwise provided in this Protocol, the provisions of the Convention relating to its protocols shall apply to this Protocol.

Article 15: Signature

This Protocol shall be open for signature by States and by regional economic integration organizations in Montreal on 16 September 1987, in Ottawa from 17 September 1987 to 16 January 1988, and at United Nations Headquarters in New York from 17 January 1988 to 15 September 1988.

Article 16: Entry into force

1. This Protocol shall enter into force on 1 January 1989, provided that at least eleven instruments of ratification, acceptance, approval of the Protocol or accession thereto have been deposited by States or regional economic integration organizations representing at least two-thirds of 1986 estimated global consumption of the controlled substances, and the provisions of paragraph 1 of Article 17 of the Convention have been fulfilled. In the event that these conditions have not been fulfilled by that date, the Protocol shall enter into force on the ninetieth day following the date on which the conditions have been fulfilled.
2. For the purposes of paragraph 1, any such instrument deposited by a regional economic integration organization shall not be counted as additional to those deposited by member States of such organization.
3. After the entry into force of this Protocol, any State or regional economic integration organization shall become a Party to it on the ninetieth day following the date of deposit of its instrument of ratification, acceptance, approval or accession.

Article 17: Parties joining after entry into force

Subject to Article 5, any State or regional economic integration organization which becomes a Party to this Protocol after the date of its entry into force, shall fulfil forthwith the sum of the obligations under Article 2, as well as under Articles 2A to 2J and Article 4, that apply at that date to the States and regional economic integration organizations that became Parties on the date the Protocol entered into force.

Article 18: Reservations

No reservations may be made to this Protocol.

Article 19: Withdrawal

Any Party may withdraw from this Protocol by giving written notification to the Depositary at any time after four years of assuming the obligations specified in paragraph 1 of Article 2A. Any such withdrawal shall take effect upon expiry of one year after the date of its receipt by the Depositary, or on such later date as may be specified in the notification of the withdrawal.

Article 20: Authentic texts

The original of this Protocol, of which the Arabic, Chinese, English, French, Russian and Spanish texts are equally authentic, shall be deposited with the Secretary-General of the United Nations.

IN WITNESS WHEREOF the undersigned, being duly authorized to that effect, have signed this protocol.

one thousand nine hundred and eighty seven.

Annex A. Controlled Substances

Group	Substance	Ozone-Depleting Potential	100-Year Global Warming Potential
Group I			
$CFCl_3$	(CFC-11)	1.0	4,750
CF_2Cl_2	(CFC-12)	1.0	10,900
$C_2F_3Cl_3$	(CFC-113)	0.8	6,130
$C_2F_4Cl_2$	(CFC-114)	1.0	7,370
C_2F_5Cl	(CFC-115)	0.6	
Group II			
CF_2BrCl	(halon-1211)	3.0	
CF_3Br	(halon-1301)	10.0	
$C_2F_4Br_2$	(halon-2402)	6.0	

6.1. UNFCCC 1992

United Nations Framework Convention on Climate Change, New York, 9 May 1992, 1771 UNTS 107

The Parties to this Convention,

Acknowledging that change in the Earth's climate and its adverse effects are a common concern of humankind,

Concerned that human activities have been substantially increasing the atmospheric concentrations of greenhouse gases, that these increases enhance the natural greenhouse effect, and that this will result on average in an additional warming of the Earth's surface and atmosphere and may adversely affect natural ecosystems and humankind,

Noting that the largest share of historical and current global emissions of greenhouse gases has originated in developed countries, that per capita emissions in developing countries are still relatively low and that the share of global emissions originating in developing countries will grow to meet their social and development needs,

Aware of the role and importance in terrestrial and marine ecosystems of sinks and reservoirs of greenhouse gases,

Noting that there are many uncertainties in predictions of climate change, particularly with regard to the timing, magnitude and regional patterns thereof,

Acknowledging that the global nature of climate change calls for the widest possible cooperation by all countries and their participation in an effective and appropriate international response, in accordance with their common but differentiated responsibilities and respective capabilities and their social and economic conditions,

Recalling the pertinent provisions of the Declaration of the United Nations Conference on the Human Environment, adopted at Stockholm on 16 June 1972,

Recalling also that States have, in accordance with the Charter of the United Nations and the principles of international law, the sovereign right to exploit their own resources pursuant to their own environmental and developmental policies, and the responsibility to ensure that activities within their jurisdiction or control do not cause damage to the environment of other States or of areas beyond the limits of national jurisdiction,

Reaffirming the principle of sovereignty of States in international cooperation to address climate change,

Recognizing that States should enact effective environmental legislation, that environmental standards, management objectives and priorities should reflect the environmental and developmental context to which they apply, and that standards applied by some countries may be inappropriate and of unwarranted economic and social cost to other countries, in particular developing countries,

Recalling the provisions of General Assembly resolution 44/228 of 22 December 1989 on the United Nations Conference on Environment and Development, and resolutions 43/53 of 6 December 1988, 44/207 of 22 December 1989, 45/212 of 21 December 1990 and 46/169 of 19 December 1991 on protection of global climate for present and future generations of mankind,

Recalling also the provisions of General Assembly resolution 44/206 of 22 December 1989 on the possible adverse effects of sea-level rise on islands and coastal areas, particularly low-lying coastal areas and the pertinent provisions of General Assembly resolution 44/172 of 19 December 1989 on the implementation of the Plan of Action to Combat Desertification,

Recalling further the Vienna Convention for the Protection of the Ozone Layer, 1985, and the Montreal Protocol on Substances that Deplete the Ozone Layer, 1987, as adjusted and amended on 29 June 1990,

Noting the Ministerial Declaration of the Second World Climate Conference adopted on 7 November 1990,

Conscious of the valuable analytical work being conducted by many States on climate change and of the important contributions of the World Meteorological Organization, the United Nations Environment Programme and other organs, organizations and bodies of the United Nations system, as well as other international and intergovernmental bodies, to the exchange of results of scientific research and the coordination of research,

Recognizing that steps required to understand and address climate change will be environmentally, socially and economically most effective if they are based on relevant scientific, technical and economic considerations and continually re-evaluated in the light of new findings in these areas,

Recognizing that various actions to address climate change can be justified economically in their own right and can also help in solving other environmental problems,

Recognizing also the need for developed countries to take immediate action in a flexible manner on the basis of clear priorities, as a first step towards comprehensive response strategies at the global, national and, where agreed, regional levels that take into account all greenhouse gases, with due consideration of their relative contributions to the enhancement of the greenhouse effect,

Recognizing further that low-lying and other small island countries, countries with low-lying coastal, arid and semi-arid areas or areas liable to floods, drought and desertification, and developing countries with fragile mountainous ecosystems are particularly vulnerable to the adverse effects of climate change,

Recognizing the special difficulties of those countries, especially developing countries, whose economies are particularly dependent on fossil fuel production, use and exportation, as a consequence of action taken on limiting greenhouse gas emissions,

Affirming that responses to climate change should be coordinated with social and economic development in an integrated manner with a view to avoiding adverse impacts on the latter, taking into full account the legitimate priority needs of developing countries for the achievement of sustained economic growth and the eradication of poverty,

Recognizing that all countries, especially developing countries, need access to resources required to achieve sustainable social and economic development and that, in order for developing countries to progress towards that goal, their energy consumption will need to grow taking into account the possibilities for achieving greater energy efficiency and for controlling greenhouse gas emissions in general, including through the application of new technologies on terms which make such an application economically and socially beneficial,

Determined to protect the climate system for present and future generations,

Have agreed as follows:

Article 1 – DEFINITIONS[1]

For the purposes of this Convention:

1. "Adverse effects of climate change" means changes in the physical environment or biota resulting from climate change which have significant deleterious effects on the composition, resilience or productivity of natural and managed ecosystems or on the operation of socio-economic systems or on human health and welfare.
2. "Climate change" means a change of climate which is attributed directly or indirectly to human activity that alters the composition of the global atmosphere and which is in addition to natural climate variability observed over comparable time periods.
3. "Climate system" means the totality of the atmosphere, hydrosphere, biosphere and geosphere and their interactions.
4. "Emissions" means the release of greenhouse gases and/or their precursors into the atmosphere over a specified area and period of time.
5. "Greenhouse gases" means those gaseous constituents of the atmosphere, both natural and anthropogenic, that absorb and re-emit infrared radiation.
6. "Regional economic integration organization" means an organization constituted by sovereign States of a given region which has competence in respect of matters governed by this Convention or its protocols and has been duly authorized, in accordance with its internal procedures, to sign, ratify, accept, approve or accede to the instruments concerned.
7. "Reservoir" means a component or components of the climate system where a greenhouse gas or a precursor of a greenhouse gas is stored.
8. "Sink" means any process, activity or mechanism which removes a greenhouse gas, an aerosol or a precursor of a greenhouse gas from the atmosphere.
9. "Source" means any process or activity which releases a greenhouse gas, an aerosol or a precursor of a greenhouse gas into the atmosphere.

Article 2 – OBJECTIVE

The ultimate objective of this Convention and any related legal instruments that the Conference of the Parties may adopt is to achieve, in accordance with the relevant provisions of the Convention, stabilization of greenhouse gas concentrations in the atmosphere at a level that would prevent dangerous anthropogenic interference with the climate system. Such a level should be achieved within a time frame sufficient to allow ecosystems to adapt naturally to climate change, to ensure that food production is not threatened and to enable economic development to proceed in a sustainable manner.

Article 3 – PRINCIPLES

In their actions to achieve the objective of the Convention and to implement its provisions, the Parties shall be guided, inter alia, by the following:

1. The Parties should protect the climate system for the benefit of present and future generations of humankind, on the basis of equity and in accordance with their common but differentiated responsibilities and respective capabilities. Accordingly, the developed country Parties should take the lead in combating climate change and the adverse effects thereof.
2. The specific needs and special circumstances of developing country Parties, especially those that are particularly vulnerable to the adverse effects of climate change, and of those Parties, especially developing country Parties, that would have to bear a disproportionate or abnormal burden under the Convention, should be given full consideration.
3. The Parties should take precautionary measures to anticipate, prevent or minimize the causes of climate change and mitigate its adverse effects. Where there are threats of serious or irreversible damage, lack of full scientific certainty should not be used as a reason for postponing such measures, taking into account that policies and measures to deal with climate change should be cost-effective so as to ensure global benefits at the lowest possible cost. To achieve this, such policies and measures should take into account different socio-economic contexts, be comprehensive, cover all relevant sources, sinks and reservoirs of greenhouse gases and adaptation, and comprise all economic sectors. Efforts to address climate change may be carried out cooperatively by interested Parties.
4. The Parties have a right to, and should, promote sustainable development. Policies and measures to protect the climate system against human-induced change should be appropriate for the specific conditions of each Party and should be integrated with

1 Titles of articles are included solely to assist the reader.

national development programmes, taking into account that economic development is essential for adopting measures to address climate change.

5. The Parties should cooperate to promote a supportive and open international economic system that would lead to sustainable economic growth and development in all Parties, particularly developing country Parties, thus enabling them better to address the problems of climate change. Measures taken to combat climate change, including unilateral ones, should not constitute a means of arbitrary or unjustifiable discrimination or a disguised restriction on international trade.

Article 4 – COMMITMENTS

1. All Parties, taking into account their common but differentiated responsibilities and their specific national and regional development priorities, objectives and circumstances, shall:
   (a) Develop, periodically update, publish and make available to the Conference of the Parties, in accordance with Article 12, national inventories of anthropogenic emissions by sources and removals by sinks of all greenhouse gases not controlled by the Montreal Protocol, using comparable methodologies to be agreed upon by the Conference of the Parties;

   (b) Formulate, implement, publish and regularly update national and, where appropriate, regional programmes containing measures to mitigate climate change by addressing anthropogenic emissions by sources and removals by sinks of all greenhouse gases not controlled by the Montreal Protocol, and measures to facilitate adequate adaptation to climate change;

   (c) Promote and cooperate in the development, application and diffusion, including transfer, of technologies, practices and processes that control, reduce or prevent anthropogenic emissions of greenhouse gases not controlled by the Montreal Protocol in all relevant sectors, including the energy, transport, industry, agriculture, forestry and waste management sectors;

   (d) Promote sustainable management, and promote and cooperate in the conservation and enhancement, as appropriate, of sinks and reservoirs of all greenhouse gases not controlled by the Montreal Protocol, including biomass, forests and oceans as well as other terrestrial, coastal and marine ecosystems;

   (e) Cooperate in preparing for adaptation to the impacts of climate change; develop and elaborate appropriate and integrated plans for coastal zone management, water resources and agriculture, and for the protection and rehabilitation of areas, particularly in Africa, affected by drought and desertification, as well as floods;

   (f) Take climate change considerations into account, to the extent feasible, in their relevant social, economic and environmental policies and actions, and employ appropriate methods, for example impact assessments, formulated and determined nationally, with a view to minimizing adverse effects on the economy, on public health and on the quality of the environment, of projects or measures undertaken by them to mitigate or adapt to climate change;

   (g) Promote and cooperate in scientific, technological, technical, socio-economic and other research, systematic observation and development of data archives related to the climate system and intended to further the understanding and to reduce or eliminate the remaining uncertainties regarding the causes, effects, magnitude and timing of climate change and the economic and social consequences of various response strategies;

   (h) Promote and cooperate in the full, open and prompt exchange of relevant scientific, technological, technical, socio-economic and legal information related to the climate system and climate change, and to the economic and social consequences of various response strategies;

   (i) Promote and cooperate in education, training and public awareness related to climate change and encourage the widest participation in this process, including that of non-governmental organizations; and

   (j) Communicate to the Conference of the Parties information related to implementation, in accordance with Article 12.

2. The developed country Parties and other Parties included in Annex I commit themselves specifically as provided for in the following:
   (a) Each of these Parties shall adopt national[1] policies and take corresponding measures on the mitigation of climate change, by limiting its anthropogenic emissions of greenhouse gases and protecting and enhancing its greenhouse gas sinks and reservoirs. These policies and measures will demonstrate that developed countries are taking the lead in modifying longer-term trends in anthropogenic emissions consistent with the objective of the Convention, recognizing that the return by the end of the present decade to earlier levels of anthropogenic emissions of carbon dioxide and other greenhouse gases not controlled by the Montreal Protocol would contribute to such modification, and taking into account the differences in these Parties' starting points and approaches, economic structures and resource bases, the need to maintain strong and sustainable economic growth, available technologies and other individual circumstances, as well as the need for equitable and appropriate contributions by each of these Parties to the global effort regarding that objective. These Parties may implement such policies and measures jointly with other Parties and may assist other Parties in contributing to the achievement of

1 This includes policies and measures adopted by regional economic integration organizations.

the objective of the Convention and, in particular, that of this subparagraph;

(b) In order to promote progress to this end, each of these Parties shall communicate, within six months of the entry into force of the Convention for it and periodically thereafter, and in accordance with Article 12, detailed information on its policies and measures referred to in subparagraph (a) above, as well as on its resulting projected anthropogenic emissions by sources and removals by sinks of greenhouse gases not controlled by the Montreal Protocol for the period referred to in subparagraph (a), with the aim of returning individually or jointly to their 1990 levels these anthropogenic emissions of carbon dioxide and other greenhouse gases not controlled by the Montreal Protocol. This information will be reviewed by the Conference of the Parties, at its first session and periodically thereafter, in accordance with Article 7;

(c) Calculations of emissions by sources and removals by sinks of greenhouse gases for the purposes of subparagraph (b) above should take into account the best available scientific knowledge, including of the effective capacity of sinks and the respective contributions of such gases to climate change. The Conference of the Parties shall consider and agree on methodologies for these calculations at its first session and review them regularly thereafter;

(d) The Conference of the Parties shall, at its first session, review the adequacy of subparagraphs (a) and (b) above. Such review shall be carried out in the light of the best available scientific information and assessment on climate change and its impacts, as well as relevant technical, social and economic information. Based on this review, the Conference of the Parties shall take appropriate action, which may include the adoption of amendments to the commitments in subparagraphs (a) and (b) above. The Conference of the Parties, at its first session, shall also take decisions regarding criteria for joint implementation as indicated in subparagraph (a) above. A second review of subparagraphs (a) and (b) shall take place not later than 31 December 1998, and thereafter at regular intervals determined by the Conference of the Parties, until the objective of the Convention is met;

(e) Each of these Parties shall:

(i) coordinate as appropriate with other such Parties, relevant economic and administrative instruments developed to achieve the objective of the Convention; and

(ii) identify and periodically review its own policies and practices which encourage activities that lead to greater levels of anthropogenic emissions of greenhouse gases not controlled by the Montreal Protocol than would otherwise occur;

(f) The Conference of the Parties shall review, not later than 31 December 1998, available information with a view to taking decisions regarding such amendments to the lists in Annexes I and II as may be appropriate, with the approval of the Party concerned;

(g) Any Party not included in Annex I may, in its instrument of ratification, acceptance, approval or accession, or at any time thereafter, notify the Depositary that it intends to be bound by subparagraphs (a) and (b) above. The Depositary shall inform the other signatories and Parties of any such notification.

3. The developed country Parties and other developed Parties included in Annex II shall provide new and additional financial resources to meet the agreed full costs incurred by developing country Parties in complying with their obligations under Article 12, paragraph 1. They shall also provide such financial resources, including for the transfer of technology, needed by the developing country Parties to meet the agreed full incremental costs of implementing measures that are covered by paragraph 1 of this Article and that are agreed between a developing country Party and the international entity or entities referred to in Article 11, in accordance with that Article. The implementation of these commitments shall take into account the need for adequacy and predictability in the flow of funds and the importance of appropriate burden sharing among the developed country Parties.

4. The developed country Parties and other developed Parties included in Annex II shall also assist the developing country Parties that are particularly vulnerable to the adverse effects of climate change in meeting costs of adaptation to those adverse effects.

5. The developed country Parties and other developed Parties included in Annex II shall take all practicable steps to promote, facilitate and finance, as appropriate, the transfer of, or access to, environmentally sound technologies and know-how to other Parties, particularly developing country Parties, to enable them to implement the provisions of the Convention. In this process, the developed country Parties shall support the development and enhancement of endogenous capacities and technologies of developing country Parties. Other Parties and organizations in a position to do so may also assist in facilitating the transfer of such technologies.

6. In the implementation of their commitments under paragraph 2 above, a certain degree of flexibility shall be allowed by the Conference of the Parties to the Parties included in Annex I undergoing the process of transition to a market economy, in order to enhance the ability of these Parties to address climate change, including with regard to the historical level of anthropogenic emissions of greenhouse gases not controlled by the Montreal Protocol chosen as a reference.

7. The extent to which developing country Parties will effectively implement their commitments under the Convention will depend on the effective implementation by developed country Parties of their commitments under the Convention related

to financial resources and transfer of technology and will take fully into account that economic and social development and poverty eradication are the first and overriding priorities of the developing country Parties.

8. In the implementation of the commitments in this Article, the Parties shall give full consideration to what actions are necessary under the Convention, including actions related to funding, insurance and the transfer of technology, to meet the specific needs and concerns of developing country Parties arising from the adverse effects of climate change and/or the impact of the implementation of response measures, especially on:
   (a) Small island countries;
   (b) Countries with low-lying coastal areas;
   (c) Countries with arid and semi-arid areas, forested areas and areas liable to forest decay;
   (d) Countries with areas prone to natural disasters;
   (e) Countries with areas liable to drought and desertification;
   (f) Countries with areas of high urban atmospheric pollution;
   (g) Countries with areas with fragile ecosystems, including mountainous ecosystems;
   (h) Countries whose economies are highly dependent on income generated from the production, processing and export, and/or on consumption of fossil fuels and associated energy-intensive products; and
   (i) Landlocked and transit countries.

   Further, the Conference of the Parties may take actions, as appropriate, with respect to this paragraph.
9. The Parties shall take full account of the specific needs and special situations of the least developed countries in their actions with regard to funding and transfer of technology.
10. The Parties shall, in accordance with Article 10, take into consideration in the implementation of the commitments of the Convention the situation of Parties, particularly developing country Parties, with economies that are vulnerable to the adverse effects of the implementation of measures to respond to climate change. This applies notably to Parties with economies that are highly dependent on income generated from the production, processing and export, and/or consumption of fossil fuels and associated energy-intensive products and/or the use of fossil fuels for which such Parties have serious difficulties in switching to alternatives.

Article 5 – RESEARCH AND SYSTEMATIC OBSERVATION

In carrying out their commitments under Article 4, paragraph 1 (g), the Parties shall:

(a) Support and further develop, as appropriate, international and intergovernmental programmes and networks or organizations aimed at defining, conducting, assessing and financing research, data collection and systematic observation, taking into account the need to minimize duplication of effort;

(b) Support international and intergovernmental efforts to strengthen systematic observation and national scientific and technical research capacities and capabilities, particularly in developing countries, and to promote access to, and the exchange of, data and analyses thereof obtained from areas beyond national jurisdiction; and

(c) Take into account the particular concerns and needs of developing countries and cooperate in improving their endogenous capacities and capabilities to participate in the efforts referred to in subparagraphs (a) and (b) above.

Article 6 – EDUCATION, TRAINING AND PUBLIC AWARENESS

In carrying out their commitments under Article 4, paragraph 1 (i), the Parties shall:

(a) Promote and facilitate at the national and, as appropriate, subregional and regional levels, and in accordance with national laws and regulations, and within their respective capacities:
   (i) the development and implementation of educational and public awareness programmes on climate change and its effects;
   (ii) public access to information on climate change and its effects;
   (iii) public participation in addressing climate change and its effects and developing adequate responses; and
   (iv) training of scientific, technical and managerial personnel;

(b) Cooperate in and promote, at the international level, and, where appropriate, using existing bodies:
   (i) the development and exchange of educational and public awareness material on climate change and its effects; and
   (ii) the development and implementation of education and training programmes, including the strengthening of national institutions and the exchange or secondment of personnel to train experts in this field, in particular for developing countries.

Climate

Article 7 – CONFERENCE OF THE PARTIES

1. A Conference of the Parties is hereby established.
2. The Conference of the Parties, as the supreme body of this Convention, shall keep under regular review the implementation of the Convention and any related legal instruments that the Conference of the Parties may adopt, and shall make, within its mandate, the decisions necessary to promote the effective implementation of the Convention. To this end, it shall:
   (a) Periodically examine the obligations of the Parties and the institutional arrangements under the Convention, in the light of the objective of the Convention, the experience gained in its implementation and the evolution of scientific and technological knowledge;

(b) Promote and facilitate the exchange of information on measures adopted by the Parties to address climate change and its effects, taking into account the differing circumstances, responsibilities and capabilities of the Parties and their respective commitments under the Convention;

(c) Facilitate, at the request of two or more Parties, the coordination of measures adopted by them to address climate change and its effects, taking into account the differing circumstances, responsibilities and capabilities of the Parties and their respective commitments under the Convention;

(d) Promote and guide, in accordance with the objective and provisions of the Convention, the development and periodic refinement of comparable methodologies, to be agreed on by the Conference of the Parties, inter alia, for preparing inventories of greenhouse gas emissions by sources and removals by sinks, and for evaluating the effectiveness of measures to limit the emissions and enhance the removals of these gases;

(e) Assess, on the basis of all information made available to it in accordance with the provisions of the Convention, the implementation of the Convention by the Parties, the overall effects of the measures taken pursuant to the Convention, in particular environmental, economic and social effects as well as their cumulative impacts and the extent to which progress towards the objective of the Convention is being achieved;

(f) Consider and adopt regular reports on the implementation of the Convention and ensure their publication;

(g) Make recommendations on any matters necessary for the implementation of the Convention;

(h) Seek to mobilize financial resources in accordance with Article 4, paragraphs 3, 4 and 5, and Article 11;

(i) Establish such subsidiary bodies as are deemed necessary for the implementation of the Convention;

(j) Review reports submitted by its subsidiary bodies and provide guidance to them;

(k) Agree upon and adopt, by consensus, rules of procedure and financial rules for itself and for any subsidiary bodies;

(l) Seek and utilize, where appropriate, the services and cooperation of, and information provided by, competent international organizations and intergovernmental and non-governmental bodies; and

(m) Exercise such other functions as are required for the achievement of the objective of the Convention as well as all other functions assigned to it under the Convention.

3. The Conference of the Parties shall, at its first session, adopt its own rules of procedure as well as those of the subsidiary bodies established by the Convention, which shall include decision-making procedures for matters not already covered by decision-making procedures stipulated in the Convention. Such procedures may include specified majorities required for the adoption of particular decisions.

4. The first session of the Conference of the Parties shall be convened by the interim secretariat referred to in Article 21 and shall take place not later than one year after the date of entry into force of the Convention. Thereafter, ordinary sessions of the Conference of the Parties shall be held every year unless otherwise decided by the Conference of the Parties.

5. Extraordinary sessions of the Conference of the Parties shall be held at such other times as may be deemed necessary by the Conference, or at the written request of any Party, provided that, within six months of the request being communicated to the Parties by the secretariat, it is supported by at least one third of the Parties.

6. The United Nations, its specialized agencies and the International Atomic Energy Agency, as well as any State member thereof or observers thereto not Party to the Convention, may be represented at sessions of the Conference of the Parties as observers. Any body or agency, whether national or international, governmental or non-governmental, which is qualified in matters covered by the Convention, and which has informed the secretariat of its wish to be represented at a session of the Conference of the Parties as an observer, may be so admitted unless at least one third of the Parties present object. The admission and participation of observers shall be subject to the rules of procedure adopted by the Conference of the Parties.

Article 8 – SECRETARIAT

1. A secretariat is hereby established.

2. The functions of the secretariat shall be:

(a) To make arrangements for sessions of the Conference of the Parties and its subsidiary bodies established under the Convention and to provide them with services as required;

(b) To compile and transmit reports submitted to it;

(c) To facilitate assistance to the Parties, particularly developing country Parties, on request, in the compilation and communication of information required in accordance with the provisions of the Convention;

(d) To prepare reports on its activities and present them to the Conference of the Parties;

(e) To ensure the necessary coordination with the secretariats of other relevant international bodies;

(f) To enter, under the overall guidance of the Conference of the Parties, into such administrative and contractual arrangements as may be required for the effective discharge of its functions; and

(g) To perform the other secretariat functions specified in the Convention and in any of its protocols and such other functions as may be determined by the Conference of the Parties.

3. The Conference of the Parties, at its first session, shall designate a permanent secretariat and make arrangements for its functioning.

Article 9 – SUBSIDIARY BODY FOR SCIENTIFIC AND TECHNOLOGICAL ADVICE

1. A subsidiary body for scientific and technological advice is hereby established to provide the Conference of the Parties and, as appropriate, its other subsidiary bodies with timely information and advice on scientific and technological matters relating to the Convention. This body shall be open to participation by all Parties and shall be multidisciplinary. It shall comprise government representatives competent in the relevant field of expertise. It shall report regularly to the Conference of the Parties on all aspects of its work.
2. Under the guidance of the Conference of the Parties, and drawing upon existing competent international bodies, this body shall:
   (a) Provide assessments of the state of scientific knowledge relating to climate change and its effects;
   (b) Prepare scientific assessments on the effects of measures taken in the implementation of the Convention;
   (c) Identify innovative, efficient and state-of-the-art technologies and know-how and advise on the ways and means of promoting development and/or transferring such technologies;
   (d) Provide advice on scientific programmes, international cooperation in research and development related to climate change, as well as on ways and means of supporting endogenous capacity-building in developing countries; and
   (e) Respond to scientific, technological and methodological questions that the Conference of the Parties and its subsidiary bodies may put to the body.
3. The functions and terms of reference of this body may be further elaborated by the Conference of the Parties.

Article 10 – SUBSIDIARY BODY FOR IMPLEMENTATION

1. A subsidiary body for implementation is hereby established to assist the Conference of the Parties in the assessment and review of the effective implementation of the Convention. This body shall be open to participation by all Parties and comprise government representatives who are experts on matters related to climate change. It shall report regularly to the Conference of the Parties on all aspects of its work.
2. Under the guidance of the Conference of the Parties, this body shall:
   (a) Consider the information communicated in accordance with Article 12, paragraph 1, to assess the overall aggregated effect of the steps taken by the Parties in the light of the latest scientific assessments concerning climate change;
   (b) Consider the information communicated in accordance with Article 12, paragraph 2, in order to assist the Conference of the Parties in carrying out the reviews required by Article 4, paragraph 2 (d); and
   (c) Assist the Conference of the Parties, as appropriate, in the preparation and implementation of its decisions.

Article 11 – FINANCIAL MECHANISM

1. A mechanism for the provision of financial resources on a grant or concessional basis, including for the transfer of technology, is hereby defined. It shall function under the guidance of and be accountable to the Conference of the Parties, which shall decide on its policies, programme priorities and eligibility criteria related to this Convention. Its operation shall be entrusted to one or more existing international entities.
2. The financial mechanism shall have an equitable and balanced representation of all Parties within a transparent system of governance.
3. The Conference of the Parties and the entity or entities entrusted with the operation of the financial mechanism shall agree upon arrangements to give effect to the above paragraphs, which shall include the following:
   (a) Modalities to ensure that the funded projects to address climate change are in conformity with the policies, programme priorities and eligibility criteria established by the Conference of the Parties;
   (b) Modalities by which a particular funding decision may be reconsidered in light of these policies, programme priorities and eligibility criteria;
   (c) Provision by the entity or entities of regular reports to the Conference of the Parties on its funding operations, which is consistent with the requirement for accountability set out in paragraph 1 above; and
   (d) Determination in a predictable and identifiable manner of the amount of funding necessary and available for the implementation of this Convention and the conditions under which that amount shall be periodically reviewed.
4. The Conference of the Parties shall make arrangements to implement the above-mentioned provisions at its first session, reviewing and taking into account the interim arrangements referred to in Article 21, paragraph 3, and shall decide whether these interim arrangements shall be maintained. Within four years thereafter, the Conference of the Parties shall review the financial mechanism and take appropriate measures.
5. The developed country Parties may also provide and developing country Parties avail themselves of, financial resources related to the implementa-

tion of the Convention through bilateral, regional and other multilateral channels.

Article 12 – COMMUNICATION OF INFORMATION RELATED TO IMPLEMENTATION

1. In accordance with Article 4, paragraph 1, each Party shall communicate to the Conference of the Parties, through the secretariat, the following elements of information:
   (a) A national inventory of anthropogenic emissions by sources and removals by sinks of all greenhouse gases not controlled by the Montreal Protocol, to the extent its capacities permit, using comparable methodologies to be promoted and agreed upon by the Conference of the Parties;
   (b) A general description of steps taken or envisaged by the Party to implement the Convention; and
   (c) Any other information that the Party considers relevant to the achievement of the objective of the Convention and suitable for inclusion in its communication, including, if feasible, material relevant for calculations of global emission trends.
2. Each developed country Party and each other Party included in Annex I shall incorporate in its communication the following elements of information:
   (a) A detailed description of the policies and measures that it has adopted to implement its commitment under Article 4, paragraphs 2 (a) and 2 (b); and
   (b) A specific estimate of the effects that the policies and measures referred to in subparagraph (a) immediately above will have on anthropogenic emissions by its sources and removals by its sinks of greenhouse gases during the period referred to in Article 4, paragraph 2 (a).
3. In addition, each developed country Party and each other developed Party included in Annex II shall incorporate details of measures taken in accordance with Article 4, paragraphs 3, 4 and 5.
4. Developing country Parties may, on a voluntary basis, propose projects for financing, including specific technologies, materials, equipment, techniques or practices that would be needed to implement such projects, along with, if possible, an estimate of all incremental costs, of the reductions of emissions and increments of removals of greenhouse gases, as well as an estimate of the consequent benefits.
5. Each developed country Party and each other Party included in Annex I shall make its initial communication within six months of the entry into force of the Convention for that Party. Each Party not so listed shall make its initial communication within three years of the entry into force of the Convention for that Party, or of the availability of financial resources in accordance with Article 4, paragraph 3. Parties that are least developed countries may make their initial communication at their discretion. The frequency of subsequent communications by all Parties shall be determined by the Conference of the Parties, taking into account the differentiated timetable set by this paragraph.
6. Information communicated by Parties under this Article shall be transmitted by the secretariat as soon as possible to the Conference of the Parties and to any subsidiary bodies concerned. If necessary, the procedures for the communication of information may be further considered by the Conference of the Parties.
7. From its first session, the Conference of the Parties shall arrange for the provision to developing country Parties of technical and financial support, on request, in compiling and communicating information under this Article, as well as in identifying the technical and financial needs associated with proposed projects and response measures under Article 4. Such support may be provided by other Parties, by competent international organizations and by the secretariat, as appropriate.
8. Any group of Parties may, subject to guidelines adopted by the Conference of the Parties, and to prior notification to the Conference of the Parties, make a joint communication in fulfilment of their obligations under this Article, provided that such a communication includes information on the fulfilment by each of these Parties of its individual obligations under the Convention.
9. Information received by the secretariat that is designated by a Party as confidential, in accordance with criteria to be established by the Conference of the Parties, shall be aggregated by the secretariat to protect its confidentiality before being made available to any of the bodies involved in the communication and review of information.
10. Subject to paragraph 9 above, and without prejudice to the ability of any Party to make public its communication at any time, the secretariat shall make communications by Parties under this Article publicly available at the time they are submitted to the Conference of the Parties.

Article 13 – RESOLUTION OF QUESTIONS REGARDING IMPLEMENTATION

The Conference of the Parties shall, at its first session, consider the establishment of a multilateral consultative process, available to Parties on their request, for the resolution of questions regarding the implementation of the Convention.

Article 14 – SETTLEMENT OF DISPUTES

1. In the event of a dispute between any two or more Parties concerning the interpretation or application of the Convention, the Parties concerned shall seek a settlement of the dispute through negotiation or any other peaceful means of their own choice.
2. When ratifying, accepting, approving or acceding to the Convention, or at any time thereafter, a Party which is not a regional economic integration organization may declare in a written instrument submitted to the Depositary that, in respect of any dispute concerning the interpretation or application

of the Convention, it recognizes as compulsory ipso facto and without special agreement, in relation to any Party accepting the same obligation:

(a) Submission of the dispute to the International Court of Justice; and/or

(b) Arbitration in accordance with procedures to be adopted by the Conference of the Parties as soon as practicable, in an annex on arbitration.

A Party which is a regional economic integration organization may make a declaration with like effect in relation to arbitration in accordance with the procedures referred to in subparagraph (b) above.

3. A declaration made under paragraph 2 above shall remain in force until it expires in accordance with its terms or until three months after written notice of its revocation has been deposited with the Depositary.
4. A new declaration, a notice of revocation or the expiry of a declaration shall not in any way affect proceedings pending before the International Court of Justice or the arbitral tribunal, unless the parties to the dispute otherwise agree.
5. Subject to the operation of paragraph 2 above, if after twelve months following notification by one Party to another that a dispute exists between them, the Parties concerned have not been able to settle their dispute through the means mentioned in paragraph 1 above, the dispute shall be submitted, at the request of any of the parties to the dispute, to conciliation.
6. A conciliation commission shall be created upon the request of one of the parties to the dispute. The commission shall be composed of an equal number of members appointed by each party concerned and a chairman chosen jointly by the members appointed by each party. The commission shall render a recommendatory award, which the parties shall consider in good faith.
7. Additional procedures relating to conciliation shall be adopted by the Conference of the Parties, as soon as practicable, in an annex on conciliation.
8. The provisions of this Article shall apply to any related legal instrument which the Conference of the Parties may adopt, unless the instrument provides otherwise.

Article 15 – AMENDMENTS TO THE CONVENTION

1. Any Party may propose amendments to the Convention.
2. Amendments to the Convention shall be adopted at an ordinary session of the Conference of the Parties. The text of any proposed amendment to the Convention shall be communicated to the Parties by the secretariat at least six months before the meeting at which it is proposed for adoption. The secretariat shall also communicate proposed amendments to the signatories to the Convention and, for information, to the Depositary.
3. The Parties shall make every effort to reach agreement on any proposed amendment to the Convention by consensus. If all efforts at consensus have been exhausted, and no agreement reached, the amendment shall as a last resort be adopted by a three-fourths majority vote of the Parties present and voting at the meeting. The adopted amendment shall be communicated by the secretariat to the Depositary, who shall circulate it to all Parties for their acceptance.
4. Instruments of acceptance in respect of an amendment shall be deposited with the Depositary. An amendment adopted in accordance with paragraph 3 above shall enter into force for those Parties having accepted it on the ninetieth day after the date of receipt by the Depositary of an instrument of acceptance by at least three fourths of the Parties to the Convention.
5. The amendment shall enter into force for any other Party on the ninetieth day after the date on which that Party deposits with the Depositary its instrument of acceptance of the said amendment.
6. For the purposes of this Article, "Parties present and voting" means Parties present and casting an affirmative or negative vote.

Article 16 – ADOPTION AND AMENDMENT OF ANNEXES TO THE CONVENTION

1. Annexes to the Convention shall form an integral part thereof and, unless otherwise expressly provided, a reference to the Convention constitutes at the same time a reference to any annexes thereto. Without prejudice to the provisions of Article 14, paragraphs 2 (b) and 7, such annexes shall be restricted to lists, forms and any other material of a descriptive nature that is of a scientific, technical, procedural or administrative character.
2. Annexes to the Convention shall be proposed and adopted in accordance with the procedure set forth in Article 15, paragraphs 2, 3 and 4.
3. An annex that has been adopted in accordance with paragraph 2 above shall enter into force for all Parties to the Convention six months after the date of the communication by the Depositary to such Parties of the adoption of the annex, except for those Parties that have notified the Depositary, in writing, within that period of their non-acceptance of the annex. The annex shall enter into force for Parties which withdraw their notification of non-acceptance on the ninetieth day after the date on which withdrawal of such notification has been received by the Depositary.
4. The proposal, adoption and entry into force of amendments to annexes to the Convention shall be subject to the same procedure as that for the proposal, adoption and entry into force of annexes to the Convention in accordance with paragraphs 2 and 3 above.
5. If the adoption of an annex or an amendment to an annex involves an amendment to the Convention, that annex or amendment to an annex shall not enter into force until such time as the amendment to the Convention enters into force.

Article 17 – PROTOCOLS

1. The Conference of the Parties may, at any ordinary session, adopt protocols to the Convention.
2. The text of any proposed protocol shall be communicated to the Parties by the secretariat at least six months before such a session.
3. The requirements for the entry into force of any protocol shall be established by that instrument.
4. Only Parties to the Convention may be Parties to a protocol.
5. Decisions under any protocol shall be taken only by the Parties to the protocol concerned.

Article 18 – RIGHT TO VOTE

1. Each Party to the Convention shall have one vote, except as provided for in paragraph 2 below.
2. Regional economic integration organizations, in matters within their competence, shall exercise their right to vote with a number of votes equal to the number of their member States that are Parties to the Convention. Such an organization shall not exercise its right to vote if any of its member States exercises its right, and vice versa.

Article 19 – DEPOSITARY

The Secretary-General of the United Nations shall be the Depositary of the Convention and of protocols adopted in accordance with Article 17.

Article 20 – SIGNATURE

This Convention shall be open for signature by States Members of the United Nations or of any of its specialized agencies or that are Parties to the Statute of the International Court of Justice and by regional economic integration organizations at Rio de Janeiro, during the United Nations Conference on Environment and Development, and thereafter at United Nations Headquarters in New York from 20 June 1992 to 19 June 1993.

Article 21 – INTERIM ARRANGEMENTS

1. The secretariat functions referred to in Article 8 will be carried out on an interim basis by the secretariat established by the General Assembly of the United Nations in its resolution 45/212 of 21 December 1990, until the completion of the first session of the Conference of the Parties.
2. The head of the interim secretariat referred to in paragraph 1 above will cooperate closely with the Intergovernmental Panel on Climate Change to ensure that the Panel can respond to the need for objective scientific and technical advice. Other relevant scientific bodies could also be consulted.
3. The Global Environment Facility of the United Nations Development Programme, the United Nations Environment Programme and the International Bank for Reconstruction and Development shall be the international entity entrusted with the operation of the financial mechanism referred to in Article 11 on an interim basis. In this connection, the Global Environment Facility should be appropriately restructured and its membership made universal to enable it to fulfil the requirements of Article 11.

Article 22 – RATIFICATION, ACCEPTANCE, APPROVAL OR ACCESSION

1. The Convention shall be subject to ratification, acceptance, approval or accession by States and by regional economic integration organizations. It shall be open for accession from the day after the date on which the Convention is closed for signature. Instruments of ratification, acceptance, approval or accession shall be deposited with the Depositary.
2. Any regional economic integration organization which becomes a Party to the Convention without any of its member States being a Party shall be bound by all the obligations under the Convention. In the case of such organizations, one or more of whose member States is a Party to the Convention, the organization and its member States shall decide on their respective responsibilities for the performance of their obligations under the Convention. In such cases, the organization and the member States shall not be entitled to exercise rights under the Convention concurrently.
3. In their instruments of ratification, acceptance, approval or accession, regional economic integration organizations shall declare the extent of their competence with respect to the matters governed by the Convention. These organizations shall also inform the Depositary, who shall in turn inform the Parties, of any substantial modification in the extent of their competence.

Article 23 – ENTRY INTO FORCE

1. The Convention shall enter into force on the ninetieth day after the date of deposit of the fiftieth instrument of ratification, acceptance, approval or accession.
2. For each State or regional economic integration organization that ratifies, accepts or approves the Convention or accedes thereto after the deposit of the fiftieth instrument of ratification, acceptance, approval or accession, the Convention shall enter into force on the ninetieth day after the date of deposit by such State or regional economic integration organization of its instrument of ratification, acceptance, approval or accession.
3. For the purposes of paragraphs 1 and 2 above, any instrument deposited by a regional economic integration organization shall not be counted as additional to those deposited by States members of the organization.

Article 24 – RESERVATIONS

No reservations may be made to the Convention.

Article 25 – WITHDRAWAL

1. At any time after three years from the date on which the Convention has entered into force for a Party, that Party may withdraw from the Convention by giving written notification to the Depositary.

2. Any such withdrawal shall take effect upon expiry of one year from the date of receipt by the Depositary of the notification of withdrawal, or on such later date as may be specified in the notification of withdrawal.
3. Any Party that withdraws from the Convention shall be considered as also having withdrawn from any protocol to which it is a Party.

Article 26 – AUTHENTIC TEXTS

The original of this Convention, of which the Arabic, Chinese, English, French, Russian and Spanish texts are equally authentic, shall be deposited with the Secretary-General of the United Nations.

IN WITNESS WHEREOF the undersigned, being duly authorized to that effect, have signed this Convention.

DONE at New York this ninth day of May one thousand nine hundred and ninety-two.

Annex I

Australia
Austria
Belarus[a]
Belgium
Bulgaria[a]
Canada
Croatia[a]
Czech Republic
Denmark
European Economic Community
Estonia[a]
Finland
France
Germany
Greece
Hungary[a]
Iceland
Ireland
Italy
Japan
Latvia[a]
Liechtenstein
Lithuania
Luxembourg
Monaco
Netherlands
New Zealand
Norway
Poland[a]
Portugal
Romania[a]
Russian Federation[a]
Slovakia[a]
Slovenia[a]
Spain
Sweden
Switzerland
Turkey
Ukraine[a]
United Kingdom of Great Britain and Northern Ireland
United States of America

Annex II

Australia
Austria
Belgium
Canada
Denmark
European Economic Community
Finland
France
Germany
Greece
Iceland
Ireland
Italy
Japan
Luxembourg
Netherland
New Zealand
Norway
Portugal
Spain
Sweden
Switzerland
United Kingdom of Great Britain and Northern Ireland
United States of America

a Countries that are undergoing the process of transition to a market economy.

6.2. Kyoto Protocol 1997

Kyoto Protocol to the United Nations Framework Convention on Climate Change, Kyoto, 11 December 1997, 2303 UNTS 148

The Parties to this Protocol,

Being Parties to the United Nations Framework Convention on Climate Change, hereinafter referred to as "the Convention",

In pursuit of the ultimate objective of the Convention as stated in its Article 2,

Recalling the provisions of the Convention,

Being guided by Article 3 of the Convention,

Pursuant to the Berlin Mandate adopted by decision 1/CP.1 of the Conference of the Parties to the Convention at its first session,

Have agreed as follows:

Article 1

For the purposes of this Protocol, the definitions contained in Article 1 of the Convention shall apply. In addition:

1. "Conference of the Parties" means the Conference of the Parties to the Convention.
2. "Convention" means the United Nations Framework Convention on Climate Change, adopted in New York on 9 May 1992.
3. "Intergovernmental Panel on Climate Change" means the Intergovernmental Panel on Climate Change established in 1988 jointly by the World Meteorological Organization and the United Nations Environment Programme.
4. "Montreal Protocol" means the Montreal Protocol on Substances that Deplete the Ozone Layer, adopted in Montreal on 16 September 1987 and as subsequently adjusted and amended.
5. "Parties present and voting" means Parties present and casting an affirmative or negative vote.
6. "Party" means, unless the context otherwise indicates, a Party to this Protocol.
7. "Party included in Annex I" means a Party included in Annex I to the Convention, as may be amended, or a Party which has made a notification under Article 4, paragraph 2 (g), of the Convention.

Article 2

1. Each Party included in Annex I, in achieving its quantified emission limitation and reduction commitments under Article 3, in order to promote sustainable development, shall:

   (a) Implement and/or further elaborate policies and measures in accordance with its national circumstances, such as:

   (i) Enhancement of energy efficiency in relevant sectors of the national economy;

   (ii) Protection and enhancement of sinks and reservoirs of greenhouse gases not controlled by the Montreal Protocol, taking into account its commitments under relevant international environmental agreements; promotion of sustainable forest management practices, afforestation and reforestation;

   (iii) Promotion of sustainable forms of agriculture in light of climate change considerations;

   (iv) Research on, and promotion, development and increased use of, new and renewable forms of energy, of carbon dioxide sequestration technologies and of advanced and innovative environmentally sound technologies;

   (v) Progressive reduction or phasing out of market imperfections, fiscal incentives, tax and duty exemptions and subsidies in all greenhouse gas emitting sectors that run counter to the objective of the Convention and application of market instruments;

   (vi) Encouragement of appropriate reforms in relevant sectors aimed at promoting policies and measures which limit or reduce emissions of greenhouse gases not controlled by the Montreal Protocol;

   (vii) Measures to limit and/or reduce emissions of greenhouse gases not controlled by the Montreal Protocol in the transport sector;

   (viii) Limitation and/or reduction of methane emissions through recovery and use in waste management, as well as in the production, transport and distribution of energy;

   (b) Cooperate with other such Parties to enhance the individual and combined effectiveness of their policies and measures adopted under this Article, pursuant to Article 4, paragraph 2 (e) (i), of the Convention. To this end, these Parties shall take steps to share their experience and exchange information on such policies and measures, including developing ways of improving their comparability, transparency and effectiveness. The Conference of the Parties serving as the meeting of the Parties to this Protocol shall, at its first session or as soon as practicable thereafter, consider ways to facilitate such cooperation, taking into account all relevant information.

2. The Parties included in Annex I shall pursue limitation or reduction of emissions of greenhouse

gases not controlled by the Montreal Protocol from aviation and marine bunker fuels, working through the International Civil Aviation Organization and the International Maritime Organization, respectively.

3. The Parties included in Annex I shall strive to implement policies and measures under this Article in such a way as to minimize adverse effects, including the adverse effects of climate change, effects on international trade, and social, environmental and economic impacts on other Parties, especially developing country Parties and in particular those identified in Article 4, paragraphs 8 and 9, of the Convention, taking into account Article 3 of the Convention. The Conference of the Parties serving as the meeting of the Parties to this Protocol may take further action, as appropriate, to promote the implementation of the provisions of this paragraph.
4. The Conference of the Parties serving as the meeting of the Parties to this Protocol, if it decides that it would be beneficial to coordinate any of the policies and measures in paragraph 1 (a) above, taking into account different national circumstances and potential effects, shall consider ways and means to elaborate the coordination of such policies and measures.

Article 3

1. The Parties included in Annex I shall, individually or jointly, ensure that their aggregate anthropogenic carbon dioxide equivalent emissions of the greenhouse gases listed in Annex A do not exceed their assigned amounts, calculated pursuant to their quantified emission limitation and reduction commitments inscribed in Annex B and in accordance with the provisions of this Article, with a view to reducing their overall emissions of such gases by at least 5 per cent below 1990 levels in the commitment period 2008 to 2012.
2. Each Party included in Annex I shall, by 2005, have made demonstrable progress in achieving its commitments under this Protocol.
3. The net changes in greenhouse gas emissions by sources and removals by sinks resulting from direct human-induced land-use change and forestry activities, limited to afforestation, reforestation and deforestation since 1990, measured as verifiable changes in carbon stocks in each commitment period, shall be used to meet the commitments under this Article of each Party included in Annex I. The greenhouse gas emissions by sources and removals by sinks associated with those activities shall be reported in a transparent and verifiable manner and reviewed in accordance with Articles 7 and 8.
4. Prior to the first session of the Conference of the Parties serving as the meeting of the Parties to this Protocol, each Party included in Annex I shall provide, for consideration by the Subsidiary Body for Scientific and Technological Advice, data to establish its level of carbon stocks in 1990 and to enable an estimate to be made of its changes in carbon stocks in subsequent years. The Conference of the Parties serving as the meeting of the Parties to this Protocol shall, at its first session or as soon as practicable thereafter, decide upon modalities, rules and guidelines as to how, and which, additional human-induced activities related to changes in greenhouse gas emissions by sources and removals by sinks in the agricultural soils and the land-use change and forestry categories shall be added to, or subtracted from, the assigned amounts for Parties included in Annex I, taking into account uncertainties, transparency in reporting, verifiability, the methodological work of the Intergovernmental Panel on Climate Change, the advice provided by the Subsidiary Body for Scientific and Technological Advice in accordance with Article 5 and the decisions of the Conference of the Parties. Such a decision shall apply in the second and subsequent commitment periods. A Party may choose to apply such a decision on these additional human-induced activities for its first commitment period, provided that these activities have taken place since 1990.
5. The Parties included in Annex I undergoing the process of transition to a market economy whose base year or period was established pursuant to decision 9/CP.2 of the Conference of the Parties at its second session shall use that base year or period for the implementation of their commitments under this Article. Any other Party included in Annex I undergoing the process of transition to a market economy which has not yet submitted its first national communication under Article 12 of the Convention may also notify the Conference of the Parties serving as the meeting of the Parties to this Protocol that it intends to use an historical base year or period other than 1990 for the implementation of its commitments under this Article. The Conference of the Parties serving as the meeting of the Parties to this Protocol shall decide on the acceptance of such notification.
6. Taking into account Article 4, paragraph 6, of the Convention, in the implementation of their commitments under this Protocol other than those under this Article, a certain degree of flexibility shall be allowed by the Conference of the Parties serving as the meeting of the Parties to this Protocol to the Parties included in Annex I undergoing the process of transition to a market economy.
7. In the first quantified emission limitation and reduction commitment period, from 2008 to 2012, the assigned amount for each Party included in Annex I shall be equal to the percentage inscribed for it in Annex B of its aggregate anthropogenic carbon dioxide equivalent emissions of the greenhouse gases listed in Annex A in 1990, or the base year or period determined in accordance with paragraph 5 above, multiplied by five. Those Parties included in Annex I for whom land-use change and forestry constituted a net source of greenhouse gas emissions in 1990 shall include in their 1990 emissions base year or period the aggregate anthropogenic carbon dioxide equivalent emissions by sources minus removals by sinks in 1990 from land-use change for the purposes of calculating their assigned amount.

8. Any Party included in Annex I may use 1995 as its base year for hydrofluorocarbons, perfluorocarbons and sulphur hexafluoride, for the purposes of the calculation referred to in paragraph 7 above.
9. Commitments for subsequent periods for Parties included in Annex I shall be established in amendments to Annex B to this Protocol, which shall be adopted in accordance with the provisions of Article 21, paragraph 7. The Conference of the Parties serving as the meeting of the Parties to this Protocol shall initiate the consideration of such commitments at least seven years before the end of the first commitment period referred to in paragraph 1 above.
10. Any emission reduction units, or any part of an assigned amount, which a Party acquires from another Party in accordance with the provisions of Article 6 or of Article 17 shall be added to the assigned amount for the acquiring Party.
11. Any emission reduction units, or any part of an assigned amount, which a Party transfers to another Party in accordance with the provisions of Article 6 or of Article 17 shall be subtracted from the assigned amount for the transferring Party.
12. Any certified emission reductions which a Party acquires from another Party in accordance with the provisions of Article 12 shall be added to the assigned amount for the acquiring Party.
13. If the emissions of a Party included in Annex I in a commitment period are less than its assigned amount under this Article, this difference shall, on request of that Party, be added to the assigned amount for that Party for subsequent commitment periods.
14. Each Party included in Annex I shall strive to implement the commitments mentioned in paragraph 1 above in such a way as to minimize adverse social, environmental and economic impacts on developing country Parties, particularly those identified in Article 4, paragraphs 8 and 9, of the Convention. In line with relevant decisions of the Conference of the Parties on the implementation of those paragraphs, the Conference of the Parties serving as the meeting of the Parties to this Protocol shall, at its first session, consider what actions are necessary to minimize the adverse effects of climate change and/or the impacts of response measures on Parties referred to in those paragraphs. Among the issues to be considered shall be the establishment of funding, insurance and transfer of technology.

Article 4

1. Any Parties included in Annex I that have reached an agreement to fulfil their commitments under Article 3 jointly, shall be deemed to have met those commitments provided that their total combined aggregate anthropogenic carbon dioxide equivalent emissions of the greenhouse gases listed in Annex A do not exceed their assigned amounts calculated pursuant to their quantified emission limitation and reduction commitments inscribed in Annex B and in accordance with the provisions of Article 3. The respective emission level allocated to each of the Parties to the agreement shall be set out in that agreement.
2. The Parties to any such agreement shall notify the secretariat of the terms of the agreement on the date of deposit of their instruments of ratification, acceptance or approval of this Protocol, or accession thereto. The secretariat shall in turn inform the Parties and signatories to the Convention of the terms of the agreement.
3. Any such agreement shall remain in operation for the duration of the commitment period specified in Article 3, paragraph 7.
4. If Parties acting jointly do so in the framework of, and together with, a regional economic integration organization, any alteration in the composition of the organization after adoption of this Protocol shall not affect existing commitments under this Protocol. Any alteration in the composition of the organization shall only apply for the purposes of those commitments under Article 3 that are adopted subsequent to that alteration.
5. In the event of failure by the Parties to such an agreement to achieve their total combined level of emission reductions, each Party to that agreement shall be responsible for its own level of emissions set out in the agreement.
6. If Parties acting jointly do so in the framework of, and together with, a regional economic integration organization which is itself a Party to this Protocol, each member State of that regional economic integration organization individually, and together with the regional economic integration organization acting in accordance with Article 24, shall, in the event of failure to achieve the total combined level of emission reductions, be responsible for its level of emissions as notified in accordance with this Article.

Article 5

1. Each Party included in Annex I shall have in place, no later than one year prior to the start of the first commitment period, a national system for the estimation of anthropogenic emissions by sources and removals by sinks of all greenhouse gases not controlled by the Montreal Protocol. Guidelines for such national systems, which shall incorporate the methodologies specified in paragraph 2 below, shall be decided upon by the Conference of the Parties serving as the meeting of the Parties to this Protocol at its first session.
2. Methodologies for estimating anthropogenic emissions by sources and removals by sinks of all greenhouse gases not controlled by the Montreal Protocol shall be those accepted by the Intergovernmental Panel on Climate Change and agreed upon by the Conference of the Parties at its third session. Where such methodologies are not used, appropriate adjustments shall be applied according to methodologies agreed upon by the Conference of the Parties serving as the meeting of the Parties to this Protocol at its first session. Based on the work of, inter alia, the Intergovernmental Panel

on Climate Change and advice provided by the Subsidiary Body for Scientific and Technological Advice, the Conference of the Parties serving as the meeting of the Parties to this Protocol shall regularly review and, as appropriate, revise such methodologies and adjustments, taking fully into account any relevant decisions by the Conference of the Parties. Any revision to methodologies or adjustments shall be used only for the purposes of ascertaining compliance with commitments under Article 3 in respect of any commitment period adopted subsequent to that revision.

3. The global warming potentials used to calculate the carbon dioxide equivalence of anthropogenic emissions by sources and removals by sinks of greenhouse gases listed in Annex A shall be those accepted by the Intergovernmental Panel on Climate Change and agreed upon by the Conference of the Parties at its third session. Based on the work of, inter alia, the Intergovernmental Panel on Climate Change and advice provided by the Subsidiary Body for Scientific and Technological Advice, the Conference of the Parties serving as the meeting of the Parties to this Protocol shall regularly review and, as appropriate, revise the global warming potential of each such greenhouse gas, taking fully into account any relevant decisions by the Conference of the Parties. Any revision to a global warming potential shall apply only to commitments under Article 3 in respect of any commitment period adopted subsequent to that revision.

Article 6

1. For the purpose of meeting its commitments under Article 3, any Party included in Annex I may transfer to, or acquire from, any other such Party emission reduction units resulting from projects aimed at reducing anthropogenic emissions by sources or enhancing anthropogenic removals by sinks of greenhouse gases in any sector of the economy, provided that:
   (a) Any such project has the approval of the Parties involved;
   (b) Any such project provides a reduction in emissions by sources, or an enhancement of removals by sinks, that is additional to any that would otherwise occur;
   (c) It does not acquire any emission reduction units if it is not in compliance with its obligations under Articles 5 and 7; and
   (d) The acquisition of emission reduction units shall be supplemental to domestic actions for the purposes of meeting commitments under Article 3.
2. The Conference of the Parties serving as the meeting of the Parties to this Protocol may, at its first session or as soon as practicable thereafter, further elaborate guidelines for the implementation of this Article, including for verification and reporting.
3. A Party included in Annex I may authorize legal entities to participate, under its responsibility, in actions leading to the generation, transfer or acquisition under this Article of emission reduction units.
4. If a question of implementation by a Party included in Annex I of the requirements referred to in this Article is identified in accordance with the relevant provisions of Article 8, transfers and acquisitions of emission reduction units may continue to be made after the question has been identified, provided that any such units may not be used by a Party to meet its commitments under Article 3 until any issue of compliance is resolved.

Article 7

1. Each Party included in Annex I shall incorporate in its annual inventory of anthropogenic emissions by sources and removals by sinks of greenhouse gases not controlled by the Montreal Protocol, submitted in accordance with the relevant decisions of the Conference of the Parties, the necessary supplementary information for the purposes of ensuring compliance with Article 3, to be determined in accordance with paragraph 4 below.
2. Each Party included in Annex I shall incorporate in its national communication, submitted under Article 12 of the Convention, the supplementary information necessary to demonstrate compliance with its commitments under this Protocol, to be determined in accordance with paragraph 4 below.
3. Each Party included in Annex I shall submit the information required under paragraph 1 above annually, beginning with the first inventory due under the Convention for the first year of the commitment period after this Protocol has entered into force for that Party. Each such Party shall submit the information required under paragraph 2 above as part of the first national communication due under the Convention after this Protocol has entered into force for it and after the adoption of guidelines as provided for in paragraph 4 below. The frequency of subsequent submission of information required under this Article shall be determined by the Conference of the Parties serving as the meeting of the Parties to this Protocol, taking into account any timetable for the submission of national communications decided upon by the Conference of the Parties.
4. The Conference of the Parties serving as the meeting of the Parties to this Protocol shall adopt at its first session, and review periodically thereafter, guidelines for the preparation of the information required under this Article, taking into account guidelines for the preparation of national communications by Parties included in Annex I adopted by the Conference of the Parties. The Conference of the Parties serving as the meeting of the Parties to this Protocol shall also, prior to the first commitment period, decide upon modalities for the accounting of assigned amounts.

Article 8

1. The information submitted under Article 7 by each Party included in Annex I shall be reviewed by expert review teams pursuant to the relevant decisions of the Conference of the Parties and in

accordance with guidelines adopted for this purpose by the Conference of the Parties serving as the meeting of the Parties to this Protocol under paragraph 4 below. The information submitted under Article 7, paragraph 1, by each Party included in Annex I shall be reviewed as part of the annual compilation and accounting of emissions inventories and assigned amounts. Additionally, the information submitted under Article 7, paragraph 2, by each Party included in Annex I shall be reviewed as part of the review of communications.

2. Expert review teams shall be coordinated by the secretariat and shall be composed of experts selected from those nominated by Parties to the Convention and, as appropriate, by intergovernmental organizations, in accordance with guidance provided for this purpose by the Conference of the Parties.
3. The review process shall provide a thorough and comprehensive technical assessment of all aspects of the implementation by a Party of this Protocol. The expert review teams shall prepare a report to the Conference of the Parties serving as the meeting of the Parties to this Protocol, assessing the implementation of the commitments of the Party and identifying any potential problems in, and factors influencing, the fulfilment of commitments. Such reports shall be circulated by the secretariat to all Parties to the Convention. The secretariat shall list those questions of implementation indicated in such reports for further consideration by the Conference of the Parties serving as the meeting of the Parties to this Protocol.
4. The Conference of the Parties serving as the meeting of the Parties to this Protocol shall adopt at its first session, and review periodically thereafter, guidelines for the review of implementation of this Protocol by expert review teams taking into account the relevant decisions of the Conference of the Parties.
5. The Conference of the Parties serving as the meeting of the Parties to this Protocol shall, with the assistance of the Subsidiary Body for Implementation and, as appropriate, the Subsidiary Body for Scientific and Technological Advice, consider:
   (a) The information submitted by Parties under Article 7 and the reports of the expert reviews thereon conducted under this Article; and
   (b) Those questions of implementation listed by the secretariat under paragraph 3 above, as well as any questions raised by Parties.
6. Pursuant to its consideration of the information referred to in paragraph 5 above, the Conference of the Parties serving as the meeting of the Parties to this Protocol shall take decisions on any matter required for the implementation of this Protocol.

Article 9

1. The Conference of the Parties serving as the meeting of the Parties to this Protocol shall periodically review this Protocol in the light of the best available scientific information and assessments on climate change and its impacts, as well as relevant technical, social and economic information. Such reviews shall be coordinated with pertinent reviews under the Convention, in particular those required by Article 4, paragraph 2 (d), and Article 7, paragraph 2 (a), of the Convention. Based on these reviews, the Conference of the Parties serving as the meeting of the Parties to this Protocol shall take appropriate action.
2. The first review shall take place at the second session of the Conference of the Parties serving as the meeting of the Parties to this Protocol. Further reviews shall take place at regular intervals and in a timely manner.

Article 10

All Parties, taking into account their common but differentiated responsibilities and their specific national and regional development priorities, objectives and circumstances, without introducing any new commitments for Parties not included in Annex I, but reaffirming existing commitments under Article 4, paragraph 1, of the Convention, and continuing to advance the implementation of these commitments in order to achieve sustainable development, taking into account Article 4, paragraphs 3, 5 and 7, of the Convention, shall:

(a) Formulate, where relevant and to the extent possible, cost-effective national and, where appropriate, regional programmes to improve the quality of local emission factors, activity data and/or models which reflect the socio-economic conditions of each Party for the preparation and periodic updating of national inventories of anthropogenic emissions by sources and removals by sinks of all greenhouse gases not controlled by the Montreal Protocol, using comparable methodologies to be agreed upon by the Conference of the Parties, and consistent with the guidelines for the preparation of national communications adopted by the Conference of the Parties;

(b) Formulate, implement, publish and regularly update national and, where appropriate, regional programmes containing measures to mitigate climate change and measures to facilitate adequate adaptation to climate change:

   (i) Such programmes would, inter alia, concern the energy, transport and industry sectors as well as agriculture, forestry and waste management. Furthermore, adaptation technologies and methods for improving spatial planning would improve adaptation to climate change; and

   (ii) Parties included in Annex I shall submit information on action under this Protocol, including national programmes, in accordance with Article 7; and other Parties shall seek to include in their national communications, as appropriate, information on programmes which contain measures that the Party believes contribute to addressing climate change and its adverse impacts, including the abatement of increases in greenhouse gas emissions, and enhancement of and removals by sinks, capacity building and adaptation measures;

(c) Cooperate in the promotion of effective modalities for the development, application and diffusion of, and take all practicable steps to promote, facilitate and finance, as appropriate, the transfer of, or access to, environmentally sound technologies, know-how, practices and processes pertinent to climate change, in particular to developing countries, including the formulation of policies and programmes for the effective transfer of environmentally sound technologies that are publicly owned or in the public domain and the creation of an enabling environment for the private sector, to promote and enhance the transfer of, and access to, environmentally sound technologies;

(d) Cooperate in scientific and technical research and promote the maintenance and the development of systematic observation systems and development of data archives to reduce uncertainties related to the climate system, the adverse impacts of climate change and the economic and social consequences of various response strategies, and promote the development and strengthening of endogenous capacities and capabilities to participate in international and intergovernmental efforts, programmes and networks on research and systematic observation, taking into account Article 5 of the Convention;

(e) Cooperate in and promote at the international level, and, where appropriate, using existing bodies, the development and implementation of education and training programmes, including the strengthening of national capacity building, in particular human and institutional capacities and the exchange or secondment of personnel to train experts in this field, in particular for developing countries, and facilitate at the national level public awareness of, and public access to information on, climate change. Suitable modalities should be developed to implement these activities through the relevant bodies of the Convention, taking into account Article 6 of the Convention;

(f) Include in their national communications information on programmes and activities undertaken pursuant to this Article in accordance with relevant decisions of the Conference of the Parties; and

(g) Give full consideration, in implementing the commitments under this Article, to Article 4, paragraph 8, of the Convention.

Article 11

1. In the implementation of Article 10, Parties shall take into account the provisions of Article 4, paragraphs 4, 5, 7, 8 and 9, of the Convention.

2. In the context of the implementation of Article 4, paragraph 1, of the Convention, in accordance with the provisions of Article 4, paragraph 3, and Article 11 of the Convention, and through the entity or entities entrusted with the operation of the financial mechanism of the Convention, the developed country Parties and other developed Parties included in Annex II to the Convention shall:

   (a) Provide new and additional financial resources to meet the agreed full costs incurred by developing country Parties in advancing the implementation of existing commitments under Article 4, paragraph 1 (a), of the Convention that are covered in Article 10, subparagraph (a); and

   (b) Also provide such financial resources, including for the transfer of technology, needed by the developing country Parties to meet the agreed full incremental costs of advancing the implementation of existing commitments under Article 4, paragraph 1, of the Convention that are covered by Article 10 and that are agreed between a developing country Party and the international entity or entities referred to in Article 11 of the Convention, in accordance with that Article. The implementation of these existing commitments shall take into account the need for adequacy and predictability in the flow of funds and the importance of appropriate burden sharing among developed country Parties. The guidance to the entity or entities entrusted with the operation of the financial mechanism of the Convention in relevant decisions of the Conference of the Parties, including those agreed before the adoption of this Protocol, shall apply mutatis mutandis to the provisions of this paragraph.

3. The developed country Parties and other developed Parties in Annex II to the Convention may also provide, and developing country Parties avail themselves of, financial resources for the implementation of Article 10, through bilateral, regional and other multilateral channels.

Article 12

1. A clean development mechanism is hereby defined.

2. The purpose of the clean development mechanism shall be to assist Parties not included in Annex I in achieving sustainable development and in contributing to the ultimate objective of the Convention, and to assist Parties included in Annex I in achieving compliance with their quantified emission limitation and reduction commitments under Article 3.

3. Under the clean development mechanism:

   (a) Parties not included in Annex I will benefit from project activities resulting in certified emission reductions; and

   (b) Parties included in Annex I may use the certified emission reductions accruing from such project activities to contribute to compliance with part of their quantified emission limitation and reduction commitments under Article 3, as determined by the Conference of the Parties serving as the meeting of the Parties to this Protocol.

4. The clean development mechanism shall be subject to the authority and guidance of the Conference of the Parties serving as the meeting of the Parties to this Protocol and be supervised by an executive board of the clean development mechanism.

5. Emission reductions resulting from each project activity shall be certified by operational entities

to be designated by the Conference of the Parties serving as the meeting of the Parties to this Protocol, on the basis of:

(a) Voluntary participation approved by each Party involved;

(b) Real, measurable, and long-term benefits related to the mitigation of climate change; and

(c) Reductions in emissions that are additional to any that would occur in the absence of the certified project activity.

6. The clean development mechanism shall assist in arranging funding of certified project activities as necessary.

7. The Conference of the Parties serving as the meeting of the Parties to this Protocol shall, at its first session, elaborate modalities and procedures with the objective of ensuring transparency, efficiency and accountability through independent auditing and verification of project activities.

8. The Conference of the Parties serving as the meeting of the Parties to this Protocol shall ensure that a share of the proceeds from certified project activities is used to cover administrative expenses as well as to assist developing country Parties that are particularly vulnerable to the adverse effects of climate change to meet the costs of adaptation.

9. Participation under the clean development mechanism, including in activities mentioned in paragraph 3 (a) above and in the acquisition of certified emission reductions, may involve private and/or public entities, and is to be subject to whatever guidance may be provided by the executive board of the clean development mechanism.

10. Certified emission reductions obtained during the period from the year 2000 up to the beginning of the first commitment period can be used to assist in achieving compliance in the first commitment period.

Article 13

1. The Conference of the Parties, the supreme body of the Convention, shall serve as the meeting of the Parties to this Protocol.

2. Parties to the Convention that are not Parties to this Protocol may participate as observers in the proceedings of any session of the Conference of the Parties serving as the meeting of the Parties to this Protocol. When the Conference of the Parties serves as the meeting of the Parties to this Protocol, decisions under this Protocol shall be taken only by those that are Parties to this Protocol.

3. When the Conference of the Parties serves as the meeting of the Parties to this Protocol, any member of the Bureau of the Conference of the Parties representing a Party to the Convention but, at that time, not a Party to this Protocol, shall be replaced by an additional member to be elected by and from amongst the Parties to this Protocol.

4. The Conference of the Parties serving as the meeting of the Parties to this Protocol shall keep under regular review the implementation of this Protocol and shall make, within its mandate, the decisions necessary to promote its effective implementation. It shall perform the functions assigned to it by this Protocol and shall:

(a) Assess, on the basis of all information made available to it in accordance with the provisions of this Protocol, the implementation of this Protocol by the Parties, the overall effects of the measures taken pursuant to this Protocol, in particular environmental, economic and social effects as well as their cumulative impacts and the extent to which progress towards the objective of the Convention is being achieved;

(b) Periodically examine the obligations of the Parties under this Protocol, giving due consideration to any reviews required by Article 4, paragraph 2 (d), and Article 7, paragraph 2, of the Convention, in the light of the objective of the Convention, the experience gained in its implementation and the evolution of scientific and technological knowledge, and in this respect consider and adopt regular reports on the implementation of this Protocol;

(c) Promote and facilitate the exchange of information on measures adopted by the Parties to address climate change and its effects, taking into account the differing circumstances, responsibilities and capabilities of the Parties and their respective commitments under this Protocol;

(d) Facilitate, at the request of two or more Parties, the coordination of measures adopted by them to address climate change and its effects, taking into account the differing circumstances, responsibilities and capabilities of the Parties and their respective commitments under this Protocol;

(e) Promote and guide, in accordance with the objective of the Convention and the provisions of this Protocol, and taking fully into account the relevant decisions by the Conference of the Parties, the development and periodic refinement of comparable methodologies for the effective implementation of this Protocol, to be agreed on by the Conference of the Parties serving as the meeting of the Parties to this Protocol;

(f) Make recommendations on any matters necessary for the implementation of this Protocol;

(g) Seek to mobilize additional financial resources in accordance with Article 11, paragraph 2;

(h) Establish such subsidiary bodies as are deemed necessary for the implementation of this Protocol;

(i) Seek and utilize, where appropriate, the services and cooperation of, and information provided by, competent international organizations and intergovernmental and non-governmental bodies; and

(j) Exercise such other functions as may be required for the implementation of this Protocol, and consider any assignment resulting from a decision by the Conference of the Parties.

5. The rules of procedure of the Conference of the Parties and financial procedures applied under the Convention shall be applied mutatis mutandis under this Protocol, except as may be otherwise decided by consensus by the Conference of the Parties serving as the meeting of the Parties to this Protocol.
6. The first session of the Conference of the Parties serving as the meeting of the Parties to this Protocol shall be convened by the secretariat in conjunction with the first session of the Conference of the Parties that is scheduled after the date of the entry into force of this Protocol. Subsequent ordinary sessions of the Conference of the Parties serving as the meeting of the Parties to this Protocol shall be held every year and in conjunction with ordinary sessions of the Conference of the Parties, unless otherwise decided by the Conference of the Parties serving as the meeting of the Parties to this Protocol.
7. Extraordinary sessions of the Conference of the Parties serving as the meeting of the Parties to this Protocol shall be held at such other times as may be deemed necessary by the Conference of the Parties serving as the meeting of the Parties to this Protocol, or at the written request of any Party, provided that, within six months of the request being communicated to the Parties by the secretariat, it is supported by at least one third of the Parties.
8. The United Nations, its specialized agencies and the International Atomic Energy Agency, as well as any State member thereof or observers thereto not party to the Convention, may be represented at sessions of the Conference of the Parties serving as the meeting of the Parties to this Protocol as observers. Any body or agency, whether national or international, governmental or non-governmental, which is qualified in matters covered by this Protocol and which has informed the secretariat of its wish to be represented at a session of the Conference of the Parties serving as the meeting of the Parties to this Protocol as an observer, may be so admitted unless at least one third of the Parties present object. The admission and participation of observers shall be subject to the rules of procedure, as referred to in paragraph 5 above.

Article 14

1. The secretariat established by Article 8 of the Convention shall serve as the secretariat of this Protocol.
2. Article 8, paragraph 2, of the Convention on the functions of the secretariat, and Article 8, paragraph 3, of the Convention on arrangements made for the functioning of the secretariat, shall apply mutatis mutandis to this Protocol. The secretariat shall, in addition, exercise the functions assigned to it under this Protocol.

Article 15

1. The Subsidiary Body for Scientific and Technological Advice and the Subsidiary Body for Implementation established by Articles 9 and 10 of the Convention shall serve as, respectively, the Subsidiary Body for Scientific and Technological Advice and the Subsidiary Body for Implementation of this Protocol. The provisions relating to the functioning of these two bodies under the Convention shall apply mutatis mutandis to this Protocol. Sessions of the meetings of the Subsidiary Body for Scientific and Technological Advice and the Subsidiary Body for Implementation of this Protocol shall be held in conjunction with the meetings of, respectively, the Subsidiary Body for Scientific and Technological Advice and the Subsidiary Body for Implementation of the Convention.
2. Parties to the Convention that are not Parties to this Protocol may participate as observers in the proceedings of any session of the subsidiary bodies. When the subsidiary bodies serve as the subsidiary bodies of this Protocol, decisions under this Protocol shall be taken only by those that are Parties to this Protocol.
3. When the subsidiary bodies established by Articles 9 and 10 of the Convention exercise their functions with regard to matters concerning this Protocol, any member of the Bureaux of those subsidiary bodies representing a Party to the Convention but, at that time, not a party to this Protocol, shall be replaced by an additional member to be elected by and from amongst the Parties to this Protocol.

Article 16

The Conference of the Parties serving as the meeting of the Parties to this Protocol shall, as soon as practicable, consider the application to this Protocol of, and modify as appropriate, the multilateral consultative process referred to in Article 13 of the Convention, in the light of any relevant decisions that may be taken by the Conference of the Parties. Any multilateral consultative process that may be applied to this Protocol shall operate without prejudice to the procedures and mechanisms established in accordance with Article 18.

Article 17

The Conference of the Parties shall define the relevant principles, modalities, rules and guidelines, in particular for verification, reporting and accountability for emissions trading. The Parties included in Annex B may participate in emissions trading for the purposes of fulfilling their commitments under Article 3. Any such trading shall be supplemental to domestic actions for the purpose of meeting quantified emission limitation and reduction commitments under that Article.

Article 18

The Conference of the Parties serving as the meeting of the Parties to this Protocol shall, at its first session, approve appropriate and effective procedures and mechanisms to determine and to address cases of non-compliance with the provisions of this Protocol, including through the development of an indicative list of consequences, taking into account the cause, type, degree and frequency of non-compliance. Any procedures and mechanisms under this Article entailing binding consequences shall be adopted by means of an amendment to this Protocol.

Article 19

The provisions of Article 14 of the Convention on settlement of disputes shall apply mutatis mutandis to this Protocol.

Article 20

1. Any Party may propose amendments to this Protocol.
2. Amendments to this Protocol shall be adopted at an ordinary session of the Conference of the Parties serving as the meeting of the Parties to this Protocol. The text of any proposed amendment to this Protocol shall be communicated to the Parties by the secretariat at least six months before the meeting at which it is proposed for adoption. The secretariat shall also communicate the text of any proposed amendments to the Parties and signatories to the Convention and, for information, to the Depositary.
3. The Parties shall make every effort to reach agreement on any proposed amendment to this Protocol by consensus. If all efforts at consensus have been exhausted, and no agreement reached, the amendment shall as a last resort be adopted by a three-fourths majority vote of the Parties present and voting at the meeting. The adopted amendment shall be communicated by the secretariat to the Depositary, who shall circulate it to all Parties for their acceptance.
4. Instruments of acceptance in respect of an amendment shall be deposited with the Depositary. An amendment adopted in accordance with paragraph 3 above shall enter into force for those Parties having accepted it on the ninetieth day after the date of receipt by the Depositary of an instrument of acceptance by at least three fourths of the Parties to this Protocol.
5. The amendment shall enter into force for any other Party on the ninetieth day after the date on which that Party deposits with the Depositary its instrument of acceptance of the said amendment.

Article 21

1. Annexes to this Protocol shall form an integral part thereof and, unless otherwise expressly provided, a reference to this Protocol constitutes at the same time a reference to any annexes thereto. Any annexes adopted after the entry into force of this Protocol shall be restricted to lists, forms and any other material of a descriptive nature that is of a scientific, technical, procedural or administrative character.
2. Any Party may make proposals for an annex to this Protocol and may propose amendments to annexes to this Protocol.
3. Annexes to this Protocol and amendments to annexes to this Protocol shall be adopted at an ordinary session of the Conference of the Parties serving as the meeting of the Parties to this Protocol. The text of any proposed annex or amendment to an annex shall be communicated to the Parties by the secretariat at least six months before the meeting at which it is proposed for adoption. The secretariat shall also communicate the text of any proposed annex or amendment to an annex to the Parties and signatories to the Convention and, for information, to the Depositary.
4. The Parties shall make every effort to reach agreement on any proposed annex or amendment to an annex by consensus. If all efforts at consensus have been exhausted, and no agreement reached, the annex or amendment to an annex shall as a last resort be adopted by a three-fourths majority vote of the Parties present and voting at the meeting. The adopted annex or amendment to an annex shall be communicated by the secretariat to the Depositary, who shall circulate it to all Parties for their acceptance.
5. An annex, or amendment to an annex other than Annex A or B, that has been adopted in accordance with paragraphs 3 and 4 above shall enter into force for all Parties to this Protocol six months after the date of the communication by the Depositary to such Parties of the adoption of the annex or adoption of the amendment to the annex, except for those Parties that have notified the Depositary, in writing, within that period of their non-acceptance of the annex or amendment to the annex. The annex or amendment to an annex shall enter into force for Parties which withdraw their notification of non-acceptance on the ninetieth day after the date on which withdrawal of such notification has been received by the Depositary.
6. If the adoption of an annex or an amendment to an annex involves an amendment to this Protocol, that annex or amendment to an annex shall not enter into force until such time as the amendment to this Protocol enters into force.
7. Amendments to Annexes A and B to this Protocol shall be adopted and enter into force in accordance with the procedure set out in Article 20, provided that any amendment to Annex B shall be adopted only with the written consent of the Party concerned.

Article 22

1. Each Party shall have one vote, except as provided for in paragraph 2 below.
2. Regional economic integration organizations, in matters within their competence, shall exercise their right to vote with a number of votes equal to the number of their member States that are Parties to this Protocol. Such an organization shall not exercise its right to vote if any of its member States exercises its right, and vice versa.

Article 23

The Secretary-General of the United Nations shall be the Depositary of this Protocol.

Article 24

1. This Protocol shall be open for signature and subject to ratification, acceptance or approval by States and regional economic integration organizations which are Parties to the Convention. It shall be open for signature at United Nations Headquar-

ters in New York from 16 March 1998 to 15 March 1999. This Protocol shall be open for accession from the day after the date on which it is closed for signature. Instruments of ratification, acceptance, approval or accession shall be deposited with the Depositary.

2. Any regional economic integration organization which becomes a Party to this Protocol without any of its member States being a Party shall be bound by all the obligations under this Protocol. In the case of such organizations, one or more of whose member States is a Party to this Protocol, the organization and its member States shall decide on their respective responsibilities for the performance of their obligations under this Protocol. In such cases, the organization and the member States shall not be entitled to exercise rights under this Protocol concurrently.
3. In their instruments of ratification, acceptance, approval or accession, regional economic integration organizations shall declare the extent of their competence with respect to the matters governed by this Protocol. These organizations shall also inform the Depositary, who shall in turn inform the Parties, of any substantial modification in the extent of their competence.

Article 25

1. This Protocol shall enter into force on the ninetieth day after the date on which not less than 55 Parties to the Convention, incorporating Parties included in Annex I which accounted in total for at least 55 per cent of the total carbon dioxide emissions for 1990 of the Parties included in Annex I, have deposited their instruments of ratification, acceptance, approval or accession.
2. For the purposes of this Article, "the total carbon dioxide emissions for 1990 of the Parties included in Annex I" means the amount communicated on or before the date of adoption of this Protocol by the Parties included in Annex I in their first national communications submitted in accordance with Article 12 of the Convention.
3. For each State or regional economic integration organization that ratifies, accepts or approves this Protocol or accedes thereto after the conditions set out in paragraph 1 above for entry into force have been fulfilled, this Protocol shall enter into force on the ninetieth day following the date of deposit of its instrument of ratification, acceptance, approval or accession.
4. For the purposes of this Article, any instrument deposited by a regional economic integration organization shall not be counted as additional to those deposited by States members of the organization.

Article 26

No reservations may be made to this Protocol.

Article 27

1. At any time after three years from the date on which this Protocol has entered into force for a Party, that Party may withdraw from this Protocol by giving written notification to the Depositary.
2. Any such withdrawal shall take effect upon expiry of one year from the date of receipt by the Depositary of the notification of withdrawal, or on such later date as may be specified in the notification of withdrawal.
3. Any Party that withdraws from the Convention shall be considered as also having withdrawn from this Protocol.

Article 28

The original of this Protocol, of which the Arabic, Chinese, English, French, Russian and Spanish texts are equally authentic, shall be deposited with the Secretary-General of the United Nations.

DONE at Kyoto this eleventh day of December one thousand nine hundred and ninety-seven.

IN WITNESS WHEREOF the undersigned, being duly authorized to that effect, have affixed their signatures to this Protocol on the dates indicated.

Annex A

Greenhouse gases

Carbon dioxide (C02)

Methane (CH4)

Nitrous oxide (N20)

Hydrofluorocarbons (HFCs)

Perfluorocarbons (PFCs)

Sulphur hexafluoride (SF6)

Sectors/source categories

- Energy
  - Fuel combustion
    - Energy industries
    - Manufacturing industries and construction
    - Transport
    - Other sectors
    - Other
  - Fugitive emissions from fuels
    - Solid fuels
    - Oil and natural gas
    - Other
- Industrial processes
  - Mineral products
  - Chemical industry
  - Metal production
  - Other production
  - Production of halocarbons and sulphur hexafluoride
  - Consumption of halocarbons and sulphur hexafluoride
  - Other
- Solvent and other product use
- Agriculture
  - Enteric fermentation
  - Manure management

Rice cultivation
Agricultural soils
Prescribed burning of savannas
Field burning of agricultural residues
Other

Waste
Solid waste disposal on land
Wastewater handling
Waste incineration
Other

Annex B

Party	Quantified emission limitation or reduction commitment (percentage of base year or period)
Australia	108
Austria	92
Belgium	92
Bulgaria*	92
Canada	94
Croatia*	95
Czech Republic*	92
Denmark	92
Estonia*	92
European Community	92
Finland	92
France	92
Germany	92
Greece	92
Hungary*	94
Iceland	110
Ireland	92
Italy	92
Japan	94
Latvia*	92

Party	Quantified emission limitation or reduction commitment (percentage of base year or period)
Liechtenstein	92
Lithuania*	92
Luxembourg	92
Monaco	92
Netherlands	92
New Zealand	100
Norway	101
Poland*	94
Portugal	92
Romania*	92
Russian Federation*	100
Slovakia*	92
Slovenia*	92
Spain	92
Sweden	92
Switzerland	92
Ukraine*	100
United Kingdom of Great Britain and Northern Ireland	92
United States of America	93

* Countries that are undergoing the process of transition to a market economy.

6.3. Doha Amendment 2012

Doha Amendment to the Kyoto Protocol, Doha, 8 December 2012, UNFCCC Doc. FCCC/KP/CMP/2012/13/Add.1, Decision 1/CMP.8

Article 1: Amendment

A. Annex B to the Kyoto Protocol

The following table shall replace the table in Annex B to the Protocol:

1	2	3	4	5	6
Party	Quantified emission limitation or reduction commitment (2008-2012) (percentage of base year or period)	Quantified emission limitation or reduction commitment (2013-2020) (percentage of base year or period)	Reference Year[1]	Quantified emission limitation or reduction commitment (2013-2020) (expressed as percentage of reference year)[1]	Pledges for the reduction of green-house gas emissions by 2020 (percentage of reference year)[2]
Australia	108	99.5	2000	98	-5 to -15% or -25%[3]
Austria	92	80[4]	NA	NA	
Belarus[5*]		88	1990	NA	-8%
Belgium	92	80[4]	NA	NA	
Bulgaria[*]	92	80[4]	NA	NA	
Croatia[*]	95	80[6]	NA	NA	-20% / -30%[7]
Cyprus		80[4]	NA	NA	
Czech Republic[*]	92	80[4]	NA	NA	
Denmark	92	80[4]	NA	NA	
Estonia[*]	92	80[4]	NA	NA	

Climate

* Countries that are undergoing the process of transition to a market economy.

1 A reference year may be used by a Party on an optional basis for its own purposes to express its quantified emission limitation or reduction commitment (QELRC) as a percentage of emissions of that year, that is not internationally binding under the Kyoto Protocol, in addition to the listing of its QELRC(s) in relation to the base year in the second and third columns of this table, which are internationally legally binding.

2 Further information on these pledges can be found in documents FCCC/SB/2011/INF.1/Rev.1 and FCCC/KP/AWG/2012/MISC.1, Add.1 and Add.2.

3 Australia's QELRC under the second commitment period of the Kyoto Protocol is consistent with the achievement of Australia's unconditional 2020 target of 5 per cent below 2000 levels. Australia retains the option later to move up within its 2020 target of 5 to 15, or 25 per cent below 2000 levels, subject to certain conditions being met. This reference retains the status of these pledges as made under the Cancun Agreements and does not amount to a new legally binding commitment under this Protocol or its associated rules and modalities.

4 The QELRCs for the European Union and its member States for a second commitment period under the Kyoto Protocol are based on the understanding that these will be fulfilled jointly with the European Union and its member States, in accordance with Article 4 of the Kyoto Protocol. The QELRCs are without prejudice to the subsequent notification by the European Union and its member States of an agreement to fulfil their commitments jointly in accordance with the provisions of the Kyoto Protocol.

5 Added to Annex B by an amendment adopted pursuant to decision 10/CMP.2. This amendment has not yet entered into force.

6 Croatia's QELRC for a second commitment period under the Kyoto Protocol is based on the understanding that it will fulfil this QELRC jointly with the European Union and its member States, in accordance with Article 4 of the Kyoto Protocol. As a consequence, Croatia's accession to the European Union shall not affect its participation in such joint fulfilment agreement pursuant to Article 4 or its QELRC.

1	2	3	4	5	6
European Union	92	80[4]	1990	NA	-20% / -30%[7]
Finland	92	80[4]	NA	NA	
France	92	80[4]	NA	NA	
Germany	92	80[4]	NA	NA	
Greece	92	80[4]	NA	NA	
Hungary*	94	80[4]	NA	NA	
Iceland	110	80[8]	NA	NA	
Ireland	92	80[4]	NA	NA	
Italy	92	80[4]	NA	NA	
Kazakhstan*		95	1990	95	-7%
Latvia*	92	80[4]	NA	NA	
Liechtenstein	92	84	1990	84	-20%/ -30%[9]
Lithuania*	92	80[4]	NA	NA	
Luxembourg	92	80[4]	NA	NA	
Malta		80[4]	NA	NA	
Monaco	92	78	1990	78	–30%
Netherlands	92	80[4]	NA	NA	
Norway	101	84	1990	84	-30% to -40%[10]
Poland*	94	80[4]	NA	NA	
Portugal	92	80[4]	NA	NA	
Romania*	92	80[4]	NA	NA	
Slovakia*	92	80[4]	NA	NA	
Slovenia*	92	80[4]	NA	NA	
Spain	92	80[4]	NA	NA	
Sweden	92	80[4]	NA	NA	
Switzerland	92	84.2	1990	NA	-20% to -30%[11]
Ukraine*	100	76[12]	1990	NA	-20%

7 As part of a global and comprehensive agreement for the period beyond 2012, the European Union reiterates its conditional offer to move to a 30 per cent reduction by 2020 compared to 1990 levels, provided that other developed countries commit themselves to comparable emission reductions and developing countries contribute adequately according to their responsibilities and respective capabilities.

8 The QELRC for Iceland for a second commitment period under the Kyoto Protocol is based on the understanding that it will be fulfilled jointly with the European Union and its member States, in accordance with Article 4 of the Kyoto Protocol.

9 The QELRC presented in column three refers to a reduction target of 20 per cent by 2020 compared to 1990 levels. Liechtenstein would consider a higher reduction target of up to 30 per cent by 2020 compared to 1990 levels under the condition that other developed countries commit themselves to comparable emission reductions and that economically more advanced developing countries contribute adequately according to their responsibilities and respective capabilities.

10 Norway's QELRC of 84 is consistent with its target of 30 per cent reduction of emissions by 2020, compared to 1990. If it can contribute to a global and comprehensive agreement where major emitting Parties agree on emission reductions in line with the 2° C target, Norway will move to a level of 40 per cent reduction for 2020 based on 1990 levels. This reference retains the status of the pledge made under the Cancun Agreements and does not amount to a new legally binding commitment under this Protocol.

11 The QELRC presented in the third column of this table refers to a reduction target of 20 per cent by 2020 compared to 1990 levels. Switzerland would consider a higher reduction target up to 30 per cent by 2020 compared to 1990 levels subject to comparable emission reduction commitments from other developed countries and adequate contribution from developing countries according to their responsibilities and capabilities in line with the 2° C target. This reference retains the status of the pledge made under the Cancun Agreements and does not amount to a new legally binding commitment under this Protocol or its associated rules and modalities.

1	2	3	4	5	6
United Kingdom of Great Britain and Northern Ireland	92	80[4]	NA	NA	

Party	Quantified emission limitation or reduction commitment (2008-2012) (percentage of base year or period)
Canada[13]	94
Japan[14]	94
New Zealand[15]	100
Russian Federation[16*]	100

Abbreviation: NA = not applicable.

All footnotes below, except for footnotes 1, 2 and 5, have been provided through communications from the respective Parties.

B. Annex A to the Kyoto Protocol

The following list shall replace the list under the heading "Greenhouse gases" in Annex A to the Protocol:

Greenhouse gases

Carbon dioxide (CO_2)

Methane (CH_4)

Nitrous oxide (N_2O)

Hydrofluorocarbons (HFCs)

Perfluorocarbons (PFCs)

Sulphur hexafluoride (SF_6)

Nitrogen trifluoride (NF_3)[1]

C. Article 3, paragraph 1 bis

The following paragraph shall be inserted after paragraph 1 of Article 3 of the Protocol:

1 bis. The Parties included in Annex I shall, individually or jointly, ensure that their aggregate anthropogenic carbon dioxide equivalent emissions of the greenhouse gases listed in Annex A do not exceed their assigned amounts, calculated pursuant to their quantified emission limitation and reduction commitments inscribed in the third column of the table contained in Annex B and in accordance with the provisions of this Article, with a view to reducing their overall emissions of such gases by at least 18 per cent below 1990 levels in the commitment period 2013 to 2020.

Climate

D. Article 3, paragraph 1 ter

The following paragraph shall be inserted after paragraph 1 bis of Article 3 of the Protocol:

1 ter. A Party included in Annex B may propose an adjustment to decrease the percentage inscribed in the third column of Annex B of its quantified emission limitation and reduction commitment inscribed in the third column of the table contained in Annex B. A proposal for such an adjustment shall be communicated to the Parties by the secretariat at least three months before the meeting of the Conference of the Parties serving as the meeting of the

13 On 15 December 2011, the Depositary received written notification of Canada's withdrawal from the Kyoto Protocol. This action will become effective for Canada on 15 December 2012.

14 In a communication dated 10 December 2010, Japan indicated that it does not have any intention to be under obligation of the second commitment period of the Kyoto Protocol after 2012.

15 New Zealand remains a Party to the Kyoto Protocol. It will be taking a quantified economy-wide emission reduction target under the United Nations Framework Convention on Climate Change in the period 2013 to 2020.

16 In a communication dated 8 December 2010 that was received by the secretariat on 9 December 2010, the Russian Federation indicated that it does not intend to assume a quantitative emission limitation or reduction commitment for the second commitment period.

1 Applies only from the beginning of the second commitment period.

Parties to this Protocol at which it is proposed for adoption.

E. Article 3, paragraph 1 quater

The following paragraph shall be inserted after paragraph 1 ter of Article 3 of the Protocol:

1quater. An adjustment proposed by a Party included in Annex I to increase the ambition of its quantified emission limitation and reduction commitment in accordance with Article 3, paragraph 1 ter, above shall be considered adopted by the Conference of the Parties serving as the meeting of the Parties to this Protocol unless more than three-fourths of the Parties present and voting object to its adoption. The adopted adjustment shall be communicated by the secretariat to the Depositary, who shall circulate it to all Parties, and shall enter into force on 1 January of the year following the communication by the Depositary. Such adjustments shall be binding upon Parties.

F. Article 3, paragraph 7 bis

The following paragraphs shall be inserted after paragraph 7 of Article 3 of the Protocol:

7bis. In the second quantified emission limitation and reduction commitment period, from 2013 to 2020, the assigned amount for each Party included in Annex I shall be equal to the percentage inscribed for it in the third column of the table contained in Annex B of its aggregate anthropogenic carbon dioxide equivalent emissions of the greenhouse gases listed in Annex A in 1990, or the base year or period determined in accordance with paragraph 5 above, multiplied by eight. Those Parties included in Annex I for whom land- use change and forestry constituted a net source of greenhouse gas emissions in 1990 shall include in their 1990 emissions base year or period the aggregate anthropogenic carbon dioxide equivalent emissions by sources minus removals by sinks in 1990 from land-use change for the purposes of calculating their assigned amount.

G. Article 3, paragraph 7 ter

The following paragraph shall be inserted after paragraph 7 bis of Article 3 of the Protocol:

7ter. Any positive difference between the assigned amount of the second commitment period for a Party included in the Annex I and average annual emissions for the first three years of the preceding commitment period multiplied by eight shall be transferred to the cancellation account of that Party.

H. Article 3, paragraph 8

In paragraph 8 of Article 3 of the Protocol, the words:

– calculation referred to in paragraph 7 above

shall be substituted by:

– calculations referred to in paragraphs 7 and 7 bis above

I. Article 3, paragraph 8 bis

The following paragraph shall be inserted after paragraph 8 of Article 3 of the Protocol:

8bis. Any Party included in Annex I may use 1995 or 2000 as its base year for nitrogen trifluoride for the purposes of the calculation referred to in paragraph 7 bis above.

J. Article 3, paragraphs 12 bis and ter

The following paragraphs shall be inserted after paragraph 12 of Article 3 of the Protocol:

12bis. Any units generated from market-based mechanisms to be established under the Convention or its instruments may be used by Parties included in Annex I to assist them in achieving compliance with their quantified emission limitation and reduction commitments under Article 3. Any such units which a Party acquires from another Party to the Convention shall be added to the assigned amount for the acquiring Party and subtracted from the quantity of units held by the transferring Party.

12ter. The Conference of the Parties serving as the meeting of the Parties to this Protocol shall ensure that, where units from approved activities under market-based mechanisms referred to in paragraph 12 bis above are used by Parties included in Annex I to assist them in achieving compliance with their quantified emission limitation and reduction commitments under Article 3, a share of these units is used to cover administrative expenses, as well as to assist developing country Parties that are particularly vulnerable to the adverse effects of climate change to meet the costs of adaptation if these units are acquired under Article 17.

K. Article 4, paragraph 2

The following words shall be added to the end of the first sentence of paragraph 2 of Article 4 of the Protocol:

, or on the date of deposit of their instruments of acceptance of any amendment to Annex B pursuant to Article 3, paragraph 9

L. Article 4, paragraph 3

In paragraph 3 of Article 4 of the Protocol, the words:

, paragraph 7

shall be substituted by:

to which it relates

Article 2: Entry into force

This amendment shall enter into force in accordance with Articles 20 and 21 of the Kyoto Protocol.

6.4. Paris Agreement 2015

Paris Agreement, 12 December 2015, Paris, 3156 UNTS 79

The Parties to this Agreement,

Being Parties to the United Nations Framework Convention on Climate Change, hereinafter referred to as "the Convention",

Pursuant to the Durban Platform for Enhanced Action established by decision l/CP.17 of the Conference of the Parties to the Convention at its seventeenth session,

In pursuit of the objective of the Convention, and being guided by its principles, including the principle of equity and common but differentiated responsibilities and respective capabilities, in the light of different national circumstances,

Recognizing the need for an effective and progressive response to the urgent threat of climate change on the basis of the best available scientific knowledge,

Also recognizing the specific needs and special circumstances of developing country Parties, especially those that are particularly vulnerable to the adverse effects of climate change, as provided for in the Convention,

Taking duly account of the specific needs and special situations of the least developed countries with regard to funding and transfer of technology,

Recognizing that Parties may be affected not only by climate change, but also by the impacts of the measures taken in response to it,

Emphasizing the intrinsic relationship that climate change actions, responses and impacts have with equitable access to sustainable development and eradication of poverty,

Recognizing the fundamental priority of safeguarding food security and ending hunger, and the particular vulnerabilities of food production systems to the adverse impacts of climate change,

Taking into account the imperatives of a just transition of the workforce and the creation of decent work and quality jobs in accordance with nationally defined development priorities,

Acknowledging that climate change is a common concern of humankind, Parties should, when taking action to address climate change, respect, promote and consider their respective obligations on human rights, the right to health, the rights of indigenous peoples, local communities, migrants, children, persons with disabilities and people in vulnerable situations and the right to development, as well as gender equality, empowerment of women and intergenerational equity,

Recognizing the importance of the conservation and enhancement, as appropriate, of sinks and reservoirs of the greenhouse gases referred to in the Convention,

Noting the importance of ensuring the integrity of all ecosystems, including oceans, and the protection of biodiversity, recognized by some cultures as Mother Earth, and noting the importance for some of the concept of "climate justice", when taking action to address climate change,

Affirming the importance of education, trammg, public awareness, public participation, public access to information and cooperation at all levels on the matters addressed in this Agreement,

Recognizing the importance of the engagements of all levels of government and various actors, in accordance with respective national legislations of Parties, in addressing climate change,

Also recognizing that sustainable lifestyles and sustainable patterns of consumption and production, with developed country Parties taking the lead, play an important role in addressing climate change,

Have agreed as follows:

Article 1

For the purpose of this Agreement, the definitions contained in Article 1 of the Convention shall apply. In addition:

(a) "Convention" means the United Nations Framework Convention on Climate Change, adopted in New York on 9 May 1992;

(b) "Conference of the Parties" means the Conference of the Parties to the Convention;

(c) "Party" means a Party to this Agreement.

Article 2

1. This Agreement, in enhancing the implementation of the Convention, including its objective, aims to strengthen the global response to the threat of climate change, in the context of sustainable development and efforts to eradicate poverty, including by:
   (a) Holding the increase in the global average temperature to well below 2°C above pre-industrial levels and pursuing efforts to limit the temperature increase to 1.5°C above pre-industrial levels, recognizing that this would significantly reduce the risks and impacts of climate change;
   (b) Increasing the ability to adapt to the adverse impacts of climate change and foster climate resilience and low greenhouse gas emissions development, in a manner that does not threaten food production; and
   (c) Making finance flows consistent with a pathway towards low greenhouse gas emissions and climate-resilient development.
2. This Agreement will be implemented to reflect equity and the principle of common but differentiated responsibilities and respective capabilities, in the light of different national circumstances.

Article 3

As nationally determined contributions to the global response to climate change, all Parties are to undertake and commhnicate ambitious efforts as defined in Articles 4, 7, 9, 10, 11 and 13 with the view to achieving the purpose of this Agreement as set out in Article 2. The efforts of all Parties will represent a progression over time, while recognizing the need to support developing country Parties for the effective implementation of this Agreement.

Article 4

1. In order to achieve the long-term temperature goal set out in Article 2, Parties aim to reach global peaking of greenhouse gas emissions as soon as possible, recognizing that peaking will take longer for developing country Parties, and to undertake rapid reductions thereafter in accordance with best available science, so as to achieve a balance between anthropogenic emissions by sources and removals by sinks of greenhouse gases in the second half of this century, on the basis of equity, and in the context of sustainable development and efforts to eradicate poverty.
2. Each Party shall prepare, communicate and maintain successive nationally determined contributions that it intends to achieve. Parties shall pursue domestic mitigation measures, with the aim of achieving the objectives of such contributions.
3. Each Party's successive nationally determined contribution will represent a progression beyond the Party's then current nationally determined contribution and reflect its highest possible ambition, reflecting its common but differentiated responsibilities and respective capabilities, in the light of different national circumstances.
4. Developed country Parties should continue taking the lead by undertaking economy-wide absolute emission reduction targets. Developing country Parties should continue enhancing their mitigation efforts, and are encouraged to move over time towards economy-wide emission reduction or limitation targets in the light of different national circumstances.
5. Support shall be provided to developing country Parties for the impl mentation of this Article, in accordance with Articles 9, 10 and 11, recognizing that enhanced support for developing country Parties will allow for higher ambition in their actions.
6. The least developed countries and small island developing States may prepare and communicate strategies, plans and actions for low greenhouse gas emissions development reflecting their special circumstances.
7. Mitigation co-benefits resulting from Parties' adaptation actions and/or economlc diversification plans can contribute to mitigation outcomes under this Article.
8. In communicating their nationally determined contributions, all Parties shall provide the information necessary for clarity, transparency and understanding in accordance with decision l/CP.21 and any relevant decisions of the Conference of the Parties serving as the meeting of the Parties to this Agreement.
9. Each Party shall communicate a nationally determined contribution every five years in accordance with decision l/CP.21 and any relevant decisions of the Conference of the Parties serving as the meeting of the Parties to this Agreement and be informed by the outcomes of the global stocktake referred to in Article 14.
10. The Conference of the Parties serving as the meeting of the Parties to this Agreement shall consider common time frames for nationally determined contributions at its first session.
11. A Party may at any time adjust its existing nationally determined contribution with a view to enhancing its level of ambition, in accordance with guidance adopted by the Conference of the Parties serving as the meeting of the Parties to this Agreement.
12. Nationally determined contributions communicated by Parties shall be recorded in a public registry maintained by the secretariat.
13. Parties shall account for their nationally determined contributions. In accounting for anthropogenic emissions and removals corresponding to their nationally determined contributions, Parties shall promote environmental integrity, transparency, accuracy, completeness, comparability and consistency, and ensure the avoidance of double counting, in accordance with guidance adopted by the Conference of the Parties serving as the meeting of the Parties to this Agreement.
14. In the context of their nationally determined contributions, when recognizing and implementing mitigation actions with respect to anthropogenic emissions and removals, Parties should take into account, as appropriate, existing methods and guidance under the Convention, in the light of the provisions of paragraph 13 of this Article.
15. Parties shall take into consideration in the implementation of this Agreement the concerns of Parties with economies most affected by the impacts of response measures, particularly developing country Parties.
16. Parties, including regional economic integration organizations and their member States, that have reached an agreement to act jointly under paragraph 2 of this Article shall notify the secretariat of the terms of that agreement, including the emission level allocated to each Party within the relevant time period, when they communicate their nationally determined contributions. The secretariat shall in turn inform the Parties and signatories to the Convention of the terms ofthat agreement.
17. Each party to such an agreement shall be responsible for its emission level as set out in the agreement referred to in paragraph 16 of this Article in accordance with paragraphs 13 and 14 of this Article and Articles 13 and 15.
18. If Parties acting jointly do so in the framework of, and together with, a regional economic integration organization which is itself a Party to this Agree-

ment, each member State of that regional economic integration organization individually, and together with the regional economic integration organization, shall be responsible for its emission level as set out in the agreement communicated under paragraph 16 of this Article in accordance with paragraphs 13 and 14 of this Article and Articles 13 and 15.

19. All Parties should strive to formulate and communicate long-term low greenhouse gas emission development strategies, mindful of Article 2 taking into account their common but differentiated responsibilities and respective capabilities, in the light of different national circumstances.

Article 5

1. Parties should take action to conserve and enhance, as appropriate, sinks and reservoirs of greenhouse gases as referred to in Article 4, paragraph 1 (d), of the Convention, including forests.
2. Parties are encouraged to take action to implement and support, including through results-based payments, the existing framework as set out in rel ted guidance and decisions already agreed under the Convention for: policy approaches and positive incentives for activities relating to reducing emissions from deforestation and forest degradation, and the role of conservation, sustainable management of forests and enhancement of forest carbon stocks in developing countries; and alternative policy approaches, such as joint mitigation and adaptation approaches for the integral and sustainable management of forests, while reaffirming the importance of incentivizing, as appropriate, non-carbon benefits associated with such approaches.

Article 6

1. Parties recognize that some Parties choose to pursue voluntary cooperation in the implementation of their nationally determined contributions to allow for higher ambition in their mitigation and adaptation actions and to promote sustainable development and environmental integrity.
2. Parties shall, where engaging on a voluntary basis in cooperative approaches that involve the use of internationally transferred mitigation outcomes towards nationally determined contributions, promote sustainable development and ensure environmental integrity and transparency, including in govemance, and shall apply robust accounting to ensure, inter alia, the avoidance of double counting, consistent with guidance adopted by the Conference of the Parties serving as the meeting of the Parties to this Agreement.
3. The use of internationally transferred mitigation outcomes to achieve nationally determined contributions under this Agreement shall be voluntary and authorized by participating Parties.
4. A mechanism to contribute to the mitigation of greenhouse gas emissions and support sustainable development is hereby established under the authority and guidance of the Conference of the Parties serving as the meeting of the Parties to this Agreement for use by Parties on a voluntary basis. It shall be supervised by a body designated by the Conference of the Parties serving as the meeting of the Partie.s to this Agreement, and shall aim:
   (a) To promote the mitigation of greenhouse gas emissions while fostering sustainable development;
   (b) To incentivize and facilitate partlc1pation in the mitigation of greenhouse gas emissions by public and private entities authorized by a Party;
   (c) To contribute to the reduction of emission levels in the host Party, which will benefit from mitigation activities resulting in emission reductions that can also be used by another Party to fulfil its nationally determined contribution; and
   (d) To deliver an overall mitigation in global emissions.
5. Emission reductions resulting from the mechanism referred to in paragraph 4 of this Article shall not be used to demonstrate achievement of the host Party's nationally determined contribution if used by another Party to demonstrate achievement of its nationally determined contribution.
6. The Conference of the Parties serving as the meeting of the Parties to this Agreement shall ensure that a share of the proceeds from activities under the mechanism referred to in paragraph 4 of this Article is used to cover administrative expenses as well as to assist developing country Parties that are particularly vulnerable to the adverse effects of climate change to meet the costs of adaptation.
7. The Conference of the Parties serving as the meeting of the Parties to this Agreement shall adopt rules, modalities and procedures for the mechanism referred to in paragraph 4 of this Article at its first sess-ion.
8. Parties recognize the importance of integrated, holistic and balanced non-market approaches being available to Parties to assist in the implementation of their nationally determined contributions, in the context of sustainable development and poverty eradication, in a coordinated and effective manner, including through, inter alia, mitigation, adaptation, finance, technology transfer and capacity building, as appropriate. These approaches shall aim to:
   (a) Promote mitigation and adaptation ambition;
   (b) Enhance public and private sector participation in the implementation of nationally determined contributions; and
   (c) Enable opportunities for coordination across instruments and relevant institutionaf arrangements.
9. A framework for non-market approaches to sustainable development is hereby defined to promote the non-market approaches referred to in paragraph 8 of this Article.

Article 7

1. Parties hereby establish the global goal on adaptation of enhancing adaptive capacity, strengthening resilience and reducing vulnerability to climate change, with a view to contributing to sustainable development and ensuring an adequate adaptation response in the context of the temperature goal referred to in Article 2.
2. Parties recognize that adaptation is a global challenge faced by all with local, subnational, national, regional and international dimensions, and that it is a key component of and makes a contribution to the long-term global response to climate change to protect people, livelihoods and ecosystems, taking into account the urgent and immediate needs of those developing country Parties that are particularly vulnerable to the adverse effects of climate change.
3. The adaptation efforts of developing country Parties shall be recognized, in accordance with the modalities to be adopted by the Conference of the Parties serving as the meeting of the Parties to this Agreement at its first session.
4. Parties recognize that the current need for adaptation is significant and that greater levels of mitigation can reduce the need for additional adaptation efforts, and that greater adaptation needs can involve greater adaptation costs.
5. Parties acknowledge that adaptation action should follow a country-driven, gender-responsive, participatory and fully transparent approach, taking into consideration vulnerable groups, communities and ecosystems, and should be based on and guided by the best available science and, as appropriate, traditional knowledge, knowledge of indigenous peoples and local knowledge systems, with a view to integrating adaptation into relevant socioeconomic and environmental policies and actions, where appropriate.
6. Parties recognize the importance of support for and international cooperation on adaptation efforts and the importance of taking into account the needs of developing country Parties, especially those that are particularly vulnerable .to the adverse effects of dimate change.
7. Parties should strengthen their cooperation on enhancing action on adaptation, taking into account the Cancun Adaptation Framework, including with regard to:
   (a) Sharing information, good practices, experiences and lessons learned, including, as appropriate, as these relate to science, planning, policies and implementation in relation to adaptation actions;
   (b) Strengthening institutional arrangements, including those under the Convention that serve this Agreement, to support the synthesis of relevant information and knowledge, and the provision of technical support and guidance to Parties;
   (c) Strengthening scientific knowledge on climate, including research, systematic observation of the climate system and early warning systems, in a manner that informs climate services and supports decision-making;
   (d) Assisting developing country Parties in identifying effective adaptation practices, adaptation needs, priorities, support provided and received for adaptation actions and efforts, and challenges and gaps, in a manner consistent with encouraging good practices; and
   (e) Improving the effectiveness and durability of adaptation actions.
8. United Nations specialized organizations and agencies are encouraged to support the efforts of Parties to implement the actions referred to in paragraph 7 of this Article, taking into account the provisions of paragraph 5 of this Article.
9. Each Party shall, as appropriate, engage in adaptation planning processes and the implementation of actions, including the development or enhancement of relevant plans, policies and/or contributions, which may include:
   (a) The implementation of adaptation actions, undertakings and/or efforts;
   (b) The process to formulate and implement national adaptation plans;
   (c) The assessment of climate change impacts and vulnerability, with a view to formulating nationally determined prioritized actions, taking into account vulnerable people, places and ecosystems;
   (d) Monitoring and evaluating and learning from adaptation plans, policies, programmes and actions; and
   (e) Building the resilience of socioeconomic and ecological systems, including through economic diversification and sustainable management of natural resources.
10. Each Party should, as appropriate, submit and update periodically an adaptation communication, which may include its priorities, implementation and support needs, plans and actions, without creating any additional burden for developing country Parties.
11. The adaptation communication referred to in paragraph 10 of this Article shall be, as appropriate, submitted and updated periodically, as a component of or in conjunction with other communications or documents, including a national adaptation plan, a nationally determined contribution as referred to in Article 4, paragraph 2, and/or a national communication.
12. The adaptation communications referred to in paragraph 10 of this Article shall be recorded in a public registry maintained by the secretariat.
13. Continuous and enhanced international support shall be provided to developing country Parties for the implementation of paragraphs 7, 9, 10 and 11 of this Article, in accordance with the provisions of Articles 9, 10 and 11.
14. The global stocktake referred to in Article 14 shall, inter alia:

(a) Recognize adaptation efforts of developing country Parties;

(b) Enhance the implementation of adaptation action taking into account the adaptation communication referred to in paragraph 10 of this Article;

(c) Review the adequacy and effectiveness of adaptation and support provided for adaptation; and

(d) Review the overall progress made in achieving the global goal on adaptation referred to in paragraph 1 of this Article.

Article 8

1. Parties recognize the importance of averting, minimizing and addressing loss and damage associated with the adverse effects of climate change, including extreme weather events and slow onset events, and the role of sustainable development in reducing the risk of loss and damage.
2. The Warsaw International Mechanism for Loss and Damage associated with Climate Change Impacts shall be subject to the authority and guidance of the Conference of the Parties serving as the meeting of the Parties to this Agreement and may be enhanced and strengthened, as determined by the Conference of the Parties serving as the meeting of the Parties to this Agreement.
3. Parties should enhance understanding, action and support, including through the Warsaw International Mechanism, as · appropriate, on a cooperative and facilitative basis with respect to loss and damage associated with the adverse effects of climate change.
4. Accordingly, areas of cooperation and facilitation to enhance understanding, action and support may include:

   (a) Early warning systems;

   (b) Emergency preparedness;

   (c) Slow onset events;

   (d) Events that may involve irreversible and permanent loss and damage;

   (e) Comprehensive risk assessment and management;

   (f) Risk insurance facilities, climate risk pooling and other insurance solutions;

   (g) Non-economic losses; and

   (h) Resilience of communities, livelihoods and ecosystems.
5. The Warsaw International Mechanism shall collaborate with existing bodies and expert groups under the Agreement, as well as relevant organizations and expert bodies outside the Agreement.

Article 9

1. Developed country Parties shall provide financial resources to assist developing country Parties with respect to both mitigation and adaptation in continuation of their existing obligations under the Convention.
2. Other Parties are encouraged to provide or continue to provide such support voluntarily.
3. As part of a global effort, developed country Parties should continue to take the lead in mobilizing climate finance from a wide variety of sources, instruments and channels, noting the significant role of public funds, through a variety of actions, including supporting country-driven strategies, and taking into account the needs and priorities of developing country Parties. Such mobilization of climate finance should represent a progression beyond previous efforts.
4. The provision of scaled-up financial resources should aim to achieve a balance between adaptation and mitigation, taking into account country-driven strategies, and the priorities and needs of developing country Parties, especially those that are particularly vulnerable to the adverse effects of climate change and have significant capacity constraints, such as the least developed countries and small island developing States, considering the need for public and grant-based resources for adaptation.
5. Developed country Parties shall biennially communicate indicative quantitative and qualitative information related to paragraphs 1 and 3 of this Article, as applicable, including, as available, projected levels of public financial resources to be provided to developing country Parties. Other Parties providing resources are encouraged to communicate biennially such information on a voluntary basis.
6. The global stocktake referred to in Article 14 shall take into account the relevant information provided by developed country Parties and/or Agreement bodies on efforts related to climate finance.
7. Developed country Parties shall provide transparent and consistent information on support for developing country Parties provided and mobilized through public interventions biennially in accordance with the modalities, procedures and guidelines to be adopted by the Conference of the Parties serving as the meeting of the Parties to this Agreement, at its first session, as stipulated in Article 13, paragraph 13. Other Parties are encouraged to do so.
8. The Financial Mechanism of the Convention, including its operating entities, shall serve as the financial mechanism of this Agreement.
9. The institutions serving this Agreement, including the operating entities of the Financial Mechanism of the Convention, shall aim to ensure efficient access to financial resources through simplified approval procedures and enhanced readiness support for developing country Parties, in particular for the least developed countries and small island developing States, in the context of their national climate strategies and plans.

Article 10

1. Parties share a long-term vision on the importance of fully realizing technology development and

transfer in order to improve resilience to climate change and to reduce greenhouse gas emissions.

2. Parties, noting the importance of technology for the implementation of mitigation and adaptation actions under this Agreement and recognizing existing technology deployment and dissemination efforts, shall strengthen cooperative action on technology development and transfer.
3. The Technology Mechanism established under the Convention shall serve this Agreement.
4. A technology framework is hereby established to provide overarching guidance to the work of the Technology Mechanism in promoting and facilitating enhanced action on technology development and transfer in order to support the implementation of this Agreement, in pursuit of the long-term vision referred to in paragraph 1 of this Article.
5. Accelerating, encouraging and enabling innovation is critical for an effective, long-term global response to climate change and promoting economic growth and sustainable development. Such effort shall be, as appropriate, supported, including by the Technology Mechanism and, through financial means, by the Financial Mechanism of the Convention, for collaborative approaches to research and development, and facilitating access to technology, in particular for early stages of the technology cycle, to developing country Parties.
6. Support, including financial support, shall be provided to developing country Parties for the implementation of this Article, including for strengthening cooperative action on technology development and transfer at different stages of the technology cycle, with a view to achieving a balance between support for mitigation and adaptation. The global stocktake referred to in Article 14 shall take into account available information on efforts related to support on technology development and transfer for developing country Parties.

Article 11

1. Capacity-building under this Agreement should enhance the capacity and ability of developing country Parties, in particular countries with the least capacity, such as the least developed countries, and those that are particularly vulnerable to the adverse effects of climate change, such as small island developing States, to take effective climate change action, including, inter alia, to implement adaptation and mitigation actions, and should facilitate technology development, dissemination and deployment, access to climate finance, relevant aspects of education, training and public awareness, and the transparent, timely and accurate communication of information.
2. Capacity-building should be country-driven, based on and responsive to national needs, and foster country ownership of Parties, in particular, for developing country Parties, including at the national, subnational and local levels. Capacity-building should be guided by lessons learned, including those from capacity-building activities under the Convention, and should be an effective, iterative process that is participatory, cross-cutting and gender-responsive.
3. All Parties should cooperate to enhance the capacity of developing country Parties to implement this Agreement. Developed country Parties should enhance support for capacity-building actions in developing country Parties.
4. All Parties enhancing the capacity of developing country Parties to implement this Agreement, including through regional, bilateral and multilateral approaches, shall regularly communicate on these actions or measures on capacity building. Developing country Parties should regularly communicate progress made on implementing capacity-building plans, policies, actions or measures to implement this Agreement.
5. Capacity-building activities shall be enhanced through appropriate institutional arrangements to support the implementation of this Agreement, including the appropriate institutional arrangements established under the Convention that serve this Agreement. The Conference of the Parties serving as the meeting of the Parties to this Agreement shall, at its first session, consider and adopt a decision on the initial institutional arrangements for capacity-building.

Article 12

Parties shall cooperate in taking measures, as appropriate, to enhance climate change education, training, public awareness, public participation and public access to information, recognizing the importance of these steps with respect to enhancing actions under this Agreement.

Article 13

1. In order to build mutual trust and confidence and to promote effective implementation, an enhanced transparency framework for action and support, with built-in flexibility which takes into account Parties' different capacities and builds upon collective experience is hereby established.
2. The transparency framework shall provide flexibility in the implementation of the provisions of this Article to those developing country Parties that need it in the light of their capacities. The modalities, procedures and guidelines referred to in paragraph 13 of this Article shall reflect such flexibility.
3. The transparency framework shall build on and enhance the transparency arrangements under the Convention, recognizing the special circumstances of the least developed countries and small island developing States, and be implemented in a facilitative, non-intrusive, non-punitive manner, respectful of national sovereignty, and avoid placing undue burden on Parties.
4. The transparency arrangements under the Convention, including national communications, biennial reports and biennial update reports, international assessment and review and international consultation and analysis, shall form part of the experience drawn upon for the development of the modalities,

procedures and guidelines under paragraph 13 of this Article.

5. The purpose of the framework for transparency of action is to provide a clear understanding of climate change action in the light of the objective of the Convention as set out in its Article 2, including clarity and tracking of progress towards achieving Parties' individual nationally determined contributions under Article 4, and Parties' adaptation actions under Article 7, including good practices, priorities, needs and gaps, to inform the global stocktake under Article 14.
6. The purpose of the framework for transparency of support is to provide clarity on support provided and received by relevant individual Parties in the context of climate change actions under Articles 4, 7, 9, 10 and 11, and, to the extent possible, to provide a full overview of aggregate financial support provided, to inform the global stocktake under Article 14.
7. Each Party shall regularly provide the following information:
   (a) A national inventory report of anthropogenic emissions by sources and removals by sinks of greenhouse gases, prepared using good practice methodologies accepted by the Intergovernmental Panel on Climate Change and agreed upon by the Conference of the Parties serving as the meeting of the Parties to this Agreement; and
   (b) Information necessary to track progress made in implementing and achieving its nationally determined contribution under Article 4.
8. Each Party should also provide information related to climate change impacts and adaptation under Article 7, as appropriate.
9. Developed country Parties shall, and other Parties that provide support should, provide information on financial, technology transfer and capacity-building support provided to developing country Parties under Articles 9, 10 and 11.
10. Developing country Parties should provide information on financial, technology transfer and capacity-building support needed and received under Articles 9, 10 and 11.
11. Information submitted by each Party under paragraphs 7 and 9 of this Article shall undergo a technical expert review, in accordance with decision 1/CP.21. For those developing country Parties that need it in the light of their capacities, the review process shall include assistance in identifying capacity-building needs. In addition, each Party shall participate in a facilitative, multilateral consideration of progress with respect to efforts under Article 9, and its respective implementation and achievement of its nationally determined contribution.
12. The technical expert review under this paragraph shall consist of a consideration of the Party's support provided, as relevant, and its implementation and achievement of its nationally determined contribution. The review shall also identify areas of improvement for the Party, and include a review of the consistency of the information with the modalities, procedures and guidelines referred to in paragraph 13 of this Article, taking into account the flexibility accorded to the Party under paragraph 2 of this Article. The review shall pay particular attention to the respective national capabilities and circumstances of developing country Parties.
13. The Conference of the Parties serving as the meeting of the Parties to this Agreement shall, at its first session, building on experience from the arrangements related to transparency under the Convention, and elaborating on the provisions in this Article, adopt common modalities, procedures and guidelines, as appropriate, for the transparency of action and support.
14. Support shall be provided to developing countries for the implementation of this Article.
15. Support shall also be provided for the building of transparency-related capacity of developing country Parties on a continuous basis.

Article 14

1. The Conference of the Parties serving as the meeting of the Parties to this Agreement shall periodically take stock of the implementation of this Agreement to assess the collective progress towards achieving the purpose of this Agreement and its long-term goals (referred to as the "global stocktake"). It shall do so in a comprehensive and facilitative manner, considering mitigation, adaptation and the means of implementation and support, and in the light of equity and the best available science.
2. The Conference of the Parties serving as the meeting of the Parties to this Agreement shall undertake its first global stocktake in 2023 and every five years thereafter unless otherwise decided by the Conference of the Parties serving as the meeting of the Parties to this Agreement.
3. The outcome of the global stocktake shall inform Parties in updating and enhancing, in a nationally determined manner, their actions and support in accordance with the relevant provisions of this Agreement, as well as in enhancing international cooperation for climate action.

Article 15

1. A mechanism to facilitate implementation of and promote compliance with the provisions of this Agreement is hereby established.
2. The mechanism referred to in paragraph 1 of this Article shall consist of a committee that shall be expert-based and facilitative in nature and function in a manner that is transparent, non-adversarial and non-punitive. The committee shall pay particular attention to the respective national capabilities and circumstances of Parties.
3. The committee shall operate under the modalities and procedures adopted by the Conference of the Parties serving as the meeting of the Parties to this Agreement at its first session and report annually to

the Conference of the Parties serving as the meeting of the Parties to this Agreement.

Article 16

1. The Conference of the Parties, the supreme body of the Convention, shall serve as the meeting of the Parties to this Agreement.
2. Parties to the Convention that are not Parties to this Agreement may participate as observers in the proceedings of any session of the Conference of the Parties serving as the meeting of the Parties to this Agreement. When the Conference of the Parties serves as the meeting of the Parties to this Agreement, decisions under this Agreement shall be taken only by those that are Parties to this Agreement.
3. When the Conference of the Parties serves as the meeting of the Parties to this Agreement, any member of tbe Bureau of the Conference of the Parties representing a Party to tbe Convention but, at that time, not a Party to this Agreement, shall be replaced by an additional member to be elected by and from amongst tbe Parties to this Agreement.
4. The Conference of the Parties serving as the meeting of the Parties to this Agreement shall keep under regular review the implementation of this Agreement and shall make, within its mandate, the decisions necessary to promote its effective implementation. lt shall perform the functions assigned to it by this Agreement and shall:
   (a) Establish such subsidiary bodies as deemed necessary for the implementation of this Agreement; and
   (b) Exercise such other functions as may be required for the implementation of this Agreement.
5. The rules of procedure of the Conference of the Parties and the financial procedures applied under the Convention shall be applied mutatis mutandis under this Agreement, except as may be otherwise decided by consensus by the Conference of the Parties serving as the meeting of the Parties to this Agreement.
6. The first session of the Conference of the Parties serving as the meeting of the Parties to this Agreement shall be convened by the secretariat in conjunction with the first session of the Conference of the Parties that is scheduled after the date of entry into force of this Agreement. Subsequent ordinary sessions of the Conference of the Parties serving as the meeting of the Parties to this Agreement shall be held in conjunction with ordinary sessions of the Conference of the Parties, unless otherwise decided by the Conference of the Parties serving as the meeting of the Parties to this Agreement.
7. Extraordinary sessions of the Conference of the Parties serving as the meeting of the Parties to this Agreement shall be held at such other times as may be deemed necessary by the Conference of the Parties serving as the meeting of the Parties to this Agreement or at the written request of any Party, provided that, within six months of the request being communicated to the Parties by the secretariat, it is supported by at least one third of the Parties.
8. The United Nations and its specialized agencies and the International Atomic Energy Agency, as well as any State member thereof or observers thereto not party to the Convention, may be represented at sessions of the Conference of the Parties serving as the meeting of the Parties to this Agreement as observers. Any body or agency, whether national or international, governmental or non-governmental, which is qualified in matters covered by this Agreement and which has informed the secretariat of its wish to be represented at a session of the Conference of the Parties serving as the meeting of the Parties to this Agreement as an observer, may be so admitted unless at least one third of the Parties present object. The admission and participation of observers shall be subject to the rules of procedure referred to in paragraph 5 of this Article.

Article 17

1. The secretariat established by Article 8 of the Convention shall serve as the secretariat of this Agreement.
2. Article 8, paragraph 2, of the Convention on the functions of the secretariat, and Article 8, paragraph 3, of the Convention, on the arrangements made for the functioning of the secretariat, shall apply mutatis mutandis to this Agreement. The secretariat shall, in addition, exercise the functions assigned to it under this Agreement and by the Conference of the Parties serving as the meeting of the Parties to this Agreement.

Article 18

1. The Subsidiary Body for Scientific and Technological Advice and the Subsidiary Body for Implementation established by Articles 9 and 10 of the Convention shall serve, respectively, as the Subsidiary Body for Scientific and Technological Advice and the Subsidiary Body for Implementation of this Agreement. The provisions of the Convention relating to the functioning of these two bodies shall apply mutatis mutandis to this Agreement. Sessions of the meetings of the Subsidiary Body for Scientific and Technological Advice and the Subsidiary Body for Implementation of this Agreement shall be held in conjunction with the meetings of, respectively, the Subsidiary Body for Scientific and Technological Advice and the Subsidiary Body for Implementation of the Convention.
2. Parties to the Convention that are not Parties to this Agreement may participate as observers in the proceedings of any session of the subsidiary bodies. When the subsidiary bodies serve as the subsidiary bodies of this Agreement, decisions under this Agreement shall be taken only by those that are Parties to this Agreement.
3. When the subsidiary bodies established by Articles 9 and 10 of the Convention exercise their functions with regard to matters concerning this Agreement, any member of the bureaux of those subsidiary bodies representing a Party to the Convention but, at that time, not a Party to this Agreement, shall be

replaced by an additional member to be elected by and from amongst the Parties to this Agreement.

Article 19

1. Subsidiary bodies or other institutional arrangements established by or under the Convention, other than those referred to in this Agreement, shall serve this Agreement upon a decision of the Conference of the Parties serving as the meeting of the Parties to this Agreement. The Conference of the Parties serving as the meeting of the Parties to this Agreement shall specify the functions to be exercised by such subsidiary bodies or arrangements.
2. The Conference of the Parties serving as the meeting of the Parties to this Agreement may provide further guidance to such subsidiary bodies and institutional arrangements.

Article 20

1. This Agreement shall be open for signature and subject to ratification, acceptance or approval by States and regional economic integration organizations that are Parties to the Convention. It shall be open for signature at the United Nations Headquarters in New York from 22 April 2016 to 21 April 2017. Thereafter, this Agreement shall be open for accession from the day following the date on which it is closed for signature. Instruments of ratification, acceptance, approval or accession shall be deposited with the Depositary.
2. Any regional economic integration organization that becomes a Party to this Agreement without any of its member States being a Party shall be bound by all the obligations under this Agreement. In the case of regional economic integration organizations with one or more member States that are Parties to this Agreement, the organization and its member States shall decide on their respective responsibilities for the performance of their obligations under this Agreement. In such cases, the organization and the member States shall not be entitled to exercise rights under this Agreement concurrently.
3. In their instruments of ratification, acceptance, approval or accession, regional economic integration organizations shall declare the extent of their competence with respect to the matters governed by this Agreement. These organizations shall also inform the Depositary, who shall in turn inform the Parties, of any substantial modification in the extent of their competence.

Article 21

1. This Agreement shall enter into force on the thirtieth day after the date on which at least 55 Parties to the Convention accounting in total for at least an estimated 55 per cent of the total global greenhouse gas emissions have deposited their instruments of ratification, acceptance, approval or accession.
2. Solely for the limited purpose of paragraph 1 of this Article, "total global greenhouse gas emissions" means the most up-to-date amount communicated on or before the date of adoption of this Agreement by the Parties to the Convention.
3. For each State or regional economic integration organization that ratifies, accepts or approves this Agreement or accedes thereto after the conditions set out in paragraph 1 of this Article for entry into force have been fulfilled, this Agreement shall enter into force on the thirtieth day after the date of deposit by such State or regional economic integration organization of its instrument of ratification, acceptance, approval or accession.
4. For the purposes of paragraph 1 of this Article, any instrument deposited by a regional economic integration organization shall not be counted as additional to those deposited by its member States.

Article 22

The provisions of Article 15 of the Convention on the adoption of amendments to the Convention shall apply mutatis mutandis to this Agreement.

Article 23

1. The provisions of Article 16 of the Convention on the adoption and amendment of annexes to the Convention shall apply mutatis mutandis to this Agreement.
2. Annexes to this Agreement shall form an integral part thereof and, unless otherwise expressly provided for, a reference to this Agreement constitutes at the same time a reference to any annexes thereto. Such annexes shall be restricted to lists, forms and any other material of a descriptive nature that is of a scientific, technical, procedural or administrative character.

Article 24

The provisions of Article 14 of the Convention on settlement of disputes shall apply mutatis mutandis to this Agreement.

Article 25

1. Each Party shall have one vote, except as provided for in paragraph 2 of this Article.
2. Regional economic integration organizations, in matters within their competence, shall exercise their right to vote with a number of votes equal to the number of their member States that are Parties to this Agreement. Such an organization shall not exercise its right to vote if any of its member States exercises its right, and vice versa.

Article 26

The Secretary-General of the United Nations shall be the Depositary of this Agreement.

Article 27

No reservations may be made to this Agreement.

Article 28

1. At any time after three years from the date on which this Agreement has entered into force for a Party, that Party may withdraw from this Agreement by giving written notification to the Depositary.
2. Any such withdrawal shall take effect upon expiry of one year from the date of receipt by the Depos-

itary of the notification of withdrawal, or on such later date as may be specified in the notification of withdrawal.

3. Any Party that withdraws from the Convention shall be considered as also having withdrawn from this Agreement.

Article 29

The original of this Agreement, of which the Arabic, Chinese, English, French, Russian and Spanish texts are equally authentic, shall be deposited with the Secretary-General of the United Nations.

DONE at Paris this twelfth day of December two thousand and fifteen.

IN WITNESS WHEREOF, the undersigned, being duly authorized to that effect, have signed this Agreement.

7.1. Helsinki Convention 1992

Convention on the Protection and Use of Transboundary Watercourses and International Lakes, Helsinki, 17 March 1992, 1936 UNTS 269

The Parties to this Convention,

Mindful that the protection and use of transboundary watercourses and international lakes are important and urgent tasks, the effective accomplishment of which can only be ensured by enhanced cooperation,

Concerned over the existence and threats of adverse effects, in the short or long term, of changes in the conditions of transboundary watercourses and international lakes on the environment, economies and well-being of the member countries of the Economic Commission for Europe (ECE),

Emphasizing the need for strengthened national and international measures to prevent, control and reduce the release of hazardous substances into the aquatic environment and to abate eutrophication and acidification, as well as pollution of the marine environment, in particular coastal areas, from land-based sources,

Commending the efforts already undertaken by the ECE Governments to strengthen cooperation, on bilateral and multilateral levels, for the prevention, control and reduction of transboundary pollution, sustainable water management, conservation of water resources and environmental protection,

Recalling the pertinent provisions and principles of the Declaration of the Stockholm Conference on the Human Environment, the Final Act of the Conference on Security and Cooperation in Europe (CSCE), the Concluding Documents of the Madrid and Vienna Meetings of Representatives of the Participating States of the CSCE, and the Regional Strategy for Environmental Protection and Rational Use of Natural Resources in ECE Member Countries covering the Period up to the Year 2000 and Beyond,

Conscious of the role of the United Nations Economic Commission for Europe in promoting international cooperation for the prevention, control and reduction of transboundary water pollution and sustainable use of transboundary waters, and in this regard recalling the ECE Declaration of Policy on Prevention and Control of Water Pollution, including Transboundary Pollution; the ECE Declaration of Policy on the Rational Use of Water; the ECE Principles Regarding Cooperation in the Field of Transboundary Waters; the ECE Charter on Groundwater Management; and the Code of Conduct on Accidental Pollution of Transboundary Inland Waters,

Referring to decisions I (42) and I (44) adopted by the Economic Commission for Europe at its forty-second and forty-fourth sessions, respectively, and the outcome of the CSCE Meeting on the Protection of the Environment (Sofia, Bulgaria, 16 October - 3 November 1989),

Emphasizing that cooperation between member countries in regard to the protection and use of transboundary waters shall be implemented primarily through the elaboration of agreements between countries bordering the same waters, especially where no such agreements have yet been reached,

Have agreed as follows:

Article 1 – DEFINITIONS

For the purposes of this Convention,

1. "Transboundary waters" means any surface or ground waters which mark, cross or are located on boundaries between two or more States; wherever transboundary waters flow directly into the sea, these transboundary waters end at a straight line across their respective mouths between points on the low-water line of their banks;
2. "Transboundary impact" means any significant adverse effect on the environment resulting from a change in the conditions of transboundary waters caused by a human activity, the physical origin of which is situated wholly or in part within an area under the jurisdiction of a Party, within an area under the jurisdiction of another Party. Such effects on the environment include effects on human health and safety, flora, fauna, soil, air, water, climate, landscape and historical monuments or other physical structures or the interaction among these factors; they also include effects on the cultural heritage or socio-economic conditions resulting from alterations to those factors;
3. "Party" means, unless the text otherwise indicates, a Contracting Party to this Convention;
4. "Riparian Parties" means the Parties bordering the same transboundary waters;
5. "Joint body" means any bilateral or multilateral commission or other appropriate institutional arrangements for cooperation between the Riparian Parties;
6. "Hazardous substances" means substances which are toxic, carcinogenic, mutagenic, teratogenic or bio-accumulative, especially when they are persistent;
7. "Best available technology" (the definition is contained in annex I to this Convention).

PART I – PROVISIONS RELATING TO ALL PARTIES

Article 2 – GENERAL PROVISIONS

1. The Parties shall take all appropriate measures to prevent, control and reduce any transboundary impact.
2. The Parties shall, in particular, take all appropriate measures:
   (a) To prevent, control and reduce pollution of waters causing or likely to cause transboundary impact;

(b) To ensure that transboundary waters are used with the aim of ecologically sound and rational water management, conservation of water resources and environmental protection;

(c) To ensure that transboundary waters are used in a reasonable and equitable way, taking into particular account their transboundary character, in the case of activities which cause or are likely to cause transboundary impact;

(d) To ensure conservation and, where necessary, restoration of ecosystems.

3. Measures for the prevention, control and reduction of water pollution shall be taken, where possible, at source.

4. These measures shall not directly or indirectly result in a transfer of pollution to other parts of the environment.

5. In taking the measures referred to in paragraphs 1 and 2 of this article, the Parties shall be guided by the following principles:

(a) The precautionary principle, by virtue of which action to avoid the potential transboundary impact of the release of hazardous substances shall not be postponed on the ground that scientific research has not fully proved a causal link between those substances, on the one hand, and the potential transboundary impact, on the other hand;

(b) The polluter-pays principle, by virtue of which costs of pollution prevention, control and reduction measures shall be borne by the polluter;

(c) Water resources shall be managed so that the needs of the present generation are met without compromising the ability of future generations to meet their own needs.

6. The Riparian Parties shall cooperate on the basis of equality and reciprocity, in particular through bilateral and multilateral agreements, in order to develop harmonized policies, programmes and strategies covering the relevant catchment areas, or parts thereof, aimed at the prevention, control and reduction of transboundary impact and aimed at the protection of the environment of transboundary waters or the environment influenced by such waters, including the marine environment.

7. The application of this Convention shall not lead to the deterioration of environmental conditions nor lead to increased transboundary impact.

8. The provisions of this Convention shall not affect the right of Parties individually or jointly to adopt and implement more stringent measures than those set down in this Convention.

Article 3 – PREVENTION, CONTROL AND REDUCTION

1. To prevent, control and reduce transboundary impact, the Parties shall develop, adopt, implement and, as far as possible, render compatible relevant legal, administrative, economic, financial and technical measures, in order to ensure, inter alia, that:

(a) The emission of pollutants is prevented, controlled and reduced at source through the application of, inter alia, low- and non-waste technology;

(b) Transboundary waters are protected against pollution from point sources through the prior licensing of waste-water discharges by the competent national authorities, and that the authorized discharges are monitored and controlled;

(c) Limits for waste-water discharges stated in permits are based on the best available technology for discharges of hazardous substances;

(d) Stricter requirements, even leading to prohibition in individual cases, are imposed when the quality of the receiving water or the ecosystem so requires;

(e) At least biological treatment or equivalent processes are applied to municipal waste water, where necessary in a step-by-step approach;

(f) Appropriate measures are taken, such as the application of the best available technology, in order to reduce nutrient inputs from industrial and municipal sources;

(g) Appropriate measures and best environmental practices are developed and implemented for the reduction of inputs of nutrients and hazardous substances from diffuse sources, especially where the main sources are from agriculture (guidelines for developing best environmental practices are given in annex II to this Convention);

(h) Environmental impact assessment and other means of assessment are applied;

(i) Sustainable water-resources management, including the application of the ecosystems approach, is promoted;

(j) Contingency planning is developed;

(k) Additional specific measures are taken to prevent the pollution of groundwaters;

(l) The risk of accidental pollution is minimized.

2. To this end, each Party shall set emission limits for discharges from point sources into surface waters based on the best available technology, which are specifically applicable to individual industrial sectors or industries from which hazardous substances derive. The appropriate measures mentioned in paragraph 1 of this article to prevent, control and reduce the input of hazardous substances from point and diffuse sources into waters, may, inter alia, include total or partial prohibition of the production or use of such substances. Existing lists of such industrial sectors or industries and of such hazardous substances in international conventions or regulations, which are applicable in the area covered by this Convention, shall be taken into account.

3. In addition, each Party shall define, where appropriate, water-quality objectives and adopt water-quality criteria for the purpose of preventing, controlling and reducing transboundary impact.

General guidance for developing such objectives and criteria is given in annex III to this Convention. When necessary, the Parties shall endeavour to update this annex.

Article 4 – MONITORING

The Parties shall establish programmes for monitoring the conditions of transboundary waters.

Article 5 – RESEARCH AND DEVELOPMENT

The Parties shall cooperate in the conduct of research into and development of effective techniques for the prevention, control and reduction of transboundary impact. To this effect, the Parties shall, on a bilateral and/or multilateral basis, taking into account research activities pursued in relevant international forums, endeavour to initiate or intensify specific research programmes, where necessary, aimed, inter alia, at:

(a) Methods for the assessment of the toxicity of hazardous substances and the noxiousness of pollutants;

(b) Improved knowledge on the occurrence, distribution and environmental effects of pollutants and the processes involved;

(c) The development and application of environmentally sound technologies, production and consumption patterns;

(d) The phasing out and/or substitution of substances likely to have transboundary impact;

(e) Environmentally sound methods of disposal of hazardous substances;

(f) Special methods for improving the conditions of transboundary waters;

(g) The development of environmentally sound water-construction works and water-regulation techniques;

(h) The physical and financial assessment of damage resulting from transboundary impact.

The results of these research programmes shall be exchanged among the Parties in accordance with article 6 of this Convention.

Article 6 – EXCHANGE OF INFORMATION

The Parties shall provide for the widest exchange of information, as early as possible, on issues covered by the provisions of this Convention.

Article 7 – RESPONSIBILITY AND LIABILITY

The Parties shall support appropriate international efforts to elaborate rules, criteria and procedures in the field of responsibility and liability.

Article 8 – PROTECTION OF INFORMATION

The provisions of this Convention shall not affect the rights or the obligations of Parties in accordance with their national legal systems and applicable supranational regulations to protect information related to industrial and commercial secrecy, including intellectual property, or national security.

PART II – PROVISIONS RELATING TO RIPARIAN PARTIES

Article 9 – BILATERAL AND MULTILATERAL COOPERATION

1. The Riparian Parties shall on the basis of equality and reciprocity enter into bilateral or multilateral agreements or other arrangements, where these do not yet exist, or adapt existing ones, where necessary to eliminate the contradictions with the basic principles of this Convention, in order to define their mutual relations and conduct regarding the prevention, control and reduction of transboundary impact. The Riparian Parties shall specify the catchment area, or part(s) thereof, subject to cooperation. These agreements or arrangements shall embrace relevant issues covered by this Convention, as well as any other issues on which the Riparian Parties may deem it necessary to cooperate.
2. The agreements or arrangements mentioned in paragraph 1 of this article shall provide for the establishment of joint bodies. The tasks of these joint bodies shall be, inter alia, and without prejudice to relevant existing agreements or arrangements, the following:
   (a) To collect, compile and evaluate data in order to identify pollution sources likely to cause transboundary impact;

   (b) To elaborate joint monitoring programmes concerning water quality and quantity;

   (c) To draw up inventories and exchange information on the pollution sources mentioned in paragraph 2 (a) of this article;

   (d) To elaborate emission limits for waste water and evaluate the effectiveness of control programmes;

   (e) To elaborate joint water-quality objectives and criteria having regard to the provisions of article 3, paragraph 3 of this Convention, and to propose relevant measures for maintaining and, where necessary, improving the existing water quality;

   (f) To develop concerted action programmes for the reduction of pollution loads from both point sources (e.g. municipal and industrial sources) and diffuse sources (particularly from agriculture);

   (g) To establish warning and alarm procedures;

   (h) To serve as a forum for the exchange of information on existing and planned uses of water and related installations that are likely to cause transboundary impact;

   (i) To promote cooperation and exchange of information on the best available technology in accordance with the provisions of article 13 of this Convention, as well as to encourage cooperation in scientific research programmes;

   (j) To participate in the implementation of environmental impact assessments relating to transboundary waters, in accordance with appropriate international regulations.

3. In cases where a coastal State, being Party to this Convention, is directly and significantly affected by transboundary impact, the Riparian Parties can, if they all so agree, invite that coastal State to be involved in an appropriate manner in the activities of multilateral joint bodies established by Parties riparian to such transboundary waters.
4. Joint bodies according to this Convention shall invite joint bodies, established by coastal States for the protection of the marine environment directly affected by transboundary impact, to cooperate in order to harmonize their work and to prevent, control and reduce the transboundary impact.
5. Where two or more joint bodies exist in the same catchment area, they shall endeavour to coordinate their activities in order to strengthen the prevention, control and reduction of transboundary impact within that catchment area.

Article 10 – CONSULTATIONS

Consultations shall be held between the Riparian Parties on the basis of reciprocity, good faith and good-neighbourliness, at the request of any such Party. Such consultations shall aim at cooperation regarding the issues covered by the provisions of this Convention. Any such consultations shall be conducted through a joint body established under article 9 of this Convention, where one exists.

Article 11 – JOINT MONITORING AND ASSESSMENT

1. In the framework of general cooperation mentioned in article 9 of this Convention, or specific arrangements, the Riparian Parties shall establish and implement joint programmes for monitoring the conditions of transboundary waters, including floods and ice drifts, as well as transboundary impact.
2. The Riparian Parties shall agree upon pollution parameters and pollutants whose discharges and concentration in transboundary waters shall be regularly monitored.
3. The Riparian Parties shall, at regular intervals, carry out joint or coordinated assessments of the conditions of transboundary waters and the effectiveness of measures taken for the prevention, control and reduction of transboundary impact. The results of these assessments shall be made available to the public in accordance with the provisions set out in article 16 of this Convention.
4. For these purposes, the Riparian Parties shall harmonize rules for the setting up and operation of monitoring programmes, measurement systems, devices, analytical techniques, data processing and evaluation procedures, and methods for the registration of pollutants discharged.

Article 12 – COMMON RESEARCH AND DEVELOPMENT

In the framework of general cooperation mentioned in article 9 of this Convention, or specific arrangements, the Riparian Parties shall undertake specific research and development activities in support of achieving and maintaining the water-quality objectives and criteria which they have agreed to set and adopt.

Article 13 – EXCHANGE OF INFORMATION BETWEEN RIPARIAN PARTIES

1. The Riparian Parties shall, within the framework of relevant agreements or other arrangements according to article 9 of this Convention, exchange reasonably available data, inter alia, on:
   (a) Environmental conditions of transboundary waters;
   (b) Experience gained in the application and operation of best available technology and results of research and development;
   (c) Emission and monitoring data;
   (d) Measures taken and planned to be taken to prevent, control and reduce transboundary impact;
   (e) Permits or regulations for waste-water discharges issued by the competent authority or appropriate body.
2. In order to harmonize emission limits, the Riparian Parties shall undertake the exchange of information on their national regulations.
3. If a Riparian Party is requested by another Riparian Party to provide data or information that is not available, the former shall endeavour to comply with the request but may condition its compliance upon the payment, by the requesting Party, of reasonable charges for collecting and, where appropriate, processing such data or information.
4. For the purposes of the implementation of this Convention, the Riparian Parties shall facilitate the exchange of best available technology, particularly through the promotion of: the commercial exchange of available technology; direct industrial contacts and cooperation, including joint ventures; the exchange of information and experience; and the provision of technical assistance. The Riparian Parties shall also undertake joint training programmes and the organization of relevant seminars and meetings.

Article 14 – WARNING AND ALARM SYSTEMS

The Riparian Parties shall without delay inform each other about any critical situation that may have transboundary impact. The Riparian Parties shall set up, where appropriate, and operate coordinated or joint communication, warning and alarm systems with the aim of obtaining and transmitting information. These systems shall operate on the basis of compatible data transmission and treatment procedures and facilities to be agreed upon by the Riparian Parties. The Riparian Parties shall inform each other about competent authorities or points of contact designated for this purpose.

Article 15 – MUTUAL ASSISTANCE

1. If a critical situation should arise, the Riparian Parties shall provide mutual assistance upon request,

following procedures to be established in accordance with paragraph 2 of this article.

2. The Riparian Parties shall elaborate and agree upon procedures for mutual assistance addressing, inter alia, the following issues:
   (a) The direction, control, coordination and supervision of assistance;
   (b) Local facilities and services to be rendered by the Party requesting assistance, including, where necessary, the facilitation of border-crossing formalities;
   (c) Arrangements for holding harmless, indemnifying and/or compensating the assisting Party and/or its personnel, as well as for transit through territories of third Parties, where necessary;
   (d) Methods of reimbursing assistance services.

Article 16 – PUBLIC INFORMATION

1. The Riparian Parties shall ensure that information on the conditions of transboundary waters, measures taken or planned to be taken to prevent, control and reduce transboundary impact, and the effectiveness of those measures, is made available to the public. For this purpose, the Riparian Parties shall ensure that the following information is made available to the public:
   (a) Water-quality objectives;
   (b) Permits issued and the conditions required to be met;
   (c) Results of water and effluent sampling carried out for the purposes of monitoring and assessment, as well as results of checking compliance with the water-quality objectives or the permit conditions.
2. The Riparian Parties shall ensure that this information shall be available to the public at all reasonable times for inspection free of charge, and shall provide members of the public with reasonable facilities for obtaining from the Riparian Parties, on payment of reasonable charges, copies of such information.

PART III – INSTITUTIONAL AND FINAL PROVISIONS

Article 17 – MEETING OF PARTIES

1. The first meeting of the Parties shall be convened no later than one year after the date of the entry into force of this Convention. Thereafter, ordinary meetings shall be held every three years, or at shorter intervals as laid down in the rules of procedure. The Parties shall hold an extraordinary meeting if they so decide in the course of an ordinary meeting or at the written request of any Party, provided that, within six months of it being communicated to all Parties, the said request is supported by at least one third of the Parties.
2. At their meetings, the Parties shall keep under continuous review the implementation of this Convention, and, with this purpose in mind, shall:
   (a) Review the policies for and methodological approaches to the protection and use of transboundary waters of the Parties with a view to further improving the protection and use of transboundary waters;
   (b) Exchange information regarding experience gained in concluding and implementing bilateral and multilateral agreements or other arrangements regarding the protection and use of transboundary waters to which one or more of the Parties are party;
   (c) Seek, where appropriate, the services of relevant ECE bodies as well as other competent international bodies and specific committees in all aspects pertinent to the achievement of the purposes of this Convention;
   (d) At their first meeting, consider and by consensus adopt rules of procedure for their meetings;
   (e) Consider and adopt proposals for amendments to this Convention;
   (f) Consider and undertake any additional action that may be required for the achievement of the purposes of this Convention.

Article 18 – RIGHT TO VOTE

1. Except as provided for in paragraph 2 of this article, each Party to this Convention shall have one vote.
2. Regional economic integration organizations, in matters within their competence, shall exercise their right to vote with a number of votes equal to the number of their member States which are Parties to this Convention. Such organizations shall not exercise their right to vote if their member States exercise theirs, and vice versa.

Article 19 – SECRETARIAT

The Executive Secretary of the Economic Commission for Europe shall carry out the following secretariat functions:

(a) The convening and preparing of meetings of the Parties;
(b) The transmission to the Parties of reports and other information received in accordance with the provisions of this Convention;
(c) The performance of such other functions as may be determined by the Parties.

Article 20 – ANNEXES

Annexes to this Convention shall constitute an integral part thereof.

Article 21 – AMENDMENTS TO THE CONVENTION

1. Any Party may propose amendments to this Convention.
2. Proposals for amendments to this Convention shall be considered at a meeting of the Parties.
3. The text of any proposed amendment to this Convention shall be submitted in writing to the Executive Secretary of the Economic Commission for

Europe, who shall communicate it to all Parties at least ninety days before the meeting at which it is proposed for adoption.

4. An amendment to the present Convention shall be adopted by consensus of the representatives of the Parties to this Convention present at a meeting of the Parties, and shall enter into force for the Parties to the Convention which have accepted it on the ninetieth day after the date on which two thirds of those Parties have deposited with the Depositary their instruments of acceptance of the amendment. The amendment shall enter into force for any other Party on the ninetieth day after the date on which that Party deposits its instrument of acceptance of the amendment.

Article 22 – SETTLEMENT OF DISPUTES

1. If a dispute arises between two or more Parties about the interpretation or application of this Convention, they shall seek a solution by negotiation or by any other means of dispute settlement acceptable to the parties to the dispute.
2. When signing, ratifying, accepting, approving or acceding to this Convention, or at any time thereafter, a Party may declare in writing to the Depositary that, for a dispute not resolved in accordance with paragraph 1 of this article, it accepts one or both of the following means of dispute settlement as compulsory in relation to any Party accepting the same obligation:
   (a) Submission of the dispute to the International Court of Justice;
   (b) Arbitration in accordance with the procedure set out in annex IV.
3. If the parties to the dispute have accepted both means of dispute settlement referred to in paragraph 2 of this article, the dispute may be submitted only to the International Court of Justice, unless the parties agree otherwise.

Article 23 – SIGNATURE

This Convention shall be open for signature at Helsinki from 17 to 18 March 1992 inclusive, and thereafter at United Nations Headquarters in New York until 18 September 1992, by States members of the Economic Commission for Europe as well as States having consultative status with the Economic Commission for Europe pursuant to paragraph 8 of Economic and Social Council resolution 36 (IV) of 28 March 1947, and by regional economic integration organizations constituted by sovereign States members of the Economic Commission for Europe to which their member States have transferred competence over matters governed by this Convention, including the competence to enter into treaties in respect of these matters.

Article 24 – DEPOSITARY

The Secretary-General of the United Nations shall act as the Depositary of this Convention.

Article 25 – RATIFICATION, ACCEPTANCE, APPROVAL AND ACCESSION

1. This Convention shall be subject to ratification, acceptance or approval by signatory States and regional economic integration organizations.
2. This Convention shall be open for accession by the States and organizations referred to in article 23.
3. Any organization referred to in article 23 which becomes a Party to this Convention without any of its member States being a Party shall be bound by all the obligations under this Convention. In the case of such organizations, one or more of whose member States is a Party to this Convention, the organization and its member States shall decide on their respective responsibilities for the performance of their obligations under this Convention. In such cases, the organization and the member States shall not be entitled to exercise rights under this Convention concurrently.
4. In their instruments of ratification, acceptance, approval or accession, the regional economic integration organizations referred to in article 23 shall declare the extent of their competence with respect to the matters governed by this Convention. These organizations shall also inform the Depositary of any substantial modification to the extent of their competence.

Article 26 – ENTRY INTO FORCE

1. This Convention shall enter into force on the ninetieth day after the date of deposit of the sixteenth instrument of ratification, acceptance, approval or accession.
2. For the purposes of paragraph 1 of this article, any instrument deposited by a regional economic integration organization shall not be counted as additional to those deposited by States members of such an organization.
3. For each State or organization referred to in article 23 which ratifies, accepts or approves this Convention or accedes thereto after the deposit of the sixteenth instrument of ratification, acceptance, approval or accession, the Convention shall enter into force on the ninetieth day after the date of deposit by such State or organization of its instrument of ratification, acceptance, approval or accession.

Article 27 – WITHDRAWAL

At any time after three years from the date on which this Convention has come into force with respect to a Party, that Party may withdraw from the Convention by giving written notification to the Depositary. Any such withdrawal shall take effect on the ninetieth day after the date of its receipt by the Depositary.

Article 28 – AUTHENTIC TEXTS

The original of this Convention, of which the English, French and Russian texts are equally authentic, shall be deposited with the Secretary-General of the United Nations.

IN WITNESS WHEREOF the undersigned, being duly authorized thereto, have signed this Convention.

DONE at Helsinki, this seventeenth day of March one thousand nine hundred and ninety-two.

ANNEX I – DEFINITION OF THE TERM "BEST AVAILABLE TECHNOLOGY"

1. The term "best available technology" is taken to mean the latest stage of development of processes, facilities or methods of operation which indicate the practical suitability of a particular measure for limiting discharges, emissions and waste. In determining whether a set of processes, facilities and methods of operation constitute the best available technology in general or individual cases, special consideration is given to:
   (a) Comparable processes, facilities or methods of operation which have recently been successfully tried out;
   (b) Technological advances and changes in scientific knowledge and understanding;
   (c) The economic feasibility of such technology;
   (d) Time limits for installation in both new and existing plants;
   (e) The nature and volume of the discharges and effluents concerned;
   (f) Low- and non-waste technology.
2. It therefore follows that what is "best available technology" for a particular process will change with time in the light of technological advances, economic and social factors, as well as in the light of changes in scientific knowledge and understanding.

ANNEX II – GUIDELINES FOR DEVELOPING BEST ENVIRONMENTAL PRACTICES

1. In selecting for individual cases the most appropriate combination of measures which may constitute the best environmental practice, the following graduated range of measures should be considered:
   (a) Provision of information and education to the public and to users about the environmental consequences of the choice of particular activities and products, their use and ultimate disposal;
   (b) The development and application of codes of good environmental practice which cover all aspects of the product's life;
   (c) Labels informing users of environmental risks related to a product, its use and ultimate disposal;
   (d) Collection and disposal systems available to the public;
   (e) Recycling, recovery and reuse;
   (f) Application of economic instruments to activities, products or groups of products;
   (g) A system of licensing, which involves a range of restrictions or a ban.
2. In determining what combination of measures constitute best environmental practices, in general or in individual cases, particular consideration should be given to:
   (a) The environmental hazard of:
      (i) The product;
      (ii) The product's production;
      (iii) The product's use;
      (iv) The product's ultimate disposal;
   (b) Substitution by less polluting processes or substances;
   (c) Scale of use;
   (d) Potential environmental benefit or penalty of substitute materials or activities;
   (e) Advances and changes in scientific knowledge and understanding;
   (f) Time limits for implementation;
   (g) Social and economic implications.
3. It therefore follows that best environmental practices for a particular source will change with time in the light of technological advances, economic and social factors, as well as in the light of changes in scientific knowledge and understanding.

ANNEX III – GUIDELINES FOR DEVELOPING WATER-QUALITY OBJECTIVES AND CRITERIA

Water-quality objectives and criteria shall:

(a) Take into account the aim of maintaining and, where necessary, improving the existing water quality;
(b) Aim at the reduction of average pollution loads (in particular hazardous substances) to a certain degree within a certain period of time;
(c) Take into account specific water-quality requirements (raw water for drinking-water purposes, irrigation, etc.);
(d) Take into account specific requirements regarding sensitive and specially protected waters and their environment, e.g. lakes and groundwater resources;
(e) Be based on the application of ecological classification methods and chemical indices for the medium- and long-term review of water-quality maintenance and improvement;
(f) Take into account the degree to which objectives are reached and the additional protective measures, based on emission limits, which may be required in individual cases.

ANNEX IV – ARBITRATION

1. In the event of a dispute being submitted for arbitration pursuant to article 22, paragraph 2 of this Convention, a party or parties shall notify the secretariat of the subject-matter of arbitration and indicate, in particular, the articles of this Convention

whose interpretation or application is at issue. The secretariat shall forward the information received to all Parties to this Convention.

2. The arbitral tribunal shall consist of three members. Both the claimant party or parties and the other party or parties to the dispute shall appoint an arbitrator, and the two arbitrators so appointed shall designate by common agreement the third arbitrator, who shall be the president of the arbitral tribunal. The latter shall not be a national of one of the parties to the dispute, nor have his or her usual place of residence in the territory of one of these parties, nor be employed by any of them, nor have dealt with the case in any other capacity.
3. If the president of the arbitral tribunal has not been designated within two months of the appointment of the second arbitrator, the Executive Secretary of the Economic Commission for Europe shall, at the request of either party to the dispute, designate the president within a further two-month period.
4. If one of the parties to the dispute does not appoint an arbitrator within two months of the receipt of the request, the other party may so inform the Executive Secretary of the Economic Commission for Europe, who shall designate the president of the arbitral tribunal within a further two-month period. Upon designation, the president of the arbitral tribunal shall request the party which has not appointed an arbitrator to do so within two months. If it fails to do so within that period, the president shall so inform the Executive Secretary of the Economic Commission for Europe, who shall make this appointment within a further two-month period.
5. The arbitral tribunal shall render its decision in accordance with international law and the provisions of this Convention.
6. Any arbitral tribunal constituted under the provisions set out in this annex shall draw up its own rules of procedure.
7. The decisions of the arbitral tribunal, both on procedure and on substance, shall be taken by majority vote of its members.
8. The tribunal may take all appropriate measures to establish the facts.
9. The parties to the dispute shall facilitate the work of the arbitral tribunal and, in particular, using all means at their disposal, shall:
   (a) Provide it with all relevant documents, facilities and information;
   (b) Enable it, where necessary, to call witnesses or experts and receive their evidence.
10. The parties and the arbitrators shall protect the confidentiality of any information they receive in confidence during the proceedings of the arbitral tribunal.
11. The arbitral tribunal may, at the request of one of the parties, recommend interim measures of protection.
12. If one of the parties to the dispute does not appear before the arbitral tribunal or fails to defend its case, the other party may request the tribunal to continue the proceedings and to render its final decision. Absence of a party or failure of a party to defend its case shall not constitute a bar to the proceedings.
13. The arbitral tribunal may hear and determine counter-claims arising directly out of the subject-matter of the dispute.
14. Unless the arbitral tribunal determines otherwise because of the particular circumstances of the case, the expenses of the tribunal, including the remuneration of its members, shall be borne by the parties to the dispute in equal shares. The tribunal shall keep a record of all its expenses, and shall furnish a final statement thereof to the parties.
15. Any Party to this Convention which has an interest of a legal nature in the subject-matter of the dispute, and which may be affected by a decision in the case, may intervene in the proceedings with the consent of the tribunal.
16. The arbitral tribunal shall render its award within five months of the date on which it is established, unless it finds it necessary to extend the time limit for a period which should not exceed five months.
17. The award of the arbitral tribunal shall be accompanied by a statement of reasons. It shall be final and binding upon all parties to the dispute. The award will be transmitted by the arbitral tribunal to the parties to the dispute and to the secretariat. The secretariat will forward the information received to all Parties to this Convention.
18. Any dispute which may arise between the parties concerning the interpretation or execution of the award may be submitted by either party to the arbitral tribunal which made the award or, if the latter cannot be seized thereof, to another tribunal constituted for this purpose in the same manner as the first.

7.2. Watercourses Convention 1997

Convention on the Law of the Non-Navigational Uses of International Watercourses, New York, 21 May 1997, 2999 UNTS 77

The Parties to the present Convention,

Conscious of the importance of international watercourses and the non-navigational uses thereof in many regions of the world,

Having in mind Article 13, paragraph 1 (a), of the Charter of the United Nations, which provides that the General Assembly shall initiate studies and make recommendations for the purpose of encouraging the progressive development of international law and its codification,

Considering that successful codification and progressive development of rules of international law regarding non-navigational uses of international watercourses would assist in promoting and implementing the purposes and principles set forth in Articles 1 and 2 of the Charter of the United Nations,

Taking into account the problems affecting many international watercourses resulting from, among other things, increasing demands and pollution,

Expressing the conviction that a framework convention will ensure the utilization, development, conservation, management and protection of international watercourses and the promotion of the optimal and sustainable utilization thereof for present and future generations,

Affirming the importance of international cooperation and good-neighbourliness in this field,

Aware of the special situation and needs of developing countries,

Recalling the principles and recommendations adopted by the United Nations Conference on Environment and Development of 1992 in the Rio Declaration and Agenda 21,

Recalling also the existing bilateral and multilateral agreements regarding the non-navigational uses of international watercourses,

Mindful of the valuable contribution of international organizations, both governmental and non-governmental, to the codification and progressive development of international law in this field,

Appreciative of the work carried out by the International Law Commission on the law of the non-navigational uses of international watercourses,

Bearing in mind United Nations General Assembly resolution 49/52 of 9 December 1994,

Have agreed as follows:

PART I. INTRODUCTION

Article 1 – Scope of the present Convention

1. The present Convention applies to uses of international watercourses and of their waters for purposes other than navigation and to measures of protection, preservation and management related to the uses of those watercourses and their waters.
2. The uses of international watercourses for navigation is not within the scope of the present Convention except insofar as other uses affect navigation or are affected by navigation.

Article 2 – Use of terms

For the purposes of the present Convention:

(a) "Watercourse" means a system of surface waters and groundwaters constituting by virtue of their physical relationship a unitary whole and normally flowing into a common terminus;

(b) "International watercourse" means a watercourse, parts of which are situated in different States;

(c) "Watercourse State" means a State Party to the present Convention in whose territory part of an international watercourse is situated, or a Party that is a regional economic integration organization, in the territory of one or more of whose Member States part of an international watercourse is situated;

(d) "Regional economic integration organization" means an organization constituted by sovereign States of a given region, to which its member States have transferred competence in respect of matters governed by this Convention and which has been duly authorized in accordance with its internal procedures, to sign, ratify, accept, approve or accede to it.

Article 3 – Watercourse agreements

1. In the absence of an agreement to the contrary, nothing in the present Convention shall affect the rights or obligations of a watercourse State arising from agreements in force for it on the date on which it became a party to the present Convention.
2. Notwithstanding the provisions of paragraph 1, parties to agreements referred to in paragraph 1 may, where necessary, consider harmonizing such agreements with the basic principles of the present Convention.
3. Watercourse States may enter into one or more agreements, hereinafter referred to as "watercourse agreements", which apply and adjust the provisions of the present Convention to the characteristics and uses of a particular international watercourse or part thereof.
4. Where a watercourse agreement is concluded between two or more watercourse States, it shall define the waters to which it applies. Such an agreement may be entered into with respect to an entire international watercourse or any part thereof or a particular project, programme or use except insofar

as the agreement adversely affects, to a significant extent, the use by one or more other watercourse States of the waters of the watercourse, without their express consent.

5. Where a watercourse State considers that adjustment and application of the provisions of the present Convention is required because of the characteristics and uses of a particular international watercourse, watercourse States shall consult with a view to negotiating in good faith for the purpose of concluding a watercourse agreement or agreements.
6. Where some but not all watercourse States to a particular international watercourse are parties to an agreement, nothing in such agreement shall affect the rights or obligations under the present Convention of watercourse States that are not parties to such an agreement.

Article 4 – Parties to watercourse agreements

1. Every watercourse State is entitled to participate in the negotiation of and to become a party to any watercourse agreement that applies to the entire international watercourse, as well as to participate in any relevant consultations.
2. A watercourse State whose use of an international watercourse may be affected to a significant extent by the implementation of a proposed watercourse agreement that applies only to a part of the watercourse or to a particular project, programme or use is entitled to participate in consultations on such an agreement and, where appropriate, in the negotiation thereof in good faith with a view to becoming a party thereto, to the extent that its use is thereby affected.

PART II. GENERAL PRINCIPLES

Article 5 – Equitable and reasonable utilization and participation

1. Watercourse States shall in their respective territories utilize an international watercourse in an equitable and reasonable manner. In particular, an international watercourse shall be used and developed by watercourse States with a view to attaining optimal and sustainable utilization thereof and benefits therefrom, taking into account the interests of the watercourse States concerned, consistent with adequate protection of the watercourse.
2. Watercourse States shall participate in the use, development and protection of an international watercourse in an equitable and reasonable manner. Such participation includes both the right to utilize the watercourse and the duty to cooperate in the protection and development thereof, as provided in the present Convention.

Article 6 – Factors relevant to equitable and reasonable utilization

1. Utilization of an international watercourse in an equitable and reasonable manner within the meaning of article 5 requires taking into account all relevant factors and circumstances, including:
   (a) Geographic, hydrographic, hydrological, climatic, ecological and other factors of a natural character;
   (b) The social and economic needs of the watercourse States concerned;
   (c) The population dependent on the watercourse in each watercourse State;
   (d) The effects of the use or uses of the watercourses in one watercourse State on other watercourse States;
   (e) Existing and potential uses of the watercourse;
   (f) Conservation, protection, development and economy of use of the water resources of the watercourse and the costs of measures taken to that effect;
   (g) The availability of alternatives, of comparable value, to a particular planned or existing use.
2. In the application of article 5 or paragraph 1 of this article, watercourse States concerned shall, when the need arises, enter into consultations in a spirit of cooperation.
3. The weight to be given to each factor is to be determined by its importance in comparison with that of other relevant factors. In determining what is a reasonable and equitable use, all relevant factors are to be considered together and a conclusion reached on the basis of the whole.

Article 7 – Obligation not to cause significant harm

1. Watercourse States shall, in utilizing an international watercourse in their territories, take all appropriate measures to prevent the causing of significant harm to other watercourse States.
2. Where significant harm nevertheless is caused to another watercourse State, the States whose use causes such harm shall, in the absence of agreement to such use, take all appropriate measures, having due regard for the provisions of articles 5 and 6, in consultation with the affected State, to eliminate or mitigate such harm and, where appropriate, to discuss the question of compensation.

Article 8 – General obligation to cooperate

1. Watercourse States shall cooperate on the basis of sovereign equality, territorial integrity, mutual benefit and good faith in order to attain optimal utilization and adequate protection of an international watercourse.
2. In determining the manner of such cooperation, watercourse States may consider the establishment of joint mechanisms or commissions, as deemed necessary by them, to facilitate cooperation on relevant measures and procedures in the light of experience gained th rough cooperation in existing joint mechanisms and commissions in various regions.

Article 9 – Regular exchange of data and information

1. Pursuant to article 8, watercourse States shall on a regular basis exchange readily available data and information on the condition of the watercourse,

in particular that of a hydrological, meteorological, hydrogeological and ecological nature and related to the water quality as well as related forecasts.

2. If a watercourse State is requested by another watercourse State to provide data or information that is not readily available, it shall employ its best efforts to comply with the request but may condition its compliance upon payment by the requesting State of the reasonable costs of collecting and, where appropriate, processing such data or information.
3. Watercourse States shall employ their best efforts to collect and, where appropriate, to process data and information in a manner which facilitates its utilization by the other watercourse States to which it is communicated.

Article 10 – Relationship between different kinds of uses

1. In the absence of agreement or custom to the contrary, no use of an international watercourse enjoys inherent priority over other uses.
2. In the event of a conflict between uses of an international watercourse, it shall be resolved with reference to articles 5 to 7, with special regard being given to the requirements of vital human needs.

PART III. PLANNED MEASURES

Article 11 – Information concerning planned measures

Watercourse States shall exchange information and consult each other and, if necessary, negotiate on the possible effects of planned measures on the condition of an international watercourse.

Article 12 – Notification concerning planned measures with possible adverse effects

Before a watercourse State implements or permits the implementation of planned measures which may have a significant adverse effect upon other watercourse States, it shall provide those States with timely notification thereof. Such notification shall be accompanied by available technical data and information, including the results of any environmental impact assessment, in order to enable the notified States to evaluate the possible effects of the planned measures.

Article 13 – Period for reply to notification

Unless otherwise agreed:

(a) A watercourse State providing a notification under article 12 shall allow the notified States a period of six months within which to study and evaluate the possible effects of the planned measures and to communicate the findings to it;

(b) This period shall, at the request of a notified State for which the evaluation of the planned measures poses special difficulty, be extended for a period of six months.

Article 14 – Obligations of the notifying State during the period for reply

During the period referred to in article 13, the notifying State:

(a) Shall cooperate with the notified States by providing them, on request, with any additional data and information that is available and necessary for an accurate evaluation; and

(b) Shall not implement or permit the implementation of the planned measures without the consent of the notified States.

Article 15 – Reply to notification

The notified States shall communicate their findings to the notifying State as early as possible within the period applicable pursuant to article 13. If a notified State finds that implementation of the planned measures would be inconsistent with the provisions of articles 5 or 7, it shall attach to its finding a documented explanation setting forth the reasons for the finding.

Article 16 – Absence of reply to notification

1. If, within the period applicable pursuant to article 13, the notifying State receives no communication under article 15, it may, subject to its obligations under articles 5 and 7, proceed with the implementation of the planned measures, in accordance with the notification and any other data and information provided to the notified States.
2. Any claim to compensation by a notified State which has failed to reply within the peri od applicable pursuant to article 13 may be offset by the costs incurred by the notifying State for action undertaken after the expiration of the time for a reply which would not have been undertaken if the notified State had objected within that period.

Article 17 – Consultations and negotiations concerning planned measures

1. If a communication is made under article 15 that implementation of the planned measures would be inconsistent with the provisions of article 5 or 7, the notifying State and the State making the communication shall enter into consultations and, if necessary, negotiations with a view to arriving at an equitable resolution of the situation.
2. The consultations and negotiations shall be conducted on the basis that each State must in goo d faith pay reasonable regard to the rights and legitimate interests of the other State.
3. During the course of the consultations and negotiations, the notifying State shall, if so requested by the notified State at the time it makes the communication, refrain from implementing or permitting the implementation of the planned measures for a period of six months unless otherwise agreed.

Article 18 – Procedures in the absence of notification

1. If a watercourse State has reasonable grounds to believe that another watercourse State is planning measures that may have a significant adverse effect upon it, the former State may request the latter to apply the provisions of article 12. The request shall be accompanied by a documented explanation setting forth its grounds.

2. In the event that the State planning the measures nevertheless finds that it is not under an obligation to provide a notification under article 12, it shall so inform the other State, providing a documented explanation setting forth the reasons for such finding. If this finding does not satisfy the other State, the two States shall, at the request of that other State, promptly enter into consultations and negotiations in the manner indicated in paragraphs 1 and 2 of article 17.
3. During the course of the consultations and negotiations, the State planning the measures shall, if so requested by the other State at the time it requests the initiation of consultations and negotiations, refrain from implementing or permitting the implementation of those measures for a period of six months unless otherwise agreed.

Article 19 – Urgent implementation of planned measures

1. In the event that the implementation of planned measures is of the utmost urgency in order to protect public health, public safety or other equally important interests, the State planning the measures may, subject to articles 5 and 7, immediately proceed to implementation, notwithstanding the provisions of article 14 and paragraph 3 of article 17.
2. In such case, a formal declaration of the urgency of the measures shall be communicated without delay to the other watercourse States referred to in article 12 together with the relevant data and information.
3. The State planning the measures shall, at the request of any of the States referred to in paragraph 2, promptly enter into consultations and negotiations with it in the manner indicated in paragraphs 1 and 2 of article 17.

PART IV. PROTECTION, PRESERVATION AND MANAGEMENT

Article 20 – Protection and preservation of ecosystems

Watercourse States shall, individually and, where appropriate, jointly, protect and preserve the ecosystems of international watercourses.

Article 21 – Prevention, reduction and control of pollution

1. For the purpose of this article, "pollution of an international watercourse" means any detrimental alteration in the composition or quality of the waters of an international watercourse which results directly or indirectly from human conduct.
2. Watercourse States shall, individually and, where appropriate, jointly, prevent, reduce and control the pollution of an international watercourse that may cause significant harm to other watercourse States or to their environment, including harm to human health or safety, to the use of the waters for any beneficial purpose or to the living resources of the watercourse. Watercourse States shall take steps to harmonize their policies in this connection.
3. Watercourse States shall, at the request of any of them, consult with a view to arriving at mutually agreeable measures and methods to prevent, reduce and control pollution of an international watercourse, such as:
   (a) Setting joint water quality objectives and criteria;
   (b) Establishing techniques and practices to address pollution from point and non -point sources;
   (c) Establishing lists of substances the introduction of which into the waters of an international watercourse is to be prohibited, limited, investigated or monitored.

Article 22 – Introduction of alien or new species

Watercourse States shall take all measures necessary to prevent the introduction of species, alien or new, into an international watercourse which may have effects detrimental to the ecosystem of the watercourse resulting in significant harm to other watercourse States.

Article 23 – Protection and preservation of the marine environment

Watercourse States shall, individually and, where appropriate, in cooperation with other States, take all measures with respect to an international watercourse that are necessary to protect and preserve the marine environment, including estuaries, taking into account generally accepted international rules and standards.

Article 24 – Management

1. Watercourse States shall, at the request of any of them, enter into consultations concerning the management of an international watercourse, which may include the establishment of a joint management mechanism.
2. For the purposes of this article, "management" refers, in particular, to:
   (a) Planning the sustainable development of an international watercourse and providing f or the implementation of any plans adopted; and
   (b) Otherwise promoting the rational and optimal utilization, protection and control of the watercourse.

Article 25 – Regulation

1. Watercourse States shall cooperate, where appropriate, to respond to needs or opportunities for regulation of the flow of the waters of an international watercourse.
2. Unless otherwise agreed, watercourse States shall participate on an equitable basis in the construction and maintenance or defrayal of the costs of such regulation works as they may have agreed to undertake.
3. For the purposes of this article, "regulation" means the use of hydraulic works or any other continuing measure to alter, vary or otherwise control the flow of the waters of an international watercourse.

Article 26 – Installations

1. Watercourse States shall, within their respective territories, employ their best efforts to maintain and protect installations, facilities and other works related to an international watercourse.
2. Watercourse States shall, at the request of any of them which has reasonable grounds to believe that it may suffer significant adverse effects, enter into consultations with regard to:
   (a) The safe operation and maintenance of installations, facilities or other works related to an international watercourse; and
   (b) The protection of installations, facilities or other works from wilful or negligent acts or the forces of nature.

PART V. HARMFUL CONDITIONS AND EMERGENCY SITUATIONS

Article 27 – Prevention and mitigation of harmful conditions

Watercourse States shall, individually and, where appropriate, jointly, take all appropriate measures to prevent or mitigate conditions related to an international watercourse that may be harmful to other watercourse States, whether resulting from natural causes or human conduct, such as flood or ice conditions, water-borne diseases, siltation, erosion, salt-water intrusion, drought or desertification.

Article 28 – Emergency situations

1. For the purposes of this article, "emergency" means a situation that causes, or poses an imminent threat of causing, serious harm to watercourse States or other States and that results suddenly from natural causes, such as floods, the breaking up of ice, landslides or earthquakes, or from human conduct, such as industrial accidents.
2. A watercourse State shall, without delay and by the most expeditious means available, notify other potentially affected States and competent international organizations of any emergency originating within its territory.
3. A watercourse State within whose territory an emergency originates shall, in cooperation with potentially affected States and, where appropriate, competent international organizations, immediately take all practicable measures necessitated by the circumstances to prevent, mitigate and eliminate harmful effects of the emergency.
4. When necessary, watercourse States shall jointly develop contingency plans for responding to emergencies, in cooperation, where appropriate, with other potentially affected States and competent international organizations.

PART VI. MISCELLANEOUS PROVISIONS

Article 29 – International watercourses and installations in time of armed conflict

International watercourses and related installations, facilities and other works shall enjoy the protection accorded by the principles and rules of international law applicable in international and non-international armed conflict and shall not be used in violation of those principles and rules.

Article 30 – Indirect procedures

In cases where there are serious obstacles to direct contacts between watercourse States, the States concerned shall fulfil their obligations of cooperation provided for in the present Convention, including exchange of data and information, notification, communication, consultations and negotiations, through any indirect procedure accepted by them.

Article 31 – Data and information vital to national defence or security

Nothing in the present Convention obliges a watercourse State to provide data or information vital to its national defence or security. Nevertheless, that State shall cooperate in good faith with the other watercourse States with a view to providing as much information as possible under the circumstances.

Article 32 – Non-discrimination

Unless the watercourse States concerned have agreed otherwise for the protection of the interests of persons, natural or juridical, who have suffered or are under a serious threat of suffering significant transboundary harm as a result of activities related to an international watercourse, a watercourse State shall not discriminate on the basis of nationality or residence or place where the injury occurred, in granting to such persons, in accordance with its legal system, access to judicial or other procedures, or a right to claim compensation or other relief in respect of significant harm caused by such activities carried on in its territory.

Article 33 – Settlement of disputes

1. In the event of a dispute between two or more parties concerning the interpretation or application of the present Convention, the parties concerned shall, in the absence of an applicable agreement between them, seek a settlement of the dispute by peaceful means in accordance with the following provisions.
2. If the parties concerned cannot reach agreement by negotiation requested by one of them, they may jointly seek the good offices of, or request mediation or conciliation by, a third party, or make use, as appropriate, of any joint watercourse institutions that may have been established by them or agree to submit the dispute to arbitration or to the International Court of Justice.
3. Subject to the operation of paragraph 10, if after six months from the time of the request for negotiations referred to in paragraph 2, the parties concerned have not been able to set tle their dispute through negotiation or any other means referred to in paragraph 2, the dispute shall be submitted, at the request of any of the parties to the dispute, to impartial fact-finding in accordance with paragraphs 4 to 9, unless the parties otherwise agree.
4. A Fact-finding Commission shall be established, composed of one member nominated by each party concerned and in addition a member not having the nationality of any of the parties concerned cho-

sen by the nominated members who shall serve as Chairman.

5. If the members nominated by the parties are unable to agree on a Chairman within three months of the request for the establishment of the Commission, any party concerned may request the Secretary-General of the United Nations to appoint the Chairman who shall not have the nationality of any of the parties to the dispute or of any riparian State of the watercourse concerned. If one of the parties fails to nominate a member within three months of the initial request pursuant to paragraph 3, an y other party concerned may request the Secretary-General of the United Nations to appoint a person who shall not have the nationality of any of the parties to the dispute or of any riparian State of the watercourse concerned. The person so appointed shall constitute a single-member Commission.
6. The Commission shall determine its own procedure.
7. The parties concerned have the obligation to provide the Commission with such information as it may require and, on request, to permit the Commission to have access to their respective territory and to inspect any facilities, plant, equipment, construction or natural feature relevant for the purpose of its inquiry.
8. The Commission shall adopt its report by a majority vote, unless it is a single -member Commission, and shall submit that report to the parties concerned setting forth its findings and the reasons therefor and such recommendations as it deems appropriate for an equitable solution of the dispute, which the parties concerned shall consider in good faith.
9. The expenses of the Commission shall be borne equally by the parties concerned.
10. When ratifying, accepting, approving or acceding to the present Convention, or at any time thereafter, a party which is not a regional economic integration organization may declare in a written instrument submitted to the depositary that, in respect of any dispute not resolved in accordance with paragraph 2, it recognizes as compulsory ipso facto, and without special agreement in relation to any party accepting the same obligation:
    (a) Submission of the dispute to the International Court of Justice; and/or
    (b) Arbitration by an arbitral tribunal established and operating, unless the parties to the dispute otherwise agreed, in accordance with the procedure laid down in the annex to the present Convention.

A party which is a regional economic integration organization may make a declaration with like effect in relation to arbitration in accordance with subparagraph (b).

PART VII. FINAL CLAUSES

Article 34 – Signature

The present Convention shall be open for signature by all States and by regional economic integration organizations from 21 May 1997 until 20 May 2000 at United Nations Headquarters in New York.

Article 35 – Ratification, acceptance, approval or accession

1. The present Convention is subject to ratification, acceptance, approval or accession by States and by regional economic integration organizations. The instruments of ratification, acceptance, approval or accession shall be deposited with the Secretary-General of the United Nations.
2. Any regional economic integration organization which becomes a Party to this Convention without any of its member States being a Party shall be bound by all the obligations under the Convention. In the case of such organizations, one or more of whose member States is a Party to this Convention, the organization and its member States shall decide on their respective responsibilities for the performance of their obligations under the Convention. In such cases, the organizat ion and the member States shall not be entitled to exercise rights under the Convention concurrently.
3. In their instruments of ratification, acceptance, approval or accession, the regional economic integration organizations shall declare the extent of their competence with respect to the matters governed by the Convention. These organizations shall also inform the Secretary-General of the United Nations of any substantial modification in the extent of their competence.

Article 36 – Entry into force

1. The present Convention shall enter into force on the ninetieth day following the date of deposit of the thirty-fifth instrument of ratification, acceptance, approval or accession with the Secretary-General of the United Nations.
2. For each State or regional economic integration organization that ratifies, accepts or approves the Convention or accedes thereto after the deposit of the thirty-fifth instrument of ratification, acceptance, approval or accession, the Convention shall enter into force on the ninet ieth day after the deposit by such State or regional economic integration organization of its instrument of ratification, acceptance, approval or accession.
3. For the purposes of paragraphs 1 and 2, any instrument deposited by a regional economic integration organization shall not be counted as additional to those deposited by States.

Article 37 – Authentic texts

The original of the present Convention, of which the Arabic, Chinese, English, French, Russian and Spanish texts are equally authentic, shall be deposited with the Secretary-General of the United Nations.

IN WITNESS WHEREOF the undersigned Plenipotentiaries, being duly authorized thereto, have signed this Convention.

DONE at New York, this twenty-first day of May one thousand nine hundred and ninety-seven.

ANNEX – ARBITRATION

Article 1

Unless the parties to the dispute otherwise agree, the arbitration pursuant to article 33 of the Convention shall take place in accordance with articles 2 to 14 of the present annex.

Article 2

The claimant party shall notify the respondent party that it is referring a dispute to arbitration pursuant to article 33 of the Convention. The notification shall state the subject matter of arbitration and include, in particular, the articles of the Convention, the interpretation or application of which are at issue. If the parties do not agree on the subject matter of the dispute, the arbitral tribunal shall determine the subject matter.

Article 3

1. In disputes between two parties, the arbitral tribunal shall consist of three members. Each of the parties to the dispute shall appoint an arbitrator and the two arbitrators so appointed shall designate by common agreement the third arbitrator, who shall be the Chairman of the tribunal. The latter shall not be a national of one of the parties to the dispute or of any riparian State of the watercourse concerned, nor have his or her usual place of residence in the territory of one of these parties or such riparian State, nor have dealt with the case in any other capacity.
2. In disputes between more than two parties, parties in the same interest shall appoint one arbitrator jointly by agreement.
3. Any vacancy shall be filled in the manner prescribed for the initial appointment.

Article 4

1. If the Chairman of the arbitral tribunal has not been designated within two months of the appointment of the second arbitrator, the President of the International Court of Justice shall, at the request of a party, designate the Chairman within a further two-month period.
2. If one of the parties to the dispute does not appoint an arbitrator within two months of receipt of the request, the other party may inform the President of the International Court of Justice, who shall make the designation within a further two-month period.

Article 5

The arbitral tribunal shall render its decisions in accordance with the provisions of this Convention and international law.

Article 6

Unless the parties to the dispute otherwise agree, the arbitral tribunal shall determine its own rules of procedure.

Article 7

The arbitral tribunal may, at the request of one of the parties, recommend essential interim measures of protection.

Article 8

1. The parties to the dispute shall facilitate the work of the arbitral tribunal and, in particular, using all means at their disposal, shall:
   (a) Provide it with all relevant documents, information and facilities; and
   (b) Enable it, when necessary, to call witnesses or experts and receive their evidence.
2. The parties and the arbitrators are under an obligation to protect the confidentiality of any information they receive in confidence during the proceedings of the arbitral tribunal.

Article 9

Unless the arbitral tribunal determines otherwise because of the particular circumstances of the case, the costs of the tribunal shall be borne by the parties to the dispute in equal shares. The tribunal shall keep a record of all its costs, and shall furnish a final statement thereof to the parties.

Article 10

Any party that has an interest of a legal nature in the subject matter of the dispute which may be affected by the decision in the case, may intervene in the proceedings with the consent of the tribunal.

Article 11

The tribunal may hear and determine counterclaims arising directly out of the subject matter of the dispute.

Article 12

Decisions both on procedure and substance of the arbitral tribunal shall be taken by a majority vote of its members.

Article 13

If one of the parties to the dispute does not appear before the arbitral tribunal or fails to defend its case, the other party may request the tribunal to continue the proceedings and to make its award. Absence of a party or a failure of a party to defend its case shall not constitute a bar to the proceedings. Before rendering its final decision, the arbitral tribunal must satisfy itself that the claim is well founded in fact and law.

Article 14

1. The tribunal shall render its final decision within five months of the date on which it is fully constituted unless it finds it necessary to extend the time l imit for a period which should not exceed five more months.
2. The final decision of the arbitral tribunal shall be confined to the subject matter of the dispute and shall state the reasons on which it is based. It shall contain the names of the members w ho have participated and the date of the final decision. Any member of the tribunal may attach a separate or dissenting opinion to the final decision.
3. The award shall be binding on the parties to the dispute. It shall be without appeal unless the parties to the dispute have agreed in advance to an appellate procedure.

4. Any controversy which may arise between the parties to the dispute as regards the interpretation or manner of implementation of the final decision may be submitted by either party for decision to the arbitral tribunal which rendered it.

7.3. ILC Draft Articles on the Law of Transboundary Aquifers 2008

Draft Articles on the Law of Transboundary Aquifers, 11 December 2008, UN Doc. A/63/10

...

Conscious of the importance for humankind of life supporting groundwater resources in all regions of the world,

Bearing in mind Article 13, paragraph 1 (a), of the Charter of the United Nations, which provides that the General Assembly shall initiate studies and make recommendations for the purpose of encouraging the progressive development of international law and its codification,

Recalling General Assembly resolution 1803 (XVII) of 14 December 1962 on permanent sovereignty over natural resources,

Reaffirming the principles and recommendations adopted by the United Nations Conference on Environment and Development of 1992 in the Rio Declaration on Environment and Development and Agenda 21,

Taking into account increasing demands for freshwater and the need to protect groundwater resources,

Mindful of the particular problems posed by the vulnerability of aquifers to pollution,

Convinced of the need to ensure the development, utilization, conservation, management and protection of groundwater resources in the context of the promotion of the optimal and sustainable development of water resources for present and future generations,

Affirming the importance of international cooperation and good neighbourliness in this field,

Emphasizing the need to take into account the special situation of developing countries,

Recognizing the necessity to promote international cooperation,

...

PART ONE – INTRODUCTION

Article 1 – Scope

The present draft articles apply to:

(a) utilization of transboundary aquifers or aquifer systems;

(b) other activities that have or are likely to have an impact upon such aquifers or aquifer systems; and

(c) measures for the protection, preservation and management of such aquifers or aquifer systems.

Article 2 – Use of terms

For the purposes of the present draft articles:

(a) "aquifer" means a permeable water-bearing geological formation underlain by a less permeable layer and the water contained in the saturated zone of the formation;

(b) "aquifer system" means a series of two or more aquifers that are hydraulically connected;

(c) "transboundary aquifer" or "transboundary aquifer system" means respectively, an aquifer or aquifer system, parts of which are situated in different States;

(d) "aquifer State" means a State in whose territory any part of a transboundary aquifer or aquifer system is situated;

(e) "utilization of transboundary aquifers or aquifer systems" includes extraction of water, heat and minerals, and storage and disposal of any substance;

(f) "recharging aquifer" means an aquifer that receives a non-negligible amount of contemporary water recharge;

(g) "recharge zone" means the zone which contributes water to an aquifer, consisting of the catchment area of rainfall water and the area where such water flows to an aquifer by runoff on the ground and infiltration through soil;

(h) "discharge zone" means the zone where water originating from an aquifer flows to its outlets, such as a watercourse, a lake, an oasis, a wetland or an ocean.

PART TWO – GENERAL PRINCIPLES

Article 3 – Sovereignty of aquifer States

Each aquifer State has sovereignty over the portion of a transboundary aquifer or aquifer system located within its territory. It shall exercise its sovereignty in accordance with international law and the present draft articles.

Article 4 – Equitable and reasonable utilization

Aquifer States shall utilize transboundary aquifers or aquifer systems according to the principle of equitable and reasonable utilization, as follows:

(a) they shall utilize transboundary aquifers or aquifer systems in a manner that is consistent with the equitable and reasonable accrual of benefits therefrom to the aquifer States concerned;

(b) they shall aim at maximizing the long-term benefits derived from the use of water contained therein;

(c) they shall establish individually or jointly a comprehensive utilization plan, taking into account present and future needs of, and alternative water sources for, the aquifer States; and

(d) they shall not utilize a recharging transboundary aquifer or aquifer system at a level that would prevent continuance of its effective functioning.

Article 5 – Factors relevant to equitable and reasonable utilization

1. Utilization of a transboundary aquifer or aquifer system in an equitable and reasonable manner within the meaning of draft article 4 requires taking into account all relevant factors, including:
   (a) the population dependent on the aquifer or aquifer system in each aquifer State;
   (b) the social, economic and other needs, present and future, of the aquifer States concerned;
   (c) the natural characteristics of the aquifer or aquifer system;
   (d) the contribution to the formation and recharge of the aquifer or aquifer system;
   (e) the existing and potential utilization of the aquifer or aquifer system;
   (f) the actual and potential effects of the utilization of the aquifer or aquifer system in one aquifer State on other aquifer States concerned;
   (g) the availability of alternatives to a particular existing and planned utilization of the aquifer or aquifer system;
   (h) the development, protection and conservation of the aquifer or aquifer system and the costs of measures to be taken to that effect;
   (i) the role of the aquifer or aquifer system in the related ecosystem.
2. The weight to be given to each factor is to be determined by its importance with regard to a specific transboundary aquifer or aquifer system in comparison with that of other relevant factors. In determining what is equitable and reasonable utilization, all relevant factors are to be considered together and a conclusion reached on the basis of all the factors. However, in weighing different kinds of utilization of a transboundary aquifer or aquifer system, special regard shall be given to vital human needs.

Article 6 – Obligation not to cause significant harm

1. Aquifer States shall, in utilizing transboundary aquifers or aquifer systems in their territories, take all appropriate measures to prevent the causing of significant harm to other aquifer States or other States in whose territory a discharge zone is located.
2. Aquifer States shall, in undertaking activities other than utilization of a transboundary aquifer or aquifer system that have, or are likely to have, an impact upon that transboundary aquifer or aquifer system, take all appropriate measures to prevent the causing of significant harm through that aquifer or aquifer system to other aquifer States or other States in whose territory a discharge zone is located.
3. Where significant harm nevertheless is caused to another aquifer State or a State in whose territory a discharge zone is located, the aquifer State whose activities cause such harm shall take, in consultation with the affected State, all appropriate response measures to eliminate or mitigate such harm, having due regard for the provisions of draft articles 4 and 5.

Article 7 – General obligation to cooperate

1. Aquifer States shall cooperate on the basis of sovereign equality, territorial integrity, sustainable development, mutual benefit and good faith in order to attain equitable and reasonable utilization and appropriate protection of their transboundary aquifers or aquifer systems.
2. For the purpose of paragraph 1, aquifer States should establish joint mechanisms of cooperation.

Article 8 – Regular exchange of data and information

1. Pursuant to draft article 7, aquifer States shall, on a regular basis, exchange readily available data and information on the condition of their transboundary aquifers or aquifer systems, in particular of a geological, hydrogeological, hydrological, meteorological and ecological nature and related to the hydrochemistry of the aquifers or aquifer systems, as well as related forecasts.
2. Where knowledge about the nature and extent of a transboundary aquifer or aquifer system is inadequate, aquifer States concerned shall employ their best efforts to collect and generate more complete data and information relating to such aquifer or aquifer system, taking into account current practices and standards. They shall take such action individually or jointly and, where appropriate, together with or through international organizations.
3. If an aquifer State is requested by another aquifer State to provide data and information relating to an aquifer or aquifer system that are not readily available, it shall employ its best efforts to comply with the request. The requested State may condition its compliance upon payment by the requesting State of the reasonable costs of collecting and, where appropriate, processing such data or information.
4. Aquifer States shall, where appropriate, employ their best efforts to collect and process data and information in a manner that facilitates their utilization by the other aquifer States to which such data and information are communicated.

Article 9 – Bilateral and regional agreements and arrangements

For the purpose of managing a particular transboundary aquifer or aquifer system, aquifer States are encouraged to enter into bilateral or regional agreements or arrangements among themselves. Such agreements or arrangements may be entered into with respect to an entire aquifer or aquifer system or any part thereof or a particular project, programme or utilization except insofar as an agreement or arrangement adversely affects, to a significant extent, the utilization, by one or more other aquifer States of the water in that aquifer or aquifer system, without their express consent.

PART THREE – PROTECTION, PRESERVATION AND MANAGEMENT

Article 10 – Protection and preservation of ecosystems

Aquifer States shall take all appropriate measures to protect and preserve ecosystems within, or dependent upon, their transboundary aquifers or aquifer systems, including measures to ensure that the quality and quantity of water retained in an aquifer or aquifer system, as well as that released through its discharge zones, are sufficient to protect and preserve such ecosystems.

Article 11 – Recharge and discharge zones

1. Aquifer States shall identify the recharge and discharge zones of transboundary aquifers or aquifer systems that exist within their territory. They shall take appropriate measures to prevent and minimize detrimental impacts on the recharge and discharge processes.
2. All States in whose territory a recharge or discharge zone is located, in whole or in part, and which are not aquifer States with regard to that aquifer or aquifer system, shall cooperate with the aquifer States to protect the aquifer or aquifer system and related ecosystems.

Article 12 – Prevention, reduction and control of pollution

Aquifer States shall, individually and, where appropriate, jointly, prevent, reduce and control pollution of their transboundary aquifers or aquifer systems, including through the recharge process, that may cause significant harm to other aquifer States. Aquifer States shall take a precautionary approach in view of uncertainty about the nature and extent of a transboundary aquifer or aquifer system and of its vulnerability to pollution.

Article 13 – Monitoring

1. Aquifer States shall monitor their transboundary aquifers or aquifer systems. They shall, wherever possible, carry out these monitoring activities jointly with other aquifer States concerned and, where appropriate, in collaboration with competent international organizations. Where monitoring activities cannot be carried out jointly, the aquifer States shall exchange the monitored data among themselves.
2. Aquifer States shall use agreed or harmonized standards and methodology for monitoring their transboundary aquifers or aquifer systems. They should identify key parameters that they will monitor based on an agreed conceptual model of the aquifers or aquifer systems. These parameters should include parameters on the condition of the aquifer or aquifer system as listed in draft article 8, paragraph 1, and also on the utilization of the aquifers or aquifer systems.

Article 14 – Management

Aquifer States shall establish and implement plans for the proper management of their transboundary aquifers or aquifer systems. They shall, at the request of any of them, enter into consultations concerning the management of a transboundary aquifer or aquifer system. A joint management mechanism shall be established, wherever appropriate.

Article 15 – Planned activities

1. When a State has reasonable grounds for believing that a particular planned activity in its territory may affect a transboundary aquifer or aquifer system and thereby may have a significant adverse effect upon another State, it shall, as far as practicable, assess the possible effects of such activity.
2. Before a State implements or permits the implementation of planned activities which may affect a transboundary aquifer or aquifer system and thereby may have a significant adverse effect upon another State, it shall provide that State with timely notification thereof. Such notification shall be accompanied by available technical data and information, including any environmental impact assessment, in order to enable the notified State to evaluate the possible effects of the planned activities.
3. If the notifying and the notified States disagree on the possible effect of the planned activities, they shall enter into consultations and, if necessary, negotiations with a view to arriving at an equitable resolution of the situation. They may utilize an independent fact-finding body to make an impartial assessment of the effect of the planned activities.

PART FOUR – MISCELLANEOUS PROVISIONS

Article 16 – Technical cooperation with developing States

States shall, directly or through competent international organizations, promote scientific, educational, legal and other cooperation with developing States for the protection and management of transboundary aquifers or aquifer systems, including, inter alia:

(a) strengthening their capacity-building in scientific, technical and legal fields;

(b) facilitating their participation in relevant international programmes;

(c) supplying them with necessary equipment and facilities;

(d) enhancing their capacity to manufacture such equipment;

(e) providing advice on and developing facilities for research, monitoring, educational and other programmes;

(f) providing advice on and developing facilities for minimizing the detrimental effects of major activities affecting their transboundary aquifer or aquifer system;

(g) providing advice in the preparation of environmental impact assessments;

(h) supporting the exchange of technical knowledge and experience among developing States with a view to strengthening cooperation among them in managing the transboundary aquifer or aquifer system.

Article 17 – Emergency situations

1. For the purpose of the present draft article, "emergency" means a situation, resulting suddenly from natural causes or from human conduct, that affects a transboundary aquifer or aquifer system and poses an imminent threat of causing serious harm to aquifer States or other States.
2. The State within whose territory the emergency originates shall:
   (a) without delay and by the most expeditious means available, notify other potentially affected States and competent international organizations of the emergency;
   (b) in cooperation with potentially affected States and, where appropriate, competent international organizations, immediately take all practicable measures necessitated by the circumstances to prevent, mitigate and eliminate any harmful effect of the emergency.
3. Where an emergency poses a threat to vital human needs, aquifer States, notwithstanding draft articles 4 and 6, may take measures that are strictly necessary to meet such needs.
4. States shall provide scientific, technical, logistical and other cooperation to other States experiencing an emergency. Cooperation may include coordination of international emergency actions and communications, making available emergency response personnel, emergency response equipment and supplies, scientific and technical expertise and humanitarian assistance.

Article 18 – Protection in time of armed conflict

Transboundary aquifers or aquifer systems and related installations, facilities and other works shall enjoy the protection accorded by the principles and rules of international law applicable in international and non-international armed conflict and shall not be used in violation of those principles and rules.

Article 19 – Data and information vital to national defence or security

Nothing in the present draft articles obliges a State to provide data or information vital to its national defence or security. Nevertheless, that State shall cooperate in good faith with other States with a view to providing as much information as possible under the circumstances.

8.1.1. London Convention 1972

Convention on the Prevention of Marine Pollution by Dumping of Wastes and Other Matter, London, 29 December 1972, 1046 UNTS 120

The Contracting Parties to this Convention,

Recognizing that the marine environment and the living organisms which it supports are of vital importance to humanity, and all people have an interest in assuring that it is so managed that its quality and resources are not impaired;

Recognizing that the capacity of the sea to assimilate wastes and render them harm less, and its ability to regenerate natural resources, is not unlimited;

Recognizing that States have, in accordance with the Charter of the United Nations and the principles of international law, the sovereign right to exploit their own resources pursuant to their own environmental policies, and the responsibility to ensure that activities within their jurisdiction or control do not cause damage to the environment of other States or of areas beyond the limits of national jurisdiction;

Recalling Resolution 2749 (XXV)1 of the General Assembly of the United Nations on the principles governing the sea-bed and the ocean floor and the subsoil thereof, beyond the limits of national jurisdiction;

Noting that marine pollution originates in many sources, such as dumping and discharges through the atmosphere, rivers, estuaries, outfalls and pipelines, and that it is important that States use the best practicable means to prevent such pollution and develop products and processes which will reduce the amount of harmful wastes to be disposed of;

Being convinced that international action to control the pollution of the sea by dumping can and must be taken without delay but that this action should not preclude discussion of measures to control other sources of marine pollution as soon as possible; and

Wishing to improve protection of the marine environment by encouraging States with a common interest in particular geographical areas to enter into appropriate agreements supplementary to this Convention;

Have agreed as follows:

Article I

Contracting Parties shall individually and collectively promote the effective control of all sources of pollution of the marine environment, and pledge them selves especially to take all practicable steps to prevent the pollution of the sea by the dumping of waste and other matter that is liable to create hazards to human health, to harm living resources and marine life, to damage amenities or to interfere with other legitimate uses of the sea.

Article II

Contracting Parties shall, as provided for in the following Articles, take effective measures individually, according to their scientific, technical and economic capabilities, and collectively, to prevent marine pollution caused by dumping and shall harmonize their policies in this regard.

Article III

For the purposes of this Convention:

1. (a) "Dumping" means:
   - (i) any deliberate disposal at sea of wastes or other matter from vessels, aircraft, platforms or other man-made structures at sea;
   - (ii) any deliberate disposal at sea of vessels, aircraft, platforms or other man-made structures at sea.

   (b) "Dumping" does not include:
   - (i) the disposal at sea of wastes or other matter incidental to, or derived from the normal operations of vessels, aircraft, platforms or other man-made structures at sea and their equipment, other than wastes or other matter transported by or to vessels, aircraft, platforms or other man-made structures at sea, operating for the purpose of disposal of such matter or derived from the treatment of such wastes or other matter on such vessels, aircraft, platforms or structures;
   - (ii) placement of matter for a purpose other than the mere disposal thereof, provided that such placement is not contrary to the aims of this Convention.

   (c) The disposal of wastes or other matter directly arising from, or related to the exploration, exploitation and associated off-shore processing of sea-bed mineral resources will not be covered by the provisions of this Convention.
2. "Vessels and aircraft" means waterborne or airborne craft of any type whatsoever. This expression includes air cushioned craft and floating craft, whether self-propelled or not.
3. "Sea" means all marine waters other than the internal waters of States.
4. "Wastes or other matter" means material and substance of any kind, form or description.
5. "Special permit" means permission granted specifically on application in advance and in accordance with Annex II and Annex III.
6. "General permit" means permission granted in advance and in accordance with Annex III.
7. "The Organization" means the Organization designated by the Contracting Parties in accordance with article XIV(2).

Article IV

1. In accordance with the provisions of this Convention, Contracting Parties shall prohibit the dumping of any wastes or other matter in whatever form or condition except as otherwise specified below:
   (a) the dumping of wastes or other matter listed in Annex I is prohibited;
   (b) the dumping of wastes or other matter listed in Annex II requires a prior special permit;
   (c) the dumping of all other wastes or matter requires a prior general permit.
2. Any permit shall be issued only after careful consideration of all the factors set forth in Annex III, including prior studies of the characteristics of the dumping site, as set forth in Sections B and C of that Annex.
3. No provision of this Convention is to be interpreted as preventing a Contracting Party from prohibiting, insofar as that Party is concerned, the dumping of wastes or other matter not mentioned in Annex I. That Party shall notify such measures to the Organisation.

Article V

1. The provisions of Article IV shall not apply when it is necessary to secure the safety of human life or of vessels, aircraft, platfolms or other man-made structures at sea in cases of force majeure caused by stress of weather, or in any case which constitutes a danger to human life or a real threat to vessels, aircraft, platforms or other man-made structures at sea, if dumping appears to be the only way of averting the threat and if there is every probability that the damage consequent upon such dumping will be less than would otherwise occur. Such dumping shall be so conducted as to minimize the likelihood of damage to human or marine life and shall be reported forthwith to the Organisation.
2. A Contracting Party may issue a special permit as an exception to Article IV(1)(a), in emergencies, posing unacceptable risk relating to human health and admitting no other feasible solution. Before doing so the Party shall consult any other country or countries that are likely to be affected and the Organisation which, after consulting other Parties, and international organisations as appropriate, shall, in accordance with Article XIV promptly recommend to the Party the most appropriate procedures to adopt. The Party shall follow these recommendations to the maximum extent feasible consistent with the time within which action must be taken and with the general obligation to avoid damage to the marine environment and shall inform the Organisation of the action it takes. The Parties pledge themselves to assist one another in such situations.
3. Any Contracting Party may waive its rights under paragraph (2) at the time of, or subsequent to ratification of, or accession to this Convention.

Article VI

1. Each Contracting Party shall designate an appropriate authority or authorities to:
   (a) issue special permits which shall be required prior to, and for, the dumping of matter listed in Annex TI and in the circumstances provided for i Article V (2);
   (b) issue general permits which shall be required prior to, and for, the dumping of all other matter;
   (c) keep records of the nature and quantities of all matter permitted to be dumped and the location, time and method of dumping;
   (d) monitor individually, or in collaboration with other Parties and competent international organisations, the condition of the seas for the purposes of this Convention.
2. The appropriate authority or authorities of a Contracting Party shall issue prior special or general permits in accordance with paragraph (1) in respect of matter intended for dumping:
   (a) loaded in its territory;
   (b) loaded by a vessel or aircraft registered in its territory or flying its flag, when the loading occurs in the territory of a State not party to this Convention.
3. In issuing permits under sub-paragraphs (1)(a) and (b) above, the appropriate authority or authorities shall comply with Annex III, together with such additional criteria, measures and requirements as they may consider relevant.
4. Each Contracting Party, directly or through a Secretariat established under a regional agreement, shall report to the Organisation, and where appropriate to other Parties, the information specified in sub-paragraphs (c) and (d) of paragraph (1) above, and the criteria, measures and requirements it adopts in accordance with paragraph (3) above. The procedure to be followed and the nature of such reports shall be agreed by the Parties in consultation.

Article VII

1. Each Contracting Party shall apply the measures required to implement the present Convention to all:
   (a) vessels and aircraft registered in its territory or flying its flag;
   (b) vessels and aircraft loading in its territory or territorial seas matter which is to be dumped;
   (c) vessels and aircraft and fixed or floating platforms under its jurisdiction believed to be engaged in dumping.
2. Each Party shall take in its territory appropriate measures to prevent and punish conduct in contravention of the provisions of this Convention.
3. The Parties agree to co-operate in the development of procedures for the effective application of this Convention particularly on the high seas, including procedures for the reporting of vessels and aircraft

observed dumping in contravention of the Convention.

4. This Convention shall not apply to those vessels and aircraft entitled to sovereign immunity under international law. However, each Party shall ensure by the adoption of appropriate measures that such vessels and aircraft owned or operated by it act in a manner consistent with the object and purpose of this Convention, and shall inform the Organisation accordingly.
5. Nothing in this Convention shall affect the right of each Party to adopt other measures, in accordance with the principles of international law, to prevent dumping at sea.

Article VIII

In order to further the objectives of this Convention, the Contracting Parties with common interests to protect in the marine environment in a given geographical area shall endeavour, taking into account characteristic regional features, to enter into regional agreements consistent with this Convention for the prevention of pollution, especially by dumping. The Contracting Parties to the present Convention shall endeavour to act consistently with the objectives and provisions of such regional agreements, which shall be notified to them by the Organisation. Contracting Parties shall seek to co-operate with the Parties to regional agreements in order to develop harnonized procedures to be followed by Contracting Parties to the different conventions concerned. Special attention shall be given to co-operation in the field of monitoring and scientific research.

Article IX

The Contracting Parties shall promote, through collaboration within the Organisation and other international bodies, support for those Parties which request it for:

(a) the training of scientific and technical personnel;

(b) the supply of necessary equipment and facilities for research and monitoring;

(c) the disposal and treatment of waste and other measures to prevent or mitigate pollution caused by dumping;

preferably within the countries concerned, so furthering the aims and purposes of this Convention.

Article X

In accordance with the principles of international law regarding State responsibility for damage to the environment of other States or to any other area of the environment, caused by dumping of wastes and other matter of all kinds, the Contracting Parties undertake to develop procedures for the assessment of liability and the settlement of disputes regarding dumping.

Article XI

The Contracting Parties shall at their first consultative meeting consider procedures for the settlement of disputes concerning the interpretation and application of this Convention.

Article XII

The Contracting Parties pledge themselves to promote, within the competent specialised agencies and other international bodies, measures to protect the marine environment against pollution caused by:

(a) hydrocarbons, including oil, and their wastes;

(b) other noxious or hazardous matter transported by vessels for purposes other than dumping;

(c) wastes generated in the course of operation of vessels, aircraft, platforms and other man-made structures at sea;

(d) radio-active pollutants from all sources, including vessels;

(e) agents of chemical and biological warfare;

(f) wastes or other matter directly arising from, or related to the exploration, exploitation and associated off-shore processing of sea-bed mineral resources.

The Parties will also promote, within the appropriate international organisation, the codification of signals to be used by vessels engaged in dumping.

Article XIII

Nothing in this Convention shall prejudice the codification and development of the law of the sea by the United Nations Conference on the Law of the Sea convened pursuant to Resolution 2750 C(XXV) of the General Assembly of the United Nations nor the present or future claims and legal views of any State concerning the law of the sea and the nature and extent of coastal and flag State jurisdiction. The Contracting Parties agree to consult at a meeting to be convened by the Organisation after the Law of the Sea Conference, and in any case not later than 1976, with a view to defining the nature and extent of the right and the responsibility of a coastal State to apply the Convention in a zone adjacent to its coast.

Article XIV

1. The Government of the United Kingdom of Great Britain and Northern Ireland as a depositary shall call a meeting of the Contracting Parties not later than three months after the entry into force of this Convention to decide on organisational matters.
2. The Contracting Parties shall designate a competent Organisation existing at the time of that meeting to be responsible for Secretariat duties in relation to this Convention. Any Party to this Convention not being a member of this Organisation shall make an appropriate contribution to the expenses incurred by the Organisation in performing these duties.
3. The Secretariat duties of the Organisation shall include:

   (a) the convening of consultative meetings of the Contracting Parties not less frequently than once every two years and of special meetings of the Parties at any time on the request of two thirds of the Parties;

   (b) preparing and assisting, in consultation with the Contracting Parties and appropriate International Organisations, in the development and implementation of procedures referred to in sub-paragraph (4)(e) of this Article;

(c) considering enquiries by, and information from the Contracting Parties, consulting with them and with the appropriate International Organisations, and providing recommendations to the Parties on questions related to, but not specifically covered by the Convention;

(d) conveying to the Parties concerned all notifications received by the Organisation in accordance with Articles IV(3), V(l) and(2), VI(4), XV, XX and XXI.

Prior to the designation of the Organisation these functions shall, as necessary, be performed by the depositary, who for this purpose shall be the Government of the United Kingdom of Great Britain and Northern Ireland.

4. Consultative or special meetings of the Contracting Parties shall keep under continuing review the implementation of this Convention and may, inter alia:

(a) review and adopt amendments to this Convention and its Annexes in accordance with Article XV;

(b) invite the appropriate scientific body or bodies to collaborate with and to advise the Parties or the Organisation on any scientific or technical aspect relevant to this Convention, including particularly the content of the Annexes;

(c) receive and consider reports made pursuant to Article VI(4);

(d) promote co-operation with and between regional organisations concerned with the prevention of marine pollution;

(e) develop or adopt, in consultation with appropriate International Organisations, procedures referred to in Article V(2), including basic criteria for determining exceptional and emergency situations, and procedures for consultative advice and the safe disposal of matter in such circumstances, including the designation of appropriate dumping areas, and recommend accordingly;

(f) consider any additional action that may be required.

5. The Contracting Parties at their first consultative meeting shall establish rules of procedure as necessary.

Article XV

1. (a) At meetings of the Contracting Parties called in accordance with Article XIV amendments to this Convention may be adopted by a two-thirds majority of those present. An amendment shall enter into force for the Parties which have accepted it on the sixtieth day after two thirds of the Parties shall have deposited an instrument of acceptance of the amendment with the Organisation. Thereafter the amendment shall enter into force for any other Party 30 days after that Party deposits its instrument of acceptance of the amendment.

(b) The Organisation shall inform all Contracting Parties of any request made for a special meeting under Article XIV and of any amendments adopted at meetings of the Parties and of the date on which each such amendment enters into force for each Party.

2. Amendments to the Annexes will be based on scientific or technical considerations. Amendments to the Annexes approved by a two-thirds majority of those present at a meeting called in accordance with Article XIV shall enter into force for each Contracting Party immediately on notification of its acceptance to the Organisation and 100 days after approval by the meeting for all other Parties except for those which before the end of the 100 days make a declaration that they are not able to accept the amendment at that time. Parties should endeavour to signify their acceptance of an amendment to the Organisation as soon as possible after approval at a meeting. A Party may at any time substitute an acceptance for a previous declaration of objection and the amendment previously objected to shall thereupon enter into force for that Party.

3. An acceptance or declaration of objection under this Article shall be made by the deposit of an instrument with the Organisation. The Organisation shall notify all Contracting Parties of the receipt of such instruments.

4. Prior to the designation of the Organisation, the Secretarial functions herein attributed to it shall be performed temporarily by the Government of the United Kingdom of Great Britain and Northern Ireland, as one of the depositaries of this Convention.

Article XVI

This Convention shall be open for signature by any State at London, Mexico City, Moscow and Washington from 29 December 1972 until 31 December 1973.

Article XVII

This Convention shall be subject to ratification. The instruments of ratification shall be deposited with the Governments of Mexico, the Union of Soviet Socialist Republics, the United Kingdom of Great Britain and Northern Ireland, and the United States of America.

Article XVIII

After 31 December 1973, this Convention shall be open for accession by any State. The instruments of accession shall be deposited with the Governments of Mexico, the Union of Soviet Socialist Republics, the United Kingdom of Great Britain and Northern Ireland, and the United States of America.

Article XIX.

1. This Convention shall enter into force on the thirtieth day following the date of deposit of the fifteenth instrument of ratification or accession.

2. For each Contracting Party ratifying or acceding to the Convention after the deposit of the fifteenth

instrument of ratification or accession, the Convention shall enter into force on the thirtieth day after deposit by such Party of its instrument of ratification or accession.

Article XX

The depositaries shall inform Contracting Parties:

(a) of signatures to this Convention and of the deposit of instruments of ratification, accession or withdrawal, in accordance with Articles XVI, XVII, XVIII and XXI, and

(b) of the date on which this Convention will enter into force, in accordance with Article XIX.

Article XXI

Any Contracting Party may withdraw from this Convention by giving six months' notice in writing to a depositary, which shall promptly inform all Parties of such notice.

Article XXII

The original of this Convention of which the English, French, Russian and Spanish texts are equally authentic, shall be deposited with the Governments of Mexico, the Union of Soviet Socialist Republics, the United Kingdom of Great Britain and Northern Ireland and the United States of America who shall send certified copies thereof to all States.

IN WITNESS WHEREOF the undersigned Plenipotentiaries, being duly authorised thereto by their respective Governments, have signed the present Convention.

DONE in quadruplicate at London, Mexico City, Moscow and Washington, this twenty-ninth day of December, 1972.

8.1.2. London Protocol 1996, as amended 2009

Protocol to the 1972 Convention on the Prevention of Marine Pollution by Dumping of Wastes and Other Matter, London, 7 November 1996, 36 ILM 7 (1997), as amended by Resolution LP.3(4)

THE CONTRACTING PARTIES TO THIS PROTOCOL,

STRESSING the need to protect the marine environment and to promote the sustainable use and conservation of marine resources,

NOTING in this regard the achievements within the framework of the Convention on the Prevention of Marine Pollution by Dumping of Wastes and Other Matter, 1972 and especially the evolution towards approaches based on precaution and prevention,

NOTING FURTHER the contribution in this regard by complementary regional and national instruments which aim to protect the marine environment and which take account of specific circumstances and needs of those regions and States,

REAFFIRMING the value of a global approach to these matters and in particular the importance of continuing co-operation and collaboration between Contracting Parties in implementing the Convention and the Protocol,

RECOGNIZING that it may be desirable to adopt, on a national or regional level, more stringent measures with respect to prevention and elimination of pollution of the marine environment from dumping at sea than are provided for in international conventions or other types of agreements with a global scope,

TAKING INTO ACCOUNT relevant international agreements and actions, especially the United Nations Convention on the Law of the Sea, 1982, the Rio Declaration on Environment and Development and Agenda 21,

RECOGNIZING ALSO the interests and capacities of developing States and in particular small island developing States,

BEING CONVINCED that further international action to prevent, reduce and where practicable eliminate pollution of the sea caused by dumping can and must be taken without delay to protect and preserve the marine environment and to manage human activities in such a manner that the marine ecosystem will continue to sustain the legitimate uses of the sea and will continue to meet the needs of present and future generations,

HAVE AGREED as follows:

ARTICLE 1 – DEFINITIONS

For the purposes of this Protocol:

1 "Convention" means the Convention on the Prevention of Marine Pollution by Dumping of Wastes and Other Matter, 1972, as amended.

2 "Organization" means the International Maritime Organization.

3 "Secretary-General" means the Secretary-General of the Organization.

4 .1 "Dumping" means:

.1 any deliberate disposal into the sea of wastes or other matter from vessels, aircraft, platforms or other man-made structures at sea;

.2 any deliberate disposal into the sea of vessels, aircraft, platforms or other man-made structures at sea;

.3 any storage of wastes or other matter in the seabed and the subsoil thereof from vessels, aircraft, platforms or other man-made structures at sea; and

.4 any abandonment or toppling at site of platforms or other man-made structures at sea, for the sole purpose of deliberate disposal.

.2 "Dumping" does not include:

.1 the disposal into the sea of wastes or other matter incidental to, or derived from the normal operations of vessels, aircraft, platforms or other man-made structures at sea and their equipment, other than wastes or other matter transported by or to vessels, aircraft, platforms or other man-made structures at sea, operating for the purpose of disposal of such matter or derived from the treatment of such wastes or other matter on such vessels, aircraft, platforms or other man-made structures;

.2 placement of matter for a purpose other than the mere disposal thereof, provided that such placement is not contrary to the aims of this Protocol; and

.3 notwithstanding paragraph 4.1.4, abandonment in the sea of matter (e.g., cables, pipelines and marine research devices) placed for a purpose other than the mere disposal thereof.

.3 The disposal or storage of wastes or other matter directly arising from, or related to the exploration, exploitation and associated off-shore processing of seabed mineral resources is not covered by the provisions of this Protocol.

5 .1 "Incineration at sea" means the combustion on board a vessel, platform or other man- made structure at sea of wastes or other matter for the purpose of their deliberate disposal by thermal destruction.

.2 "Incineration at sea" does not include the incineration of wastes or other matter on board a vessel, platform, or other man-made structure at sea if such wastes or other matter were generated during the normal operation of that vessel, platform or other man-made structure at sea.

6 "Vessels and aircraft" means waterborne or airborne craft of any type whatsoever. This expression includes air-cushioned craft and floating craft, whether self-propelled or not.

7 "Sea" means all marine waters other than the internal waters of States, as well as the seabed and the subsoil thereof; it does not include sub-seabed repositories accessed only from land.

8 "Wastes or other matter" means material and substance of any kind, form or description.

9 "Permit" means permission granted in advance and in accordance with relevant measures adopted pursuant to article 4.1.2 or 8.2.

10 "Pollution" means the introduction, directly or indirectly, by human activity, of wastes or other matter into the sea which results or is likely to result in such deleterious effects as harm to living resources and marine ecosystems, hazards to human health, hindrance to marine activities, including fishing and other legitimate uses of the sea, impairment of quality for use of sea water and reduction of amenities.

ARTICLE 2 – OBJECTIVES

Contracting Parties shall individually and collectively protect and preserve the marine environment from all sources of pollution and take effective measures, according to their scientific, technical and economic capabilities, to prevent, reduce and where practicable eliminate pollution caused by dumping or incineration at sea of wastes or other matter. Where appropriate, they shall harmonize their policies in this regard.

ARTICLE 3 – GENERAL OBLIGATIONS

1 In implementing this Protocol, Contracting Parties shall apply a precautionary approach to environmental protection from dumping of wastes or other matter whereby appropriate preventative measures are taken when there is reason to believe that wastes or other matter introduced into the marine environment are likely to cause harm even when there is no conclusive evidence to prove a causal relation between inputs and their effects.

2 Taking into account the approach that the polluter should, in principle, bear the cost of pollution, each Contracting Party shall endeavour to promote practices whereby those it has authorized to engage in dumping or incineration at sea bear the cost of meeting the pollution prevention and control requirements for the authorized activities, having due regard to the public interest.

3 In implementing the provisions of this Protocol, Contracting Parties shall act so as not to transfer, directly or indirectly, damage or likelihood of damage from one part of the environment to another or transform one type of pollution into another.

4 No provision of this Protocol shall be interpreted as preventing Contracting Parties from taking, individually or jointly, more stringent measures in accordance with international law with respect to the prevention, reduction and where practicable elimination of pollution.

ARTICLE 4 – DUMPING OF WASTES OR OTHER MATTER

1 .1 Contracting Parties shall prohibit the dumping of any wastes or other matter with the exception of those listed in Annex 1.

.2 The dumping of wastes or other matter listed in Annex 1 shall require a permit. Contracting Parties shall adopt administrative or legislative measures to ensure that issuance of permits and permit conditions comply with provisions of Annex 2. Particular attention shall be paid to opportunities to avoid dumping in favour of environmentally preferable alternatives.

2 No provision of this Protocol shall be interpreted as preventing a Contracting Party from prohibiting, insofar as that Contracting Party is concerned, the dumping of wastes or other matter mentioned in Annex 1. That Contracting Party shall notify the Organization of such measures.

ARTICLE 5 – INCINERATION AT SEA

Contracting Parties shall prohibit incineration at sea of wastes or other matter.

ARTICLE 6 – EXPORT OF WASTES OR OTHER MATTER

1 Contracting Parties shall not allow the export of wastes or other matter to other countries for dumping or incineration at sea.

2 Notwithstanding paragraph 1, the export of carbon dioxide streams for disposal in accordance with Annex 1 may occur, provided that an agreement or arrangement has been entered into by the countries concerned. Such an agreement or arrangement shall include:

.1 confirmation and allocation of permitting responsibilities between the exporting and receiving countries, consistent with the provisions of this Protocol and other applicable international law; and

.2 in the case of export to non-Contracting Parties, provisions at a minimum equivalent to those contained in this Protocol, including those relating to the issuance of permits and permit conditions for complying with the provisions of Annex 2, to ensure that the agreement or arrangement does not derogate from the obligations of Contracting Parties under this Protocol to protect and preserve the marine environment.

A Contracting Party entering into such an agreement or arrangement shall notify it to the Organization.

ARTICLE 7 – INTERNAL WATERS

1 Notwithstanding any other provision of this Protocol, this Protocol shall relate to internal waters only to the extent provided for in paragraphs 2 and 3.

2 Each Contracting Party shall at its discretion either apply the provisions of this Protocol or adopt other effective permitting and regulatory measures to control the deliberate disposal of wastes or other matter in marine internal waters where such disposal would be "dumping" or "incineration at sea" within the meaning of article 1, if conducted at sea.

3 Each Contracting Party should provide the Organization with information on legislation and institutional mechanisms regarding implementation, compliance and enforcement in marine internal waters. Contracting Parties should also use their best efforts to provide on a voluntary basis summary reports on the type and nature of the materials dumped in marine internal waters.

ARTICLE 8 – EXCEPTIONS

1 The provisions of articles 4.1 and 5 shall not apply when it is necessary to secure the safety of human life or of vessels, aircraft, platforms or other man-made structures at sea in cases of force majeure caused by stress of weather, or in any case which constitutes a danger to human life or a real threat to vessels, aircraft, platforms or other man-made structures at sea, if dumping or incineration at sea appears to be the only way of averting the threat and if there is every probability that the damage consequent upon such dumping or incineration at sea will be less than would otherwise occur. Such dumping or incineration at sea shall be conducted so as to minimize the likelihood of damage to human or marine life and shall be reported forthwith to the Organization.

2 A Contracting Party may issue a permit as an exception to articles 4.1 and 5, in emergencies posing an unacceptable threat to human health, safety, or the marine environment and admitting of no other feasible solution. Before doing so the Contracting Party shall consult any other country or countries that are likely to be affected and the Organization which, after consulting other Contracting Parties, and competent international organizations as appropriate, shall, in accordance with article 18.1.6 promptly recommend to the Contracting Party the most appropriate procedures to adopt. The Contracting Party shall follow these recommendations to the maximum extent feasible consistent with the time within which action must be taken and with the general obligation to avoid damage to the marine environment and shall inform the Organization of the action it takes. The Contracting Parties pledge themselves to assist one another in such situations.

3 Any Contracting Party may waive its rights under paragraph 2 at the time of, or subsequent to ratification of, or accession to this Protocol.

ARTICLE 9 – ISSUANCE OF PERMITS AND REPORTING

1 Each Contracting Party shall designate an appropriate authority or authorities to:

.1 issue permits in accordance with this Protocol;

.2 keep records of the nature and quantities of all wastes or other matter for which dumping permits have been issued and where practicable the quantities actually dumped and the location, time and method of dumping; and

.3 monitor individually, or in collaboration with other Contracting Parties and competent international organizations, the condition of the sea for the purposes of this Protocol.

2 The appropriate authority or authorities of a Contracting Party shall issue permits in accordance with this Protocol in respect of wastes or other matter intended for dumping or, as provided for in article 8.2, incineration at sea:

.1 loaded in its territory; and

.2 loaded onto a vessel or aircraft registered in its territory or flying its flag, when the loading occurs in the territory of a State not a Contracting Party to this Protocol.

3 In issuing permits, the appropriate authority or authorities shall comply with the requirements of article 4, together with such additional criteria, measures and requirements as they may consider relevant.

4 Each Contracting Party, directly or through a secretariat established under a regional agreement, shall report to the Organization and where appropriate to other Contracting Parties:

.1 the information specified in paragraphs 1.2 and 1.3;

.2 the administrative and legislative measures taken to implement the provisions of this Protocol, including a summary of enforcement measures; and

.3 the effectiveness of the measures referred to in paragraph 4.2 and any problems encountered in their application.

The information referred to in paragraphs 1.2 and 1.3 shall be submitted on an annual basis. The information referred to in paragraphs 4.2 and 4.3 shall be submitted on a regular basis.

5 Reports submitted under paragraphs 4.2 and 4.3 shall be evaluated by an appropriate subsidiary body as determined by the Meeting of Contracting Parties. This body will report its conclusions to an appropriate Meeting or Special Meeting of Contracting Parties.

ARTICLE 10 – APPLICATION AND ENFORCEMENT

1 Each Contracting Party shall apply the measures required to implement this Protocol to all:

.1 vessels and aircraft registered in its territory or flying its flag;

.2 vessels and aircraft loading in its territory the wastes or other matter which are to be dumped or incinerated at sea; and

.3 vessels, aircraft and platforms or other man-made structures believed to be engaged in dumping or incineration at sea in areas within which it is entitled to exercise jurisdiction in accordance with international law.

2 Each Contracting Party shall take appropriate measures in accordance with international law to prevent and if necessary punish acts contrary to the provisions of this Protocol.

3 Contracting Parties agree to co-operate in the development of procedures for the effective application of this Protocol in areas beyond the jurisdiction of any State, including procedures for the reporting of vessels and aircraft observed dumping or incinerating at sea in contravention of this Protocol.

4 This Protocol shall not apply to those vessels and aircraft entitled to sovereign immunity under international law. However, each Contracting Party shall ensure by the adoption of appropriate measures that such vessels and aircraft owned or operated by it act in a manner consistent with the object and purpose of this Protocol and shall inform the Organization accordingly.

5 A State may, at the time it expresses its consent to be bound by this Protocol, or at any time thereafter, declare that it shall apply the provisions of this Protocol to its vessels and aircraft referred to in paragraph 4, recognising that only that State may enforce those provisions against such vessels and aircraft.

ARTICLE 11 – COMPLIANCE PROCEDURES

1 No later than two years after the entry into force of this Protocol, the Meeting of Contracting Parties shall establish those procedures and mechanisms necessary to assess and promote compliance with this Protocol. Such procedures and mechanisms shall be developed with a view to allowing for the full and open exchange of information, in a constructive manner.

2 After full consideration of any information submitted pursuant to this Protocol and any recommendations made through procedures or mechanisms established under paragraph 1, the Meeting of Contracting Parties may offer advice, assistance or co-operation to Contracting Parties and non-Contracting Parties.

ARTICLE 12 – REGIONAL CO-OPERATION

In order to further the objectives of this Protocol, Contracting Parties with common interests to protect the marine environment in a given geographical area shall endeavour, taking into account characteristic regional features, to enhance regional co-operation including the conclusion of regional agreements consistent with this Protocol for the prevention, reduction and where practicable elimination of pollution caused by dumping or incineration at sea of wastes or other matter. Contracting Parties shall seek to co-operate with the parties to regional agreements in order to develop harmonized procedures to be followed by Contracting Parties to the different conventions concerned.

ARTICLE 13 – TECHNICAL CO-OPERATION AND ASSISTANCE

1 Contracting Parties shall, through collaboration within the Organization and in co-ordination with other competent international organizations, promote bilateral and multilateral support for the prevention, reduction and where practicable elimination of pollution caused by dumping as provided for in this Protocol to those Contracting Parties that request it for:

.1 training of scientific and technical personnel for research, monitoring and enforcement, including as appropriate the supply of necessary equipment and facilities, with a view to strengthening national capabilities;

.2 advice on implementation of this Protocol;

.3 information and technical co-operation relating to waste minimization and clean production processes;

.4 information and technical co-operation relating to the disposal and treatment of waste and other measures to prevent, reduce and where practicable eliminate pollution caused by dumping; and

.5 access to and transfer of environmentally sound technologies and corresponding know-how, in particular to developing countries and countries in transition to market economies, on favourable terms, including on concessional and preferential terms, as mutually agreed, taking into account the need to protect intellectual property rights as well as the special needs of developing countries and countries in transition to market economies.

2 The Organization shall perform the following functions:

.1 forward requests from Contracting Parties for technical co-operation to other Contracting Parties, taking into account such factors as technical capabilities;

.2 co-ordinate requests for assistance with other competent international organizations, as appropriate; and

.3 subject to the availability of adequate resources, assist developing countries and those in transition to market economies, which have declared their intention to become Contracting Parties to this Protocol, to examine the means necessary to achieve full implementation.

ARTICLE 14 – SCIENTIFIC AND TECHNICAL RESEARCH

1 Contracting Parties shall take appropriate measures to promote and facilitate scientific and technical research on the prevention, reduction and where practicable elimination of pollution by dumping and other sources of marine pollution relevant to

this Protocol. In particular, such research should include observation, measurement, evaluation and analysis of pollution by scientific methods.

2 Contracting Parties shall, to achieve the objectives of this Protocol, promote the availability of relevant information to other Contracting Parties who request it on:

.1 scientific and technical activities and measures undertaken in accordance with this Protocol;

.2 marine scientific and technological programmes and their objectives; and

.3 the impacts observed from the monitoring and assessment conducted pursuant to article 9.1.3.

ARTICLE 15 – RESPONSIBILITY AND LIABILITY

In accordance with the principles of international law regarding State responsibility for damage to the environment of other States or to any other area of the environment, the Contracting Parties undertake to develop procedures regarding liability arising from the dumping or incineration at sea of wastes or other matter.

ARTICLE 16 – SETTLEMENT OF DISPUTES

1 Any disputes regarding the interpretation or application of this Protocol shall be resolved in the first instance through negotiation, mediation or conciliation, or other peaceful means chosen by parties to the dispute.

2 If no resolution is possible within twelve months after one Contracting Party has notified another that a dispute exists between them, the dispute shall be settled, at the request of a party to the dispute, by means of the Arbitral Procedure set forth in Annex 3, unless the parties to the dispute agree to use one of the procedures listed in paragraph 1 of Article 287 of the 1982 United Nations Convention on the Law of the Sea. The parties to the dispute may so agree, whether or not they are also States Parties to the 1982 United Nations Convention on the Law of the Sea.

3 In the event an agreement to use one of the procedures listed in paragraph 1 of Article 287 of the 1982 United Nations Convention on the Law of the Sea is reached, the provisions set forth in Part XV of that Convention that are related to the chosen procedure would also apply, mutatis mutandis.

4 The twelve month period referred to in paragraph 2 may be extended for another twelve months by mutual consent of the parties concerned.

5 Notwithstanding paragraph 2, any State may, at the time it expresses its consent to be bound by this Protocol, notify the Secretary-General that, when it is a party to a dispute about the interpretation or application of article 3.1 or 3.2, its consent will be required before the dispute may be settled by means of the Arbitral Procedure set forth in Annex 3.

ARTICLE 17 – INTERNATIONAL CO-OPERATION

Contracting Parties shall promote the objectives of this Protocol within the competent international organizations.

ARTICLE 18 – MEETINGS OF CONTRACTING PARTIES

1 Meetings of Contracting Parties or Special Meetings of Contracting Parties shall keep under continuing review the implementation of this Protocol and evaluate its effectiveness with a view to identifying means of strengthening action, where necessary, to prevent, reduce and where practicable eliminate pollution caused by dumping and incineration at sea of wastes or other matter. To these ends, Meetings of Contracting Parties or Special Meetings of Contracting Parties may:

.1 review and adopt amendments to this Protocol in accordance with articles 21 and 22;

.2 establish subsidiary bodies, as required, to consider any matter with a view to facilitating the effective implementation of this Protocol;

.3 invite appropriate expert bodies to advise the Contracting Parties or the Organization on matters relevant to this Protocol;

.4 promote co-operation with competent international organizations concerned with the prevention and control of pollution;

.5 consider the information made available pursuant to article 9.4;

.6 develop or adopt, in consultation with competent international organizations, procedures referred to in article 8.2, including basic criteria for determining exceptional and emergency situations, and procedures for consultative advice and the safe disposal of matter at sea in such circumstances;

.7 consider and adopt resolutions; and

.8 consider any additional action that may be required.

2 The Contracting Parties at their first Meeting shall establish rules of procedure as necessary.

ARTICLE 19 – DUTIES OF THE ORGANIZATION

1 The Organization shall be responsible for Secretariat duties in relation to this Protocol. Any Contracting Party to this Protocol not being a member of this Organization shall make an appropriate contribution to the expenses incurred by the Organization in performing these duties.

2 Secretariat duties necessary for the administration of this Protocol include:

.1 convening Meetings of Contracting Parties once per year, unless otherwise decided by Contracting Parties, and Special Meetings of Contracting Parties at any time on the request of two-thirds of the Contracting Parties;

.2 providing advice on request on the implementation of this Protocol and on guidance and procedures developed thereunder;

.3 considering enquiries by, and information from Contracting Parties, consulting with them and with the competent international organizations, and providing recommendations to Contracting Parties on questions related to, but not specifically covered by, this Protocol;

.4 preparing and assisting, in consultation with Contracting Parties and the competent international organizations, in the development and implementation of procedures referred to in article 18.1.6;

.5 conveying to the Contracting Parties concerned all notifications received by the Organization in accordance with this Protocol; and

.6 preparing, every two years, a budget and a financial account for the administration of this Protocol which shall be distributed to all Contracting Parties.

3 The Organization shall, subject to the availability of adequate resources, in addition to the requirements set out in article 13.2.3.

.1 collaborate in assessments of the state of the marine environment; and

.2 co-operate with competent international organizations concerned with the prevention and control of pollution.

ARTICLE 20 – ANNEXES

Annexes to this Protocol form an integral part of this Protocol.

ARTICLE 21 – AMENDMENT OF THE PROTOCOL

1 Any Contracting Party may propose amendments to the articles of this Protocol. The text of a proposed amendment shall be communicated to Contracting Parties by the Organization at least six months prior to its consideration at a Meeting of Contracting Parties or a Special Meeting of Contracting Parties.

2 Amendments to the articles of this Protocol shall be adopted by a two-thirds majority vote of the Contracting Parties which are present and voting at the Meeting of Contracting Parties or Special Meeting of Contracting Parties designated for this purpose.

3 An amendment shall enter into force for the Contracting Parties which have accepted it on the sixtieth day after two-thirds of the Contracting Parties shall have deposited an instrument of acceptance of the amendment with the Organization. Thereafter the amendment shall enter into force for any other Contracting Party on the sixtieth day after the date on which that Contracting Party has deposited its instrument of acceptance of the amendment.

4 The Secretary-General shall inform Contracting Parties of any amendments adopted at Meetings of Contracting Parties and of the date on which such amendments enter into force generally and for each Contracting Party.

5 After entry into force of an amendment to this Protocol, any State that becomes a Contracting Party to this Protocol shall become a Contracting Party to this Protocol as amended, unless two-thirds of the Contracting Parties present and voting at the Meeting or Special Meeting of Contracting Parties adopting the amendment agree otherwise.

ARTICLE 22 – AMENDMENT OF THE ANNEXES

1 Any Contracting Party may propose amendments to the Annexes to this Protocol. The text of a proposed amendment shall be communicated to Contracting Parties by the Organization at least six months prior to its consideration by a Meeting of Contracting Parties or Special Meeting of Contracting Parties.

2 Amendments to the Annexes other than Annex 3 will be based on scientific or technical considerations and may take into account legal, social and economic factors as appropriate. Such amendments shall be adopted by a two-thirds majority vote of the Contracting Parties present and voting at a Meeting of Contracting Parties or Special Meeting of Contracting Parties designated for this purpose.

3 The Organization shall without delay communicate to Contracting Parties amendments to the Annexes that have been adopted at a Meeting of Contracting Parties or Special Meeting of Contracting Parties.

4 Except as provided in paragraph 7, amendments to the Annexes shall enter into force for each Contracting Party immediately on notification of its acceptance to the Organization or 100 days after the date of their adoption at a Meeting of Contracting Parties, if that is later, except for those Contracting Parties which before the end of the 100 days make a declaration that they are not able to accept the amendment at that time. A Contracting Party may at any time substitute an acceptance for a previous declaration of objection and the amendment previously objected to shall thereupon enter into force for that Contracting Party.

5 The Secretary-General shall without delay notify Contracting Parties of instruments of acceptance or objection deposited with the Organization.

6 A new Annex or an amendment to an Annex which is related to an amendment to the articles of this Protocol shall not enter into force until such time as the amendment to the articles of this Protocol enters into force.

7 With regard to amendments to Annex 3 concerning the Arbitral Procedure and with regard to the adoption and entry into force of new Annexes the procedures on amendments to the articles of this Protocol shall apply.

ARTICLE 23 – RELATIONSHIP BETWEEN THE PROTOCOL AND THE CONVENTION

This Protocol will supersede the Convention as between Contracting Parties to this Protocol which are also Parties to the Convention.

ARTICLE 24 – SIGNATURE, RATIFICATION, ACCEPTANCE, APPROVAL AND ACCESSION

1 This Protocol shall be open for signature by any State at the Headquarters of the Organization from 1 April 1997 to 31 March 1998 and shall thereafter remain open for accession by any State.

2 States may become Contracting Parties to this Protocol by:

.1 signature not subject to ratification, acceptance or approval; or

.2 signature subject to ratification, acceptance or approval, followed by ratification, acceptance or approval; or

.3 accession.

3 Ratification, acceptance, approval or accession shall be effected by the deposit of an instrument to that effect with the Secretary-General.

ARTICLE 25 – ENTRY INTO FORCE

1 This Protocol shall enter into force on the thirtieth day following the date on which:

.1 at least 26 States have expressed their consent to be bound by this Protocol in accordance with article 24; and

.2 at least 15 Contracting Parties to the Convention are included in the number of States referred to in paragraph 1.1.

2 For each State that has expressed its consent to be bound by this Protocol in accordance with article 24 following the date referred to in paragraph 1, this Protocol shall enter into force on the thirtieth day after the date on which such State expressed its consent.

ARTICLE 26 – TRANSITIONAL PERIOD

1 Any State that was not a Contracting Party to the Convention before 31 December 1996 and that expresses its consent to be bound by this Protocol prior to its entry into force or within five years after its entry into force may, at the time it expresses its consent, notify the Secretary-General that, for reasons described in the notification, it will not be able to comply with specific provisions of this Protocol other than those provided in paragraph 2, for a transitional period that shall not exceed that described in paragraph 4.

2 No notification made under paragraph 1 shall affect the obligations of a Contracting Party to this Protocol with respect to incineration at sea or the dumping of radioactive wastes or other radioactive matter.

3 Any Contracting Party to this Protocol that has notified the Secretary-General under paragraph 1 that, for the specified transitional period, it will not be able to comply, in part or in whole, with article 4.1 or article 9 shall nonetheless during that period prohibit the dumping of wastes or other matter for which it has not issued a permit, use its best efforts to adopt administrative or legislative measures to ensure that issuance of permits and permit conditions comply with the provisions of Annex 2, and notify the Secretary-General of any permits issued.

4 Any transitional period specified in a notification made under paragraph 1 shall not extend beyond five years after such notification is submitted.

5 Contracting Parties that have made a notification under paragraph 1 shall submit to the first Meeting of Contracting Parties occurring after deposit of their instrument of ratification, acceptance, approval or accession a programme and timetable to achieve full compliance with this Protocol, together with any requests for relevant technical co-operation and assistance in accordance with article 13 of this Protocol.

6 Contracting Parties that have made a notification under paragraph 1 shall establish procedures and mechanisms for the transitional period to implement and monitor submitted programmes designed to achieve full compliance with this Protocol. A report on progress toward compliance shall be submitted by such Contracting Parties to each Meeting of Contracting Parties held during their transitional period for appropriate action.

ARTICLE 27 – WITHDRAWAL

1 Any Contracting Party may withdraw from this Protocol at any time after the expiry of two years from the date on which this Protocol enters into force for that Contracting Party.

2 Withdrawal shall be effected by the deposit of an instrument of withdrawal with the Secretary-General.

3 A withdrawal shall take effect one year after receipt by the Secretary-General of the instrument of withdrawal or such longer period as may be specified in that instrument.

ARTICLE 28 – DEPOSITARY

1 This Protocol shall be deposited with the Secretary-General.

2 In addition to the functions specified in articles 10.5, 16.5, 21.4, 22.5 and 26.5, the Secretary- General shall:

.1 inform all States which have signed this Protocol or acceded thereto of:

.1 each new signature or deposit of an instrument of ratification, acceptance, approval or accession, together with the date thereof;

.2 the date of entry into force of this Protocol; and

.3 the deposit of any instrument of withdrawal from this Protocol together with the date on which it was received and the date on which the withdrawal takes effect.

.2 transmit certified copies of this Protocol to all States which have signed this Protocol or acceded thereto.

3 As soon as this Protocol enters into force, a certified true copy thereof shall be transmitted by the Secretary-General to the Secretariat of the United Nations for registration and publication in accordance with Article 102 of the Charter of the United Nations.

ARTICLE 29 – AUTHENTIC TEXTS

This Protocol is established in a single original in the Arabic, Chinese, English, French, Russian and Spanish languages, each text being equally authentic.

IN WITNESS WHEREOF the undersigned being duly authorized by their respective Governments for that purpose have signed this Protocol[1].

DONE AT LONDON, this seventh day of November, one thousand nine hundred and ninety-six.

ANNEX 1 – WASTES OR OTHER MATTER THAT MAY BE CONSIDERED FOR DUMPING

1 The following wastes or other matter are those that may be considered for dumping being mindful of the Objectives and General Obligations of this Protocol set out in articles 2 and 3:

.1 dredged material;

.2 sewage sludge;

.3 fish waste, or material resulting from industrial fish processing operations;

.4 vessels and platforms or other man-made structures at sea;

.5 inert, inorganic geological material;

.6 organic material of natural origin;

.7 bulky items primarily comprising iron, steel, concrete and similarly unharmful materials for which the concern is physical impact, and limited to those circumstances where such wastes are generated at locations, such as small islands with isolated communities, having no practicable access to disposal options other than dumping; and

.8 Carbon dioxide streams from carbon dioxide capture processes for sequestration.

2 The wastes or other matter listed in paragraphs 1.4 and 1.7 may be considered for dumping, provided that material capable of creating floating debris or otherwise contributing to pollution of the marine environment has been removed to the maximum extent and provided that the material dumped poses no serious obstacle to fishing or navigation.

3 Notwithstanding the above, materials listed in paragraphs 1.1 to 1.8 containing levels of radioactivity greater than de minimis (exempt) concentrations as defined by the IAEA and adopted by Contracting Parties, shall not be considered eligible for dumping; provided further that within 25 years of 20 February 1994, and at each 25 year interval thereafter, Contracting Parties shall complete a scientific study relating to all radioactive wastes and other radioactive matter other than high level wastes or matter, taking into account such other factors as Contracting Parties consider appropriate and shall review the prohibition on dumping of such substances in accordance with the procedures set forth in article 22.

4 Carbon dioxide streams referred to in paragraph 1.8 may only be considered for dumping, if:

.1 disposal is into a sub-seabed geological formation; and

.2 they consist overwhelmingly of carbon dioxide. They may contain incidental associated substances derived from the source material and the capture and sequestration processes used; and

.3 no wastes or other matter are added for the purpose of disposing of those wastes or other matter.

ANNEX 2 – ASSESSMENT OF WASTES OR OTHER MATTER THAT MAY BE CONSIDERED FOR DUMPING

GENERAL

1 The acceptance of dumping under certain circumstances shall not remove the obligations under this Annex to make further attempts to reduce the necessity for dumping.

WASTE PREVENTION AUDIT

2 The initial stages in assessing alternatives to dumping should, as appropriate, include an evaluation of:

.1 types, amounts and relative hazard of wastes generated;

.2 details of the production process and the sources of wastes within that process; and

.3 feasibility of the following waste reduction/prevention techniques:

.1 product reformulation;

.2 clean production technologies;

.3 process modification;

.4 input substitution; and

.5 on-site, closed-loop recycling.

3 In general terms, if the required audit reveals that opportunities exist for waste prevention at source, an applicant is expected to formulate and implement a waste prevention strategy, in collaboration with relevant local and national agencies, which includes specific waste reduction targets and provision for further waste prevention audits to ensure that these targets are being met. Permit issuance or renewal decisions shall assure compliance with any resulting waste reduction and prevention requirements.

1 Signatures omitted.

4 For dredged material and sewage sludge, the goal of waste management should be to identify and control the sources of contamination. This should be achieved through implementation of waste prevention strategies and requires collaboration between the relevant local and national agencies involved with the control of point and non-point sources of pollution. Until this objective is met, the problems of contaminated dredged material may be addressed by using disposal management techniques at sea or on land.

CONSIDERATION OF WASTE MANAGEMENT OPTIONS

5 Applications to dump wastes or other matter shall demonstrate that appropriate consideration has been given to the following hierarchy of waste management options, which implies an order of increasing environmental impact:

.1 re-use;

.2 off-site recycling;

.3 destruction of hazardous constituents;

.4 treatment to reduce or remove the hazardous constituents; and

.5 disposal on land, into air and in water.

6 A permit to dump wastes or other matter shall be refused if the permitting authority determines that appropriate opportunities exist to re-use, recycle or treat the waste without undue risks to human health or the environment or disproportionate costs. The practical availability of other means of disposal should be considered in the light of a comparative risk assessment involving both dumping and the alternatives.

CHEMICAL, PHYSICAL AND BIOLOGICAL PROPERTIES

7 A detailed description and characterization of the waste is an essential precondition for the consideration of alternatives and the basis for a decision as to whether a waste may be dumped. If a waste is so poorly characterized that proper assessment cannot be made of its potential impacts on human health and the environment, that waste shall not be dumped.

8 Characterization of the wastes and their constituents shall take into account:

.1 origin, total amount, form and average composition;

.2 properties: physical, chemical, biochemical and biological;

.3 toxicity;

.4 persistence: physical, chemical and biological; and

.5 accumulation and biotransformation in biological materials or sediments.

ACTION LIST

9 Each Contracting Party shall develop a national Action List to provide a mechanism for screening candidate wastes and their constituents on the basis of their potential effects on human health and the marine environment. In selecting substances for consideration in an Action List, priority shall be given to toxic, persistent and bioaccumulative substances from anthropogenic sources (e.g., cadmium, mercury, organohalogens, petroleum hydrocarbons, and, whenever relevant, arsenic, lead, copper, zinc, beryllium, chromium, nickel and vanadium, organosilicon compounds, cyanides, fluorides and pesticides or their by-products other than organohalogens). An Action List can also be used as a trigger mechanism for further waste prevention considerations.

10 An Action List shall specify an upper level and may also specify a lower level. The upper level should be set so as to avoid acute or chronic effects on human health or on sensitive marine organisms representative of the marine ecosystem. Application of an Action List will result in three possible categories of waste:

.1 wastes which contain specified substances, or which cause biological responses, exceeding the relevant upper level shall not be dumped, unless made acceptable for dumping through the use of management techniques or processes;

.2 wastes which contain specified substances, or which cause biological responses, below the relevant lower levels should be considered to be of little environmental concern in relation to dumping; and

.3 wastes which contain specified substances, or which cause biological responses, below the upper level but above the lower level require more detailed assessment before their suitability for dumping can be determined.

DUMP-SITE SELECTION

11 Information required to select a dump-site shall include:

.1 physical, chemical and biological characteristics of the water-column and the seabed;

.2 location of amenities, values and other uses of the sea in the area under consideration;

.3 assessment of the constituent fluxes associated with dumping in relation to existing fluxes of substances in the marine environment; and

.4 economic and operational feasibility.

ASSESSMENT OF POTENTIAL EFFECTS

12 Assessment of potential effects should lead to a concise statement of the expected consequences of the sea or land disposal options, i.e., the "Impact Hypothesis". It provides a basis for deciding whether to approve or reject the proposed disposal option and for defining environmental monitoring requirements.

13 The assessment for dumping should integrate information on waste characteristics, conditions at the proposed dump-site(s), fluxes, and proposed disposal techniques and specify the potential effects on human health, living resources, ameni-

ties and other legitimate uses of the sea. It should define the nature, temporal and spatial scales and duration of expected impacts based on reasonably conservative assumptions.

14 An analysis of each disposal option should be considered in the light of a comparative assessment of the following concerns: human health risks, environmental costs, hazards, (including accidents), economics and exclusion of future uses. If this assessment reveals that adequate information is not available to determine the likely effects of the proposed disposal option then this option should not be considered further. In addition, if the interpretation of the comparative assessment shows the dumping option to be less preferable, a permit for dumping should not be given.

15 Each assessment should conclude with a statement supporting a decision to issue or refuse a permit for dumping.

MONITORING

16 Monitoring is used to verify that permit conditions are met – compliance monitoring – and that the assumptions made during the permit review and site selection process were correct and sufficient to protect the environment and human health - field monitoring. It is essential that such monitoring programmes have clearly defined objectives.

PERMIT AND PERMIT CONDITIONS

17 A decision to issue a permit should only be made if all impact evaluations are completed and the monitoring requirements are determined. The provisions of the permit shall ensure, as far as practicable, that environmental disturbance and detriment are minimized and the benefits maximized. Any permit issued shall contain data and information specifying:

.1 the types and sources of materials to be dumped;

.2 the location of the dump-site(s);

.3 the method of dumping; and

.4 monitoring and reporting requirements.

18 Permits should be reviewed at regular intervals, taking into account the results of monitoring and the objectives of monitoring programmes. Review of monitoring results will indicate whether field programmes need to be continued, revised or terminated and will contribute to informed decisions regarding the continuance, modification or revocation of permits. This provides an important feedback mechanism for the protection of human health and the marine environment.

ANNEX 3 – ARBITRAL PROCEDURE

Article 1

1 An Arbitral Tribunal (hereinafter referred to as the "Tribunal") shall be established upon the request of a Contracting Party addressed to another Contracting Party in application of article 16 of this Protocol. The request for arbitration shall consist of a statement of the case together with any supporting documents.

2 The requesting Contracting Party shall inform the Secretary-General of:

.1 its request for arbitration; and

.2 the provisions of this Protocol the interpretation or application of which is, in its opinion, the subject of disagreement.

3 The Secretary-General shall transmit this information to all Contracting States.

Article 2

1 The Tribunal shall consist of a single arbitrator if so agreed between the parties to the dispute within 30 days from the date of receipt of the request for arbitration.

2 In the case of the death, disability or default of the arbitrator, the parties to a dispute may agree upon a replacement within 30 days of such death, disability or default.

Article 3

1 Where the parties to a dispute do not agree upon a Tribunal in accordance with article 2 of this Annex, the Tribunal shall consist of three members:

.1 one arbitrator nominated by each party to the dispute; and

.2 a third arbitrator who shall be nominated by agreement between the two first named and who shall act as its Chairman.

2 If the Chairman of a Tribunal is not nominated within 30 days of nomination of the second arbitrator, the parties to a dispute shall, upon the request of one party, submit to the Secretary-General within a further period of 30 days an agreed list of qualified persons. The Secretary-General shall select the Chairman from such list as soon as possible. He shall not select a Chairman who is or has been a national of one party to the dispute except with the consent of the other party to the dispute.

3 If one party to a dispute fails to nominate an arbitrator as provided in paragraph 1.1 within 60 days from the date of receipt of the request for arbitration, the other party may request the submission to the Secretary-General within a period of 30 days of an agreed list of qualified persons. The Secretary-General shall select the Chairman of the Tribunal from such list as soon as possible. The Chairman shall then request the party which has not nominated an arbitrator to do so. If this party does not nominate an arbitrator within 15 days of such request, the Secretary-General shall, upon request of the Chairman, nominate the arbitrator from the agreed list of qualified persons.

4 In the case of the death, disability or default of an arbitrator, the party to the dispute who nominated him shall nominate a replacement within 30 days of such death, disability or default. If the party does not nominate a replacement, the arbitration shall proceed with the remaining arbitrators. In the case of the death, disability or default of the Chairman, a replacement shall be nominated in accord-

ance with the provision of paragraphs 1.2 and 2 within 90 days of such death, disability or default.

5 A list of arbitrators shall be maintained by the Secretary-General and composed of qualified persons nominated by the Contracting Parties. Each Contracting Party may designate for inclusion in the list four persons who shall not necessarily be its nationals. If the parties to the dispute have failed within the specified time limits to submit to the Secretary-General an agreed list of qualified persons as provided for in paragraphs 2, 3 and 4, the Secretary-General shall select from the list maintained by him the arbitrator or arbitrators not yet nominated.

Article 4

The Tribunal may hear and determine counter-claims arising directly out of the subject matter of the dispute.

Article 5

Each party to the dispute shall be responsible for the costs entailed by the preparation of its own case. The remuneration of the members of the Tribunal and of all general expenses incurred by the arbitration shall be borne equally by the parties to the dispute. The Tribunal shall keep a record of all its expenses and shall furnish a final statement thereof to the parties.

Article 6

Any Contracting Party which has an interest of a legal nature which may be affected by the decision in the case may, after giving written notice to the parties to the dispute which have originally initiated the procedure, intervene in the arbitration procedure with the consent of the Tribunal and at its own expense. Any such intervenor shall have the right to present evidence, briefs and oral argument on the matters giving rise to its intervention, in accordance with procedures established pursuant to article 7 of this Annex, but shall have no rights with respect to the composition of the Tribunal.

Article 7

A Tribunal established under the provisions of this Annex shall decide its own rules of procedure.

Article 8

1 Unless a Tribunal consists of a single arbitrator, decisions of the Tribunal as to its procedure, its place of meeting, and any question related to the dispute laid before it, shall be taken by majority vote of its members. However, the absence or abstention of any member of the Tribunal who was nominated by a party to the dispute shall not constitute an impediment to the Tribunal reaching a decision. In case of equal voting, the vote of the Chairman shall be decisive.

2 The parties to the dispute shall facilitate the work of the Tribunal and in particular shall, in accordance with their legislation and using all means at their disposal:

.1 provide the Tribunal with all necessary documents and information; and

.2 enable the Tribunal to enter their territory, to hear witnesses or experts, and to visit the scene.

3 The failure of a party to the dispute to comply with the provisions of paragraph 2 shall not preclude the Tribunal from reaching a decision and rendering an award.

Article 9

The Tribunal shall render its award within five months from the time it is established unless it finds it necessary to extend that time limit for a period not to exceed five months. The award of the Tribunal shall be accompanied by a statement of reasons for the decision. It shall be final and without appeal and shall be communicated to the Secretary-General who shall inform the Contracting Parties. The parties to the dispute shall immediately comply with the award.

8.2. MARPOL 1973, as modified by the Protocol of 1978

International Convention for the Prevention of Pollution from Ships, 1973, Final Act of the International Conference on Marine Pollution, London, 2 November 1973; 1978 Protocol Relating to the 1973 International Convention for the Prevention of Pollution from Ships, London, 17 February 1978, 1340 UNTS 61

International Convention for the Prevention of Pollution from Ships, 1973, as modified

The Parties to the Convention

Being conscious of the need to preserve the human environment in general and the marine environment in particular,

Recognizing that deliberate, negligent or accidental release of oil and other harmful substances from ships constitutes a serious source of pollution,

Recognizing also the importance of the International Convention for the Prevention of Pollution of the Sea by Oil 1954, as being the first multilateral instrument to be concluded with the prime objective of protecting the environment, and appreciating the significant contribution which that Convention has made in preserving the seas and coastal environment from pollution,

Desiring to achieve the complete elimination of intentional pollution of the marine environment by oil and other harmful substances and the minimization of accidental discharge of such substances,

Considering that this object may best be achieved by establishing rules not limited to oil pollution having a universal purport,

Have agreed as follows:

Article 1 – General obligations under the Convention

1. The Parties to the Convention undertake to give effect to the provisions of the present Convention and those Annexes thereto by which they are bound, in order to prevent the pollution of the marine environment by the discharge of harmful substances or effluents containing such substances in contravention of the present Convention.
2. Unless expressly provided otherwise, a reference to the present Convention constitutes at the same time a reference to its Protocols and to the Annexes.

Article 2 – Definitions

For the purposes of the present Convention, unless expressly provided otherwise:

1. "Regulations" means the Regulations contained in the Annexes to the present Convention.
2. "Harmful substance" means any substance which, if introduced into the sea, is liable to create hazards to human health, to harm living resources and marine life, to damage amenities or to interfere with other legitimate uses of the sea, and includes any substance subject to control by the present Convention.
3. (a) "Discharge", in relation to harmful substances or effluents containing such substances, means any release howsoever caused from a ship and includes any escape, disposal, spilling, leaking, pumping, emitting or emptying;
   (b) "Discharge" does not include:
      (i) dumping within the meaning of the Convention on the Prevention of Marine Pollution by Dumping of Wastes and Other Matter, done at London on 13 November 1972; or
      (ii) release of harmful substances directly arising from the exploration, exploitation and associated off-shore processing of sea-bed mineral resources; or
      (iii) release of harmful substances for purposes of legitimate scientific research into pollution abatement or control.
4. "Ship" means a vessel of any type whatsoever operating in the marine environment and includes hydrofoil boats, air-cushion vehicles, submersibles, floating craft and fixed or floating platforms.
5. "Administration" means the Government of the State under whose authority the ship is operating. With respect to a ship entitled to fly a flag of any State, the Administration is the Government of that State. With respect to fixed or floating platforms engaged in exploration and exploitation of the sea-bed and subsoil thereof adjacent to the coast over which the coastal State exercises sovereign rights for the purposes of exploration and exploitation of their natural resources, the Administration is the Government of the coastal State concerned.
6. "Incident" means an event involving the actual or probably discharge into the sea of a harmful substance, or effluents containing such a substance.
7. "Organization" means the Inter-Governmental Maritime Consultative Organization.

Article 3 – Application

1. The present Convention shall apply to:
   (a) ships entitled to fly the flag of a Party to the Convention; and
   (b) ships not entitled to fly the flag of a party but which operate under the authority of a Party.

2. Nothing in the present Article shall be construed as derogating from or extending the sovereign rights of the Parties under international law over the sea-bed and subsoil thereof adjacent to their coasts for the purposes of exploration and exploitation of their natural resources.
3. The present Convention shall not apply to any warship, naval auxiliary or other ship owned or operated by a State and used, for the time being, only on government non-commercial service. However, each Party shall ensure by the adoption of appropriate measures not impairing the operations or operational capabilities of such ships owned or operated by it, that such ships act in a manner consistent, so far as is reasonable and practicable, with the present Convention.

Article 4 – Violation

1. Any violation of the requirements of the present Convention shall be prohibited and sanctions shall be established therefor under the law of the Administration of the ship concerned wherever the violation occurs. If the Administration is informed of such a violation and is satisfied that sufficient evidence is available to enable proceedings to be brought in respect of the alleged violation, it shall cause such proceedings to be taken as soon as possible, in accordance with its law.
2. Any violation of the requirements of the present Convention within the jurisdiction of any Party to the Convention shall be prohibited and sanctions shall be established therefor under the law of that Party. Whenever such a violation occurs, that Party shall either:
   (a) cause proceedings to be taken in accordance with its law; or
   (b) furnish to the Administration of the ship such information and evidence as may be in its possession that a violation has occurred.
3. Where information or evidence with respect to any violation of the present Convention by a ship is furnished to the Administration of that ship, the Administration shall promptly inform the Party which has furnished the information or evidence, and the Organization, of the action taken.
4. The penalties specified under the law of a Party pursuant to the present Article shall be adequate in severity to discourage violations of the present Convention and shall be equally severe irrespective of where the violations occur.

Article 5 – Certificates and special rules on inspection of ships

1. Subject to the provisions of paragraph (2) of the present Article a certificate issued under the authority of a Party to the Convention in accordance with the provisions of the Regulations shall be accepted by the other Parties and regarded for all purposes covered by the present Convention as having the same validity as a certificate issued by them.
2. A ship required to hold a certificate in accordance with the provisions of the Regulations is subject, while in the ports or off-shore terminals under the jurisdiction of a Party, to inspection by officers duly authorized by that Party. Any such inspection shall be limited to verifying that there is on board a valid certificate, unless there are clear grounds for believing that the condition of the ship or its equipment does not correspond substantially with the particulars of that certificate. In that case, or if the ship does not carry a valid certificate, the Party carrying out the inspection shall take such steps as will ensure that the ship shall not sail until it can proceed to sea without presenting an unreasonable threat of harm to the marine environment. That Party may, however, grant such a ship permission to leave the port or off-shore terminal for the purpose of proceeding to the nearest appropriate repair yard available.
3. If a Party denies a foreign ship entry to the ports or off-shore terminals under its jurisdiction or takes any action against such a ship for the reasons that the ship does not comply with the provisions of the present Convention, the Party shall immediately inform the consul or diplomatic representative of the Party whose flag the ship is entitled to fly, or if this is not possible, the Administration of the ship concerned. Before denying entry or taking such action the Party may request consultation with the Administration of the ship concerned. Information shall also be given to the Administration when a ship does not carry a valid certificate in accordance with the provisions of the Regulations.
4. With respect to the ships of non-Parties to the Convention, Parties shall apply the requirements of the present Convention as may be necessary to ensure that no more favourable treatment is given to such ships.

Article 6 – Detection of violations and enforcement of the Convention

1. Parties to the Convention shall co-operate in the detection of violations and the enforcement of the provisions of the present Convention, using all appropriate and practicable measures of detection and environmental monitoring, adequate procedures for reporting and accumulation of evidence.
2. A ship to which the present Convention applies may, in any port or off-shore terminal of a Party, be subject to inspection by officers appointed or authorized by that Party for the purpose of verifying whether the ship has discharged any harmful substances in violation of the provisions of the Regulations. If an inspection indicates a violation of the Convention, a report shall be forwarded to the Administration for any appropriate action.
3. Any Party shall furnish to the Administration evidence, if any, that the ship has discharged harmful substances or effluents containing such substances in violation of the provisions of the Regulations. If it is practicable to do so, the competent authority of the former Party shall notify the Master of the ship of the alleged violation.
4. Upon receiving such evidence, the Administration so informed shall investigate the matter, and may request the other Party to furnish further or better

evidence of the alleged contravention. If the Administration is satisfied that sufficient evidence is available to enable proceedings to be brought in respect of the alleged violation, it shall cause such proceedings to be taken in accordance with its law as soon as possible. The Administration shall promptly inform the Party which has reported the alleged violation, as well as the Organization, of the action taken.

5. A Party may also inspect a ship to which the present Convention applies when it enters the ports or off-shore terminals under its jurisdiction, if a request for an investigation is received from any Party together with sufficient evidence that the ship has discharged harmful substances or effluents containing such substances in any place. The report of such investigation shall be sent to the Party requesting it and to the Administration so that the appropriate action may be taken under the present Convention.

Article 7 – Undue delay to ships

1. All possible efforts shall be made to avoid a ship being unduly detained or delayed under Article 4, 5 or 6 of the present Convention.
2. When a ship is unduly detained or delayed under Article 4, 5 or 6 of the present Convention, it shall be entitled to compensation for any loss or damage suffered.

Article 8 – Reports on incidents involving harmful substances

1. A report of an incident shall be made without delay to the fullest extent possible in accordance with the provisions of Protocol I to the present Convention.
2. Each Party to the Convention shall:
   (a) make all arrangements necessary for an appropriate officer or agency to receive and process all reports on incidents; and
   (b) notify the Organization with complete details of such arrangements for circulation to other Parties and Member States of the Organization.
3. Whenever a Party receives a report under the provisions of the present Article, that Party shall relay the report without delay to:
   (a) the Administration of the ship involved; and
   (b) any other State which may be affected.
4. Each Party to the Convention undertakes to issue instructions to its maritime inspection vessels and aircraft and to other appropriate services, to report to its authorities any incident referred to in Protocol I to the present Convention. That Party shall, if it considers it appropriate, report accordingly to the Organization and to any other party concerned.

Article 9 – Other treaties and interpretation

1. Upon its entry into force, the present Convention supersedes the International Convention for the Prevention of Pollution of the Sea by Oil, 1954, as amended, as between Parties to that Convention.
2. Nothing in the present Convention shall prejudice the codification and development of the law of the sea by the United Nations Conference on the Law of the Sea convened pursuant to Resolution 2750C(XXV) of the General Assembly of the United Nations nor the present or future claims and legal views of any State concerning the law of the sea and the nature and extent of coastal and flag State jurisdiction.
3. The term "jurisdiction" in the present Convention shall be construed in the light of international law in force at the time of application or interpretation of the present Convention.

Article 10 – Settlement of disputes

Any dispute between two or more Parties to the Convention concerning the interpretation or application of the present Convention shall, if settlement by negotiation between the Parties involved has not been possible, and if these Parties do not otherwise agree, be submitted upon request of any of them to arbitration as set out in Protocol II to the present Convention.

Article 11 – Communication of information

1. The Parties to the Convention undertake to communicate to the Organization:
   (a) the text of laws, orders, decrees and regulations and other instruments which have been promulgated on the various matters within the scope of the present Convention;
   (b) a list of nominated surveyors or recognized organizations which are authorized to act on their behalf in the administration of matters relating to the design, construction, equipment and operation of ships carrying harmful substances in accordance with the provisions of the Regulations for circulation to the Parties for information of their officers. The Administration shall therefore notify the Organization of the specific responsibilities and conditions of the authority delegated to nominated surveyors or recognized organizations.[1]
   (c) a sufficient number of specimens of their certificates issued under the provisions of the Regulations;
   (d) a list of reception facilities including their location, capacity and available facilities and other characteristics;
   (e) official reports or summaries of official reports in so far as they show the results of the application of the present Convention; and
   (f) an annual statistical report, in a form standardized by the Organization, of penalties actually imposed for infringement of the present Convention.
2. The Organization shall notify Parties of the receipt of any communications under the present Article

1 The original provision prior to the 1978 amendment reads "a list of non-governmental agencies which are authorized to act on their behalf in matters relating to the design, construction and equipment of ships carrying harmful substances in accordance with the provisions of the regulations" [the editors].

and circulate to all Parties any information communicated to it under sub-paragraphs (1)(b) to (f) of the present Article.

Article 12 – Casualties to ships

1. Each Administration undertakes to conduct an investigation of any casualty occurring to any of its ships subject to the provisions of the Regulations if such casualty has produced a major deleterious effect upon the marine environment.
2. Each Party to the Convention undertakes to supply the Organization with information concerning the findings of such investigation, when it judges that such information may assist in determining what changes in the present Convention might be desirable.

Article 13 – Signature, ratification, acceptance, approval and accession

1. The present Convention shall remain open for signature at the Headquarters of the Organization from 15 January 1974 until 31 December 1974 and shall thereafter remain open for accession. States may become Parties to the present Convention by:
   (a) signature without reservation as to ratification, acceptance or approval; or
   (b) signature subject to ratification, acceptance or approval, followed by ratification, acceptance or approval; or
   (c) accession.
2. Ratification, acceptance, approval or accession shall be effected by the deposit of an instrument to that effect with the Secretary-General of the Organization.
3. The Secretary-General of the Organization shall inform all States which have signed the present Convention or acceded to it of any signature or of the deposit of any new instrument of ratification, acceptance, approval or accession and the date of its deposit.

Article 14 – Optional Annexes

1. A State may at the time of signing, ratifying, accepting, approving or acceding to the present Convention declare that it does not accept any one or all of Annexes III, IV and V (hereinafter referred to as "Optional Annexes") to the present Convention. Subject to the above, Parties to the Convention shall be bound by any Annex in its entirety.
2. A State which has declared that it is not bound by an Optional Annex may at any time accept such Annex by depositing with the Organization an instrument of the kind referred to in Article 13(2) of the present Convention.
3. A State which makes a declaration under paragraph (1) of the present Article in respect of an Optional Annex and which has not subsequently accepted that Annex in accordance with paragraph (2) of the present Article shall not be under any obligation nor entitled to claim any privileges under the present Convention in respect of matters related to such Annex and all references to Parties in the present Convention shall not include that State in so far as matters related to such Annex are concerned.
4. The Organization shall inform the States which have signed or acceded to the present Convention of any declaration under the present Article as well as the receipt of any instrument deposited in accordance with the provisions of paragraph (2) of the present Article.

Article 15 – Entry into force

1. The present Convention shall enter into force twelve months after the date on which not less than fifteen States, the combined merchant fleets of which constitute not less than fifty per cent of the gross tonnage of the world's merchant shipping, have become parties to it in accordance with Article 13 of the present Convention.
2. An Optional Annex shall enter into force twelve months after the date on which the conditions stipulated in paragraph (1) of the present Article have been satisfied in relation to that Annex.
3. The Organization shall inform the States which have signed the present Convention or acceded to it of the date on which it enters into force and of the date on which an Optional Annex enters into force in accordance with paragraph (2) of the present Article.
4. For States which have deposited an instrument of ratification, acceptance, approval or accession in respect of the present Convention or any Optional Annex after the requirements for entry into force thereof have been met but prior to the date of entry into force, the ratification, acceptance, approval or accession shall take effect on the date of entry into force of the Convention or such Annex or three months after the date of deposit of the instrument whichever is the later date.
5. For States which have deposited an instrument of ratification, acceptance, approval or accession after the date on which the Convention or an Optional Annex entered into force, the Convention or the Optional Annex shall become effective three months after the date of deposit of the instrument.
6. After the date on which all the conditions required under Article 16 to bring an amendment to the present Convention or an Optional Annex into force have been fulfilled, any instrument of ratification, acceptance, approval or accession deposited shall apply to the Convention or Annex as amended.

Article 16 – Amendments

1. The present Convention may be amended by any of the procedures specified in the following paragraphs.
2. Amendments after consideration by the Organization:
   (a) any amendment proposed by a Party to the Convention shall be submitted to the Organization and circulated by its Secretary-General to all Members of the Organization and all Parties at least six months prior to its consideration;

(b) any amendment proposed and circulated as above shall be submitted to an appropriate body by the Organization for consideration;

(c) Parties to the Convention, whether or not Members of the Organization, shall be entitled to participate in the proceedings of the appropriate body;

(d) amendments shall be adopted by a two-thirds majority of only the Parties to the Convention present and voting;

(e) if adopted in accordance with sub-paragraph (d) of this paragraph, amendments shall be communicated by the Secretary-General of the Organization to all the Parties to the Convention for acceptance;

(f) an amendment shall be deemed to have been accepted in the following circumstances:

(i) an amendment to an Article of the Convention shall be deemed to have been accepted on the date on which it is accepted by two-thirds of the Parties, the combined merchant fleets of which constitute not less than fifty per cent of the gross tonnage of the world's merchant fleet;

(ii) an amendment to an Annex to the Convention shall be deemed to have been accepted in accordance with the procedures specified in sub-paragraph (f)(iii) of this paragraph unless the appropriate body, at the time of its adoption, determines that the amendment shall be deemed to have been accepted on the date on which it is accepted by two-thirds of the Parties, the combined merchant fleets of which constitute not less than fifty per cent of the gross tonnage of the world's merchant fleet. Nevertheless, at any time before the entry into force of an amendment to an Annex to the Convention, a Party may notify the Secretary-General of the Organization that its express approval will be necessary before the amendment enters into force for it. The latter shall bring such notification and the date of its receipt to the notice of Parties;

(iii) an amendment to an Appendix to an Annex to the Convention shall be deemed to have been accepted at the end of a period to be determined by the appropriate body at the time of its adoption, which period shall not be less than ten months, unless within that period an objection is communicated to the Organization by not less than one-third of the Parties or by Parties the combined merchant fleets of which constitute not less than fifty per cent of the gross tonnage of the world's merchant fleet whichever condition is fulfilled;

(iv) an amendment to Protocol I to the Convention shall be subject to the same procedures as for the amendments to the Annexes to the Convention, as provided for in sub-paragraphs (f)(ii) or (f)(iii) of this paragraph;

(v) an amendment to Protocol II to the Convention shall be subject to the same procedures as for the amendments to an Article of the Convention, as provided for in sub-paragraph (f)(i) of this paragraph;

(g) the amendment shall enter into force under the following conditions:

(i) in the case of an amendment to an Article of the Convention, to Protocol II, or to Protocol I or to an Annex to the Convention not under the procedure specified in sub-paragraph (f)(iii) of this paragraph, the amendment accepted in conformity with the foregoing provisions shall enter into force six months after the date of its acceptance with respect to the Parties which have declared that they have accepted it;

(ii) in the case of an amendment to Protocol I, to an Appendix to an Annex or to an Annex to the Convention under the procedure specified in sub-paragraph (f)(iii) of this paragraph, the amendment deemed to have been accepted in accordance with the foregoing conditions shall enter into force six months after its acceptance for all the Parties with the exception of those which, before that date, have made a declaration that they do not accept it, or a declaration under sub-paragraph (f)(ii) of this paragraph, that their express approval is necessary.

3. Amendment by a Conference:

(a) Upon the request of a Party, concurred in by at least one-third of the Parties, the Organization shall convene a Conference of Parties to the Convention to consider amendments to the present Convention.

(b) Every amendment adopted by such a Conference by a two-thirds majority of those present and voting of the Parties shall be communicated by the Secretary-General of the Organization to all Contracting Parties for their acceptance.

(c) Unless the Conference decides otherwise, the amendment shall be deemed to have been accepted and to have entered into force in accordance with the procedures specified for that purpose in sub-paragraphs (2)(f) and (g) of the present Article.

4. (a) In the case of an amendment to an Optional Annex, a reference in the present Article to a "Party to the Convention" shall be deemed to mean a reference to a Party bound by that Annex.

(b) Any Party which has declined to accept an amendment to an Annex shall be treated as a non-Party only for the purpose of application of that Amendment.

5. The adoption and entry into force of a new Annex shall be subject to the same procedures as for the adoption and entry into force of an amendment to an Article of the Convention.
6. Unless expressly provided otherwise, any amendment to the present Convention made under this Article, which relates to the structure of a ship, shall apply only to ships for which the building contract is placed, or in the absence of a building contract, the keel of which is laid, on or after the date on which the amendment comes into force.
7. Any amendment to a Protocol or to an Annex shall relate to the substance of that Protocol or Annex and shall be consistent with the Articles of the present Convention.
8. The Secretary-General of the Organization shall inform all Parties of any amendments which enter into force under the present Article, together with the date on which each such amendment enters into force.
9. Any declaration of acceptance or of objection to an amendment under the present Article shall be notified in writing to the Secretary-General of the Organization. The latter shall bring such notification and the date of its receipt to the notice of the Parties to the Convention.

Article 17 – Promotion of technical co-operation

The Parties to the Convention shall promote, in consultation with the Organization and other international bodies, with assistance and co-ordination by the Executive Director of the United Nations Environment Programme, support for those Parties which request technical assistance for:

a. the training of scientific and technical personnel;
b. the supply of necessary equipment and facilities for reception and monitoring;
c. the facilitation of other measures and arrangements to prevent or mitigate pollution of the marine environment by ships; and
d. the encouragement of research;

preferably within the countries concerned, so furthering the aims and purposes of the present Convention.

Article 18 – Denunciation

The present convention or any Optional Annex may be denounced by any Parties to the Convention at any time after the expiry of five years from the date on which the Convention or such Annex enters into force for that Party.

2. Denunciation shall be effected by notification in writing to the Secretary-General of the Organization who shall inform all the other Parties of any such notification received and of the date of its receipt as well as the date on which such denunciation takes effect.
3. A denunciation shall take effect twelve months after receipt of the notification of denunciation by the Secretary-General of the Organization or after the expiry of any other longer period which may be indicated in the notification.

Article 19 – Deposit and registration

1. The present Convention shall be deposited with the Secretary-General of the Organization who shall transmit certified true copies thereof to all States which have signed the present Convention or acceded to it.
2. As soon as the present Convention enters into force, the text shall be transmitted by the Secretary-General of the Organization to the Secretary-General of the United Nations for registration and publication, in accordance with Article 102 of the Charter of the United Nations.

Article 20 – Languages

The present Convention is established in a single copy in the English, French, Russian and Spanish languages, each text being equally authentic. Official translations in the Arabic, German, Italian and Japanese languages shall be prepared and deposited with the signed original.

In witness whereof the undersigned being duly authorized by their respective Governments for that purpose have signed the present Convention.

Done at London this second day of November, one thousand nine hundred and seventy-three.

Protocol I - Provisions concerning reports on incidents involving harmful substances

(in accordance with Article 8 of the Convention)

Article I – Duty to report

1. The Master or other person having charge of any ship involved in an incident referred to in Article II of this Protocol shall report the particulars of such incident without delay and to the fullest extent possible in accordance with the provisions of this Protocol.
2. In the event of the ship referred to in paragraph (1) of this Article being abandoned, or in the event of a report from such a ship being incomplete or unobtainable, the owner, charterer, manager or operator of the ship, or their agent shall, to the fullest extent possible, assume the obligations placed upon the Master under the provisions of this Protocol.

Article II – When to make reports

1. The report shall be made when an incident involves:
   (a) a discharge or probable discharge of oil, or noxious liquid substances carried in bulk, resulting from damage to the ship or its equipment, or for the purpose of securing the safety of a ship or saving life at sea; or
   (b) a discharge or probable discharge of harmful substances in packaged form, including those in freight containers, portable tanks, road and rail vehicles and shipborne barges; or
   (c) a discharge during the operation of the ship of oil or noxious liquid substances in excess of the

quantity or instantaneous rate permitted under the present Convention.

2. For the purposes of this Protocol:
   (a) "Oil" referred to in sub-paragraph 1(a) of this Article means oil as defined in Regulation 1(1) of Annex I of the Convention.
   (b) "Noxious liquid substances" referred to in sub-paragraph 1(a) of this Article means noxious liquid substances as defined in Regulation 1(6) of Annex II of the Convention.
   (c) "Harmful substances" in packaged form referred to in sub-paragraph 1(b) of this Article means substances which are identified as marine pollutants in the International Maritime Dangerous Goods (IMDG) Code.

Article III – Contents of report

Reports shall in any case include:

a. identity of ships involved;
b. time, type and location of incident;
c. quantity and type of harmful substance involved;
d. assistance and salvage measures.

Article IV – Supplementary report

Any person who is obliged under the provisions of this Protocol to send a report shall, when possible:

a. supplement the initial report, as necessary, and provide information concerning further developments; and
b. comply as fully as possible with requests from affected States for additional information.

Article V – Reporting procedures

1. Reports shall be made by the fastest telecommunications channels available with the highest possible priority to the nearest coastal State.
2. In order to implement the provisions of this Protocol, Parties to the present Convention shall issue, or cause to be issued, regulations or instructions on the procedures to be followed in reporting incidents involving harmful substances, based on guidelines developed by the Organization.

Protocol II - Arbitration (in accordance with Article 10 of the Convention)

Article I

Arbitration procedure, unless the Parties to the dispute decide otherwise, shall be in accordance with the rules set out in this Protocol.

Article II

1. An Arbitration Tribunal shall be established upon the request of one Party to the Convention addressed to another in application of Article 10 of the present Convention. The request for arbitration shall consist of a statement of the case together with any supporting documents.
2. The requesting Party shall inform the Secretary-General of the Organization of the fact that it has applied for the establishment of a Tribunal, of the names of the Parties to the dispute, and of the Articles of the Convention or Regulations over which there is in its opinion disagreement concerning their interpretation or application. The Secretary-General shall transmit this information to all Parties.

Article III

The Tribunal shall consist of three members: one Arbitrator nominated by each Party to the dispute and a third Arbitrator who shall be nominated by agreement between the two first named, and shall act as its Chairman.

Article IV

1. If, at the end of a period of sixty days from the nomination of the second Arbitrator, the Chairman of the Tribunal shall not have been nominated, the Secretary-General of the Organization upon request of either Party shall within a further period of sixty days proceed to such nomination, selecting him from a list of qualified persons previously drawn up by the Council of the Organization.
2. If, within a period of sixty days from the date of receipt of the request, one of the Parties shall not have nominated the member of the Tribunal for whose designation it is responsible, the other party may directly inform the Secretary-General of the Organization who shall nominate the Chairman of the Tribunal within a period of sixty days, selecting him from the list prescribed in paragraph (1) of the present Article.
3. The Chairman of the Tribunal shall, upon nomination, request the Party which has not provided an Arbitrator, to do so in the same manner and under the same conditions. If the Party does not make the required nomination, the Chairman of the Tribunal shall request the Secretary-General of the Organization to make the nomination in the form and conditions prescribed in the preceding paragraph.
4. The Chairman of the Tribunal, if nominated under the provisions of the present Article, shall not be or have been a national of one of the Parties concerned, except with the consent of the other Party.
5. In the case of the decease or default of an Arbitrator for whose nomination one of the Parties is responsible, the said Party shall nominate a replacement within a period of sixty days from the date of decease or default. Should the said Party not make the nomination, the arbitration shall proceed under the remaining Arbitrators. In case of the decease or default of the Chairman of the Tribunal, a replacement shall be nominated in accordance with the provisions of Article III above, or in the absence of agreement between the members of the Tribunal within a period of sixty days of the decease or default, according to the provisions of the present Article.

Article V

The Tribunal may hear and determine counter-claims arising directly out of the subject matter of the dispute.

Article VI

Each Party shall be responsible for the remuneration of its Arbitrator and connected costs and for the costs entailed by the preparation of its own case. The remuneration of the Chairman of the Tribunal and of all general expenses incurred by the Arbitration shall be borne equally by the Parties. The Tribunal shall keep a record of all its expenses and shall furnish a final statement thereof.

Article VII

Any Party to the Convention which has an interest of a legal nature and which may be affected by the decision in the case may, after giving written notice to the Parties which have originally initiated the procedure, join in the arbitration procedure with the consent of the Tribunal.

Article VIII

Any Arbitration Tribunal established under the provisions of the present Protocol shall decide its own rules of procedure.

Article IX

1. Decisions of the Tribunal both as to its procedure and its place of meeting and as to any question laid before it, shall be taken by majority votes of its members; the absence or abstention of one of the members of the Tribunal for whose nomination the Parties were responsible, shall not constitute an impediment to the Tribunal reaching a decision. In cases of equal voting, the vote of the Chairman shall be decisive.
2. The Parties shall facilitate the work of the Tribunal and in particular, in accordance with their legislation, and using all means at their disposal:
   (a) provide the Tribunal with the necessary documents and information;
   (b) enable the Tribunal to enter their territory, to hear witnesses or experts, and to visit the scene.
3. Absence or default of one Party shall not constitute an impediment to the procedure.

Article X

1. The Tribunal shall render its award within a period of five months from the time it is established unless it decides, in the case of necessity, to extend the time limit for a further period not exceeding three months. The award of the Tribunal shall be accompanied by a statement of reasons. It shall be final and without appeal and shall be communicated to the Secretary-General of the Organization. The Parties shall immediately comply with the award.
2. Any controversy which may arise between the Parties as regards interpretation or execution of the award may be submitted by either Party for judgment to the Tribunal which made the award, or, if it is not available to another Tribunal constituted for this purpose, in the same manner as the original Tribunal.

1978 Protocol Relating to the 1973 International Convention for the Prevention of Pollution from Ships

The Parties to the present Protocol,

Recognizing the significant contribution which can be made by the International Convention for the Prevention of Pollution from Ships, 1973, to the protection of the marine environment from pollution from ships,

Recognizing also the need to improve further the prevention and control of marine pollution from ships, particularly oil tankers,

Recognizing further the need for implementing the Regulations for the Prevention of Pollution by Oil contained in Annex I of that Convention as early and as widely as possible,

Acknowledging however the need to defer the application of Annex II of that Convention until certain technical problems have been satisfactorily resolved,

Considering that these objectives may best be achieved by the conclusion of a Protocol relating to the International Convention for the Prevention of Pollution from Ships, 1973,

Have agreed as follows:

Article I. GENERAL OBLIGATIONS

1. The Parties to the present Protocol undertake to give effect to the provisions of:
   (a) The present Protocol and the Annex hereto which shall constitute an integral part of the present Protocol; and
   (b) The International Convention for the Prevention of Pollution from Ships, 1973 (hereinafter referred to as "the Convention"), subject to the modifications and additions set out in the present Protocol.
2. The provisions of the Convention and the present Protocol shall be read and interpreted together as one single instrument.
3. Every reference to the present Protocol constitutes at the same time a reference to the Annex hereto.

Article II. IMPLEMENTATION OF ANNEX II OF THE CONVENTION

1. Notwithstanding the provisions of Article 14(1) of the Convention, the Parties to the present Protocol agree that they shall not be bound by the provisions of Annex II of the Convention for a period of three years from the date of entry into force of the present Protocol or for such longer period as may be decided by a two-thirds majority of the Parties to the present Protocol in the Marine Environment Protection Committee (hereinafter referred to as "the Committee") of the Inter-Governmental Maritime Consultative Organization (hereinafter referred to as "the Organization").
2. During the period specified in paragraph I of this Article, the Parties to the present Protocol shall not be under any obligations nor entitled to claim any privileges under the Convention in respect of matters relating to Annex II of the Convention and

all reference to Parties in the Convention shall not include the Parties to the present Protocol in so far as matters relating to that Annex are concerned.

Article III. COMMUNICATION OF INFORMATION

The text of Article II (1) (b) of the Convention is replaced by the following: "A list of nominated surveyors or recognized organizations which are authorized to act on their behalf in the administration of matters relating to the design, construction, equipment and operation of ships carrying harmful substances in accordance with the provisions of the Regulations for circulation to the Parties for information of their officers. The Administration shall therefore notify the Organization of the specific responsibilities and conditions of the authority delegated to nominated surveyors or recognized organizations."

Article IV. SIGNATURE, RATIFICATION, ACCEPTANCE, APPROVAL AND ACCESSION

1. The present Protocol shall be open for signature at the Headquarters of the Organization from 1 June 1978 to 31 May 1979 and shall thereafter remain open for accession. States may become Parties to the present Protocol by:
   (a) Signature without reservation as to ratification, acceptance or approval; or
   (b) Signature, subject to ratification, acceptance or approval, followed by ratification, acceptance or approval; or
   (c) Accession.
2. Ratification, acceptance, approval or accession shall be effected by the deposit of an instrument to that effect with the Secretary-General of the Organization.

Article V. ENTRY INTO FORCE

1. The present Protocol shall enter into force twelve months after the date on which not less than fifteen States, the combined merchant fleets of which constitute not less than fifty per cent of the gross tonnage of the world's merchant shipping, have become Parties to it in accordance with Article IV of the present Protocol.
2. Any instrument of ratification, acceptance, approval or accession deposited after the date on which the present Protocol enters into force shall take effect three months after the date of deposit.
3. After the date on which an amendment to the present Protocol is deemed to have been accepted in accordance with Article 16 of the Convention, any instrument of ratification, acceptance, approval or accession deposited shall apply to the present Protocol as amended.

Article VI. AMENDMENTS

The procedures set out in Article 16 of the Convention in respect of amend ments to the Articles, an Annex and an Appendix to an Annex of the Convention shall apply respectively to amendments to the Articles, the Annex and an Appendix to the Annex of the present Protocol.

Article VII. DENUNCIATION

1. The present Protocol may be denounced by any Party to the present Protocol at any time after the expiry of five years from the date on which the Protocol enters into force for that Party.
2. Denunciation shall be effected by the deposit of an instrument of denunciation with the Secretary-General of the Organization.
3. A denunciation shall take effect twelve months after receipt of the notification by the Secretary-General of the Organization or after the expiry of any other longer period which may be indicated in the notification.

Article VIII. DEPOSITARY

1. The present Protocol shall be deposited with the Secretary-General of the Organization (hereinafter referred to as "the Depositary").
2. The Depositary shall:
   (a) Inform all States which have signed the present Protocol or acceded thereto of:
      (i) Each new signature or deposit of an instrument of ratification, acceptance, approval or accession, together with the date thereof;
      (ii) The date of entry into force of the present Protocol;
      (iii) The deposit of any instrument of denunciation of the present Protocol together with the date on which it was received and the date on which the denunciation takes effect;
      (iv) Any decision made in accordance with Article II(1) of the present Protocol;
   (b) Transmit certified true copies of the present Protocol to all States which have signed the present Protocol or acceded thereto.
3. As soon as the present Protocol enters into force, a certified true copy thereof shall be transmitted by the Depositary to the Secretariat of the United Nations for registration and publication in accordance with Article 102 of the Charter of the United Nations.

Article IX. LANGUAGES

The present Protocol is established in a single original in the English, French, Russian and Spanish languages, each text being equally authentic. Official translations in the Arabic, German, Italian and Japanese languages shall be prepared and deposited with the signed original.

IN WITNESS WHEREOF the undersigned being duly authorized by their respective Governments for that purpose have signed the present Protocol. DONE at London this seventeenth day of February one thousand nine hundred and seventy-eight.

8.3.1. UNCLOS 1982

United Nations Convention on the Law of the Sea, Montego Bay, 10 December 1982, 1833 UNTS 397

The States Parties to this Convention,

Prompted by the desire to settle, in a spirit of mutual understanding and cooperation, all issues relating to the law of the sea and aware of the historic significance of this Convention as an important contribution to the maintenance of peace, justice and progress for all peoples of the world,

Noting that developments since the United Nations Conferences on the Law of the Sea held at Geneva in 1958 and 1960 have accentuated the need for a new and generally acceptable Convention on the law of the sea,

Conscious that the problems of ocean space are closely interrelated and need to be considered as a whole,

Recognizing the desirability of establishing through this Convention, with due regard for the sovereignty of all States, a legal order for the seas and oceans which will facilitate international communication, and will promote the peaceful uses of the seas and oceans, the equitable and efficient utilization of their resources, the conservation of their living resources, and the study, protection and preservation of the marine environment,

Bearing in mind that the achievement of these goals will contribute to the realization of a just and equitable international economic order which takes into account the interests and needs of mankind as a whole and, in particular, the special interests and needs of developing countries, whether coastal or land-locked,

Desiring by this Convention to develop the principles embodied in resolution 2749 (XXV) of 17 December 1970 in which the General Assembly of the United Nations solemnly declared inter alia that the area of the seabed and ocean floor and the subsoil thereof, beyond the limits of national jurisdiction, as well as its resources, are the common heritage of mankind, the exploration and exploitation of which shall be carried out for the benefit of mankind as a whole, irrespective of the geographical location of States,

Believing that the codification and progressive development of the law of the sea achieved in this Convention will contribute to the strengthening of peace, security, cooperation and friendly relations among all nations in conformity with the principles of justice and equal rights and will promote the economic and social advancement of all peoples of the world, in accordance with the Purposes and Principles of the United Nations as set forth in the Charter,

Affirming that matters not regulated by this Convention continue to be governed by the rules and principles of general international law,

Have agreed as follows:

PART I – INTRODUCTION

Article 1 – Use of terms and scope

1. For the purposes of this Convention:

   (1) "Area" means the seabed and ocean floor and subsoil thereof, beyond the limits of national jurisdiction;

   (2) "Authority" means the International Seabed Authority;

   (3) "activities in the Area" means all activities of exploration for, and exploitation of, the resources of the Area;

   (4) "pollution of the marine environment" means the introduction by man, directly or indirectly, of substances or energy into the marine environment, including estuaries, which results or is likely to result in such deleterious effects as harm to living resources and marine life, hazards to human health, hindrance to marine activities, including fishing and other legitimate uses of the sea, impairment of quality for use of sea water and reduction of amenities;

   (5) (a) "dumping" means:

   (i) any deliberate disposal of wastes or other matter from vessels, aircraft, platforms or other man-made structures at sea;

   (ii) any deliberate disposal of vessels, aircraft, platforms or other man-made structures at sea;

   (b) "dumping" does not include:

   (i) the disposal of wastes or other matter incidental to, or derived from the normal operations of vessels, aircraft, platforms or other man-made structures at sea and their equipment, other than wastes or other matter transported by or to vessels, aircraft, platforms or other man-made structures at sea, operating for the purpose of disposal of such matter or derived from the treatment of such wastes or other matter on such vessels, aircraft, platforms or structures;

   (ii) placement of matter for a purpose other than the mere disposal thereof, provided that such placement is not contrary to the aims of this Convention.

2. (1) "States Parties" means States which have consented to be bound by this Convention and for which this Convention is in force.

   (2) This Convention applies mutatis mutandis to the entities referred to in article 305, paragraph l(b), (c), (d), (e) and (f), which become Par-

ties to this Convention in accordance with the conditions relevant to each, and to that extent "States Parties" refers to those entities.

PART II – TERRITORIAL SEA AND CONTIGUOUS ZONE

SECTION 1. GENERAL PROVISIONS

Article 2 – Legal status of the territorial sea, of the air space over the territorial sea and of its bed and subsoil

1. The sovereignty of a coastal State extends, beyond its land territory and internal waters and, in the case of an archipelagic State, its archipelagic waters, to an adjacent belt of sea, described as the territorial sea.
2. This sovereignty extends to the air space over the territorial sea as well as to its bed and subsoil.
3. The sovereignty over the territorial sea is exercised subject to this Convention and to other rules of international law.

SECTION 2. LIMITS OF THE TERRITORIAL SEA

Article 3 – Breadth of the territorial sea

Every State has the right to establish the breadth of its territorial sea up to a limit not exceeding 12 nautical miles, measured from baselines determined in accordance with this Convention.

Article 4 – Outer limit of the territorial sea

The outer limit of the territorial sea is the line every point of which is at a distance from the nearest point of the baseline equal to the breadth of the territorial sea.

Article 5 – Normal baseline

Except where otherwise provided in this Convention, the normal baseline for measuring the breadth of the territorial sea is the low-water line along the coast as marked on large-scale charts officially recognized by the coastal State.

Article 6 – Reefs

In the case of islands situated on atolls or of islands having fringing reefs, the baseline for measuring the breadth of the territorial sea is the seaward low-water line of the reef, as shown by the appropriate symbol on charts officially recognized by the coastal State.

Article 7 – Straight baselines

1. In localities where the coastline is deeply indented and cut into, or if there is a fringe of islands along the coast in its immediate vicinity, the method of straight baselines joining appropriate points may be employed in drawing the baseline from which the breadth of the territorial sea is measured.
2. Where because of the presence of a delta and other natural conditions the coastline is highly unstable, the appropriate points may be selected along the furthest seaward extent of the low-water line and, notwithstanding subsequent regression of the low-water line, the straight baselines shall remain effective until changed by the coastal State in accordance with this Convention.
3. The drawing of straight baselines must not depart to any appreciable extent from the general direction of the coast, and the sea areas lying within the lines must be sufficiently closely linked to the land domain to be subject to the regime of internal waters.
4. Straight baselines shall not be drawn to and from low-tide elevations, unless lighthouses or similar installations which are permanently above sea level have been built on them or except in instances where the drawing of baselines to and from such elevations has received general international recognition.
5. Where the method of straight baselines is applicable under paragraph 1, account may be taken, in determining particular baselines, of economic interests peculiar to the region concerned, the reality and the importance of which are clearly evidenced by long usage.
6. The system of straight baselines may not be applied by a State in such a manner as to cut off the territorial sea of another State from the high seas or an exclusive economic zone.

Article 8 – Internal waters

1. Except as provided in Part IV, waters on the landward side of the baseline of the territorial sea form part of the internal waters of the State.
2. Where the establishment of a straight baseline in accordance with the method set forth in article 7 has the effect of enclosing as internal waters areas which had not previously been considered as such, a right of innocent passage as provided in this Convention shall exist in those waters.

Article 9 – Mouths of rivers

If a river flows directly into the sea, the baseline shall be a straight line across the mouth of the river between points on the low-water line of its banks.

Article 10 – Bays

1. This article relates only to bays the coasts of which belong to a single State.
2. For the purposes of this Convention, a bay is a well-marked indentation whose penetration is in such proportion to the width of its mouth as to contain land-locked waters and constitute more than a mere curvature of the coast. An indentation shall not, however, be regarded as a bay unless its area is as large as, or larger than, that of the semi-circle whose diameter is a line drawn across the mouth of that indentation.
3. For the purpose of measurement, the area of an indentation is that lying between the low-water mark around the shore of the indentation and a line joining the low-water mark of its natural entrance points. Where, because of the presence of islands, an indentation has more than one mouth, the semi-circle shall be drawn on a line as long as the sum total of the lengths of the lines across the different mouths. Islands within an indentation

shall be included as if they were part of the water area of the indentation.

4. If the distance between the low-water marks of the natural entrance points of a bay does not exceed 24 nautical miles, a closing line may be drawn between these two low-water marks, and the waters enclosed thereby shall be considered as internal waters.
5. Where the distance between the low-water marks of the natural entrance points of a bay exceeds 24 nautical miles, a straight baseline of 24 nautical miles shall be drawn within the bay in such a manner as to enclose the maximum area of water that is possible with a line of that length.
6. The foregoing provisions do not apply to so-called "historic" bays, or in any case where the system of straight baselines provided for in article 7 is applied.

Article 11 – Ports

For the purpose of delimiting the territorial sea, the outermost permanent harbour works which form an integral part of the harbour system are regarded as forming part of the coast. Off-shore installations and artificial islands shall not be considered as permanent harbour works.

Article 12 – Roadsteads

Roadsteads which are normally used for the loading, unloading and anchoring of ships, and which would otherwise be situated wholly or partly outside the outer limit of the territorial sea, are included in the territorial sea.

Article 13 – Low-tide elevations

1. A low-tide elevation is a naturally formed area of land which is surrounded by and above water at low tide but submerged at high tide. Where a low-tide elevation is situated wholly or partly at a distance not exceeding the breadth of the territorial sea from the mainland or an island, the low-water line on that elevation may be used as the baseline for measuring the breadth of the territorial sea.
2. Where a low-tide elevation is wholly situated at a distance exceeding the breadth of the territorial sea from the mainland or an island, it has no territorial sea of its own.

Article 14 – Combination of methods for determining baselines

The coastal State may determine baselines in turn by any of the methods provided for in the foregoing articles to suit different conditions.

Article 15 – Delimitation of the territorial sea between States with opposite or adjacent coasts

Where the coasts of two States are opposite or adjacent to each other, neither of the two States is entitled, failing agreement between them to the contrary, to extend its territorial sea beyond the median line every point of which is equidistant from the nearest points on the baselines from which the breadth of the territorial seas of each of the two States is measured. The above provision does not apply, however, where it is necessary by reason of historic title or other special circumstances to delimit the territorial seas of the two States in a way which is at variance therewith.

Article 16 – Charts and lists of geographical coordinates

1. The baselines for measuring the breadth of the territorial sea determined in accordance with articles 7, 9 and 10, or the limits derived therefrom, and the lines of delimitation drawn in accordance with articles 12 and 15 shall be shown on charts of a scale or scales adequate for ascertaining their position. Alternatively, a list of geographical coordinates of points, specifying the geodetic datum, may be substituted.
2. The coastal State shall give due publicity to such charts or lists of geographical coordinates and shall deposit a copy of each such chart or list with the Secretary-General of the United Nations

SECTION 3. INNOCENT PASSAGE IN THE TERRITORIAL SEA

SUBSECTION A. RULES APPLICABLE TO ALL SHIPS

Article 17 – Right of innocent passage

Subject to this Convention, ships of all States, whether coastal or land-locked, enjoy the right of innocent passage through the territorial sea.

Article 18 – Meaning of passage

1. Passage means navigation through the territorial sea for the purpose of:
   (a) traversing that sea without entering internal waters or calling at a roadstead or port facility outside internal waters; or
   (b) proceeding to or from internal waters or a call at such roadstead or port facility.
2. Passage shall be continuous and expeditious. However, passage includes stopping and anchoring, but only in so far as the same are incidental to ordinary navigation or are rendered necessary by force majeure or distress or for the purpose of rendering assistance to persons, ships or aircraft in danger or distress.

Article 19 – Meaning of innocent passage

1. Passage is innocent so long as it is not prejudicial to the peace, good order or security of the coastal State. Such passage shall take place in conformity with this Convention and with other rules of international law.
2. Passage of a foreign ship shall be considered to be prejudicial to the peace, good order or security of the coastal State if in the territorial sea it engages in any of the following activities:
   (a) any threat or use of force against the sovereignty, territorial integrity or political independence of the coastal State, or in any other manner in violation of the principles of international law embodied in the Charter of the United Nations;
   (b) any exercise or practice with weapons of any kind;

(c) any act aimed at collecting information to the prejudice of the defence or security of the coastal State;

(d) any act of propaganda aimed at affecting the defence or security of the coastal State;

(e) the launching, landing or taking on board of any aircraft;

(f) the launching, landing or taking on board of any military device;

(g) the loading or unloading of any commodity, currency or person contrary to the customs, fiscal, immigration or sanitary laws and regulations of the coastal State;

(h) any act of wilful and serious pollution contrary to this Convention;

(i) any fishing activities;

(j) the carrying out of research or survey activities;

(k) any act aimed at interfering with any systems of communication or any other facilities or installations of the coastal State;

(l) any other activity not having a direct bearing on passage.

Article 20 – Submarines and other underwater vehicles

In the territorial sea, submarines and other underwater vehicles are required to navigate on the surface and to show their flag.

Article 21 – Laws and regulations of the coastal State relating to innocent passage

1. The coastal State may adopt laws and regulations, in conformity with the provisions of this Convention and other rules of international law, relating to innocent passage through the territorial sea, in respect of all or any of the following:

   (a) the safety of navigation and the regulation of maritime traffic;

   (b) the protection of navigational aids and facilities and other facilities or installations;

   (c) the protection of cables and pipelines;

   (d) the conservation of the living resources of the sea;

   (e) the prevention of infringement of the fisheries laws and regulations of the coastal State;

   (f) the preservation of the environment of the coastal State and the prevention, reduction and control of pollution thereof;

   (g) marine scientific research and hydrographic surveys;

   (h) the prevention of infringement of the customs, fiscal, immigration or sanitary laws and regulations of the coastal State.

2. Such laws and regulations shall not apply to the design, construction, manning or equipment of foreign ships unless they are giving effect to generally accepted international rules or standards.

3. The coastal State shall give due publicity to all such laws and regulations.

4. Foreign ships exercising the right of innocent passage through the territorial sea shall comply with all such laws and regulations and all generally accepted international regulations relating to the prevention of collisions at sea.

Article 22 – Sea lanes and traffic separation schemes in the territorial sea

1. The coastal State may, where necessary having regard to the safety of navigation, require foreign ships exercising the right of innocent passage through its territorial sea to use such sea lanes and traffic separation schemes as it may designate or prescribe for the regulation of the passage of ships.

2. In particular, tankers, nuclear-powered ships and ships carrying nuclear or other inherently dangerous or noxious substances or materials may be required to confine their passage to such sea lanes.

3. In the designation of sea lanes and the prescription of traffic separation schemes under this article, the coastal State shall take into account:

   (a) the recommendations of the competent international organization;

   (b) any channels customarily used for international navigation;

   (c) the special characteristics of particular ships and channels; and

   (d) the density of traffic.

4. The coastal State shall clearly indicate such sea lanes and traffic separation schemes on charts to which due publicity shall be given.

Article 23 – Foreign nuclear-powered ships and ships carrying nuclear or other inherently dangerous or noxious substances

Foreign nuclear-powered ships and ships carrying nuclear or other inherently dangerous or noxious substances shall, when exercising the right of innocent passage through the territorial sea, carry documents and observe special precautionary measures established for such ships by international agreements.

Article 24 – Duties of the coastal State

1. The coastal State shall not hamper the innocent passage of foreign ships through the territorial sea except in accordance with this Convention. In particular, in the application of this Convention or of any laws or regulations adopted in conformity with this Convention, the coastal State shall not:

   (a) impose requirements on foreign ships which have the practical effect of denying or impairing the right of innocent passage; or

   (b) discriminate in form or in fact against the ships of any State or against ships carrying cargoes to, from or on behalf of any State.

2. The coastal State shall give appropriate publicity to any danger to navigation, of which it has knowledge, within its territorial sea.

Article 25 – Rights of protection of the coastal State

1. The coastal State may take the necessary steps in its territorial sea to prevent passage which is not innocent.
2. In the case of ships proceeding to internal waters or a call at a port facility outside internal waters, the coastal State also has the right to take the necessary steps to prevent any breach of the conditions to which admission of those ships to internal waters or such a call is subject.
3. The coastal State may, without discrimination in form or in fact among foreign ships, suspend temporarily in specified areas of its territorial sea the innocent passage of foreign ships if such suspension is essential for the protection of its security, including weapons exercises. Such suspension shall take effect only after having been duly published.

Article 26 – Charges which may be levied upon foreign ships

1. No charge may be levied upon foreign ships by reason only of their passage through the territorial sea.
2. Charges may be levied upon a foreign ship passing through the territorial sea as payment only for specific services rendered to the ship. These charges shall be levied without discrimination.

SUBSECTION B. RULES APPLICABLE TO MERCHANT SHIPS AND GOVERNMENT SHIPS OPERATED FOR COMMERCIAL PURPOSES

Article 27 – Criminal jurisdiction on board a foreign ship

1. The criminal jurisdiction of the coastal State should not be exercised on board a foreign ship passing through the territorial sea to arrest any person or to conduct any investigation in connection with any crime committed on board the ship during its passage, save only in the following cases:
   (a) if the consequences of the crime extend to the coastal State;
   (b) if the crime is of a kind to disturb the peace of the country or the good order of the territorial sea;
   (c) if the assistance of the local authorities has been requested by the master of the ship or by a diplomatic agent or consular officer of the flag State; or
   (d) if such measures are necessary for the suppression of illicit traffic in narcotic drugs or psychotropic substances.
2. The above provisions do not affect the right of the coastal State to take any steps authorized by its laws for the purpose of an arrest or investigation on board a foreign ship passing through the territorial sea after leaving internal waters.
3. In the cases provided for in paragraphs 1 and 2, the coastal State shall, if the master so requests, notify a diplomatic agent or consular officer of the flag State before taking any steps, and shall facilitate contact between such agent or officer and the ship's crew. In cases of emergency this notification may be communicated while the measures are being taken.
4. In considering whether or in what manner an arrest should be made, the local authorities shall have due regard to the interests of navigation.
5. Except as provided in Part XII or with respect to violations of laws and regulations adopted in accordance with Part V, the coastal State may not take any steps on board a foreign ship passing through the territorial sea to arrest any person or to conduct any investigation in connection with any crime committed before the ship entered the territorial sea, if the ship, proceeding from a foreign port, is only passing through the territorial sea without entering internal waters.

Article 28 – Civil jurisdiction in relation to foreign ships

1. The coastal State should not stop or divert a foreign ship passing through the territorial sea for the purpose of exercising civil jurisdiction in relation to a person on board the ship.
2. The coastal State may not levy execution against or arrest the ship for the purpose of any civil proceedings, save only in respect of obligations or liabilities assumed or incurred by the ship itself in the course or for the purpose of its voyage through the waters of the coastal State.
3. Paragraph 2 is without prejudice to the right of the coastal State, in accordance with its laws, to levy execution against or to arrest, for the purpose of any civil proceedings, a foreign ship lying in the territorial sea, or passing through the territorial sea after leaving internal waters.

[…]

SECTION 4. CONTIGUOUS ZONE

Article 33 – Contiguous zone

1. In a zone contiguous to its territorial sea, described as the contiguous zone, the coastal State may exercise the control necessary to:
   (a) prevent infringement of its customs, fiscal, immigration or sanitary laws and regulations within its territory or territorial sea;
   (b) punish infringement of the above laws and regulations committed within its territory or territorial sea.
2. The contiguous zone may not extend beyond 24 nautical miles from the baselines from which the breadth of the territorial sea is measured.

PART III – STRAITS USED FOR INTERNATIONAL NAVIGATION

SECTION 1. GENERAL PROVISIONS

Article 34 – Legal status of waters forming straits used for international navigation

1. The regime of passage through straits used for international navigation established in this Part shall not in other respects affect the legal status of the waters forming such straits or the exercise by the States bordering the straits of their sovereignty or jurisdiction over such waters and their air space, bed and subsoil.
2. The sovereignty or jurisdiction of the States bordering the straits is exercised subject to this Part and to other rules of international law.

Article 35 – Scope of this Part

Nothing in this Part affects:

(a) any areas of internal waters within a strait, except where the establishment of a straight baseline in accordance with the method set forth in article 7 has the effect of enclosing as internal waters areas which had not previously been considered as such;

(b) the legal status of the waters beyond the territorial seas of States bordering straits as exclusive economic zones or high seas; or

(c) the legal regime in straits in which passage is regulated in whole or in part by long-standing international conventions in force specifically relating to such straits.

Article 36 – High seas routes or routes through exclusive economic zones through straits used for international navigation

This Part does not apply to a strait used for international navigation if there exists through the strait a route through the high seas or through an exclusive economic zone of similar convenience with respect to navigational and hydrographical characteristics; in such routes, the other relevant Parts of this Convention, including the provisions regarding the freedoms of navigation and overflight, apply.

SECTION 2. TRANSIT PASSAGE

Article 37 – Scope of this section

This section applies to straits which are used for international navigation between one part of the high seas or an exclusive economic zone and another part of the high seas or an exclusive economic zone.

Article 38 – Right of transit passage

1. In straits referred to in article 37, all ships and aircraft enjoy the right of transit passage, which shall not be impeded; except that, if the strait is formed by an island of a State bordering the strait and its mainland, transit passage shall not apply if there exists seaward of the island a route through the high seas or through an exclusive economic zone of similar convenience with respect to navigational and hydrographical characteristics.
2. Transit passage means the exercise in accordance with this Part of the freedom of navigation and overflight solely for the purpose of continuous and expeditious transit of the strait between one part of the high seas or an exclusive economic zone and another part of the high seas or an exclusive economic zone. However, the requirement of continuous and expeditious transit does not preclude passage through the strait for the purpose of entering, leaving or returning from a State bordering the strait, subject to the conditions of entry to that State.
3. Any activity which is not an exercise of the right of transit passage through a strait remains subject to the other applicable provisions of this Convention.

Article 39 – Duties of ships and aircraft during transit passage

1. Ships and aircraft, while exercising the right of transit passage, shall:

   (a) proceed without delay through or over the strait;

   (b) refrain from any threat or use of force against the sovereignty, territorial integrity or political independence of States bordering the strait, or in any other manner in violation of the principles of international law embodied in the Charter of the United Nations;

   (c) refrain from any activities other than those incident to their normal modes of continuous and expeditious transit unless rendered necessary by force majeure or by distress;

   (d) comply with other relevant provisions of this Part.

2. Ships in transit passage shall:

   (a) comply with generally accepted international regulations, procedures and practices for safety at sea, including the International Regulations for Preventing Collisions at Sea;

   (b) comply with generally accepted international regulations, procedures and practices for the prevention, reduction and control of pollution from ships.

3. Aircraft in transit passage shall:

   (a) observe the Rules of the Air established by the International Civil Aviation Organization as they apply to civil aircraft; state aircraft will normally comply with such safety measures and will at all times operate with due regard for the safety of navigation;

   (b) at all times monitor the radio frequency assigned by the competent internationally designated air traffic control authority or the appropriate international distress radio frequency.

Article 40 – Research and survey activities

During transit passage, foreign ships, including marine scientific research and hydrographic survey ships, may not carry out any research or survey activities without the prior authorization of the States bordering straits.

Article 41 – Sea lanes and traffic separation schemes in straits used for international navigation

1. In conformity with this Part, States bordering straits may designate sea lanes and prescribe traffic separation schemes for navigation in straits where necessary to promote the safe passage of ships.
2. Such States may, when circumstances require, and after giving due publicity thereto, substitute other sea lanes or traffic separation schemes for any sea lanes or traffic separation schemes previously designated or prescribed by them.
3. Such sea lanes and traffic separation schemes shall conform to generally accepted international regulations.
4. Before designating or substituting sea lanes or prescribing or substituting traffic separation schemes, States bordering straits shall refer proposals to the competent international organization with a view to their adoption. The organization may adopt only such sea lanes and traffic separation schemes as may be agreed with the States bordering the straits, after which the States may designate, prescribe or substitute them.
5. In respect of a strait where sea lanes or traffic separation schemes through the waters of two or more States bordering the strait are being proposed, the States concerned shall cooperate in formulating proposals in consultation with the competent international organization.
6. States bordering straits shall clearly indicate all sea lanes and traffic separation schemes designated or prescribed by them on charts to which due publicity shall be given.
7. Ships in transit passage shall respect applicable sea lanes and traffic separation schemes established in accordance with this article.

Article 42 – Laws and regulations of States bordering straits relating to transit passage

1. Subject to the provisions of this section, States bordering straits may adopt laws and regulations relating to transit passage through straits, in respect of all or any of the following:
   (a) the safety of navigation and the regulation of maritime traffic, as provided in article 41;
   (b) the prevention, reduction and control of pollution, by giving effect to applicable international regulations regarding the discharge of oil, oily wastes and other noxious substances in the strait;
   (c) with respect to fishing vessels, the prevention of fishing, including the stowage of fishing gear;
   (d) the loading or unloading of any commodity, currency or person in contravention of the customs, fiscal, immigration or sanitary laws and regulations of States bordering straits.
2. Such laws and regulations shall not discriminate in form or in fact among foreign ships or in their application have the practical effect of denying, hampering or impairing the right of transit passage as defined in this section.
3. States bordering straits shall give due publicity to all such laws and regulations.
4. Foreign ships exercising the right of transit passage shall comply with such laws and regulations.
5. The flag State of a ship or the State of registry of an aircraft entitled to sovereign immunity which acts in a manner contrary to such laws and regulations or other provisions of this Part shall bear international responsibility for any loss or damage which results to States bordering straits.

Article 43 – Navigational and safety aids and other improvements and the prevention, reduction and control of pollution

User States and States bordering a strait should by agreement cooperate:

(a) in the establishment and maintenance in a strait of necessary navigational and safety aids or other improvements in aid of international navigation; and

(b) for the prevention, reduction and control of pollution from ships.

Article 44 – Duties of States bordering straits

States bordering straits shall not hamper transit passage and shall give appropriate publicity to any danger to navigation or overflight within or over the strait of which they have knowledge. There shall be no suspension of transit passage.

SECTION 3. INNOCENT PASSAGE

Article 45 – Innocent passage

1. The regime of innocent passage, in accordance with Part II, section 3, shall apply in straits used for international navigation:
   (a) excluded from the application of the regime of transit passage under article 38, paragraph 1; or
   (b) between a part of the high seas or an exclusive economic zone and the territorial sea of a foreign State.
2. There shall be no suspension of innocent passage through such straits.

PART IV – ARCHIPELAGIC STATES

Article 46 – Use of terms

For the purposes of this Convention:

(a) "archipelagic State" means a State constituted wholly by one or more archipelagos and may include other islands;

(b) "archipelago" means a group of islands, including parts of islands, interconnecting waters and other natural features which are so closely interrelated that such islands, waters and other natural features form an intrinsic geographical, economic and political entity, or which historically have been regarded as such.

Article 47 – Archipelagic baselines

1. An archipelagic State may draw straight archipelagic baselines joining the outermost points of

the outermost islands and drying reefs of the archipelago provided that within such baselines are included the main islands and an area in which the ratio of the area of the water to the area of the land, including atolls, is between 1 to 1 and 9 to 1.

2. The length of such baselines shall not exceed 100 nautical miles, except that up to 3 per cent of the total number of baselines enclosing any archipelago may exceed that length, up to a maximum length of 125 nautical miles.
3. The drawing of such baselines shall not depart to any appreciable extent from the general configuration of the archipelago.
4. Such baselines shall not be drawn to and from low-tide elevations, unless lighthouses or similar installations which are permanently above sea level have been built on them or where a low-tide elevation is situated wholly or partly at a distance not exceeding the breadth of the territorial sea from the nearest island.
5. The system of such baselines shall not be applied by an archipelagic State in such a manner as to cut off from the high seas or the exclusive economic zone the territorial sea of another State.
6. If a part of the archipelagic waters of an archipelagic State lies between two parts of an immediately adjacent neighbouring State, existing rights and all other legitimate interests which the latter State has traditionally exercised in such waters and all rights stipulated by agreement between those States shall continue and be respected.
7. For the purpose of computing the ratio of water to land under paragraph l, land areas may include waters lying within the fringing reefs of islands and atolls, including that part of a steep-sided oceanic plateau which is enclosed or nearly enclosed by a chain of limestone islands and drying reefs lying on the perimeter of the plateau.
8. The baselines drawn in accordance with this article shall be shown on charts of a scale or scales adequate for ascertaining their position. Alternatively, lists of geographical coordinates of points, specifying the geodetic datum, may be substituted.
9. The archipelagic State shall give due publicity to such charts or lists of geographical coordinates and shall deposit a copy of each such chart or list with the Secretary-General of the United Nations.

Article 48 – Measurement of the breadth of the territorial sea, the contiguous zone, the exclusive economic zone and the continental shelf

The breadth of the territorial sea, the contiguous zone, the exclusive economic zone and the continental shelf shall be measured from archipelagic baselines drawn in accordance with article 47.

Article 49 – Legal status of archipelagic waters, of the air space over archipelagic waters and of their bed and subsoil

1. The sovereignty of an archipelagic State extends to the waters enclosed by the archipelagic baselines drawn in accordance with article 47, described as archipelagic waters, regardless of their depth or distance from the coast.
2. This sovereignty extends to the air space over the archipelagic waters, as well as to their bed and subsoil, and the resources contained therein.
3. This sovereignty is exercised subject to this Part.
4. The regime of archipelagic sea lanes passage established in this Part shall not in other respects affect the status of the archipelagic waters, including the sea lanes, or the exercise by the archipelagic State of its sovereignty over such waters and their air space, bed and subsoil, and the resources contained therein.

Article 50 – Delimitation of internal waters

Within its archipelagic waters, the archipelagic State may draw closing lines for the delimitation of internal waters, in accordance with articles 9, 10 and 11.

Article 51 – Existing agreements, traditional fishing rights and existing submarine cables

1. Without prejudice to article 49, an archipelagic State shall respect existing agreements with other States and shall recognize traditional fishing rights and other legitimate activities of the immediately adjacent neighbouring States in certain areas falling within archipelagic waters. The terms and conditions for the exercise of such rights and activities, including the nature, the extent and the areas to which they apply, shall, at the request of any of the States concerned, be regulated by bilateral agreements between them. Such rights shall not be transferred to or shared with third States or their nationals.
2. An archipelagic State shall respect existing submarine cables laid by other States and passing through its waters without making a landfall. An archipelagic State shall permit the maintenance and replacement of such cables upon receiving due notice of their location and the intention to repair or replace them.

Article 52 – Right of innocent passage

1. Subject to article 53 and without prejudice to article 50, ships of all States enjoy the right of innocent passage through archipelagic waters, in accordance with Part II, section 3.
2. The archipelagic State may, without discrimination in form or in fact among foreign ships, suspend temporarily in specified areas of its archipelagic waters the innocent passage of foreign ships if such suspension is essential for the protection of its security. Such suspension shall take effect only after having been duly published.

Article 53 – Right of archipelagic sea lanes passage

1. An archipelagic State may designate sea lanes and air routes thereabove, suitable for the continuous and expeditious passage of foreign ships and aircraft through or over its archipelagic waters and the adjacent territorial sea.

2. All ships and aircraft enjoy the right of archipelagic sea lanes passage in such sea lanes and air routes.
3. Archipelagic sea lanes passage means the exercise in accordance with this Convention of the rights of navigation and overflight in the normal mode solely for the purpose of continuous, expeditious and unobstructed transit between one part of the high seas or an exclusive economic zone and another part of the high seas or an exclusive economic zone.
4. Such sea lanes and air routes shall traverse the archipelagic waters and the adjacent territorial sea and shall include all normal passage routes used as routes for international navigation or overflight through or over archipelagic waters and, within such routes, so far as ships are concerned, all normal navigational channels, provided that duplication of routes of similar convenience between the same entry and exit points shall not be necessary.
5. Such sea lanes and air routes shall be defined by a series of continuous axis lines from the entry points of passage routes to the exit points. Ships and aircraft in archipelagic sea lanes passage shall not deviate more than 25 nautical miles to either side of such axis lines during passage, provided that such ships and aircraft shall not navigate closer to the coasts than 10 per cent of the distance between the nearest points on islands bordering the sea lane.
6. An archipelagic State which designates sea lanes under this article may also prescribe traffic separation schemes for the safe passage of ships through narrow channels in such sea lanes.
7. An archipelagic State may, when circumstances require, after giving due publicity thereto, substitute other sea lanes or traffic separation schemes for any sea lanes or traffic separation schemes previously designated or prescribed by it.
8. Such sea lanes and traffic separation schemes shall conform to generally accepted international regulations.
9. In designating or substituting sea lanes or prescribing or substituting traffic separation schemes, an archipelagic State shall refer proposals to the competent international organization with a view to their adoption. The organization may adopt only such sea lanes and traffic separation schemes as may be agreed with the archipelagic State, after which the archipelagic State may designate, prescribe or substitute them.
10. The archipelagic State shall clearly indicate the axis of the sea lanes and the traffic separation schemes designated or prescribed by it on charts to which due publicity shall be given.
11. Ships in archipelagic sea lanes passage shall respect applicable sea lanes and traffic separation schemes established in accordance with this article.
12. If an archipelagic State does not designate sea lanes or air routes, the right of archipelagic sea lanes passage may be exercised through the routes normally used for international navigation.

Article 54 – Duties of ships and aircraft during their passage, research and survey activities, duties of the archipelagic State and laws and regulations of the archipelagic State relating to archipelagic sea lanes passage

Articles 39, 40, 42 and 44 apply mutatis mutandis to archipelagic sea lanes passage.

PART V – EXCLUSIVE ECONOMIC ZONE

Article 55 – Specific legal regime of the exclusive economic zone

The exclusive economic zone is an area beyond and adjacent to the territorial sea, subject to the specific legal regime established in this Part, under which the rights and jurisdiction of the coastal State and the rights and freedoms of other States are governed by the relevant provisions of this Convention.

Article 56 – Rights, jurisdiction and duties of the coastal State in the exclusive economic zone

1. In the exclusive economic zone, the coastal State has:
    (a) sovereign rights for the purpose of exploring and exploiting, conserving and managing the natural resources, whether living or non-living, of the waters superjacent to the seabed and of the seabed and its subsoil, and with regard to other activities for the economic exploitation and exploration of the zone, such as the production of energy from the water, currents and winds;
    (b) jurisdiction as provided for in the relevant provisions of this Convention with regard to:
        (i) the establishment and use of artificial islands, installations and structures;
        (ii) marine scientific research;
        (iii) the protection and preservation of the marine environment;
    (c) other rights and duties provided for in this Convention.
2. In exercising its rights and performing its duties under this Convention in the exclusive economic zone, the coastal State shall have due regard to the rights and duties of other States and shall act in a manner compatible with the provisions of this Convention.
3. The rights set out in this article with respect to the seabed and subsoil shall be exercised in accordance with Part VI.

Article 57 – Breadth of the exclusive economic zone

The exclusive economic zone shall not extend beyond 200 nautical miles from the baselines from which the breadth of the territorial sea is measured.

Article 58 – Rights and duties of other States in the exclusive economic zone

1. In the exclusive economic zone, all States, whether coastal or land-locked, enjoy, subject to the relevant provisions of this Convention, the freedoms referred to in article 87 of navigation and overflight and of the laying of submarine cables and pipelines, and other internationally lawful uses of the sea related to these freedoms, such as those associated with the operation of ships, aircraft and submarine cables and pipelines, and compatible with the other provisions of this Convention.
2. Articles 88 to 115 and other pertinent rules of international law apply to the exclusive economic zone in so far as they are not incompatible with this Part.
3. In exercising their rights and performing their duties under this Convention in the exclusive economic zone, States shall have due regard to the rights and duties of the coastal State and shall comply with the laws and regulations adopted by the coastal State in accordance with the provisions of this Convention and other rules of international law in so far as they are not incompatible with this Part.

Article 59 – Basis for the resolution of conflicts regarding the attribution of rights and jurisdiction in the exclusive economic zone

In cases where this Convention does not attribute rights or jurisdiction to the coastal State or to other States within the exclusive economic zone, and a conflict arises between the interests of the coastal State and any other State or States, the conflict should be resolved on the basis of equity and in the light of all the relevant circumstances, taking into account the respective importance of the interests involved to the parties as well as to the international community as a whole.

Article 60 – Artificial islands, installations and structures in the exclusive economic zone

1. In the exclusive economic zone, the coastal State shall have the exclusive right to construct and to authorize and regulate the construction, operation and use of:
   (a) artificial islands;
   (b) installations and structures for the purposes provided for in article 56 and other economic purposes;
   (c) installations and structures which may interfere with the exercise of the rights of the coastal State in the zone.
2. The coastal State shall have exclusive jurisdiction over such artificial islands, installations and structures, including jurisdiction with regard to customs, fiscal, health, safety and immigration laws and regulations.
3. Due notice must be given of the construction of such artificial islands, installations or structures, and permanent means for giving warning of their presence must be maintained. Any installations or structures which are abandoned or disused shall be removed to ensure safety of navigation, taking into account any generally accepted international standards established in this regard by the competent international organization. Such removal shall also have due regard to fishing, the protection of the marine environment and the rights and duties of other States. Appropriate publicity shall be given to the depth, position and dimensions of any installations or structures not entirely removed.
4. The coastal State may, where necessary, establish reasonable safety zones around such artificial islands, installations and structures in which it may take appropriate measures to ensure the safety both of navigation and of the artificial islands, installations and structures.
5. The breadth of the safety zones shall be determined by the coastal State, taking into account applicable international standards. Such zones shall be designed to ensure that they are reasonably related to the nature and function of the artificial islands, installations or structures, and shall not exceed a distance of 500 metres around them, measured from each point of their outer edge, except as authorized by generally accepted international standards or as recommended by the competent international organization. Due notice shall be given of the extent of safety zones.
6. All ships must respect these safety zones and shall comply with generally accepted international standards regarding navigation in the vicinity of artificial islands, installations, structures and safety zones.
7. Artificial islands, installations and structures and the safety zones around them may not be established where interference may be caused to the use of recognized sea lanes essential to international navigation.
8. Artificial islands, installations and structures do not possess the status of islands. They have no territorial sea of their own, and their presence does not affect the delimitation of the territorial sea, the exclusive economic zone or the continental shelf.

Article 61 – Conservation of the living resources

1. The coastal State shall determine the allowable catch of the living resources in its exclusive economic zone.
2. The coastal State, taking into account the best scientific evidence available to it, shall ensure through proper conservation and management measures that the maintenance of the living resources in the exclusive economic zone is not endangered by over-exploitation. As appropriate, the coastal State and competent international organizations, whether subregional, regional or global, shall cooperate to this end.
3. Such measures shall also be designed to maintain or restore populations of harvested species at levels which can produce the maximum sustainable yield, as qualified by relevant environmental and economic factors, including the economic needs of coastal fishing communities and the special requirements of developing States, and taking into

account fishing patterns, the interdependence of stocks and any generally recommended international minimum standards, whether subregional, regional or global.

4. In taking such measures the coastal State shall take into consideration the effects on species associated with or dependent upon harvested species with a view to maintaining or restoring populations of such associated or dependent species above levels at which their reproduction may become seriously threatened.
5. Available scientific information, catch and fishing effort statistics, and other data relevant to the conservation of fish stocks shall be contributed and exchanged on a regular basis through competent international organizations, whether subregional, regional or global, where appropriate and with participation by all States concerned, including States whose nationals are allowed to fish in the exclusive economic zone.

Article 62 – Utilization of the living resources

1. The coastal State shall promote the objective of optimum utilization of the living resources in the exclusive economic zone without prejudice to article 61.
2. The coastal State shall determine its capacity to harvest the living resources of the exclusive economic zone. Where the coastal State does not have the capacity to harvest the entire allowable catch, it shall, through agreements or other arrangements and pursuant to the terms, conditions, laws and regulations referred to in paragraph 4, give other States access to the surplus of the allowable catch, having particular regard to the provisions of articles 69 and 70, especially in relation to the developing States mentioned therein.
3. In giving access to other States to its exclusive economic zone under this article, the coastal State shall take into account all relevant factors, including, inter alia, the significance of the living resources of the area to the economy of the coastal State concerned and its other national interests, the provisions of articles 69 and 70, the requirements of developing States in the subregion or region in harvesting part of the surplus and the need to minimize economic dislocation in States whose nationals have habitually fished in the zone or which have made substantial efforts in research and identification of stocks.
4. Nationals of other States fishing in the exclusive economic zone shall comply with the conservation measures and with the other terms and conditions established in the laws and regulations of the coastal State. These laws and regulations shall be consistent with this Convention and may relate, inter alia, to the following:
   (a) licensing of fishermen, fishing vessels and equipment, including payment of fees and other forms of remuneration, which, in the case of developing coastal States, may consist of adequate compensation in the field of financing, equipment and technology relating to the fishing industry;
   (b) determining the species which may be caught, and fixing quotas of catch, whether in relation to particular stocks or groups of stocks or catch per vessel over a period of time or to the catch by nationals of any State during a specified period;
   (c) regulating seasons and areas of fishing, the types, sizes and amount of gear, and the types, sizes and number of fishing vessels that may be used;
   (d) fixing the age and size of fish and other species that may be caught;
   (e) specifying information required of fishing vessels, including catch and effort statistics and vessel position reports;
   (f) requiring, under the authorization and control of the coastal State, the conduct of specified fisheries research programmes and regulating the conduct of such research, including the sampling of catches, disposition of samples and reporting of associated scientific data;
   (g) the placing of observers or trainees on board such vessels by the coastal State;
   (h) the landing of all or any part of the catch by such vessels in the ports of the coastal State;
   (i) terms and conditions relating to joint ventures or other cooperative arrangements;
   (j) requirements for the training of personnel and the transfer of fisheries technology, including enhancement of the coastal State's capability of undertaking fisheries research;
   (k) enforcement procedures.
5. Coastal States shall give due notice of conservation and management laws and regulations.

Article 63 – Stocks occurring within the exclusive economic zones of two or more coastal States or both within the exclusive economic zone and in an area beyond and adjacent to it

1. Where the same stock or stocks of associated species occur within the exclusive economic zones of two or more coastal States, these States shall seek, either directly or through appropriate subregional or regional organizations, to agree upon the measures necessary to coordinate and ensure the conservation and development of such stocks without prejudice to the other provisions of this Part.
2. Where the same stock or stocks of associated species occur both within the exclusive economic zone and in an area beyond and adjacent to the zone, the coastal State and the States fishing for such stocks in the adjacent area shall seek, either directly or through appropriate subregional or regional organizations, to agree upon the measures necessary for the conservation of these stocks in the adjacent area.

Article 64 – Highly migratory species

1. The coastal State and other States whose nationals fish in the region for the highly migratory species listed in Annex I shall cooperate directly or through appropriate international organizations with a view to ensuring conservation and promoting the objective of optimum utilization of such species throughout the region, both within and beyond the exclusive economic zone. In regions for which no appropriate international organization exists, the coastal State and other States whose nationals harvest these species in the region shall cooperate to establish such an organization and participate in its work.
2. The provisions of paragraph 1 apply in addition to the other provisions of this Part.

Article 65 – Marine mammals

Nothing in this Part restricts the right of a coastal State or the competence of an international organization, as appropriate, to prohibit, limit or regulate the exploitation of marine mammals more strictly than provided for in this Part. States shall cooperate with a view to the conservation of marine mammals and in the case of cetaceans shall in particular work through the appropriate international organizations for their conservation, management and study.

Article 66 – Anadromous stocks

1. States in whose rivers anadromous stocks originate shall have the primary interest in and responsibility for such stocks.
2. The State of origin of anadromous stocks shall ensure their conservation by the establishment of appropriate regulatory measures for fishing in all waters landward of the outer limits of its exclusive economic zone and for fishing provided for in paragraph 3(b). The State of origin may, after consultations with the other States referred to in paragraphs 3 and 4 fishing these stocks, establish total allowable catches for stocks originating in its rivers.
3. (a) Fisheries for anadromous stocks shall be conducted only in waters landward of the outer limits of exclusive economic zones, except in cases where this provision would result in economic dislocation for a State other than the State of origin. With respect to such fishing beyond the outer limits of the exclusive economic zone, States concerned shall maintain consultations with a view to achieving agreement on terms and conditions of such fishing giving due regard to the conservation requirements and the needs of the State of origin in respect of these stocks.
   (b) The State of origin shall cooperate in minimizing economic dislocation in such other States fishing these stocks, taking into account the normal catch and the mode of operations of such States, and all the areas in which such fishing has occurred.
   (c) States referred to in subparagraph (b), participating by agreement with the State of origin in measures to renew anadromous stocks, particularly by expenditures for that purpose, shall be given special consideration by the State of origin in the harvesting of stocks originating in its rivers.
   (d) Enforcement of regulations regarding anadromous stocks beyond the exclusive economic zone shall be by agreement between the State of origin and the other States concerned.
4. In cases where anadromous stocks migrate into or through the waters landward of the outer limits of the exclusive economic zone of a State other than the State of origin, such State shall cooperate with the State of origin with regard to the conservation and management of such stocks.
5. The State of origin of anadromous stocks and other States fishing these stocks shall make arrangements for the implementation of the provisions of this article, where appropriate, through regional organizations.

Article 67 – Catadromous species

1. A coastal State in whose waters catadromous species spend the greater part of their life cycle shall have responsibility for the management of these species and shall ensure the ingress and egress of migrating fish.
2. Harvesting of catadromous species shall be conducted only in waters landward of the outer limits of exclusive economic zones. When conducted in exclusive economic zones, harvesting shall be subject to this article and the other provisions of this Convention concerning fishing in these zones.
3. In cases where catadromous fish migrate through the exclusive economic zone of another State, whether as juvenile or maturing fish, the management, including harvesting, of such fish shall be regulated by agreement between the State mentioned in paragraph 1 and the other State concerned. Such agreement shall ensure the rational management of the species and take into account the responsibilities of the State mentioned in paragraph 1 for the maintenance of these species.

Article 68 – Sedentary species

This Part does not apply to sedentary species as defined in article 77, paragraph 4.

Article 69 – Right of land-locked States

1. Land-locked States shall have the right to participate, on an equitable basis, in the exploitation of an appropriate part of the surplus of the living resources of the exclusive economic zones of coastal States of the same subregion or region, taking into account the relevant economic and geographical circumstances of all the States concerned and in conformity with the provisions of this article and of articles 61 and 62.
2. The terms and modalities of such participation shall be established by the States concerned through bilateral, subregional or regional agreements taking into account, inter alia:

(a) the need to avoid effects detrimental to fishing communities or fishing industries of the coastal State;

(b) the extent to which the land-locked State, in accordance with the provisions of this article, is participating or is entitled to participate under existing bilateral, subregional or regional agreements in the exploitation of living resources of the exclusive economic zones of other coastal States;

(c) the extent to which other land-locked States and geographically disadvantaged States are participating in the exploitation of the living resources of the exclusive economic zone of the coastal State and the consequent need to avoid a particular burden for any single coastal State or a part of it;

(d) the nutritional needs of the populations of the respective States.

3. When the harvesting capacity of a coastal State approaches a point which would enable it to harvest the entire allowable catch of the living resources in its exclusive economic zone, the coastal State and other States concerned shall cooperate in the establishment of equitable arrangements on a bilateral, subregional or regional basis to allow for participation of developing land-locked States of the same subregion or region in the exploitation of the living resources of the exclusive economic zones of coastal States of the subregion or region, as may be appropriate in the circumstances and on terms satisfactory to all parties. In the implementation of this provision the factors mentioned in paragraph 2 shall also be taken into account.

4. Developed land-locked States shall, under the provisions of this article, be entitled to participate in the exploitation of living resources only in the exclusive economic zones of developed coastal States of the same subregion or region having regard to the extent to which the coastal State, in giving access to other States to the living resources of its exclusive economic zone, has taken into account the need to minimize detrimental effects on fishing communities and economic dislocation in States whose nationals have habitually fished in the zone.

5. The above provisions are without prejudice to arrangements agreed upon in subregions or regions where the coastal States may grant to land-locked States of the same subregion or region equal or preferential rights for the exploitation of the living resources in the exclusive economic zones.

Article 70 – Right of geographically disadvantaged States

1. Geographically disadvantaged States shall have the right to participate, on an equitable basis, in the exploitation of an appropriate part of the surplus of the living resources of the exclusive economic zones of coastal States of the same subregion or region, taking into account the relevant economic and geographical circumstances of all the States concerned and in conformity with the provisions of this article and of articles 61 and 62.

2. For the purposes of this Part, "geographically disadvantaged States" means coastal States, including States bordering enclosed or semi-enclosed seas, whose geographical situation makes them dependent upon the exploitation of the living resources of the exclusive economic zones of other States in the subregion or region for adequate supplies of fish for the nutritional purposes of their populations or parts thereof, and coastal States which can claim no exclusive economic zones of their own.

3. The terms and modalities of such participation shall be established by the States concerned through bilateral, subregional or regional agreements taking into account, inter alia:

(a) the need to avoid effects detrimental to fishing communities or fishing industries of the coastal State;

(b) the extent to which the geographically disadvantaged State, in accordance with the provisions of this article, is participating or is entitled to participate under existing bilateral, subregional or regional agreements in the exploitation of living resources of the exclusive economic zones of other coastal States;

(c) the extent to which other geographically disadvantaged States and land-locked States are participating in the exploitation of the living resources of the exclusive economic zone of the coastal State and the consequent need to avoid a particular burden for any single coastal State or a part of it;

(d) the nutritional needs of the populations of the respective States.

4. When the harvesting capacity of a coastal State approaches a point which would enable it to harvest the entire allowable catch of the living resources in its exclusive economic zone, the coastal State and other States concerned shall cooperate in the establishment of equitable arrangements on a bilateral, subregional or regional basis to allow for participation of developing geographically disadvantaged States of the same subregion or region in the exploitation of the living resources of the exclusive economic zones of coastal States of the subregion or region, as may be appropriate in the circumstances and on terms satisfactory to all parties. In the implementation of this provision the factors mentioned in paragraph 3 shall also be taken into account.

5. Developed geographically disadvantaged States shall, under the provisions of this article, be entitled to participate in the exploitation of living resources only in the exclusive economic zones of developed coastal States of the same subregion or region having regard to the extent to which the coastal State, in giving access to other States to the living resources of its exclusive economic zone, has taken into account the need to minimize detrimental effects on fishing communities and economic dislocation in States whose nationals have habitually fished in the zone.

6. The above provisions are without prejudice to arrangements agreed upon in subregions or regions where the coastal States may grant to geographically disadvantaged States of the same subregion or region equal or preferential rights for the exploitation of the living resources in the exclusive economic zones.

Article 71 – Non-applicability of articles 69 and 70

The provisions of articles 69 and 70 do not apply in the case of a coastal State whose economy is overwhelmingly dependent on the exploitation of the living resources of its exclusive economic zone.

Article 72 – Restrictions on transfer of rights

1. Rights provided under articles 69 and 70 to exploit living resources shall not be directly or indirectly transferred to third States or their nationals by lease or licence, by establishing joint ventures or in any other manner which has the effect of such transfer unless otherwise agreed by the States concerned.
2. The foregoing provision does not preclude the States concerned from obtaining technical or financial assistance from third States or international organizations in order to facilitate the exercise of the rights pursuant to articles 69 and 70, provided that it does not have the effect referred to in paragraph 1.

Article 73 – Enforcement of laws and regulations of the coastal State

1. The coastal State may, in the exercise of its sovereign rights to explore, exploit, conserve and manage the living resources in the exclusive economic zone, take such measures, including boarding, inspection, arrest and judicial proceedings, as may be necessary to ensure compliance with the laws and regulations adopted by it in conformity with this Convention.
2. Arrested vessels and their crews shall be promptly released upon the posting of reasonable bond or other security.
3. Coastal State penalties for violations of fisheries laws and regulations in the exclusive economic zone may not include imprisonment, in the absence of agreements to the contrary by the States concerned, or any other form of corporal punishment.
4. In cases of arrest or detention of foreign vessels the coastal State shall promptly notify the flag State, through appropriate channels, of the action taken and of any penalties subsequently imposed.

Article 74 – Delimitation of the exclusive economic zone between States with opposite or adjacent coasts

1. The delimitation of the exclusive economic zone between States with opposite or adjacent coasts shall be effected by agreement on the basis of international law, as referred to in Article 38 of the Statute of the International Court of Justice, in order to achieve an equitable solution.
2. If no agreement can be reached within a reasonable period of time, the States concerned shall resort to the procedures provided for in Part XV.
3. Pending agreement as provided for in paragraph 1, the States concerned, in a spirit of understanding and cooperation, shall make every effort to enter into provisional arrangements of a practical nature and, during this transitional period, not to jeopardize or hamper the reaching of the final agreement. Such arrangements shall be without prejudice to the final delimitation.
4. Where there is an agreement in force between the States concerned, questions relating to the delimitation of the exclusive economic zone shall be determined in accordance with the provisions of that agreement.

Article 75 – Charts and lists of geographical coordinates

1. Subject to this Part, the outer limit lines of the exclusive economic zone and the lines of delimitation drawn in accordance with article 74 shall be shown on charts of a scale or scales adequate for ascertaining their position. Where appropriate, lists of geographical coordinates of points, specifying the geodetic datum, may be substituted for such outer limit lines or lines of delimitation.
2. The coastal State shall give due publicity to such charts or lists of geographical coordinates and shall deposit a copy of each such chart or list with the Secretary-General of the United Nations.

PART VI – CONTINENTAL SHELF

Article 76 – Definition of the continental shelf

1. The continental shelf of a coastal State comprises the seabed and subsoil of the submarine areas that extend beyond its territorial sea throughout the natural prolongation of its land territory to the outer edge of the continental margin, or to a distance of 200 nautical miles from the baselines from which the breadth of the territorial sea is measured where the outer edge of the continental margin does not extend up to that distance.
2. The continental shelf of a coastal State shall not extend beyond the limits provided for in paragraphs 4 to 6.
3. The continental margin comprises the submerged prolongation of the land mass of the coastal State, and consists of the seabed and subsoil of the shelf, the slope and the rise. It does not include the deep ocean floor with its oceanic ridges or the subsoil thereof.
4. (a) For the purposes of this Convention, the coastal State shall establish the outer edge of the continental margin wherever the margin extends beyond 200 nautical miles from the baselines from which the breadth of the territorial sea is measured, by either:
    (i) a line delineated in accordance with paragraph 7 by reference to the outermost fixed points at each of which the thickness of sedimentary rocks is at least 1 per cent

of the shortest distance from such point to the foot of the continental slope; or

(ii) a line delineated in accordance with paragraph 7 by reference to fixed points not more than 60 nautical miles from the foot of the continental slope.

(b) In the absence of evidence to the contrary, the foot of the continental slope shall be determined as the point of maximum change in the gradient at its base.

5. The fixed points comprising the line of the outer limits of the continental shelf on the seabed, drawn in accordance with paragraph 4 (a)(i) and (ii), either shall not exceed 350 nautical miles from the baselines from which the breadth of the territorial sea is measured or shall not exceed 100 nautical miles from the 2,500 metre isobath, which is a line connecting the depth of 2,500 metres.
6. Notwithstanding the provisions of paragraph 5, on submarine ridges, the outer limit of the continental shelf shall not exceed 350 nautical miles from the baselines from which the breadth of the territorial sea is measured. This paragraph does not apply to submarine elevations that are natural components of the continental margin, such as its plateaux, rises, caps, banks and spurs.
7. The coastal State shall delineate the outer limits of its continental shelf, where that shelf extends beyond 200 nautical miles from the baselines from which the breadth of the territorial sea is measured, by straight lines not exceeding 60 nautical miles in length, connecting fixed points, defined by coordinates of latitude and longitude.
8. Information on the limits of the continental shelf beyond 200 nautical miles from the baselines from which the breadth of the territorial sea is measured shall be submitted by the coastal State to the Commission on the Limits of the Continental Shelf set up under Annex II on the basis of equitable geographical representation. The Commission shall make recommendations to coastal States on matters related to the establishment of the outer limits of their continental shelf. The limits of the shelf established by a coastal State on the basis of these recommendations shall be final and binding.
9. The coastal State shall deposit with the Secretary-General of the United Nations charts and relevant information, including geodetic data, permanently describing the outer limits of its continental shelf. The Secretary-General shall give due publicity thereto.
10. The provisions of this article are without prejudice to the question of delimitation of the continental shelf between States with opposite or adjacent coasts.

Article 77 – Rights of the coastal State over the continental shelf

1. The coastal State exercises over the continental shelf sovereign rights for the purpose of exploring it and exploiting its natural resources.
2. The rights referred to in paragraph 1 are exclusive in the sense that if the coastal State does not explore the continental shelf or exploit its natural resources, no one may undertake these activities without the express consent of the coastal State.
3. The rights of the coastal State over the continental shelf do not depend on occupation, effective or notional, or on any express proclamation.
4. The natural resources referred to in this Part consist of the mineral and other non-living resources of the seabed and subsoil together with living organisms belonging to sedentary species, that is to say, organisms which, at the harvestable stage, either are immobile on or under the seabed or are unable to move except in constant physical contact with the seabed or the subsoil.

Article 78 – Legal status of the superjacent waters and air space and the rights and freedoms of other States

1. The rights of the coastal State over the continental shelf do not affect the legal status of the superjacent waters or of the air space above those waters.
2. The exercise of the rights of the coastal State over the continental shelf must not infringe or result in any unjustifiable interference with navigation and other rights and freedoms of other States as provided for in this Convention.

Article 79 – Submarine cables and pipelines on the continental shelf

1. All States are entitled to lay submarine cables and pipelines on the continental shelf, in accordance with the provisions of this article.
2. Subject to its right to take reasonable measures for the exploration of the continental shelf, the exploitation of its natural resources and the prevention, reduction and control of pollution from pipelines, the coastal State may not impede the laying or maintenance of such cables or pipelines.
3. The delineation of the course for the laying of such pipelines on the continental shelf is subject to the consent of the coastal State.
4. Nothing in this Part affects the right of the coastal State to establish conditions for cables or pipelines entering its territory or territorial sea, or its jurisdiction over cables and pipelines constructed or used in connection with the exploration of its continental shelf or exploitation of its resources or the operations of artificial islands, installations and structures under its jurisdiction.
5. When laying submarine cables or pipelines, States shall have due regard to cables or pipelines already in position. In particular, possibilities of repairing existing cables or pipelines shall not be prejudiced.

Article 80 – Artificial islands, installations and structures on the continental shelf

Article 60 applies mutatis mutandis to artificial islands, installations and structures on the continental shelf.

Article 81 – Drilling on the continental shelf

The coastal State shall have the exclusive right to authorize and regulate drilling on the continental shelf for all purposes.

Article 82 – Payments and contributions with respect to the exploitation of the continental shelf beyond 200 nautical miles

1. The coastal State shall make payments or contributions in kind in respect of the exploitation of the non-living resources of the continental shelf beyond 200 nautical miles from the baselines from which the breadth of the territorial sea is measured.
2. The payments and contributions shall be made annually with respect to all production at a site after the first five years of production at that site. For the sixth year, the rate of payment or contribution shall be 1 per cent of the value or volume of production at the site. The rate shall increase by 1 per cent for each subsequent year until the twelfth year and shall remain at 7 per cent thereafter. Production does not include resources used in connection with exploitation.
3. A developing State which is a net importer of a mineral resource produced from its continental shelf is exempt from making such payments or contributions in respect of that mineral resource.
4. The payments or contributions shall be made through the Authority, which shall distribute them to States Parties to this Convention, on the basis of equitable sharing criteria, taking into account the interests and needs of developing States, particularly the least developed and the land-locked among them.

Article 83 – Delimitation of the continental shelf between States with opposite or adjacent coasts

1. The delimitation of the continental shelf between States with opposite or adjacent coasts shall be effected by agreement on the basis of international law, as referred to in Article 38 of the Statute of the International Court of Justice, in order to achieve an equitable solution.
2. If no agreement can be reached within a reasonable period of time, the States concerned shall resort to the procedures provided for in Part XV.
3. Pending agreement as provided for in paragraph 1, the States concerned, in a spirit of understanding and cooperation, shall make every effort to enter into provisional arrangements of a practical nature and, during this transitional period, not to jeopardize or hamper the reaching of the final agreement. Such arrangements shall be without prejudice to the final delimitation.
4. Where there is an agreement in force between the States concerned, questions relating to the delimitation of the continental shelf shall be determined in accordance with the provisions of that agreement.

Article 84 – Charts and lists of geographical coordinates

1. Subject to this Part, the outer limit lines of the continental shelf and the lines of delimitation drawn in accordance with article 83 shall be shown on charts of a scale or scales adequate for ascertaining their position. Where appropriate, lists of geographical coordinates of points, specifying the geodetic datum, may be substituted for such outer limit lines or lines of delimitation.
2. The coastal State shall give due publicity to such charts or lists of geographical coordinates and shall deposit a copy of each such chart or list with the Secretary-General of the United Nations and, in the case of those showing the outer limit lines of the continental shelf, with the Secretary-General of the Authority.

Article 85 – Tunnelling

This Part does not prejudice the right of the coastal State to exploit the subsoil by means of tunnelling, irrespective of the depth of water above the subsoil.

PART VII – HIGH SEAS

SECTION 1. GENERAL PROVISIONS

Article 86 – Application of the provisions of this Part

The provisions of this Part apply to all parts of the sea that are not included in the exclusive economic zone, in the territorial sea or in the internal waters of a State, or in the archipelagic waters of an archipelagic State. This article does not entail any abridgement of the freedoms enjoyed by all States in the exclusive economic zone in accordance with article 58.

Article 87 – Freedom of the high seas

1. The high seas are open to all States, whether coastal or land-locked. Freedom of the high seas is exercised under the conditions laid down by this Convention and by other rules of international law. It comprises, inter alia, both for coastal and land-locked States:
   (a) freedom of navigation;
   (b) freedom of overflight;
   (c) freedom to lay submarine cables and pipelines, subject to Part VI;
   (d) freedom to construct artificial islands and other installations permitted under international law, subject to Part VI;
   (e) freedom of fishing, subject to the conditions laid down in section 2;
   (f) freedom of scientific research, subject to Parts VI and XIII.
2. These freedoms shall be exercised by all States with due regard for the interests of other States in their exercise of the freedom of the high seas, and also with due regard for the rights under this Convention with respect to activities in the Area.

Article 88 – Reservation of the high seas for peaceful purposes

The high seas shall be reserved for peaceful purposes.

Article 89 – Invalidity of claims of sovereignty over the high seas

No State may validly purport to subject any part of the high seas to its sovereignty.

Article 90 – Right of navigation

Every State, whether coastal or land-locked, has the right to sail ships flying its flag on the high seas.

Article 91 – Nationality of ships

1. Every State shall fix the conditions for the grant of its nationality to ships, for the registration of ships in its territory, and for the right to fly its flag. Ships have the nationality of the State whose flag they are entitled to fly. There must exist a genuine link between the State and the ship.
2. Every State shall issue to ships to which it has granted the right to fly its flag documents to that effect.

Article 92 – Status of ships

1. Ships shall sail under the flag of one State only and, save in exceptional cases expressly provided for in international treaties or in this Convention, shall be subject to its exclusive jurisdiction on the high seas. A ship may not change its flag during a voyage or while in a port of call, save in the case of a real transfer of ownership or change of registry.
2. A ship which sails under the flags of two or more States, using them according to convenience, may not claim any of the nationalities in question with respect to any other State, and may be assimilated to a ship without nationality.

Article 93 – Ships flying the flag of the United Nations, its specialized agencies and the International Atomic Energy Agency

The preceding articles do not prejudice the question of ships employed on the official service of the United Nations, its specialized agencies or the International Atomic Energy Agency, flying the flag of the organization.

Article 94 – Duties of the flag State

1. Every State shall effectively exercise its jurisdiction and control in administrative, technical and social matters over ships flying its flag.
2. In particular every State shall:
   (a) maintain a register of ships containing the names and particulars of ships flying its flag, except those which are excluded from generally accepted international regulations on account of their small size; and
   (b) assume jurisdiction under its internal law over each ship flying its flag and its master, officers and crew in respect of administrative, technical and social matters concerning the ship.
3. Every State shall take such measures for ships flying its flag as are necessary to ensure safety at sea with regard, inter alia, to:
   (a) the construction, equipment and seaworthiness of ships;
   (b) the manning of ships, labour conditions and the training of crews, taking into account the applicable international instruments;
   (c) the use of signals, the maintenance of communications and the prevention of collisions.
4. Such measures shall include those necessary to ensure:
   (a) that each ship, before registration and thereafter at appropriate intervals, is surveyed by a qualified surveyor of ships, and has on board such charts, nautical publications and navigational equipment and instruments as are appropriate for the safe navigation of the ship;
   (b) that each ship is in the charge of a master and officers who possess appropriate qualifications, in particular in seamanship, navigation, communications and marine engineering, and that the crew is appropriate in qualification and numbers for the type, size, machinery and equipment of the ship;
   (c) that the master, officers and, to the extent appropriate, the crew are fully conversant with and required to observe the applicable international regulations concerning the safety of life at sea, the prevention of collisions, the prevention, reduction and control of marine pollution, and the maintenance of communications by radio.
5. In taking the measures called for in paragraphs 3 and 4 each State is required to conform to generally accepted international regulations, procedures and practices and to take any steps which may be necessary to secure their observance.
6. A State which has clear grounds to believe that proper jurisdiction and control with respect to a ship have not been exercised may report the facts to the flag State. Upon receiving such a report, the flag State shall investigate the matter and, if appropriate, take any action necessary to remedy the situation.
7. Each State shall cause an inquiry to be held by or before a suitably qualified person or persons into every marine casualty or incident of navigation on the high seas involving a ship flying its flag and causing loss of life or serious injury to nationals of another State or serious damage to ships or installations of another State or to the marine environment. The flag State and the other State shall cooperate in the conduct of any inquiry held by that other State into any such marine casualty or incident of navigation.

Article 95 – Immunity of warships on the high seas

Warships on the high seas have complete immunity from the jurisdiction of any State other than the flag State.

Article 96 – Immunity of ships used only on government non-commercial service

Ships owned or operated by a State and used only on government non-commercial service shall, on the high seas, have complete immunity from the jurisdiction of any State other than the flag State.

Article 97 – Penal jurisdiction in matters of collision or any other incident of navigation

1. In the event of a collision or any other incident of navigation concerning a ship on the high seas, involving the penal or disciplinary responsibility of the master or of any other person in the service of the ship, no penal or disciplinary proceedings may be instituted against such person except before the judicial or administrative authorities either of the flag State or of the State of which such person is a national.
2. In disciplinary matters, the State which has issued a master's certificate or a certificate of competence or licence shall alone be competent, after due legal process, to pronounce the withdrawal of such certificates, even if the holder is not a national of the State which issued them.
3. No arrest or detention of the ship, even as a measure of investigation, shall be ordered by any authorities other than those of the flag State.

Article 98 – Duty to render assistance

1. Every State shall require the master of a ship flying its flag, in so far as he can do so without serious danger to the ship, the crew or the passengers:
   (a) to render assistance to any person found at sea in danger of being lost;
   (b) to proceed with all possible speed to the rescue of persons in distress, if informed of their need of assistance, in so far as such action may reasonably be expected of him;
   (c) after a collision, to render assistance to the other ship, its crew and its passengers and, where possible, to inform the other ship of the name of his own ship, its port of registry and the nearest port at which it will call.
2. Every coastal State shall promote the establishment, operation and maintenance of an adequate and effective search and rescue service regarding safety on and over the sea and, where circumstances so require, by way of mutual regional arrangements cooperate with neighbouring States for this purpose.

Article 99 – Prohibition of the transport of slaves

Every State shall take effective measures to prevent and punish the transport of slaves in ships authorized to fly its flag and to prevent the unlawful use of its flag for that purpose. Any slave taking refuge on board any ship, whatever its flag, shall ipso facto be free.

Article 100 – Duty to cooperate in the repression of piracy

All States shall cooperate to the fullest possible extent in the repression of piracy on the high seas or in any other place outside the jurisdiction of any State.

Article 101 – Definition of piracy

Piracy consists of any of the following acts:

(a) any illegal acts of violence or detention, or any act of depredation, committed for private ends by the crew or the passengers of a private ship or a private aircraft, and directed:

(i) on the high seas, against another ship or aircraft, or against persons or property on board such ship or aircraft;

(ii) against a ship, aircraft, persons or property in a place outside the jurisdiction of any State;

(b) any act of voluntary participation in the operation of a ship or of an aircraft with knowledge of facts making it a pirate ship or aircraft;

(c) any act of inciting or of intentionally facilitating an act described in subparagraph (a) or (b).

Article 102 – Piracy by a warship, government ship or government aircraft whose crew has mutinied

The acts of piracy, as defined in article 101, committed by a warship, government ship or government aircraft whose crew has mutinied and taken control of the ship or aircraft are assimilated to acts committed by a private ship or aircraft.

Article 103 – Definition of a pirate ship or aircraft

A ship or aircraft is considered a pirate ship or aircraft if it is intended by the persons in dominant control to be used for the purpose of committing one of the acts referred to in article 101. The same applies if the ship or aircraft has been used to commit any such act, so long as it remains under the control of the persons guilty of that act.

Article 104 – Retention or loss of the nationality of a pirate ship or aircraft

A ship or aircraft may retain its nationality although it has become a pirate ship or aircraft. The retention or loss of nationality is determined by the law of the State from which such nationality was derived.

Article 105 – Seizure of a pirate ship or aircraft

On the high seas, or in any other place outside the jurisdiction of any State, every State may seize a pirate ship or aircraft, or a ship or aircraft taken by piracy and under the control of pirates, and arrest the persons and seize the property on board. The courts of the State which carried out the seizure may decide upon the penalties to be imposed, and may also determine the action to be taken with regard to the ships, aircraft or property, subject to the rights of third parties acting in good faith.

Article 106 – Liability for seizure without adequate grounds

Where the seizure of a ship or aircraft on suspicion of piracy has been effected without adequate grounds, the State making the seizure shall be liable to the State the nationality of which is possessed by the ship or aircraft for any loss or damage caused by the seizure.

Article 107 – Ships and aircraft which are entitled to seize on account of piracy

A seizure on account of piracy may be carried out only by warships or military aircraft, or other ships or aircraft clearly marked and identifiable as being on government service and authorized to that effect.

Article 108 – Illicit traffic in narcotic drugs or psychotropic substances

1. All States shall cooperate in the suppression of illicit traffic in narcotic drugs and psychotropic substances engaged in by ships on the high seas contrary to international conventions.
2. Any State which has reasonable grounds for believing that a ship flying its flag is engaged in illicit traffic in narcotic drugs or psychotropic substances may request the cooperation of other States to suppress such traffic.

Article 109 – Unauthorized broadcasting from the high seas

1. All States shall cooperate in the suppression of unauthorized broadcasting from the high seas.
2. For the purposes of this Convention, "unauthorized broadcasting" means the transmission of sound radio or television broadcasts from a ship or installation on the high seas intended for reception by the general public contrary to international regulations, but excluding the transmission of distress calls.
3. Any person engaged in unauthorized broadcasting may be prosecuted before the court of:
   (a) the flag State of the ship;
   (b) the State of registry of the installation;
   (c) the State of which the person is a national;
   (d) any State where the transmissions can be received; or
   (e) any State where authorized radio communication is suffering interference.
4. On the high seas, a State having jurisdiction in accordance with paragraph 3 may, in conformity with article 110, arrest any person or ship engaged in unauthorized broadcasting and seize the broadcasting apparatus.

Article 110 – Right of visit

1. Except where acts of interference derive from powers conferred by treaty, a warship which encounters on the high seas a foreign ship, other than a ship entitled to complete immunity in accordance with articles 95 and 96, is not justified in boarding it unless there is reasonable ground for suspecting that:
   (a) the ship is engaged in piracy;
   (b) the ship is engaged in the slave trade;
   (c) the ship is engaged in unauthorized broadcasting and the flag State of the warship has jurisdiction under article 109;
   (d) the ship is without nationality; or
   (e) though flying a foreign flag or refusing to show its flag, the ship is, in reality, of the same nationality as the warship.
2. In the cases provided for in paragraph 1, the warship may proceed to verify the ship's right to fly its flag. To this end, it may send a boat under the command of an officer to the suspected ship. If suspicion remains after the documents have been checked, it may proceed to a further examination on board the ship, which must be carried out with all possible consideration.
3. If the suspicions prove to be unfounded, and provided that the ship boarded has not committed any act justifying them, it shall be compensated for any loss or damage that may have been sustained.
4. These provisions apply mutatis mutandis to military aircraft.
5. These provisions also apply to any other duly authorized ships or aircraft clearly marked and identifiable as being on government service.

Article 111 – Right of hot pursuit

1. The hot pursuit of a foreign ship may be undertaken when the competent authorities of the coastal State have good reason to believe that the ship has violated the laws and regulations of that State. Such pursuit must be commenced when the foreign ship or one of its boats is within the internal waters, the archipelagic waters, the territorial sea or the contiguous zone of the pursuing State, and may only be continued outside the territorial sea or the contiguous zone if the pursuit has not been interrupted. It is not necessary that, at the time when the foreign ship within the territorial sea or the contiguous zone receives the order to stop, the ship giving the order should likewise be within the territorial sea or the contiguous zone. If the foreign ship is within a contiguous zone, as defined in article 33, the pursuit may only be undertaken if there has been a violation of the rights for the protection of which the zone was established.
2. The right of hot pursuit shall apply mutatis mutandis to violations in the exclusive economic zone or on the continental shelf, including safety zones around continental shelf installations, of the laws and regulations of the coastal State applicable in accordance with this Convention to the exclusive economic zone or the continental shelf, including such safety zones.
3. The right of hot pursuit ceases as soon as the ship pursued enters the territorial sea of its own State or of a third State.
4. Hot pursuit is not deemed to have begun unless the pursuing ship has satisfied itself by such practicable means as may be available that the ship pursued or one of its boats or other craft working

as a team and using the ship pursued as a mother ship is within the limits of the territorial sea, or, as the case may be, within the contiguous zone or the exclusive economic zone or above the continental shelf. The pursuit may only be commenced after a visual or auditory signal to stop has been given at a distance which enables it to be seen or heard by the foreign ship.

5. The right of hot pursuit may be exercised only by warships or military aircraft, or other ships or aircraft clearly marked and identifiable as being on government service and authorized to that effect.
6. Where hot pursuit is effected by an aircraft:
   (a) the provisions of paragraphs 1 to 4 shall apply mutatis mutandis;
   (b) the aircraft giving the order to stop must itself actively pursue the ship until a ship or another aircraft of the coastal State, summoned by the aircraft, arrives to take over the pursuit, unless the aircraft is itself able to arrest the ship. It does not suffice to justify an arrest outside the territorial sea that the ship was merely sighted by the aircraft as an offender or suspected offender, if it was not both ordered to stop and pursued by the aircraft itself or other aircraft or ships which continue the pursuit without interruption.
7. The release of a ship arrested within the jurisdiction of a State and escorted to a port of that State for the purposes of an inquiry before the competent authorities may not be claimed solely on the ground that the ship, in the course of its voyage, was escorted across a portion of the exclusive economic zone or the high seas, if the circumstances rendered this necessary.
8. Where a ship has been stopped or arrested outside the territorial sea in circumstances which do not justify the exercise of the right of hot pursuit, it shall be compensated for any loss or damage that may have been thereby sustained.

Article 112 – Right to lay submarine cables and pipelines

1. All States are entitled to lay submarine cables and pipelines on the bed of the high seas beyond the continental shelf.
2. Article 79, paragraph 5, applies to such cables and pipelines.

Article 113 – Breaking or injury of a submarine cable or pipeline

Every State shall adopt the laws and regulations necessary to provide that the breaking or injury by a ship flying its flag or by a person subject to its jurisdiction of a submarine cable beneath the high seas done wilfully or through culpable negligence, in such a manner as to be liable to interrupt or obstruct telegraphic or telephonic communications, and similarly the breaking or injury of a submarine pipeline or high-voltage power cable, shall be a punishable offence. This provision shall apply also to conduct calculated or likely to result in such breaking or injury. However, it shall not apply to any break or injury caused by persons who acted merely with the legitimate object of saving their lives or their ships, after having taken all necessary precautions to avoid such break or injury.

Article 114 – Breaking or injury by owners of a submarine cable or pipeline of another submarine cable or pipeline

Every State shall adopt the laws and regulations necessary to provide that, if persons subject to its jurisdiction who are the owners of a submarine cable or pipeline beneath the high seas, in laying or repairing that cable or pipeline, cause a break in or injury to another cable or pipeline, they shall bear the cost of the repairs.

Article 115 – Indemnity for loss incurred in avoiding injury to a submarine cable or pipeline

Every State shall adopt the laws and regulations necessary to ensure that the owners of ships who can prove that they have sacrificed an anchor, a net or any other fishing gear, in order to avoid injuring a submarine cable or pipeline, shall be indemnified by the owner of the cable or pipeline, provided that the owner of the ship has taken all reasonable precautionary measures beforehand.

SECTION 2. CONSERVATION AND MANAGEMENT OF THE LIVING RESOURCES OF THE HIGH SEAS

Article 116 – Right to fish on the high seas

All States have the right for their nationals to engage in fishing on the high seas subject to:

(a) their treaty obligations;

(b) the rights and duties as well as the interests of coastal States provided for, inter alia, in article 63, paragraph 2, and articles 64 to 67; and

(c) the provisions of this section.

Article 117 – Duty of States to adopt with respect to their nationals measures for the conservation of the living resources of the high seas

All States have the duty to take, or to cooperate with other States in taking, such measures for their respective nationals as may be necessary for the conservation of the living resources of the high seas.

Article 118 – Cooperation of States in the conservation and management of living resources

States shall cooperate with each other in the conservation and management of living resources in the areas of the high seas. States whose nationals exploit identical living resources, or different living resources in the same area, shall enter into negotiations with a view to taking the measures necessary for the conservation of the living resources concerned. They shall, as appropriate, cooperate to establish subregional or regional fisheries organizations to this end.

Article 119 – Conservation of the living resources of the high seas

1. In determining the allowable catch and establishing other conservation measures for the living resources in the high seas, States shall:
   (a) take measures which are designed, on the best scientific evidence available to the States concerned, to maintain or restore populations of harvested species at levels which can produce the maximum sustainable yield, as qualified by relevant environmental and economic factors, including the special requirements of developing States, and taking into account fishing patterns, the interdependence of stocks and any generally recommended international minimum standards, whether subregional, regional or global;
   (b) take into consideration the effects on species associated with or dependent upon harvested species with a view to maintaining or restoring populations of such associated or dependent species above levels at which their reproduction may become seriously threatened.
2. Available scientific information, catch and fishing effort statistics, and other data relevant to the conservation of fish stocks shall be contributed and exchanged on a regular basis through competent international organizations, whether subregional, regional or global, where appropriate and with participation by all States concerned.
3. States concerned shall ensure that conservation measures and their implementation do not discriminate in form or in fact against the fishermen of any State.

Article 120 – Marine mammals

Article 65 also applies to the conservation and management of marine mammals in the high seas.

PART VIII – REGIME OF ISLANDS

Article 121 – Regime of islands

1. An island is a naturally formed area of land, surrounded by water, which is above water at high tide.
2. Except as provided for in paragraph 3, the territorial sea, the contiguous zone, the exclusive economic zone and the continental shelf of an island are determined in accordance with the provisions of this Convention applicable to other land territory.
3. Rocks which cannot sustain human habitation or economic life of their own shall have no exclusive economic zone or continental shelf.

PART IX – ENCLOSED OR SEMI-ENCLOSED SEAS

Article 122 – Definition

For the purposes of this Convention, "enclosed or semi-enclosed sea" means a gulf, basin or sea surrounded by two or more States and connected to another sea or the ocean by a narrow outlet or consisting entirely or primarily of the territorial seas and exclusive economic zones of two or more coastal States.

Article 123 – Cooperation of States bordering enclosed or semi-enclosed seas

States bordering an enclosed or semi-enclosed sea should cooperate with each other in the exercise of their rights and in the performance of their duties under this Convention. To this end they shall endeavour, directly or through an appropriate regional organization:

(a) to coordinate the management, conservation, exploration and exploitation of the living resources of the sea;

(b) to coordinate the implementation of their rights and duties with respect to the protection and preservation of the marine environment;

(c) to coordinate their scientific research policies and undertake where appropriate joint programmes of scientific research in the area;

(d) to invite, as appropriate, other interested States or international organizations to cooperate with them in furtherance of the provisions of this article.

PART X – RIGHT OF ACCESS OF LAND-LOCKED STATES TO AND FROM THE SEA AND FREEDOM OF TRANSIT

Article 124 – Use of terms

1. For the purposes of this Convention:
   (a) "land-locked State" means a State which has no sea-coast;
   (b) "transit State" means a State, with or without a sea-coast, situated between a land-locked State and the sea, through whose territory traffic in transit passes;
   (c) "traffic in transit" means transit of persons, baggage, goods and means of transport across the territory of one or more transit States, when the passage across such territory, with or without trans-shipment, warehousing, breaking bulk or change in the mode of transport, is only a portion of a complete journey which begins or terminates within the territory of the land-locked State;
   (d) "means of transport" means:
      (i) railway rolling stock, sea, lake and river craft and road vehicles;
      (ii) where local conditions so require, porters and pack animals.
2. Land-locked States and transit States may, by agreement between them, include as means of transport pipelines and gas lines and means of transport other than those included in paragraph 1.

Article 125 – Right of access to and from the sea and freedom of transit

1. Land-locked States shall have the right of access to and from the sea for the purpose of exercising the rights provided for in this Convention including those relating to the freedom of the high seas and the common heritage of mankind. To this end, land-locked States shall enjoy freedom of transit through the territory of transit States by all means of transport.

2. The terms and modalities for exercising freedom of transit shall be agreed between the land-locked States and transit States concerned through bilateral, subregional or regional agreements.
3. Transit States, in the exercise of their full sovereignty over their territory, shall have the right to take all measures necessary to ensure that the rights and facilities provided for in this Part for land-locked States shall in no way infringe their legitimate interests.

Article 126 – Exclusion of application of the most-favoured-nation clause

The provisions of this Convention, as well as special agreements relating to the exercise of the right of access to and from the sea, establishing rights and facilities on account of the special geographical position of land-locked States, are excluded from the application of the most-favoured-nation clause.

Article 127 – Customs duties, taxes and other charges

1. Traffic in transit shall not be subject to any customs duties, taxes or other charges except charges levied for specific services rendered in connection with such traffic.
2. Means of transport in transit and other facilities provided for and used by land-locked States shall not be subject to taxes or charges higher than those levied for the use of means of transport of the transit State.

Article 128 – Free zones and other customs facilities

For the convenience of traffic in transit, free zones or other customs facilities may be provided at the ports of entry and exit in the transit States, by agreement between those States and the land-locked States.

Article 129 – Cooperation in the construction and improvement of means of transport

Where there are no means of transport in transit States to give effect to the freedom of transit or where the existing means, including the port installations and equipment, are inadequate in any respect, the transit States and land-locked States concerned may cooperate in constructing or improving them.

Article 130 – Measures to avoid or eliminate delays or other difficulties of a technical nature in traffic in transit

1. Transit States shall take all appropriate measures to avoid delays or other difficulties of a technical nature in traffic in transit.
2. Should such delays or difficulties occur, the competent authorities of the transit States and land-locked States concerned shall cooperate towards their expeditious elimination.

Article 131 – Equal treatment in maritime ports

Ships flying the flag of land-locked States shall enjoy treatment equal to that accorded to other foreign ships in maritime ports.

Article 132 – Grant of greater transit facilities

This Convention does not entail in any way the withdrawal of transit facilities which are greater than those provided for in this Convention and which are agreed between States Parties to this Convention or granted by a State Party. This Convention also does not preclude such grant of greater facilities in the future.

PART XI – THE AREA

SECTION 1. GENERAL PROVISIONS

Article 133 – Use of terms

For the purposes of this Part:

(a) “resources” means all solid, liquid or gaseous mineral resources in situ in the Area at or beneath the seabed, including polymetallic nodules;

(b) resources, when recovered from the Area, are referred to as “minerals”.

Article 134 – Scope of this Part

1. This Part applies to the Area.
2. Activities in the Area shall be governed by the provisions of this Part.
3. The requirements concerning deposit of, and publicity to be given to, the charts or lists of geographical coordinates showing the limits referred to in article l, paragraph l(1), are set forth in Part VI.
4. Nothing in this article affects the establishment of the outer limits of the continental shelf in accordance with Part VI or the validity of agreements relating to delimitation between States with opposite or adjacent coasts.

Article 135 – Legal status of the superjacent waters and air space

Neither this Part nor any rights granted or exercised pursuant thereto shall affect the legal status of the waters superjacent to the Area or that of the air space above those waters.

SECTION 2. PRINCIPLES GOVERNING THE AREA

Article 136 – Common heritage of mankind

The Area and its resources are the common heritage of mankind.

Article 137 – Legal status of the Area and its resources

1. No State shall claim or exercise sovereignty or sovereign rights over any part of the Area or its resources, nor shall any State or natural or juridical person appropriate any part thereof. No such claim or exercise of sovereignty or sovereign rights nor such appropriation shall be recognized.
2. All rights in the resources of the Area are vested in mankind as a whole, on whose behalf the Au-

thority shall act. These resources are not subject to alienation. The minerals recovered from the Area, however, may only be alienated in accordance with this Part and the rules, regulations and procedures of the Authority.

3. No State or natural or juridical person shall claim, acquire or exercise rights with respect to the minerals recovered from the Area except in accordance with this Part. Otherwise, no such claim, acquisition or exercise of such rights shall be recognized.

Article 138 – General conduct of States in relation to the Area

The general conduct of States in relation to the Area shall be in accordance with the provisions of this Part, the principles embodied in the Charter of the United Nations and other rules of international law in the interests of maintaining peace and security and promoting international cooperation and mutual understanding.

Article 139 – Responsibility to ensure compliance and liability for damage

1. States Parties shall have the responsibility to ensure that activities in the Area, whether carried out by States Parties, or state enterprises or natural or juridical persons which possess the nationality of States Parties or are effectively controlled by them or their nationals, shall be carried out in conformity with this Part. The same responsibility applies to international organizations for activities in the Area carried out by such organizations.
2. Without prejudice to the rules of international law and Annex III, article 22, damage caused by the failure of a State Party or international organization to carry out its responsibilities under this Part shall entail liability; States Parties or international organizations acting together shall bear joint and several liability. A State Party shall not however be liable for damage caused by any failure to comply with this Part by a person whom it has sponsored under article 153, paragraph 2(b), if the State Party has taken all necessary and appropriate measures to secure effective compliance under article 153, paragraph 4, and Annex III, article 4, paragraph 4.
3. States Parties that are members of international organizations shall take appropriate measures to ensure the implementation of this article with respect to such organizations.

Article 140 – Benefit of mankind

1. Activities in the Area shall, as specifically provided for in this Part, be carried out for the benefit of mankind as a whole, irrespective of the geographical location of States, whether coastal or land-locked, and taking into particular consideration the interests and needs of developing States and of peoples who have not attained full independence or other self-governing status recognized by the United Nations in accordance with General Assembly resolution 1514 (XV) and other relevant General Assembly resolutions.
2. The Authority shall provide for the equitable sharing of financial and other economic benefits derived from activities in the Area through any appropriate mechanism, on a non-discriminatory basis, in accordance with article 160, paragraph 2(f)(i).

Article 141 – Use of the Area exclusively for peaceful purposes

The Area shall be open to use exclusively for peaceful purposes by all States, whether coastal or land-locked, without discrimination and without prejudice to the other provisions of this Part.

Article 142 – Rights and legitimate interests of coastal States

1. Activities in the Area, with respect to resource deposits in the Area which lie across limits of national jurisdiction, shall be conducted with due regard to the rights and legitimate interests of any coastal State across whose jurisdiction such deposits lie.
2. Consultations, including a system of prior notification, shall be maintained with the State concerned, with a view to avoiding infringement of such rights and interests. In cases where activities in the Area may result in the exploitation of resources lying within national jurisdiction, the prior consent of the coastal State concerned shall be required.
3. Neither this Part nor any rights granted or exercised pursuant thereto shall affect the rights of coastal States to take such measures consistent with the relevant provisions of Part XII as may be necessary to prevent, mitigate or eliminate grave and imminent danger to their coastline, or related interests from pollution or threat thereof or from other hazardous occurrences resulting from or caused by any activities in the Area.

Article 143 – Marine scientific research

1. Marine scientific research in the Area shall be carried out exclusively for peaceful purposes and for the benefit of mankind as a whole, in accordance with Part XIII.
2. The Authority may carry out marine scientific research concerning the Area and its resources, and may enter into contracts for that purpose. The Authority shall promote and encourage the conduct of marine scientific research in the Area, and shall coordinate and disseminate the results of such research and analysis when available.
3. States Parties may carry out marine scientific research in the Area. States Parties shall promote international cooperation in marine scientific research in the Area by:
   (a) participating in international programmes and encouraging cooperation in marine scientific research by personnel of different countries and of the Authority;
   (b) ensuring that programmes are developed through the Authority or other international organizations as appropriate for the benefit of developing States and technologically less developed States with a view to:
      (i) strengthening their research capabilities;

(ii) training their personnel and the personnel of the Authority in the techniques and applications of research;

(iii) fostering the employment of their qualified personnel in research in the Area;

(c) effectively disseminating the results of research and analysis when available, through the Authority or other international channels when appropriate.

Article 144 – Transfer of technology

1. The Authority shall take measures in accordance with this Convention:

   (a) to acquire technology and scientific knowledge relating to activities in the Area; and

   (b) to promote and encourage the transfer to developing States of such technology and scientific knowledge so that all States Parties benefit therefrom.

2. To this end the Authority and States Parties shall cooperate in promoting the transfer of technology and scientific knowledge relating to activities in the Area so that the Enterprise and all States Parties may benefit therefrom. In particular they shall initiate and promote:

   (a) programmes for the transfer of technology to the Enterprise and to developing States with regard to activities in the Area, including, inter alia, facilitating the access of the Enterprise and of developing States to the relevant technology, under fair and reasonable terms and conditions;

   (b) measures directed towards the advancement of the technology of the Enterprise and the domestic technology of developing States, particularly by providing opportunities to personnel from the Enterprise and from developing States for training in marine science and technology and for their full participation in activities in the Area.

Article 145 – Protection of the marine environment

Necessary measures shall be taken in accordance with this Convention with respect to activities in the Area to ensure effective protection for the marine environment from harmful effects which may arise from such activities. To this end the Authority shall adopt appropriate rules, regulations and procedures for inter alia:

(a) the prevention, reduction and control of pollution and other hazards to the marine environment, including the coastline, and of interference with the ecological balance of the marine environment, particular attention being paid to the need for protection from harmful effects of such activities as drilling, dredging, excavation, disposal of waste, construction and operation or maintenance of installations, pipelines and other devices related to such activities;

(b) the protection and conservation of the natural resources of the Area and the prevention of damage to the flora and fauna of the marine environment.

Article 146 – Protection of human life

With respect to activities in the Area, necessary measures shall be taken to ensure effective protection of human life. To this end the Authority shall adopt appropriate rules, regulations and procedures to supplement existing international law as embodied in relevant treaties.

Article 147 – Accommodation of activities in the Area and in the marine environment

1. Activities in the Area shall be carried out with reasonable regard for other activities in the marine environment.

2. Installations used for carrying out activities in the Area shall be subject to the following conditions:

   (a) such installations shall be erected, emplaced and removed solely in accordance with this Part and subject to the rules, regulations and procedures of the Authority. Due notice must be given of the erection, emplacement and removal of such installations, and permanent means for giving warning of their presence must be maintained;

   (b) such installations may not be established where interference may be caused to the use of recognized sea lanes essential to international navigation or in areas of intense fishing activity;

   (c) safety zones shall be established around such installations with appropriate markings to ensure the safety of both navigation and the installations. The configuration and location of such safety zones shall not be such as to form a belt impeding the lawful access of shipping to particular maritime zones or navigation along international sea lanes;

   (d) such installations shall be used exclusively for peaceful purposes;

   (e) such installations do not possess the status of islands. They have no territorial sea of their own, and their presence does not affect the delimitation of the territorial sea, the exclusive economic zone or the continental shelf.

3. Other activities in the marine environment shall be conducted with reasonable regard for activities in the Area.

Article 148 – Participation of developing States in activities in the Area

The effective participation of developing States in activities in the Area shall be promoted as specifically provided for in this Part, having due regard to their special interests and needs, and in particular to the special need of the land-locked and geographically disadvantaged among them to overcome obstacles arising from their disadvantaged location, including remoteness from the Area and difficulty of access to and from it.

Article 149 – Archaeological and historical objects

All objects of an archaeological and historical nature found in the Area shall be preserved or disposed of for the benefit of mankind as a whole, particular regard being paid to the preferential rights of the State or country of origin, or the State of cultural origin, or the State of historical and archaeological origin.

SECTION 3. DEVELOPMENT OF RESOURCES OF THE AREA

Article 150 – Policies relating to activities in the Area

Activities in the Area shall, as specifically provided for in this Part, be carried out in such a manner as to foster healthy development of the world economy and balanced growth of international trade, and to promote international cooperation for the over-all development of all countries, especially developing States, and with a view to ensuring:

(a) the development of the resources of the Area;

(b) orderly, safe and rational management of the resources of the Area, including the efficient conduct of activities in the Area and, in accordance with sound principles of conservation, the avoidance of unnecessary waste;

(c) the expansion of opportunities for participation in such activities consistent in particular with articles 144 and 148;

(d) participation in revenues by the Authority and the transfer of technology to the Enterprise and developing States as provided for in this Convention;

(e) increased availability of the minerals derived from the Area as needed in conjunction with minerals derived from other sources, to ensure supplies to consumers of such minerals;

(f) the promotion of just and stable prices remunerative to producers and fair to consumers for minerals derived both from the Area and from other sources, and the promotion of long-term equilibrium between supply and demand;

(g) the enhancement of opportunities for all States Parties, irrespective of their social and economic systems or geographical location, to participate in the development of the resources of the Area and the prevention of monopolization of activities in the Area;

(h) the protection of developing countries from adverse effects on their economies or on their export earnings resulting from a reduction in the price of an affected mineral, or in the volume of exports of that mineral, to the extent that such reduction is caused by activities in the Area, as provided in article 151;

(i) the development of the common heritage for the benefit of mankind as a whole; and

(j) conditions of access to markets for the imports of minerals produced from the resources of the Area and for imports of commodities produced from such minerals shall not be more favourable than the most favourable applied to imports from other sources.

Article 151 – Production policies

1. (a) Without prejudice to the objectives set forth in article 150 and for the purpose of implementing subparagraph (h) of that article, the Authority, acting through existing forums or such new arrangements or agreements as may be appropriate, in which all interested parties, including both producers and consumers, participate, shall take measures necessary to promote the growth, efficiency and stability of markets for those commodities produced from the minerals derived from the Area, at prices remunerative to producers and fair to consumers. All States Parties shall cooperate to this end.

   (b) The Authority shall have the right to participate in any commodity conference dealing with those commodities and in which all interested parties including both producers and consumers participate. The Authority shall have the right to become a party to any arrangement or agreement resulting from such conferences. Participation of the Authority in any organs established under those arrangements or agreements shall be in respect of production in the Area and in accordance with the relevant rules of those organs.

   (c) The Authority shall carry out its obligations under the arrangements or agreements referred to in this paragraph in a manner which assures a uniform and non-discriminatory implementation in respect of all production in the Area of the minerals concerned. In doing so, the Authority shall act in a manner consistent with the terms of existing contracts and approved plans of work of the Enterprise.

2. (a) During the interim period specified in paragraph 3, commercial production shall not be undertaken pursuant to an approved plan of work until the operator has applied for and has been issued a production authorization by the Authority. Such production authorizations may not be applied for or issued more than five years prior to the planned commencement of commercial production under the plan of work unless, having regard to the nature and timing of project development, the rules, regulations and procedures of the Authority prescribe another period.

   (b) In the application for the production authorization, the operator shall specify the annual quantity of nickel expected to be recovered under the approved plan of work. The application shall include a schedule of expenditures to be made by the operator after he has received the authorization which are reasonably calculated to allow him to begin commercial production on the date planned.

   (c) For the purposes of subparagraphs (a) and (b), the Authority shall establish appropriate performance requirements in accordance with Annex III, article 17.

(d) The Authority shall issue a production authorization for the level of production applied for unless the sum of that level and the levels already authorized exceeds the nickel production ceiling, as calculated pursuant to paragraph 4 in the year of issuance of the authorization, during any year of planned production falling within the interim period.

(e) When issued, the production authorization and approved application shall become a part of the approved plan of work.

(f) If the operator's application for a production authorization is denied pursuant to subparagraph (d), the operator may apply again to the Authority at any time.

3. The interim period shall begin five years prior to 1 January of the year in which the earliest commercial production is planned to commence under an approved plan of work. If the earliest commercial production is delayed beyond the year originally planned, the beginning of the interim period and the production ceiling originally calculated shall be adjusted accordingly. The interim period shall last 25 years or until the end of the Review Conference referred to in article 155 or until the day when such new arrangements or agreements as are referred to in paragraph 1 enter into force, whichever is earliest. The Authority shall resume the power provided in this article for the remainder of the interim period if the said arrangements or agreements should lapse or become ineffective for any reason whatsoever.

4. (a) The production ceiling for any year of the interim period shall be the sum of:

   (i) the difference between the trend line values for nickel consumption, as calculated pursuant to subparagraph (b), for the year immediately prior to the year of the earliest commercial production and the year immediately prior to the commencement of the interim period; and

   (ii) sixty per cent of the difference between the trend line values for nickel consumption, as calculated pursuant to subparagraph (b), for the year for which the production authorization is being applied for and the year immediately prior to the year of the earliest commercial production.

   (b) For the purposes of subparagraph (a):

   (i) trend line values used for computing the nickel production ceiling shall be those annual nickel consumption values on a trend line computed during the year in which a production authorization is issued. The trend line shall be derived from a linear regression of the logarithms of actual nickel consumption for the most recent 15-year period for which such data are available, time being the independent variable. This trend line shall be referred to as the original trend line;

   (ii) if the annual rate of increase of the original trend line is less than 3 per cent, then the trend line used to determine the quantities referred to in subparagraph (a) shall instead be one passing through the original trend line at the value for the first year of the relevant 15-year period, and increasing at 3 per cent annually; provided however that the production ceiling established for any year of the interim period may not in any case exceed the difference between the original trend line value for that year and the original trend line value for the year immediately prior to the commencement of the interim period.

5. The Authority shall reserve to the Enterprise for its initial production a quantity of 38,000 metric tonnes of nickel from the available production ceiling calculated pursuant to paragraph 4.

6. (a) An operator may in any year produce less than or up to 8 per cent more than the level of annual production of minerals from polymetallic nodules specified in his production authorization, provided that the over-all amount of production shall not exceed that specified in the authorization. Any excess over 8 per cent and up to 20 per cent in any year, or any excess in the first and subsequent years following two consecutive years in which excesses occur, shall be negotiated with the Authority, which may require the operator to obtain a supplementary production authorization to cover additional production.

   (b) Applications for such supplementary production authorizations shall be considered by the Authority only after all pending applications by operators who have not yet received production authorizations have been acted upon and due account has been taken of other likely applicants. The Authority shall be guided by the principle of not exceeding the total production allowed under the production ceiling in any year of the interim period. It shall not authorize the production under any plan of work of a quantity in excess of 46,500 metric tonnes of nickel per year.

7. The levels of production of other metals such as copper, cobalt and manganese extracted from the polymetallic nodules that are recovered pursuant to a production authorization should not be higher than those which would have been produced had the operator produced the maximum level of nickel from those nodules pursuant to this article. The Authority shall establish rules, regulations and procedures pursuant to Annex III, article 17, to implement this paragraph.

8. Rights and obligations relating to unfair economic practices under relevant multilateral trade agreements shall apply to the exploration for and exploitation of minerals from the Area. In the settlement of disputes arising under this provision, States Parties which are Parties to such multilateral trade agreements shall have recourse to the dispute settlement procedures of such agreements.

9. The Authority shall have the power to limit the level of production of minerals from the Area, other than minerals from polymetallic nodules, under such conditions and applying such methods as may be appropriate by adopting regulations in accordance with article 161, paragraph 8.
10. Upon the recommendation of the Council on the basis of advice from the Economic Planning Commission, the Assembly shall establish a system of compensation or take other measures of economic adjustment assistance including cooperation with specialized agencies and other international organizations to assist developing countries which suffer serious adverse effects on their export earnings or economies resulting from a reduction in the price of an affected mineral or in the volume of exports of that mineral, to the extent that such reduction is caused by activities in the Area. The Authority on request shall initiate studies on the problems of those States which are likely to be most seriously affected with a view to minimizing their difficulties and assisting them in their economic adjustment.

Article 152 – Exercise of powers and functions by the Authority

1. The Authority shall avoid discrimination in the exercise of its powers and functions, including the granting of opportunities for activities in the Area.
2. Nevertheless, special consideration for developing States, including particular consideration for the land-locked and geographically disadvantaged among them, specifically provided for in this Part shall be permitted.

Article 153 – System of exploration and exploitation

1. Activities in the Area shall be organized, carried out and controlled by the Authority on behalf of mankind as a whole in accordance with this article as well as other relevant provisions of this Part and the relevant Annexes, and the rules, regulations and procedures of the Authority.
2. Activities in the Area shall be carried out as prescribed in paragraph 3:
   (a) by the Enterprise, and
   (b) in association with the Authority by States Parties, or state enterprises or natural or juridical persons which possess the nationality of States Parties or are effectively controlled by them or their nationals, when sponsored by such States, or any group of the foregoing which meets the requirements provided in this Part and in Annex III.
3. Activities in the Area shall be carried out in accordance with a formal written plan of work drawn up in accordance with Annex III and approved by the Council after review by the Legal and Technical Commission. In the case of activities in the Area carried out as authorized by the Authority by the entities specified in paragraph 2(b), the plan of work shall, in accordance with Annex III, article 3, be in the form of a contract. Such contracts may provide for joint arrangements in accordance with Annex III, article 11.
4. The Authority shall exercise such control over activities in the Area as is necessary for the purpose of securing compliance with the relevant provisions of this Part and the Annexes relating thereto, and the rules, regulations and procedures of the Authority, and the plans of work approved in accordance with paragraph 3. States Parties shall assist the Authority by taking all measures necessary to ensure such compliance in accordance with article 139.
5. The Authority shall have the right to take at any time any measures provided for under this Part to ensure compliance with its provisions and the exercise of the functions of control and regulation assigned to it thereunder or under any contract. The Authority shall have the right to inspect all installations in the Area used in connection with activities in the Area.
6. A contract under paragraph 3 shall provide for security of tenure. Accordingly, the contract shall not be revised, suspended or terminated except in accordance with Annex III, articles 18 and 19.

Article 154 – Periodic review

Every five years from the entry into force of this Convention, the Assembly shall undertake a general and systematic review of the manner in which the international regime of the Area established in this Convention has operated in practice. In the light of this review the Assembly may take, or recommend that other organs take, measures in accordance with the provisions and procedures of this Part and the Annexes relating thereto which will lead to the improvement of the operation of the regime.

Article 155 – The Review Conference

1. Fifteen years from 1 January of the year in which the earliest commercial production commences under an approved plan of work, the Assembly shall convene a conference for the review of those provisions of this Part and the relevant Annexes which govern the system of exploration and exploitation of the resources of the Area. The Review Conference shall consider in detail, in the light of the experience acquired during that period:
   (a) whether the provisions of this Part which govern the system of exploration and exploitation of the resources of the Area have achieved their aims in all respects, including whether they have benefited mankind as a whole;
   (b) whether, during the 15-year period, reserved areas have been exploited in an effective and balanced manner in comparison with non-reserved areas;
   (c) whether the development and use of the Area and its resources have been undertaken in such a manner as to foster healthy development of the world economy and balanced growth of international trade;
   (d) whether monopolization of activities in the Area has been prevented;

(e) whether the policies set forth in articles 150 and 151 have been fulfilled; and

(f) whether the system has resulted in the equitable sharing of benefits derived from activities in the Area, taking into particular consideration the interests and needs of the developing States.

2. The Review Conference shall ensure the maintenance of the principle of the common heritage of mankind, the international regime designed to ensure equitable exploitation of the resources of the Area for the benefit of all countries, especially the developing States, and an Authority to organize, conduct and control activities in the Area. It shall also ensure the maintenance of the principles laid down in this Part with regard to the exclusion of claims or exercise of sovereignty over any part of the Area, the rights of States and their general conduct in relation to the Area, and their participation in activities in the Area in conformity with this Convention, the prevention of monopolization of activities in the Area, the use of the Area exclusively for peaceful purposes, economic aspects of activities in the Area, marine scientific research, transfer of technology, protection of the marine environment, protection of human life, rights of coastal States, the legal status of the waters superjacent to the Area and that of the air space above those waters and accommodation between activities in the Area and other activities in the marine environment.

3. The decision-making procedure applicable at the Review Conference shall be the same as that applicable at the Third United Nations Conference on the Law of the Sea. The Conference shall make every effort to reach agreement on any amendments by way of consensus and there should be no voting on such matters until all efforts at achieving consensus have been exhausted.

4. If, five years after its commencement, the Review Conference has not reached agreement on the system of exploration and exploitation of the resources of the Area, it may decide during the ensuing 12 months, by a three-fourths majority of the States Parties, to adopt and submit to the States Parties for ratification or accession such amendments changing or modifying the system as it determines necessary and appropriate. Such amendments shall enter into force for all States Parties 12 months after the deposit of instruments of ratification or accession by three fourths of the States Parties.

5. Amendments adopted by the Review Conference pursuant to this article shall not affect rights acquired under existing contracts.

[…]

SECTION 5. SETTLEMENT OF DISPUTES AND ADVISORY OPINIONS

Article 186 – Seabed Disputes Chamber of the International Tribunal for the Law of the Sea

The establishment of the Seabed Disputes Chamber and the manner in which it shall exercise its jurisdiction shall be governed by the provisions of this section, of Part XV and of Annex VI.

Article 187 – Jurisdiction of the Seabed Disputes Chamber

The Seabed Disputes Chamber shall have jurisdiction under this Part and the Annexes relating thereto in disputes with respect to activities in the Area falling within the following categories:

(a) disputes between States Parties concerning the interpretation or application of this Part and the Annexes relating thereto;

(b) disputes between a State Party and the Authority concerning:

(i) acts or omissions of the Authority or of a State Party alleged to be in violation of this Part or the Annexes relating thereto or of rules, regulations and procedures of the Authority adopted in accordance therewith; or

(ii) acts of the Authority alleged to be in excess of jurisdiction or a misuse of power;

(c) disputes between parties to a contract, being States Parties, the Authority or the Enterprise, state enterprises and natural or juridical persons referred to in article 153, paragraph 2(b), concerning:

(i) the interpretation or application of a relevant contract or a plan of work; or

(ii) acts or omissions of a party to the contract relating to activities in the Area and directed to the other party or directly affecting its legitimate interests;

(d) disputes between the Authority and a prospective contractor who has been sponsored by a State as provided in article 153, paragraph 2(b), and has duly fulfilled the conditions referred to in Annex III, article 4, paragraph 6, and article 13, paragraph 2, concerning the refusal of a contract or a legal issue arising in the negotiation of the contract;

(e) disputes between the Authority and a State Party, a state enterprise or a natural or juridical person sponsored by a State Party as provided for in article 153, paragraph 2(b), where it is alleged that the Authority has incurred liability as provided in Annex III, article 22;

(f) any other disputes for which the jurisdiction of the Chamber is specifically provided in this Convention.

Article 188 – Submission of disputes to a special chamber of the International Tribunal for the Law of the Sea or an ad hoc chamber of the Seabed Disputes Chamber or to binding commercial arbitration

1. Disputes between States Parties referred to in article 187, subparagraph (a), may be submitted:

(a) at the request of the parties to the dispute, to a special chamber of the International Tribunal for the Law of the Sea to be formed in accordance with Annex VI, articles 15 and 17; or

(b) at the request of any party to the dispute, to an ad hoc chamber of the Seabed Disputes Chamber to be formed in accordance with Annex VI, article 36.

2. (a) Disputes concerning the interpretation or application of a contract referred to in article 187, subparagraph (c)(i), shall be submitted, at the request of any party to the dispute, to binding commercial arbitration, unless the parties otherwise agree. A commercial arbitral tribunal to which the dispute is submitted shall have no jurisdiction to decide any question of interpretation of this Convention. When the dispute also involves a question of the interpretation of Part XI and the Annexes relating thereto, with respect to activities in the Area, that question shall be referred to the Seabed Disputes Chamber for a ruling.
   (b) If, at the commencement of or in the course of such arbitration, the arbitral tribunal determines, either at the request of any party to the dispute or proprio motu, that its decision depends upon a ruling of the Seabed Disputes Chamber, the arbitral tribunal shall refer such question to the Seabed Disputes Chamber for such ruling. The arbitral tribunal shall then proceed to render its award in conformity with the ruling of the Seabed Disputes Chamber.
   (c) In the absence of a provision in the contract on the arbitration procedure to be applied in the dispute, the arbitration shall be conducted in accordance with the UNCITRAL Arbitration Rules or such other arbitration rules as may be prescribed in the rules, regulations and procedures of the Authority, unless the parties to the dispute otherwise agree.

Article 189 – Limitation on jurisdiction with regard to decisions of the Authority

The Seabed Disputes Chamber shall have no jurisdiction with regard to the exercise by the Authority of its discretionary powers in accordance with this Part; in no case shall it substitute its discretion for that of the Authority. Without prejudice to article 191, in exercising its jurisdiction pursuant to article 187, the Seabed Disputes Chamber shall not pronounce itself on the question of whether any rules, regulations and procedures of the Authority are in conformity with this Convention, nor declare invalid any such rules, regulations and procedures. Its jurisdiction in this regard shall be confined to deciding claims that the application of any rules, regulations and procedures of the Authority in individual cases would be in conflict with the contractual obligations of the parties to the dispute or their obligations under this Convention, claims concerning excess of jurisdiction or misuse of power, and to claims for damages to be paid or other remedy to be given to the party concerned for the failure of the other party to comply with its contractual obligations or its obligations under this Convention.

Article 190 – Participation and appearance of sponsoring States Parties in proceedings

1. If a natural or juridical person is a party to a dispute referred to in article 187, the sponsoring State shall be given notice thereof and shall have the right to participate in the proceedings by submitting written or oral statements.
2. If an action is brought against a State Party by a natural or juridical person sponsored by another State Party in a dispute referred to in article 187, subparagraph (c), the respondent State may request the State sponsoring that person to appear in the proceedings on behalf of that person. Failing such appearance, the respondent State may arrange to be represented by a juridical person of its nationality.

Article 191 – Advisory opinions

The Seabed Disputes Chamber shall give advisory opinions at the request of the Assembly or the Council on legal questions arising within the scope of their activities. Such opinions shall be given as a matter of urgency.

PART XII – PROTECTION AND PRESERVATION OF THE MARINE ENVIRONMENT

SECTION 1. GENERAL PROVISIONS

Article 192 – General obligation

States have the obligation to protect and preserve the marine environment.

Article 193 – Sovereign right of States to exploit their natural resources

States have the sovereign right to exploit their natural resources pursuant to their environmental policies and in accordance with their duty to protect and preserve the marine environment.

Article 194 – Measures to prevent, reduce and control pollution of the marine environment

1. States shall take, individually or jointly as appropriate, all measures consistent with this Convention that are necessary to prevent, reduce and control pollution of the marine environment from any source, using for this purpose the best practicable means at their disposal and in accordance with their capabilities, and they shall endeavour to harmonize their policies in this connection.
2. States shall take all measures necessary to ensure that activities under their jurisdiction or control are so conducted as not to cause damage by pollution to other States and their environment, and that pollution arising from incidents or activities under their jurisdiction or control does not spread beyond the areas where they exercise sovereign rights in accordance with this Convention.
3. The measures taken pursuant to this Part shall deal with all sources of pollution of the marine environment. These measures shall include, inter alia, those designed to minimize to the fullest possible extent:
   (a) the release of toxic, harmful or noxious substances, especially those which are persistent, from land-based sources, from or through the atmosphere or by dumping;
   (b) pollution from vessels, in particular measures for preventing accidents and dealing with emergencies, ensuring the safety of operations

at sea, preventing intentional and unintentional discharges, and regulating the design, construction, equipment, operation and manning of vessels;

(c) pollution from installations and devices used in exploration or exploitation of the natural resources of the seabed and subsoil, in particular measures for preventing accidents and dealing with emergencies, ensuring the safety of operations at sea, and regulating the design, construction, equipment, operation and manning of such installations or devices;

(d) pollution from other installations and devices operating in the marine environment, in particular measures for preventing accidents and dealing with emergencies, ensuring the safety of operations at sea, and regulating the design, construction, equipment, operation and manning of such installations or devices.

4. In taking measures to prevent, reduce or control pollution of the marine environment, States shall refrain from unjustifiable interference with activities carried out by other States in the exercise of their rights and in pursuance of their duties in conformity with this Convention.

5. The measures taken in accordance with this Part shall include those necessary to protect and preserve rare or fragile ecosystems as well as the habitat of depleted, threatened or endangered species and other forms of marine life.

Article 195 – Duty not to transfer damage or hazards or transform one type of pollution into another

In taking measures to prevent, reduce and control pollution of the marine environment, States shall act so as not to transfer, directly or indirectly, damage or hazards from one area to another or transform one type of pollution into another.

Article 196 – Use of technologies or introduction of alien or new species

1. States shall take all measures necessary to prevent, reduce and control pollution of the marine environment resulting from the use of technologies under their jurisdiction or control, or the intentional or accidental introduction of species, alien or new, to a particular part of the marine environment, which may cause significant and harmful changes thereto.

2. This article does not affect the application of this Convention regarding the prevention, reduction and control of pollution of the marine environment.

SECTION 2. GLOBAL AND REGIONAL COOPERATION

Article 197 – Cooperation on a global or regional basis

States shall cooperate on a global basis and, as appropriate, on a regional basis, directly or through competent international organizations, in formulating and elaborating international rules, standards and recommended practices and procedures consistent with this Convention, for the protection and preservation of the marine environment, taking into account characteristic regional features.

Article 198 – Notification of imminent or actual damage

When a State becomes aware of cases in which the marine environment is in imminent danger of being damaged or has been damaged by pollution, it shall immediately notify other States it deems likely to be affected by such damage, as well as the competent international organizations.

Article 199 – Contingency plans against pollution

In the cases referred to in article 198, States in the area affected, in accordance with their capabilities, and the competent international organizations shall cooperate, to the extent possible, in eliminating the effects of pollution and preventing or minimizing the damage. To this end, States shall jointly develop and promote contingency plans for responding to pollution incidents in the marine environment.

Article 200 – Studies, research programmes and exchange of information and data

States shall cooperate, directly or through competent international organizations, for the purpose of promoting studies, undertaking programmes of scientific research and encouraging the exchange of information and data acquired about pollution of the marine environment. They shall endeavour to participate actively in regional and global programmes to acquire knowledge for the assessment of the nature and extent of pollution, exposure to it, and its pathways, risks and remedies.

Article 201 – Scientific criteria for regulations

In the light of the information and data acquired pursuant to article 200, States shall cooperate, directly or through competent international organizations, in establishing appropriate scientific criteria for the formulation and elaboration of rules, standards and recommended practices and procedures for the prevention, reduction and control of pollution of the marine environment.

SECTION 3. TECHNICAL ASSISTANCE

Article 202 – Scientific and technical assistance to developing States

States shall, directly or through competent international organizations:

(a) promote programmes of scientific, educational, technical and other assistance to developing States for the protection and preservation of the marine environment and the prevention, reduction and control of marine pollution. Such assistance shall include, inter alia:

(i) training of their scientific and technical personnel;

(ii) facilitating their participation in relevant international programmes;

(iii) supplying them with necessary equipment and facilities;

(iv) enhancing their capacity to manufacture such equipment;

(v) advice on and developing facilities for research, monitoring, educational and other programmes;

(b) provide appropriate assistance, especially to developing States, for the minimization of the effects of major incidents which may cause serious pollution of the marine environment;

(c) provide appropriate assistance, especially to developing States, concerning the preparation of environmental assessments.

Article 203 – Preferential treatment for developing States

Developing States shall, for the purposes of prevention, reduction and control of pollution of the marine environment or minimization of its effects, be granted preference by international organizations in:

(a) the allocation of appropriate funds and technical assistance; and

(b) the utilization of their specialized services.

SECTION 4. MONITORING AND ENVIRONMENTAL ASSESSMENT

Article 204 – Monitoring of the risks or effects of pollution

1. States shall, consistent with the rights of other States, endeavour, as far as practicable, directly or through the competent international organizations, to observe, measure, evaluate and analyse, by recognized scientific methods, the risks or effects of pollution of the marine environment.
2. In particular, States shall keep under surveillance the effects of any activities which they permit or in which they engage in order to determine whether these activities are likely to pollute the marine environment.

Article 205 – Publication of reports

States shall publish reports of the results obtained pursuant to article 204 or provide such reports at appropriate intervals to the competent international organizations, which should make them available to all States.

Article 206 – Assessment of potential effects of activities

When States have reasonable grounds for believing that planned activities under their jurisdiction or control may cause substantial pollution of or significant and harmful changes to the marine environment, they shall, as far as practicable, assess the potential effects of such activities on the marine environment and shall communicate reports of the results of such assessments in the manner provided in article 205.

SECTION 5. INTERNATIONAL RULES AND NATIONAL LEGISLATION TO PREVENT, REDUCE AND CONTROL POLLUTION OF THE MARINE ENVIRONMENT

Article 207 – Pollution from land-based sources

1. States shall adopt laws and regulations to prevent, reduce and control pollution of the marine environment from land-based sources, including rivers, estuaries, pipelines and outfall structures, taking into account internationally agreed rules, standards and recommended practices and procedures.
2. States shall take other measures as may be necessary to prevent, reduce and control such pollution.
3. States shall endeavour to harmonize their policies in this connection at the appropriate regional level.
4. States, acting especially through competent international organizations or diplomatic conference, shall endeavour to establish global and regional rules, standards and recommended practices and procedures to prevent, reduce and control pollution of the marine environment from land-based sources, taking into account characteristic regional features, the economic capacity of developing States and their need for economic development. Such rules, standards and recommended practices and procedures shall be re-examined from time to time as necessary.
5. Laws, regulations, measures, rules, standards and recommended practices and procedures referred to in paragraphs 1, 2 and 4 shall include those designed to minimize, to the fullest extent possible, the release of toxic, harmful or noxious substances, especially those which are persistent, into the marine environment.

Article 208 – Pollution from seabed activities subject to national jurisdiction

1 Coastal States shall adopt laws and regulations to prevent, reduce and control pollution of the marine environment arising from or in connection with seabed activities subject to their jurisdiction and from artificial islands, installations and structures under their jurisdiction, pursuant to articles 60 and 80.

2. States shall take other measures as may be necessary to prevent, reduce and control such pollution.
3. Such laws, regulations and measures shall be no less effective than international rules, standards and recommended practices and procedures.
4. States shall endeavour to harmonize their policies in this connection at the appropriate regional level.
5. States, acting especially through competent international organizations or diplomatic conference, shall establish global and regional rules, standards and recommended practices and procedures to prevent, reduce and control pollution of the marine environment referred to in paragraph l. Such rules, standards and recommended practices and procedures shall be re-examined from time to time as necessary.

Article 209 – Pollution from activities in the Area

1. International rules, regulations and procedures shall be established in accordance with Part XI to prevent, reduce and control pollution of the marine environment from activities in the Area. Such rules, regulations and procedures shall be re-examined from time to time as necessary.
2. Subject to the relevant provisions of this section, States shall adopt laws and regulations to prevent, reduce and control pollution of the marine environment from activities in the Area undertaken by vessels, installations, structures and other devices flying their flag or of their registry or operating under their authority, as the case may be. The requirements of such laws and regulations shall be no less effective than the international rules, regulations and procedures referred to in paragraph 1.

Article 210 – Pollution by dumping

1. States shall adopt laws and regulations to prevent, reduce and control pollution of the marine environment by dumping.
2. States shall take other measures as may be necessary to prevent, reduce and control such pollution.
3. Such laws, regulations and measures shall ensure that dumping is not carried out without the permission of the competent authorities of States.
4. States, acting especially through competent international organizations or diplomatic conference, shall endeavour to establish global and regional rules, standards and recommended practices and procedures to prevent, reduce and control such pollution. Such rules, standards and recommended practices and procedures shall be re-examined from time to time as necessary.
5. Dumping within the territorial sea and the exclusive economic zone or onto the continental shelf shall not be carried out without the express prior approval of the coastal State, which has the right to permit, regulate and control such dumping after due consideration of the matter with other States which by reason of their geographical situation may be adversely affected thereby.
6. National laws, regulations and measures shall be no less effective in preventing, reducing and controlling such pollution than the global rules and standards.

Article 211 – Pollution from vessels

1. States, acting through the competent international organization or general diplomatic conference, shall establish international rules and standards to prevent, reduce and control pollution of the marine environment from vessels and promote the adoption, in the same manner, wherever appropriate, of routeing systems designed to minimize the threat of accidents which might cause pollution of the marine environment, including the coastline, and pollution damage to the related interests of coastal States. Such rules and standards shall, in the same manner, be re-examined from time to time as necessary.
2. States shall adopt laws and regulations for the prevention, reduction and control of pollution of the marine environment from vessels flying their flag or of their registry. Such laws and regulations shall at least have the same effect as that of generally accepted international rules and standards established through the competent international organization or general diplomatic conference.
3. States which establish particular requirements for the prevention, reduction and control of pollution of the marine environment as a condition for the entry of foreign vessels into their ports or internal waters or for a call at their off-shore terminals shall give due publicity to such requirements and shall communicate them to the competent international organization. Whenever such requirements are established in identical form by two or more coastal States in an endeavour to harmonize policy, the communication shall indicate which States are participating in such cooperative arrangements. Every State shall require the master of a vessel flying its flag or of its registry, when navigating within the territorial sea of a State participating in such cooperative arrangements, to furnish, upon the request of that State, information as to whether it is proceeding to a State of the same region participating in such cooperative arrangements and, if so, to indicate whether it complies with the port entry requirements of that State. This article is without prejudice to the continued exercise by a vessel of its right of innocent passage or to the application of article 25, paragraph 2.
4. Coastal States may, in the exercise of their sovereignty within their territorial sea, adopt laws and regulations for the prevention, reduction and control of marine pollution from foreign vessels, including vessels exercising the right of innocent passage. Such laws and regulations shall, in accordance with Part II, section 3, not hamper innocent passage of foreign vessels.
5. Coastal States, for the purpose of enforcement as provided for in section 6, may in respect of their exclusive economic zones adopt laws and regulations for the prevention, reduction and control of pollution from vessels conforming to and giving effect to generally accepted international rules and standards established through the competent international organization or general diplomatic conference.
6. (a) Where the international rules and standards referred to in paragraph 1 are inadequate to meet special circumstances and coastal States have reasonable grounds for believing that a particular, clearly defined area of their respective exclusive economic zones is an area where the adoption of special mandatory measures for the prevention of pollution from vessels is required for recognized technical reasons in relation to its oceanographical and ecological conditions, as well as its utilization or the protection of its resources and the particular character of its traffic, the coastal States, after appropriate consultations through the competent international organization with any other States concerned,

may, for that area, direct a communication to that organization, submitting scientific and technical evidence in support and information on necessary reception facilities. Within 12 months after receiving such a communication, the organization shall determine whether the conditions in that area correspond to the requirements set out above. If the organization so determines, the coastal States may, for that area, adopt laws and regulations for the prevention, reduction and control of pollution from vessels implementing such international rules and standards or navigational practices as are made applicable, through the organization, for special areas. These laws and regulations shall not become applicable to foreign vessels until 15 months after the submission of the communication to the organization.

(b) The coastal States shall publish the limits of any such particular, clearly defined area.

(c) If the coastal States intend to adopt additional laws and regulations for the same area for the prevention, reduction and control of pollution from vessels, they shall, when submitting the aforesaid communication, at the same time notify the organization thereof. Such additional laws and regulations may relate to discharges or navigational practices but shall not require foreign vessels to observe design, construction, manning or equipment standards other than generally accepted international rules and standards; they shall become applicable to foreign vessels 15 months after the submission of the communication to the organization, provided that the organization agrees within 12 months after the submission of the communication.

7. The international rules and standards referred to in this article should include inter alia those relating to prompt notification to coastal States, whose coastline or related interests may be affected by incidents, including maritime casualties, which involve discharges or probability of discharges.

Article 212 – Pollution from or through the atmosphere

1. States shall adopt laws and regulations to prevent, reduce and control pollution of the marine environment from or through the atmosphere, applicable to the air space under their sovereignty and to vessels flying their flag or vessels or aircraft of their registry, taking into account internationally agreed rules, standards and recommended practices and procedures and the safety of air navigation.
2. States shall take other measures as may be necessary to prevent, reduce and control such pollution.
3. States, acting especially through competent international organizations or diplomatic conference, shall endeavour to establish global and regional rules, standards and recommended practices and procedures to prevent, reduce and control such pollution.

SECTION 6. ENFORCEMENT

Article 213 – Enforcement with respect to pollution from land-based sources

States shall enforce their laws and regulations adopted in accordance with article 207 and shall adopt laws and regulations and take other measures necessary to implement applicable international rules and standards established through competent international organizations or diplomatic conference to prevent, reduce and control pollution of the marine environment from land-based sources.

Article 214 – Enforcement with respect to pollution from seabed activities

States shall enforce their laws and regulations adopted in accordance with article 208 and shall adopt laws and regulations and take other measures necessary to implement applicable international rules and standards established through competent international organizations or diplomatic conference to prevent, reduce and control pollution of the marine environment arising from or in connection with seabed activities subject to their jurisdiction and from artificial islands, installations and structures under their jurisdiction, pursuant to articles 60 and 80.

Article 215 – Enforcement with respect to pollution from activities in the Area

Enforcement of international rules, regulations and procedures established in accordance with Part XI to prevent, reduce and control pollution of the marine environment from activities in the Area shall be governed by that Part.

Article 216 – Enforcement with respect to pollution by dumping

1. Laws and regulations adopted in accordance with this Convention and applicable international rules and standards established through competent international organizations or diplomatic conference for the prevention, reduction and control of pollution of the marine environment by dumping shall be enforced:

   (a) by the coastal State with regard to dumping within its territorial sea or its exclusive economic zone or onto its continental shelf;

   (b) by the flag State with regard to vessels flying its flag or vessels or aircraft of its registry;

   (c) by any State with regard to acts of loading of wastes or other matter occurring within its territory or at its off-shore terminals.
2. No State shall be obliged by virtue of this article to institute proceedings when another State has already instituted proceedings in accordance with this article.

Article 217 – Enforcement by flag States

1. States shall ensure compliance by vessels flying their flag or of their registry with applicable international rules and standards, established through the competent international organization or general diplomatic conference, and with their laws and regulations adopted in accordance with this Con-

vention for the prevention, reduction and control of pollution of the marine environment from vessels and shall accordingly adopt laws and regulations and take other measures necessary for their implementation. Flag States shall provide for the effective enforcement of such rules, standards, laws and regulations, irrespective of where a violation occurs.

2. States shall, in particular, take appropriate measures in order to ensure that vessels flying their flag or of their registry are prohibited from sailing, until they can proceed to sea in compliance with the requirements of the international rules and standards referred to in paragraph 1, including requirements in respect of design, construction, equipment and manning of vessels.
3. States shall ensure that vessels flying their flag or of their registry carry on board certificates required by and issued pursuant to international rules and standards referred to in paragraph 1. States shall ensure that vessels flying their flag are periodically inspected in order to verify that such certificates are in conformity with the actual condition of the vessels. These certificates shall be accepted by other States as evidence of the condition of the vessels and shall be regarded as having the same force as certificates issued by them, unless there are clear grounds for believing that the condition of the vessel does not correspond substantially with the particulars of the certificates.
4. If a vessel commits a violation of rules and standards established through the competent international organization or general diplomatic conference, the flag State, without prejudice to articles 218, 220 and 228, shall provide for immediate investigation and where appropriate institute proceedings in respect of the alleged violation irrespective of where the violation occurred or where the pollution caused by such violation has occurred or has been spotted.
5. Flag States conducting an investigation of the violation may request the assistance of any other State whose cooperation could be useful in clarifying the circumstances of the case. States shall endeavour to meet appropriate requests of flag States.
6. States shall, at the written request of any State, investigate any violation alleged to have been committed by vessels flying their flag. If satisfied that sufficient evidence is available to enable proceedings to be brought in respect of the alleged violation, flag States shall without delay institute such proceedings in accordance with their laws.
7. Flag States shall promptly inform the requesting State and the competent international organization of the action taken and its outcome. Such information shall be available to all States.
8. Penalties provided for by the laws and regulations of States for vessels flying their flag shall be adequate in severity to discourage violations wherever they occur.

Article 218 – Enforcement by port States

1. When a vessel is voluntarily within a port or at an off-shore terminal of a State, that State may undertake investigations and, where the evidence so warrants, institute proceedings in respect of any discharge from that vessel outside the internal waters, territorial sea or exclusive economic zone of that State in violation of applicable international rules and standards established through the competent international organization or general diplomatic conference.
2. No proceedings pursuant to paragraph 1 shall be instituted in respect of a discharge violation in the internal waters, territorial sea or exclusive economic zone of another State unless requested by that State, the flag State, or a State damaged or threatened by the discharge violation, or unless the violation has caused or is likely to cause pollution in the internal waters, territorial sea or exclusive economic zone of the State instituting the proceedings.
3. When a vessel is voluntarily within a port or at an off-shore terminal of a State, that State shall, as far as practicable, comply with requests from any State for investigation of a discharge violation referred to in paragraph 1, believed to have occurred in, caused, or threatened damage to the internal waters, territorial sea or exclusive economic zone of the requesting State. It shall likewise, as far as practicable, comply with requests from the flag State for investigation of such a violation, irrespective of where the violation occurred.
4. The records of the investigation carried out by a port State pursuant to this article shall be transmitted upon request to the flag State or to the coastal State. Any proceedings instituted by the port State on the basis of such an investigation may, subject to section 7, be suspended at the request of the coastal State when the violation has occurred within its internal waters, territorial sea or exclusive economic zone. The evidence and records of the case, together with any bond or other financial security posted with the authorities of the port State, shall in that event be transmitted to the coastal State. Such transmittal shall preclude the continuation of proceedings in the port State.

Article 219 – Measures relating to seaworthiness of vessels to avoid pollution

Subject to section 7, States which, upon request or on their own initiative, have ascertained that a vessel within one of their ports or at one of their off-shore terminals is in violation of applicable international rules and standards relating to seaworthiness of vessels and thereby threatens damage to the marine environment shall, as far as practicable, take administrative measures to prevent the vessel from sailing. Such States may permit the vessel to proceed only to the nearest appropriate repair yard and, upon removal of the causes of the violation, shall permit the vessel to continue immediately.

Article 220 – Enforcement by coastal States

1. When a vessel is voluntarily within a port or at an off-shore terminal of a State, that State may, subject to section 7, institute proceedings in respect of any violation of its laws and regulations adopted in accordance with this Convention or applicable international rules and standards for the prevention, reduction and control of pollution from vessels when the violation has occurred within the territorial sea or the exclusive economic zone of that State.
2. Where there are clear grounds for believing that a vessel navigating in the territorial sea of a State has, during its passage therein, violated laws and regulations of that State adopted in accordance with this Convention or applicable international rules and standards for the prevention, reduction and control of pollution from vessels, that State, without prejudice to the application of the relevant provisions of Part II, section 3, may undertake physical inspection of the vessel relating to the violation and may, where the evidence so warrants, institute proceedings, including detention of the vessel, in accordance with its laws, subject to the provisions of section 7.
3. Where there are clear grounds for believing that a vessel navigating in the exclusive economic zone or the territorial sea of a State has, in the exclusive economic zone, committed a violation of applicable international rules and standards for the prevention, reduction and control of pollution from vessels or laws and regulations of that State conforming and giving effect to such rules and standards, that State may require the vessel to give information regarding its identity and port of registry, its last and its next port of call and other relevant information required to establish whether a violation has occurred.
4. States shall adopt laws and regulations and take other measures so that vessels flying their flag comply with requests for information pursuant to paragraph 3.
5. Where there are clear grounds for believing that a vessel navigating in the exclusive economic zone or the territorial sea of a State has, in the exclusive economic zone, committed a violation referred to in paragraph 3 resulting in a substantial discharge causing or threatening significant pollution of the marine environment, that State may undertake physical inspection of the vessel for matters relating to the violation if the vessel has refused to give information or if the information supplied by the vessel is manifestly at variance with the evident factual situation and if the circumstances of the case justify such inspection.
6. Where there is clear objective evidence that a vessel navigating in the exclusive economic zone or the territorial sea of a State has, in the exclusive economic zone, committed a violation referred to in paragraph 3 resulting in a discharge causing major damage or threat of major damage to the coastline or related interests of the coastal State, or to any resources of its territorial sea or exclusive economic zone, that State may, subject to section 7, provided that the evidence so warrants, institute proceedings, including detention of the vessel, in accordance with its laws.
7. Notwithstanding the provisions of paragraph 6, whenever appropriate procedures have been established, either through the competent international organization or as otherwise agreed, whereby compliance with requirements for bonding or other appropriate financial security has been assured, the coastal State if bound by such procedures shall allow the vessel to proceed.
8. The provisions of paragraphs 3, 4, 5, 6and 7 also apply in respect of national laws and regulations adopted pursuant to article 211, paragraph 6.

Article 221 – Measures to avoid pollution arising from maritime casualties

1. Nothing in this Part shall prejudice the right of States, pursuant to international law, both customary and conventional, to take and enforce measures beyond the territorial sea proportionate to the actual or threatened damage to protect their coastline or related interests, including fishing, from pollution or threat of pollution following upon a maritime casualty or acts relating to such a casualty, which may reasonably be expected to result in major harmful consequences.
2. For the purposes of this article, "maritime casualty" means a collision of vessels, stranding or other incident of navigation, or other occurrence on board a vessel or external to it resulting in material damage or imminent threat of material damage to a vessel or cargo.

Article 222 – Enforcement with respect to pollution from or through the atmosphere

States shall enforce, within the air space under their sovereignty or with regard to vessels flying their flag or vessels or aircraft of their registry, their laws and regulations adopted in accordance with article 212, paragraph 1, and with other provisions of this Convention and shall adopt laws and regulations and take other measures necessary to implement applicable international rules and standards established through competent international organizations or diplomatic conference to prevent, reduce and control pollution of the marine environment from or through the atmosphere, in conformity with all relevant international rules and standards concerning the safety of air navigation.

SECTION 7. SAFEGUARDS

Article 223 – Measures to facilitate proceedings

In proceedings instituted pursuant to this Part, States shall take measures to facilitate the hearing of witnesses and the admission of evidence submitted by authorities of another State, or by the competent international organization, and shall facilitate the attendance at such proceedings of official representatives of the competent international organization, the flag State and any State affected by pollution arising out of any violation. The official representatives attending such proceedings shall have such rights and duties as may be provided under national laws and regulations or international law.

Article 224 – Exercise of powers of enforcement

The powers of enforcement against foreign vessels under this Part may only be exercised by officials or by warships, military aircraft, or other ships or aircraft clearly marked and identifiable as being on government service and authorized to that effect.

Article 225 – Duty to avoid adverse consequences in the exercise of the powers of enforcement

In the exercise under this Convention of their powers of enforcement against foreign vessels, States shall not endanger the safety of navigation or otherwise create any hazard to a vessel, or bring it to an unsafe port or anchorage, or expose the marine environment to an unreasonable risk.

Article 226 – Investigation of foreign vessels

1. (a) States shall not delay a foreign vessel longer than is essential for purposes of the investigations provided for in articles 216, 218 and 220. Any physical inspection of a foreign vessel shall be limited to an examination of such certificates, records or other documents as the vessel is required to carry by generally accepted international rules and standards or of any similar documents which it is carrying; further physical inspection of the vessel may be undertaken only after such an examination and only when:
   - (i) there are clear grounds for believing that the condition of the vessel or its equipment does not correspond substantially with the particulars of those documents;
   - (ii) the contents of such documents are not sufficient to confirm or verify a suspected violation; or
   - (iii) the vessel is not carrying valid certificates and records.

   (b) If the investigation indicates a violation of applicable laws and regulations or international rules and standards for the protection and preservation of the marine environment, release shall be made promptly subject to reasonable procedures such as bonding or other appropriate financial security.

   (c) Without prejudice to applicable international rules and standards relating to the seaworthiness of vessels, the release of a vessel may, whenever it would present an unreasonable threat of damage to the marine environment, be refused or made conditional upon proceeding to the nearest appropriate repair yard. Where release has been refused or made conditional, the flag State of the vessel must be promptly notified, and may seek release of the vessel in accordance with Part XV.
2. States shall cooperate to develop procedures for the avoidance of unnecessary physical inspection of vessels at sea.

Article 227 – Non-discrimination with respect to foreign vessels

In exercising their rights and performing their duties under this Part, States shall not discriminate in form or in fact against vessels of any other State.

Article 228 – Suspension and restrictions on institution of proceedings

1. Proceedings to impose penalties in respect of any violation of applicable laws and regulations or international rules and standards relating to the prevention, reduction and control of pollution from vessels committed by a foreign vessel beyond the territorial sea of the State instituting proceedings shall be suspended upon the taking of proceedings to impose penalties in respect of corresponding charges by the flag State within six months of the date on which proceedings were first instituted, unless those proceedings relate to a case of major damage to the coastal State or the flag State in question has repeatedly disregarded its obligation to enforce effectively the applicable international rules and standards in respect of violations committed by its vessels. The flag State shall in due course make available to the State previously instituting proceedings a full dossier of the case and the records of the proceedings, whenever the flag State has requested the suspension of proceedings in accordance with this article. When proceedings instituted by the flag State have been brought to a conclusion, the suspended proceedings shall be terminated. Upon payment of costs incurred in respect of such proceedings, any bond posted or other financial security provided in connection with the suspended proceedings shall be released by the coastal State.
2. Proceedings to impose penalties on foreign vessels shall not be instituted after the expiry of three years from the date on which the violation was committed, and shall not be taken by any State in the event of proceedings having been instituted by another State subject to the provisions set out in paragraph 1.
3. The provisions of this article are without prejudice to the right of the flag State to take any measures, including proceedings to impose penalties, according to its laws irrespective of prior proceedings by another State.

Article 229 – Institution of civil proceedings

Nothing in this Convention affects the institution of civil proceedings in respect of any claim for loss or damage resulting from pollution of the marine environment.

Article 230 – Monetary penalties and the observance of recognized rights of the accused

1. Monetary penalties only may be imposed with respect to violations of national laws and regulations or applicable international rules and standards for the prevention, reduction and control of pollution of the marine environment, committed by foreign vessels beyond the territorial sea.

2. Monetary penalties only may be imposed with respect to violations of national laws and regulations or applicable international rules and standards for the prevention, reduction and control of pollution of the marine environment, committed by foreign vessels in the territorial sea, except in the case of a wilful and serious act of pollution in the territorial sea.
3. In the conduct of proceedings in respect of such violations committed by a foreign vessel which may result in the imposition of penalties, recognized rights of the accused shall be observed.

Article 231 – Notification to the flag State and other States concerned

States shall promptly notify the flag State and any other State concerned of any measures taken pursuant to section 6 against foreign vessels, and shall submit to the flag State all official reports concerning such measures. However, with respect to violations committed in the territorial sea, the foregoing obligations of the coastal State apply only to such measures as are taken in proceedings. The diplomatic agents or consular officers and where possible the maritime authority of the flag State, shall be immediately informed of any such measures taken pursuant to section 6 against foreign vessels.

Article 232 – Liability of States arising from enforcement measures

States shall be liable for damage or loss attributable to them arising from measures taken pursuant to section 6 when such measures are unlawful or exceed those reasonably required in the light of available information. States shall provide for recourse in their courts for actions in respect of such damage or loss.

Article 233 – Safeguards with respect to straits used for international navigation

Nothing in sections 5, 6 and 7 affects the legal regime of straits used for international navigation. However, if a foreign ship other than those referred to in section 10 has committed a violation of the laws and regulations referred to in article 42, paragraph 1(a) and (b), causing or threatening major damage to the marine environment of the straits, the States bordering the straits may take appropriate enforcement measures and if so shall respect mutatis mutandis the provisions of this section.

SECTION 8. ICE-COVERED AREAS

Article 234 – Ice-covered areas

Coastal States have the right to adopt and enforce non-discriminatory laws and regulations for the prevention, reduction and control of marine pollution from vessels in ice-covered areas within the limits of the exclusive economic zone, where particularly severe climatic conditions and the presence of ice covering such areas for most of the year create obstructions or exceptional hazards to navigation, and pollution of the marine environment could cause major harm to or irreversible disturbance of the ecological balance. Such laws and regulations shall have due regard to navigation and the protection and preservation of the marine environment based on the best available scientific evidence.

SECTION 9. RESPONSIBILITY AND LIABILITY

Article 235 – Responsibility and liability

1. States are responsible for the fulfilment of their international obligations concerning the protection and preservation of the marine environment. They shall be liable in accordance with international law.
2. States shall ensure that recourse is available in accordance with their legal systems for prompt and adequate compensation or other relief in respect of damage caused by pollution of the marine environment by natural or juridical persons under their jurisdiction.
3. With the objective of assuring prompt and adequate compensation in respect of all damage caused by pollution of the marine environment, States shall cooperate in the implementation of existing international law and the further development of international law relating to responsibility and liability for the assessment of and compensation for damage and the settlement of related disputes, as well as, where appropriate, development of criteria and procedures for payment of adequate compensation, such as compulsory insurance or compensation funds.

SECTION 10. SOVEREIGN IMMUNITY

Article 236 – Sovereign immunity

The provisions of this Convention regarding the protection and preservation of the marine environment do not apply to any warship, naval auxiliary, other vessels or aircraft owned or operated by a State and used, for the time being, only on government non-commercial service. However, each State shall ensure, by the adoption of appropriate measures not impairing operations or operational capabilities of such vessels or aircraft owned or operated by it, that such vessels or aircraft act in a manner consistent, so far as is reasonable and practicable, with this Convention.

SECTION 11. OBLIGATIONS UNDER OTHER CONVENTIONS ON THE PROTECTION AND PRESERVATION OF THE MARINE ENVIRONMENT

Article 237 – Obligations under other conventions on the protection and preservation of the marine environment

1. The provisions of this Part are without prejudice to the specific obligations assumed by States under special conventions and agreements concluded previously which relate to the protection and preservation of the marine environment and to agreements which may be concluded in furtherance of the general principles set forth in this Convention.
2. Specific obligations assumed by States under special conventions, with respect to the protection and preservation of the marine environment, should be carried out in a manner consistent with the general principles and objectives of this Convention.

PART XIII – MARINE SCIENTIFIC RESEARCH

SECTION 1. GENERAL PROVISIONS

Article 238 – Right to conduct marine scientific research

All States, irrespective of their geographical location, and competent international organizations have the right to conduct marine scientific research subject to the rights and duties of other States as provided for in this Convention.

Article 239 – Promotion of marine scientific research

States and competent international organizations shall promote and facilitate the development and conduct of marine scientific research in accordance with this Convention.

Article 240 – General principles for the conduct of marine scientific research

In the conduct of marine scientific research the following principles shall apply:

(a) marine scientific research shall be conducted exclusively for peaceful purposes;

(b) marine scientific research shall be conducted with appropriate scientific methods and means compatible with this Convention;

(c) marine scientific research shall not unjustifiably interfere with other legitimate uses of the sea compatible with this Convention and shall be duly respected in the course of such uses;

(d) marine scientific research shall be conducted in compliance with all relevant regulations adopted in conformity with this Convention including those for the protection and preservation of the marine environment.

Article 241 – Non-recognition of marine scientific research activities as the legal basis for claims

Marine scientific research activities shall not constitute the legal basis for any claim to any part of the marine environment or its resources.

SECTION 2. INTERNATIONAL COOPERATION

Article 242 – Promotion of international cooperation

1. States and competent international organizations shall, in accordance with the principle of respect for sovereignty and jurisdiction and on the basis of mutual benefit, promote international cooperation in marine scientific research for peaceful purposes.
2. In this context, without prejudice to the rights and duties of States under this Convention, a State, in the application of this Part, shall provide, as appropriate, other States with a reasonable opportunity to obtain from it, or with its cooperation, information necessary to prevent and control damage to the health and safety of persons and to the marine environment.

Article 243 Creation of favourable conditions

States and competent international organizations shall cooperate, through the conclusion of bilateral and multilateral agreements, to create favourable conditions for the conduct of marine scientific research in the marine environment and to integrate the efforts of scientists in studying the essence of phenomena and processes occurring in the marine environment and the interrelations between them.

Article 244 – Publication and dissemination of information and knowledge

1. States and competent international organizations shall, in accordance with this Convention, make available by publication and dissemination through appropriate channels information on proposed major programmes and their objectives as well as knowledge resulting from marine scientific research.
2. For this purpose, States, both individually and in cooperation with other States and with competent international organizations, shall actively promote the flow of scientific data and information and the transfer of knowledge resulting from marine scientific research, especially to developing States, as well as the strengthening of the autonomous marine scientific research capabilities of developing States through, inter alia, programmes to provide adequate education and training of their technical and scientific personnel.

SECTION 3. CONDUCT AND PROMOTION OF MARINE SCIENTIFIC RESEARCH

Article 245 – Marine scientific research in the territorial sea

Coastal States, in the exercise of their sovereignty, have the exclusive right to regulate, authorize and conduct marine scientific research in their territorial sea. Marine scientific research therein shall be conducted only with the express consent of and under the conditions set forth by the coastal State.

Article 246 – Marine scientific research in the exclusive economic zone and on the continental shelf

1. Coastal States, in the exercise of their jurisdiction, have the right to regulate, authorize and conduct marine scientific research in their exclusive economic zone and on their continental shelf in accordance with the relevant provisions of this Convention.
2. Marine scientific research in the exclusive economic zone and on the continental shelf shall be conducted with the consent of the coastal State.
3. Coastal States shall, in normal circumstances, grant their consent for marine scientific research projects by other States or competent international organizations in their exclusive economic zone or on their continental shelf to be carried out in accordance with this Convention exclusively for peaceful purposes and in order to increase scientific knowledge of the marine environment for the benefit of all mankind. To this end, coastal States

shall establish rules and procedures ensuring that such consent will not be delayed or denied unreasonably.

4. For the purposes of applying paragraph 3, normal circumstances may exist in spite of the absence of diplomatic relations between the coastal State and the researching State.
5. Coastal States may however in their discretion withhold their consent to the conduct of a marine scientific research project of another State or competent international organization in the exclusive economic zone or on the continental shelf of the coastal State if that project:
   (a) is of direct significance for the exploration and exploitation of natural resources, whether living or non-living;
   (b) involves drilling into the continental shelf, the use of explosives or the introduction of harmful substances into the marine environment;
   (c) involves the construction, operation or use of artificial islands, installations and structures referred to in articles 60 and 80;
   (d) contains information communicated pursuant to article 248 regarding the nature and objectives of the project which is inaccurate or if the researching State or competent international organization has outstanding obligations to the coastal State from a prior research project.
6. Notwithstanding the provisions of paragraph 5, coastal States may not exercise their discretion to withhold consent under subparagraph (a) of that paragraph in respect of marine scientific research projects to be undertaken in accordance with the provisions of this Part on the continental shelf, beyond 200 nautical miles from the baselines from which the breadth of the territorial sea is measured, outside those specific areas which coastal States may at any time publicly designate as areas in which exploitation or detailed exploratory operations focused on those areas are occurring or will occur within a reasonable period of time. Coastal States shall give reasonable notice of the designation of such areas, as well as any modifications thereto, but shall not be obliged to give details of the operations therein.
7. The provisions of paragraph 6 are without prejudice to the rights of coastal States over the continental shelf as established in article 77.
8. Marine scientific research activities referred to in this article shall not unjustifiably interfere with activities undertaken by coastal States in the exercise of their sovereign rights and jurisdiction provided for in this Convention.

Article 247 – Marine scientific research projects undertaken by or under the auspices of international organizations

A coastal State which is a member of or has a bilateral agreement with an international organization, and in whose exclusive economic zone or on whose continental shelf that organization wants to carry out a marine scientific research project, directly or under its auspices, shall be deemed to have authorized the project to be carried out in conformity with the agreed specifications if that State approved the detailed project when the decision was made by the organization for the undertaking of the project, or is willing to participate in it, and has not expressed any objection within four months of notification of the project by the organization to the coastal State.

Article 248 – Duty to provide information to the coastal State

States and competent international organizations which intend to undertake marine scientific research in the exclusive economic zone or on the continental shelf of a coastal State shall, not less than six months in advance of the expected starting date of the marine scientific research project, provide that State with a full description of:

(a) the nature and objectives of the project;
(b) the method and means to be used, including name, tonnage, type and class of vessels and a description of scientific equipment;
(c) the precise geographical areas in which the project is to be conducted;
(d) the expected date of first appearance and final departure of the research vessels, or deployment of the equipment and its removal, as appropriate;
(e) the name of the sponsoring institution, its director, and the person in charge of the project; and
(f) the extent to which it is considered that the coastal State should be able to participate or to be represented in the project.

Article 249 – Duty to comply with certain conditions

1. States and competent international organizations when undertaking marine scientific research in the exclusive economic zone or on the continental shelf of a coastal State shall comply with the following conditions:
   (a) ensure the right of the coastal State, if it so desires, to participate or be represented in the marine scientific research project, especially on board research vessels and other craft or scientific research installations, when practicable, without payment of any remuneration to the scientists of the coastal State and without obligation to contribute towards the costs of the project;
   (b) provide the coastal State, at its request, with preliminary reports, as soon as practicable, and with the final results and conclusions after the completion of the research;
   (c) undertake to provide access for the coastal State, at its request, to all data and samples derived from the marine scientific research project and likewise to furnish it with data which may be copied and samples which may be divided without detriment to their scientific value;
   (d) if requested, provide the coastal State with an assessment of such data, samples and research

results or provide assistance in their assessment or interpretation;

(e) ensure, subject to paragraph 2, that the research results are made internationally available through appropriate national or international channels, as soon as practicable;

(f) inform the coastal State immediately of any major change in the research programme;

(g) unless otherwise agreed, remove the scientific research installations or equipment once the research is completed.

2. This article is without prejudice to the conditions established by the laws and regulations of the coastal State for the exercise of its discretion to grant or withhold consent pursuant to article 246, paragraph 5, including requiring prior agreement for making internationally available the research results of a project of direct significance for the exploration and exploitation of natural resources.

Article 250 – Communications concerning marine scientific research projects

Communications concerning the marine scientific research projects shall be made through appropriate official channels, unless otherwise agreed.

Article 251 – General criteria and guidelines

States shall seek to promote through competent international organizations the establishment of general criteria and guidelines to assist States in ascertaining the nature and implications of marine scientific research.

Article 252 – Implied consent

States or competent international organizations may proceed with a marine scientific research project six months after the date upon which the information required pursuant to article 248 was provided to the coastal State unless within four months of the receipt of the communication containing such information the coastal State has informed the State or organization conducting the research that:

(a) it has withheld its consent under the provisions of article 246; or

(b) the information given by that State or competent international organization regarding the nature or objectives of the project does not conform to the manifestly evident facts; or

(c) it requires supplementary information relevant to conditions and the information provided for under articles 248 and 249; or

(d) outstanding obligations exist with respect to a previous marine scientific research project carried out by that State or organization, with regard to conditions established in article 249.

Article 253 – Suspension or cessation of marine scientific research activities

1. A coastal State shall have the right to require the suspension of any marine scientific research activities in progress within its exclusive economic zone or on its continental shelf if:

   (a) the research activities are not being conducted in accordance with the information communicated as provided under article 248 upon which the consent of the coastal State was based; or

   (b) the State or competent international organization conducting the research activities fails to comply with the provisions of article 249 concerning the rights of the coastal State with respect to the marine scientific research project.

2. A coastal State shall have the right to require the cessation of any marine scientific research activities in case of any non-compliance with the provisions of article 248 which amounts to a major change in the research project or the research activities.

3. A coastal State may also require cessation of marine scientific research activities if any of the situations contemplated in paragraph 1 are not rectified within a reasonable period of time.

4. Following notification by the coastal State of its decision to order suspension or cessation, States or competent international organizations authorized to conduct marine scientific research activities shall terminate the research activities that are the subject of such a notification.

5. An order of suspension under paragraph 1 shall be lifted by the coastal State and the marine scientific research activities allowed to continue once the researching State or competent international organization has complied with the conditions required under articles 248 and 249.

Article 254 – Rights of neighbouring land-locked and geographically disadvantaged States

1. States and competent international organizations which have submitted to a coastal State a project to undertake marine scientific research referred to in article 246, paragraph 3, shall give notice to the neighbouring land-locked and geographically disadvantaged States of the proposed research project, and shall notify the coastal State thereof.

2. After the consent has been given for the proposed marine scientific research project by the coastal State concerned, in accordance with article 246 and other relevant provisions of this Convention, States and competent international organizations undertaking such a project shall provide to the neighbouring land-locked and geographically disadvantaged States, at their request and when appropriate, relevant information as specified in article 248 and article 249, paragraph 1(f).

3. The neighbouring land-locked and geographically disadvantaged States referred to above shall, at their request, be given the opportunity to participate, whenever feasible, in the proposed marine scientific research project through qualified experts appointed by them and not objected to by the coastal State, in accordance with the conditions agreed for the project, in conformity with the provisions of this Convention, between the coastal State concerned and the State or competent international organizations conducting the marine scientific research.

4. States and competent international organizations referred to in paragraph 1 shall provide to the above-mentioned land-locked and geographically disadvantaged States, at their request, the information and assistance specified in article 249, paragraph 1(d), subject to the provisions of article 249, paragraph 2.

Article 255 – Measures to facilitate marine scientific research and assist research vessels

States shall endeavour to adopt reasonable rules, regulations and procedures to promote and facilitate marine scientific research conducted in accordance with this Convention beyond their territorial sea and, as appropriate, to facilitate, subject to the provisions of their laws and regulations, access to their harbours and promote assistance for marine scientific research vessels which comply with the relevant provisions of this Part.

Article 256 – Marine scientific research in the Area

All States, irrespective of their geographical location, and competent international organizations have the right, in conformity with the provisions of Part XI, to conduct marine scientific research in the Area.

Article 257 – Marine scientific research in the water column beyond the exclusive economic zone

All States, irrespective of their geographical location, and competent international organizations have the right, in conformity with this Convention, to conduct marine scientific research in the water column beyond the limits of the exclusive economic zone.

SECTION 4. SCIENTIFIC RESEARCH INSTALLATIONS OR EQUIPMENT IN THE MARINE ENVIRONMENT

Article 258 – Deployment and use

The deployment and use of any type of scientific research installations or equipment in any area of the marine environment shall be subject to the same conditions as are prescribed in this Convention for the conduct of marine scientific research in any such area.

Article 259 – Legal status

The installations or equipment referred to in this section do not possess the status of islands. They have no territorial sea of their own, and their presence does not affect the delimitation of the territorial sea, the exclusive economic zone or the continental shelf.

Article 260 – Safety zones

Safety zones of a reasonable breadth not exceeding a distance of 500 metres may be created around scientific research installations in accordance with the relevant provisions of this Convention. All States shall ensure that such safety zones are respected by their vessels.

Article 261 – Non-interference with shipping routes

The deployment and use of any type of scientific research installations or equipment shall not constitute an obstacle to established international shipping routes.

Article 262 – Identification markings and warning signals

Installations or equipment referred to in this section shall bear identification markings indicating the State of registry or the international organization to which they belong and shall have adequate internationally agreed warning signals to ensure safety at sea and the safety of air navigation, taking into account rules and standards established by competent international organizations.

SECTION 5. RESPONSIBILITY AND LIABILITY

Article 263 – Responsibility and liability

1. States and competent international organizations shall be responsible for ensuring that marine scientific research, whether undertaken by them or on their behalf, is conducted in accordance with this Convention.
2. States and competent international organizations shall be responsible and liable for the measures they take in contravention of this Convention in respect of marine scientific research conducted by other States, their natural or juridical persons or by competent international organizations, and shall provide compensation for damage resulting from such measures.
3. States and competent international organizations shall be responsible and liable pursuant to article 235 for damage caused by pollution of the marine environment arising out of marine scientific research undertaken by them or on their behalf.

SECTION 6. SETTLEMENT OF DISPUTES AND INTERIM MEASURES

Article 264 – Settlement of disputes

Disputes concerning the interpretation or application of the provisions of this Convention with regard to marine scientific research shall be settled in accordance with Part XV, sections 2 and 3.

Article 265 – Interim measures

Pending settlement of a dispute in accordance with Part XV, sections 2 and 3, the State or competent international organization authorized to conduct a marine scientific research project shall not allow research activities to commence or continue without the express consent of the coastal State concerned.

PART XIV – DEVELOPMENT AND TRANSFER OF MARINE TECHNOLOGY

SECTION 1. GENERAL PROVISIONS

Article 266 – Promotion of the development and transfer of marine technology

1. States, directly or through competent international organizations, shall cooperate in accordance with their capabilities to promote actively the development and transfer of marine science and marine technology on fair and reasonable terms and conditions.
2. States shall promote the development of the marine scientific and technological capacity of States which may need and request technical assistance in this field, particularly developing States, including land-locked and geographically disadvantaged States, with regard to the exploration, exploitation, conservation and management of marine resources, the protection and preservation of the marine environment, marine scientific research and other activities in the marine environment compatible with this Convention, with a view to accelerating the social and economic development of the developing States.
3. States shall endeavour to foster favourable economic and legal conditions for the transfer of marine technology for the benefit of all parties concerned on an equitable basis.

Article 267 – Protection of legitimate interests

States, in promoting cooperation pursuant to article 266, shall have due regard for all legitimate interests including, inter alia, the rights and duties of holders, suppliers and recipients of marine technology.

Article 268 – Basic objectives

States, directly or through competent international organizations, shall promote:

(a) the acquisition, evaluation and dissemination of marine technological knowledge and facilitate access to such information and data;

(b) the development of appropriate marine technology;

(c) the development of the necessary technological infrastructure to facilitate the transfer of marine technology;

(d) the development of human resources through training and education of nationals of developing States and countries and especially the nationals of the least developed among them;

(e) international cooperation at all levels, particularly at the regional, subregional and bilateral levels.

Article 269 – Measures to achieve the basic objectives

In order to achieve the objectives referred to in article 268, States, directly or through competent international organizations, shall endeavour, inter alia, to:

(a) establish programmes of technical cooperation for the effective transfer of all kinds of marine technology to States which may need and request technical assistance in this field, particularly the developing land-locked and geographically disadvantaged States, as well as other developing States which have not been able either to establish or develop their own technological capacity in marine science and in the exploration and exploitation of marine resources or to develop the infrastructure of such technology;

(b) promote favourable conditions for the conclusion of agreements, contracts and other similar arrangements, under equitable and reasonable conditions;

(c) hold conferences, seminars and symposia on scientific and technological subjects, in particular on policies and methods for the transfer of marine technology;

(d) promote the exchange of scientists and of technological and other experts;

(e) undertake projects and promote joint ventures and other forms of bilateral and multilateral cooperation.

SECTION 2. INTERNATIONAL COOPERATION

Article 270 – Ways and means of international cooperation

International cooperation for the development and transfer of marine technology shall be carried out, where feasible and appropriate, through existing bilateral, regional or multilateral programmes, and also through expanded and new programmes in order to facilitate marine scientific research, the transfer of marine technology, particularly in new fields, and appropriate international funding for ocean research and development.

Article 271 – Guidelines, criteria and standards

States, directly or through competent international organizations, shall promote the establishment of generally accepted guidelines, criteria and standards for the transfer of marine technology on a bilateral basis or within the framework of international organizations and other fora, taking into account, in particular, the interests and needs of developing States.

Article 272 – Coordination of international programmes

In the field of transfer of marine technology, States shall endeavour to ensure that competent international organizations coordinate their activities, including any regional or global programmes, taking into account the interests and needs of developing States, particularly land-locked and geographically disadvantaged States.

Article 273 – Cooperation with international organizations and the Authority

States shall cooperate actively with competent international organizations and the Authority to encourage and facilitate the transfer to developing States, their nationals and the Enterprise of skills and marine technology with regard to activities in the Area.

Article 274 – Objectives of the Authority

Subject to all legitimate interests including, inter alia, the rights and duties of holders, suppliers and recipients of technology, the Authority, with regard to activities in the Area, shall ensure that:

(a) on the basis of the principle of equitable geographical distribution, nationals of developing States, whether coastal, land-locked or geographically disadvantaged, shall be taken on for the purposes of training as members of the managerial, research and technical staff constituted for its undertakings;

(b) the technical documentation on the relevant equipment, machinery, devices and processes is made available to all States, in particular developing States which may need and request technical assistance in this field;

(c) adequate provision is made by the Authority to facilitate the acquisition of technical assistance in the field of marine technology by States which may need and request it, in particular developing States, and the acquisition by their nationals of the necessary skills and know-how, including professional training;

(d) States which may need and request technical assistance in this field, in particular developing States, are assisted in the acquisition of necessary equipment, processes, plant and other technical know-how through any financial arrangements provided for in this Convention.

SECTION 3. NATIONAL AND REGIONAL MARINE SCIENTIFIC AND TECHNOLOGICAL CENTRES

Article 275 – Establishment of national centres

1. States, directly or through competent international organizations and the Authority, shall promote the establishment, particularly in developing coastal States, of national marine scientific and technological research centres and the strengthening of existing national centres, in order to stimulate and advance the conduct of marine scientific research by developing coastal States and to enhance their national capabilities to utilize and preserve their marine resources for their economic benefit.
2. States, through competent international organizations and the Authority, shall give adequate support to facilitate the establishment and strengthening of such national centres so as to provide for advanced training facilities and necessary equipment, skills and know-how as well as technical experts to such States which may need and request such assistance.

Article 276 – Establishment of regional centres

1. States, in coordination with the competent international organizations, the Authority and national marine scientific and technological research institutions, shall promote the establishment of regional marine scientific and technological research centres, particularly in developing States, in order to stimulate and advance the conduct of marine scientific research by developing States and foster the transfer of marine technology.
2. All States of a region shall cooperate with the regional centres therein to ensure the more effective achievement of their objectives.

Article 277 – Functions of regional centres

The functions of such regional centres shall include, inter alia:

(a) training and educational programmes at all levels on various aspects of marine scientific and technological research, particularly marine biology, including conservation and management of living resources, oceanography, hydrography, engineering, geological exploration of the seabed, mining and desalination technologies;

(b) management studies;

(c) study programmes related to the protection and preservation of the marine environment and the prevention, reduction and control of pollution;

(d) organization of regional conferences, seminars and symposia;

(e) acquisition and processing of marine scientific and technological data and information;

(f) prompt dissemination of results of marine scientific and technological research in readily available publications;

(g) publicizing national policies with regard to the transfer of marine technology and systematic comparative study of those policies;

(h) compilation and systematization of information on the marketing of technology and on contracts and other arrangements concerning patents;

(i) technical cooperation with other States of the region.

SECTION 4. COOPERATION AMONG INTERNATIONAL ORGANIZATIONS

Article 278 – Cooperation among international organizations

The competent international organizations referred to in this Part and in Part XIII shall take all appropriate measures to ensure, either directly or in close cooperation among themselves, the effective discharge of their functions and responsibilities under this Part.

PART XV – SETTLEMENT OF DISPUTES

SECTION 1. GENERAL PROVISIONS

Article 279 – Obligation to settle disputes by peaceful means

States Parties shall settle any dispute between them concerning the interpretation or application of this Convention by peaceful means in accordance with article 2, paragraph 3, of the Charter of the United Nations and, to this end, shall seek a solution by the means indicated in article 33, paragraph 1, of the Charter.

Article 280 – Settlement of disputes by any peaceful means chosen by the parties

Nothing in this Part impairs the right of any States Parties to agree at any time to settle a dispute between them concerning the interpretation or application of this Convention by any peaceful means of their own choice.

Article 281 – Procedure where no settlement has been reached by the parties

1. If the States Parties which are parties to a dispute concerning the interpretation or application of this Convention have agreed to seek settlement of the dispute by a peaceful means of their own choice, the procedures provided for in this Part apply only where no settlement has been reached by recourse to such means and the agreement between the parties does not exclude any further procedure.
2. If the parties have also agreed on a time-limit, paragraph 1 applies only upon the expiration of that time-limit.

Article 282 – Obligations under general, regional or bilateral agreements

If the States Parties which are parties to a dispute concerning the interpretation or application of this Convention have agreed, through a general, regional or bilateral agreement or otherwise, that such dispute shall, at the request of any party to the dispute, be submitted to a procedure that entails a binding decision, that procedure shall apply in lieu of the procedures provided for in this Part, unless the parties to the dispute otherwise agree.

Article 283 – Obligation to exchange views

1. When a dispute arises between States Parties concerning the interpretation or application of this Convention, the parties to the dispute shall proceed expeditiously to an exchange of views regarding its settlement by negotiation or other peaceful means.
2. The parties shall also proceed expeditiously to an exchange of views where a procedure for the settlement of such a dispute has been terminated without a settlement or where a settlement has been reached and the circumstances require consultation regarding the manner of implementing the settlement.

Article 284 – Conciliation

1. A State Party which is a party to a dispute concerning the interpretation or application of this Convention may invite the other party or parties to submit the dispute to conciliation in accordance with the procedure under Annex V, section 1, or another conciliation procedure.
2. If the invitation is accepted and if the parties agree upon the conciliation procedure to be applied, any party may submit the dispute to that procedure.
3. If the invitation is not accepted or the parties do not agree upon the procedure, the conciliation proceedings shall be deemed to be terminated.
4. Unless the parties otherwise agree, when a dispute has been submitted to conciliation, the proceedings may be terminated only in accordance with the agreed conciliation procedure.

Article 285 – Application of this section to disputes submitted pursuant to Part XI

This section applies to any dispute which pursuant to Part XI, section 5, is to be settled in accordance with procedures provided for in this Part. If an entity other than a State Party is a party to such a dispute, this section applies mutatis mutandis.

SECTION 2. COMPULSORY PROCEDURES ENTAILING BINDING DECISIONS

Article 286 – Application of procedures under this section

Subject to section 3, any dispute concerning the interpretation or application of this Convention shall, where no settlement has been reached by recourse to section 1, be submitted at the request of any party to the dispute to the court or tribunal having jurisdiction under this section.

Article 287 – Choice of procedure

1. When signing, ratifying or acceding to this Convention or at any time thereafter, a State shall be free to choose, by means of a written declaration, one or more of the following means for the settlement of disputes concerning the interpretation or application of this Convention:
   (a) the International Tribunal for the Law of the Sea established in accordance with Annex VI;
   (b) the International Court of Justice;
   (c) an arbitral tribunal constituted in accordance with Annex VII;
   (d) a special arbitral tribunal constituted in accordance with Annex VIII for one or more of the categories of disputes specified therein.
2. A declaration made under paragraph 1 shall not affect or be affected by the obligation of a State Party to accept the jurisdiction of the Seabed Disputes Chamber of the International Tribunal for the Law of the Sea to the extent and in the manner provided for in Part XI, section 5.
3. A State Party, which is a party to a dispute not covered by a declaration in force, shall be deemed to have accepted arbitration in accordance with Annex VII.
4. If the parties to a dispute have accepted the same procedure for the settlement of the dispute, it may be submitted only to that procedure, unless the parties otherwise agree.
5. If the parties to a dispute have not accepted the same procedure for the settlement of the dispute, it may be submitted only to arbitration in accordance with Annex VII, unless the parties otherwise agree.
6. A declaration made under paragraph 1 shall remain in force until three months after notice of revocation has been deposited with the Secretary-General of the United Nations.
7. A new declaration, a notice of revocation or the expiry of a declaration does not in any way affect proceedings pending before a court or tribunal having jurisdiction under this article, unless the parties otherwise agree.

8. Declarations and notices referred to in this article shall be deposited with the Secretary-General of the United Nations, who shall transmit copies thereof to the States Parties.

Article 288 – Jurisdiction

1. A court or tribunal referred to in article 287 shall have jurisdiction over any dispute concerning the interpretation or application of this Convention which is submitted to it in accordance with this Part.
2. A court or tribunal referred to in article 287 shall also have jurisdiction over any dispute concerning the interpretation or application of an international agreement related to the purposes of this Convention, which is submitted to it in accordance with the agreement.
3. The Seabed Disputes Chamber of the International Tribunal for the Law of the Sea established in accordance with Annex VI, and any other chamber or arbitral tribunal referred to in Part XI, section 5, shall have jurisdiction in any matter which is submitted to it in accordance therewith.
4. In the event of a dispute as to whether a court or tribunal has jurisdiction, the matter shall be settled by decision of that court or tribunal.

Article 289 – Experts

In any dispute involving scientific or technical matters, a court or tribunal exercising jurisdiction under this section may, at the request of a party or proprio motu, select in consultation with the parties no fewer than two scientific or technical experts chosen preferably from the relevant list prepared in accordance with Annex VIII, article 2, to sit with the court or tribunal but without the right to vote.

Article 290 – Provisional measures

1. If a dispute has been duly submitted to a court or tribunal which considers that prima facie it has jurisdiction under this Part or Part XI, section 5, the court or tribunal may prescribe any provisional measures which it considers appropriate under the circumstances to preserve the respective rights of the parties to the dispute or to prevent serious harm to the marine environment, pending the final decision.
2. Provisional measures may be modified or revoked as soon as the circumstances justifying them have changed or ceased to exist.
3. Provisional measures may be prescribed, modified or revoked under this article only at the request of a party to the dispute and after the parties have been given an opportunity to be heard.
4. The court or tribunal shall forthwith give notice to the parties to the dispute, and to such other States Parties as it considers appropriate, of the prescription, modification or revocation of provisional measures.
5. Pending the constitution of an arbitral tribunal to which a dispute is being submitted under this section, any court or tribunal agreed upon by the parties or, failing such agreement within two weeks from the date of the request for provisional measures, the International Tribunal for the Law of the Sea or, with respect to activities in the Area, the Seabed Disputes Chamber, may prescribe, modify or revoke provisional measures in accordance with this article if it considers that prima facie the tribunal which is to be constituted would have jurisdiction and that the urgency of the situation so requires. Once constituted, the tribunal to which the dispute has been submitted may modify, revoke or affirm those provisional measures, acting in conformity with paragraphs 1 to 4.
6. The parties to the dispute shall comply promptly with any provisional measures prescribed under this article.

Article 291 – Access

1. All the dispute settlement procedures specified in this Part shall be open to States Parties.
2. The dispute settlement procedures specified in this Part shall be open to entities other than States Parties only as specifically provided for in this Convention.

Article 292 – Prompt release of vessels and crews

1. Where the authorities of a State Party have detained a vessel flying the flag of another State Party and it is alleged that the detaining State has not complied with the provisions of this Convention for the prompt release of the vessel or its crew upon the posting of a reasonable bond or other financial security, the question of release from detention may be submitted to any court or tribunal agreed upon by the parties or, failing such agreement within 10 days from the time of detention, to a court or tribunal accepted by the detaining State under article 287 or to the International Tribunal for the Law of the Sea, unless the parties otherwise agree.
2. The application for release may be made only by or on behalf of the flag State of the vessel.
3. The court or tribunal shall deal without delay with the application for release and shall deal only with the question of release, without prejudice to the merits of any case before the appropriate domestic forum against the vessel, its owner or its crew. The authorities of the detaining State remain competent to release the vessel or its crew at any time.
4. Upon the posting of the bond or other financial security determined by the court or tribunal, the authorities of the detaining State shall comply promptly with the decision of the court or tribunal concerning the release of the vessel or its crew.

Article 293 – Applicable law

1. A court or tribunal having jurisdiction under this section shall apply this Convention and other rules of international law not incompatible with this Convention.
2. Paragraph 1 does not prejudice the power of the court or tribunal having jurisdiction under this section to decide a case ex aequo et bono, if the parties so agree.

Article 294 – Preliminary proceedings

1. A court or tribunal provided for in article 287 to which an application is made in respect of a dispute referred to in article 297 shall determine at the request of a party, or may determine proprio motu, whether the claim constitutes an abuse of legal process or whether prima facie it is well founded. If the court or tribunal determines that the claim constitutes an abuse of legal process or is prima facie unfounded, it shall take no further action in the case.
2. Upon receipt of the application, the court or tribunal shall immediately notify the other party or parties of the application, and shall fix a reasonable time-limit within which they may request it to make a determination in accordance with paragraph 1.
3. Nothing in this article affects the right of any party to a dispute to make preliminary objections in accordance with the applicable rules of procedure.

Article 295 – Exhaustion of local remedies

Any dispute between States Parties concerning the interpretation or application of this Convention may be submitted to the procedures provided for in this section only after local remedies have been exhausted where this is required by international law.

Article 296 – Finality and binding force of decisions

1. Any decision rendered by a court or tribunal having jurisdiction under this section shall be final and shall be complied with by all the parties to the dispute.
2. Any such decision shall have no binding force except between the parties and in respect of that particular dispute.

SECTION 3. LIMITATIONS AND EXCEPTIONS TO APPLICABILITY OF SECTION 2

Article 297 – Limitations on applicability of section 2

1. Disputes concerning the interpretation or application of this Convention with regard to the exercise by a coastal State of its sovereign rights or jurisdiction provided for in this Convention shall be subject to the procedures provided for in section 2 in the following cases:
   (a) when it is alleged that a coastal State has acted in contravention of the provisions of this Convention in regard to the freedoms and rights of navigation, overflight or the laying of submarine cables and pipelines, or in regard to other internationally lawful uses of the sea specified in article 58;
   (b) when it is alleged that a State in exercising the aforementioned freedoms, rights or uses has acted in contravention of this Convention or of laws or regulations adopted by the coastal State in conformity with this Convention and other rules of international law not incompatible with this Convention; or
   (c) when it is alleged that a coastal State has acted in contravention of specified international rules and standards for the protection and preservation of the marine environment which are applicable to the coastal State and which have been established by this Convention or through a competent international organization or diplomatic conference in accordance with this Convention.
2. (a) Disputes concerning the interpretation or application of the provisions of this Convention with regard to marine scientific research shall be settled in accordance with section 2, except that the coastal State shall not be obliged to accept the submission to such settlement of any dispute arising out of:
      (i) the exercise by the coastal State of a right or discretion in accordance with article 246; or
      (ii) a decision by the coastal State to order suspension or cessation of a research project in accordance with article 253.
   (b) A dispute arising from an allegation by the researching State that with respect to a specific project the coastal State is not exercising its rights under articles 246 and 253 in a manner compatible with this Convention shall be submitted, at the request of either party, to conciliation under Annex V, section 2, provided that the conciliation commission shall not call in question the exercise by the coastal State of its discretion to designate specific areas as referred to in article 246, paragraph 6, or of its discretion to withhold consent in accordance with article 246, paragraph 5.
3. (a) Disputes concerning the interpretation or application of the provisions of this Convention with regard to fisheries shall be settled in accordance with section 2, except that the coastal State shall not be obliged to accept the submission to such settlement of any dispute relating to its sovereign rights with respect to the living resources in the exclusive economic zone or their exercise, including its discretionary powers for determining the allowable catch, its harvesting capacity, the allocation of surpluses to other States and the terms and conditions established in its conservation and management laws and regulations.
   (b) Where no settlement has been reached by recourse to section 1 of this Part, a dispute shall be submitted to conciliation under Annex V, section 2, at the request of any party to the dispute, when it is alleged that:
      (i) a coastal State has manifestly failed to comply with its obligations to ensure through proper conservation and management measures that the maintenance of the living resources in the exclusive economic zone is not seriously endangered;
      (ii) a coastal State has arbitrarily refused to determine, at the request of another State, the allowable catch and its capacity to har-

vest living resources with respect to stocks which that other State is interested in fishing; or

(iii) a coastal State has arbitrarily refused to allocate to any State, under articles 62, 69 and 70 and under the terms and conditions established by the coastal State consistent with this Convention, the whole or part of the surplus it has declared to exist.

(c) In no case shall the conciliation commission substitute its discretion for that of the coastal State.

(d) The report of the conciliation commission shall be communicated to the appropriate international organizations.

(e) In negotiating agreements pursuant to articles 69 and 70, States Parties, unless they otherwise agree, shall include a clause on measures which they shall take in order to minimize the possibility of a disagreement concerning the interpretation or application of the agreement, and on how they should proceed if a disagreement nevertheless arises.

Article 298 – Optional exceptions to applicability of section 2

1. When signing, ratifying or acceding to this Convention or at any time thereafter, a State may, without prejudice to the obligations arising under section 1, declare in writing that it does not accept any one or more of the procedures provided for in section 2 with respect to one or more of the following categories of disputes:

(a) (i) disputes concerning the interpretation or application of articles 15, 74 and 83 relating to sea boundary delimitations, or those involving historic bays or titles, provided that a State having made such a declaration shall, when such a dispute arises subsequent to the entry into force of this Convention and where no agreement within a reasonable period of time is reached in negotiations between the parties, at the request of any party to the dispute, accept submission of the matter to conciliation under Annex V, section 2; and provided further that any dispute that necessarily involves the concurrent consideration of any unsettled dispute concerning sovereignty or other rights over continental or insular land territory shall be excluded from such submission;

(ii) after the conciliation commission has presented its report, which shall state the reasons on which it is based, the parties shall negotiate an agreement on the basis of that report; if these negotiations do not result in an agreement, the parties shall, by mutual consent, submit the question to one of the procedures provided for in section 2, unless the parties otherwise agree;

(iii) this subparagraph does not apply to any sea boundary dispute finally settled by an arrangement between the parties, or to any such dispute which is to be settled in accordance with a bilateral or multilateral agreement binding upon those parties;

(b) disputes concerning military activities, including military activities by government vessels and aircraft engaged in non-commercial service, and disputes concerning law enforcement activities in regard to the exercise of sovereign rights or jurisdiction excluded from the jurisdiction of a court or tribunal under article 297, paragraph 2 or 3;

(c) disputes in respect of which the Security Council of the United Nations is exercising the functions assigned to it by the Charter of the United Nations, unless the Security Council decides to remove the matter from its agenda or calls upon the parties to settle it by the means provided for in this Convention.

2. A State Party which has made a declaration under paragraph 1 may at any time withdraw it, or agree to submit a dispute excluded by such declaration to any procedure specified in this Convention.
3. A State Party which has made a declaration under paragraph 1 shall not be entitled to submit any dispute falling within the excepted category of disputes to any procedure in this Convention as against another State Party, without the consent of that party.
4. If one of the States Parties has made a declaration under paragraph 1(a), any other State Party may submit any dispute falling within an excepted category against the declarant party to the procedure specified in such declaration.
5. A new declaration, or the withdrawal of a declaration, does not in any way affect proceedings pending before a court or tribunal in accordance with this article, unless the parties otherwise agree.
6. Declarations and notices of withdrawal of declarations under this article shall be deposited with the Secretary-General of the United Nations, who shall transmit copies thereof to the States Parties.

Article 299 – Right of the parties to agree upon a procedure

1. A dispute excluded under article 297 or excepted by a declaration made under article 298 from the dispute settlement procedures provided for in section 2 may be submitted to such procedures only by agreement of the parties to the dispute.
2. Nothing in this section impairs the right of the parties to the dispute to agree to some other procedure for the settlement of such dispute or to reach an amicable settlement.

PART XVI – GENERAL PROVISIONS

Article 300 – Good faith and abuse of rights

States Parties shall fulfil in good faith the obligations assumed under this Convention and shall exercise the rights, jurisdiction and freedoms recognized in this Convention in a manner which would not constitute an abuse of right.

Article 301 – Peaceful uses of the seas

In exercising their rights and performing their duties under this Convention, States Parties shall refrain from any threat or use of force against the territorial integrity or political independence of any State, or in any other manner inconsistent with the principles of international law embodied in the Charter of the United Nations.

Article 302 – Disclosure of information

Without prejudice to the right of a State Party to resort to the procedures for the settlement of disputes provided for in this Convention, nothing in this Convention shall be deemed to require a State Party, in the fulfilment of its obligations under this Convention, to supply information the disclosure of which is contrary to the essential interests of its security.

Article 303 – Archaeological and historical objects found at sea

1. States have the duty to protect objects of an archaeological and historical nature found at sea and shall cooperate for this purpose.
2. In order to control traffic in such objects, the coastal State may, in applying article 33, presume that their removal from the seabed in the zone referred to in that article without its approval would result in an infringement within its territory or territorial sea of the laws and regulations referred to in that article.
3. Nothing in this article affects the rights of identifiable owners, the law of salvage or other rules of admiralty, or laws and practices with respect to cultural exchanges.
4. This article is without prejudice to other international agreements and rules of international law regarding the protection of objects of an archaeological and historical nature.

Article 304 – Responsibility and liability for damage

The provisions of this Convention regarding responsibility and liability for damage are without prejudice to the application of existing rules and the development of further rules regarding responsibility and liability under international law.

PART XVII – FINAL PROVISIONS

Article 305 – Signature

1. This Convention shall be open for signature by:
   (a) all States;
   (b) Namibia, represented by the United Nations Council for Namibia;
   (c) all self-governing associated States which have chosen that status in an act of self-determination supervised and approved by the United Nations in accordance with General Assembly resolution 1514 (XV) and which have competence over the matters governed by this Convention, including the competence to enter into treaties in respect of those matters;
   (d) all self-governing associated States which, in accordance with their respective instruments of association, have competence over the matters governed by this Convention, including the competence to enter into treaties in respect of those matters;
   (e) all territories which enjoy full internal self-government, recognized as such by the United Nations, but have not attained full independence in accordance with General Assembly resolution 1514 (XV) and which have competence over the matters governed by this Convention, including the competence to enter into treaties in respect of those matters;
   (f) international organizations, in accordance with Annex IX.
2. This Convention shall remain open for signature until 9 December 1984 at the Ministry of Foreign Affairs of Jamaica and also, from 1 July 1983 until 9 December 1984, at United Nations Headquarters in New York.

Article 306 – Ratification and formal confirmation

This Convention is subject to ratification by States and the other entities referred to in article 305, paragraph l(b), (c), (d) and (e), and to formal confirmation, in accordance with Annex IX, by the entities referred to in article 305, paragraph l(f). The instruments of ratification and of formal confirmation shall be deposited with the Secretary-General of the United Nations.

Article 307 – Accession

This Convention shall remain open for accession by States and the other entities referred to in article 305. Accession by the entities referred to in article 305, paragraph l(f), shall be in accordance with Annex IX. The instruments of accession shall be deposited with the Secretary-General of the United Nations.

Article 308 – Entry into force

1. This Convention shall enter into force 12 months after the date of deposit of the sixtieth instrument of ratification or accession.
2. For each State ratifying or acceding to this Convention after the deposit of the sixtieth instrument of ratification or accession, the Convention shall enter into force on the thirtieth day following the deposit of its instrument of ratification or accession, subject to paragraph 1.
3. The Assembly of the Authority shall meet on the date of entry into force of this Convention and shall elect the Council of the Authority. The first Council shall be constituted in a manner consistent with the purpose of article 161 if the provisions of that article cannot be strictly applied.
4. The rules, regulations and procedures drafted by the Preparatory Commission shall apply provisionally pending their formal adoption by the Authority in accordance with Part XI.
5. The Authority and its organs shall act in accordance with resolution II of the Third United Nations Conference on the Law of the Sea relating

to preparatory investment and with decisions of the Preparatory Commission taken pursuant to that resolution.

Article 309 – Reservations and exceptions

No reservations or exceptions may be made to this Convention unless expressly permitted by other articles of this Convention.

Article 310 – Declarations and statements

Article 309 does not preclude a State, when signing, ratifying or acceding to this Convention, from making declarations or statements, however phrased or named, with a view, inter alia, to the harmonization of its laws and regulations with the provisions of this Convention, provided that such declarations or statements do not purport to exclude or to modify the legal effect of the provisions of this Convention in their application to that State.

Article 311 – Relation to other conventions and international agreements

1. This Convention shall prevail, as between States Parties, over the Geneva Conventions on the Law of the Sea of 29 April 1958.
2. This Convention shall not alter the rights and obligations of States Parties which arise from other agreements compatible with this Convention and which do not affect the enjoyment by other States Parties of their rights or the performance of their obligations under this Convention.
3. Two or more States Parties may conclude agreements modifying or suspending the operation of provisions of this Convention, applicable solely to the relations between them, provided that such agreements do not relate to a provision derogation from which is incompatible with the effective execution of the object and purpose of this Convention, and provided further that such agreements shall not affect the application of the basic principles embodied herein, and that the provisions of such agreements do not affect the enjoyment by other States Parties of their rights or the performance of their obligations under this Convention.
4. States Parties intending to conclude an agreement referred to in paragraph 3 shall notify the other States Parties through the depositary of this Convention of their intention to conclude the agreement and of the modification or suspension for which it provides.
5. This article does not affect international agreements expressly permitted or preserved by other articles of this Convention.
6. States Parties agree that there shall be no amendments to the basic principle relating to the common heritage of mankind set forth in article 136 and that they shall not be party to any agreement in derogation thereof.

Article 312 – Amendment

1. After the expiry of a period of 10 years from the date of entry into force of this Convention, a State Party may, by written communication addressed to the Secretary-General of the United Nations, propose specific amendments to this Convention, other than those relating to activities in the Area, and request the convening of a conference to consider such proposed amendments. The Secretary-General shall circulate such communication to all States Parties. If, within 12 months from the date of the circulation of the communication, not less than one half of the States Parties reply favourably to the request, the Secretary-General shall convene the conference.
2. The decision-making procedure applicable at the amendment conference shall be the same as that applicable at the Third United Nations Conference on the Law of the Sea unless otherwise decided by the conference. The conference should make every effort to reach agreement on any amendments by way of consensus and there should be no voting on them until all efforts at consensus have been exhausted.

Article 313 – Amendment by simplified procedure

1. A State Party may, by written communication addressed to the Secretary-General of the United Nations, propose an amendment to this Convention, other than an amendment relating to activities in the Area, to be adopted by the simplified procedure set forth in this article without convening a conference. The Secretary-General shall circulate the communication to all States Parties.
2. If, within a period of 12 months from the date of the circulation of the communication, a State Party objects to the proposed amendment or to the proposal for its adoption by the simplified procedure, the amendment shall be considered rejected. The Secretary-General shall immediately notify all States Parties accordingly.
3. If, 12 months from the date of the circulation of the communication, no State Party has objected to the proposed amendment or to the proposal for its adoption by the simplified procedure, the proposed amendment shall be considered adopted. The Secretary-General shall notify all States Parties that the proposed amendment has been adopted.

Article 314 – Amendments to the provisions of this Convention relating exclusively to activities in the Area

1. A State Party may, by written communication addressed to the Secretary-General of the Authority, propose an amendment to the provisions of this Convention relating exclusively to activities in the Area, including Annex VI, section 4. The Secretary-General shall circulate such communication to all States Parties. The proposed amendment shall be subject to approval by the Assembly following its approval by the Council. Representatives of States Parties in those organs shall have full powers to consider and approve the proposed amendment. The proposed amendment as approved by the Council and the Assembly shall be considered adopted.

2. Before approving any amendment under paragraph 1, the Council and the Assembly shall ensure that it does not prejudice the system of exploration for and exploitation of the resources of the Area, pending the Review Conference in accordance with article 155.

Article 315 – Signature, ratification of, accession to and authentic texts of amendments

1. Once adopted, amendments to this Convention shall be open for signature by States Parties for 12 months from the date of adoption, at United Nations Headquarters in New York, unless otherwise provided in the amendment itself.
2. Articles 306, 307 and 320 apply to all amendments to this Convention.

Article 316 – Entry into force of amendments

1. Amendments to this Convention, other than those referred to in paragraph 5, shall enter into force for the States Parties ratifying or acceding to them on the thirtieth day following the deposit of instruments of ratification or accession by two thirds of the States Parties or by 60 States Parties, whichever is greater. Such amendments shall not affect the enjoyment by other States Parties of their rights or the performance of their obligations under this Convention.
2. An amendment may provide that a larger number of ratifications or accessions shall be required for its entry into force than are required by this article.
3. For each State Party ratifying or acceding to an amendment referred to in paragraph 1 after the deposit of the required number of instruments of ratification or accession, the amendment shall enter into force on the thirtieth day following the deposit of its instrument of ratification or accession.
4. A State which becomes a Party to this Convention after the entry into force of an amendment in accordance with paragraph 1 shall, failing an expression of a different intention by that State:
   (a) be considered as a Party to this Convention as so amended; and
   (b) be considered as a Party to the unamended Convention in relation to any State Party not bound by the amendment.
5. Any amendment relating exclusively to activities in the Area and any amendment to Annex VI shall enter into force for all States Parties one year following the deposit of instruments of ratification or accession by three fourths of the States Parties.
6. A State which becomes a Party to this Convention after the entry into force of amendments in accordance with paragraph 5 shall be considered as a Party to this Convention as so amended.

Article 317 – Denunciation

1. A State Party may, by written notification addressed to the Secretary-General of the United Nations, denounce this Convention and may indicate its reasons. Failure to indicate reasons shall not affect the validity of the denunciation. The denunciation shall take effect one year after the date of receipt of the notification, unless the notification specifies a later date.
2. A State shall not be discharged by reason of the denunciation from the financial and contractual obligations which accrued while it was a Party to this Convention, nor shall the denunciation affect any right, obligation or legal situation of that State created through the execution of this Convention prior to its termination for that State.
3. The denunciation shall not in any way affect the duty of any State Party to fulfil any obligation embodied in this Convention to which it would be subject under international law independently of this Convention.

Article 318 – Status of Annexes

The Annexes form an integral part of this Convention and, unless expressly provided otherwise, a reference to this Convention or to one of its Parts includes a reference to the Annexes relating thereto.

Article 319 – Depositary

1. The Secretary-General of the United Nations shall be the depositary of this Convention and amendments thereto.
2. In addition to his functions as depositary, the Secretary-General shall:
   (a) report to all States Parties, the Authority and competent international organizations on issues of a general nature that have arisen with respect to this Convention;
   (b) notify the Authority of ratifications and formal confirmations of and accessions to this Convention and amendments thereto, as well as of denunciations of this Convention;
   (c) notify States Parties of agreements in accordance with article 311, paragraph 4;
   (d) circulate amendments adopted in accordance with this Convention to States Parties for ratification or accession;
   (e) convene necessary meetings of States Parties in accordance with this Convention.
3. (a) The Secretary-General shall also transmit to the observers referred to in article 156:
      (i) reports referred to in paragraph 2(a);
      (ii) notifications referred to in paragraph 2(b) and (c); and
      (iii) texts of amendments referred to in paragraph 2(d), for their information.
   (b) The Secretary-General shall also invite those observers to participate as observers at meetings of States Parties referred to in paragraph 2(e).

Article 320 – Authentic texts

The original of this Convention, of which the Arabic, Chinese, English, French, Russian and Spanish texts are equally authentic, shall, subject to article 305, paragraph 2, be deposited with the Secretary-General of the United Nations.

IN WITNESS WHEREOF, the undersigned Plenipotentiaries, being duly authorized thereto, have signed this Convention.

DONE AT MONTEGO BAY, this tenth day of December, one thousand nine hundred and eighty-two.

ANNEX I. HIGHLY MIGRATORY SPECIES

1. Albacore tuna: Thunnus alalunga.
2. Bluefin tuna: Thunnus thynnus.
3. Bigeye tuna: Thunnus obesus.
4. Skipjack tuna: Katsuwonus pelamis.
5. Yellowfin tuna: Thunnus albacares.
6. Blackfin tuna: Thunnus atlanticus.
7. Little tuna: Euthynnus alletteratus; Euthynnus affinis.
8. Southern bluefin tuna: Thunnus maccoyii.
9. Frigate mackerel: Auxis thazard; Auxis rochei.
10. Pomfrets: Family Bramidae.
11. Marlins: Tetrapturus angustirostris; Tetrapturus belone; Tetrapturus pfluegeri; Tetrapturus albidus; Tetrapturus audax; Tetrapturus georgei; Makaira mazara; Makaira indica; Makaira nigricans.
12. Sail-fishes: Istiophorus platypterus; Istiophorus albicans.
13. Swordfish: Xiphias gladius.
14. Sauries: Scomberesox saurus; Cololabis saira; Cololabis adocetus; Scomberesox saurus scombroides.
15. Dolphin: Coryphaena hippurus; Coryphaena equiselis.
16. Oceanic sharks: Hexanchus griseus; Cetorhinus maximus; Family Alopiidae; Rhincodon typus; Family Carcharhinidae; Family Sphyrnidae; Family Isurida.
17. Cetaceans: Family Physeteridae; Family Balaenopteridae; Family Balaenidae; Family Eschrichtiidae; Family Monodontidae; Family Ziphiidae; Family Delphinidae.

ANNEX II. COMMISSION ON THE LIMITS OF THE CONTINENTAL SHELF

Article 1

In accordance with the provisions of article 76, a Commission on the Limits of the Continental Shelf beyond 200 nautical miles shall be established in conformity with the following articles.

Article 2

1. The Commission shall consist of 21 members who shall be experts in the field of geology, geophysics or hydrography, elected by States Parties to this Convention from among their nationals, having due regard to the need to ensure equitable geographical representation, who shall serve in their personal capacities.
2. The initial election shall be held as soon as possible but in any case within 18 months after the date of entry into force of this Convention. At least three months before the date of each election, the Secretary-General of the United Nations shall address a letter to the States Parties, inviting the submission of nominations, after appropriate regional consultations, within three months. The Secretary-General shall prepare a list in alphabetical order of all persons thus nominated and shall submit it to all the States Parties.
3. Elections of the members of the Commission shall be held at a meeting of States Parties convened by the Secretary-General at United Nations Headquarters. At that meeting, for which two thirds of the States Parties shall constitute a quorum, the persons elected to the Commission shall be those nominees who obtain a two-thirds majority of the votes of the representatives of States Parties present and voting. Not less than three members shall be elected from each geographical region.
4. The members of the Commission shall be elected for a term of five years. They shall be eligible for re-election.
5. The State Party which submitted the nomination of a member of the Commission shall defray the expenses of that member while in performance of Commission duties. The coastal State concerned shall defray the expenses incurred in respect of the advice referred to in article 3, paragraph 1(b), of this Annex. The secretariat of the Commission shall be provided by the Secretary-General of the United Nations.

Article 3

1. The functions of the Commission shall be:
   (a) to consider the data and other material submitted by coastal States concerning the outer limits of the continental shelf in areas where those limits extend beyond 200 nautical miles, and to make recommendations in accordance with article 76 and the Statement of Understanding adopted on 29 August 1980 by the Third United Nations Conference on the Law of the Sea;
   (b) to provide scientific and technical advice, if requested by the coastal State concerned during the preparation of the data referred to in subparagraph (a).
2. The Commission may cooperate, to the extent considered necessary and useful, with the Intergovernmental Oceanographic Commission of UNESCO, the International Hydrographic Organization and other competent international organizations with a view to exchanging scientific and technical information which might be of assistance in discharging the Commission's responsibilities.

Article 4

Where a coastal State intends to establish, in accordance with article 76, the outer limits of its continental shelf beyond 200 nautical miles, it shall submit particulars of such limits to the Commission along with supporting scientific and technical data as soon as possible but in any case within 10 years of the entry into force of this Convention for that State. The coastal State shall at the same time give the names of any Commission members who have provided it with scientific and technical advice.

Article 5

Unless the Commission decides otherwise, the Commission shall function by way of sub-commissions composed of seven members, appointed in a balanced manner taking into account the specific elements of each submission by a coastal State. Nationals of the coastal State making the submission who are members of the Commission and any Commission member who has assisted a coastal State by providing scientific and technical advice with respect to the delineation shall not be a member of the sub-commission dealing with that submission but has the right to participate as a member in the proceedings of the Commission concerning the said submission. The coastal State which has made a submission to the Commission may send its representatives to participate in the relevant proceedings without the right to vote.

Article 6

1. The sub-commission shall submit its recommendations to the Commission.
2. Approval by the Commission of the recommendations of the sub-commission shall be by a majority of two thirds of Commission members present and voting.
3. The recommendations of the Commission shall be submitted in writing to the coastal State which made the submission and to the Secretary-General of the United Nations.

Article 7

Coastal States shall establish the outer limits of the continental shelf in conformity with the provisions of article 76, paragraph 8, and in accordance with the appropriate national procedures.

Article 8

In the case of disagreement by the coastal State with the recommendations of the Commission, the coastal State shall, within a reasonable time, make a revised or new submission to the Commission.

Article 9

The actions of the Commission shall not prejudice matters relating to delimitation of boundaries between States with opposite or adjacent coasts.

ANNEX III. BASIC CONDITIONS OF PROSPECTING, EXPLORATION AND EXPLOITATION

Article 1 – Title to minerals

Title to minerals shall pass upon recovery in accordance with this Convention.

Article 2 – Prospecting

1. (a) The Authority shall encourage prospecting in the Area.
   (b) Prospecting shall be conducted only after the Authority has received a satisfactory written undertaking that the proposed prospector will comply with this Convention and the relevant rules, regulations and procedures of the Authority concerning cooperation in the training programmes referred to in articles 143 and 144 and the protection of the marine environment, and will accept verification by the Authority of compliance therewith. The proposed prospector shall, at the same time, notify the Authority of the approximate area or areas in which prospecting is to be conducted.
   (c) Prospecting may be conducted simultaneously by more than one prospector in the same area or areas.
2. Prospecting shall not confer on the prospector any rights with respect to resources. A prospector may, however, recover a reasonable quantity of minerals to be used for testing.

Article 3 – Exploration and exploitation

1. The Enterprise, States Parties, and the other entities referred to in article 153, paragraph 2(b), may apply to the Authority for approval of plans of work for activities in the Area.
2. The Enterprise may apply with respect to any part of the Area, but applications by others with respect to reserved areas are subject to the additional requirements of article 9 of this Annex.
3. Exploration and exploitation shall be carried out only in areas specified in plans of work referred to in article 153, paragraph 3, and approved by the Authority in accordance with this Convention and the relevant rules, regulations and procedures of the Authority.
4. Every approved plan of work shall:
   (a) be in conformity with this Convention and the rules, regulations and procedures of the Authority;
   (b) provide for control by the Authority of activities in the Area in accordance with article 153, paragraph 4;
   (c) confer on the operator, in accordance with the rules, regulations and procedures of the Authority, the exclusive right to explore for and exploit the specified categories of resources in the area covered by the plan of work. If, however, the applicant presents for approval a plan of work covering only the stage of exploration or the stage of exploitation, the approved plan of work shall confer such exclusive right with respect to that stage only.
5. Upon its approval by the Authority, every plan of work, except those presented by the Enterprise, shall be in the form of a contract concluded between the Authority and the applicant or applicants.

Article 4 – Qualifications of applicants

1. Applicants, other than the Enterprise, shall be qualified if they have the nationality or control and sponsorship required by article 153, paragraph 2(b), and if they follow the procedures and meet the qualification standards set forth in the rules, regulations and procedures of the Authority.
2. Except as provided in paragraph 6, such qualification standards shall relate to the financial and technical capabilities of the applicant and his performance under any previous contracts with the Authority.
3. Each applicant shall be sponsored by the State Party of which it is a national unless the applicant has more than one nationality, as in the case of a partnership or consortium of entities from several States, in which event all States Parties involved shall sponsor the application, or unless the applicant is effectively controlled by another State Party or its nationals, in which event both States Parties shall sponsor the application. The criteria and procedures for implementation of the sponsorship requirements shall be set forth in the rules, regulations and procedures of the Authority.
4. The sponsoring State or States shall, pursuant to article 139, have the responsibility to ensure, within their legal systems, that a contractor so sponsored shall carry out activities in the Area in conformity with the terms of its contract and its obligations under this Convention. A sponsoring State shall not, however, be liable for damage caused by any failure of a contractor sponsored by it to comply with its obligations if that State Party has adopted laws and regulations and taken administrative measures which are, within the framework of its legal system, reasonably appropriate for securing compliance by persons under its jurisdiction.
5. The procedures for assessing the qualifications of States Parties which are applicants shall take into account their character as States.
6. The qualification standards shall require that every applicant, without exception, shall as part of his application undertake:
   (a) to accept as enforceable and comply with the applicable obligations created by the provisions of Part XI, the rules, regulations and procedures of the Authority, the decisions of the organs of the Authority and terms of his contracts with the Authority;
   (b) to accept control by the Authority of activities in the Area, as authorized by this Convention;
   (c) to provide the Authority with a written assurance that his obligations under the contract will be fulfilled in good faith;
   (d) to comply with the provisions on the transfer of technology set forth in article 5 of this Annex.

Article 5 – Transfer of technology

1. When submitting a plan of work, every applicant shall make available to the Authority a general description of the equipment and methods to be used in carrying out activities in the Area, and other relevant non-proprietary information about the characteristics of such technology and information as to where such technology is available.
2. Every operator shall inform the Authority of revisions in the description and information made available pursuant to paragraph 1 whenever a substantial technological change or innovation is introduced.
3. Every contract for carrying out activities in the Area shall contain the following undertakings by the contractor:
   (a) to make available to the Enterprise on fair and reasonable commercial terms and conditions, whenever the Authority so requests, the technology which he uses in carrying out activities in the Area under the contract, which the contractor is legally entitled to transfer. This shall be done by means of licences or other appropriate arrangements which the contractor shall negotiate with the Enterprise and which shall be set forth in a specific agreement supplementary to the contract. This undertaking may be invoked only if the Enterprise finds that it is unable to obtain the same or equally efficient and useful technology on the open market on fair and reasonable commercial terms and conditions;
   (b) to obtain a written assurance from the owner of any technology used in carrying out activities in the Area under the contract, which is not generally available on the open market and which is not covered by subparagraph (a), that the owner will, whenever the Authority so requests, make that technology available to the Enterprise under licence or other appropriate arrangements and on fair and reasonable commercial terms and conditions, to the same extent as made available to the contractor. If this assurance is not obtained, the technology in question shall not be used by the contractor in carrying out activities in the Area;
   (c) to acquire from the owner by means of an enforceable contract, upon the request of the Enterprise and if it is possible to do so without substantial cost to the contractor, the legal right to transfer to the Enterprise any technology used by the contractor, in carrying out activities in the Area under the contract, which the contractor is otherwise not legally entitled to transfer and which is not generally available on the open market. In cases where there is a substantial corporate relationship between the contractor and the owner of the technology, the closeness of this relationship and the degree of control or influence shall be relevant to the determination whether all feasible measures have been taken to acquire such a right. In cases where the contractor exercises effective control over the owner, failure to acquire from the owner the legal right shall be considered relevant to the contractor's qualification for any subsequent application for approval of a plan of work;

(d) to facilitate, upon the request of the Enterprise, the acquisition by the Enterprise of any technology covered by subparagraph (b), under licence or other appropriate arrangements and on fair and reasonable commercial terms and conditions, if the Enterprise decides to negotiate directly with the owner of the technology;

(e) to take the same measures as are prescribed in subparagraphs (a), (b), (c) and (d) for the benefit of a developing State or group of developing States which has applied for a contract under article 9 of this Annex, provided that these measures shall be limited to the exploitation of the part of the area proposed by the contractor which has been reserved pursuant to article 8 of this Annex and provided that activities under the contract sought by the developing State or group of developing States would not involve transfer of technology to a third State or the nationals of a third State. The obligation under this provision shall only apply with respect to any given contractor where technology has not been requested by the Enterprise or transferred by that contractor to the Enterprise.

4. Disputes concerning undertakings required by paragraph 3, like other provisions of the contracts, shall be subject to compulsory settlement in accordance with Part XI and, in cases of violation of these undertakings, suspension or termination of the contract or monetary penalties may be ordered in accordance with article 18 of this Annex. Disputes as to whether offers made by the contractor are within the range of fair and reasonable commercial terms and conditions may be submitted by either party to binding commercial arbitration in accordance with the UNCITRAL Arbitration Rules or such other arbitration rules as may be prescribed in the rules, regulations and procedures of the Authority. If the finding is that the offer made by the contractor is not within the range of fair and reasonable commercial terms and conditions, the contractor shall be given 45 days to revise his offer to bring it within that range before the Authority takes any action in accordance with article 18 of this Annex.

5. If the Enterprise is unable to obtain on fair and reasonable commercial terms and conditions appropriate technology to enable it to commence in a timely manner the recovery and processing of minerals from the Area, either the Council or the Assembly may convene a group of States Parties composed of those which are engaged in activities in the Area, those which have sponsored entities which are engaged in activities in the Area and other States Parties having access to such technology. This group shall consult together and shall take effective measures to ensure that such technology is made available to the Enterprise on fair and reasonable commercial terms and conditions. Each such State Party shall take all feasible measures to this end within its own legal system.

6. In the case of joint ventures with the Enterprise, transfer of technology will be in accordance with the terms of the joint venture agreement.

7. The undertakings required by paragraph 3 shall be included in each contract for the carrying out of activities in the Area until 10 years after the commencement of commercial production by the Enterprise, and may be invoked during that period.

8. For the purposes of this article, "technology" means the specialized equipment and technical know-how, including manuals, designs, operating instructions, training and technical advice and assistance, necessary to assemble, maintain and operate a viable system and the legal right to use these items for that purpose on a non-exclusive basis.

Article 6 – Approval of plans of work

1. Six months after the entry into force of this Convention, and thereafter each fourth month, the Authority shall take up for consideration proposed plans of work.

2. When considering an application for approval of a plan of work in the form of a contract, the Authority shall first ascertain whether:

   (a) the applicant has complied with the procedures established for applications in accordance with article 4 of this Annex and has given the Authority the undertakings and assurances required by that article. In cases of non-compliance with these procedures or in the absence of any of these undertakings and assurances, the applicant shall be given 45 days to remedy these defects;

   (b) the applicant possesses the requisite qualifications provided for in article 4 of this Annex.

3. All proposed plans of work shall be taken up in the order in which they are received. The proposed plans of work shall comply with and be governed by the relevant provisions of this Convention and the rules, regulations and procedures of the Authority, including those on operational requirements, financial contributions and the undertakings concerning the transfer of technology. If the proposed plans of work conform to these requirements, the Authority shall approve them provided that they are in accordance with the uniform and non-discriminatory requirements set forth in the rules, regulations and procedures of the Authority, unless:

   (a) part or all of the area covered by the proposed plan of work is included in an approved plan of work or a previously submitted proposed plan of work which has not yet been finally acted on by the Authority;

   (b) part or all of the area covered by the proposed plan of work is disapproved by the Authority pursuant to article 162, paragraph 2(x); or

   (c) the proposed plan of work has been submitted or sponsored by a State Party which already holds:

      (i) plans of work for exploration and exploitation of polymetallic nodules in non-reserved areas that, together with either part of the area covered by the application for a plan of work, exceed in size 30 per cent of a circular area of 400,000 square kilometres surrounding the centre of either part of the area covered by the proposed plan of work;

(ii) plans of work for the exploration and exploitation of polymetallic nodules in non-reserved areas which, taken together, constitute 2 per cent of the total seabed area which is not reserved or disapproved for exploitation pursuant to article 162, paragraph (2)(x).

4. For the purpose of the standard set forth in paragraph 3(c), a plan of work submitted by a partnership or consortium shall be counted on a pro rata basis among the sponsoring States Parties involved in accordance with article 4, paragraph 3, of this Annex. The Authority may approve plans of work covered by paragraph 3(c) if it determines that such approval would not permit a State Party or entities sponsored by it to monopolize the conduct of activities in the Area or to preclude other States Parties from activities in the Area.

5. Notwithstanding paragraph 3(a), after the end of the interim period specified in article 151, paragraph 3, the Authority may adopt by means of rules, regulations and procedures other procedures and criteria consistent with this Convention for deciding which applicants shall have plans of work approved in cases of selection among applicants for a proposed area. These procedures and criteria shall ensure approval of plans of work on an equitable and non-discriminatory basis.

Article 7 – Selection among applicants for production authorizations

1. Six months after the entry into force of this Convention, and thereafter each fourth month, the Authority shall take up for consideration applications for production authorizations submitted during the immediately preceding period. The Authority shall issue the authorizations applied for if all such applications can be approved without exceeding the production limitation or contravening the obligations of the Authority under a commodity agreement or arrangement to which it has become a party, as provided in article 151.

2. When a selection must be made among applicants for production authorizations because of the production limitation set forth in article 151, paragraphs 2 to 7, or because of the obligations of the Authority under a commodity agreement or arrangement to which it has become a party, as provided for in article 151, paragraph 1, the Authority shall make the selection on the basis of objective and non-discriminatory standards set forth in its rules, regulations and procedures.

3. In the application of paragraph 2, the Authority shall give priority to those applicants which:

   (a) give better assurance of performance, taking into account their financial and technical qualifications and their performance, if any, under previously approved plans of work;

   (b) provide earlier prospective financial benefits to the Authority, taking into account when commercial production is scheduled to begin;

   (c) have already invested the most resources and effort in prospecting or exploration.

4. Applicants which are not selected in any period shall have priority in subsequent periods until they receive a production authorization.

5. Selection shall be made taking into account the need to enhance opportunities for all States Parties, irrespective of their social and economic systems or geographical locations so as to avoid discrimination against any State or system, to participate in activities in the Area and to prevent monopolization of those activities.

6. Whenever fewer reserved areas than non-reserved areas are under exploitation, applications for production authorizations with respect to reserved areas shall have priority.

7. The decisions referred to in this article shall be taken as soon as possible after the close of each period.

Article 8 – Reservation of areas

Each application, other than those submitted by the Enterprise or by any other entities for reserved areas, shall cover a total area, which need not be a single continuous area, sufficiently large and of sufficient estimated commercial value to allow two mining operations. The applicant shall indicate the coordinates dividing the area into two parts of equal estimated commercial value and submit all the data obtained by him with respect to both parts. Without prejudice to the powers of the Authority pursuant to article 17 of this Annex, the data to be submitted concerning polymetallic nodules shall relate to mapping, sampling, the abundance of nodules, and their metal content. Within 45 days of receiving such data, the Authority shall designate which part is to be reserved solely for the conduct of activities by the Authority through the Enterprise or in association with developing States. This designation may be deferred for a further period of 45 days if the Authority requests an independent expert to assess whether all data required by this article has been submitted. The area designated shall become a reserved area as soon as the plan of work for the non-reserved area is approved and the contract is signed.

Article 9 – Activities in reserved areas

1. The Enterprise shall be given an opportunity to decide whether it intends to carry out activities in each reserved area. This decision may be taken at any time, unless a notification pursuant to paragraph 4 is received by the Authority, in which event the Enterprise shall take its decision within a reasonable time. The Enterprise may decide to exploit such areas in joint ventures with the interested State or entity.

2. The Enterprise may conclude contracts for the execution of part of its activities in accordance with Annex IV, article 12. It may also enter into joint ventures for the conduct of such activities with any entities which are eligible to carry out activities in

the Area pursuant to article 153, paragraph 2(b). When considering such joint ventures, the Enterprise shall offer to States Parties which are developing States and their nationals the opportunity of effective participation.

3. The Authority may prescribe, in its rules, regulations and procedures, substantive and procedural requirements and conditions with respect to such contracts and joint ventures.
4. Any State Party which is a developing State or any natural or juridical person sponsored by it and effectively controlled by it or by other developing State which is a qualified applicant, or any group of the foregoing, may notify the Authority that it wishes to submit a plan of work pursuant to article 6 of this Annex with respect to a reserved area. The plan of work shall be considered if the Enterprise decides, pursuant to paragraph 1, that it does not intend to carry out activities in that area.

Article 10 – Preference and priority among applicants

An operator who has an approved plan of work for exploration only, as provided in article 3, paragraph 4(c), of this Annex shall have a preference and a priority among applicants for a plan of work covering exploitation of the same area and resources. However, such preference or priority may be withdrawn if the operator's performance has not been satisfactory.

Article 11 – Joint arrangements

1. Contracts may provide for joint arrangements between the contractor and the Authority through the Enterprise, in the form of joint ventures or production sharing, as well as any other form of joint arrangement, which shall have the same protection against revision, suspension or termination as contracts with the Authority.
2. Contractors entering into such joint arrangements with the Enterprise may receive financial incentives as provided for in article 13 of this Annex.
3. Partners in joint ventures with the Enterprise shall be liable for the payments required by article 13 of this Annex to the extent of their share in the joint ventures, subject to financial incentives as provided for in that article.

Article 12 – Activities carried out by the Enterprise

1. Activities in the Area carried out by the Enterprise pursuant to article 153, paragraph 2(a), shall be governed by Part XI, the rules, regulations and procedures of the Authority and its relevant decisions.
2. Any plan of work submitted by the Enterprise shall be accompanied by evidence supporting its financial and technical capabilities.

Article 13 – Financial terms of contracts

1. In adopting rules, regulations and procedures concerning the financial terms of a contract between the Authority and the entities referred to in article 153, paragraph 2(b), and in negotiating those financial terms in accordance with Part XI and those rules, regulations and procedures, the Authority shall be guided by the following objectives:
   (a) to ensure optimum revenues for the Authority from the proceeds of commercial production;
   (b) to attract investments and technology to the exploration and exploitation of the Area;
   (c) to ensure equality of financial treatment and comparable financial obligations for contractors;
   (d) to provide incentives on a uniform and non-discriminatory basis for contractors to undertake joint arrangements with the Enterprise and developing States or their nationals, to stimulate the transfer of technology thereto, and to train the personnel of the Authority and of developing States;
   (e) to enable the Enterprise to engage in seabed mining effectively at the same time as the entities referred to in article 153, paragraph 2(b); and
   (f) to ensure that, as a result of the financial incentives provided to contractors under paragraph 14, under the terms of contracts reviewed in accordance with article 19 of this Annex or under the provisions of article 11 of this Annex with respect to joint ventures, contractors are not subsidized so as to be given an artificial competitive advantage with respect to land-based miners.
2. A fee shall be levied for the administrative cost of processing an application for approval of a plan of work in the form of a contract and shall be fixed at an amount of $US 500,000 per application. The amount of the fee shall be reviewed from time to time by the Council in order to ensure that it covers the administrative cost incurred. If such administrative cost incurred by the Authority in processing an application is less than the fixed amount, the Authority shall refund the difference to the applicant.
3. A contractor shall pay an annual fixed fee of $US 1 million from the date of entry into force of the contract. If the approved date of commencement of commercial production is postponed because of a delay in issuing the production authorization, in accordance with article 151, the annual fixed fee shall be waived for the period of postponement. From the date of commencement of commercial production, the contractor shall pay either the production charge or the annual fixed fee, whichever is greater.
4. Within a year of the date of commencement of commercial production, in conformity with paragraph 3, a contractor shall choose to make his financial contribution to the Authority by either:
   (a) paying a production charge only; or
   (b) paying a combination of a production charge and a share of net proceeds.
5. (a) If a contractor chooses to make his financial contribution to the Authority by paying a production charge only, it shall be fixed at a per-

centage of the market value of the processed metals produced from the polymetallic nodules recovered from the area covered by the contract. This percentage shall be fixed as follows:

(i) years 1-10 of commercial production 5 per cent

(ii) years 11 to the end of commercial production 12 per cent

(b) The said market value shall be the product of the quantity of the processed metals produced from the polymetallic nodules extracted from the area covered by the contract and the average price for those metals during the relevant accounting year, as defined in paragraphs 7 and 8.

6. If a contractor chooses to make his financial contribution to the Authority by paying a combination of a production charge and a share of net proceeds, such payments shall be determined as follows:

(a) The production charge shall be fixed at a percentage of the market value, determined in accordance with subpara-graph (b), of the processed metals produced from the polymetallic nodules recovered from the area covered by the contract. This percentage shall be fixed as follows:

(i) first period of commercial production 2 per cent

(ii) second period of commercial production 4 per cent If, in the second period of commercial production, as defined in subparagraph (d), the return on investment in any accounting year as defined in subparagraph (m) falls below 15 per cent as a result of the payment of the production charge at 4 per cent, the production charge shall be 2 per cent instead of 4 per cent in that accounting year.

(b) The said market value shall be the product of the quantity of the processed metals produced from the polymetallic nodules recovered from the area covered by the contract and the average price for those metals during the relevant accounting year as defined in paragraphs 7 and 8.

(c) (i) The Authority's share of net proceeds shall be taken out of that portion of the contractor's net proceeds which is attributable to the mining of the resources of the area covered by the contract, referred to hereinafter as attributable net proceeds.

(ii) The Authority's share of attributable net proceeds shall be determined in accordance with the following incremental schedule:

Portion of attributable net proceeds	Share of the Authority	
	First period of commercial production	Second period of commercial production
That portion representing a return on investment which is greater than 0 per cent, but less than 10 per cent	35 per cent	40 per cent
That portion representing a return on investment which is 10 per cent or greater, but less than 20 per cent	42.5 per cent	50 per cent
That portion representing a return on investment which is 20 per cent or greater	50 per cent	70 per cent

(d) (i) The first period of commercial production referred to in subparagraphs (a) and (c) shall commence in the first accounting year of commercial production and terminate in the accounting year in which the contractor's development costs with interest on the unrecovered portion thereof are fully recovered by his cash surplus, as follows:

In the first accounting year during which development costs are incurred, unrecovered development costs shall equal the development costs less cash surplus in that year. In each subsequent accounting year, unrecovered development costs shall equal the unrecovered development costs at the end of the preceding accounting year, plus interest thereon at the rate of 10 per cent per annum, plus development costs incurred in the current accounting year and less contractor's cash surplus in the current accounting year. The accounting year in which unrecovered development costs become zero for the first time shall be the accounting year in which the contractor's development costs with interest on the unrecovered portion thereof are fully recovered by his cash surplus. The contractor's cash surplus in any accounting year shall be his gross proceeds less his operating costs and less his payments to the Authority under subparagraph (c).

(ii) The second period of commercial production shall commence in the accounting year following the termination of the first period of commercial production and shall continue until the end of the contract.

(e) "Attributable net proceeds" means the product of the contractor's net proceeds and the ratio of the development costs in the mining sector to the contractor's development costs. If the contractor engages in mining, transporting polymetallic nodules and production primarily of three processed metals, namely, cobalt, copper and nickel, the amount of attributable net proceeds shall not be less than 25 per cent of the contractor's net proceeds. Subject to subparagraph (n), in all other cases, including those where the contractor engages in mining, transporting polymetallic nodules, and production primarily of four processed metals, namely, cobalt, copper, manganese and nickel, the Authority may, in its rules, regulations and procedures, prescribe appropriate floors which shall bear the same relationship to each case as the 25 per cent floor does to the three-metal case.

(f) "Contractor's net proceeds" means the contractor's gross proceeds less his operating costs and less the recovery of his development costs as set out in subparagraph (j).

(g) (i) If the contractor engages in mining, transporting polymetallic nodules and production of processed metals, "contractor's gross proceeds" means the gross revenues from the sale of the processed metals and any other monies deemed reasonably attributable to operations under the contract in accordance with the financial rules, regulations and procedures of the Authority.

(ii) In all cases other than those specified in subparagraphs (g)(i) and (n)(iii), "contractor's gross proceeds" means the gross revenues from the sale of the semi-processed metals from the polymetallic nodules recovered from the area covered by the contract, and any other monies deemed reasonably attributable to operations under the contract in accordance with the financial rules, regulations and procedures of the Authority.

(h) "Contractor's development costs" means:

(i) all expenditures incurred prior to the commencement of commercial production which are directly related to the development of the productive capacity of the area covered by the contract and the activities related thereto for operations under the contract in all cases other than that specified in subparagraph (n), in conformity with generally recognized accounting principles, including, inter alia, costs of machinery, equipment, ships, processing plant, construction, buildings, land, roads, prospecting and exploration of the area covered by the contract, research and development, interest, required leases, licences and fees; and

(ii) expenditures similar to those set forth in (i) above incurred subsequent to the commencement of commercial production and necessary to carry out the plan of work, except those chargeable to operating costs.

(i) The proceeds from the disposal of capital assets and the market value of those capital assets which are no longer required for operations under the contract and which are not sold shall be deducted from the contractor's development costs during the relevant accounting year. When these deductions exceed the contractor's development costs the excess shall be added to the contractor's gross proceeds.

(j) The contractor's development costs incurred prior to the commencement of commercial production referred to in subparagraphs (h)(i) and (n)(iv) shall be recovered in 10 equal annual instalments from the date of commencement of commercial production. The contractor's development costs incurred subsequent to the commencement of commercial production referred to in subparagraphs (h)(ii) and (n)(iv) shall be recovered in 10 or fewer equal annual instalments so as to ensure their complete recovery by the end of the contract.

(k) "Contractor's operating costs" means all expenditures incurred after the commencement of commercial production in the operation of the productive capacity of the area covered by the contract and the activities related thereto for operations under the contract, in conformity with generally recognized accounting principles, including, inter alia, the annual fixed fee or the production charge, whichever is greater, expenditures for wages, salaries, employee benefits, materials, services, transporting, processing and marketing costs, interest, utilities, preservation of the marine environment, overhead and administrative costs specifically related to operations under the contract, and any net operating losses carried forward or backward as specified herein. Net operating losses may be carried forward for two consecutive years except in the last two years of the contract in which case they may be carried backward to the two preceding years.

(l) If the contractor engages in mining, transporting of polymetallic nodules, and production of processed and semi-processed metals, "development costs of the mining sector" means the portion of the contractor's development costs which is directly related to the mining of the resources of the area covered by the contract, in conformity with generally recognized accounting principles, and the financial rules, regulations and procedures of the Authority, including, inter alia, application fee, annual fixed fee and, where applicable, costs of prospecting and exploration of the area covered by the contract, and a portion of research and development costs.

(m) "Return on investment" in any accounting year means the ratio of attributable net proceeds in that year to the development costs of the mining sector. For the purpose of computing this ratio the development costs of the mining sector shall include expenditures on new or replacement equipment in the mining sector less the original cost of the equipment replaced.

(n) If the contractor engages in mining only:

(i) "attributable net proceeds" means the whole of the contractor's net proceeds;

(ii) "contractor's net proceeds" shall be as defined in subparagraph (f);

(iii) "contractor's gross proceeds" means the gross revenues from the sale of the polymetallic nodules, and any other monies deemed reasonably attributable to operations under the contract in accordance with the financial rules, regulations and procedures of the Authority;

(iv) "contractor's development costs" means all expenditures incurred prior to the commencement of commercial production as set forth in subparagraph (h)(i), and all expenditures incurred subsequent to the commencement of commercial production as set forth in subparagraph (h)(ii), which are directly related to the mining of the resources of the area covered by the contract, in conformity with generally recognized accounting principles;

(v) "contractor's operating costs" means the contractor's operating costs as in subparagraph (k) which are directly related to the mining of the resources of the area covered by the contract in conformity with generally recognized accounting principles;

(vi) "return on investment" in any accounting year means the ratio of the contractor's net proceeds in that year to the contractor's development costs. For the purpose of computing this ratio, the contractor's development costs shall include expenditures on new or replacement equipment less the original cost of the equipment replaced.

(o) The costs referred to in subparagraphs (h), (k), (l) and (n) in respect of interest paid by the contractor shall be allowed to the extent that, in all the circumstances, the Authority approves, pursuant to article 4, paragraph 1, of this Annex, the debt-equity ratio and the rates of interest as reasonable, having regard to existing commercial practice.

(p) The costs referred to in this paragraph shall not be interpreted as including payments of corporate income taxes or similar charges levied by States in respect of the operations of the contractor.

7. (a) "Processed metals", referred to in paragraphs 5 and 6, means the metals in the most basic form in which they are customarily traded on international terminal markets. For this purpose, the Authority shall specify, in its financial rules, regulations and procedures, the relevant international terminal market. For the metals which are not traded on such markets, "processed metals" means the metals in the most basic form in which they are customarily traded in representative arm's length transactions.

(b) If the Authority cannot otherwise determine the quantity of the processed metals produced from the polymetallic nodules recovered from the area covered by the contract referred to in paragraphs 5(b) and 6(b), the quantity shall be determined on the basis of the metal content of the nodules, processing recovery efficiency and other relevant factors, in accordance with the rules, regulations and procedures of the Authority and in conformity with generally recognized accounting principles.

8. If an international terminal market provides a representative pricing mechanism for processed metals, polymetallic nodules and semi-processed metals from the nodules, the average price on that market shall be used. In all other cases, the Authority shall, after consulting the contractor, determine a fair price for the said products in accordance with paragraph 9.

9. (a) All costs, expenditures, proceeds and revenues and all determinations of price and value referred to in this article shall be the result of free market or arm's length transactions. In the absence thereof, they shall be determined by the Authority, after consulting the contractor, as though they were the result of free market or arm's length transactions, taking into account relevant transactions in other markets.

(b) In order to ensure compliance with and enforcement of the provisions of this paragraph, the Authority shall be guided by the principles adopted for, and the interpretation given to, arm's length transactions by the Commission on Transnational Corporations of the United Nations, the Group of Experts on Tax Treaties between Developing and Developed Countries and other international organizations, and shall, in its rules, regulations and procedures, specify uniform and internationally acceptable accounting rules and procedures, and the means of selection by the contractor of certified independent accountants acceptable to the Authority for the purpose of carrying out auditing in compliance with those rules, regulations and procedures.

10. The contractor shall make available to the accountants, in accordance with the financial rules, regulations and procedures of the Authority, such financial data as are required to determine compliance with this article.

11. All costs, expenditures, proceeds and revenues, and all prices and values referred to in this article, shall be determined in accordance with generally recognized accounting principles and the financial rules, regulations and procedures of the Authority.

12. Payments to the Authority under paragraphs 5 and 6 shall be made in freely usable currencies or cur-

rencies which are freely available and effectively usable on the major foreign exchange markets or, at the contractor's option, in the equivalents of processed metals at market value. The market value shall be determined in accordance with paragraph 5(b). The freely usable currencies and currencies which are freely available and effectively usable on the major foreign exchange markets shall be defined in the rules, regulations and procedures of the Authority in accordance with prevailing international monetary practice.

13. All financial obligations of the contractor to the Authority, as well as all his fees, costs, expenditures, proceeds and revenues referred to in this article, shall be adjusted by expressing them in constant terms relative to a base year.
14. The Authority may, taking into account any recommendations of the Economic Planning Commission and the Legal and Technical Commission, adopt rules, regulations and procedures that provide for incentives, on a uniform and non-discriminatory basis, to contractors to further the objectives set out in paragraph 1.
15. In the event of a dispute between the Authority and a contractor over the interpretation or application of the financial terms of a contract, either party may submit the dispute to binding commercial arbitration, unless both parties agree to settle the dispute by other means, in accordance with article 188, paragraph 2.

Article 14 – Transfer of data

1. The operator shall transfer to the Authority, in accordance with its rules, regulations and procedures and the terms and conditions of the plan of work, at time intervals determined by the Authority all data which are both necessary for and relevant to the effective exercise of the powers and functions of the principal organs of the Authority in respect of the area covered by the plan of work.
2. Transferred data in respect of the area covered by the plan of work, deemed proprietary, may only be used for the purposes set forth in this article. Data necessary for the formulation by the Authority of rules, regulations and procedures concerning protection of the marine environment and safety, other than equipment design data, shall not be deemed proprietary.
3. Data transferred to the Authority by prospectors, applicants for contracts or contractors, deemed proprietary, shall not be disclosed by the Authority to the Enterprise or to anyone external to the Authority, but data on the reserved areas may be disclosed to the Enterprise. Such data transferred by such persons to the Enterprise shall not be disclosed by the Enterprise to the Authority or to anyone external to the Authority.

Article 15 – Training programmes

The contractor shall draw up practical programmes for the training of personnel of the Authority and developing States, including the participation of such personnel in all activities in the Area which are covered by the contract, in accordance with article 144, paragraph 2.

Article 16 – Exclusive right to explore and exploit

The Authority shall, pursuant to Part XI and its rules, regulations and procedures, accord the operator the exclusive right to explore and exploit the area covered by the plan of work in respect of a specified category of resources and shall ensure that no other entity operates in the same area for a different category of resources in a manner which might interfere with the operations of the operator. The operator shall have security of tenure in accordance with article 153, paragraph 6.

Article 17 – Rules, regulations and procedures of the Authority

1. The Authority shall adopt and uniformly apply rules, regulations and procedures in accordance with article 160, paragraph 2(f)(ii), and article 162, paragraph 2(o)(ii), for the exercise of its functions as set forth in Part XI on, inter alia, the following matters:
   (a) administrative procedures relating to prospecting, exploration and exploitation in the Area;
   (b) operations:
      (i) size of area;
      (ii) duration of operations;
      (iii) performance requirements including assurances pursuant to article 4, paragraph 6(c), of this Annex;
      (iv) categories of resources;
      (v) renunciation of areas;
      (vi) progress reports;
      (vii) submission of data;
      (viii) inspection and supervision of operations;
      (ix) prevention of interference with other activities in the marine environment;
      (x) transfer of rights and obligations by a contractor;
      (xi) procedures for transfer of technology to developing States in accordance with article 144 and for their direct participation;
      (xii) mining standards and practices, including those relating to operational safety, conservation of the resources and the protection of the marine environment;
      (xiii) definition of commercial production;
      (xiv) qualification standards for applicants;
   (c) financial matters:
      (i) establishment of uniform and non-discriminatory costing and accounting rules and the method of selection of auditors;
      (ii) apportionment of proceeds of operations;

(iii) the incentives referred to in article 13 of this Annex;

(d) implementation of decisions taken pursuant to article 151, paragraph 10, and article 164, paragraph 2(d).

2. Rules, regulations and procedures on the following items shall fully reflect the objective criteria set out below:

(a) Size of areas:

The Authority shall determine the appropriate size of areas for exploration which may be up to twice as large as those for exploitation in order to permit intensive exploration operations. The size of area shall be calculated to satisfy the requirements of article 8 of this Annex on reservation of areas as well as stated production requirements consistent with article 151 in accordance with the terms of the contract taking into account the state of the art of technology then available for seabed mining and the relevant physical characteristics of the areas. Areas shall be neither smaller nor larger than are necessary to satisfy this objective.

(b) Duration of operations:

(i) Prospecting shall be without time-limit;

(ii) Exploration should be of sufficient duration to permit a thorough survey of the specific area, the design and construction of mining equipment for the area and the design and construction of small and medium-size processing plants for the purpose of testing mining and processing systems;

(iii) The duration of exploitation should be related to the economic life of the mining project, taking into consideration such factors as the depletion of the ore, the useful life of mining equipment and processing facilities and commercial viability. Exploitation should be of sufficient duration to permit commercial extraction of minerals of the area and should include a reasonable time period for construction of commercial-scale mining and processing systems, during which period commercial production should not be required. The total duration of exploitation, however, should also be short enough to give the Authority an opportunity to amend the terms and conditions of the plan of work at the time it considers renewal in accordance with rules, regulations and procedures which it has adopted subsequent to approving the plan of work.

(c) Performance requirements:

The Authority shall require that during the exploration stage periodic expenditures be made by the operator which are reasonably related to the size of the area covered by the plan of work and the expenditures which would be expected of a bona fide operator who intended to bring the area into commercial production within the time-limits established by the Authority. The required expenditures should not be established at a level which would discourage prospective operators with less costly technology than is prevalently in use. The Authority shall establish a maximum time interval, after the exploration stage is completed and the exploitation stage begins, to achieve commercial production. To determine this interval, the Authority should take into consideration that construction of large-scale mining and processing systems cannot be initiated until after the termination of the exploration stage and the commencement of the exploitation stage. Accordingly, the interval to bring an area into commercial production should take into account the time necessary for this construction after the completion of the exploration stage and reasonable allowance should be made for unavoidable delays in the construction schedule. Once commercial production is achieved, the Authority shall within reasonable limits and taking into consideration all relevant factors require the operator to maintain commercial production throughout the period of the plan of work.

(d) Categories of resources:

In determining the category of resources in respect of which a plan of work may be approved, the Authority shall give emphasis inter alia to the following characteristics:

(i) that certain resources require the use of similar mining methods; and

(ii) that some resources can be developed simultaneously without undue interference between operators developing different resources in the same area.

Nothing in this subparagraph shall preclude the Authority from approving a plan of work with respect to more than one category of resources in the same area to the same applicant.

(e) Renunciation of areas:

The operator shall have the right at any time to renounce without penalty the whole or part of his rights in the area covered by a plan of work.

(f) Protection of the marine environment:

Rules, regulations and procedures shall be drawn up in order to secure effective protection of the marine environment from harmful effects directly resulting from activities in the Area or from shipboard processing immediately above a mine site of minerals derived from that mine site, taking into account the extent to which such harmful effects may directly result from drilling, dredging, coring and excavation and from disposal, dumping and discharge into the marine environment of sediment, wastes or other effluents.

(g) Commercial production:

Commercial production shall be deemed to have begun if an operator engages in sustained large-scale recovery operations which yield a quantity of materials sufficient to indicate clearly that the principal purpose is large-scale production rather than production intended for information gathering, analysis or the testing of equipment or plant.

Article 18 – Penalties

1. A contractor's rights under the contract may be suspended or terminated only in the following cases:
   (a) if, in spite of warnings by the Authority, the contractor has conducted his activities in such a way as to result in serious, persistent and wilful violations of the fundamental terms of the contract, Part XI and the rules, regulations and procedures of the Authority; or
   (b) if the contractor has failed to comply with a final binding decision of the dispute settlement body applicable to him.
2. In the case of any violation of the contract not covered by paragraph 1(a), or in lieu of suspension or termination under paragraph 1(a), the Authority may impose upon the contractor monetary penalties proportionate to the seriousness of the violation.
3. Except for emergency orders under article 162, paragraph 2(w), the Authority may not execute a decision involving monetary penalties, suspension or termination until the contractor has been accorded a reasonable opportunity to exhaust the judicial remedies available to him pursuant to Part XI, section 5.

Article 19 – Revision of contract

1. When circumstances have arisen or are likely to arise which, in the opinion of either party, would render the contract inequitable or make it impracticable or impossible to achieve the objectives set out in the contract or in Part XI, the parties shall enter into negotiations to revise it accordingly.
2. Any contract entered into in accordance with article 153, paragraph 3, may be revised only with the consent of the parties.

Article 20 – Transfer of rights and obligations

The rights and obligations arising under a contract may be transferred only with the consent of the Authority, and in accordance with its rules, regulations and procedures. The Authority shall not unreasonably withhold consent to the transfer if the proposed transferee is in all respects a qualified applicant and assumes all of the obligations of the transferor and if the transfer does not confer to the transferee a plan of work, the approval of which would be forbidden by article 6, paragraph 3(c), of this Annex.

Article 21 – Applicable law

1. The contract shall be governed by the terms of the contract, the rules, regulations and procedures of the Authority, Part XI and other rules of international law not incompatible with this Convention.
2. Any final decision rendered by a court or tribunal having jurisdiction under this Convention relating to the rights and obligations of the Authority and of the contractor shall be enforceable in the territory of each State Party.
3. No State Party may impose conditions on a contractor that are inconsistent with Part XI. However, the application by a State Party to contractors sponsored by it, or to ships flying its flag, of environmental or other laws and regulations more stringent than those in the rules, regulations and procedures of the Authority adopted pursuant to article 17, paragraph 2(f), of this Annex shall not be deemed inconsistent with Part XI.

Article 22 – Responsibility

The contractor shall have responsibility or liability for any damage arising out of wrongful acts in the conduct of its operations, account being taken of contributory acts or omissions by the Authority. Similarly, the Authority shall have responsibility or liability for any damage arising out of wrongful acts in the exercise of its powers and functions, including violations under article 168, paragraph 2, account being taken of contributory acts or omissions by the contractor. Liability in every case shall be for the actual amount of damage.

ANNEX IV. STATUTE OF THE ENTERPRISE

Article 1 – Purposes

1. The Enterprise is the organ of the Authority which shall carry out activities in the Area directly, pursuant to article 153, paragraph 2 (a), as well as the transporting, processing and marketing of minerals recovered from the Area.
2. In carrying out its purposes and in the exercise of its functions, the Enterprise shall act in accordance with this Convention and the rules, regulations and procedures of the Authority.
3. In developing the resources of the Area pursuant to paragraph 1, the Enterprise shall, subject to this Convention, operate in accordance with sound commercial principles.

Article 2 – Relationship to the Authority

1. Pursuant to article 170, the Enterprise shall act in accordance with the general policies of the Assembly and the directives of the Council.
2. Subject to paragraph l, the Enterprise shall enjoy autonomy in the conduct of its operations.
3. Nothing in this Convention shall make the Enterprise liable for the acts or obligations of the Authority, or make the Authority liable for the acts or obligations of the Enterprise.

Article 3 – Limitation of liability

Without prejudice to article 11, paragraph 3, of this Annex, no member of the Authority shall be liable by reason only of its membership for the acts or obligations of the Enterprise.

Article 4 – Structure

The Enterprise shall have a Governing Board, a Director-General and the staff necessary for the exercise of its functions.

Article 5 – Governing Board

1. The Governing Board shall be composed of 15 members elected by the Assembly in accordance with article 160, paragraph 2(c). In the election of the members of the Board, due regard shall be paid to the principle of equitable geographical distribution. In submitting nominations of candidates for election to the Board, members of the Authority shall bear in mind the need to nominate candidates of the highest standard of competence, with qualifications in relevant fields, so as to ensure the viability and success of the Enterprise.
2. Members of the Board shall be elected for four years and may be re-elected; and due regard shall be paid to the principle of rotation of membership.
3. Members of the Board shall continue in office until their successors are elected. If the office of a member of the Board becomes vacant, the Assembly shall, in accordance with article 160, paragraph 2(c), elect a new member for the remainder of his predecessor's term.
4. Members of the Board shall act in their personal capacity. In the performance of their duties they shall not seek or receive instructions from any government or from any other source. Each member of the Authority shall respect the independent character of the members of the Board and shall refrain from all attempts to influence any of them in the discharge of their duties.
5. Each member of the Board shall receive remuneration to be paid out of the funds of the Enterprise. The amount of remuneration shall be fixed by the Assembly, upon the recommendation of the Council.
6. The Board shall normally function at the principal office of the Enterprise and shall meet as often as the business of the Enterprise may require.
7. Two thirds of the members of the Board shall constitute a quorum.
8. Each member of the Board shall have one vote. All matters before the Board shall be decided by a majority of its members. If a member has a conflict of interest on a matter before the Board he shall refrain from voting on that matter.
9. Any member of the Authority may ask the Board for information in respect of its operations which particularly affect that member. The Board shall endeavour to provide such information.

Article 6 – Powers and functions of the Governing Board

The Governing Board shall direct the operations of the Enterprise. Subject to this Convention, the Governing Board shall exercise the powers necessary to fulfil the purposes of the Enterprise, including powers:

(a) to elect a Chairman from among its members;

(b) to adopt its rules of procedure;

(c) to draw up and submit formal written plans of work to the Council in accordance with article 153, paragraph 3, and article 162, paragraph 2(j);

(d) to develop plans of work and programmes for carrying out the activities specified in article 170;

(e) to prepare and submit to the Council applications for production authorizations in accordance with article 151, paragraphs 2 to 7;

(f) to authorize negotiations concerning the acquisition of technology, including those provided for in Annex III, article 5, paragraph 3(a), (c) and (d), and to approve the results of those negotiations;

(g) to establish terms and conditions, and to authorize negotiations, concerning joint ventures and other forms of joint arrangements referred to in Annex III, articles 9 and 11, and to approve the results of such negotiations;

(h) to recommend to the Assembly what portion of the net income of the Enterprise should be retained as its reserves in accordance with article 160, paragraph 2(f), and article 10 of this Annex;

(i) to approve the annual budget of the Enterprise;

(j) to authorize the procurement of goods and services in accordance with article 12, paragraph 3, of this Annex;

(k) to submit an annual report to the Council in accordance with article 9 of this Annex;

(l) to submit to the Council for the approval of the Assembly draft rules in respect of the organization, management, appointment and dismissal of the staff of the Enterprise and to adopt regulations to give effect to such rules;

(m) to borrow funds and to furnish such collateral or other security as it may determine in accordance with article 11, paragraph 2, of this Annex;

(n) to enter into any legal proceedings, agreements and transactions and to take any other actions in accordance with article 13 of this Annex;

(o) to delegate, subject to the approval of the Council, any non-discretionary powers to the Director-General and to its committees.

Article 7 – Director-General and staff of the Enterprise

1. The Assembly shall, upon the recommendation of the Council and the nomination of the Governing Board, elect the Director-General of the Enterprise who shall not be a member of the Board. The Director-General shall hold office for a fixed term, not exceeding five years, and may be re-elected for further terms.
2. The Director-General shall be the legal representative and chief executive of the Enterprise and shall be directly responsible to the Board for the conduct of the operations of the Enterprise. He shall be responsible for the organization, management,

appointment and dismissal of the staff of the Enterprise in accordance with the rules and regulations referred to in article 6, subparagraph (l), of this Annex. He shall participate, without the right to vote, in the meetings of the Board and may participate, without the right to vote, in the meetings of the Assembly and the Council when these organs are dealing with matters concerning the Enterprise.

3. The paramount consideration in the recruitment and employment of the staff and in the determination of their conditions of service shall be the necessity of securing the highest standards of efficiency and of technical competence. Subject to this consideration, due regard shall be paid to the importance of recruiting the staff on an equitable geographical basis.
4. In the performance of their duties the Director-General and the staff shall not seek or receive instructions from any government or from any other source external to the Enterprise. They shall refrain from any action which might reflect on their position as international officials of the Enterprise responsible only to the Enterprise. Each State Party undertakes to respect the exclusively international character of the responsibilities of the Director-General and the staff and not to seek to influence them in the discharge of their responsibilities.
5. The responsibilities set forth in article 168, paragraph 2, are equally applicable to the staff of the Enterprise.

Article 8 – Location

The Enterprise shall have its principal office at the seat of the Authority. The Enterprise may establish other offices and facilities in the territory of any State Party with the consent of that State Party.

Article 9 – Reports and financial statements

1. The Enterprise shall, not later than three months after the end of each financial year, submit to the Council for its consideration an annual report containing an audited statement of its accounts and shall transmit to the Council at appropriate intervals a summary statement of its financial position and a profit and loss statement showing the results of its operations.
2. The Enterprise shall publish its annual report and such other reports as it finds appropriate.
3. All reports and financial statements referred to in this article shall be distributed to the members of the Authority.

Article 10 – Allocation of net income

1. Subject to paragraph 3, the Enterprise shall make payments to the Authority under Annex III, article 13, or their equivalent.
2. The Assembly shall, upon the recommendation of the Governing Board, determine what portion of the net income of the Enterprise shall be retained as reserves of the Enterprise. The remainder shall be transferred to the Authority.
3. During an initial period required for the Enterprise to become self-supporting, which shall not exceed 10 years from the commencement of commercial production by it, the Assembly shall exempt the Enterprise from the payments referred to in paragraph 1, and shall leave all of the net income of the Enterprise in its reserves.

Article 11 – Finances

1. The funds of the Enterprise shall include:
   (a) amounts received from the Authority in accordance with article 173, paragraph 2(b);
   (b) voluntary contributions made by States Parties for the purpose of financing activities of the Enterprise;
   (c) amounts borrowed by the Enterprise in accordance with paragraphs 2 and 3;
   (d) income of the Enterprise from its operations;
   (e) other funds made available to the Enterprise to enable it to commence operations as soon as possible and to carry out its functions.
2. (a) The Enterprise shall have the power to borrow funds and to furnish such collateral or other security as it may determine. Before making a public sale of its obligations in the financial markets or currency of a State Party, the Enterprise shall obtain the approval of that State Party. The total amount of borrowings shall be approved by the Council upon the recommendation of the Governing Board.
   (b) States Parties shall make every reasonable effort to support applications by the Enterprise for loans on capital markets and from international financial institutions.
3. (a) The Enterprise shall be provided with the funds necessary to explore and exploit one mine site, and to transport, process and market the minerals recovered therefrom and the nickel, copper, cobalt and manganese obtained, and to meet its initial administrative expenses. The amount of the said funds, and the criteria and factors for its adjustment, shall be included by the Preparatory Commission in the draft rules, regulations and procedures of the Authority.
   (b) All States Parties shall make available to the Enterprise an amount equivalent to one half of the funds referred to in subparagraph (a) by way of long-term interest-free loans in accordance with the scale of assessments for the United Nations regular budget in force at the time when the assessments are made, adjusted to take into account the States which are not members of the United Nations. Debts incurred by the Enterprise in raising the other half of the funds shall be guaranteed by all States Parties in accordance with the same scale.
   (c) If the sum of the financial contributions of States Parties is less than the funds to be provided to the Enterprise under subparagraph (a), the Assembly shall, at its first session, consider the extent of the shortfall and adopt by consensus measures for dealing with this

shortfall, taking into account the obligation of States Parties under subparagraphs (a) and (b) and any recommendations of the Preparatory Commission.

(d) (i) Each State Party shall, within 60 days after the entry into force of this Convention, or within 30 days after the deposit of its instrument of ratification or accession, whichever is later, deposit with the Enterprise irrevocable, non-negotiable, non-interest-bearing promissory notes in the amount of the share of such State Party of interest-free loans pursuant to subparagraph (b).

(ii) The Board shall prepare, at the earliest practicable date after this Convention enters into force, and thereafter at annual or other appropriate intervals, a schedule of the magnitude and timing of its requirements for the funding of its administrative expenses and for activities carried out by the Enterprise in accordance with article 170 and article 12 of this Annex.

(iii) The States Parties shall, thereupon, be notified by the Enterprise, through the Authority, of their respective shares of the funds in accordance with subparagraph (b), required for such expenses. The Enterprise shall encash such amounts of the promissory notes as may be required to meet the expenditure referred to in the schedule with respect to interest-free loans.

(iv) States Parties shall, upon receipt of the notification, make available their respective shares of debt guarantees for the Enterprise in accordance with subparagraph (b).

(e) (i) If the Enterprise so requests, State Parties may provide debt guarantees in addition to those provided in accordance with the scale referred to in subparagraph (b).

(ii) In lieu of debt guarantees, a State Party may make a voluntary contribution to the Enterprise in an amount equivalent to that portion of the debts which it would otherwise be liable to guarantee.

(f) Repayment of the interest-bearing loans shall have priority over the repayment of the interest-free loans. Repayment of interest-free loans shall be in accordance with a schedule adopted by the Assembly, upon the recommendation of the Council and the advice of the Board. In the exercise of this function the Board shall be guided by the relevant provisions of the rules, regulations and procedures of the Authority, which shall take into account the paramount importance of ensuring the effective functioning of the Enterprise and, in particular, ensuring its financial independence.

(g) Funds made available to the Enterprise shall be in freely usable currencies or currencies which are freely available and effectively usable in the major foreign exchange markets. These currencies shall be defined in the rules, regulations and procedures of the Authority in accordance with prevailing international monetary practice. Except as provided in paragraph 2, no State Party shall maintain or impose restrictions on the holding, use or exchange by the Enterprise of these funds.

(h) "Debt guarantee" means a promise of a State Party to creditors of the Enterprise to pay, pro rata in accordance with the appropriate scale, the financial obligations of the Enterprise covered by the guarantee following notice by the creditors to the State Party of a default by the Enterprise. Procedures for the payment of those obligations shall be in conformity with the rules, regulations and procedures of the Authority.

4. The funds, assets and expenses of the Enterprise shall be kept separate from those of the Authority. This article shall not prevent the Enterprise from making arrangements with the Authority regarding facilities, personnel and services and arrangements for reimbursement of administrative expenses paid by either on behalf of the other.

5. The records, books and accounts of the Enterprise, including its annual financial statements, shall be audited annually by an independent auditor appointed by the Council.

Article 12 – Operations

1. The Enterprise shall propose to the Council projects for carrying out activities in accordance with article 170. Such proposals shall include a formal written plan of work for activities in the Area in accordance with article 153, paragraph 3, and all such other information and data as may be required from time to time for its appraisal by the Legal and Technical Commission and approval by the Council.

2. Upon approval by the Council, the Enterprise shall execute the project on the basis of the formal written plan of work referred to in paragraph 1.

3. (a) If the Enterprise does not possess the goods and services required for its operations it may procure them. For that purpose, it shall issue invitations to tender and award contracts to bidders offering the best combination of quality, price and delivery time.

(b) If there is more than one bid offering such a combination, the contract shall be awarded in accordance with:

(i) the principle of non-discrimination on the basis of political or other considerations not relevant to the carrying out of operations with due diligence and efficiency; and

(ii) guidelines approved by the Council with regard to the preferences to be accorded to goods and services originating in developing States, including the land-locked and geographically disadvantaged among them.

(c) The Governing Board may adopt rules determining the special circumstances in which the requirement of invitations to bid may, in the best interests of the Enterprise, be dispensed with.

4. The Enterprise shall have title to all minerals and processed substances produced by it.
5. The Enterprise shall sell its products on a non-discriminatory basis. It shall not give non-commercial discounts.
6. Without prejudice to any general or special power conferred on the Enterprise under any other provision of this Convention, the Enterprise shall exercise such powers incidental to its business as shall be necessary.
7. The Enterprise shall not interfere in the political affairs of any State Party; nor shall it be influenced in its decisions by the political character of the State Party concerned. Only commercial considerations shall be relevant to its decisions, and these considerations shall be weighed impartially in order to carry out the purposes specified in article 1 of this Annex.

Article 13 – Legal status, privileges and immunities

1. To enable the Enterprise to exercise its functions, the status, privileges and immunities set forth in this article shall be accorded to the Enterprise in the territories of States Parties. To give effect to this principle the Enterprise and States Parties may, where necessary, enter into special agreements.
2. The Enterprise shall have such legal capacity as is necessary for the exercise of its functions and the fulfilment of its purposes and, in particular, the capacity:
   (a) to enter into contracts, joint arrangements or other arrangements, including agreements with States and international organizations;
   (b) to acquire, lease, hold and dispose of immovable and movable property;
   (c) to be a party to legal proceedings.
3. (a) Actions may be brought against the Enterprise only in a court of competent jurisdiction in the territory of a State Party in which the Enterprise:
      (i) has an office or facility;
      (ii) has appointed an agent for the purpose of accepting service or notice of process;
      (iii) has entered into a contract for goods or services;
      (iv) has issued securities; or
      (v) is otherwise engaged in commercial activity.
   (b) The property and assets of the Enterprise, wherever located and by whomsoever held, shall be immune from all forms of seizure, attachment or execution before the delivery of final judgment against the Enterprise.
4. (a) The property and assets of the Enterprise, wherever located and by whomsoever held, shall be immune from requisition, confiscation, expropriation or any other form of seizure by executive or legislative action.
   (b) The property and assets of the Enterprise, wherever located and by whomsoever held, shall be free from discriminatory restrictions, regulations, controls and moratoria of any nature.
   (c) The Enterprise and its employees shall respect local laws and regulations in any State or territory in which the Enterprise or its employees may do business or otherwise act.
   (d) States Parties shall ensure that the Enterprise enjoys all rights, privileges and immunities accorded by them to entities conducting commercial activities in their territories. These rights, privileges and immunities shall be accorded to the Enterprise on no less favourable a basis than that on which they are accorded to entities engaged in similar commercial activities. If special privileges are provided by States Parties for developing States or their commercial entities, the Enterprise shall enjoy those privileges on a similarly preferential basis.
   (e) States Parties may provide special incentives, rights, privileges and immunities to the Enterprise without the obligation to provide such incentives, rights, privileges and immunities to other commercial entities.
5. The Enterprise shall negotiate with the host countries in which its offices and facilities are located for exemption from direct and indirect taxation.
6. Each State Party shall take such action as is necessary for giving effect in terms of its own law to the principles set forth in this Annex and shall inform the Enterprise of the specific action which it has taken.
7. The Enterprise may waive any of the privileges and immunities conferred under this article or in the special agreements referred to in paragraph 1 to such extent and upon such conditions as it may determine.

ANNEX V. CONCILIATION

SECTION 1. CONCILIATION PROCEDURE PURSUANT TO SECTION 1 OF PART XV

Article 1 – Institution of proceedings

If the parties to a dispute have agreed, in accordance with article 284, to submit it to conciliation under this section, any such party may institute the proceedings by written notification addressed to the other party or parties to the dispute.

Article 2 – List of conciliators

A list of conciliators shall be drawn up and maintained by the Secretary-General of the United Nations. Every State Party shall be entitled to nominate four conciliators, each of whom shall be a person enjoying the highest reputation for fairness, competence and integrity. The names of the persons so nominated shall constitute the list. If at any time the conciliators nominated by a State Party in the list so constituted shall be fewer than four, that State Party shall be entitled to make further nominations as necessary. The name of a conciliator shall remain on the list until withdrawn by the State Party which made the nomination, provided that such conciliator shall continue to serve on any conciliation commission to which that conciliator has been appointed until the completion of the proceedings before that commission.

Article 3 – Constitution of conciliation commission

The conciliation commission shall, unless the parties otherwise agree, be constituted as follows:

(a) Subject to subparagraph (g), the conciliation commission shall consist of five members.

(b) The party instituting the proceedings shall appoint two conciliators to be chosen preferably from the list referred to in article 2 of this Annex, one of whom may be its national, unless the parties otherwise agree. Such appointments shall be included in the notification referred to in article 1 of this Annex.

(c) The other party to the dispute shall appoint two conciliators in the manner set forth in subparagraph (b) within 21 days of receipt of the notification referred to in article 1 of this Annex. If the appointments are not made within that period, the party instituting the proceedings may, within one week of the expiration of that period, either terminate the proceedings by notification addressed to the other party or request the Secretary-General of the United Nations to make the appointments in accordance with subparagraph (e).

(d) Within 30 days after all four conciliators have been appointed, they shall appoint a fifth conciliator chosen from the list referred to in article 2 of this Annex, who shall be chairman. If the appointment is not made within that period, either party may, within one week of the expiration of that period, request the Secretary-General of the United Nations to make the appointment in accordance with subparagraph (e).

(e) Within 30 days of the receipt of a request under subparagraph (c) or (d), the Secretary-General of the United Nations shall make the necessary appointments from the list referred to in article 2 of this Annex in consultation with the parties to the dispute.

(f) Any vacancy shall be filled in the manner prescribed for the initial appointment.

(g) Two or more parties which determine by agreement that they are in the same interest shall appoint two conciliators jointly. Where two or more parties have separate interests or there is a disagreement as to whether they are of the same interest, they shall appoint conciliators separately.

(h) In disputes involving more than two parties having separate interests, or where there is disagreement as to whether they are of the same interest, the parties shall apply subparagraphs (a) to (f) in so far as possible.

Article 4 – Procedure

The conciliation commission shall, unless the parties otherwise agree, determine its own procedure. The commission may, with the consent of the parties to the dispute, invite any State Party to submit to it its views orally or in writing. Decisions of the commission regarding procedural matters, the report and recommendations shall be made by a majority vote of its members.

Article 5 – Amicable settlement

The commission may draw the attention of the parties to any measures which might facilitate an amicable settlement of the dispute.

Article 6 – Functions of the commission

The commission shall hear the parties, examine their claims and objections, and make proposals to the parties with a view to reaching an amicable settlement.

Article 7 – Report

1. The commission shall report within 12 months of its constitution. Its report shall record any agreements reached and, failing agreement, its conclusions on all questions of fact or law relevant to the matter in dispute and such recommendations as the commission may deem appropriate for an amicable settlement. The report shall be deposited with the Secretary-General of the United Nations and shall immediately be transmitted by him to the parties to the dispute.
2. The report of the commission, including its conclusions or recommendations, shall not be binding upon the parties.

Article 8 – Termination

The conciliation proceedings are terminated when a settlement has been reached, when the parties have accepted or one party has rejected the recommendations of the report by written notification addressed to the Secretary-General of the United Nations, or when a period of three months has expired from the date of transmission of the report to the parties.

Article 9 – Fees and expenses

The fees and expenses of the commission shall be borne by the parties to the dispute.

Article 10 – Right of parties to modify procedure

The parties to the dispute may by agreement applicable solely to that dispute modify any provision of this Annex.

SECTION 2. COMPULSORY SUBMISSION TO CONCILIATION PROCEDURE PURSUANT TO SECTION 3 OF PART XV

Article 11 – Institution of proceedings

1. Any party to a dispute which, in accordance with Part XV, section 3, may be submitted to conciliation under this section, may institute the proceed-

ings by written notification addressed to the other party or parties to the dispute.

2. Any party to the dispute, notified under paragraph 1, shall be obliged to submit to such proceedings.

Article 12 – Failure to reply or to submit to conciliation

The failure of a party or parties to the dispute to reply to notification of institution of proceedings or to submit to such proceedings shall not constitute a bar to the proceedings.

Article 13 – Competence

A disagreement as to whether a conciliation commission acting under this section has competence shall be decided by the commission.

Article 14 – Application of section 1

Articles 2 to 10 of section 1 of this Annex apply subject to this section.

ANNEX VI. STATUTE OF THE INTERNATIONAL TRIBUNAL FOR THE LAW OF THE SEA

Article 1 – General provisions

1. The International Tribunal for the Law of the Sea is constituted and shall function in accordance with the provisions of this Convention and this Statute.
2. The seat of the Tribunal shall be in the Free and Hanseatic City of Hamburg in the Federal Republic of Germany.
3. The Tribunal may sit and exercise its functions elsewhere whenever it considers this desirable.
4. A reference of a dispute to the Tribunal shall be governed by the provisions of Parts XI and XV.

SECTION 1. ORGANIZATION OF THE TRIBUNAL

Article 2 – Composition

1. The Tribunal shall be composed of a body of 21 independent members, elected from among persons enjoying the highest reputation for fairness and integrity and of recognized competence in the field of the law of the sea.
2. In the Tribunal as a whole the representation of the principal legal systems of the world and equitable geographical distribution shall be assured.

Article 3 – Membership

1. No two members of the Tribunal may be nationals of the same State. A person who for the purposes of membership in the Tribunal could be regarded as a national of more than one State shall be deemed to be a national of the one in which he ordinarily exercises civil and political rights.
2. There shall be no fewer than three members from each geographical group as established by the General Assembly of the United Nations.

Article 4 – Nominations and elections

1. Each State Party may nominate not more than two persons having the qualifications prescribed in article 2 of this Annex. The members of the Tribunal shall be elected from the list of persons thus nominated.
2. At least three months before the date of the election, the Secretary-General of the United Nations in the case of the first election and the Registrar of the Tribunal in the case of subsequent elections shall address a written invitation to the States Parties to submit their nominations for members of the Tribunal within two months. He shall prepare a list in alphabetical order of all the persons thus nominated, with an indication of the States Parties which have nominated them, and shall submit it to the States Parties before the seventh day of the last month before the date of each election.
3. The first election shall be held within six months of the date of entry into force of this Convention.
4. The members of the Tribunal shall be elected by secret ballot. Elections shall be held at a meeting of the States Parties convened by the Secretary-General of the United Nations in the case of the first election and by a procedure agreed to by the States Parties in the case of subsequent elections. Two thirds of the States Parties shall constitute a quorum at that meeting. The persons elected to the Tribunal shall be those nominees who obtain the largest number of votes and a two-thirds majority of the States Parties present and voting, provided that such majority includes a majority of the States Parties.

Article 5 – Term of office

1. The members of the Tribunal shall be elected for nine years and may be re-elected; provided, however, that of the members elected at the first election, the terms of seven members shall expire at the end of three years and the terms of seven more members shall expire at the end of six years.
2. The members of the Tribunal whose terms are to expire at the end of the above-mentioned initial periods of three and six years shall be chosen by lot to be drawn by the Secretary-General of the United Nations immediately after the first election.
3. The members of the Tribunal shall continue to discharge their duties until their places have been filled. Though replaced, they shall finish any proceedings which they may have begun before the date of their replacement.
4. In the case of the resignation of a member of the Tribunal, the letter of resignation shall be addressed to the President of the Tribunal. The place becomes vacant on the receipt of that letter.

Article 6 – Vacancies

1. Vacancies shall be filled by the same method as that laid down for the first election, subject to the following provision: the Registrar shall, within one month of the occurrence of the vacancy, proceed to issue the invitations provided for in article 4 of this Annex, and the date of the election shall be fixed

by the President of the Tribunal after consultation with the States Parties.

2. A member of the Tribunal elected to replace a member whose term of office has not expired shall hold office for the remainder of his predecessor's term.

Article 7 – Incompatible activities

1. No member of the Tribunal may exercise any political or administrative function, or associate actively with or be financially interested in any of the operations of any enterprise concerned with the exploration for or exploitation of the resources of the sea or the seabed or other commercial use of the sea or the seabed.
2. No member of the Tribunal may act as agent, counsel or advocate in any case.
3. Any doubt on these points shall be resolved by decision of the majority of the other members of the Tribunal present.

Article 8 – Conditions relating to participation of members in a particular case

1. No member of the Tribunal may participate in the decision of any case in which he has previously taken part as agent, counsel or advocate for one of the parties, or as a member of a national or international court or tribunal, or in any other capacity.
2. If, for some special reason, a member of the Tribunal considers that he should not take part in the decision of a particular case, he shall so inform the President of the Tribunal.
3. If the President considers that for some special reason one of the members of the Tribunal should not sit in a particular case, he shall give him notice accordingly.
4. Any doubt on these points shall be resolved by decision of the majority of the other members of the Tribunal present.

Article 9 – Consequence of ceasing to fulfil required conditions

If, in the unanimous opinion of the other members of the Tribunal, a member has ceased to fulfil the required conditions, the President of the Tribunal shall declare the seat vacant.

Article 10 – Privileges and immunities

The members of the Tribunal, when engaged on the business of the Tribunal, shall enjoy diplomatic privileges and immunities.

Article 11 – Solemn declaration by members

Every member of the Tribunal shall, before taking up his duties, make a solemn declaration in open session that he will exercise his powers impartially and conscientiously.

Article 12 – President, Vice-President and Registrar

1. The Tribunal shall elect its President and Vice-President for three years; they may be re-elected.
2. The Tribunal shall appoint its Registrar and may provide for the appointment of such other officers as may be necessary.
3. The President and the Registrar shall reside at the seat of the Tribunal.

Article 13 – Quorum

1. All available members of the Tribunal shall sit; a quorum of 11 elected members shall be required to constitute the Tribunal.
2. Subject to article 17 of this Annex, the Tribunal shall determine which members are available to constitute the Tribunal for the consideration of a particular dispute, having regard to the effective functioning of the chambers as provided for in articles 14 and 15 of this Annex.
3. All disputes and applications submitted to the Tribunal shall be heard and determined by the Tribunal, unless article 14 of this Annex applies, or the parties request that it shall be dealt with in accordance with article 15 of this Annex.

Article 14 – Seabed Disputes Chamber

A Seabed Disputes Chamber shall be established in accordance with the provisions of section 4 of this Annex. Its jurisdiction, powers and functions shall be as provided for in Part XI, section 5.

Article 15 – Special chambers

1. The Tribunal may form such chambers, composed of three or more of its elected members, as it considers necessary for dealing with particular categories of disputes.
2. The Tribunal shall form a chamber for dealing with a particular dispute submitted to it if the parties so request. The composition of such a chamber shall be determined by the Tribunal with the approval of the parties.
3. With a view to the speedy dispatch of business, the Tribunal shall form annually a chamber composed of five of its elected members which may hear and determine disputes by summary procedure. Two alternative members shall be selected for the purpose of replacing members who are unable to participate in a particular proceeding.
4. Disputes shall be heard and determined by the chambers provided for in this article if the parties so request.
5. A judgment given by any of the chambers provided for in this article and in article 14 of this Annex shall be considered as rendered by the Tribunal.

Article 16 – Rules of the Tribunal

The Tribunal shall frame rules for carrying out its functions. In particular it shall lay down rules of procedure.

Article 17 – Nationality of members

1. Members of the Tribunal of the nationality of any of the parties to a dispute shall retain their right to participate as members of the Tribunal.

2. If the Tribunal, when hearing a dispute, includes upon the bench a member of the nationality of one of the parties, any other party may choose a person to participate as a member of the Tribunal.
3. If the Tribunal, when hearing a dispute, does not include upon the bench a member of the nationality of the parties, each of those parties may choose a person to participate as a member of the Tribunal.
4. This article applies to the chambers referred to in articles 14 and 15 of this Annex. In such cases, the President, in consultation with the parties, shall request specified members of the Tribunal forming the chamber, as many as necessary, to give place to the members of the Tribunal of the nationality of the parties concerned, and, failing such, or if they are unable to be present, to the members specially chosen by the parties.
5. Should there be several parties in the same interest, they shall, for the purpose of the preceding provisions, be considered as one party only. Any doubt on this point shall be settled by the decision of the Tribunal.
6. Members chosen in accordance with paragraphs 2, 3 and 4 shall fulfil the conditions required by articles 2, 8 and 11 of this Annex. They shall participate in the decision on terms of complete equality with their colleagues.

Article 18 – Remuneration of members

1. Each elected member of the Tribunal shall receive an annual allowance and, for each day on which he exercises his functions, a special allowance, provided that in any year the total sum payable to any member as special allowance shall not exceed the amount of the annual allowance.
2. The President shall receive a special annual allowance.
3. The Vice-President shall receive a special allowance for each day on which he acts as President.
4. The members chosen under article 17 of this Annex, other than elected members of the Tribunal, shall receive compensation for each day on which they exercise their functions.
5. The salaries, allowances and compensation shall be determined from time to time at meetings of the States Parties, taking into account the workload of the Tribunal. They may not be decreased during the term of office.
6. The salary of the Registrar shall be determined at meetings of the States Parties, on the proposal of the Tribunal.
7. Regulations adopted at meetings of the States Parties shall determine the conditions under which retirement pensions may be given to members of the Tribunal and to the Registrar, and the conditions under which members of the Tribunal and Registrar shall have their travelling expenses refunded.
8. The salaries, allowances, and compensation shall be free of all taxation.

Article 19 – Expenses of the Tribunal

1. The expenses of the Tribunal shall be borne by the States Parties and by the Authority on such terms and in such a manner as shall be decided at meetings of the States Parties.
2. When an entity other than a State Party or the Authority is a party to a case submitted to it, the Tribunal shall fix the amount which that party is to contribute towards the expenses of the Tribunal.

SECTION 2. COMPETENCE

Article 20 – Access to the Tribunal

1. The Tribunal shall be open to States Parties.
2. The Tribunal shall be open to entities other than States Parties in any case expressly provided for in Part XI or in any case submitted pursuant to any other agreement conferring jurisdiction on the Tribunal which is accepted by all the parties to that case.

Article 21 – Jurisdiction

The jurisdiction of the Tribunal comprises all disputes and all applications submitted to it in accordance with this Convention and all matters specifically provided for in any other agreement which confers jurisdiction on the Tribunal.

Article 22 – Reference of disputes subject to other agreements

If all the parties to a treaty or convention already in force and concerning the subject-matter covered by this Convention so agree, any disputes concerning the interpretation or application of such treaty or convention may, in accordance with such agreement, be submitted to the Tribunal.

Article 23 – Applicable law

The Tribunal shall decide all disputes and applications in accordance with article 293.

SECTION 3. PROCEDURE

Article 24 – Institution of proceedings

1. Disputes are submitted to the Tribunal, as the case may be, either by notification of a special agreement or by written application, addressed to the Registrar. In either case, the subject of the dispute and the parties shall be indicated.
2. The Registrar shall forthwith notify the special agreement or the application to all concerned.
3. The Registrar shall also notify all States Parties.

Article 25 – Provisional measures

1. In accordance with article 290, the Tribunal and its Seabed Disputes Chamber shall have the power to prescribe provisional measures.
2. If the Tribunal is not in session or a sufficient number of members is not available to constitute a quorum, the provisional measures shall be prescribed by the chamber of summary procedure formed under article 15, paragraph 3, of this Annex. Notwithstanding article 15, paragraph 4, of this Annex, such provisional measures may be adopted at the

request of any party to the dispute. They shall be subject to review and revision by the Tribunal.

Article 26 – Hearing

1. The hearing shall be under the control of the President or, if he is unable to preside, of the Vice-President. If neither is able to preside, the senior judge present of the Tribunal shall preside.
2. The hearing shall be public, unless the Tribunal decides otherwise or unless the parties demand that the public be not admitted.

Article 27 – Conduct of case

The Tribunal shall make orders for the conduct of the case, decide the form and time in which each party must conclude its arguments, and make all arrangements connected with the taking of evidence.

Article 28 – Default

When one of the parties does not appear before the Tribunal or fails to defend its case, the other party may request the Tribunal to continue the proceedings and make its decision. Absence of a party or failure of a party to defend its case shall not constitute a bar to the proceedings. Before making its decision, the Tribunal must satisfy itself not only that it has jurisdiction over the dispute, but also that the claim is well founded in fact and law.

Article 29 – Majority for decision

1. All questions shall be decided by a majority of the members of the Tribunal who are present.
2. In the event of an equality of votes, the President or the member of the Tribunal who acts in his place shall have a casting vote.

Article 30 – Judgment

1. The judgment shall state the reasons on which it is based.
2. It shall contain the names of the members of the Tribunal who have taken part in the decision.
3. If the judgment does not represent in whole or in part the unanimous opinion of the members of the Tribunal, any member shall be entitled to deliver a separate opinion.
4. The judgment shall be signed by the President and by the Registrar. It shall be read in open court, due notice having been given to the parties to the dispute.

Article 31 – Request to intervene

1. Should a State Party consider that it has an interest of a legal nature which may be affected by the decision in any dispute, it may submit a request to the Tribunal to be permitted to intervene.
2. It shall be for the Tribunal to decide upon this request.
3. If a request to intervene is granted, the decision of the Tribunal in respect of the dispute shall be binding upon the intervening State Party in so far as it relates to matters in respect of which that State Party intervened.

Article 32 – Right to intervene in cases of interpretation or application

1. Whenever the interpretation or application of this Convention is in question, the Registrar shall notify all States Parties forthwith.
2. Whenever pursuant to article 21 or 22 of this Annex the interpretation or application of an international agreement is in question, the Registrar shall notify all the parties to the agreement.
3. Every party referred to in paragraphs 1 and 2 has the right to intervene in the proceedings; if it uses this right, the interpretation given by the judgment will be equally binding upon it.

Article 33 – Finality and binding force of decisions

1. The decision of the Tribunal is final and shall be complied with by all the parties to the dispute.
2. The decision shall have no binding force except between the parties in respect of that particular dispute.
3. In the event of dispute as to the meaning or scope of the decision, the Tribunal shall construe it upon the request of any party.

Article 34 – Costs

Unless otherwise decided by the Tribunal, each party shall bear its own costs.

SECTION 4. SEABED DISPUTES CHAMBER

Article 35 – Composition

1. The Seabed Disputes Chamber referred to in article 14 of this Annex shall be composed of 11 members, selected by a majority of the elected members of the Tribunal from among them.
2. In the selection of the members of the Chamber, the representation of the principal legal systems of the world and equitable geographical distribution shall be assured. The Assembly of the Authority may adopt recommendations of a general nature relating to such representation and distribution.
3. The members of the Chamber shall be selected every three years and may be selected for a second term.
4. The Chamber shall elect its President from among its members, who shall serve for the term for which the Chamber has been selected.
5. If any proceedings are still pending at the end of any three-year period for which the Chamber has been selected, the Chamber shall complete the proceedings in its original composition.
6. If a vacancy occurs in the Chamber, the Tribunal shall select a successor from among its elected members, who shall hold office for the remainder of his predecessor's term.
7. A quorum of seven of the members selected by the Tribunal shall be required to constitute the Chamber.

Article 36 – Ad hoc chambers

1. The Seabed Disputes Chamber shall form an ad hoc chamber, composed of three of its members, for dealing with a particular dispute submitted to it in accordance with article 188, paragraph 1(b). The composition of such a chamber shall be determined by the Seabed Disputes Chamber with the approval of the parties.
2. If the parties do not agree on the composition of an ad hoc chamber, each party to the dispute shall appoint one member, and the third member shall be appointed by them in agreement. If they disagree, or if any party fails to make an appointment, the President of the Seabed Disputes Chamber shall promptly make the appointment or appointments from among its members, after consultation with the parties.
3. Members of the ad hoc chamber must not be in the service of, or nationals of, any of the parties to the dispute.

Article 37 – Access

The Chamber shall be open to the States Parties, the Authority and the other entities referred to in Part XI, section 5.

Article 38 – Applicable law

In addition to the provisions of article 293, the Chamber shall apply:

(a) the rules, regulations and procedures of the Authority adopted in accordance with this Convention; and

(b) the terms of contracts concerning activities in the Area in matters relating to those contracts.

Article 39 – Enforcement of decisions of the Chamber

The decisions of the Chamber shall be enforceable in the territories of the States Parties in the same manner as judgments or orders of the highest court of the State Party in whose territory the enforcement is sought.

Article 40 – Applicability of other sections of this Annex

1. The other sections of this Annex which are not incompatible with this section apply to the Chamber.
2. In the exercise of its functions relating to advisory opinions, the Chamber shall be guided by the provisions of this Annex relating to procedure before the Tribunal to the extent to which it recognizes them to be applicable.

SECTION 5. AMENDMENTS

Article 41 – Amendments

1. Amendments to this Annex, other than amendments to section 4, may be adopted only in accordance with article 313 or by consensus at a conference convened in accordance with this Convention.
2. Amendments to section 4 may be adopted only in accordance with article 314.
3. The Tribunal may propose such amendments to this Statute as it may consider necessary, by written communications to the States Parties for their consideration in conformity with paragraphs 1 and 2.

ANNEX VII. ARBITRATION

Article 1 – Institution of proceedings

Subject to the provisions of Part XV, any party to a dispute may submit the dispute to the arbitral procedure provided for in this Annex by written notification addressed to the other party or parties to the dispute. The notification shall be accompanied by a statement of the claim and the grounds on which it is based.

Article 2 – List of arbitrators

1. A list of arbitrators shall be drawn up and maintained by the Secretary-General of the United Nations. Every State Party shall be entitled to nominate four arbitrators, each of whom shall be a person experienced in maritime affairs and enjoying the highest reputation for fairness, competence and integrity. The names of the persons so nominated shall constitute the list.
2. If at any time the arbitrators nominated by a State Party in the list so constituted shall be fewer than four, that State Party shall be entitled to make further nominations as necessary.
3. The name of an arbitrator shall remain on the list until withdrawn by the State Party which made the nomination, provided that such arbitrator shall continue to serve on any arbitral tribunal to which that arbitrator has been appointed until the completion of the proceedings before that arbitral tribunal.

Article 3 – Constitution of arbitral tribunal

For the purpose of proceedings under this Annex, the arbitral tribunal shall, unless the parties otherwise agree, be constituted as follows:

(a) Subject to subparagraph (g), the arbitral tribunal shall consist of five members.

(b) The party instituting the proceedings shall appoint one member to be chosen preferably from the list referred to in article 2 of this Annex, who may be its national. The appointment shall be included in the notification referred to in article 1 of this Annex.

(c) The other party to the dispute shall, within 30 days of receipt of the notification referred to in article 1 of this Annex, appoint one member to be chosen preferably from the list, who may be its national. If the appointment is not made within that period, the party instituting the proceedings may, within two weeks of the expiration of that period, request that the appointment be made in accordance with subparagraph (e).

(d) The other three members shall be appointed by agreement between the parties. They shall be chosen preferably from the list and shall be nationals of third States unless the parties otherwise agree. The parties to the dispute shall appoint the President of the arbitral tribunal from among those three members. If, within 60 days of receipt of the notification referred to in article 1 of this Annex, the parties are unable to reach agreement on the appointment of one or more of the members of the tribunal to be appointed by agreement, or on the appointment of the President, the remaining appointment or appointments shall be made in accordance with subparagraph (e), at the request of a party to the dispute. Such request shall be made within two weeks of the expiration of the aforementioned 60-day period.

(e) Unless the parties agree that any appointment under subparagraphs (c) and (d) be made by a person or a third State chosen by the parties, the President of the International Tribunal for the Law of the Sea shall make the necessary appointments. If the President is unable to act under this subparagraph or is a national of one of the parties to the dispute, the appointment shall be made by the next senior member of the International Tribunal for the Law of the Sea who is available and is not a national of one of the parties. The appointments referred to in this subparagraph shall be made from the list referred to in article 2 of this Annex within a period of 30 days of the receipt of the request and in consultation with the parties. The members so appointed shall be of different nationalities and may not be in the service of, ordinarily resident in the territory of, or nationals of, any of the parties to the dispute.

(f) Any vacancy shall be filled in the manner prescribed for the initial appointment.

(g) Parties in the same interest shall appoint one member of the tribunal jointly by agreement. Where there are several parties having separate interests or where there is disagreement as to whether they are of the same interest, each of them shall appoint one member of the tribunal. The number of members of the tribunal appointed separately by the parties shall always be smaller by one than the number of members of the tribunal to be appointed jointly by the parties.

(h) In disputes involving more than two parties, the provisions of subparagraphs (a) to (f) shall apply to the maximum extent possible.

Article 4 – Functions of arbitral tribunal

An arbitral tribunal constituted under article 3 of this Annex shall function in accordance with this Annex and the other provisions of this Convention.

Article 5 – Procedure

Unless the parties to the dispute otherwise agree, the arbitral tribunal shall determine its own procedure, assuring to each party a full opportunity to be heard and to present its case.

Article 6 – Duties of parties to a dispute

The parties to the dispute shall facilitate the work of the arbitral tribunal and, in particular, in accordance with their law and using all means at their disposal, shall:

(a) provide it with all relevant documents, facilities and information; and

(b) enable it when necessary to call witnesses or experts and receive their evidence and to visit the localities to which the case relates.

Article 7 – Expenses

Unless the arbitral tribunal decides otherwise because of the particular circumstances of the case, the expenses of the tribunal, including the remuneration of its members, shall be borne by the parties to the dispute in equal shares.

Article 8 – Required majority for decisions

Decisions of the arbitral tribunal shall be taken by a majority vote of its members. The absence or abstention of less than half of the members shall not constitute a bar to the tribunal reaching a decision. In the event of an equality of votes, the President shall have a casting vote.

Article 9 – Default of appearance

If one of the parties to the dispute does not appear before the arbitral tribunal or fails to defend its case, the other party may request the tribunal to continue the proceedings and to make its award. Absence of a party or failure of a party to defend its case shall not constitute a bar to the proceedings. Before making its award, the arbitral tribunal must satisfy itself not only that it has jurisdiction over the dispute but also that the claim is well founded in fact and law.

Article 10 – Award

The award of the arbitral tribunal shall be confined to the subject-matter of the dispute and state the reasons on which it is based. It shall contain the names of the members who have participated and the date of the award. Any member of the tribunal may attach a separate or dissenting opinion to the award.

Article 11 – Finality of award

The award shall be final and without appeal, unless the parties to the dispute have agreed in advance to an appellate procedure. It shall be complied with by the parties to the dispute.

Article 12 – Interpretation or implementation of award

1. Any controversy which may arise between the parties to the dispute as regards the interpretation or manner of implementation of the award may be submitted by either party for decision to the arbitral tribunal which made the award. For this purpose, any vacancy in the tribunal shall be filled in the manner provided for in the original appointments of the members of the tribunal.
2. Any such controversy may be submitted to another court or tribunal under article 287 by agreement of all the parties to the dispute.

Article 13 – Application to entities other than States Parties

The provisions of this Annex shall apply mutatis mutandis to any dispute involving entities other than States Parties.

ANNEX VIII. SPECIAL ARBITRATION

Article 1 – Institution of proceedings

Subject to Part XV, any party to a dispute concerning the interpretation or application of the articles of this Convention relating to (1) fisheries, (2) protection and preservation of the marine environment, (3) marine scientific research, or (4) navigation, including pollution from vessels and by dumping, may submit the dispute to the special arbitral procedure provided for in this Annex by written notification addressed to the other party or parties to the dispute. The notification shall be accompanied by a statement of the claim and the grounds on which it is based.

Article 2 – Lists of experts

1. A list of experts shall be established and maintained in respect of each of the fields of (1) fisheries, (2) protection and preservation of the marine environment, (3) marine scientific research, and (4) navigation, including pollution from vessels and by dumping.
2. The lists of experts shall be drawn up and maintained, in the field of fisheries by the Food and Agriculture Organization of the United Nations, in the field of protection and preservation of the marine environment by the United Nations Environment Programme, in the field of marine scientific research by the Intergovernmental Oceanographic Commission, in the field of navigation, including pollution from vessels and by dumping, by the International Maritime Organization, or in each case by the appropriate subsidiary body concerned to which such organization, programme or commission has delegated this function.
3. Every State Party shall be entitled to nominate two experts in each field whose competence in the legal, scientific or technical aspects of such field is established and generally recognized and who enjoy the highest reputation for fairness and integrity. The names of the persons so nominated in each field shall constitute the appropriate list.
4. If at any time the experts nominated by a State Party in the list so constituted shall be fewer than two, that State Party shall be entitled to make further nominations as necessary.
5. The name of an expert shall remain on the list until withdrawn by the State Party which made the nomination, provided that such expert shall continue to serve on any special arbitral tribunal to which that expert has been appointed until the completion of the proceedings before that special arbitral tribunal.

Article 3 – Constitution of special arbitral tribunal

For the purpose of proceedings under this Annex, the special arbitral tribunal shall, unless the parties otherwise agree, be constituted as follows:

(a) Subject to subparagraph (g), the special arbitral tribunal shall consist of five members.

(b) The party instituting the proceedings shall appoint two members to be chosen preferably from the appropriate list or lists referred to in article 2 of this Annex relating to the matters in dispute, one of whom may be its national. The appointments shall be included in the notification referred to in article 1 of this Annex.

(c) The other party to the dispute shall, within 30 days of receipt of the notification referred to in article 1 of this Annex, appoint two members to be chosen preferably from the appropriate list or lists relating to the matters in dispute, one of whom may be its national. If the appointments are not made within that period, the party instituting the proceedings may, within two weeks of the expiration of that period, request that the appointments be made in accordance with subparagraph (e).

(d) The parties to the dispute shall by agreement appoint the President of the special arbitral tribunal, chosen preferably from the appropriate list, who shall be a national of a third State, unless the parties otherwise agree. If, within 30 days of receipt of the notification referred to in article 1 of this Annex, the parties are unable to reach agreement on the appointment of the President, the appointment shall be made in accordance with subparagraph (e), at the request of a party to the dispute. Such request shall be made within two weeks of the expiration of the aforementioned 30-day period.

(e) Unless the parties agree that the appointment be made by a person or a third State chosen by the parties, the Secretary-General of the United Nations shall make the necessary appointments within 30 days of receipt of a request under subparagraphs (c) and (d). The appointments referred to in this subparagraph shall be made from the appropriate list or lists of experts referred to in article 2 of this Annex and in consultation with the parties to the dispute and the appropriate international organization. The members so appointed shall be of different nationalities and may not be in the service of, ordinarily resident in the territory of, or nationals of, any of the parties to the dispute.

(f) Any vacancy shall be filled in the manner prescribed for the initial appointment.

(g) Parties in the same interest shall appoint two members of the tribunal jointly by agreement. Where there are several parties having separate interests or where there is disagreement as to whether they are of the same interest, each of them shall appoint one member of the tribunal.

(h) In disputes involving more than two parties, the provisions of subparagraphs (a) to (f) shall apply to the maximum extent possible.

Article 4 – General provisions

Annex VII, articles 4 to 13, apply mutatis mutandis to the special arbitration proceedings in accordance with this Annex.

Article 5 – Fact finding

1. The parties to a dispute concerning the interpretation or application of the provisions of this Convention relating to (l) fisheries, (2) protection and preservation of the marine environment, (3) marine

scientific research, or (4) navigation, including pollution from vessels and by dumping, may at any time agree to request a special arbitral tribunal constituted in accordance with article 3 of this Annex to carry out an inquiry and establish the facts giving rise to the dispute.

2. Unless the parties otherwise agree, the findings of fact of the special arbitral tribunal acting in accordance with paragraph 1, shall be considered as conclusive as between the parties.
3. If all the parties to the dispute so request, the special arbitral tribunal may formulate recommendations which, without having the force of a decision, shall only constitute the basis for a review by the parties of the questions giving rise to the dispute.
4. Subject to paragraph 2, the special arbitral tribunal shall act in accordance with the provisions of this Annex, unless the parties otherwise agree.

ANNEX IX. PARTICIPATION BY INTERNATIONAL ORGANIZATIONS

Article 1 – Use of terms

For the purposes of article 305 and of this Annex, "international organization" means an intergovernmental organization constituted by States to which its member States have transferred competence over matters governed by this Convention, including the competence to enter into treaties in respect of those matters.

Article 2 – Signature

An international organization may sign this Convention if a majority of its member States are signatories of this Convention. At the time of signature an international organization shall make a declaration specifying the matters governed by this Convention in respect of which competence has been transferred to that organization by its member States which are signatories, and the nature and extent of that competence.

Article 3 – Formal confirmation and accession

1. An international organization may deposit its instrument of formal confirmation or of accession if a majority of its member States deposit or have deposited their instruments of ratification or accession.
2. The instruments deposited by the international organization shall contain the undertakings and declarations required by articles 4 and 5 of this Annex.

Article 4 – Extent of participation and rights and obligations

1. The instrument of formal confirmation or of accession of an international organization shall contain an undertaking to accept the rights and obligations of States under this Convention in respect of matters relating to which competence has been transferred to it by its member States which are Parties to this Convention.
2. An international organization shall be a Party to this Convention to the extent that it has competence in accordance with the declarations, communications of information or notifications referred to in article 5 of this Annex.
3. Such an international organization shall exercise the rights and perform the obligations which its member States which are Parties would otherwise have under this Convention, on matters relating to which competence has been transferred to it by those member States. The member States of that international organization shall not exercise competence which they have transferred to it.
4. Participation of such an international organization shall in no case entail an increase of the representation to which its member States which are States Parties would otherwise be entitled, including rights in decision-making.
5. Participation of such an international organization shall in no case confer any rights under this Convention on member States of the organization which are not States Parties to this Convention.
6. In the event of a conflict between the obligations of an international organization under this Convention and its obligations under the agreement establishing the organization or any acts relating to it, the obligations under this Convention shall prevail.

Article 5 – Declarations, notifications and communications

1. The instrument of formal confirmation or of accession of an international organization shall contain a declaration specifying the matters governed by this Convention in respect of which competence has been transferred to the organization by its member States which are Parties to this Convention.
2. A member State of an international organization shall, at the time it ratifies or accedes to this Convention or at the time when the organization deposits its instrument of formal confirmation or of accession, whichever is later, make a declaration specifying the matters governed by this Convention in respect of which it has transferred competence to the organization.
3. States Parties which are member States of an international organization which is a Party to this Convention shall be presumed to have competence over all matters governed by this Convention in respect of which transfers of competence to the organization have not been specifically declared, notified or communicated by those States under this article.
4. The international organization and its member States which are States Parties shall promptly notify the depositary of this Convention of any changes to the distribution of competence, including new transfers of competence, specified in the declarations under paragraphs 1 and 2.
5. Any State Party may request an international organization and its member States which are States Parties to provide information as to which, as between the organization and its member States, has competence in respect of any specific question which has arisen. The organization and the member States concerned shall provide this information

within a reasonable time. The international organization and the member States may also, on their own initiative, provide this information.

6. Declarations, notifications and communications of information under this article shall specify the nature and extent of the competence transferred.

Article 6 – Responsibility and liability

1. Parties which have competence under article 5 of this Annex shall have responsibility for failure to comply with obligations or for any other violation of this Convention.
2. Any State Party may request an international organization or its member States which are States Parties for information as to who has responsibility in respect of any specific matter. The organization and the member States concerned shall provide this information. Failure to provide this information within a reasonable time or the provision of contradictory information shall result in joint and several liability.

Article 7 – Settlement of disputes

1. At the time of deposit of its instrument of formal confirmation or of accession, or at any time thereafter, an international organization shall be free to choose, by means of a written declaration, one or more of the means for the settlement of disputes concerning the interpretation or application of this Convention, referred to in article 287, paragraph 1(a), (c) or (d).
2. Part XV applies mutatis mutandis to any dispute between Parties to this Convention, one or more of which are international organizations.
3. When an international organization and one or more of its member States are joint parties to a dispute, or parties in the same interest, the organization shall be deemed to have accepted the same procedures for the settlement of disputes as the member States; when, however, a member State has chosen only the International Court of Justice under article 287, the organization and the member State concerned shall be deemed to have accepted arbitration in accordance with Annex VII, unless the parties to the dispute otherwise agree.

Article 8 – Applicability of Part XVII

Part XVII applies mutatis mutandis to an international organization, except in respect of the following:

(a) the instrument of formal confirmation or of accession of an international organization shall not be taken into account in the application of article 308, paragraph 1;

(b) (i) an international organization shall have exclusive capacity with respect to the application of articles 312 to 315, to the extent that it has competence under article 5 of this Annex over the entire subject-matter of the amendment;

(ii) the instrument of formal confirmation or of accession of an international organization to an amendment, the entire subject-matter over which the international organization has competence under article 5 of this Annex, shall be considered to be the instrument of ratification or accession of each of the member States which are States Parties, for the purposes of applying article 316, paragraphs 1, 2 and 3;

(iii) the instrument of formal confirmation or of accession of the international organization shall not be taken into account in the application of article 316, paragraphs 1 and 2, with regard to all other amendments;

(c) (i) an international organization may not denounce this Convention in accordance with article 317 if any of its member States is a State Party and if it continues to fulfil the qualifications specified in article 1 of this Annex;

(ii) an international organization shall denounce this Convention when none of its member States is a State Party or if the international organization no longer fulfils the qualifications specified in article 1 of this Annex. Such denunciation shall take effect immediately.

Final Act of the Third United Nations Conference on the Law of the Sea (excerpts)

ANNEX I

RESOLUTION I – ESTABLISHMENT OF THE PREPARATORY COMMISSION FOR THE INTERNATIONAL SEA-BED AUTHORITY AND FOR THE INTERNATIONAL TRIBUNAL FOR THE LAW OF THE SEA

The Third United Nations Conference on the Law of the Sea,

Having adopted the Convention on the Law of the Sea which provides for the establishment of the International Seabed Authority and the International Tribunal for the Law of the Sea,

Having decided to take all possible measures to ensure the entry into effective operation without undue delay of the Authority and the Tribunal and to make the necessary arrangements for the commencement of their functions,

Having decided that a Preparatory Commission should be established for the fulfilment of these purposes,

Decides as follows:

1. There is hereby established the Preparatory Commission for the International Seabed Authority and for the International Tribunal for the Law of the Sea. Upon signature of or accession to the Convention by 50 States, the Secretary-General of the United Nations shall convene the Commission, and it shall meet no sooner than 60 days and no later than 90 days thereafter.
2. The Commission shall consist of the representatives of States and of Namibia, represented by the United Nations Council for Namibia, which have signed the Convention or acceded to it. The representatives of signatories of the Final Act may participate fully in the deliberations of the Commission as observers but shall not be entitled to participate in the taking of decisions.

3. The Commission shall elect its Chairman and other officers.
4. The Rules of Procedure of the Third United Nations Conference on the Law of the Sea shall apply mutatis mutandis to the adoption of the rules of procedure of the Commission.
5. The Commission shall:
   (a) prepare the provisional agenda for the first session of the Assembly and of the Council and, as appropriate, make recommendations relating to items thereon;
   (b) prepare draft rules of procedure of the Assembly and of the Council;
   (c) make recommendations concerning the budget for the first financial period of the Authority;
   (d) make recommendations concerning the relationship between the Authority and the United Nations and other international organizations;
   (e) make recommendations concerning the Secretariat of the Authority in accordance with the relevant provisions of the Convention;
   (f) undertake studies, as necessary, concerning the establishment of the headquarters of the Authority, and make recommendations relating thereto;
   (g) prepare draft rules, regulations and procedures, as necessary, to enable the Authority to commence its functions, including draft regulations concerning the financial management and the internal administration of the Authority;
   (h) exercise the powers and functions assigned to it by resolution II of the Third United Nations Conference on the Law of the Sea relating to preparatory investment;
   (i) undertake studies on the problems which would be encountered by developing land-based producer States likely to be most seriously affected by the production of minerals derived from the Area with a view to minimizing their difficulties and helping them to make the necessary economic adjustment, including studies on the establishment of a compensation fund, and submit recommendations to the Authority thereon.
6. The Commission shall have such legal capacity as may be necessary for the exercise of its functions and the fulfilment of its purposes as set forth in this resolution.
7. The Commission may establish such subsidiary bodies as are necessary for the exercise of its functions and shall determine their functions and rules of procedure. It may also make use, as appropriate, of outside sources of expertise in accordance with United Nations practice to facilitate the work of bodies so established.
8. The Commission shall establish a special commission for the Enterprise and entrust to it the functions referred to in paragraph 12 of resolution II of the Third United Nations Conference on the Law of the Sea relating to preparatory investment. The special commission shall take all measures necessary for the early entry into effective operation of the Enterprise.
9. The Commission shall establish a special commission on the problems which would be encountered by developing land-based producer States likely to be most seriously affected by the production of minerals derived from the Area and entrust to it the functions referred to in paragraph 5(i).
10. The Commission shall prepare a report containing recommendations for submission to the meeting of the States Parties to be convened in accordance with Annex VI, article 4, of the Convention regarding practical arrangements for the establishment of the International Tribunal for the Law of the Sea.
11. The Commission shall prepare a final report on all matters within its mandate, except as provided in paragraph 10, for the presentation to the Assembly at its first session. Any action which may be taken on the basis of the report must be in conformity with the provisions of the Convention concerning the powers and functions entrusted to the respective organs of the Authority.
12. The Commission shall meet at the seat of the Authority if facilities are available; it shall meet as often as necessary for the expeditious exercise of its functions.
13. The Commission shall remain in existence until the conclusion of the first session of the Assembly, at which time its property and records shall be transferred to the Authority.
14. The expenses of the Commission shall be met from the regular budget of the United Nations, subject to the approval of the General Assembly of the United Nations.
15. The Secretary-General of the United Nations shall make available to the Commission such secretariat services as may be required.
16. The Secretary-General of the United Nations shall bring this resolution, in particular paragraphs 14 and 15, to the attention of the General Assembly for necessary action.

RESOLUTION II – GOVERNING PREPARATORY INVESTMENT IN PIONEER ACTIVITIES RELATING TO POLYMETALLIC NODULES

The Third United Nations Conference on the Law of the Sea,

Having adopted the Convention on the Law of the Sea (the "Convention"),

Having established by resolution I the Preparatory Commission for the International Seabed Authority and for the International Tribunal for the Law of the Sea (the "Commission") and directed it to prepare draft rules, regulations and procedures, as necessary to enable the Authority to commence its functions, as well as to make recommendations for the early entry into effective operation of the Enterprise,

Desirous of making provision for investments by States and other entities made in a manner compatible with the international regime set forth in Part XI of the

Convention and the Annexes relating thereto, before the entry into force of the Convention,

Recognizing the need to ensure that the Enterprise will be provided with the funds, technology and expertise necessary to enable it to keep pace with the States and other entities referred to in the preceding paragraph with respect to activities in the Area,

Decides as follows:

1. For the purposes of this resolution:
   (a) "pioneer investor" refers to:
      (i) France, India, Japan and the Union of Soviet Socialist Republics, or a state enterprise of each of those States or one natural or juridical person which possesses the nationality of or is effectively controlled by each of those States, or their nationals, provided that the State concerned signs the Convention and the State or state enterprise or natural or juridical person has expended, before 1 January 1983, an amount equivalent to at least $US 30 million (United States dollars calculated in constant dollars relative to 1982) in pioneer activities and has expended no less than 10 per cent of that amount in the location, survey and evaluation of the area referred to in paragraph 3(a);
      (ii) four entities, whose components being natural or juridical persons 1 possess the nationality of one or more of the following States, or are effectively controlled by one or more of them or their nationals: Belgium, Canada, the Federal Republic of Germany, Italy, Japan, the Netherlands, the United Kingdom of Great Britain and Northern Ireland, and the United States of America, provided that the certifying State or States sign the Convention and the entity concerned has expended, before 1 January 1983, the levels of expenditure for the purpose stated in subparagraph (i);
      (iii) any developing State which signs the Convention or any state enterprise or natural or juridical person which possesses the nationality of such State or is effectively controlled by it or its nationals, or any group of the foregoing, which, before 1 January 1985, has expended the levels of expenditure for the purpose stated in subparagraph (i);

      The rights of the pioneer investor may devolve upon its successor in interest.
   (b) "pioneer activities" means undertakings, commitments of financial and other assets, investigations, findings, research, engineering development and other activities relevant to the identification, discovery, and systematic analysis and evaluation of polymetallic nodules and to the determination of the technical and economic feasibility of exploitation. Pioneer activities include:
      (i) any at-sea observation and evaluation activity which has as its objective the establishment and documentation of the nature, shape, concentration, location and grade of polymetallic nodules and of the environmental, technical and other appropriate factors which must be taken into account before exploitation;
      (ii) the recovery from the Area of polymetallic nodules with a view to the designing, fabricating and testing of equipment which is intended to be used in the exploitation of polymetallic nodules;
   (c) "certifying State" means a State which signs the Convention, standing in the same relation to a pioneer investor as would a sponsoring State pursuant to Annex III, article 4, of the Convention and which certifies the levels of expenditure specified in subparagraph (a);
   (d) "polymetallic nodules" means one of the resources of the Area consisting of any deposit or accretion of nodules, on or just below the surface of the deep seabed, which contain manganese, nickel, cobalt and copper;
   (e) "pioneer area" means an area allocated by the Commission to a pioneer investor for pioneer activities pursuant to this resolution. A pioneer area shall not exceed 150,000 square kilometres. The pioneer investor shall relinquish portions of the pioneer area to revert to the Area, in accordance with the following schedule:
      (i) 20 per cent of the area allocated by the end of the third year from the date of the allocation;
      (ii) an additional 10 per cent of the area allocated by the end of the fifth year from the date of the allocation;
      (iii) an additional 20 per cent of the area allocated or such larger amount as would exceed the exploitation area decided upon by the Authority in its rules, regulations and procedures, after eight years from the date of the allocation of the area or the date of the award of a production authorization, whichever is earlier;
   (f) "Area", "Authority", "activities in the Area" and "resources" have the meanings assigned to those terms in the Convention.
2. As soon as the Commission begins to function, any State which has signed the Convention may apply to the Commission on its behalf or on behalf of any state enterprise or entity or natural or juridical person specified in paragraph 1(a) for registration as a pioneer investor. The Commission shall register the applicant as a pioneer investor if the application:
   (a) is accompanied, in the case of a State which has signed the Convention, by a statement certifying the level of expenditure made in accordance with paragraph 1(a), and, in all other cases, a certificate concerning such level of ex-

penditure issued by a certifying State or States; and

(b) is in conformity with the other provisions of this resolution, including paragraph 5.

3. (a) Every application shall cover a total area which need not be a single continuous area, sufficiently large and of sufficient estimated commercial value to allow two mining operations. The application shall indicate the coordinates of the area defining the total area and dividing it into two parts of equal estimated commercial value and shall contain all the data available to the applicant with respect to both parts of the area. Such data shall include, inter alia, information relating to mapping, testing, the density of polymetallic nodules and their metal content. In dealing with such data, the Commission and its staff shall act in accordance with the relevant provisions of the Convention and its Annexes concerning the confidentiality of data.

(b) Within 45 days of receiving the data required by subparagraph (a), the Commission shall designate the part of the area which is to be reserved in accordance with the Convention for the conduct of activities in the Area by the Authority through the Enterprise or in association with developing States. The other part of the area shall be allocated to the pioneer investor as a pioneer area.

4. No pioneer investor may be registered in respect of more than one pioneer area. In the case of a pioneer investor which is made up of two or more components, none of such components may apply to be registered as a pioneer investor in its own right or under paragraph 1(a)(iii).

5. (a) Any State which has signed the Convention and which is a prospective certifying State shall ensure, before making applications to the Commission under paragraph 2, that areas in respect of which applications are made do not overlap one another or areas previously allocated as pioneer areas. The States concerned shall keep the Commission currently and fully informed of any efforts to resolve conflicts with respect to overlapping claims and of the results thereof.

(b) Certifying States shall ensure, before the entry into force of the Convention, that pioneer activities are conducted in a manner compatible with it.

(c) The prospective certifying States, including all potential claimants, shall resolve their conflicts as required under subparagraph (a) by negotiations within a reasonable period. If such conflicts have not been resolved by 1 March 1983, the prospective certifying States shall arrange for the submission of all such claims to binding arbitration in accordance with UNCITRAL Arbitration Rules to commence not later than 1 May 1983 and to be completed by 1 December 1984. If one of the States concerned does not wish to participate in the arbitration, it shall arrange for a juridical person of its nationality to represent it in the arbitration. The arbitral tribunal may, for good cause, extend the deadline for the making of the award for one or more 30-day periods.

(d) In determining the issue as to which applicant involved in a conflict shall be awarded all or part of each area in conflict, the arbitral tribunal shall find a solution which is fair and equitable, having regard, with respect to each applicant involved in the conflict, to the following factors:

(i) the deposit of the list of relevant coordinates with the prospective certifying State or States not later than the date of adoption of the Final Act or 1 January 1983, whichever is earlier;

(ii) the continuity and extent of past activities relevant to each area in conflict and to the application area of which it is a part;

(iii) the date on which each pioneer investor concerned or predecessor in interest or component organization thereof commenced activities at sea in the application area;

(iv) the financial cost of activities measured in constant United States dollars relevant to each area in conflict and to the application area of which it is a part; and

(v) the time when those activities were carried out and the quality of activities.

6. A pioneer investor registered pursuant to this resolution shall, from the date of registration, have the exclusive right to carry out pioneer activities in the pioneer area allocated to it.

7. (a) Every applicant for registration as a pioneer investor shall pay to the Commission a fee of $US 250,000. When the pioneer investor applies to the Authority for a plan of work for exploration and exploitation the fee referred to in Annex III, article 13, paragraph 2, of the Convention shall be $US 250,000.

(b) Every registered pioneer investor shall pay an annual fixed fee of $US 1 million commencing from the date of the allocation of the pioneer area. The payments shall be made by the pioneer investor to the Authority upon the approval of its plan of work for exploration and exploitation. The financial arrangements undertaken pursuant to such plan of work shall be adjusted to take account of the payments made pursuant to this paragraph.

(c) Every registered pioneer investor shall agree to incur periodic expenditures, with respect to the pioneer area allocated to it, until approval of its plan of work pursuant to paragraph 8, of an amount to be determined by the Commission. The amount should be reasonably related to the size of the pioneer area and the expenditures which would be expected of a bona fide operator who intends to bring that area into commercial production within a reasonable time.

8. (a) Within six months of the entry into force of the Convention and certification by the Commission in accordance with paragraph 11, of compliance with this resolution, the pioneer investor so registered shall apply to the Authority for approval of a plan of work for exploration and exploitation, in accordance with the Convention. The plan of work in respect of such application shall comply with and be governed by the relevant provisions of the Convention and the rules, regulations and procedures of the Authority, including those on the operational requirements, the financial requirements and the undertakings concerning the transfer of technology. Accordingly, the Authority shall approve such application.

   (b) When an application for approval of a plan of work is submitted by an entity other than a State, pursuant to subparagraph (a), the certifying State or States shall be deemed to be the sponsoring State for the purposes of Annex III, article 4, of the Convention, and shall thereupon assume such obligations.

   (c) No plan of work for exploration and exploitation shall be approved unless the certifying State is a Party to the Convention. In the case of the entities referred to in paragraph 1(a)(ii), the plan of work for exploration and exploitation shall not be approved unless all the States whose natural or juridical persons comprise those entities are Parties to the Convention. If any such State fails to ratify the Convention within six months after it has received a notification from the Authority that an application by it, or sponsored by it, is pending, its status as a pioneer investor or certifying State, as the case may be, shall terminate, unless the Council, by a majority of three fourths of its members present and voting, decides to postpone the terminal date for a period not exceeding six months.

9. (a) In the allocation of production authorizations, in accordance with article 151 and Annex III, article 7, of the Convention, the pioneer investors who have obtained approval of plans of work for exploration and exploitation shall have priority over all applicants other than the Enterprise which shall be entitled to production authorizations for two mine sites including that referred to in article 151, paragraph 5, of the Convention. After each of the pioneer investors has obtained production authorization for its first mine site, the priority for the Enterprise contained in Annex III, article 7, paragraph 6, of the Convention shall apply.

   (b) Production authorizations shall be issued to each pioneer investor within 30 days of the date on which that pioneer investor notifies the Authority that it will commence commercial production within five years. If a pioneer investor is unable to begin production within the period of five years for reasons beyond its control, it shall apply to the Legal and Technical Commission for an extension of time. That Commission shall grant the extension of time, for a period not exceeding five years and not subject to further extension, if it is satisfied that the pioneer investor cannot begin on an economically viable basis at the time originally planned. Nothing in this subparagraph shall prevent the Enterprise or any other pioneer applicant, who has notified the Authority that it will commence commercial production within five years, from being given a priority over any applicant who has obtained an extension of time under this subparagraph.

   (c) If the Authority, upon being given notice, pursuant to subparagraph (b), determines that the commencement of commercial production within five years would exceed the production ceiling in article 151, paragraphs 2 to 7, of the Convention, the applicant shall hold a priority over any other applicant for the award of the next production authorization allowed by the production ceiling.

   (d) If two or more pioneer investors apply for production authorizations to begin commercial production at the same time and article 151, paragraphs 2 to 7, of the Convention, would not permit all such production to commence simultaneously, the Authority shall notify the pioneer investors concerned. Within three months of such notification, they shall decide whether and, if so, to what extent they wish to apportion the allowable tonnage among themselves.

   (e) If, pursuant to subparagraph (d), the pioneer investors concerned decide not to apportion the available production among themselves they shall agree on an order of priority for production authorizations and all subsequent applications for production authorizations will be granted after those referred to in this subparagraph have been approved.

   (f) If, pursuant to subparagraph (d), the pioneer investors concerned decide to apportion the available production among themselves, the Authority shall award each of them a production authorization for such lesser quantity as they have agreed. In each case the stated production requirements of the applicant will be approved and their full production will be allowed as soon as the production ceiling admits of additional capacity sufficient for the applicants involved in the competition. All subsequent applications for production authorizations will only be granted after the requirements of this subparagraph have been met and the applicant is no longer subject to the reduction of production provided for in this subparagraph.

   (g) If the parties fail to reach agreement within the stated time period, the matter shall be decided immediately by the means provided for in paragraph 5(c) in accordance with the criteria set forth in Annex III, article 7, paragraphs 3 and 5, of the Convention.

10. (a) Any rights acquired by entities or natural or juridical persons which possess the nationality of or are effectively controlled by a State or States whose status as certifying State has been terminated, shall lapse unless the pioneer investor changes its nationality and sponsorship within six months of the date of such termination, as provided for in subparagraph (b).

    (b) A pioneer investor may change its nationality and sponsorship from that existing at the time of its registration as a pioneer investor to that of any State Party to the Convention which has effective control over the pioneer investor in terms of paragraph 1(a).

    (c) Changes of nationality and sponsorship pursuant to this paragraph shall not affect any right or priority conferred on a pioneer investor pursuant to paragraphs 6 and 8.

11. The Commission shall:

    (a) provide each pioneer investor with the certificate of compliance with the provisions of this resolution referred to in paragraph 8; and

    (b) include in its final report required by paragraph 11 of resolution I of the Conference details of all registrations of pioneer investors and allocations of pioneer areas pursuant to this resolution.

12. In order to ensure that the Enterprise is able to carry out activities in the Area in such a manner as to keep pace with States and other entities:

    (a) every registered pioneer investor shall:

        (i) carry out exploration, at the request of the Commission, in the area reserved, pursuant to paragraph 3 in connection with its application, for activities in the Area by the Authority through the Enterprise or in association with developing States, on the basis that the costs so incurred plus interest thereon at the rate of 10 per cent per annum shall be reimbursed;

        (ii) provide training at all levels for personnel designated by the Commission;

        (iii) undertake before the entry into force of the Convention, to perform the obligations prescribed in the Convention relating to transfer of technology;

    (b) every certifying State shall:

        (i) ensure that the necessary funds are made available to the Enterprise in a timely manner in accordance with the Convention, upon its entry into force; and

        (ii) report periodically to the Commission on the activities carried out by it, by its entities or natural or juridical persons.

13. The Authority and its organs shall recognize and honour the rights and obligations arising from this resolution and the decisions of the Commission taken pursuant to it.

14. Without prejudice to paragraph 13, this resolution shall have effect until the entry into force of the Convention.

15. Nothing in this resolution shall derogate from Annex III, article 6, paragraph 3(c), of the Convention.

RESOLUTION III

The Third United Nations Conference on the Law of the Sea, Having regard to the Convention on the Law of the Sea,

Bearing in mind the Charter of the United Nations, in particular article 73,

1. Declares that:

    (a) In the case of a territory whose people have not attained full independence or other self-governing status recognized by the United Nations, or a territory under colonial domination, provisions concerning rights and interests under the Convention shall be implemented for the benefit of the people of the territory with a view to promoting their well-being and development.

    (b) Where a dispute exists between States over the sovereignty of a territory to which this resolution applies, in respect of which the United Nations has recommended specific means of settlement, there shall be consultations between the parties to that dispute regarding the exercise of the rights referred to in subparagraph (a). In such consultations the interests of the people of the territory concerned shall be a fundamental consideration. Any exercise of those rights shall take into account the relevant resolutions of the United Nations and shall be without prejudice to the position of any party to the dispute. The States concerned shall make every effort to enter into provisional arrangements of a practical nature and shall not jeopardize or hamper the reaching of a final settlement of the dispute.

2. Requests the Secretary-General of the United Nations to bring this resolution to the attention of all Members of the United Nations and the other participants in the Conference, as well as the principal organs of the United Nations, and to request their compliance with it.

RESOLUTION IV

The Third United Nations Conference on the Law of the Sea,

Bearing in mind that national liberation movements have been invited to participate in the Conference as observers in accordance with rule 62 of its rules of procedure,

Decides that the national liberation movements, which have been participating in the Third United Nations Conference on the Law of the Sea, shall be entitled to sign the Final Act of the Conference, in their capacity as observers.

ANNEX II – STATEMENT OF UNDERSTANDING CONCERNING A SPECIFIC METHOD TO BE USED IN ESTABLISHING THE OUTER EDGE OF THE CONTINENTAL MARGIN

The Third United Nations Conference on the Law of the Sea,

Considering the special characteristics of a State's continental margin where: (1) the average distance at which the 200 metre isobath occurs is not more than 20 nautical miles; (2) the greater proportion of the sedimentary rock of the continental margin lies beneath the rise; and

Taking into account the inequity that would result to that State from the application to its continental margin of article 76 of the Convention, in that, the mathematical average of the thickness of sedimentary rock along a line established at the maximum distance permissible in accordance with the provisions of paragraph 4(a)(i) and (ii) of that article as representing the entire outer edge of the continental margin would not be less than 3.5 kilometres; and that more than half of the margin would be excluded thereby;

Recognizes that such State may, notwithstanding the provisions of article 76, establish the outer edge of its continental margin by straight lines not exceeding 60 nautical miles in length connecting fixed points, defined by latitude and longitude, at each of which the thickness of sedimentary rock is not less than 1 kilometre,

Where a State establishes the outer edge of its continental margin by applying the method set forth in the preceding paragraph of this statement, this method may also be utilized by a neighbouring State for delineating the outer edge of its continental margin on a common geological feature, where its outer edge would lie on such feature on a line established at the maximum distance permissible in accordance with article 76, paragraph 4(a)(i) and (ii), along which the mathematical average of the thickness of sedimentary rock is not less than 3.5 kilometres,

The Conference requests the Commission on the Limits of the Continental Shelf set up pursuant to Annex II of the Convention, to be governed by the terms of this Statement when making its recommendations on matters related to the establishment of the outer edge of the continental margins of these States in the southern part of the Bay of Bengal.

ANNEX VI – RESOLUTION ON DEVELOPMENT OF NATIONAL MARINE SCIENCE, TECHNOLOGY AND OCEAN SERVICE INFRASTRUCTURES

The Third United Nations Conference on the Law of the Sea,

Recognizing that the Convention on the Law of the Sea is intended to establish a new regime for the seas and oceans which will contribute to the realization of a just and equitable international economic order through making provision for the peaceful use of ocean space, the equitable and efficient management and utilization of its resources, and the study, protection and preservation of the marine environment,

Bearing in mind that the new regime must take into account, in particular, the special needs and interests of the developing countries, whether coastal, land-locked, or geographically disadvantaged,

Aware of the rapid advances being made in the field of marine science and technology, and the need for the developing countries, whether coastal, land-locked, or geographically disadvantaged, to share in these achievements if the aforementioned goals are to be met,

Convinced that, unless urgent measures are taken, the marine scientific and technological gap between the developed and the developing countries will widen further and thus endanger the very foundations of the new regime, Believing that optimum utilization of the new opportunities for social and economic development offered by the new regime will be facilitated through action at the national and international level aimed at strengthening national capabilities in marine science, technology and ocean services, particularly in the developing countries, with a view to ensuring the rapid absorption and efficient application of technology and scientific knowledge available to them,

Considering that national and regional marine scientific and technological centres would be the principal institutions through which States and, in particular, the developing countries, foster and conduct marine scientific research, and receive and disseminate marine technology,

Recognizing the special role of the competent international organizations envisaged by the Convention on the Law of the Sea, especially in relation to the establishment and development of national and regional marine scientific and technological centres,

Noting that present efforts undertaken within the United Nations system in training, education and assistance in the field of marine science and technology and ocean services are far below current requirements and would be particularly inadequate to meet the demands generated through operation of the Convention on the Law of the Sea,

Welcoming recent initiatives within international organizations to promote and coordinate their major international assistance programmes aimed at strengthening marine science infrastructures in developing countries,

1. Calls upon all Member States to determine appropriate priorities in their development plans for the strengthening of their marine science, technology and ocean services;
2. Calls upon the developing countries to establish programmes for the promotion of technical cooperation among themselves in the field of marine science, technology and ocean service development;
3. Urges the industrialized countries to assist the developing countries in the preparation and implementation of their marine science, technology and ocean service development programmes;
4. Recommends that the World Bank, the regional banks, the United Nations Development Programme, the United Nations Financing System

for Science and Technology and other multilateral funding agencies augment and coordinate their operations for the provision of funds to developing countries for the preparation and implementation of major programmes of assistance in strengthening their marine science, technology and ocean services;

5. Recommends that all competent international organizations within the United Nations system expand programmes within their respective fields of competence for assistance to developing countries in the field of marine science, technology and ocean services and coordinate their efforts on a system-wide basis in the implementation of such programmes, paying particular attention to the special needs of the developing countries, whether coastal, land-locked or geographically disadvantaged;

6. Requests the Secretary-General of the United Nations to transmit this resolution to the General Assembly at its thirty-seventh session.

8.3.2. Fish Stocks Agreement 1995

Agreement for the Implementation of the Provisions of the United Nations Convention on the Law of the Sea of 10 December 1982 relating to the Conservation and Management of Straddling Fish Stocks and Highly Migratory Fish Stocks, New York, 4 August 1995, 2167 UNTS 3

The States Parties to this Agreement,

Recalling the relevant provisions of the United Nations Convention on the Law of the Sea of 10 December 1982,

Determined to ensure the long-term conservation and sustainable use of straddling fish stocks and highly migratory fish stocks,

Resolved to improve cooperation between States to that end,

Calling for more effective enforcement by flag States, port States and coastal States of the conservation and management measures adopted for such stocks,

Seeking to address in particular the problems identified in Chapter 17, programme area C, of Agenda 21 adopted by the United Nations Conference on Environment and Development, namely, that the management of high seas fisheries is inadequate in many areas and that some resources are over-utilised; noting that there are problems of unregulated fishing, over-capitalisation, excessive fleet size, vessel reflagging to escape controls, insufficiently selective gear, unreliable databases and lack of sufficient cooperation between States,

Committing themselves to responsible fisheries,

Conscious of the need to avoid adverse impacts on the marine environment, preserve biodiversity, maintain the integrity of marine ecosystems and minimise the risk of long-term or irreversible effects of fishing operations,

Recognising the need for specific assistance, including financial, scientific and technological assistance, in order that developing States can participate effectively in the conservation, management and sustainable use of straddling fish stocks and highly migratory fish stocks,

Convinced that an agreement for the implementation of the relevant provisions of the Convention would best serve these purposes and contribute to the maintenance of international peace and security,

Affirming that matters not regulated by the Convention or by this Agreement continue to be governed by the rules and principles of general international law,

Have agreed as follows:

PART I – GENERAL PROVISIONS

Article 1 – Use of terms and scope

1. For the purposes of this Agreement:
   (a) 'Convention' means the United Nations Convention on the Law of the Sea of 10 December 1982;
   (b) 'conservation and management measures' means measures to conserve and manage one or more species of living marine resources that are adopted and applied consistent with the relevant rules of international law as reflected in the Convention and this Agreement;
   (c) 'fish' includes molluscs and crustaceans except those belonging to sedentary species as defined in article 77 of the Convention; and
   (d) 'arrangement' means a cooperative mechanism established in accordance with the Convention and this Agreement by two or more States for the purpose, inter alia, of establishing conservation and management measures in a subregion or region for one or more straddling fish stocks or highly migratory fish stocks.
2. (a) 'States Parties' means States which have consented to be bound by this Agreement and for which the Agreement is in force.
   (b) This Agreement applies mutatis mutandis:
      (i) to any entity referred to in article 305, paragraph 1 (c), (d), and (e), of the Convention and
      (ii) subject to article 47, to any entity referred to as an 'international organisation' in Annex IX, article 1, of the Convention which becomes a Party to this Agreement, and to that extent 'States Parties' refers to those entities.
3. This Agreement applies mutatis mutandis to other fishing entities whose vessels fish on the high seas.

Article 2 – Objective

The objective of this Agreement is to ensure the long-term conservation and sustainable use of straddling fish stocks and highly migratory fish stocks through effective implementation of the relevant provisions of the Convention.

Article 3 – Application

1. Unless otherwise provided, this Agreement applies to the conservation and management of straddling fish stocks and highly migratory fish stocks beyond areas under national jurisdiction, except that articles 6 and 7 apply also to the conservation and management of such stocks within areas under national jurisdiction, subject to the different legal regimes that apply within areas under national jurisdiction and in areas beyond national jurisdiction as provided for in the Convention.
2. In the exercise of its sovereign rights for the purpose of exploring and exploiting, conserving and

managing straddling fish stocks and highly migratory fish stocks within areas under national jurisdiction, the coastal State shall apply mutatis mutandis the general principles enumerated in article 5.

3. States shall give due consideration to the respective capacities of developing States to apply articles 5, 6 and 7 within areas under national jurisdiction and their need for assistance as provided for in this Agreement. To this end, Part VII applies mutatis mutandis in respect of areas under national jurisdiction.

Article 4 – Relationship between this Agreement and the Convention

Nothing in this Agreement shall prejudice the rights, jurisdiction and duties of States under the Convention. This Agreement shall be interpreted and applied in the context of and in a manner consistent with the Convention.

PART II – CONSERVATION AND MANAGEMENT OF STRADDLING FISH STOCKS AND HIGHLY MIGRATORY FISH STOCKS

Article 5 – General principles

In order to conserve and manage straddling fish stocks and highly migratory fish stocks, coastal States and States fishing on the high seas shall, in giving effect to their duty to cooperate in accordance with the Convention:

(a) adopt measures to ensure long-term sustainability of straddling fish stocks and highly migratory fish stocks and promote the objective of their optimum utilisation;

(b) ensure that such measures are based on the best scientific evidence available and are designed to maintain or restore stocks at levels capable of producing maximum sustainable yield, as qualified by relevant environmental and economic factors, including the special requirements of developing States, and taking into account fishing patterns, the interdependence of stocks and any generally recommended international minimum standards, whether subregional, regional or global;

(c) apply the precautionary approach in accordance with article 6;

(d) assess the impacts of fishing, other human activities and environmental factors on target stocks and species belonging to the same ecosystem or associated with or dependent on the target stocks;

(e) adopt, where necessary, conservation and management measures for species belonging to the same ecosystem or associated with or dependent on the target stocks, with a view to maintaining or restoring populations of such species above levels at which their reproduction may become seriously threatened;

(f) minimise pollution, waste, discards, catch by lost or abandoned gear, catch of non-target species, both fish and non-fish species, (hereinafter referred to as 'non-target species') and impacts on associated or dependent species, in particular endangered species, through measures including, to the extent practicable, the development and use of selective, environmentally safe and cost-effective fishing gear and techniques;

(g) protect biodiversity in the marine environment;

(h) take measures to prevent or eliminate overfishing and excess fishing capacity and to ensure that levels of fishing effort do not exceed those commensurate with the sustainable use of fishery resources;

(i) take into account the interests of artisanal and subsistence fishers;

(j) collect and share, in a timely manner, complete and accurate data concerning fishing activities on, inter alia, vessel position, catch of target and non-target species and fishing effort, as set out in Annex I, as well as information from national and international research programmes;

(k) promote and conduct scientific research and develop appropriate technologies in support of fishery conservation and management, and

(l) implement and enforce conservation and management measures through effective monitoring, control and surveillance.

Article 6 – Application of the precautionary approach

1. States shall apply the precautionary approach widely to conservation, management and exploitation of straddling fish stocks and highly migratory fish stocks in order to protect the living marine resources and preserve the marine environment.

2. States shall be more cautions when information is uncertain, unreliable or inadequate. The absence of adequate scientific information shall not be used as a reason for postponing or failing to take conservation and management measures.

3. In implementing the precautionary approach, States shall:

   (a) improve decision-making for fishery resource conservation and management by obtaining and sharing the best scientific information available and implementing improved techniques for dealing with risk and uncertainty,

   (b) apply the guidelines set out in Annex II and determine, on the basis of the best scientific information available, stock-specific reference points and the action to be taken if they are exceeded;

   (c) take into account, inter alia, uncertainties relating to the size and productivity of the stocks, reference points, stock condition in relation to such reference points, levels and distribution of fishing mortality and the impact of fishing activities on non-target and associated or dependent species, as well as existing and predicted oceanic, environmental and socioeconomic conditions, and

   (d) develop data-collection and research programmes to assess the impact of fishing on non-target and associated or dependent species and their environment, and adopt plans which are necessary to ensure the conservation of such species and to protect habitats of special concern.

4. State shall take measures to ensure that, when reference points are approached, they will not be exceeded. In the event that they are exceeded, States shall, without delay, take the action determined under paragraph 3(b) to restore the stocks.
5. Where the status of target stocks or non-target or associated or dependent species is of concern, States shall subject such stocks and species to enhanced monitoring in order to review their status and the efficacy of conservation and management measures. They shall revise those measures regularly in the light of new information.
6. For new or exploratory fisheries, States shall adopt as soon as possible cautious conservation and management measures, including, inter alia, catch limits and effort limits. Such measures shall remain in force until there are sufficient data to allow assessment of the impact of the fisheries on the long-term sustainability of the stocks, whereupon conservation and management measures based on that assessment shall be implemented. The latter measures shall, if appropriate, allow for the gradual development of the fisheries.
7. If a natural phenomenon has a significant adverse impact on the status of straddling fish stocks or highly migratory fish stocks, States shall adopt conservation and management measures on an emergency basis to ensure that fishing activity does not exacerbate such adverse impact. States shall also adopt such measures on an emergency basis where fishing activity presents a serious threat to the sustainability of such stocks. Measures taken on an emergency basis shall be temporary and shall be based on the best scientific evidence available.

Article 7 – Compatibility of conservation and management measures

1. Without prejudice to the sovereign rights of coastal States for the purpose of exploring and exploiting, conserving and managing the living marine resources within areas under national jurisdiction as provided for in the Convention, and the right of all States for their nationals to engage in fishing on the high seas in accordance with the Convention:
   (a) with respect to straddling fish stocks, the relevant coastal States and the States whose nationals fish for such stocks in the adjacent high seas area shall seek, either directly or through the appropriate mechanisms for cooperation provided for in Part III, to agree upon the measures necessary for the conservation of these stocks in the adjacent high seas area;
   (b) with respect to highly migratory fish stocks, the relevant coastal States and other States whose nationals fish for such stocks in the region shall cooperate, either directly or through the appropriate mechanisms for cooperation provided for in Part III, with a view to ensuring conservation and promoting the objective of optimum utilisation of such stocks throughout the region, both within and beyond the areas under national jurisdiction.
2. Conservation and management measures established for the high seas and those adopted for areas under national jurisdiction shall be compatible in order to ensure conservation and management of the straddling fish stocks and highly migratory fish stocks in their entirety. To this end, coastal States and States fishing on the high seas have a duty to cooperate for the purpose of achieving compatible measures in respect of such stocks. In determining compatible conservation and management measures, States shall:
   (a) take into account the conservation and management measures adopted and applied in accordance with article 61 of the Convention in respect of the same stocks by coastal States within areas under national jurisdiction and ensure that measures established in respect of such stocks for the high seas do not undermine the effectiveness of such measures;
   (b) take into account previously agreed measures established and applied for the high seas in accordance with the Convention in respect of the same stocks by relevant coastal States and States fishing on the high seas;
   (c) take into account previously agreed measures established and applied in accordance with the Convention in respect of the same stocks by a subregional or regional fisheries management organisation or arrangement;
   (d) take into account the biological unity and other biological characteristics of the stocks and the relationships between the distribution of the stocks, the fisheries and the geographical particularities of the region concerned, including the extent to which the stocks occur and are fished in areas under national jurisdiction;
   (e) take into account the respective dependence of the coastal States and the States fishing on the high seas on the stocks concerned, and
   (f) ensure that such measures do not result in harmful impact on the living marine resources as a whole.
3. In giving effect to their duty to cooperate, States shall make every effort to agree on compatible conservation and management measures within a reasonable period of time.
4. If no agreement can be reached within a reasonable period of time, any of the States concerned may invoke the procedures for the settlement of disputes provided for in Part VIII.
5. Pending agreement on compatible conservation and management measures, the States concerned, in a spirit of understanding and cooperation, shall make every effort to enter into provisional arrangements of a practical nature. In the event that they are unable to agree on such arrangements, any of the States concerned may, for the purpose of obtaining provisional measures, submit the dispute to a court or tribunal in accordance with the proce-

dures for the settlement of disputes provided for in Part VIII.

6. Provisional arrangements or measures entered into or prescribed pursuant to paragraph 5 shall take into account the provisions of this Part, shall have due regard to the rights and obligations of all States concerned, shall not jeopardize or hamper the reaching of final agreement on compatible conservation and management measures and shall be without prejudice to the final outcome of any dispute settlement procedure.
7. Coastal States shall regularly inform States fishing on the high seas in the subregion or region, either directly or through appropriate subregional or regional fisheries management organisations or arrangements, or through other appropriate means, of the measures they have adopted for straddling fish stocks and highly migratory fish stocks within areas under their national jurisdiction.
8. States fishing on the high seas shall regularly inform other interested States, either directly or through appropriate subregional or regional fisheries management organisations or arrangements, or through other appropriate means, of the measures they have adopted for regulating the activities of vessels flying their flag which fish for such stocks on the high seas.

PART III – MECHANISMS FOR INTERNATIONAL COOPERATION CONCERNING STRADDLING FISH STOCKS AND HIGHLY MIGRATORY FISH STOCKS

Article 8 – Cooperation for conservation and management

1. Coastal States and States fishing on the high seas shall, in accordance with the Convention, pursue cooperation in relation to straddling fish stocks and highly migratory fish stocks either directly or through appropriate subregional or regional fisheries management organisations or arrangements, taking into account the specific characteristics of the subregion or region, to ensure effective conservation and management of such stocks.
2. States shall enter into consultations in good faith and without delay, particularly where there is evidence that the straddling fish stocks and highly migratory fish stocks concerned may be under threat of overexploitation or where a new fishery is being developed for such stocks. To this end, consultations may be initiated at the request of any interested State with a view to establishing appropriate arrangements to ensure conservation and management of the stocks. Pending agreement on such arrangements, States shall observe the provisions of this Agreement and shall act in good faith and with due regard to the rights, interests and duties of other States.
3. Where a subregional or regional fisheries management organisation or arrangement has the competence to establish conservation and management measures for particular straddling fish stocks or highly migratory fish stocks, States fishing for the stocks on the high seas and relevant coastal States shall give effect to their duty to cooperate by becoming members of such organisation or participants in such arrangement, or by agreeing to apply the conservation and management measures established by such organisation or arrangement. States having a real interest in the fisheries concerned may become members of such organisation or participants in such arrangement. The terms of participation in such organisation or arrangement shall not preclude such States from membership or participation; nor shall they be applied in a manner which discriminates against any State or group of States having a real interest in the fisheries concerned.
4. Only those States which are members of such an organisation or participants in such an arrangement, or which agree to apply the conservation and management measures established by such organisation or arrangement, shall have access to the fishery resources to which those measures apply.
5. Where there is no subregional or regional fisheries management organisation or arrangement to establish conservation and management measures for a particular straddling fish stock or highly migratory fish stock, relevant coastal States and States fishing on the high seas for such stock in the subregion or region shall cooperate to establish such an organisation or enter into other appropriate arrangements to ensure conservation and management of such stock and shall participate in the work of the organisation or arrangement.
6. Any State intending to propose that action be taken by an intergovernmental organisation having competence with respect to living resources should, where such action would have a significant effect on conservation and management measures already established by a competent subregional or regional fisheries management organisation or arrangement, consult through that organisation or arrangement with its members or participants. To the extent practicable, such consultation should take place prior to the submission of the proposal to the intergovernmental organisation.

Article 9 – Subregional and regional fisheries management organisations and arrangements

1. In establishing subregional or regional fisheries management organisations or in entering into subregional or regional fisheries management arrangements for straddling fish stocks and highly migratory fish stocks, States shall agree, inter alia, on:
   (a) the stocks to which conservation and management measures apply, taking into account the biological characteristics of the stocks concerned and the nature of the fisheries involved;
   (b) the area of application, taking into account article 7, paragraph 1, and the characteristics of the subregion or region, including socioeconomic, geographical and environmental factors;
   (c) the relationship between the work of the new organisation or arrangement and the role, objectives and operations of any relevant exist-

ing fisheries management organisations or arrangements, and

(d) the mechanisms by which the organisation or arrangement will obtain scientific advice and review the status of the stocks, including, where appropriate, the establishment of a scientific advisory body.

2. States cooperating in the formation of a subregional or regional fisheries management organisation or arrangement shall inform other States which they are aware have a real interest in the work of the proposed organisation or arrangement of such cooperation.

Article 10 – Functions of subregional and regional fisheries management organisations and arrangements

In fulfilling their obligation to cooperate through subregional or regional fisheries management organisations or arrangements, States shall:

(a) agree on and comply with conservation and management measures to ensure the long-term sustainability of straddling fish stocks and highly migratory fish stocks;

(b) agree, as appropriate, on participatory rights such as allocations of allowable catch or levels of fishing effort;

(c) adopt and apply any generally recommended international minimum standards for the responsible conduct of fishing operations;

(d) obtain and evaluate scientific advice, review the status of the stocks and assess the impact of fishing on non-target and associated or dependent species;

(e) agree on standards for collection, reporting, verification and exchange of data on fisheries for the stocks;

(f) compile and disseminate accurate and complete statistical data, as described in Annex I, to ensure that the best scientific evidence is available, while maintaining confidentiality where appropriate;

(g) promote and conduct scientific assessments of the stocks and relevant research and disseminate the results thereof;

(h) establish appropriate cooperative mechanisms for effective monitoring, control, surveillance and enforcement;

(i) agree on means by which the fishing interests of new members of the organisation or new participants in the arrangement will be accommodated;

(j) agree on decision-making procedures which facilitate the adoption of conservation and management measures in a timely and effective manner,

(k) promote the peaceful settlement of disputes in accordance with Part VIII;

(l) ensure the full cooperation of their relevant national agencies and industries in implementing the recommendations and decisions of the organisation or arrangement, and

(m) give due publicity to the conservation and management measures established by the organisation or arrangement.

Article 11 – New members or participants

In determining the nature and extent of participatory rights for new members of a subregional or regional fisheries management organisation, or for new participants in a subregional or regional fisheries management arrangement, States shall take into account, inter alia:

(a) the status of the straddling fish stocks and highly migratory fish stocks and the existing level of fishing effort in the fishery;

(b) the respective interests, fishing patterns and fishing practices of new and existing members or participants;

(c) the respective contributions of new and existing members or participants to conservation and management of the stocks, to the collection and provision of accurate data and to the conduct of scientific research on the stocks;

(d) the needs of coastal fishing communities which are dependent mainly on fishing for the stocks;

(e) the needs of coastal States whose economies are overwhelmingly dependent on the exploitation of living marine resources, and

(f) the interests of developing States from the subregion or region in whose areas of national jurisdiction the stocks also occur.

Article 12 – Transparency in activities of subregional and regional fisheries management organisations and arrangements

1. States shall provide for transparency in the decision-making process and other activities of subregional and regional fisheries management organisations and arrangements.

2. Representatives from other intergovernmental organisations and representatives from non-governmental organisations concerned with straddling fish stocks and highly migratory fish stocks shall be afforded the opportunity to take part in meetings of subregional and regional fisheries management organisations and arrangements as observers or otherwise, as appropriate, in accordance with the procedures of the organisation or arrangement concerned. Such procedures shall not be unduly restrictive in this respect. Such intergovernmental organisations and non-governmental organisations shall have timely access to the records and reports of such organisations and arrangements, subject to the procedural rules on access to them.

Article 13 – Strengthening of existing organisations and arrangements

States shall cooperate to strengthen existing subregional and regional fisheries management organisations and arrangements in order to improve their effectiveness in establishing and implementing conservation and management measures for straddling fish stocks and highly migratory fish stocks.

Article 14 – Collection and provision of information and cooperation in scientific research

1. States shall ensure that fishing vessels flying their flag provide such information as may be necessary in order to fulfil their obligations under this Agreement. To this end, States shall in accordance with Annex I:
   (a) collect and exchange scientific, technical and statistical data with respect to fisheries for straddling fish stocks and highly migratory fish stocks;
   (b) ensure that data are collected in sufficient detail to facilitate effective stock assessment and are provided in a timely manner to fulfil the requirements of subregional or regional fisheries management organisations or arrangements, and
   (c) take appropriate measures to verify the accuracy of such data.
2. States shall cooperate, either directly or through sub regional or regional fisheries management organisations or arrangements:
   (a) to agree on the specification of data and the format in which they are to be provided to such organisations or arrangements, taking into account the nature of the stocks and the fisheries for those stocks, and
   (b) to develop and share analytical techniques and stock assessment methodologies to improve measures for the conservation and management of straddling fish stocks and highly migratory fish stocks.
3. Consistent with Part XIII of the Convention, States shall cooperate, either directly or through competent international organisations, to strengthen scientific research capacity in the field of fisheries and promote scientific research related to the conservation and management of straddling fish stocks and highly migratory fish stocks for the benefit of all. To this end, a State or the competent international organisation conducting such research beyond areas under national jurisdiction shall actively promote the publication and dissemination to any interested States of the results of that research and information relating to its objectives and methods and, to the extent practicable, shall facilitate the participation of scientists from those States in such research.

Article 15 – Enclosed and semi-enclosed seas

In implementing this Agreement in an enclosed or semi-enclosed sea, States shall take into account the natural characteristics of that sea and shall also act in a manner consistent with Part IX of the Convention and other relevant provisions thereof.

Article 16 – Areas of high seas surrounded entirely by an area under the national jurisdiction of a single State

1. States fishing for straddling fish stocks and highly migratory fish stocks in an area of the high seas surrounded entirely by an area under the national jurisdiction of a single State and the latter State shall cooperate to establish conservation and management measures in respect of those stocks in the high seas area. Having regard to the natural characteristics of the area, States shall pay special attention to the establishment of compatible conservation and management measures for such stocks pursuant to article 7. Measures taken in respect of the high seas shall take into account the rights, duties and interests of the coastal State under the Convention, shall be based on the best scientific evidence available and shall also take into account any conservation and management measures adopted and applied in respect of the same stocks in accordance with article 61 of the Convention by the coastal State in the area under national jurisdiction. States shall also agree on measures for monitoring, control, surveillance and enforcement to ensure compliance with the conservation and management measures in respect of the high seas.
2. Pursuant to article 8, States shall act in good faith and make every effort to agree without delay on conservation and management measures to be applied in the carrying out of fishing operations in the area referred to in paragraph 1. If, within a reasonable period of time, the fishing States concerned and the coastal State are unable to agree on such measures, they shall, having regard to paragraph 1, apply article 7, paragraphs 4, 5 and 6, relating to provisional arrangements or measures. Pending the establishment of such provisional arrangements or measures, the States concerned shall take measures in respect of vessels flying their flag in order that they not engage in fisheries which could undermine the stocks concerned.

PART IV – NON-MEMBERS AND NON-PARTICIPANTS

Article 17 – Non-members of organisations and non-participants in arrangements

1. A State which is not a member of a subregional or regional fisheries management organisation or is not a participant in a subregional or regional fisheries management arrangement, and which does not otherwise agree to apply the conservation and management measures established by such organisation or arrangement, is not discharged from the obligation to cooperate, in accordance with the Convention and this Agreement, in the conservation and management of the relevant straddling fish stocks and highly migratory fish stocks.
2. Such State shall not authorise vessels flying its flag to engage in fishing operations for the straddling fish stocks or highly migratory fish stocks which are subject to the conservation and management measures established by such organisation or arrangement.
3. States which are members of a subregional or regional fisheries management organisation or participants in a subregional or regional fisheries management arrangement shall, individually or jointly, request the fishing entities referred to in article 1, paragraph 3, which have fishing vessels in the relevant area to cooperate fully with such organisation

or arrangement in implementing the conservation and management measures it has established, with a view to having such measures applied de facto as extensively as possible to fishing activities in the relevant area. Such fishing entities shall enjoy benefits from participation in the fishery commensurate with their commitment to comply with conservation and management measures in respect of the stocks.

4. States which are members of such organisation or participants in such arrangement shall exchange information with respect to the activities of fishing vessels flying the flags of States which are neither members of the organisation nor participants in the arrangement and which are engaged in fishing operations for the relevant stocks. They shall take measures consistent with this Agreement and international law to deter activities of such vessels which undermine the effectiveness of subregional or regional conservation and management measures.

PART V – DUTIES OF THE FLAG STATE

Article 18 – Duties of the flag State

1. A State whose vessels fish on the high seas shall take such measures as may be necessary to ensure that vessels flying its flag comply with subregional and regional conservation and management measures and that such vessels do not engage in any activity which undermines the effectiveness of such measures.
2. A State shall authorise the use of vessels flying its flag for fishing on the high seas only where it is able to exercise effectively its responsibilities in respect of such vessels under the Convention and this Agreement.
3. Measures to be taken by a State in respect of vessels flying its flag shall include:
   (a) control of such vessels on the high seas by means of fishing licences, authorisations or permits, in accordance with any applicable procedures agreed at the subregional, regional or global level;
   (b) establishment of regulations:
      (i) to apply terms and conditions to the licence, authorisation or permit sufficient to fulfil any subregional, regional or global obligations of the flag State,
      (ii) to prohibit fishing on the high seas by vessels which are not duly licensed or authorised to fish, or fishing on the high seas by vessels otherwise than in accordance with the terms and conditions of a licence, authorisation or permit,
      (iii) to require vessels fishing on the high seas to carry the licence, authorisation or permit on board at all times and to produce it on demand for inspection by a duly authorised person,
      (iv) to ensure that vessels flying its flag do not conduct unauthorised fishing within areas under the national jurisdiction of other States;
   (c) establishment of a national record of fishing vessels authorised to fish on the high seas and provision of access to the information contained in that record on request by directly interested States, taking into account any national laws of the flag State regarding the release of such information;
   (d) requirements for marking of fishing vessels and fishing gear for identification in accordance with uniform and internationally recognisable vessel and gear marking systems, such as the Food and Agriculture Organisation of the United Nations Standard Specifications for the Marking and Identification of Fishing Vessels;
   (e) requirements for recording and timely reporting of vessel position, catch of target and non-target species, fishing effort and other relevant fisheries data in accordance with subregional, regional and global standards for collection of such data;
   (f) requirements for verifying the catch of target and non-target species through such means as observer programmes, inspection schemes, unloading reports, supervision of transhipment and monitoring of landed catches and market statistics;
   (g) monitoring, control and surveillance of such vessels, their fishing operations and related activities by, inter alia:
      (i) the implementation of national inspection schemes and subregional and regional schemes for cooperation in enforcement pursuant to articles 21 and 22, including requirements for such vessels to permit access by duly authorised inspectors from other States,
      (ii) the implementation of national observer programmers and subregional and regional observer programmes in which the flag State is a participant, including requirements for such vessels to permit access by observers from other States to carry out the functions agreed under the programmes,
      (iii) the development and implementation of vessel monitoring systems, including, as appropriate, satellite transmitter systems, in accordance with any national programmes and those which have been subregionally, regionally or globally agreed among the States concerned;
   (h) regulation of transhipment on the high seas to ensure that the effectiveness of conservation and management measures is not undermined;
   (i) regulation of fishing activities to ensure compliance with subregional, regional or global measures, including those aimed at minimising catches of non-target species.

4. Where there is a subregionally, regionally or globally agreed system of monitoring, control and surveillance in effect, States shall ensure that the measures they impose on vessels flying their flag are compatible with that system.

PART VI – COMPLIANCE AND ENFORCEMENT

Article 19 – Compliance and enforcement by the flag State

1. A State shall ensure compliance by vessels flying its flag with subregional and regional conservation and management measures for straddling fish stocks and highly migratory fish stocks. To this end, that State shall:
   (a) enforce such measures irrespective of where violations occur,
   (b) investigate immediately and fully any alleged violation of subregional or regional conservation and management measures, which may include the physical inspection of the vessels concerned, and report promptly to the State alleging the violation and the relevant subregional or regional organisation or arrangements on the progress and outcome of the investigation;
   (c) require any vessel flying its flag to give information to the investigating authority regarding vessel position, catches, fishing gear, fishing operations and related activities in the area of an alleged violation;
   (d) if satisfied that sufficient evidence is available in respect of an alleged violation, refer the case to its authorities with a view to instituting proceedings without delay in accordance with its laws and, where appropriate, detain the vessel concerned;
   (e) ensure that, where it has been established, in accordance with its laws, a vessel has been involved in the commission of a serious violation of such measures, the vessel does not engage in fishing operations on the high seas until such time as all outstanding sanctions imposed by the flag State in respect of the violation have been complied with.
2. All investigations and judicial proceedings shall be carried out expeditiously. Sanctions applicable in respect of violations shall be adequate in severity to be effective in securing compliance and to discourage violations wherever they occur and shall deprive offenders of the benefits accruing from their illegal activities. Measures applicable in respect of masters and other officers of fishing vessels shall include provisions which may permit, inter alia, refusal, withdrawal or suspension of authorisations to serve as masters or officers on such vessels.

Article 20 – International cooperation in enforcement

1. States shall cooperate, either directly or through subregional or regional fisheries management organisations or arrangements, to ensure compliance with and enforcement of subregional and regional conservation and management measures for straddling fish stocks and highly migratory fish stocks.
2. A flag State conducting an investigation of an alleged violation of conservation and management measures for straddling fish stocks or highly migratory fish stocks may request the assistance of any other State whose cooperation may be useful in the conduct of that investigation. All States shall endeavour to meet reasonable requests made by a flag State in connection with such investigations.
3. A flag State may undertake such investigations directly, in cooperation with other interested States or through the relevant subregional or regional fisheries management organisation or arrangement. Information on the progress and outcome of the investigations shall be provided to all States having an interest in, or affected by, the alleged violation.
4. States shall assist each other in identifying vessels reported to have engaged in activities undermining the effectiveness of subregional, regional or global conservation and management measures.
5. States shall, to the extent permitted by national laws and regulations, establish arrangements for making available to prosecuting authorities in other States evidence relating to alleged violations of such measures.
6. Where there are reasonable grounds for believing that a vessel on the high seas has been engaged in unauthorised fishing within an area under the jurisdiction of a coastal State, the flag State of that vessel, at the request of the coastal State concerned, shall immediately and fully investigate the matter. The flag State shall cooperate with the coastal State in taking appropriate enforcement action in such cases and may authorise the relevant authorities of the coastal State to board and inspect the vessel on the high seas. This paragraph is without prejudice to article 111 of the Convention.
7. States Parties which are members of a subregional or regional fisheries management organisation or participants in a subregional or regional fisheries management arrangement may take action in accordance with international law, including through recourse to subregional or regional procedures established for this purpose, to deter vessels which have engaged in activities which undermine the effectiveness of or otherwise violate the conservation and management measures established by that organisation or arrangement from fishing on the high seas in the subregion or region until such time as appropriate action is taken by the flag State.

Article 21 – Subregional and regional cooperation in enforcement

1. In any high seas area covered by a subregional or regional fisheries management organisation or arrangement, a State Party which is a member of such organisation or a participant in such arrangement may, through its duly authorised inspectors, board and inspect, in accordance with paragraph 2, fishing vessels flying the flag of another State Party to this Agreement, whether or not such State

Party is also a member of the organisation or a participant in the arrangement, for the purpose of ensuring compliance with conservation and management measures for straddling fish stocks and highly migratory fish stocks established by that organisation or arrangement.

2. States shall establish, through subregional or regional fisheries management organisations or arrangements, procedures for boarding and inspection pursuant to paragraph 1, as well as procedures to implement other provisions of this article. Such procedures shall be consistent with this article and the basic procedures set out in article 22 and shall not discriminate against non-members of the organisation or non-participants in the arrangement. Boarding and inspection as well as any subsequent enforcement action shall be conducted in accordance with such procedures. States shall give due publicity to procedures established pursuant to this paragraph.
3. If, within two years of the adoption of this Agreement, any organisation or arrangement has not established such procedures, boarding and inspection pursuant to paragraph 1, as well as any subsequent enforcement action, shall, pending the establishment of such procedures, be conducted in accordance with this article and the basic procedures set out in article 22.
4. Prior to taking action under this article, inspecting States shall, either directly or through the relevant subregional or regional fisheries management organisation or arrangement, inform all States whose vessels fish on the high seas in the subregion or region of the form of identification issued to their duly authorised inspectors. The vessels used for boarding and inspection shall be clearly marked and identifiable as being on government service. At the time of becoming a Party to this Agreement, a State shall designate an appropriate authority to receive notifications pursuant to this article and shall give due publicity of such designation through the relevant subregional or regional fisheries management organisation or arrangement.
5. Where, following a boarding and inspection, there are clear grounds for believing that a vessel has engaged in any activity contrary to the conservation and management measures referred to in paragraph 1, the inspecting State shall, where appropriate, secure evidence and shall promptly notify the flag State of the alleged violation.
6. The flag State shall respond to the notification referred to in paragraph 5 within three working days of its receipt, or such other period as may be prescribed in procedures established in accordance with paragraph 2, and shall either:
   (a) fulfil, without delay, its obligations under article 19 to investigate and, if evidence so warrants, take enforcement action with respect to the vessel, in which case it shall promptly inform the inspecting State of the results of the investigation and of any enforcement action taken; or
   (b) authorise the inspecting State to investigate.
7. Where the flag State authorises the inspecting State to investigate an alleged violation, the inspecting State shall, without delay, communicate the results of that investigation to the flag State. The flag State shall, if evidence so warrants, fulfil its obligations to take enforcement action with respect to the vessel. Alternatively, the flag State may authorise the inspecting State to take such enforcement action as the flag State may specify with respect to the vessel, consistent with the rights and obligations of the flag State under this Agreement.
8. Where, following boarding and inspection, there are clear grounds for believing that a vessel has committed a serious violation, and the flag State has either failed to respond or failed to take action as required under paragraphs 6 or 7, the inspectors may remain on board and secure evidence and may require the master to assist in further investigation including, where appropriate, by bringing the vessel without delay to the nearest appropriate port, or to such other port as may be specified in procedures established in accordance with paragraph 2. The inspecting State shall immediately inform the flag State of the name of the port to which the vessel is to proceed. The inspecting State and the flag State and, as appropriate, the port State shall take all necessary steps to ensure the well-being of the crew regardless of their nationality.
9. The inspecting State shall inform the flag State and the relevant organisation or the participants in the relevant arrangement of the results of any further investigation.
10. The inspecting State shall require its inspectors to observe generally accepted international regulations, procedures and practices relating to the safety of the vessel and the crew, minimise interference with fishing operations and, to the extent practicable, avoid action which would adversely affect the quality of the catch on board. The inspecting State shall ensure that boarding and inspection is not conducted in a manner that would constitute harassment of any fishing vessel.
11. For the purposes of this article, a serious violation means:
    (a) fishing without a valid licence, authorisation or permit issued by the flag State in accordance with article 18, paragraph 3 (a);
    (b) failing to maintain accurate records of catch and catch-related data, as required by the relevant subregional or regional fisheries management organisation or arrangement, or serious misreporting of catch, contrary to the catch reporting requirements of such organisation or arrangement;
    (c) fishing in a closed area, fishing during a closed season or fishing without, or after attainment of, a quota established by the relevant subregional or regional fisheries management organisation or arrangement;
    (d) directed fishing for a stock which is subject to a moratorium or for which fishing is prohibited;
    (e) using prohibited fishing gear,

(f) falsifying or concealing the markings, identity or registration of a fishing vessel;

(g) concealing, tampering with or disposing of evidence relating to an investigation;

(h) multiple violations which together constitute a serious disregard of conservation and management measures; or

(i) such other violations as may be specified in procedures established by the relevant subregional or regional fisheries management organisation or arrangement.

12. Notwithstanding the other provisions of this article, the flag State may, at any time, take action to fulfil its obligations under article 19 with respect to an alleged violation. Where the vessel is under the direction of the inspecting State, the inspecting State shall, at the request of the flag State, release the vessel to the flag State along with full information on the progress and outcome of its investigation.

13. This article is without prejudice to the right of the flag State to take any measures, including proceedings to impose penalties, according to its laws.

14. This article applies mutatis mutandis to boarding and inspection by a State Party which is a member of a subregional or regional fisheries management organisation or a participant in a subregional or regional fisheries management arrangement and which has clear grounds for believing that a fishing vessel flying the flag of another State Party has engaged in any activity contrary to relevant conservation and management measures referred to in paragraph 1 in the high seas area covered by such organisation or arrangement, and such vessel has subsequently, during the same fishing trip, entered into an area under the national jurisdiction of the inspecting State.

15. Where a subregional or regional fisheries management organisation or arrangement has established an alternative mechanism which effectively discharges the obligation under this Agreement of its members or participants to ensure compliance with the conservation and management measures established by the organisation or arrangement, members of such organisation or participants in such arrangement may agree to limit the application of paragraph 1 as between themselves in respect of the conservation and management measures which have been established in the relevant high seas area.

16. Action taken by States other than the flag State in respect of vessels having engaged in activities contrary to subregional or regional conservation and management measures shall be proportionate to the seriousness of the violation.

17. Where there are reasonable grounds for suspecting that a fishing vessel on the high seas is without nationality, a State may board and inspect the vessel. Where evidence so warrants, the State may take such action as may be appropriate in accordance with international law.

18. States shall be liable for damage or loss attributable to them arising from action taken pursuant to this article when such action is unlawful or exceeds that reasonably required in the light of available information to implement the provisions of this article.

Article 22 – Basic procedures for boarding and inspection pursuant to Article 21

1. The inspecting State shall ensure that its duly authorised inspectors:

(a) present credentials to the master of the vessel and produce a copy of the text of the relevant conservation and management measures or rules and regulations in force in the high seas area in question, pursuant to those measures;

(b) initiate notice to the flag State at the time of the boarding and inspection;

(c) do not interfere with the master's ability to communicate with the authorities of the flag State during the boarding and inspection;

(d) provide a copy of a report on the boarding and inspection to the master and to the authorities of the flag State, noting therein any objection or statement which the master wishes to have included in the report;

(e) promptly leave the vessel following completion of the inspection if they find no evidence of a serious violation; and

(f) avoid the use of force except when and to the degree necessary to ensure the safety of the inspectors and where the inspectors are obstructed in the execution of their duties. The degree of force used shall not exceed that reasonably required in the circumstances.

2. The duly authorised inspectors of an inspecting State shall have the authority to inspect the vessel, its licence, gear, equipment, records, facilities, fish and fish products and any relevant documents necessary to verify compliance with the relevant conservation and management measures.

3. The flag State shall ensure that vessel masters:

(a) accept and facilitate prompt and safe boarding by the inspectors;

(b) cooperate with and assist in the inspection of the vessel conducted pursuant to these procedures;

(c) do not obstruct, intimidate or interfere with the inspectors in the performance of their duties;

(d) allow the inspectors to communicate with the authorities of the flag State and the inspecting State during the boarding and inspection;

(e) provide reasonable facilities, including, where appropriate, food and accommodation, to the inspectors;

(f) facilitate safe disembarkation by the inspectors.

4. In the event that the master of a vessel refuses to accept boarding and inspection in accordance with this article and article 21, the flag State shall, ex-

cept in circumstances where, in accordance with generally accepted international regulations, procedures and practices relating to safety at sea, it is necessary to delay the boarding and inspection, direct the master of the vessel to submit immediately to boarding and inspection and, if the master does not comply with such direction, shall suspend the vessel's authorisation to fish and order the vessel to return immediately to port. The flag State shall advise the inspecting State of the action it has taken when the circumstances referred to in this paragraph arise.

Article 23 – Measures taken by a port State

1. A port State has the right and the duty to take measures, in accordance with international law, to promote the effectiveness of subregional, regional and global conservation and management measures. When taking such measures a port State shall not discriminate in form or in fact against the vessels of any State.
2. A port State may, inter alia, inspect documents, fishing gear and catch on board fishing vessels, when such vessels are voluntarily in its ports or at its offshore terminals.
3. States may adopt regulations empowering the relevant national authorities to prohibit landings and transhipments where it has been established that the catch has been taken in a manner which undermines the effectiveness of subregional, regional or global conservation and management measures on the high seas.
4. Nothing in this article affects the exercise by States of their sovereignty over ports in their territory in accordance with international law.

PART VII – REQUIREMENTS OF DEVELOPING STATES

Article 24 – Recognition of the special requirements of developing States

1. States shall give full recognition to the special requirements of developing States in relation to conservation and management of straddling fish stocks and highly migratory fish stocks and development of fisheries for such stocks. To this end, States shall, either directly or through the United Nations Development Programme, the Food and Agriculture Organisation of the United Nations and other specialised agencies, the Global Environment Facility, the Commission on Sustainable Development and other appropriate international and regional organisations and bodies, provide assistance to developing States.
2. In giving effect to the duty to cooperate in the establishment of conservation and management measures for straddling fish stocks and highly migratory fish stocks, States shall take into account the special requirements of developing States, in particular:
   (a) the vulnerability of developing States which are dependent on the exploitation of living marine resources, including for meeting the nutritional requirements of their populations or parts thereof;
   (b) the need to avoid adverse impacts on, and ensure access to fisheries by, subsistence, small-scale and artisanal fishers and women fishworkers, as well as indigenous people in developing States, particularly small island developing States;
   (c) the need to ensure that such measures do not result in transferring, directly or indirectly, a disproportionate burden of conservation action onto developing States.

Article 25 – Forms of cooperation with developing States

1. States shall cooperate, either directly or through subregional, regional or global organisations:
   (a) to enhance the ability of developing States, in particular the least-developed among them and small island developing States, to conserve and manage straddling fish stocks and highly migratory fish stocks and to develop their own fisheries for such stocks;
   (b) to assist developing States, in particular the least-developed among them and small island developing States, to enable them to participate in high seas fisheries for such stocks, including facilitating access to such fisheries subject to articles 5 and 11;
   (c) to facilitate the participation of developing States in subregional and regional fisheries management organisations and arrangements.
2. Cooperation with developing States for the purposes set out in this article shall include the provision of financial assistance, assistance relating to human resources development, technical assistance, transfer of technology, including through joint-venture arrangements, and advisory and consultative services.
3. Such assistance shall, inter alia, be directed specifically towards:
   (a) improved conservation and management of straddling fish stocks and highly migratory fish stocks through collection, reporting, verification, exchange and analysis of fisheries data and related information;
   (b) stock assessment and scientific research;
   (c) monitoring, control, surveillance, compliance and enforcement, including training and capacity-building at the local level, development and funding of national and regional observer programmes and access to technology and equipment.

Article 26 – Special assistance in the implementation of this Agreement

1. States shall cooperate to establish special funds to assist developing States in the implementation of this Agreement, including assisting developing States to meet the costs involved in any proceedings for the settlement of disputes to which they may be parties.

2. States and international organisations should assist developing States in establishing new subregional or regional fisheries management organisations or arrangements, or in strengthening existing organisations or arrangements, for the conservation and management of straddling fish stocks and highly migratory fish stocks.

PART VIII – PEACEFUL SETTLEMENT OF DISPUTES

Article 27 – Obligation to settle disputes by peaceful means

States have the obligation to settle their disputes by negotiation, inquiry, mediation, conciliation, arbitration, judicial settlement, resort to regional agencies or arrangements, or other peaceful means of their own choice.

Article 28 – Prevention of disputes

States shall cooperate in order to prevent disputes. To this end, States shall agree on efficient and expeditious decision-making procedures within subregional and regional fisheries management organisations and arrangements and shall strengthen existing decision-making procedures as necessary.

Article 29 – Disputes of a technical nature

Where a dispute concerns a matter of a technical nature, the States concerned may refer the dispute to an ad hoc expert panel established by them. The panel shall confer with the States concerned and shall endeavour to resolve the dispute expeditiously without recourse to binding procedures for the settlement of disputes.

Article 30 – Procedures for the settlement of disputes

1. The provisions relating to the settlement of disputes set out in Part XV of the Convention apply mutatis mutandis to any dispute between States Parties to this Agreement concerning the interpretation or application of this Agreement, whether or not they are also Parties to the Convention.
2. The provisions relating to the settlement of disputes set out in Part XV of the Convention apply mutatis mutandis to any dispute between States Parties to this Agreement concerning the interpretation or application of a subregional, regional or global fisheries agreement relating to straddling fish stocks or highly migratory fish stocks to which they are parties, including any dispute concerning the conservation and management of such stocks, whether or not they are also Parties to the Convention.
3. Any procedure accepted by a State Party to this Agreement and the Convention pursuant to article 287 of the Convention shall apply to the settlement of disputes under this Part, unless that State Party, when signing, ratifying or acceding to this Agreement, or at any time thereafter, has accepted another procedure pursuant to article 287 for the settlement of disputes under this Part.
4. A State Party to this Agreement which is not a Party to the Convention, when signing, ratifying or acceding to this Agreement, or at any time thereafter, shall be free to choose, by means of a written declaration, one or more of the means set out in article 287(1), of the Convention for the settlement of disputes under this Part. article 287 shall apply to such a declaration, as well as to any dispute to which such State is a party which is not covered by a declaration in force. For the purposes of conciliation and arbitration in accordance with Annexes V, VII and VIII to the Convention, such State shall be entitled to nominate conciliators, arbitrators and experts to be included in the lists referred to in Annex V, article 2, Annex VII, article 2, and Annex VIII, article 2, for the settlement of disputes under this Part.
5. Any court or tribunal to which a dispute has been submitted under this Part shall apply the relevant provisions of the Convention, of this Agreement and of any relevant subregional, regional or global fisheries agreement, as well as generally accepted standards for the conservation and management of living marine resources and other rules of international law not incompatible with the Convention, with a view to ensuring the conservation of the straddling fish stocks and highly migratory fish stocks concerned.

Article 31 – Provisional measures

1. Pending the settlement of a dispute in accordance with this Part, the parties to the dispute shall make every effort to enter into provisional arrangements of a practical nature.
2. Without prejudice to article 290 of the Convention, the court or tribunal to which the dispute has been submitted under this Part may prescribe any provisional measures which it considers appropriate under the circumstances to preserve the respective rights of the parties to the dispute or to prevent damage to the stocks in question, as well as in the circumstances referred to in article 7, paragraph 5, and article 16, paragraph 2.
3. A State Party to this Agreement which is not a Party to the Convention may declare that, notwithstanding article 290(5), of the Convention, the International Tribunal for the Law of the Sea shall not be entitled to prescribe, modify or revoke provisional measures without the agreement of such State.

Article 32 – Limitations on applicability of procedures for the settlement of disputes

Article 297, paragraph 3, of the Convention applies also to this Agreement.

PART IX – NON-PARTIES TO THIS AGREEMENT

Article 33 – Non-parties to this Agreement

1. States Parties shall encourage non-parties to this Agreement to become parties thereto and to adopt laws and regulations consistent with its provisions.

2. States Parties shall take measures consistent with this Agreement and international law to deter the activities of vessels flying the flag of non-parties which undermine the effective implementation of this Agreement.

PART X – GOOD FAITH AND ABUSE OF RIGHTS

Article 34 – Good faith and abuse of rights

States Parties shall fulfil in good faith the obligations assumed under this Agreement and shall exercise the rights recognised in this Agreement in a manner which would not constitute an abuse of right.

PART XI – RESPONSIBILITY AND LIABILITY

Article 35 – Responsibility and liability

States Parties are liable in accordance with international law for damage or loss attributable to them in regard to this Agreement.

PART XII – REVIEW CONFERENCE

Article 36 – Review conference

1. Four years after the date of entry into force of this Agreement, the Secretary-General of the United Nations shall convene a conference with a view to assessing the effectiveness of this Agreement in securing the conservation and management of straddling fish stocks and highly migratory fish stocks. The Secretary-General shall invite to the conference all States Parties and those States and entities which are entitled to become Parties to this Agreement as well as those intergovernmental and non-governmental organisations entitled to participate as observers.
2. The Conference shall review and assess the adequacy of the provisions of this Agreement and, if necessary, propose means of strengthening the substance and methods of implementation of those provisions in order better to address any continuing problems in the conservation and management of straddling fish stocks and highly migratory fish stocks.

PART XIII – FINAL PROVISIONS

Article 37 – Signature

This Agreement shall be open for signature by all States and the other entities referred to in article 1, paragraph 2 (b), and shall remain open for signature at United Nations Headquarters for 12 months from the 4 December 1995.

Article 38 – Ratification

This Agreement is subject to ratification by States and the other entities referred to in article 1, paragraph 2 (b). The instruments of ratification shall be deposited with the Secretary-General of the United Nations.

Article 39 – Accession

This Agreement shall remain open for accession by States and the other entities referred to in article 1, paragraph 2 (b). The instruments of accession shall be deposited with the Secretary-General of the United Nations.

Article 40 – Entry into force

1. This Agreement shall enter into force 30 days after the date of deposit of the 30th instrument of ratification or accession.
2. For each State or entity which ratifies the Agreement or accedes thereto after the deposit of the 30th instrument of ratification or accession, this Agreement shall enter into force on the 30th day following the deposit of its instrument of ratification or accession.

Article 41 – Provisional application

1. This Agreement shall be applied provisionally by a State or entity which consents to its provisional application by so notifying the depositary in writing. Such provisional application shall become effective from the date of receipt of the notification.
2. Provisional application by a State or entity shall terminate on the entry into force of this agreement for that State or entity or on notification by that State or entity to the depositary in writing of its intention to terminate provisional application.

Article 42 – Reservations and exceptions

No reservations or exceptions may be made to this Agreement.

Article 43 – Declarations and statements

Article 42 does not preclude a State or entity, when signing, ratifying or acceding to this Agreement, from making declarations or statements, however phrased or named, with a view, inter alia, to the harmonisation of its laws and regulations with the provisions of this Agreement, provided that such declarations or statements do not purport to exclude or to modify the legal effect of the provisions of this Agreement in their application to that State or entity.

Article 44 – Relation to other agreements

1. This Agreement shall not alter the rights and obligations of States Parties which arise from other agreements compatible with this Agreement and which do not affect the enjoyment by other States Parties of their rights or the performance of their obligations under this Agreement.
2. Two or more States Parties may conclude agreements modifying or suspending the operation of provisions of this Agreement, applicable solely to the relations between them, provided that such agreements do not relate to a provision derogation from which is incompatible with the effective execution of the object and purpose of this Agreement, and provided further that such agreements shall not affect the application of the basic principles embodied herein, and that the provisions of such agreements do not affect the enjoyment by other States Parties of their rights or the performance of their obligations under this Agreement.
3. States Parties intending to conclude an agreement referred to in paragraph 2 shall notify the other States Parties through the depositary of this Agree-

ment of their intention to conclude the agreement and of the modification or suspension for which it provides.

Article 45 – Amendment

1. A State Party may, by written communication addressed to the Secretary-General of the United Nations, propose amendments to this Agreement and request the convening of a conference to consider such proposed amendments. The Secretary-General shall circulate such communication to all States Parties. If, within six months from the date of the circulation of the communication, not less than one half of the States Parties reply favourably to the request, the Secretary-General shall convene the conference.
2. The decision-making procedure applicable at the amendment conference convened pursuant to paragraph 1 shall be the same as that applicable at the United Nations Conference on Straddling Fish Stocks and Highly Migratory Fish Stocks, unless otherwise decided by the conference. The conference should make every effort to reach agreement on any amendments by way of consensus and there should be no voting on them until all efforts at consensus have been exhausted.
3. Once adopted, amendments to this agreement shall be open for signature at United Nations Headquarters by States Parties for 12 months from the date of adoption, unless otherwise provided in the amendment itself.
4. Articles 38, 39, 47 and 50 apply to all amendments to this Agreement.
5. Amendments to this Agreement shall enter into force for the States Parties ratifying or acceding to them on the 30th day following the deposit of instruments of ratification or accession by two thirds of the States Parties. Thereafter, for each State Party ratifying or acceding to an amendment after the deposit of the required number of such instruments, the amendment shall enter into force on the 30th day following the deposit of its instrument of ratification or accession.
6. An amendment may provide that a smaller or a larger number of ratifications or accessions shall be required for its entry into force than are required by this article.
7. A State which becomes a Party to this Agreement after the entry into force of amendments in accordance with paragraph 5 shall, failing an expression of a different intention by that State:
   (a) be considered as a Party to this Agreement as so amended;
   (b) be considered as a Party to the unamended Agreement in relation to any State Party not bound by the amendment.

Article 46 – Denunciation

1. A State Party may, by written notification addressed to the Secretary-General of the United Nations, denounce this Agreement and may indicate its reasons. Failure to indicate reasons shall not affect the validity of the denunciation. The denunciation shall take effect one year after the date of receipt of the notification, unless the notification specifies a later date.
2. The denunciation shall not in any way affect the duty of any State Party to fulfil any obligation embodied in this Agreement to which it would be subject under international law independently of this Agreement.

Article 47 – Participation by international organisations

1. In cases where an international organisation referred to in Annex IX, article 1, of the Convention does not have competence over all the matters governed by this Agreement, Annex IX to the Convention shall apply mutatis mutandis to participation by such international organisation in this Agreement, except that the following provisions of that Annex shall not apply:
   (a) article 2, first sentence;
   (b) article 3, paragraph 1.
2. In cases where an international organisation referred to in Annex IX, article 1, of the Convention has competence over all the matters governed by this Agreement, the following provisions shall apply to participation by such international organisation in this Agreement:
   (a) at the time of signature or accession, such international organisation shall make a declaration stating:
      (i) that it has competence over all the matters governed by this Agreement;
      (ii) that, for this reason, its Member States shall not become States Parties, except in respect of their territories for which the international organisation has no responsibility;
      (iii) that it accepts the rights and obligations of States under this Agreement;
   (b) participation of such an international organisation shall in no case confer any rights under this Agreement on Member States of the international organisation;
   (c) in the event of a conflict between the obligations of an international organisation under this Agreement and its obligations under the agreement establishing the international organisation or any acts relating to it, the obligations under this Agreement shall prevail.

Article 48 – Annexes

1. The Annexes form an integral part of this Agreement and, unless expressly provided otherwise, a reference to this Agreement or to one of its Parts includes a reference to the Annexes relating thereto.
2. The Annexes may be revised from time to time by States Parties. Such revisions shall be based on scientific and technical considerations. Notwithstanding the provisions of article 45, if a revision

to an Annex is adopted by consensus at a meeting of States Parties, it shall be incorporated in this Agreement and shall take effect from the date of its adoption or from such other date as may be specified in the revision. If a revision to an Annex is not adopted by consensus at such a meeting, the amendment procedures set out in article 45 shall apply.

Article 49 – Depositary

The Secretary-General of the United Nations shall be the depositary of this Agreement and any amendments or revisions thereto.

Article 50 – Authentic texts

The Arabic, Chinese, English, French, Russian and Spanish texts of this Agreement are equally authentic.

In witness whereof, the undersigned Plenipotentiaries, being duly authorised thereto, have signed this Agreement.

Opened for signature at New York, this fourth day of December, one thousand nine hundred and ninety-five, in a single original, in the Arabic, Chinese, English, French, Russian and Spanish languages.

Annex I – STANDARD REQUIREMENTS FOR THE COLLECTION AND SHARING OF DATA

Article 1 – General principles

1. The timely collection, compilation and analysis of data are fundamental to the effective conservation and management of straddling fish stocks and highly migratory fish stocks. To this end, data from fisheries for these stocks on the high seas and those in areas under national jurisdiction are required and should be collected and compiled in such a way as to enable statistically meaningful analysis for the purposes of fishery resource conservation and management. These data include catch and fishing effort statistics and other fishery-related information, such as vessel-related and other data for standardising fishing effort. Data collected should also include information on non-target and associated or dependent species. All data should be verified to ensure accuracy. Confidentiality of non-aggregated data shall be maintained. The dissemination of such data shall be subject to the terms on which they have been provided.
2. Assistance, including training as well as financial and technical assistance, shall be provided to developing States in order to build capacity in the field of conservation and management of living marine resources. Assistance should focus on enhancing capacity to implement data collection and verification, observer programmes, data analysis and research projects supporting stock assessments. The fullest possible involvement of developing State scientists and managers in conservation and management of straddling fish stocks and highly migratory fish stocks should be promoted.

Article 2 – Principles of data collection, compilation and exchange

The following general principles should be considered in defining the parameters for collection, compilation and exchange of data from fishing operations for straddling fish stocks and highly migratory fish stocks:

(a) States should ensure that data are collected from vessels flying their flag on fishing activities according to the operational characteristics of each fishing method (e.g., each individual tow for trawl, each set for long-line and purse-seine, each school fished for pole-and-line and each day fished for troll) and in sufficient detail to facilitate effective stock assessment;

(b) States should ensure that fishery data are verified through an appropriate system;

(c) States should compile fishery-related and other supporting scientific data and provide them in an agreed format and in a timely manner to the relevant subregional or regional fisheries management organisation or arrangement where one exists. Otherwise, States should cooperate to exchange data either directly or through such other cooperative mechanisms as may be agreed among them;

(d) States should agree, within the framework of subregional or regional fisheries management organisations or arrangements, or otherwise, on the specification of data and the format in which they are to be provided, in accordance with this Annex and taking into account the nature of the stocks and the fisheries for those stocks in the region. Such organisations or arrangements should request non-members or non-participants to provide data concerning relevant fishing activities by vessels flying their flag;

(e) such organisations or arrangements shall compile data and make them available in a timely manner and in an agreed format to all interested States under the terms and conditions established by the organisation or arrangement; and

(f) scientists of the flag State and from the relevant subregional or regional fisheries management organisation or arrangement should analyse the data separately or jointly, as appropriate.

Article 3 – Basic fishery data

1. States shall collect and make available to the relevant subregional or regional fisheries management organisation or arrangement the following types of data in sufficient detail to facilitate effective stock assessment in accordance with agreed procedures:
   (a) time series of catch and effort statistics by fishery and fleet;
   (b) total catch in number, nominal weight, or both, by species (both target and non-target) as is appropriate to each fishery. (Nominal weight is defined by the Food and Agriculture Organisation of the United Nations as the live-weight equivalent of the landings);
   (c) discard statistics, including estimates where necessary, reported as number or nominal

weight by species, as is appropriate to each fishery;

(d) effort statistics appropriate to each fishing method;

(e) fishing location, date and time fished and other statistics on fishing operations as appropriate.

2. States shall also collect where appropriate and provide to the relevant subregional or regional fisheries management organisation or arrangement information to support stock assessment, including:

(a) composition of the catch according to length, weight and sex;

(b) other biological information supporting stock assessments, such as information on age, growth, recruitment, distribution and stock identity;

(c) other relevant research, including surveys of abundance, biomass surveys, hydro-acoustic surveys, research on environmental factors affecting stock abundance, and oceanographic and ecological studies.

Article 4 – Vessel data and information

1. States should collect the following types of vessel-related data for standardising fleet composition and vessel fishing power and for converting between different measures of effort in the analysis of catch and effort data:

(a) vessel identification, flag and port of registry;

(b) vessel type;

(c) vessel specifications (e.g., material of construction, date built, registered length, gross registered tonnage, power of main engines, hold capacity and catch storage methods);

(d) fishing gear description (e.g., types, gear specifications and quantity).

2. The flag State will collect the following information:

(a) navigation and position fixing aids;

(b) communication equipment and international radio call sign;

(c) crew size.

Article 5 – Reporting

A State shall ensure that vessels flying its flag sends to its national fisheries administration and, where agreed, to the relevant sub regional or regional fisheries management organisation or arrangement, logbook-data on catch and effort, including data on fishing operations on the high seas, at sufficiently frequent intervals to meet national requirements and regional and international obligations. Such data shall be transmitted, where necessary, by radio, telex, fax or satellite transmission or by other means.

Article 6 – Data verification

States or, as appropriate, subregional or regional fisheries management organisations or arrangements should establish mechanisms for verifying fishery data, such as:

(a) position verification through vessel monitoring systems;

(b) scientific observer programmes to monitor catch, effort, catch composition (target and non-target) and other details of fishing operations;

(c) vessel trip, landing and transshipment reports;

(d) port sampling.

Article 7 – Data exchange

1. Data collected by flag States must be shared with other flag States and relevant coastal States through appropriate subregional or regional fisheries management organisations or arrangements. Such organisations or arrangements shall compile data and make them available in a timely manner and in an agreed format to all interested States under the terms and conditions established by the organisation or arrangement, while maintaining confidentiality of non-aggregated data, and should, to the extent feasible, develop database systems which provide efficient access to data.

2. At the global level, collection and dissemination of data should be effected through the Food and Agriculture Organisation of the United Nations. Where a subregional or regional fisheries management organisation or arrangement does not exist, that organization may also do the same at the subregional or regional level by arrangement with the States concerned.

Annex II – GUIDELINES FOR THE APPLICATION OF PRECAUTIONARY REFERENCE POINTS IN CONSERVATION AND MANAGEMENT OF STRADDLING FISH STOCKS AND HIGHLY MIGRATORY FISH STOCKS

1. A precautionary reference point is an estimated value derived through an agreed scientific procedure, which corresponds to the state of the resource and of the fishery, and which can be used as a guide for fisheries management.

2. Two types of precautionary reference points should be used: conservation, or limit, reference points and management, or target, reference points. Limit reference points set boundaries which are intended to constrain harvesting within safe biological limits within which the stocks can produce maximum sustainable yield. Target reference points are intended to meet management objectives.

3. Precautionary reference points should be stock-specific to account, inter alia, for the reproductive capacity, the resilience of each stock and the characteristics of fisheries exploiting the stock, as well as other sources of mortality and major sources of uncertainty.

4. Management strategies shall seek to maintain or restore populations of harvested stocks, and where necessary associated or dependent species, at levels consistent with previously agreed precautionary reference points. Such reference points shall be used to trigger pre-agreed conservation and

management action. Management strategies shall include measures which can be implemented when precautionary reference points are approached.

5. Fishery management strategies shall ensure that the risk of exceeding limit reference points is very low. If a stock falls below a limit reference point or is at risk of falling below such a reference point, conservation and management action should be initiated to facilitate stock recovery. Fishery management strategies shall ensure that target reference points are not exceeded on average.
6. When information for determining reference points for a fishery is poor or absent, provisional reference points shall be set. Provisional reference points may be established by analogy to similar and better-known stocks. In such situations, the fishery shall be subject to enhanced monitoring so as to enable revision of provisional reference points as improved information becomes available.
7. The fishing mortality rate which generates maximum sustainable yield should be regarded as a minimum standard for limit reference points. For stocks which are not overfished, fishery management strategies shall ensure that fishing mortality does not exceed that which corresponds to maximum sustainable yield, and that the biomass does not fall below a predefined threshold. For overfished stocks, the biomass which would produce maximum sustainable yield can serve as a rebuilding target.

8.3.3. BBNJ Treaty 2023

Agreement under the United Nations Convention on the Law of the Sea on the Conservation and Sustainable Use of Marine Biological Diversity of Areas beyond National Jurisdiction, 19 June 2023, UN Doc. A/CONF.232/2023/4

The Parties to this Agreement,

Recalling the relevant provisions of the United Nations Convention on the Law of the Sea of 10 December 1982, including the obligation to protect and preserve the marine environment,

Stressing the need to respect the balance of rights, obligations and interests se t out in the Convention,

Recognizing the need to address, in a coherent and cooperative manner, biological diversity loss and degradation of ecosystems of the ocean, due, in particular, to climate change impacts on marine ecosystems, such as warming and ocean deoxygenation, as well as ocean acidification, pollution, including plastic pollution, and unsustainable use,

Conscious of the need for the comprehensive global regime under the Convention to better address the conservation and sustainable use of marine biological diversity of areas beyond national jurisdiction,

Recognizing the importance of contributing to the realization of a just and equitable international economic order which takes into account the interests and needs of humankind as a whole and, in particular, the special interests and needs of developing States, whether coastal or landlocked,

Recognizing also that support for developing States Parties through capacity-building and the development and transfer of marine technology are essential elements for the attainment of the objectives of the conservation and sustainable use of marine biological diversity of areas beyond national jurisdiction,

Recalling the United Nations Declaration on the Rights of Indigenous Peoples,

Affirming that nothing in this Agreement shall be construed as diminishing or extinguishing the existing rights of Indigenous Peoples, including as set out in the United Nations Declaration on the Rights of Indigenous Peoples, or of, as appropriate, local communities,

Recognizing the obligation set out in the Convention to assess, as far as practicable, the potential effects on the marine environment of activities under a State's jurisdiction or control when the State has reasonable grounds for believing that such activities may cause substantial pollution of or significant and harmful changes to the marine environment,

Mindful of the obligation set out in the Convention to take all measures necessary to ensure that pollution arising from incidents or activities does not spread beyond the areas where sovereign rights are exercised in accordance with the Convention,

Desiring to act as stewards of the ocean in areas beyond national jurisdiction on behalf of present and future generations by protecting, caring for and ensuring responsible use of the marine environment, maintaining the integrity of ocean ecosystems and conserving the inherent value of biological diversity of areas beyond national jurisdiction,

Acknowledging that the generation of, access to and utilization of digital sequence information on marine genetic resources of areas beyond national jurisdiction, together with the fair and equitable sharing of benefits arising from its utilization, contribute to research and innovation and to the genera l objective of this Agreement,

Respecting the sovereignty, territorial integrity and political independence of all States,

Recalling that the legal status of non-parties to the Convention or any other related agreements is governed by the rules of the law of treaties,

Recalling also that, as set out in the Convention, States are responsible for the fulfilment of their international obligations concerning the protection and preservation of the marine environment and may be liable in accordance with international law,

Committed to achieving sustainable development,

Aspiring to achieve universal participation,

Have agreed as follows:

PART I – GENERAL PROVISIONS

Article 1 – Use of terms

For the purposes of this Agreement:

1. "Area-based management tool" means a tool, including a marine protected area, for a geographically defined area through which one or several sectors or activities are managed with the aim of achieving particular conservation and sustainable use objectives in accordance with this Agreement.
2. "Areas beyond national jurisdiction" means the high seas and the Area.
3. "Biotechnology" means any technological application that uses biological systems, living organisms, or derivatives thereof, to make or modify products or processes for specific use.
4. "Collection in situ", in relation to marine genetic resources, means the collection or sampling of marine genetic resources in areas beyond national jurisdiction.
5. "Convention" means the United Nations Convention on the Law of the Sea of 10 December 1982.
6. "Cumulative impacts" means the combined and incremental impacts resulting from different activities, including known past and present and reasonably foreseeable activities, or from the repetition of similar activities over time, and the consequences

of climate change, ocean acidification and related impacts .

7. "Environmental impact assessment" means a process to identify and evaluate the potential impacts of an activity to inform decision-making.
8. "Marine genetic resources" means any material of marine plant, animal, microbial or other origin containing functional units of heredity of actual or potential value.
9. "Marine protected area" means a geographically defined marine area that is designated and managed to achieve specific long-term biological diversity conservation objectives and may allow, where appropriate, sustainable use provided it is consistent with the conservation objectives.
10. "Marine technology" includes, inter alia, information and data, provided in a user-friendly format, on marine sciences and related marine operations and services; manuals, guidelines, criteria, standards and reference materials; sampling and methodology equipment; observation facilities and equipment for in situ and laboratory observations, analysis and experimentation; computer and computer software, including models and modelling techniques; related biotechnology; and expertise, knowledge, skills, technical, scientific and legal know-how and analytical methods related to the conservation and sustainable use of marine biological diversity.
11. "Party" means a State or regional economic integration organization that has consented to be bound by this Agreement and for which this Agreement is in force.
12. "Regional economic integration organization" means an organization constituted by sovereign States of a given region to which its member States have transferred competence in respect of matters governed by this Agreement and which has been duly authorized, in accordance with its internal procedures, to sign, ratify, approve, accept or accede to this Agreement.
13. "Sustainable use" means the use of components of biological diversity in a way and at a rate that does not lead to a long-term decline of biological diversity, thereby maintaining its potential to meet the needs and aspirations of prese nt and future generations.
14. "Utilization of marine genetic resources" means to conduct research and development on the genetic and/or biochemical composition of marine genetic resources, including through the application of biotechnology, as defined in paragraph 3 above.

Article 2 – General objective

The objective of this Agreement is to ensure the conservation and sustainable use of marine biological diversity of areas beyond national jurisdiction, for the present and in the long term, through effective implementation of the relevant provisions of the Convention and further international cooperation and coordination.

Article 3 – Scope of application

This Agreement applies to areas beyond national jurisdiction.

Article 4 – Exceptions

This Agreement does not apply to any warship, military aircraft or naval auxiliary. Except for Part II, this Agreement does not apply to other vessels or aircraft owned or operated by a Party and used, for the time being, only on government non-commercial service. However, each Party shall ensure, by the adoption of appropriate measures not impairing the operations or operational capabilities of such vessels or aircraft owned or operated by it, that such vessels or aircraft act in a manner consistent, so far as is reasonable and practicable, with this Agreement.

Article 5 – Relationship between this Agreement and the Convention and relevant legal instruments and frameworks and relevant global, regional, subregional and sectoral bodies

1. This Agreement shall be interpreted and applied in the context of and in a manner consistent with the Convention. Nothing in this Agreement shall prejudice the rights, jurisdiction and duties of States under the Convention, including in respect of the exclusive economic zone and the continental shelf within and beyond 200 nautical miles.
2. This Agreement shall be interpreted and applied in a manner that does not undermine relevant legal instruments and frameworks and relevant global, regional, subregional and sectoral bodies and that promotes coherence and coordination with those instruments, frameworks and bodies.
3. The legal status of non-parties to the Convention or any other related agreements with regard to those instruments is not affected by this Agreement.

Article 6 – Without prejudice

This Agreement, including any decision or recommendation of the Conference of the Parties or any of its subsidiary bodies, and any acts, measures or activities undertaken on the basis thereof, shall be without prejudice to, and shall not be relied upon as a basis for asserting or denying any claims to, sovereignty, sovereign rights or jurisdiction, including in respect of any disputes relating thereto .

Article 7 – General principles and approaches

In order to achieve the objectives of this Agreement, Parties shall be guided by the following principles and approaches:

(a) The polluter-pays principle;

(b) The principle of the common heritage of humankind which is set out in the Convention;

(c) The freedom of marine scientific research, together with other freedoms of the high seas;

(d) The principle of equity and the fair and equitable sharing of benefits;

(e) The precautionary principle or precautionary approach, as appropriate;

(f) An ecosystem approach;

(g) An integrated approach to ocean management;

(h) An approach that builds ecosystem resilience, including to adverse effects of climate change and ocean acidification, and also maintains and restores ecosystem integrity, including the carbon cycling services that underpin the role of the ocean in climate;

(i) The use of the best available science and scientific information;

(j) The use of relevant traditional knowledge of Indigenous Peoples and local communities, where available;

(k) The respect, promotion and consideration of their respective obligations, as applicable, relating to the rights of Indigenous Peoples or of, as appropriate, local communities when taking action to address the conservation and sustainable use of marine biological diversity of areas beyond national jurisdiction;

(l) The non-transfer, directly or indirectly, of damage or hazards from one area to another and the non-transformation of one type of pollution into another in taking measures to prevent, reduce and control pollution of the marine environment;

(m) Full recognition of the special circumstances of small island developing States and of least developed countries;

(n) Acknowledgement of the special interests and needs of landlocked developing countries.

Article 8 – International cooperation

1. Parties shall cooperate under this Agreement for the conservation and sustainable use of marine biological diversity of areas beyond national jurisdiction, including through strengthening and enhancing cooperation with and promoting cooperation among relevant legal instruments and frameworks and relevant global, regional, subregional and sectoral bodies in the achievement of the objective s of this Agreement.
2. Parties shall endeavour to promote, as appropriate, the objectives of this Agreement when participating in decision-making under other relevant legal instruments, frameworks, or global, regional, subregional or sectoral bodies .
3. Parties shall promote international cooperation in marine scientific research and in the development and transfer of marine technology consistent with the Convention in support of the objectives of this Agreement.

PART II – MARINE GENETIC RESOURCES, INCLUDING THE FAIR AND EQUITABLE SHARING OF BENEFITS

Article 9 – Objectives

The objectives of this Part are:

(a) The fair and equitable sharing of benefits arising from activities with respect to marine genetic resources and digital sequence information on marine genetic resources of areas beyond national jurisdiction for the conservation and sustainable use of marine biological diversity of areas beyond national jurisdiction;

(b) The building and development of the capacity of Parties, particularly developing States Parties, in particular the least developed countries, landlocked developing countries, geographically disadvantaged States, small island developing States, coastal African States, archipelagic States and developing middle-income countries, to carry out activities with respect to marine genetic resources and digital sequence information on marine genetic resources of areas beyond national jurisdiction;

(c) The generation of knowledge, scientific understanding and technological innovation, including through the development and conduct of marine scientific research, as fundamental contributions to the implementation of this Agreement;

(d) The development and transfer of marine technology in accordance with this Agreement.

Article 10 – Application

1. The provisions of this Agreement shall apply to activities with respect to marine genetic resources and digital sequence information on marine genetic resources of areas beyond national jurisdiction collected and generated after the entry into force of this Agreement for the respective Party. The application of the pro visions of this Agreement shall extend to the utilization of marine genetic resources and digital sequence information on marine genetic resources of areas beyond national jurisdiction collected or generated before entry into force, unless a Party makes an exception in writing under article 70 when signing, ratifying, approving, accepting or acceding to this Agreement.
2. The provisions of this Part shall not apply to:
   (a) Fishing regulated under relevant international law and fishing -related activities; or
   (b) Fish or other living marine resources known to have been taken in fishing and fishing-related activities from areas beyond national jurisdiction, except where such fish or other living marine resources are regulated as utilization under this Part.
3. The obligations in this Part shall not apply to a Party's military activities, including military activities by government vessels and aircraft engaged in non-commercial service. The obligations in this Part with respect to the utilization of marine genetic resources and digital sequence information on marine genetic resources of areas beyond national jurisdiction shall apply to a Party's non -military activities.

Article 11 – Activities with respect to marine genetic resources of areas beyond national jurisdiction

1. Activities with respect to marine genetic resources and digital sequence information on marine genetic resources of areas beyond national jurisdiction may be carried out by all Parties, irrespective of their geographical location, and by natural or juridical persons under the jurisdiction of the Parties.

Such activities shall be carried out in accordance with this Agreement.

2. Parties shall promote cooperation in all activities with respect to marine genetic resources and digital sequence information on marine genetic resources of areas beyond national jurisdiction.
3. Collection in situ of marine genetic resources of areas beyond national jurisdiction shall be carried out with due regard for the rights and legitimate interests of coastal States in areas within their national jurisdiction and with due regard for the interests of other States in areas beyond national jurisdiction, in accordance with the Convention. To this end, Parties shall endeavour to cooperate, as appropriate, including through specific modalities for the operation of the Clearing-House Mechanism determined under article 51, with a view to implementing this Agreement.
4. No State shall claim or exercise sovereignty or sovereign rights over marine genetic resources of areas beyond national jurisdiction. No such claim or exercise of sovereignty or sovereign rights shall be recognized.
5. Collection in situ of marine genetic resources of areas beyond national jurisdiction shall not constitute the legal basis for any claim to any part of the marine environment or its resources.
6. Activities with respect to marine genetic resources and digital sequence information on marine genetic resources of areas beyond national jurisdiction are in the interests of all States and for the benefit of all humanity, particularly for the benefit of advancing the scientific knowledge of humanity and promoting the conservation and sustainable use of marine biological diversity, taking into particular consideration the interests and needs of developing States.
7. Activities with respect to marine genetic resources and digital sequence information on marine genetic resources of areas beyond national jurisdiction shall be carried out exclusively for peaceful purposes.

Article 12 – Notification on activities with respect to marine genetic resources and digital sequence information on marine genetic resources of areas beyond national jurisdiction

1. Parties shall take the necessary legislative, administrative or policy measures to ensure that information is notified to the Clearing-House Mechanism in accordance with this Part.
2. The following information shall be notified to the Clearing -House Mechanism six months or as early as possible prior to the collection in situ of marine genetic resources of areas beyond national jurisdiction:
   (a) The nature and objectives under which the collection is carried out, including, as appropriate, any programme(s) of which it forms part;
   (b) The subject matter of the research or, if known, the marine genetic resources to be targeted or collected, and the purposes for which such resources will be collected;
   (c) The geographical areas in which the collection is to be undertaken;
   (d) A summary of the method and means to be used for collection, including the name, tonnage, type and class of vessels, scientific equipment and/or study methods employed;
   (e) Information concerning any other contributions to proposed major programmes;
   (f) The expected date of first appearance and final departure of the research vessels, or deployment of the equipment and its removal, as appropriate;
   (g) The name(s) of the sponsoring institution(s) and the person in charge of the project;
   (h) Opportunities for scientists of all States, in particular scientists from developing States, to be involved in or associated with the project;
   (i) The extent to which it is considered that States that may need and request technical assistance, in particular developing States, should be able to participate or to be represented in the project;
   (j) A data management plan prepared according to open and responsible data governance, taking into account current international practice.
3. Upon notification referred to in paragraph 2 above, the Clearing -House Mechanism shall automatically generate a "BBNJ" standardized batch identifier.
4. Where there is a material change to the information provided to the Clearing - House Mechanism prior to the planned collection, updated information shall be notified to the Clearing-House Mechanism within a reasonable period of time and no later than the start of collection in situ, when practicable.
5. Parties shall ensure that the following information, along with the "BBNJ" standardized batch identifier, is notified to the Clearing-House Mechanism as soon as it becomes available, but no later than one year from the collection in situ of marine genetic resources of areas beyond national jurisdiction:
   (a) The repository or database where digital sequence information on marine genetic resources is or will be deposited;
   (b) Where all marine genetic resources collected in situ are or will be deposited or held;
   (c) A report detailing the geographical area from which marine genetic resources were collected, including information on the latitude, longitude and depth of collection, and, to the extent available, the findings from the activity undertaken;
   (d) Any necessary updates to the data management plan provided under paragraph (2) (j) above.
6. Parties shall ensure that samples of marine genetic resources and digital sequence information on marine genetic resources of areas beyond national jurisdiction that are in repositories or databases under their jurisdiction can be identified as origi-

nating from areas beyond national jurisdiction, in accordance with current international practice and to the extent practicable.

7. Parties shall ensure that repositories, to the extent practicable, and databases under their jurisdiction prepare, on a biennial basis, an aggregate report on access to marine genetic resources and digital sequence information linked to their "BBNJ" standardized batch identifier, and make the report available to the access and benefit-sharing committee established under article 15.
8. Where marine genetic resources of areas beyond national jurisdiction, and where practicable, the digital sequence information on such resources are subject to utilization, including commercialization, by natural or juridical persons under their jurisdiction, Parties shall ensure that the following information, including the "BBNJ" standardized batch identifier, if available, be notified to the Clearing-House Mechanism as soon as such information becomes available:
   (a) Where the results of the utilization, such as publications, patents granted, if available and to the extent possible, and products developed, can be found;
   (b) Where available, details of the post-collection notification to the Clearing- House Mechanism related to the marine genetic resources that were the subject of utilization;
   (c) Where the original sample that is the subject of utilization is held;
   (d) The modalities envisaged for access to marine genetic resources and digital sequence information on marine genetic resources being utilized, and a data management plan for the same;
   (e) Once marketed, information, if available, on sales of relevant products and any further development.

Article 13 – Traditional knowledge of Indigenous Peoples and local communities associated with marine genetic resources in areas beyond national jurisdiction

Parties shall take legislative, administrative or policy measures, where relevant and as appropriate, with the aim of ensuring that traditional knowledge associated with marine genetic resources in areas beyond national jurisdiction that is held by Indigenous Peoples and local communities shall only be accessed with the free, prior and informed consent or approval and involvement of these Indigenous Peoples and local communities. Access to such traditional knowledge may be facilitated by the Clearing-House Mechanism. Access to and use of such traditional knowledge shall be on mutually agreed terms.

Article 14 – Fair and equitable sharing of benefits

1. The benefits arising from activities with respect to marine genetic resources and digital sequence information on marine genetic resources of areas beyond national jurisdiction shall be shared in a fair and equitable manner in accordance with this Part and contribute to the conservation and sustainable use of marine biological diversity of areas beyond national jurisdiction.
2. Non-monetary benefits shall be shared in accordance with this Agreement in the form of, inter alia:
   (a) Access to samples and sample collections in accordance with current international practice;
   (b) Access to digital sequence information in accordance with current international practice;
   (c) Open access to findable, accessible, interoperable and reusable (FAIR) scientific data in accordance with current international practice and open and responsible data governance;
   (d) Information contained in the notifications, along with "BBNJ" standardized batch identifiers, provided in accordance with article 12, in publicly searchable and accessible forms;
   (e) Transfer of marine technology in line with relevant modalities provided under Part V of this Agreement;
   (f) Capacity-building, including by financing research programmes, and partnership opportunities, particularly directly relevant and substantial ones, for scientists and researchers in research projects, as well as dedicated initiatives, in particular for developing States, taking into account the special circumstances of small island developing States and of least developed countries;
   (g) Increased technical and scientific cooperation, in particular with scientists from and scientific institutions in developing States;
   (h) Other forms of benefits as determined by the Conference of the Parties, taking into account recommendations of the access and benefit-sharing committee established under article 15.
3. Parties shall take the necessary legislative, administrative or policy measures to ensure that marine genetic resources and digital sequence information on marine genetic resources of areas beyond national jurisdiction, together with their "BBNJ" standardized batch identifiers, subject to utilization by natural or juridical persons under their jurisdiction are deposited in publicly accessible repositories and databases, maintained either nationally or internationally, no later than three years from the start of such utilization, or as soon as they become available, taking into account current international practice.
4. Access to marine genetic resources and digital sequence information on marine genetic resources of areas beyond national jurisdiction in the repositories and databases under a Party's jurisdiction may be subject to reasonable conditions, as follows:
   (a) The need to preserve the physical integrity of marine genetic resources;
   (b) The reasonable costs associated with maintaining the relevant gene bank, biorepository or da-

tabase in which the sample, data or information is held;

(c) The reasonable costs associated with providing access to the marine genetic resource, data or information;

(d) Other reasonable conditions in line with the objectives of this Agreement;

and opportunities for such access on fair and most favourable terms, including on concessional and preferential terms, may be provided to researchers and research institutions from developing States.

5. Monetary benefits from the utilization of marine genetic resources and digital sequence information on marine genetic resources of areas beyond national jurisdiction, including commercialization, shall be shared fairly and equitably, through the financial mechanism established under article 52, for the conservation and sustainable use of marine biological diversity of areas beyond national jurisdiction.

6. After the entry into force of this Agreement, developed Parties shall make annual contributions to the special fund referred to in article 52. A Party's rate of contribution shall be 50 per cent of that Party's assessed contribution to the budget adopted by the Conference of the Parties under article 47, paragraph 6 (e). Such payment shall continue until a decision is taken by the Conference of the Parties under paragraph 7 below.

7. The Conference of the Parties shall decide on the modalities for the sharing of monetary benefits from the utilization of marine genetic resources and digital sequence information on marine genetic resources of areas beyond national jurisdiction, taking into account the recommendations of the access and benefit-sharing committee established under article 15. If all efforts to reach consensus have been exhausted, a decision shall be adopted by a three-fourths majority of the Parties present and voting. The payments shall be made through the special fund established under article 52. The modalities may include the following:

   (a) Milestone payments;

   (b) Payments or contributions related to the commercialization of products, including payment of a percentage of the revenue from sales of products;

   (c) A tiered fee, paid on a periodic basis, based on a diversified set of indicators measuring the aggregate level of activities by a Party;

   (d) Other forms as decided by the Conference of the Parties, taking into account recommendations of the access and benefit-sharing committee.

8. A Party may make a declaration at the time the Conference of the Parties adopts the modalities stating that those modalities shall not take effect for that Party for a period of up to four years, in order to allow time for necessary implementation. A Party that makes such a declaration shall continue to make the payment set out in paragraph 6 above until the new modalities take effect.

9. In deciding on the modalities for the sharing of monetary benefits from the use of digital sequence information on marine genetic resources of areas beyond national jurisdiction under paragraph 7 above, the Conference of the Parties shall take into account the recommendations of the access and benefit-sharing committee, recognizing that such modalities should be mutually supportive of and adaptable to other access and benefit-sharing instruments.

10. The Conference of the Parties, taking into account recommendations of the access and benefit-sharing committee established under article 15, shall review and assess, on a biennial basis, the monetary benefits from the utilization of marine genetic resources and digital sequence information on marine genetic resources of areas beyond national jurisdiction. The first review shall take place no later than five years after the entry into force of this Agreement. The review shall include consideration of the annual contributions referred to in paragraph 6 above.

11. Parties shall take the necessary legislative, administrative or policy measures, as appropriate, with the aim of ensuring that benefits arising from activities with respect to marine genetic resources and digital sequence information on marine genetic resources of areas beyond national jurisdiction by natural or juridical persons under their jurisdiction are shared in accordance with this Agreement.

Article 15 – Access and benefit-sharing committee

1. An access and benefit-sharing committee is hereby established. It shall serve, inter alia, as a means for establishing guidelines for benefit-sharing, in accordance with article 14, providing transparency and ensuring a fair and equitable sharing of both monetary and non-monetary benefits.

2. The access and benefit-sharing committee shall be composed of 15 members possessing appropriate qualifications in related fields, so as to ensure the effective exercise of the functions of the committee. The members shall be nominated by Parties and elected by the Conference of the Parties, taking into account gender balance and equitable geographical distribution and providing for representation on the committee from developing States, including from the least developed countries, from small island developing States and from landlocked developing countries. The terms of reference and modalities for the operation of the committee shall be determined by the Conference of the Parties.

3. The committee may make recommendations to the Conference of the Parties on matters relating to this Part, including on the following matters:

   (a) Guidelines or a code of conduct for activities with respect to marine genetic resources and digital sequence information on marine genetic resources of areas beyond national jurisdiction in accordance with this Part;

(b) Measures to implement decisions taken in accordance with this Part;

(c) Rates or mechanisms for the sharing of monetary benefits in accordance with article 14;

(d) Matters relating to this Part in relation to the Clearing-House Mechanism;

(e) Matters relating to this Part in relation to the financial mechanism established under article 52;

(f) Any other matters relating to this Part that the Conference of the Parties may request the access and benefit-sharing committee to address.

4. Each Party shall make available to the access and benefit-sharing committee, through the Clearing-House Mechanism, the information required under this Agreement, which shall include:

(a) Legislative, administrative and policy measures on access and benefit- sharing;

(b) Contact details and other relevant information on national focal points;

(c) Other information required pursuant to the decisions taken by the Conference of the Parties.

5. The access and benefit-sharing committee may consult and facilitate the exchange of information with relevant legal instruments and frameworks and relevant global, regional, subregional and sectoral bodies on activities under its mandate, including benefit-sharing, the use of digital sequence information on marine genetic resources, best practices, tools and methodologies, data governance and lessons learned.

6. The access and benefit-sharing committee may make recommendations to the Conference of the Parties in relation to information obtained under paragraph 5 above.

Article 16 – Monitoring and transparency

1. Monitoring and transparency of activities with respect to marine genetic resources and digital sequence information on marine genetic resources of areas beyond national jurisdiction shall be achieved through notification to the Clearing-House Mechanism, through the use of "BBNJ" standardized batch identifiers in accordance with this Part and according to procedures adopted by the Conference of the Parties as recommended by the access and benefit-sharing committee.

2. Parties shall periodically submit reports to the access and benefit-sharing committee on their implementation of the provisions in this Part on activities with respect to marine genetic resources and digital sequence information on marine genetic resources of areas beyond national jurisdiction and the sharing of benefits therefrom, in accordance with this Part.

3. The access and benefit-sharing committee shall prepare a report based on the information received through the Clearing-House Mechanism and make it available to Parties, which may submit comments. The access and benefit-sharing committee shall submit the report, including comments received, for the consideration of the Conference of the Parties. The Conference of the Parties, taking into account t he recommendation of the access and benefit-sharing committee, may determine appropriate guidelines for the implementation of this article, which shall take into account the national capabilities and circumstances of Parties.

PART III – MEASURES SUCH AS AREA-BASED MANAGEMENT TOOLS, INCLUDING MARINE PROTECTED AREAS

Article 17 – Objectives

The objectives of this Part are to:

(a) Conserve and sustainably use areas requiring protection, including through the establishment of a comprehensive system of area-based management tools, with ecologically representative and well-connected networks of marine protected areas;

(b) Strengthen cooperation and coordination in the use of area-based management tools, including marine protected areas, among States, relevant legal instruments and frameworks and relevant global, regional, subregional and sectoral bodies;

(c) Protect, preserve, restore and maintain biological diversity and ecosystems, including with a view to enhancing their productivity and health, and strengthen resilience to stressors, including those related to climate change, ocean acidification and marine pollution;

(d) Support food security and other socioeconomic objectives, including the protection of cultural values;

(e) Support developing States Parties, in particular the least developed countries, landlocked developing countries, geographically disadvantaged States, small island developing States, coastal African States, archipelagic States and developing middle-income countries, taking into account the special circumstances of small island developing States, through capacity-building and the development and transfer of marine technology in developing, implementing, monitoring, managing and enforcing area-based management tools, including marine protected areas.

Article 18 – Area of application

The establishment of area-based management tools, including marine protected areas, shall not include any areas within national jurisdiction and shall not be relied upon as a basis for asserting or denying any claims to sovereignty, sovereign rights or jurisdiction, including in respect of any disputes relating thereto. The Conference of the Parties shall not consider for decision proposals for the establishment of such area-based management tools, including marine protected areas, and in no case shall such proposals be interpreted as recognition or non-recognition of any claims to sovereignty, sovereign rights or jurisdiction.

Article 19 – Proposals

1. Proposals regarding the establishment of area-based management tools, including marine pro-

tected areas, under this Part shall be submitted by Parties, individually or collectively, to the secretariat.

2. Parties shall collaborate and consult, as appropriate, with relevant stakeholders, including States and global, regional, subregional and sectoral bodies, as well as civil society, the scientific community, the private sector, Indigenous Peoples and local communities, for the development of proposals, as set out in this Part.
3. Proposals shall be formulated on the basis of the best available science and scientific information and, where available, relevant traditional knowledge of Indigenous Peoples and local communities, taking into account the precautionary approach and an ecosystem approach.
4. Proposals with regard to identified areas shall include the following key elements:
   (a) A geographic or spatial description of the area that is the subject of the proposal by reference to the indicative criteria specified in Annex I;
   (b) Information on any of the criteria specified in Annex I, as well as any criteria that may be further developed and revised in accordance with paragraph 5 below applied in identifying the area;
   (c) Human activities in the area, including uses by Indigenous Peoples and local communities, and their possible impact, if any;
   (d) A description of the state of the marine environment and biological diversity in the identified area;
   (e) A description of the conservation and, where appropriate, sustainable use objectives that are to be applied to the area;
   (f) A draft management plan encompassing the proposed measures and outlining proposed monitoring, research and review activities to achieve the specified objectives;
   (g) The duration of the proposed area and measures, if any;
   (h) Information on any consultations undertaken with States, including adjacent coastal States and/or relevant global, regional, subregional and sectoral bodies, if any;
   (i) Information on area-based management tools, including marine protected areas, implemented under relevant legal instruments and frameworks and relevant global, regional, subregional and sectoral bodies;
   (j) Relevant scientific input and, where available, traditional knowledge of Indigenous Peoples and local communities.
5. Indicative criteria for the identification of such areas shall include, as relevant, those specified in Annex I and may be further developed and revised as necessary by the Scientific and Technical Body for consideration and adoption by the Conference of the Parties.
6. Further requirements regarding the contents of proposals, including the modalities for the application of indicative criteria as specified in paragraph 5 above, and guidance on proposals specified in paragraph 4 (b) above shall be elaborated by the Scientific and Technical Body, as necessary, for consideration and adoption by the Conference of the Parties.

Article 20 – Publicity and preliminary review of proposals

Upon receipt of a proposal in writing, the secretariat shall make the proposal publicly available and transmit it to the Scientific and Technical Body for a preliminary review. The purpose of the review is to ascertain that the proposal contains the information required under article 19, including indicative criteria described in this Part and in Annex I. The outcome of that review shall be made publicly available and shall be conveyed to the proponent by the secretariat. The proponent shall retransmit the proposal to the secretariat, having taken into account the preliminary review by the Scientific and Technical Body. The secretariat shall notify the Parties and make that retransmitted proposal publicly available and facilitate consultations pursuant to article 21.

Article 21 – Consultations on and assessment of proposals

1. Consultations on proposals submitted under article 19 shall be inclusive, transparent and open to all relevant stakeholders, including States and global, regional, subregional and sectoral bodies, as well as civil society, the scientific community, Indigenous Peoples and local communities.
2. The secretariat shall facilitate consultations and gather input as follows:
   (a) States, in particular adjacent coastal States, shall be notified and invited to submit, inter alia:
      (i) Views on the merits and geographic scope of the proposal;
      (ii) Any other relevant scientific input;
      (iii) Information regarding any existing measures or activities in adjacent or related areas within national jurisdiction and beyond national jurisdiction;
      (iv) Views on the potential implications of the proposal for areas within national jurisdiction;
      (v) Any other relevant information;
   (b) Bodies of relevant legal instruments and frameworks and relevant global, regional, subregional and sectoral bodies shall be notified and invited to submit, inter alia:
      (i) Views on the merits of the proposal;
      (ii) Any other relevant scientific input;
      (iii) Information regarding any existing measures adopted by that instrument, framework or body for the relevant area or for adjacent areas;

(iv) Views regarding any aspects of the measures and other elements for a draft management plan identified in the proposal that fall within the competence of that body;

(v) Views regarding any relevant additional measures that fall within the competence of that instrument, framework or body;

(vi) Any other relevant information;

(c) Indigenous Peoples and local communities with relevant traditional knowledge, the scientific community, civil society and other relevant stakeholders shall be invited to submit, inter alia:

(i) Views on the merits of the proposal;

(ii) Any other relevant scientific input;

(iii) Any relevant traditional knowledge of Indigenous Peoples and local communities;

(iv) Any other relevant information.

3. Contributions received pursuant to paragraph 2 above shall be made publicly available by the secretariat.

4. In cases where the proposed measure affects areas that are entirely surrounded by the exclusive economic zones of States, proponents shall:

(a) Undertake targeted and proactive consultations, including prior notification, with such States;

(b) Consider the views and comments of such States on the proposed measure and provide written responses specifically addressing such views and comments and, where appropriate, revise the proposed measure accordingly.

5. The proponent shall consider the contributions received during the consultation period, as well as the views of and information from the Scientific and Technical Body, and, as appropriate, revise the proposal accordingly or respond to substantive contributions not reflected in the proposal.

6. The consultation period shall be time-bound.

7. The revised proposal shall be submitted to the Scientific and Technical Body, which shall assess the proposal and make recommendations to the Conference of the Parties.

8. The modalities for the consultation and assessment process, including duration, shall be further elaborated by the Scientific and Technical Body, as necessary, at its first meeting, for consideration and adoption by the Conference of the Parties, taking into account the special circumstances of small island developing States.

Article 22 – Establishment of area-based management tools, including marine protected areas

1. The Conference of the Parties, on the basis of the final proposal and the draft management plan, taking into account the contributions and scientific input received during the consultation process established under this Part, and the scientific advice and recommendations of the Scientific and Technical Body:

(a) Shall take decisions on the establishment of area-based management tools, including marine protected areas, and related measures;

(b) May take decisions on measures compatible with those adopted by relevant legal instruments and frameworks and relevant global, regional, subregional and sectoral bodies, in cooperation and coordination with those instruments, frameworks and bodies;

(c) May, where proposed measures are within the competences of other global, regional, subregional or sectoral bodies, make recommendations to Parties to this Agreement and to global, regional, subregional and sectoral bodies to promote the adoption of relevant measures through such instruments, frameworks and bodies, in accordance with their respective mandates.

2. In taking decisions under this article, the Conference of the Parties shall respect the competences of, and not undermine, relevant legal instruments and frameworks and relevant global, regional, subregional and sectoral bodies.

3. The Conference of the Parties shall make arrangements for regular consultations to enhance cooperation and coordination with and among relevant legal instruments and frameworks and relevant global, regional, subregional and sectoral bodies with regard to area-based management tools, including marine protected areas, as well as coordination with regard to related measures adopted under such instruments and frameworks and by such bodies.

4. Where the achievement of the objectives and the implementation of this Part so requires, to further international cooperation and coordination with respect to the conservation and sustainable use of marine biological diversity of areas beyond national jurisdiction, the Conference of the Parties may consider and, subject to paragraphs 1 and 2 above, may decide, as appropriate, to develop a mechanism regarding existing area-based management tools, including marine protected areas, adopted by relevant legal instruments and frameworks or relevant global, regional, subregional or sectoral bodies.

5. Decisions and recommendations adopted by the Conference of the Parties in accordance with this Part shall not undermine the effectiveness of measures adopted in respect of areas within national jurisdiction and shall be made with due regard for the rights and duties of all States, in accordance with the Convention. In cases where measures proposed under this Part would affect or could reasonably be expected to affect the superjacent water above the seabed and subsoil of submarine areas over which a coastal State exercises sovereign rights in accordance with the Convention, such measures shall have due regard to the sovereign rights of such coastal States . Consultations shall be under-

taken to that end, in accordance with the provisions of this Part.

6. In cases where an area-based management tool, including a marine protected area, established under this Part subsequently falls, either wholly or in part, within the national jurisdiction of a coastal State, the part within national jurisdiction shall immediately cease to be in force. The part remaining in areas beyond national jurisdiction shall remain in force until the Conference of the Parties, at its following meeting, reviews and decides whether to amend or revoke the area-based management tool, including a marine protected area, as necessary.
7. Upon the establishment of, or amendment to the competence of, a relevant legal instrument or framework or a relevant global, regional, subregional or sectoral body, any area-based management tool, including a marine protected area, or related measures adopted by the Conference of the Parties under this Part that subsequently falls within the competence of such instrument, framework or body, either wholly or in part, shall remain in force until the Conference of the Parties reviews and decides, in close cooperation and coordination with that instrument, framework or body, to maintain, amend or revoke the area-based management tool, including a marine protected area, and related measures, as appropriate.

Article 23 – Decision-making

1. As a general rule, the decisions and recommendations under this Part shall be taken by consensus.
2. If no consensus is reached, decisions and recommendations under this Part shall be taken by a three-fourths majority of the Parties present and voting, before which the Conference of the Parties shall decide, by a two-thirds majority of the Parties present and voting that all efforts to reach consensus have been exhausted .
3. Decisions taken under this Part shall enter into force 120 days after t he meeting of the Conference of the Parties at which they were taken and shall be binding on all Parties.
4. During the period of 120 days provided for in paragraph 3 above, any Party may, by notification in writing to the secretariat, make an objection with respect to a decision adopted under this Part, and that decision shall not be binding on that Party. An objection to a decision may be withdrawn at any time by written notification to the secretariat and, thereupon, the decision shall be binding for that Party 90 days following the date of the notification stating that the objection is withdrawn.
5. A Party making an objection under paragraph 4 above shall provide to the secretariat, in writing, at the time of making its objection, the explanation of the grounds for its objection, which shall be based on one or more of the following grounds:
   (a) The decision is inconsistent with this Agreement or the rights and duties of the objecting Party in accordance with the Convention;
   (b) The decision unjustifiably discriminates in form or in fact against the objecting Party;
   (c) The Party cannot practicably comply with the decision at the time of the objection after making all reasonable efforts to do so.
6. A Party making an objection under paragraph 4 above shall, to the extent practicable, adopt alternative measures or approaches that are equivalent in effect to the decision to which it has objected and shall not adopt measures nor take actions that would undermine the effectiveness of the decision to which it has objected unless such measures or actions are essential for the exercise of rights and duties of the objecting Party in accordance with the Convention.
7. The objecting Party shall report to the next ordinary meeting of the Conference of the Parties following its notification under paragraph 4 above, and periodically thereafter, on its implementation of paragraph 6 above, to inform the monitoring and review under article 26.
8. An objection to a decision made in accordance with paragraph 4 above may only be renewed if the objecting Party considers it still necessary, every three years after the entry into force of the decision, by written notification to the secretariat. Such written notification shall include an explanation of the grounds of its initial objection.
9. If no notification of renewal pursuant to paragraph 8 above is received, the objection shall be considered automatically withdrawn and, thereupon, the decision shall be binding for that Party 120 days after that objection is automatically withdrawn. The secretariat shall notify the Party 60 days prior to the date on which the objection will be automatically withdrawn.
10. Decisions of the Conference of the Parties adopted under this Part, and objections to those decisions, shall be made publicly available by the secretariat and shall be transmitted to all States and relevant legal instruments and frameworks and relevant global, regional, subregional and sectoral bodies.

Article 24 – Emergency measures

1. The Conference of the Parties shall take decisions to adopt measures in areas beyond national jurisdiction, to be applied on an emergency basis, if necessary, when a natural phenomenon or human-caused disaster has caused, or is likely to cause, serious or irreversible harm to marine biological diversity of areas beyond national jurisdiction, to ensure that the serious or irreversible harm is not exacerbated.
2. Measures adopted under this article shall be considered necessary only if, following consultation with relevant legal instruments or frameworks or relevant global, regional, subregional or sectoral bodies, the serious or irreversible harm cannot be managed in a timely manner through the application of the other articles of this Agreement or by a relevant legal instrument or framework or a relevant global, regional, subregional or sectoral body.
3. Measures adopted on an emergency basis shall be based on the best available science and scientific information and, where available, relevant

traditional knowledge of Indigenous Peoples and local communities and shall take into account the precautionary approach. Such measures may be proposed by Parties or recommended by the Scientific and Technical Body and may be adopted intersessionally. The measures shall be temporary and must be reconsidered for decision at the next meeting of the Conference of the Parties following their adoption.

4. The measures shall terminate two years following their entry into force or shall be terminated earlier by the Conference of the Parties upon being replaced by area-based management tools, including marine protected areas, and related measures established in accordance with this Part, or by measures adopted by a relevant legal instrument or framework or relevant global, regional, subregional or sectoral body, or by a decision of the Conference of the Parties when the circumstances that necessitated the measure cease to exist.
5. Procedures and guidance for the establishment of emergency measures, including consultation procedures, shall be elaborated by the Scientific and Technical Body, as necessary, for consideration and adoption by the Conference of the Parties at its earliest opportunity. Such procedures shall be inclusive and transparent.

Article 25 – Implementation

1. Parties shall ensure that activities under their jurisdiction or control that take place in areas beyond national jurisdiction are conducted consistently with the decisions adopted under this Part.
2. Nothing in this Agreement shall prevent a Party from adopting more stringent measures with respect to its nationals and vessels or with regard to activities under its jurisdiction or control in addition to those adopted under this Part, in accordance with international law and in support of the objectives of the Agreement.
3. The implementation of the measures adopted under this Part should not impose a disproportionate burden on Parties that are small island developing States or least developed countries, directly or indirectly.
4. Parties shall promote, as appropriate, the adoption of measures within relevant legal instruments and frameworks and relevant global, regional, subregional and sectoral bodies of which they are members, to support the implementation of the decisions and recommendations made by the Conference of the Parties under this Part.
5. Parties shall encourage those States that are entitled to become Parties to this Agreement, in particular those whose activities, vessels or nationals operate in an area that is the subject of an established area-based management tool, including a marine protected area, to adopt measures supporting the decisions and recommendations of the Conference of the Parties on area-based management tools, including marine protected areas, established under this Part.
6. A Party that is not a party to or a participant in a relevant legal instrument or framework, or a member of a relevant global, regional, subregional or sectoral body, and that does not otherwise agree to apply the measures established under such instruments and frameworks and by such bodies shall not be discharged from the obligation to cooperate, in accordance with the Convention and this Agreement, in the conservation and sustainable use of marine biological diversity of areas beyond national jurisdiction.

Article 26 – Monitoring and review

1. Parties shall, individually or collectively, report to the Conference of the Parties on the implementation of area-based management tools, including marine protected areas, established under this Part and related measures. Such reports, as well as the information and the review referred to in paragraphs 2 and 3 below, respectively, shall be made publicly available by the secretariat.
2. The relevant legal instruments and frameworks and relevant global, regional, subregional and sectoral bodies shall be invited to provide information to the Conference of the Parties on the implementation of measures that they have adopted to achieve the objectives of area-based management tools, including marine protected areas, established under this Part.
3. Area-based management tools, including marine protected areas, established under this Part, including related measures, shall be monitored and periodically reviewed by the Scientific and Technical Body, taking into account the reports and information referred to in paragraphs 1 and 2 above, respectively.
4. In the review referred to in paragraph 3 above, the Scientific and Technical Body shall assess the effectiveness of area-based management tools, including marine protected areas, established under this Part, including related measures and the progress made in achieving their objectives, and provide advice and recommendations to the Conference of the Parties.
5. Following the review, the Conference of the Parties shall, as necessary, take decisions or recommendations on the amendment, extension or revocation of area - based management tools, including marine protected areas, and any related measures adopted by the Conference of the Parties, on the basis of the best available science and scientific information and, where available, relevant traditional knowledge of Indigenous Peoples and local communities, taking into account the precautionary approach and an ecosystem approach.

PART IV – ENVIRONMENTAL IMPACT ASSESSMENTS

Article 27 – Objectives

The objectives of this Part are to:

(a) Operationalize the provisions of the Convention on environmental impact assessment for areas beyond national jurisdiction by establishing processes, thresholds and other requirements for conducting and reporting assessments by Parties;

(b) Ensure that activities covered by this Part are assessed and conducted to prevent, mitigate and manage significant adverse impacts for the purpose of protecting and preserving the marine environment;

(c) Support the consideration of cumulative impacts and impacts in areas within national jurisdiction;

(d) Provide for strategic environmental assessments;

(e) Achieve a coherent environmental impact assessment frame work for activities in areas beyond national jurisdiction;

(f) Build and strengthen the capacity of Parties, particularly developing States Parties, in particular the least developed countries, landlocked developing countries, geographically disadvantaged States, small island developing States, coastal African States, archipelagic States and developing middle-income countries, to prepare, conduct and evaluate environmental impact assessments and strategic environmental assessments in support of the objectives of this Agreement.

Article 28 – Obligation to conduct environmental impact assessments

1. Parties shall ensure that the potential impacts on the marine environment of planned activities under their jurisdiction or control that take place in areas beyond national jurisdiction are assessed as set out in this Part before they are authorized.
2. When a Party with jurisdiction or control over a planned activity that is to be conducted in marine areas within national jurisdiction determines that the activity may cause substantial pollution of or significant and harmful changes to the marine environment in areas beyond national jurisdiction, that Party shall ensure that an environmental impact assessment of such activity is conducted in accordance with this Part or that an environmental impact assessment is conducted under the Party's national process. A Party conducting such an assessment under its national process shall:
   (a) Make relevant information available through the Clearing-House Mechanism, in a timely manner, during the national process;
   (b) Ensure that the activity is monitored in a manner consistent with the requirements of its national process;
   (c) Ensure that environmental impact assessment reports and any relevant monitoring reports are made available through the Clearing-House Mechanism as set out in this Agreement.
3. Upon receiving the information referred to in paragraph 2 (a) above, the Scientific and Technical Body may provide comments to the Party with jurisdiction or control over the planned activity.

Article 29 – Relationship between this Agreement and environmental impact assessment processes under relevant legal instruments and frameworks and relevant global, regional, subregional and sectoral bodies

1. Parties shall promote the use of environmental impact assessments and the adoption and implementation of the standards and/or guidelines developed under article 38 in relevant legal instruments and frameworks and relevant global, regional, subregional and sectoral bodies of which they are members.
2. The Conference of the Parties shall develop mechanisms under this Part for the Scientific and Technical Body to collaborate with relevant legal instruments and frameworks and relevant global, regional, subregional and sectoral bodies that regulate activities in areas beyond national jurisdiction or protect the marine environment.
3. When developing or updating standards or guidelines for the conduct of environmental impact assessments of activities in areas beyond national jurisdiction by Parties to this Agreement under article 38, the Scientific and Technical Body shall, as appropriate, collaborate with relevant legal instruments and frameworks and relevant global, regional, subregional and sectoral bodies.
4. It is not necessary to conduct a screening or an environmental impact assessment of a planned activity in areas beyond national jurisdiction, provided that the Party with jurisdiction or control over the planned activity determines:
   (a) That the potential impacts of the planned activity or category of activity have been assessed in accordance with the requirements of other relevant legal instruments or frameworks or by relevant global, regional, subregional or sectoral bodies;
   (b) That:
      (i) the assessment already undertaken for the planned activity is equivalent to the one required under this Part, and the results of the assessment are taken into account; or
      (ii) the regulations or standards of the relevant legal instruments or frameworks or relevant global, regional, subregional or sectoral bodies arising from the assessment were designed to prevent, mitigate or manage potential impacts below the threshold for environmental impact assessments under this Part, and they have been complied with.
5. When an environmental impact assessment for a planned activity in areas beyond national jurisdiction has been conducted under a relevant legal instrument or framework or a relevant global, regional, subregional or sectoral body, the Party concerned shall ensure that the environmental impact assessment report is published through the Clearing-House Mechanism.
6. Unless the planned activities that meet the criteria set out in paragraph 4 (b) (i) above are subject

to monitoring and review under a relevant legal instrument or framework or relevant global, regional, subregional or sectoral body, Parties shall monitor and review the activities and ensure that the monitoring and review reports are published through the Clearing-House Mechanism.

Article 30 – Thresholds and factors for conducting environmental impact assessments

1. When a planned activity may have more than a minor or transitory effect on the marine environment, or the effects of the activity are unknown or poorly understood, the Party with jurisdiction or control of the activity shall conduct a screening of the activity under article 31, using the factors set out in paragraph 2 below, and:
   - (a) The screening shall be sufficiently detailed for the Party to assess whether it has reasonable grounds for believing that the planned activity may cause substantial pollution of or significant and harmful changes to the marine environment and shall include:
     - (i) A description of the planned activity, including its purpose, location, duration and intensity; and
     - (ii) An initial analysis of the potential impacts, including consideration of cumulative impacts and, as appropriate, alternatives to the planned activity;
   - (b) If it is determined on the basis of the screening that the Party has reasonable grounds for believing that the activity may cause substantial pollution of or significant and harmful changes to the marine environment, an environmental impact assessment shall be conducted in accordance with the provisions of this Part.
2. When determining whether planned activities under their jurisdiction or control meet the threshold set out in paragraph 1 above, Parties shall consider the following non-exhaustive factors:
   - (a) The type of and technology used for the activity and the manner in which it is to be conducted;
   - (b) The duration of the activity;
   - (c) The location of the activity;
   - (d) The characteristics and ecosystem of the location (including areas of particular ecological or biological significance or vulnerability);
   - (e) The potential impacts of the activity, including the potential cumulative impacts and the potential impacts in areas within national jurisdiction;
   - (f) The extent to which the effects of the activity are unknown or poorly understood;
   - (g) Other relevant ecological or biological criteria.

Article 31 – Process for environmental impact assessments

1. Parties shall ensure that the process for conducting an environmental impact assessment pursuant to this Part includes the following steps:
   - (a) Screening. Parties shall undertake screening, in a timely manner, to determine whether an environmental impact assessment is required in respect of a planned activity under its jurisdiction or control, in accordance with article 30, and make its determination publicly available:
     - (i) If a Party determines that an environmental impact assessment is not required for a planned activity under its jurisdiction or control, it shall make relevant information, including under article 30, paragraph 1 (a), publicly available through the Clearing-House Mechanism under this Agreement;
     - (ii) On the basis of the best available science and scientific information and, where available, relevant traditional knowledge of Indigenous Peoples and local communities, a Party may register its views on the potential impacts of a planned activity on which a determination has been made in accordance with subparagraph (a) (i) above with the Party that made the determination and the Scientific and Technical Body, within 40 days of the publication thereof;
     - (iii) If the Party that registered its views expressed concerns on the potential impacts of a planned activity on which the determination was made, the Party that made that determination shall give consideration to such concerns and may review its determination;
     - (iv) Upon consideration of the concerns registered by a Party under subparagraph (a) (ii) above, the Scientific and Technical Body shall consider and may evaluate the potential impacts of the planned activity on the basis of the best available science and scientific information and, where available, relevant traditional knowledge of Indigenous Peoples and local communities and, as appropriate, may make recommendations to the Party that made the determination after giving that Party an opportunity to respond to the concerns registered and taking into account such response;
     - (v) The Party that made the determination under subparagraph (a) (i) above shall give consideration to any recommendations of the Scientific and Technical Body;
     - (vi) The registration of views and the recommendations of the Scientific and Technical Body shall be made publicly available, including through the Clearing-House Mechanism;
   - (b) Scoping. Parties shall ensure that key environmental and any associated impacts, such as economic, social, cultural and human health impacts, including potential cumulative impacts and impacts in areas within national jurisdiction, as well as alternatives to the

planned activity, if any, to be included in the environmental impact assessments that shall be conducted under this Part, are identified. The scope shall be defined by using the best available science and scientific information and, where available, relevant traditional knowledge of Indigenous Peoples and local communities;

(c) Impact assessment and evaluation. Parties shall ensure that the impacts of planned activities, including cumulative impacts and impacts in areas within national jurisdiction, are assessed and evaluated using the best available science and scientific information and, where available, relevant traditional knowledge of Indigenous Peoples and local communities;

(d) Prevention, mitigation and management of potential adverse effects. Parties shall ensure that:

(i) Measures to prevent, mitigate and manage potential adverse effects of the planned activities under their jurisdiction or control are identified and analysed to avoid significant adverse impacts. Such measures may include the consideration of alternatives to the planned activity under their jurisdiction or control;

(ii) Where appropriate, these measures are incorporated into an environmental management plan;

(e) Parties shall ensure public notification and consultation in accordance with article 32;

(f) Parties shall ensure the preparation and publication of an environmental impact assessment report in accordance with article 33.

2. Parties may conduct joint environmental impact assessments, in particular for planned activities under the jurisdiction or control of small island developing States.

3. A roster of experts shall be created under the Scientific and Technical Body. Parties with capacity constraints may request advice and assistance from those experts to conduct and evaluate screenings and environmental impact assessments for a planned activity under their jurisdiction or control. The experts cannot be appointed to another part of the environmental impact assessment process of the same activity. The Party that requested the advice and assistance shall ensure that such environmental impact assessments are submitted to it for review and decision-making.

Article 32 – Public notification and consultation

1. Parties shall ensure timely public notification of a planned activity, including by publication through the Clearing-House Mechanism and through the secretariat, and planned and effective time-bound opportunities, as far as practicable, for participation by all States, in particular adjacent coastal States and any other States adjacent to the activity when they are potentially most affected States, and stakeholders in the environmental impact assessment process. Notification and opportunities for participation, including through the submission of comments, shall take place throughout the environmental impact assessment process, as appropriate, including when identifying the scope of an environmental impact assessment under article 31, paragraph 1 (b), and when a draft environmental impact assessment report has been prepared under article 33, before a decision is made as to whether to authorize the activity.

2. Potentially most affected States shall be determined by taking into account the nature and potential effects on the marine environment of the planned activity and shall include:

(a) Coastal States whose exercise of sovereign rights for the purpose of exploring, exploiting, conserving or managing natural resources may reasonably be believed to be affected by the activity;

(b) States that carry out, in the area of the planned activity, human activities, including economic activities, that may reasonably be believed to be affected.

3. Stakeholders in this process include Indigenous Peoples and local communities with relevant traditional knowledge, relevant global, regional, subregional and sectoral bodies, civil society, the scientific community and the public.

4. Public notification and consultation shall, in accordance with article 48, paragraph 3, be inclusive and transparent, be conducted in a timely manner and be targeted and proactive when involving small island developing States.

5. Substantive comments received during the consultation process, including from adjacent coastal States and any other States adjacent to the planned activity when they are potentially most affected States, shall be considered and responded to or addressed by Parties. Parties shall give particular regard to comments concerning potential impacts in areas within national jurisdiction and provide written responses, as appropriate, specifically addressing such comments, including regarding any additional measures meant to address those potential impacts. Parties shall make public the comments received and the responses or descriptions of the manner in which they were addressed.

6. Where a planned activity affects areas of the high seas that are entirely surrounded by the exclusive economic zones of States, Parties shall:

(a) Undertake targeted and proactive consultations, including prior notification, with such surrounding States;

(b) Consider the views and comments of those surrounding States on the planned activity and provide written responses specifically addressing such views and comments and, as appropriate, revise the planned activity accordingly.

7. Parties shall ensure access to information related to the environmental impact assessment process under this Agreement. Notwithstanding this, Parties shall not be required to disclose confidential or proprietary information. The fact that confidential

or proprietary information has been redacted shall be indicated in public documents.

Article 33 – Environmental impact assessment reports

1. Parties shall ensure the preparation of an environmental impact assessment report for any such assessment undertaken pursuant to this Part.
2. The environmental impact assessment report shall include, at a minimum, the following information: a description of the planned activity, including its location; a description of the results of the scoping exercise; a baseline assessment of the marine environment likely to be affected; a description of potential impacts, including potential cumulative impacts and any impacts in areas within national jurisdiction; a description of potential prevention, mitigation and management measures; a description of uncertainties and gaps in knowledge; information on the public consultation process; a description of the consideration of reasonable alternatives to the planned activity; a description of follow-up actions, including an environmental management plan; and a non-technical summary.
3. The Party shall make the draft environmental impact assessment report available through the Clearing-House Mechanism during the public consultation process, to provide an opportunity for the Scientific and Technical Body to consider and evaluate the report.
4. The Scientific and Technical Body, as appropriate and in a timely manner, may make comments to the Party on the draft environmental impact assessment report. The Party shall give consideration to any comments made by the Scientific and Technical Body.
5. Parties shall publish the reports of the environmental impact assessments, including through the Clearing-House Mechanism. The secretariat shall ensure that all Parties are notified in a timely manner when reports are published through the Clearing-House Mechanism.
6. Final environmental impact assessment reports shall be considered by the Scientific and Technical Body, on the basis of relevant practices, procedures and knowledge under this Agreement, for the purpose of developing guidelines, including the identification of best practices.
7. A selection of the published information used in the screening process to make decisions on whether to conduct an environmental impact assessment, in accordance with articles 30 and 31, shall be considered and reviewed by the Scientific and Technical Body, on the basis of relevant practices, procedures and knowledge under this Agreement, for the purpose of developing guidelines, including the identification of best practices.

Article 34 – Decision-making

1. A Party under whose jurisdiction or control a planned activity falls shall be responsible for determining if it may proceed.
2. When determining whether the planned activity may proceed under this Part, full account shall be taken of an environmental impact assessment conducted in accordance with this Part. A decision to authorize the planned activity under the jurisdiction or control of a Party shall only be made when, taking into account mitigation or management measures, the Party has determined that it has made all reasonable efforts to ensure that the activity can be conducted in a manner consistent with the prevention of significant adverse impacts on the marine environment.
3. Decision documents shall clearly outline any conditions of approval related to mitigation measures and follow-up requirements. Decision documents shall be made public, including through the Clearing-House Mechanism.
4. At the request of a Party, the Conference of the Parties may provide advice and assistance to that Party when determining whether a planned activity under its jurisdiction or control may proceed.

Article 35 – Monitoring of impacts of authorized activities

Parties shall, by using the best available science and scientific information and, where available, the relevant traditional knowledge of Indigenous Peoples and local communities, keep under surveillance the impacts of any activities in areas beyond national jurisdiction that they permit or in which they engage in order to determine whether these activities are likely to pollute or have adverse impacts on the marine environment. In particular, each Party shall monitor the environmental and any associated impacts, such as economic, social, cultural and human health impacts, of an authorized activity under their jurisdiction or control in accordance with the conditions set out in the approval of the activity.

Article 36 – Reporting on impacts of authorized activities

1. Parties, whether acting individually or collectively, shall periodically report on the impacts of the authorized activity and the results of the monitoring required under article 35.
2. Monitoring reports shall be made public, including through the Clearing-House Mechanism, and the Scientific and Technical Body may consider and evaluate the monitoring reports.
3. Monitoring reports shall be considered by the Scientific and Technical Body, on the basis of relevant practices, procedures and knowledge under this Agreement, for the purpose of developing guidelines on the monitoring of impacts of authorized activities, including the identification of best practices.

Article 37 – Review of authorized activities and their impacts

1. Parties shall ensure that the impacts of the authorized activity monitored pursuant to article 35 are reviewed.

2. Should the Party with jurisdiction or control over the activity identify significant adverse impacts that either were not foreseen in the environmental impact assessment, in nature or severity, or that arise from a breach of any of the conditions set out in the approval of the activity, the Party shall review its decision authorizing the activity, notify the Conference of the Parties, other Parties and the public, including through the Clearing-House Mechanism, and:
   (a) Require that measures be proposed and implemented to prevent, mitigate and/or manage those impacts or take any other necessary action and/or halt the activity, as appropriate; and
   (b) Evaluate, in a timely manner, any measures implemented or actions taken under subparagraph (a) above.
3. On the basis of the reports received under article 36, the Scientific and Technical Body may notify the Party that authorized the activity if it considers that the activity may have significant adverse impacts that were either not foreseen in the environmental impact assessment or that arise from a breach of any conditions of approval of the authorized activity and, as appropriate, may make recommendations to the Party.
4. (a) On the basis of the best available science and scientific information and, where available, relevant traditional knowledge of Indigenous Peoples and local communities, a Party may register its concerns, with the Party that authorized the activity and with the Scientific and Technical Body, that the authorized activity may have significant adverse impacts that were either not foreseen in the environmental impact assessment, in nature or severity, or that arise from a breach of any conditions of approval of the authorized activity;
   (b) The Party that authorized the activity shall give consideration to such concerns;
   (c) Upon consideration of the concerns registered by a Party, the Scientific and Technical Body shall consider and may evaluate the matter based on the best available science and scientific information and, where available, relevant traditional knowledge of Indigenous Peoples and local communities and may notify the Party that authorized the activity, if it considers that such activity may have significant adverse impacts that were either not foreseen in the environmental impact assessment or that arise from a breach of any conditions of approval of the authorized activity and, after giving that Party an opportunity to respond to the concerns registered and taking into account such response and as appropriate, may make recommendations to the Party that authorized the activity;
   (d) The registration of concerns, any notifications issued and any recommendations made by the Scientific and Technical Body shall be made publicly available, including through the Clearing-House Mechanism;
   (e) The Party that authorized the activity shall give consideration to any notifications issued and any recommendations made by the Scientific and Technical Body.
5. All States, in particular adjacent coastal States and any other States adjacent to the activity when they are potentially most affected States, and stakeholders shall be kept informed through the Clearing-House Mechanism and may be consulted in the monitoring, reporting and review processes in respect of an activity authorized under this Agreement.
6. Parties shall publish, including through the Clearing-House Mechanism:
   (a) Reports on the review of the impacts of the authorized activity;
   (b) Decision documents, including a record of the reasons for the decision by the Party, when a Party has changed its decision authorizing the activity.

Article 38 – Standards and/or guidelines to be developed by the Scientific and Technical Body related to environmental impact assessments

1. The Scientific and Technical Body shall develop standards or guidelines for consideration and adoption by the Conference of the Parties on:
   (a) The determination of whether the thresholds for the conduct of a screening or an environmental impact assessment under article 30 have been met or exceeded for planned activities, including on the basis of the non-exhaustive factors set out in paragraph 2 of that article;
   (b) The assessment of cumulative impacts in areas beyond national jurisdiction and how those impacts should be taken into account in the environmental impact assessment process;
   (c) The assessment of impacts, in areas within national jurisdiction, of planned activities in areas beyond national jurisdiction and how those impacts should be taken into account in the environmental impact assessment process;
   (d) The public notification and consultation process under article 32, including the determination of what constitutes confidential or proprietary information;
   (e) The required content of environmental impact assessment reports and published information used in the screening process pursuant to article 33, including best practices;
   (f) The monitoring of and reporting on the impacts of authorized activities as set out in articles 35 and 36, including the identification of best practices;
   (g) The conduct of strategic environmental assessments.
2. The Scientific and Technical Body may also develop standards and guidelines for consideration and adoption by the Conference of the Parties, including on:

(a) An indicative non-exhaustive list of activities that require or do not require an environmental impact assessment, as well as any criteria related to those activities, which shall be periodically updated;

(b) The conduct of environmental impact assessments by Parties to this Agreement in areas identified as requiring protection or special attention.

3. Any standard shall be set out in an annex to this Agreement, in accordance with article 74.

Article 39 – Strategic environmental assessments

1. Parties shall, individually or in cooperation with other Parties, consider conducting strategic environmental assessments for plans and programmes relating to activities under their jurisdiction or control, to be conducted in areas beyond national jurisdiction, in order to assess the potential effects of such plans or programmes, as well as of alternatives, on the marine environment.
2. The Conference of the Parties may conduct a strategic environmental assessment of an area or region to collate and synthesize the best available information about the area or region, assess current and potential future impacts and identify data gaps and research priorities.
3. When undertaking environmental impact assessments pursuant to this Part, Parties shall take into account the results of relevant strategic environmental assessments carried out under paragraphs 1 and 2 above, where available.
4. The Conference of the Parties shall develop guidance on the conduct of each category of strategic environmental assessment described in this article.

PART V – CAPACITY-BUILDING AND THE TRANSFER OF MARINE TECHNOLOGY

Article 40 – Objectives

The objectives of this Part are to:

(a) Assist Parties, in particular developing States Parties, in implementing the provisions of this Agreement, to achieve its objectives;

(b) Enable inclusive, equitable and effective cooperation and participation in the activities undertaken under this Agreement;

(c) Develop the marine scientific and technological capacity, including with respect to research, of Parties, in particular developing States Parties, with regard to the conservation and sustainable use of marine biological diversity of areas beyond national jurisdiction, including through access to marine technology by, and the transfer of marine technology to, developing States Parties;

(d) Increase, disseminate and share knowledge on the conservation and sustainable use of marine biological diversity of areas beyond national jurisdiction;

(e) More specifically, support developing States Parties, in particular the least developed countries, landlocked developing countries, geographically disadvantaged States, small island developing States, coastal African States, archipelagic States and developing middle-income countries, through capacity-building and the development and transfer of marine technology under this Agreement, in achieving the objectives relating to:

(i) Marine genetic resources, including the sharing of benefits, as reflected in article 9;

(ii) Measures such as area-based management tools, including marine protected areas, as reflected in article 17;

(iii) Environmental impact assessments, as reflected in article 27.

Article 41 – Cooperation in capacity-building and the transfer of marine technology

1. Parties shall cooperate, directly or through relevant legal instruments and frameworks and relevant global, regional, subregional and sectoral bodies, to assist Parties, in particular developing States Parties, in achieving the objectives of this Agreement through capacity-building and the development and transfer of marine science and marine technology.
2. In providing capacity-building and the transfer of marine technology under this Agreement, Parties shall cooperate at all levels and in all forms, including through partnerships with and involving all relevant stakeholders, such as, where appropriate, the private sector, civil society, and Indigenous Peoples and local communities as holders of traditional knowledge, as well as through strengthening cooperation and coordination between relevant legal instruments and frameworks and relevant global, regional, subregional and sectoral bodies.
3. In giving effect to this Part, Parties shall give full recognition to the special requirements of developing States Parties, in particular the least developed countries, landlocked developing countries, geographically disadvantaged States, small island developing States, coastal African States, archipelagic States and developing middle-income countries. Parties shall ensure that the provision of capacity-building and the transfer of marine technology is not conditional on onerous reporting requirements.

Article 42 – Modalities for capacity-building and for the transfer of marine technology

1. Parties, within their capabilities, shall ensure capacity-building for developing States Parties and shall cooperate to achieve the transfer of marine technology, in particular to developing States Parties that need and request it, taking into account the special circumstances of small island developing States and of least developed countries, in accordance with the provisions of this Agreement.
2. Parties shall provide, within their capabilities, resources to support such capacity- building and the development and transfer of marine technology and to facilitate access to other sources of support, taking into account their national policies, priorities, plans and programmes.

3. Capacity-building and the transfer of marine technology should be a country-driven, transparent, effective and iterative process that is participatory, cross-cutting and gender- responsive. It shall build upon, as appropriate, and not duplicate existing programmes and be guided by lessons learned, including those from capacity-building and transfer of marine technology activities under relevant legal instruments and frameworks and relevant global, regional, subregional and sectoral bodies. Insofar as possible, it shall take into account these activities with a view to maximizing efficiency and results.
4. Capacity-building and the transfer of marine technology shall be based on and be responsive to the needs and priorities of developing States Parties, taking into account the special circumstances of small island developing States and of least developed countries, identified through needs assessments on an individual case-by-case, subregional or regional basis. Such needs and priorities may be self-assessed or facilitated through the capacity-building and transfer of marine technology committee and the Clearing-House Mechanism.

Article 43 – Additional modalities for the transfer of marine technology

1. Parties share a long-term vision of the importance of fully realizing technology development and transfer for inclusive, equitable and effective cooperation and participation in the activities undertaken under this Agreement and in order to fully achieve its objectives.
2. The transfer of marine technology undertaken under this Agreement shall take place on fair and most favourable terms, including on concessional and preferential terms, and in accordance with mutually agreed terms and conditions as well as the objectives of this Agreement.
3. Parties shall promote and encourage economic and legal conditions for the transfer of marine technology to developing States Parties, taking into account the special circumstances of small island developing States and of least developed countries, which may include providing incentives to enterprises and institutions.
4. The transfer of marine technology shall take into account all rights over such technologies and be carried out with due regard for all legitimate interests, including, inter alia, the rights and duties of holders, suppliers and recipients of marine technology and taking into particular consideration the interests and needs of developing States for the attainment of the objectives of this Agreement.
5. Marine technology transferred pursuant to this Part shall be appropriate, relevant and, to the extent possible, reliable, affordable, up to date, environmentally sound and available in an accessible form for developing States Parties, taking into account the special circumstances of small island developing States and of least developed countries.

Article 44 – Types of capacity-building and of the transfer of marine technology

1. In support of the objectives set out in article 40, the types of capacity-building and of the transfer of marine technology may include, but are not limited to, support for the creation or enhancement of the human, financial management, scientific, technological, organizational, institutional and other resource capabilities of Parties, such as:
   (a) The sharing and use of relevant data, information, knowledge and research results;
   (b) Information dissemination and awareness-raising, including with respect to relevant traditional knowledge of Indigenous Peoples and local communities, in line with the free, prior and informed consent of these Indigenous Peoples and, as appropriate, local communities;
   (c) The development and strengthening of relevant infrastructure, including equipment and capacity of personnel for its use and maintenance;
   (d) The development and strengthening of institutional capacity and national regulatory frameworks or mechanisms;
   (e) The development and strengthening of human and financial management resource capabilities and of technical expertise through exchanges, research collaboration, technical support, education and training and the transfer of marine technology;
   (f) The development and sharing of manuals, guidelines and standards;
   (g) The development of technical, scientific and research and development programmes;
   (h) The development and strengthening of capacities and technological tools for effective monitoring, control and surveillance of activities within the scope of this Agreement.
2. Further details concerning the types of capacity-building and of the transfer of marine technology identified in this article are elaborated in Annex II.
3. The Conference of the Parties, taking account of the recommendations of the capacity-building and transfer of marine technology committee, shall periodically, as necessary, review, assess and further develop and provide guidance on the indicative and non-exhaustive list of types of capacity-building and of transfer of marine technology elaborated in Annex II, to reflect technological progress and innovation and to respond and adapt to the evolving needs of States, subregions and regions.

Article 45 – Monitoring and review

1. Capacity-building and the transfer of marine technology undertaken in accordance with the provisions of this Part shall be monitored and reviewed periodically.
2. The monitoring and review referred to in paragraph 1 above shall be carried out by the capacity-building and transfer of marine technology

committee under the authority of the Conference of the Parties and shall be aimed at:

(a) Assessing and reviewing the needs and priorities of developing States Parties in terms of capacity-building and the transfer of marine technology, paying particular attention to the special requirements of developing States Parties and to the special circumstances of small island developing States and of least developed countries, in accordance with article 42, paragraph 4;

(b) Reviewing the support required, provided and mobilized, as well as gaps in meeting the assessed needs of developing States Parties in relation to this Agreement;

(c) Identifying and mobilizing funds under the financial mechanism established under article 52 to develop and implement capacity-building and the transfer of marine technology, including for the conduct of needs assessments;

(d) Measuring performance on the basis of agreed indicators and reviewing results-based analyses, including on the output, outcomes, progress and effectiveness of capacity-building and transfer of marine technology under this Agreement, as well as successes and challenges;

(e) Making recommendations for follow-up activities, including on how capacity-building and the transfer of marine technology could be further enhanced to allow developing States Parties, taking into account the special circumstances of small island developing States and of least developed countries, to strengthen their implementation of the Agreement in order to achieve its objectives.

3. In supporting the monitoring and review of capacity-building and the transfer of marine technology, Parties shall submit reports to the capacity-building and transfer of marine technology committee. Those reports should be in a format and at intervals to be determined by the Conference of the Parties, taking into account the recommendations of the capacity-building and transfer of marine technology committee. In submitting their reports, Parties shall take into account, where applicable, input from regional and subregional bodies on capacity-building and the transfer of marine technology. The reports submitted by Parties, as well as any input from regional and subregional bodies on capacity-building and the transfer of marine technology, should be made publicly available. The Conference of the Parties shall ensure that reporting requirements should be streamlined and not onerous, in particular for developing States Parties, including in terms of costs and time requirements.

Article 46 – Capacity-building and transfer of marine technology committee

1. A capacity-building and transfer of marine technology committee is hereby established.
2. The committee shall consist of members possessing appropriate qualifications and expertise, to serve objectively in the best interest of the Agreement, nominated by Parties and elected by the Conference of the Parties, taking into account gender balance and equitable geographical distribution and providing for representation on the committee from the least developed countries, from the small island developing States and from the landlocked developing countries. The terms of reference and modalities for the operation of the committee shall be decided by the Conference of the Parties at its first meeting.
3. The committee shall submit reports and recommendations that the Conference of the Parties shall consider and take action on as appropriate.

PART VI – INSTITUTIONAL ARRANGEMENTS

Article 47 – Conference of the Parties

1. A Conference of the Parties is hereby established.
2. The first meeting of the Conference of the Parties shall be convened by the Secretary-General of the United Nations no later than one year after the entry into force of this Agreement. Thereafter, ordinary meetings of the Conference of the Parties shall be held at regular intervals to be determined by the Conference of the Parties. Extraordinary meetings of the Conference of the Parties may be held at other times, in accordance with the rules of procedure.
3. The Conference of the Parties shall ordinarily meet at the seat of the secretariat or at United Nations Headquarters.
4. The Conference of the Parties shall by consensus adopt, at its first meeting, rules of procedure for itself and its subsidiary bodies, financial rules governing its funding and the funding of the secretariat and any subsidiary bodies and, thereafter, rules of procedure and financial rules for any further subsidiary body that it may establish. Until such time as the rules of procedure have been adopted, the rules of procedure of the intergovernmental conference on an international legally binding instrument under the United Nations Convention on the Law of the Sea on the conservation and sustainable use of marine biological diversity of areas beyond national jurisdiction shall apply.
5. The Conference of the Parties shall make every effort to adopt decisions and recommendations by consensus. Except as otherwise provided in this Agreement, if all efforts to reach consensus have been exhausted, decisions and recommendations of the Conference of the Parties on questions of substance shall be adopted by a two-thirds majority of the Parties present and voting, and decisions on questions of procedure shall be adopted by a majority of the Parties present and voting.
6. The Conference of the Parties shall keep under review and evaluation the implementation of this Agreement and, for this purpose, shall:

(a) Adopt decisions and recommendations related to the implementation of this Agreement;

(b) Review and facilitate the exchange of information among Parties relevant to the implementation of this Agreement;

(c) Promote, including by establishing appropriate processes, cooperation and coordination with and among relevant legal instruments and frameworks and relevant global, regional, subregional and sectoral bodies, with a view to promoting coherence among efforts towards the conservation and sustainable use of marine biological diversity of areas beyond national jurisdiction;

(d) Establish such subsidiary bodies as deemed necessary to support the implementation of this Agreement;

(e) Adopt a budget by a three-fourths majority of the Parties present and voting if all efforts to reach consensus have been exhausted, at such frequency and for such a financial period as it may determine;

(f) Undertake other functions identified in this Agreement or as may be required for its implementation.

7. The Conference of the Parties may decide to request the International Tribunal for the Law of the Sea to give an advisory opinion on a legal question on the conformity with this Agreement of a proposal before the Conference of the Parties on any matter within its competence. A request for an advisory opinion shall not be sought on a matter within the competences of other global, regional, subregional or sectoral bodies, or on a matter that necessarily involves the concurrent consideration of any dispute concerning sovereignty or other rights over continental or insular land territory or a claim thereto, or the legal status of an area as within national jurisdiction. The request shall indicate the scope of the legal question on which the advisory opinion is sought. The Conference of the Parties may request that such opinion be given as a matter of urgency.

8. The Conference of the Parties shall, within five years of the entry into force of this Agreement and thereafter at intervals to be determined by it, assess and review the adequacy and effectiveness of the provisions of this Agreement and, if necessary, propose means of strengthening the implementation of those provisions in order to better address the conservation and sustainable use of marine biological diversity of areas beyond national jurisdiction.

Article 48 – Transparency

1. The Conference of the Parties shall promote transparency in decision-making processes and other activities carried out under this Agreement.

2. All meetings of the Conference of the Parties and its subsidiary bodies shall be open to observers participating in accordance with the rules of procedure unless otherwise decided by the Conference of the Parties. The Conference of the Parties shall publish and maintain a public record of its decisions.

3. The Conference of the Parties shall promote transparency in the implementation of this Agreement, including through the public dissemination of information and the facilitation of the participation of, and consultation with, relevant global, regional, subregional and sectoral bodies, Indigenous Peoples and local communities with relevant traditional knowledge, the scientific community, civil society and other relevant stakeholders, as appropriate and in accordance with the provisions of this Agreement.

4. Representatives of States not party to this Agreement, relevant global, regional, subregional and sectoral bodies, Indigenous Peoples and local communities with relevant traditional knowledge, the scientific community, civil society and other relevant stakeholders with an interest in matters pertaining to the Conference of the Parties may request to participate as observers in the meetings of the Conference of the Parties and of its subsidiary bodies. The rules of procedure of the Conference of the Parties shall provide for modalities for such participation and shall not be unduly restrictive in this respect. The rules of procedure shall also provide for such representatives to have timely access to all relevant information.

Article 49 – Scientific and Technical Body

1. A Scientific and Technical Body is hereby established.

2. The Scientific and Technical Body shall be composed of members serving in their expert capacity and in the best interest of the Agreement, nominated by Parties and elected by the Conference of the Parties, with suitable qualifications, taking into account the need for multidisciplinary expertise, including relevant scientific and technical expertise and expertise in relevant traditional knowledge of Indigenous Peoples and local communities, gender balance and equitable geographical representation. The terms of reference and modalities for the operation of the Scientific and Technical Body, including its selection process and the terms of members' mandates, shall be determined by the Conference of the Parties at its first meeting.

3. The Scientific and Technical Body may draw on appropriate advice emanating from relevant legal instruments and frameworks and relevant global, regional, subregional and sectoral bodies, as well as from other scientists and experts, as may be required.

4. Under the authority and guidance of the Conference of the Parties, and taking into account the multidisciplinary expertise referenced in paragraph 2 above, the Scientific and Technical Body shall provide scientific and technical advice to the Conference of the Parties, perform the functions assigned to it under this Agreement and such other functions as may be determined by the Conference of the Parties and provide reports to the Conference of the Parties on its work.

Article 50 – Secretariat

1. A secretariat is hereby established. The Conference of the Parties, at its first meeting, shall make arrangements for the functioning of the secretariat, including deciding on its seat.
2. Until such time as the secretariat commences its functions, the Secretary-General of the United Nations, through the Division for Ocean Affairs and the Law of the Sea of the Office of Legal Affairs of the United Nations Secretariat, shall perform the secretariat functions under this Agreement.
3. The secretariat and the host State may conclude a headquarters agreement. The secretariat shall enjoy legal capacity in the territory of the host State and be granted such privileges and immunities by the host State as are necessary for the exercise of its functions.
4. The secretariat shall:
   (a) Provide administrative and logistical support to the Conference of the Parties and its subsidiary bodies for the purposes of the implementation of this Agreement;
   (b) Arrange and service the meetings of the Conference of the Parties and of any other bodies as may be established under this Agreement or by the Conference of the Parties;
   (c) Circulate information relating to the implementation of this Agreement in a timely manner, including making decisions of the Conference of the Parties publicly available and transmitting them to all Parties, as well as to relevant legal instruments and frameworks and relevant global, regional, subregional and sectoral bodies;
   (d) Facilitate cooperation and coordination, as appropriate, with the secretariats of other relevant international bodies and, in particular, enter into such administrative and contractual arrangements as may be required for that purpose and for the effective discharge of its functions, subject to approval by the Conference of the Parties;
   (e) Prepare reports on the execution of its functions under this Agreement and submit them to the Conference of the Parties;
   (f) Provide assistance with the implementation of this Agreement and perform such other functions as may be determined by the Conference of the Parties or assigned to it under this Agreement.

Article 51 – Clearing-House Mechanism

1. A Clearing-House Mechanism is hereby established.
2. The Clearing-House Mechanism shall consist primarily of an open-access platform. The specific modalities for the operation of the Clearing-House Mechanism shall be determined by the Conference of the Parties.
3. The Clearing-House Mechanism shall:
   (a) Serve as a centralized platform to enable Parties to access, provide and disseminate information with respect to activities taking place pursuant to the provisions of this Agreement, including information relating to:
      (i) Marine genetic resources of areas beyond national jurisdiction, as set out in Part II of this Agreement;
      (ii) The establishment and implementation of area-based management tools, including marine protected areas;
      (iii) Environmental impact assessments;
      (iv) Requests for capacity-building and the transfer of marine technology and opportunities with respect thereto, including research collaboration and training opportunities, information on sources and availability of technological information and data for the transfer of marine technology, opportunities for facilitated access to marine technology and the availability of funding;
   (b) Facilitate the matching of capacity-building needs with the support available and with providers for the transfer of marine technology, including governmental, non- governmental or private entities interested in participating as donors in the transfer of marine technology, and facilitate access to related know-how and expertise;
   (c) Provide links to relevant global, regional, subregional, national and sectoral clearing-house mechanisms and other gene banks, repositories and databases, including those pertaining to relevant traditional knowledge of Indigenous Peoples and local communities, and promote, where possible, links with publicly available private and non- governmental platforms for the exchange of information;
   (d) Build on global, regional and subregional clearing-house institutions, where applicable, when establishing regional and subregional mechanisms under the global mechanism;
   (e) Foster enhanced transparency, including by facilitating the sharing of environmental baseline data and information relating to the conservation and sustainable use of marine biological diversity of areas beyond national jurisdiction between Parties and other relevant stakeholders;
   (f) Facilitate international cooperation and collaboration, including scientific and technical cooperation and collaboration;
   (g) Perform such other functions as may be determined by the Conference of the Parties or assigned to it under this Agreement.
4. The Clearing-House Mechanism shall be managed by the secretariat, without prejudice to possible cooperation with other relevant legal instruments and frameworks and relevant global, regional, subregional and sectoral bodies as determined by the Conference of the Parties, including the Intergovernmental Oceanographic Commission of the United Nations Educational, Scientific and Cultur-

al Organization, the International Seabed Authority, the International Maritime Organization and the Food and Agriculture Organization of the United Nations.

5. In the management of the Clearing-House Mechanism, full recognition shall be given to the special requirements of developing States Parties, as well as the special circumstances of small island developing States Parties, and their access to the mechanism shall be facilitated to enable those States to utilize it without undue obstacles or administrative burdens. Information shall be included on activities to promote information- sharing, awareness-raising and dissemination in and with those States, as well as to provide specific programmes for those States.
6. The confidentiality of information provided under this Agreement and rights thereto shall be respected. Nothing under this Agreement shall be interpreted as requiring the sharing of information that is protected from disclosure under the domestic law of a Party or other applicable law.

PART VII – FINANCIAL RESOURCES AND MECHANISM

Article 52 – Funding

1. Each Party shall provide, within its capabilities, resources in respect of those activities that are intended to achieve the objectives of this Agreement, taking into account its national policies, priorities, plans and programmes.
2. The institutions established under this Agreement shall be funded through assessed contributions of the Parties.
3. A mechanism for the provision of adequate, accessible, new and additional and predictable financial resources under this Agreement is hereby established. The mechanism shall assist developing States Parties in implementing this Agreement, including through funding in support of capacity-building and the transfer of marine technology, and perform other functions as set out in this article for the conservation and sustainable use of marine biological diversity.
4. The mechanism shall include:
   (a) A voluntary trust fund established by the Conference of the Parties to facilitate the participation of representatives of developing States Parties, in particular least developed countries, landlocked developing countries and small island developing States, in the meetings of the bodies established under this Agreement;
   (b) A special fund that shall be funded through the following sources:
      (i) Annual contributions in accordance with article 14, paragraph 6;
      (ii) Payments in accordance with article 14, paragraph 7;
      (iii) Additional contributions from Parties and private entities wishing to provide financial resources to support the conservation and sustainable use of marine biological diversity of areas beyond national jurisdiction;
   (c) The Global Environment Facility trust fund.
5. The Conference of the Parties may consider the possibility of establishing additional funds, as part of the financial mechanism, to support the conservation and sustainable use of marine biological diversity of areas beyond national jurisdiction, to finance rehabilitation and ecological restoration of marine biological diversity of areas beyond national jurisdiction.
6. The special fund and the Global Environment Facility trust fund shall be utilized in order to:
   (a) Fund capacity-building projects under this Agreement, including effective projects on the conservation and sustainable use of marine biological diversity and activities and programmes, including training related to the transfer of marine technology;
   (b) Assist developing States Parties in implementing this Agreement;
   (c) Support conservation and sustainable use programmes by Indigenous Peoples and local communities as holders of traditional knowledge;
   (d) Support public consultations at the national, subregional and regional levels;
   (e) Fund the undertaking of any other activities as decided by the Conference of the Parties.
7. The financial mechanism should seek to ensure that duplication is avoided, and complementarity and coherence promoted, among the utilization of the funds within the mechanism.
8. Financial resources mobilized in support of the implementation of this Agreement may include funding provided through public and private sources, both national and international, including, but not limited to, contributions from States, international financial institutions, existing funding mechanisms under global and regional instruments, donor agencies, intergovernmental organizations, non-governmental organizations and natural and juridical persons, and through public-private partnerships.
9. For the purposes of this Agreement, the mechanism shall function under the authority, where appropriate, and guidance of the Conference of the Parties and shall be accountable thereto. The Conference of the Parties shall provide guidance on overall strategies, policies, programme priorities and eligibility for access to and utilization of financial resources.
10. The Conference of the Parties and the Global Environment Facility shall agree upon arrangements to give effect to the above paragraphs at the first meeting of the Conference of the Parties.
11. In recognition of the urgency to address the conservation and sustainable use of marine biological diversity of areas beyond national jurisdiction, the Conference of the Parties shall determine an initial resource mobilization goal through 2030 for the

special fund from all sources, taking into account, inter alia, the institutional modalities of the special fund and the information provided through the capacity-building and transfer of marine technology committee.

12. Eligibility for access to funding under this Agreement shall be open to developing States Parties on the basis of need. Funding under the special fund shall be distributed according to equitable sharing criteria, taking into account the needs for assistance of Parties with special requirements, in particular the least developed countries, landlocked developing countries, geographically disadvantaged States, small island developing States and coastal African States, archipelagic States and developing middle-income countries, and taking into account the special circumstances of small island developing States and of least developed countries. The special fund shall be aimed at ensuring efficient access to funding through simplified application and approval procedures and enhanced readiness of support for such developing States Parties.
13. In the light of capacity constraints, Parties shall encourage international organizations to grant preferential treatment to, and consider the specific needs and special requirements of developing States Parties, in particular the least developed countries, landlocked developing countries and small island developing States, and taking into account the special circumstances of small island developing States and of least developed countries, in the allocation of appropriate funds and technical assistance and the utilization of their specialized services for the purposes of the conservation and sustainable use of marine biological diversity of areas beyond national jurisdiction.
14. The Conference of the Parties shall establish a finance committee on financial resources. It shall be composed of members possessing appropriate qualifications and expertise, taking into account gender balance and equitable geographical distribution. The terms of reference and modalities for the operation of the committee shall be decided by the Conference of the Parties. The committee shall periodically report and make recommendations on the identification and mobilization of funds under the mechanism. It shall also collect information and report on funding under other mechanisms and instruments contributing directly or indirectly to the achievement of the objectives of this Agreement. In addition to the considerations provided in this article, the committee shall consider, inter alia:
    (a) The assessment of the needs of the Parties, in particular developing States Parties;
    (b) The availability and timely disbursement of funds;
    (c) The transparency of decision-making and management processes concerning fundraising and allocations;
    (d) The accountability of the recipient developing States Parties with respect to the agreed use of funds.
15. The Conference of the Parties shall consider the reports and recommendations of the finance committee and take appropriate action.
16. The Conference of the Parties shall, in addition, undertake a periodic review of the financial mechanism to assess the adequacy, effectiveness and accessibility of financial resources, including for the delivery of capacity-building and the transfer of marine technology, in particular for developing States Parties.

PART VIII – IMPLEMENTATION AND COMPLIANCE

Article 53 – Implementation

Parties shall take the necessary legislative, administrative or policy measures, as appropriate, to ensure the implementation of this Agreement.

Article 54 – Monitoring of implementation

Each Party shall monitor the implementation of its obligations under this Agreement and shall, in a format and at intervals to be determined by the Conference of the Parties, report to the Conference on measures that it has taken to implement this Agreement.

Article 55 – Implementation and Compliance Committee

1. An Implementation and Compliance Committee to facilitate and consider the implementation of and promote compliance with the provisions of this Agreement is hereby established. The Implementation and Compliance Committee shall be facilitative in nature and function in a manner that is transparent, non-adversarial and non-punitive.
2. The Implementation and Compliance Committee shall consist of members possessing appropriate qualifications and experience nominated by Parties and elected by the Conference of the Parties, with due consideration given to gender balance and equitable geographical representation.
3. The Implementation and Compliance Committee shall operate under the modalities and rules of procedure adopted by the Conference of the Parties at its first meeting. The Implementation and Compliance Committee shall consider issues of implementation and compliance at the individual and systemic levels, inter alia, and report periodically and make recommendations, as appropriate while cognizant of respective national circumstances, to the Conference of the Parties.
4. In the course of its work, the Implementation and Compliance Committee may draw on appropriate information from bodies established under this Agreement, as well as relevant legal instruments and frameworks and relevant global, regional, subregional and sectoral bodies, as may be required.

PART IX – SETTLEMENT OF DISPUTES

Article 56 – Prevention of disputes

Parties shall cooperate in order to prevent disputes.

Article 57 – Obligation to settle disputes by peaceful means

Parties have the obligation to settle their disputes concerning the interpretation or application of this Agreement by negotiation, inquiry, mediation, conciliation, arbitration, judicial settlement, resort to regional agencies or arrangements, or other peaceful means of their own choice.

Article 58 – Settlement of disputes by any peaceful means chosen by the Parties

Nothing in this Part impairs the right of any Party to this Agreement to agree at any time to settle a dispute between them concerning the interpretation or application of this Agreement by any peaceful means of their own choice.

Article 59 – Disputes of a technical nature

Where a dispute concerns a matter of a technical nature, the Parties concerned may refer the dispute to an ad hoc expert panel established by them. The panel shall confer with the Parties concerned and shall endeavour to resolve the dispute expeditiously without recourse to binding procedures for the settlement of disputes under article 60 of this Agreement.

Article 60 – Procedures for the settlement of disputes

1. Disputes concerning the interpretation or application of this Agreement shall be settled in accordance with the provisions for the settlement of disputes provided for in Part XV of the Convention.
2. The provisions of Part XV of and Annexes V, VI, VII and VIII to the Convention shall be deemed to be replicated for the purpose of the settlement of disputes involving a Party to this Agreement that is not a Party to the Convention.
3. Any procedure accepted by a Party to this Agreement that is also a Party to the Convention pursuant to article 287 of the Convention shall apply to the settlement of disputes under this Part, unless that Party, when signing, ratifying, approving, accepting or acceding to this Agreement, or at any time thereafter, has accepted another procedure pursuant to article 287 of the Convention for the settlement of disputes under this Part.
4. Any declaration made by a Party to this Agreement that is also a Party to the Convention pursuant to article 298 of the Convention shall apply to the settlement of disputes under this Part, unless that Party, when signing, ratifying, approving, accepting or acceding to this Agreement, or at any time thereafter, has made a different declaration pursuant to article 298 of the Convention for the settlement of disputes under this Part.
5. Pursuant to paragraph 2 above, a Party to this Agreement that is not a Party to the Convention, when signing, ratifying, approving, accepting or acceding to this Agreement, or at any time thereafter, shall be free to choose, by means of a written declaration, submitted to the depositary, one or more of the following means for the settlement of disputes concerning the interpretation or application of this Agreement:
   (a) The International Tribunal for the Law of the Sea;
   (b) The International Court of Justice;
   (c) An Annex VII arbitral tribunal;
   (d) An Annex VIII special arbitral tribunal for one or more of the categories of disputes specified in said Annex.
6. A Party to this Agreement that is not a Party to the Convention that has not issued a declaration shall be deemed to have accepted the option in paragraph 5 (c) above. If the parties to a dispute have accepted the same procedure for the settlement of the dispute, it may be submitted only to that procedure, unless the parties otherwise agree. If the parties to a dispute have not accepted the same procedure for the settlement of the dispute, it may be submitted only to arbitration under Annex VII to the Convention, unless the parties otherwise agree. Article 287, paragraphs 6 to 8, of the Convention shall apply to declarations made under paragraph 5 above.
7. A Party to this Agreement that is not a Party to the Convention may, when signing, ratifying, approving, accepting or acceding to this Agreement, or at any time thereafter, without prejudice to the obligations arising under this Part, declare in writing that it does not accept any or more of the procedures provided for in Part XV, section 2, of the Convention with respect to one or more of the categories of disputes set out in article 298 of the Convention for the settlement of disputes under this Part. Article 298 of the Convention shall apply to such a declaration.
8. The provisions of this article shall be without prejudice to the procedures on the settlement of disputes to which Parties have agreed as participants in a relevant legal instrument or framework, or as members of a relevant global, regional, subregional or sectoral body concerning the interpretation or application of such instruments and frameworks.
9. Nothing in this Agreement shall be interpreted as conferring jurisdiction upon a court or tribunal over any dispute that concerns or necessarily involves the concurrent consideration of the legal status of an area as within national jurisdiction, nor over any dispute concerning sovereignty or other rights over continental or insular land territory or a claim thereto of a Party to this Agreement, provided that nothing in this paragraph shall be interpreted as limiting the jurisdiction of a court or tribunal under Part XV, section 2, of the Convention.
10. For the avoidance of doubt, nothing in this Agreement shall be relied upon as a basis for asserting or denying any claims to sovereignty, sovereign rights or jurisdiction over land or maritime areas, including in respect to any disputes relating thereto.

Article 61 – Provisional arrangements

Pending the settlement of a dispute in accordance with this Part, the parties to the dispute shall make every effort to enter into provisional arrangements of a practical nature.

PART X – NON-PARTIES TO THIS AGREEMENT

Article 62 – Non-parties to this Agreement

Parties shall encourage non-parties to this Agreement to become Parties thereto and to adopt laws and regulations consistent with its provisions.

PART XI – GOOD FAITH AND ABUSE OF RIGHTS

Article 63 – Good faith and abuse of rights

Parties shall fulfil in good faith the obligations assumed under this Agreement and exercise the rights recognized therein in a manner that would not constitute an abuse of right.

PART XII – FINAL PROVISIONS

Article 64 – Right to vote

1. Each Party to this Agreement shall have one vote, except as provided for in paragraph 2 below.
2. A regional economic integration organization Party to this Agreement, on matters within its competence, shall exercise its right to vote with a number of votes equal to the number of its member States that are Parties to this Agreement. Such an organization shall not exercise its right to vote if any of its member States exercises its right to vote, and vice versa.

Article 65 – Signature

This Agreement shall be open for signature by all States and regional economic integration organizations from 20 September 2023 and shall remain open for signature at United Nations Headquarters in New York until 20 September 2025.

Article 66 – Ratification, approval, acceptance and accession

This Agreement shall be subject to ratification, approval or acceptance by States and regional economic integration organizations. It shall be open for accession by States and regional economic integration organizations from the day after the date on which the Agreement is closed for signature. Instruments of ratification, approval, acceptance and accession shall be deposited with the Secretary-General of the United Nations.

Article 67 – Division of the competence of regional economic integration organizations and their member States in respect of the matters governed by this Agreement

1. Any regional economic integration organization that becomes a Party to this Agreement without any of its member States being a Party shall be bound by all the obligations under this Agreement. In the case of such organizations, one or more of whose member States is a Party to this Agreement, the organization and its member States shall decide on their respective responsibilities for the performance of their obligations under this Agreement. In such cases, the organization and the member States shall not be entitled to exercise rights under this Agreement concurrently.
2. In its instrument of ratification, approval, acceptance or accession, a regional economic integration organization shall declare the extent of its competence in respect of the matters governed by this Agreement. Any such organization shall also inform the depositary, who shall in turn inform the Parties, of any relevant modification of the extent of its competence.

Article 68 – Entry into force

1. This Agreement shall enter into force 120 days after the date of deposit of the sixtieth instrument of ratification, approval, acceptance or accession.
2. For each State or regional economic integration organization that ratifies, approves or accepts this Agreement or accedes thereto after the deposit of the sixtieth instrument of ratification, approval, acceptance or accession, this Agreement shall enter into force on the thirtieth day following the deposit of its instrument of ratification, approval, acceptance or accession, subject to paragraph 1 above.
3. For the purposes of paragraphs 1 and 2 above, any instrument deposited by a regional economic integration organization shall not be counted as additional to those deposited by the member States of that organization.

Article 69 – Provisional application

1. This Agreement may be applied provisionally by a State or regional economic integration organization that consents to its provisional application by so notifying the depositary in writing at the time of signature or deposit of its instrument of ratification, approval, acceptance or accession. Such provisional application shall become effective from the date of receipt of the notification by the depositary.
2. Provisional application by a State or regional economic integration organization shall terminate upon the entry into force of this Agreement for that State or regional economic integration organization or upon notification by that State or regional economic integration organization to the depositary in writing of its intention to terminate its provisional application.

Article 70 – Reservations and exceptions

No reservations or exceptions may be made to this Agreement, unless expressly permitted by other articles of this Agreement.

Article 71 – Declarations and statements

Article 70 does not preclude a State or regional economic integration organization, when signing, ratifying, approving, accepting or acceding to this Agreement, from making declarations or statements, however phrased or named, with a view, inter alia, to the harmonization of its laws and regulations with the provisions of this Agreement, provided that such declarations or statements do not purport to exclude or to modify the legal effect of the provisions of this Agreement in their application to that State or regional economic integration organization.

Article 72 – Amendment

1. A Party may, by written communication addressed to the secretariat, propose amendments to this Agreement. The secretariat shall circulate such a communication to all Parties. If, within six months from the date of the circulation of the communication, not less than one half of the Parties reply favourably to the request, the proposed amendment shall be considered at the following meeting of the Conference of the Parties.
2. An amendment to this Agreement adopted in accordance with article 47 shall be communicated by the depositary to all Parties for ratification, approval or acceptance.
3. Amendments to this Agreement shall enter into force for the Parties ratifying, approving or accepting them on the thirtieth day following the deposit of instruments of ratification, approval or acceptance by two thirds of the number of Parties to this Agreement as at the time of adoption of the amendment. Thereafter, for each Party depositing its instrument of ratification, approval or acceptance of an amendment after the deposit of the required number of such instruments, the amendment shall enter into force on the thirtieth day following the deposit of its instrument of ratification, approval or acceptance.
4. An amendment may provide, at the time of its adoption, that a smaller or larger number of ratifications, approvals or acceptances shall be required for its entry into force than required under this article.
5. For the purposes of paragraphs 3 and 4 above, any instrument deposited by a regional economic integration organization shall not be counted as additional to those deposited by the member States of that organization.
6. A State or regional economic integration organization that becomes a Party to this Agreement after the entry into force of amendments in accordance with paragraph 3 above shall, failing an expression of a different intention by that State or regional economic integration organization:
   (a) Be considered as a Party to this Agreement as so amended;
   (b) Be considered as a Party to the unamended Agreement in relation to any Party not bound by the amendment.

Article 73 – Denunciation

1. A Party may, by written notification addressed to the Secretary-General of the United Nations, denounce this Agreement and may indicate its reasons. Failure to indicate reasons shall not affect the validity of the denunciation. The denunciation shall take effect one year after the date of receipt of the notification, unless the notification specifies a later date.
2. The denunciation shall not in any way affect the duty of any Party to fulfil any obligation embodied in this Agreement to which it would be subject under international law independently of this Agreement.

Article 74 – Annexes

1. The annexes form an integral part of this Agreement and, unless expressly provided otherwise, a reference to this Agreement or to one of its parts includes a reference to the annexes relating thereto.
2. The provisions of article 72 relating to the amendment of this Agreement shall also apply to the proposal, adoption and entry into force of a new annex to the Agreement.
3. Any Party may propose an amendment to any annex to this Agreement for consideration at the next meeting of the Conference of the Parties. The annexes may be amended by the Conference of the Parties. Notwithstanding the provisions of article 72, the following provisions shall apply in relation to amendments to annexes to this Agreement:
   (a) The text of the proposed amendment shall be communicated to the secretariat at least 150 days before the meeting. The secretariat shall, upon receiving the text of the proposed amendment, communicate it to the Parties. The secretariat shall consult relevant subsidiary bodies, as required, and shall communicate any response to all Parties not later than 30 days before the meeting;
   (b) Amendments adopted at a meeting shall enter into force 180 days after the close of that meeting for all Parties, except those that make an objection in accordance with paragraph 4 below.
4. During the period of 180 days provided for in paragraph 3 (b) above, any Party may, by notification in writing to the depositary, make an objection with respect to the amendment. Such objection may be withdrawn at any time by written notification to the depositary and, thereupon, the amendment to the annex shall enter into force for that Party on the thirtieth day after the date of withdrawal of the objection.

Article 75 – Depositary

The Secretary-General of the United Nations shall be the depositary of this Agreement and any amendments or revisions thereto.

Article 76 – Authentic texts

The Arabic, Chinese, English, French, Russian and Spanish texts of this Agreement are equally authentic.

ANNEX I – Indicative criteria for identification of areas

(a) Uniqueness;
(b) Rarity;

(c) Special importance for the life history stages of species;

(d) Special importance of the species found therein;

(e) The importance for threatened, endangered or declining species or habitats;

(f) Vulnerability, including to climate change and ocean acidification;

(g) Fragility;

(h) Sensitivity;

(i) Biological diversity and productivity;

(j) Representativeness;

(k) Dependency;

(l) Naturalness;

(m) Ecological connectivity;

(n) Important ecological processes occurring therein;

(o) Economic and social factors;

(p) Cultural factors;

(q) Cumulative and transboundary impacts;

(r) Slow recovery and resilience;

(s) Adequacy and viability;

(t) Replication;

(u) Sustainability of reproduction;

(v) Existence of conservation and management measures.

ANNEX II – Types of capacity-building and of the transfer of marine technology

Under this Agreement, capacity-building and transfer of marine technology initiatives may include but are not limited to:

(a) The sharing of relevant data, information, knowledge and research, in user- friendly formats, including:

  (i) The sharing of marine scientific and technological knowledge;

  (ii) The exchange of information on the conservation and sustainable use of marine biological diversity of areas beyond national jurisdiction;

  (iii) The sharing of research and development results;

(b) Information dissemination and awareness-raising, including with regard to:

  (i) Marine scientific research, marine sciences and related marine operations and services;

  (ii) Environmental and biological information collected through research conducted in areas beyond national jurisdiction;

  (iii) Relevant traditional knowledge in line with the free, prior and informed consent of the holders of such knowledge;

  (iv) Stressors on the ocean that affect marine biological diversity of areas beyond national jurisdiction, including the adverse effects of climate change, such as warming and ocean deoxygenation, as well as ocean acidification;

  (v) Measures such as area-based management tools, including marine protected areas;

  (vi) Environmental impact assessments;

(c) The development and strengthening of relevant infrastructure, including equipment, such as:

  (i) The development and establishment of necessary infrastructure;

  (ii) The provision of technology, including sampling and methodology equipment (e.g., for water, geological, biological or chemical samples);

  (iii) The acquisition of the equipment necessary to support and further develop research and development capabilities, including in data management, in the context of activities with respect to marine genetic resources and digital sequence information on marine genetic resources of areas beyond national jurisdiction, measures such as area-based management tools, including marine protected areas, and the conduct of environmental impact assessments;

(d) The development and strengthening of institutional capacity and national regulatory frameworks or mechanisms, including:

  (i) Governance, policy and legal frameworks and mechanisms;

  (ii) Assistance in the development, implementation and enforcement of national legislative, administrative or policy measures, including associated regulatory, scientific and technical requirements at the national, subregional or regional level;

  (iii) Technical support for the implementation of the provisions of this Agreement, including for data monitoring and reporting;

  (iv) Capacity to translate information and data into effective and efficient policies, including by facilitating access to and the acquisition of knowledge necessary to inform decision makers in developing States Parties;

  (v) The establishment or strengthening of the institutional capacities of relevant national and regional organizations and institutions;

  (vi) The establishment of national and regional scientific centres, including as data repositories;

  (vii) The development of regional centres of excellence;

  (viii) The development of regional centres for skills development;

  (ix) Increasing cooperative links between regional institutions, for example, North-South and South-South collaboration and collaboration among regional seas organizations and regional fisheries management organizations;

(e) The development and strengthening of human and financial management resource capabilities and of technical expertise through exchanges, research collaboration, technical support, education and training and the transfer of marine technology, such as:

(i) Collaboration and cooperation in marine science, including through data collection, technical exchange, scientific research projects and programmes, and the development of joint scientific research projects in cooperation with institutions in developing States;

(ii) Education and training in:

a. The natural and social sciences, both basic and applied, to develop scientific and research capacity;

b. Technology, and the application of marine science and technology, to develop scientific and research capacities;

c. Policy and governance;

d. The relevance and application of traditional knowledge;

(iii) The exchange of experts, including experts on traditional knowledge;

(iv) The provision of funding for the development of human resources and technical expertise, including through:

a. The provision of scholarships or other grants for representatives of small island developing States Parties in workshops, training programmes or other relevant programmes to develop their specific capacities;

b. The provision of financial and technical expertise and resources, in particular for small island developing States, concerning environmental impact assessments;

(v) The establishment of a networking mechanism among trained human resources;

(f) The development and sharing of manuals, guidelines and standards, including:

(i) Criteria and reference materials;

(ii) Technology standards and rules;

(iii) A repository for manuals and relevant information to share knowledge and capacity on how to conduct environmental impact assessments, lessons learned and best practices;

(g) The development of technical, scientific and research and development programmes, including biotechnological research activities.

8.4. OSPAR Convention 1992

Convention for the Protection of the Marine Environment of the North-East Atlantic, Paris, 22 September 1992, 2354 UNTS 67

THE CONTRACTING PARTIES,

RECOGNISING that the marine environment and the fauna and flora which it supports are of vital importance to all nations;

RECOGNISING the inherent worth of the marine environment of the North-East Atlantic and the necessity for providing coordinated protection for it;

RECOGNISING that concerted action at national, regional and global levels is essential to prevent and eliminate marine pollution and to achieve sustainable management of the maritime area, that is, the management of human activities in such a manner that the marine ecosystem will continue to sustain the legitimate uses of the sea and will continue to meet the needs of present and future generations;

MINDFUL that the ecological equilibrium and the legitimate uses of the sea are threatened by pollution;

CONSIDERING the recommendations of the United Nations Conference on the Human Environment, held in Stockholm in June 1972;

CONSIDERING also the results of the United Nations Conference on the Environment and Development held in Rio de Janeiro in June 1992;

RECALLING the relevant provisions of customary international law reflected in Part XII of the United Nations Law of the Sea Convention and, in particular, Article 197 on global and regional cooperation for the protection and preservation of the marine environment;

CONSIDERING that the common interests of States concerned with the same marine area should induce them to cooperate at regional or sub-regional levels;

RECALLING the positive results obtained within the context of the Convention for the prevention of marine pollution by dumping from ships and aircraft signed in Oslo on 15th February 1972, as amended by the protocols of 2nd March 1983 and 5th December 1989, and the Convention for the prevention of marine pollution from land-based sources signed in Paris on 4th June 1974, as amended by the protocol of 26th March 1986;

CONVINCED that further international action to prevent and eliminate pollution of the sea should be taken without delay, as part of progressive and coherent measures to protect the marine environment;

RECOGNISING that it may be desirable to adopt, on the regional level, more stringent measures with respect to the prevention and elimination of pollution of the marine environment or with respect to the protection of the marine environment against the adverse effects of human activities than are provided for in international conventions or agreements with a global scope;

RECOGNISING that questions relating to the management of fisheries are appropriately regulated under international and regional agreements dealing specifically with such questions;

CONSIDERING that the present Oslo and Paris Conventions do not adequately control some of the many sources of pollution, and that it is therefore justifiable to replace them with the present Convention, which addresses all sources of pollution of the marine environment and the adverse effects of human activities upon it, takes into account the precautionary principle and strengthens regional cooperation;

HAVE AGREED as follows:

ARTICLE 1 – DEFINITIONS

For the purposes of the Convention:

(a) "Maritime area" means the internal waters and the territorial seas of the Contracting Parties, the sea beyond and adjacent to the territorial sea under the jurisdiction of the coastal state to the extent recognised by international law, and the high seas, including the bed of all those waters and its sub-soil, situated within the following limits:

  (i) those parts of the Atlantic and Arctic Oceans and their dependent seas which lie north of 36° north latitude and between 42° west longitude and 51° east longitude, but excluding:

    (1) the Baltic Sea and the Belts lying to the south and east of lines drawn from Hasenore Head to Gniben Point, from Korshage to Spodsbjerg and from Gilbjerg Head to Kullen,

    (2) the Mediterranean Sea and its dependent seas as far as the point of intersection of the parallel of 36° north latitude and the meridian of 5° 36' west longitude;

  (ii) that part of the Atlantic Ocean north of 59° north latitude and between 44° west longitude and 42° west longitude.

(b) "Internal waters" means the waters on the landward side of the baselines from which the breadth of the territorial sea is measured, extending in the case of watercourses up to the freshwater limit.

(c) "Freshwater limit" means the place in a watercourse where, at low tide and in a period of low freshwater flow, there is an appreciable increase in salinity due to the presence of seawater.

(d) "Pollution" means the introduction by man, directly or indirectly, of substances or energy into the maritime area which results, or is likely to result, in hazards to human health, harm to living resources and marine ecosystems, damage to amenities or interference with other legitimate uses of the sea.

(e) "Land-based sources" means point and diffuse sources on land from which substances or energy reach the maritime area by water, through the air, or directly from the coast. It includes sources associated with any deliberate disposal under the seabed made accessible from land by tunnel, pipeline or other means and sources associated with man-made structures placed, in the maritime area under the jurisdiction of a Contracting Party, other than for the purpose of offshore activities.

(f) "Dumping" means

  (i) any deliberate disposal in the maritime area of wastes or other matter

    (1) from vessels or aircraft;

    (2) from offshore installations;

  (ii) any deliberate disposal in the maritime area of

    (1) vessels or aircraft;

    (2) offshore installations and offshore pipelines.

(g) "Dumping" does not include:

  (i) the disposal in accordance with the International Convention for the Prevention of Pollution from Ships, 1973, as modified by the Protocol of 1978 relating thereto, or other applicable international law, of wastes or other matter incidental to, or derived from, the normal operations of vessels or aircraft or offshore installations other than wastes or other matter transported by or to vessels or aircraft or offshore installations for the purpose of disposal of such wastes or other matter or derived from the treatment of such wastes or other matter on such vessels or aircraft or offshore installations;

  (ii) placement of matter for a purpose other than the mere disposal thereof, provided that, if the placement is for a purpose other than that for which the matter was originally designed or constructed, it is in accordance with the relevant provisions of the Convention; and

  (iii) for the purposes of Annex III, the leaving wholly or partly in place of a disused offshore installation or disused offshore pipeline, provided that any such operation takes place in accordance with any relevant provision of the Convention and with other relevant international law.

(h) "Incineration" means any deliberate combustion of wastes or other matter in the maritime area for the purpose of their thermal destruction.

(i) "Incineration" does not include the thermal destruction of wastes or other matter in accordance with applicable international law incidental to, or derived from the normal operation of vessels or aircraft, or offshore installations other than the thermal destruction of wastes or other matter on vessels or aircraft or offshore installations operating for the purpose of such thermal destruction.

(j) "Offshore activities" means activities carried out in the maritime area for the purposes of the exploration, appraisal or exploitation of liquid and gaseous hydrocarbons.

(k) "Offshore sources" means offshore installations and offshore pipelines from which substances or energy reach the maritime area.

(l) "Offshore installation" means any man-made structure, plant or vessel or parts thereof, whether floating or fixed to the seabed, placed within the maritime area for the purpose of offshore activities.

(m) "Offshore pipeline" means any pipeline which has been placed in the maritime area for the purpose of offshore activities.

(n) "Vessels or aircraft" means waterborne or airborne craft of any type whatsoever, their parts and other fittings. This expression includes air-cushion craft, floating craft whether self-propelled or not, and other man-made structures in the maritime area and their equipment, but excludes offshore installations and offshore pipelines.

(o) "Wastes or other matter" does not include:

  (i) human remains;

  (ii) offshore installations;

  (iii) offshore pipelines;

  (iv) unprocessed fish and fish offal discarded from fishing vessels.

(p) "Convention" means, unless the text otherwise indicates, the Convention for the Protection of the Marine Environment of the North-East Atlantic, its Annexes and Appendices.

(q) "Oslo Convention" means the Convention for the Prevention of Marine Pollution by Dumping from Ships and Aircraft signed in Oslo on 15th February 1972, as amended by the protocols of 2nd March 1983 and 5th December 1989.

(r) "Paris Convention" means the Convention for the Prevention of Marine Pollution from Land-based Sources, signed in Paris on 4th June 1974, as amended by the protocol of 26th March 1986.

(s) "Regional economic integration organisation" means an organisation constituted by sovereign States of a given region which has competence in respect of matters governed by the Convention and has been duly authorised, in accordance with its internal procedures, to sign, ratify, accept, approve or accede to the Convention.

ARTICLE 2 – GENERAL OBLIGATIONS

1. (a) The Contracting Parties shall, in accordance with the provisions of the Convention, take all possible steps to prevent and eliminate pollution and shall take the necessary measures to protect the maritime area against the adverse effects of human activities so as to safeguard human health and to conserve marine ecosystems and, when practicable, restore marine areas which have been adversely affected.

   (b) To this end Contracting Parties shall, individually and jointly, adopt programmes and measures and shall harmonise their policies and strategies.

2. The Contracting Parties shall apply:

(a) the precautionary principle, by virtue of which preventive measures are to be taken when there are reasonable grounds for concern that substances or energy introduced, directly or indirectly, into the marine environment may bring about hazards to human health, harm living resources and marine ecosystems, damage amenities or interfere with other legitimate uses of the sea, even when there is no conclusive evidence of a causal relationship between the inputs and the effects;

(b) the polluter pays principle, by virtue of which the costs of pollution prevention, control and reduction measures are to be borne by the polluter.

3. (a) In implementing the Convention, Contracting Parties shall adopt programmes and measures which contain, where appropriate, time-limits for their completion and which take full account of the use of the latest technological developments and practices designed to prevent and eliminate pollution fully.

   (b) To this end they shall:

   (i) taking into account the criteria set forth in Appendix 1, define with respect to programmes and measures the application of, inter alia,

   – best available techniques

   – best environmental practice including, where appropriate, clean technology;

   (ii) in carrying out such programmes and measures, ensure the application of best available techniques and best environmental practice as so defined, including, where appropriate, clean technology.

4. The Contracting Parties shall apply the measures they adopt in such a way as to prevent an increase in pollution of the sea outside the maritime area or in other parts of the environment.

5. No provision of the Convention shall be interpreted as preventing the Contracting Parties from taking, individually or jointly, more stringent measures with respect to the prevention and elimination of pollution of the maritime area or with respect to the protection of the maritime area against the adverse effects of human activities.

ARTICLE 3 – POLLUTION FROM LAND-BASED SOURCES

The Contracting Parties shall take, individually and jointly, all possible steps to prevent and eliminate pollution from land-based sources in accordance with the provisions of the Convention, in particular as provided for in Annex I.

ARTICLE 4 – POLLUTION BY DUMPING OR INCINERATION

The Contracting Parties shall take, individually and jointly, all possible steps to prevent and eliminate pollution by dumping or incineration of wastes or other matter in accordance with the provisions of the Convention, in particular as provided for in Annex II.

ARTICLE 5 – POLLUTION FROM OFF-SHORE SOURCES

The Contracting Parties shall take, individually and jointly, all possible steps to prevent and eliminate pollution from offshore sources in accordance with the provisions of the Convention, in particular as provided for in Annex III.

ARTICLE 6 – ASSESSMENT OF THE QUALITY OF THE MARINE ENVIRONMENT

The Contracting Parties shall, in accordance with the provisions of the Convention, in particular as provided for in Annex IV:

(a) undertake and publish at regular intervals joint assessments of the quality status of the marine environment and of its development, for the maritime area or for regions or sub-regions thereof;

(b) include in such assessments both an evaluation of the effectiveness of the measures taken and planned for the protection of the marine environment and the identification of priorities for action.

ARTICLE 7 – POLLUTION FROM OTHER SOURCES

The Contracting Parties shall cooperate with a view to adopting Annexes, in addition to the Annexes mentioned in Articles 3, 4, 5 and 6 above, prescribing measures, procedures and standards to protect the maritime area against pollution from other sources, to the extent that such pollution is not already the subject of effective measures agreed by other international organisations or prescribed by other international conventions.

ARTICLE 8 – SCIENTIFIC AND TECHNICAL RESEARCH

1. To further the aims of the Convention, the Contracting Parties shall establish complementary or joint programmes of scientific or technical research and, in accordance with a standard procedure, to transmit to the Commission:

   (a) the results of such complementary, joint or other relevant research;

   (b) details of other relevant programmes of scientific and technical research.

2. In so doing, the Contracting Parties shall have regard to the work carried out, in these fields, by the appropriate international organisations and agencies.

ARTICLE 9 – ACCESS TO INFORMATION

1. The Contracting Parties shall ensure that their competent authorities are required to make available the information described in paragraph 2 of this Article to any natural or legal person, in response to any reasonable request, without that person's having to prove an interest, without unreasonable charges, as soon as possible and at the latest within two months.

2. The information referred to in paragraph 1 of this Article is any available information in written, visual, aural or data-base form on the state of the maritime area, on activities or measures adversely

affecting or likely to affect it and on activities or measures introduced in accordance with the Convention.

3. The provisions of this Article shall not affect the right of Contracting Parties, in accordance with their national legal systems and applicable international regulations, to provide for a request for such information to be refused where it affects:
   (a) the confidentiality of the proceedings of public authorities, international relations and national defence;
   (b) public security;
   (c) matters which are, or have been, sub judice, or under enquiry (including disciplinary enquiries), or which are the subject of preliminary investigation proceedings;
   (d) commercial and industrial confidentiality, including intellectual property;
   (e) the confidentiality of personal data and/or files;
   (f) material supplied by a third party without that party being under a legal obligation to do so;
   (g) material, the disclosure of which would make it more likely that the environment to which such material related would be damaged.
4. The reasons for a refusal to provide the information requested must be given.

ARTICLE 10 – COMMISSION

1. A Commission, made up of representatives of each of the Contracting Parties, is hereby established. The Commission shall meet at regular intervals and at any time when, due to special circumstances, it is so decided in accordance with the Rules of Procedure.
2. It shall be the duty of the Commission:
   (a) to supervise the implementation of the Convention;
   (b) generally to review the condition of the maritime area, the effectiveness of the measures being adopted, the priorities and the need for any additional or different measures;
   (c) to draw up, in accordance with the General Obligations of the Convention, programmes and measures for the prevention and elimination of pollution and for the control of activities which may, directly or indirectly, adversely affect the maritime area; such programmes and measure may, when appropriate, include economic instruments;
   (d) to establish at regular intervals its programme of work;
   (e) to set up such subsidiary bodies as it considers necessary and to define their terms of reference;
   (f) to consider and, where appropriate, adopt proposals for the amendment of the Convention in accordance with Articles 15, 16, 17, 18, 19 and 27;
   (g) to discharge the functions conferred by Articles 21 and 23 and such other functions as may be appropriate under the terms of the Convention;
3. To these ends the Commission may, inter alia, adopt decisions and recommendations in accordance with Article 13.
4. The Commission shall draw up its Rules of Procedure which shall be adopted by unanimous vote of the Contracting Parties.
5. The Commission shall draw up its Financial Regulations which shall be adopted by unanimous vote of the Contracting Parties.

ARTICLE 11 – OBSERVERS

1. The Commission may, by unanimous vote of the Contracting Parties, decide to admit as an observer:
   (a) any State which is not a Contracting Party to the Convention;
   (b) any international governmental or any non-governmental organisation the activities of which are related to the Convention.
2. Such observers may participate in meetings of the Commission but without the right to vote and may present to the Commission any information or reports relevant to the objectives of the Convention.
3. The conditions for the admission and the participation of observers shall be set in the Rules of Procedure of the Commission.

ARTICLE 12 – SECRETARIAT

1. A permanent Secretariat is hereby established.
2. The Commission shall appoint an Executive Secretary and determine the duties of that post and the terms and conditions upon which it is to be held.
3. The Executive Secretary shall perform the functions that are necessary for the administration of the Convention and for the work of the Commission as well as the other tasks entrusted to the Executive Secretary by the Commission in accordance with its Rules of Procedure and its Financial Regulations.

ARTICLE 13 – DECISIONS AND RECOMMENDATIONS

1. Decisions and recommendations shall be adopted by unanimous vote of the Contracting Parties. Should unanimity not be attainable, and unless otherwise provided in the Convention, the Commission may nonetheless adopt decisions or recommendations by a three-quarters majority vote of the Contracting Parties.
2. A decision shall be binding on the expiry of a period of two hundred days after its adoption for those Contracting Parties that voted for it and have not within that period notified the Executive Secretary in writing that they are unable to accept the decision, provided that at the expiry of that period three-quarters of the Contracting Parties have either voted for the decision and not withdrawn their acceptance or notified the Executive Secretary in writing that they are able to accept the decision.

Such a decision shall become binding on any other Contracting Party which has notified the Executive Secretary in writing that it is able to accept the decision from the moment of that notification or after the expiry of a period of two hundred days after the adoption of the decision, whichever is later.

3. A notification under paragraph 2 of this Article to the Executive Secretary may indicate that a Contracting Party is unable to accept a decision insofar as it relates to one or more of its dependent or autonomous territories to which the Convention applies.
4. All decisions adopted by the Commission shall, where appropriate, contain provisions specifying the timetable by which the decision shall be implemented.
5. Recommendations shall have no binding force.
6. Decisions concerning any Annex or Appendix shall be taken only by the Contracting Parties bound by the Annex or Appendix concerned.

ARTICLE 14 – STATUS OF ANNEXES AND APPENDICES

1. The Annexes and Appendices form an integral part of the Convention.
2. The Appendices shall be of a scientific, technical or administrative nature.

ARTICLE 15 – AMENDMENT OF THE CONVENTION

1. Without prejudice to the provisions of paragraph 2 of Article 27 and to specific provisions applicable to the adoption or amendment of Annexes or Appendices, an amendment to the Convention shall be governed by the present Article.
2. Any Contracting Party may propose an amendment to the Convention. The text of the proposed amendment shall be communicated to the Contracting Parties by the Executive Secretary of the Commission at least six months before the meeting of the Commission at which it is proposed for adoption. The Executive Secretary shall also communicate the proposed amendment to the signatories to the Convention for information.
3. The Commission shall adopt the amendment by unanimous vote of the Contracting Parties.
4. The adopted amendment shall be submitted by the Depositary Government to the Contracting Parties for ratification, acceptance or approval. Ratification, acceptance or approval of the amendment shall be notified to the Depositary Government in writing.
5. The amendment shall enter into force for those Contracting Parties which have ratified, accepted or approved it on the thirtieth day after receipt by the Depositary Government of notification of its ratification, acceptance or approval by at least seven Contracting Parties. Thereafter the amendment shall enter into force for any other Contracting Party on the thirtieth day after that Contracting Party has deposited its instrument of ratification, acceptance or approval of the amendment.

ARTICLE 16 – ADOPTION OF ANNEXES

The provisions of Article 15 relating to the amendment of the Convention shall also apply to the proposal, adoption and entry into force of an Annex to the Convention, except that the Commission shall adopt any Annex referred to in Article 7 by a three-quarters majority vote of the Contracting Parties.

ARTICLE 17 – AMENDMENT OF ANNEXES

1. The provisions of Article 15 relating to the amendment of the Convention shall also apply to an amendment to an Annex to the Convention, except that the Commission shall adopt amendments to any Annex referred to in Articles 3, 4, 5, 6 or 7 by a three-quarters majority vote of the Contracting Parties bound by that Annex.
2. If the amendment of an Annex is related to an amendment to the Convention, the amendment of the Annex shall be governed by the same provisions as apply to the amendment to the Convention.

ARTICLE 18 – ADOPTION OF APPENDICES

1. If a proposed Appendix is related to an amendment to the Convention or an Annex, proposed for adoption in accordance with Article 15 or Article 17, the proposal, adoption and entry into force of that Appendix shall be governed by the same provisions as apply to the proposal, adoption and entry into force of that amendment.
2. If a proposed Appendix is related to an Annex to the Convention, proposed for adoption in accordance with Article 16, the proposal, adoption and entry into force of that Appendix shall be governed by the same provisions as apply to the proposal, adoption and entry into force of that Annex.

ARTICLE 19 – AMENDMENT OF APPENDICES

1. Any Contracting Party bound by an Appendix may propose an amendment to that Appendix. The text of the proposed amendment shall be communicated to all Contracting Parties to the Convention by the Executive Secretary of the Commission as provided for in paragraph 2 of Article 15.
2. The Commission shall adopt the amendment to an Appendix by a three-quarters majority vote of the Contracting Parties bound by that Appendix.
3. An amendment to an Appendix shall enter into force on the expiry of a period of two hundred days after its adoption for those Contracting Parties which are bound by that Appendix and have not within that period notified the Depositary Government in writing that they are unable to accept that amendment, provided that at the expiry of that period three-quarters of the Contracting Parties bound by that Appendix have either voted for the amendment and not withdrawn their acceptance or have notified the Depositary Government in writing that they are able to accept the amendment.
4. A notification under paragraph 3 of this Article to the Depositary Government may indicate that a Contracting Party is unable to accept the amend-

ment insofar as it relates to one or more of its dependent or autonomous territories to which the Convention applies.

5. An amendment to an Appendix shall become binding on any other Contracting Party bound by the Appendix which has notified the Depositary Government in writing that it is able to accept the amendment from the moment of that notification or after the expiry of a period of two hundred days after the adoption of the amendment, whichever is later.
6. The Depositary Government shall without delay notify all Contracting Parties of any such notification received.
7. If the amendment of an Appendix is related to an amendment to the Convention or an Annex, the amendment of the Appendix shall be governed by the same provisions as apply to the amendment to the Convention or that Annex.

ARTICLE 20 – RIGHT TO VOTE

1. Each Contracting Party shall have one vote in the Commission.
2. Notwithstanding the provisions of paragraph 1 of this Article, the European Economic Community and other regional economic integration organisations, within the areas of their competence, are entitled to a number of votes equal to the number of their Member States which are Contracting Parties to the Convention. Those organisations shall not exercise their right to vote in cases where their Member States exercise theirs and conversely.

ARTICLE 21 – TRANSBOUNDARY POLLUTION

1. When pollution originating from a Contracting Party is likely to prejudice the interests of one or more of the other Contracting Parties to the Convention, the Contracting Parties concerned shall enter into consultation, at the request of any one of them, with a view to negotiating a cooperation agreement.
2. At the request of any Contracting Party concerned, the Commission shall consider the question and may make recommendations with a view to reaching a satisfactory solution.
3. An agreement referred to in paragraph 1 of this Article may, inter alia, define the areas to which it shall apply, the quality objectives to be achieved and the methods for achieving these objectives, including methods for the application of appropriate standards and the scientific and technical information to be collected.
4. The Contracting Parties signatory to such an agreement shall, through the medium of the Commission, inform the other Contracting Parties of its purport and of the progress made in putting it into effect.

ARTICLE 22 – REPORTING TO THE COMMISSION

The Contracting Parties shall report to the Commission at regular intervals on:

(a) the legal, regulatory, or other measures taken by them for the implementation of the provisions of the Convention and of decisions and recommendations adopted thereunder, including in particular measures taken to prevent and punish conduct in contravention of those provisions;

(b) the effectiveness of the measures referred to in subparagraph (a) of this Article;

(c) problems encountered in the implementation of the provisions referred to in subparagraph (a) of this Article.

ARTICLE 23 – COMPLIANCE

The Commission shall:

(a) on the basis of the periodical reports referred to in Article 22 and any other report submitted by the Contracting Parties, assess their compliance with the Convention and the decisions and recommendations adopted thereunder;

(b) when appropriate, decide upon and call for steps to bring about full compliance with the Convention, and decisions adopted thereunder, and promote the implementation of recommendations, including measures to assist a Contracting Party to carry out its obligations.

ARTICLE 24 – REGIONALISATION

The Commission may decide that any decision or recommendation adopted by it shall apply to all, or a specified part, of the maritime area and may provide for different timetables to be applied, having regard to the differences between ecological and economic conditions in the various regions and sub-regions covered by the Convention.

ARTICLE 25 – SIGNATURE

The Convention shall be open for signature at Paris from 22nd September 1992 to 30th June 1993 by:

(a) the Contracting Parties to the Oslo Convention or the Paris Convention;

(b) any other coastal State bordering the maritime area;

(c) any State located upstream on watercourses reaching the maritime area;

(d) any regional economic integration organisation having as a member at least one State to which any of the subparagraphs (a) to (c) of this Article applies.

ARTICLE 26 – RATIFICATION, ACCEPTANCE OR APPROVAL

The Convention shall be subject to ratification, acceptance or approval. The instruments of ratification, acceptance or approval shall be deposited with the Government of the French Republic.

ARTICLE 27 – ACCESSIONS

1. After 30th June 1993, the Convention shall be open for accession by the States and regional economic integration organisations referred to in Article 25.
2. The Contracting Parties may unanimously invite States or regional economic integration organi-

sations not referred to in Article 25 to accede to the Convention. In the case of such an accession, the definition of the maritime area shall, if necessary, be amended by a decision of the Commission adopted by unanimous vote of the Contracting Parties. Any such amendment shall enter into force after unanimous approval of all the Contracting Parties on the thirtieth day after the receipt of the last notification by the Depositary Government.

3. Any such accession shall relate to the Convention including any Annex and any Appendix that have been adopted at the date of such accession, except when the instrument of accession contains an express declaration of non-acceptance of one or several Annexes other than Annexes I, II, III and IV.
4. The instruments of accession shall be deposited with the Government of the French Republic.

ARTICLE 28 – RESERVATIONS

No reservation to the Convention may be made.

ARTICLE 29 – ENTRY INTO FORCE

1. The Convention shall enter into force on the thirtieth day following the date on which all Contracting Parties to the Oslo Convention and all Contracting Parties to the Paris Convention have deposited their instrument of ratification, acceptance, approval or accession.
2. For any State or regional economic integration organisation not referred to in paragraph 1 of this Article, the Convention shall enter into force in accordance with paragraph 1 of this Article, or on the thirtieth day following the date of the deposit of the instrument of ratification, acceptance, approval or accession by that State or regional economic integration organisations, whichever is later.

ARTICLE 30 – WITHDRAWAL

1. At any time after the expiry of two years from the date of entry into force of the Convention for a Contracting Party, that Contracting Party may withdraw from the Convention by notification in writing to the Depositary Government.
2. Except as may be otherwise provided in an Annex other than Annexes I to IV to the Convention, any Contracting Party may at any time after the expiry of two years from the date of entry into force of such Annex for that Contracting Party withdraw from such Annex by notification in writing to the Depositary Government.
3. Any withdrawal referred to in paragraphs 1 and 2 of this Article shall take effect one year after the date on which the notification of that withdrawal is received by the Depositary Government.

ARTICLE 31 – REPLACEMENT OF THE OSLO AND PARIS CONVENTIONS

1. Upon its entry into force, the Convention shall replace the Oslo and Paris Conventions as between the Contracting Parties.
2. Notwithstanding paragraph 1 of this Article, decisions, recommendations and all other agreements adopted under the Oslo Convention or the Paris Convention shall continue to be applicable, unaltered in their legal nature, to the extent that they are compatible with, or not explicitly terminated by, the Convention, any decisions or, in the case of existing recommendations, any recommendations adopted thereunder.

ARTICLE 32 – SETTLEMENT OF DISPUTES

1. Any disputes between Contracting Parties relating to the interpretation or application of the Convention, which cannot be settled otherwise by the Contracting Parties concerned, for instance by means of inquiry or conciliation within the Commission, shall at the request of any of those Contracting Parties, be submitted to arbitration under the conditions laid down in this Article.
2. Unless the parties to the dispute decide otherwise, the procedure of the arbitration referred to in paragraph 1 of this Article shall be in accordance with paragraphs 3 to 10 of this Article.
3. (a) At the request addressed by one Contracting Party to another Contracting Party in accordance with paragraph 1 of this Article, an arbitral tribunal shall be constituted. The request for arbitration shall state the subject matter of the application including in particular the Articles of the Convention, the interpretation or application of which is in dispute.

   (b) The applicant party shall inform the Commission that it has requested the setting up of an arbitral tribunal, stating the name of the other party to the dispute and the Articles of the Convention the interpretation or application of which, in its opinion, is in dispute. The Commission shall forward the information thus received to all Contracting Parties to the Convention.
4. The arbitral tribunal shall consist of three members: each of the parties to the dispute shall appoint an arbitrator; the two arbitrators so appointed shall designate by common agreement the third arbitrator who shall be the chairman of the tribunal. The latter shall not be a national of one of the parties to the dispute, nor have his usual place of residence in the territory of one of these parties, nor be employed by any of them, nor have dealt with the case in any other capacity.
5. (a) If the chairman of the arbitral tribunal has not been designated within two months of the appointment of the second arbitrator, the President of the International Court of Justice shall, at the request of either party, designate him within a further two months' period.

   (b) If one of the parties to the dispute does not appoint an arbitrator within two months of receipt of the request, the other party may inform the President of the International Court of Justice who shall designate the chairman of the arbitral tribunal within a further two months' period. Upon designation, the chairman of the arbitral tribunal shall request the party which has not appointed an arbitrator to do so within two months. After such period, he shall inform the

President of the International Court of Justice who shall make this appointment within a further two months' period.

6. (a) The arbitral tribunal shall decide according to the rules of international law and, in particular, those of the Convention.
   (b) Any arbitral tribunal constituted under the provisions of this Article shall draw up its own rules of procedure.
   (c) In the event of a dispute as to whether the arbitral tribunal has jurisdiction, the matter shall be decided by the decision of the arbitral tribunal.
7. (a) The decisions of the arbitral tribunal, both on procedure and on substance, shall be taken by majority voting of its members.
   (b) The arbitral tribunal may take all appropriate measures in order to establish the facts. It may, at the request of one of the parties, recommend essential interim measures of protection.
   (c) If two or more arbitral tribunals constituted under the provisions of this Article are seized of requests with identical or similar subjects, they may inform themselves of the procedures for establishing the facts and take them into account as far as possible.
   (d) The parties to the dispute shall provide all facilities necessary for the effective conduct of the proceedings.
   (e) The absence or default of a party to the dispute shall not constitute an impediment to the proceedings.
8. Unless the arbitral tribunal determines otherwise because of the particular circumstances of the case, the expenses of the tribunal, including the remuneration of its members, shall be borne by the parties to the dispute in equal shares. The tribunal shall keep a record of all its expenses, and shall furnish a final statement thereof to the parties.
9. Any Contracting Party that has an interest of a legal nature in the subject matter of the dispute which may be affected by the decision in the case, may intervene in the proceedings with the consent of the tribunal.
10. (a) The award of the arbitral tribunal shall be accompanied by a statement of reasons. It shall be final and binding upon the parties to the dispute.
    (b) Any dispute which may arise between the parties concerning the interpretation or execution of the award may be submitted by either party to the arbitral tribunal which made the award or, if the latter cannot be seized thereof, to another arbitral tribunal constituted for this purpose in the same manner as the first.

ARTICLE 33 – DUTIES OF THE DEPOSITARY GOVERNMENT

The Depositary Government shall inform the Contracting Parties and the signatories to the Convention:

(a) of the deposit of instruments of ratification, acceptance, approval or accession, of declarations of non-acceptance and of notifications of withdrawal in accordance with Articles 26, 27 and 30;

(b) of the date on which the Convention comes into force in accordance with Article 29;

(c) of the receipt of notifications of acceptance, of the deposit of instruments of ratification, acceptance, approval or accession and of the entry into force of amendments to the Convention and of the adoption and amendment of Annexes or Appendices, in accordance with Articles 15, 16, 17, 18 and 19.

ARTICLE 34 – ORIGINAL TEXT

The original of the Convention, of which the French and English texts shall be equally authentic, shall be deposited with the Government of the French Republic which shall send certified copies thereof to the Contracting Parties and the signatories to the Convention and shall deposit a certified copy with the Secretary General of the United Nations for registration and publication in accordance with Article 102 of the United Nations Charter.

IN WITNESS WHEREOF, the undersigned, being duly authorised by their respective Governments, have signed this Convention.

DONE at Paris, on the twenty-second day of September 1992.

ANNEX I ON THE PREVENTION AND ELIMINATION OF POLLUTION FROM LAND-BASED SOURCES

ARTICLE 1

1. When adopting programmes and measures for the purpose of this Annex, the Contracting Parties shall require, either individually or jointly, the use of
   - best available techniques for point sources
   - best environmental practice for point and diffuse sources including, where appropriate, clean technology.
2. When setting priorities and in assessing the nature and extent of the programmes and measures and their time scales, the Contracting Parties shall use the criteria given in Appendix 2.
3. The Contracting Parties shall take preventive measures to minimise the risk of pollution caused by accidents.
4. When adopting programmes and measures in relation to radioactive substances, including waste, the Contracting Parties shall also take account of:
   (a) the recommendations of the other appropriate international organisations and agencies;
   (b) the monitoring procedures recommended by these international organisations and agencies.

ARTICLE 2

1. Point source discharges to the maritime area, and releases into water or air which reach and may affect the maritime area, shall be strictly subject to authorisation or regulation by the competent authorities of the Contracting Parties. Such author-

isation or regulation shall, in particular, implement relevant decisions of the Commission which bind the relevant Contracting Party.

2. The Contracting Parties shall provide for a system of regular monitoring and inspection by their competent authorities to assess compliance with authorisations and regulations of releases into water or air.

ARTICLE 3

For the purposes of this Annex, it shall, inter alia, be the duty of the Commission to draw up:

(a) plans for the reduction and phasing out of substances that are toxic, persistent and liable to bioaccumulate arising from land-based sources;

(b) when appropriate, programmes and measures for the reduction of inputs of nutrients from urban, municipal, industrial, agricultural and other sources.

ANNEX II ON THE PREVENTION AND ELIMINATION OF POLLUTION BY DUMPING OR INCINERATION

ARTICLE 1

This Annex shall not apply to any deliberate disposal in the maritime area of:

(a) wastes or other matter from offshore installations;

(b) offshore installations and offshore pipelines.

ARTICLE 2

Incineration is prohibited.

ARTICLE 3

1. The dumping of all wastes or other matter is prohibited, except for those wastes or other matter listed in paragraphs 2 and 3 of this Article.

2. The list referred to in paragraph 1 of this Article is as follows:

   (a) dredged material;

   (b) inert materials of natural origin, that is solid, chemically unprocessed geological material the chemical constituents of which are unlikely to be released into the marine environment;

   (c) sewage sludge until 31st December 1998;

   (d) fish waste from industrial fish processing operations;

   (e) vessels or aircraft until, at the latest, 31st December 2004;

   (f)[1] carbon dioxide streams from carbon dioxide capture processes for storage, provided:

      i. disposal is into a sub-soil geological formation;

      ii. the streams consist overwhelmingly of carbon dioxide. They may contain incidental associated substances derived from the source material and the capture, transport and storage processes used;

      iii. no wastes or other matter are added for the purpose of disposing of those wastes or other matter;

      iv. they are intended to be retained in these formations permanently and will not lead to significant adverse consequences for the marine environment, human health and other legitimate uses of the maritime area.

3. (a) The dumping of low and intermediate level radioactive substances, including wastes, is prohibited.

   (b)[2] As an exception to subparagraph 3(a) of this Article, those Contracting Parties, the United Kingdom and France, who wish to retain the option of an exception to subparagraph 3(a) in any case not before the expiry of a period of 15 years from 1st January 1993, shall report to the meeting of the Commission at Ministerial level in 1997 on the steps taken to explore alternative land-based options.

   (c) Unless, at or before the expiry of this period of 15 years, the Commission decides by a unanimous vote not to continue the exception provided in subparagraph 3(b), it shall take a decision pursuant to Article 13 of the Convention on the prolongation for a period of 10 years after 1st January 2008 of the prohibition, after which another meeting of the Commission at Ministerial level shall be held. Those Contracting Parties mentioned in subparagraph 3(b) of this Article still wishing to retain the option mentioned in subparagraph 3(b) shall report to the Commission meetings to be held at Ministerial level at two yearly intervals from 1999 onwards about the progress in establishing alternative land-based options and on the results of scientific studies which show that any potential dumping operations would not result in hazards to human health, harm to living resources or marine ecosystems, damage to amenities or interference with other legitimate uses of the sea.

ARTICLE 4

1. The Contracting Parties shall ensure that:

   (a) no wastes or other matter listed in paragraph 2 of Article 3 of this Annex shall be dumped without authorisation by their competent authorities, or regulation;

1 Sub-paragraph (f) was introduced by amendment to the Annex agreed by OSPAR 2007. The amendment will enter into force for those Contracting Parties which have ratified, accepted or approved it on the thirtieth day after receipt by the Depositary Government of notification of its ratification, acceptance or approval by at least seven Contracting Parties. Thereafter the amendment will enter into force for any other Contracting Party on the thirtieth day after that Contracting Party has deposited its instrument of ratification, acceptance or approval of the amendment.

2 After the entry into force of OSPAR Decision 98/2 on Dumping of Radioactive Waste on 9 February 1999, subparagraphs (b) and (c) of this paragraph ceased to have effect.

(b) such authorisation or regulation is in accordance with the relevant applicable criteria, guidelines and procedures adopted by the Commission in accordance with Article 6 of this Annex;

(c) with the aim of avoiding situations in which the same dumping operation is authorised or regulated by more than one Contracting Party, their competent authorities shall, as appropriate, consult before granting an authorisation or applying regulation.

2. Any authorisation or regulation under paragraph 1 of this Article shall not permit the dumping of vessels or aircraft containing substances which result or are likely to result in hazards to human health, harm to living resources and marine ecosystems, damage to amenities or interference with other legitimate uses of the sea.

3. Each Contracting Party shall keep, and report to the Commission records of the nature and the quantities of wastes or other matter dumped in accordance with paragraph 1 of this Article, and of the dates, places and methods of dumping.

ARTICLE 5

No placement of matter in the maritime area for a purpose other than that for which it was originally designed or constructed shall take place without authorisation or regulation by the competent authority of the relevant Contracting Party. Such authorisation or regulation shall be in accordance with the relevant applicable criteria, guidelines and procedures adopted by the Commission in accordance with Article 6 of this Annex. This provision shall not be taken to permit the dumping of wastes or other matter otherwise prohibited under this Annex.

ARTICLE 6

For the purposes of this Annex, it shall, inter alia, be the duty of the Commission to draw up and adopt criteria, guidelines and procedures relating to the dumping of wastes or other matter listed in paragraph 2 of Article 3, and to the placement of matter referred to in Article 5, of this Annex, with a view to preventing and eliminating pollution.

ARTICLE 7

The provisions of this Annex concerning dumping shall not apply in case of force majeure, due to stress of weather or any other cause, when the safety of human life or of a vessel or aircraft is threatened. Such dumping shall be so conducted as to minimise the likelihood of damage to human or marine life and shall immediately be reported to the Commission, together with full details of the circumstances and of the nature and quantities of the wastes or other matter dumped.

ARTICLE 8

The Contracting Parties shall take appropriate measures, both individually and within relevant international organisations, to prevent and eliminate pollution resulting from the abandonment of vessels or aircraft in the maritime area caused by accidents. In the absence of relevant guidance from such international organisations, the measures taken by individual Contracting Parties should be based on such guidelines as the Commission may adopt.

ARTICLE 9

In an emergency, if a Contracting Party considers that wastes or other matter the dumping of which is prohibited under this Annex cannot be disposed of on land without unacceptable danger or damage, it shall forthwith consult other Contracting Parties with a view to finding the most satisfactory methods of storage or the most satisfactory means of destruction or disposal under the prevailing circumstances. The Contracting Party shall inform the Commission of the steps adopted following this consultation. The Contracting Parties pledge themselves to assist one another in such situations.

ARTICLE 10

1. Each Contracting Party shall ensure compliance with the provisions of this Annex:

(a) by vessels or aircraft registered in its territory;

(b) by vessels or aircraft loading in its territory the wastes or other matter which are to be dumped or incinerated;

(c) by vessels or aircraft believed to be engaged in dumping or incineration within its internal waters or within its territorial sea or within that part of the sea beyond and adjacent to the territorial sea under the jurisdiction of the coastal state to the extent recognised by international law.

2. Each Contracting Party shall issue instructions to its maritime inspection vessels and aircraft and to other appropriate services to report to its authorities any incidents or conditions in the maritime area which give rise to suspicions that dumping in contravention of the provisions of the present Annex has occurred or is about to occur. Any Contracting Party whose authorities receive such a report shall, if it considers it appropriate, accordingly inform any other Contracting Party concerned.

3. Nothing in this Annex shall abridge the sovereign immunity to which certain vessels are entitled under international law.

ANNEX III ON THE PREVENTION AND ELIMINATION OF POLLUTION FROM OFFSHORE SOURCES

ARTICLE 1

This Annex shall not apply to any deliberate disposal in the maritime area of:

(a) wastes or other matter from vessels or aircraft;

(b) vessels or aircraft.

ARTICLE 2

1. When adopting programmes and measures for the purpose of this Annex, the Contracting Parties shall require, either individually or jointly, the use of:

(a) best available techniques

(b) best environmental practice including, where appropriate, clean technology.

2. When setting priorities and in assessing the nature and extent of the programmes and measures and their time scales, the Contracting Parties shall use the criteria given in Appendix 2.

ARTICLE 3

1. Any dumping of wastes or other matter from offshore installations is prohibited.
2. This prohibition does not relate to discharges or emissions from offshore sources.
3.[1] The prohibition referred to in paragraph 1 of this Article does not apply to carbon dioxide streams from carbon dioxide capture processes for storage, provided
   (a) disposal is into a sub-soil geological formation;
   (b) the streams consist overwhelmingly of carbon dioxide. They may contain incidental associated substances derived from the source material and the capture, transport and storage processes used;
   (c) no wastes or other matter are added for the purpose of disposing of those wastes or other matter;
   (d) they are intended to be retained in these formations permanently and will not lead to significant adverse consequences for the marine environment, human health and other legitimate uses of the maritime area.
4. The Contracting Parties shall ensure that no streams referred to in paragraph 3 shall be disposed of in sub-soil geological formations without authorisation or regulation by their competent authorities. Such authorisation or regulation shall, in particular, implement the relevant applicable decisions, recommendations and all other agreements adopted under the Convention.

ARTICLE 4

1. The use on, or the discharge or emission from, offshore sources of substances which may reach and affect the maritime area shall be strictly subject to authorisation or regulation by the competent authorities of the Contracting Parties. Such authorisation or regulation shall, in particular, implement the relevant applicable decisions, recommendations and all other agreements adopted under the Convention.
2. The competent authorities of the Contracting Parties shall provide for a system of monitoring and inspection to assess compliance with authorisation or regulation as provided for in paragraph 1 of Article 4 of this Annex.

ARTICLE 5

1. No disused offshore installation or disused offshore pipeline shall be dumped and no disused offshore installation shall be left wholly or partly in place in the maritime area without a permit issued by the competent authority of the relevant Contracting Party on a case-by-case basis. The Contracting Parties shall ensure that their authorities, when granting such permits, shall implement the relevant applicable decisions, recommendations and all other agreements adopted under the Convention.
2. No such permit shall be issued if the disused offshore installation or disused offshore pipeline contains substances which result or are likely to result in hazards to human health, harm to living resources and marine ecosystems, damage to amenities or interference with other legitimate uses of the sea.
3. Any Contracting Party which intends to take the decision to issue a permit for the dumping of a disused offshore installation or a disused offshore pipeline placed in the maritime area after 1st January 1998 shall, through the medium of the Commission, inform the other Contracting Parties of its reasons for accepting such dumping, in order to make consultation possible.
4. Each Contracting Party shall keep, and report to the Commission, records of the disused offshore installations and disused offshore pipelines dumped and of the disused offshore installations left in place in accordance with the provisions of this Article, and of the dates, places and methods of dumping.

ARTICLE 6

Articles 3 and 5 of this Annex shall not apply in case of force majeure, due to stress of weather or any other cause, when the safety of human life or of an offshore installation is threatened. Such dumping shall be so conducted as to minimise the likelihood of damage to human or marine life and shall immediately be reported to the Commission, together with full details of the circumstances and of the nature and quantities of the matter dumped.

ARTICLE 7

The Contracting Parties shall take appropriate measures, both individually and within relevant international organisations, to prevent and eliminate pollution resulting from the abandonment of offshore installations in the maritime area caused by accidents. In the absence of relevant guidance from such international organisations, the measures taken by individual Contracting Parties should be based on such guidelines as the Commission may adopt.

ARTICLE 8

No placement of a disused offshore installation or a disused offshore pipeline in the maritime area for

1 Paragraphs 3 and 4 were introduced by amendment to the Annex agreed by OSPAR 2007. The amendment will enter into force for those Contracting Parties which have ratified, accepted or approved it on the thirtieth day after receipt by the Depositary Government of notification of its ratification, acceptance or approval by at least seven Contracting Parties. Thereafter the amendment will enter into force for any other Contracting Party on the thirtieth day after that Contracting Party has deposited its instrument of ratification, acceptance or approval of the amendment.

a purpose other than that for which it was originally designed or constructed shall take place without authorisation or regulation by the competent authority of the relevant Contracting Party. Such authorisation or regulation shall be in accordance with the relevant applicable criteria, guidelines and procedures adopted by the Commission in accordance with subparagraph (d) of Article 10 of this Annex. This provision shall not be taken to permit the dumping of disused offshore installations or disused offshore pipelines in contravention of the provisions of this Annex.

ARTICLE 9

1. Each Contracting Party shall issue instructions to its maritime inspection vessels and aircraft and to other appropriate services to report to its authorities any incidents or conditions in the maritime area which give rise to suspicions that a contravention of the provisions of the present Annex has occurred or is about to occur. Any Contracting Party whose authorities receive such a report shall, if it considers it appropriate, accordingly inform any other Contracting Party concerned.
2. Nothing in this Annex shall abridge the sovereign immunity to which certain vessels are entitled under international law.

ARTICLE 10

For the purposes of this Annex, it shall, inter alia, be the duty of the Commission:

(a) to collect information about substances which are used in offshore activities and, on the basis of that information, to agree lists of substances for the purposes of paragraph 1 of Article 4 of this Annex;

(b) to list substances which are toxic, persistent and liable to bioaccumulate and to draw up plans for the reduction and phasing out of their use on, or discharge from, offshore sources;

(c) to draw up criteria, guidelines and procedures for the prevention of pollution from dumping of disused offshore installations and of disused offshore pipelines, and the leaving in place of offshore installations, in the maritime area;

(d) to draw up criteria, guidelines and procedures relating to the placement of disused offshore installations and disused offshore pipelines referred to in Article 8 of this Annex, with a view to preventing and eliminating pollution.

ANNEX IV ON THE ASSESSMENT OF THE QUALITY OF THE MARINE ENVIRONMENT

ARTICLE 1

1. For the purposes of this Annex "monitoring" means the repeated measurement of:
   (a) the quality of the marine environment and each of its compartments, that is, water, sediments and biota;
   (b) activities or natural and anthropogenic inputs which may affect the quality of the marine environment;
   (c) the effects of such activities and inputs.
2. Monitoring may be undertaken either for the purposes of ensuring compliance with the Convention, with the objective of identifying patterns and trends or for research purposes.

ARTICLE 2

For the purposes of this Annex, the Contracting Parties shall:

(a) cooperate in carrying out monitoring programmes and submit the resulting data to the Commission;

(b) comply with quality assurance prescriptions and participate in intercalibration exercises;

(c) use and develop, individually or preferably jointly, other duly validated scientific assessment tools, such as modelling, remote sensing and progressive risk assessment strategies;

(d) carry out, individually or preferably jointly, research which is considered necessary to assess the quality of the marine environment, and to increase knowledge and scientific understanding of the marine environment and, in particular, of the relationship between inputs, concentration and effects;

(e) take into account scientific progress which is considered to be useful for such assessment purposes and which has been made elsewhere either on the initiative of individual researchers and research institutions, or through other national and international research programmes or under the auspices of the European Economic Community or other regional economic integration organisations.

ARTICLE 3

For the purposes of this Annex, it shall, inter alia, be the duty of the Commission:

(a) to define and implement programmes of collaborative monitoring and assessment-related research, to draw up codes of practice for the guidance of participants in carrying out these monitoring programmes and to approve the presentation and interpretation of their results;

(b) to carry out assessments taking into account the results of relevant monitoring and research and the data relating to inputs of substances or energy into the maritime area which are provided by virtue of other Annexes to the Convention, as well as other relevant information;

(c) to seek, where appropriate, the advice or services of competent regional organisations and other competent international organisations and competent bodies with a view to incorporating the latest results of scientific research;

(d) to cooperate with competent regional organisations and other competent international organisations in carrying out quality status assessments.

ANNEX V ON THE PROTECTION AND CONSERVATION OF THE ECOSYSTEMS AND BIOLOGICAL DIVERSITY OF THE MARITIME AREA[1][2][3]

ARTICLE 1

For the purposes of this Annex and of Appendix 3 the definitions of "biological diversity", "ecosystem" and "habitat" are those contained in the Convention on Biological Diversity of 5 June 1992.

ARTICLE 2

In fulfilling their obligation under the Convention to take, individually and jointly, the necessary measures to protect the maritime area against the adverse effects of human activities so as to safeguard human health and to conserve marine ecosystems and, when practicable, restore marine areas which have been adversely affected, as well as their obligation under the Convention on Biological Diversity of 5 June 1992 to develop strategies, plans or programmes for the conservation and sustainable use of biological diversity, Contracting Parties shall:

a. take the necessary measures to protect and conserve the ecosystems and the biological diversity of the maritime area, and to restore, where practicable, marine areas which have been adversely affected; and

b. cooperate in adopting programmes and measures for those purposes for the control of the human activities identified by the application of the criteria in Appendix 3.

ARTICLE 3

1. For the purposes of this Annex, it shall inter alia be the duty of the Commission:

   a. to draw up programmes and measures for the control of the human activities identified by the application of the criteria in Appendix 3;

   b. in doing so:

      (i) to collect and review information on such activities and their effects on ecosystems and biological diversity;

      (ii) to develop means, consistent with international law, for instituting protective, conservation, restorative or precautionary measures related to specific areas or sites or related to particular species or habitats;

      (iii) subject to Article 4 of this Annex, to consider aspects of national strategies and guidelines on the sustainable use of components of biological diversity of the maritime area as they affect the various regions and sub-regions of that area;

      (iv) subject to Article 4 of this Annex, to aim for the application of an integrated ecosystem approach.

   c. also in doing so, to take account of programmes and measures adopted by Contracting Parties for the protection and conservation of ecosystems within waters under their sovereignty or jurisdiction.

2. In the adoption of such programmes and measures, due consideration shall be given to the question whether any particular programme or measure should apply to all, or a specified part, of the maritime area.

ARTICLE 4

1. In accordance with the penultimate recital of the Convention, no programme or measure concerning a question relating to the management of fisheries shall be adopted under this Annex. However where the Commission considers that action is desirable in relation to such a question, it shall draw that question to the attention of the authority or international body competent for that question. Where action within the competence of the Commission is desirable to complement or support action by those authorities or bodies, the Commission shall endeavour to cooperate with them.

2. Where the Commission considers that action under this Annex is desirable in relation to a question concerning maritime transport, it shall draw that question to the attention of the International Maritime Organisation. The Contracting Parties who are members of the International Maritime Organisation shall endeavour to cooperate within that Organisation in order to achieve an appropriate response, including in relevant cases that Organisation's agreement to regional or local action, taking account of any guidelines developed by that Organisation on the designation of special areas, the identification of particularly sensitive areas or other matters.

APPENDIX 1 – CRITERIA FOR THE DEFINITION OF PRACTICES AND TECHNIQUES MENTIONED IN PARAGRAPH 3(B) (I) OF ARTICLE 2 OF THE CONVENTION

BEST AVAILABLE TECHNIQUES

1. The use of the best available techniques shall emphasise the use of non-waste technology, if available.

2. The term "best available techniques" means the latest stage of development (state of the art) of processes, of facilities or of methods of operation which indicate the practical suitability of a particu-

1 On the adoption of the new Annex V in 1998, Ministers also reached agreement on the meaning of certain concepts given in this new Annex V (see OSPAR Agreement 1998-15.2)

2 In accordance with Article 15.5 of the Convention, Annex V and Appendix 3 has entered into force: on 30 August 2000 for Finland, Spain, Switzerland, Luxembourg, European Community, United Kingdom and Denmark; on 5 October 2000 for Sweden; on 18 July 2001 for Iceland; on 22 July 2001 for Norway; on 24 August 2001 for the Netherlands; on 13 January 2002 for Germany; on 21 June 2003 for Ireland; on 24 November 2004 for France; on 28 August 2005 for Belgium; on 25 March 2006 for Portugal.

3 In a Note Verbale dated 26 July 2005, the Embassy of Great Britain in Paris informed the French Government that the British government wished to extend the ratification of Annex V and Appendix 3 to the Isle of Man.

lar measure for limiting discharges, emissions and waste. In determining whether a set of processes, facilities and methods of operation constitute the best available techniques in general or individual cases, special consideration shall be given to:

(a) comparable processes, facilities or methods of operation which have recently been successfully tried out;

(b) technological advances and changes in scientific knowledge and understanding;

(c) the economic feasibility of such techniques;

(d) time limits for installation in both new and existing plants;

(e) the nature and volume of the discharges and emissions concerned.

3. It therefore follows that what is "best available techniques" for a particular process will change with time in the light of technological advances, economic and social factors, as well as changes in scientific knowledge and understanding.

4. If the reduction of discharges and emissions resulting from the use of best available techniques does not lead to environmentally acceptable results, additional measures have to be applied.

5. "Techniques" include both the technology used and the way in which the installation is designed, built, maintained, operated and dismantled.

BEST ENVIRONMENTAL PRACTICE

6. The term "best environmental practice" means the application of the most appropriate combination of environmental control measures and strategies. In making a selection for individual cases, at least the following graduated range of measures should be considered:

(a) the provision of information and education to the public and to users about the environmental consequences of choice of particular activities and choice of products, their use and ultimate disposal;

(b) the development and application of codes of good environmental practice which covers all aspect of the activity in the product's life;

(c) the mandatory application of labels informing users of environmental risks related to a product, its use and ultimate disposal;

(d) saving resources, including energy;

(e) making collection and disposal systems available to the public;

(f) avoiding the use of hazardous substances or products and the generation of hazardous waste;

(g) recycling, recovery and re-use;

(h) the application of economic instruments to activities, products or groups of products;

(i) establishing a system of licensing, involving a range of restrictions or a ban.

7. In determining what combination of measures constitute best environmental practice, in general or individual cases, particular consideration should be given to:

(a) the environmental hazard of the product and its production, use and ultimate disposal;

(b) the substitution by less polluting activities or substances;

(c) the scale of use;

(d) the potential environmental benefit or penalty of substitute materials or activities;

(e) advances and changes in scientific knowledge and understanding;

(f) time limits for implementation;

(g) social and economic implications.

8. It therefore follows that best environmental practice for a particular source will change with time in the light of technological advances, economic and social factors, as well as changes in scientific knowledge and understanding.

9. If the reduction of inputs resulting from the use of best environmental practice does not lead to environmentally acceptable results, additional measures have to be applied and best environmental practice redefined.

APPENDIX 2 – CRITERIA MENTIONED IN PARAGRAPH 2 OF ARTICLE 1 OF ANNEX I AND IN PARAGRAPH 2 OF ARTICLE 2 OF ANNEX III

1. When setting priorities and in assessing the nature and extent of the programmes and measures and their time scales, the Contracting Parties shall use the criteria given below:

(a) persistency;

(b) toxicity or other noxious properties;

(c) tendency to bioaccumulation;

(d) radioactivity;

(e) the ratio between observed or (where the results of observations are not yet available) predicted concentrations and no observed effect concentrations;

(f) anthropogenically caused risk of eutrophication;

(g) transboundary significance;

(h) risk of undesirable changes in the marine ecosystem and irreversibility or durability of effects;

(i) interference with harvesting of sea-foods or with other legitimate uses of the sea;

(j) effects on the taste and/or smell of products for human consumption from the sea, or effects on smell, colour, transparency or other characteristics of the water in the marine environment;

(k) distribution pattern (i.e., quantities involved, use pattern and liability to reach the marine environment);

(l) non-fulfilment of environmental quality objectives.

2. These criteria are not necessarily of equal importance for the consideration of a particular substance or group of substances.

3. The above criteria indicate that substances which shall be subject to programmes and measures include:

   (a) heavy metals and their compounds;

   (b) organohalogen compounds (and substances which may form such compounds in the marine environment);

   (c) organic compounds of phosphorus and silicon;

   (d) biocides such as pesticides, fungicides, herbicides, insecticides, slimicides and chemicals used, inter alia, for the preservation of wood, timber, wood pulp, cellulose, paper, hides and textiles;

   (e) oils and hydrocarbons of petroleum origin;

   (f) nitrogen and phosphorus compounds;

   (g) radioactive substances, including wastes;

   (h) persistent synthetic materials which may float, remain in suspension or sink.

APPENDIX 3 – CRITERIA FOR IDENTIFYING HUMAN ACTIVITIES FOR THE PURPOSE OF ANNEX V

1. The criteria to be used, taking into account regional differences, for identifying human activities for the purposes of Annex V are:

   a. the extent, intensity and duration of the human activity under consideration;

   b. actual and potential adverse effects of the human activity on specific species, communities and habitats;

   c. actual and potential adverse effects of the human activity on specific ecological processes;

   d. irreversibility or durability of these effects.

2. These criteria are not necessarily exhaustive or of equal importance for the consideration of a particular activity.

9.1. ICRW / Whaling Convention 1946 and Protocol 1956

International Convention for the Regulation of Whaling, Washington, 2 December 1946, 161 UNTS 72; Protocol, 19 November 1956, 338 UNTS 366

The Governments whose duly authorised representatives have subscribed hereto,

Recognizing the interest of the nations of the world in safeguarding for future generations the great natural resources represented by the whale stocks;

Considering that the history of whaling has seen over-fishing of one area after another and of one species of whale after another to such a degree that it is essential to protect all species of whales from further over-fishing;

Recognizing that the whale stocks are susceptible of natural increases if whaling is properly regulated, and that increases in the size of whale stocks will permit increases in the number of whales which may be captured without endangering these natural resources;

Recognizing that it is in the common interest to achieve the optimum level of whale stocks as rapidly as possible without causing widespread economic and nutritional distress;

Recognizing that in the course of achieving these objectives, whaling operations should be confined to those species best able to sustain exploitation in order to give an interval for recovery to certain species of whales now depleted in numbers;

Desiring to establish a system of international regulation for the whale fisheries to ensure proper and effective conservation and development of whale stocks on the basis of the principles embodied in the provisions of the International Agreement for the Regulation of Whaling, signed in London on 8th June, 1937, and the protocols to that Agreement signed in London on 24th June, 1938, and 26th November, 1945; and

Having decided to conclude a convention to provide for the proper conservation of whale stocks and thus make possible the orderly development of the whaling industry;

Have agreed as follows:

ARTICLE I

1. This Convention includes the Schedule attached thereto which forms an integral part thereof. All references to "Convention" shall be understood as including the said Schedule either in its present terms or as amended in accordance with the provisions of Article V.
2. This Convention applies to factory ships, land stations, and whale catchers under the jurisdiction of the Contracting Governments and to all waters in which whaling is prosecuted by such factory ships, land stations, and whale catchers.

ARTICLE II

As used in this Convention:

1. "Factory ship" means a ship in which or on which whales are treated either wholly or in part;
2. "Land station" means a factory on the land at which whales are treated whether wholly or in part;
3. "Whale catcher" means a ship used for the purpose of hunting, taking, towing, holding on to, or scouting for whales;
4. "Contracting Government" means any Government which has deposited an instrument of ratification or has given notice of adherence to this Convention.

ARTICLE III

1. The Contracting Governments agree to establish an International Whaling Commission, hereinafter referred to as the Commission, to be composed of one member from each Contracting Government. Each member shall have one vote and may be accompanied by one or more experts and advisers.
2. The Commission shall elect from its own members a Chairman and Vice-Chairman and shall determine its own Rules of Procedure. Decisions of the Commission shall be taken by a simple majority of those members voting except that a three-fourths majority of those members voting shall be required for action in pursuance of Article V. The Rules of Procedure may provide for decisions otherwise than at meetings of the Commission.
3. The Commission may appoint its own Secretary and staff.
4. The Commission may set up, from among its own members and experts or advisers, such committees as it considers desirable to perform such functions as it may authorize.
5. The expenses of each member of the Commission and of his experts and advisers shall be determined and paid by his own Government.
6. Recognizing that specialized agencies related to the United Nations will be concerned with the conservation and development of whale fisheries and the products arising therefrom and desiring to avoid duplication of functions, the Contracting Governments will consult among themselves within two years after the coming into force of this Convention to decide whether the Commission shall be brought within the framework of a specialized agency related to the United Nations.
7. In the meantime the Government of the United Kingdom of Great Britain and Northern Ireland shall arrange, in consultation with the other Con-

tracting Governments, to convene the first meeting of the Commission, and shall initiate the consultation referred to in paragraph 6 above.

8. Subsequent meetings of the Commission shall be convened as the Commission may determine.

ARTICLE IV

1. The Commission may either in collaboration with or through independent agencies of the Contracting Governments or other public or private agencies, establishments, or organizations, or independently
   (a) encourage, recommend, or if necessary, organize studies and investigations relating to whales and whaling;
   (b) collect and analyze statistical information concerning the current condition and trend of the whale stocks and the effects of whaling activities thereon;
   (c) study, appraise, and disseminate information concerning methods of maintaining and increasing the populations of whale stocks.
2. The Commission shall arrange for the publication of reports of its activities, and it may publish independently or in collaboration with the International Bureau for Whaling Statistics at Sandefjord in Norway and other organizations and agencies such reports as it deems appropriate, as well as statistical, scientific, and other pertinent information relating to whales and whaling.

ARTICLE V

1. The Commission may amend from time to time the provisions of the Schedule by adopting regulations with respect to the conservation and utilization of whale resources, fixing
   (a) protected and unprotected species;
   (b) open and closed seasons;
   (c) open and closed waters, including the designation of sanctuary areas;
   (d) size limits for each species;
   (e) time, methods, and intensity of whaling (including the maximum catch of whales to be taken in any one season);
   (f) types and specifications of gear and apparatus and appliances which may be used;
   (g) methods of measurement; and
   (h) catch returns and other statistical and biological records.
2. These amendments of the Schedule
   (a) shall be such as are necessary to carry out the objectives and purposes of this Convention and to provide for the conservation, development, and optimum utilization of the whale resources;
   (b) shall be based on scientific findings;
   (c) shall not involve restrictions on the number or nationality of factory ships or land stations, nor allocate specific quotas to any factory ship or land station or to any group of factory ships or land stations; and
   (d) shall take into consideration the interests of the consumers of whale products and the whaling industry.
3. Each of such amendments shall become effective with respect to the Contracting Governments ninety days following notification of the amendment by the Commission to each of the Contracting Governments, except that
   (a) if any Government presents to the Commission objection to any amendment prior to the expiration of this ninety-day period, the amendment shall not become effective with respect to any of the Governments for an additional ninety days;
   (b) thereupon, any other Contracting Government may present objection to the amendment at any time prior to the expiration of the additional ninety-day period, or before the expiration of thirty days from the date of receipt of the last objection received during such additional ninety-day period, whichever date shall be the later; and
   (c) thereafter, the amendment shall become effective with respect to all Contracting Governments which have not presented objection but shall not become effective with respect to any Government which has so objected until such date as the objection is withdrawn. The Commission shall notify each Contracting Government immediately upon receipt of each objection and withdrawal and each Contracting Government shall acknowledge receipt of all notifications of amendments, objections, and withdrawals.
4. No amendments shall become effective before 1st July, 1949.

ARTICLE VI

The Commission may from time to time make recommendations to any or all Contracting Governments on any matters which relate to whales or whaling and to the objectives and purposes of this Convention.

ARTICLE VII

The Contracting Government shall ensure prompt transmission to the International Bureau for Whaling Statistics at Sandefjord in Norway, or to such other body as the Commission may designate, of notifications and statistical and other information required by this Convention in such form and manner as may be prescribed by the Commission.

ARTICLE VIII

1. Notwithstanding anything contained in this Convention any Contracting Government may grant to any of its nationals a special permit authorizing that national to kill, take and treat whales for purposes of scientific research subject to such restrictions as to number and subject to such other conditions as the Contracting Government thinks fit, and the killing, taking, and treating of whales in

accordance with the provisions of this Article shall be exempt from the operation of this Convention. Each Contracting Government shall report at once to the Commission all such authorizations which it has granted. Each Contracting Government may at any time revoke any such special permit which it has granted.

2. Any whales taken under these special permits shall so far as practicable be processed and the proceeds shall be dealt with in accordance with directions issued by the Government by which the permit was granted.
3. Each Contracting Government shall transmit to such body as may be designated by the Commission, in so far as practicable, and at intervals of not more than one year, scientific information available to that Government with respect to whales and whaling, including the results of research conducted pursuant to paragraph 1 of this Article and to Article IV.
4. Recognizing that continuous collection and analysis of biological data in connection with the operations of factory ships and land stations are indispensable to sound and constructive management of the whale fisheries, the Contracting Governments will take all practicable measures to obtain such data.

ARTICLE IX

1. Each Contracting Government shall take appropriate measures to ensure the application of the provisions of this Convention and the punishment of infractions against the said provisions in operations carried out by persons or by vessels under its jurisdiction.
2. No bonus or other remuneration calculated with relation to the results of their work shall be paid to the gunners and crews of whale catchers in respect of any whales the taking of which is forbidden by this Convention.
3. Prosecution for infractions against or contraventions of this Convention shall be instituted by the Government having jurisdiction over the offence.
4. Each Contracting Government shall transmit to the Commission full details of each infraction of the provisions of this Convention by persons or vessels under the jurisdiction of that Government as reported by its inspectors. This information shall include a statement of measures taken for dealing with the infraction and of penalties imposed.

ARTICLE X

1. This Convention shall be ratified and the instruments of ratifications shall be deposited with the Government of the United States of America.
2. Any Government which has not signed this Convention may adhere thereto after it enters into force by a notification in writing to the Government of the United States of America.
3. The Government of the United States of America shall inform all other signatory Governments and all adhering Governments of all ratifications deposited and adherences received.
4. This Convention shall, when instruments of ratification have been deposited by at least six signatory Governments, which shall include the Governments of the Netherlands, Norway, the Union of Soviet Socialist Republics, the United Kingdom of Great Britain and Northern Ireland, and the United States of America, enter into force with respect to those Governments and shall enter into force with respect to each Government which subsequently ratifies or adheres on the date of the deposit of its instrument of ratification or the receipt of its notification of adherence.
5. The provisions of the Schedule shall not apply prior to 1st July, 1948. Amendments to the Schedule adopted pursuant to Article V shall not apply prior to 1st July, 1949.

ARTICLE XI

Any Contracting Government may withdraw from this Convention on 30th June, of any year by giving notice on or before 1st January, of the same year to the depository Government, which upon receipt of such a notice shall at once communicate it to the other Contracting Governments. Any other Contracting Government may, in like manner, within one month of the receipt of a copy of such a notice from the depository Government give notice of withdrawal, so that the Convention shall cease to be in force on 30th June, of the same year with respect to the Government giving such notice of withdrawal.

The Convention shall bear the date on which it is opened for signature and shall remain open for signature for a period of fourteen days thereafter.

In witness whereof the undersigned, being duly authorized, have signed this Convention.

Done in Washington this second day of December, 1946, in the English language, the original of which shall be deposited in the archives of the Government of the United States of America. The Government of the United States of America shall transmit certified copies thereof to all the other signatory and adhering Governments.

Protocol

The Contracting Governments to the International Convention for the Regulation of Whaling signed at Washington under date of 2nd December, 1946 which Convention is hereinafter referred to as the 1946 Whaling Convention, desiring to extend the application of that Convention to helicopters and other aircraft and to include provisions on methods of inspection among those Schedule provisions which may be amended by the Commission, agree as follows:

ARTICLE I

Subparagraph 3 of the Article II of the 1946 Whaling Convention shall be amended to read as follows: "3. 'whale catcher' means a helicopter, or other aircraft, or a ship, used for the purpose of hunting, taking, killing, towing, holding on to, or scouting for whales."

ARTICLE II

Paragraph 1 of Article V of the 1946 Whaling Convention shall be amended by deleting the word "and" preceding clause (h), substituting a semicolon for the period at the end of the paragraph, and adding the following language: "and (i) methods of inspection".

ARTICLE III

1. This Protocol shall be open for signature and ratification or for adherence on behalf of any Contracting Government to the 1946 Whaling Convention.
2. This Protocol shall enter into force on the date upon which instruments of ratification have been deposited with, or written notifications of adherence have been received by, the Government of the United States of America on behalf of all the Contracting Governments to the 1946 Whaling Convention.
3. The Government of the United States of America shall inform all Governments signatory or adhering to the 1946 Whaling Convention of all ratifications deposited and adherences received.
4. This Protocol shall bear the date on which it is opened for signature and shall remain open for signature for a period of fourteen days thereafter, following which period it shall be open for adherence.

IN WITNESS WHEREOF the undersigned, being duly authorized, have signed this Protocol.

DONE in Washington this nineteenth day of November, 1956, in the English Language, the original of which shall be deposited in the archives of the Government of the United States of America. The Government of the United States of America shall transmit certified copies thereof to all Governments signatory or adhering to the 1946 Whaling Convention.

9.2. Ramsar Convention 1971

Convention on Wetlands of International Importance especially as Waterfowl Habitat, Ramsar, 2 February 1971, 996 UNTS 245

The Contracting Parties,

Recognizing the interdependence of man and his environment;

Considering the fundamental ecological functions of wetlands as regulators of water regimes and as habitats supporting a characteristic flora and fauna, especially waterfowl;

Being convinced that wetlands constitute a resource of great economic, cultural, scientific and recreational value, the lass of which would be irreparable;

Desiring to stem the progressive encroachment on and lass of wetlands now and in the future;

Recognizing that waterfowl in their seasonal migrations may transcend frontiers and so should be regarded as an international resource;

Being confident that the conservation of wetlands and their flora and fauna can be ensured by combining far-sighted national policies with co-ordinated international action;

Have agreed as follows:

Article 1

1. For the purpose of this Convention, wetlands are areas of marsh, fen, peatland or water, whether natural or artificial, permanent or temporary, with water that is static or flowing, fresh, brackish or salt, including areas of marine water the depth of which at low tide does not exceed six metres.
2. For the purpose of this Convention waterfowl are birds ecologically dependent on wetlands.

Article 2

1. Each Contracting Party shall designate suitable wetlands within its territory for inclusion in a List of Wetlands of International Importance, hereinafter referred to as "the List" which is maintained by the bureau established under Article 8. The boundaries of each wetland shall be precisely described and also delimited on a map and they may incorporate riparian and coastal zones adjacent to the wetlands, and islands or bodies of marine water deeper than six metres at low tide lying within the wetlands, especially where these have importance as waterfowl habitat.
2. Wetlands should be selected for the List on account of their international significance in terms of ecology, botany, zoology, limnology or hydrology. In the first instance wetlands of international importance to waterfowl at any season should be included.
3. The inclusion of a wetland in the List does not prejudice the exclusive sovereign rights of the Contracting Party in whose territory the wetland is situated.
4. Each Contracting Party shall designate at least one wetland to be included in the List when signing this Convention or when depositing its instrument of ratification or accession, as provided in Article 9.
5. Any Contracting Party shall have the right to add to the List further wetlands situated within its territory, to extend the boundaries of those wetlands already included by it in the List, or, because of its urgent national interests, to delete or restrict the boundaries of wetlands already included by it in the List and shall, at the earliest possible time, inform the organization or government responsible for the continuing bureau duties specified in Article 8 of any such changes.
6. Each Contracting Party shall consider its international responsibilities for the conservation, management and wise use of migratory stocks of waterfowl, both when designating entries for the List and when exercising its right to change entries in the List relating to wetlands within its territory.

Article 3

1. The Contracting Parties shall formulate and implement their planning so as to promote the conservation of the wetlands included in the List, and as Jar as possible the wise use of wetlands in their territory.
2. Each Contracting Party shall arrange to be informed at the earliest possible time if the ecological character of any wetland in its territory and included in the List has changed, is changing or is likely to change as the result of technological developments, pollution or other human interference. Information on such changes shall be passed without delay to the organization or government responsible for the continuing bureau duties specified in Article 8.

Article 4

1. Each Contracting Party shall promote the conservation of wetlands and waterfowl by establishing nature reserves on wetlands, whether they are included in the List or not, and provide adequately for their wardening.
2. Where a Contracting Party in its urgent national interest, deletes or restricts the boundaries of a wetland included in the List, it should as far as possible compensate for any loss of wetland resources, and in particular it should create additional nature reserves for waterfowl and for the protection, either in the same area or elsewhere, of an adequate portion of the original habitat.
3. The Contracting Parties shall encourage research and the exchange of data and publications regarding wetlands and their flora and fauna.

4. The Contracting Parties shall endeavour through management to increase waterfowl populations on appropriate wetlands.
5. The Contracting Parties shall promote the training of personnel competent in the fields of wetland research, management and wardening.

Article 5

The Contracting Parties shall consult with each other about implementing obligations arising from the Convention especially in the case of a wetland extending over the territories of more than one Contracting Party or where a water system is shared by Contracting Parties.

They shall at the same time endeavour to co-ordinate and support present and future policies and regulations concerning the conservation of wetlands and their flora and fauna.

Article 6

1. The Contracting Parties shall, as the necessity arises, convene Conferences on the Conservation of Wetlands and Waterfowl.
2. These Conferences shall have an advisory character and shall be competent inter alia:
   (a) to discuss the implementation of this Convention;
   (b) to discuss additions to and changes in the List;
   (c) to consider information regarding changes in the ecological character of wetlands included in the List provided in accordance with paragraph 2 of Article 3;
   (d) to make general or specific recommendations to the Contracting Parties regarding the conservation, management and wise use of wetlands and their flora and fauna;
   (e) to request relevant international bodies to prepare reports and statistics on matters which are essentially international in character affecting wetlands,
3. The Contracting Parties shall ensure that those responsible at all levels for wetlands management shall be informed of, and take into consideration, recommendations of such Conferences concerning the conservation, management and wise use of wetlands and their flora and fauna.

Article 7

1. The representatives of the Contracting Parties at such Conferences should include persons who are experts on wetlands or waterfowl by reason of knowledge and experience gained in scientific, administrative or other ap propriate capacities.
2. Each of the Contracting Parties represented at a Conference shall have one vote, recommendations being adopted by a simple majority of the votes cast, provided that not less than half the Contracting Parties cast votes.

Article 8

1. The International Union for the Conservation of Nature and Natural Resources shall perform the continuing bureau duties under this Convention until such time as another organization or government is appointed by a majority of two-thirds of all Contracting Parties.
2. The continuing bureau duties shall be, inter alia:
   (a) to assist in the convening and organizing of Conferences specified in Article 6;
   (b) to maintain the List of Wetlands of International Importance and to be in formed by the Contracting Parties of any additions, extensions, deletions or restrictions concerning wetlands included in the List provided in accordance with paragraph 5 of Article 2;
   (c) to be informed by the Contracting Parties of any changes in the ecological character of wetlands included in the List provided in accordance with paragraph 2 of Article 3;
   (d) to forward notification of any alterations to the List, or changes in character of wetlands included therein, to all Contracting Parties and to arrange for these matters to be discussed at the next Conference;
   (e) to make known to the Contracting Party concerned, the recommendations of the Conferences in respect of such alterations to the List or of changes in the character of wetlands included therein.

Article 9

1. This Convention shall remain open for signature indefinitely.
2. Any member of the United Nations or of one of the Specialized Agencies or of the International Atomic Energy Agency or Party to the Statute of the International Court of Justice may become a party to this Convention by:
   (a) signature without reservation as to ratification;
   (b) signature subject to ratification followed by ratification;
   (c) accession.
3. Ratification or accession shall be effected by the deposit of an instrument of ratification or accession with the Director-General of the United Nations Educational, Scientific and Cultural Organization (hereinafter referred to as “the Depository”).

Article 10

1. This Convention shall enter into force four months after seven States have become Parties to this Convention in accordance with paragraph 2 of Article 9.
2. Thereafter this Convention shall enter into force for each Contracting Party four months after the day of its signature without reservation as to ratification, or its deposit of an instrument of ratification or accession.

Article 11

1. This Convention shall continue in force for an indefinite period.

2. Any Contracting Party may denounce this Convention after a period of five years from the date on which it entered into force for that Party by giving writ ten notice thereof to the Depository. Denunciation shall take effect four months after the day on which notice thereof is received by the Depository.

Article 12

1. The Depository shall inform all States that have signed and acceded to this Convention as soon as possible of:
   (a) signatures to the Convention;
   (b) deposits of instruments of ratification of this Convention;
   (c) deposits of instruments of accession to this Convention;
   (d) the date of entry into force of this Convention;
   (e) notifications of denunciation of this Convention.
2. When this Convention has entered into force, the Depository shall have it registered with the Secretariat of the United Nations in accordance with Article 102 of the Charter.

IN WITNESS WHEREOF, the undersigned, being duly authorized to that effect, have signed this Convention.

DONE at Ramsar this 2nd day of February 1971, in a single original in the English, French, German and Russian languages, in any case of divergency the English text prevailing, which shall be deposited with the Depository which shall send true copies thereof to all Contracting Parties.

9.3. World Heritage Convention1972

Convention for the Protection of the World Cultural and Natural Heritage, Paris, 17 December 1972, 1037 UNTS 151

The General Conference of the United Nations Educational, Scientific and Cultural Organization meeting in Paris from 17 October to 21 November 1972, at its seventeenth session,

Noting that the cultural heritage and the natural heritage are increasingly threatened with destruction not only by the traditional causes of decay, but also by changing social and economic conditions which aggravate the situation with even more formidable phenomena of damage or destruction,

Considering that deterioration or disappearance of any item of the cultural or natural heritage constitutes a harmful impoverishment of the heritage of all the nations of the world,

Considering that protection of this heritage at the national level often remains incomplete because of the scale of the resources which it requires and of the insufficient economic, scientific, and technological resources of the country where the property to be protected is situated,

Recalling that the Constitution of the Organization provides that it will maintain, increase, and diffuse knowledge by assuring the conservation and protection of the world's heritage, and recommending to the nations concerned the necessary international conventions,

Considering that the existing international conventions, recommendations and resolutions concerning cultural and natural property demonstrate the importance, for all the peoples of the world, of safeguarding this unique and irreplaceable property, to whatever people it may belong,

Considering that parts of the cultural or natural heritage are of outstanding interest and therefore need to be preserved as part of the world heritage of mankind as a whole,

Considering that, in view of the magnitude and gravity of the new dangers threatening them, it is incumbent on the international community as a whole to participate in the protection of the cultural and natural heritage of outstanding universal value, by the granting of collective assistance which, although not taking the place of action by the State concerned, will serve as an efficient complement thereto,

Considering that it is essential for this purpose to adopt new provisions in the form of a convention establishing an effective system of collective protection of the cultural and natural heritage of outstanding universal value, organized on a permanent basis and in accordance with modern scientific methods,

Having decided, at its sixteenth session, that this question should be made the subject of an international convention,

Adopts this sixteenth day of November 1972 this Convention.

I. DEFINITION OF THE CULTURAL AND NATURAL HERITAGE

Article 1

For the purpose of this Convention, the following shall be considered as "cultural heritage":

monuments: architectural works, works of monumental sculpture and painting, elements or structures of an archaeological nature, inscriptions, cave dwellings and combinations of features, which are of outstanding universal value from the point of view of history, art or science;

groups of buildings: groups of separate or connected buildings which, because of their architecture, their homogeneity or their place in the landscape, are of outstanding universal value from the point of view of history, art or science;

sites: works of man or the combined works of nature and man, and areas including archaeological sites which are of outstanding universal value from the historical, aesthetic, ethnological or anthropological point of view.

Article 2

For the purposes of this Convention, the following shall be considered as "natural heritage":

natural features consisting of physical and biological formations or groups of such formations, which are of outstanding universal value from the aesthetic or scientific point of view;

geological and physiographical formations and precisely delineated areas which constitute the habitat of threatened species of animals and plants of outstanding universal value from the point of view of science or conservation;

natural sites or precisely delineated natural areas of outstanding universal value from the point of view of science, conservation or natural beauty.

Article 3

It is for each State Party to this Convention to identify and delineate the different properties situated on its territory mentioned in Articles 1 and 2 above.

II. NATIONAL PROTECTION AND INTERNATIONAL PROTECTION OF THE CULTURAL AND NATURAL HERITAGE

Article 4

Each State Party to this Convention recognizes that the duty of ensuring the identification, protection, conservation, presentation and transmission to future generations of the cultural and natural heritage referred to in Articles 1 and 2 and situated on its territory, belongs primarily to that State. It will do all it can to this end, to the utmost of its own resources and, where appropriate, with any international assistance and co-operation, in particular, financial, artistic, scientific and technical, which it may be able to obtain.

Article 5

To ensure that effective and active measures are taken for the protection, conservation and presentation of the cultural and natural heritage situated on its territory, each State Party to this Convention shall endeavor, in so far as possible, and as appropriate for each country:

(a) to adopt a general policy which aims to give the cultural and natural heritage a function in the life of the community and to integrate the protection of that heritage into comprehensive planning programmes;

(b) to set up within its territories, where such services do not exist, one or more services for the protection, conservation and presentation of the cultural and natural heritage with an appropriate staff and possessing the means to discharge their functions;

(c) to develop scientific and technical studies and research and to work out such operating methods as will make the State capable of counteracting the dangers that threaten its cultural or natural heritage;

(d) to take the appropriate legal, scientific, technical, administrative and financial measures necessary for the identification, protection, conservation, presentation and rehabilitation of this heritage; and

(e) to foster the establishment or development of national or regional centres for training in the protection, conservation and presentation of the cultural and natural heritage and to encourage scientific research in this field.

Article 6

1. Whilst fully respecting the sovereignty of the States on whose territory the cultural and natural heritage mentioned in Articles 1 and 2 is situated, and without prejudice to property right provided by national legislation, the States Parties to this Convention recognize that such heritage constitutes a world heritage for whose protection it is the duty of the international community as a whole to co-operate.
2. The States Parties undertake, in accordance with the provisions of this Convention, to give their help in the identification, protection, conservation and presentation of the cultural and natural heritage referred to in paragraphs 2 and 4 of Article 11 if the States on whose territory it is situated so request.
3. Each State Party to this Convention undertakes not to take any deliberate measures which might damage directly or indirectly the cultural and natural heritage referred to in Articles 1 and 2 situated on the territory of other States Parties to this Convention.

Article 7

For the purpose of this Convention, international protection of the world cultural and natural heritage shall be understood to mean the establishment of a system of international co- operation and assistance designed to support States Parties to the Convention in their efforts to conserve and identify that heritage.

III. INTERGOVERNMENTAL COMMITTEE FOR THE PROTECTION OF THE WORLD CULTURAL AND NATURAL HERITAGE

Article 8

1. An Intergovernmental Committee for the Protection of the Cultural and Natural Heritage of Outstanding Universal Value, called "the World Heritage Committee", is hereby established within the United Nations Educational, Scientific and Cultural Organization. It shall be composed of 15 States Parties to the Convention, elected by States Parties to the Convention meeting in general assembly during the ordinary session of the General Conference of the United Nations Educational, Scientific and Cultural Organization. The number of States members of the Committee shall be increased to 21 as from the date of the ordinary session of the General Conference following the entry into force of this Convention for at least 40 States.
2. Election of members of the Committee shall ensure an equitable representation of the different regions and cultures of the world.
3. A representative of the International Centre for the Study of the Preservation and Restoration of Cultural Property (Rome Centre), a representative of the International Council of Monuments and Sites (ICOMOS) and a representative of the International Union for Conservation of Nature and Natural Resources (IUCN), to whom may be added, at the request of States Parties to the Convention meeting in general assembly during the ordinary sessions of the General Conference of the United Nations Educational, Scientific and Cultural Organization, representatives of other intergovernmental or non-governmental organizations, with similar objectives, may attend the meetings of the Committee in an advisory capacity.

Article 9

1. The term of office of States members of the World Heritage Committee shall extend from the end of the ordinary session of the General Conference during which they are elected until the end of its third subsequent ordinary session.
2. The term of office of one-third of the members designated at the time of the first election shall, however, cease at the end of the first ordinary session of the General Conference following that at which they were elected; and the term of office of a further third of the members designated at the same time shall cease at the end of the second ordinary session of the General Conference following that at which they were elected. The names of these members shall be chosen by lot by the President of the General Conference of the United Nations

Educational, Scientific and Cultural Organization after the first election.

3. States members of the Committee shall choose as their representatives persons qualified in the field of the cultural or natural heritage.

Article 10

1. The World Heritage Committee shall adopt its Rules of Procedure.
2. The Committee may at any time invite public or private organizations or individuals to participate in its meetings for consultation on particular problems.
3. The Committee may create such consultative bodies as it deems necessary for the performance of its functions.

Article 11

1. Every State Party to this Convention shall, in so far as possible, submit to the World Heritage Committee an inventory of property forming part of the cultural and natural heritage, situated in its territory and suitable for inclusion in the list provided for in paragraph 2 of this Article. This inventory, which shall not be considered exhaustive, shall include documentation about the location of the property in question and its significance.
2. On the basis of the inventories submitted by States in accordance with paragraph 1, the Committee shall establish, keep up to date and publish, under the title of "World Heritage List," a list of properties forming part of the cultural heritage and natural heritage, as defined in Articles 1 and 2 of this Convention, which it considers as having outstanding universal value in terms of such criteria as it shall have established. An updated list shall be distributed at least every two years.
3. The inclusion of a property in the World Heritage List requires the consent of the State concerned. The inclusion of a property situated in a territory, sovereignty or jurisdiction over which is claimed by more than one State shall in no way prejudice the rights of the parties to the dispute.
4. The Committee shall establish, keep up to date and publish, whenever circumstances shall so require, under the title of "list of World Heritage in Danger", a list of the property appearing in the World Heritage List for the conservation of which major operations are necessary and for which assistance has been requested under this Convention. This list shall contain an estimate of the cost of such operations. The list may include only such property forming part of the cultural and natural heritage as is threatened by serious and specific dangers, such as the threat of disappearance caused by accelerated deterioration, large-scale public or private projects or rapid urban or tourist development projects; destruction caused by changes in the use or ownership of the land; major alterations due to unknown causes; abandonment for any reason whatsoever; the outbreak or the threat of an armed conflict; calamities and cataclysms; serious fires, earthquakes, landslides; volcanic eruptions; changes in water level, floods and tidal waves. The Committee may at any time, in case of urgent need, make a new entry in the List of World Heritage in Danger and publicize such entry immediately.
5. The Committee shall define the criteria on the basis of which a property belonging to the cultural or natural heritage may be included in either of the lists mentioned in paragraphs 2 and 4 of this article.
6. Before refusing a request for inclusion in one of the two lists mentioned in paragraphs 2 and 4 of this article, the Committee shall consult the State Party in whose territory the cultural or natural property in question is situated.
7. The Committee shall, with the agreement of the States concerned, co-ordinate and encourage the studies and research needed for the drawing up of the lists referred to in paragraphs 2 and 4 of this article.

Article 12

The fact that a property belonging to the cultural or natural heritage has not been included in either of the two lists mentioned in paragraphs 2 and 4 of Article 11 shall in no way be construed to mean that it does not have an outstanding universal value for purposes other than those resulting from inclusion in these lists.

Article 13

1. The World Heritage Committee shall receive and study requests for international assistance formulated by States Parties to this Convention with respect to property forming part of the cultural or natural heritage, situated in their territories, and included or potentially suitable for inclusion in the lists mentioned referred to in paragraphs 2 and 4 of Article 11. The purpose of such requests may be to secure the protection, conservation, presentation or rehabilitation of such property.
2. Requests for international assistance under paragraph 1 of this article may also be concerned with identification of cultural or natural property defined in Articles 1 and 2, when preliminary investigations have shown that further inquiries would be justified.
3. The Committee shall decide on the action to be taken with regard to these requests, determine where appropriate, the nature and extent of its assistance, and authorize the conclusion, on its behalf, of the necessary arrangements with the government concerned.
4. The Committee shall determine an order of priorities for its operations. It shall in so doing bear in mind the respective importance for the world cultural and natural heritage of the property requiring protection, the need to give international assistance to the property most representative of a natural environment or of the genius and the history of the peoples of the world, the urgency of the work to be done, the resources available to the States on whose territory the threatened property is situated and in particular the extent to which they are able to safeguard such property by their own means.

5. The Committee shall draw up, keep up to date and publicize a list of property for which international assistance has been granted.
6. The Committee shall decide on the use of the resources of the Fund established under Article 15 of this Convention. It shall seek ways of increasing these resources and shall take all useful steps to this end.
7. The Committee shall co-operate with international and national governmental and non-governmental organizations having objectives similar to those of this Convention. For the implementation of its programmes and projects, the Committee may call on such organizations, particularly the International Centre for the Study of the Preservation and Restoration of Cultural Property (the Rome Centre), the International Council of Monuments and Sites (ICOMOS) and the International Union for Conservation of Nature and Natural Resources (IUCN), as well as on public and private bodies and individuals.
8. Decisions of the Committee shall be taken by a majority of two-thirds of its members present and voting. A majority of the members of the Committee shall constitute a quorum.

Article 14

1. The World Heritage Committee shall be assisted by a Secretariat appointed by the Director-General of the United Nations Educational, Scientific and Cultural Organization.
2. The Director-General of the United Nations Educational, Scientific and Cultural Organization, utilizing to the fullest extent possible the services of the International Centre for the Study of the Preservation and the Restoration of Cultural Property (the Rome Centre), the International Council of Monuments and Sites (ICOMOS) and the International Union for Conservation of Nature and Natural Resources (IUCN) in their respective areas of competence and capability, shall prepare the Committee's documentation and the agenda of its meetings and shall have the responsibility for the implementation of its decisions.

IV. FUND FOR THE PROTECTION OF THE WORLD CULTURAL AND NATURAL HERITAGE

Article 15

1. A Fund for the Protection of the World Cultural and Natural Heritage of Outstanding Universal Value, called "the World Heritage Fund", is hereby established.
2. The Fund shall constitute a trust fund, in conformity with the provisions of the Financial Regulations of the United Nations Educational, Scientific and Cultural Organization.
3. The resources of the Fund shall consist of:
   (a) compulsory and voluntary contributions made by States Parties to this Convention,
   (b) Contributions, gifts or bequests which may be made by:
      (i) other States;
      (ii) the United Nations Educational, Scientific and Cultural Organization, other organizations of the United Nations system, particularly the United Nations Development Programme or other intergovernmental organizations;
      (iii) public or private bodies or individuals;
   (c) any interest due on the resources of the Fund;
   (d) funds raised by collections and receipts from events organized for the benefit of the fund; and
   (e) all other resources authorized by the Fund's regulations, as drawn up by the World Heritage Committee.
4. Contributions to the Fund and other forms of assistance made available to the Committee may be used only for such purposes as the Committee shall define. The Committee may accept contributions to be used only for a certain programme or project, provided that the Committee shall have decided on the implementation of such programme or project. No political conditions may be attached to contributions made to the Fund.

Article 16

1. Without prejudice to any supplementary voluntary contribution, the States Parties to this Convention undertake to pay regularly, every two years, to the World Heritage Fund, contributions, the amount of which, in the form of a uniform percentage applicable to all States, shall be determined by the General Assembly of States Parties to the Convention, meeting during the sessions of the General Conference of the United Nations Educational, Scientific and Cultural Organization. This decision of the General Assembly requires the majority of the States Parties present and voting, which have not made the declaration referred to in paragraph 2 of this Article. In no case shall the compulsory contribution of States Parties to the Convention exceed 1% of the contribution to the regular budget of the United Nations Educational, Scientific and Cultural Organization.
2. However, each State referred to in Article 31 or in Article 32 of this Convention may declare, at the time of the deposit of its instrument of ratification, acceptance or accession, that it shall not be bound by the provisions of paragraph 1 of this Article.
3. A State Party to the Convention which has made the declaration referred to in paragraph 2 of this Article may at any time withdraw the said declaration by notifying the Director-General of the United Nations Educational, Scientific and Cultural Organization. However, the withdrawal of the declaration shall not take effect in regard to the compulsory contribution due by the State until the date of the subsequent General Assembly of States parties to the Convention.
4. In order that the Committee may be able to plan its operations effectively, the contributions of States Parties to this Convention which have made the

declaration referred to in paragraph 2 of this Article, shall be paid on a regular basis, at least every two years, and should not be less than the contributions which they should have paid if they had been bound by the provisions of paragraph 1 of this Article.

5. Any State Party to the Convention which is in arrears with the payment of its compulsory or voluntary contribution for the current year and the calendar year immediately preceding it shall not be eligible as a Member of the World Heritage Committee, although this provision shall not apply to the first election.

The terms of office of any such State which is already a member of the Committee shall terminate at the time of the elections provided for in Article 8, paragraph 1 of this Convention.

Article 17

The States Parties to this Convention shall consider or encourage the establishment of national public and private foundations or associations whose purpose is to invite donations for the protection of the cultural and natural heritage as defined in Articles 1 and 2 of this Convention.

Article 18

The States Parties to this Convention shall give their assistance to international fund-raising campaigns organized for the World Heritage Fund under the auspices of the United Nations Educational, Scientific and Cultural Organization. They shall facilitate collections made by the bodies mentioned in paragraph 3 of Article 15 for this purpose.

V. CONDITIONS AND ARRANGEMENTS FOR INTERNATIONAL ASSISTANCE

Article 19

Any State Party to this Convention may request international assistance for property forming part of the cultural or natural heritage of outstanding universal value situated within its territory. It shall submit with its request such information and documentation provided for in Article 21 as it has in its possession and as will enable the Committee to come to a decision.

Article 20

Subject to the provisions of paragraph 2 of Article 13, sub-paragraph (c) of Article 22 and Article 23, international assistance provided for by this Convention may be granted only to property forming part of the cultural and natural heritage which the World Heritage Committee has decided, or may decide, to enter in one of the lists mentioned in paragraphs 2 and 4 of Article 11.

Article 21

1. The World Heritage Committee shall define the procedure by which requests to it for international assistance shall be considered and shall specify the content of the request, which should define the operation contemplated, the work that is necessary, the expected cost thereof, the degree of urgency and the reasons why the resources of the State requesting assistance do not allow it to meet all the expenses. Such requests must be supported by experts' reports whenever possible.
2. Requests based upon disasters or natural calamities should, by reasons of the urgent work which they may involve, be given immediate, priority consideration by the Committee, which should have a reserve fund at its disposal against such contingencies.
3. Before coming to a decision, the Committee shall carry out such studies and consultations as it deems necessary.

Article 22

Assistance granted by the World Heritage Fund may take the following forms:

(a) studies concerning the artistic, scientific and technical problems raised by the protection, conservation, presentation and rehabilitation of the cultural and natural heritage, as defined in paragraphs 2 and 4 of Article 11 of this Convention;

(b) provisions of experts, technicians and skilled labour to ensure that the approved work is correctly carried out;

(c) training of staff and specialists at all levels in the field of identification, protection, conservation, presentation and rehabilitation of the cultural and natural heritage;

(d) supply of equipment which the State concerned does not possess or is not in a position to acquire;

(e) low-interest or interest-free loans which might be repayable on a long-term basis;

(f) the granting, in exceptional cases and for special reasons, of non-repayable subsidies.

Article 23

The World Heritage Committee may also provide international assistance to national or regional centres for the training of staff and specialists at all levels in the field of identification, protection, conservation, presentation and rehabilitation of the cultural and natural heritage.

Article 24

International assistance on a large scale shall be preceded by detailed scientific, economic and technical studies. These studies shall draw upon the most advanced techniques for the protection, conservation, presentation and rehabilitation of the natural and cultural heritage and shall be consistent with the objectives of this Convention. The studies shall also seek means of making rational use of the resources available in the State concerned.

Article 25

As a general rule, only part of the cost of work necessary shall be borne by the international community. The contribution of the State benefiting from international assistance shall constitute a substantial share of the resources devoted to each programme or project, unless its resources do not permit this.

Article 26

The World Heritage Committee and the recipient State shall define in the agreement they conclude the conditions in which a programme or project for which international assistance under the terms of this Convention is provided, shall be carried out. It shall be the responsibility of the State receiving such international assistance to continue to protect, conserve and present the property so safeguarded, in observance of the conditions laid down by the agreement.

VI. EDUCATIONAL PROGRAMMES

Article 27

1. The States Parties to this Convention shall endeavor by all appropriate means, and in particular by educational and information programmes, to strengthen appreciation and respect by their peoples of the cultural and natural heritage defined in Articles 1 and 2 of the Convention.
2. They shall undertake to keep the public broadly informed of the dangers threatening this heritage and of the activities carried on in pursuance of this Convention.

Article 28

States Parties to this Convention which receive international assistance under the Convention shall take appropriate measures to make known the importance of the property for which assistance has been received and the role played by such assistance.

VII. REPORTS

Article 29

1. The States Parties to this Convention shall, in the reports which they submit to the General Conference of the United Nations Educational, Scientific and Cultural Organization on dates and in a manner to be determined by it, give information on the legislative and administrative provisions which they have adopted and other action which they have taken for the application of this Convention, together with details of the experience acquired in this field.
2. These reports shall be brought to the attention of the World Heritage Committee.
3. The Committee shall submit a report on its activities at each of the ordinary sessions of the General Conference of the United Nations Educational, Scientific and Cultural Organization.

VIII. FINAL CLAUSES

Article 30

This Convention is drawn up in Arabic, English, French, Russian and Spanish, the five texts being equally authoritative.

Article 31

1. This Convention shall be subject to ratification or acceptance by States members of the United Nations Educational, Scientific and Cultural Organization in accordance with their respective constitutional procedures.
2. The instruments of ratification or acceptance shall be deposited with the Director- General of the United Nations Educational, Scientific and Cultural Organization.

Article 32

1. This Convention shall be open to accession by all States not members of the United Nations Educational, Scientific and Cultural Organization which are invited by the General Conference of the Organization to accede to it.
2. Accession shall be effected by the deposit of an instrument of accession with the Director-General of the United Nations Educational, Scientific and Cultural Organization.

Article 33

This Convention shall enter into force three months after the date of the deposit of the twentieth instrument of ratification, acceptance or accession, but only with respect to those States which have deposited their respective instruments of ratification, acceptance or accession on or before that date. It shall enter into force with respect to any other State three months after the deposit of its instrument of ratification, acceptance or accession.

Article 34

The following provisions shall apply to those States Parties to this Convention which have a federal or non-unitary constitutional system:

(a) with regard to the provisions of this Convention, the implementation of which comes under the legal jurisdiction of the federal or central legislative power, the obligations of the federal or central government shall be the same as for those States parties which are not federal States;

(b) with regard to the provisions of this Convention, the implementation of which comes under the legal jurisdiction of individual constituent States, countries, provinces or cantons that are not obliged by the constitutional system of the federation to take legislative measures, the federal government shall inform the competent authorities of such States, countries, provinces or cantons of the said provisions, with its recommendation for their adoption.

Article 35

1. Each State Party to this Convention may denounce the Convention.
2. The denunciation shall be notified by an instrument in writing, deposited with the Director-General of the United Nations Educational, Scientific and Cultural Organization.
3. The denunciation shall take effect twelve months after the receipt of the instrument of denunciation. It shall not affect the financial obligations of the denouncing State until the date on which the withdrawal takes effect.

Article 36

The Director-General of the United Nations Educational, Scientific and Cultural Organization shall inform the States members of the Organization, the States not members of the Organization which are referred to in Article 32, as well as the United Nations, of the deposit of all the instruments of ratification, acceptance, or accession provided for in Articles 31 and 32, and of the denunciations provided for in Article 35.

Article 37

1. This Convention may be revised by the General Conference of the United Nations Educational, Scientific and Cultural Organization. Any such revision shall, however, bind only the States which shall become Parties to the revising convention.
2. If the General Conference should adopt a new convention revising this Convention in whole or in part, then, unless the new convention otherwise provides, this Convention shall cease to be open to ratification, acceptance or accession, as from the date on which the new revising convention enters into force.

Article 38

In conformity with Article 102 of the Charter of the United Nations, this Convention shall be registered with the Secretariat of the United Nations at the request of the Director-General of the United Nations Educational, Scientific and Cultural Organization.

Done in Paris, this twenty-third day of November 1972, in two authentic copies bearing the signature of the President of the seventeenth session of the General Conference and of the Director-General of the United Nations Educational, Scientific and Cultural Organization, which shall be deposited in the archives of the United Nations Educational, Scientific and Cultural Organization, and certified true copies of which shall be delivered to all the States referred to in Articles 31 and 32 as well as to the United Nations.

9.4. CITES / Washington Convention 1973, as amended 1983

Convention on International Trade in Endangered Species of Wild Fauna and Flora, Washington, 3 March 1973, 993 UNTS 243; Amendment to article XI (3)(a), Bonn, 22 June 1979, 1459 UNTS 369; Amendment to Article XXI of the Convention Of 3 March 1973 on International Trade In Endangered Species Of Wild Fauna And Flora (with Corrigendum), Gaborone, 30 April 1983, 2993 UNTS 78

The Contracting States,

Recognizing that wild fauna and flora in their many beautiful and varied forms are an irreplaceable part of the natural systems of the earth which must be protected for this and the generations to come;

Conscious of the ever-growing value of wild fauna and flora from aesthetic, scientific, cultural, recreational and economic points of view;

Recognizing that peoples and States are and should be the best protectors of their own wild fauna and flora;

Recognizing, in addition, that international co-operation is essential for the protection of certain species of wild fauna and flora against over-exploitation through international trade;

Convinced of the urgency of taking appropriate measures to this end;

Have agreed as follows:

Article I – Definitions

For the purpose of the present Convention, unless the context otherwise requires:

(a) "Species" means any species, subspecies, or geographically separate population thereof;

(b) "Specimen" means:

(i) any animal or plant, whether alive or dead;

(ii) in the case of an animal: for species included in Appendices I and II, any readily recognizable part or derivative thereof; and for species included in Appendix III, any readily recognizable part or derivative thereof specified in Appendix III in relation to the species; and

(iii)in the case of a plant: for species included in Appendix I, any readily recognizable part or derivative thereof; and for species included in Appendices II and III, any readily recognizable part or derivative thereof specified in Appendices II and III in relation to the species;

(c) "Trade" means export, re-export, import and introduction from the sea;

(d) "Re-export" means export of any specimen that has previously been imported;

(e) "Introduction from the sea" means transportation into a State of specimens of any species which were taken in the marine environment not under the jurisdiction of any State;

(f) "Scientific Authority" means a national scientific authority designated in accordance with Article IX;

(g) "Management Authority" means a national management authority designated in accordance with Article IX;

(h) "Party" means a State for which the present Convention has entered into force.

Article II – Fundamental principles

1. Appendix I shall include all species threatened with extinction which are or may be affected by trade. Trade in specimens of these species must be subject to particularly strict regulation in order not to endanger further their survival and must only be authorized in exceptional circumstances.
2. Appendix II shall include:

   (a) all species which although not necessarily now threatened with extinction may become so unless trade in specimens of such species is subject to strict regulation in order to avoid utilization incompatible with their survival; and

   (b) other species which must be subject to regulation in order that trade in specimens of certain species referred to in sub-paragraph (a) of this paragraph may be brought under effective control.
3. Appendix III shall include all species which any Party identifies as being subject to regulation within its jurisdiction for the purpose of preventing or restricting exploitation, and as needing the co-operation of other Parties in the control of trade.
4. The Parties shall not allow trade in specimens of species included in Appendices I, II and III except in accordance with the provisions of the present Convention.

Article III – Regulation of trade in specimens of species included in Appendix I

1. All trade in specimens of species included in Appendix I shall be in accordance with the provisions of this Article.
2. The export of any specimen of a species included in Appendix I shall require the prior grant and presentation of an export permit. An export permit shall only be granted when the following conditions have been met:

   (a) a Scientific Authority of the State of export has advised that such export will not be detrimental to the survival of that species;

   (b) a Management Authority of the State of export is satisfied that the specimen was not obtained in contravention of the laws of that State for the protection of fauna and flora;

(c) a Management Authority of the State of export is satisfied that any living specimen will be so prepared and shipped as to minimize the risk of injury, damage to health or cruel treatment; and

(d) a Management Authority of the State of export is satisfied that an import permit has been granted for the specimen.

3. The import of any specimen of a species included in Appendix I shall require the prior grant and presentation of an import permit and either an export permit or a re-export certificate. An import permit shall only be granted when the following conditions have been met:

   (a) a Scientific Authority of the State of import has advised that the import will be for purposes which are not detrimental to the survival of the species involved;

   (b) a Scientific Authority of the State of import is satisfied that the proposed recipient of a living specimen is suitably equipped to house and care for it; and

   (c) a Management Authority of the State of import is satisfied that the specimen is not to be used for primarily commercial purposes.

4. The re-export of any specimen of a species included in Appendix I shall require the prior grant and presentation of a re-export certificate. A re-export certificate shall only be granted when the following conditions have been met:

   (a) a Management Authority of the State of re-export is satisfied that the specimen was imported into that State in accordance with the provisions of the present Convention;

   (b) a Management Authority of the State of re-export is satisfied that any living specimen will be so prepared and shipped as to minimize the risk of injury, damage to health or cruel treatment; and

   (c) a Management Authority of the State of re-export is satisfied that an import permit has been granted for any living specimen.

5. The introduction from the sea of any specimen of a species included in Appendix I shall require the prior grant of a certificate from a Management Authority of the State of introduction. A certificate shall only be granted when the following conditions have been met:

   (a) a Scientific Authority of the State of introduction advises that the introduction will not be detrimental to the survival of the species involved;

   (b) a Management Authority of the State of introduction is satisfied that the proposed recipient of a living specimen is suitably equipped to house and care for it; and

   (c) a Management Authority of the State of introduction is satisfied that the specimen is not to be used for primarily commercial purposes.

Article IV – Regulation of trade in specimens of species included in Appendix II

1. All trade in specimens of species included in Appendix II shall be in accordance with the provisions of this Article.

2. The export of any specimen of a species included in Appendix II shall require the prior grant and presentation of an export permit. An export permit shall only be granted when the following conditions have been met:

   (a) a Scientific Authority of the State of export has advised that such export will not be detrimental to the survival of that species;

   (b) a Management Authority of the State of export is satisfied that the specimen was not obtained in contravention of the laws of that State for the protection of fauna and flora; and

   (c) a Management Authority of the State of export is satisfied that any living specimen will be so prepared and shipped as to minimize the risk of injury, damage to health or cruel treatment.

3. A Scientific Authority in each Party shall monitor both the export permits granted by that State for specimens of species included in Appendix II and the actual exports of such specimens. Whenever a Scientific Authority determines that the export of specimens of any such species should be limited in order to maintain that species throughout its range at a level consistent with its role in the ecosystems in which it occurs and well above the level at which that species might become eligible for inclusion in Appendix I, the Scientific Authority shall advise the appropriate Management Authority of suitable measures to be taken to limit the grant of export permits for specimens of that species.

4. The import of any specimen of a species included in Appendix II shall require the prior presentation of either an export permit or a re-export certificate.

5. The re-export of any specimen of a species included in Appendix II shall require the prior grant and presentation of a re-export certificate. A re-export certificate shall only be granted when the following conditions have been met:

   (a) a Management Authority of the State of re-export is satisfied that the specimen was imported into that State in accordance with the provisions of the present Convention; and

   (b) a Management Authority of the State of re-export is satisfied that any living specimen will be so prepared and shipped as to minimize the risk of injury, damage to health or cruel treatment.

6. The introduction from the sea of any specimen of a species included in Appendix II shall require the prior grant of a certificate from a Management Authority of the State of introduction. A certificate shall only be granted when the following conditions have been met:

   (a) a Scientific Authority of the State of introduction advises that the introduction will not be detrimental to the survival of the species involved; and

(b) a Management Authority of the State of introduction is satisfied that any living specimen will be so handled as to minimize the risk of injury, damage to health or cruel treatment.

7. Certificates referred to in paragraph 6 of this Article may be granted on the advice of a Scientific Authority, in consultation with other national scientific authorities or, when appropriate, international scientific authorities, in respect of periods not exceeding one year for total numbers of specimens to be introduced in such periods.

Article V – Regulation of trade in specimens of species included in Appendix III

1. All trade in specimens of species included in Appendix III shall be in accordance with the provisions of this Article.
2. The export of any specimen of a species included in Appendix III from any State which has included that species in Appendix III shall require the prior grant and presentation of an export permit. An export permit shall only be granted when the following conditions have been met:
   (a) a Management Authority of the State of export is satisfied that the specimen was not obtained in contravention of the laws of that State for the protection of fauna and flora; and
   (b) a Management Authority of the State of export is satisfied that any living specimen will be so prepared and shipped as to minimize the risk of injury, damage to health or cruel treatment.
3. The import of any specimen of a species included in Appendix III shall require, except in circumstances to which paragraph 4 of this Article applies, the prior presentation of a certificate of origin and, where the import is from a State which has included that species in Appendix III, an export permit.
4. In the case of re-export, a certificate granted by the Management Authority of the State of re- export that the specimen was processed in that State or is being re-exported shall be accepted by the State of import as evidence that the provisions of the present Convention have been complied with in respect of the specimen concerned.

Article VI Permits and certificates

1. Permits and certificates granted under the provisions of Articles III, IV, and V shall be in accordance with the provisions of this Article.
2. An export permit shall contain the information specified in the model set forth in Appendix IV, and may only be used for export within a period of six months from the date on which it was granted.
3. Each permit or certificate shall contain the title of the present Convention, the name and any identifying stamp of the Management Authority granting it and a control number assigned by the Management Authority.
4. Any copies of a permit or certificate issued by a Management Authority shall be clearly marked as copies only and no such copy may be used in place of the original, except to the extent endorsed thereon.
5. A separate permit or certificate shall be required for each consignment of specimens.
6. A Management Authority of the State of import of any specimen shall cancel and retain the export permit or re-export certificate and any corresponding import permit presented in respect of the import of that specimen.
7. Where appropriate and feasible a Management Authority may affix a mark upon any specimen to assist in identifying the specimen. For these purposes "mark" means any indelible imprint, lead seal or other suitable means of identifying a specimen, designed in such a way as to render its imitation by unauthorized persons as difficult as possible.

Article VII – Exemptions and other special provisions relating to trade

1. The provisions of Articles III, IV and V shall not apply to the transit or transhipment of specimens through or in the territory of a Party while the specimens remain in Customs control.
2. Where a Management Authority of the State of export or re-export is satisfied that a specimen was acquired before the provisions of the present Convention applied to that specimen, the provisions of Articles III, IV and V shall not apply to that specimen where the Management Authority issues a certificate to that effect.
3. The provisions of Articles III, IV and V shall not apply to specimens that are personal or household effects. This exemption shall not apply where:
   (a) in the case of specimens of a species included in Appendix I, they were acquired by the owner outside his State of usual residence, and are being imported into that State; or
   (b) in the case of specimens of species included in Appendix II:
      (i) they were acquired by the owner outside his State of usual residence and in a State where removal from the wild occurred;
      (ii) they are being imported into the owner's State of usual residence; and
      (iii) the State where removal from the wild occurred requires the prior grant of export permits before any export of such specimens;

   unless a Management Authority is satisfied that the specimens were acquired before the provisions of the present Convention applied to such specimens.
4. Specimens of an animal species included in Appendix I bred in captivity for commercial purposes, or of a plant species included in Appendix I artificially propagated for commercial purposes, shall be deemed to be specimens of species included in Appendix II.
5. Where a Management Authority of the State of export is satisfied that any specimen of an animal species was bred in captivity or any specimen of a plant species was artificially propagated, or is

a part of such an animal or plant or was derived therefrom, a certificate by that Management Authority to that effect shall be accepted in lieu of any of the permits or certificates required under the provisions of Article III, IV or V.

6. The provisions of Articles III, IV and V shall not apply to the non-commercial loan, donation or exchange between scientists or scientific institutions registered by a Management Authority of their State, of herbarium specimens, other preserved, dried or embedded museum specimens, and live plant material which carry a label issued or approved by a Management Authority.
7. A Management Authority of any State may waive the requirements of Articles III, IV and V and allow the movement without permits or certificates of specimens which form part of a travelling zoo, circus, menagerie, plant exhibition or other travelling exhibition provided that:
   (a) the exporter or importer registers full details of such specimens with that Management Authority;
   (b) the specimens are in either of the categories specified in paragraph 2 or 5 of this Article; and
   (c) the Management Authority is satisfied that any living specimen will be so transported and cared for as to minimize the risk of injury, damage to health or cruel treatment.

Article VIII – Measures to be taken by the Parties

1. The Parties shall take appropriate measures to enforce the provisions of the present Convention and to prohibit trade in specimens in violation thereof. These shall include measures:
   (a) to penalize trade in, or possession of, such specimens, or both; and
   (b) to provide for the confiscation or return to the State of export of such specimens.
2. In addition to the measures taken under paragraph 1 of this Article, a Party may, when it deems it necessary, provide for any method of internal reimbursement for expenses incurred as a result of the confiscation of a specimen traded in violation of the measures taken in the application of the provisions of the present Convention.
3. As far as possible, the Parties shall ensure that specimens shall pass through any formalities required for trade with a minimum of delay. To facilitate such passage, a Party may designate ports of exit and ports of entry at which specimens must be presented for clearance. The Parties shall ensure further that all living specimens, during any period of transit, holding or shipment, are properly cared for so as to minimize the risk of injury, damage to health or cruel treatment.
4. Where a living specimen is confiscated as a result of measures referred to in paragraph 1 of this Article:
   (a) the specimen shall be entrusted to a Management Authority of the State of confiscation;
   (b) the Management Authority shall, after consultation with the State of export, return the specimen to that State at the expense of that State, or to a rescue centre or such other place as the Management Authority deems appropriate and consistent with the purposes of the present Convention; and
   (c) the Management Authority may obtain the advice of a Scientific Authority, or may, whenever it considers it desirable, consult the Secretariat in order to facilitate the decision under sub- paragraph (b) of this paragraph, including the choice of a rescue centre or other place.
5. A rescue centre as referred to in paragraph 4 of this Article means an institution designated by a Management Authority to look after the welfare of living specimens, particularly those that have been confiscated.
6. Each Party shall maintain records of trade in specimens of species included in Appendices I, II and III which shall cover:
   (a) the names and addresses of exporters and importers; and
   (b) the number and type of permits and certificates granted; the States with which such trade occurred; the numbers or quantities and types of specimens, names of species as included in Appendices I, II and III and, where applicable, the size and sex of the specimens in question.
7. Each Party shall prepare periodic reports on its implementation of the present Convention and shall transmit to the Secretariat:
   (a) an annual report containing a summary of the information specified in sub-paragraph (b) of paragraph 6 of this Article; and
   (b) a biennial report on legislative, regulatory and administrative measures taken to enforce the provisions of the present Convention.
8. The information referred to in paragraph 7 of this Article shall be available to the public where this is not inconsistent with the law of the Party concerned.

Article IX – Management and Scientific Authorities

1. Each Party shall designate for the purposes of the present Convention:
   (a) one or more Management Authorities competent to grant permits or certificates on behalf of that Party; and
   (b) one or more Scientific Authorities.
2. A State depositing an instrument of ratification, acceptance, approval or accession shall at that time inform the Depositary Government of the name and address of the Management Authority authorized to communicate with other Parties and with the Secretariat.
3. Any changes in the designations or authorizations under the provisions of this Article shall be communicated by the Party concerned to the Secretariat for transmission to all other Parties.

4. Any Management Authority referred to in paragraph 2 of this Article shall, if so requested by the Secretariat or the Management Authority of another Party, communicate to it impression of stamps, seals or other devices used to authenticate permits or certificates.

Article X – Trade with States not party to the Convention

Where export or re-export is to, or import is from, a State not a Party to the present Convention, comparable documentation issued by the competent authorities in that State which substantially conforms with the requirements of the present Convention for permits and certificates may be accepted in lieu thereof by any Party.

Article XI – Conference of the Parties

1. The Secretariat shall call a meeting of the Conference of the Parties not later than two years after the entry into force of the present Convention.
2. Thereafter the Secretariat shall convene regular meetings at least once every two years, unless the Conference decides otherwise, and extraordinary meetings at any time on the written request of at least one-third of the Parties.
3. At meetings, whether regular or extraordinary, the Parties shall review the implementation of the present Convention and may:
   (a) make such provision as may be necessary to enable the Secretariat to carry out its duties, and adopt financial provisions;
   (b) consider and adopt amendments to Appendices I and II in accordance with Article XV;
   (c) review the progress made towards the restoration and conservation of the species included in Appendices I, II and III;
   (d) receive and consider any reports presented by the Secretariat or by any Party; and
   (e) where appropriate, make recommendations for improving the effectiveness of the present Convention.
4. At each regular meeting, the Parties may determine the time and venue of the next regular meeting to be held in accordance with the provisions of paragraph 2 of this Article.
5. At any meeting, the Parties may determine and adopt rules of procedure for the meeting.
6. The United Nations, its Specialized Agencies and the International Atomic Energy Agency, as well as any State not a Party to the present Convention, may be represented at meetings of the Conference by observers, who shall have the right to participate but not to vote.
7. Any body or agency technically qualified in protection, conservation or management of wild fauna and flora, in the following categories, which has informed the Secretariat of its desire to be represented at meetings of the Conference by observers, shall be admitted unless at least one- third of the Parties present object:
   (a) international agencies or bodies, either governmental or non-governmental, and national governmental agencies and bodies; and
   (b) national non-governmental agencies or bodies which have been approved for this purpose by the State in which they are located.

Once admitted, these observers shall have the right to participate but not to vote.

Article XII – The Secretariat

1. Upon entry into force of the present Convention, a Secretariat shall be provided by the Executive Director of the United Nations Environment Programme. To the extent and in the manner he considers appropriate, he may be assisted by suitable inter-governmental or non-governmental international or national agencies and bodies technically qualified in protection, conservation and management of wild fauna and flora.
2. The functions of the Secretariat shall be:
   (a) to arrange for and service meetings of the Parties;
   (b) to perform the functions entrusted to it under the provisions of Articles XV and XVI of the present Convention;
   (c) to undertake scientific and technical studies in accordance with programmes authorized by the Conference of the Parties as will contribute to the implementation of the present Convention, including studies concerning standards for appropriate preparation and shipment of living specimens and the means of identifying specimens;
   (d) to study the reports of Parties and to request from Parties such further information with respect thereto as it deems necessary to ensure implementation of the present Convention;
   (e) to invite the attention of the Parties to any matter pertaining to the aims of the present Convention;
   (f) to publish periodically and distribute to the Parties current editions of Appendices I, II and III together with any information which will facilitate identification of specimens of species included in those Appendices;
   (g) to prepare annual reports to the Parties on its work and on the implementation of the present Convention and such other reports as meetings of the Parties may request;
   (h) to make recommendations for the implementation of the aims and provisions of the present Convention, including the exchange of information of a scientific or technical nature;
   (i) to perform any other function as may be entrusted to it by the Parties.

Article XIII – International measures

1. When the Secretariat in the light of information received is satisfied that any species included in Appendix I or II is being affected adversely by trade in specimens of that species or that the provisions

of the present Convention are not being effectively implemented, it shall communicate such information to the authorized Management Authority of the Party or Parties concerned.

2. When any Party receives a communication as indicated in paragraph 1 of this Article, it shall, as soon as possible, inform the Secretariat of any relevant facts insofar as its laws permit and, where appropriate, propose remedial action. Where the Party considers that an inquiry is desirable, such inquiry may be carried out by one or more persons expressly authorized by the Party.
3. The information provided by the Party or resulting from any inquiry as specified in paragraph 2 of this Article shall be reviewed by the next Conference of the Parties which may make whatever recommendations it deems appropriate.

Article XIV – Effect on domestic legislation and international conventions

1. The provisions of the present Convention shall in no way affect the right of Parties to adopt:
   (a) stricter domestic measures regarding the conditions for trade, taking, possession or transport of specimens of species included in Appendices I, II and III, or the complete prohibition thereof; or
   (b) domestic measures restricting or prohibiting trade, taking, possession or transport of species not included in Appendix I, II or III.
2. The provisions of the present Convention shall in no way affect the provisions of any domestic measures or the obligations of Parties deriving from any treaty, convention, or international agreement relating to other aspects of trade, taking, possession or transport of specimens which is in force or subsequently may enter into force for any Party including any measure pertaining to the Customs, public health, veterinary or plant quarantine fields.
3. The provisions of the present Convention shall in no way affect the provisions of, or the obligations deriving from, any treaty, convention or international agreement concluded or which may be concluded between States creating a union or regional trade agreement establishing or maintaining a common external Customs control and removing Customs control between the parties thereto insofar as they relate to trade among the States members of that union or agreement.
4. A State party to the present Convention, which is also a party to any other treaty, convention or international agreement which is in force at the time of the coming into force of the present Convention and under the provisions of which protection is afforded to marine species included in Appendix II, shall be relieved of the obligations imposed on it under the provisions of the present Convention with respect to trade in specimens of species included in Appendix II that are taken by ships registered in that State and in accordance with the provisions of such other treaty, convention or international agreement.
5. Notwithstanding the provisions of Articles III, IV and V, any export of a specimen taken in accordance with paragraph 4 of this Article shall only require a certificate from a Management Authority of the State of introduction to the effect that the specimen was taken in accordance with the provisions of the other treaty, convention or international agreement in question.
6. Nothing in the present Convention shall prejudice the codification and development of the law of the sea by the United Nations Conference on the Law of the Sea convened pursuant to Resolution 2750 C (XXV) of the General Assembly of the United Nations nor the present or future claims and legal views of any State concerning the law of the sea and the nature and extent of coastal and flag State jurisdiction.

Article XV – Amendments to Appendices I and II

1. The following provisions shall apply in relation to amendments to Appendices I and II at meetings of the Conference of the Parties:
   (a) Any Party may propose an amendment to Appendix I or II for consideration at the next meeting. The text of the proposed amendment shall be communicated to the Secretariat at least 150 days before the meeting. The Secretariat shall consult the other Parties and interested bodies on the amendment in accordance with the provisions of sub- paragraphs (b) and (c) of paragraph 2 of this Article and shall communicate the response to all Parties not later than 30 days before the meeting.
   (b) Amendments shall be adopted by a two-thirds majority of Parties present and voting. For these purposes "Parties present and voting" means Parties present and casting an affirmative or negative vote. Parties abstaining from voting shall not be counted among the two-thirds required for adopting an amendment.
   (c) Amendments adopted at a meeting shall enter into force 90 days after that meeting for all Parties except those which make a reservation in accordance with paragraph 3 of this Article.
2. The following provisions shall apply in relation to amendments to Appendices I and II between meetings of the Conference of the Parties:
   (a) Any Party may propose an amendment to Appendix I or II for consideration between meetings by the postal procedures set forth in this paragraph.
   (b) For marine species, the Secretariat shall, upon receiving the text of the proposed amendment, immediately communicate it to the Parties. It shall also consult inter- governmental bodies having a function in relation to those species especially with a view to obtaining scientific data these bodies may be able to provide and to ensuring co-ordination with any conservation measures enforced by such bodies. The Secretariat shall communicate the views expressed and data provided by these bodies and its own

findings and recommendations to the Parties as soon as possible.

(c) For species other than marine species, the Secretariat shall, upon receiving the text of the proposed amendment, immediately communicate it to the Parties, and, as soon as possible thereafter, its own recommendations.

(d) Any Party may, within 60 days of the date on which the Secretariat communicated its recommendations to the Parties under sub-paragraph (b) or (c) of this paragraph, transmit to the Secretariat any comments on the proposed amendment together with any relevant scientific data and information.

(e) The Secretariat shall communicate the replies received together with its own recommendations to the Parties as soon as possible.

(f) If no objection to the proposed amendment is received by the Secretariat within 30 days of the date the replies and recommendations were communicated under the provisions of sub-paragraph (e) of this paragraph, the amendment shall enter into force 90 days later for all Parties except those which make a reservation in accordance with paragraph 3 of this Article.

(g) If an objection by any Party is received by the Secretariat, the proposed amendment shall be submitted to a postal vote in accordance with the provisions of sub-paragraphs (h), (i) and (j) of this paragraph.

(h) The Secretariat shall notify the Parties that notification of objection has been received.

(i) Unless the Secretariat receives the votes for, against or in abstention from at least one-half of the Parties within 60 days of the date of notification under sub-paragraph (h) of this paragraph, the proposed amendment shall be referred to the next meeting of the Conference for further consideration.

(j) Provided that votes are received from one-half of the Parties, the amendment shall be adopted by a two-thirds majority of Parties casting an affirmative or negative vote.

(k) The Secretariat shall notify all Parties of the result of the vote.

(l) If the proposed amendment is adopted it shall enter into force 90 days after the date of the notification by the Secretariat of its acceptance for all Parties except those which make a reservation in accordance with paragraph 3 of this Article.

3. During the period of 90 days provided for by sub-paragraph (c) of paragraph 1 or sub- paragraph (l) of paragraph 2 of this Article any Party may by notification in writing to the Depositary Government make a reservation with respect to the amendment. Until such reservation is withdrawn the Party shall be treated as a State not a Party to the present Convention with respect to trade in the species concerned.

Article XVI – Appendix III and amendments thereto

1. Any Party may at any time submit to the Secretariat a list of species which it identifies as being subject to regulation within its jurisdiction for the purpose mentioned in paragraph 3 of Article II. Appendix III shall include the names of the Parties submitting the species for inclusion therein, the scientific names of the species so submitted, and any parts or derivatives of the animals or plants concerned that are specified in relation to the species for the purposes of sub- paragraph (b) of Article I.
2. Each list submitted under the provisions of paragraph 1 of this Article shall be communicated to the Parties by the Secretariat as soon as possible after receiving it. The list shall take effect as part of Appendix III 90 days after the date of such communication. At any time after the communication of such list, any Party may by notification in writing to the Depositary Government enter a reservation with respect to any species or any parts or derivatives, and until such reservation is withdrawn, the State shall be treated as a State not a Party to the present Convention with respect to trade in the species or part or derivative concerned.
3. A Party which has submitted a species for inclusion in Appendix III may withdraw it at any time by notification to the Secretariat which shall communicate the withdrawal to all Parties. The withdrawal shall take effect 30 days after the date of such communication.
4. Any Party submitting a list under the provisions of paragraph 1 of this Article shall submit to the Secretariat a copy of all domestic laws and regulations applicable to the protection of such species, together with any interpretations which the Party may deem appropriate or the Secretariat may request. The Party shall, for as long as the species in question is included in Appendix III, submit any amendments of such laws and regulations or any interpretations as they are adopted.

Article XVII – Amendment of the Convention

1. An extraordinary meeting of the Conference of the Parties shall be convened by the Secretariat on the written request of at least one-third of the Parties to consider and adopt amendments to the present Convention. Such amendments shall be adopted by a two-thirds majority of Parties present and voting. For these purposes "Parties present and voting" means Parties present and casting an affirmative or negative vote. Parties abstaining from voting shall not be counted among the two-thirds required for adopting an amendment.
2. The text of any proposed amendment shall be communicated by the Secretariat to all Parties at least 90 days before the meeting.
3. An amendment shall enter into force for the Parties which have accepted it 60 days after two- thirds of the Parties have deposited an instrument of acceptance of the amendment with the Depositary Government. Thereafter, the amendment shall enter into force for any other Party 60 days after that

Party deposits its instrument of acceptance of the amendment.

Article XVIII – Resolution of disputes

1. Any dispute which may arise between two or more Parties with respect to the interpretation or application of the provisions of the present Convention shall be subject to negotiation between the Parties involved in the dispute.
2. If the dispute can not be resolved in accordance with paragraph 1 of this Article, the Parties may, by mutual consent, submit the dispute to arbitration, in particular that of the Permanent Court of Arbitration at The Hague, and the Parties submitting the dispute shall be bound by the arbitral decision.

Article XIX – Signature

The present Convention shall be open for signature at Washington until 30th April 1973 and thereafter at Berne until 31st December 1974.

Article XX – Ratification, acceptance, approval

The present Convention shall be subject to ratification, acceptance or approval. Instruments of ratification, acceptance or approval shall be deposited with the Government of the Swiss Confederation which shall be the Depositary Government.

Article XXI – Accession

1. The present Convention shall be open indefinitely for accession. Instruments of accession shall be deposited with the Depositary Government.
2. This Convention shall be open for accession by regional economic integration organizations constituted by sovereign States which have competence in respect of the negotiation, conclusion and implementation of international agreements in matters transferred to them by their Member States and covered by this Convention.
3. In their instruments of accession, such organizations shall declare the extent of their competence with respect to the matters governed by the Convention. These organizations shall also inform the Depositary Government of any substantial modification in the extent of their competence. Notifications by regional economic integration organizations concerning their competence with respect to matters governed by this Convention and modifications thereto shall be distributed to the Parties by the Depositary Government.
4. In matters within their competence, such regional economic integration organizations shall exercise the rights and fulfil the obligations which this Convention attributes to their Member States, which are Parties to the Convention. In such cases the Member States of the organizations shall not be entitled to exercise such rights individually.
5. In the fields of their competence, regional economic integration organizations shall exercise their right to vote with a number of votes equal to the number of their Member States which are Parties to the Convention. Such organizations shall not exercise their right to vote if their Member States exercise theirs, and vice versa.
6. Any reference to "Party" in the sense used in Article I (h) of this Convention to "State"/"States" or to "State Party"/"State Parties" to the Convention shall be construed as including a reference to any regional economic integration organization having competence in respect of the negotiation, conclusion and application of international agreements in matters covered by this Convention.

Article XXII – Entry into force

1. The present Convention shall enter into force 90 days after the date of deposit of the tenth instrument of ratification, acceptance, approval or accession, with the Depositary Government.
2. For each State which ratifies, accepts or approves the present Convention or accedes thereto after the deposit of the tenth instrument of ratification, acceptance, approval or accession, the present Convention shall enter into force 90 days after the deposit by such State of its instrument of ratification, acceptance, approval or accession.

Article XXIII – Reservations

1. The provisions of the present Convention shall not be subject to general reservations. Specific reservations may be entered in accordance with the provisions of this Article and Articles XV and XVI.
2. Any State may, on depositing its instrument of ratification, acceptance, approval or accession, enter a specific reservation with regard to:
   (a) any species included in Appendix I, II or III; or
   (b) any parts or derivatives specified in relation to a species included in Appendix III.
3. Until a Party withdraws its reservation entered under the provisions of this Article, it shall be treated as a State not a Party to the present Convention with respect to trade in the particular species or parts or derivatives specified in such reservation.

Article XXIV – Denunciation

Any Party may denounce the present Convention by written notification to the Depositary Government at any time. The denunciation shall take effect twelve months after the Depositary Government has received the notification.

Article XXV – Depositary

1. The original of the present Convention, in the Chinese, English, French, Russian and Spanish languages, each version being equally authentic, shall be deposited with the Depositary Government, which shall transmit certified copies thereof to all States that have signed it or deposited instruments of accession to it.
2. The Depositary Government shall inform all signatory and acceding States and the Secretariat of signatures, deposit of instruments of ratification, acceptance, approval or accession, entry into force of the present Convention, amendments thereto, entry and withdrawal of reservations and notifications of denunciation.

3. As soon as the present Convention enters into force, a certified copy thereof shall be transmitted by the Depositary Government to the Secretariat of the United Nations for registration and publication in accordance with Article 102 of the Charter of the United Nations.

In witness whereof the undersigned Plenipotentiaries, being duly authorized to that effect, have signed the present Convention.

Done at Washington this third day of March, One Thousand Nine Hundred and Seventy-three.

9.5. CMS / Bonn Convention 1979

Convention on the Conservation of Migratory Species of Wild Animals, Bonn, 23 June 1979, 1651 UNTS 333

THE CONTRACTING PARTIES,

RECOGNIZING that wild animals in their innumerable forms are an irreplaceable part of the earth's natural system which must be conserved for the good of mankind;

AWARE that each generation of man holds the resources of the earth for future generations and has an obligation to ensure that this legacy is conserved and, where utilized, is used wisely;

CONSCIOUS of the ever-growing value of wild animals from environmental, ecological, genetic, scientific, aesthetic, recreational, cultural, educational, social and economic points of view;

CONCERNED particularly with those species of wild animals that migrate across or outside national jurisdictional boundaries;

RECOGNIZING that the States are and must be the protectors of the migratory species of wild animals that live within or pass through their national jurisdictional boundaries;

CONVINCED that conservation and effective management of migratory species of wild animals require the concerted action of all States within the national jurisdictional boundaries of which such species spend any part of their life cycle;

RECALLING Recommendation 32 of the Action Plan adopted by the United Nations Conference on the Human Environment (Stockholm,1972) and noted with satisfaction at the Twenty-seventh Session of the General Assembly of the United Nations,

HAVE AGREED as follows:

Article I – Interpretation

1. For the purpose of this Convention:
   a) "Migratory species" means the entire population or any geographically separate part of the population of any species or lower taxon of wild animals, a significant proportion of whose members cyclically and predictably cross one or more national jurisdictional boundaries;
   b) "Conservation status of a migratory species" means the sum of the influences acting on the migratory species that may affect its long-term distribution and abundance;
   c) "Conservation status" will be taken as "favourable" when:
      (1) population dynamics data indicate that the migratory species is maintaining itself on a long-term basis as a viable component of its ecosystems;
      (2) the range of the migratory species is neither currently being reduced, nor is likely to be reduced, on a long-term basis;
      (3) there is, and will be in the foreseeable future, sufficient habitat to maintain the population of the migratory species on a long-term basis; and
      (4) the distribution and abundance of the migratory species approach historic coverage and levels to the extent that potentially suitable ecosystems exist and to the extent consistent with wise wildlife management;
   d) "Conservation status" will be taken as "unfavourable" if any of the conditions set out in sub-paragraph (c) of this paragraph is not met;
   e) "Endangered" in relation to a particular migratory species means that the migratory species is in danger of extinction throughout all or a significant portion of its range;
   f) "Range" means all the areas of land or water that a migratory species inhabits, stays in temporarily, crosses or overflies at any time on its normal migration route;
   g) "Habitat" means any area in the range of a migratory species which contains suitable living conditions for that species;
   h) "Range State" in relation to a particular migratory species means any State (and where appropriate any other Party referred to under sub-paragraph (k) of this paragraph) that exercises jurisdiction over any part of the range of that migratory species, or a State, flag vessels of which are engaged outside national jurisdictional limits in taking that migratory species;
   i) "Taking" means taking, hunting, fishing, capturing, harassing, deliberate killing, or attempting to engage in any such conduct;
   j) "AGREEMENT" means an international agreement relating to the conservation of one or more migratory species as provided for in Articles IV and V of this Convention; and
   k) "Party" means a State or any regional economic integration organization constituted by sovereign States which has competence in respect of the negotiation, conclusion and application of international agreements in matters covered by this Convention for which this Convention is in force.
2. In matters within their competence, the regional economic integration organizations which are Parties to this Convention shall in their own name exercise the rights and fulfil the responsibilities which this Convention attributes to their member States. In such cases the member States of these organizations shall not be entitled to exercise such rights individually.

3. Where this Convention provides for a decision to be taken by either a two-thirds majority or a unanimous decision of "the Parties present and voting" this shall mean "the Parties present and casting an affirmative or negative vote". Those abstaining from voting shall not be counted amongst "the Parties present and voting" in determining the majority.

Article II – Fundamental Principles

1. The Parties acknowledge the importance of migratory species being conserved and of Range States agreeing to take action to this end whenever possible and appropriate, paying special attention to migratory species the conservation status of which is unfavourable, and taking individually or in co-operation appropriate and necessary steps to conserve such species and their habitat.
2. The Parties acknowledge the need to take action to avoid any migratory species becoming endangered.
3. In particular, the Parties:
   a) should promote, co-operate in and support research relating to migratory species;
   b) shall endeavour to provide immediate protection for migratory species included in Appendix I; and
   c) shall endeavour to conclude AGREEMENTS covering the conservation and management of migratory species included in Appendix II.

Article III – Endangered Migratory Species: Appendix I

1. Appendix I shall list migratory species which are endangered.
2. A migratory species may be listed in Appendix I provided that reliable evidence, including the best scientific evidence available, indicates that the species is endangered.
3. A migratory species may be removed from Appendix I when the Conference of the Parties determines that:
   a) reliable evidence, including the best scientific evidence available, indicates that the species is no longer endangered, and
   b) the species is not likely to become endangered again because of loss of protection due to its removal from Appendix I.
4. Parties that are Range States of a migratory species listed in Appendix I shall endeavour:
   a) to conserve and, where feasible and appropriate, restore those habitats of the species which are of importance in removing the species from danger of extinction;
   b) to prevent, remove, compensate for or minimize, as appropriate, the adverse effects of activities or obstacles that seriously impede or prevent the migration of the species; and
   c) to the extent feasible and appropriate, to prevent, reduce or control factors that are endangering or are likely to further endanger the species, including strictly controlling the introduction of, or controlling or eliminating, already introduced exotic species.
5. Parties that are Range States of a migratory species listed in Appendix I shall prohibit the taking of animals belonging to such species. Exceptions may be made to this prohibition only if:
   a) the taking is for scientific purposes;
   b) the taking is for the purpose of enhancing the propagation or survival of the affected species;
   c) the taking is to accommodate the needs of traditional subsistence users of such species; or
   d) extraordinary circumstances so require;

   provided that such exceptions are precise as to content and limited in space and time. Such taking should not operate to the disadvantage of the species.
6. The Conference of the Parties may recommend to the Parties that are Range States of a migratory species listed in Appendix I that they take further measures considered appropriate to benefit the species.
7. The Parties shall as soon as possible inform the Secretariat of any exceptions made pursuant to paragraph 5 of this Article.

Article IV – Migratory Species to Be the Subject of AGREEMENTS: Appendix II

1. Appendix II shall list migratory species which have an unfavourable conservation status and which require international agreements for their conservation and management, as well as those which have a conservation status which would significantly benefit from the international co-operation that could be achieved by an international agreement.
2. If the circumstances so warrant, a migratory species may be listed both in Appendix I and Appendix II.
3. Parties that are Range States of migratory species listed in Appendix II shall endeavour to conclude AGREEMENTS where these would benefit the species and should give priority to those species in an unfavourable conservation status.
4. Parties are encouraged to take action with a view to concluding agreements for any population or any geographically separate part of the population of any species or lower taxon of wild animals, members of which periodically cross one or more national jurisdictional boundaries.
5. The Secretariat shall be provided with a copy of each AGREEMENT concluded pursuant to the provisions of this Article.

Article V – Guidelines for AGREEMENTS

1. The object of each AGREEMENT shall be to restore the migratory species concerned to a favourable conservation status or to maintain it in such a status. Each AGREEMENT should deal with those aspects of the conservation and management

of the migratory species concerned which serve to achieve that object.

2. Each AGREEMENT should cover the whole of the range of the migratory species concerned and should be open to accession by all Range States of that species, whether or not they are Parties to this Convention.
3. An AGREEMENT should, wherever possible, deal with more than one migratory species.
4. Each AGREEMENT should:
   a) identify the migratory species covered;
   b) describe the range and migration route of the migratory species;
   c) provide for each Party to designate its national authority concerned with the implementation of the AGREEMENT;
   d) establish, if necessary, appropriate machinery to assist in carrying out the aims of the AGREEMENT, to monitor its effectiveness, and to prepare reports for the Conference of the Parties;
   e) provide for procedures for the settlement of disputes between Parties to the AGREEMENT; and
   f) at a minimum, prohibit, in relation to a migratory species of the Order Cetacea, any taking that is not permitted for that migratory species under any other multilateral agreement and provide for accession to the AGREEMENT by States that are not Range States of that migratory species.
5. Where appropriate and feasible, each AGREEMENT should provide for, but not be limited to:
   a) periodic review of the conservation status of the migratory species concerned and the identification of the factors which may be harmful to that status;
   b) co-ordinated conservation and management plans;
   c) research into the ecology and population dynamics of the migratory species concerned, with special regard to migration;
   d) the exchange of information on the migratory species concerned, special regard being paid to the exchange of the results of research and of relevant statistics;
   e) conservation and, where required and feasible, restoration of the habitats of importance in maintaining a favourable conservation status, and protection of such habitats from disturbances, including strict control of the introduction of, or control of already introduced, exotic species detrimental to the migratory species;
   f) maintenance of a network of suitable habitats appropriately disposed in relation to the migration routes;
   g) where it appears desirable, the provision of new habitats favourable to the migratory species or reintroduction of the migratory species into favourable habitats;
   h) elimination of, to the maximum extent possible, or compensation for activities and obstacles which hinder or impede migration;
   i) prevention, reduction or control of the release into the habitat of the migratory species of substances harmful to that migratory species;
   j) measures based on sound ecological principles to control and manage the taking of the migratory species;
   k) procedures for co-ordinating action to suppress illegal taking;
   l) exchange of information on substantial threats to the migratory species;
   m) emergency procedures whereby conservation action would be considerably and rapidly strengthened when the conservation status of the migratory species is seriously affected; and
   n) making the general public aware of the contents and aims of the AGREEMENT.

Article VI – Range States

1. A list of the Range States of migratory species listed in Appendices I and II shall be kept up to date by the Secretariat using information it has received from the Parties.
2. The Parties shall keep the Secretariat informed in regard to which of the migratory species listed in Appendices I and II they consider themselves to be Range States, including provision of information on their flag vessels engaged outside national jurisdictional limits in taking the migratory species concerned and, where possible, future plans in respect of such taking.
3. The Parties which are Range States for migratory species listed in Appendix I or Appendix II should inform the Conference of the Parties through the Secretariat, at least six months prior to each ordinary meeting of the Conference, on measures that they are taking to implement the provisions of this Convention for these species.

Article VII – The Conference of the Parties

1. The Conference of the Parties shall be the decision-making organ of this Convention.
2. The Secretariat shall call a meeting of the Conference of the Parties not later than two years after the entry into force of this Convention.
3. Thereafter the Secretariat shall convene ordinary meetings of the Conference of the Parties at intervals of not more than three years, unless the Conference decides otherwise, and extraordinary meetings at any time on the written request of at least one-third of the Parties.
4. The Conference of the Parties shall establish and keep under review the financial regulations of this Convention. The Conference of the Parties shall, at each of its ordinary meetings, adopt the budget for the next financial period. Each Party shall contribute to this budget according to a scale to be agreed upon by the Conference. Financial regulations, including the provisions on the budget and the scale

of contributions as well as their modifications, shall be adopted by unanimous vote of the Parties present and voting.

5. At each of its meetings the Conference of the Parties shall review the implementation of this Convention and may in particular:
   a) review and assess the conservation status of migratory species;
   b) review the progress made towards the conservation of migratory species, especially those listed in Appendices I and II;
   c) make such provision and provide such guidance as may be necessary to enable the Scientific Council and the Secretariat to carry out their duties;
   d) receive and consider any reports presented by the Scientific Council, the Secretariat, any Party or any standing body established pursuant to an AGREEMENT;
   e) make recommendations to the Parties for improving the conservation status of migratory species and review the progress being made under AGREEMENTS;
   f) in those cases where an AGREEMENT has not been concluded, make recommendations for the convening of meetings of the Parties that are Range States of a migratory species or group of migratory species to discuss measures to improve the conservation status of the species;
   g) make recommendations to the Parties for improving the effectiveness of this Convention; and
   h) decide on any additional measure that should be taken to implement the objectives of this Convention.
6. Each meeting of the Conference of the Parties should determine the time and venue of the next meeting.
7. Any meeting of the Conference of the Parties shall determine and adopt rules of procedure for that meeting. Decisions at a meeting of the Conference of the Parties shall require a two-thirds majority of the Parties present and voting, except where otherwise provided for by this Convention.
8. The United Nations, its Specialized Agencies, the International Atomic Energy Agency, as well as any State not a party to this Convention and, for each AGREEMENT, the body designated by the parties to that AGREEMENT, may be represented by observers at meetings of the Conference of the Parties.
9. Any agency or body technically qualified in protection, conservation and management of migratory species, in the following categories, which has informed the Secretariat of its desire to be represented at meetings of the Conference of the Parties by observers, shall be admitted unless at least one-third of the Parties present object:
   a) international agencies or bodies, either governmental or non-governmental, and national governmental agencies and bodies; and
   b) national non-governmental agencies or bodies which have been approved for this purpose by the State in which they are located.

   Once admitted, these observers shall have the right to participate but not to vote.

Article VIII – The Scientific Council

1. At its first meeting, the Conference of the Parties shall establish a Scientific Council to provide advice on scientific matters.
2. Any Party may appoint a qualified expert as a member of the Scientific Council. In addition, the Scientific Council shall include as members qualified experts selected and appointed by the Conference of the Parties; the number of these experts, the criteria for their selection and the terms of their appointments shall be as determined by the Conference of the Parties.
3. The Scientific Council shall meet at the request of the Secretariat as required by the Conference of the Parties.
4. Subject to the approval of the Conference of the Parties, the Scientific Council shall establish its own rules of procedure.
5. The Conference of the Parties shall determine the functions of the Scientific Council, which may include:
   a) providing scientific advice to the Conference of the Parties, to the Secretariat, and, if approved by the Conference of the Parties, to any body set up under this Convention or an AGREEMENT or to any Party;
   b) recommending research and the co-ordination of research on migratory species, evaluating the results of such research in order to ascertain the conservation status of migratory species and reporting to the Conference of the Parties on such status and measures for its improvement;
   c) making recommendations to the Conference of the Parties as to the migratory species to be included in Appendices I or II, together with an indication of the range of such migratory species;
   d) making recommendations to the Conference of the Parties as to specific conservation and management measures to be included in AGREEMENTS on migratory species; and
   e) recommending to the Conference of the Parties solutions to problems relating to the scientific aspects of the implementation of this Convention, in particular with regard to the habitats of migratory species.

Article IX – The Secretariat

1. For the purposes of this Convention a Secretariat shall be established.
2. Upon entry into force of this Convention, the Secretariat is provided by the Executive Director of

the United Nations Environment Programme. To the extent and in the manner he considers appropriate, he may be assisted by suitable intergovernmental or non-governmental, international or national agencies and bodies technically qualified in protection, conservation and management of wild animals.

3. If the United Nations Environment Programme is no longer able to provide the Secretariat, the Conference of the Parties shall make alternative arrangements for the Secretariat.
4. The functions of the Secretariat shall be:
   a) to arrange for and service meetings:
      i) of the Conference of the Parties, and
      ii) of the Scientific Council;
   b) to maintain liaison with and promote liaison between the Parties, the standing bodies set up under AGREEMENTS and other international organizations concerned with migratory species;
   c) to obtain from any appropriate source reports and other information which will further the objectives and implementation of this Convention and to arrange for the appropriate dissemination of such information;
   d) to invite the attention of the Conference of the Parties to any matter pertaining to the objectives of this Convention;
   e) to prepare for the Conference of the Parties reports on the work of the Secretariat and on the implementation of this Convention;
   f) to maintain and publish a list of Range States of all migratory species included in Appendices I and II;
   g) to promote, under the direction of the Conference of the Parties, the conclusion of AGREEMENTS;
   h) to maintain and make available to the Parties a list of AGREEMENTS and, if so required by the Conference of the Parties, to provide any information on such AGREEMENTS;
   i) to maintain and publish a list of the recommendations made by the Conference of the Parties pursuant to subparagraphs (e), (f) and (g) of paragraph 5 of Article VII or of decisions made pursuant to sub-paragraph (h) of that paragraph;
   j) to provide for the general public information concerning this Convention and its objectives; and
   k) to perform any other function entrusted to it under this Convention or by the Conference of the Parties.

Article X – Amendment of the Convention

1. This Convention may be amended at any ordinary or extraordinary meeting of the Conference of the Parties.
2. Proposals for amendment may be made by any Party.
3. The text of any proposed amendment and the reasons for it shall be communicated to the Secretariat at least one hundred and fifty days before the meeting at which it is to be considered and shall promptly be communicated by the Secretariat to all Parties. Any comments on the text by the Parties shall be communicated to the Secretariat not less than sixty days before the meeting begins. The Secretariat shall, immediately after the last day for submission of comments, communicate to the Parties all comments submitted by that day.
4. Amendments shall be adopted by a two-thirds majority of Parties present and voting.
5. An amendment adopted shall enter into force for all Parties which have accepted it on the first day of the third month following the date on which two-thirds of the Parties have deposited an instrument of acceptance with the Depositary. For each Party which deposits an instrument of acceptance after the date on which two-thirds of the Parties have deposited an instrument of acceptance, the amendment shall enter into force for that Party on the first day of the third month following the deposit of its instrument of acceptance.

Article XI – Amendment of the Appendices

1. Appendices I and II may be amended at any ordinary or extraordinary meeting of the Conference of the Parties.
2. Proposals for amendment may be made by any Party.
3. The text of any proposed amendment and the reasons for it, based on the best scientific evidence available, shall be communicated to the Secretariat at least one hundred and fifty days before the meeting and shall promptly be communicated by the Secretariat to all Parties. Any comments on the text by the Parties shall be communicated to the Secretariat not less than sixty days before the meeting begins. The Secretariat shall, immediately after the last day for submission of comments, communicate to the Parties all comments submitted by that day.
4. Amendments shall be adopted by a two-thirds majority of Parties present and voting.
5. An amendment to the Appendices shall enter into force for all Parties ninety days after the meeting of the Conference of the Parties at which it was adopted, except for those Parties which make a reservation in accordance with paragraph 6 of this Article.
6. During the period of ninety days provided for in paragraph 5 of this Article, any Party may by notification in writing to the Depositary make a reservation with respect to the amendment. A reservation to an amendment may be withdrawn by written notification to the Depositary and thereupon the amendment shall enter into force for that Party ninety days after the reservation is withdrawn.

Article XII – Effect on International Conventions and Other Legislation

1. Nothing in this Convention shall prejudice the codification and development of the law of the sea by the United Nations Conference on the Law of the Sea convened pursuant to Resolution 2750 C (XXV) of the General Assembly of the United Nations nor the present or future claims and legal views of any State concerning the law of the sea and the nature and extent of coastal and flag State jurisdiction.
2. The provisions of this Convention shall in no way affect the rights or obligations of any Party deriving from any existing treaty, convention or agreement.
3. The provisions of this Convention shall in no way affect the right of Parties to adopt stricter domestic measures concerning the conservation of migratory species listed in Appendices I and II or to adopt domestic measures concerning the conservation of species not listed in Appendices I and II.

Article XIII – Settlement of Disputes

1. Any dispute which may arise between two or more Parties with respect to the interpretation or application of the provisions of this Convention shall be subject to negotiation between the Parties involved in the dispute.
2. If the dispute cannot be resolved in accordance with paragraph 1 of this Article, the Parties may, by mutual consent, submit the dispute to arbitration, in particular that of the Permanent Court of Arbitration at The Hague, and the Parties submitting the dispute shall be bound by the arbitral decision.

Article XIV – Reservations

1. The provisions of this Convention shall not be subject to general reservations. Specific reservations may be entered in accordance with the provisions of this Article and Article XI.
2. Any State or any regional economic integration organization may, on depositing its instrument of ratification, acceptance, approval or accession, enter a specific reservation with regard to the presence on either Appendix I or Appendix II or both, of any migratory species and shall then not be regarded as a Party in regard to the subject of that reservation until ninety days after the Depositary has transmitted to the Parties notification that such reservation has been withdrawn.

Article XV – Signature

This Convention shall be open for signature at Bonn for all States and any regional economic integration organization until the twenty-second day of June 1980.

Article XVI – Ratification, Acceptance, Approval

This Convention shall be subject to ratification, acceptance or approval. Instruments of ratification, acceptance or approval shall be deposited with the Government of the Federal Republic of Germany, which shall be the Depositary.

Article XVII – Accession

After the twenty-second day of June 1980 this Convention shall be open for accession by all non-signatory States and any regional economic integration organization. Instruments of accession shall be deposited with the Depositary.

Article XVIII – Entry into Force

1. This Convention shall enter into force on the first day of the third month following the date of deposit of the fifteenth instrument of ratification, acceptance, approval or accession with the Depositary.
2. For each State or each regional economic integration organization which ratifies, accepts or approves this Convention or accedes thereto after the deposit of the fifteenth instrument of ratification, acceptance, approval or accession, this Convention shall enter into force on the first day of the third month following the deposit by such State or such organization of its instrument of ratification, acceptance, approval or accession.

Article XIX – Denunciation

Any Party may denounce this Convention by written notification to the Depositary at any time. The denunciation shall take effect twelve months after the Depositary has received the notification.

Article XX – Depositary

1. The original of this Convention, in the English, French, German, Russian and Spanish languages, each version being equally authentic, shall be deposited with the Depositary. The Depositary shall transmit certified copies of each of these versions to all States and all regional economic integration organizations that have signed the Convention or deposited instruments of accession to it.
2. The Depositary shall, after consultation with the Governments concerned, prepare official versions of the text of this Convention in the Arabic and Chinese languages.
3. The Depositary shall inform all signatory and acceding States and all signatory and acceding regional economic integration organizations and the Secretariat of signatures, deposit of instruments of ratification, acceptance, approval or accession, entry into force of this Convention, amendments thereto, specific reservations and notifications of denunciation.
4. As soon as this Convention enters into force, a certified copy thereof shall be transmitted by the Depositary to the Secretariat of the United Nations for registration and publication in accordance with Article 102 of the Charter of the United Nations.

IN WITNESS WHEREOF the undersigned, being duly authorized to that effect, have signed this Convention.

DONE at Bonn on 23 June 1979.

9.6. Bern Convention 1979

Convention on the Conservation of European Wildlife and Natural Habitats, Bern, 19 September 1979, ETS 104

The member States of the Council of Europe and the other signatories hereto,

Considering that the aim of the Council of Europe is to achieve a greater unity between its members;

Considering the wish of the Council of Europe to co-operate with other States in the field of nature conservation;

Recognising that wild flora and fauna constitute a natural heritage of aesthetic, scientific, cultural, recreational, economic and intrinsic value that needs to be preserved and handed on to future generations;

Recognising the essential role played by wild flora and fauna in maintaining biological balances;

Noting that numerous species of wild flora and fauna are being seriously depleted and that some of them are threatened with extinction;

Aware that the conservation of natural habitats is a vital component of the protection and conservation of wild flora and fauna;

Recognising that the conservation of wild flora and fauna should be taken into consideration by the governments in their national goals and programmes, and that international co-operation should be established to protect migratory species in particular;

Bearing in mind the widespread requests for common action made by governments or by international bodies, in particular the requests expressed by the United Nations Conference on the Human Environment 1972 and the Consultative Assembly of the Council of Europe;

Desiring particularly to follow, in the field of wildlife conservation, the recommendations of Resolution No. 2 of the Second European Ministerial Conference on the Environment,

Have agreed as follows:

Chapter I – General provisions

Article 1

1 The aims of this Convention are to conserve wild flora and fauna and their natural habitats, especially those species and habitats whose conservation requires the co-operation of several States, and to promote such co-operation.

2 Particular emphasis is given to endangered and vulnerable species, including endangered and vulnerable migratory species.

Article 2

The Contracting Parties shall take requisite measures to maintain the population of wild flora and fauna at, or adapt it to, a level which corresponds in particular to ecological, scientific and cultural requirements, while taking account of economic and recreational requirements and the needs of sub-species, varieties or forms at risk locally.

Article 3

1 Each Contracting Party shall take steps to promote national policies for the conservation of wild flora, wild fauna and natural habitats, with particular attention to endangered and vulnerable species, especially endemic ones, and endangered habitats, in accordance with the provisions of this Convention.

2 Each Contracting Party undertakes, in its planning and development policies and in its measures against pollution, to have regard to the conservation of wild flora and fauna.

3 Each Contracting Party shall promote education and disseminate general information on the need to conserve species of wild flora and fauna and their habitats.

Chapter II – Protection of habitats

Article 4

1 Each Contracting Party shall take appropriate and necessary legislative and administrative measures to ensure the conservation of the habitats of the wild flora and fauna species, especially those specified in Appendices I and II, and the conservation of endangered natural habitats.

2 The Contracting Parties in their planning and development policies shall have regard to the conservation requirements of the areas protected under the preceding paragraph, so as to avoid or minimise as far as possible any deterioration of such areas.

3 The Contracting Parties undertake to give special attention to the protection of areas that are of importance for the migratory species specified in Appendices II and III and which are appropriately situated in relation to migration routes, as wintering, staging, feeding, breeding or moulting areas.

4 The Contracting Parties undertake to co-ordinate as appropriate their efforts for the protection of the natural habitats referred to in this article when these are situated in frontier areas.

Chapter III – Protection of species

Article 5

Each Contracting Party shall take appropriate and necessary legislative and administrative measures to ensure the special protection of the wild flora species specified in Appendix I. Deliberate picking, collecting, cutting or uprooting of such plants shall be prohibited. Each Contracting Party shall, as appropriate, prohibit the possession or sale of these species.

Article 6

Each Contracting Party shall take appropriate and necessary legislative and administrative measures to ensure the special protection of the wild fauna species specified in Appendix II. The following will in particular be prohibited for these species:

a all forms of deliberate capture and keeping and deliberate killing;

b the deliberate damage to or destruction of breeding or resting sites;

c the deliberate disturbance of wild fauna, particularly during the period of breeding, rearing and hibernation, insofar as disturbance would be significant in relation to the objectives of this Convention;

d the deliberate destruction or taking of eggs from the wild or keeping these eggs even if empty;

e the possession of and internal trade in these animals, alive or dead, including stuffed animals and any readily recognisable part or derivative thereof, where this would contribute to the effectiveness of the provisions of this article.

Article 7

1 Each Contracting Party shall take appropriate and necessary legislative and administrative measures to ensure the protection of the wild fauna species specified in Appendix III.

2 Any exploitation of wild fauna specified in Appendix III shall be regulated in order to keep the populations out of danger, taking into account the requirements of Article 2.

3 Measures to be taken shall include:

  a closed seasons and/or other procedures regulating the exploitation;

  b the temporary or local prohibition of exploitation, as appropriate, in order to restore satisfactory population levels;

  c the regulation as appropriate of sale, keeping for sale, transport for sale or offering for sale of live and dead wild animals.

Article 8

In respect of the capture or killing of wild fauna species specified in Appendix III and in cases where, in accordance with Article 9, exceptions are applied to species specified in Appendix II, Contracting Parties shall prohibit the use of all indiscriminate means of capture and killing and the use of all means capable of causing local disappearance of, or serious disturbance to, populations of a species, and in particular, the means specified in Appendix IV.

Article 9

1 Each Contracting Party may make exceptions from the provisions of Articles 4, 5, 6, 7 and from the prohibition of the use of the means mentioned in Article 8 provided that there is no other satisfactory solution and that the exception will not be detrimental to the survival of the population concerned:

- for the protection of flora and fauna;
- to prevent serious damage to crops, livestock, forests, fisheries, water and other forms of property;
- in the interests of public health and safety, air safety or other overriding public interests;
- for the purposes of research and education, of repopulation, of reintroduction and for the necessary breeding;
- to permit, under strictly supervised conditions, on a selective basis and to a limited extent, the taking, keeping or other judicious exploitation of certain wild animals and plants in small numbers.

2 The Contracting Parties shall report every two years to the Standing Committee on the exceptions made under the preceding paragraph. These reports must specify:

- the populations which are or have been subject to the exceptions and, when practical, the number of specimens involved;
- the means authorised for the killing or capture;
- the conditions of risk and the circumstances of time and place under which such exceptions were granted;
- the authority empowered to declare that these conditions have been fulfilled, and to take decisions in respect of the means that may be used, their limits and the persons instructed to carry them out;
- the controls involved.

Chapter IV – Special provisions for migratory species

Article 10

1 The Contracting Parties undertake, in addition to the measures specified in Articles 4, 6, 7 and 8, to co-ordinate their efforts for the protection of the migratory species specified in Appendices II and III whose range extends into their territories.

2 The Contracting Parties shall take measures to seek to ensure that the closed seasons and/or other procedures regulating the exploitation established under paragraph 3.a of Article 7 are adequate and appropriately disposed to meet the requirements of the migratory species specified in Appendix III.

Chapter V – Supplementary provisions

Article 11

1 In carrying out the provisions of this Convention, the Contracting Parties undertake:

  a to co-operate whenever appropriate and in particular where this would enhance the effectiveness of measures taken under other articles of this Convention;

  b to encourage and co-ordinate research related to the purposes of this Convention.

2 Each Contracting Party undertakes:

  a to encourage the reintroduction of native species of wild flora and fauna when this would contribute to the conservation of an endangered species, provided that a study is first made in the light of the experiences of other Contracting Parties to establish that such reintroduction would be effective and acceptable;

b to strictly control the introduction of non-native species.

3 Each Contracting Party shall inform the Standing Committee of the species receiving complete protection on its territory and not included in Appendices I and II.

Article 12

The Contracting Parties may adopt stricter measures for the conservation of wild flora and fauna and their natural habitats than those provided under this Convention.

Chapter VI – Standing Committee

Article 13

1 For the purposes of this Convention, a Standing Committee shall be set up.

2 Any Contracting Party may be represented on the Standing Committee by one or more delegates. Each delegation shall have one vote. Within the areas of its competence, the European Economic Community shall exercise its right to vote with a number of votes equal to the number of its member States which are Contracting Parties to this Convention; the European Economic Community shall not exercise its right to vote in cases where the member States concerned exercise theirs, and conversely.

3 Any member State of the Council of Europe which is not a Contracting Party to the Convention may be represented on the committee as an observer.

The Standing Committee may, by unanimous decision, invite any non-member State of the Council of Europe which is not a Contracting Party to the Convention to be represented by an observer at one of its meetings.

Any body or agency technically qualified in the protection, conservation or management of wild fauna and flora and their habitats, and belonging to one of the following categories:

a international agencies or bodies, either governmental or non-governmental, and national governmental agencies or bodies;

b national non-governmental agencies or bodies which have been approved for this purpose by the State in which they are located,

may inform the Secretary General of the Council of Europe, at least three months before the meeting of the Committee, of its wish to be represented at that meeting by observers. They shall be admitted unless, at least one month before the meeting, one-third of the Contracting Parties have informed the Secretary General of their objection.

4 The Standing Committee shall be convened by the Secretary General of the Council of Europe. Its first meeting shall be held within one year of the date of the entry into force of the Convention. It shall subsequently meet at least every two years and whenever a majority of the Contracting Parties so request.

5 A majority of the Contracting Parties shall constitute a quorum for holding a meeting of the Standing Committee.

6 Subject to the provisions of this Convention, the Standing Committee shall draw up its own Rules of Procedure.

Article 14

1 The Standing Committee shall be responsible for following the application of this Convention. It may in particular:

- keep under review the provisions of this Convention, including its appendices, and examine any modifications necessary;
- make recommendations to the Contracting Parties concerning measures to be taken for the purposes of this Convention;
- recommend the appropriate measures to keep the public informed about the activities undertaken within the framework of this Convention;
- make recommendations to the Committee of Ministers concerning non-member States of the Council of Europe to be invited to accede to this Convention;
- make any proposal for improving the effectiveness of this Convention, including proposals for the conclusion, with the States which are not Contracting Parties to the Convention, of agreements that would enhance the effective conservation of species or groups of species.

2 In order to discharge its functions, the Standing Committee may, on its own initiative, arrange for meetings of groups of experts.

Article 15

After each meeting, the Standing Committee shall forward to the Committee of Ministers of the Council of Europe a report on its work and on the functioning of the Convention.

Chapter VII – Amendments

Article 16

1 Any amendment to the articles of this Convention proposed by a Contracting Party or the Committee of Ministers shall be communicated to the Secretary General of the Council of Europe and forwarded by him at least two months before the meeting of the Standing Committee to the member States of the Council of Europe, to any signatory, to any Contracting Party, to any State invited to sign this Convention in accordance with the provisions of Article 19 and to any State invited to accede to it in accordance with the provisions of Article 20.

2 Any amendment proposed in accordance with the provisions of the preceding paragraph shall be examined by the Standing Committee which:

a for amendments to Articles 1 to 12, shall submit the text adopted by a three-quarters majority of the votes cast to the Contracting Parties for acceptance;

b for amendments to Articles 13 to 24, shall submit the text adopted by a three-quarters majority of the votes cast to the Committee of Ministers for approval. After its approval, this text shall be forwarded to the Contracting Parties for acceptance.

3 Any amendment shall enter into force on the thirtieth day after all the Contracting Parties have informed the Secretary General that they have accepted it.

4 The provisions of paragraphs 1, 2.a and 3 of this article shall apply to the adoption of new appendices to this Convention.

Article 17

1 Any amendment to the appendices of this Convention proposed by a Contracting Party or the Committee of Ministers shall be communicated to the Secretary General of the Council of Europe and forwarded by him at least two months before the meeting of the Standing Committee to the member States of the Council of Europe, to any signatory, to any Contracting Party, to any State invited to sign this Convention in accordance with the provisions of Article 19 and to any State invited to accede to it in accordance with the provisions of Article 20.

2 Any amendment proposed in accordance with the provisions of the preceding paragraph shall be examined by the Standing Committee, which may adopt it by a two-thirds majority of the Contracting Parties. The text adopted shall be forwarded to the Contracting Parties.

3 Three months after its adoption by the Standing Committee and unless one-third of the Contracting Parties have notified objections, any amendment shall enter into force for those Contracting Parties which have not notified objections.

Chapter VIII – Settlement of disputes

Article 18

1 The Standing Committee shall use its best endeavours to facilitate a friendly settlement of any difficulty to which the execution of this Convention may give rise.

2 Any dispute between Contracting Parties concerning the interpretation or application of this Convention which has not been settled on the basis of the provisions of the preceding paragraph or by negotiation between the parties concerned shall, unless the said parties agree otherwise, be submitted, at the request of one of them, to arbitration. Each party shall designate an arbitrator and the two arbitrators shall designate a third arbitrator. Subject to the provisions of paragraph 3 of this article, if one of the parties has not designated its arbitrator within the three months following the request for arbitration, he shall be designated at the request of the other party by the President of the European Court of Human Rights within a further three months' period. The same procedure shall be observed if the arbitrators cannot agree on the choice of the third arbitrator within the three months following the designation of the two first arbitrators.

3 In the event of a dispute between two Contracting Parties one of which is a member State of the European Economic Community, the latter itself being a Contracting Party, the other Contracting Party shall address the request for arbitration both to the member State and to the Community, which jointly shall notify it, within two months of receipt of the request, whether the member State or the Community, or the member and the Community jointly, shall be party to the dispute. In the absence of such notification within the said time limit, the member State and the Community shall be considered as being one and the same party to the dispute for the purposes of the application of the provisions governing the constitution and procedure of the arbitration tribunal. The same shall apply when the member State and the Community jointly present themselves as party to the dispute.

4 The arbitration tribunal shall draw up its own Rules of Procedure. Its decisions shall be taken by majority vote. Its award shall be final and binding.

5 Each party to the dispute shall bear the expenses of the arbitrator designated by it and the parties shall share equally the expenses of the third arbitrator, as well as other costs entailed by the arbitration.

Chapter IX – Final provisions

Article 19

1 This Convention shall be open for signature by the member States of the Council of Europe and non-member States which have participated in its elaboration and by the European Economic Community.

Up until the date when the Convention enters into force, it shall also be open for signature by any other State so invited by the Committee of Ministers.

The Convention is subject to ratification, acceptance or approval. Instruments of ratification, acceptance or approval shall be deposited with the Secretary General of the Council of Europe.

2 The Convention shall enter into force on the first day of the month following the expiry of a period of three months after the date on which five States, including at least four member States of the Council of Europe, have expressed their consent to be bound by the Convention in accordance with the provisions of the preceding paragraph.

3 In respect of any signatory State or the European Economic Community which subsequently express their consent to be bound by it, the Convention shall enter into force on the first day of the month following the expiry of a period of three months after the date of the deposit of the instrument of ratification, acceptance or approval.

Article 20

1 After the entry into force of this Convention, the Committee of Ministers of the Council of Europe, after consulting the Contracting Parties, may invite to accede to the Convention any non-member State of the Council which, invited to sign in accordance with the provisions of Article 19, has not yet done so, and any other non-member State.

2 In respect of any acceding State, the Convention shall enter into force on the first day of the month following the expiry of a period of three months after the date of the deposit of the instrument of accession with the Secretary General of the Council of Europe.

Article 21

1 Any State may, at the time of signature or when depositing its instrument of ratification, acceptance, approval or accession, specify the territory or territories to which this Convention shall apply.

2 Any Contracting Party may, when depositing its instrument of ratification, acceptance, approval or accession or at any later date, by declaration addressed to the Secretary General of the Council of Europe, extend the application of this Convention to any other territory specified in the declaration and for whose international relations it is responsible or on whose behalf it is authorised to give undertakings.

3 Any declaration made under the preceding paragraph may, in respect of any territory mentioned in such declaration, be withdrawn by notification addressed to the Secretary General. Such withdrawal shall become effective on the first day of the month following the expiry of a period of six months after the date of receipt of the notification by the Secretary General.

Article 22

1 Any State may, at the time of signature or when depositing its instrument of ratification, acceptance, approval or accession, make one or more reservations regarding certain species specified in Appendices I to III and/or, for certain species mentioned in the reservation or reservations, regarding certain means or methods of killing, capture and other exploitation listed in Appendix IV. No reservations of a general nature may be made.

2 Any Contracting Party which extends the application of this Convention to a territory mentioned in the declaration referred to in paragraph 2 of Article 21 may, in respect of the territory concerned, make one or more reservations in accordance with the provisions of the preceding paragraph.

3 No other reservation may be made.

4 Any Contracting Party which has made a reservation under paragraphs 1 and 2 of this article may wholly or partly withdraw it by means of a notification addressed to the Secretary General of the Council of Europe. Such withdrawal shall take effect as from the date of receipt of the notification by the Secretary General.

Article 23

1 Any Contracting Party may, at any time, denounce this Convention by means of a notification addressed to the Secretary General of the Council of Europe.

2 Such denunciation shall become effective on the first day of the month following the expiry of a period of six months after the date of receipt of the notification by the Secretary General.

Article 24

The Secretary General of the Council of Europe shall notify the member States of the Council of Europe, any signatory State, the European Economic Community if a signatory of this Convention and any Contracting Party of:

a any signature;

b the deposit of any instrument of ratification, acceptance, approval or accession;

c any date of entry into force of this Convention in accordance with Articles 19 and 20;

d any information forwarded under the provisions of paragraph 3 of Article 13;

e any report established in pursuance of the provisions of Article 15;

f any amendment or any new appendix adopted in accordance with Articles 16 and 17 and the date on which the amendment or new appendix comes into force;

g any declaration made under the provisions of paragraphs 2 and 3 of Article 21;

h any reservation made under the provisions of paragraphs 1 and 2 of Article 22;

i the withdrawal of any reservation carried out under the provisions of paragraph 4 of Article 22;

j any notification made under the provisions of Article 23 and the date on which the denunciation takes effect.

In witness whereof the undersigned, being duly authorised thereto, have signed this Convention.

Done at Bern, this 19th day of September 1979, in English and French, both texts being equally authentic, in a single copy which shall be deposited in the archives of the Council of Europe. The Secretary General of the Council of Europe shall transmit certified copies to each member State of the Council of Europe, to any signatory State, to the European Economic Community if a signatory and to any State invited to sign this Convention or to accede thereto.

9.7. CBD / Biodiversity Convention 1992

Convention on Biological Diversity, Rio de Janeiro, 5 June 1992, 1760 UNTS 79

The Contracting Parties,

Conscious of the intrinsic value of biological diversity and of the ecological, genetic, social, economic, scientific, educational, cultural, recreational and aesthetic values of biological diversity and its components,

Conscious also of the importance of biological diversity for evolution and for maintaining life sustaining systems of the biosphere,

Affirming that the conservation of biological diversity is a common concern of humankind,

Reaffirming that States have sovereign rights over their own biological resources,

Reaffirming also that States are responsible for conserving their biological diversity and for using their biological resources in a sustainable manner,

Concerned that biological diversity is being significantly reduced by certain human activities,

Aware of the general lack of information and knowledge regarding biological diversity and of the urgent need to develop scientific, technical and institutional capacities to provide the basic understanding upon which to plan and implement appropriate measures,

Noting that it is vital to anticipate, prevent and attack the causes of significant reduction or loss of biological diversity at source,

Noting also that where there is a threat of significant reduction or loss of biological diversity, lack of full scientific certainty should not be used as a reason for postponing measures to avoid or minimize such a threat,

Noting further that the fundamental requirement for the conservation of biological diversity is the in-situ conservation of ecosystems and natural habitats and the maintenance and recovery of viable populations of species in their natural surroundings,

Noting further that ex-situ measures, preferably in the country of origin, also have an important role to play,

Recognizing the close and traditional dependence of many indigenous and local communities embodying traditional lifestyles on biological resources, and the desirability of sharing equitably benefits arising from the use of traditional knowledge, innovations and practices relevant to the conservation of biological diversity and the sustainable use of its components,

Recognizing also the vital role that women play in the conservation and sustainable use of biological diversity and affirming the need for the full participation of women at all levels of policy-making and implementation for biological diversity conservation,

Stressing the importance of, and the need to promote, international, regional and global cooperation among States and intergovernmental organizations and the non-governmental sector for the conservation of biological diversity and the sustainable use of its components,

Acknowledging that the provision of new and additional financial resources and appropriate access to relevant technologies can be expected to make a substantial difference in the world's ability to address the loss of biological diversity,

Acknowledging further that special provision is required to meet the needs of developing countries, including the provision of new and additional financial resources and appropriate access to relevant technologies,

Noting in this regard the special conditions of the least developed countries and small island States,

Acknowledging that substantial investments are required to conserve biological diversity and that there is the expectation of a broad range of environmental, economic and social benefits from those investments,

Recognizing that economic and social development and poverty eradication are the first and overriding priorities of developing countries,

Aware that conservation and sustainable use of biological diversity is of critical importance for meeting the food, health and other needs of the growing world population, for which purpose access to and sharing of both genetic resources and technologies are essential,

Noting that, ultimately, the conservation and sustainable use of biological diversity will strengthen friendly relations among States and contribute to peace for humankind,

Desiring to enhance and complement existing international arrangements for the conservation of biological diversity and sustainable use of its components, and

Determined to conserve and sustainably use biological diversity for the benefit of present and future generations,

Have agreed as follows:

Article 1. Objectives

The objectives of this Convention, to be pursued in accordance with its relevant provisions, are the conservation of biological diversity, the sustainable use of its components and the fair and equitable sharing of the benefits arising out of the utilization of genetic resources, including by appropriate access to genetic resources and by appropriate transfer of relevant technologies, taking into account all rights over those resources and to technologies, and by appropriate funding.

Article 2. Use of Terms

For the purposes of this Convention:

"Biological diversity" means the variability among living organisms from all sources including, inter alia, terrestrial, marine and other aquatic ecosystems and the ecological complexes of which they are part; this includes diversity within species, between species and of ecosystems.

"Biological resources" includes genetic resources, organisms or parts thereof, populations, or any other biotic component of ecosystems with actual or potential use or value for humanity.

"Biotechnology" means any technological application that uses biological systems, living organisms, or derivatives thereof, to make or modify products or processes for specific use.

"Country of origin of genetic resources" means the country which possesses those genetic resources in in-situ conditions.

"Country providing genetic resources" means the country supplying genetic resources collected from in-situ sources, including populations of both wild and domesticated species, or taken from ex-situ sources, which may or may not have originated in that country.

"Domesticated or cultivated species" means species in which the evolutionary process has been influenced by humans to meet their needs.

"Ecosystem" means a dynamic complex of plant, animal and micro-organism communities and their non-living environment interacting as a functional unit.

"Ex-situ conservation" means the conservation of components of biological diversity outside their natural habitats.

"Genetic material" means any material of plant, animal, microbial or other origin containing functional units of heredity.

"Genetic resources" means genetic material of actual or potential value.

"Habitat" means the place or type of site where an organism or population naturally occurs.

"In-situ conditions" means conditions where genetic resources exist within ecosystems and natural habitats, and, in the case of domesticated or cultivated species, in the surroundings where they have developed their distinctive properties.

"In-situ conservation" means the conservation of ecosystems and natural habitats and the maintenance and recovery of viable populations of species in their natural surroundings and, in the case of domesticated or cultivated species, in the surroundings where they have developed their distinctive properties.

"Protected area" means a geographically defined area which is designated or regulated and managed to achieve specific conservation objectives.

"Regional economic integration organization" means an organization constituted by sovereign States of a given region, to which its member States have transferred competence in respect of matters governed by this Convention and which has been duly authorized, in accordance with its internal procedures, to sign, ratify, accept, approve or accede to it.

"Sustainable use" means the use of components of biological diversity in a way and at a rate that does not lead to the long-term decline of biological diversity, thereby maintaining its potential to meet the needs and aspirations of present and future generations.

"Technology" includes biotechnology.

Article 3. Principle

States have, in accordance with the Charter of the United Nations and the principles of international law, the sovereign right to exploit their own resources pursuant to their own environmental policies, and the responsibility to ensure that activities within their jurisdiction or control do not cause damage to the environment of other States or of areas beyond the limits of national jurisdiction.

Article 4. Jurisdictional Scope

Subject to the rights of other States, and except as otherwise expressly provided in this Convention, the provisions of this Convention apply, in relation to each Contracting Party:

(a) In the case of components of biological diversity, in areas within the limits of its national jurisdiction; and

(b) In the case of processes and activities, regardless of where their effects occur, carried out under its jurisdiction or control, within the area of its national jurisdiction or beyond the limits of national jurisdiction.

Article 5. Cooperation

Each Contracting Party shall, as far as possible and as appropriate, cooperate with other Contracting Parties, directly or, where appropriate, through competent international organizations, in respect of areas beyond national jurisdiction and on other matters of mutual interest, for the conservation and sustainable use of biological diversity.

Article 6. General Measures for Conservation and Sustainable Use

Each Contracting Party shall, in accordance with its particular conditions and capabilities:

(a) Develop national strategies, plans or programmes for the conservation and sustainable use of biological diversity or adapt for this purpose existing strategies, plans or programmes which shall reflect, inter alia, the measures set out in this Convention relevant to the Contracting Party concerned; and

(b) Integrate, as far as possible and as appropriate, the conservation and sustainable use of biological diversity into relevant sectoral or cross-sectoral plans, programmes and policies.

Article 7. Identification and Monitoring

Each Contracting Party shall, as far as possible and as appropriate, in particular for the purposes of Articles 8 to 10:

(a) Identify components of biological diversity important for its conservation and sustainable use having regard to the indicative list of categories set down in Annex I;

(b) Monitor, through sampling and other techniques, the components of biological diversity identified pursuant to subparagraph (a) above, paying particular attention to those requiring urgent conservation measures and those which offer the greatest potential for sustainable use;

(c) Identify processes and categories of activities which have or are likely to have significant adverse impacts on the conservation and sustainable use of biological diversity, and monitor their effects through sampling and other techniques; and

(d) Maintain and organize, by any mechanism data, derived from identification and monitoring activities pursuant to subparagraphs (a), (b) and (c) above.

Article 8. In-situ Conservation

Each Contracting Party shall, as far as possible and as appropriate:

(a) Establish a system of protected areas or areas where special measures need to be taken to conserve biological diversity;

(b) Develop, where necessary, guidelines for the selection, establishment and management of protected areas or areas where special measures need to be taken to conserve biological diversity;

(c) Regulate or manage biological resources important for the conservation of biological diversity whether within or outside protected areas, with a view to ensuring their conservation and sustainable use;

(d) Promote the protection of ecosystems, natural habitats and the maintenance of viable populations of species in natural surroundings;

(e) Promote environmentally sound and sustainable development in areas adjacent to protected areas with a view to furthering protection of these areas;

(f) Rehabilitate and restore degraded ecosystems and promote the recovery of threatened species, inter alia, through the development and implementation of plans or other management strategies;

(g) Establish or maintain means to regulate, manage or control the risks associated with the use and release of living modified organisms resulting from biotechnology which are likely to have adverse environmental impacts that could affect the conservation and sustainable use of biological diversity, taking also into account the risks to human health;

(h) Prevent the introduction of, control or eradicate those alien species which threaten ecosystems, habitats or species;

(i) Endeavour to provide the conditions needed for compatibility between present uses and the conservation of biological diversity and the sustainable use of its components;

(j) Subject to its national legislation, respect, preserve and maintain knowledge, innovations and practices of indigenous and local communities embodying traditional lifestyles relevant for the conservation and sustainable use of biological diversity and promote their wider application with the approval and involvement of the holders of such knowledge, innovations and practices and encourage the equitable sharing of the benefits arising from the utilization of such knowledge, innovations and practices;

(k) Develop or maintain necessary legislation and/or other regulatory provisions for the protection of threatened species and populations;

(l) Where a significant adverse effect on biological diversity has been determined pursuant to Article 7, regulate or manage the relevant processes and categories of activities; and

(m) Cooperate in providing financial and other support for in-situ conservation outlined in subparagraphs (a) to (l) above, particularly to developing countries.

Article 9. Ex-situ Conservation

Each Contracting Party shall, as far as possible and as appropriate, and predominantly for the purpose of complementing in-situ measures:

(a) Adopt measures for the ex-situ conservation of components of biological diversity, preferably in the country of origin of such components;

(b) Establish and maintain facilities for ex-situ conservation of and research on plants, animals and micro- organisms, preferably in the country of origin of genetic resources;

(c) Adopt measures for the recovery and rehabilitation of threatened species and for their reintroduction into their natural habitats under appropriate conditions;

(d) Regulate and manage collection of biological resources from natural habitats for ex-situ conservation purposes so as not to threaten ecosystems and in-situ populations of species, except where special temporary ex-situ measures are required under subparagraph (c) above; and

(e) Cooperate in providing financial and other support for ex-situ conservation outlined in subparagraphs (a) to (d) above and in the establishment and maintenance of ex- situ conservation facilities in developing countries.

Article 10. Sustainable Use of Components of Biological Diversity

Each Contracting Party shall, as far as possible and as appropriate:

(a) Integrate consideration of the conservation and sustainable use of biological resources into national decision-making;

(b) Adopt measures relating to the use of biological resources to avoid or minimize adverse impacts on biological diversity;

(c) Protect and encourage customary use of biological resources in accordance with traditional cultural practices that are compatible with conservation or sustainable use requirements;

(d) Support local populations to develop and implement remedial action in degraded areas where biological diversity has been reduced; and

(e) Encourage cooperation between its governmental authorities and its private sector in developing methods for sustainable use of biological resources.

Article 11. Incentive Measures

Each Contracting Party shall, as far as possible and as appropriate, adopt economically and socially sound measures that act as incentives for the conservation and sustainable use of components of biological diversity.

Article 12. Research and Training

The Contracting Parties, taking into account the special needs of developing countries, shall:

(a) Establish and maintain programmes for scientific and technical education and training in measures for the identification, conservation and sustainable use of biological diversity and its components and provide support for such education and training for the specific needs of developing countries;

(b) Promote and encourage research which contributes to the conservation and sustainable use of biological diversity, particularly in developing countries, inter alia, in accordance with decisions of the Conference of the Parties taken in consequence of recommendations of the Subsidiary Body on Scientific, Technical and Technological Advice; and

(c) In keeping with the provisions of Articles 16, 18 and 20, promote and cooperate in the use of scientific advances in biological diversity research in developing methods for conservation and sustainable use of biological resources.

Article 13. Public Education and Awareness

The Contracting Parties shall:

(a) Promote and encourage understanding of the importance of, and the measures required for, the conservation of biological diversity, as well as its propagation through media, and the inclusion of these topics in educational programmes; and

(b) Cooperate, as appropriate, with other States and international organizations in developing educational and public awareness programmes, with respect to conservation and sustainable use of biological diversity.

Article 14. Impact Assessment and Minimizing Adverse Impacts

1. Each Contracting Party, as far as possible and as appropriate, shall:

   (a) Introduce appropriate procedures requiring environmental impact assessment of its proposed projects that are likely to have significant adverse effects on biological diversity with a view to avoiding or minimizing such effects and, where appropriate, allow for public participation in such procedures;

   (b) Introduce appropriate arrangements to ensure that the environmental consequences of its programmes and policies that are likely to have significant adverse impacts on biological diversity are duly taken into account;

   (c) Promote, on the basis of reciprocity, notification, exchange of information and consultation on activities under their jurisdiction or control which are likely to significantly affect adversely the biological diversity of other States or areas beyond the limits of national jurisdiction, by encouraging the conclusion of bilateral, regional or multilateral arrangements, as appropriate;

   (d) In the case of imminent or grave danger or damage, originating under its jurisdiction or control, to biological diversity within the area under jurisdiction of other States or in areas beyond the limits of national jurisdiction, notify immediately the potentially affected States of such danger or damage, as well as initiate action to prevent or minimize such danger or damage; and

   (e) Promote national arrangements for emergency responses to activities or events, whether caused naturally or otherwise, which present a grave and imminent danger to biological diversity and encourage international cooperation to supplement such national efforts and, where appropriate and agreed by the States or regional economic integration organizations concerned, to establish joint contingency plans.

2. The Conference of the Parties shall examine, on the basis of studies to be carried out, the issue of liability and redress, including restoration and compensation, for damage to biological diversity, except where such liability is a purely internal matter.

Article 15. Access to Genetic Resources

1. Recognizing the sovereign rights of States over their natural resources, the authority to determine access to genetic resources rests with the national governments and is subject to national legislation.
2. Each Contracting Party shall endeavour to create conditions to facilitate access to genetic resources for environmentally sound uses by other Contracting Parties and not to impose restrictions that run counter to the objectives of this Convention.
3. For the purpose of this Convention, the genetic resources being provided by a Contracting Party, as referred to in this Article and Articles 16 and 19, are only those that are provided by Contracting Parties that are countries of origin of such resources or by the Parties that have acquired the genetic resources in accordance with this Convention.
4. Access, where granted, shall be on mutually agreed terms and subject to the provisions of this Article.
5. Access to genetic resources shall be subject to prior informed consent of the Contracting Party providing such resources, unless otherwise determined by that Party.
6. Each Contracting Party shall endeavour to develop and carry out scientific research based on genetic resources provided by other Contracting Parties with the full participation of, and where possible in, such Contracting Parties.

7. Each Contracting Party shall take legislative, administrative or policy measures, as appropriate, and in accordance with Articles 16 and 19 and, where necessary, through the financial mechanism established by Articles 20 and 21 with the aim of sharing in a fair and equitable way the results of research and development and the benefits arising from the commercial and other utilization of genetic resources with the Contracting Party providing such resources. Such sharing shall be upon mutually agreed terms.

Article 16. Access to and Transfer of technology

1. Each Contracting Party, recognizing that technology includes biotechnology, and that both access to and transfer of technology among Contracting Parties are essential elements for the attainment of the objectives of this Convention, undertakes subject to the provisions of this Article to provide and/or facilitate access for and transfer to other Contracting Parties of technologies that are relevant to the conservation and sustainable use of biological diversity or make use of genetic resources and do not cause significant damage to the environment.
2. Access to and transfer of technology referred to in paragraph 1 above to developing countries shall be provided and/or facilitated under fair and most favourable terms, including on concessional and preferential terms where mutually agreed, and, where necessary, in accordance with the financial mechanism established by Articles 20 and 21. In the case of technology subject to patents and other intellectual property rights, such access and transfer shall be provided on terms which recognize and are consistent with the adequate and effective protection of intellectual property rights. The application of this paragraph shall be consistent with paragraphs 3, 4 and 5 below.
3. Each Contracting Party shall take legislative, administrative or policy measures, as appropriate, with the aim that Contracting Parties, in particular those that are developing countries, which provide genetic resources are provided access to and transfer of technology which makes use of those resources, on mutually agreed terms, including technology protected by patents and other intellectual property rights, where necessary, through the provisions of Articles 20 and 21 and in accordance with international law and consistent with paragraphs 4 and 5 below.
4. Each Contracting Party shall take legislative, administrative or policy measures, as appropriate, with the aim that the private sector facilitates access to, joint development and transfer of technology referred to in paragraph 1 above for the benefit of both governmental institutions and the private sector of developing countries and in this regard shall abide by the obligations included in paragraphs 1, 2 and 3 above.
5. The Contracting Parties, recognizing that patents and other intellectual property rights may have an influence on the implementation of this Convention, shall cooperate in this regard subject to national legislation and international law in order to ensure that such rights are supportive of and do not run counter to its objectives.

Article 17. Exchange of Information

1. The Contracting Parties shall facilitate the exchange of information, from all publicly available sources, relevant to the conservation and sustainable use of biological diversity, taking into account the special needs of developing countries.
2. Such exchange of information shall include exchange of results of technical, scientific and socio-economic research, as well as information on training and surveying programmes, specialized knowledge, indigenous and traditional knowledge as such and in combination with the technologies referred to in Article 16, paragraph 1. It shall also, where feasible, include repatriation of information.

Article 18. Technical and Scientific Cooperation

1. The Contracting Parties shall promote international technical and scientific cooperation in the field of conservation and sustainable use of biological diversity, where necessary, through the appropriate international and national institutions.
2. Each Contracting Party shall promote technical and scientific cooperation with other Contracting Parties, in particular developing countries, in implementing this Convention, inter alia, through the development and implementation of national policies. In promoting such cooperation, special attention should be given to the development and strengthening of national capabilities, by means of human resources development and institution building.
3. The Conference of the Parties, at its first meeting, shall determine how to establish a clearing-house mechanism to promote and facilitate technical and scientific cooperation.
4. The Contracting Parties shall, in accordance with national legislation and policies, encourage and develop methods of cooperation for the development and use of technologies, including indigenous and traditional technologies, in pursuance of the objectives of this Convention. For this purpose, the Contracting Parties shall also promote cooperation in the training of personnel and exchange of experts.
5. The Contracting Parties shall, subject to mutual agreement, promote the establishment of joint research programmes and joint ventures for the development of technologies relevant to the objectives of this Convention.

Article 19. Handling of Biotechnology and Distribution of its Benefits

1. Each Contracting Party shall take legislative, administrative or policy measures, as appropriate, to provide for the effective participation in biotechnological research activities by those Contracting Parties, especially developing countries, which provide the genetic resources for such research, and where feasible in such Contracting Parties.
2. Each Contracting Party shall take all practicable measures to promote and advance priority access

on a fair and equitable basis by Contracting Parties, especially developing countries, to the results and benefits arising from biotechnologies based upon genetic resources provided by those Contracting Parties. Such access shall be on mutually agreed terms.

3. The Parties shall consider the need for and modalities of a protocol setting out appropriate procedures, including, in particular, advance informed agreement, in the field of the safe transfer, handling and use of any living modified organism resulting from biotechnology that may have adverse effect on the conservation and sustainable use of biological diversity.
4. Each Contracting Party shall, directly or by requiring any natural or legal person under its jurisdiction providing the organisms referred to in paragraph 3 above, provide any available information about the use and safety regulations required by that Contracting Party in handling such organisms, as well as any available information on the potential adverse impact of the specific organisms concerned to the Contracting Party into which those organisms are to be introduced.

Article 20. Financial Resources

1. Each Contracting Party undertakes to provide, in accordance with its capabilities, financial support and incentives in respect of those national activities which are intended to achieve the objectives of this Convention, in accordance with its national plans, priorities and programmes.
2. The developed country Parties shall provide new and additional financial resources to enable developing country Parties to meet the agreed full incremental costs to them of implementing measures which fulfil the obligations of this Convention and to benefit from its provisions and which costs are agreed between a developing country Party and the institutional structure referred to in Article 21, in accordance with policy, strategy, programme priorities and eligibility criteria and an indicative list of incremental costs established by the Conference of the Parties. Other Parties, including countries undergoing the process of transition to a market economy, may voluntarily assume the obligations of the developed country Parties. For the purpose of this Article, the Conference of the Parties, shall at its first meeting establish a list of developed country Parties and other Parties which voluntarily assume the obligations of the developed country Parties. The Conference of the Parties shall periodically review and if necessary amend the list. Contributions from other countries and sources on a voluntary basis would also be encouraged. The implementation of these commitments shall take into account the need for adequacy, predictability and timely flow of funds and the importance of burden-sharing among the contributing Parties included in the list.
3. The developed country Parties may also provide, and developing country Parties avail themselves of, financial resources related to the implementation of this Convention through bilateral, regional and other multilateral channels.
4. The extent to which developing country Parties will effectively implement their commitments under this Convention will depend on the effective implementation by developed country Parties of their commitments under this Convention related to financial resources and transfer of technology and will take fully into account the fact that economic and social development and eradication of poverty are the first and overriding priorities of the developing country Parties.
5. The Parties shall take full account of the specific needs and special situation of least developed countries in their actions with regard to funding and transfer of technology.
6. The Contracting Parties shall also take into consideration the special conditions resulting from the dependence on, distribution and location of, biological diversity within developing country Parties, in particular small island States.
7. Consideration shall also be given to the special situation of developing countries, including those that are most environmentally vulnerable, such as those with arid and semi- arid zones, coastal and mountainous areas.

Article 21. Financial Mechanism

1. There shall be a mechanism for the provision of financial resources to developing country Parties for purposes of this Convention on a grant or concessional basis the essential elements of which are described in this Article. The mechanism shall function under the authority and guidance of, and be accountable to, the Conference of the Parties for purposes of this Convention. The operations of the mechanism shall be carried out by such institutional structure as may be decided upon by the Conference of the Parties at its first meeting. For purposes of this Convention, the Conference of the Parties shall determine the policy, strategy, programme priorities and eligibility criteria relating to the access to and utilization of such resources. The contributions shall be such as to take into account the need for predictability, adequacy and timely flow of funds referred to in Article 20 in accordance with the amount of resources needed to be decided periodically by the Conference of the Parties and the importance of burden-sharing among the contributing Parties included in the list referred to in Article 20, paragraph 2. Voluntary contributions may also be made by the developed country Parties and by other countries and sources. The mechanism shall operate within a democratic and transparent system of governance.
2. Pursuant to the objectives of this Convention, the Conference of the Parties shall at its first meeting determine the policy, strategy and programme priorities, as well as detailed criteria and guidelines for eligibility for access to and utilization of the financial resources including monitoring and evaluation on a regular basis of such utilization. The Conference of the Parties shall decide on the arrangements to give effect to paragraph 1 above

after consultation with the institutional structure entrusted with the operation of the financial mechanism.

3. The Conference of the Parties shall review the effectiveness of the mechanism established under this Article, including the criteria and guidelines referred to in paragraph 2 above, not less than two years after the entry into force of this Convention and thereafter on a regular basis. Based on such review, it shall take appropriate action to improve the effectiveness of the mechanism if necessary.
4. The Contracting Parties shall consider strengthening existing financial institutions to provide financial resources for the conservation and sustainable use of biological diversity.

Article 22. Relationship with Other International Conventions

1. The provisions of this Convention shall not affect the rights and obligations of any Contracting Party deriving from any existing international agreement, except where the exercise of those rights and obligations would cause a serious damage or threat to biological diversity.
2. Contracting Parties shall implement this Convention with respect to the marine environment consistently with the rights and obligations of States under the law of the sea.

Article 23. Conference of the Parties

1. A Conference of the Parties is hereby established. The first meeting of the Conference of the Parties shall be convened by the Executive Director of the United Nations Environment Programme not later than one year after the entry into force of this Convention. Thereafter, ordinary meetings of the Conference of the Parties shall be held at regular intervals to be determined by the Conference at its first meeting.
2. Extraordinary meetings of the Conference of the Parties shall be held at such other times as may be deemed necessary by the Conference, or at the written request of any Party, provided that, within six months of the request being communicated to them by the Secretariat, it is supported by at least one third of the Parties.
3. The Conference of the Parties shall by consensus agree upon and adopt rules of procedure for itself and for any subsidiary body it may establish, as well as financial rules governing the funding of the Secretariat. At each ordinary meeting, it shall adopt a budget for the financial period until the next ordinary meeting.
4. The Conference of the Parties shall keep under review the implementation of this Convention, and, for this purpose, shall:
   (a) Establish the form and the intervals for transmitting the information to be submitted in accordance with Article 26 and consider such information as well as reports submitted by any subsidiary body;
   (b) Review scientific, technical and technological advice on biological diversity provided in accordance with Article 25;
   (c) Consider and adopt, as required, protocols in accordance with Article 28;
   (d) Consider and adopt, as required, in accordance with Articles 29 and 30, amendments to this Convention and its annexes;
   (e) Consider amendments to any protocol, as well as to any annexes thereto, and, if so decided, recommend their adoption to the parties to the protocol concerned;
   (f) Consider and adopt, as required, in accordance with Article 30, additional annexes to this Convention;
   (g) Establish such subsidiary bodies, particularly to provide scientific and technical advice, as are deemed necessary for the implementation of this Convention;
   (h) Contact, through the Secretariat, the executive bodies of conventions dealing with matters covered by this Convention with a view to establishing appropriate forms of cooperation with them; and
   (i) Consider and undertake any additional action that may be required for the achievement of the purposes of this Convention in the light of experience gained in its operation.
5. The United Nations, its specialized agencies and the International Atomic Energy Agency, as well as any State not Party to this Convention, may be represented as observers at meetings of the Conference of the Parties. Any other body or agency, whether governmental or non-governmental, qualified in fields relating to conservation and sustainable use of biological diversity, which has informed the Secretariat of its wish to be represented as an observer at a meeting of the Conference of the Parties, may be admitted unless at least one third of the Parties present object. The admission and participation of observers shall be subject to the rules of procedure adopted by the Conference of the Parties.

Article 24. Secretariat

1. A secretariat is hereby established. Its functions shall be:
   (a) To arrange for and service meetings of the Conference of the Parties provided for in Article 23;
   (b) To perform the functions assigned to it by any protocol;
   (c) To prepare reports on the execution of its functions under this Convention and present them to the Conference of the Parties;
   (d) To coordinate with other relevant international bodies and, in particular to enter into such administrative and contractual arrangements as may be required for the effective discharge of its functions; and

(e) To perform such other functions as may be determined by the Conference of the Parties.

2. At its first ordinary meeting, the Conference of the Parties shall designate the secretariat from amongst those existing competent international organizations which have signified their willingness to carry out the secretariat functions under this Convention.

Article 25. Subsidiary Body on Scientific, Technical and Technological Advice

1. A subsidiary body for the provision of scientific, technical and technological advice is hereby established to provide the Conference of the Parties and, as appropriate, its other subsidiary bodies with timely advice relating to the implementation of this Convention. This body shall be open to participation by all Parties and shall be multidisciplinary. It shall comprise government representatives competent in the relevant field of expertise. It shall report regularly to the Conference of the Parties on all aspects of its work.
2. Under the authority of and in accordance with guidelines laid down by the Conference of the Parties, and upon its request, this body shall:
   (a) Provide scientific and technical assessments of the status of biological diversity;
   (b) Prepare scientific and technical assessments of the effects of types of measures taken in accordance with the provisions of this Convention;
   (c) Identify innovative, efficient and state-of-the-art technologies and know-how relating to the conservation and sustainable use of biological diversity and advise on the ways and means of promoting development and/or transferring such technologies;
   (d) Provide advice on scientific programmes and international cooperation in research and development related to conservation and sustainable use of biological diversity; and
   (e) Respond to scientific, technical, technological and methodological questions that the Conference of the Parties and its subsidiary bodies may put to the body.
3. The functions, terms of reference, organization and operation of this body may be further elaborated by the Conference of the Parties.

Article 26. Reports

Each Contracting Party shall, at intervals to be determined by the Conference of the Parties, present to the Conference of the Parties, reports on measures which it has taken for the implementation of the provisions of this Convention and their effectiveness in meeting the objectives of this Convention.

Article 27. Settlement of Disputes

1. In the event of a dispute between Contracting Parties concerning the interpretation or application of this Convention, the parties concerned shall seek solution by negotiation.
2. If the parties concerned cannot reach agreement by negotiation, they may jointly seek the good offices of, or request mediation by, a third party.
3. When ratifying, accepting, approving or acceding to this Convention, or at any time thereafter, a State or regional economic integration organization may declare in writing to the Depositary that for a dispute not resolved in accordance with paragraph 1 or paragraph 2 above, it accepts one or both of the following means of dispute settlement as compulsory:
   (a) Arbitration in accordance with the procedure laid down in Part 1 of Annex II;
   (b) Submission of the dispute to the International Court of Justice.
4. If the parties to the dispute have not, in accordance with paragraph 3 above, accepted the same or any procedure, the dispute shall be submitted to conciliation in accordance with Part 2 of Annex II unless the parties otherwise agree.
5. The provisions of this Article shall apply with respect to any protocol except as otherwise provided in the protocol concerned.

Article 28. Adoption of Protocols

1. The Contracting Parties shall cooperate in the formulation and adoption of protocols to this Convention.
2. Protocols shall be adopted at a meeting of the Conference of the Parties.
3. The text of any proposed protocol shall be communicated to the Contracting Parties by the Secretariat at least six months before such a meeting.

Article 29. Amendment of the Convention or Protocols

1. Amendments to this Convention may be proposed by any Contracting Party. Amendments to any protocol may be proposed by any Party to that protocol.
2. Amendments to this Convention shall be adopted at a meeting of the Conference of the Parties. Amendments to any protocol shall be adopted at a meeting of the Parties to the Protocol in question. The text of any proposed amendment to this Convention or to any protocol, except as may otherwise be provided in such protocol, shall be communicated to the Parties to the instrument in question by the secretariat at least six months before the meeting at which it is proposed for adoption. The secretariat shall also communicate proposed amendments to the signatories to this Convention for information.
3. The Parties shall make every effort to reach agreement on any proposed amendment to this Convention or to any protocol by consensus. If all efforts at consensus have been exhausted, and no agreement reached, the amendment shall as a last resort be adopted by a two-third majority vote of the Parties to the instrument in question present and voting at the meeting, and shall be submitted by the

Depositary to all Parties for ratification, acceptance or approval.

4. Ratification, acceptance or approval of amendments shall be notified to the Depositary in writing. Amendments adopted in accordance with paragraph 3 above shall enter into force among Parties having accepted them on the ninetieth day after the deposit of instruments of ratification, acceptance or approval by at least two thirds of the Contracting Parties to this Convention or of the Parties to the protocol concerned, except as may otherwise be provided in such protocol. Thereafter the amendments shall enter into force for any other Party on the ninetieth day after that Party deposits its instrument of ratification, acceptance or approval of the amendments.
5. For the purposes of this Article, "Parties present and voting" means Parties present and casting an affirmative or negative vote.

Article 30. Adoption and Amendment of Annexes

1. The annexes to this Convention or to any protocol shall form an integral part of the Convention or of such protocol, as the case may be, and, unless expressly provided otherwise, a reference to this Convention or its protocols constitutes at the same time a reference to any annexes thereto. Such annexes shall be restricted to procedural, scientific, technical and administrative matters.
2. Except as may be otherwise provided in any protocol with respect to its annexes, the following procedure shall apply to the proposal, adoption and entry into force of additional annexes to this Convention or of annexes to any protocol:
   (a) Annexes to this Convention or to any protocol shall be proposed and adopted according to the procedure laid down in Article 29;
   (b) Any Party that is unable to approve an additional annex to this Convention or an annex to any protocol to which it is Party shall so notify the Depositary, in writing, within one year from the date of the communication of the adoption by the Depositary. The Depositary shall without delay notify all Parties of any such notification received. A Party may at any time withdraw a previous declaration of objection and the annexes shall thereupon enter into force for that Party subject to subparagraph (c) below;
   (c) On the expiry of one year from the date of the communication of the adoption by the Depositary, the annex shall enter into force for all Parties to this Convention or to any protocol concerned which have not submitted a notification in accordance with the provisions of subparagraph (b) above.
3. The proposal, adoption and entry into force of amendments to annexes to this Convention or to any protocol shall be subject to the same procedure as for the proposal, adoption and entry into force of annexes to the Convention or annexes to any protocol.
4. If an additional annex or an amendment to an annex is related to an amendment to this Convention or to any protocol, the additional annex or amendment shall not enter into force until such time as the amendment to the Convention or to the protocol concerned enters into force.

Article 31. Right to Vote

1. Except as provided for in paragraph 2 below, each Contracting Party to this Convention or to any protocol shall have one vote.
2. Regional economic integration organizations, in matters within their competence, shall exercise their right to vote with a number of votes equal to the number of their member States which are Contracting Parties to this Convention or the relevant protocol. Such organizations shall not exercise their right to vote if their member States exercise theirs, and vice versa.

Article 32. Relationship between this Convention and Its Protocols

1. A State or a regional economic integration organization may not become a Party to a protocol unless it is, or becomes at the same time, a Contracting Party to this Convention.
2. Decisions under any protocol shall be taken only by the Parties to the protocol concerned. Any Contracting Party that has not ratified, accepted or approved a protocol may participate as an observer in any meeting of the parties to that protocol.

Article 33. Signature

This Convention shall be open for signature at Rio de Janeiro by all States and any regional economic integration organization from 5 June 1992 until 14 June 1992, and at the United Nations Headquarters in New York from 15 June 1992 to 4 June 1993.

Article 34. Ratification, Acceptance or Approval

1. This Convention and any protocol shall be subject to ratification, acceptance or approval by States and by regional economic integration organizations. Instruments of ratification, acceptance or approval shall be deposited with the Depositary.
2. Any organization referred to in paragraph 1 above which becomes a Contracting Party to this Convention or any protocol without any of its member States being a Contracting Party shall be bound by all the obligations under the Convention or the protocol, as the case may be. In the case of such organizations, one or more of whose member States is a Contracting Party to this Convention or relevant protocol, the organization and its member States shall decide on their respective responsibilities for the performance of their obligations under the Convention or protocol, as the case may be. In such cases, the organization and the member States shall not be entitled to exercise rights under the Convention or relevant protocol concurrently.
3. In their instruments of ratification, acceptance or approval, the organizations referred to in paragraph 1 above shall declare the extent of their

competence with respect to the matters governed by the Convention or the relevant protocol. These organizations shall also inform the Depositary of any relevant modification in the extent of their competence.

Article 35. Accession

1. This Convention and any protocol shall be open for accession by States and by regional economic integration organizations from the date on which the Convention or the protocol concerned is closed for signature. The instruments of accession shall be deposited with the Depositary.
2. In their instruments of accession, the organizations referred to in paragraph 1 above shall declare the extent of their competence with respect to the matters governed by the Convention or the relevant protocol. These organizations shall also inform the Depositary of any relevant modification in the extent of their competence.
3. The provisions of Article 34, paragraph 2, shall apply to regional economic integration organizations which accede to this Convention or any protocol.

Article 36. Entry Into Force

1. This Convention shall enter into force on the ninetieth day after the date of deposit of the thirtieth instrument of ratification, acceptance, approval or accession.
2. Any protocol shall enter into force on the ninetieth day after the date of deposit of the number of instruments of ratification, acceptance, approval or accession, specified in that protocol, has been deposited.
3. For each Contracting Party which ratifies, accepts or approves this Convention or accedes thereto after the deposit of the thirtieth instrument of ratification, acceptance, approval or accession, it shall enter into force on the ninetieth day after the date of deposit by such Contracting Party of its instrument of ratification, acceptance, approval or accession.
4. Any protocol, except as otherwise provided in such protocol, shall enter into force for a Contracting Party that ratifies, accepts or approves that protocol or accedes thereto after its entry into force pursuant to paragraph 2 above, on the ninetieth day after the date on which that Contracting Party deposits its instrument of ratification, acceptance, approval or accession, or on the date on which this Convention enters into force for that Contracting Party, whichever shall be the later.
5. For the purposes of paragraphs 1 and 2 above, any instrument deposited by a regional economic integration organization shall not be counted as additional to those deposited by member States of such organization.

Article 37. Reservations

No reservations may be made to this Convention.

Article 38. Withdrawals

1. At any time after two years from the date on which this Convention has entered into force for a Contracting Party, that Contracting Party may withdraw from the Convention by giving written notification to the Depositary.
2. Any such withdrawal shall take place upon expiry of one year after the date of its receipt by the Depositary, or on such later date as may be specified in the notification of the withdrawal.
3. Any Contracting Party which withdraws from this Convention shall be considered as also having withdrawn from any protocol to which it is party.

Article 39. Financial Interim Arrangements

Provided that it has been fully restructured in accordance with the requirements of Article 21, the Global Environment Facility of the United Nations Development Programme, the United Nations Environment Programme and the International Bank for Reconstruction and Development shall be the institutional structure referred to in Article 21 on an interim basis, for the period between the entry into force of this Convention and the first meeting of the Conference of the Parties or until the Conference of the Parties decides which institutional structure will be designated in accordance with Article 21.

Article 40. Secretariat Interim Arrangements

The secretariat to be provided by the Executive Director of the United Nations Environment Programme shall be the secretariat referred to in Article 24, paragraph 2, on an interim basis for the period between the entry into force of this Convention and the first meeting of the Conference of the Parties.

Article 41. Depositary

The Secretary-General of the United Nations shall assume the functions of Depositary of this Convention and any protocols.

Article 42. Authentic texts

The original of this Convention, of which the Arabic, Chinese, English, French, Russian and Spanish texts are equally authentic, shall be deposited with the Secretary General of the United Nations.

IN WITNESS WHEREOF the undersigned, being duly authorized to that effect, have signed this Convention.

Done at Rio de Janeiro on this fifth day of June, one thousand nine hundred and ninety- two.

Annex I. Identification and Monitoring

1. Ecosystems and habitats: containing high diversity, large numbers of endemic or threatened species, or wilderness; required by migratory species; of social, economic, cultural or scientific importance; or, which are representative, unique or associated with key evolutionary or other biological processes;
2. Species and communities which are: threatened; wild relatives of domesticated or cultivated species; of medicinal, agricultural or other economic value; or social, scientific or cultural importance;

or importance for research into the conservation and sustainable use of biological diversity, such as indicator species; and

3. Described genomes and genes of social, scientific or economic importance.

Annex II - Part 1. Arbitration

Article 1

The claimant party shall notify the secretariat that the parties are referring a dispute to arbitration pursuant to Article 27. The notification shall state the subject-matter of arbitration and include, in particular, the articles of the Convention or the protocol, the interpretation or application of which are at issue. If the parties do not agree on the subject matter of the dispute before the President of the tribunal is designated, the arbitral tribunal shall determine the subject matter. The secretariat shall forward the information thus received to all Contracting Parties to this Convention or to the protocol concerned.

Article 2

1. In disputes between two parties, the arbitral tribunal shall consist of three members. Each of the parties to the dispute shall appoint an arbitrator and the two arbitrators so appointed shall designate by common agreement the third arbitrator who shall be the President of the tribunal. The latter shall not be a national of one of the parties to the dispute, nor have his or her usual place of residence in the territory of one of these parties, nor be employed by any of them, nor have dealt with the case in any other capacity.
2. In disputes between more than two parties, parties in the same interest shall appoint one arbitrator jointly by agreement.
3. Any vacancy shall be filled in the manner prescribed for the initial appointment.

Article 3

1. If the President of the arbitral tribunal has not been designated within two months of the appointment of the second arbitrator, the Secretary-General of the United Nations shall, at the request of a party, designate the President within a further two-month period.
2. If one of the parties to the dispute does not appoint an arbitrator within two months of receipt of the request, the other party may inform the Secretary-General who shall make the designation within a further two-month period.

Article 4

The arbitral tribunal shall render its decisions in accordance with the provisions of this Convention, any protocols concerned, and international law.

Article 5

Unless the parties to the dispute otherwise agree, the arbitral tribunal shall determine its own rules of procedure.

Article 6

The arbitral tribunal may, at the request of one of the parties, recommend essential interim measures of protection.

Article 7

The parties to the dispute shall facilitate the work of the arbitral tribunal and, in particular, using all means at their disposal, shall:

(a) Provide it with all relevant documents, information and facilities; and

(b) Enable it, when necessary, to call witnesses or experts and receive their evidence.

Article 8

The parties and the arbitrators are under an obligation to protect the confidentiality of any information they receive in confidence during the proceedings of the arbitral tribunal.

Article 9

Unless the arbitral tribunal determines otherwise because of the particular circumstances of the case, the costs of the tribunal shall be borne by the parties to the dispute in equal shares. The tribunal shall keep a record of all its costs, and shall furnish a final statement thereof to the parties.

Article 10

Any Contracting Party that has an interest of a legal nature in the subject-matter of the dispute which may be affected by the decision in the case, may intervene in the proceedings with the consent of the tribunal.

Article 11

The tribunal may hear and determine counterclaims arising directly out of the subject-matter of the dispute.

Article 12

Decisions both on procedure and substance of the arbitral tribunal shall be taken by a majority vote of its members.

Article 13

If one of the parties to the dispute does not appear before the arbitral tribunal or fails to defend its case, the other party may request the tribunal to continue the proceedings and to make its award. Absence of a party or a failure of a party to defend its case shall not constitute a bar to the proceedings. Before rendering its final decision, the arbitral tribunal must satisfy itself that the claim is well founded in fact and law.

Article 14

The tribunal shall render its final decision within five months of the date on which it is fully constituted unless it finds it necessary to extend the time-limit for a period which should not exceed five more months.

Article 15

The final decision of the arbitral tribunal shall be confined to the subject-matter of the dispute and shall state the reasons on which it is based. It shall contain the names of the members who have participated and the date of the final decision. Any member of the tribunal may attach a separate or dissenting opinion to the final decision.

Article 16

The award shall be binding on the parties to the dispute. It shall be without appeal unless the parties to the dispute have agreed in advance to an appellate procedure.

Article 17

Any controversy which may arise between the parties to the dispute as regards the interpretation or manner of implementation of the final decision may be submitted by either party for decision to the arbitral tribunal which rendered it.

Annex II - Part 2. Conciliation

Article 1

A conciliation commission shall be created upon the request of one of the parties to the dispute. The commission shall, unless the parties otherwise agree, be composed of five members, two appointed by each Party concerned and a President chosen jointly by those members.

Article 2

In disputes between more than two parties, parties in the same interest shall appoint their members of the commission jointly by agreement. Where two or more parties have separate interests or there is a disagreement as to whether they are of the same interest, they shall appoint their members separately.

Article 3

If any appointments by the parties are not made within two months of the date of the request to create a conciliation commission, the Secretary-General of the United Nations shall, if asked to do so by the party that made the request, make those appointments within a further two-month period.

Article 4

If a President of the conciliation commission has not been chosen within two months of the last of the members of the commission being appointed, the Secretary-General of the United Nations shall, if asked to do so by a party, designate a President within a further two-month period.

Article 5

The conciliation commission shall take its decisions by majority vote of its members. It shall, unless the parties to the dispute otherwise agree, determine its own procedure. It shall render a proposal for resolution of the dispute, which the parties shall consider in good faith.

Article 6

A disagreement as to whether the conciliation commission has competence shall be decided by the commission.

9.8. Convention to Combat Desertification 1994

United Nations Convention to Combat Desertification in those Countries Experiencing Serious Drought and/or Desertification, Particularly in Africa, Paris, 14 October 1994, 1954 UNTS 3

The Parties to this Convention,

Affirming that human beings in affected or threatened areas are at the centre of concerns to combat desertification and mitigate the effects of drought,

Reflecting the urgent concern of the international community, including States and international organizations, about the adverse impacts of desertification and drought,

Aware that arid, semi-arid and dry sub-humid areas together account for a significant proportion of the Earth's land area and are the habitat and source of livelihood for a large segment of its population,

Acknowledging that desertification and drought are problems of global dimension in that they affect all regions of the world and that joint action of the international community is needed to combat desertification and/or mitigate the effects of drought,

Noting the high concentration of developing countries, notably the least developed countries, among those experiencing serious drought and/or desertification, and the particularly tragic consequences of these phenomena in Africa,

Noting also that desertification is caused by complex interactions among physical, biological, political, social, cultural and economic factors,

Considering the impact of trade and relevant aspects of international economic relations on the ability of affected countries to combat desertification adequately,

Conscious that sustainable economic growth, social development and poverty eradication are priorities of affected developing countries, particularly in Africa, and are essential to meeting sustainability objectives,

Mindful that desertification and drought affect sustainable development through their interrelationships with important social problems such as poverty, poor health and nutrition, lack of food security, and those arising from migration, displacement of persons and demographic dynamics,

Appreciating the significance of the past efforts and experience of States and international organizations in combating desertification and mitigating the effects of drought, particularly in implementing the Plan of Action to Combat Desertification which was adopted at the United Nations Conference on Desertification in 1977,

Realizing that, despite efforts in the past, progress in combating desertification and mitigating the effects of drought has not met expectations and that a new and more effective approach is needed at all levels within the framework of sustainable development,

Recognizing the validity and relevance of decisions adopted at the United Nations Conference on Environment and Development, particularly of Agenda 21 and its chapter 12, which provide a basis for combating desertification,

Reaffirming in this light the commitments of developed countries as contained in paragraph 13 of chapter 33 of Agenda 21,

Recalling General Assembly resolution 47/188, particularly the priority in it prescribed for Africa, and all other relevant United Nations resolutions, decisions and programmes on desertification and drought, as well as relevant declarations by African countries and those from other regions,

Reaffirming the Rio Declaration on Environment and Development which states, in its Principle 2, that States have, in accordance with the Charter of the United Nations and the principles of international law, the sovereign right to exploit their own resources pursuant to their own environmental and developmental policies, and the responsibility to ensure that activities within their jurisdiction or control do not cause damage to the environment of other States or of areas beyond the limits of national jurisdiction,

Recognizing that national Governments play a critical role in combating desertification and mitigating the effects of drought and that progress in that respect depends on local implementation of action programmes in affected areas,

Recognizing also the importance and necessity of international cooperation and partnership in combating desertification and mitigating the effects of drought,

Recognizing further the importance of the provision to affected developing countries, particularly in Africa, of effective means, inter alia substantial financial resources, including new and additional funding, and access to technology, without which it will be difficult for them to implement fully their commitments under this Convention,

Expressing concern over the impact of desertification and drought on affected countries in Central Asia and the Transcaucasus,

Stressing the important role played by women in regions affected by desertification and/or drought, particularly in rural areas of developing countries, and the importance of ensuring the full participation of both men and women at all levels in programmes to combat desertification and mitigate the effects of drought,

Emphasizing the special role of non-governmental organizations and other major groups in programmes to combat desertification and mitigate the effects of drought,

Bearing in mind the relationship between desertification and other environmental problems of global dimension facing the international and national communities,

Bearing also in mind the contribution that combating desertification can make to achieving the objectives of the United Nations Framework Convention on Climate Change, the Convention on Biological Diversity and other related environmental conventions,

Believing that strategies to combat desertification and mitigate the effects of drought will be most effective if they are based on sound systematic observation and rigorous scientific knowledge and if they are continuously reevaluated,

Recognizing the urgent need to improve the effectiveness and coordination of international cooperation to facilitate the implementation of national plans and priorities,

Determined to take appropriate action in combating desertification and mitigating the effects of drought for the benefit of present and future generations,

Have agreed as follows:

PART I – INTRODUCTION

Article 1 – Use of terms

For the purposes of this Convention:

(a) "desertification" means land degradation in arid, semi-arid and dry sub-humid areas resulting from various factors, including climatic variations and human activities;

(b) "combating desertification" includes activities which are part of the integrated development of land in arid, semi-arid and dry sub-humid areas for sustainable development which are aimed at:
- prevention and/or reduction of land degradation;
- rehabilitation of partly degraded land; and
- reclamation of desertified land;

(c) "drought" means the naturally occurring phenomenon that exists when precipitation has been significantly below normal recorded levels, causing serious hydrological imbalances that adversely affect land resource production systems;

(d) "mitigating the effects of drought" means activities related to the prediction of drought and intended to reduce the vulnerability of society and natural systems to drought as it relates to combating desertification;

(e) "land" means the terrestrial bio-productive system that comprises soil, vegetation, other biota, and the ecological and hydrological processes that operate within the system;

(f) "land degradation" means reduction or loss, in arid, semi-arid and dry sub-humid areas, of the biological or economic productivity and complexity of rainfed cropland, irrigated cropland, or range, pasture, forest and woodlands resulting from land uses or from a process or combination of processes, including processes arising from human activities and habitation patterns, such as:
- soil erosion caused by wind and/or water;
- deterioration of the physical, chemical and biological or economic properties of soil; and
- long-term loss of natural vegetation;

(g) "arid, semi-arid and dry sub-humid areas" means areas, other than polar and sub-polar regions, in which the ratio of annual precipitation to potential evapotranspiration falls within the range from 0.05 to 0.65;

(h) "affected areas" means arid, semi-arid and/or dry sub-humid areas affected or threatened by desertification;

(i) "affected countries" means countries whose lands include, in whole or in part, affected areas;

(j) "regional economic integration organization" means an organization constituted by sovereign States of a given region which has competence in respect of matters governed by this Convention and has been duly authorized, in accordance with its internal procedures, to sign, ratify, accept, approve or accede to this Convention;

(k) "developed country Parties" means developed country Parties and regional economic integration organizations constituted by developed countries.

Article 2 – Objective

1. The objective of this Convention is to combat desertification and mitigate the effects of drought in countries experiencing serious drought and/or desertification, particularly in Africa, through effective action at all levels, supported by international cooperation and partnership arrangements, in the framework of an integrated approach which is consistent with Agenda 21, with a view to contributing to the achievement of sustainable development in affected areas.
2. Achieving this objective will involve long-term integrated strategies that focus simultaneously, in affected areas, on improved productivity of land, and the rehabilitation, conservation and sustainable management of land and water resources, leading to improved living conditions, in particular at the community level.

Article 3 – Principles

In order to achieve the objective of this Convention and to implement its provisions, the Parties shall be guided, inter alia, by the following:

(a) the Parties should ensure that decisions on the design and implementation of programmes to combat desertification and/or mitigate the effects of drought are taken with the participation of populations and local communities and that an enabling environment is created at higher levels to facilitate action at national and local levels;

(b) the Parties should, in a spirit of international solidarity and partnership, improve cooperation and coordination at subregional, regional and international levels, and better focus financial, human, organizational and technical resources where they are needed;

(c) the Parties should develop, in a spirit of partnership, cooperation among all levels of government, communities, non-governmental organizations and landholders to establish a better understanding of the nature and value of land and scarce water resources in affected areas and to work towards their sustainable use; and

(d) the Parties should take into full consideration the special needs and circumstances of affected developing country Parties, particularly the least developed among them.

PART II – GENERAL PROVISIONS

Article 4 – General obligations

1. The Parties shall implement their obligations under this Convention, individually or jointly, either through existing or prospective bilateral and multilateral arrangements or a combination thereof, as appropriate, emphasizing the need to coordinate efforts and develop a coherent long-term strategy at all levels.
2. In pursuing the objective of this Convention, the Parties shall:
   (a) adopt an integrated approach addressing the physical, biological and socio-economic aspects of the processes of desertification and drought;
   (b) give due attention, within the relevant international and regional bodies, to the situation of affected developing country Parties with regard to international trade, marketing arrangements and debt with a view to establishing an enabling international economic environment conducive to the promotion of sustainable development;
   (c) integrate strategies for poverty eradication into efforts to combat desertification and mitigate the effects of drought;
   (d) promote cooperation among affected country Parties in the fields of environmental protection and the conservation of land and water resources, as they relate to desertification and drought;
   (e) strengthen subregional, regional and international cooperation;
   (f) cooperate within relevant intergovernmental organizations;
   (g) determine institutional mechanisms, if appropriate, keeping in mind the need to avoid duplication; and
   (h) promote the use of existing bilateral and multilateral financial mechanisms and arrangements that mobilize and channel substantial financial resources to affected developing country Parties in combating desertification and mitigating the effects of drought.
3. Affected developing country Parties are eligible for assistance in the implementation of the Convention.

Article 5 – Obligations of affected country Parties

In addition to their obligations pursuant to article 4, affected country Parties undertake to:

(a) give due priority to combating desertification and mitigating the effects of drought, and allocate adequate resources in accordance with their circumstances and capabilities;

(b) establish strategies and priorities, within the framework of sustainable development plans and/ or policies, to combat desertification and mitigate the effects of drought;

(c) address the underlying causes of desertification and pay special attention to the socio- economic factors contributing to desertification processes;

(d) promote awareness and facilitate the participation of local populations, particularly women and youth, with the support of nongovernmental organizations, in efforts to combat desertification and mitigate the effects of drought; and

(e) provide an enabling environment by strengthening, as appropriate, relevant existing legislation and, where they do not exist, enacting new laws and establishing long-term policies and action programmes.

Article 6 – Obligations of developed country Parties

In addition to their general obligations pursuant to article 4, developed country Parties under- take to:

(a) actively support, as agreed, individually or jointly, the efforts of affected developing country Parties, particularly those in Africa, and the least developed countries, to combat desertification and mitigate the effects of drought;

(b) provide substantial financial resources and other forms of support to assist affected developing country Parties, particularly those in Africa, effectively to develop and implement their own long-term plans and strategies to combat desertification and mitigate the effects of drought;

(c) promote the mobilization of new and additional funding pursuant to article 20, paragraph 2 (b);

(d) encourage the mobilization of funding from the private sector and other non-governmental sources; and

(e) promote and facilitate access by affected country Parties, particularly affected developing country Parties, to appropriate technology, knowledge and know-how.

Article 7 – Priority for Africa

In implementing this Convention, the Parties shall give priority to affected African country Parties, in the light of the particular situation prevailing in that region, while not neglecting affected developing country Parties in other regions.

Article 8 – Relationship with other conventions

1. The Parties shall encourage the coordination of activities carried out under this Convention and, if

they are Parties to them, under other relevant international agreements, particularly the United Nations Framework Convention on Climate Change and the Convention on Biological Diversity, in order to derive maximum benefit from activities under each agreement while avoiding duplication of effort. The Parties shall encourage the conduct of joint programmes, particularly in the fields of research, training, systematic observation and information collection and exchange, to the extent that such activities may contribute to achieving the objectives of the agreements concerned.

2. The provisions of this Convention shall not affect the rights and obligations of any Party deriving from a bilateral, regional or international agreement into which it has entered prior to the entry into force of this Convention for it.

PART III – ACTION PROGRAMMES, SCIENTIFIC AND TECHNICAL COOPERATION AND SUPPORTING MEASURES

Section 1: Action programmes

Article 9 – Basic approach

1. In carrying out their obligations pursuant to article 5, affected developing country Parties and any other affected country Party in the framework of its regional implementation annex or, otherwise, that has notified the Permanent Secretariat in writing of its intention to prepare a national action A/AC.241/27 page 10 programme, shall, as appropriate, prepare, make public and implement national action programmes, utilizing and building, to the extent possible, on existing relevant successful plans and programmes, and subregional and regional action programmes, as the central element of the strategy to combat desertification and mitigate the effects of drought. Such programmes shall be updated through a continuing participatory process on the basis of lessons from field action, as well as the results of research. The preparation of national action programmes shall be closely interlinked with other efforts to formulate national policies for sustainable development.
2. In the provision by developed country Parties of different forms of assistance under the terms of article 6, priority shall be given to supporting, as agreed, national, subregional and regional action programmes of affected developing country Parties, particularly those in Africa, either directly or through relevant multilateral organizations or both.
3. The Parties shall encourage organs, funds and programmes of the United Nations system and other relevant intergovernmental organizations, academic institutions, the scientific community and non-governmental organizations in a position to cooperate, in accordance with their mandates and capabilities, to support the elaboration, implementation and follow-up of action programmes.

Article 10 – National action programmes

1. The purpose of national action programmes is to identify the factors contributing to desertification and practical measures necessary to combat desertification and mitigate the effects of drought.
2. National action programmes shall specify the respective roles of government, local communities and land users and the resources available and needed. They shall, inter alia:
   (a) incorporate long-term strategies to combat desertification and mitigate the effects of drought, emphasize implementation and be integrated with national policies for sustainable development;
   (b) allow for modifications to be made in response to changing circumstances and be sufficiently flexible at the local level to cope with different socio-economic, biological and geo-physical conditions;
   (c) give particular attention to the implementation of preventive measures for lands that are not yet degraded or which are only slightly degraded;
   (d) enhance national climatological, meteorological and hydrological capabilities and the means to provide for drought early warning;
   (e) promote policies and strengthen institutional frameworks which develop cooperation and coordination, in a spirit of partnership, between the donor community, governments at all levels, local populations and community groups, and facilitate access by local populations to appropriate information and technology;
   (f) provide for effective participation at the local, national and regional levels of non-governmental organizations and local populations, both women and men, particularly resource users, including farmers and pastoralists and their representative organizations, in policy planning, decision-making, and implementation and review of national action programmes; and
   (g) require regular review of, and progress reports on, their implementation.
3. National action programmes may include, inter alia, some or all of the following measures to prepare for and mitigate the effects of drought:
   (a) establishment and/or strengthening, as appropriate, of early warning systems, including local and national facilities and joint systems at the subregional and regional levels, and mechanisms for assisting environmentally displaced persons;
   (b) strengthening of drought preparedness and management, including drought contingency plans at the local, national, subregional and regional levels, which take into consideration seasonal to interannual climate predictions;
   (c) establishment and/or strengthening, as appropriate, of food security systems, including storage and marketing facilities, particularly in rural areas;

(d) establishment of alternative livelihood projects that could provide incomes in drought prone areas; and

(e) development of sustainable irrigation programmes for both crops and livestock.

4. Taking into account the circumstances and requirements specific to each affected country Party, national action programmes include, as appropriate, inter alia, measures in some or all of the following priority fields as they relate to combating desertification and mitigating the effects of drought in affected areas and to their populations: promotion of alternative livelihoods and improvement of national economic environments with a view to strengthening programmes aimed at the eradication of poverty and at ensuring food security; demographic dynamics; sustainable management of natural resources; sustainable agricultural practices; development and efficient use of various energy sources; institutional and legal frameworks; strengthening of capabilities for assessment and systematic observation, including hydrological and meteorological services, and capacity building, education and public awareness.

Article 11 – Subregional and regional action programmes

Affected country Parties shall consult and cooperate to prepare, as appropriate, in accordance with relevant regional implementation annexes, subregional and/or regional action programmes to harmonize, complement and increase the efficiency of national programmes. The provisions of article 10 shall apply mutatis mutandis to subregional and regional programmes. Such cooperation may include agreed joint programmes for the sustainable management of transboundary natural resources, scientific and technical cooperation, and strengthening of relevant institutions.

Article 12 – International cooperation

Affected country Parties, in collaboration with other Parties and the international community, should cooperate to ensure the promotion of an enabling international environment in the implementation of the Convention. Such cooperation should also cover fields of technology transfer as well as scientific research and development, information collection and dissemination and financial resources.

Article 13 – Support for the elaboration and implementation of action programmes

1. Measures to support action programmes pursuant to article 9 include, inter alia:

(a) financial cooperation to provide predictability for action programmes, allowing for necessary long-term planning;

(b) elaboration and use of cooperation mechanisms which better enable support at the local level, including action through non-governmental organizations, in order to promote the replicability of successful pilot programme activities where relevant;

(c) increased flexibility in project design, funding and implementation in keeping with the experimental, iterative approach indicated for participatory action at the local community level; and

(d) as appropriate, administrative and budgetary procedures that increase the efficiency of cooperation and of support programmes.

2. In providing such support to affected developing country Parties, priority shall be given to African country Parties and to least developed country Parties.

Article 14 – Coordination in the elaboration and implementation of action programmes

1. The Parties shall work closely together, directly and through relevant intergovernmental organizations, in the elaboration and implementation of action programmes.

2. The Parties shall develop operational mechanisms, particularly at the national and field levels, to ensure the fullest possible coordination among developed country Parties, developing country Parties and relevant intergovernmental and non-governmental organizations, in order to avoid duplication, harmonize interventions and approaches, and maximize the impact of assistance. In affected developing country Parties, priority will be given to coordinating activities related to international cooperation in order to maximize the efficient use of resources, to ensure responsive assistance, and to facilitate the implementation of national action programmes and priorities under this Convention.

Article 15 – Regional implementation annexes

Elements for incorporation in action programmes shall be selected and adapted to the socio- economic, geographical and climatic factors applicable to affected country Parties or regions, as well as to their level of development. Guidelines for the preparation of action programmes and their exact focus and content for particular subregions and regions are set out in the regional implementation annexes.

Section 2: Scientific and technical cooperation

Article 16 – Information collection, analysis and exchange

The Parties agree, according to their respective capabilities, to integrate and coordinate the collection, analysis and exchange of relevant short term and long term data and information to ensure systematic observation of land degradation in affected areas and to understand better and assess the processes and effects of drought and desertification. This would help accomplish, inter alia, early warning and advance planning for periods of adverse climatic variation in a form suited for practical application by users at all levels, including especially local populations. To this end, they shall, as appropriate:

(a) facilitate and strengthen the functioning of the global network of institutions and facilities for the collection, analysis and exchange of information, as well as for systematic observation at all levels, which shall, inter alia:

- aim to use compatible standards and systems;
- encompass relevant data and stations, including in remote areas;
- use and disseminate modern technology for data collection, transmission and assessment on land degradation; and
- link national, subregional and regional data and information centres more closely with global information sources;

(b) ensure that the collection, analysis and exchange of information address the needs of local communities and those of decision makers, with a view to resolving specific problems, and that local communities are involved in these activities;

(c) support and further develop bilateral and multilateral programmes and projects aimed at defining, conducting, assessing and financing the collection, analysis and exchange of data and information, including, inter alia, integrated sets of physical, biological, social and economic indicators;

(d) make full use of the expertise of competent intergovernmental and nongovernmental organizations, particularly to disseminate relevant information and experiences among target groups in different regions;

(e) give full weight to the collection, analysis and exchange of socioeconomic data, and their integration with physical and biological data;

(f) exchange and make fully, openly and promptly available information from all publicly avail- able sources relevant to combating desertification and mitigating the effects of drought; and

(g) subject to their respective national legislation and/or policies, exchange information on local and traditional knowledge, ensuring adequate protection for it and providing appropriate return from the benefits derived from it, on an equitable basis and on mutually agreed terms, to the local populations concerned.

Article 17 – Research and development

1. The Parties undertake, according to their respective capabilities, to promote technical and scientific cooperation in the fields of combating desertification and mitigating the effects of drought through appropriate national, subregional, regional and international institutions. To this end, they shall support research activities that:

   (a) contribute to increased knowledge of the processes leading to desertification and drought and the impact of, and distinction between, causal factors, both natural and human, with a view to combating desertification and mitigating the effects of drought, and achieving improved productivity as well as sustainable use and management of resources;

   (b) respond to well defined objectives, address the specific needs of local populations and lead to the identification and implementation of solutions that improve the living standards of people in affected areas;

   (c) protect, integrate, enhance and validate traditional and local knowledge, know-how and practices, ensuring, subject to their respective national legislation and/or policies, that the owners of that knowledge will directly benefit on an equitable basis and on mutually agreed terms from any commercial utilization of it or from any technological development derived from that knowledge;

   (d) develop and strengthen national, subregional and regional research capabilities in affected developing country Parties, particularly in Africa, including the development of local skills and the strengthening of appropriate capacities, especially in countries with a weak research base, giving particular attention to multidisciplinary and participative socio-economic research;

   (e) take into account, where relevant, the relationship between poverty, migration caused by environmental factors, and desertification;

   (f) promote the conduct of joint research programmes between national, subregional, regional and international research organizations, in both the public and private sectors, for the development of improved, affordable and accessible technologies for sustainable development through effective participation of local populations and communities; and

   (g) enhance the availability of water resources in affected areas, by means of, inter alia, cloud-seeding.

2. Research priorities for particular regions and subregions, reflecting different local conditions, should be included in action programmes. The Conference of the Parties shall review research priorities periodically on the advice of the Committee on Science and Technology.

Article 18 – Transfer, acquisition, adaptation and development of technology

1. The Parties undertake, as mutually agreed and in accordance with their respective national legislation and/or policies, to promote, finance and/or facilitate the financing of the transfer, acquisition, adaptation and development of environmentally sound, economically viable and socially acceptable A/AC.241/27 page 16 technologies relevant to combating desertification and/or mitigating the effects of drought, with a view to contributing to the achievement of sustainable development in affected areas. Such cooperation shall be conducted bilaterally or multilaterally, as appropriate, making full use of the expertise of intergovernmental and non- governmental organizations. The Parties shall, in particular:

   (a) fully utilize relevant existing national, subregional, regional and international information systems and clearing-houses for the dissemination of information on available technologies, their sources, their environmental risks and the broad terms under which they may be acquired;

(b) facilitate access, in particular by affected developing country Parties, on favourable terms, including on concessional and preferential terms, as mutually agreed, taking into account the need to protect intellectual property rights, to technologies most suitable to practical application for specific needs of local populations, paying special attention to the social, cultural, economic and environmental impact of such technology;

(c) facilitate technology cooperation among affected country Parties through financial assistance or other appropriate means;

(d) extend technology cooperation with affected developing country Parties, including, where relevant, joint ventures, especially to sectors which foster alternative livelihoods; and

(e) take appropriate measures to create domestic market conditions and incentives, fiscal or otherwise, conducive to the development, transfer, acquisition and adaptation of suitable technology, knowledge, know-how and practices, including measures to ensure adequate and effective protection of intellectual property rights.

2. The Parties shall, according to their respective capabilities, and subject to their respective national legislation and/or policies, protect, promote and use in particular relevant traditional and local technology, knowledge, know-how and practices and, to that end, they undertake to:

(a) make inventories of such technology, knowledge, know-how and practices and their potential uses with the participation of local populations, and disseminate such information, where appropriate, in cooperation with relevant intergovernmental and non-governmental organizations;

(b) ensure that such technology, knowledge, know-how and practices are adequately protected and that local populations benefit directly, on an equitable basis and as mutually agreed, from any commercial utilization of them or from any technological development derived therefrom;

(c) encourage and actively support the improvement and dissemination of such technology, knowledge, know-how and practices or of the development of new technology based on them; and

(d) facilitate, as appropriate, the adaptation of such technology, knowledge, know-how and practices to wide use and integrate them with modern technology, as appropriate.

Section 3: Supporting measures

Article 19 – Capacity building, education and public awareness

1. The Parties recognize the significance of capacity building -- that is to say, institution building, training and development of relevant local and national capacities -- in efforts to combat desertification and mitigate the effects of drought. They shall promote, as appropriate, capacity- building:

(a) through the full participation at all levels of local people, particularly at the local level, especially women and youth, with the cooperation of non-governmental and local organizations;

(b) by strengthening training and research capacity at the national level in the field of desertification and drought;

(c) by establishing and/or strengthening support and extension services to disseminate relevant technology methods and techniques more effectively, and by training field agents and members of rural organizations in participatory approaches for the conservation and sustainable use of natural resources;

(d) by fostering the use and dissemination of the knowledge, know-how and practices of local people in technical cooperation programmes, wherever possible;

(e) by adapting, where necessary, relevant environmentally sound technology and traditional methods of agriculture and pastoralism to modern socio-economic conditions;

(f) by providing appropriate training and technology in the use of alternative energy sources, particularly renewable energy resources, aimed particularly at reducing dependence on wood for fuel;

(g) through cooperation, as mutually agreed, to strengthen the capacity of affected developing country Parties to develop and implement programmes in the field of collection, analysis and exchange of information pursuant to article 16;

(h) through innovative ways of promoting alternative livelihoods, including training in new skills;

(i) by training of decision makers, managers, and personnel who are responsible for the collection and analysis of data for the dissemination and use of early warning information on drought conditions and for food production;

(j) through more effective operation of existing national institutions and legal frameworks and, where necessary, creation of new ones, along with strengthening of strategic planning and management; and

(k) by means of exchange visitor programmes to enhance capacity building in affected country Parties through a long-term, interactive process of learning and study.

2. Affected developing country Parties shall conduct, in cooperation with other Parties and competent intergovernmental and non-governmental organizations, as appropriate, an interdisciplinary review of available capacity and facilities at the local and national levels, and the potential for strengthening them.

3. The Parties shall cooperate with each other and through competent intergovernmental organizations, as well as with non-governmental organizations, in undertaking and supporting public awareness and educational programmes in both affected

and, where relevant, unaffected country Parties to promote understanding of the causes and effects of desertification and drought and of the importance of meeting the objective of this Convention. To that end, they shall:

(a) organize awareness campaigns for the general public;

(b) promote, on a permanent basis, access by the public to relevant information, and wide public participation in education and awareness activities;

(c) encourage the establishment of associations that contribute to public awareness;

(d) develop and exchange educational and public awareness material, where possible in local languages, exchange and second experts to train personnel of affected developing country Parties in carrying out relevant education and awareness programmes, and fully utilize relevant educational material available in competent international bodies;

(e) assess educational needs in affected areas, elaborate appropriate school curricula and expand, as needed, educational and adult literacy programmes and opportunities for all, in particular for girls and women, on the identification, conservation and sustainable use and management of the natural resources of affected areas; and

(f) develop interdisciplinary participatory programmes integrating desertification and drought awareness into educational systems and in non-formal, adult, distance and practical educational programmes.

4. The Conference of the Parties shall establish and/ or strengthen networks of regional education and training centres to combat desertification and mitigate the effects of drought. These networks shall be coordinated by an institution created or designated for that purpose, in order to train scientific, technical and management personnel and to strengthen existing institutions responsible for education and training in affected country Parties, where appropriate, with a view to harmonizing programmes and to organizing exchanges A/AC.241/27 page 19 of experience among them. These networks shall cooperate closely with relevant intergovernmental and non- governmental organizations to avoid duplication of effort.

Article 20 – Financial resources

1. Given the central importance of financing to the achievement of the objective of the Convention, the Parties, taking into account their capabilities, shall make every effort to ensure that adequate financial resources are available for programmes to combat desertification and mitigate the effects of drought.

2. In this connection, developed country Parties, while giving priority to affected African country Parties without neglecting affected developing country Parties in other regions, in accordance with article 7, undertake to:

(a) mobilize substantial financial resources, including grants and concessional loans, in order to support the implementation of programmes to combat desertification and mitigate the effects of drought;

(b) promote the mobilization of adequate, timely and predictable financial resources, including new and additional funding from the Global Environment Facility of the agreed incremental costs of those activities concerning desertification that relate to its four focal areas, in conformity with the relevant provisions of the Instrument establishing the Global Environment Facility;

(c) facilitate through international cooperation the transfer of technology, knowledge and know-how; and

(d) explore, in cooperation with affected developing country Parties, innovative methods and incentives for mobilizing and channelling resources, including those of foundations, non-governmental organizations and other private sector entities, particularly debt swaps and other innovative means which increase financing by reducing the external debt burden of affected developing country Parties, particularly those in Africa.

3. Affected developing country Parties, taking into account their capabilities, undertake to mobilize adequate financial resources for the implementation of their national action programmes.

4. In mobilizing financial resources, the Parties shall seek full use and continued qualitative improvement of all national, bilateral and multilateral funding sources and mechanisms, using consortia, joint programmes and parallel financing, and shall seek to involve private sector funding sources and mechanisms, including those of non-governmental organizations. To this end, the Parties shall fully utilize the operational mechanisms developed pursuant to article 14.

5. In order to mobilize the financial resources necessary for affected developing country Parties to combat desertification and mitigate the effects of drought, the Parties shall:

(a) rationalize and strengthen the management of resources already allocated for combating desertification and mitigating the effects of drought by using them more effectively and efficiently, assessing their successes and shortcomings, removing hindrances to their effective use and, where necessary, reorienting programmes in light of the integrated long- term approach adopted pursuant to this Convention;

(b) give due priority and attention within the governing bodies of multilateral financial institutions, facilities and funds, including regional development banks and funds, to supporting affected developing country Parties, particularly those in Africa, in activities which advance implementation of the Convention, notably action programmes they undertake in the framework of regional implementation annexes; and

(c) examine ways in which regional and subregional cooperation can be strengthened to support efforts undertaken at the national level.

6. Other Parties are encouraged to provide, on a voluntary basis, knowledge, know-how and techniques related to desertification and/or financial resources to affected developing country Parties.

7. The full implementation by affected developing country Parties, particularly those in Africa, of their obligations under the Convention will be greatly assisted by the fulfilment by developed country Parties of their obligations under the Convention, including in particular those regarding financial resources and transfer of technology. In fulfilling their obligations, developed country Parties should take fully into account that economic and social development and poverty eradication are the first priorities of affected developing country Parties, particularly those in Africa.

Article 21 – Financial mechanisms

1. The Conference of the Parties shall promote the availability of financial mechanisms and shall encourage such mechanisms to seek to maximize the availability of funding for affected developing country Parties, particularly those in Africa, to implement the Convention. To this end, the Conference of the Parties shall consider for adoption inter alia approaches and policies that:

   (a) facilitate the provision of necessary funding at the national, subregional, regional and global levels for activities pursuant to relevant provisions of the Convention;

   (b) promote multiple-source funding approaches, mechanisms and arrangements and their assessment, consistent with article 20;

   (c) provide on a regular basis, to interested Parties and relevant intergovernmental and non- governmental organizations, information on available sources of funds and on funding patterns in order to facilitate coordination among them;

   (d) facilitate the establishment, as appropriate, of mechanisms, such as national desertification funds, including those involving the participation of non-governmental organizations, to channel financial resources rapidly and efficiently to the local level in affected developing country Parties; and

   (e) strengthen existing funds and financial mechanisms at the subregional and regional levels, particularly in Africa, to support more effectively the implementation of the Convention.

2. The Conference of the Parties shall also encourage the provision, through various mechanisms within the United Nations system and through multilateral financial institutions, of support at the national, subregional and regional levels to activities that enable developing country Parties to meet their obligations under the Convention.

3. Affected developing country Parties shall utilize, and where necessary, establish and/or strengthen, national coordinating mechanisms, integrated in national development programmes, that would ensure the efficient use of all available financial resources. They shall also utilize participatory processes involving non-governmental organizations, local groups and the private sector, in raising funds, in elaborating as well as implementing programmes and in assuring access to funding by groups at the local level. These actions can be enhanced by improved coordination and flexible programming on the part of those providing assistance.

4. In order to increase the effectiveness and efficiency of existing financial mechanisms, a Global Mechanism to promote actions leading to the mobilization and channelling of substantial financial resources, including for the transfer of technology, on a grant basis, and/or on concessional or other terms, to affected developing country Parties, is hereby established. This Global Mechanism shall function under the authority and guidance of the Conference of the Parties and be accountable to it.

5. The Conference of the Parties shall identify, at its first ordinary session, an organization to house the Global Mechanism. The Conference of the Parties and the organization it has identified shall agree upon modalities for this Global Mechanism to ensure inter alia that such Mechanism:

   (a) identifies and draws up an inventory of relevant bilateral and multilateral cooperation programmes that are available to implement the Convention;

   (b) provides advice, on request, to Parties on innovative methods of financing and sources of financial assistance and on improving the coordination of cooperation activities at the national level;

   (c) provides interested Parties and relevant intergovernmental and nongovernmental organizations with information on available sources of funds and on funding patterns in order to facilitate coordination among them; and

   (d) reports to the Conference of the Parties, beginning at its second ordinary session, on its activities.

6. The Conference of the Parties shall, at its first session, make appropriate arrangements with the organization it has identified to house the Global Mechanism for the administrative operations of such Mechanism, drawing to the extent possible on existing budgetary and human resources.

7. The Conference of the Parties shall, at its third ordinary session, review the policies, operational modalities and activities of the Global Mechanism accountable to it pursuant to paragraph 4, taking into account the provisions of article 7. On the basis of this review, it shall consider and take appropriate action.

PART IV – INSTITUTIONS

Article 22 – Conference of the Parties

1. A Conference of the Parties is hereby established.

2. The Conference of the Parties is the supreme body of the Convention. It shall make, within its mandate, the decisions necessary to promote its effective implementation. In particular, it shall:
   (a) regularly review the implementation of the Convention and the functioning of its institutional arrangements in the light of the experience gained at the national, subregional, regional and international levels and on the basis of the evolution of scientific and technological knowledge;
   (b) promote and facilitate the exchange of information on measures adopted by the Parties, and determine the form and timetable for transmitting the information to be submitted pursuant to article 26, review the reports and make recommendations on them;
   (c) establish such subsidiary bodies as are deemed necessary for the implementation of the Convention;
   (d) review reports submitted by its subsidiary bodies and provide guidance to them;
   (e) agree upon and adopt, by consensus, rules of procedure and financial rules for itself and any subsidiary bodies;
   (f) adopt amendments to the Convention pursuant to articles 30 and 31;
   (g) approve a programme and budget for its activities, including those of its subsidiary bodies, and undertake necessary arrangements for their financing;
   (h) as appropriate, seek the cooperation of, and utilize the services of and information provided by, competent bodies or agencies, whether national or international, intergovernmental or non-governmental;
   (i) promote and strengthen the relationship with other relevant conventions while avoiding duplication of effort; and
   (j) exercise such other functions as may be necessary for the achievement of the objective of the Convention.
3. The Conference of the Parties shall, at its first session, adopt its own rules of procedure, by consensus, which shall include decision-making procedures for matters not already covered by decision-making procedures stipulated in the Convention. Such procedures may include specified majorities required for the adoption of particular decisions.
4. The first session of the Conference of the Parties shall be convened by the interim secretariat referred to in article 35 and shall take place not later than one year after the date of entry into force of the Convention. Unless otherwise decided by the Conference of the Parties, the second, third and fourth ordinary sessions shall be held yearly, and thereafter, ordinary sessions shall be held every two years.
5. Extraordinary sessions of the Conference of the Parties shall be held at such other times as may be decided either by the Conference of the Parties in ordinary session or at the written request of any Party, provided that, within three months of the request being communicated to the Parties by the Permanent Secretariat, it is supported by at least one third of the Parties.
6. At each ordinary session, the Conference of the Parties shall elect a Bureau. The structure and functions of the Bureau shall be determined in the rules of procedure. In appointing the Bureau, due regard shall be paid to the need to ensure equitable geographical distribution and adequate representation of affected country Parties, particularly those in Africa.
7. The United Nations, its specialized agencies and any State member thereof or observers thereto not Party to the Convention, may be represented at sessions of the Conference of the Parties as observers. Any body or agency, whether national or international, governmental or non-governmental, which is qualified in matters covered by the Convention, and which has informed the Permanent Secretariat of its wish to be represented at a session of the Conference of the Parties as an observer, may be so admitted unless at least one third of the Parties present object. The admission and participation of observers shall be subject to the rules of procedure adopted by the Conference of the Parties.
8. The Conference of the Parties may request competent national and international organizations which have relevant expertise to provide it with information relevant to article 16, paragraph (g), article 17, paragraph 1 (c) and article 18, paragraph 2(b).

Article 23 – Permanent Secretariat

1. A Permanent Secretariat is hereby established.
2. The functions of the Permanent Secretariat shall be:
   (a) to make arrangements for sessions of the Conference of the Parties and its subsidiary bodies established under the Convention and to provide them with services as required;
   (b) to compile and transmit reports submitted to it;
   (c) to facilitate assistance to affected developing country Parties, on request, particularly those in Africa, in the compilation and communication of information required under the Convention;
   (d) to coordinate its activities with the secretariats of other relevant international bodies and conventions;
   (e) to enter, under the guidance of the Conference of the Parties, into such administrative and contractual arrangements as may be required for the effective discharge of its functions;
   (f) to prepare reports on the execution of its functions under this Convention and present them to the Conference of the Parties; and
   (g) to perform such other secretariat functions as may be determined by the Conference of the Parties.

3. The Conference of the Parties, at its first session, shall designate a Permanent Secretariat and make arrangements for its functioning.

Article 24 – Committee on Science and Technology

1. A Committee on Science and Technology is hereby established as a subsidiary body of the Conference of the Parties to provide it with information and advice on scientific and technological matters relating to combating desertification and mitigating the effects of drought. The Committee shall meet in conjunction with the ordinary sessions of the Conference of the Parties and shall be multidisciplinary and open to the participation of all Parties. It shall be composed of government representatives competent in the relevant fields of expertise. The Conference of the Parties shall decide, at its first session, on the terms of reference of the Committee.
2. The Conference of the Parties shall establish and maintain a roster of independent experts with expertise and experience in the relevant fields. The roster shall be based on nominations received in writing from the Parties, taking into account the need for a multidisciplinary approach and broad geographical representation.
3. The Conference of the Parties may, as necessary, appoint ad hoc panels to provide it, through the Committee, with information and advice on specific issues regarding the state of the art in fields of science and technology relevant to combating desertification and mitigating the effects of drought. These panels shall be composed of experts whose names are taken from the roster, taking into account the need for a multidisciplinary approach and broad geographical representation. These experts shall have scientific backgrounds and field experience and shall be appointed by the Conference of the Parties on the recommendation of the Committee. The Conference of the Parties shall decide on the terms of reference and the modalities of work of these panels.

Article 25 – Networking of institutions, agencies and bodies

1. The Committee on Science and Technology shall, under the supervision of the Conference of the Parties, make provision for the undertaking of a survey and evaluation of the relevant existing networks, institutions, agencies and bodies willing to become units of a network. Such a network shall support the implementation of the Convention.
2. On the basis of the results of the survey and evaluation referred to in paragraph 1, the Committee on Science and Technology shall make recommendations to the Conference of the Parties on ways and means to facilitate and strengthen networking of the units at the local, national and other levels, with a view to ensuring that the thematic needs set out in articles 16 to 19 are addressed.
3. Taking into account these recommendations, the Conference of the Parties shall:
   (a) identify those national, subregional, regional and international units that are most appropriate for networking, and recommend operational procedures, and a time frame, for them; and
   (b) identify the units best suited to facilitating and strengthening such networking at all levels.

PART V – PROCEDURES

Article 26 – Communication of information

1. Each Party shall communicate to the Conference of the Parties for consideration at its ordinary sessions, through the Permanent Secretariat, reports on the measures which it has taken for the implementation of the Convention. The Conference of the Parties shall determine the timetable for submission and the format of such reports.
2. Affected country Parties shall provide a description of the strategies established pursuant to article 5 and of any relevant information on their implementation.
3. Affected country Parties which implement action programmes pursuant to articles 9 to 15 shall provide a detailed description of the programmes and of their implementation.
4. Any group of affected country Parties may make a joint communication on measures taken at the subregional and/or regional levels in the framework of action programmes.
5. Developed country Parties shall report on measures taken to a sist in the preparation and implementation of action programmes, including information on the financial resources they have provided, or are providing, under the Convention.
6. Information communicated pursuant to paragraphs 1 to 4 shall be transmitted by the Permanent Secretariat as soon as possible to the Conference of the Parties and to any relevant subsidiary body.
7. The Conference of the Parties shall facilitate the provision to affected developing countries, particularly those in Africa, on request, of technical and financial support in compiling and communicating information in accordance with this article, as well as identifying the technical and financial needs associated with action programmes.

Article 27 – Measures to resolve questions on implementation

The Conference of the Parties shall consider and adopt procedures and institutional mechanisms for the resolution of questions that may arise with regard to the implementation of the Convention.

Article 28 – Settlement of disputes

1. Parties shall settle any dispute between them concerning the interpretation or application of the Convention through negotiation or other peaceful means of their own choice.
2. When ratifying, accepting, approving, or acceding to the Convention, or at any time thereafter, a Party which is not a regional economic integration organization may declare in a written instrument submitted to the Depositary that, in respect of any

dispute concerning the interpretation or application of the Convention, it recognizes one or both of the following means of dispute settlement as compulsory in relation to any Party accepting the same obligation:

(a) arbitration in accordance with procedures adopted by the Conference of the Parties in an annex as soon as practicable;

(b) submission of the dispute to the International Court of Justice.

3. A Party which is a regional economic integration organization may make a declaration with like effect in relation to arbitration in accordance with the procedure referred to in paragraph 2 (a).

4. A declaration made pursuant to paragraph 2 shall remain in force until it expires in accordance with its terms or until three months after written notice of its revocation has been deposited with the Depositary.

5. The expiry of a declaration, a notice of revocation or a new declaration shall not in any way affect proceedings pending before an arbitral tribunal or the International Court of Justice unless the Parties to the dispute otherwise agree.

6. If the Parties to a dispute have not accepted the same or any procedure pursuant to paragraph 2 and if they have not been able to settle their dispute within twelve months following notification by one Party to another that a dispute exists between them, the dispute shall be submitted to conciliation at the request of any Party to the dispute, in accordance with procedures adopted by the Conference of the Parties in an annex as soon as practicable.

Article 29 – Status of annexes

1. Annexes form an integral part of the Convention and, unless expressly provided otherwise, a reference to the Convention also constitutes a reference to its annexes.

2. The Parties shall interpret the provisions of the annexes in a manner that is in conformity with their rights and obligations under the articles of this Convention.

Article 30 – Amendments to the Convention

1. Any Party may propose amendments to the Convention.

2. Amendments to the Convention shall be adopted at an ordinary session of the Conference of the Parties. The text of any proposed amendment shall be communicated to the Parties by the Permanent Secretariat at least six months before the meeting at which it is proposed for adoption. The Permanent Secretariat shall also communicate proposed amendments to the signatories to the Convention.

3. The Parties shall make every effort to reach agreement on any proposed amendment to the Convention by consensus. If all efforts at consensus have been exhausted and no agreement reached, the amendment shall, as a last resort, be adopted by a two-thirds majority vote of the Parties present and voting at the meeting. The adopted amendment shall be communicated by the Permanent Secretariat to the Depositary, who shall circulate it to all Parties for their ratification, acceptance, approval or accession.

4. Instruments of ratification, acceptance, approval or accession in respect of an amendment shall be deposited with the Depositary. An amendment adopted pursuant to paragraph 3 shall enter into force for those Parties having accepted it on the ninetieth day after the date of receipt by the Depositary of an instrument of ratification, acceptance, approval or accession by at least two thirds of the Parties to the Convention which were Parties at the time of the adoption of the amendment.

5. The amendment shall enter into force for any other Party on the ninetieth day after the date on which that Party deposits with the Depositary its instrument of ratification, acceptance or approval of, or accession to the said amendment.

6. For the purposes of this article and article 31, "Parties present and voting" means Parties present and casting an affirmative or negative vote.

Article 31 – Adoption and amendment of annexes

1. Any additional annex to the Convention and any amendment to an annex shall be proposed and adopted in accordance with the procedure for amendment of the Convention set forth in article 30, provided that, in adopting an additional regional implementation annex or amendment to any regional implementation annex, the majority provided for in that article shall include a two- thirds majority vote of the Parties of the region concerned present and voting. The adoption or amendment of an annex shall be communicated by the Depositary to all Parties.

2. An annex, other than an additional regional implementation annex, or an amendment to an annex, other than an amendment to any regional implementation annex, that has been adopted in accordance with paragraph 1, shall enter into force for all Parties to the Convention six months after the date of communication by the Depositary to such Parties of the adoption of such annex or amendment, except for those Parties that have notified the Depositary in writing within that period of their non-acceptance of such annex or amendment. Such annex or amendment shall enter into force for Parties which withdraw their notification of non-acceptance on the ninetieth day after the date on which withdrawal of such notification has been received by the Depositary.

3. An additional regional implementation annex or amendment to any regional implementation annex that has been adopted in accordance with paragraph 1, shall enter into force for all Parties to the Convention six months after the date of the communication by the Depositary to such Parties of the adoption of such annex or amendment, except with respect to:

(a) any Party that has notified the Depositary in writing, within such six month period, of its non- acceptance of that additional regional implementation annex or of the amendment to the regional implementation annex, in which case such annex or amendment shall enter into force for Parties which withdraw their notification of nonacceptance on the ninetieth day after the date on which withdrawal of such notification has been received by the Depositary; and

(b) any Party that has made a declaration with respect to additional regional implementation annexes or amendments to regional implementation annexes in accordance with article 34, paragraph 4, in which case any such annex or amendment shall enter into force for such a Party on the ninetieth day after the date of deposit with the Depositary of its instrument of ratification, acceptance, approval or accession with respect to such annex or amendment.

4. If the adoption of an annex or an amendment to an annex involves an amendment to the Convention, that annex or amendment to an annex shall not enter into force until such time as the amendment to the Convention enters into force.

Article 32 – Right to vote

1. Except as provided for in paragraph 2, each Party to the Convention shall have one vote.
2. Regional economic integration organizations, in matters within their competence, shall exercise their right to vote with a number of votes equal to the number of their member States that are Parties to the Convention. Such an organization shall not exercise its right to vote if any of its member States exercises its right, and vice versa.

PART VI – FINAL PROVISIONS

Article 33 – Signature

This Convention shall be opened for signature at Paris, on 14-15 October 1994, by States Members of the United Nations or any of its specialized agencies or that are Parties to the Statute of the International Court of Justice and by regional economic integration organizations. It shall remain open for signature, thereafter, at the United Nations Headquarters in New York until 13 October 1995.

Article 34 – Ratification, acceptance, approval and accession

1. The Convention shall be subject to ratification, acceptance, approval or accession by States and by regional economic integration organizations. It shall be open for accession from the day after the date on which the Convention is closed for signature. Instruments of ratification, acceptance, approval or accession shall be deposited with the Depositary.
2. Any regional economic integration organization which becomes a Party to the Convention without any of its member States being a Party to the Convention shall be bound by all the obligations under the Convention. Where one or more member States of such an organization are also Party to the Convention, the organization and its member States shall decide on their respective responsibilities for the performance of their obligations under the Convention. In such cases, the organization and the member States shall not be entitled to exercise rights under the Convention concurrently.
3. In their instruments of ratification, acceptance, approval or accession, regional economic integration organizations shall declare the extent of their competence with respect to the matters governed by the Convention. They shall also promptly inform the Depositary, who shall in turn inform the Parties, of any substantial modification in the extent of their competence.
4. In its instrument of ratification, acceptance, approval or accession, any Party may declare that, with respect to it, any additional regional implementation annex or any amendment to any regional implementation annex shall enter into force only upon the deposit of its instrument of ratification, acceptance, approval or accession with respect thereto.

Article 35 – Interim arrangements

The secretariat functions referred to in article 23 will be carried out on an interim basis by the secretariat established by the General Assembly of the United Nations in its resolution 47/188 of 22 December 1992, until the completion of the first session of the Conference of the Parties.

Article 36 – Entry into force

1. The Convention shall enter into force on the ninetieth day after the date of deposit of the fiftieth instrument of ratification, acceptance, approval or accession.
2. For each State or regional economic integration organization ratifying, accepting, approving or acceding to the Convention after the deposit of the fiftieth instrument of ratification, acceptance, approval or accession, the Convention shall enter into force on the ninetieth day after the date of deposit by such State or regional economic integration organization of its instrument of ratification, acceptance, approval or accession.
3. For the purposes of paragraphs 1 and 2, any instrument deposited by a regional economic integration organization shall not be counted as additional to those deposited by States members of the organization.

Article 37 – Reservations

No reservations may be made to this Convention.

Article 38 – Withdrawal

1. At any time after three years from the date on which the Convention has entered into force for a Party, that Party may withdraw from the Convention by giving written notification to the Depositary.
2. Any such withdrawal shall take effect upon expiry of one year from the date of receipt by the Depositary of the notification of withdrawal, or on such

later date as may be specified in the notification of withdrawal.

Article 39 – Depositary

The Secretary-General of the United Nations shall be the Depositary of the Convention.

Article 40 – Authentic texts

The original of the present Convention, of which the Arabic, Chinese, English, French, Russian and Spanish texts are equally authentic, shall be deposited with the Secretary-General of the United Nations.

IN WITNESS WHEREOF the undersigned, being duly authorized to that effect, have signed the present Convention.

DONE AT Paris, this 17th day of June one thousand nine hundred and ninety four.

Annex I – Regional implementation annex for Africa

Article 1 – Scope

This Annex applies to Africa, in relation to each Party and in conformity with the Convention, in particular its article 7, for the purpose of combating desertification and/or mitigating the effects of drought in its arid, semi-arid and dry sub-humid areas.

Article 2 – Purpose

The purpose of this Annex, at the national, subregional and regional levels in Africa and in the light of its particular conditions, is to:

(a) identify measures and arrangements, including the nature and processes of assistance provided by developed country Parties, in accordance with the relevant provisions of the Convention;

(b) provide for the efficient and practical implementation of the Convention to address conditions specific to Africa; and

(c) promote processes and activities relating to combating desertification and/or mitigating the effects of drought within the arid, semi-arid and dry sub-humid areas of Africa.

Article 3 – Particular conditions of the African region

In carrying out their obligations under the Convention, the Parties shall, in the implementation of this Annex, adopt a basic approach that takes into consideration the following particular conditions of Africa:

(a) the high proportion of arid, semi-arid and dry sub-humid areas;

(b) the substantial number of countries and populations adversely affected by desertification and by the frequent recurrence of severe drought;

(c) the large number of affected countries that are landlocked;

(d) the widespread poverty prevalent in most affected countries, the large number of least developed countries among them, and their need for significant amounts of external assistance, in the form of grants and loans on concessional terms, to pursue their development objectives;

(e) the difficult socio-economic conditions, exacerbated by deteriorating and fluctuating terms of trade, external indebtedness and political instability, which induce internal, regional and international migrations;

(f) the heavy reliance of populations on natural resources for subsistence which, compounded by the effects of demographic trends and factors, a weak technological base and unsustainable production practices, contributes to serious resource degradation;

(g) the insufficient institutional and legal frameworks, the weak infrastructural base and the insufficient scientific, technical and educational capacity, leading to substantial capacity building requirements; and

(h) the central role of actions to combat desertification and/or mitigate the effects of drought in the national development priorities of affected African countries.

Article 4 – Commitments and obligations of African country Parties

1. In accordance with their respective capabilities, African country Parties undertake to:

   (a) adopt the combating of desertification and/or the mitigation of the effects of drought as a central strategy in their efforts to eradicate poverty;

   (b) promote regional cooperation and integration, in a spirit of solidarity and partnership based on mutual interest, in programmes and activities to combat desertification and/or mitigate the effects of drought;

   (c) rationalize and strengthen existing institutions concerned with desertification and drought and involve other existing institutions, as appropriate, in order to make them more effective and to ensure more efficient use of resources;

   (d) promote the exchange of information on appropriate technology, knowledge, know-how and practices between and among them; and

   (e) develop contingency plans for mitigating the effects of drought in areas degraded by desertification and/or drought.

2. Pursuant to the general and specific obligations set out in articles 4 and 5 of the Convention, affected African country Parties shall aim to:

   (a) make appropriate financial allocations from their national budgets consistent with national conditions and capabilities and reflecting the new priority Africa has accorded to the phenomenon of desertification and/or drought;

   (b) sustain and strengthen reforms currently in progress toward greater decentralization and resource tenure as well as reinforce participation of local populations and communities; and

   (c) identify and mobilize new and additional national financial resources, and expand, as a matter of priority, existing national capabilities and facilities to mobilize domestic financial resources.

Article 5 – Commitments and obligations of developed country Parties

1. In fulfilling their obligations pursuant to articles 4, 6 and 7 of the Convention, developed country Parties shall give priority to affected African country Parties and, in this context, shall:
   (a) assist them to combat desertification and/or mitigate the effects of drought by, inter alia, providing and/or facilitating access to financial and/or other resources, and promoting, financing and/or facilitating the financing of the transfer, adaptation and access to appropriate environmental technologies and know-how, as mutually agreed and in accordance with national policies, taking into account their adoption of poverty eradication as a central strategy;
   (b) continue to allocate significant resources and/or increase resources to combat desertification and/or mitigate the effects of drought; and
   (c) assist them in strengthening capacities to enable them to improve their institutional frameworks, as well as their scientific and technical capabilities, information collection and analysis, and research and development for the purpose of combating desertification and/or mitigating the effects of drought.
2. Other country Parties may provide, on a voluntary basis, technology, knowledge and know-how relating to desertification and/or financial resources, to affected African country Parties. The transfer of such knowledge, know-how and techniques is facilitated by international cooperation.

Article 6 – Strategic planning framework for sustainable development

1. National action programmes shall be a central and integral part of a broader process of formulating national policies for the sustainable development of affected African country Parties.
2. A consultative and participatory process involving appropriate levels of government, local populations, communities and non-governmental organizations shall be undertaken to provide guidance on a strategy with flexible planning to allow maximum participation from local populations and communities. As appropriate, bilateral and multilateral assistance agencies may be involved in this process at the request of an affected African country Party.

Article 7 – Timetable for preparation of action programmes

Pending entry into force of this Convention, the African country Parties, in cooperation with other members of the international community, as appropriate, shall, to the extent possible, provisionally apply those provisions of the Convention relating to the preparation of national, subregional and regional action programmes.

Article 8 – Content of national action programmes

1. Consistent with article 10 of the Convention, the overall strategy of national action programmes shall emphasize integrated local development programmes for affected areas, based on participatory mechanisms and on integration of strategies for poverty eradication into efforts to combat desertification and mitigate the effects of drought. The programmes shall aim at strengthening the capacity of local authorities and ensuring the active involvement of local populations, communities and groups, with emphasis on education and training, mobilization of non-governmental organizations with proven expertise and strengthening of decentralized governmental structures.
2. National action programmes shall, as appropriate, include the following general features:
   (a) the use, in developing and implementing national action programmes, of past experiences in combating desertification and/or mitigating the effects of drought, taking into account social, economic and ecological conditions;
   (b) the identification of factors contributing to desertification and/or drought and the resources and capacities available and required, and the setting up of appropriate policies and institutional and other responses and measures necessary to combat those phenomena and/or mitigate their effects; and
   (c) the increase in participation of local populations and communities, including women, farmers and pastoralists, and delegation to them of more responsibility for management.
3. National action programmes shall also, as appropriate, include the following:
   (a) measures to improve the economic environment with a view to eradicating poverty:
      – increasing incomes and employment opportunities, especially for the poorest members of the community, by:
      – developing markets for farm and livestock products;
      – creating financial instruments suited to local needs;
      – encouraging diversification in agriculture and the setting-up of agricultural enter prises; and
      – developing economic activities of a paraa-gricultural or non-agricultural type;
      – improving the long-term prospects of rural economies by the creation of:
      – incentives for productive investment and access to the means of production; and
      – price and tax policies and commercial practices that promote growth;

Biodiversity

- defining and applying population and migration policies to reduce population pressure on land; and
- promoting the use of drought resistant crops and the application of integrated dry-land farming systems for food security purposes;

(b) measures to conserve natural resources:

- ensuring integrated and sustainable management of natural resources, including:
- agricultural land and pastoral land;
- vegetation cover and wildlife;
- forests;
- water resources; and
- biological diversity;
- training with regard to, and strengthening, public awareness and environmental education campaigns and disseminating knowledge of techniques relating to the sustainable management of natural resources; and
- ensuring the development and efficient use of diverse energy sources, the promotion of alternative sources of energy, particularly solar energy, wind energy and biogas, and specific arrangements for the transfer, acquisition and adaptation of relevant technology to alleviate the pressure on fragile natural resources;

(c) measures to improve institutional organization:

- defining the roles and responsibilities of central government and local authorities within the framework of a land use planning policy;
- encouraging a policy of active decentralization, devolving responsibility for management and decision-making to local authorities, and encouraging initiatives and the assumption of responsibility by local communities and the establishment of local structures; and
- adjusting, as appropriate, the institutional and regulatory framework of natural resource management to provide security of land tenure for local populations;

(d) measures to improve knowledge of desertification:

- promoting research and the collection, processing and exchange of information on the scientific, technical and socio-economic aspects of desertification;
- improving national capabilities in research and in the collection, processing, exchange and analysis of information so as to increase understanding and to translate the results of the analysis into operational terms; and
- encouraging the medium and long term study of:
- socio-economic and cultural trends in affected areas;
- qualitative and quantitative trends in natural resources; and
- the interaction between climate and desertification; and

(e) measures to monitor and assess the effects of drought:

- developing strategies to evaluate the impacts of natural climate variability on regional drought and desertification and/or to utilize predictions of climate variability on seasonal to interannual time scales in efforts to mitigate the effects of drought;
- improving early warning and response capacity, efficiently managing emergency relief and food aid, and improving food stocking and distribution systems, cattle protection schemes and public works and alternative livelihoods for drought prone areas; and
- monitoring and assessing ecological degradation to provide reliable and timely information on the process and dynamics of resource degradation in order to facilitate better policy formulations and responses.

Article 9 – Preparation of national action programmes and implementation and evaluation indicators

Each affected African country Party shall designate an appropriate national coordinating body to function as a catalyst in the preparation, implementation and evaluation of its national action programme. This coordinating body shall, in the light of article 3 and as appropriate:

(a) undertake an identification and review of actions, beginning with a locally driven consultation process, involving local populations and communities and with the cooperation of local administrative authorities, developed country Parties and intergovernmental and nongovernmental organizations, on the basis of initial consultations of those concerned at the national level;

(b) identify and analyze the constraints, needs and gaps affecting development and sustainable land use and recommend practical measures to avoid duplication by making full use of relevant ongoing efforts and promote implementation of results;

(c) facilitate, design and formulate project activities based on interactive, flexible approaches in order to ensure active participation of the population in affected areas, to minimize the negative impact of such activities, and to identify and prioritize requirements for financial assistance and technical cooperation;

(d) establish pertinent, quantifiable and readily verifiable indicators to ensure the assessment and evaluation of national action programmes, which encompass actions in the short, medium and long terms, and of the implementation of such programmes; and

(e) prepare progress reports on the implementation of the national action programmes.

Article 10 – Organizational framework of subregional action programmes

1. Pursuant to article 4 of the Convention, African country Parties shall cooperate in the preparation and implementation of subregional action programmes for central, eastern, northern, southern and western Africa and, in that regard, may delegate the following responsibilities to relevant subregional intergovernmental organizations:
   (a) acting as focal points for preparatory activities and coordinating the implementation of the subregional action programmes;
   (b) assisting in the preparation and implementation of national action programmes;
   (c) facilitating the exchange of information, experience and know-how as well as providing advice on the review of national legislation; and
   (d) any other responsibilities relating to the implementation of subregional action programmes.
2. Specialized subregional institutions may provide support, upon request, and/or be entrusted with the responsibility to coordinate activities in their respective fields of competence.

Article 11 – Content and preparation of subregional action programmes

Subregional action programmes shall focus on issues that are better addressed at the subregional level. They shall establish, where necessary, mechanisms for the management of shared natural resources. Such mechanisms shall effectively handle transboundary problems associated with desertification and/or drought and shall provide support for the harmonious implementation of national action programmes. Priority areas for subregional action programmes shall, as appropriate, focus on:

(a) joint programmes for the sustainable management of transboundary natural resources through bilateral and multilateral mechanisms, as appropriate;

(b) coordination of programmes to develop alternative energy sources;

(c) cooperation in the management and control of pests as well as of plant and animal diseases;

(d) capacity building, education and public awareness activities that are better carried out or supported at the subregional level;

(e) scientific and technical cooperation, particularly in the climatological, meteorological and hydrological fields, including networking for data collection and assessment, information sharing and project monitoring, and coordination and prioritization of research and development activities;

(f) early warning systems and joint planning for mitigating the effects of drought, including measures to address the problems resulting from environmentally induced migrations;

(g) exploration of ways of sharing experiences, particularly regarding participation of local populations and communities, and creation of an enabling environment for improved land use management and for use of appropriate technologies;

(h) strengthening of the capacity of subregional organizations to coordinate and provide technical services, as well as establishment, reorientation and strengthening of subregional centres and institutions; and

(i) development of policies in fields, such as trade, which have impact upon affected areas and populations, including policies for the coordination of regional marketing regimes and for common infrastructure.

Article 12 – Organizational framework of the regional action programme

1. Pursuant to article 11 of the Convention, African country Parties shall jointly determine the procedures for preparing and implementing the regional action programme.
2. The Parties may provide appropriate support to relevant African regional institutions and organizations to enable them to assist African country Parties to fulfil their responsibilities under the Convention.

Article 13 – Content of the regional action programme

The regional action programme includes measures relating to combating desertification and/or mitigating the effects of drought in the following priority areas, as appropriate:

(a) development of regional cooperation and coordination of sub-regional action programmes for building regional consensus on key policy areas, including through regular consultations of sub-regional organizations;

(b) promotion of capacity building in activities which are better implemented at the regional level;

(c) the seeking of solutions with the international community to global economic and social issues that have an impact on affected areas taking into account article 4, paragraph 2 (b) of the Convention;

(d) promotion among the affected country Parties of Africa and its subregions, as well as with other affected regions, of exchange of information and appropriate techniques, technical know-how and relevant experience; promotion of scientific and technological cooperation particularly in the fields of climatology, meteorology, hydrology, water resource development and alternative energy sources; coordination of sub-regional and regional research activities; and identification of regional priorities for research and development;

(e) coordination of networks for systematic observation and assessment and information exchange, as well as their integration into world wide networks; and

(f) coordination of and reinforcement of sub-regional and regional early warning systems and drought contingency plans.

Article 14 – Financial resources

1. Pursuant to article 20 of the Convention and article 4, paragraph 2, affected African country Parties shall endeavour to provide a macroeconomic framework conducive to the mobilization of financial resources and shall develop policies and establish procedures to channel resources more effectively to local development programmes, including through non-governmental organizations, as appropriate.
2. Pursuant to article 21, paragraphs 4 and 5 of the Convention, the Parties agree to establish an inventory of sources of funding at the national, subregional, regional and international levels to ensure the rational use of existing resources and to identify gaps in resource allocation, to facilitate implementation of the action programmes. The inventory shall be regularly reviewed and updated.
3. Consistent with article 7 of the Convention, the developed country Parties shall continue to allocate significant resources and/or increased resources as well as other forms of assistance to affected African country Parties on the basis of partnership agreements and arrangements referred to in article 18, giving, inter alia, due attention to matters related to debt, international trade and marketing arrangements in accordance with article 4, paragraph 2 (b) of the Convention.

Article 15 – Financial Mechanisms

1. Consistent with article 7 of the Convention underscoring the priority to affected African country Parties and considering the particular situation prevailing in this region, the Parties shall pay special attention to the implementation in Africa of the provisions of article 21, paragraph 1 (d) and (e) of the Convention, notably by:
   (a) facilitating the establishment of mechanisms, such as national desertification funds, to channel financial resources to the local level; and
   (b) strengthening existing funds and financial mechanisms at the subregional and regional levels.
2. Consistent with articles 20 and 21 of the Convention, the Parties which are also members of the governing bodies of relevant regional and subregional financial institutions, including the African Development Bank and the African Development Fund, shall promote efforts to give due priority and attention to the activities of those institutions that advance the implementation of this Annex.
3. The Parties shall streamline, to the extent possible, procedures for channelling funds to affected African country Parties.

Article 16 – Technical assistance and cooperation

The Parties undertake, in accordance with their respective capabilities, to rationalize technical assistance to, and cooperation with, African country Parties with a view to increasing project and programme effectiveness by, inter alia:

(a) limiting the costs of support measures and backstopping, especially overhead costs; in any case, such costs shall only represent an appropriately low percentage of the total cost of the project so as to maximize project efficiency;

(b) giving preference to the utilization of competent national experts or, where necessary, competent experts from within the subregion and/or region, in project design, preparation and implementation, and to the building of local expertise where it does not exist; and

(c) effectively managing and coordinating, as well as efficiently utilizing, technical assistance to be provided.

Article 17 – Transfer, acquisition, adaptation and access to environmentally sound technology

In implementing article 18 of the Convention relating to transfer, acquisition, adaptation and development of technology, the Parties undertake to give priority to African country Parties and, as necessary, to develop with them new models of partnership and cooperation with a view to strengthening capacity building in the fields of scientific research and development and information collection and dissemination to enable them to implement their strategies to combat desertification and mitigate the effects of drought.

Article 18 – Coordination and partnership agreements

1. African country Parties shall coordinate the preparation, negotiation and implementation of national, subregional and regional action programmes. They may involve, as appropriate, other Parties and relevant intergovernmental and non-governmental organizations in this process.
2. The objectives of such coordination shall be to ensure that financial and technical cooperation is consistent with the Convention and to provide the necessary continuity in the use and administration of resources.
3. African country Parties shall organize consultative processes at the national, subregional and regional levels. These consultative processes may:
   (a) serve as a forum to negotiate and conclude partnership agreements based on national, subregional and regional action programmes; and
   (b) specify the contribution of African country Parties and other members of the consultative groups to the programmes and identify priorities and agreements on implementation and evaluation indicators, as well as funding arrangements for implementation.
4. The Permanent Secretariat may, at the request of African country Parties, pursuant to article 23 of the Convention, facilitate the convocation of such consultative processes by:
   (a) providing advice on the organization of effective consultative arrangements, drawing on experiences from other such arrangements;

(b) providing information to relevant bilateral and multilateral agencies concerning consultative meetings or processes, and encouraging their active involvement; and

(c) providing other information that may be relevant in establishing or improving consultative arrangements.

5. The subregional and regional coordinating bodies shall, inter alia:

(a) recommend appropriate adjustments to partnership agreements;

(b) monitor, assess and report on the implementation of the agreed subregional and regional programmes; and

(c) aim to ensure efficient communication and cooperation among African country Parties.

6. Participation in the consultative groups shall, as appropriate, be open to Governments, interested groups and donors, relevant organs, funds and programmes of the United Nations system, relevant subregional and regional organizations, and representatives of relevant non- governmental organizations. Participants of each consultative group shall determine the modalities of its management and operation.

7. Pursuant to article 14 of the Convention, developed country Parties are encouraged to develop, on their own initiative, an informal process of consultation and coordination among themselves, at the national, subregional and regional levels, and, at the request of an affected African country Party or of an appropriate subregional or regional organization, to participate in a national, subregional or regional consultative process that would evaluate and respond to assistance needs in order to facilitate implementation.

Article 19 – Follow-up arrangements

Follow-up of this Annex shall be carried out by African country Parties in accordance with the Convention as follows:

(a) at the national level, by a mechanism the composition of which should be determined by each affected African country Party and which shall include representatives of local communities and shall function under the supervision of the national coordinating body referred to in article 9;

(b) at the subregional level, by a multidisciplinary scientific and technical consultative committee, the composition and modalities of operation of which shall be determined by the African country Parties of the subregion concerned; and

(c) at the regional level, by mechanisms defined in accordance with the relevant provisions of the Treaty establishing the African Economic Community, and by an African Scientific and Technical Advisory Committee.

Annex II – Regional implementation annex for Asia

Article 1 – Purpose

The purpose of this Annex is to provide guidelines and arrangements for the effective implementation of the Convention in the affected country Parties of the Asian region in the light of its particular conditions.

Article 2 – Particular conditions of the Asian region

In carrying out their obligations under the Convention, the Parties shall, as appropriate, take into consideration the following particular conditions which apply in varying degrees to the affected country Parties of the region:

(a) the high proportion of areas in their territories affected by, or vulnerable to, desertification and drought and the broad diversity of these areas with regard to climate, topography, land use and socio-economic systems;

(b) the heavy pressure on natural resources for livelihoods;

(c) the existence of production systems, directly related to widespread poverty, leading to land degradation and to pressure on scarce water resources;

(d) the significant impact of conditions in the world economy and social problems such as poverty, poor health and nutrition, lack of food security, migration, displaced persons and demographic dynamics;

(e) their expanding, but still insufficient, capacity and institutional frameworks to deal with national desertification and drought problems; and

(f) their need for international cooperation to pursue sustainable development objectives relating to combating desertification and mitigating the effects of drought.

Article 3 – Framework for national action programmes

1. National action programmes shall be an integral part of broader national policies for sustainable development of the affected country Parties of the region.

2. The affected country Parties shall, as appropriate, develop national action programmes pursuant to articles 9 to 11 of the Convention, paying special attention to article 10, paragraph 2 (f). As appropriate, bilateral and multilateral cooperation agencies may be involved in this process at the request of the affected country Party concerned.

Article 4 – National action programmes

1. In preparing and implementing national action programmes, the affected country Parties of the region, consistent with their respective circumstances and policies, may, inter alia, as appropriate:

(a) designate appropriate bodies responsible for the preparation, coordination and implementation of their action programmes;

(b) involve affected populations, including local communities, in the elaboration, coordination and implementation of their action programmes through a locally driven consultative process, with the cooperation of local authorities and relevant national and nongovernmental organizations;

(c) survey the state of the environment in affected areas to assess the causes and consequences of desertification and to determine priority areas for action;

(d) evaluate, with the participation of affected populations, past and current programmes for combating desertification and mitigating the effects of drought, in order to design a strategy and elaborate activities in their action programmes;

(e) prepare technical and financial programmes based on the information derived from the activities in subparagraphs (a) to (d);

(f) develop and utilize procedures and benchmarks for evaluating implementation of their ac- tion programmes;

(g) promote the integrated management of drainage basins, the conservation of soil resources, and the enhancement and efficient use of water resources;

(h) strengthen and/or establish information, evaluation and follow up and early warning systems in regions prone to desertification and drought, taking account of climatological, meteorological, hydrological, biological and other relevant factors; and

(i) formulate in a spirit of partnership, where international cooperation, including financial and technical resources, is involved, appropriate arrangements supporting their action programmes.

2. Consistent with article 10 of the Convention, the overall strategy of national action programmes shall emphasize integrated local development programmes for affected areas, based on participatory mechanisms and on the integration of strategies for poverty eradication into efforts to combat desertification and mitigate the effects of drought. Sectoral measures in the action programmes shall be grouped in priority fields which take account of the broad diversity of affected areas in the region referred to in article 2 (a).

Article 5 – Subregional and joint action programmes

1. Pursuant to article 11 of the Convention, affected country Parties in Asia may mutually agree to consult and cooperate with other Parties, as appropriate, to prepare and implement subregional or joint action programmes, as appropriate, in order to complement, and increase effectiveness in the implementation of, national action programmes. In either case, the relevant Parties may jointly agree to entrust subregional, including bilateral or national organizations, or specialized institutions, with responsibilities relating to the preparation, coordination and implementation of programmes. Such organizations or institutions may also act as focal points for the promotion and coordination of actions pursuant to articles 16 to 18 of the Convention.

2. In preparing and implementing subregional or joint action programmes, the affected country Parties of the region shall, inter alia, as appropriate:

(a) identify, in cooperation with national institutions, priorities relating to combating desertification and mitigating the effects of drought which can better be met by such programmes, as well as relevant activities which could be effectively carried out through them;

(b) evaluate the operational capacities and activities of relevant regional, subregional and national institutions;

(c) assess existing programmes relating to desertification and drought among all or some parties of the region or subregion and their relationship with national action programmes; and

(d) formulate in a spirit of partnership, where international cooperation, including financial and technical resources, is involved, appropriate bilateral and/or multilateral arrangements supporting the programmes.

3. Subregional or joint action programmes may include agreed joint programmes for the sustainable management of transboundary natural resources relating to desertification, priorities for coordination and other activities in the fields of capacity building, scientific and technical cooperation, particularly drought early warning systems and information sharing, and means of strengthening the relevant subregional and other organizations or institutions.

Article 6 – Regional activities

Regional activities for the enhancement of subregional or joint action programmes may include, inter alia, measures to strengthen institutions and mechanisms for coordination and cooperation at the national, subregional and regional levels, and to promote the implementation of articles 16 to 19 of the Convention. These activities may also include:

(a) promoting and strengthening technical cooperation networks;

(b) preparing inventories of technologies, knowledge, know-how and practices, as well as traditional and local technologies and know-how, and promoting their dissemination and use;

(c) evaluating the requirements for technology transfer and promoting the adaptation and use of such technologies; and

(d) encouraging public awareness programmes and promoting capacity building at all levels, strengthening training, research and development and building systems for human resource development.

Article 7 – Financial resources and mechanisms

1. The Parties shall, in view of the importance of combating desertification and mitigating the effects of drought in the Asian region, promote the mobilization of substantial financial resources and the availability of financial mechanisms, pursuant to articles 20 and 21 of the Convention.
2. In conformity with the Convention and on the basis of the coordinating mechanism provided for in article 8 and in accordance with their national development policies, affected country Parties of the region shall, individually or jointly:
   (a) adopt measures to rationalize and strengthen mechanisms to supply funds through public and private investment with a view to achieving specific results in action to combat desertification and mitigate the effects of drought;
   (b) identify international cooperation requirements in support of national efforts, particularly financial, technical and technological; and
   (c) promote the participation of bilateral and/or multilateral financial cooperation institutions with a view to ensuring implementation of the Convention.
3. The Parties shall streamline, to the extent possible, procedures for channelling funds to affected country Parties in the region.

Article 8 – Cooperation and coordination mechanisms

1. Affected country Parties, through the appropriate bodies designated pursuant to article 4, paragraph 1 (a), and other Parties in the region, may, as appropriate, set up a mechanism for, inter alia, the following purposes:
   (a) exchange of information, experience, knowledge and know-how;
   (b) cooperation and coordination of actions, including bilateral and multilateral arrangements, at the subregional and regional levels;
   (c) promotion of scientific, technical, technological and financial cooperation pursuant to articles 5 to 7;
   (d) identification of external cooperation requirements; and
   (e) follow-up and evaluation of the implementation of action programmes.
2. Affected country Parties, through the appropriate bodies designated pursuant to article 4, paragraph 1 (a), and other Parties in the region, may also, as appropriate, consult and coordinate as regards the national, subregional and joint action programmes. They may involve, as appropriate, other Parties and relevant intergovernmental and non-governmental organizations in this process. Such coordination shall, inter alia, seek to secure agreement on opportunitiesfor international cooperation in accordance with articles 20 and 21 of the Convention, enhance technical cooperation and channel resources so that they are used effectively.
3. Affected country Parties of the region shall hold periodic coordination meetings, and the Permanent Secretariat may, at their request, pursuant to article 23 of the Convention, facilitate the convocation of such coordination meetings by:
   (a) providing advice on the organization of effective coordination arrangements, drawing on experience from other such arrangements;
   (b) providing information to relevant bilateral and multilateral agencies concerning coordination meetings, and encouraging their active involvement; and
   (c) providing other information that may be relevant in establishing or improving coordination processes.

Annex III – Regional implementation annex for Latin America and the Caribbean

Article 1 – Purpose

The purpose of this Annex is to provide general guidelines for the implementation of the Convention in the Latin American and Caribbean region, in light of its particular conditions.

Article 2 – Particular conditions of the Latin American and Caribbean region

The Parties shall, in accordance with the provisions of the Convention, take into consideration the following particular conditions of the region:

(a) the existence of broad expanses which are vulnerable and have been severely affected by desertification and/or drought and in which diverse characteristics may be observed, depending on the area in which they occur; this cumulative and intensifying process has negative social, cultural, economic and environmental effects which are all the more serious in that the region contains one of the largest resources of biological diversity in the world;

(b) the frequent use of unsustainable development practices in affected areas as a result of complex interactions among physical, biological, political, social, cultural and economic factors, including international economic factors such as external indebtedness, deteriorating terms of trade and trade practices which affect markets for agricultural, fishery and forestry products; and

(c) a sharp drop in the productivity of ecosystems being the main consequence of desertification and drought, taking the form of a decline in agricultural, livestock and forestry yields and a loss of biological diversity; from the social point of view, the results are impoverishment, migration, internal population movements, and the deterioration of the quality of life; the region will therefore have to adopt an integrated approach to problems of desertification and drought by promoting sustainable development models that are in keeping with the environmental, economic and social situation in each country.

Article 3 – Action programmes

1. In conformity with the Convention, in particular its articles 9 to 11, and in accordance with their national development policies, affected country Parties of the region shall, as appropriate, prepare and implement national action programmes to combat desertification and mitigate the effects of drought as an integral part of their national policies for sustainable development. Subregional and regional programmes may be prepared and implemented in accordance with the requirements of the region.
2. In the preparation of their national action programmes, affected country Parties of the region shall pay particular attention to article 10, paragraph 2 (f) of the Convention.

Article 4 – Content of national action programmes

In the light of their respective situations, the affected country Parties of the region may take account, inter alia, of the following thematic issues in developing their national strategies for action to combat desertification and/or mitigate the effects of drought, pursuant to article 5 of the Convention:

(a) increasing capacities, education and public awareness, technical, scientific and technological cooperation and financial resources and mechanisms;

(b) eradicating poverty and improving the quality of human life;

(c) achieving food security and sustainable development and management of agricultural, livestock-rearing, forestry and multipurpose activities;

(d) sustainable management of natural resources, especially the rational management of drainage basins;

(e) sustainable management of natural resources in high-altitude areas;

(f) rational management and conservation of soil resources and exploitation and efficient use of water resources;

(g) formulation and application of emergency plans to mitigate the effects of drought;

(h) strengthening and/or establishing information, evaluation and follow-up and early warning systems in areas prone to desertification and drought, taking account of climatological, meteorological, hydrological, biological, soil, economic and social factors;

(i) developing, managing and efficiently using diverse sources of energy, including the promotion of alternative sources;

(j) conservation and sustainable use of biodiversity in accordance with the provisions of the Convention on Biological Diversity;

(k) consideration of demographic aspects related to desertification and drought; and

(l) establishing or strengthening institutional and legal frameworks permitting application of the Convention and aimed, inter alia, at decentralizing administrative structures and functions relating to desertification and drought, with the participation of affected communities and society in general.

Article 5 – Technical, scientific and technological cooperation

In conformity with the Convention, in particular its articles 16 to 18, and on the basis of the coordinating mechanism provided for in article 7, affected country Parties of the region shall, individually or jointly:

(a) promote the strengthening of technical cooperation networks and national, subregional and regional information systems, as well as their integration, as appropriate, in worldwide sources of information;

(b) prepare an inventory of available technologies and know-how and promote their dissemination and use;

(c) promote the use of traditional technology, knowledge, know-how and practices pursuant to article 18, paragraph 2 (b), of the Convention;

(d) identify transfer of technology requirements; and

(e) promote the development, adaptation, adoption and transfer of relevant existing and new environmentally sound technologies.

Article 6 – Financial resources and mechanisms

In conformity with the Convention, in particular its articles 20 and 21, on the basis of the coordinating mechanism provided for in article 7 and in accordance with their national development policies, affected country Parties of the region shall, individually or jointly:

(a) adopt measures to rationalize and strengthen mechanisms to supply funds through public and private investment with a view to achieving specific results in action to combat desertification and mitigate the effects of drought;

(b) identify international cooperation requirements in support of national efforts; and

(c) promote the participation of bilateral and/or multilateral financial cooperation institutions with a view to ensuring implementation of the Convention.

Article 7 – Institutional framework

1. In order to give effect to this Annex, affected country Parties of the region shall:
   (a) establish and/or strengthen national focal points to coordinate action to combat desertification and/or mitigate the effects of drought; and
   (b) set up a mechanism to coordinate the national focal points for the following purposes:
      - exchanges of information and experience;
      - coordination of activities at the subregional and regional levels;
      - promotion of technical, scientific, technological and financial cooperation;
      - identification of external cooperation requirements; and

- follow-up and evaluation of the implementation of action programmes.

2. Affected country Parties of the region shall hold periodic coordination meetings and the Permanent Secretariat may, at their request, pursuant to article 23 of the Convention, facilitate the convocation of such coordination meetings, by:
   (a) providing advice on the organization of effective coordination arrangements, drawing on experience from other such arrangements;
   (b) providing information to relevant bilateral and multilateral agencies concerning coordination meetings, and encouraging their active involvement; and
   (c) providing other information that may be relevant in establishing or improving coordination processes.

Annex IV – Regional implementation annex for the northern Mediterranean

Article 1 – Purpose

The purpose of this Annex is to provide guidelines and arrangements necessary for the effective implementation of the Convention in affected country Parties of the northern Mediterranean region in the light of its particular conditions.

Article 2 – Particular conditions of the northern Mediterranean region

The particular conditions of the northern Mediterranean region referred to in article 1 include:

(a) semi-arid climatic conditions affecting large areas, seasonal droughts, very high rainfall variability and sudden and high-intensity rainfall;

(b) poor and highly erodible soils, prone to develop surface crusts;

(c) uneven relief with steep slopes and very diversified landscapes;

(d) extensive forest coverage losses due to frequent wildfires;

(e) crisis conditions in traditional agriculture with associated land abandonment and deterioration of soil and water conservation structures;

(f) unsustainable exploitation of water resources leading to serious environmental damage, including chemical pollution, salinization and exhaustion of aquifers; and

(g) concentration of economic activity in coastal areas as a result of urban growth, industrial activities, tourism and irrigated agriculture.

Article 3 – Strategic planning framework for sustainable development

1. National action programmes shall be a central and integral part of the strategic planning framework for sustainable development of the affected country Parties of the northern Mediterranean.
2. A consultative and participatory process, involving appropriate levels of government, local communities and non-governmental organizations, shall be undertaken to provide guidance on a strategy with flexible planning to allow maximum local participation, pursuant to article 10, paragraph 2 (f) of the Convention.

Article 4 – Obligation to prepare national action programmes and timetable

Affected country Parties of the northern Mediterranean region shall prepare national action programmes and, as appropriate, subregional, regional or joint action programmes. The preparation of such programmes shall be finalized as soon as practicable.

Article 5 – Preparation and implementation of national action programmes

In preparing and implementing national action programmes pursuant to articles 9 and 10 of the Convention, each affected country Party of the region shall, as appropriate:

(a) designate appropriate bodies responsible for the preparation, coordination and implementation of its programme;

(b) involve affected populations, including local communities, in the elaboration, coordination and implementation of the programme through a locally driven consultative process, with the cooperation of local authorities and relevant non-governmental organizations;

(c) survey the state of the environment in affected areas to assess the causes and consequences of desertification and to determine priority areas for action;

(d) evaluate, with the participation of affected populations, past and current programmes in order to design a strategy and elaborate activities in the action programme;

(e) prepare technical and financial programmes based on the information gained through the activities in subparagraphs (a) to (d); and

(f) develop and utilize procedures and benchmarks for monitoring and evaluating the implementation of the programme.

Article 6 – Content of national action programmes

Affected country Parties of the region may include, in their national action programmes, measures relating to:

(a) legislative, institutional and administrative areas;

(b) land use patterns, management of water resources, soil conservation, forestry, agricultural activities and pasture and range management;

(c) management and conservation of wildlife and other forms of biological diversity;

(d) protection against forest fires;

(e) promotion of alternative livelihoods; and

(f) research, training and public awareness.

Article 7 – Subregional, regional and joint action programmes

1. Affected country Parties of the region may, in accordance with article 11 of the Convention, prepare and implement subregional and/or regional action programmes in order to complement and increase the efficiency of national action programmes. Two or more affected country Parties of the region, may similarly agree to prepare a joint action programme between or among them.
2. The provisions of articles 5 and 6 shall apply mutatis mutandis to the preparation and implementation of subregional, regional and joint action programmes. In addition, such programmes may include the conduct of research and development activities concerning selected ecosystems in affected areas.
3. In preparing and implementing subregional, regional or joint action programmes, affected country Parties of the region shall, as appropriate:
   (a) identify, in cooperation with national institutions, national objectives relating to desertification which can better be met by such programmes and relevant activities which could be effectively carried out through them;
   (b) evaluate the operational capacities and activities of relevant regional, subregional and national institutions; and
   (c) assess existing programmes relating to desertification among Parties of the region and their relationship with national action programmes.

Article 8 – Coordination of subregional, regional and joint action programmes

Affected country Parties preparing a subregional, regional or joint action programme may establish a coordination committee composed of representatives of each affected country Party concerned to review progress in combating desertification, harmonize national action programmes, make recommendations at the various stages of preparation and implementation of the subregional, regional or joint action programme, and act as a focal point for the promotion and coordination of technical cooperation pursuant to articles 16 to 19 of the Convention.

Article 9 – Non-eligibility for financial assistance

In implementing national, subregional, regional and joint action programmes, affected developed country Parties of the region are not eligible to receive financial assistance under this Convention.

Article 10 – Coordination with other subregions and regions

Subregional, regional and joint action programmes in the northern Mediterranean region may be prepared and implemented in collaboration with those of other subregions or regions, particularly with those of the subregion of northern Africa.

Annex V – Regional implementation annex for Central and Eastern Europe

Article 1 – Purpose

The purpose of this Annex is to provide guidelines and arrangements for the effective implementation of the Convention in affected country Parties of the Central and Eastern European region, in the light of its particular conditions.

Article 2 – Particular conditions of the Central and Eastern European region

The particular conditions of the Central and Eastern European region referred to in article 1, which apply in varying degrees to the affected country Parties of the region, include:

(a) specific problems and challenges related to the current process of economic transition, including macroeconomic and financial problems and the need for strengthening the social and political framework for economic and market reforms;

(b) the variety of forms of land degradation in the different ecosystems of the region, including the effects of drought and the risks of desertification in regions prone to soil erosion caused by water and wind;

(c) crisis conditions in agriculture due, inter alia, to depletion of arable land, problems related to inappropriate irrigation systems and gradual deterioration of soil and water conservation structures;

(d) unsustainable exploitation of water resources leading to serious environmental damage, including chemical pollution, salinisation and exhaustion of aquifers;

(e) forest coverage losses due to climatic factors, consequences of air pollution and frequent wildfires;

(f) the use of unsustainable development practices in affected areas as a result of complex interactions among physical, biological, political, social and economic factors;

(g) the risks of growing economic hardships and deteriorating social conditions in areas affected by land degradation, desertification and drought;

(h) the need to review research objectives and the policy and legislative framework for the sustainable management of natural resources; and

(i) the opening up of the region to wider international cooperation and the pursuit of broad objectives of sustainable development.

Article 3 – Action programmes

1. National action programmes shall be an integral part of the policy framework for sustainable development and address in an appropriate manner the various forms of land degradation, desertification and drought affecting the Parties of the region.
2. A consultative and participatory process, involving appropriate levels of government, local communities and non-governmental organizations, shall be undertaken to provide guidance on a strategy with flexible planning to allow maximum local participation, pursuant to article 10, paragraph 2(f), of

the Convention. As appropriate, bilateral and multilateral cooperation agencies may be involved in this process at the request of the affected country Party concerned.

Article 4 – Preparation and implementation of national action programmes

In preparing and implementing national action programmes pursuant to articles 9 and 10 of the Convention, each affected country Party of the region shall, as appropriate:

(a) designate appropriate bodies responsible for the preparation, coordination and implementation of its programme;

(b) involve affected populations, including local communities, in the elaboration, coordination and implementation of the programme through a locally driven consultative process, with the cooperation of local authorities and relevant non-governmental organizations;

(c) survey the state of the environment in affected areas to assess the causes and consequences of desertification and to determine priority areas for action;

(d) evaluate, with the participation of affected populations, past and current programmes in order to design a strategy and elaborate actions in the action programme;

(e) prepare technical and financial programmes based on the information gained through the activities in subparagraphs (a) to (d); and

(f) develop and utilize procedures and benchmarks for monitoring and evaluating the implementation of the programme.

Article 5 – Subregional, regional and joint action programmes

1. Affected country Parties of the region, in accordance with articles 11 and 12 of the Convention, may prepare and implement subregional and/or regional action programmes in order to complement and increase the effectiveness and efficiency of national action programmes. Two or more affected country Parties of the region may similarly agree to prepare a joint action programme between or among them.

2. Such programmes may be prepared and implemented in collaboration with other Parties or regions. The objective of such collaboration would be to secure an enabling international environment and to facilitate financial and/or technical support or other forms of assistance to address more effectively desertification and drought issues at different levels.

3. The provisions of articles 3 and 4 shall apply, mutatis mutandis, to the preparation and implementation of subregional, regional and joint action programmes. In addition, such programmes may include the conduct of research and development activities concerning selected ecosystems in affected areas.

4. In preparing and implementing subregional, regional or joint action programmes, affected country Parties of the region shall, as appropriate:

   (a) identify, in cooperation with national institutions, national objectives relating to desertification which can better be met by such programmes, and relevant activities, which could be effectively carried out through them;

   (b) evaluate the operational capacities and activities of relevant regional, subregional and national institutions;

   (c) assess existing programmes relating to desertification among Parties of the region and their relationship with national action programmes; and

   (d) consider action for the coordination of subregional, regional and joint action programmes, including, as appropriate, the establishment of coordination committees composed of representatives of each affected country Party concerned to review progress in combating desertification, harmonize national action programmes, make recommendations at the various stages of preparation and implementation of the subregional, regional or joint action programmes, and act as focal points for the promotion and coordination of technical cooperation pursuant to articles 16 to 19 of the Convention.

Article 6 – Technical, scientific and technological cooperation

In conformity with the objective and principles of the Convention, Parties of the region shall, individually or jointly:

(a) promote the strengthening of scientific and technical cooperation networks, of monitoring indicators and of information systems at all levels, as well as their integration, as appropriate, in worldwide systems of information; and

(b) promote the development, adaptation and transfer of relevant existing and new environmentally sound technologies within and outside the region.

Article 7 – Financial resources and mechanisms

In conformity with the objective and principles of the Convention, affected country Parties of the region shall, individually or jointly:

(a) adopt measures to rationalize and strengthen mechanisms to supply funds through public and private investment with a view to achieving concrete results in action to combat land degradation and desertification and mitigate the effects of drought;

(b) identify international cooperation requirements in support of national efforts, thereby creating, in particular, an enabling environment for investments and encouraging active investment policies and an integrated approach to effectively combating desertification, including early identification of the problems caused by this process;

(c) seek the participation of bilateral and/or multilateral partners and financial cooperation institutions with a view to ensuring implementation of the Convention, including programme activities which take into account the specific needs of affected country Parties of the region; and

(d) assess the possible impact of article 2(a) on the implementation of articles 6, 13 and 20 and other related provisions of the Convention.

Article 8 – Institutional framework

1. In order to give effect to this Annex, Parties of the region shall:

   (a) establish and/or strengthen national focal points to coordinate action to combat desertification and/or mitigate the effects of drought; and

   (b) consider mechanisms to strengthen regional cooperation, as appropriate.

2. The Permanent Secretariat may, at the request of Parties of the region and pursuant to article 23 of the Convention, facilitate the convocation of coordination meetings in the region by:

   (a) providing advice on the organization of effective coordination arrangements, drawing on experience from other such arrangements; and

   (b) providing other information that may be relevant in establishing or improving coordination processes.

10.1. Basel Convention 1989, revised 2019

Basel Convention on the Control of Transboundary Movements of Hazardous Wastes and their Disposal, Basel, Switzerland, 22 March 1989, 1673 UNTS 57, C.N.302.1992.TREATIES-9 of 25 November 1992, C.N.77.1998.TREATIES-2 of 6 May 1998, C.N.399.2003.TREATIES-9 of 20 May 2003, C.N.1314.2003.TREATIES-12 of 20 November 2003, C.N.263.2005.TREATIES-4 of 8 April 2005, C.N.263.2005. TREATIES-4 of 13 June 2005, C.N.1044.2005.TREATIES-7 of 10 October 2005, C.N.1038.2007.TREATIES-5 of 14 November 2007, C.N.119.2008.TREATIES-1 of 26 February 2008, C.N.125.2008.TREATIES-2 of 26 February 2008, C.N.243.2008. TREATIES-3 of 7 April 2008, C.N.397.2008.TREATIES-4 of 27 May 2008, C.N.609.2008.TREATIES-8 of 28 August 2008, C.N.644.2008.TREATIES-9 of 18 September 2008, C.N.778.2008.TREATIES-10 of 28 October 2008, C.N.760.2011. TREATIES-6 of 28 November 2011, C.N.824.2011.TREATIES-7 of 30 December 2011, C.N.965.2013.TREATIES-XXVII-3 of 26 November 2013, C.N.304.2014.TREATIES-XXVII-3 of 28 May 2014, C.N.432.2019.TREATIES-XXVII.3 of 24 September 2019, C.N.116.2020.TREATIES-XXVII-3 of 30 March 2020

The Parties to this Convention,[1]

Aware of the risk of damage to human health and the environment caused by hazardous wastes and other wastes and the transboundary movement thereof,

Mindful of the growing threat to human health and the environment posed by the increased generation and complexity, and transboundary movement of hazardous wastes and other wastes,

Mindful also that the most effective way of protecting human health and the environment from the dangers posed by such wastes is the reduction of their generation to a minimum in terms of quantity and/or hazard potential,

Convinced that States should take necessary measures to ensure that the management of hazardous wastes and other wastes including their transboundary movement and disposal is consistent with the protection of human health and the environment whatever the place of disposal,

Noting that States should ensure that the generator should carry out duties with regard to the transport and disposal of hazardous wastes and other wastes in a manner that is consistent with the protection of the environment, whatever the place of disposal,

Fully recognizing that any State has the sovereign right to ban the entry or disposal of foreign hazardous wastes and other wastes in its territory,

Recognizing also the increasing desire for the prohibition of transboundary movements of hazardous wastes and their disposal in other States, especially developing countries,

Recognizing that transboundary movements of hazardous wastes, especially to developing countries, have a high risk of not constituting an environmentally sound management of hazardous wastes as required by this Convention,[2]

Convinced that hazardous wastes and other wastes should, as far as is compatible with environmentally sound and efficient management, be disposed of in the State where they were generated,

Aware also that transboundary movements of such wastes from the State of their generation to any other State should be permitted only when conducted under conditions which do not endanger human health and the environment, and under conditions in conformity with the provisions of this Convention,

Considering that enhanced control of transboundary movement of hazardous wastes and other wastes will act as an incentive for their environmentally sound management and for the reduction of the volume of such transboundary movement,

Convinced that States should take measures for the proper exchange of information on and control of the transboundary movement of hazardous wastes and other wastes from and to those States,

Noting that a number of international and regional agreements have addressed the issue of protection and preservation of the environment with regard to the transit of dangerous goods,

Taking into account the Declaration of the United Nations Conference on the Human Environment (Stockholm, 1972), the Cairo Guidelines and Principles for the Environmentally Sound Management of Hazardous Wastes adopted by the Governing Council of the United Nations Environment Programme (UNEP) by decision 14/30 of 17 June 1987, the Recommendations of the United Nations Commit-

1 The present text incorporates amendments to the Convention adopted subsequent to its entry into force and that are in force as at 31 March 2020. Only the text of the Convention as kept in the custody of the Secretary-General of the United Nations in his capacity as Depositary constitutes the authentic version of the Convention, as modified by any amendments and/or corrections thereto. This publication is issued for information purposes only.

2 The Conference of the Parties adopted Decision III/1 at its third meeting to amend the Convention by adding, inter alia, a new preambular paragraph 7 bis. This amendment entered into force on 5 December 2019 (depositary notification C.N.420.2019).

tee of Experts on the Transport of Dangerous Goods (formulated in 1957 and updated biennially), relevant recommendations, declarations, instruments and regulations adopted within the United Nations system and the work and studies done within other international and regional organizations,

Mindful of the spirit, principles, aims and functions of the World Charter for Nature adopted by the General Assembly of the United Nations at its thirty-seventh session (1982) as the rule of ethics in respect of the protection of the human environment and the conservation of natural resources,

Affirming that States are responsible for the fulfilment of their international obligations concerning the protection of human health and protection and preservation of the environment, and are liable in accordance with international law,

Recognizing that in the case of a material breach of the provisions of this Convention or any protocol thereto the relevant international law of treaties shall apply,

Aware of the need to continue the development and implementation of environmentally sound low-waste technologies, recycling options, good house-keeping and management systems with a view to reducing to a minimum the generation of hazardous wastes and other wastes,

Aware also of the growing international concern about the need for stringent control of transboundary movement of hazardous wastes and other wastes, and of the need as far as possible to reduce such movement to a minimum,

Concerned about the problem of illegal transboundary traffic in hazardous wastes and other wastes,

Taking into account also the limited capabilities of the developing countries to manage hazardous wastes and other wastes,

Recognizing the need to promote the transfer of technology for the sound management of hazardous wastes and other wastes produced locally, particularly to the developing countries in accordance with the spirit of the Cairo Guidelines and decision 14/16 of the Governing Council of UNEP on Promotion of the transfer of environmental protection technology,

Recognizing also that hazardous wastes and other wastes should be transported in accordance with relevant international conventions and recommendations,

Convinced also that the transboundary movement of hazardous wastes and other wastes should be permitted only when the transport and the ultimate disposal of such wastes is environmentally sound, and

Determined to protect, by strict control, human health and the environment against the adverse effects which may result from the generation and management of hazardous wastes and other wastes,

Have agreed as follows:

Article 1 – Scope of the Convention

1. The following wastes that are subject to transboundary movement shall be "hazardous wastes" for the purposes of this Convention:
   (a) Wastes that belong to any category contained in Annex I, unless they do not possess any of the characteristics contained in Annex III; and
   (b) Wastes that are not covered under paragraph (a) but are defined as, or are considered to be, hazardous wastes by the domestic legislation of the Party of export, import or transit.
2. Wastes that belong to any category contained in Annex II that are subject to transboundary movement shall be "other wastes" for the purposes of this Convention.
3. Wastes which, as a result of being radioactive, are subject to other international control systems, including international instruments, applying specifically to radioactive materials, are excluded from the scope of this Convention.
4. Wastes which derive from the normal operations of a ship, the discharge of which is covered by another international instrument, are excluded from the scope of this Convention.

Article 2 – Definitions

For the purposes of this Convention:

1. "Wastes" are substances or objects which are disposed of or are intended to be disposed of or are required to be disposed of by the provisions of national law;
2. "Management" means the collection, transport and disposal of hazardous wastes or other wastes, including after-care of disposal sites;
3. "Transboundary movement" means any movement of hazardous wastes or other wastes from an area under the national jurisdiction of one State to or through an area under the national jurisdiction of another State or to or through an area not under the national jurisdiction of any State, provided at least two States are involved in the movement;
4. "Disposal" means any operation specified in Annex IV to this Convention;
5. "Approved site or facility" means a site or facility for the disposal of hazardous wastes or other wastes which is authorized or permitted to operate for this purpose by a relevant authority of the State where the site or facility is located;
6. "Competent authority" means one governmental authority designated by a Party to be responsible, within such geographical areas as the Party may think fit, for receiving the notification of a transboundary movement of hazardous wastes or other wastes, and any information related to it, and for responding to such a notification, as provided in Article 6;
7. "Focal point" means the entity of a Party referred to in Article 5 responsible for receiving and submitting information as provided for in Articles 13 and 16;
8. "Environmentally sound management of hazardous wastes or other wastes" means taking all practicable steps to ensure that hazardous wastes or other wastes are managed in a manner which will protect human health and the environment against

the adverse effects which may result from such wastes;

9. "Area under the national jurisdiction of a State" means any land, marine area or airspace within which a State exercises administrative and regulatory responsibility in accordance with international law in regard to the protection of human health or the environment;
10. "State of export" means a Party from which a transboundary movement of hazardous wastes or other wastes is planned to be initiated or is initiated;
11. "State of import" means a Party to which a transboundary movement of hazardous wastes or other wastes is planned or takes place for the purpose of disposal therein or for the purpose of loading prior to disposal in an area not under the national jurisdiction of any State;
12. "State of transit" means any State, other than the State of export or import, through which a movement of hazardous wastes or other wastes is planned or takes place;
13. "States concerned" means Parties which are States of export or import, or transit States, whether or not Parties;
14. "Person" means any natural or legal person;
15. "Exporter" means any person under the jurisdiction of the State of export who arranges for hazardous wastes or other wastes to be exported;
16. "Importer" means any person under the jurisdiction of the State of import who arranges for hazardous wastes or other wastes to be imported;
17. "Carrier" means any person who carries out the transport of hazardous wastes or other wastes;
18. "Generator" means any person whose activity produces hazardous wastes or other wastes or, if that person is not known, the person who is in possession and/or control of those wastes;
19. "Disposer" means any person to whom hazardous wastes or other wastes are shipped and who carries out the disposal of such wastes;
20. "Political and/or economic integration organization" means an organization constituted by sovereign States to which its member States have transferred competence in respect of matters governed by this Convention and which has been duly authorized, in accordance with its internal procedures, to sign, ratify, accept, approve, formally confirm or accede to it;
21. "Illegal traffic" means any transboundary movement of hazardous wastes or other wastes as specified in Article 9.

Article 3 – National Definitions of Hazardous Wastes

1. Each Party shall, within six months of becoming a Party to this Convention, inform the Secretariat of the Convention of the wastes, other than those listed in Annexes I and II, considered or defined as hazardous under its national legislation and of any requirements concerning transboundary movement procedures applicable to such wastes.
2. Each Party shall subsequently inform the Secretariat of any significant changes to the information it has provided pursuant to paragraph 1.
3. The Secretariat shall forthwith inform all Parties of the information it has received pursuant to paragraphs 1 and 2.
4. Parties shall be responsible for making the information transmitted to them by the Secretariat under paragraph 3 available to their exporters.

Article 4 – General Obligations

1. (a) Parties exercising their right to prohibit the import of hazardous wastes or other wastes for disposal shall inform the other Parties of their decision pursuant to Article 13.
   (b) Parties shall prohibit or shall not permit the export of hazardous wastes and other wastes to the Parties which have prohibited the import of such wastes, when notified pursuant to subparagraph (a) above.
   (c) Parties shall prohibit or shall not permit the export of hazardous wastes and other wastes if the State of import does not consent in writing to the specific import, in the case where that State of import has not prohibited the import of such wastes.
2. Each Party shall take the appropriate measures to:
   (a) Ensure that the generation of hazardous wastes and other wastes within it is reduced to a minimum, taking into account social, technological and economic aspects;
   (b) Ensure the availability of adequate disposal facilities, for the environ- mentally sound management of hazardous wastes and other wastes, that shall be located, to the extent possible, within it, whatever the place of their disposal;
   (c) Ensure that persons involved in the management of hazardous wastes or other wastes within it take such steps as are necessary to prevent pollution due to hazardous wastes and other wastes arising from such management and, if such pollution occurs, to minimize the consequences thereof for human health and the environment;
   (d) Ensure that the transboundary movement of hazardous wastes and other wastes is reduced to the minimum consistent with the environmentally sound and efficient management of such wastes, and is conducted in a manner which will protect human health and the environment against the adverse effects which may result from such movement;
   (e) Not allow the export of hazardous wastes or other wastes to a State or group of States belonging to an economic and/or political integration organization that are Parties, particularly developing countries, which have prohibited by their legislation all imports, or if it has reason to believe that the wastes in question will not be managed in an environmentally sound

manner, according to criteria to be decided on by the Parties at their first meeting;

(f) Require that information about a proposed transboundary movement of hazardous wastes and other wastes be provided to the States concerned, according to Annex V A, to state clearly the effects of the proposed movement on human health and the environment;

(g) Prevent the import of hazardous wastes and other wastes if it has reason to believe that the wastes in question will not be managed in an environ- mentally sound manner;

(h) Co-operate in activities with other Parties and interested organizations, directly and through the Secretariat, including the dissemination of information on the transboundary movement of hazardous wastes and other wastes, in order to improve the environmentally sound management of such wastes and to achieve the prevention of illegal traffic.

3. The Parties consider that illegal traffic in hazardous wastes or other wastes is criminal.

4. Each Party shall take appropriate legal, administrative and other measures to implement and enforce the provisions of this Convention, including measures to prevent and punish conduct in contravention of the Convention.

5. A Party shall not permit hazardous wastes or other wastes to be exported to a non-Party or to be imported from a non-Party.

6. The Parties agree not to allow the export of hazardous wastes or other wastes for disposal within the area south of 60° South latitude, whether or not such wastes are subject to transboundary movement.

7. Furthermore, each Party shall:

(a) Prohibit all persons under its national jurisdiction from transporting or disposing of hazardous wastes or other wastes unless such persons are authorized or allowed to perform such types of operations;

(b) Require that hazardous wastes and other wastes that are to be the subject of a transboundary movement be packaged, labelled, and transported in conformity with generally accepted and recognized international rules and standards in the field of packaging, labelling, and transport, and that due account is taken of relevant internationally recognized practices;

(c) Require that hazardous wastes and other wastes be accompanied by a movement document from the point at which a transboundary movement commences to the point of disposal.

8. Each Party shall require that hazardous wastes or other wastes, to be exported, are managed in an environmentally sound manner in the State of import or elsewhere. Technical guidelines for the environmentally sound management of wastes subject to this Convention shall be decided by the Parties at their first meeting.

9. Parties shall take the appropriate measures to ensure that the transboundary movement of hazardous wastes and other wastes only be allowed if:

(a) The State of export does not have the technical capacity and the necessary facilities, capacity or suitable disposal sites in order to dispose of the wastes in question in an environmentally sound and efficient manner; or

(b) The wastes in question are required as a raw material for recycling or recovery industries in the State of import; or

(c) The transboundary movement in question is in accordance with other criteria to be decided by the Parties, provided those criteria do not differ from the objectives of this Convention.

10. The obligation under this Convention of States in which hazardous wastes and other wastes are generated to require that those wastes are managed in an environmentally sound manner may not under any circumstances be transferred to the States of import or transit.

11. Nothing in this Convention shall prevent a Party from imposing additional requirements that are consistent with the provisions of this Convention, and are in accordance with the rules of international law, in order better to protect human health and the environment.

12. Nothing in this Convention shall affect in any way the sovereignty of States over their territorial sea established in accordance with international law, and the sovereign rights and the jurisdiction which States have in their exclusive economic zones and their continental shelves in accordance with international law, and the exercise by ships and aircraft of all States of navigational rights and freedoms as provided for in international law and as reflected in relevant international instruments.

13. Parties shall undertake to review periodically the possibilities for the reduction of the amount and/or the pollution potential of hazardous wastes and other wastes which are exported to other States, in particular to developing countries.

Article 4A – General Obligations[1]

1. Each Party listed in Annex VII shall prohibit all transboundary movements of hazardous wastes which are destined for operations according to Annex IV A to States not listed in Annex VII.

2. Each Party listed in Annex VII shall phase out by 31 December 1997, and prohibit as of that date, all transboundary movements of hazardous wastes under Article 1(1)(a) of the Convention which are destined for operations according to Annex IV B to States not listed in Annex VII. Such transboundary movement shall not be prohibited unless the

1 The Conference of the Parties adopted Decision III/1 at its third meeting to amend the Convention by adding, inter alia, a new Article 4A. This amendment entered into force on 5 December 2019 (depositary notification C.N.420.2019). For information on the status of individual Parties in relation to the amendment/s, please see the Status of Ratifications page on the Basel Convention website.

wastes in question are characterized as hazardous under the Convention.

Article 5 – Designation of Competent Authorities and Focal Point

To facilitate the implementation of this Convention, the Parties shall:

1. Designate or establish one or more competent authorities and one focal point. One competent authority shall be designated to receive the notification in case of a State of transit.
2. Inform the Secretariat, within three months of the date of the entry into force of this Convention for them, which agencies they have designated as their focal point and their competent authorities.
3. Inform the Secretariat, within one month of the date of decision, of any changes regarding the designation made by them under paragraph 2 above.

Article 6 – Transboundary Movement between Parties

1. The State of export shall notify, or shall require the generator or exporter to notify, in writing, through the channel of the competent authority of the State of export, the competent authority of the States concerned of any proposed transboundary movement of hazardous wastes or other wastes. Such notification shall contain the declarations and information specified in Annex V A, written in a language acceptable to the State of import. Only one notification needs to be sent to each State concerned.
2. The State of import shall respond to the notifier in writing, consenting to the movement with or without conditions, denying permission for the movement, or requesting additional information. A copy of the final response of the State of import shall be sent to the competent authorities of the States concerned which are Parties.
3. The State of export shall not allow the generator or exporter to commence the transboundary movement until it has received written confirmation that:
   (a) The notifier has received the written consent of the State of import; and
   (b) The notifier has received from the State of import confirmation of the existence of a contract between the exporter and the disposer specifying environmentally sound management of the wastes in question.
4. Each State of transit which is a Party shall promptly acknowledge to the notifier receipt of the notification. It may subsequently respond to the notifier in writing, within 60 days, consenting to the movement with or without conditions, denying permission for the movement, or requesting additional information. The State of export shall not allow the transboundary movement to commence until it has received the written consent of the State of transit. However, if at any time a Party decides not to require prior written consent, either generally or under specific conditions, for transit transboundary movements of hazardous wastes or other wastes, or modifies its requirements in this respect, it shall forthwith inform the other Parties of its decision pursuant to Article 13. In this latter case, if no response is received by the State of export within 60 days of the receipt of a given notification by the State of transit, the State of export may allow the export to proceed through the State of transit.
5. In the case of a transboundary movement of wastes where the wastes are legally defined as or considered to be hazardous wastes only:
   (a) By the State of export, the requirements of paragraph 9 of this Article that apply to the importer or disposer and the State of import shall apply mutatis mutandis to the exporter and State of export, respectively;
   (b) By the State of import, or by the States of import and transit which are Parties, the requirements of paragraphs 1, 3, 4 and 6 of this Article that apply to the exporter and State of export shall apply mutatis mutandis to the importer or disposer and State of import, respectively; or
   (c) By any State of transit which is a Party, the provisions of paragraph 4 shall apply to such State.
6. The State of export may, subject to the written consent of the States concerned, allow the generator or the exporter to use a general notification where hazardous wastes or other wastes having the same physical and chemical characteristics are shipped regularly to the same disposer via the same customs office of exit of the State of export via the same customs office of entry of the State of import, and, in the case of transit, via the same customs office of entry and exit of the State or States of transit.
7. The States concerned may make their written consent to the use of the general notification referred to in paragraph 6 subject to the supply of certain information, such as the exact quantities or periodical lists of hazardous wastes or other wastes to be shipped.
8. The general notification and written consent referred to in paragraphs 6 and 7 may cover multiple shipments of hazardous wastes or other wastes during a maximum period of 12 months.
9. The Parties shall require that each person who takes charge of a transboundary movement of hazardous wastes or other wastes sign the movement document either upon delivery or receipt of the wastes in question. They shall also require that the disposer inform both the exporter and the competent authority of the State of export of receipt by the disposer of the wastes in question and, in due course, of the completion of disposal as specified in the notification. If no such information is received within the State of export, the competent authority of the State of export or the exporter shall so notify the State of import.
10. The notification and response required by this Article shall be transmitted to the competent authority

of the Parties concerned or to such governmental authority as may be appropriate in the case of non-Parties.

11. Any transboundary movement of hazardous wastes or other wastes shall be covered by insurance, bond or other guarantee as may be required by the State of import or any State of transit which is a Party.

Article 7 – Transboundary Movement from a Party through States which are not Parties

Paragraph 1 of Article 6 of the Convention shall apply mutatis mutandis to transboundary movement of hazardous wastes or other wastes from a Party through a State or States which are not Parties.

Article 8 – Duty to Re-import

When a transboundary movement of hazardous wastes or other wastes to which the consent of the States concerned has been given, subject to the provisions of this Convention, cannot be completed in accordance with the terms of the contract, the State of export shall ensure that the wastes in question are taken back into the State of export, by the exporter, if alternative arrangements cannot be made for their disposal in an environmentally sound manner, within 90 days from the time that the importing State informed the State of export and the Secretariat, or such other period of time as the States concerned agree. To this end, the State of export and any Party of transit shall not oppose, hinder or prevent the return of those wastes to the State of export.

Article 9 – Illegal Traffic

1. For the purpose of this Convention, any transboundary movement of hazardous wastes or other wastes:
   (a) without notification pursuant to the provisions of this Convention to all States concerned; or
   (b) without the consent pursuant to the provisions of this Convention of a State concerned; or
   (c) with consent obtained from States concerned through falsification, misrepresentation or fraud; or
   (d) that does not conform in a material way with the documents; or
   (e) that results in deliberate disposal (e.g. dumping) of hazardous wastes or other wastes in contravention of this Convention and of general principles of international law, shall be deemed to be illegal traffic.
2. In case of a transboundary movement of hazardous wastes or other wastes deemed to be illegal traffic as the result of conduct on the part of the exporter or generator, the State of export shall ensure that the wastes in question are:
   (a) taken back by the exporter or the generator or, if necessary, by itself into the State of export, or, if impracticable,
   (b) are otherwise disposed of in accordance with the provisions of this Convention, within 30 days from the time the State of export has been informed about the illegal traffic or such other period of time as States concerned may agree. To this end the Parties concerned shall not oppose, hinder or prevent the return of those wastes to the State of export.
3. In the case of a transboundary movement of hazardous wastes or other wastes deemed to be illegal traffic as the result of conduct on the part of the importer or disposer, the State of import shall ensure that the wastes in question are disposed of in an environmentally sound manner by the importer or disposer or, if necessary, by itself within 30 days from the time the illegal traffic has come to the attention of the State of import or such other period of time as the States concerned may agree. To this end, the Parties concerned shall co-operate, as necessary, in the disposal of the wastes in an environmentally sound manner.
4. In cases where the responsibility for the illegal traffic cannot be assigned either to the exporter or generator or to the importer or disposer, the Parties concerned or other Parties, as appropriate, shall ensure, through co-operation, that the wastes in question are disposed of as soon as possible in an environmentally sound manner either in the State of export or the State of import or elsewhere as appropriate.
5. Each Party shall introduce appropriate national/domestic legislation to prevent and punish illegal traffic. The Parties shall co-operate with a view to achieving the objects of this Article.

Article 10 – International Co-operation

1. The Parties shall co-operate with each other in order to improve and achieve environmentally sound management of hazardous wastes and other wastes.
2. To this end, the Parties shall:
   (a) Upon request, make available information, whether on a bilateral or multilateral basis, with a view to promoting the environmentally sound management of hazardous wastes and other wastes, including harmonization of technical standards and practices for the adequate management of hazardous wastes and other wastes;
   (b) Co-operate in monitoring the effects of the management of hazardous wastes on human health and the environment;
   (c) Co-operate, subject to their national laws, regulations and policies, in the development and implementation of new environmentally sound low-waste technologies and the improvement of existing technologies with a view to eliminating, as far as practicable, the generation of hazardous wastes and other wastes and achieving more effective and efficient methods of ensuring their management in an environmentally sound manner, including the study of the economic, social and environmental effects of the adoption of such new or improved technologies;

(d) Co-operate actively, subject to their national laws, regulations and policies, in the transfer of technology and management systems related to the environmentally sound management of hazardous wastes and other wastes. They shall also co-operate in developing the technical capacity among Parties, especially those which may need and request technical assistance in this field;

(e) Co-operate in developing appropriate technical guidelines and/or codes of practice.

3. The Parties shall employ appropriate means to co-operate in order to assist developing countries in the implementation of subparagraphs a, b, c and d of paragraph 2 of Article 4.

4. Taking into account the needs of developing countries, co-operation between Parties and the competent international organizations is encouraged to promote, inter alia, public awareness, the development of sound management of hazardous wastes and other wastes and the adoption of new low-waste technologies.

Article 11 – Bilateral, Multilateral and Regional Agreements

1. Notwithstanding the provisions of Article 4 paragraph 5, Parties may enter into bilateral, multilateral, or regional agreements or arrangements regarding transboundary movement of hazardous wastes or other wastes with Parties or non-Parties provided that such agreements or arrangements do not derogate from the environmentally sound management of hazardous wastes and other wastes as required by this Convention. These agreements or arrangements shall stipulate provisions which are not less environmentally sound than those provided for by this Convention in particular taking into account the interests of developing countries.

2. Parties shall notify the Secretariat of any bilateral, multilateral or regional agreements or arrangements referred to in paragraph 1 and those which they have entered into prior to the entry into force of this Convention for them, for the purpose of controlling transboundary movements of hazardous wastes and other wastes which take place entirely among the Parties to such agreements. The provisions of this Convention shall not affect transboundary movements which take place pursuant to such agreements provided that such agreements are compatible with the environmentally sound management of hazardous wastes and other wastes as required by this Convention.

Article 12 – Consultations on Liability

The Parties shall co-operate with a view to adopting, as soon as practicable, a protocol setting out appropriate rules and procedures in the field of liability and compensation for damage resulting from the transboundary movement and disposal of hazardous wastes and other wastes.

Article 13 – Transmission of Information

1. The Parties shall, whenever it comes to their knowledge, ensure that, in the case of an accident occurring during the transboundary movement of hazardous wastes or other wastes or their disposal, which are likely to present risks to human health and the environment in other States, those States are immediately informed.

2. The Parties shall inform each other, through the Secretariat, of:

(a) Changes regarding the designation of competent authorities and/or focal points, pursuant to Article 5;

(b) Changes in their national definition of hazardous wastes, pursuant to Article 3;

and, as soon as possible,

(c) Decisions made by them not to consent totally or partially to the import of hazardous wastes or other wastes for disposal within the area under their national jurisdiction;

(d) Decisions taken by them to limit or ban the export of hazardous wastes or other wastes;

(e) Any other information required pursuant to paragraph 4 of this Article.

3. The Parties, consistent with national laws and regulations, shall transmit, through the Secretariat, to the Conference of the Parties established under Article 15, before the end of each calendar year, a report on the previous calendar year, containing the following information:

(a) Competent authorities and focal points that have been designated by them pursuant to Article 5;

(b) Information regarding transboundary movements of hazardous wastes or other wastes in which they have been involved, including:

(i) The amount of hazardous wastes and other wastes exported, their category, characteristics, destination, any transit country and disposal method as stated on the response to notification;

(ii) The amount of hazardous wastes and other wastes imported, their category, characteristics, origin, and disposal methods;

(iii) Disposals which did not proceed as intended;

(iv) Efforts to achieve a reduction of the amount of hazardous wastes or other wastes subject to transboundary movement;

(c) Information on the measures adopted by them in implementation of this Convention;

(d) Information on available qualified statistics which have been compiled by them on the effects on human health and the environment of the generation, transportation and disposal of hazardous wastes or other wastes;

(e) Information concerning bilateral, multilateral and regional agreements and arrangements entered into pursuant to Article 11 of this Convention;

(f) Information on accidents occurring during the transboundary movement and disposal of hazardous wastes and other wastes and on the measures undertaken to deal with them;

(g) Information on disposal options operated within the area of their national jurisdiction;

(h) Information on measures undertaken for development of technologies for the reduction and/or elimination of production of hazardous wastes and other wastes; and

(i) Such other matters as the Conference of the Parties shall deem relevant.

4. The Parties, consistent with national laws and regulations, shall ensure that copies of each notification concerning any given transboundary movement of hazardous wastes or other wastes, and the response to it, are sent to the Secretariat when a Party considers that its environment may be affected by that transboundary movement has requested that this should be done.

Article 14 – Financial Aspects

1. The Parties agree that, according to the specific needs of different regions and subregions, regional or sub-regional centres for training and technology transfers regarding the management of hazardous wastes and other wastes and the minimization of their generation should be established. The Parties shall decide on the establishment of appropriate funding mechanisms of a voluntary nature.

2. The Parties shall consider the establishment of a revolving fund to assist on an interim basis in case of emergency situations to minimize damage from accidents arising from transboundary movements of hazardous wastes and other wastes or during the disposal of those wastes.

Article 15 – Conference of the Parties

1. A Conference of the Parties is hereby established. The first meeting of the Conference of the Parties shall be convened by the Executive Director of UNEP not later than one year after the entry into force of this Convention. Thereafter, ordinary meetings of the Conference of the Parties shall be held at regular intervals to be determined by the Conference at its first meeting.

2. Extraordinary meetings of the Conference of the Parties shall be held at such other times as may be deemed necessary by the Conference, or at the written request of any Party, provided that, within six months of the request being communicated to them by the Secretariat, it is supported by at least one third of the Parties.

3. The Conference of the Parties shall by consensus agree upon and adopt rules of procedure for itself and for any subsidiary body it may establish, as well as financial rules to determine in particular the financial participation of the Parties under this Convention.

4. The Parties at their first meeting shall consider any additional measures needed to assist them in fulfilling their responsibilities with respect to the protection and the preservation of the marine environment in the context of this Convention.

5. The Conference of the Parties shall keep under continuous review and evaluation the effective implementation of this Convention, and, in addition, shall:

(a) Promote the harmonization of appropriate policies, strategies and measures for minimizing harm to human health and the environment by hazardous wastes and other wastes;

(b) Consider and adopt, as required, amendments to this Convention and its annexes, taking into consideration, inter alia, available scientific, technical, economic and environmental information;

(c) Consider and undertake any additional action that may be required for the achievement of the purposes of this Convention in the light of experience gained in its operation and in the operation of the agreements and arrangements envisaged in Article 11;

(d) Consider and adopt protocols as required; and

(e) Establish such subsidiary bodies as are deemed necessary for the implementation of this Convention.

6. The United Nations, its specialized agencies, as well as any State not Party to this Convention, may be represented as observers at meetings of the Conference of the Parties. Any other body or agency, whether national or international, governmental or non-governmental, qualified in fields relating to hazardous wastes or other wastes which has informed the Secretariat of its wish to be represented as an observer at a meeting of the Conference of the Parties, may be admitted unless at least one third of the Parties present object. The admission and participation of observers shall be subject to the rules of procedure adopted by the Conference of the Parties.

7. The Conference of the Parties shall undertake three years after the entry into force of this Convention, and at least every six years thereafter, an evaluation of its effectiveness and, if deemed necessary, to consider the adoption of a complete or partial ban of transboundary movements of hazardous wastes and other wastes in light of the latest scientific, environmental, technical and economic information.

Article 16 – Secretariat

1. The functions of the Secretariat shall be:

(a) To arrange for and service meetings provided for in Articles 15 and 17;

(b) To prepare and transmit reports based upon information received in accordance with Articles 3, 4, 6, 11 and 13 as well as upon information derived from meetings of subsidiary bodies established under Article 15 as well as upon, as appropriate, information provided by relevant intergovernmental and non-governmental entities;

(c) To prepare reports on its activities carried out in implementation of its functions under this Convention and present them to the Conference of the Parties;

(d) To ensure the necessary coordination with relevant international bodies, and in particular to enter into such administrative and contractual arrangements as may be required for the effective discharge of its function;

(e) To communicate with focal points and competent authorities established by the Parties in accordance with Article 5 of this Convention;

(f) To compile information concerning authorized national sites and facilities of Parties available for the disposal of their hazardous wastes and other wastes and to circulate this information among Parties;

(g) To receive and convey information from and to Parties on:

- sources of technical assistance and training;
- available technical and scientific know-how;
- sources of advice and expertise; and
- availability of resources with a view to assisting them, upon request, in such areas as:
- the handling of the notification system of this Convention;
- the management of hazardous wastes and other wastes;
- environmentally sound technologies relating to hazardous wastes and other wastes, such as low- and non-waste technology;
- the assessment of disposal capabilities and sites;
- the monitoring of hazardous wastes and other wastes; and
- emergency responses;

(h) To provide Parties, upon request, with information on consultants or consulting firms having the necessary technical competence in the field, which can assist them to examine a notification for a transboundary movement, the concurrence of a shipment of hazardous wastes or other wastes with the relevant notification, and/or the fact that the proposed disposal facilities for hazardous wastes or other wastes are environmentally sound, when they have reason to believe that the wastes in question will not be managed in an environmentally sound manner. Any such examination would not be at the expense of the Secretariat;

(i) To assist Parties upon request in their identification of cases of illegal traffic and to circulate immediately to the Parties concerned any information it has received regarding illegal traffic;

(j) To co-operate with Parties and with relevant and competent international organizations and agencies in the provision of experts and equipment for the purpose of rapid assistance to States in the event of an emergency situation; and

(k) To perform such other functions relevant to the purposes of this Convention as may be determined by the Conference of the Parties.

2. The secretariat functions will be carried out on an interim basis by UNEP until the completion of the first meeting of the Conference of the Parties held pursuant to Article 15.

3. At its first meeting, the Conference of the Parties shall designate the Secretariat from among those existing competent intergovernmental organizations which have signified their willingness to carry out the secretariat functions under this Convention. At this meeting, the Conference of the Parties shall also evaluate the implementation by the interim Secretariat of the functions assigned to it, in particular under paragraph 1 above, and decide upon the structures appropriate for those functions.

Article 17 – Amendment of the Convention

1. Any Party may propose amendments to this Convention and any Party to a protocol may propose amendments to that protocol. Such amendments shall take due account, inter alia, of relevant scientific and technical considerations.

2. Amendments to this Convention shall be adopted at a meeting of the Conference of the Parties. Amendments to any protocol shall be adopted at a meeting of the Parties to the protocol in question. The text of any proposed amendment to this Convention or to any protocol, except as may otherwise be provided in such protocol, shall be communicated to the Parties by the Secretariat at least six months before the meeting at which it is proposed for adoption. The Secretariat shall also communicate proposed amendments to the Signatories to this Convention for information.

3. The Parties shall make every effort to reach agreement on any proposed amendment to this Convention by consensus. If all efforts at consensus have been exhausted, and no agreement reached, the amendment shall as a last resort be adopted by a three-fourths majority vote of the Parties present and voting at the meeting, and shall be submitted by the Depositary to all Parties for ratification, approval, formal confirmation or acceptance.

4. The procedure mentioned in paragraph 3 above shall apply to amendments to any protocol, except that a two-thirds majority of the Parties to that protocol present and voting at the meeting shall suffice for their adoption.

5. Instruments of ratification, approval, formal confirmation or acceptance of amendments shall be deposited with the Depositary. Amendments adopted in accordance with paragraphs 3 or 4 above shall enter into force between Parties having accepted them on the ninetieth day after the receipt by the Depositary of their instrument of ratification, approval, formal confirmation or acceptance by at least three-fourths of the Parties who accepted

them or by at least two thirds of the Parties to the protocol concerned who accepted them, except as may otherwise be provided in such protocol. The amendments shall enter into force for any other Party on the ninetieth day after that Party deposits its instrument of ratification, approval, formal confirmation or acceptance of the amendments.

6. For the purpose of this Article, "Parties present and voting" means Parties present and casting an affirmative or negative vote.

Article 18 – Adoption and Amendment of Annexes

1. The annexes to this Convention or to any protocol shall form an integral part of this Convention or of such protocol, as the case may be and, unless expressly provided otherwise, a reference to this Convention or its protocols constitutes at the same time a reference to any annexes thereto. Such annexes shall be restricted to scientific, technical and administrative matters.
2. Except as may be otherwise provided in any protocol with respect to its annexes, the following procedure shall apply to the proposal, adoption and entry into force of additional annexes to this Convention or of annexes to a protocol:
   (a) Annexes to this Convention and its protocols shall be proposed and adopted according to the procedure laid down in Article 17, paragraphs 2, 3 and 4;
   (b) Any Party that is unable to accept an additional annex to this Convention or an annex to any protocol to which it is party shall so notify the Depositary, in writing, within six months from the date of the communication of the adoption by the Depositary. The Depositary shall without delay notify all Parties of any such notification received. A Party may at any time substitute an acceptance for a previous declaration of objection and the annexes shall thereupon enter into force for that Party;
   (c) On the expiry of six months from the date of the circulation of the communication by the Depositary, the annex shall become effective for all Parties to this Convention or to any protocol concerned, which have not submitted a notification in accordance with the provision of subparagraph (b) above.
3. The proposal, adoption and entry into force of amendments to annexes to this Convention or to any protocol shall be subject to the same procedure as for the proposal, adoption and entry into force of annexes to the Convention or annexes to a protocol. Annexes and amendments thereto shall take due account, inter alia, of relevant scientific and technical considerations.
4. If an additional annex or an amendment to an annex involves an amendment to this Convention or to any protocol, the additional annex or amended annex shall not enter into force until such time the amendment to this Convention or to the protocol enters into force.

Article 19 – Verification

Any Party which has reason to believe that another Party is acting or has acted in breach of its obligations under this Convention may inform the Secretariat thereof, and in such an event, shall simultaneously and immediately inform, directly or through the Secretariat, the Party against whom the allegations are made. All relevant information should be submitted by the Secretariat to the Parties.

Article 20 – Settlement of Disputes

1. In case of a dispute between Parties as to the interpretation or application of, or compliance with, this Convention or any protocol thereto, they shall seek a settlement of the dispute through negotiation or any other peaceful means of their own choice.
2. If the Parties concerned cannot settle their dispute through the means mentioned in the preceding paragraph, the dispute, if the Parties to the dispute agree, shall be submitted to the International Court of Justice or to arbitration under the conditions set out in Annex VI on Arbitration. However, failure to reach common agreement on submission of the dispute to the International Court of Justice or to arbitration shall not absolve the Parties from the responsibility of continuing to seek to resolve it by the means referred to in paragraph 1.
3. When ratifying, accepting, approving, formally confirming or acceding to this Convention, or at any time thereafter, a State or political and/or economic integration organization may declare that it recognizes as compulsory ipso facto and without special agreement, in relation to any Party accepting the same obligation:
   (a) submission of the dispute to the International Court of Justice; and/or
   (b) arbitration in accordance with the procedures set out in Annex VI.

   Such declaration shall be notified in writing to the Secretariat which shall communicate it to the Parties.

Article 21 – Signature

This Convention shall be open for signature by States, by Namibia, represented by the United Nations Council for Namibia, and by political and/or economic integration organizations, in Basel on 22 March 1989, at the Federal Department of Foreign Affairs of Switzerland in Berne from 23 March 1989 to 30 June 1989 and at United Nations Headquarters in New York from 1 July 1989 to 22 March 1990.

Article 22 – Ratification, Acceptance, Formal Confirmation or Approval

1. This Convention shall be subject to ratification, acceptance or approval by States and by Namibia, represented by the United Nations Council for Namibia, and to formal confirmation or approval by political and/or economic integration organizations. Instruments of ratification, acceptance, formal confirmation, or approval shall be deposited with the Depositary.

2. Any organization referred to in paragraph 1 above which becomes a Party to this Convention without any of its member States being a Party shall be bound by all the obligations under the Convention. In the case of such organizations, one or more of whose member States is a Party to the Convention, the organization and its member States shall decide on their respective responsibilities for the performance of their obligations under the Convention. In such cases, the organization and the member States shall not be entitled to exercise rights under the Convention concurrently.
3. In their instruments of formal confirmation or approval, the organizations referred to in paragraph 1 above shall declare the extent of their competence with respect to the matters governed by the Convention. These organizations shall also inform the Depositary, who will inform the Parties of any substantial modification in the extent of their competence.

Article 23 – Accession

1. This Convention shall be open for accession by States, by Namibia, represented by the United Nations Council for Namibia, and by political and/or economic integration organizations from the day after the date on which the Convention is closed for signature. The instruments of accession shall be deposited with the Depositary.
2. In their instruments of accession, the organizations referred to in paragraph 1 above shall declare the extent of their competence with respect to the matters governed by the Convention. These organizations shall also inform the Depositary of any substantial modification in the extent of their competence.
3. The provisions of Article 22, paragraph 2, shall apply to political and/or economic integration organizations which accede to this Convention.

Article 24 – Right to Vote

1. Except as provided for in paragraph 2 below, each Contracting Party to this Convention shall have one vote.
2. Political and/or economic integration organizations, in matters within their competence, in accordance with Article 22, paragraph 3, and Article 23, paragraph 2, shall exercise their right to vote with a number of votes equal to the number of their member States which are Parties to the Convention or the relevant protocol. Such organizations shall not exercise their right to vote if their member States exercise theirs, and vice versa.

Article 25 – Entry into Force

1. This Convention shall enter into force on the ninetieth day after the date of deposit of the twentieth instrument of ratification, acceptance, formal confirmation, approval or accession.
2. For each State or political and/or economic integration organization which ratifies, accepts, approves or formally confirms this Convention or accedes thereto after the date of the deposit of the twentieth instrument of ratification, acceptance, approval, formal confirmation or accession, it shall enter into force on the ninetieth day after the date of deposit by such State or political and/or economic integration organization of its instrument of ratification, acceptance, approval, formal confirmation or accession.
3. For the purpose of paragraphs 1 and 2 above, any instrument deposited by a political and/or economic integration organization shall not be counted as additional to those deposited by member States of such organization.

Article 26 – Reservations and Declarations

1. No reservation or exception may be made to this Convention.
2. Paragraph 1 of this Article does not preclude a State or political and/or economic integration organization, when signing, ratifying, accepting, approving, formally confirming or acceding to this Convention, from making declarations or statements, however phrased or named, with a view, inter alia, to the harmonization of its laws and regulations with the provisions of this Convention, provided that such declarations or statements do not purport to exclude or to modify the legal effects of the provisions of the Convention in their application to that State.

Article 27 – Withdrawal

1. At any time after three years from the date on which this Convention has entered into force for a Party, that Party may withdraw from the Convention by giving written notification to the Depositary.
2. Withdrawal shall be effective one year from receipt of notification by the Depositary, or on such later date as may be specified in the notification.

Article 28 – Depository

The Secretary-General of the United Nations shall be the Depository of this Convention and of any protocol thereto.

Article 29 – Authentic texts

The original Arabic, Chinese, English, French, Russian and Spanish texts of this Convention are equally authentic.

IN WITNESS WHEREOF the undersigned, being duly authorized to that effect, have signed this Convention.

Done at Basel on the 22 day of March 1989.

Annex I – Categories of wastes to be controlled

Waste Streams

Y1	Clinical wastes from medical care in hospitals, medical centers and clinics
Y2	Wastes from the production and preparation of pharmaceutical products
Y3	Waste pharmaceuticals, drugs and medicines
Y4	Wastes from the production, formulation and use of biocides and phytopharmaceuticals
Y5	Wastes from the manufacture, formulation and use of wood preserving chemicals
Y6	Wastes from the production, formulation and use of organic solvents
Y7	Wastes from heat treatment and tempering operations containing cyanides
Y8	Waste mineral oils unfit for their originally intended use
Y9	Waste oils/water, hydrocarbons/water mixtures, emulsions
Y10	Waste substances and articles containing or contaminated with polychlorinated biphenyls (PCBs) and/or polychlorinated terphenyls (PCTs) and/or polybrominated biphenyls (PBBs)
Y11	Waste tarry residues arising from refining, distillation and any pyrolytic treatment
Y12	Wastes from production, formulation and use of inks, dyes, pigments, paints, lacquers, varnish
Y13	Wastes from production, formulation and use of resins, latex, plasticizers, glues/adhesives
Y14	Waste chemical substances arising from research and development or teaching activities which are not identified and/or are new and whose effects on man and/or the environment are not known
Y15	Wastes of an explosive nature not subject to other legislation
Y16	Wastes from production, formulation and use of photographic chemicals and processing materials
Y17	Wastes resulting from surface treatment of metals and plastics
Y18	Residues arising from industrial waste disposal operations

Waste having as constituents:

Y19	Metal carbonyls
Y20	Beryllium; beryllium compounds
Y21	Hexavalent chromium compounds
Y22	Copper compounds
Y23	Zinc compounds
Y24	Arsenic; arsenic compounds
Y25	Selenium; selenium compounds
Y26	Cadmium; cadmium compounds
Y27	Antimony; antimony compounds
Y28	Tellurium; tellurium compounds
Y29	Mercury; mercury compounds
Y30	Thallium; thallium compounds
Y31	Lead; lead compounds
Y32	Inorganic fluorine compounds excluding calcium fluoride
Y33	Inorganic cyanides
Y34	Acidic solutions or acids in solid form
Y35	Basic solutions or bases in solid form
Y36	Asbestos (dust and fibres)
Y37	Organic phosphorus compounds
Y38	Organic cyanides
Y39	Phenols; phenol compounds including chlorophenols
Y40	Ethers
Y41	Halogenated organic solvents
Y42	Organic solvents excluding halogenated solvents
Y43	Any congenor of polychlorinated dibenzo-furan
Y44	Any congenor of polychlorinated dibenzo-p-dioxin
Y45	Organohalogen compounds other than substances referred to in this Annex (e.g. Y39, Y41, Y42, Y43, Y44)

(a) To facilitate the application of this Convention, and subject to paragraphs (b), (c) and (d), wastes listed in Annex VIII are characterized as hazardous pursuant to Article 1, paragraph 1 (a), of this Convention, and wastes listed in Annex IX are not covered by Article 1, paragraph 1 (a), of this Convention.

(b) Designation of a waste on Annex VIII does not preclude, in a particular case, the use of Annex III to demonstrate that a waste is not hazardous pursuant to Article 1, paragraph 1 (a), of this Convention.

(c) Designation of a waste on Annex IX does not preclude, in a particular case, characterization of such a waste as hazardous pursuant to Article 1, paragraph 1 (a), of this Convention if it contains Annex I material to an extent causing it to exhibit an Annex III characteristic.

(d) Annexes VIII and IX do not affect the application of Article 1, paragraph 1 (a), of this Convention for the purpose of characterization of wastes.[4]

Annex II – Categories of wastes requiring special consideration[5]

Y46	Wastes collected from households
Y47	Residues arising from the incineration of household wastes

4 The amendment whereby paragraphs (a), (b), (c) and (d) were added to at the end of Annex I entered into force on 6 November 1998, six months following the issuance of depositary notification C.N.77.1998 of 6 May 1998 (reflecting Decision IV/9, adopted by the Conference of the Parties at its fourth meeting).

5 This amendment to Annex II whereby one new entry was added entered into force on 24 March 2020 (depositary notification C.N. 432.2019), reflecting decision BC-14/12 adopted by the Conference of the Parties at its fourteenth meeting. For information on the status of individual Parties in relation to the amendment/s, please see the Status of Ratifications page on the Basel Convention website.

Y48[6,7]	Plastic waste, including mixtures of such waste, with the exception of the following: – Plastic waste that is hazardous waste pursuant to paragraph 1 (a) of Article 1[8] – Plastic waste listed below, provided it is destined for recycling[9] in an environmentally sound manner and almost free from contamination and other types of wastes:[10] – Plastic waste almost exclusively[6] consisting of one non-halogenated polymer, including but not limited to the following polymers: – Polyethylene (PE) – Polypropylene (PP) – Polystyrene (PS) – Acrylonitrile butadiene styrene (ABS) – Polyethylene terephthalate (PET) – Polycarbonates (PC) – Polyethers – Plastic waste almost exclusively[11] consisting of one cured resin or condensation product, including but not limited to the following resins: – Urea formaldehyde resins – Phenol formaldehyde resins – Melamine formaldehyde resins – Epoxy resins – Alkyd resins – Plastic waste almost exclusively[11] consisting of one of the following fluorinated polymers:[12] – Perfluoroethylene/propylene (FEP) – Perfluoroalkoxy alkanes: – Tetrafluoroethylene/ –perfluoroalkyl vinyl ether (PFA) – Tetrafluoroethylene/–perfluoromethyl vinyl ether (MFA) – Polyvinylfluoride (PVF) – Polyvinylidenefluoride (PVDF) – Mixtures of plastic waste, consisting of polyethylene (PE), polypropylene (PP) and/or polyethylene terephthalate (PET), provided they are destined for separate recycling[13] of each material and in an environmentally sound manner and almost free from contamination and other types of wastes.[10]

Annex III – List of hazardous characteristics

UN Class[14]	Code	Characteristic
1	H1	Explosive
		An explosive substance or waste is a solid or liquid substance or waste (or mixture of substances or wastes) which is in itself capable by chemical reaction of producing gas at such a temperature and pressure and at such a speed as to cause damage to the surroundings.

6 This entry becomes effective as of 1 January 2021.
7 Parties can impose stricter requirements in relation to this entry.
8 Note the related entry on list A A3210 in Annex VIII.
9 Recycling/reclamation of organic substances that are not used as solvents (R3 in Annex IV, sect. B) or, if needed, temporary storage limited to one instance, provided that it is followed by operation R3 and evidenced by contractual or relevant official documentation.
10 In relation to "almost free from contamination and other types of wastes", international and national specifications may offer a point of reference.
11 In relation to "almost exclusively", international and national specifications may offer a point of reference.
12 Post-consumer wastes are excluded.
13 Recycling/reclamation of organic substances that are not used as solvents (R3 in Annex IV, sect. B), with prior sorting and, if needed, temporary storage limited to one instance, provided that it is followed by operation R3 and evidenced by contractual or relevant official documentation.
14 Corresponds to the hazard classification system included in the United Nations Recommendations on the Transport of Dangerous Goods (ST/SG/AC.10/1Rev.5, United Nations, New York, 1988).

UN Class[14]	Code	Characteristic
3	H3	Flammable liquids
		The word "flammable" has the same meaning as "inflammable". Flammable liquids are liquids, or mixtures of liquids, or liquids containing solids in solution or suspension (for example, paints, varnishes, lacquers, etc., but not including substances or wastes otherwise classified on account of their dangerous characteristics) which give off a flammable vapour at temperatures of not more than 60.5°C, closed-cup test, or not more than 65.6°C, open-cup test. (Since the results of open-cup tests and of closed-cup tests are not strictly comparable and even individual results by the same test are often variable, regulations varying from the above figures to make allowance for such differences would be within the spirit of this definition.)
4.1	H4.1	Flammable solids
		Solids, or waste solids, other than those classed as explosives, which under conditions encountered in transport are readily combustible, or may cause or contribute to fire through friction.
4.2	H4.2	Substances or wastes liable to spontaneous combustion
		Substances or wastes which are liable to spontaneous heating under normal conditions encountered in transport, or to heating up on contact with air, and being then liable to catch fire.
4.3	H4.3	Substances or wastes which, in contact with water emit flammable gases
		Substances or wastes which, by interaction with water, are liable to become spontaneously flammable or to give off flammable gases in dangerous quantities.
5.1	H5.1	Oxidizing
		Substances or wastes which, while in themselves not necessarily combustible, may, generally by yielding oxygen cause, or contribute to, the combustion of other materials.
5.2	H5.2	Organic Peroxides
		Organic substances or wastes which contain the bivalent-o-o-structure are thermally unstable substances which may undergo exothermic self-accelerating decomposition.
6.1	H6.1	Poisonous (Acute)
		Substances or wastes liable either to cause death or serious injury or to harm human health if swallowed or inhaled or by skin contact.
6.2	H6.2	Infectious substances
		Substances or wastes containing viable micro organisms or their toxins which are known or suspected to cause disease in animals or humans.
8	H8	Corrosives
		Substances or wastes which, by chemical action, will cause severe damage when in contact with living tissue, or, in the case of leakage, will materially damage, or even destroy, other goods or the means of transport; they may also cause other hazards.
9	H10	Liberation of toxic gases in contact with air or water
		Substances or wastes which, by interaction with air or water, are liable to give off toxic gases in dangerous quantities.
9	H11	Toxic (Delayed or chronic)
		Substances or wastes which, if they are inhaled or ingested or if they penetrate the skin, may involve delayed or chronic effects, including carcinogenicity.
9	H12	Ecotoxic
		Substances or wastes which if released present or may present immediate or delayed adverse impacts to the environment by means of bioaccumulation and/or toxic effects upon biotic systems.

UN Class[14]	Code	Characteristic
9	H13	Capable, by any means, after disposal, of yielding another material, e.g., leachate, which possesses any of the characteristics listed above.

Tests

The potential hazards posed by certain types of wastes are not yet fully documented; tests to define quantitatively these hazards do not exist. Further research is necessary in order to develop means to characterise potential hazards posed to man and/or the environment by these wastes. Standardized tests have been derived with respect to pure substances and materials. Many countries have developed national tests which can be applied to materials listed in Annex I, in order to decide if these materials exhibit any of the characteristics listed in this Annex.

Annex IV – Disposal Operations

A. Operations which do not lead to the possibility of resource recovery, recycling, reclamation, direct re-use or alternative uses

Section A encompasses all such disposal operations which occur in practice.

D1	Deposit into or onto land, (e.g., landfill, etc.)
D2	Land treatment, (e.g., biodegradation of liquid or sludgy discards in soils, etc.)
D3	Deep injection, (e.g., injection of pumpable discards into wells, salt domes of naturally occurring repositories, etc.)
D4	Surface impoundment, (e.g., placement of liquid or sludge discards into pits, ponds or lagoons, etc.)
D5	Specially engineered landfill, (e.g., placement into lined discrete cells which are capped and isolated from one another and the environment, etc.)
D6	Release into a water body except seas/oceans
D7	Release into seas/oceans including sea-bed insertion
D8	Biological treatment not specified elsewhere in this Annex which results in final compounds or mixtures which are discarded by means of any of the operations in Section A
D9	Physico chemical treatment not specified elsewhere in this Annex which results in final compounds or mixtures which are discarded by means of any of the operations in Section A, (e.g., evaporation, drying, calcination, neutralization, precipitation, etc.)
D10	Incineration on land
D11	Incineration at sea
D12	Permanent storage (e.g., emplacement of containers in a mine, etc.)
D13	Blending or mixing prior to submission to any of the operations in Section A
D14	Repackaging prior to submission to any of the operations in Section A
D15	Storage pending any of the operations in Section A

B. Operations which may lead to resource recovery, recycling reclamation, direct re-use or alternative uses

Section B encompasses all such operations with respect to materials legally defined as or considered to be hazardous wastes and which otherwise would have been destined for operations included in Section A

R1	Use as a fuel (other than in direct incineration) or other means to generate energy
R2	Solvent reclamation/regeneration
R3	Recycling/reclamation of organic substances which are not used as solvents
R4	Recycling/reclamation of metals and metal compounds
R5	Recycling/reclamation of other inorganic materials
R6	Regeneration of acids or bases
R7	Recovery of components used for pollution abatement
R8	Recovery of components from catalysts
R9	Used oil re-refining or other reuses of previously used oil
R10	Land treatment resulting in benefit to agriculture or ecological improvement
R11	Uses of residual materials obtained from any of the operations numbered R1-R10

R12	Exchange of wastes for submission to any of the operations numbered R1-R11
R13	Accumulation of material intended for any operation in Section B

Annex V A – Information to be provided on notification

1. Reason for waste export
2. Exporter of the waste[1]
3. Generator(s) of the waste and site of generation[1]
4. Disposer of the waste and actual site of disposal[1]
5. Intended carrier(s) of the waste or their agents, if known[1]
6. Country of export of the waste Competent authority[2]
7. Expected countries of transit Competent authority[2]
8. Country of import of the waste Competent authority[2]
9. General or single notification
10. Projected date(s) of shipment(s) and period of time over which waste is to be exported and proposed itinerary (including point of entry and exit)[3]
11. Means of transport envisaged (road, rail, sea, air, inland waters)
12. Information relating to insurance[4]
13. Designation and physical description of the waste including Y number and UN number and its composition[5] and information on any special handling requirements including emergency provisions in case of accidents
14. Type of packaging envisaged (e.g. bulk, drummed, tanker)
15. Estimated quantity in weight/volume[6]
16. Process by which the waste is generated[7]
17. For wastes listed in Annex I, classifications from Annex III: hazardous characteristic, H number, and UN class
18. Method of disposal as per Annex IV
19. Declaration by the generator and exporter that the information is correct
20. Information transmitted (including technical description of the plant) to the exporter or generator from the disposer of the waste upon which the latter has based his assessment that there was no reason to believe that the wastes will not be managed in an environmentally sound manner in accordance with the laws and regulations of the country of import
21. Information concerning the contract between the exporter and disposer.

Annex V B – Information to be provided on the movement document

1. Exporter of the waste[1]
2. Generator(s) of the waste and site of generation[1]
3. Disposer of the waste and actual site of disposal[1]
4. Carrier(s) of the waste[1] or his agent(s)
5. Subject of general or single notification
6. The date the transboundary movement started and date(s) and signature on receipt by each person who takes charge of the waste
7. Means of transport (road, rail, inland waterway, sea, air) including countries of export, transit and import, also point of entry and exit where these have been designated
8. General description of the waste (physical state, proper UN shipping name and class, UN number, Y number and H number as applicable)
9. Information on special handling requirements including emergency provision in case of accidents
10. Type and number of packages
11. Quantity in weight/volume
12. Declaration by the generator or exporter that the information is correct
13. Declaration by the generator or exporter indicating no objection from the competent authorities of all States concerned which are Parties
14. Certification by disposer of receipt at designated disposal facility and indication of method of disposal and of the approximate date of disposal.

The information required on the movement document shall where possible be integrated in one document with that required under transport rules. Where this is not possible the information should complement rather than duplicate that required under the transport rules. The movement document shall carry instructions as to who is to provide information and fill-out any form.

---

1 Full name and address, telephone, telex or telefax number and the name, address, telephone, telex or telefax number of the person to be contacted.
2 Full name and address, telephone, telex or telefax number.
3 In the case of a general notification covering several shipments, either the expected dates of each shipment or, if this is not known, the expected frequency of the shipments will be required.
4 Information to be provided on relevant insurance requirements and how they are met by exporter, carrier and disposer.
5 The nature and the concentration of the most hazardous components, in terms of toxicity and other dangers presented by the waste both in handling and in relation to the proposed disposal method.
6 In the case of a general notification covering several shipments, both the estimated total quantity and the estimated quantities for each individual shipment will be required.
7 Insofar as this is necessary to assess the hazard and determine the appropriateness of the proposed disposal operation.

1 Full name and address, telephone, telex or telefax number and the name, address, telephone, telex or telefax number of the person to be contacted in case of emergency.

Annex VI – Arbitration

Article 1

Unless the agreement referred to in Article 20 of the Convention provides otherwise, the arbitration procedure shall be conducted in accordance with Articles 2 to 10 below.

Article 2

The claimant Party shall notify the Secretariat that the Parties have agreed to submit the dispute to arbitration pursuant to paragraph 2 or paragraph 3 of Article 20 and include, in particular, the Articles of the Convention the interpretation or application of which are at issue. The Secretariat shall forward the information thus received to all Parties to the Convention.

Article 3

The arbitral tribunal shall consist of three members. Each of the Parties to the dispute shall appoint an arbitrator, and the two arbitrators so appointed shall designate by common agreement the third arbitrator, who shall be the chairman of the tribunal. The latter shall not be a national of one of the Parties to the dispute, nor have his usual place of residence in the territory of one of these Parties, nor be employed by any of them, nor have dealt with the case in any other capacity.

Article 4

1. If the chairman of the arbitral tribunal has not been designated within two months of the appointment of the second arbitrator, the Secretary-General of the United Nations shall, at the request of either Party, designate him within a further two months period.
2. If one of the Parties to the dispute does not appoint an arbitrator within two months of the receipt of the request, the other Party may inform the Secretary- General of the United Nations who shall designate the chairman of the arbitral tribunal within a further two months' period. Upon designation, the chairman of the arbitral tribunal shall request the Party which has not appointed an arbitrator to do so within two months. After such period, he shall inform the Secretary-General of the United Nations, who shall make this appointment within a further two months' period.

Article 5

1. The arbitral tribunal shall render its decision in accordance with international law and in accordance with the provisions of this Convention.
2. Any arbitral tribunal constituted under the provisions of this Annex shall draw up its own rules of procedure.

Article 6

1. The decisions of the arbitral tribunal both on procedure and on substance, shall be taken by majority vote of its members.
2. The tribunal may take all appropriate measures in order to establish the facts. It may, at the request of one of the Parties, recommend essential interim measures of protection.
3. The Parties to the dispute shall provide all facilities necessary for the effective conduct of the proceedings.
4. The absence or default of a Party in the dispute shall not constitute an impediment to the proceedings.

Article 7

The tribunal may hear and determine counter-claims arising directly out of the subject-matter of the dispute.

Article 8

Unless the arbitral tribunal determines otherwise because of the particular circumstances of the case, the expenses of the tribunal, including the remuneration of its members, shall be borne by the Parties to the dispute in equal shares. The tribunal shall keep a record of all its expenses, and shall furnish a final statement thereof to the Parties.

Article 9

Any Party that has an interest of a legal nature in the subject-matter of the dispute which may be affected by the decision in the case, may intervene in the proceedings with the consent of the tribunal.

Article 10

1. The tribunal shall render its award within five months of the date on which it is established unless it finds it necessary to extend the time-limit for a period which should not exceed five months.
2. The award of the arbitral tribunal shall be accompanied by a statement of reasons. It shall be final and binding upon the Parties to the dispute.
3. Any dispute which may arise between the Parties concerning the interpretation or execution of the award may be submitted by either Party to the arbitral tribunal which made the award or, if the latter cannot be seized thereof, to another tribunal constituted for this purpose in the same manner as the first.

Annex VII[15]

Parties and other States which are members of OECD, EC, Liechtenstein

15 The amendment whereby Annex VII was added to the Convention entered into force on 5 December 2019, in accordance with article 17(5) of the Convention (depositary notification C.N.420.2019), reflecting decision III/1 adopted by the Conference of the Parties at its third meeting.

Annex VIII[16] – List A

Wastes contained in this Annex are characterized as hazardous under Article 1, paragraph 1 (a), of this Convention, and their designation on this Annex does not preclude the use of Annex III to demonstrate that a waste is not hazardous.

A1. Metal and metal-bearing wastes

A1010	Metal wastes and waste consisting of alloys of any of the following: – Antimony – Arsenic – Beryllium – Cadmium – Lead – Mercury – Selenium – Tellurium – Thallium but excluding such wastes specifically listed on list B.
A1020	Waste having as constituents or contaminants, excluding metal waste in massive form, any of the following: – Antimony; antimony compounds – Beryllium; beryllium compounds – Cadmium; cadmium compounds – Lead; lead compounds – Selenium; selenium compounds – Tellurium; tellurium compounds
A1030	Wastes having as constituents or contaminants any of the following: – Arsenic; arsenic compounds – Mercury; mercury compounds – Thallium; thallium compounds
A1040	Wastes having as constituents any of the following: – Metal carbonyls – Hexavalent chromium compounds
A1050	Galvanic sludges
A1060	Waste liquors from the pickling of metals
A1070	Leaching residues from zinc processing, dust and sludges such as jarosite, hematite, etc.
A1080	Waste zinc residues not included on list B, containing lead and cadmium in concentrations sufficient to exhibit Annex III characteristics
A1090	Ashes from the incineration of insulated copper wire
A1100	Ashes from the incineration of insulated copper wire
A1110	Spent electrolytic solutions from copper electrorefining and electrowinning operations
A1120	Waste sludges, excluding anode slimes, from electrolyte purification systems in copper electrorefining and electrowinning operations
A1130	Spent etching solutions containing dissolved copper
A1140	Waste cupric chloride and copper cyanide catalysts
A1150	Precious metal ash from incineration of printed circuit boards not included on list B[27]

16 The amendment whereby Annex VIII was added to the Convention entered into force on 6 November 1998, six months following the issuance of depositary notification C.N.77.1998 of 6 May 1998 (reflecting Decision IV/9 adopted by the Conference of the Parties at its fourth meeting). The amendment to Annex VIII whereby new entries were added entered into force on 20 November 2003 (depositary notification C.N.1314.2003), six months following the issuance of depositary notification C.N.399.2003 of 20 May 2003 (reflecting Decision VI/35 adopted by the Conference of the Parties at its sixth meeting). The amendment to Annex VIII whereby one new entry was added entered into force on 8 October 2005 (depositary notification C.N.1044.2005), six months following the issuance of depositary notification C.N.263.2005 of 8 April 2005 (re-issued on 13 June 2005, reflecting Decision VII/19 adopted by the Conference of the Parties at its seventh meeting). The amendment to Annex VIII whereby one new entry was added entered into force on 24 March 2020, six months following the issuance of depositary notification C.N.432.2019 of 24 September 2019 (reflecting decision BC-14/12 adopted by the Conference of the Parties at its fourteenth meeting). The present text includes all amendments. For information on the status of individual Parties in relation to the amendment/s, please see the Status of Ratifications page on the Basel Convention website.

17 Note that mirror entry on list B (B1160) does not specify exceptions.

A1160	Waste lead-acid batteries, whole or crushed
A1170	Unsorted waste batteries excluding mixtures of only list B batteries. Waste batteries not specified on list B containing Annex I constituents to an extent to render them hazardous
A1180	Waste electrical and electronic assemblies or scrap[18] containing components such as accumulators and other batteries included on list A, mercury-switches, glass from cathode-ray tubes and other activated glass and PCB-capacitors, or contaminated with Annex I constituents (e.g., cadmium, mercury, lead, polychlorinated biphenyl) to an extent that they possess any of the characteristics contained in Annex III (note the related entry on list B B1110)[19]
A1190	Waste metal cables coated or insulated with plastics containing or contaminated with coal tar, PCB20[20], lead, cadmium, other organohalogen compounds or other Annex I constituents to an extent that they exhibit Annex III characteristics.

A2. Wastes containing principally inorganic constituents, which may contain metals and organic materials

A2010	Glass waste from cathode-ray tubes and other activated glasses
A2020	Waste inorganic fluorine compounds in the form of liquids or sludges but excluding such wastes specified on list B
A2030	Waste catalysts but excluding such wastes specified on list B
A2040	Waste gypsum arising from chemical industry processes, when containing Annex I constituents to the extent that it exhibits an Annex III hazardous characteristic (note the related entry on list B B2080)
A2050	Waste asbestos (dusts and fibres)
A2060	Coal-fired power plant fly-ash containing Annex I substances in concentrations sufficient to exhibit Annex III characteristics (note the related entry on list B B2050)

A3. Wastes containing principally organic constituents, which may contain metals and inorganic materials

A3010	Waste from the production or processing of petroleum coke and bitumen
A3020	Waste mineral oils unfit for their originally intended use
A3030	Wastes that contain, consist of or are contaminated with leaded anti-knock compound sludges
A3040	Waste thermal (heat transfer) fluids
A3050	Wastes from production, formulation and use of resins, latex, plasticizers, glues/adhesives excluding such wastes specified on list B (note the related entry on list B B4020)
A3060	Waste nitrocellulose
A3070	Waste phenols, phenol compounds including chlorophenol in the form of liquids or sludges
A3080	Waste ethers not including those specified on list B
A3090	Waste leather dust, ash, sludges and flours when containing hexavalent chromium compounds or biocides (note the related entry on list B B3100)
A3100	Waste paring and other waste of leather or of composition leather not suitable for the manufacture of leather articles containing hexavalent chromium compounds or biocides (note the related entry on list B B3090)
A3110	Fellmongery wastes containing hexavalent chromium compounds or biocides or infectious substances (note the related entry on list B B3110)
A3120	Fluff - light fraction from shredding
A3130	Waste organic phosphorous compounds
A3140	Waste non-halogenated organic solvents but excluding such wastes specified on list B
A3150	Waste halogenated organic solvents

18 This entry does not include scrap assemblies from electric power generation.
19 PCBs are at concentration level of 50 mg/kg or more.
20 PCBs are at concentration level of 50 mg/kg or more.

A3160	Waste halogenated or unhalogenated non-aqueous distillation residues arising from organic solvent recovery operations
A3170	Wastes arising from the production of aliphatic halogenated hydrocarbons (such as chloromethane, dichloro-ethane, vinyl chloride, vinylidene chloride, allyl chloride and epichlorhydrin)
A3180	Wastes, substances and articles containing, consisting of or contaminated with polychlorinated biphenyl (PCB), polychlorinated terphenyl (PCT), polychlorinated naphthalene (PCN) or polybrominated biphenyl (PBB), or any other polybrominated analogues of these compounds, at a concentration level of 50 mg/kg or more[21]
A3190	Waste tarry residues (excluding asphalt cements) arising from refining, distillation and any pyrolitic treatment of organic materials
A3200	Bituminous material (asphalt waste) from road construction and maintenance, containing tar (note the related entry on list B, B2130)
A3210[22]	Plastic waste, including mixtures of such waste, containing or contaminated with Annex I constituents, to an extent that it exhibits an Annex III characteristic (note the related entries Y48 in Annex II and on list B B3011).

A4. Wastes which may contain either inorganic or organic constituents

A4010	Wastes from the production, preparation and use of pharmaceutical products but excluding such wastes specified on list B
A4020	Clinical and related wastes; that is wastes arising from medical, nursing, dental, veterinary, or similar practices, and wastes generated in hospitals or other facilities during the investigation or treatment of patients, or research projects
A4030	Wastes from the production, formulation and use of biocides and phytopharmaceuticals, including waste pesticides and herbicides which are off-specification, outdated,[23] or unfit for their originally intended use
A4040	Wastes from the manufacture, formulation and use of wood-preserving chemicals[24]
A4050	Wastes that contain, consist of or are contaminated with any of the following: – Inorganic cyanides, excepting precious-metal-bearing residues in solid form containing traces of inorganic cyanides – Organic cyanides
A4060	Waste oils/water, hydrocarbons/water mixtures, emulsions
A4070	Wastes from the production, formulation and use of inks, dyes, pigments, paints, lacquers, varnish excluding any such waste specified on list B (note the related entry on list B B4010)
A4080	Wastes of an explosive nature (but excluding such wastes specified on list B)
A4090	Waste acidic or basic solutions, other than those specified in the corresponding entry on list B (note the related entry on list B B2120)
A4100	Wastes from industrial pollution control devices for cleaning of industrial off-gases but excluding such wastes specified on list B
A4110	Wastes that contain, consist of or are contaminated with any of the following: – Any congenor of polychlorinated dibenzo-furan – Any congenor of polychlorinated dibenzo-p-dioxin
A4120	Wastes that contain, consist of or are contaminated with peroxides
A4130	Waste packages and containers containing Annex I substances in concentrations sufficient to exhibit Annex III hazard characteristics
A4140	Waste consisting of or containing off specification or outdated[25] chemicals corresponding to Annex I categories and exhibiting Annex III hazard characteristics

21 The 50 mg/kg level is considered to be an internationally practical level for all wastes. However, many individual countries have established lower regulatory levels (e.g., 20 mg/kg) for specific wastes.
22 This entry becomes effective as of 1 January 2021.
23 "Outdated" means unused within the period recommended by the manufacturer.
24 This entry does not include wood treated with wood preserving chemicals.
25 "Outdated" means unused within the period recommended by the manufacturer.

A4150	Waste chemical substances arising from research and development or teaching activities which are not identified and/or are new and whose effects on human health and/or the environment are not known
A4160	Spent activated carbon not included on list B (note the related entry on list B B2060).

Annex IX[26] – List B

Wastes contained in the Annex will not be wastes covered by Article 1, paragraph 1 (a), of this Convention unless they contain Annex I material to an extent causing them to exhibit an Annex III characteristic.

B1. Metal and metal-bearing wastes

B1010	Metal and metal-alloy wastes in metallic, non-dispersible form: – Precious metals (gold, silver, the platinum group, but not mercury) – Iron and steel scrap – Copper scrap – Nickel scrap – Aluminium scrap – Zinc scrap – Tin scrap – Tungsten scrap – Molybdenum scrap – Tantalum scrap – Magnesium scrap – Cobalt scrap – Bismuth scrap – Titanium scrap – Zirconium scrap – Manganese scrap – Germanium scrap – Vanadium scrap – Scrap of hafnium, indium, niobium, rhenium and gallium – Thorium scrap – Rare earths scrap – Chromium scrap
B1020	Clean, uncontaminated metal scrap, including alloys, in bulk finished form (sheet, plate, beams, rods, etc), of: – Antimony scrap – Beryllium scrap – Cadmium scrap – Lead scrap (but excluding lead-acid batteries) – Selenium scrap – Tellurium scrap
B1030	Refractory metals containing residues
B1031	Molybdenum, tungsten, titanium, tantalum, niobium and rhenium metal and metal alloy wastes in metallic dispersible form (metal powder), excluding such wastes as specified in list A under entry A1050, Galvanic sludges
B1040	Scrap assemblies from electrical power generation not contaminated with lubricating oil, PCB or PCT to an extent to render them hazardous

26 The amendment whereby Annex IX was added to the Convention entered into force on 6 November 1998, six months following the issuance of depositary notification C.N.77.1998 (reflecting Decision IV/9 adopted by the Conference of the Parties at its fourth meeting). The amendment to Annex IX whereby new entries were added entered into force on 20 November 2003 (depositary notification C.N.1314.2003), six months following the issuance of depositary notification C.N.399.2003 of 20 May 2003 (reflecting Decision VI/35 adopted by the Conference of the Parties at its sixth meeting). The amendment to Annex IX whereby one entry was added entered into force on 8 October 2005 (depositary notification C.N.1044.2005) six months following the issuance of depositary notification C.N.263.2005 of 8 April 2005 (re-issued on 13 June 2005, reflecting Decision VII/19 adopted by the Conference of the Parties at its seventh meeting). The amendment to Annex IX whereby new entries where added entered into force on 27 May 2014 (depositary notification C.N. 304.2014) six months following the issuance of depositary notification C.N. 965.2013 of 26 November 2013 (reflecting decision BC-11/6 adopted by the Conference of the Parties at its eleventh meeting). Amendments to Annex IX entered into force on 24 March 2020, six months following the issuance of depositary notification C.N.432.2019 of 24 September 2019 (reflecting decision BC-14/12 adopted by the Conference of the Parties at its fourteenth meeting). The present text includes all amendments. For information on the status of individual Parties in relation to the amendment/s, please see the Status of Ratifications page on the Basel Convention website.

B1050	Mixed non-ferrous metal, heavy fraction scrap, not containing Annex I materials in concentrations sufficient to exhibit Annex III characteristics[27]
B1060	Waste selenium and tellurium in metallic elemental form including powder
B1070	Waste of copper and copper alloys in dispersible form, unless they contain Annex I constituents to an extent that they exhibit Annex III characteristics
B1080	Zinc ash and residues including zinc alloys residues in dispersible form unless containing Annex I constituents in concentration such as to exhibit Annex III characteristics[28]
B1090	Waste batteries conforming to a specification, excluding those made with lead, cadmium or mercury

B1100	Metal-bearing wastes arising from melting, smelting and refining of metals:
	– Hard zinc spelter
	– Zinc-containing drosses:
	  – Galvanizing slab zinc top dross (>90% Zn)
	  – Galvanizing slab zinc bottom dross (>92% Zn)
	  – Zinc die casting dross
	    – (>85% Zn)
	  – Hot dip galvanizers slab zinc dross (batch) (>92% Zn)
	  – Zinc skimmings
	– Aluminium skimmings (or skims) excluding salt slag
	– Slags from copper processing for further processing or refining not containing arsenic, lead or cadmium to an extent that they exhibit Annex III hazard characteristics
	– Wastes of refractory linings, including crucibles, originating from copper smelting
	– Slags from precious metals processing for further refining
	– Tantalum-bearing tin slags with less than 0.5% tin

B1110	Electrical and electronic assemblies: – Electronic assemblies consisting only of metals or alloys – Waste electrical and electronic assemblies or scrap[29] (including printed circuit boards) not containing components such as accumulators and other batteries included on list A, mercury-switches, glass from cathode-ray tubes and other activated glass and PCB-capacitors, or not contaminated with Annex I constituents (e.g., cadmium, mercury, lead, polychlorinated biphenyl) or from which these have been removed, to an extent that they do not possess any of the characteristics contained in Annex III (note the related entry on list A A1180) – Electrical and electronic assemblies (including printed circuit boards, electronic components and wires) destined for direct reuse,[30] and not for recycling or final disposal[31]
B1115	Waste metal cables coated or insulated with plastics, not included in list A A1190, excluding those destined for Annex IVA operations or any other disposal operations involving, at any stage, uncontrolled thermal processes, such as open-burning.

27 Note that even where low level contamination with Annex I materials initially exists, subsequent processes, including recycling processes, may result in separated fractions containing significantly enhanced concentrations of those Annex I materials.
28 The status of zinc ash is currently under review and there is a recommendation with the United Nations Conference on Trade and Development (UNCTAD) that zinc ashes should not be dangerous goods.
29 This entry does not include scrap from electrical power generation.
30 Reuse can include repair, refurbishment or upgrading, but not major reassembly.
31 In some countries these materials destined for direct re-use are not considered wastes.

B1120	Spent catalysts excluding liquids used as catalysts, containing any of: Transition metals, excluding waste catalysts (spent catalysts, liquid used catalysts or other catalysts) on list A: – Scandium – Vanadium – Manganese – Cobalt – Copper – Yttrium – Niobium – Hafnium – Tungsten – Titanium – Chromium – Iron – Nickel – Zinc – Zirconium – Molybdenum – Tantalum – Rhenium Lanthanides (rare earth metals): – Lanthanum – Praseodymium – Samarium – Gadolinium – Dysprosium – Erbium – Ytterbium – Cerium – Neodymium – Europium – Terbium – Holmium – Thulium – Lutetium
B1130	Cleaned spent precious-metal-bearing catalysts
B1140	Precious-metal-bearing residues in solid form which contain traces of inorganic cyanides
B1150	Precious metals and alloy wastes (gold, silver, the platinum group, but not mercury) in a dispersible, non-liquid form with appropriate packaging and labelling
B1160	Precious-metal ash from the incineration of printed circuit boards (note the related entry on list A A1150)
B1170	Precious-metal ash from the incineration of photographic film
B1180	Waste photographic film containing silver halides and metallic silver
B1190	Waste photographic paper containing silver halides and metallic silver
B1200	Granulated slag arising from the manufacture of iron and steel
B1210	Slag arising from the manufacture of iron and steel including slags as a source of TiO_2 and vanadium
B1220	Slag from zinc production, chemically stabilized, having a high iron content (above 20%) and processed according to industrial specifications (e.g., DIN 4301) mainly for construction
B1230	Mill scaling arising from the manufacture of iron and steel
B1240	Copper oxide mill-scale
B1250	Waste end-of-life motor vehicles, containing neither liquids nor other hazardous components

B2. Wastes containing principally inorganic constituents, which may contain metals and organic materials

B2010	Wastes from mining operations in non-dispersible form: – Natural graphite waste – Slate waste, whether or not roughly trimmed or merely cut, by sawing or otherwise – Mica waste – Leucite, nepheline and nepheline syenite waste – Feldspar waste – Fluorspar waste – Silica wastes in solid form excluding those used in foundry operations
B2020	Glass waste in non-dispersible form: – Cullet and other waste and scrap of glass except for glass from cathode-ray tubes and other activated glasses
B2030	Ceramic wastes in non-dispersible form: – Cermet wastes and scrap (metal ceramic composites) – Ceramic based fibres not elsewhere specified or included
B2040	Other wastes containing principally inorganic constituents: – Partially refined calcium sulphate produced from flue-gas desulphurization (FGD) – Waste gypsum wallboard or plasterboard arising from the demolition of buildings – Slag from copper production, chemically stabilized, having a high iron content (above 20%) and processed according to industrial specifications (e.g., DIN 4301 and DIN 8201) mainly for construction and abrasive applications – Sulphur in solid form – Limestone from the production of calcium cyanamide (having a pH less than 9) – Sodium, potassium, calcium chlorides – Carborundum (silicon carbide) – Broken concrete – Lithium-tantalum and lithium-niobium containing glass scraps
B2050	Coal-fired power plant fly-ash, not included on list A (note the related entry on list A A2060)
B2060	Spent activated carbon not containing any Annex I constituents to the extent they exhibit Annex III characteristics, for example, carbon resulting from the treatment of potable water and processes of the food industry and vitamin production (note the related entry on list A A4160)
B2070	Calcium fluoride sludge
B2080	Waste gypsum arising from chemical industry processes not included on list A (note the related entry on list A A2040)
B2090	Waste anode butts from steel or aluminium production made of petroleum coke or bitumen and cleaned to normal industry specifications (excluding anode butts from chlor alkali electrolyses and from metallurgical industry)
B2100	Waste hydrates of aluminium and waste alumina and residues from alumina production excluding such materials used for gas cleaning, flocculation or filtration processes
B2110	Bauxite residue ("red mud") (pH moderated to less than 11.5)
B2120	Waste acidic or basic solutions with a pH greater than 2 and less than 11.5, which are not corrosive or otherwise hazardous (note the related entry on list A A4090)
B2130	Bituminous material (asphalt waste) from road construction and maintenance, not containing tar[32] (note the related entry on list A, A3200).

32 The concentration level of Benzol (a) pyrene should not be 50mg/kg or more.

B3. Wastes containing principally organic constituents, which may contain metals and inorganic materials

B3010[33]	Solid plastic waste: The following plastic or mixed plastic materials, provided they are not mixed with other wastes and are prepared to a specification: – Scrap plastic of non-halogenated polymers and co-polymers, including but not limited to the following:[34] – ethylene – styrene – polypropylene – polyethylene terephthalate – acrylonitrile – butadiene – polyacetals – polyamides – polybutylene terephthalate – polycarbonates – polyethers – polyphenylene sulphides – acrylic polymers – alkanes C10-C13 (plasticiser) – polyurethane (not containing CFCs) – polysiloxanes – polymethyl methacrylate – polyvinyl alcohol – polyvinyl butyral – polyvinyl acetate – Cured waste resins or condensation products including the following: – urea formaldehyde resins – phenol formaldehyde resins – melamine formaldehyde resins – epoxy resins – alkyd resins – polyamides – The following fluorinated polymer wastes:[35] – perfluoroethylene/propylene (FEP) – perfluoro alkoxyl alkane: – tetrafluoroethylene/per – fluoro vinyl ether (PFA) – tetrafluoroethylene/per – fluoro methylvinyl ether (MFA) – polyvinylfluoride (PVF) – polyvinylidenefluoride (PVDF)

33 Entry B3010 is effective until 31 December 2020. Entry B3011 becomes effective as of 1 January 2021.
34 It is understood that such scraps are completely polymerized.
35 Post-consumer wastes are excluded from this entry:Wastes shall not be mixedProblems arising from open-burning practices to be considered.

<table>
<tr><td>B3011[36]</td><td>Plastic waste (note the related entries Y48 in Annex II and on list A A3210):
– Plastic waste listed below, provided it is destined for recycling[37] in an environmentally sound manner and almost free from contamination and other types of wastes:[38]
– Plastic waste almost exclusively[39] consisting of one non-halogenated polymer, including but not limited to the following polymers:
– Polyethylene (PE)
– Polypropylene (PP)
– Polystyrene (PS)
– Acrylonitrile butadiene styrene (ABS)
– Polyethylene terephthalate (PET)
– Polycarbonates (PC)
– Polyethers
– Plastic waste almost exclusively[39] consisting of one cured resin or condensation product, including but not limited to the following resins:
– Urea formaldehyde resins
– Phenol formaldehyde resins
– Melamine formaldehyde resins
– Epoxy resins
– Alkyd resins
– Plastic waste almost exclusively[39] consisting of one of the following fluorinated polymers:[40]
– Perfluoroethylene/ propylene (FEP)
– Perfluoroalkoxy alkanes:
– Tetrafluoroethylene/ perfluoroalkyl vinyl ether (PFA)
– Tetrafluoroethylene/ – perfluoromethyl vinyl ether (MFA)
– Polyvinylfluoride (PVF)
– Polyvinylidenefluoride (PVDF)
– Mixtures of plastic waste, consisting of polyethylene (PE), polypropylene (PP) and/ or polyethylene terephthalate (PET), provided they are destined for separate recycling[41] of each material and in an environmentally sound manner, and almost free from contamination and other types of wastes.[38]</td></tr>
<tr><td>B3020</td><td>Paper, paperboard and paper product wastes
The following materials, provided they are not mixed with hazardous wastes:
Waste and scrap of paper or paperboard of:
– unbleached paper or paperboard or of corrugated paper or paperboard
– other paper or paperboard, made mainly of bleached chemical pulp, not coloured in the mass
– paper or paperboard made mainly of mechanical pulp (for example, newspapers, journals and similar printed matter)
– other, including but not limited to 1) laminated paperboard 2) unsorted scrap</td></tr>
</table>

36 This entry becomes effective as of 1 January 2021. Entry B3010 is effective until 31 December 2020.
37 Recycling/reclamation of organic substances that are not used as solvents (R3 in Annex IV, sect. B) or, if needed, temporary storage limited to one instance, provided that it is followed by operation R3 and evidenced by contractual or relevant official documentation.
38 In relation to "almost free from contamination and other types of wastes", international and national specifications may offer a point of reference.
39 In relation to "almost exclusively", international and national specifications may offer a point of reference.
40 Post-consumer wastes are excluded.
41 Recycling/reclamation of organic substances that are not used as solvents (R3 in Annex IV, sect. B), with prior sorting and, if needed, temporary storage limited to one instance, provided that it is followed by operation R3 and evidenced by contractual or relevant official documentation.

B3026	The following waste from the pre-treatment of composite packaging for liquids, not containing Annex I materials in concentrations sufficient to exhibit Annex III characteristics: • Non-separable plastic fraction • Non-separable plastic-aluminium fraction
B3027	Self-adhesive label laminate waste containing raw materials used in label material production

B3030	Textile wastes
	The following materials, provided they are not mixed with other wastes and are prepared to a specification:
	– Silk waste (including cocoons unsuitable for reeling, yarn waste and garnetted stock)
	  – not carded or combed
	  – other
	– Waste of wool or of fine or coarse animal hair, including yarn waste but excluding garnetted stock
	  – noils of wool or of fine animal hair
	  – other waste of wool or of fine animal hair
	  – waste of coarse animal hair
	– Cotton waste (including yarn waste and garnetted stock)
	  – yarn waste (including thread waste)
	  – garnetted stock
	  – other
	– Flax tow and waste
	– Tow and waste (including yarn waste and garnetted stock) of true hemp (Cannabis sativa L.)
	– Tow and waste (including yarn waste and garnetted stock) of jute and other textile bast fibres (excluding flax, true hemp and ramie)
	– Tow and waste (including yarn waste and garnetted stock) of sisal and other textile fibres of the genus Agave
	– Tow, noils and waste (including yarn waste and garneted stock) of coconut
	– Tow, noils and waste (including yarn waste and garnetted stock) of abaca (Manila hemp or Musa textilis Nee)
	– Tow, noils and waste (including yarn waste and garneted stock) of ramie and other vegetable textile fibres, not elsewhere specified or included
	– Waste (including noils, yarn waste and garnetted stock) of man-made fibres
	  – of synthetic fibres
	  – of artificial fibres
	– Worn clothing and other worn textile articles
	– Used rags, scrap twine, cordage, rope and cables and worn out articles of twine, cordage, rope or cables of textile materials
	  – sorted
	  – other

B3035	Waste textile floor coverings, carpets
B3040	Rubber wastes The following materials, provided they are not mixed with other wastes: – Waste and scrap of hard rubber (e.g., ebonite) – Other rubber wastes (excluding such wastes specified elsewhere)

B3050	Untreated cork and wood waste: – Wood waste and scrap, whether or not agglomerated in logs, briquettes, pellets or similar forms – Cork waste: crushed, granulated or ground cork
B3060	Wastes arising from agro-food industries provided it is not infectious: – Wine lees – Dried and sterilized vegetable waste, residues and byproducts, whether or not in the form of pellets, of a kind used in animal feeding, not elsewhere specified or included – Degras: residues resulting from the treatment of fatty substances or animal or vegetable waxes – Waste of bones and horn-cores, unworked, defatted, simply prepared (but not cut to shape), treated with acid or degelatinised – Fish waste – Cocoa shells, husks, skins and other cocoa waste – Other wastes from the agro-food industry excluding by-products which meet national and international requirements and standards for human or animal consumption
B3065	Waste edible fats and oils of animal or vegetable origin (e.g. frying oils), provided they do not exhibit an Annex III characteristic
B3070	The following wastes: – Waste of human hair – Waste straw – Deactivated fungus mycelium from penicillin production to be used as animal feed
B3080	Waste parings and scrap of rubber
B3090	Paring and other wastes of leather or of composition leather not suitable for the manufacture of leather articles, excluding leather sludges, not containing hexavalent chromium compounds and biocides (note the related entry on list A A3100)
B3100	Leather dust, ash, sludges or flours not containing hexavalent chromium compounds or biocides (note the related entry on list A A3090)
B3110	Fellmongery wastes not containing hexavalent chromium compounds or biocides or infectious substances (note the related entry on list A A3110)
B3120	Wastes consisting of food dyes
B3130	Waste polymer ethers and waste non-hazardous monomer ethers incapable of forming peroxides
B3140	Waste pneumatic tyres, excluding those destined for Annex IVA operations

B4. Wastes which may contain either inorganic or organic constituents

B4010	Wastes consisting mainly of water-based/latex paints, inks and hardened varnishes not containing organic solvents, heavy metals or biocides to an extent to render them hazardous (note the related entry on list A A4070)
B4020	Wastes from production, formulation and use of resins, latex, plasticizers, glues/adhesives, not listed on list A, free of solvents and other contaminants to an extent that they do not exhibit Annex III characteristics, e.g., water-based, or glues based on casein starch, dextrin, cellulose ethers, polyvinyl alcohols (note the related entry on list A A3050)
B4030	Used single-use cameras, with batteries not included on list A

10.2. Rotterdam Convention 1998, as amended 2022

Rotterdam Convention on the Prior Informed Consent Procedure for Certain Hazardous Chemicals and Pesticides in International Trade, 10 September 1998, 2244 UNTS 337, C.N.846.2002.TREATIES-8 of 20 August 2002, C.N.1029.2002. TREATIES-18 of 23 September 2002, C.N.10.2005.TREATIES-1 of 11 January 2005, C.N.11.2005.TREATIES-2 of 11 January 2005, C.N.83.2009.TREATIES-1 of 5 February 2009, C.N.139.2012.TREATIES-XXVII.14 of 8 March 2012, C.N.973.2013.TREATIES-XXVII.14 of 6 December 2013, C.N.696.2015.TREATIES-XXVII.14 of 21 December 2015, C.N.489.2017.TREATIES-XXVII.14 of 24 August 2017, C.N.397.2019. TREATIES-XXVII.14 of 28 August 2019, C.N.574.2019.TREATIES-XXVII.14 of 8 November 2019, C.N.530.2020.TREATIES-XXVII.14 of 16 November 2020, C.N.315.2022.TREATIES-XXVII.14 of 28 September 2022

The Parties to this Convention,

Aware of the harmful impact on human health and the environment from certain hazardous chemicals and pesticides in international trade,

Recalling the pertinent provisions of the Rio Declaration on Environment and Development and chapter 19 of Agenda 21 on "Environmentally sound management of toxic chemicals, including prevention of illegal international traffic in toxic and dangerous products",

Mindful of the work undertaken by the United Nations Environment Programme (UNEP) and the Food and Agriculture Organization of the United Nations (FAO) in the operation of the voluntary Prior Informed Consent procedure, as set out in the UNEP Amended London Guidelines for the Exchange of Information on Chemicals in International Trade (hereinafter referred to as the "Amended London Guidelines") and the FAO International Code of Conduct on the Distribution and Use of Pesticides (hereinafter referred to as the "International Code of Conduct"),

Taking into account the circumstances and particular requirements of developing countries and countries with economies in transition, in particular the need to strengthen national capabilities and capacities for the management of chemicals, including transfer of technology, providing financial and technical assistance and promoting cooperation among the Parties,

Noting the specific needs of some countries for information on transit movements,

Recognizing that good management practices for chemicals should be promoted in all countries, taking into account, inter alia, the voluntary standards laid down in the International Code of Conduct and the UNEP Code of Ethics on the International Trade in Chemicals,

Desiring to ensure that hazardous chemicals that are exported from their territory are packaged and labelled in a manner that is adequately protective of human health and the environment, consistent with the principles of the Amended London Guidelines and the International Code of Conduct,

Recognizing that trade and environmental policies should be mutually supportive with a view to achieving sustainable development,

Emphasizing that nothing in this Convention shall be interpreted as implying in any way a change in the rights and obligations of a Party under any existing international agreement applying to chemicals in international trade or to environmental protection,

Understanding that the above recital is not intended to create a hierarchy between this Convention and other international agreements,

Determined to protect human health, including the health of consumers and workers, and the environment against potentially harmful impacts from certain hazardous chemicals and pesticides in international trade,

Have agreed as follows:

Article 1 – Objective

The objective of this Convention is to promote shared responsibility and cooperative efforts among Parties in the international trade of certain hazardous chemicals in order to protect human health and the environment from potential harm and to contribute to their environmentally sound use, by facilitating information exchange about their characteristics, by providing for a national decision-making process on their import and export and by disseminating these decisions to Parties.

Article 2 – Definitions

For the purposes of this Convention:

(a) "Chemical" means a substance whether by itself or in a mixture or preparation and whether manufactured or obtained from nature, but does not include any living organism. It consists of the following categories: pesticide (including severely hazardous pesticide formulations) and industrial;

(b) "Banned chemical" means a chemical all uses of which within one or more categories have been prohibited by final regulatory action, in order to protect human health or the environment. It includes a chemical that has been refused approval for first-time use or has been withdrawn by industry either from the domestic market or from further consideration in the domestic approval process and where there is clear evidence that such action has been taken in order to protect human health or the environment;

(c) "Severely restricted chemical" means a chemical virtually all use of which within one or more categories has been prohibited by final regulatory action in order to protect human health or the environment, but for which certain specific uses remain allowed. It includes a chemical that has, for virtually all use, been refused for approval or been withdrawn by industry either from the domestic market or from further consideration in the domestic approval process, and where there is clear evidence that such action has been taken in order to protect human health or the environment;

(d) "Severely hazardous pesticide formulation" means a chemical formulated for pesticidal use that produces severe health or environmental effects observable within a short period of time after single or multiple exposure, under conditions of use;

(e) "Final regulatory action" means an action taken by a Party, that does not require subsequent regulatory action by that Party, the purpose of which is to ban or severely restrict a chemical;

(f) "Export" and "import" mean, in their respective connotations, the movement of a chemical from one Party to another Party, but exclude mere transit operations;

(g) "Party" means a State or regional economic integration organization that has consented to be bound by this Convention and for which the Convention is in force;

(h) "Regional economic integration organization" means an organization constituted by sovereign States of a given region to which its member States have transferred competence in respect of matters governed by this Convention and which has been duly authorized, in accordance with its internal procedures, to sign, ratify, accept, approve or accede to this Convention;

(i) "Chemical Review Committee" means the subsidiary body referred to in paragraph 6 of Article 18.

Article 3 – Scope of the Convention

1. This Convention applies to:
   (a) Banned or severely restricted chemicals; and
   (b) Severely hazardous pesticide formulations.
2. This Convention does not apply to:
   (a) Narcotic drugs and psychotropic substances;
   (b) Radioactive materials;
   (c) Wastes;
   (d) Chemical weapons;
   (e) Pharmaceuticals, including human and veterinary drugs;
   (f) Chemicals used as food additives;
   (g) Food;
   (h) Chemicals in quantities not likely to affect human health or the environment provided they are imported:
      (i) For the purpose of research or analysis; or
      (ii) By an individual for his or her own personal use in quantities reasonable for such use.

Article 4 – Designated national authorities

1. Each Party shall designate one or more national authorities that shall be authorized to act on its behalf in the performance of the administrative functions required by this Convention.
2. Each Party shall seek to ensure that such authority or authorities have sufficient resources to perform their tasks effectively.
3. Each Party shall, no later than the date of the entry into force of this Convention for it, notify the name and address of such authority or authorities to the Secretariat. It shall forthwith notify the Secretariat of any changes in the name and address of such authority or authorities.
4. The Secretariat shall forthwith inform the Parties of the notifications it receives under paragraph 3.

Article 5 – Procedures for banned or severely restricted chemicals

1. Each Party that has adopted a final regulatory action shall notify the Secretariat in writing of such action. Such notification shall be made as soon as possible, and in any event no later than ninety days after the date on which the final regulatory action has taken effect, and shall contain the information required by Annex I, where available.
2. Each Party shall, at the date of entry into force of this Convention for it, notify the Secretariat in writing of its final regulatory actions in effect at that time, except that each Party that has submitted notifications of final regulatory actions under the Amended London Guidelines or the International Code of Conduct need not resubmit those notifications.
3. The Secretariat shall, as soon as possible, and in any event no later than six months after receipt of a notification under paragraphs 1 and 2, verify whether the notification contains the information required by Annex I. If the notification contains the information required, the Secretariat shall forthwith forward to all Parties a summary of the information received. If the notification does not contain the information required, it shall inform the notifying Party accordingly.
4. The Secretariat shall every six months communicate to the Parties a synopsis of the information received pursuant to paragraphs 1 and 2, including information regarding those notifications which do not contain all the information required by Annex I.
5. When the Secretariat has received at least one notification from each of two Prior Informed Consent regions regarding a particular chemical that it has verified meet the requirements of Annex I, it shall

forward them to the Chemical Review Committee. The composition of the Prior Informed Consent regions shall be defined in a decision to be adopted by consensus at the first meeting of the Conference of the Parties.

6. The Chemical Review Committee shall review the information provided in such notifications and, in accordance with the criteria set out in Annex II, recommend to the Conference of the Parties whether the chemical in question should be made subject to the Prior Informed Consent procedure and, accordingly, be listed in Annex III.

Article 6 – Procedures for severely hazardous pesticide formulations

1. Any Party that is a developing country or a country with an economy in transition and that is experiencing problems caused by a severely hazardous pesticide formulation under conditions of use in its territory, may propose to the Secretariat the listing of the severely hazardous pesticide formulation in Annex III. In developing a proposal, the Party may draw upon technical expertise from any relevant source. The proposal shall contain the information required by part 1 of Annex IV.
2. The Secretariat shall, as soon as possible, and in any event no later than six months after receipt of a proposal under paragraph 1, verify whether the proposal contains the information required by part 1 of Annex IV. If the proposal contains the information required, the Secretariat shall forthwith forward to all Parties a summary of the information received. If the proposal does not contain the information required, it shall inform the proposing Party accordingly.
3. The Secretariat shall collect the additional information set out in part 2 of Annex IV regarding the proposal forwarded under paragraph 2.
4. When the requirements of paragraphs 2 and 3 above have been fulfilled with regard to a particular severely hazardous pesticide formulation, the Secretariat shall forward the proposal and the related information to the Chemical Review Committee.
5. The Chemical Review Committee shall review the information provided in the proposal and the additional information collected and, in accordance with the criteria set out in part 3 of Annex IV, recommend to the Conference of the Parties whether the severely hazardous pesticide formulation in question should be made subject to the Prior Informed Consent procedure and, accordingly, be listed in Annex III.

Article 7 – Listing of chemicals in Annex III

1. For each chemical that the Chemical Review Committee has decided to recommend for listing in Annex III, it shall prepare a draft decision guidance document. The decision guidance document should, at a minimum, be based on the information specified in Annex I, or, as the case may be, Annex IV, and include information on uses of the chemical in a category other than the category for which the final regulatory action applies.
2. The recommendation referred to in paragraph 1 together with the draft decision guidance document shall be forwarded to the Conference of the Parties. The Conference of the Parties shall decide whether the chemical should be made subject to the Prior Informed Consent procedure and, accordingly, list the chemical in Annex III and approve the draft decision guidance document.
3. When a decision to list a chemical in Annex III has been taken and the related decision guidance document has been approved by the Conference of the Parties, the Secretariat shall forthwith communicate this information to all Parties.

Article 8 – Chemicals in the voluntary Prior Informed Consent procedure

For any chemical, other than a chemical listed in Annex III, that has been included in the voluntary Prior Informed Consent procedure before the date of the first meeting of the Conference of the Parties, the Conference of the Parties shall decide at that meeting to list the chemical in Annex III, provided that it is satisfied that all the requirements for listing in that Annex have been fulfilled.

Article 9 – Removal of chemicals from Annex III

1. If a Party submits to the Secretariat information that was not available at the time of the decision to list a chemical in Annex III and that information indicates that its listing may no longer be justified in accordance with the relevant criteria in Annex II or, as the case may be, Annex IV, the Secretariat shall forward the information to the Chemical Review Committee.
2. The Chemical Review Committee shall review the information it receives under paragraph 1. For each chemical that the Chemical Review Committee decides, in accordance with the relevant criteria in Annex II or, as the case may be, Annex IV, to recommend for removal from Annex III, it shall prepare a revised draft decision guidance document.
3. A recommendation referred to in paragraph 2 shall be forwarded to the Conference of the Parties and be accompanied by a revised draft decision guidance document. The Conference of the Parties shall decide whether the chemical should be removed from Annex III and whether to approve the revised draft decision guidance document.
4. When a decision to remove a chemical from Annex III has been taken and the revised decision guidance document has been approved by the Conference of the Parties, the Secretariat shall forthwith communicate this information to all Parties.

Article 10 – Obligations in relation to imports of chemicals listed in Annex III

1. Each Party shall implement appropriate legislative or administrative measures to ensure timely decisions with respect to the import of chemicals listed in Annex III.

2. Each Party shall transmit to the Secretariat, as soon as possible, and in any event no later than nine months after the date of dispatch of the decision guidance document referred to in paragraph 3 of Article 7, a response concerning the future import of the chemical concerned. If a Party modifies this response, it shall forthwith submit the revised response to the Secretariat.
3. The Secretariat shall, at the expiration of the time period in paragraph 2, forthwith address to a Party that has not provided such a response, a written request to do so. Should the Party be unable to provide a response, the Secretariat shall, where appropriate, help it to provide a response within the time period specified in the last sentence of paragraph 2 of Article 11.
4. A response under paragraph 2 shall consist of either:
   (a) A final decision, pursuant to legislative or administrative measures:
      (i) To consent to import;
      (ii) Not to consent to import; or
      (iii) To consent to import only subject to specified conditions; or
   (b) An interim response, which may include:
      (i) An interim decision consenting to import with or without specified conditions, or not consenting to import during the interim period;
      (ii) A statement that a final decision is under active consideration;
      (iii) A request to the Secretariat, or to the Party that notified the final regulatory action, for further information;
      (iv) A request to the Secretariat for assistance in evaluating the chemical.
5. A response under subparagraphs (a) or (b) of paragraph 4 shall relate to the category or categories specified for the chemical in Annex III.
6. A final decision should be accompanied by a description of any legislative or administrative measures upon which it is based.
7. Each Party shall, no later than the date of entry into force of this Convention for it, transmit to the Secretariat responses with respect to each chemical listed in Annex III. A Party that has provided such responses under the Amended London Guidelines or the International Code of Conduct need not resubmit those responses.
8. Each Party shall make its responses under this Article available to those concerned within its jurisdiction, in accordance with its legislative or administrative measures.
9. A Party that, pursuant to paragraphs 2 and 4 above and paragraph 2 of Article 11, takes a decision not to consent to import of a chemical or to consent to its import only under specified conditions shall, if it has not already done so, simultaneously prohibit or make subject to the same conditions:
   (a) Import of the chemical from any source; and
   (b) Domestic production of the chemical for domestic use.
10. Every six months the Secretariat shall inform all Parties of the responses it has received. Such information shall include a description of the legislative or administrative measures on which the decisions have been based, where available. The Secretariat shall, in addition, inform the Parties of any cases of failure to transmit a response.

Article 11 – Obligations in relation to exports of chemicals listed in Annex III

1. Each exporting Party shall:
   (a) Implement appropriate legislative or administrative measures to communicate the responses forwarded by the Secretariat in accordance with paragraph 10 of Article 10 to those concerned within its jurisdiction;
   (b) Take appropriate legislative or administrative measures to ensure that exporters within its jurisdiction comply with decisions in each response no later than six months after the date on which the Secretariat first informs the Parties of such response in accordance with paragraph 10 of Article 10;
   (c) Advise and assist importing Parties, upon request and as appropriate:
      (i) To obtain further information to help them to take action in accordance with paragraph 4 of Article 10 and paragraph 2 (c) below; and
      (ii) To strengthen their capacities and capabilities to manage chemicals safely during their life-cycle.
2. Each Party shall ensure that a chemical listed in Annex III is not exported from its territory to any importing Party that, in exceptional circumstances, has failed to transmit a response or has transmitted an interim response that does not contain an interim decision, unless:
   (a) It is a chemical that, at the time of import, is registered as a chemical in the importing Party; or
   (b) It is a chemical for which evidence exists that it has previously been used in, or imported into, the importing Party and in relation to which no regulatory action to prohibit its use has been taken; or
   (c) Explicit consent to the import has been sought and received by the exporter through a designated national authority of the importing Party. The importing Party shall respond to such a request within sixty days and shall promptly notify the Secretariat of its decision.

   The obligations of exporting Parties under this paragraph shall apply with effect from the expiration of a period of six months from the date on which the Secretariat first informs the Parties, in accordance with paragraph 10 of Article 10, that a Party has failed to transmit a response or has transmitted an interim response that does not contain an interim decision, and shall apply for one year.

Article 12 – Export notification

1. Where a chemical that is banned or severely restricted by a Party is exported from its territory, that Party shall provide an export notification to the importing Party. The export notification shall include the information set out in Annex V.
2. The export notification shall be provided for that chemical prior to the first export following adoption of the corresponding final regulatory action. Thereafter, the export notification shall be provided before the first export in any calendar year. The requirement to notify before export may be waived by the designated national authority of the importing Party.
3. An exporting Party shall provide an updated export notification after it has adopted a final regulatory action that results in a major change concerning the ban or severe restriction of that chemical.
4. The importing Party shall acknowledge receipt of the first export notification received after the adoption of the final regulatory action. If the exporting Party does not receive the acknowledgement within thirty days of the dispatch of the export notification, it shall submit a second notification. The exporting Party shall make reasonable efforts to ensure that the importing Party receives the second notification.
5. The obligations of a Party set out in paragraph 1 shall cease when:
   (a) The chemical has been listed in Annex III;
   (b) The importing Party has provided a response for the chemical to the Secretariat in accordance with paragraph 2 of Article 10; and
   (c) The Secretariat has distributed the response to the Parties in accordance with paragraph 10 of Article 10.

Article 13 – Information to accompany exported chemicals

1. The Conference of the Parties shall encourage the World Customs Organization to assign specific Harmonized System customs codes to the individual chemicals or groups of chemicals listed in Annex III, as appropriate. Each Party shall require that, whenever a code has been assigned to such a chemical, the shipping document for that chemical bears the code when exported.
2. Without prejudice to any requirements of the importing Party, each Party shall require that both chemicals listed in Annex III and chemicals banned or severely restricted in its territory are, when exported, subject to labelling requirements that ensure adequate availability of information with regard to risks and/or hazards to human health or the environment, taking into account relevant international standards.
3. Without prejudice to any requirements of the importing Party, each Party may require that chemicals subject to environmental or health labelling requirements in its territory are, when exported, subject to labelling requirements that ensure adequate availability of information with regard to risks and/or hazards to human health or the environment, taking into account relevant international standards.
4. With respect to the chemicals referred to in paragraph 2 that are to be used for occupational purposes, each exporting Party shall require that a safety data sheet that follows an internationally recognized format, setting out the most up-to-date information available, is sent to each importer.
5. The information on the label and on the safety data sheet should, as far as practicable, be given in one or more of the official languages of the importing Party.

Article 14 – Information exchange

1. Each Party shall, as appropriate and in accordance with the objective of this Convention, facilitate:
   (a) The exchange of scientific, technical, economic and legal information concerning the chemicals within the scope of this Convention, including toxicological, ecotoxicological and safety information;
   (b) The provision of publicly available information on domestic regulatory actions relevant to the objectives of this Convention; and
   (c) The provision of information to other Parties, directly or through the Secretariat, on domestic regulatory actions that substantially restrict one or more uses of the chemical, as appropriate.
2. Parties that exchange information pursuant to this Convention shall protect any confidential information as mutually agreed.
3. The following information shall not be regarded as confidential for the purposes of this Convention:
   (a) The information referred to in Annexes I and IV, submitted pursuant to Articles 5 and 6 respectively;
   (b) The information contained in the safety data sheet referred to in paragraph 4 of Article 13;
   (c) The expiry date of the chemical;
   (d) Information on precautionary measures, including hazard classification, the nature of the risk and the relevant safety advice; and
   (e) The summary results of the toxicological and ecotoxicological tests.
4. The production date of the chemical shall generally not be considered confidential for the purposes of this Convention.
5. Any Party requiring information on transit movements through its territory of chemicals listed in Annex III may report its need to the Secretariat, which shall inform all Parties accordingly.

Article 15 – Implementation of the Convention

1. Each Party shall take such measures as may be necessary to establish and strengthen its national

infrastructures and institutions for the effective implementation of this Convention. These measures may include, as required, the adoption or amendment of national legislative or administrative measures and may also include:

(a) The establishment of national registers and databases including safety information for chemicals;

(b) The encouragement of initiatives by industry to promote chemical safety; and

(c) The promotion of voluntary agreements, taking into consideration the provisions of Article 16.

2. Each Party shall ensure, to the extent practicable, that the public has appropriate access to information on chemical handling and accident management and on alternatives that are safer for human health or the environment than the chemicals listed in Annex III.

3. The Parties agree to cooperate, directly or, where appropriate, through competent international organizations, in the implementation of this Convention at the subregional, regional and global levels.

4. Nothing in this Convention shall be interpreted as restricting the right of the Parties to take action that is more stringently protective of human health and the environment than that called for in this Convention, provided that such action is consistent with the provisions of this Convention and is in accordance with international law.

Article 16 – Technical assistance

The Parties shall, taking into account in particular the needs of developing countries and countries with economies in transition, cooperate in promoting technical assistance for the development of the infrastructure and the capacity necessary to manage chemicals to enable implementation of this Convention. Parties with more advanced programmes for regulating chemicals should provide technical assistance, including training, to other Parties in developing their infrastructure and capacity to manage chemicals throughout their life-cycle.

Article 17 – Non-Compliance

The Conference of the Parties shall, as soon as practicable, develop and approve procedures and institutional mechanisms for determining non-compliance with the provisions of this Convention and for treatment of Parties found to be in non- compliance.

Article 18 – Conference of the Parties

1. A Conference of the Parties is hereby established.

2. The first meeting of the Conference of the Parties shall be convened by the Executive Director of UNEP and the Director-General of FAO, acting jointly, no later than one year after the entry into force of this Convention. Thereafter, ordinary meetings of the Conference of the Parties shall be held at regular intervals to be determined by the Conference.

3. Extraordinary meetings of the Conference of the Parties shall be held at such other times as may be deemed necessary by the Conference, or at the written request of any Party provided that it is supported by at least one third of the Parties.

4. The Conference of the Parties shall by consensus agree upon and adopt at its first meeting rules of procedure and financial rules for itself and any subsidiary bodies, as well as financial provisions governing the functioning of the Secretariat.

5. The Conference of the Parties shall keep under continuous review and evaluation the implementation of this Convention. It shall perform the functions assigned to it by the Convention and, to this end, shall:

(a) Establish, further to the requirements of paragraph 6 below, such subsidiary bodies as it considers necessary for the implementation of the Convention;

(b) Cooperate, where appropriate, with competent international organizations and intergovernmental and non-governmental bodies; and

(c) Consider and undertake any additional action that may be required for the achievement of the objectives of the Convention.

6. The Conference of the Parties shall, at its first meeting, establish a subsidiary body, to be called the Chemical Review Committee, for the purposes of performing the functions assigned to that Committee by this Convention. In this regard:

(a) The members of the Chemical Review Committee shall be appointed by the Conference of the Parties. Membership of the Committee shall consist of a limited number of government-designated experts in chemicals management. The members of the Committee shall be appointed on the basis of equitable geographical distribution, including ensuring a balance between developed and developing Parties;

(b) The Conference of the Parties shall decide on the terms of reference, organization and operation of the Committee;

(c) The Committee shall make every effort to make its recommendations by consensus. If all efforts at consensus have been exhausted, and no consensus reached, such recommendation shall as a last resort be adopted by a two-thirds majority vote of the members present and voting.

7. The United Nations, its specialized agencies and the International Atomic Energy Agency, as well as any State not Party to this Convention, may be represented at meetings of the Conference of the Parties as observers. Any body or agency, whether national or international, governmental or non-governmental, qualified in matters covered by the Convention, and which has informed the Secretariat of its wish to be represented at a meeting of the Conference of the Parties as an observer may be admitted unless at least one third of the Parties present object. The admission and participation of observers shall be subject to the rules of procedure adopted by the Conference of the Parties.

Article 19 – Secretariat

1. A Secretariat is hereby established.
2. The functions of the Secretariat shall be:
   (a) To make arrangements for meetings of the Conference of the Parties and its subsidiary bodies and to provide them with services as required;
   (b) To facilitate assistance to the Parties, particularly developing Parties and Parties with economies in transition, on request, in the implementation of this Convention;
   (c) To ensure the necessary coordination with the Secretariats of other relevant international bodies;
   (d) To enter, under the overall guidance of the Conference of the Parties, into such administrative and contractual arrangements as may be required for the effective discharge of its functions; and
   (e) To perform the other secretariat functions specified in this Convention and such other functions as may be determined by the Conference of the Parties.
3. The secretariat functions for this Convention shall be performed jointly by the Executive Director of UNEP and the Director-General of FAO, subject to such arrangements as shall be agreed between them and approved by the Conference of the Parties.
4. The Conference of the Parties may decide, by a three-fourths majority of the Parties present and voting, to entrust the secretariat functions to one or more other competent international organizations, should it find that the Secretariat is not functioning as intended.

Article 20 – Settlement of disputes

1. Parties shall settle any dispute between them concerning the interpretation or application of this Convention through negotiation or other peaceful means of their own choice.
2. When ratifying, accepting, approving or acceding to this Convention, or at any time thereafter, a Party that is not a regional economic integration organization may declare in a written instrument submitted to the Depositary that, with respect to any dispute concerning the interpretation or application of the Convention, it recognizes one or both of the following means of dispute settlement as compulsory in relation to any Party accepting the same obligation:
   (a) Arbitration in accordance with procedures to be adopted by the Conference of the Parties in an annex as soon as practicable; and
   (b) Submission of the dispute to the International Court of Justice.
3. A Party that is a regional economic integration organization may make a declaration with like effect in relation to arbitration in accordance with the procedure referred to in paragraph 2 (a).
4. A declaration made pursuant to paragraph 2 shall remain in force until it expires in accordance with its terms or until three months after written notice of its revocation has been deposited with the Depositary.
5. The expiry of a declaration, a notice of revocation or a new declaration shall not in any way affect proceedings pending before an arbitral tribunal or the International Court of Justice unless the parties to the dispute otherwise agree.
6. If the parties to a dispute have not accepted the same or any procedure pursuant to paragraph 2, and if they have not been able to settle their dispute within twelve months following notification by one party to another that a dispute exists between them, the dispute shall be submitted to a conciliation commission at the request of any party to the dispute. The conciliation commission shall render a report with recommendations. Additional procedures relating to the conciliation commission shall be included in an annex to be adopted by the Conference of the Parties no later than the second meeting of the Conference.

Article 21 – Amendments to the Convention

1. Amendments to this Convention may be proposed by any Party.
2. Amendments to this Convention shall be adopted at a meeting of the Conference of the Parties. The text of any proposed amendment shall be communicated to the Parties by the Secretariat at least six months before the meeting at which it is proposed for adoption. The Secretariat shall also communicate the proposed amendment to the signatories to this Convention and, for information, to the Depositary.
3. The Parties shall make every effort to reach agreement on any proposed amendment to this Convention by consensus. If all efforts at consensus have been exhausted, and no agreement reached, the amendment shall as a last resort be adopted by a three-fourths majority vote of the Parties present and voting at the meeting.
4. The amendment shall be communicated by the Depositary to all Parties for ratification, acceptance or approval.
5. Ratification, acceptance or approval of an amendment shall be notified to the Depositary in writing. An amendment adopted in accordance with paragraph 3 shall enter into force for the Parties having accepted it on the ninetieth day after the date of deposit of instruments of ratification, acceptance or approval by at least three fourths of the Parties. Thereafter, the amendment shall enter into force for any other Party on the ninetieth day after the date on which that Party deposits its instrument of ratification, acceptance or approval of the amendment.

Article 22 – Adoption and amendment of annexes

1. Annexes to this Convention shall form an integral part thereof and, unless expressly provided other-

wise, a reference to this Convention constitutes at the same time a reference to any annexes thereto.

2. Annexes shall be restricted to procedural, scientific, technical or administrative matters.
3. The following procedure shall apply to the proposal, adoption and entry into force of additional annexes to this Convention:
   (a) Additional annexes shall be proposed and adopted according to the procedure laid down in paragraphs 1, 2 and 3 of Article 21;
   (b) Any Party that is unable to accept an additional annex shall so notify the Depositary, in writing, within one year from the date of communication of the adoption of the additional annex by the Depositary. The Depositary shall without delay notify all Parties of any such notification received. A Party may at any time withdraw a previous notification of non-acceptance in respect of an additional annex and the annex shall thereupon enter into force for that Party subject to subparagraph (c) below; and
   (c) On the expiry of one year from the date of the communication by the Depositary of the adoption of an additional annex, the annex shall enter into force for all Parties that have not submitted a notification in accordance with the provisions of subparagraph (b) above.
4. Except in the case of Annex III, the proposal, adoption and entry into force of amendments to annexes to this Convention shall be subject to the same procedures as for the proposal, adoption and entry into force of additional annexes to the Convention.
5. The following procedure shall apply to the proposal, adoption and entry into force of amendments to Annex III:
   (a) Amendments to Annex III shall be proposed and adopted according to the procedure laid down in Articles 5 to 9 and paragraph 2 of Article 21;
   (b) The Conference of the Parties shall take its decisions on adoption by consensus;
   (c) A decision to amend Annex III shall forthwith be communicated to the Parties by the Depositary. The amendment shall enter into force for all Parties on a date to be specified in the decision.
6. If an additional annex or an amendment to an annex is related to an amendment to this Convention, the additional annex or amendment shall not enter into force until such time as the amendment to the Convention enters into force.

Article 23 – Voting

1. Each Party to this Convention shall have one vote, except as provided for in paragraph 2 below.
2. A regional economic integration organization, on matters within its competence, shall exercise its right to vote with a number of votes equal to the number of its member States that are Parties to this Convention. Such an organization shall not exercise its right to vote if any of its member States exercises its right to vote, and vice versa.
3. For the purposes of this Convention, "Parties present and voting" means Parties present and casting an affirmative or negative vote.

Article 24 – Signature

This Convention shall be open for signature at Rotterdam by all States and regional economic integration organizations on 11 September 1998, and at United Nations Headquarters in New York from 12 September 1998 to 10 September 1999.

Article 25 – Ratification, acceptance, approval or accession

1. This Convention shall be subject to ratification, acceptance or approval by States and by regional economic integration organizations. It shall be open for accession by States and by regional economic integration organizations from the day after the date on which the Convention is closed for signature. Instruments of ratification, acceptance, approval or accession shall be deposited with the Depositary.
2. Any regional economic integration organization that becomes a Party to this Convention without any of its member States being a Party shall be bound by all the obligations under the Convention. In the case of such organizations, one or more of whose member States is a Party to this Convention, the organization and its member States shall decide on their respective responsibilities for the performance of their obligations under the Convention. In such cases, the organization and the member States shall not be entitled to exercise rights under the Convention concurrently.
3. In its instrument of ratification, acceptance, approval or accession, a regional economic integration organization shall declare the extent of its competence in respect of the matters governed by this Convention. Any such organization shall also inform the Depositary, who shall in turn inform the Parties, of any relevant modification in the extent of its competence.

Article 26 – Entry into force

1. This Convention shall enter into force on the ninetieth day after the date of deposit of the fiftieth instrument of ratification, acceptance, approval or accession.
2. For each State or regional economic integration organization that ratifies, accepts or approves this Convention or accedes thereto after the deposit of the fiftieth instrument of ratification, acceptance, approval or accession, the Convention shall enter into force on the ninetieth day after the date of deposit by such State or regional economic integration organization of its instrument of ratification, acceptance, approval or accession.
3. For the purpose of paragraphs 1 and 2, any instrument deposited by a regional economic integration organization shall not be counted as additional to

those deposited by member States of that organization.

Article 27 – Reservations

No reservations may be made to this Convention.

Article 28 – Withdrawal

1. At any time after three years from the date on which this Convention has entered into force for a Party, that Party may withdraw from the Convention by giving written notification to the Depositary.
2. Any such withdrawal shall take effect upon expiry of one year from the date of receipt by the Depositary of the notification of withdrawal, or on such later date as may be specified in the notification of withdrawal.

Article 29 – Depositary

The Secretary-General of the United Nations shall be the Depositary of this Convention.

Article 30 – Authentic texts

The original of this Convention, of which the Arabic, Chinese, English, French, Russian and Spanish texts are equally authentic, shall be deposited with the Secretary-General of the United Nations.

IN WITNESS WHEREOF the undersigned, being duly authorized to that effect, have signed this Convention.

Done at Rotterdam on this tenth day of September, one thousand nine hundred and ninety-eight.

Annex I – Information requirements for notifications made pursuant to Article 5

Notifications shall include:

1. Properties, identification and uses
   - (a) Common name;
   - (b) Chemical name according to an internationally recognized nomenclature (for example, International Union of Pure and Applied Chemistry (IUPAC)), where such nomenclature exists;
   - (c) Trade names and names of preparations;
   - (d) Code numbers: Chemical Abstracts Service (CAS) number, Harmonized System customs code and other numbers;
   - (e) Information on hazard classification, where the chemical is subject to classification requirements;
   - (f) Use or uses of the chemical;
   - (g) Physico-chemical, toxicological and ecotoxicological properties.
2. Final regulatory action
   - (a) Information specific to the final regulatory action:
     - (i) Summary of the final regulatory action;
     - (ii) Reference to the regulatory document;
     - (iii) Date of entry into force of the final regulatory action;
     - (iv) Indication of whether the final regulatory action was taken on the basis of a risk or hazard evaluation and, if so, information on such evaluation, covering a reference to the relevant documentation;
     - (v) Reasons for the final regulatory action relevant to human health, including the health of consumers and workers, or the environment;
     - (vi) Summary of the hazards and risks presented by the chemical to human health, including the health of consumers and workers, or the environment and the expected effect of the final regulatory action;
   - (b) Category or categories where the final regulatory action has been taken, and for each category:
     - (i) Use or uses prohibited by the final regulatory action;
     - (ii) Use or uses that remain allowed;
     - (iii) Estimation, where available, of quantities of the chemical produced, imported, exported and used;
   - (c) An indication, to the extent possible, of the likely relevance of the final regulatory action to other States and regions;
   - (d) Other relevant information that may cover:
     - (i) Assessment of socio-economic effects of the final regulatory action;
     - (ii) Information on alternatives and their relative risks, where available, such as:
       - Integrated pest management strategies;
       - Industrial practices and processes, including cleaner technology.

Annex II – Criteria for listing banned or severely restricted chemicals in Annex III

In reviewing the notifications forwarded by the Secretariat pursuant to paragraph 5 of Article 5, the Chemical Review Committee shall:

- (a) Confirm that the final regulatory action has been taken in order to protect human health or the environment;
- (b) Establish that the final regulatory action has been taken as a consequence of a risk evaluation. This evaluation shall be based on a review of scientific data in the context of the conditions prevailing in the Party in question. For this purpose, the documentation provided shall demonstrate that:
  - (i) Data have been generated according to scientifically recognized methods;
  - (ii) Data reviews have been performed and documented according to generally recognized scientific principles and procedures;

(iii) The final regulatory action was based on a risk evaluation involving prevailing conditions within the Party taking the action;

(c) Consider whether the final regulatory action provides a sufficiently broad basis to merit listing of the chemical in Annex III, by taking into account:

(i) Whether the final regulatory action led, or would be expected to lead, to a significant decrease in the quantity of the chemical used or the number of its uses;

(ii) Whether the final regulatory action led to an actual reduction of risk or would be expected to result in a significant reduction of risk for human health or the environment of the Party that submitted the notification;

(iii) Whether the considerations that led to the final regulatory action being taken are applicable only in a limited geographical area or in other limited circumstances;

(iv) Whether there is evidence of ongoing international trade in the chemical;

(d) Take into account that intentional misuse is not in itself an adequate reason to list a chemical in Annex III.

Annex III – Chemicals subject to the prior informed consent procedure

[...]

Annex IV – Information and criteria for listing severely hazardous pesticide formulations in Annex III

Part 1. Documentation required from a proposing Party

Proposals submitted pursuant to paragraph 1 of Article 6 shall include adequate documentation containing the following information:

(a) Name of the hazardous pesticide formulation;

(b) Name of the active ingredient or ingredients in the formulation;

(c) Relative amount of each active ingredient in the formulation;

(d) Type of formulation;

(e) Trade names and names of the producers, if available;

(f) Common and recognized patterns of use of the formulation within the proposing Party;

(g) A clear description of incidents related to the problem, including the adverse effects and the way in which the formulation was used;

(h) Any regulatory, administrative or other measure taken, or intended to be taken, by the proposing Party in response to such incidents.

Part 2. Information to be collected by the Secretariat

Pursuant to paragraph 3 of Article 6, the Secretariat shall collect relevant information relating to the formulation, including:

(a) The physico-chemical, toxicological and ecotoxicological properties of the formulation;

(b) The existence of handling or applicator restrictions in other States;

(c) Information on incidents related to the formulation in other States;

(d) Information submitted by other Parties, international organizations, non- governmental organizations or other relevant sources, whether national or international;

(e) Risk and/or hazard evaluations, where available;

(f) Indications, if available, of the extent of use of the formulation, such as the number of registrations or production or sales quantity;

(g) Other formulations of the pesticide in question, and incidents, if any, relating to these formulations;

(h) Alternative pest-control practices;

(i) Other information which the Chemical Review Committee may identify as relevant.

Part 3. Criteria for listing severely hazardous pesticide formulations in Annex III

In reviewing the proposals forwarded by the Secretariat pursuant to paragraph 5 of Article 6, the Chemical Review Committee shall take into account:

(a) The reliability of the evidence indicating that use of the formulation, in accordance with common or recognized practices within the proposing Party, resulted in the reported incidents;

(b) The relevance of such incidents to other States with similar climate, conditions and patterns of use of the formulation;

(c) The existence of handling or applicator restrictions involving technology or techniques that may not be reasonably or widely applied in States lacking the necessary infrastructure;

(d) The significance of reported effects in relation to the quantity of the formulation used;

(e) That intentional misuse is not in itself an adequate reason to list a formulation in Annex III.

Annex V – Information requirements for export notification

1. Export notifications shall contain the following information:

(a) Name and address of the relevant designated national authorities of the exporting Party and the importing Party;

(b) Expected date of export to the importing Party;

(c) Name of the banned or severely restricted chemical and summary of the information specified in Annex I that is to be provided to the Secretariat in accordance with Article 5.

Where more than one such chemical is included in a mixture or preparation, such information shall be provided for each chemical;

(d) A statement indicating, if known, the foreseen category of the chemical and its foreseen use within that category in the importing Party;

(e) Information on precautionary measures to reduce exposure to and emission of, the chemical;

(f) In case of a mixture or a preparation, the concentration of the banned or severely restricted chemical or chemicals in question;

(g) Name and address of the importer;

(h) Any additional information that is readily available to the relevant designated national authority of the exporting Party that would be of assistance to the designated national authority of the importing Party.

2. In addition to the information referred to in paragraph 1, the exporting Party shall provide such further information specified in Annex I as may be requested by the importing Party.

Annex VI[1] – Settlements of disputes

A. Rules on arbitration

The arbitration procedure for purposes of paragraph 2 (a) of article 20 of the Rotterdam Convention on the Prior Informed Consent Procedure for Certain Hazardous Chemicals and Pesticides in International Trade shall be as follows:

Article 1

1. A Party may initiate recourse to arbitration in accordance with article 20 of the Convention by written notification addressed to the other Party to the dispute. The notification shall be accompanied by a statement of the claim, together with any supporting documents, and shall state the subject matter for arbitration including, in particular, the articles of the Convention the interpretation or application of which are at issue.
2. The claimant Party shall notify the Secretariat that the Parties are referring a dispute to arbitration pursuant to Article 20. The written notification of the claimant Party shall be accompanied by the statement of claim and the supporting documents referred to in paragraph 1 above. The Secretariat shall forward the information thus received to all Parties.

Article 2

1. In disputes between two Parties, an Arbitral Tribunal shall be established. It shall consist of three members.
2. Each of the Parties to the dispute shall appoint an arbitrator and the two arbitrators so appointed shall designate by common agreement the third arbitrator, who shall be the President of the Tribunal. The President of the Tribunal shall not be a national of one of the Parties to the dispute, nor have his or her usual place of residence in the territory of one of these Parties, nor be employed by any of them, nor have dealt with the case in any other capacity.
3. In disputes between more than two Parties, Parties in the same interest shall appoint one arbitrator jointly by agreement.
4. Any vacancy shall be filled in the manner prescribed for the initial appointment.
5. If the Parties do not agree on the subject matter of the dispute before the President of the Arbitral Tribunal is designated, the Arbitral Tribunal shall determine the subject matter.

Article 3

1. If one of the Parties to the dispute does not appoint an arbitrator within two months of the date on which the respondent Party receives the notification of the arbitration, the other Party may inform the Secretary-General of the United Nations who shall make the designation within a further two-month period.
2. If the President of the Arbitral Tribunal has not been designated within two months of the date of the appointment of the second arbitrator, the Secretary-General of the United Nations shall, at the request of a Party, designate the President within a further two-month period.

Article 4

The Arbitral Tribunal shall render its decisions in accordance with the provisions of the Convention and international law.

Article 5

Unless the parties to the dispute agree otherwise, the Arbitral Tribunal shall determine its own rules of procedure.

Article 6

The Arbitral Tribunal may, at the request of one of the Parties, recommend essential interim measures of protection.

Article 7

The Parties to the dispute shall facilitate the work of the Arbitral Tribunal and, in particular, using all means at their disposal, shall:

(a) Provide it with all relevant documents, information and facilities; and

(b) Enable it, when necessary, to call witnesses or experts and receive their evidence.

Article 8

The Parties and the arbitrators are under an obligation to protect the confidentiality of any information they receive in confidence during the proceedings of the Arbitral Tribunal.

1 The amendment whereby Annex VI was added to the Convention entered into force on 11 January 2006, on expiry of one year from the date of the communication of its adoption by the depositary (C.N.10.2005 reflecting decision RC-1/11 adopted by the first meeting of the Conference of the Parties).

Article 9

Unless the Arbitral Tribunal determines otherwise because of the particular circumstances of the case, the costs of the Tribunal shall be borne by the Parties to the dispute in equal shares. The Tribunal shall keep a record of all its costs and shall furnish a final statement thereof to the Parties.

Article 10

A Party that has an interest of a legal nature in the subject matter of the dispute which may be affected by the decision in the case, may intervene in the proceedings with the consent of the Arbitral Tribunal.

Article 11

The Arbitral Tribunal may hear and determine counterclaims arising directly out of the subject matter of the dispute.

Article 12

Decisions of the Arbitral Tribunal on both procedure and substance shall be taken by a majority vote of its members.

Article 13

1. If one of the Parties to the dispute does not appear before the Arbitral Tribunal or fails to defend its case, the other Party may request the Tribunal to continue the proceedings and to render its decision. Absence of a Party or failure of a Party to defend its case shall not constitute a bar to the proceedings.
2. Before rendering its final decision, the Arbitral Tribunal must satisfy itself that the claim is well founded in fact and law.

Article 14

The Arbitral Tribunal shall render its final decision within five months of the date on which it is fully constituted, unless it finds it necessary to extend the time limit for a period which should not exceed five more months.

Article 15

The final decision of the Arbitral Tribunal shall be confined to the subject matter of the dispute and shall state the reasons on which it is based. It shall contain the names of the members who have participated and the date of the final decision. Any member of the Tribunal may attach a separate or dissenting opinion to the final decision.

Article 16

The award shall be binding on the parties to the dispute. The interpretation of the Convention given by the award shall also be binding upon a Party intervening under Article 10 above insofar as it relates to matters in respect of which that Party intervened. The award shall be without appeal unless the parties to the dispute have agreed in advance to an appellate procedure.

Article 17

Any controversy which may arise between those bound by the final decision in accordance with Article 16 above, as regards the interpretation or manner of implementation of that decision, may be submitted by any of them for decision to the Arbitral Tribunal which rendered it.

B. Rules on conciliation

The conciliation procedure for purposes of paragraph 6 of article 20 of the Convention shall be as follows.

Article 1

1. A request by a party to a dispute to establish a conciliation commission in consequence of paragraph 6 of Article 20 shall be addressed in writing to the Secretariat. The Secretariat shall forthwith inform all Parties accordingly.
2. The conciliation commission shall, unless the parties otherwise agree, be composed of five members, two appointed by each Party concerned and a President chosen jointly by those members.

Article 2

In disputes between more than two parties, parties in the same interest shall appoint their members of the commission jointly by agreement.

Article 3

If any appointments by the parties are not made within two months of the date of receipt by the Secretariat of the written request referred to in article 1, the Secretary-General of the United Nations shall, upon request by a party, make those appointments within a further two-month period.

Article 4

If the President of the conciliation commission has not been chosen within two months of the fourth member of the commission being appointed, the Secretary-General of the United Nations shall, upon request by a party, designate the President within a further two-month period.

Article 5

1. The conciliation commission shall, unless the parties to the dispute otherwise agree, determine its own rules of procedure.
2. The parties and members of the commission are under an obligation to protect the confidentiality of any information they receive in confidence during the proceedings of the commission.

Article 6

The conciliation commission shall take its decisions by a majority vote of its members.

Article 7

The conciliation commission shall render a report with recommendations for resolution of the dispute within twelve months of being established, which the parties shall consider in good faith.

Article 8

Any disagreement as to whether the conciliation commission has competence to consider a matter referred to it shall be decided by the commission.

Article 9

The costs of the Commission shall be borne by the parties to the dispute in shares agreed by them. The Commission shall keep the record of all its costs and shall furnish a final statement thereof to the parties.

Annex VII[1] – Procedures and mechanisms on compliance with the Rotterdam Convention

1. A compliance committee (hereinafter referred to as "the Committee") is hereby established.

Members

2. The Committee shall consist of 15 members. Members shall be nominated by Parties and elected by the Conference of the Parties on the basis of equitable geographical representation of the five regional groups of the United Nations.
3. Members shall have expertise and specific qualifications in the subject matter covered by the Convention. They shall serve objectively and in the best interest of the Convention.

Election of members

4. At its first meeting after the entry into force of the present annex, the Conference of the Parties shall elect eight members of the Committee for one term and seven members for two terms. The Conference of the Parties shall, at each ordinary meeting thereafter, elect for two full terms new members to replace those members whose period of office as expired or is about to expire. Members shall not serve for more than two consecutive terms. For the purpose of the present annex, "term" shall mean the period that begins at the end of one ordinary meeting of the Conference of the Parties and ends at the end of the next ordinary meeting of the Conference of the Parties.
5. If a member of the Committee resigns or is otherwise unable to complete his or her term of office or to perform his or her functions, the Party that nominated that member shall nominate an alternate to serve for the remainder of the term.

Officers

6. The Committee shall elect its own chair. A vice-chair and a rapporteur shall be elected, on a rotating basis, by the Committee in accordance with rule 30 of the rules of procedure of the Conference of the Parties.

Meetings

7. The Committee shall hold meetings as necessary and wherever possible in conjunction with meetings of the Conference of the Parties or other Convention bodies.
8. Subject to paragraph 9 below, the meetings of the Committee shall be open to Parties and the public unless the Committee decides otherwise. When the Committee is dealing with submissions pursuant to paragraph 12 or 13 below, the meetings of the Committee shall be open to Parties and closed to the public unless the Party whose compliance is in question agrees otherwise. The Parties or observers to whom the meeting is open shall not have the right to participate in the meeting unless the Committee and the Party whose compliance is in question agree otherwise.
9. Where a submission is made with regard to the possible non-compliance of a Party, it shall be invited to participate in the consideration of the submission by the Committee. Such a Party, however, may not take part in the elaboration and adoption of a recommendation or conclusion of the Committee in relation to the matter.
10. The Committee shall make every effort to reach agreement on all matters of substance by consensus. Where this is not possible, the report shall reflect the views of all Committee members. If all efforts to reach consensus have been exhausted and no agreement has been reached, any decision shall, as a last resort, be taken by a four-fifths majority of the members present and voting or by eight members, whichever is greater. Ten members of the Committee shall constitute a quorum.
11. Each member of the Committee shall, in respect of any matter that is under consideration by the Committee, avoid direct or indirect conflicts of interest. When a member finds himself or herself faced with a direct or indirect conflict of interest, or is a citizen of a Party whose compliance is in question, that member shall bring the issue to the attention of the Committee before consideration of the matter. The concerned member shall not participate in the elaboration and adoption of a recommendation of the Committee in relation to that matter.
12. Submissions may be made in writing, through the Secretariat, by:
    (a) A Party that believes that, despite its best endeavours, it is, or will be, unable to comply with certain obligations under the Convention. Such a submission should include details as to which specific obligations are concerned and an assessment of the reason why the Party may be unable to meet those obligations. Where possible, substantiating information, or advice as to where such substantiating information may be found, may be provided. The submission may include suggestions for solutions which the Party considers may be most appropriate to its particular needs;
    (b) A Party that is directly affected or likely to be directly affected by another Party's alleged failure to comply with the obligations of the Convention. A Party intending to make a submission under the present subparagraph

1 The amendment whereby Annex VII was added to the Convention entered into force on 6 November 2020, on expiry of one year from the date of the communication of its adoption by the depositary (C.N.574.2019 reflecting decision RC-9/7 adopted by the ninth meeting of the Conference of the Parties).

should, before so doing, undertake consultations with the Party whose compliance is in question. The submission should include details as to which specific obligations are concerned, and information substantiating the submission, including how the Party is affected or likely to be affected.

13. The Committee, in order to assess possible difficulties faced by Parties in fulfilling their obligations under Articles 4 (1), 5 (1), 5 (2) and 10 of the Convention, upon receipt of information from the Secretariat provided by such Parties pursuant to those provisions, shall notify the Party in writing regarding the matter of concern. If the matter has not been resolved within 90 days by consultation through the Secretariat with the Party concerned and the Committee considers the matter further, it shall do so in accordance with paragraphs 16 to 24 below.
14. The Secretariat shall forward submissions made under subparagraph 12 (a) above, within two weeks of receiving such submissions, to the members of the Committee for consideration at the Committee's next meeting.
15. The Secretariat shall, within two weeks of its receiving any submission made under subparagraph 12 (b) or in furtherance to paragraph 13 above, send a copy to the Party whose compliance with the Convention is in question and to the members of the Committee for consideration at the Committee's next meeting.
16. A Party whose compliance is in question may present responses or comments at every step of the proceedings described in the present annex.
17. Without prejudice to paragraph 16 above, additional information, provided by a Party whose compliance is in question in response to a submission, should be forwarded to the Secretariat within three months of the date of receipt of the submission by that Party, unless the circumstances of a particular case require an extended period of time. Such information shall be immediately transmitted to the members of the Committee for consideration at the Committee's next meeting. Where a submission has been made pursuant to subparagraph 12 (b) above, the information shall be forwarded by the Secretariat also to the Party that made the submission.
18. The Committee may decide not to proceed with submissions which it considers to be:
    (a) De minimis;
    (b) Manifestly ill-founded.

Facilitation

19. The Committee shall consider any submission made to it in accordance with paragraph 12 or in furtherance of paragraph 13 above, with a view to establishing the facts and the root causes of the matter of concern and to assisting in its resolution, taking into account Article 16 of the Convention. To that end, the Committee may provide a Party with:
    (a) Advice;
    (b) Non-binding recommendations;
    (c) Any further information required to assist the Party in developing a compliance plan, including timelines and targets.

Possible measures to address compliance issues

20. If, after undertaking the facilitation procedure set forth in paragraph 19 above and taking into account the cause, type, degree and frequency of compliance difficulties, including financial and technical capacities of the Parties whose compliance is in question, the Committee considers it necessary to propose further measures to address a Party's compliance problems, the Committee may recommend to the Conference of the Parties, bearing in mind its ability under Article 18 (5) (c) of the Convention, that it consider the following measures, to be taken in accordance with international law, to attain compliance:
    (a) Further support under the Convention for the Party concerned, including facilitation, as appropriate, of access to financial resources, technical assistance and capacity-building;
    (b) Providing advice regarding future compliance in order to help Parties to implement the provisions of the Convention and to promote cooperation among all Parties;
    (c) Requesting the Party concerned to provide an update on its efforts;
    (d) Issuing a statement of concern regarding possible future non-compliance;
    (e) Issuing a statement of concern regarding current non-compliance;
    (f) Requesting the Executive Secretary to make public cases of non- compliance;
    (g) Recommending that a non-compliance situation be addressed by the non-compliant Party with the aim of resolving the situation.

Handling of information

21. (1) The Committee may receive relevant information, through the Secretariat, from:
    (a) The Parties;
    (b) Relevant sources, as it considers necessary and appropriate, with the prior consent of the Party concerned or as directed by the Conference of the Parties;
    (c) The Convention clearing-house mechanism and relevant intergovernmental organizations. The Committee shall provide the Party concerned with such information and invite it to present comments thereon.
    (2) The Committee may also request information from the Secretariat, where appropriate, in the form of a report, on matters under the Committee's consideration.
22. For the purpose of examining systemic issues of general compliance under paragraph 25 below, the Committee may:

(a) Request information from all Parties;

(b) In accordance with relevant guidance by the Conference of the Parties, request relevant information from any reliable sources and outside experts;

(c) Consult with the Secretariat and draw upon its experience and knowledge base.

23. Subject to Article 14 of the Convention, the Committee, any Party or any person involved in the deliberations of the Committee shall protect the confidentiality of information received in confidence.

Monitoring

24. The Committee should monitor the consequences of action taken in pursuance of paragraph 19 or 20 above. General compliance issues

25. The Committee may examine systemic issues of general compliance of interest to all Parties where:

(a) The Conference of the Parties so requests;

(b) The Committee, on the basis of information obtained by the Secretariat, while acting pursuant to its functions under the Convention, from Parties and submitted to the Committee by the Secretariat, decides that there is a need for an issue of general non-compliance to be examined and for a report on it to be made to the Conference of the Parties.

Reports to the Conference of the Parties

26. The Committee shall submit a report to each ordinary meeting of the Conference of the Parties reflecting:

(a) The work that the Committee has undertaken;

(b) The conclusions or recommendations of the Committee;

(c) The future programme of work of the Committee, including the schedule of expected meetings which it considers necessary for the fulfilment of its programme of work, for the consideration and approval of the Conference of the Parties.

Other subsidiary bodies

27. Where the activities of the Committee in respect of particular issues overlap with the responsibilities of another Rotterdam Convention body, the Conference of the Parties may direct the Committee to consult with that body. Information-sharing with compliance committees under relevant multilateral environmental agreements

28. Where relevant, the Committee may solicit specific information, upon request by the Conference of the Parties or at its own initiative, from compliance committees dealing with hazardous substances and wastes under the auspices of relevant multilateral environmental agreements and report on these activities to the Conference of the Parties.

Review of the compliance mechanism

29. The Conference of the Parties shall regularly review the implementation of the procedures and mechanisms set forth in the present annex.

Relationship with settlement of disputes

30. These procedures and mechanisms shall be without prejudice to Article 20 of the Convention